The Legislative Process, Statutory Interpretation, and Administrative Agencies

The Legislative Process, Statutory Interpretation, and Administrative Agencies

Linda D. Jellum
ELLISON CAPERS PALMER SR. PROFESSOR OF LAW
MERCER UNIVERSITY SCHOOL OF LAW

CAROLINA ACADEMIC PRESS
Durham, North Carolina

Print ISBN 978-1-61163-877-6
e-Book ISBN 978-1-61163-977-3
LCCN 2016944760

Carolina Academic Press, LLC
700 Kent Street
Durham, North Carolina 27701
Telephone (919) 489-7486
Fax (919) 493-5668
www.cap-press.com

Printed in the United States of America

This book is dedicated to my children, Chris and Kaylee. You have turned into wonderful young adults despite my less than perfect parenting. I'm extremely proud of you both.

Contents

Table of Cases

Table of Secondary Authorities

Publications

(sorted by author)

Robert A. Anthony, *Which Agency Interpretations Should Bind Citizens & the Courts?*, 7 YALE J. ON REG. 1 (1990)

Aharon Barak, *Foreword: A Judge on Judging: The Role of a Supreme Court in a Democracy*, 116 HARV. L. REV. 16 (2002)

Kent Barnett, *Resolving the ALJ Quandary*, 66 VAND. L. REV. 797, 812 (2013)

MICHAEL J. BEAN & MELANIE J. ROWLAND, THE EVOLUTION OF NATIONAL WILDLIFE LAW (1997)

Bernard Bell, *"No More Vehicles in the Park"*: *Reviving the Hart-Fuller Debate to Introduce Statutory Construction*, 48 J. LEGAL EDUCATION 88, (1998) (citing H.L.A. Hart, *Positivism & the Separation of Law & Morals*, 71 HARV. L. REV. 593, 607 (1958); Lon L. Fuller, *Positivism & Fidelity to Law—A Reply to Professor Hart*, 71 HARV. L. REV. 630, 663 (1958))

RONALD B. BROWN & SHARON J. BROWN, STATUTORY INTERPRETATION: THE SEARCH FOR LEGISLATIVE INTENT (2d ed. 2011

Lisa Schultz Bressman, *How* Mead *Has Muddled Judicial Review of Agency Action*, 58 VAND. L. REV. 1443 (2005)

Stephen Breyer, *On the Uses of Legislative History in Interpreting Statutes*, 65 S. CAL. L. REV. 845 (1992)

James J. Brudney & Corey Ditsler, *Canons of Construction & the Elusive Search for Neutral Reasoning*, 58 VAND. L. REV. 1 (2005)

Aaron-Andrew P. Bruhl, *Hierarchically Variable Deference to Agency Interpretations*, 89 NOTRE DAME L. REV. 728 (2013)

GUIDO CALABRESI, A COMMON LAW FOR THE AGE OF STATUTES (1985)

Carol Chomsky, *Unlocking the Mysteries of Holy Trinity: Spirit, Letter, & History in Statutory Interpretation*, 100 COLUM. L. REV. 901 (2000)

BARBARA H. CRAIG, CHADHA: THE STORY OF AN EPIC CONSTITUTIONAL STRUGGLE 25 (1988)

JACK DAVIES, LEGISLATIVE LAW & PROCESS IN A NUTSHELL (3d ed. 2007)

A. CONAN DOYLE, SILVER BLAZE, IN THE COMPLETE SHERLOCK HOLMES (1927)

Frank H. Easterbrook, *Statutes' Domains*, 50 U. CHI. L. REV. 533 (1983)

Linda D. Jellum, *The Impact of the Rise & Fall of* Chevron *on the Executive's Power to Make & Interpret Law*, 44 Loy. U. Chi. L.J. 141 (2012)

Linda D. Jellum, *"Which is to be Master," the Judiciary or the Legislature? When Statutory Directives Violate Separation of Powers*, 56 UCLA L. Rev. 837 (2009)

Fred Kameny, *Are Inseverability Clauses Constitutional?*, 68 Alb. L. Rev. 997 (2005)

John M. Kernochan, *Statutory Interpretation: An Outline of Method*, 3 Dalhousie L.J. 333 (1976)

Orin S. Kerr, *Shedding Light on* Chevron: *An Empirical Study of the* Chevron *Doctrine in the United States Courts of Appeals*, 15 Yale J. Reg. 1 (1998)

Ronald J. Krotoszynski, *On the Danger of Wearing Two Hats: Mistretta & Morrison Revisited*, 38 Wm. & Mary L. Rev. 417 (1997)

Gary Lawson, *Mostly Unconstitutional: The Case Against Precedent Revisited*, 5 Ave Maria L. Rev. 1 (2007)

Hillel Y. Levin, *Everything I need to Know About Statutory Interpretation I learned by the Time I was Nine*, 12 The Green Bag 357 (2009)

Ronald M. Levin, *The Anatomy of* Chevron: *Step Two Reconsidered*, 72 Chi.-Kent L. Rev. 1253 (1997)

Karl N. Llewellyn, *Remarks on the Theory of Appellate Decision & the Rules of Cannon about How Statutes are to be Construed*, 3 Vand. L. Rev. 395 (1949)

Jeffrey Lubbers, *"If It Didn't Exist, It Would Have to Be Invented" — Reviving the Administrative Conference*, 30 Ariz. St. L.J. 147 (1998)

Bradford C. Mank, *Legal Context: Reading Statutes in Light of Prevailing Legal Precedent*, 34 Ariz. St. L.J. 815 (2002)

John F. Manning, *Clear Statement Rules & the Constitution*, 100 Colum. L. Rev. 101 (2010)

John F. Manning, *Federalism & the Generality Problem in Constitutional Interpretation*, 122 Harv. L. Rev. 2004 (2009)

Peter B. McCutchen, *Mistakes, Precedent, & The Rise of the Administrative State: Toward a Constitutional Theory of the Second Best*, 80 Cornell L. Rev. 1 (1994)

Thomas W. Merrill, *Textualism & the Future of the* Chevron *Doctrine*, 72 Wash. U. L.Q. 351 (1994)

Erica Newland, Note, *Executive Orders in Court*, 124 Yale L.J. 2026

Lars Noah, *The Executive Line Item Veto & the Judicial Power to Sever: What's The Difference?*, 56 Wash. & Lee L. Rev. 235 (1999)

Richard Posner, *How Nuanced is Justice Scalia's Judicial Philosophy? An Exchange* (September 10, 2012)

Richard A. Posner, *Statutory Interpretation — In the Classroom & the Courtroom*, 50 U. Chi. L. Rev. 800 (1983)

Roscoe Pound, *Spurious Interpretation*, 7 Colum. L. Rev. 379 (1907)

Martin H. Redish & Elizabeth J. Cisar, *"If Angels Were to Govern": The Need for Pragmatic Formalism in Separation of Powers Theory*, 41 Duke L.J. 449 (1991)

Preface

Leg/Reg courses, as they are colloquially known, are multiplying as law schools incorporate them into the first year required curriculum. The practice of law today involves statutory interpretation and regulatory work. Hence, students need to know both subjects, and leg/reg courses are thus critically important.

However, law professors often struggle to identify what topics within these three areas (legislative process, interpretation, and administrative law) to cover and how deeply to cover those they do select. At this point in a student's education, too much information distracts students from what they need to know to become better students, but two little leaves students without the background they need to be successful as students and, ultimately, as lawyers. I have chosen to focus more attention on interpretation and agencies and less on the legislative process, because I believe more of our graduates will work in these areas. Of the two, I sink deeper into interpretation because every lawyer will encounter this topic and it is easier to grasp in the first year, while not all of them will interact with agencies, particularly federal agencies.

Hence, this text is organized as follows. Chapter 1 introduces the legislative and interpretive processes with the well-known ambulances in the park hypothetical. Chapter 2 explains separation of powers, which underlies statutory interpretation and the administrative state. Chapter 3 describes the legislative process and legal process theories. Chapter 4 explores the theories of, or approaches to, statutory interpretation and the sources of meaning: intrinsic sources, extrinsic sources, and policy-based sources. The next eleven chapters are organized around these sources. Thus, Chapters 5-9 cover the intrinsic sources, including the words, grammar, punctuation, linguistic canons, and statutory components. Chapters 10-13 cover the extrinsic sources, including conflicting statutes, legislative history, statutory purpose, legislative acquiescence, and post enactment activities. Chapters 14-15 cover the policy based sources, including both constitutional ones, such as the rule of lenity, and prudential ones, such as the remedial canon. Chapters 16-19 turn to agencies, what they are, why they regulate, how they regulate, and what deference they receive when they do regulate. Finally, Chapter 20 provides a brief review and organizational approach to the course (if you are a student reading this preface, you might wish to glance at Chapter 20 before you get started).

Within each chapter, I have tried to do a number of things. First, I begin each section by explaining the relevant canons in detail; I do not use cases to explain the basics. Instead, I include the highly edited cases to explore the canons and concepts in more detail. Many of the cases illustrate instances in which the court did not apply the canons or concepts accurately. It can be frustrating for students to read cases in which the judges got it wrong. But doing so helps students learn how to argue and critique. Lawyering, after all, is about learning how to make convincing arguments of your own while fairly criticizing those of your opponent. Statutory interpretation is no different. Lawyers do not want to know what a statute means as much as they want to know how to convince a judge that the statute means what their client says it means. Hence, critiquing judicial opinions is valuable and educational.

Unlike most textbooks, I have identified the justices who joined the majority and dissenting opinions in every Supreme Court case and many lower court opinions. These cases can make for strange bedfellows; it can be interesting to see when judges abandon their approach to interpretation or separation of powers to join an opinion that is more consistent with their political views or less consistent with them. The agency deference cases are particularly relevant here.

Like most textbooks, I have removed extraneous information using ellipses, and I have removed citations without any reference to keep clutter at a minimum. While lawyers do not have the luxury of having cases edited for them in this way, and for this reason some professors prefer less edited cases, at this early stage of student learning I prefer to help students swim in the relevant immediately without forcing them to first drown in the irrelevant.

At the end of every case, I have included notes and focused questions (*Points for Discussion*) to help students prepare the case for class discussion. For example, for cases involving interpretation issues, I suggest to students that they always ask themselves the following three questions: (1) What is the language at issue; (2) what does each party want that language to mean; and (3) how does each judge interpret that language and why? In answering that third question, it can be helpful to ask further, (a) what intrinsic sources did the judge consider or fail to consider; (b) what extrinsic sources did the judge consider or fail to consider; (c) what policy-based sources did the judge consider or fail to consider.

Finally, at the end of every chapter and sometimes at the end of a section, I have included problems that address one or more topics in the chapter. The problems are optional and can be assigned for out of class work or even review, if preferred. One of the most important skills that students learn by tackling the problems is to identify the relevant language or section of a law. When students simply read cases, the judges do this important work for them. But judges will not be pointing the way when our students practice. Hence, the problems are an important way to develop this important skill. The problems vary in their complexity, so judicious use is advised.

I have included a few additional things. First, in the appendices, I included a very simple sample bill (both the original house bill and the companion senate bill) and some of the legislative history for this bill. The bill was never enacted, so it never became an act, but it is instructive for students to see the differences between a bill and a statute (codified sections of an act). I have also included a glossary. Words that are included in the glossary are italicized in the text the first time they appear.

I look forward to hearing from you regarding ways to improve this text for the next edition. I particularly love to hear about the wonderful local cases you find. Too many of these textbooks are overly focused on Supreme Court cases, as if no other courts are interpreting statutes. Yet state case are often more accessible and tend to be more interesting (*see Ohio Division of Wildlife v. Clifton,* 692 N.E.2d 253 (Ohio Mun. Ct. 1997) in Chapter 12). Indeed, some of these cases were contributed by my former students.

In closing, I note that this book would not have been possible without the help of many. First, I would like to thank the Mercer Law Students from my 2015 course, who served as guinea pigs for this project and never complained. Additionally, Whit Cameron '16 and Joshua Pico '17 were wonderful research assistants. The text is better for their help. I appreciate the financial support Mercer Law School provided to make their help available. Also, David Pope, Keith Sipe, Linda Lacy, and Grace Pledger provided much needed support to help make this text a reality.

Finally, I would not be nearly as productive in life without my husband, Lee, who understands me when I say, "Git yer arse in the truck!"

Linda Jellum
Hilton Head Island, SC
June 2016

The Legislative Process, Statutory Interpretation, and Administrative Agencies

Chapter 1

Preliminary Matters

A. Introduction to This Chapter

While this is a book about the legislative process, statutory interpretation, and agencies, this chapter focuses primarily on statutory interpretation—what it is and why you as a future lawyer need to understand it. You will learn that statutes (and other written laws) generally work well and need little interpreting. But sometimes laws are unclear. This book describes the methods for interpreting unclear laws. To understand how to interpret unclear laws, you will learn about the legislative process and the role that agencies play in interpreting statutes and regulations.

This chapter will help you understand your starting point. You do not come to these topics as a neophyte. Rather, you bring beliefs about the proper way to interpret statutes; about the interpretive role of judges, legislatures, and agencies; and about the use of materials generated during the legislative process. This chapter will help you identify your beliefs before we get started.

As you read this text, keep in mind that judges interpret language in documents other than statutes. Because the canons that you will learn in this text are useful to anyone interpreting written language, you will find judges using the canons for more than statutory interpretation. For example, judges often interpret contracts, constitutions, and regulations, both state and federal. Judges use many of the same interpretation techniques to interpret these types of documents. However, each of these documents may have unique interpretation rules as well. For example, contracts are to be construed against the drafter. *Klapp v. United Ins. Group Agency, Inc.*, 663 N.W.2d 447, 454 (Mich. 2003) ("In interpreting a contract whose language is ambiguous, the jury should also consider that ambiguities are to be construed against the drafter of the contract."). Agencies have broad power to interpret their own regulations. *Auer v. Robbins*, 519 U.S. 452 (1997). Additionally, substantive law areas may have unique interpretive rules. For example, tax statutes are generally construed in favor of the taxpayer. *Travelscape, LLC v. South Carolina Dept. of Revenue*, 705 S.E.2d 28, 112 (2011) (Pleicones, J., dissenting) (noting the "well-recognized rule of statutory construction, that in the enforcement of tax statutes, the taxpayer should receive the benefit in cases of doubt."). Thus, there are some differences in interpretation techniques based on the text and subject matter being interpreted. This is true for constitutional interpretation as well.

B. Why Law Works Well Most of the Time

You may wonder why interpretation is necessary. After all, ordinary citizens obey laws every day. How is this possible if laws are so unclear? Most citizens do not have the luxury of hiring lawyers to help them understand the law, nor do they have the time to study statutory interpretation in the detail you are doing. Yet, they are expected to know the law, whether they have read it or not, and conform their actions accordingly. And they do so more often than not. How can ordinary citizens know whether their actions conform to legal requirements if a lawyer has to read books like this one to learn how to read statutes and has to take three years of law school to learn how to "think like a lawyer"?

Simply put, many laws are intuitive and conform to societal expectations. Most of us do not need a law to tell us that killing, assaulting, or stealing from someone is wrong. We also understand that there may be times when doing one of these actions, though usually wrong, would not be wrong given the particular circumstances (self-defense, for example). While most of us do not need laws to conform our behavior to societal norms, some outliers and sociopaths may need laws to prevent, or at least allow society to punish, their behavior. Legislators write statutes (and judges make common law) to define law clearly for the outliers and enforcers, to enable those in authority to punish wrongdoers, and to identify the boundaries of that law.

Let's focus on statutes. How do legislators write clear statutes? Statutes follow familiar patterns. Statutes are understandable both because they conform—much of the time—to societal expectations and because they have a familiar format. As one scholar has noted, statutes resemble dictionary definitions. Lawrence M. Solan, The Language of Statutes 18 (2010). For example, the definition of the verb "lie" is "to make an untrue statement with intent to deceive." Merriam-Webster's online dictionary (http://www.merriam-webster.com/ dictionary/lie). If we unpack this definition, we see that people lie when they 1) make an untrue statement, and 2) have the intent to deceive. Let's compare the federal statute criminalizing perjury:

> Whoever ... having taken an oath before a competent tribunal, officer, or person, in any case in which a law of the United States authorizes an oath to be administered, that he will testify, declare, depose, or certify truly, ... and contrary to such oath states or subscribes any material matter which he does not believe to be true ... is guilty of perjury.

18 USC § 1621 (1). If we unpack this definition, people commit perjury when they 1) take an oath promising to testify truthfully, and 2) state something material that they do not believe to be true. Do you see the similarity between this statute and the definition of "lie" above?

When statutes conform to societal expectations and define conduct in expected ways, they generally need be less clear as most individuals will follow the statute without inducement. But when statutes do not conform to societal expectations or do not define conduct in expected ways, individuals and their lawyers fight back by holding the legislature to the precise words it used. For example, a statute that states,

"Whoever shall willfully take the life of another shall be punished by death" is probably both expected and clear. But a statute that requires individuals to pay thirty percent of their "income" to the federal government better define "income" very clearly.

Let's look at another example, one closer to home. Consider your commute to work or school. You leave your house, drive a car that meets state safety standards, fill it with the appropriate kind of gas, drive on the correct side of the road, stop at stop signs, stay reasonably close to the speed limit, pay to park your car legally, and turn on headlights when it grows dark. Daily, like all other ordinary citizens, you follow laws without thinking about whether you are doing so. You may not follow the laws perfectly (note the speed limit example), but you will follow the laws well enough to help society run smoothly. Thus, laws generally work well.

From these examples, you can see that it is usually the hard cases that wind up in court and only the toughest of cases that are resolved at the Supreme Court. Remember that fact, because after reading this text, you will be warped into thinking that statutes are malleable and ambiguous and that ambiguity is resolved depending upon the judge's whim. This is not the case: Most statutes are clear and work well. But because language is imprecise—precision is impossible with a limited number of symbols representing a multitude of concepts—ambiguity and vagueness are unavoidable. When ambiguity and vagueness arise, the question becomes how should they be resolved? That is the question that this text answers.

Below is a fun introduction to the various interpretive approaches and canons.

The Food Stays in the Kitchen:
Everything I Needed to Know About Statutory Interpretation I Learned by the Time I Was Nine*

Hillel Y. Levin
Originally published in 12 The Green Bag 357 (2009)

On March 23, 1986, the following proclamation, henceforth known as Ordinance 7.3, was made by the Supreme Lawmaker, MOTHER: I am tired of finding popcorn kernels, pretzel crumbs, and pieces of cereal all over the family room. From now on, no food may be eaten outside the kitchen. Thereupon, litigation arose.

———————

FATHER, C.J. issued the following ruling on March 30, 1986:

Defendant Anne, age 14, was seen carrying a glass of water into the family room. She was charged with violating Ordinance 7.3 ("the Rule"). We hold that drinking water outside of the kitchen does not violate the Rule.

The Rule prohibits "food" from being eaten outside of the kitchen. This prohibition does not extend to water, which is a beverage rather than food. Our interpretation is confirmed by Webster's Dictionary, which defines food to mean, in relevant part,

———————

* Copyright Professor Hillel Y. Levin. Used with permission of the author.

a "material consisting essentially of protein, carbohydrate, and fat used in the body of an organism to sustain growth, repair, and vital processes and to furnish energy ..." and "nutriment in solid form." Plainly, water, which contains no protein, carbohydrate, or fat, and which is not in solid form, is not a food.

Customary usage further substantiates this interpretation of food to exclude water. Ordinance 6.2, authored by the very same Supreme Lawmaker, declares that "[a]fter you get home from school, have some food and something to drink, and then do your homework." This demonstrates that the Supreme Lawmaker speaks of food and drink separately and is fully capable of identifying one or both as appropriate. After all, if "food," as used in the Code, included beverages, then the word "drink" in Ordinance 6.2 would be redundant and mere surplusage. Thus, had the Supreme Lawmaker wished to prohibit beverages from being taken out of the kitchen, she could easily have done so by declaring that "no food *or drink* is permitted outside the kitchen."

Our understanding of the word "food" to exclude water is further buttressed by the evident purpose of the Ordinance. The Supreme Lawmaker enacted the Rule as a response to the mess produced by solid foods. Water, even when spilled, does not produce a similar kind of mess. Some may argue that the cup in which the Defendant was drinking water may, if left in the family room, itself be a mess. But we are not persuaded. The language of the Rule speaks to the Supreme Lawmaker's concern with small particles of food rather than to a more generalized concern with the containers in which food is held. A cup or other container is more similar to other bric-a-brac, such as toys and backpacks, to which the Rule does not speak, than it is to the food spoken of in the Rule. Although we need not divine the Supreme Lawmaker's reasons for such a distinction, there are at least two plausible explanations. First, it could be that small particles of food left around the house are more problematic than the stray cup or bowl because they find their way into hard-to reach places and may lead to rodent infestation. Second, it is possible that the Supreme Lawmaker was unconcerned with containers being left in the family room because citizens of this jurisdiction have been meticulous about removing such containers.

BABYSITTER SUE, J., issued the following ruling on April 12, 1986:

Defendant Beatrice, age, 12, is charged with violating Ordinance 7.3 by drinking a beverage, to wit: orange juice, in the family room. The Defendant relies on our ruling of March 30, 1986, and urges us to conclude that all beverages are permitted in the family room under Ordinance 7.3. While we believe this is a difficult case, we agree. As we have previously held, the term "food" does not extend to beverages.

Our hesitation stems not from the literal meaning of the Ordinance, which strongly supports the Defendant's claim, but rather from an understanding of its purpose. As we have previously stated, and as evidenced by the language of the Ordinance itself, the Ordinance was enacted as a result of the Supreme Lawmaker's concern with mess. As is not the case with water, if the Defendant were to spill orange juice on the couch or rug in the family room, the mess would be problematic—perhaps even more so than the mess produced by crumbs of food. We cannot see any rational reason that the Supreme Lawmaker would choose to prohibit solid foods outside of the kitchen but to permit orange juice. Nevertheless, we are bound by the plain language of the Ordinance and by precedent. We are confident that if the Supreme Lawmaker disagrees with the outcome in this case, she can change or clarify the law accordingly.

GRANDMA, Senior J., issued the following ruling on May 3, 1986:

Defendant Charlie, age 10, is charged with violating Ordinance 7.3 by eating popcorn in the family room. The Defendant contends, and we agree, that the Ordinance does not apply in this case.

Ordinance 7.3 was enacted to prevent messes outside of the kitchen. This purpose is demonstrated by the language of the Ordinance itself, which refers to food being left all over the family room as the immediate cause of its adoption. Such messes are produced only when one transfers food from a container to his or her mouth outside of the kitchen. During that process—what the Ordinance refers to as "eat[ing]"—crumbs and other food particles often fall out of the eater's hand and onto the floor or sofa. As the record shows, the Defendant placed all of the popcorn into his mouth prior to leaving the kitchen. He merely masticated and swallowed while in the family room. At no time was there any danger that a mess would be produced.

We are certain that there was no intent to prohibit merely the chewing or swallowing of food outside of the kitchen. After all, the Supreme Lawmaker has expressly permitted the chewing of gum in the family room. It would be senseless and absurd to treat gum differently from popcorn that has been ingested prior to leaving the kitchen. If textual support is necessary to support this obvious and commonsensical interpretation, abundant support is available. First, the Ordinance prohibits food from being "eaten" outside of the kitchen. The term "eat" is defined to mean "to take in through the mouth as food: ingest, chew, *and* swallow in turn." The Defendant, having only chewed and swallowed, did not "eat." Further, the statute prohibits the "eating" rather than the "bringing" of food outside of the kitchen; and indeed, food is often *brought* out of the kitchen and through the family room, as when school lunches are delivered to the front door for carpool pickup. There is no reason to treat food enclosed in a brown bag any differently from food enclosed within the Defendant's mouth. Finally, if any doubt remains as to the meaning of this Ordinance as it pertains to the chewing and swallowing food, we cannot punish the Defendant for acting reasonably and in good faith reliance upon the statute and our past pronouncements as to its meaning and intent.

UNCLE RICK, J., issued the following ruling on May 20, 1986:

Defendant Charlie, age 10, is charged with violating Ordinance 7.3 ("the Rule") by bringing a double thick mint chocolate chip milkshake into the living room.

Were I writing on a clean slate, I would surely conclude that the Defendant has violated the Rule. A double thick milkshake is "food" because it contains protein, carbohydrate, and/or fat. Further, the purpose of the Rule—to prevent messes—would be undermined by permitting a double thick milkshake to be brought in the family room. Indeed, it makes little sense to treat a milkshake differently from a pretzel or a scoop of ice cream. However, I am not writing on a clean slate. Our precedents have now developed such that all beverages are permitted outside of the kitchen under the Rule. Our Defendant relied on those precedents in good faith. Further, the Supreme Lawmaker has had ample opportunity to clarify or change the law to prohibit any or all beverages from being brought out of the kitchen, and she has elected not to exercise that authority. I can only conclude that she is satisfied with the status quo.

––––––––––

GRANDMA, Senior J., issued the following ruling on July 2, 1986:

Defendant Anne, age 14, is charged with violating Ordinance 7.3 by eating apple slices in the family room. As we have repeatedly held, the Ordinance only pertains to messy foods. Moreover, the Ordinance explicitly refers to "popcorn kernels, pretzel crumbs, and pieces of cereal." Sliced apples, not being messy (and certainly being no worse than orange juice and milkshakes, which are permitted), and being wholly dissimilar from the crumbly foods listed in the Ordinance, do not come within the meaning of the Ordinance. We also find it significant that the consumption of healthy foods such as sliced apples is a behavior that this jurisdiction supports and encourages. It would be odd to read the Ordinance in a way that would reduce such healthy behaviors.

––––––––––

AUNT SARAH, J., issued the following ruling on August 12, 1986:

Defendant Beatrice, age 13, is charged with violating Ordinance 7.3 by eating pretzels, popcorn, cereal, and birthday cake in the family room. Under ordinary circumstances, the Defendant would clearly be subject to the Ordinance. However, the circumstances giving rise to the Defendant's action in this case are far from ordinary.

The Defendant celebrated her thirteenth birthday on August 10, 1986. For the celebration, she invited four of her closest friends to sleep over. During the evening, and as part of the festivities, the celebrants watched a movie in the family room. CHIEF JUSTICE FATHER provided those present with drinks and snacks, including the aforesaid pretzels, popcorn, and cereal, for consumption during the movie-watching. FATHER admonished the Defendant to clean up after the movie, and there is no evidence in the record suggesting that the Defendant failed to do so.

We frankly concede that the Defendant's action were violative of the plain meaning of the Ordinance. However, given the special and unique nature of the occasion, the fact that FATHER, a representative of the Supreme Lawmaker—as well as of this Court—approved of the Defendant's actions, and the apparent efforts of the Defendant in upholding the spirit of the Ordinance by cleaning up after her friends, we believe that the best course of action is to release the Defendant. In light of the growing confusion in the interpretation of this ambiguous Ordinance, we urge the Supreme Lawmaker to exercise her authority to clarify and/or change the law if and as she deems it appropriate.

FATHER, C.J., issued the following ruling on September 17, 1986:

Defendant Derek, age 9, was charged with violating Ordinance 7.3 ("the Rule") by eating pretzels, potato chips, popcorn, a bagel with cream cheese, cottage cheese, and a chocolate bar in the family room. The Defendant argues that our precedents have clearly established a pattern permitting food to be eaten in the family room so long as the eater cleans up any mess. He further maintains that it would be unjust for this Court to punish him after having permitted past actions such as drinking water, orange juice, and a milkshake, as well as swallowing popcorn, eating apple slices, and eating pretzels, popcorn, and cereal on a special occasion. The Defendant avers that there is no rational distinction between eating foods in the family room during a movie on a special occasion from his eating foods in the family room during a weekly television show. We agree. The citizens of this jurisdiction look to the rulings of this Court, as well as to general practice, to understand their rights and obligations as citizens. In the many months since the Rule was originally announced, the cumulative rulings of this Court on the subject would signify to any citizen that, whatever the technical language of the Rule, the *real* Rule is that they must clean up after eating any food outside of the kitchen. Any other line that we were now to draw would be arbitrary and, as such, unjust.

On November 4, 1986, the following proclamation, henceforth known as The New Ordinance 7.3, was made by the Supreme Lawmaker:

MOTHER: Over the past few months, I have found empty cups, orange juice stains, milkshake spills, slimy spots of unknown origin, all manner of crumbs, melted chocolate, and icing from cake in the family room. I thought I was clear the first time! And you've all had a chance to show me that you could use your common sense and clean up after yourselves. So now let me be clearer: No food, gum, or drink of any kind, on any occasion or in any form, is permitted in the family room. Ever. Seriously. I mean it!

* * *

Points for Discussion

1. *Statutory Language*: What written law, or "statute," is being interpreted? What word or words in that statute are the law interpreters, "judges," interpreting?

2. *Arguments*: In ordinary parlance, is any of the following food: water, orange juice, popcorn, milkshake, apple slices, pretzels, cereal, birthday cake, potato chips, bagel with cream cheese, cottage cheese, and a chocolate bar? Assuming

so, why did the various judges conclude that they were not prohibited by the "statute"? *literal meaning of the word "food" & Reasons to Prohibit*

3. *Test the Reasoning*: Which judicial interpretations, "opinions," do you find most persuasive? Least persuasive? Which judges most digressed from the law maker's, "legislative," intent? *water, Apple Slices & Birthday*.

C. An Introduction to Statutory Interpretation

If a client came to your office wanting to open a local restaurant, your first step should be to see if there is a local, state, or federal statute or regulation on point. Assuming you find one, you will need to understand what that statute says. Sure, you think, that is easy. I'll just read it. Not so fast. Even if the statute appears clear, it may not be. As you will learn, reading a statute's text is only the first step to understanding what that statute means. Because language is inherently ambiguous (for example, is "blue" a state of being or a color? Is dust a verb or noun?), interpreting statutes is more complex than it would seem.

Statutory interpretation, also called statutory construction, is the process of determining the meaning of a legislative act called a statute. Interpreting a statute is more than simply reading the text. Statutes are the product of a long, legislative process that includes the reconciling of competing interests. The final product — the statute — is a compromise arrived at only after a long, political, and often controversial, process. Hence, statutes may have gaps, ambiguities, errors, or omissions. The tools and canons (or rules of thumb) of interpretation help lawyers understand and argue about those gaps, ambiguities, errors, and omissions. Statutory interpretation is an art, not a science, a language, not a set of rules. Knowing how to interpret statutes in light of these imperfections will be critical to your practice, because most of the work lawyers do today centers on statutes and regulations, whether federal or state. Because statutes and regulations have proliferated, reading and understanding statutes is a basic legal skill and, thus, is essential to your success as a lawyer.

This book will help you learn the art of statutory interpretation. Because different scholars and courts use different approaches to statutory interpretation (*See* Chapter 4), this text cannot definitively explain how a judge or court will interpret a statute. But it will help you learn to make arguments for your client, speak this new language, and anticipate how statutes are likely to be interpreted. At the conclusion of this text, you should: (1) be familiar with the canons of interpretation, knowing how to use them and how to counter your opponent's use of them, (2) have an understanding of the various theories of interpretation judges use in interpreting statutes, and (3) be aware of the breadth of arguments that can be made about seemingly clear language. In short, this text will help you master the art of statutory interpretation.

Let's start with an example. The facts from a recent Supreme Court case are excerpted below. Before you study this subject any further, read the excerpt and think about how you would decide the case: should the Court find the defendant, Yates, guilty of violating 18 U.S.C. § 1519 for throwing under-sized fish overboard? Note your gut reaction. How would you rule?

Yates v. United States

Supreme Court of the United States

135 S. Ct. 1074 (2015)

tends to be conservitave

◆ JUSTICE GINSBURG delivered the opinion of the Court [in which ROBERTS, C.J., and BREYER and SOTOMAYOR, JJ., concur]. ← *Tend to be liberal*

John Yates, a commercial fisherman, caught undersized red grouper in federal waters in the Gulf of Mexico. To prevent federal authorities from confirming that he had harvested undersized fish, Yates ordered a crew member to toss the suspect catch into the sea. For this offense, he was charged with, and convicted of, violating 18 U.S.C. § 1519, which provides:

Captain throws original fish over & replaced with other

> Whoever knowingly alters, destroys, mutilates, conceals, covers up, falsifies, or makes a false entry in any record, document, or tangible object with the intent to impede, obstruct, or influence the investigation or proper administration of any matter within the jurisdiction of any department or agency of the United States or any case filed under title 11, or in relation to or contemplation of any such matter or case, shall be fined under this title, imprisoned not more than 20 years, or both....

Yates ... maintains that fish are not trapped within the term "tangible object," as that term is used in § 1519....

[Facts:] On August 23, 2007, the *Miss Katie*, a commercial fishing boat, was six days into an expedition in the Gulf of Mexico. Her crew numbered three, including Yates, the captain. Engaged in a routine offshore patrol to inspect both recreational and commercial vessels, Officer John Jones of the Florida Fish and Wildlife Conservation Commission [a state agency] decided to board the *Miss Katie* to check on the vessel's compliance with fishing rules....

Upon boarding the *Miss Katie*, Officer Jones noticed three red grouper that appeared to be undersized hanging from a hook on the deck. At the time, federal conservation regulations required immediate release of red grouper less than 20 inches long. Violation of those regulations is a civil offense punishable by a fine or fishing license suspension.

Suspecting that other undersized fish might be onboard, Officer Jones proceeded to inspect the ship's catch.... Officer Jones ultimately determined that 72 fish fell short of the 20-inch mark. A fellow officer recorded the length of each of the undersized fish on a catch measurement verification form. With few exceptions, the measured fish were between 19 and 20 inches; three were less than 19 inches; none were less than 18.75 inches. After separating the fish measuring below 20 inches from the rest of the catch by placing them in wooden crates, Officer Jones directed Yates to leave the fish, thus segregated, in the crates until the *Miss Katie* returned to port....

Handwritten margin note (top left): Δ moved for Aquital
—denied
11ᵗʰ : Affirmed
SC: granted cert

Four days later, after the *Miss Katie* had docked in Cortez, Florida, Officer Jones measured the fish contained in the wooden crates. This time, however, the measured fish, although still less than 20 inches, slightly exceeded the lengths recorded on board. Jones surmised that the fish brought to port were not the same as those he had detected during his initial inspection. Under questioning, one of the crew members admitted that, at Yates's direction, he had thrown overboard the fish Officer Jones had measured at sea, and that he and Yates had replaced the tossed grouper with fish from the rest of the catch.

… On May 5, 2010, [Yates] was indicted for destroying property to prevent a federal seizure, in violation of § 2232(a),* and for destroying, concealing, and covering up undersized fish to impede a federal investigation, in violation of § 1519.… Yates was tried on the criminal charges in August 2011. At the end of the Government's case in chief, he moved for a judgment of acquittal [arguing] that the section sets forth "a documents offense" and that its reference to "tangible object[s]" subsumes "computer hard drives, logbooks, [and] things of that nature," not fish.… The Government countered that a "tangible object" within § 1519's compass is "simply something other than a document or record." … [The defendant moved for acquittal on this charge. The trial court denied the motion. The Eleventh Circuit affirmed. The Supreme Court granted certiorari.] [The remainder of the opinion has been omitted.]

Handwritten margin note (left): 5ᵗʰ & conserv.

[JUSTICE ALITO's concurrence JUSTICE KAGAN's dissent, in which SCALIA, KENNEDY, and THOMAS, JJ., joined, have been omitted.]

Handwritten note: Not very cons.

* * *

Points for Discussion

1. *Statutory Language*: The first question you should ask yourself in every case involving interpretation of a statute (or regulation or other written law) is "what is the language at issue?" In this case, the language being interpreted is "tangible object." It is much easier to identify the relevant language when a court has done so for you. Identifying the language without this help is significantly more difficult; however, identifying the statutory language in dispute is a critical skill that you will need to develop as a lawyer. This text will help you do so.

2. *Competing Interpretations*: After you have identified the relevant language, ask yourself "how does each party want that language to be interpreted?" You need to be specific. It is not enough to say, "My client believes that tangible object does not include fish." Give the court an alternative meaning. For example, the defendant might argue that "tangible object" includes only those items that are either similar to records and documents or hold written information. In contrast, the government might argue "tangible object" includes any item that is touchable, including fish. Generally, one side will want a narrower interpretation, while the other side will want a broader interpretation. But each side needs to be specific with its alternate interpretation.

---

* Editor's footnote: Yates did not dispute his conviction on this charge.

Handwritten note: — he did throw the fish over

3. *How Would You Rule*: Finally, determine what meaning the court (majority and dissent, if there are both) gave to the language and why. Determine which arguments the court makes that you find persuasive and which you find unpersuasive. You cannot do that step here because you only have the facts. But, how would you decide this case and why?

[handwritten: Purpose of the statute – Reading the language]

4. *Size Matters*: Why do you think Justice Ginsburg included in the opinion the size of the fish both times they were measured? Is not the only relevant fact about size that 72 were smaller than 20 inches? Good lawyers put their clients in as favorable light as possible. While the size of the fish was irrelevant to the legal issue (because the "new" fish were still too short), the fact that the difference was so small allows the reader to have more sympathy for the defendant. It is an effective persuasive technique. From this one fact, can you guess which way the majority ruled?

* * * *[handwritten: Persuasive technique → its minor]*

D. Vehicles in the Park

Let's turn to a hypothetical example to practice. Is an ambulance a motor vehicle? This question may sound silly. Of course an ambulance is a motor vehicle. It has a motor, drives on the roads, and transports people and things. But is it really? You might be surprised to learn that very intelligent people disagree about whether an ambulance is a vehicle, at least within the context of a statute prohibiting "vehicles in the park." Indeed, this question is so famous and contentious that former Justice Antonin Scalia and Judge Richard Posner had a very public falling out based, in part, on their approach to resolving this very issue. Richard A. Posner, *The Incoherence of Antonin Scalia*, (August 24, 2012), http://www.newrepublic.com/article/magazine/books-and-arts/106441/scalia-garner-reading-the-law-textual-originalism; Bryan A. Garner, *How Nuanced is Justice Scalia's Judicial Philosophy? An Exchange* (September 10, 2012), http://www.newrepublic.com/article/politics/107001/how-nuanced-justice-scalias-judicial-philosophy-exchange; Richard Posner, *How Nuanced is Justice Scalia's Judicial Philosophy? An Exchange* (September 10, 2012), http://www.newrepublic.com/article/politics/107001/how-nuanced-justice-scalias-judicial-philosophy-exchange.

A hypothetical local city ordinance is included below. After you read the hypothetical city ordinance and its "legislative history," you will be asked to consider some hypothetical scenarios and decide whether you, as a new prosecutor for the city, would prosecute the individuals involved for violating the ordinance. When you answer the questions, consider how, if you would prosecute, you would explain to a judge that the defendant's actions violated the ordinance. What might a defense attorney argue in response? What materials do you find helpful, relevant, and appropriate to consider in making your decisions as a prosecutor? What materials do you consider unhelpful, irrelevant, or inappropriate to consider? Why? Does it matter which side of the argument you are on? You should think about how you would resolve these questions before you read the rest of this text. This hypothetical will test your beliefs about statutory interpretation while you are still an ordinary citizen, albeit one already influenced by some legal training.

Do not worry if you do not understand everything included in the problem at this point. Just do your best by reading the ordinance, the accompanying legislative history, and the mayor's signing statement. Then answer the questions that follow, noting your conclusions and reasoning in the margins. You will want to come back to your conclusions as you begin to master the material in this text. Assume as you think about this problem that this ordinance was enacted in the same way that federal legislation is enacted (which you will learn in Chapter 3) and that the methods for interpreting ordinances are the same as the methods for interpreting federal statutes (they mostly are).

You may be tempted to skip this step and just read the hypothetical quickly; after all, no one will test you on your answers, and law school is time consuming enough. But you will learn a lot from actually attempting the hypothetical questions and noting your answers in the margins. How do you distinguish any vehicles you allow into the park from those you exclude? Do your answers have consistency, or do you fall down the rabbit hole like the judges in the "*The Food Stays in the Kitchen*" example? If you take the time, likely less than thirty minutes at most, to jot down your answers to these questions, you will learn quickly how you naturally approach interpretation issues, a topic we explore in some detail in Chapter 4.

So much of interpretation is intuitive and happens without your conscious thought. As you learn the rules of thumb, the canons of interpretation, you will be tempted to think of these canons as legal rules. They are not! Legal rules are mandatory. The parole evidence rule is a legal rule. It prevents a party to a written contract from presenting extrinsic evidence in court if that evidence would vary the written terms of a contract. The parole evidence rule is not malleable; it applies in every case involving a contract and extra-textual evidence. In contrast, the canons of interpretation are not legal rules; rather, they are guidelines, suggestions, or even a legal language that lawyers and judges use to justify outcomes. As such, they are malleable, and for every canon that supports one party's interpretation, there is a canon that supports the opposing party's interpretation. Karl N. Llewellyn, *Remarks on the Theory of Appellate Decision and the Rules of Cannon about How Statutes are to be Construed*, 3 VAND. L. REV. 395, 401 (1949) (identifying the competing canons as thrusts and parrys). Thus, know now that you are not learning law *per se*; instead, you are learning a new language; one that will provide powerful arguments for your clients.

*Hypothetical Problem**

Assuming the following citation for the ordinance below: 27 P.P.C. § 120(B). Note that a marked-up version of this ordinance has been provided. (A marked-up version

---

* Bernard Bell graciously provided a modified version of this hypothetical to me and has graciously allowed me to include it here. He describes how he uses the hypothetical in class in his article, Bernard Bell, "*No More Vehicles in the Park*": *Reviving the Hart-Fuller Debate to Introduce Statutory Construction*, 48 J. LEGAL EDUC. 88, (1998) (citing H.L.A. Hart, *Positivism and the Separation of Law and Morals*, shows amendments made during the enactment process in italics and deletions in strike-though font. After the law is codified, the italics and strike-through are removed). Assume further that there are no other applicable or relevant laws—common, regulatory, or statutory (in other words, no cheating!).

An Ordinance
To Prohibit Motor Vehicles in Pioneer Park
Be it enacted by the Council of the City of Pioneer assembled,

(1) The short title of this ordinance shall be the Pioneer Park Safety Ordinance.

(2) No cars, motorcycles, or other motor vehicles may enter or remain in Pioneer Park, except as provided in section 3 hereof.

(3) Motor vehicles may be used by authorized public groups:

    a. in maintaining Pioneer Park, and

    b. in placing barricades for parades, concerts, or other entertainment in Pioneer Park.

(4) Anyone violating this ordinance shall be subject to a $1,000 fine, provided no injuries occurred. If any injury occurred, the fine shall be doubled.

Effective: August 15, 1998.

Public Parks Committee Report: March 7, 1998

Unlike other local parks, motor vehicles are currently allowed unrestricted access to Pioneer Park. This ordinance will address the recent concerns created by a spat of accidents in Pioneer Park. In two of these accidents, a car struck a pedestrian and another struck a bicyclist on park roads. In the third, a motorcyclist drove off road and hit a pedestrian. This ordinance thus bans all vehicles from entering the park, except for vehicles used in park maintenance and in setting up barricades to control crowds at park festivities and parades. All parades must be authorized before the ordinance allows the use of motor vehicles to place barricades.

The Public Parks Committee recommends that the ordinance be adopted. (mark-up attached).

Marked-up Version of Ordinance:

An Ordinance
To Prohibit Motor Vehicles in Pioneer Park
Be it enacted by the Council of the City of Pioneer assembled,

(1) The short title of this ordinance shall be the Pioneer Park Safety Ordinance.

(2) No cars, motorcycles, or other *motor* vehicles may enter or remain in Pioneer Park, except as provided in section 3 hereof.

---

71 Harv. L. Rev. 593, 607 (1958); Lon L. Fuller, *Positivism and Fidelity to Law—A Reply to Professor Hart*, 71 Harv. L. Rev. 630, 663 (1958)).

(3) *Motor* vehicles may be used by authorized public groups:

    a. in maintaining Pioneer Park, *and*

    b. in placing barricades for parades, concerts, or other entertainment in Pioneer Park.~~, and.~~

    c. ~~Mopeds, skateboards, bicycles, and other such vehicles are exempt.~~

(4) Anyone violating this ordinance shall be subject to a $1,000 fine, provided no injuries occurred. If any injury occurred, the fine shall be doubled.

Summary of the City Council Floor Debate: June 1, 1998

Debate was short and sweet. The majority of council members were in favor of the ordinance. Some discussion arose as to why bicycles, skateboards, and mopeds should be specifically exempted. For reasons that are unclear, that section was eliminated. An amendment was offered to include the word "motor" before "vehicles" in subsections (2) and (3). That amendment passed overwhelmingly. The effects on park revenue, noise, and pollution were briefly discussed. One member was concerned that waterskiing may not be able to continue on Crockett Lake.

A vote was taken; the ordinance passed.

Mayor Poordue's Signing Statement: August 14, 1998

This ordinance directly addresses the noise and pollution concerns that have increased in recent years and will make our public park much safer. The ordinance continues to allow boaters to enjoy water-skiing on the lake, but bans noisy, dangerous vehicles. I am delighted to sign it.

Hypothetical Questions

Assume that you are a prosecutor for the city, it is your first day on the job, and you have been asked to review the following cases to decide whether to prosecute or dismiss the citations. How would you resolve each of them and why? Do you need any more information to decide whether to prosecute? If so, what information do you need?

1. An ambulance entered Pioneer Park to pick up, and take to the hospital, a man who had just suffered a heart attack. Did the ambulance driver violate the Pioneer Park Safety Ordinance (PPSO)? What about the man who suffered the heart attack?

2. A helicopter hovered over Pioneer Park for an hour. Was this a violation of the PPSO? What about a private jet that came in low over Pioneer Park as it approached the local airport? What about someone flying a drone in the park?

3. A chapter of the local Veterans of Foreign Wars wants to put an Iraq War tank in Pioneer Park as a monument. Will this violate the PPSO? Does it matter whether the tank is operable? What if the city council enacted an ordinance after the PPSO was enacted assisting the VFW in the purchase of the tank on the condition that the tank be used as a monument in Pioneer Park?

4. The local utility company enters the park in a utility truck to fix an electrical wire? Does it matter whether the wire issue poses an emergency?

5. Motorboats have been used on the lake within the park (Crockett Lake) for years. The city installed two jumps for water-skiers in 2010, and the city continues to maintain them. The jumps draw a number of water-skiers, and there is a summer competition that brings a lot of revenue into the city. Can motorboats be operated in Crockett Lake after the PPSO was enacted? If motorboats are okay, could someone use a car to bring a boat to the lake? (Assume that using some sort of land-based motorized vehicle is necessary to get a boat into the lake.)

6. Celebration Inc. scheduled a parade in Pioneer Park. The organization failed to apply for the permit required to hold the parade. Celebration Inc. used a truck to place barricades for the parade. Has Celebration Inc. violated the PPSO?

7. Citizens for a Clean Pioneer Park, a group authorized to perform maintenance work, used a riding lawnmower to cut grass in Pioneer Park. Has CCPP violated the PPSO? What if the president of CCPP drove into Pioneer Park to inspect the maintenance work performed by members of CCPP? Did the president violate the PPSO? What if an employee from TreeTrimming, Inc., a company not yet authorized to perform tree-trimming work, drove a maintenance vehicle into the park to provide a bid for the tree trimming and removal? Has the TreeTrimming employee violated the PPSO?

8. A police car entered Pioneer Park while it was chasing a car containing two people who had just robbed a bank. Have the officers violated the PPSO? What about the bank robbers?

* * *

Chapter 2

Separation of Powers

A. Introduction to This Chapter

This chapter introduces you to an important constitutional principle: separation of powers. The Court's jurisprudence in this area neither definitively defines separation of powers, nor consistently applies it. Hence, you will learn about both the formalistic and functionalist approaches the justices have used either to validate or strike down innovative power arrangements. Separation of powers plays an enormously important role in statutory interpretation. Hence, we end the chapter by looking at the role of separation of powers in a statutory interpretation case.

B. Separation of Powers

What is separation of powers? Separation of powers is the idea that the powers of a government should be split between two or more independent groups so that no one group or person can gain too much power. The vesting clauses of the U.S. Federal Constitution split the federal governmental powers among the legislative, executive, and judicial branches. No one branch is more powerful than any other. Legislators make laws, the president executes laws, and judges interpret laws. U.S. CONST. art. 1, §1 ("All legislative Powers herein granted shall be vested in a Congress of the United States, which shall consist of a Senate and House of Representatives."); U.S. CONST. art. II, §1, Cl. 1 ("The executive Power shall be vested in a President of the United States of America."); U.S. CONST. art. III, §1 ("The judicial Power of the United States, shall be vested in one supreme Court, and in such inferior Courts as the Congress may from time to time ordain and establish."). Yet there is overlap. Some overlap is valid. Indeed, our constitutional system is one of checks and balances. Too much overlap is invalid. Just where to draw the line is an issue that implicates separation of powers.

The Supreme Court has approached questions involving separation of powers issues in two different ways, one of which is more accepting of overlap, the other of which is not. Legal scholars have identified these two approaches as *formalism* and *functionalism*. As we begin this discussion of separation of powers, be aware that these categories, as well as the Court's jurisprudence in this area, are imperfect. We will touch just the surface; for additional background on the difference between formalism and functionalism, *see* M. Elizabeth Magill, *The Real Separation in Separation of Powers Law*, 86 VA. L. REV. 1127 (2000) (describing the formalist and functionalist approaches to separation of powers). Let's begin with formalism.

1. Formalism

The *formalist* approach to separation of powers emphasizes the necessity of maintaining three distinct branches of government, each with delegated powers: one branch legislates, one branch executes, and one branch adjudicates. These powers come from the vesting clauses of the U.S. Constitution. Article I vests in Congress "[a]ll legislative Powers herein granted." U.S. Const. art. 1, § 1. Legislative power is the power "to promulgate generalized standards and requirements of citizen behavior or to dispense benefits — to achieve, maintain, or avoid particular social policy results." Martin H. Redish & Elizabeth J. Cisar, *"If Angels Were to Govern": The Need for Pragmatic Formalism in Separation of Powers Theory*, 41 Duke L.J. 449, 479 (1991). Congress therefore not only has the power to create law, but also has the power to create procedural rules to ensure enforcement of those laws. Laws "alter[] the legal rights, duties, and relations of persons ... outside the Legislative Branch." *INS v. Chadha*, 462 U.S. 919, 952 (1983). Congress alters legal rights through enacting, amending, and repealing statutes.

Article II of the Constitution vests "[t]he executive Power ... in a President of the United States of America." U.S. Const. art. II, § 1, cl. 1. Executive acts are those in which an executive official exercises judgment about how to apply law to a given situation. *Bowsher v. Synar*, 478 U.S. 714, 732–33 (1986). For the executive to execute the law there must be existing law to execute. In other words, while the legislature enacts laws, the executive enforces those laws.

Article III of the Constitution vests "[t]he judicial Power of the United States, ... in one supreme Court, and in such inferior Courts as the Congress may from time to time ordain and establish." U.S. Const. art. III, § 1. Judicial power is the power to interpret laws and resolve legal disputes. "[T]o declare what the law is, or has been, is a judicial power, to declare what the law shall be is legislative." *Koshkonong v. Burton*, 104 U.S. 668, 678 (1881) (quoting *Ogden v. Blackledge*, 6 U.S. 272, 277 (1804)). In other words, while the legislature enacts laws, the executive enforces those laws, and the judiciary interprets those laws. Thus, "the interpretation of the laws is the proper and peculiar province of the courts." The Federalist No. 78, at 523, 525 (Alexander Hamilton) (J. Cooke ed. 1961). The judiciary interprets laws by adjudicating cases and rendering dispositive judgments based on findings of law and fact; indeed, this is a court's primary power.

When confronting an issue raising separation of powers concerns, a formalist judge will use a two-step, rule-based approach. First, the judge will identify the power being exercised: legislative, judicial, or executive. Second, the judge will determine whether the appropriate branch is exercising that power in accordance with the Constitution. A formalist judge will therefore focus on the activity at issue by first categorizing it as legislative, executive, or judicial. Next, a judge will analyze whether the appropriate branch is performing the activity. The chart below illustrates formalism in a very simplified way. Each branch may constitutionally perform any function that falls within its corresponding "Acts Circle," but may not constitutionally perform any function that falls within another branch's "Acts Circle."

Formalism

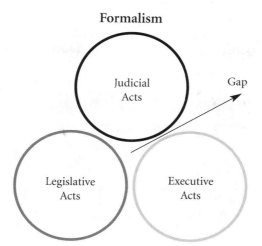

Scalia, thomas, roberts

Under formalism, a branch violates separation of powers when it attempts to exercise a power that is not constitutionally delegated to it (or not within its Acts Circle). Overlap is permitted only when constitutionally prescribed. So, for example, the president and Senate both play a role in appointing principal officers without violating separation of powers, because the Constitution delegates this power to both the executive and legislative branches. U.S. Const. art. II § 2 cl. 2.

When the Supreme Court approaches a separation of powers issue under a formalist approach, the Court regularly strikes down that exercise of power. For example, in *Clinton v. New York*, 524 U.S. 417 (1998), the Court applied a formalist approach to hold that the line-item veto was unconstitutional, because it enabled the executive to unilaterally amend and repeal legislation, a power delegated to the legislature. *Id.* at 447–49. Similarly, the Court struck down legislative veto provisions in *INS v. Chadha*, 462 U.S. 919 (1983). The legislative veto allowed Congress to delegate lawmaking authority to the executive, but reserved, either to a single chamber or to a committee from a single chamber, the power to oversee and veto the executive's use of this delegated authority. Because legislative veto provisions allowed one chamber of Congress to unilaterally amend legislation and, thereby, avoid constitutionally required bicameral passage and presentment, the Court held that these provisions were unconstitutional. *Id.* at 954–55. Justice Burger's majority opinion approached the issue in a classically formalist way.

Additionally, in *Youngstown Sheet & Tube Co. v. Sawyer*, 343 U.S. 579 (1952) (the Steel Seizure Case), the Court held that President Truman's executive order seizing private steel mills during the Korean War was unconstitutional, because it altered private property rights, a power reserved exclusively for Congress. *Id.* at 588–89. To prevent the steel industry from striking and potentially shutting down during the Korean War, President Truman had requested from Congress the authority to seize the mills. Congress refused. The President, in the absence of any specific statutory or constitutional authority, issued the order anyway. Industry sued. The issue for the Court was whether the President, absent any specific authority, had the *inherent* power to issue the order under his constitutional authority to act as Commander-in-Chief and to faithfully execute the laws. In an opinion written by Justice Black, the Court held that the President did not have this power. *Id.* at 582–87.

Under a formalist approach, the Court will generally reject any attempt by one branch to usurp, or take, power from another branch. For example, in *Bowsher v. Synar*, 478 U.S. 714 (1986), the Court held that Congress could not keep removal power over an agency official working within the Government Accountability Office because the agency official exercised executive authority. *Id.* at 726–27. And in *Stern v. Marshall*, 131 S. Ct. 2594 (2011), the Court held that a Bankruptcy Court — an Article I (executive) Court — lacked constitutional power under Article III to resolve a counterclaim based on state law. *Id.* at 2620. The counter-claim involved a long-running inheritance dispute regarding the estate of Texas Billionaire, J. Howard Marshall. Marshall's wife of fourteen months, Anna Nicole Smith, sued Marshall's heir alleging that the 90 year-old billionaire promised her more than $3 million.

Similarly, in *Plaut v. Spendthrift Farm, Inc.*, 514 U.S. 211, 240 (1995), the Court held that Congress could not retroactively require federal courts to reopen a judgment once it was final. Finally, in *United States v. Klein*, 80 U.S. 128, 146 (1871), the Court invalidated a statute that "prescribe[d] rules of decision" for a specific type of case. According to the Court, by prescribing a rule of decision — or an outcome — in a pending case, "Congress [] inadvertently passed the limit which separate[d] the legislative from the judicial power." *Id.* at 147. Although Congress may amend the underlying substantive law to accomplish policy objectives, Congress may not dictate outcomes in particular cases. Because the power to decide cases by interpreting and applying existing law to a specific, factual situation is delegated to the judiciary, Congress violates separation of powers when it attempts to decide cases, reopen final cases, or interfere with a federal court's decision-making process.

As these cases show, formalists are concerned about undue accretion of power to any one branch, no matter how small. The concentration of power in any one branch is viewed as unconstitutional regardless of whether that power is being misused. Formalists believe that accretion of power in and of itself is unacceptable because once power is acquired, it can be difficult to determine whether too much power has been ceded. Perhaps, more critically, formalists are worried that once a branch acquires too much power, it would be too late to remedy the situation. Thus, formalists view separation of powers as a doctrine that is "prophylactic in nature ... designed to avoid a situation in which one might even debate whether an undue accretion of power has taken place." Redish & Cisar, *supra* at 476.

In sum, formalism is an approach that focuses on the separate, constitutionally enumerated powers delegated to each branch in the vesting clauses of the Constitution. Overlap is not permitted for fear that one branch may accrete too much power. When the Court resolves a separation of powers issue using formalism, inevitably, the Court finds the exercise of power unconstitutional.

2. Functionalism

The Supreme Court Justices have never collectively embraced formalism. Rather, the Court has oscillated between formalism and functionalism throughout its history. Indeed, with a government adapted to the complexities of the twenty-first century, functionalism seems to be winning the war. *See, e.g., King v. Burwell*, 135 S. Ct. 2480 (2015) (using a functionalist approach to interpret the Affordable Care Act).

Functionalism's focus differs from that of formalism. While formalists focus on strict separation, functionalists focus on balancing the inevitable overlap of powers to preserve the core *functions* the Constitution assigns to each branch. To maintain a relatively balanced power distribution, functionalists believe that a complete bar against any encroachment between the branches is unnecessary. Instead, functionalists focus on limiting encroachments into the core, constitutionally-appointed functions of each branch. For example, the executive's power of appointment is a core function. U.S. Const. art. II, §2, cl. 2. However, the appointment power is not absolute, as the power applies only to the appointment of *principal* not *inferior* executive officers and is subject to senate approval. Similarly, the Constitution implicitly gives the executive the power to remove executive officers subject to conditions Congress imposes. This power, therefore, is not absolute. Note, however, that although Congress has the authority to place limits on the executive's removal power, Congress does not have the authority to eliminate that power altogether. *Bowsher v. Synar*, 478 U.S. 714, 725–26 (1986); *Myers v. United States*, 272 U.S. 52, 126–27 (1926). We will cover the appointment power more specifically in Chapter 17.

Like formalists, functionalists turn to the vesting clauses of the Constitution to define the most central, core functions of each branch: the legislature legislates, the judiciary adjudicates, and the executive enforces the law. But unlike formalists, functionalists do not compartmentalize these core functions. For example, the legislature's power to make law is a core function. The judiciary, however, also makes law, both by developing common law and by interpreting statutes. Under formalism, this encroachment would likely be sufficient to trigger a separation of powers concern. In contrast, under functionalism, the judiciary's encroachment into a core function of the legislature does not raise concern. To trigger a separation of powers concern under functionalism, one branch would have to *unduly* encroach and aggrandize a core function of another branch.

Functionalists believe that overlap between the branches is practically necessary and even desirable. Functionalists emphasize the need to maintain pragmatic flexibility to respond to the needs of modern government. Indeed, the existence of the administrative system is an example of functionalism. Agencies, which are part of the executive branch, perform all of the functions separately delegated to each of the three branches in the Constitution. (See Chapter 16). Yet, few today would suggest that the exercise of authority by agencies violate separation of powers. *But see* Peter B. McCutchen, *Mistakes, Precedent, and The Rise of the Administrative State: Toward a Constitutional Theory of the Second Best*, 80 Cornell L. Rev. 1, 11 (1994) (arguing that "[u]nder a pure formalist approach, most, if not all, of the administrative state is unconstitutional.").

While both formalism and functionalism share a common goal — to ensure that no one branch acquires too much unilateral power — these approaches go about meeting this goal in different ways. Whereas formalists use a two-step, bright-line-rule approach to categorize acts as legislative, judicial, or executive — functionalists use a factors approach, balancing the competing power interests with the pragmatic need for innovation. Functionalists recognize the government's need for flexibility to create new power-sharing arrangements to address the evolving needs of the modern century. Functionalists do not want to "unduly constrict Congress's ability to take needed and innovative action...." *Commodity Futures Trading Comm'n v. Schor*, 478 U.S. 833, 851 (1986).

To foster flexibility, functionalists focus less on maintaining the separateness of each branch and instead favor the independence of each branch, with oversight from the other branches. This independence is achieved if each branch is able to perform its core functions while also being able to limit the accretion of power by the other branches. Justice Jackson's tripartite framework from his concurrence in *Youngstown Sheet & Tube Co. v. Sawyer*, 343 U.S. 579 (1952), is informative. Justice Jackson suggested that the Court review separation of powers issues differently, based upon the level of cooperation among the branches. Because the case involved President Truman's seizure of the steel mills, the framework specifically addressed executive power, but the analysis applies to all:

> First, "[w]hen the President acts pursuant to an express or implied authorization of Congress, his authority is at its maximum, for it includes all that he possesses in his own right plus all that Congress can delegate." Second, "[w]hen the President acts in absence of either a congressional grant or denial of authority, he can only rely upon his own independent powers, but there is a zone of twilight in which he and Congress may have concurrent authority, or in which its distribution is uncertain." In such a circumstance, Presidential authority can derive support from "congressional inertia, indifference or quiescence." Finally, "[w]hen the President takes measures incompatible with the expressed or implied will of Congress, his power is at its lowest ebb," and the Court can sustain his actions "only by disabling the Congress from acting upon the subject."

Medellín v. Texas, 552 U.S. 491, 494 (2008) (quoting *Youngstown Sheet & Tube Co. v. Sawyer*, 343 U.S. at 635–38 (Jackson, J., concurring)). Simply put: when one branch unilaterally acts against the express or implied will of the other branches, the risk of tyranny is greatest.

While formalism was depicted above as a series of separate circles with no overlap, functionalism might be pictured as a set of interlocking circles, as in the chart below.

Functionalism

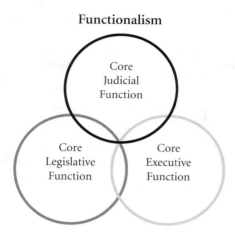

From this chart, it becomes clear that each branch possesses separate, constitutionally assigned, core functions. At the same time, each branch also has a penumbra of overlap (the zone of twilight) that shades gradually into the core functions of the other two branches. So long as the branches steer relatively clear of the other branches' core functions, and so long as the branches do not enlarge the size of their own circle at the expense of another branch's circle, functionalist separation of powers is maintained.

With this visual, you may also notice that there is a gap inside the three separate, formalism circles. This gap disappears in the interlocking circles of functionalism. Agencies are often thought of as gap-fillers: agencies act in the interstitial gaps left by Congress.

Almost exclusively, when the Court approaches a separation of powers issue under a functionalist approach, the Court approves the exercise of that branch's power. For example, in *Commodity Futures Trading Commission v. Schor*, 478 U.S. 833 (1986), the Court held that Congress can delegate to the executive the power to adjudicate a "particularized area of law," specifically common law counterclaims. *Id.* at 852–57. According to the Court, the power arrangement "raise[ed] no question of the aggrandizement of congressional power at the expense of a coordinate branch." *Id.* at 856. In other words, separation of powers was not violated simply because Congress enabled the executive to encroach on a judicial function. The Court required a concurrent finding that Congress had correspondingly expanded, or aggrandized, the executive's power before finding a separation of powers violation. *Id.* at 856–57. To illustrate, under a formalist approach, the Court had earlier denied a broader judicial power grant to a non-Article III bankruptcy court. *Northern Pipeline Constr. Co. v. Marathon Pipe Line Co.*, 458 U.S. 50, 57–58 (1982). But in *Schor*, the Court distinguished *Northern Pipeline* by saying that "the [Act at issue] leaves far more of the "'essential attributes of judicial power' to Article III courts than did that portion of the Bankruptcy Act found unconstitutional in *Northern Pipeline*." *Schor*, 478 U.S. at 852. In short, the power transfer in *Schor* was not intrusive enough to raise concerns about aggrandizement.

To illustrate further, the Court has approved Congress's delegation of limited legislative-like powers to the judiciary. In *Mistretta v. United States*, 488 U.S. 361, 368 (1989), the Court upheld the constitutionality of the U.S. Sentencing Commission, even though three of the seven proposed commissioners were sitting federal judges. The Court was unconcerned that members of the judiciary would be making law by drafting sentencing guidelines. The Court reasoned that drafting sentencing guidelines was similar to establishing court rules; therefore, "the Commission's functions ... [were] clearly attendant to a central element of the historically acknowledged mission of the Judicial Branch." *Id.* at 391. Hence, the intrusion was acceptable because it was minimal and already tolerated in other areas. *See, e.g., Free Enterprise Fund v. Public Co. Accounting Oversight Bd.*, 561 U.S. 477, 520 (2010) (Breyer, J., dissenting) (noting that the Court has "looked to function and context, and not to bright-line rules" when resolving separation of powers cases).

In summary, functionalists take a pragmatic view of separation of powers and seek to avoid the aggrandizement of a branch at the expense of another branch. Whereas formalists ask what kind of power is being wielded and whether the appropriate branch is wielding that power, functionalists ask whether one branch has encroached into the core functions of another branch and thereby aggrandized power for itself. To illustrate:

> [I]f the Supreme Court were to void a presidential pardon because it was given for improper motives, ... if the Court were to void a Senate impeachment proceeding because it had defects, ... [i]f the Court were to order the President to dismiss a Secretary of State who was facing criminal proceedings, the Court would violate the principal of separation of powers.

Aharon Barak, *Foreword: A Judge on Judging: The Role of a Supreme Court in a Democracy*, 116 HARV. L. REV. 16, 122 (2002). In all of these examples, the issue would not be whether the Court had the power to act. The Court likely has the power to require the executive and legislature to obey the Constitution. Rather, the issue would be whether, in doing so, the Court would impede the executive or legislature's ability to carry out their respective core functions and, in the process, aggrandize the Court's own role. At bottom, power given or taken by one branch must not "intru[de] on the authority and functions of [another] Branch." *Nixon v. Fitzgerald*, 457 U.S. 731, 754 (1982). Intrusions that impair another branch's ability to perform core functions are unconstitutional unless the "impact is justified by an overriding need to promote objectives within the constitutional authority of Congress." *Nixon v. Administrator of General Servs.*, 433 U.S. 425, 433 (1977).

Finally, it is important to know that, while the Founders were indeed concerned about the concentration of governmental power in any one of the three branches, they were primarily concerned with congressional self-aggrandizement. In keeping with this concern, the Court more closely scrutinizes legislation that expands Congress's authority rather than the authority of the other branches. The Court has been more accepting of judicial and executive aggrandizement. Indeed, at least one commentator has suggested that the Court uses formalism when Congress overreaches and uses functionalism when the judiciary or executive overreach. Ronald J. Kroto-szynski, *On the Danger of Wearing Two Hats: Mistretta and Morrison Revisited*, 38 Wm. & Mary L. Rev. 417, 460 (1997). In the case below, see if you can identify the formalist and functionalist reasoning of the justices. Is this an instance of congressional aggrandizement or another form of aggrandizement?

INS v. Chadha

Formalist Supreme Court of the United States
462 U.S. 919 (1983)

♦ Justice Burger delivered the opinion of the Court [in which Brennan, Marshall, Blackmun, Stevens, and O'Connor, JJ., concur].

[This case] presents a challenge to the constitutionality of the provision in § 244(c)(2) of the Immigration and Nationality Act, 8 U.S.C. § 1254(c)(2), authorizing one House of Congress, by resolution, to invalidate the decision of the Executive Branch ... to allow a particular deportable alien to remain in the United States.

[Chadha was an East Indian, born in Kenya. After his student visa expired, the Immigration and Naturalization Service (INS) began deportation proceedings. Chadha conceded that he was deportable for overstaying his visa; however, he applied to INS to suspend his deportation under § 244(a)(1), which permits a person to remain in the Country in cases of extreme hardship. After a hearing, the INS granted the application. The Attorney General accepted the decision and submitted it to Congress for possible "veto" under § 244(c)(2).]

Section 244(c)(2) provides:

"(2) In the case of an alien specified in paragraph (1) of subsection (a) of this subsection —

if ... either the Senate or the House of Representatives passes a resolution stating in substance that it does not favor the suspension of such deportation, the Attorney General shall thereupon deport such alien or authorize the alien's voluntary departure at his own expense....

[The House, without debate or recorded vote, passed a resolution of disapproval of the Attorney General's decision regarding Chadha.]. Since the House action was pursuant to § 244(c)(2), the resolution was not treated as an Article I legislative act; it was not submitted to the Senate or presented to the President for his action....

... [Chadha challenged the constitutionality of the provision both before the INS, and then to the appellate court. T]he Court of Appeals held that the House was without constitutional authority to order Chadha's deportation.... The essence of its holding was that § 244(c)(2) violates the constitutional doctrine of separation of powers. We granted certiorari ... and we now affirm....

Justice White undertakes to make a case for the proposition that the one-House veto is a useful "political invention," and we need not challenge that assertion. We can even concede this utilitarian argument although the long range political wisdom of this "invention" is arguable.... But policy arguments supporting even useful "political inventions" are subject to the demands of the Constitution which defines powers and, with respect to this subject, sets out just how those powers are to be exercised.

Explicit and unambiguous provisions of the Constitution prescribe and define the respective functions of the Congress and of the Executive in the legislative process. Since the precise terms of those familiar provisions are critical to the resolution of this case, we set them out verbatim. Art. I provides:

> "All legislative Powers herein granted shall be vested in a Congress of the United States, which shall consist of a Senate *and* a House of Representatives." Art. I, § 1. (Emphasis added).

> "Every Bill which shall have passed the House of Representatives *and* the Senate, *shall,* before it becomes a Law, be presented to the President of the United States; ..." Art. I, § 7, cl. 2. (Emphasis added).

> "*Every* Order, Resolution, or Vote to which the Concurrence of the Senate and House of Representatives may be necessary (except on a question of Adjournment) *shall be* presented to the President of the United States; and before the Same shall take Effect, *shall be* approved by him, or being disapproved by him, *shall be* repassed by two thirds of the Senate and House of Representatives, according to the Rules and Limitations prescribed in the Case of a Bill." Art. I, § 7, cl. 3. (Emphasis added).

These provisions of Art. I are integral parts of the constitutional design for the separation of powers. We have recently noted that "[t]he principle of separation of powers was not simply an abstract generalization in the minds of the Framers: it was woven into the documents that they drafted in Philadelphia in the summer of 1787." ... [W]e find that the purposes underlying the Presentment Clauses, Art. I, § 7, cls. 2, 3, and the bicameral requirement of Art. I, § 1 and § 7, cl. 2, guide our resolution of the important question presented in this case. The very structure of the articles delegating and separating powers under Arts. I, II, and III exemplify the concept of separation of powers and we now turn to Art. I.

The Presentment Clauses

The records of the Constitutional Convention reveal that the requirement that all legislation be presented to the President before becoming law was uniformly accepted by the Framers. Presentment to the President and the Presidential veto were considered so imperative that the draftsmen took special pains to assure that these requirements could not be circumvented. During the final debate on Art. I, § 7, cl. 2, James Madison expressed concern that it might easily be evaded by the simple expedient of calling a proposed law a "resolution" or "vote" rather than a "bill." As a consequence, Art. I, § 7, cl. 3 was added.

The decision to provide the President with a limited and qualified power to nullify proposed legislation by veto was based on the profound conviction of the Framers that the powers conferred on Congress were the powers to be most carefully circumscribed. It is beyond doubt that lawmaking was a power to be shared by both Houses and the President....

The President's role in the lawmaking process also reflects the Framers' careful efforts to check whatever propensity a particular Congress might have to enact oppressive, improvident, or ill-considered measures....

Bicameralism

The bicameral requirement of Art. I, §§ 1, 7 was of scarcely less concern to the Framers than was the Presidential veto and indeed the two concepts are interdependent. By providing that no law could take effect without the concurrence of the prescribed majority of the Members of both Houses, the Framers reemphasized their belief, already remarked upon in connection with the Presentment Clauses, that legislation should not be enacted unless it has been carefully and fully considered by the Nation's elected officials....

... The division of the Congress into two distinctive bodies assures that the legislative power would be exercised only after opportunity for full study and debate in separate settings.... It emerges clearly that the prescription for legislative action in Art. I, §§ 1, 7 represents the Framers' decision that the legislative power of the Federal government be exercised in accord with a single, finely wrought and exhaustively considered, procedure.

The Constitution sought to divide the delegated powers of the new federal government into three defined categories, legislative, executive and judicial, to assure, as nearly as possible, that each Branch of government would confine itself to its assigned responsibility. The hydraulic pressure inherent within each of the separate Branches to exceed the outer limits of its power, even to accomplish desirable objectives, must be resisted.

Although not "hermetically" sealed from one another, the powers delegated to the three Branches are functionally identifiable. When any Branch acts, it is presumptively exercising the power the Constitution has delegated to it. When the Executive acts, it presumptively acts in an executive or administrative capacity as defined in Art. II. And when, as here, one House of Congress purports to act, it is presumptively acting within its assigned sphere.

Beginning with this presumption, we must nevertheless establish that the challenged action under § 244(c)(2) is of the kind to which the procedural requirements of Art. I, § 7 apply. Not every action taken by either House is subject to the bicameralism and presentment requirements of Art. I. Whether actions taken by either House are, in law and fact, an exercise of legislative power depends not on their form but upon "whether they contain matter which is properly to be regarded as legislative in its character and effect."

Examination of the action taken here by one House pursuant to § 244(c)(2) reveals that it was essentially legislative in purpose and effect. In purporting to exercise power defined in Art. I, § 8, cl. 4 to "establish an uniform Rule of Naturalization," the House took action that had the purpose and effect of altering the legal rights, duties and relations of persons.... Congress has *acted* and its action has altered Chadha's status....

There is no case in controversy

The nature of the decision implemented by the one-House veto in this case further manifests its legislative character. After long experience with the clumsy, time consuming private bill procedure, Congress made a deliberate choice to delegate to the Executive Branch, and specifically to the Attorney General, the authority to allow deportable aliens to remain in this country in certain specified circumstances. It is not disputed that this choice to delegate authority is precisely the kind of decision that can be implemented only in accordance with the procedures set out in Art. I. Disagreement with the Attorney General's decision on Chadha's deportation — that is, Congress' decision to deport Chadha — no less than Congress' original choice to delegate to the Attorney General the authority to make that decision, involves determinations of policy that Congress can implement in only one way; bicameral passage followed by presentment to the President. Congress must abide by its delegation of authority until that delegation is legislatively altered or revoked....

Since it is clear that the action by the House under §244(c)(2) was not within any of the express constitutional exceptions authorizing one House to act alone, and equally clear that it was an exercise of legislative power, that action was subject to the standards prescribed in Article I.[22] ...

The choices we discern as having been made in the Constitutional Convention impose burdens on governmental processes that often seem clumsy, inefficient, even unworkable, but those hard choices were consciously made by men who had lived under a form of government that permitted arbitrary governmental acts to go unchecked. There is no support in the Constitution or decisions of this Court for the proposition that the cumbersomeness and delays often encountered in complying with explicit Constitutional standards may be avoided, either by the Congress or by the President. With all the obvious flaws of delay, untidiness, and potential for abuse, we have not yet found a better way to preserve freedom than by making the exercise of power subject to the carefully crafted restraints spelled out in the Constitution.

We hold that the Congressional veto provision in §244(c)(2) ... is unconstitutional. Accordingly, the judgment of the Court of Appeals is

---

22. Justice Powell's position is that the one-House veto in this case is a *judicial* act and therefore unconstitutional as beyond the authority vested in Congress by the Constitution. We agree that there is a sense in which one-House action pursuant to §244(c)(2) has a judicial cast, since it purports to "review" Executive action.... But the attempted analogy between judicial action and the one-House veto is less than perfect. Federal courts do not enjoy a roving mandate to correct alleged excesses of administrative agencies; we are limited by Art. III to hearing cases and controversies and no justiciable case or controversy was presented by the Attorney General's decision to allow Chadha to remain in this country. We are aware of no decision, and Justice POWELL has cited none, where a federal court has reviewed a decision of the Attorney General suspending deportation of an alien pursuant to the standards set out in §244(a)(1). This is not surprising, given that no party to such action has either the motivation or the right to appeal from it.... Thus, Justice Powell's statement that the one-House veto in this case is "clearly adjudicatory," simply is not supported by his accompanying assertion that the House has "assumed a function ordinarily entrusted to the federal courts." We are satisfied that the one-House veto is legislative in purpose and effect and subject to the procedures set out in Art. I.

House of Reps.

Affirmed.

♦ JUSTICE POWELL, concurring in the judgment.

The Court's decision … apparently will invalidate every use of the legislative veto. The breadth of this holding gives one pause. Congress has included the veto in literally hundreds of statutes, dating back to the 1930s. Congress clearly views this procedure as essential to controlling the delegation of power to administrative agencies. One reasonably may disagree with Congress' assessment of the veto's utility, but the respect due its judgment as a coordinate branch of Government cautions that our holding should be no more extensive than necessary to decide this case. In my view, the case may be decided on a narrower ground. When Congress finds that a particular person does not satisfy the statutory criteria for permanent residence in this country it has assumed a judicial function in violation of the principle of separation of powers. Accordingly, I concur only in the judgment. …

The Constitution does not establish three branches with precisely defined boundaries. Rather, as Justice Jackson wrote, "[w]hile the Constitution diffuses power the better to secure liberty, it also contemplates that practice will integrate the dispersed powers into a workable government. It enjoins upon its branches separateness but interdependence, autonomy but reciprocity." *Youngstown Sheet & Tube Co. v. Sawyer,* 343 U.S. 579, 635 (1952) (concurring opinion). The Court thus has been mindful that the boundaries between each branch should be fixed "according to common sense and the inherent necessities of the governmental co-ordination." But where one branch has impaired or sought to assume a power central to another branch, the Court has not hesitated to enforce the doctrine. …

On its face, the House's action appears clearly adjudicatory. The House did not enact a general rule; rather it made its own determination that [Chadha] did not comply with certain statutory criteria. It thus undertook the type of decision that traditionally has been left to other branches. Even if the House did not make a *de novo* determination, but simply reviewed the Immigration and Naturalization Service's findings, it still assumed a function ordinarily entrusted to the federal courts.[8] Where, as here, Congress has exercised a power "that cannot possibly be regarded as merely in aid of the legislative function of Congress," the decisions of this Court have held that Congress impermissibly assumed a function that the Constitution entrusted to another branch.

---

8. The Court reasons in response to this argument that the one-house veto exercised in this case was not judicial in nature because the decision of the Immigration and Naturalization Service did not present a justiciable issue that could have been reviewed by a court on appeal. The Court notes that since the administrative agency decided the case in favor of Chadha, there was no aggrieved party who could appeal. Reliance by the Court on this fact misses the point. Even if review of the particular decision to suspend deportation is not committed to the courts, the House of Representatives assumed a function that generally is entrusted to an impartial tribunal. In my view, the legislative branch in effect acted as an appellate court by overruling the Service's application of established law to Chadha. And unlike a court or an administrative agency, it did not provide Chadha with the right to counsel or a hearing before acting. …

The impropriety of the House's assumption of this function is confirmed by the fact that its action raises the very danger the Framers sought to avoid—the exercise of unchecked power. In deciding whether Chadha deserves to be deported, Congress is not subject to any internal constraints that prevent it from arbitrarily depriving him of the right to remain in this country. Unlike the judiciary or an administrative agency, Congress is not bound by established substantive rules. Nor is it subject to the procedural safeguards, such as the right to counsel and a hearing before an impartial tribunal, that are present when a court or an agency adjudicates individual rights. The only effective constraint on Congress' power is political, but Congress is most accountable politically when it prescribes rules of general applicability. When it decides rights of specific persons, those rights are subject to "the tyranny of a shifting majority."

... In my view, when Congress undertook to apply its rules to Chadha, it exceeded the scope of its constitutionally prescribed authority....

• JUSTICE WHITE, dissenting. Functionalist

Today the Court not only invalidates § 244(c)(2) of the Immigration and Nationality Act, but also sounds the death knell for nearly 200 other statutory provisions in which Congress has reserved a "legislative veto." For this reason, the Court's decision is of surpassing importance. And it is for this reason that the Court would have been well-advised to decide the case, if possible, on the narrower grounds of separation of powers....

The prominence of the legislative veto mechanism in our contemporary political system and its importance to Congress can hardly be overstated. It has become a central means by which Congress secures the accountability of executive and independent agencies. Without the legislative veto, Congress is faced with a Hobson's choice: either to refrain from delegating the necessary authority, leaving itself with a hopeless task of writing laws with the requisite specificity to cover endless special circumstances across the entire policy landscape, or in the alternative, to abdicate its law-making function to the executive branch and independent agencies. To choose the former leaves major national problems unresolved; to opt for the latter risks unaccountable policymaking by those not elected to fill that role. Accordingly, over the past five decades, the legislative veto has been placed in nearly 200 statutes....

... [T]he legislative veto is more than "efficient, convenient, and useful." It is an important if not indispensable political invention that allows the President and Congress to resolve major constitutional and policy differences, assures the accountability of independent regulatory agencies, and preserves Congress' control over lawmaking. Perhaps there are other means of accommodation and accountability, but the increasing reliance of Congress upon the legislative veto suggests that the alternatives to which Congress must now turn are not entirely satisfactory.

The history of the legislative veto also makes clear that it has not been a sword with which Congress has struck out to aggrandize itself at the expense of the other branches—the concerns of Madison and Hamilton. Rather, the veto has been a means of defense, a reservation of ultimate authority necessary if Congress is to fulfill its designated role under Article I as the nation's lawmaker. While the President has often objected to particular legislative vetoes, generally those left in the hands of congressional committees, the Executive has more often agreed to legislative review as the price for a broad delegation of authority. To be sure, the President may have preferred unrestricted power, but that could be precisely why Congress thought it essential to retain a check on the exercise of delegated authority.

For all these reasons, the apparent sweep of the Court's decision today is regrettable. The Court's Article I analysis appears to invalidate all legislative vetoes irrespective of form or subject. Because the legislative veto is commonly found as a check upon rulemaking by administrative agencies and upon broad-based policy decisions of the Executive Branch, it is particularly unfortunate that the Court reaches its decision in a case involving the exercise of a veto over deportation decisions regarding particular individuals. Courts should always be wary of striking statutes as unconstitutional; to strike an entire class of statutes based on consideration of a somewhat atypical and more-readily indictable exemplar of the class is irresponsible....

If the legislative veto were as plainly unconstitutional as the Court strives to suggest, its broad ruling today would be more comprehensible. But, the constitutionality of the legislative veto is anything but clearcut. The issue divides scholars, courts, attorneys general, and the two other branches of the National Government....

The ... constitutional question posed today is one of immense difficulty over which the executive and legislative branches — as well as scholars and judges — have understandably disagreed. That disagreement stems from the silence of the Constitution on the precise question: The Constitution does not directly authorize or prohibit the legislative veto. Thus, our task should be to determine whether the legislative veto is consistent with the purposes of Art. I and the principles of Separation of Powers which are reflected in that Article and throughout the Constitution....

The Court holds that the disapproval of a suspension of deportation by the resolution of one House of Congress is an exercise of legislative power without compliance with the prerequisites for lawmaking set forth in Art. I of the Constitution. Specifically, the Court maintains that the provisions of § 244(c)(2) are inconsistent with the requirement of bicameral approval, implicit in Art. I, § 1, and the requirement that all bills and resolutions that require the concurrence of both Houses be presented to the President, Art. I, § 7, cl. 2 and 3.

I do not dispute the Court's truismatic exposition of these clauses ...

It does not, however, answer the constitutional question before us. The power to exercise a legislative veto is not the power to write new law without bicameral approval or presidential consideration. The veto must be authorized by statute and may only negative what an Executive department or independent agency has proposed. On its face, the legislative veto no more allows one House of Congress to make law than does the presidential veto confer such power upon the President....

[Our earlier cases] establish that by virtue of congressional delegation, legislative power can be exercised by independent agencies and Executive departments without the passage of new legislation. For some time, the sheer amount of law—the substantive rules that regulate private conduct and direct the operation of government—made by the agencies has far outnumbered the lawmaking engaged in by Congress through the traditional process....

If Congress may delegate lawmaking power to independent and executive agencies, it is most difficult to understand Article I as forbidding Congress from also reserving a check on legislative power for itself. Absent the veto, the agencies receiving delegations of legislative or quasi-legislative power may issue regulations having the force of law without bicameral approval and without the President's signature. It is thus not apparent why the reservation of a veto over the exercise of that legislative power must be subject to a more exacting test. In both cases, it is enough that the initial statutory authorizations comply with the Article I requirements....

The central concern of the presentation and bicameralism requirements of Article I is ... fully satisfied by the operation of § 244(c)(2). The President's approval is found in the Attorney General's action in recommending to Congress that the deportation order for a given alien be suspended. The House and the Senate indicate their approval of the Executive's action by not passing a resolution of disapproval within the statutory period.... Thus understood, § 244(c)(2) fully effectuates the purposes of the bicameralism and presentation requirements....

I regret that I am in disagreement with my colleagues on the fundamental questions that this case presents. But even more I regret the destructive scope of the Court's holding. It reflects a profoundly different conception of the Constitution than that held by the Courts which sanctioned the modern administrative state. Today's decision strikes down in one fell swoop provisions in more laws enacted by Congress than the Court has cumulatively invalidated in its history. I fear it will now be more difficult "to insure that the fundamental policy decisions in our society will be made not by an appointed official but by the body immediately responsible to the people," I must dissent.

◆ [JUSTICE REHNQUIST's dissenting opinion, with which JUSTICE WHITE joins, is omitted.]

* * *

Points for Discussion

1. *Formalism & Functionalism*: Which opinions used formalistic analysis? Which used functionalist analysis?

2. *Types of Violations*: As Justice Powell noted, separation of powers may be violated in two ways. One branch may interfere impermissibly with the other's performance of its constitutionally assigned function. *See, e.g., Nixon v. Administrator of General Servs.,* 433 U.S. 425 (1974). Alternatively, the doctrine may be violated when one branch assumes a function that more properly is entrusted to another.

See, e.g., Youngstown Sheet & Tube Co. v. Sawyer, 343 U.S., at 587. Which intrusion was at issue in this case?

3. *Holding*: Why did the legislative veto violate separation of powers, according to the majority? Why was the legislative veto legitimate according to the dissent? Why, according to Justice White, was the legislative veto practically necessary?

4. *Legislative or Judicial Power*: The majority categorized the legislative veto as a legislative power. Why? Justice Powell categorized the power as judicial. Why? Given that the majority and Justice Powell reached the same result, does their disagreement on this issue matter?

5. *Narrowing the Holding*: Both Justice Powell and Justice White urged the majority to decide the case more narrowly. Justice White lamented the overruling of more than 200 such provisions in statutes enacted for the prior fifty years. Given the majority's reasoning, could the majority have decided the case more narrowly? Assuming the majority's opinion is the correct one, should it matter that Congress enacted so many such provisions?

6. *Corrections Day*: Justice White was concerned about congressional delegation as a result of this opinion. He need not have worried. After *Chadha*, Congress made some changes to reassert its authority over agency decision-making. In 1995, the House instituted the now largely defunct process known as "Corrections Day." The purpose of Corrections day, or the corrections calendar, was to allow the House to correct expeditiously errors made by both Congress and agencies. The process is straightforward: After a House committee approves a bill, the committee can request that the bill be placed on the corrections calendar. The corrections calendar occurs once a month; amendments and debate are limited to allow expeditious review. The Senate has no comparable procedure. "Announced to great fanfare … [i]t has had virtually no effect on agency regulations and certainly did not reestablish any form of legislative check on [agency] regulations." WILLIAM F. FUNK, ET AL., ADMINISTRATIVE PROCEDURE AND PRACTICE: PROBLEMS AND CASES 582 (5th 2014).

7. *Congressional Review Act*: In 1996, Congress enacted the Congressional Review Act, under which agencies must send all new rules to the Comptroller General. 5 U.S.C. §§ 801–08 (1996). Major rules are stayed for sixty days, subject to some exceptions. A major rule is one whose annual economic impact is greater than $100 million. If desired, the Congress can use a fast-track process to pass a joint resolution disapproving the rule, which must be signed by the president. Since its enactment, Congress has only "vetoed" one agency regulation: a regulation adopted by the Secretary of Labor in the final days of the Clinton administration. The regulation would have required workplaces to address ergonomic issues such as carpal tunnel syndrome. When Republicans assumed control of the white house and Congress, they killed the regulation.

Senator Rand Paul introduced legislation in the House known as the REINS Act (Regulations from the Executive in Need of Scrutiny Act), which would amend

[handwritten margin note: equivalent to Leg. veto Just with both*]*

the Congressional Review Act such that Congress would have to approve all major agency rules before they took effect. While the republican controlled House passed this bill in 2011, 2013, and 2015, it has so far not passed in the Senate. The Senate recently turned republican too, so passage is now more likely; however, the White House has threatened to veto the act if passed.

* * *

C. Separation of Powers and Statutory Interpretation

Above, you learned about separation of powers in general. Now, let's explore the role that separation of powers plays in statutory interpretation. Separation of powers underlies all aspects of statutory interpretation. While separation of powers does not inform the meaning of a statute *per se*, it plays a strong supporting role. Let's return to the excerpt from *Yates v. United States*, 135 S. Ct. 1074 (2015), contained in Chapter 1. A brief section of Justice Ginsburg's majority opinion is included below to help you remember the facts. Focus your attention, however, on Justice Kagan's dissent. Notice how she explains what she believes is the proper judicial role during statutory interpretation.

Yates v. United States

Supreme Court of the United States
135 S. Ct. 1074 (2015)

◆ Justice Ginsburg delivered the opinion of the Court [in which Roberts, C.J., and Breyer and Sotomayor, JJ., joined].

John Yates, a commercial fisherman, caught undersized red grouper in federal waters in the Gulf of Mexico. To prevent federal authorities from confirming that he had harvested undersized fish, Yates ordered a crew member to toss the suspect catch into the sea. For this offense, he was charged with, and convicted of, violating 18 U. S. C. § 1519, which provides:

> "Whoever knowingly alters, destroys, mutilates, conceals, covers up, falsifies, or makes a false entry in any record, document, or tangible object with the intent to impede, obstruct, or influence the investigation or proper administration of any matter within the jurisdiction of any department or agency of the United States or any case filed under title 11, or in relation to or contemplation of any such matter or case, shall be fined under this title, imprisoned not more than 20 years, or both." ...

... Finally, if our recourse to traditional tools of statutory construction leaves any doubt about the meaning of "tangible object," as that term is used in § 1519, we would invoke the rule that "ambiguity concerning the ambit of criminal statutes should be resolved in favor of lenity." That interpretative principle is relevant here, where the

Government urges a reading of § 1519 that exposes individuals to 20-year prison sentences for tampering with *any* physical object that *might* have evidentiary value in *any* federal investigation into *any* offense, no matter whether the investigation is pending or merely contemplated, or whether the offense subject to investigation is criminal or civil. In determining the meaning of "tangible object" in § 1519, "it is appropriate, before we choose the harsher alternative, to require that Congress should have spoken in language that is clear and definite."[8] ...

♦ [JUSTICE ALITO's concurring opinion of is omitted.].

♦ KAGAN, J., with whom JUSTICES SCALIA, KENNEDY, AND THOMAS join, dissenting.

If none of the traditional tools of statutory interpretation can produce [the plurality's] result [that fish are not tangible objects], then what accounts for it? The plurality offers a clue when it emphasizes the disproportionate penalties § 1519 imposes if the law is read broadly. Section 1519, the plurality objects, would then "expose[] individuals to 20-year prison sentences for tampering with *any* physical object that *might* have evidentiary value in *any* federal investigation into *any* offense." That brings to the surface the real issue: over criminalization and excessive punishment in the U. S. Code. Now as to this statute, I think the plurality somewhat—though only somewhat—exaggerates the matter. The plurality omits from its description of § 1519 the requirement that a person act "knowingly" and with "the intent to impede, obstruct, or influence" federal law enforcement. And in highlighting § 1519's maximum penalty, the plurality glosses over the absence of any prescribed minimum. (Let's not forget that Yates's sentence was not 20 years, but 30 days.) Congress presumably enacts laws with high maximums and no minimums when it thinks the prohibited conduct may run the gamut from major to minor. That is assuredly true of acts obstructing justice. Compare this case with the following, all of which properly come within, but now fall outside, § 1519: *McRae*, (burning human body to thwart murder investigation); *Maury*, (altering cement mixer to impede inquiry into amputation of employee's fingers); *United States* v. *Natal*, (repainting van to cover up evidence of fatal arson). Most district judges, as Congress knows, will recognize differences between such cases and prosecutions like this one, and will try to make the punishment fit the crime. Still and all, I tend to think, for the reasons the plurality gives, that § 1519 is a bad law—too broad and undifferentiated, with too-high maximum penalties, which give

---

8. The dissent cites *United States* v. *McRae*, *United States* v. *Maury*, and *United States* v. *Natal*, as cases that would not be covered by § 1519 as we read it. Those cases supply no cause for concern that persons who commit "major" obstructive acts will go unpunished. The defendant in *McRae*, a police officer who seized a car containing a corpse and then set it on fire, was also convicted for that conduct under 18 U. S. C. §844(h) and sentenced to a term of 120 months' imprisonment for that offense. The defendant in *Natal*, who repainted a van to cover up evidence of a fatal arson, was also convicted of three counts of violating 18 U. S. C. §3 and sentenced to concurrent terms of 174 months' imprisonment. And the defendant in *Maury*, a company convicted under § 1519 of concealing evidence that a cement mixer's safety lock was disabled when a worker's fingers were amputated, was also convicted of numerous other violations, including three counts of violating 18 U. S. C. § 1505 for concealing evidence of other worker safety violations. For those violations, the company was fined millions of dollars and ordered to operate under the supervision of a court-appointed monitor.

prosecutors too much leverage and sentencers too much discretion. And I'd go further: In those ways, § 1519 is unfortunately not an outlier, but an emblem of a deeper pathology in the federal criminal code.

But whatever the wisdom or folly of § 1519, this Court does not get to rewrite the law. "Resolution of the pros and cons of whether a statute should sweep broadly or narrowly is for Congress." If judges disagree with Congress's choice, we are perfectly entitled to say so—in lectures, in law review articles, and even in dicta. But we are not entitled to replace the statute Congress enacted with an alternative of our own design.

I respectfully dissent.

* * *

Points for Discussion

1. *Statutory Language*: What is the language at issue? What did Yates argue that language means? What did the government argue that language means? What interpretation did the plurality adopt? The dissent?

2. *Rule of Lenity*: Justice Ginsburg pointed to the rule of lenity to support the plurality's decision. The rule of lenity is a policy-based canon that is based on Constitutional due process concerns. The rule of lenity directs that when there is more than one reasonable interpretation of an ambiguous statute, the court should adopt the less penal interpretation. *See Liparota* v. *United States*, 471 U. S. 419, 427 (1985) ("Application of the rule of lenity ensures that criminal statutes will provide fair warning concerning conduct rendered illegal and strikes the appropriate balance between the legislature, the prosecutor, and the court in defining criminal liability."). We cover the rule of lenity in Chapter 15. Justice Kagan did not actually respond to Justice Ginsburg's rule of lenity argument, likely because Justice Kagan did not find the statutory language to be ambiguous. Instead, Justice Kagan accused Justice Ginsburg of rewriting a law she did not like to reach a better outcome. Is Justice Kagan's criticism fair? Is not Justice Kagan ignoring the rule of lenity?

3. *Footnote 8*: What was the point that Justice Ginsburg made in footnote 8? Do you find that it answers Justice Kagan's concerns about separation of powers?

4. *Bad Laws*: Who should fix "bad" laws? Justice Kagan agreed with Justice Ginsburg that this law is overly broad and poorly drafted. Why was that not enough in Justice Kagan's opinion to interpret the law narrowly or, at least, to find Yates innocent? Does it matter why a law is "bad"?

5. *Formalism & Functionalism*: Does Justice Kagan's dissent sound more formalistic or functional? Why?

* * *

Let's dig a little deeper. To understand the role of separation of powers in statutory interpretation, a little history is in order. England's system of government is very different from ours. In early English history, judges created law. The King and Parliament ran the country and only rarely enacted statutes to modify judge-made common law. The American system is based, in part, on the English system; thus, early American judges similarly developed law through the courts. In the nineteenth century, law developed almost exclusively in this way. Judge-made law, known as common law,* was the norm. Statutes were uncommon; those statutes that did exist were private (meaning they applied only to specific individuals) not public (meaning they applied to all individuals). Legislators, who worked primarily part-time, were considered to be uneducated, unsophisticated, and subject to political pressure. Indeed, a holdover custom from these early days is that a bill must be read three times before it is enacted to ensure that any representatives who are illiterate know what they are enacting! Thus, in early American history, statutes were viewed with hostility and suspicion. It was during this time that the judiciary developed the canon that statutes in derogation of the common law should be strictly construed (*See* Chapter 15). Also during this time, United States legal education was developing into its current form: the case method. The "inventor" of case method instruction, Christopher Langdell, believed that statutes were not true "law" and that only judicially created common law was worthy enough to be studied.

Things quickly changed. In the late nineteenth century, legislatures became more prolific, and legislation became more generally applicable. Today, legislation is pervasive and detailed. For example, let's compare the Sherman Act, which was enacted in 1890, with the Patient Protection and Affordable Care Act (known pejoratively as "Obamacare" or "the ACA"), which was enacted in 2010. The Sherman Act is a comprehensive and expansive act regulating federal antitrust activity, and yet it fits onto a single page. Congress left significant room for judicial development. In contrast, the ACA spans 906 pages. Congress left little room for judicial development.

> Statutes like the Sherman Act, the civil rights legislation, and the mail fraud statute were written in broad general language on the understanding that the courts would have wide latitude in construing them to achieve the remedial purposes that Congress had identified. The wide open spaces in statutes such as these are most appropriately interpreted as implicit delegations of authority to the courts to fill in the gaps in the common-law tradition of case-by-case adjudication.

McNally v. United States, 483 U.S. 350, 372–73 (1987) (Stevens, J., dissenting). Notice that Justice Stevens says that gaps in statutes are implicit delegations to *courts* to fill in the gaps. Later, in Chapter 17 we will see that implicit delegation also serves as a rational for allowing agencies to fill in the gaps pursuant to the *Chevron* doctrine (and Justice Stevens wrote that opinion as well).

---

* Technically, "'Common law' refers to that body of governing principles, mainly substantive, expounded by the common-law courts of England in deciding cases before them." William Stoebuck, *Reception of English Common Law in the American Colonies*, 10 Wm. & Mary L. Rev. 393, 393 (1968). In this sentence, I use the term more colloquially to mean simply judge made legal doctrine.

As legislation proliferated, statutes began to abrogate common law. This evolution intensified during the New Deal when Congress used legislation to solve social and economic problems. Additionally, as legislators became more skilled at their jobs, distrust of legislators started to fade. By the mid-twentieth century, the Supreme Court regularly heard cases involving statutes, and so statutory interpretation became increasingly important. Similarly, during this time, regulatory agencies proliferated. As more and more agencies drafted more and more regulations, agencies' authority to interpret statutes added to the debate.

Today, the dividing line between making law and interpreting law is blurred: Is implying a cause of action in a statute "making" or "interpreting" law? Some judges believe it is interpreting law, while others would say it is making law. A judge's theory of statutory interpretation is based in large part on that judge's view about the proper relationship between the judiciary and the legislature—or separation of powers. When judges decide cases involving statutes, judges fill gaps, resolve ambiguities, and identify statutory boundaries. Indeed, every case requires a judge to adopt one meaning and reject at least one other meaning. Because of *stare decisis*—the prudential consideration that similar cases should be decided similarly—interpretations judges make regarding statutes will have future application. Thus, it is simply wrong to suggest that judges just interpret law; rather, they act in concert with the legislature to develop law.

Yet legislative supremacy is a cornerstone in our system of government. You saw that recognition reflected in Justice Kagan's dissent in *Yates*. The exact relationship between the legislature and judiciary is at the heart of the academic and judicial debates about statutory interpretation. At one end of this continuum is the view that only the enacted text of a statute is relevant to interpretation. This view may elevate the role of the legislature at the expense of the judiciary. At the other end of the spectrum is the view that either expressed or unexpressed statutory purpose or legislative intent as discerned by the judiciary is most relevant. This view may elevate the judiciary at the expense of the legislature. The truth, of course, lies somewhere in the middle; where exactly is the basis of many scholarly articles and judicial debates, as we will see in the next opinion, *King v. Burwell*, 135 S. Ct. 2480 (2015).

It is undoubtedly true that the appropriate way to interpret a statute is far from settled. Indeed, statutory interpretation has become the focus of scholarly debate as experts disagree about the importance to be placed on the ordinary meaning of the text, the legislative history surrounding enactment, and the purpose of the statute. Former Justice Scalia can be credited, or perhaps blamed, for the reemergence of this controversy; as we will learn, he adheres to a strict approach to interpretation that ignores legislative history and unexpressed purpose. He has been credited with returning the judiciary's focus to the text of the statute. His approach, known as "new textualism," and other various theories of interpretation, will be explained in more detail in Chapter 4.

The next opinion, *King v. Burwell*, 135 S. Ct. 2480 (2015), addressed language in the ACA. The opinion pitted the liberal judges against the conservative judges as the

Court for the second time addressed the validity of President Obama's signature health care act. In the excerpt below, notice how Justices Roberts and Scalia define the judicial role during statutory interpretation.

King v. Burwell

Supreme Court of the United States

135 S. Ct. 2480 (2015)

◆ CHIEF JUSTICE ROBERTS, delivered the opinion of the Court [in which KENNEDY, GINSBURG, BREYER, SOTOMAYOR, and KAGAN, JJ., joined].

[Congress enacted the Patient Protection and Affordable Care Act after a long history of failed health insurance reform. In the 1990s, several States had tried to expand access to health insurance coverage by imposing two insurance market regulations. The first such regulation was known as the "guaranteed issue" requirement; it barred insurers from denying coverage to any person because of his or her existing health issues. The second such regulation was known as the "community rating" requirement. It barred insurers from charging a person higher premiums due to factors unique to a particular community. These two requirements helped expand access to health insurance coverage, but unexpectedly they encouraged people to wait until they got sick to buy insurance. The result was an economic "death spiral": health insurance premiums rose, while the number of people buying insurance declined. Many insurers left the market entirely. In 2006, however, Massachusetts discovered a way to make the guaranteed issue and community rating requirements work as intended—that state required individuals to buy insurance and then provided tax credits to make health insurance more affordable. The combination of these three reforms—(1) insurance market regulations, (2) required coverage, and (3) tax credits—helped Massachusetts to drastically reduce its uninsured rate.

The Affordable Care Act adopted these three key reforms. First, the Act includes the guaranteed issue and community rating requirements. Second, the Act requires individuals to maintain health insurance coverage or pay a tax to the IRS, unless the cost of buying insurance would exceed eight percent of that individual's income. And third, the Act provides refundable tax credits to individuals near the poverty line.

The language challenged in this case relates to the Act's requirement that each state establish an "Exchange"—a marketplace that allows people to compare and purchase insurance plans. The Act gives each State the opportunity to establish its own Exchange, but provides that the Federal Government will establish "such Exchange" if the State does not. 42 U. S. C. §§ 18031, 18041.

Importantly, the Act provides that tax credits "shall be allowed" for any "applicable taxpayer," 26 U.S.C. § 36B(a), but only if the taxpayer has enrolled in an insurance plan through "an Exchange established by the State under [42 U. S. C. § 18031]."

The Department of Treasury promulgated a regulation interpreting "an Exchange established by the State" in one definition of the Act as allowing tax credits "regardless of whether the Exchange is established and operated by a State ... or by HHS." 45 CFR § 155.20.

Petitioners argued that Virginia's Exchange does not qualify as "an Exchange established by the State under [42 U. S. C. § 18031]," so they should not receive any tax credits. That would make the cost of buying insurance so expensive they would be exempt from the Act's coverage requirement. As a result of the regulation, however, petitioners would have to buy insurance.]

... The issue in this case is whether the [The Patient Protection and Affordable Care] Act's tax credits are available in States that have a Federal Exchange rather than a State Exchange. The Act initially provides that tax credits "shall be allowed" for any "applicable taxpayer." 26 U.S.C. § 36B(a). The Act then provides that the amount of the tax credit depends in part on whether the taxpayer has enrolled in an insurance plan through "an Exchange *established by the State* under section 1311 of the Patient Protection and Affordable Care Act [hereinafter 42 U.S.C. § 18031]." 26 U.S.C. §§ 36B(b)–(c) (emphasis added)....

Petitioners are four individuals who live in Virginia, which has a Federal Exchange. They do not wish to purchase health insurance. In their view, Virginia's Exchange does not qualify as "an Exchange established by the State under [42 U. S. C. § 18031]".... [The Government argues that] Virginia's Exchange *would* qualify as "an Exchange established by the State under [42 U. S. C. § 18031]," so petitioners would [have to pay taxes if they do not purchase health insurance].... The [Government's interpretation] therefore requires petitioners to either buy health insurance they do not want, or make a payment to the IRS.... The District Court dismissed the suit, holding that the Act unambiguously made tax credits available to individuals enrolled through a Federal Exchange.... The Fourth Circuit [affirmed].... *

It is ... our task to determine the correct reading of Section 36B. If the statutory language is plain, we must enforce it according to its terms. But often times the "meaning — or ambiguity — of certain words or phrases may only become evident when placed in context." So when deciding whether the language is plain, we must read the words "in their context and with a view to their place in the overall statutory scheme." Our duty, after all, is "to construe statutes, not isolated provisions." ...

[We find that] the phrase "an Exchange established by the State under [42 U. S. C. § 18031]" is properly viewed as ambiguous. The phrase may be limited in its reach to State Exchanges. But it is also possible that the phrase refers to *all* Exchanges — both State and Federal....

The Affordable Care Act contains more than a few examples of inartful drafting. (To cite just one, the Act creates three separate Section 1563s. See 124 Stat. 270,

---

* Editor's footnote: In contrast, the Court of Appeals for the District of Columbia Circuit held that the phrase referred to only state exchanges. *Halbig v. Burwell*, 758 F.3d 390 (D.C. Cir. 2014), *reh'g en banc granted, judgment vacated*, No. 14–5018, 2014 WL 4627181 (D.C. Cir. Sept. 4, 2014). After the Supreme Court granted certiorari in *King*, the D.C. Circuit agreed to hold the case in abeyance pending the Supreme Court's decision in *King*.

911, 912.) Several features of the Act's passage contributed to that unfortunate reality. Congress wrote key parts of the Act behind closed doors, rather than through "the traditional legislative process." And Congress passed much of the Act using a complicated budgetary procedure known as "reconciliation," which limited opportunities for debate and amendment, and bypassed the Senate's normal 60-vote filibuster requirement. As a result, the Act does not reflect the type of care and deliberation that one might expect of such significant legislation. Cf. Frankfurter, *Some Reflections on the Reading of Statutes*, 47 Colum. L. Rev. 527, 545 (1947) (describing a cartoon "in which a senator tells his colleagues 'I admit this new bill is too complicated to understand. We'll just have to pass it to find out what it means.'")....

Given that the text is ambiguous, we must turn to the broader structure of the Act to determine the meaning of Section 36B. "A provision that may seem ambiguous in isolation is often clarified by the remainder of the statutory scheme ... because only one of the permissible meanings produces a substantive effect that is compatible with the rest of the law." Here, the statutory scheme compels us to reject petitioners' interpretation because it would destabilize the individual insurance market in any State with a Federal Exchange, and likely create the very "death spirals" that Congress designed the Act to avoid.

... Congress based the Affordable Care Act on three major reforms: first, the guaranteed issue and community rating requirements; second, a requirement that individuals maintain health insurance coverage or make a payment to the IRS; and third, the tax credits for individuals with household incomes between 100 percent and 400 percent of the federal poverty line. In a State that establishes its own Exchange, these three reforms work together to expand insurance coverage. The guaranteed issue and community rating requirements ensure that anyone can buy insurance; the coverage requirement creates an incentive for people to do so before they get sick; and the tax credits — it is hoped — make insurance more affordable. Together, those reforms "minimize ... adverse selection and broaden the health insurance risk pool to include healthy individuals, which will lower health insurance premiums."

Under petitioners' reading, however, the Act would operate quite differently in a State with a Federal Exchange. As they see it, one of the Act's three major reforms — the tax credits — would not apply. And a second major reform — the coverage requirement — would not apply in a meaningful way.... without the tax credits, the coverage requirement would apply to fewer individuals. And it would be a *lot* fewer....

The combination of no tax credits and an ineffective coverage requirement could well push a State's individual insurance market into a death spiral.... It is implausible that Congress meant the Act to operate in this manner. Congress made the guaranteed issue and community rating requirements applicable in every State in the Nation. But those requirements only work when combined with the coverage requirement and the tax credits. So it stands to reason that Congress meant for those provisions to apply in every State as well....

Petitioners' arguments about the plain meaning of Section 36B are strong. But while the meaning of the phrase "an Exchange established by the State under [42 U. S. C. § 18031]" may seem plain "when viewed in isolation," such a reading turns out to be "untenable in light of [the statute] as a whole." In this instance, the context and structure of the Act compel us to depart from what would otherwise be the most natural reading of the pertinent statutory phrase.

Reliance on context and structure in statutory interpretation is a "subtle business, calling for great wariness lest what professes to be mere rendering becomes creation and attempted interpretation of legislation becomes legislation itself." For the reasons we have given, however, such reliance is appropriate in this case, and leads us to conclude that Section 36B allows tax credits for insurance purchased on any Exchange created under the Act. Those credits are necessary for the Federal Exchanges to function like their State Exchange counterparts, and to avoid the type of calamitous result that Congress plainly meant to avoid.

In a democracy, the power to make the law rests with those chosen by the people. Our role is more confined — "to say what the law is." *Marbury v. Madison*, 1 Cranch 137, 177 (1803). That is easier in some cases than in others. But in every case we must respect the role of the Legislature, and take care not to undo what it has done. A fair reading of legislation demands a fair understanding of the legislative plan. Congress passed the Affordable Care Act to improve health insurance markets, not to destroy them. If at all possible, we must interpret the Act in a way that is consistent with the former, and avoids the latter. Section 36B can fairly be read consistent with what we see as Congress's plan, and that is the reading we adopt. The judgment of the United States Court of Appeals for the Fourth Circuit is

Affirmed.

◆ JUSTICE SCALIA filed a dissenting opinion [in which THOMAS and ALITO, JJ., joined].

The Court holds that when the Patient Protection and Affordable Care Act says "Exchange established by the State" it means "Exchange established by the State or the Federal Government." That is of course quite absurd, and the Court's 21 pages of explanation make it no less so....

I wholeheartedly agree with the Court that sound interpretation requires paying attention to the whole law, not homing in on isolated words or even isolated sections. Context always matters. Let us not forget, however, *why* context matters: It is a tool for understanding the terms of the law, not an excuse for rewriting them....

The Court protests that without the tax credits, the number of people covered by the individual mandate shrinks, and without a broadly applicable individual mandate the guaranteed-issue and community-rating requirements "would destabilize the individual insurance market." If true, these projections would show only that the statutory scheme contains a flaw; they would not show that the statute means the opposite of what it says....

Perhaps sensing the dismal failure of its efforts to show that "established by the State" means "established by the State or the Federal Government," the Court tries to palm off the pertinent statutory phrase as "inartful drafting." This Court, however, has no free-floating power "to rescue Congress from its drafting errors." Only when it is patently obvious to a reasonable reader that a drafting mistake has occurred may a court correct the mistake. The occurrence of a misprint may be apparent from the face of the law, as it is where the Affordable Care Act "creates three separate Section 1563s." But the Court does not pretend that there is any such indication of a drafting error on the face of § 36B....

The Court's decision reflects the philosophy that judges should endure whatever interpretive distortions it takes in order to correct a supposed flaw in the statutory machinery. That philosophy ignores the American people's decision to give Congress "[a]ll legislative Powers" enumerated in the Constitution. Art. I, § 1. They made Congress, not this Court, responsible for both making laws and mending them. This Court holds only the judicial power—the power to pronounce the law as Congress has enacted it. We lack the prerogative to repair laws that do not work out in practice, just as the people lack the ability to throw us out of office if they dislike the solutions we concoct. We must always remember, therefore, that "[o]ur task is to apply the text, not to improve upon it."

Trying to make its judge-empowering approach seem respectful of congressional authority, the Court asserts that its decision merely ensures that the Affordable Care Act operates the way Congress "meant [it] to operate."

First of all, what makes the Court so sure that Congress "meant" tax credits to be available everywhere? Our only evidence of what Congress meant comes from the terms of the law, and those terms show beyond all question that tax credits are available only on state Exchanges. More importantly, the Court forgets that ours is a government of laws and not of men. That means we are governed by the terms of our laws, not by the unenacted will of our lawmakers. "If Congress enacted into law something different from what it intended, then it should amend the statute to conform to its intent." In the meantime, this Court "has no roving license ... to disregard clear language simply on the view that ... Congress 'must have intended' something broader."

Even less defensible, if possible, is the Court's claim that its interpretive approach is justified because this Act "does not reflect the type of care and deliberation that one might expect of such significant legislation." It is not our place to judge the quality of the care and deliberation that went into this or any other law. A law enacted by voice vote with no deliberation whatever is fully as binding upon us as one enacted after years of study, months of committee hearings, and weeks of debate. Much less is it our place to make everything come out right when Congress does not do its job properly. It is up to Congress to design its laws with care, and it is up to the people to hold them to account if they fail to carry out that responsibility.

Rather than rewriting the law under the pretense of interpreting it, the Court should have left it to Congress to decide what to do about the Act's limitation of tax credits to state Exchanges.... The Court's insistence on making a choice that should be made by Congress both aggrandizes judicial power and encourages congressional lassitude....

Today's opinion changes the usual rules of statutory interpretation for the sake of the Affordable Care Act.... The Act that Congress passed makes tax credits available only on an "Exchange established by the State." This Court, however, concludes that this limitation would prevent the rest of the Act from working as well as hoped. So it rewrites the law to make tax credits available everywhere. We should start calling this law SCOTUScare.

Perhaps the Patient Protection and Affordable Care Act will attain the enduring status of the Social Security Act or the Taft-Hartley Act; perhaps not. But this Court's two decisions on the Act will surely be remembered through the years. The somersaults of statutory interpretation they have performed ... will be cited by litigants endlessly, to the confusion of honest jurisprudence. And the cases will publish forever the discouraging truth that the Supreme Court of the United States favors some laws over others, and is prepared to do whatever it takes to uphold and assist its favorites.

I dissent.

* * *

Points for Discussion

1. *Statutory Language*: What was the language at issue? What did King argue that language meant? What did the government argue that language meant? What interpretation did Justice Roberts adopt? Justice Scalia?

2. *Formalism & Functionalism*: Describe how Justice Robert's and Justice Scalia's view of the judicial role in statutory interpretation differ.

3. *Fixing Errors*: It is difficult, even impossible in today's political climate, for Congress to quickly correct drafting mistakes. If Congress clearly errs when enacting a statute, who should fix the mistake, according to Justice Roberts? Justice Scalia? What if the error is less obvious? In Chapter 6, we will talk about the scrivener's error doctrine, pursuant to which judges may "correct" obviously erroneous statutory language. Would that doctrine have fit here?

4. *Statutory Interpretation Continuum*: As noted earlier: At one end of this continuum is the view that only the enacted text of a statute is relevant to interpretation. This view may elevate the role of the legislature at the expense of the judiciary. At the other end of the spectrum is the view that either expressed or unexpressed statutory purpose or legislative intent as discerned by the judiciary is most relevant. This view may elevate the judiciary's role at the expense of the legislature. At which end of this continuum does Justice Roberts fall? Justice Scalia?

5. *In Pari Materia*: Both Justices Roberts and Scalia agreed that statutory provisions should not be looked at in isolation. Rather, judges should consider the textual context of those provisions. This approach is known as "*in pari materia*," which means "part of the same material" in Latin. Statutory provisions are enacted as

part of a larger act. Pursuant to *in pari materia*, judges look at the act as a whole to determine how the provision at issue fits into the statutory scheme (*See* Chapter 8). How do Justice Roberts and Justice Scalia use this canon differently?

* * *

D. A Note about Civil Law Systems

The U.S. legal system is understood to be part of the common law tradition. It derived, adapted, and evolved from the English legal system, which was familiar to the British colonists who arrived in the New World. Although both countries use a common law system, our current approach to law is quite different—one obvious and very superficial difference is that few U.S. lawyers or judges wear wigs to court. But we share a common legal heritage with our friends in England, and that heritage plays a role in statutory interpretation, as we shall see throughout this text. Other common law countries include Australia, India, Canada, Hong Kong, Ireland, and Pakistan.

Common law, however, is not the only legal system. Many countries in continental Europe and South America follow a legal system referred to as "civil" or "civilian." Indeed, it is the most common legal system in the world. Countries that follow this legal system include most of the European Union countries, Brazil, China, Japan, Mexico, Russia, Switzerland, Turkey, Quebec, Georgia, and Louisiana. Civil law and common law systems differ in many ways. One important difference between them is the weight they give to judicial opinions and statutes. For common law systems, judicial opinions are controlling. The common law system developed initially with judges deciding cases that became precedents. These precedents were eventually synthesized into legal doctrines (for example common law assault). Many of these legal doctrines were eventually codified, but we still hear the echo of judicial doctrine in these common-law-turned-statutes. Moreover, in a common law system the opinions of appellate courts typically bind lower courts in the same jurisdiction that address similar issues.

In contrast, civil law typically starts with more abstract principles, which a legislature enacts as a code of laws. The role of the judiciary is to interpret and apply these legislative enactments. A civil law judge may have more latitude with interpretation and application of a statute than a common law judge, because precedents may be non-binding and, therefore, are only (potentially) persuasive. In other words, the starting point and center of civil law analysis is the code (the statutes), not case law.

There are other systems as well, including Islamic Law and Socialist Law. This book, of course, focuses on the U.S. common law system and its approaches to statutory interpretation. However, it can be useful for you to remember that lawyers from other parts of the world may approach the statutory interpretation process quite differently.

* * *

Problem 2

Deborah Peterson and several individuals (collectively "Peterson") are victims or family members of victims of a 1983 Marine barracks bombing in Beirut, Lebanon, which was attributed to Iran. Peterson obtained a judgment again Iran, which has been unsatisfied.

A New York City branch of Citibank was holding the $1.7 billion in assets belonging to the Bank Markazi, the Central Bank of Iran. In 2010, Peterson sued Citibank and the government-owned Central Bank of Iran under the Terrorism Risk Insurance Act, which provides that, in judgments obtained against terrorists, blocked assets belonging to the terrorist group or its agents are subject to garnishment or attachment. While the action was pending, President Obama issued an Executive Order freezing the assets.

Subsequently, while the lawsuit was pending, Congress enacted the Iran Threat Reduction Act of 2012 (TRA). Section 502 of that Act (codified at 28 U.S.C. §8772) provides as follows:

SEC. 502. INTERESTS IN CERTAIN FINANCIAL ASSETS OF IRAN.

(a) INTERESTS IN BLOCKED ASSETS. —

(1) IN GENERAL. — Subject to paragraph (2) ... and preempting any inconsistent provision of State law, a financial asset that is —

(A) held in the United States for a foreign securities intermediary doing business in the United States;

(B) a blocked asset ... that is property described in subsection (b); and

(C) equal in value to a financial asset of Iran, including an asset of the central bank or monetary authority of the Government of Iran..., that such foreign securities intermediary or a related intermediary holds abroad,

shall be subject to execution or attachment in aid of execution in order to satisfy any judgment to the extent of any compensatory damages awarded against Iran for damages for personal injury or death caused by an act of torture, extrajudicial killing, aircraft sabotage, or hostage-taking, or the provision of material support or resources for such an act.

(2) COURT DETERMINATION REQUIRED. — In order to ensure that Iran is held accountable for paying the judgments described in paragraph (1) and in furtherance of the broader goals of this Act to sanction Iran, prior to an award turning over any asset pursuant to execution or attachment in aid of execution with respect to any judgments against Iran described in paragraph (1), the court shall determine whether Iran holds equitable title to, or the beneficial interest in, the assets described in subsection (b) and that no other person possesses a constitutionally protected interest in the assets described in subsection (b) under the Fifth Amendment to the Constitution of the United States. ...

(b) FINANCIAL ASSETS DESCRIBED. — The financial assets described in this section are the financial assets that are identified in and the subject of proceedings in the United States District Court for the Southern District of New York in *Peterson et al. v. Islamic Republic of Iran et al.*, Case No. 10 Civ. 4518 (BSJ) (GWG), that were restrained by restraining notices and levies secured by the plaintiffs in those proceedings, as modified by court order dated June 27, 2008, and extended by court orders dated June 23, 2009, May 10, 2010, and June 11, 2010, so long as such assets remain restrained by court order.

Under § 502 of the TRA, courts must determine (1) whether the identified assets are assets "held in the [U.S.] for a foreign securities intermediary doing business in the United States," (2) whether the assets are "blocked" assets under U.S. law, and (3) whether the assets are "equal in value to a financial asset" held abroad by a financial securities intermediary on behalf of Bank Markazi. Note that section 502 applies only to Petersons' judgment, even though other claims were pending when the Act was passed. § 502(b).

After the TRA was enacted, the district court reasoned that section 502 specifically allowed the funds in Citibank to be attached to satisfy the Petersons' judgment. The court granted summary judgment to Peterson and ordered the banks to turn over the blocked assets. Citibank settled, however, Bank Markazi has appealed. Recall that in the case of *United States v. Klein*, 80 U.S. 128 (1872), the Supreme Court held that Congress acts unconstitutionally when it directs a federal court on how to resolve a pending case. On appeal, Bank Markazi argues that section 502 has the effect of dictating the outcome of a single case pending before the courts, which renders the law an impermissible intrusion on the judiciary's proper role and a violation of separation of powers. Peterson responds that Bank Markazi's attack on the statute is unwarranted, because Congress has the constitutional authority to modify the governing law for pending civil litigation in outcome-determinative ways. Peterson cites *Plaut v. Spendthrift Farm, Inc.*, 514 U.S. 211 (1995), for the point that Congress has the power to amend existing law even if that amendment changes the outcome of the case. Thus, Peterson argues that Congress merely amended the applicable law, but left it to the courts to make the necessary factual findings supporting the appropriateness of attachment.

If the court applies a formalist approach to separation of powers, how will the court likely rule? If instead the court applies a functionalist approach to separation of powers, how will the court likely rule? What role do you think the sympathetic nature of the claims will play in the court's resolution of this case? *will move you a lot to a certain case*

Chapter 3

The Legislative Process

A. Introduction to This Chapter

This chapter explains basic legislative enactment and the role the various individuals in the process play, from legislators to lobbyists. Next, we examine some of the legislative process theories. Finally, as you learn how a bill becomes a law, you will discover the many ways that legislative history is created. We will return to this topic in Chapter 11, when we talk about the role legislative history plays in statutory interpretation. When you finish this chapter, you should have a basic understanding of how a bill is enacted, the importance of the constitutional processes of bicameralism and presentment, and the role that politics play. Let's start with the players.

B. The Legislative Movers and Shakers

Before we discuss the legislative process, you need to know who the players are in that process. This section explains those players: their roles, qualifications, and interests.

1. Legislatures and Legislators

Members of a legislature, such as Congress, are generally known as legislators, or representatives. (The word "representatives" has two meanings, one specific and one general. The specific meaning is members of the House of Representatives or members of a state's general assembly. The general meaning is senators and representatives collectively.) Representatives pass federal laws, not citizens. While the Framers could have chosen a system that would have allowed citizens to enact laws directly (and some states did make that choice), the Framers opted instead for a representative system to better ensure that laws would protect all citizens, not just those in power: "Under such a regulation, it may well happen that the public voice pronounced by the representatives of the people, will be more consonant to the public good, than if pronounced by the people themselves convened for that purpose." THE FEDERALIST No. 10 (James Madison) (Clinton Rossiter ed., 1961).

Under the Articles of Confederation (which preceded the Constitution), the legislature was a unicameral body in which each state held one vote. But the larger states were not happy with the one-vote-per-state system. When the Framers drafted the Constitution, the legislature's structure was one of the most divisive issues of the Constitutional Convention of 1787. Ultimately, the Framers selected bicameralism, a system in which there are two chambers, or houses, constituting the legislative body. Thus, the one federal legislature, Congress, is made up of two chambers: the House of Representatives and the Senate. The Framers chose bicameralism as a compromise: One chamber would represent public opinion (the House), and a second chamber would represent the views of the governments of the individual states (the Senate). State legislatures originally selected members of this latter chamber, who, as a result, were expected to be less susceptible to mass public sentiment. But today, citizens of the state they represent elect senators, just like they elect their representatives.

There are also fifty state legislatures, often called general assemblies. For the most part, the state legislatures are also bicameral, but Nebraska's legislature is unicameral. While this section will focus on Congress, its legislators, and its legislative processes, you should learn about the process in your state. It likely differs in some way from the federal process. For example, the state legislature in Georgia operates only for part of the year, with senators and representatives who have other full-time jobs.

Because Congress is made up of two separate chambers, each has its own procedures, politics, and qualifications, all of which impact the legislative process. Because these differences affect the enactment process, let's explore them for a moment. The Senate is the smaller of the two bodies. There are 100 senators, two for every state. In contrast, the House is much larger. There are 435 representatives; each represents a Congressional District made up of about 700,000 people. The number of representatives is currently fixed at 435 (Public L. No. 62-5, ch. 5, §§ 1–2, 37 Stat. 13 (1911)), although there is a bill currently pending to increase that number so that the District of Columbia can have representation. Each state is represented proportionally in the House based on that state's population. California has the most representatives: fifty-three, but every state has at least one representative. Currently, seven states have only one: Delaware, Montana, North Dakota, Vermont, South Dakota, Alaska, and Wyoming. In contrast, every state has two senators, both of whom represent the entire state. Senators serve a large constituency—constituents are the residents of a state that elected the senator—with many varied interests. The Senate is sometimes thought to be more deliberative than the House because the Senate has fewer members. Because senators serve longer terms, they are more insulated from public opinion than members of the House. Both of these factors—size and term length—encourage collegiality and discourage partisanship within the Senate. In contrast, representatives are elected from smaller (approximately 700,000 residents) and more homogenous districts than senators. The House has historically been the more partisan chamber.

2. Legislator Qualifications

Not everyone can be a legislator. The Constitution requires that senators be thirty years old, citizens for at least nine years, and "[i]nhabitant[s]" of the state from which elected. U.S. Const. art. 1. § 3. Similarly, representatives must be twenty-five years old, citizens for at least seven years, and "[i]nhabitant[s]" of the state from which elected. U.S. CONST. art. I. §2. There is no requirement that representatives actually live in the district they represent. These minimal requirements cannot be augmented. *Powell v. McCormack*, 395 U.S. 486, 550 (1969) (rejecting Congress's attempt to refuse to seat a representative who met these qualifications but was not trustworthy). Because neither Congress nor the states can alter or add to these Constitutional requirements, term limits imposed by many states on federal representatives in the 1990s were held to be unconstitutional. *U.S. Term Limits, Inc. v. Thorton*, 514 U.S. 779, 837 (1995).

Many things motivate legislators, including reelection:

> Although reelection and financial considerations are important to lawmakers, most are also motivated by the desire for status and reputation and the objective of affecting policy and the national agenda in ways consistent with their ideological commitments. Empirical studies have found that a legislator's voting behavior is most related to her constituents' interests.

WILLIAM N. ESKRIDGE, JR. *ET AL.*, LEGISLATION AND STATUTORY INTERPRETATION 98 (2d 2006) (citations omitted). Representatives are up for reelection every two years, (always in an even-numbered year). In contrast, senators are elected for six-year, staggered terms. Unlike the House, where every representative is up for re-election simultaneously, only one-third of the senators are up for reelection at any one time. Because a senator's tenure in office is longer than representatives in the House, representatives may be more risk averse when it comes to passing new legislation than senators. Moreover, because it is considered more prestigious to be a senator, representatives from the House regularly want to "move up" to the Senate. The desire to move up may affect a representative's willingness to support unpopular legislation. Also, regular turnover negatively impacts the institutional memory of the House.

3. Leadership

Politics matter, particularly in the House. Pursuant to the Constitution, approval of both chambers is required for legislation to become law. Indeed, the legislative veto, in which one chamber could unilaterally vacate decisions of the executive, was held to be unconstitutional because such a process allowed Congress to act without following the "single, finely wrought and exhaustively considered, procedure[s]" of Article I. *INS v. Chadha*, 462 U.S. 919, 951 (1983).

The party with the most seats in the House, the majority party, has the political power to get things done. The leader in the House is the Speaker of the House, whom the members elect. House rules and custom, not the Constitution, identify the powers and duties of the speaker. Thus, these powers and duties may change over time as one party attempts to expand or reign in the speaker's political power, which can be tremendous. The speaker has many powers that affect the legislative process. For example, the speaker has the power to control the order in which members of the House speak during debate on a bill. No representative may speak or bring a motion until the speaker permits.

This rule gives the speaker of the House tremendous power to control the course of the debate. Additionally, the speaker rules on representatives' objections that a rule has been breached (called points of order), but the speaker's decision is subject to appeal, which the whole House resolves. Further, the speaker is the chair of the Steering Committee, which chooses the chair of the other standing committees; these standing committees are responsible for doing the preliminary work on all bills and, thus, hold tremendous power. The speaker also decides which committee should consider bills, appoints members of the Rules Committee, and appoints members of conference committees (which reconcile different versions of a bill passed by the House and Senate). All in all, the speaker has enormous political power.

After the speaker, the majority party leader, also elected by his or her party, has the most political power. The majority leader decides which legislation members of that party should support and which legislation the membership should oppose. There is also a minority party leader who, not surprisingly, holds much less political power. Both parties also elect "whips," who try to ensure that the party's members vote as the party leadership desires. Representatives generally vote as the leadership directs because otherwise they may be threatened with reduced support for reelection campaigns, for pet legislation, and for committee chair positions.

Leadership is slightly different in the Senate; there is no speaker. Instead, the vice president of the United States is the presiding officer, or president, of the Senate. The vice president is not a senator and does not regularly vote. But in the case of a tie, the vice president may cast the tie-breaking vote. For example, John Adams, the first Vice President and President of the Senate cast tie-breaking votes twenty-nine times (more than any other vice president). He voted to protect the executive's sole authority to remove appointees, and he influenced the location of the national capital. Because the vice president does not always attend legislative sessions, the duty of presiding often falls to the president *pro tempore,* usually the most senior senator in the majority party, who may choose to delegate this task to a junior senator. Similar to the House, the Senate has both majority and minority party leaders and whips.

4. The Important Role of Committees

Both the House and Senate operate via committee and subcommittee, each of which is responsible for a particular jurisdiction or subject area. House Rule X, clause 1, and Senate Rule XXV, clause 1, specify the permanent standing committees in the chambers. All legislators serve on one or more committees. Because there are so many of them, representatives often specialize. In contrast, because of the Senate's small size, its members do not specialize in the same way. Commonly, committees are broken into subcommittees, which do the majority of the legislative work: they hold hearings, take testimony, draft and amend bill language, and recommend whether to pass a bill on to full committee consideration. Not all committees have subcommittees.

While all bills do not reach the floor for vote, all bills that do reach the floor are first screened by the appropriate committee or committees. While legislators are free to sponsor a bill that will be examined by any committee and advocate for that bill once it reaches the floor, in reality, legislators can most effectively influence the passage of bills that come before the committee of which the legislators are members. Moreover, legislators will be most successful when chairing that committee or, at least, when having a majority of the committee members in their party. Because the party in political power selects the chair and members of each committee, it is difficult for the party not in power to enact legislation. Party loyalty is strong. Legislators who adhere to the party line are rewarded, while those who stray are penalized. PROFILES IN COURAGE, by John F. Kennedy, is a Pulitzer Prize-winning biography that details the bravery and integrity of eight United States Senators who suffered because of their decision to cross party lines. The book demonstrates that politics greatly influence bill passage.

5. Staffers and Lobbyists

It is not just legislators who make up Congress. Staff members surround each chamber. These staff members also influence the legislative process; they may draft bills and committee reports, write amendments to bills, and provide other relevant information.

Additionally, lobbyists, people who are generally paid to represent a particular point of view for a specific industry or organization, may also influence the legislative process. Interestingly, "[t]he term 'lobbying' arose from the practice of people waiting in the legislature's lobby to intercept legislators to attempt to win them over to a particular position." RONALD BENTON BROWN & SHARON JACOBS BROWN, STATUTORY INTERPRETATION: THE SEARCH FOR LEGISLATIVE INTENT 143 (2d 2011). Often, lobbyists draft bills, present information during hearings, craft amendments, advocate for passage, and argue against passage. These non-legislator players also affect legislation.

Just how much of a role lobbyists should play is the subject of some debate. Lobbying can be defined as providing information to influence a lawmaker's decision. If you have written your congress member to advocate a position or signed a Facebook petition, you have lobbied. But *lobbyists* are paid experts in navigating the hurdles in the legislative process; they are professionals hired to represent industries or companies to influence legislation and policy. They do not further the public interest. They have both beneficial and pernicious effects on the legislative process. "Lobbyists inform lawmakers about constituent preferences and interests; they inform legislators about the effects of particular policies and problems that demand government solutions; they inform lawmakers about the preference of other lawmakers so that proponents of policy change can successfully negotiate the vetogates of Congress; and they inform the public about lawmakers' views and efforts regarding policies." ESKRIDGE ET AL., LEGISLATION AND STATUTORY INTERPRETATION, *supra*, at 197. Lobbying is increasing exponentially. Lobbyists must register with Congress and regularly file reports disclosing the identity of their clients, the issues for which they lobbied, and the amount of money received for all lobbying efforts. 2 U.S.C. § 1603-04.

Lobbyists can affect the legislative process. For example, the biotechnology industry influenced the record of the historic House debate on the Affordable Care Act. The *New York Times* obtained emails showing that the lobbyists drafted one statement for Democrats and another for Republicans. These remarks were then printed in the extension of remarks section* of the Congressional Record under the names of forty-two different members of Congress: twenty-two Republicans and twenty Democrats. While it is not unusual for members of Congress to submit revised or extended statements for publication in the Congressional Record after the debate, it is unusual that so many of the statements matched word for word. It is even more unusual to find clear evidence that the statements originated with lobbyists. When asked in an interview about remarks added under his name, Representative William Pascrell Jr., a Democrat of New Jersey, said: "I regret that the language was the same. I did not know it was." He said his statement came from staff members, and he "did not know where they got the information from." For the full story, see http://www.nytimes.com/2009/11/15/us/politics/15health.html?pagewanted=1&_r=2&hp&adxnnl=1&adxnnlx=1356177854-OfyR2geHJXzm3KGEGksiiA.

Now that you know who the players are, let's talk about what those players do. How does a bill become law, or an act?

C. How a Bill Becomes an Act

This section explains the constitutionally proscribed legislative process—the steps that a legislature takes to enact a bill; second, it identifies the legislative history developed along the way. This section explains the *federal* legislative process rather than the state process, but there are many similarities. Not all bills follow the path outlined here; for example, many legislatures have a shortcut for non-controversial bills: the consent calendar. Bills on the consent calendar are briefly explained to the members and then voted on. They do not go through the process described below.

The flowchart on the next page summarizes the legislative process.

As you read this section, you should notice that the legislative process is not an easy one. Indeed, it is much easier for a bill to fail than to be enacted. The Framers of our Constitution chose this balance because "[t]he injury which may possibly be done by defeating a few good laws, will be amply compensated by the advantage of preventing a number of bad ones." The Federalist No. 73 (Alexander Hamilton), (Clinton Rossiter ed., 1961). Difficult passage promotes consistency, avoiding dramatic changes in the law. William N. Eskridge, Jr. et al., Legislation and Statutory Interpretation, *supra,* at 79. Thus, in many ways, one might say that the purpose of legislatures is to kill bills not to pass them. Recent congressional activity supports this point: the 112th Congress enacted only 284 bills and 722 resolutions of the 10,865

---

* The extension of remarks section is supposed to identify when information was not considered during debate. But there are concerns that Congress may not be enforcing these marking rules. *See Gregg v. Barrett*, 771 F.2d 539 (D.C.Cir.1985) (dismissing claim without addressing the merits).

bills and resolutions introduced, while the 113th Congress enacted 296 bills and 663 resolutions of the 9,184 introduced. Bovtrack.us, Statistics and Historical Comparison, available at https://www.govtrack.us/congress/bills/statistics.

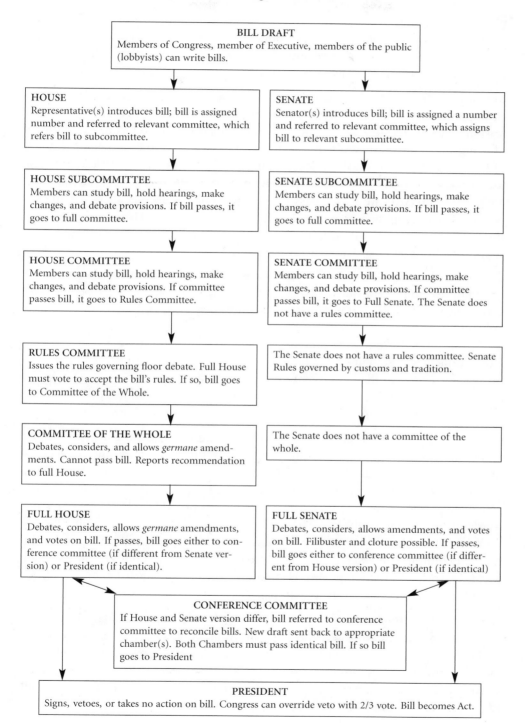

1. Congress's Role—Bicameral Passage

Now let's talk about the role of Congress and the president in the legislative process. You must understand the legislative process to understand the role legislative history plays in interpretation. Keep in mind that behind the neat progression described below is an "often-chaotic process of lobbying by interest groups and of assessments by legislators of the public interest and of their own, sometimes less public-regarding needs (such as reelection)." ESKRIDGE *ET AL.*, LEGISLATION AND STATUTORY INTER- PRETATION, *supra,* at 3.

Congress holds two legislative sessions per year. Occasionally, an extra or special session is called. The first step in the enactment of a law is for one or more members of Congress to introduce a bill or resolution in one of the two chambers. Members of Congress often introduce bills on behalf of lobbyists, because only a member of Congress can introduce legislation, but anyone can draft a bill. Recall that lobbyists are people who advocate for the passage (or rejection) of bills that affect the interest of a particular group, such as an environmental advocacy group. They do not represent the public as a whole. Often, lobbyists write the initial draft of the bill and then submit the draft to a legislator for introduction.

Proposed legislation is generally introduced as a bill, but some legislation is introduced as a joint resolution. For our purposes, there is little practical difference between the two. Concurrent resolutions, which both chambers pass, and simple resolutions, which only one chamber passes, are not used for this purpose because they do not have the force of law. Instead, concurrent and simple resolutions regulate procedure (for example, House Concurrent Resolution 123 directs the Clerk of the House of Representatives to make a correction in the enrollment of a specific bill) or simply express Congress's opinion on a relevant issue (for example, House Concurrent Resolution 107 denounces the use of civilians as human shields by Hamas and other terrorist organizations).

Generally, a bill can originate in either chamber, unless it is a tax or an appropri- ations bill—in which case the bill must originate in the House pursuant to the Orig- ination, or Revenue, Clause of the U.S. Constitution. U.S. CONST. art. I, §7, cl. 1 ("All Bills for raising Revenue shall originate in the House of Representatives; but the Senate may propose or concur with Amendments as on other Bills."). One or more legislators must sponsor the bill. The main sponsor is responsible for moving the bill through the legislative process; hence, choosing sponsors is critical. The chair of the relevant committee is often a good first choice because of the power that the chair wields in getting legislation passed. Having co-sponsors with varied political and ge- ographical interests can also help with passage.

All bills go through several steps within each chamber. The first step is generally committee and subcommittee consideration. After a bill is introduced, the Speaker of the House or the presiding officer of the Senate (depending on where the bill orig- inated) will refer the bill to the appropriate standing (meaning existing) committee or committees. Having the speaker or presiding member of the Senate refer one's bill to a supportive committee is helpful.

There are twenty standing committees in the House and sixteen in the Senate, each of which has a specified jurisdiction, such as foreign relations or finance. Standing committees have subcommittees that do the majority of the work. Subcommittees consider, amend, table, reject, and report bills to the full committee, which then considers, amends, tables, rejects, and reports bills that come within their purview to the full chamber. A bill may fall within the jurisdiction of more than one standing committee. Committees and subcommittees have extensive power over bills; indeed, these committees may block legislation from ever reaching the floor of the chamber. In addition to their legislative responsibilities, standing committees also oversee federal agencies.

Standing committees and subcommittees may hold hearings, subpoena witnesses, and collect evidence. Each committee and subcommittee has one chair and one ranking member; the chair is from the majority party, while the ranking member is from the minority party. The chair has extensive power over bills because the chair controls the committee's agenda. Thus, chairs can prevent a committee from ever debating a bill. Chairs used to be awarded by seniority. Today, a standing committee known as the Steering Committee selects chairs. Chairs are often awarded to members who faithfully follow the party direction, rather than to those with expertise.

Committees have a tremendous impact on the future of a bill. Only one out of every ten bills referred to committee becomes law. BURDETT LOOMIS, THE CONTEMPORARY CONGRESS 156 (1996). The committee chair decides whether to add the bill to the committee's agenda or to refer the bill to subcommittee. The chair also decides whether to hold public hearings on the bill. If public hearings are to be held, notice of the time and location of the meeting is published. Interested lobbyists and members of the public may attend; however, testimony is severely limited. Hearings are held, meetings occur, amendments may or may not be made, and finally, action is taken: The committee can vote to table the bill, amend (or "mark-up" the bill, see the hypothetical in Chapter 1), not report the bill, or approve the bill and forward it to the House or the Senate floor. A decision not to report the bill is the equivalent of killing the bill. If the bill is approved and forwarded to the full chamber, staff members prepare a committee report, describing the details of the committee's work. This report accompanies the bill to the floor; it may be the only part of the proposed legislation the voting members read! The committee process is basically identical in both houses.

Assuming the bill is forwarded to the full chamber, the legislative process continues. The Senate and House vary somewhat in scheduling bills for a full chamber vote. In the House, the chair of the committee that is forwarding the bill to the full House must first ask the House Rules Committee to schedule the bill for floor consideration. The Rules Committee plays a strong role in the passage of a proposed bill because the Rules Committee passes the rules governing debate on each bill, such as the time allowed for debate, how that time is allocated to each side, and the scope of possible amendments. For example, the Rules Committee can choose to schedule "closed rule" allowing no amendments to the bill, "modified closed rule" allowing limited amendments, or "open rule" allowing all *germane* amendments. The Rules Committee can recommend that consideration of a bill be expedited. The Rules Committee process provides another opportunity for derailment.

Assuming a bill is called up before the members of the House, the House must first vote on and debate the bill's rule. If the rule is accepted, the House dissolves into the Committee of the Whole. The Committee of the Whole is not a committee in the usual sense but is simply a committee consisting of all 435 members of the House, which follows simplified procedures to debate the bill. The Committee of the Whole was developed to expedite House action. It is the largest House standing committee and offers a forum for debating, considering, and amending proposed legislation. The Committee of the Whole debates the bill for an amount of time the House Rules Committee previously determined, usually one to several hours. Amendments may only be offered during this time. Debate and amendments must be *germane* to the bill being considered. Debate on proposed amendments is subject to the "five-minute rule," a House rule that in theory limits debate for and against an amendment offered in the Committee of the Whole to ten minutes, five minutes in support and five minutes in opposition. The Committee of the Whole may consider bills and amend them, *but it cannot pass a bill.* Instead, when the Committee of the Whole is done debating and amending a bill, the committee "rises" and reports its recommendations on the bill to the full House. Votes of the Committee of the Whole are not recorded; thus, legislators may feel free at this time to vote as they wish with less fear of political pressure or reprisal.

Assuming the bill is forwarded to the full House (the same individuals who just debated the bill as the Committee of the Whole), more debate may ensue. Eventually, debate concludes, and the House votes on the bill or recommits (refers) the bill back to the legislative committee from which it was reported. Referral back to committee generally means the bill dies. Voting of the full House usually takes fifteen minutes, but this time limit may be extended if the leadership needs time to "whip" its members into shape. For example, the 2003 vote on the Prescription Drug Benefit bill was open for three hours while the leadership worked to find the necessary votes for passage. Ties signal defeat for the bill; there is no casting (tie-breaking) vote in the House. Unlike votes in the Committee of the Whole, votes in the full House are recorded; thus, representatives may feel somewhat less free to vote against the party line.

In the Senate, a slightly different process ensues. First, the Senate does not have a rules committee. Rather, senate procedure is governed by established rules, customs, and traditions. In many cases, the Senate will waive some of the rules by unanimous consent. Party leaders typically negotiate unanimous consent agreements before a bill reaches the floor. Any senator may block such an agreement; thus, while the majority party still has more power in the Senate, a single senator can, theoretically, singlehandedly kill a bill. In reality, such objections are uncommon.

Also, unlike the House, there is no committee of the whole in the Senate; rather, the full Senate can debate and amend the bill on the floor. Like representatives, senators may speak during floor debates only when the presiding officer permits. But unlike the speaker of the House, the presiding officer of the Senate is required to recognize the first senator who rises to speak and, thus, has little control over the course of the debate. Moreover, unlike members of the House, senators may offer to amend bills at any time during floor debate. Sometimes senators offer amendments simply to kill a bill. For example, Representative Judge Howard W. Smith offered an amendment to the bill that became Title VII of the Civil Rights Act, in part, to kill it. His amendment added sex to the topics protected from employment discrimination. He added this amendment partly due to his own commitment to equal opportunities for women, but he also believed that the bill would then become so controversial that it would fail. Indeed, his amendment was welcomed with laughter from his fellow representatives. Despite this laughter, the amendment did not have the effect he was after; the bill passed with the amendment intact (with a vote of 168–133).

In addition, and unlike the House, there is no germaneness rule in the Senate. Indeed, there are few restrictions on what senators may say during debate and no time limits; senators may speak for as long as they please. The Senate may adopt time limits by a unanimous consent agreement, but unlimited debate is generally protected. Limits come from a unique, Senate procedural tool: the *filibuster*. The Senate first allowed filibusters in 1806, although the process was not actually used until 1837, thirty years later. The filibuster was originally conceived as a way to ensure that minority opinions would be heard before the full Senate could vote. The concept was simple: so long as a senator continued talking on the floor, a bill could not move forward. In fact, nothing could be done in the Senate during a filibuster. Hence, the filibuster, as originally conceived, was a tool designed to ensure minority participation in the debate.

However, the filibuster became a tool used by the minority to prevent the deliberative process altogether. For legislation and political appointments to pass, they had to have the support of sixty senators. Southern Democrats used the filibuster to block civil rights and anti-lynching legislation. For example, Senator Strom Thurmond delivered one of the longest filibuster speeches in the history of the Senate when he spoke for more than twenty-four hours in an unsuccessful attempt to block a vote on the Civil Rights Act of 1957.* Today, senators need not actually physically "filibuster"; a threat to filibuster ("virtual filibustering") is sufficient to stop debate. However, some senators physically filibuster anyway; in 2015, Senator Rand Paul physically filibustered for more than ten hours to protest renewal of the Patriot Act.

Originally, the only way to end a filibuster was to wait for the "filibustering" senator to feel heard (or reach physical exhaustion) and cede the floor. To respond to the challenges the filibuster wrought, the Senate has modified the process three times since its creation. The first change came in 1917 when the Senate adopted Rule XXII,

---

* Similarly, in the famous movie "Mr. Smith Goes to Washington," Jimmy Stewart stood on the floor of the Senate reciting the Declaration of Independence for twenty-three hours to prevent the Senate from voting on a proposed bill.

a procedure known as cloture ("clôture" in French means "ending" or "conclusion"). Under cloture the Senate — originally two-thirds of "presenting and voting" senators; today, three-fifths (60) of senators "duly chosen and sworn" — can vote to limit debate to thirty additional hours.

The second change came in 1975 when the Senate changed the rules to allow Senate business to continue during a filibuster; as a result, use of the filibuster increased dramatically. The Senate became increasingly politically-divided and ineffective; senate republicans were refusing to confirm executive appointments. Hence, in 2013, the third change came when senate democrats eliminated filibusters for executive branch nominations and federal judicial appointments (other than the Supreme Court appointments). They did so using the nuclear option, a procedure that allows the Senate to override a rule using just a majority vote.

Assuming there is no filibuster or cloture occurs, the bill is voted on or sent back to committee. If there is a tie, the vice-president breaks it. Votes are recorded. The Senate process is temporarily complete.

Once a bill has passed one chamber, it is less than half-way towards passage, because both chambers must pass the identical version of the bill and either the president must sign it or the president's veto must be overridden. Once the first chamber passes a bill, it is *engrossed* and passed to the other chamber. The term "engrossed" is left over from a time when important documents such as statutes were copied onto parchment paper in large, clear handwriting. Today, bills are simply printed with a laser printer. The second chamber must pass the engrossed bill, no amendments or changes are allowed. If the second chamber passes the engrossed bill, the bill returns to the first chamber where it is then *enrolled*, signed, and transmitted to the president for approval or veto. The National Archives is the depository for the original bills.

Commonly, the second chamber will pass a similar, but not identical, bill (not the *engrossed* bill). Because the second bill is not identical, the two houses must consult in a conference committee, which is an ad hoc committee of select senators and representatives. The conference committee is made up of three to five members of each chamber, usually the senior members of the standing committees of each chamber that originally considered the legislation. Members of the minority party must also be included. The committee meets, discusses the differences in the bills, resolves those differences, recommends action, and writes a report analyzing those differences. While the conference committee is not supposed to substantially alter the bill language, in many cases conference committees have departed significantly from both the House and Senate versions. *See, e.g., Boyd v. Magee*, 2014 WL 2404288 (Ala. Cir. Ct.) (criticizing a conference committee compromise bill that "was three times as long as the prior version, adding two entirely new sections to the bill"). President Ronald Reagan once joked, "If an orange and an apple went into conference consultations, it might come out a pear." *The 7-step towards formalisation of Indo-US nuke Bill*, Yahoo! News India (ANI), http://zeenews.india.com/news/nation/7-step-towards-formalisation-of-indo-us-nuke-bill_336236.html.

Once the conference committee reaches a compromise bill, it submits the bill along with its committee report to the chamber that first passed the bill for approval. If that chamber approves the report, then the chamber votes on the compromise bill. If the new vote is favorable, the bill is sent to the other chamber, where the same process ensues. Once both chambers pass the compromise bill, the bill is returned to the first chamber, enrolled, signed by members of both chambers, and sent to the president for approval.

2. The President's Role — Presentment and Signing

The final step in the legislative process is the president's approval or veto. If the president signs the enrolled bill, it becomes law. Once signed, the secretary of state files the act (it is no longer a bill).

If the president vetoes the bill, returning it to Congress with objections, the bill only becomes law if two-thirds of the legislators of each chamber vote to override the president's veto. Finally, if the president chooses not to act — neither signing nor vetoing the bill — the bill automatically becomes law after ten days (excluding Sundays). U.S. Const. art. 1, §7, cl. 2. However, if Congress adjourns during this ten day period, then the bill lapses and does not become law. This lapse, which serves to veto the bill, is known as a pocket veto. Because Congress was adjourned, it would not have been able to override the president's veto.

If vetoed, the bill is returned to the legislature, often with a veto message. *See, e.g.,* John Tyler, Protest (Aug. 30, 1842), *in* 4 A Compilation of the Messages and Papers of the Presidents 1789–1897, 190–93 (James D. Richardson ed., 1897), *also available at* http://www.presidency.ucsb.edu/ws/index.php?pid=67561&st=unconstitutional &st1=signing. The legislature may override the president's veto only with a favorable, two-thirds vote from each chamber. Overrides are rare: Less than seven percent of vetoes are successfully overridden. Eskridge et al., Legislation and Statutory Interpretation, *supra,* at 76. Indeed, as of September 2015, there have been 2,566 vetoes (both regular and pocket) with 110 overrides (four percent). Interestingly, Franklin Roosevelt had the most vetoes (635); Harry Truman was second (250). In contrast, President George W. Bush vetoed twelve bills, none by pocket veto, and President Obama has vetoed nine so far (February 15, 2016) in his presidency. Unites States Senate, Summary of Bills Vetoed, 1789–present, http://www.senate.gov/ reference/Legislation/Vetoes/vetoCounts.htm.

The president must veto a bill in its entirety; the line item veto was held to be unconstitutional. *Clinton v. City of New York,* 524 U.S. 417 (1998) (finding the line item veto for appropriations bills unconstitutional). But note that forty-three states' constitutions allow governors the right to veto "items" in appropriation bills; "items" has been defined differently by each of the state courts. Eskridge et al., Legislation and Statutory Interpretation, *supra,* at 204.

Occasionally, when a president signs legislation, the president issues a signing statement. Signing statements, which were once obscure, have become commonplace.

In the box below is a signing statement from President Obama. Chapter 17 discusses the role these statements play in interpretation. Here, we focus on their development and constitutional legitimacy.

President Obama's signing statement on H.R. 1540

Today I have signed into law H.R. 1540, the "National Defense Authorization Act for Fiscal Year 2012." . . . .

The fact that I support this bill as a whole does not mean I agree with everything in it. In particular, I have ... serious reservations with certain provisions that regulate the detention, interrogation, and prosecution of suspected terrorists. . . .

... [S]ome in Congress continue to insist upon restricting the options available to our counterterrorism professionals and interfering with the very operations that have kept us safe. My Administration has consistently opposed such measures. Ultimately, I decided to sign this bill not only because of the critically important services it provides for our forces and their families and the national security programs it authorizes, but also because the Congress revised provisions that otherwise would have jeopardized the safety, security, and liberty of the American people. Moving forward, my Administration will interpret and implement the provisions described below in a manner that best preserves the flexibility on which our safety depends and upholds the values on which this country was founded. . . .

BARACK OBAMA

THE WHITE HOUSE, December 31, 2011.

President James Monroe was the first to issue a signing statement in 1822, in which he argued that the president, not Congress, held the constitutional power to appoint military officers. *Special Message to the Senate of the United States* (Jan. 17, 1822), *in* 2 A Compilation of the Messages and Papers of the Presidents 1789–1897, 111–13 (James D. Richardson ed., 1896), *also available at* http://www.presidency.ucsb.edu/ws/?pid=66281. Initially, presidents used signing statements to give notice of the way they intended to implement a law. President Tyler was the first to express concern regarding the constitutionality of a bill in a signing statement. *Special Message to the House of Representatives* (June 25, 1842) in 4 A Compilation of the Messages and Papers of the Presidents 1789–1897, 159–160 (James D. Richardson ed., 1896). Despite his doubts, which he wanted "left on the record," he decided to defer to "the solemnly pronounced opinion of the representatives of the people and of the States." *Id.* These "reluctant" signing statements became increasingly common.

President Reagan first decided that these statements could be used to enhance the executive's influence over statutory interpretation. Under the direction of Attorney General Edwin Meese, an assistant attorney general for the Department of Justice,

Samuel Alito, authored a memorandum titled "*Using Presidential Signing Statement to Make Fuller Use of the President's Constitutionally Assigned Role in the Process of Enacting Law.*" (*See* Chapter 17). In his memo, then Assistant Attorney General Alito reasoned that because bills require presidential approval in addition to approval by both houses to become law, "it seems to follow that the President's understanding of the bill should be just as important as that of Congress." *Id.* He suggested that signing statements could be used to "increase the power of the Executive to shape the law" and, further, "help curb some of the prevalent abuses of legislative history." *Id.* Attorney General Meese then convinced West Publishing Company to include signing statements in the legislative history section of the UNITED STATES CODE CONGRESSIONAL AND ADMINISTRATIVE NEWS (USCCAN), stating that inclusion would assist courts in the future to determine what the statute actually means. TODD GARVEY, CONG. RESEARCH SERV., RL33667, PRESIDENTIAL SIGNING STATEMENTS: CONSTITUTIONAL AND INSTITUTIONAL IMPLICATIONS 2–3 (2012). Since 1986, signing statements have been published in USCCAN. As a result, presidential use of signing statements to impact interpretation increased dramatically.

In 2012, the Congressional Research Service (a legislative branch agency located within the Library of Congress, which provides policy and legal analysis to both the House and Senate) counted the percentage of signing statements that contained "objections" to provisions of a bill being signed into law and concluded as follows:

> While the history of presidential issuance of signing statements dates to the early 19th century, the practice has become the source of significant controversy in the modern era as Presidents have increasingly employed the statements to assert constitutional and legal objections to congressional enactments. President Reagan initiated this practice in earnest, transforming the signing statement into a mechanism for the assertion of presidential authority and intent. President Reagan issued 250 signing statements, 86 of which (34%) contained provisions objecting to one or more of the statutory provisions signed into law. President George H. W. Bush continued this practice, issuing 228 signing statements, 107 of which (47%) raised objections. President Clinton's conception of presidential power proved to be largely consonant with that of the preceding two administrations. In turn, President Clinton made aggressive use of the signing statement, issuing 381 statements, 70 of which (18%) raised constitutional or legal objections. President George W. Bush has continued this practice, issuing 152 signing statements, 118 of which (78%) contain some type of challenge or objection. The significant rise in the proportion of constitutional objections made by President George W. Bush was compounded by the fact that his statements were typified by multiple objections, resulting in more than 1,000 challenges to distinct provisions of law. Although President Barack Obama has continued to use presidential signing statements, the Obama Administration has used the interpretive tools with less frequency than previous administrations — issuing 20 signing statements, of which 10 (50%) contain constitutional challenges to an enacted statutory provision.

Todd Garvey, Cong. Research Serv., RL33667, Presidential Signing Statements: Constitutional and Institutional Implications summary (2012).

Are signing statements legitimate? No constitutional provision, statute, or case explicitly permits or prohibits signing statements (or veto messages). While signing statements that indicate support for the bill are unobjectionable, reluctant and limiting signing statements are more problematic. Critics argue that these signing statements are unconstitutional, because the constitution provides only that the president may veto legislation with which he disagrees (U.S. Const., art. I § 7) or faithfully execute the laws she signs (U.S. Const., art. II § 3). Signing statements do neither and may intrude on the judicial role.

The use of signing statements crosses party lines. While President Clinton issued the most signing statements, President George W. Bush issued the most controversial ones. Bush routinely asserted that he would construe certain provisions in an act as advisory rather than mandatory "because such provisions, if construed as mandatory, would impermissibly interfere with the President's exercise of his constitutional [authority to] supervise the unitary executive branch." *See, e.g., Presidential Statement on Signing the Sudan Peace Act*, 2 Pub. Papers 1852–53 (Oct. 21, 2002). In essence, Bush was claiming that Congress could not pass a law that undercut the constitutionally granted authorities of the President. This articulation actually originated with President Reagan and was parroted by George H. W. Bush. *See, e.g., Presidential Statement on Signing the Bill to Increase the Federal Debt Ceiling*, 2 Pub. Papers 1096–97 (Sept. 29, 1987) (Reagan); *Presidential Statement on Signing the Energy and Water Development Appropriations Act*, 1991, 2 Pub. Papers 1561–62 (Nov. 5, 1990) (Bush).

President Bush's signing statement on the Sudan Peace Act

I have today signed into law H.R. 5531, the "Sudan Peace Act."....

Section 6(b) of the Act purports to direct or burden the conduct of negotiations by the executive branch with foreign governments, international financial institutions, and the United Nations Security Council and purports to establish U.S. foreign policy objectives. The executive branch shall construe these provisions as advisory because such provisions, if construed as mandatory, would impermissibly interfere with the President's exercise of his constitutional authorities to conduct the Nation's foreign affairs, participate in international negotiations, and supervise the unitary executive branch....

A provision of the Act defines a particular entity as the "Government of Sudan" for purposes of implementing the Act. The executive branch shall construe the Act in a manner consistent with the President's constitutional authority for the United States to recognize foreign states and to determine what constitutes the governments of such foreign states.

GEORGE W. BUSH

In July 2006, a bipartisan commission of the American Bar Association concluded that "the misuse of presidential signing statements by claiming the authority or stating the intention to disregard or decline to enforce all or part of a law the President has signed, or to interpret such a law in a manner inconsistent with the clear intent of Congress" is "contrary to the rule of law and our constitutional system of separation of powers." American Bar Association, House of Delegates Recommendation, August 7–8, 2006 (http://www.americanbar.org/content/dam/aba/migrated/leadership/2006/annual/dailyjournal/20060823144113.authcheckdam.pdf). While this criticism was directed at then President Bush, in 2011, the President of the ABA sent a letter to President Obama criticizing his use of signing statements as well. "Although during your 2008 Presidential campaign you said you would not use signing statements 'as a way to do an end run around Congress,' your statement accompanying your signing last week of the Consolidated Appropriations Act for 2012 is reported to be the nearly 20th such signing statement you have made since taking office.... [and] we must again voice the ABA's policy opposing this practice." Letter from Wm. T. (Bill) Robinson III to President Barak Obama dated December 30, 2011 (http://www.americanbar.org/content/dam/aba/administrative/litigation/materials/sac_2012/52-5_agr_2011_12_30_aba_letter_to_obama_re_signing_statements.authcheckdam.pdf).

Assuming the president signs a bill, it is then filed. Perhaps surprisingly, once an *enrolled* bill is filed, it is conclusively presumed to have been validly adopted—this rule is known as the *enrolled bill rule*. Courts will generally not entertain challenges to the legitimacy of the procedure used to enact the bill.

Some states follow the *journal entry rule* instead, which allows a court to determine whether constitutional requirements were met solely by looking at the journal entry. For example, under the journal entry rule, a judge could determine whether identical bills were passed, whether there were sufficient affirmative votes to override a veto, and whether a bill was subject to three readings (a holdover procedure from when some legislators were illiterate). However, because there is such a strong presumption that legislative acts are valid, the differences in the two rules are minor. Generally, courts will not entertain challenges to the legislative process of a particular bill. This rule (1) respects the division of labor among the branches by not allowing the judiciary to police the legislature's activity; (2) promotes stability by allowing citizens to assume that filed acts are law; and (3) promotes harmony by keeping the legislative and judicial functions separate. Arguably, a legislature could choose to ignore the constitutionally required process, knowing its choice will not be subject to judicial review, but legislatures rarely do so.

D. Legislative Process Theories

Scholars have advanced several theories to help explain the legislative process and its role in interpretation. For example, *pluralist theories* focus on the role special interest groups play in setting legislative policy. Interest group politics leads to "pluralism"—the spreading of political power across multiple political actors. The legislative process is one area in which conflicting interest groups' desires are resolved. Examples of special interest groups include political parties, churches, unions, businesses, and environmental organizations—among others. Interest groups can often accomplish what an individual cannot. Because there is strength in numbers, interest groups offer individual citizens the best possibility for meaningful participation in the legislative process. Theoretically, one benefit of a robustly pluralist system should be moderate, balanced, and well-considered legislation.

One pluralist theory is *bargaining theory*, which proposes that statutes are a compromise between these various interest groups. Individual interest groups seek a particular benefit or protection from government but often lack the clout to enact legislation absent support from other interest groups. Hence, interest groups work together to increase their political power and get bills enacted; yet, in doing so, these groups must compromise their goals. Pursuant to bargaining theory, judges should focus on furthering the compromises that produced the necessary votes for passage of the compromise legislation. For example, Title VII of the Civil Rights Act prohibits discrimination in the workplace on the basis of race. One compromise necessary to ensure the bill's passage was that white workers would not be disadvantaged to advantage minority workers. Bargaining theorists would expect judges to interpret the statute to not allow voluntary affirmative action programs, because such programs disadvantage white workers even while helping African-American workers.

Public choice theory is another pluralist theory. Public-choice theorists use economics to explain legislators' behavior. These theorists believe that statutes are the result of compromises among legislators that come about as a result of private interest groups lobbying. These private interest groups seek the best result for their members without regard for others. Access to the political process is disparate. Business interests tend to be overrepresented, while the broad public and the less advantaged interests tend to be underrepresented. For this reason, public choice theory helps explain the success of distributive legislation, legislation that rewards multiple special interests simultaneously. For example, tax bills that offer loopholes to many specialized groups or defense appropriation bills that send money to a variety of districts both are likely to be enacted because they benefit multiple groups. Under public choice theory, special-interest legislation and pork-barrel projects (a bridge to nowhere) should enjoy limited support, because these laws benefit very few special interest groups. However, legislators may choose to support special projects for a variety of reasons, such as to gain political capital with other legislators for the future, to pay back special interest groups for financial or other support, or to increase the chances of reelection or movement within the party.

Public-choice theorists believe that there can be no single legislative intent for enactment of legislation; rather, each legislator may have a multitude of reasons for voting for a particular bill. Given the possibility of multiple reasons, public-choice theorists urge judges to narrowly interpret statutes. Additionally, these theorists suggest that judges should not fill in the statutory gaps, because legislatures do not act for the public as a whole, but rather act to reward special-interest groups, and legislators act to maximize their own reelection potential. Public-choice theorists believe that judges should ignore legislative history when determining statutory meaning, because legislative history is irrelevant. Legislation is a compromise of intentions; therefore, they posit that no one can know exactly why legislators vote the way they do.

Public choice theory can be criticized for its skepticism. Not all legislators are opportunists looking for financial rewards from special interest groups; many are honest and have independent beliefs and goals that direct their legislative behavior. Thus, interest groups may be less effective at changing lawmakers' minds than public choice theory would have us believe. Finally, interest groups are better at blocking legislation than passing it, especially when legislation has low visibility. Hence, the theory may be inapposite for enacted legislation.

A second group of legislative theories, *proceduralist theories*, focuses on the legislative process and the political obstacles a bill must hurdle to become law. We just studied this process and its hurdles. One such theory focuses on the "vetogates" of the legislative process. Eskridge *et al.*, Legislation And Statutory Interpretation, *supra*, at 190. The legislative process is complex, and it is easier kill a bill than to pass one. At any one step, the bill might be stopped, or choked, from passage. Vetogates are the chokepoints that can prevent a bill from becoming law. For example, each chamber sends bills to standing committees, such as the Senate Judiciary Committee. The bill must be referred out of the committee to the full chamber, the Senate or House, before the bill can continue the enactment process. The committee is, thus, a vetogate, while the members of the committee (especially the chair) are gatekeepers: legislators that hold power at these vetogates.

Vetogates are important for two reasons. First, gatekeepers can simply block a bill's passage at any vetogate. Second, courts often reason that statements from gatekeepers, which can be found in the legislative history, reflect the intent of the legislative body because the gatekeepers' support would have been essential to the bill's passage. Yet this reasoning may be flawed. Because these gatekeepers have such power, they may abuse their position. For example, the Alaska National Interest Lands Conservation Act altered the rules for access to all non-federally-owned land within the boundaries of the National Forest System. In *Montana Wilderness Ass'n v. U.S. Forest Service*, the question for the court was whether a subsection of the Act applied nationwide or just in Alaska. 655 F.2d 951, 953 (9th Cir.), *cert. denied*, 455 U.S. 898 (1981). Congressman Udall, a key gatekeeper at the time the bill was enacted, had claimed while proposing an amendment that the subsection of the Act applied only to Alaska and had inserted a statement to this effect in the prepared remarks section. *Id.* at 956 n.9 (citing 127 Cong. Rec. 10376 & 126 Cong. Rec. H10549). However, other factors suggested that it was more likely that Congress intended the Act to apply nationally; thus, the court rejected the argument that Udall's comments showed congressional intent to limit the Act's application to Alaska. *Id.* at 957 n.11.

Our final legislative theory, the "*Best Answer Theory*," urges judges to interpret statutes to promote an "optimal state of affairs." Such a theory views judges as protectors of the minority, those individuals not in political power. Pursuant to this theory, a judge would likely find that Title VII of the Civil Rights Act does allow voluntary affirmative action programs, because such programs would remedy employment practices that had had a disparate impact on a less powerful group, racial minorities. Allowing an employer to enact voluntary affirmative action programs, rather than wait for possible litigation, would promote harmony, lead to positive social change, and protect minority interests. Thus, in this example, promoting the "optimal state of affairs" would support allowing affirmative action programs.

E. Direct Democracy: The Referendum and Initiative Process

In contrast to the legislative process described above, about one-half of the states and many local governments allow their citizens to adopt laws or amend their constitution directly using the *initiative process*. Additionally, almost all states allow their citizens to reject laws and constitutional amendments proposed by their state's legislatures via *referendums*. In this Country, the initiative process is more common than the referendum process and is, thus, the more important process. Both of these processes are examples of direct democracy. Each of these two processes is somewhat different, but both have in common the notion that law should come directly from the people. Note that there is no similar process at the federal level, where the legislature drafts and enacts all statutory law.

The initiative process is available in twenty-four states (mostly the Western states). An initiative is a citizen-drafted statute or constitutional amendment placed on the ballot for popular vote. The process is relatively simple. First, someone drafts an initiative. After the initiative is drafted, the proponents of the initiative must obtain the requisite number of signatures by petition to have the initiative placed on the ballot. After the initiative is placed on the ballot, the voters either approve or reject it. This is the direct initiative process, in which the legislature and executive play no role. In contrast, some states require that initiatives be submitted to the legislature before being placed on the ballot. If the legislature fails to approve the measure or amends it unsatisfactorily, then the initiative proponents must secure more petition signatures to get the measure on the ballot. This is an indirect, as opposed to direct, initiative process because the state legislature is involved. One of the more well-known state initiatives was California's Proposition 13, which reduced property taxes to 1976 rates and severely limited the ability of state government to increase them in the future. CA CONST., art. 13A. More recently, many states have had initiatives addressing the use of medical and recreational marijuana. *See, e.g.*, Montana Medical Marijuana Act. Initiative No. 148.

The referendum process is similar to the initiative process, but the referendum process is generally used to reject proposed legislation rather than to pass new legislation. Almost every state allows some form of referendum process. There are two different kinds of referendum—popular and legislative. *Popular referendum* refers to the right of the voters, by collecting signatures on a petition, to refer specific legislation the legislature passed to the voters for approval or rejection. In contrast, *legislative referendum* refers to the ability of elected officials to submit proposed legislation or constitutional amendments to the voters for approval or rejection. Legislative referendum is constitutionally required for constitutional amendments in all states but Delaware.

As you can imagine, statutes that come about as a result of these direct voting methods present particular interpretation and validity problems. If statutory interpretation is the art of discerning the intent of the enacting legislature (*See* Chapter 4), then whose intent matters when citizens draft the statute? Those courts addressing the issue have concluded that the voters' intent controls. *In re Littlefield*, 851 P.2d 42, 48 (Cal. 1993); *State v. Guzek*, 906 P.2d 272, 284 (Or. 1995); *Lynch v. State*, 145 P.2d 265, 270 (Wash. 1944). But which voters: those who drafted the initiative, those who petitioned to get the initiative on the ballot, or those who voted for it? Many voters are unable to understand complex, lengthy initiatives. Should their intent really matter? Concerns that we may have about legislators actually reading bills should be multiplied in the initiative arena. Moreover, voters' opinions may be formed from media portrayals, whether by news or political advertising. Indeed, some courts have looked at these sources when interpreting initiatives. *See, e.g., Lipscomb v. State Bd. of Higher Educ.*, 753 P.2d 939, 943–947 (Or. 1988) (en banc) (using newspaper and magazine articles, *inter alia*, to determine intent behind constitutional amendment adopted by popular initiative); *Lemon v. United States*, 564 A.2d 1368, 1379–81 (D.C. 1989) (considering newspaper article and voters' pamphlet to determine purpose of legislation adopted by the initiative process). *But See* Jane S. Schacter, *The Pursuit of "Popular Intent": Interpretive Dilemmas in Direct Democracy*, 105 YALE L.J. 107, 131 (1995) (noting "judicial disregard" of mass media sources and political advertising for finding popular intent behind initiative measures).

Even assuming you can decide which group's intent matters, discerning that intent can be trickier than discerning the intent of a legislative body that leaves a voluminous historical record in one location. For this reason, at least one scholar has suggested that courts should focus on the sponsor's intent. Glenn Smith, *Solving the Initiatory Construction Puzzle (and Improving Direct Democracy) by Appropriate Refocusing on Sponsor Intent*, 78 U. COLO. L. REV. 257 (2007).

At bottom, judges are skeptical about direct democracy processes: "[for] its lack of filters to calm the momentary passions of the people and its susceptibility to use by majorities to harm disfavored groups." ESKRIDGE *ET AL.*, LEGISLATION AND STATUTORY INTERPRETATION, *supra*, at 35. This skepticism can be seen in the case below. *Romer v. Evans*, 517 U.S. 620 (1996), in which the Supreme Court invalidated a state initiative that targeted LBG individuals because the initiative was based on a "desire to harm a politically unpopular group...." *Id.* at 632.

Romer v. Evans

Supreme Court of the United States
517 U.S. 620 (1996)

◆ JUSTICE KENNEDY delivered the opinion of the Court [in which STEVENS, O'CONNOR, SOUTER, GINSBURG, and BREYER, JJ., concur].

... The enactment challenged in this case is an amendment to the Constitution of the State of Colorado, adopted in a 1992 statewide referendum. The parties and the state courts refer to it as "Amendment 2," its designation when submitted to the voters. The impetus for the amendment and the contentious campaign that preceded its adoption came in large part from ordinances that had been passed in various Colorado municipalities[,] ... which banned discrimination in many transactions and activities, including housing, employment, education, public accommodations, and health and welfare services. What gave rise to the statewide controversy was the protection the ordinances afforded to persons discriminated against by reason of their sexual orientation. Amendment 2 repeals these ordinances to the extent they prohibit discrimination on the basis of "homosexual, lesbian or bisexual orientation, conduct, practices or relationships." Colo. Const., art. II, § 30b.

Yet Amendment 2, in explicit terms, does more than repeal or rescind these provisions. It prohibits all legislative, executive or judicial action at any level of state or local government designed to protect the named class, a class we shall refer to as homosexual persons or gays and lesbians. The amendment reads:

> "*No Protected Status Based on Homosexual, Lesbian or Bisexual Orientation.* Neither the State of Colorado, through any of its branches or departments, nor any of its agencies, political subdivisions, municipalities or school districts, shall enact, adopt or enforce any statute, regulation, ordinance or policy whereby homosexual, lesbian or bisexual orientation, conduct, practices or relationships shall constitute or otherwise be the basis of or entitle any person or class of persons to have or claim any minority status, quota preferences, protected status or claim of discrimination...."

... The trial court granted a preliminary injunction to stay enforcement of Amendment 2, and an appeal was taken to the Supreme Court of Colorado. Sustaining the interim injunction and remanding the case for further proceedings, the State Supreme Court held that Amendment 2 was subject to strict scrutiny under the Fourteenth Amendment because it infringed the fundamental right of gays and lesbians to participate in the political process. On remand, the State advanced various arguments in an effort to show that Amendment 2 was narrowly tailored to serve compelling interests, but the trial court found none sufficient. It enjoined enforcement of Amendment 2, and the Supreme Court of Colorado, in a second opinion, affirmed the ruling. We granted certiorari and now affirm the judgment, but on a rationale different from that adopted by the State Supreme Court.

The State's principal argument in defense of Amendment 2 is that it puts gays and lesbians in the same position as all other persons. So, the State says, the measure does no more than deny homosexuals special rights. This reading of the amendment's language is implausible....

... [W]e cannot accept the view that Amendment 2's prohibition on specific legal protections does no more than deprive homosexuals of special rights. To the contrary, the amendment imposes a special disability upon those persons alone. Homosexuals are forbidden the safeguards that others enjoy or may seek without constraint. They can obtain specific protection against discrimination only by enlisting the citizenry of Colorado to amend the State Constitution or perhaps, on the State's view, by trying to pass helpful laws of general applicability. This is so no matter how local or discrete the harm, no matter how public and widespread the injury. We find nothing special in the protections Amendment 2 withholds. These are protections taken for granted by most people either because they already have them or do not need them; these are protections against exclusion from an almost limitless number of transactions and endeavors that constitute ordinary civic life in a free society.

The Fourteenth Amendment's promise that no person shall be denied the equal protection of the laws must coexist with the practical necessity that most legislation classifies for one purpose or another, with resulting disadvantage to various groups or persons. We have attempted to reconcile the principle with the reality by stating that, if a law neither burdens a fundamental right nor targets a suspect class, we will uphold the legislative classification so long as it bears a rational relation to some legitimate end.

Amendment 2 fails, indeed defies, even this conventional inquiry. First, the amendment has the peculiar property of imposing a broad and undifferentiated disability on a single named group, an exceptional and ... invalid form of legislation. Second, its sheer breadth is so discontinuous with the reasons offered for it that the amendment seems inexplicable by anything but animus toward the class it affects; it lacks a rational relationship to legitimate state interests....

Davis v. Beason, 133 U.S. 333 (1890), not cited by the parties but relied upon by the dissent, is not evidence that Amendment 2 is within our constitutional tradition, and any reliance upon it as authority for sustaining the amendment is misplaced. In *Davis,* the Court approved an Idaho territorial statute denying Mormons, polygamists, and advocates of polygamy the right to vote and to hold office because, as the Court construed the statute, it "simply excludes from the privilege of voting, or of holding any office of honor, trust or profit, those who have been convicted of certain offences, and those who advocate a practical resistance to the laws of the Territory and justify and approve the commission of crimes forbidden by it." To the extent *Davis* held that persons advocating a certain practice may be denied the right to vote, it is no longer good law. To the extent it held that the groups designated in the statute may be deprived of the right to vote because of their status, its ruling could not stand without surviving strict scrutiny, a most doubtful outcome....

A second and related point is that laws of the kind now before us raise the inevitable inference that the disadvantage imposed is born of animosity toward the class of persons affected. "[I]f the constitutional conception of 'equal protection of the laws' means anything, it must at the very least mean that a bare ... desire to harm a politically unpopular group cannot constitute a *legitimate* governmental interest." Even laws enacted for broad and ambitious purposes often can be explained by reference to legitimate public policies which justify the incidental disadvantages they impose on certain persons. Amendment 2, however, in making a general announcement that gays and lesbians shall not have any particular protections from the law, inflicts on them immediate, continuing, and real injuries that outrun and belie any legitimate justifications that may be claimed for it. We conclude that, in addition to the far-reaching deficiencies of Amendment 2 that we have noted, the principles it offends, in another sense, are conventional and venerable; a law must bear a rational relationship to a legitimate governmental purpose, and Amendment 2 does not.

The primary rationale the State offers for Amendment 2 is respect for other citizens' freedom of association, and in particular the liberties of landlords or employers who have personal or religious objections to homosexuality. Colorado also cites its interest in conserving resources to fight discrimination against other groups. The breadth of the amendment is so far removed from these particular justifications that we find it impossible to credit them. We cannot say that Amendment 2 is directed to any identifiable legitimate purpose or discrete objective. It is a status-based enactment divorced from any factual context from which we could discern a relationship to legitimate state interests; it is a classification of persons undertaken for its own sake, something the Equal Protection Clause does not permit. "[C]lass legislation ... [is] obnoxious to the prohibitions of the Fourteenth Amendment...."

We must conclude that Amendment 2 classifies homosexuals not to further a proper legislative end but to make them unequal to everyone else. This Colorado cannot do. A State cannot so deem a class of persons a stranger to its laws....

♦ Justice Scalia filed a dissenting opinion, in which Rehnquist, C.J., and Thomas, J., joined.

The Court has mistaken a Kulturkampf* for a fit of spite. The constitutional amendment before us here is not the manifestation of a "'bare ... desire to harm'" homosexuals, but is rather a modest attempt by seemingly tolerant Coloradans to preserve traditional sexual mores against the efforts of a politically powerful minority to revise those mores through use of the laws. That objective, and the means chosen to achieve it, are not only unimpeachable under any constitutional doctrine hitherto pronounced (hence the opinion's heavy reliance upon principles of righteousness rather than judicial holdings); they have been specifically approved by the Congress of the United States and by this Court.

---

* Editor's footnote: "Kulturkampf" refers to the conflict between the German imperial government and the Roman Catholic Church in the late 1800s, concerning control of education and ecclesiastical appointments. It is used more broadly today to refer to a conflict between civil government and religious authorities.

In holding that homosexuality cannot be singled out for disfavorable treatment, the Court contradicts a decision, unchallenged here, pronounced only 10 years ago, see *Bowers v. Hardwick,* 478 U.S. 186 (1986),** and places the prestige of this institution behind the proposition that opposition to homosexuality is as reprehensible as racial or religious bias. Whether it is or not is *precisely* the cultural debate that gave rise to the Colorado constitutional amendment (and to the preferential laws against which the amendment was directed). Since the Constitution of the United States says nothing about this subject, it is left to be resolved by normal democratic means, including the democratic adoption of provisions in state constitutions. This Court has no business imposing upon all Americans the resolution favored by the elite class from which the Members of this institution are selected, pronouncing that "animosity" toward homosexuality is evil. I vigorously dissent....

... The only denial of equal treatment [the Court] contends homosexuals have suffered is this: They may not obtain *preferential* treatment without amending the State Constitution. That is to say, the principle underlying the Court's opinion is that one who is accorded equal treatment under the laws, but cannot as readily as others obtain *preferential* treatment under the laws, has been denied equal protection of the laws. If merely stating this alleged "equal protection" violation does not suffice to refute it, our constitutional jurisprudence has achieved terminal silliness.

The central thesis of the Court's reasoning is that any group is denied equal protection when, to obtain advantage (or, presumably, to avoid disadvantage), it must have recourse to a more general and hence more difficult level of political decisionmaking than others. The world has never heard of such a principle, which is why the Court's opinion is so long on emotive utterance and so short on relevant legal citation....

... The Court's entire novel theory rests upon the proposition that there is something *special*—something that cannot be justified by normal "rational basis" analysis—in making a disadvantaged group (or a nonpreferred group) resort to a higher decisionmaking level. That proposition finds no support in law or logic.

I turn next to whether there was a legitimate rational basis for the substance of the constitutional amendment—for the prohibition of special protection for homosexuals. It is unsurprising that the Court avoids discussion of this question, since the answer is so obviously yes. The case most relevant to the issue before us today is not even mentioned in the Court's opinion: In *Bowers v. Hardwick,* 478 U.S. 186 (1986), we held that the Constitution does not prohibit what virtually all States had done from the founding of the Republic until very recent years—making homosexual conduct a crime. That holding is unassailable, except by those who think that the Constitution changes to suit current fashions.... If it is constitutionally permissible for a State to make homosexual conduct criminal, surely it is constitutionally permissible for a State to enact other laws merely *disfavoring* homosexual conduct. And *a fortiori*

** Editor's footnote: Seventeen years later, this case was overruled by *Lawrence v. Texas,* 539 U.S. 558 (2003).

it is constitutionally permissible for a State to adopt a provision *not even* disfavoring homosexual conduct, but merely prohibiting all levels of state government from bestowing *special protections* upon homosexual conduct....

But assuming that, in Amendment 2, a person of homosexual "orientation" is someone who does not engage in homosexual conduct but merely has a tendency or desire to do so, *Bowers* still suffices to establish a rational basis for the provision. If it is rational to criminalize the conduct, surely it is rational to deny special favor and protection to those with a self-avowed tendency or desire to engage in the conduct.... Amendment 2 is not constitutionally invalid simply because it could have been drawn more precisely so as to withdraw special antidiscrimination protections only from those of homosexual "orientation" who actually engage in homosexual conduct." ...

... What [Colorado] has done is not only unprohibited, but eminently reasonable, with close, congressionally approved precedent in earlier constitutional practice.

First, as to its eminent reasonableness. The Court's opinion contains grim, disapproving hints that Coloradans have been guilty of "animus" or "animosity" toward homosexuality, as though that has been established as un-American. Of course it is our moral heritage that one should not hate any human being or class of human beings. But I had thought that one could consider certain conduct reprehensible—murder, for example, or polygamy, or cruelty to animals—and could exhibit even "animus" toward such conduct. Surely that is the only sort of "animus" at issue here: moral disapproval of homosexual conduct, the same sort of moral disapproval that produced the centuries-old criminal laws that we held constitutional in *Bowers*. The Colorado amendment does not, to speak entirely precisely, prohibit giving favored status to people who are *homosexuals;* they can be favored for many reasons—for example, because they are senior citizens or members of racial minorities. But it prohibits giving them favored status *because of their homosexual conduct*—that is, it prohibits favored status *for homosexuality*.

But though Coloradans are, as I say, *entitled* to be hostile toward homosexual conduct, the fact is that the degree of hostility reflected by Amendment 2 is the smallest conceivable. The Court's portrayal of Coloradans as a society fallen victim to pointless, hate-filled "gay-bashing" is so false as to be comical. Colorado not only is one of the 25 States that have repealed their antisodomy laws, but was among the first to do so. But the society that eliminates criminal punishment for homosexual acts does not necessarily abandon the view that homosexuality is morally wrong and socially harmful; often, abolition simply reflects the view that enforcement of such criminal laws involves unseemly intrusion into the intimate lives of citizens.

There is a problem, however, which arises when criminal sanction of homosexuality is eliminated but moral and social disapprobation of homosexuality is meant to be retained. The Court cannot be unaware of that problem; it is evident in many cities of the country, and occasionally bubbles to the surface of the news, in heated political disputes over such matters as the introduction into local schools of books teaching that homosexuality is an optional and fully acceptable "alternative life style." The problem (a problem, that is, for those who wish to retain social disapprobation of homosexuality) is that, because those who engage in homosexual conduct tend to reside in disproportionate numbers in certain communities and, of course, care about homosexual-rights issues much more ardently than the public at large, they possess political power much greater than their numbers, both locally and statewide. Quite understandably, they devote this political power to achieving not merely a grudging social toleration, but full social acceptance, of homosexuality.

By the time Coloradans were asked to vote on Amendment 2, their exposure to homosexuals' quest for social endorsement was not limited to newspaper accounts of happenings in places such as New York, Los Angeles, San Francisco, and Key West. Three Colorado cities—Aspen, Boulder, and Denver—had enacted ordinances that listed "sexual orientation" as an impermissible ground for discrimination, equating the moral disapproval of homosexual conduct with racial and religious bigotry. The phenomenon had even appeared statewide: The Governor of Colorado had signed an executive order pronouncing that "in the State of Colorado we recognize the diversity in our pluralistic society and strive to bring an end to discrimination in any form," and directing state agency-heads to "ensure non-discrimination" in hiring and promotion based on, among other things, "sexual orientation." I do not mean to be critical of these legislative successes; homosexuals are as entitled to use the legal system for reinforcement of their moral sentiments as is the rest of society. But they are subject to being countered by lawful, democratic countermeasures as well.

That is where Amendment 2 came in. It sought to counter both the geographic concentration and the disproportionate political power of homosexuals by (1) resolving the controversy at the statewide level, and (2) making the election a single-issue contest for both sides. It put directly, to all the citizens of the State, the question: Should homosexuality be given special protection? They answered no....

But there is a ... close[] analogy, one that involves precisely the effort by the majority of citizens to preserve its view of sexual morality statewide, against the efforts of a geographically concentrated and politically powerful minority to undermine it. The Constitutions of the States of Arizona, Idaho, New Mexico, Oklahoma, and Utah *to this day* contain provisions stating that polygamy is "forever prohibited." Polygamists, and those who have a polygamous "orientation," have been "singled out" by these provisions for much more severe treatment than merely denial of favored status; and that treatment can only be changed by achieving amendment of the state constitutions. The Court's disposition today suggests that these provisions are unconstitutional, and that polygamy must be permitted in these States on a state-legislated, or perhaps even local-option, basis—unless, of course, polygamists for some reason have fewer constitutional rights than homosexuals.

The United States Congress, by the way, *required* the inclusion of these antipolygamy provisions in the Constitutions of [these states] as a condition of their admission to statehood.... Thus, this "singling out" of the sexual practices of a single group for statewide, democratic vote—so utterly alien to our constitutional system, the Court would have us believe—has not only happened, but has received the explicit approval of the United States Congress.

I cannot say that this Court has explicitly approved any of these state constitutional provisions; but it has approved a territorial statutory provision that went even further, depriving polygamists of the ability even to achieve a constitutional amendment, by depriving them of the power to vote. [*Davis v. Beason*, 133 U.S. 333 (1890)] ...

To the extent, if any, that this opinion permits the imposition of adverse consequences upon mere abstract advocacy of polygamy, it has, of course, been overruled by later cases. But the proposition that polygamy can be criminalized, and those engaging in that crime deprived of the vote, remains good law. *Beason* rejected the argument that "such discrimination is a denial of the equal protection of the laws."[3] ...

... It remains to be explained how [the polygamy statute] was not an "impermissible targeting" of polygamists, but (the much more mild) Amendment 2 is an "impermissible targeting" of homosexuals. Has the Court concluded that the perceived social harm of polygamy is a "legitimate concern of government," and the perceived social harm of homosexuality is not?

I strongly suspect that the answer to the last question is yes, which leads me to the last point I wish to make: The Court today, announcing that Amendment 2 "defies ... conventional (constitutional) inquiry" and "confounds (the) normal process of judicial review" employs a constitutional theory heretofore unknown to frustrate Colorado's reasonable effort to preserve traditional American moral values....

I would not myself indulge in such official praise for heterosexual monogamy, because I think it no business of the courts (as opposed to the political branches) to take sides in this culture war.

But the Court today has done so, not only by inventing a novel and extravagant constitutional doctrine to take the victory away from traditional forces, but even by verbally disparaging as bigotry adherence to traditional attitudes. To suggest, for ex-

---

3. The Court labors mightily to get around *Beason*, but cannot escape the central fact that this Court found the statute at issue—which went much further than Amendment 2, denying polygamists not merely special treatment but the right *to vote*—"not open to any constitutional or legal objection," rejecting the appellant's argument (much like the argument of respondents today) that the statute impermissibly "single[d] him out." The Court adopts my conclusion[] that... insofar as *Beason* permits the imposition of adverse consequences based upon mere advocacy, it has been overruled by subsequent cases.... To [this conclusion], it adds something new: the claim that "[t]o the extent (*Beason*) held that the groups designated in the statute may be deprived of the right to vote because of their status, its ruling could not stand without surviving strict scrutiny, a most doubtful outcome." But if that is so, it is only because we have declared the right *to vote* to be a "fundamental political right," deprivation of which triggers strict scrutiny. Amendment 2, of course, does not deny the fundamental right to vote, and the Court rejects the Colorado court's view that there exists a fundamental right to participate in the political process. Strict scrutiny is thus not in play here....

ample, that this constitutional amendment springs from nothing more than "'a bare ... desire to harm a politically unpopular group,'" is nothing short of insulting. (It is also nothing short of preposterous to call "politically unpopular" a group which enjoys enormous influence in American media and politics, and which, as the trial court here noted, though composing no more than 4% of the population had the support of 46% of the voters on Amendment 2.) ...

Today's opinion has no foundation in American constitutional law, and barely pretends to. The people of Colorado have adopted an entirely reasonable provision which does not even disfavor homosexuals in any substantive sense, but merely denies them preferential treatment. Amendment 2 is designed to prevent piecemeal deterioration of the sexual morality favored by a majority of Coloradans, and is not only an appropriate means to that legitimate end, but a means that Americans have employed before. Striking it down is an act, not of judicial judgment, but of political will. I dissent.

* * *

Points for Discussion

1. *Rational Basis Review*: This case was unprecedented in its time. The Court held that discrimination against members of the LGB community violated the equal protection clause of the U.S. Constitution and did so using rational basis review. The rational basis review test is generally considered relatively easy for the government to meet; hence, the case is one of a very few in which the Court held that the government had not met its burden of showing a legitimate state interest. More commonly, litigants challenging the government will try to argue that a higher level of scrutiny should apply. Notice that the Colorado Supreme Court applied a stricter test known as strict scrutiny by finding that LGB individuals are a suspect class. Justice Kennedy chose to sidestep this designation.

2. *Rational Basis Application*: Justices Kennedy and Scalia both agreed that the appropriate test was whether there was a rational relationship to some legitimate end. Why then did they disagree? Given that rational basis review is very differential, why did Justice Kennedy conclude that the government failed to meet its burden?

3. *The Relevance of Bigamists and Polygamists*: Justice Kennedy argued that the citizens of Colorado enacted Amendment 2 out of animosity towards LGB people and concluded that animosity was an unacceptable reason for legislation. Justice Scalia noted that the states and federal governments have enacted similar laws targeting bigamists and polygamists, and yet the Court upheld the validity of those laws in *Davis v. Beason*, 133 U.S. 333 (1890). Would Justice Kennedy have held differently if the Colorado legislature had enacted a statute similar to Amendment 2 rather than the citizens?

4. *Bowers v. Hardwick*: Justice Scalia found *Bowers v. Hardwick*, 478 U.S. 186 (1986), to be controlling, yet Justice Kennedy never mentioned the case, even though it was the only Supreme Court case addressing homosexuality. Why might Justice

Kennedy have ignored it? Regardless, *Bowers* was overruled in 2003 by *Lawrence v. Texas*, 539 U.S. 558 (2003). Justice Kennedy wrote the majority opinion in *Lawrence*; Justice Scalia issued a strongly worded dissent in which he argued that gays should promote their "agenda" through "democratic means." *Id.* at 604 (Scalia, J., dissenting). Notice that Justice Scalia similarly mentioned the LGB agenda and its success in *Romer* as legitimate reasons for the Colorado citizenry to respond as it did.

5. *Regulating Conduct or Status*: Justice Scalia argued that because *Bowers* held that states had a legitimate interest in criminalizing homosexual *conduct*, states have a legitimate interest in regulating homosexual *orientation*. In other words, he equates sexual orientation with sexual activity. Do you find his argument persuasive?

6. *Animus as Illegitimate*: The Court used this "animus towards a socially undesirable group is illegitimate" rationale in two other cases: *USDA v. Moreno*, 413 U.S. 528, 534–36 (1973) (invalidating legislation targeting "hippies"); *City of Cleburne v. Cleburne Living Center, Inc.*, 473 U.S. 432, 445–46 (1985) (invaliding application of an ordinance to the disabled).

Problem 3

You are a staff attorney for a majority member of the Senate Department of Homeland Security Committee. Your boss sponsored a bill that was thought to be relatively straightforward. The Department of Homeland Security (DHS) has one of the largest automobile fleets in the federal government with 56,000 vehicles costing $534 million. That equates to about 4.5 DHS employees to every car the department owns. A DHS audit discovered that DHS was not effectively tracking Home-to-Work transportation—a program that allows over 17,000 DHS employees to use government vehicles to drive from their homes to their place of work. The audit examined whether DHS had authorized and properly justified employees' use of the program. It found, among other things, that DHS did not have reliable and accurate data on program costs, such as miles driven and fuel costs. The result is that DHS has little ability to identify fraud, waste, and abuse in the program. The bill you helped draft suspends the program until such time as DHS can provide clear evidence that it has addressed these deficiencies.

When the bill was debated in committee, there was strong opposition to it, especially by the chair of the committee; however, the committee reached a compromise. The committee has now marked-up the bill pursuant to this compromise and issued a final committee report. The bill has not yet been referred out of committee. In reading through the bill, you notice an ambiguity that you had not identified earlier and that has not been addressed by the committee. What do you do? Do you notify your boss? If so, do you advise your boss to raise the concern with the minority co-sponsor? Should your boss raise the concern with the committee chair—who would likely send the bill back to committee—thereby risking the possibility that the bill will fail? Should you suggest that your boss raise the concern during the floor debate and, if necessary, offer an amendment? Should you simply remain quiet or suggest that your boss do so, let the bill pass, and then let the courts resolve the ambiguity or seek an amendment in a future legislative session? If you let the bill pass out of committee, should you advise your boss to talk about what the bill means during the floor debate so that these comments will be included in the legislative history in case a judge were willing to consider that information?

Chapter 4

The Sources and Theories
of Interpretation

A. Introduction to This Chapter

This chapter introduces the building blocks underlying statutory interpretation: the sources of evidence judges use to find the meaning of statutes and the theories of interpretation judges use when approaching an interpretation question. While at first glance, this chapter may seem to be one designed for academics and theorists, it is not. Grasping the building blocks of statutory interpretation is essential for anyone wishing to make statutory arguments to a judge. Theory matters, but it matters in unusual ways. These sources and theories will enable you to "talk the talk," so to speak. You will not win your case simply because you talk about the text to a textualist judge, but at least that judge will understand what you are saying. Thus, in this chapter, you will learn a new language, one with which you are likely already somewhat familiar.

B. The Art of Statutory Interpretation

In its most basic form, statutory interpretation is the art of discerning the intent of the enacting legislature, for it is the enacting legislature that has the constitutional authority to make law. *See, e.g.*, U.S. Const. art. 1, § 1. Theoretically then, judges should interpret statutes as the enacting legislature expected, or intended. But discerning an enacting legislature's intent is extremely difficult; how does one discern the intent of a group of individuals all having potentially different goals? One cannot simply contact the legislators after the fact and ask them what they intended to accomplish. Even if they were still alive, even if they remembered having a specific intent on the issue before the court, and even if they remembered accurately, such after-the-fact rationalizations are not considered valid evidence of the intent of the legislature as a whole.

Perhaps more importantly, the idea that there can be one, unified "meeting of the minds" is fiction. While members of the legislature may share the goal of passing a bill to address a particular problem, rarely will all members have the same reason for voting in favor of a bill or even the same expectations regarding the bill's effects. Rather, bills are the result of committee work and political compromise. A bill "emerges from the hubbub of legislative struggle, from the drafts of beginning lawyers, from the work of lobbyists who are casual about clarity but forceful about policy, from the chaos of adjournment deadlines." Jack Davies, Legislative Law and Process in a

NUTSHELL 307–08 (3d ed. 2007). Because of the enactment process, bills regularly contain ambiguity, absurdity, lack of clarity, obscurity, mistakes, and omissions. Legislators do not intend to be ambiguous, absurd, unclear, obscure, mistaken, or incomplete — but they often are.

Because of the difficulty of discerning legislative intent, judges have adopted a number of ways to resolve statutory interpretation issues. Some judges focus on the words of the statute, believing that when a judge gives words their ordinary, public meaning, the judge will best further the legislative agenda. Other judges also focus on the stated or unstated purpose of the bill, believing that when a judge furthers that purpose, the judge will best further the legislative agenda. And other judges focus on the piecemeal nature of the legislative process, believing that when a judge compares various versions of the bill and the legislators' statements accompanying the enactment of that bill, that judge will best further the legislative agenda. Legal scholars have named these methods the "theories of interpretation" and have exhaustively argued about which theory best accomplishes the goal of statutory interpretation.

Understanding these theories is critical. Perhaps more than in any other area of law, understanding theory is critical to understanding statutory interpretation because theory drives every aspect of statutory interpretation. A judge's theory of interpretation determines what information a judge will consider when searching for a statute's meaning. For example, some judges will not consider legislative history or social context unless the text of the statute is ambiguous. *See, e.g., Entergy Gulf States, Inc. v. Summers*, 282 S.W.3d 433, 472–73 (Tex. 2009). To convince one of these judges to consider a bill's legislative history, you must first explain why it is necessary to go beyond the text for meaning. In other words, you need to learn to "talk the talk" of statutory interpretation. Indeed, you will likely lose your case unless you master this skill. Hence, this book covers theory early and in detail.

The theories derive from the three sources of information, or evidence, judges consider in construing statutory language: (1) intrinsic sources of meaning, (2) extrinsic sources of meaning, and (3) policy-based sources of meaning. These three sources are briefly explained below. The sources of statutory interpretation and the theories of statutory interpretation are interrelated but different. The theories, which we will study next, are based on the relevance of the sources to the interpreter.

C. The Evidentiary Sources of Meaning

To interpret a statute, a judge will look at a variety of sources of information, including intrinsic (or textual) sources, extrinsic sources, and policy-based sources.

1. Intrinsic Sources

Intrinsic sources can be defined as those materials that are part of the official act being interpreted. The first step in the interpretation process for all theorists is always

"Read the statute. Read the Statute. Read the Statute." John M. Kernochan, *Statutory Interpretation: An Outline of Method*, 3 DALHOUSIE L.J. 333, 338 (1976) (citing HENRY J. FRIENDLY, BENCHMARKS 202 (1967)). Certainly, the words, or text, of the statute in dispute are the most important intrinsic source. But the words are not the only intrinsic source. Other intrinsic sources include the grammar and punctuation; the components of the act, including purpose and findings clauses, titles, and definition sections; and the linguistic canons of statutory construction. Think of intrinsic sources as those coming from the pen of the legislature that are directly related to the bill as it was actually enacted.

The use of intrinsic sources is mostly non-controversial. One issue that arises is whether a judge should consider all of the relevant intrinsic sources in every case or just those cases in which the text is ambiguous or absurd. *See, e.g., State v. Courchesne*, 816 A.2d 562, 617 (Conn. 2003) (Zarella, J., dissenting) (arguing that "[i]f the language of a statute is plain and unambiguous, we need look no further than the words themselves, unless such an interpretation produces an absurd result."). As we will see in a moment, a judge's theory of interpretation helps resolve this question.

2. Extrinsic Sources

A second category of sources that judges may consider to discern meaning is the extrinsic sources—materials outside of the official act but part of the legislative process that created the act. Extrinsic sources include earlier drafts of the bill; legislative history (written and oral statements made during the enactment process); statutory purpose; legislative silence in response to judicial interpretation of a statute; interpretations from other jurisdictions of statutes patterned and borrowed from that jurisdiction; and interpretations by agencies of the ambiguous statutes they administer. Think of extrinsic sources as those sources related to the process of enactment and subsequent interpretation of the act.

The appropriate role for some of these sources—such as borrowed statutes—is relatively non-controversial. The use of others—such as legislative history—is highly controversial. Historically, intrinsic sources were regularly used to aid interpretation, while extrinsic sources were used more sparingly. After the New Deal, this historical custom relaxed, and judges turned to extrinsic sources, especially legislative history, more readily. Today, as a result of the reemergence of a text-focused approach, consideration of extrinsic sources is once again controversial.

3. Policy-Based Sources

Third, and finally, are policy-based sources. These sources are separate from both the act and the legislative (enactment) process and subsequent interpretation. These sources reflect important social and legal choices derived from the Constitution, common law, or prudence. Policy-based sources include, among others, the constitutional avoidance doctrine (the canon that if two reasonable or fair interpretations exist, one of which raises constitutional issues, the other interpretation should control); the rule of lenity (the canon that if two reasonable interpretations of a penal statute exist, the court should adopt the less penal interpretation); the remedial and derogation canons (the canon that statutes in derogation of the common law should be strictly construed, while remedial statutes should be broadly construed); and clear statement rules (the presumption that in some situations, such as ones raising federalism concerns, Congress would not intentionally alter the status quo absent a clear statement to that effect). Additionally, certain areas of substantive law have their own policy-based sources. For example, judges should construe ambiguities in tax statutes in favor of the taxpayer, and judges should construe insurance contracts to protect the reasonable expectations of the parties. *Travelscape, LLC v. South Carolina Dep't of Revenue*, 705 S.E.2d 28, 40 (2011) (Pleicones, J., dissenting) (interpreting a tax statute) *Phoenix Control Systems, Inc. v. Insurance Co. of North America,* 796 P.2d 463, 466 (Az. 1990) (interpreting an insurance contract). Think of policy-based sources as generally applicable doctrines not related to the act's text or enactment process (although exclude agency deference doctrines).

Reliance on policy-based sources comes in and out of vogue. For example, the rule of lenity, which arises from constitutional due process concerns about providing adequate notice, has been relegated to a rule of last resort with society's current focus on penalizing criminals. Some state legislatures, such as California, have attempted to abolish the rule of lenity by statute. *See, e.g.,* Cal. Penal Code § 4 ("The rule of the common law, that penal statutes are to be strictly construed, has no application to this Code. All its provisions are to be construed according to the fair import of their terms, with a view to effect its objects and to promote justice."); N.Y. Penal Law § 5.00. However, because the rule of lenity is derived, in part, from constitutional procedural due process concerns, these state legislatures have had limited success in abolishing the rule. *See, e.g., People v. Ditta*, 422 N.E.2d 515, 517 (N.Y. 1981) ("Although [Penal Law § 5.00] obviously does not justify the imposition of criminal sanctions for conduct that falls beyond the scope of the Penal Law, it does authorize a court to dispense with hypertechnical or strained interpretations...."); *People ex rel. Lungren v. Superior Court*, 926 P.2d 1042, 1053–54 (Cal. 1996) (noting that while the rule of lenity "has been abrogated ... the defendant is entitled to the benefit of every reasonable doubt ... as to the true interpretation of words or the construction of language used in a statute.").

While it would be nice if the above categories were consistently and clearly defined in judicial opinions and academic circles, they are not. What one person calls a policy-based source, another might identify as an extrinsic source (agency deference, for example). Understanding exactly which category a source falls within is less important than understanding (1) that there is a breadth of sources available to judges for understating a statute's meaning, and (2) that judges vary in their willingness to look at more than intrinsic sources. What sources a judge will consider depends on that judge's theory of statutory interpretation.

D. The Theories of Interpretation

Former Justice Scalia pushed hard for a specific method of statutory interpretation:

> I thought we had adopted a regular method for interpreting the meaning of language in a statute: first, find the ordinary meaning of the language in its textual context; and second, using established canons of construction, ask whether there is any clear indication that some permissible meaning other than the ordinary one applies. If not—and especially if a good reason for the ordinary meaning appears plain—we apply that ordinary meaning.

Chisom v. Roemer, 501 U.S. 380, 404 (1991) (Scalia, J., dissenting). "The hard truth of the matter is that American courts have no intelligible, generally accepted, and consistently applied theory of statutory interpretation." WILLIAM N. ESKRIDGE, JR. & PHILIP P. FRICKEY, INTRODUCTION TO HENRY M. HART, JR. & ALBERT M. SACKS, THE LEGAL PROCESS 1169 (William N. Eskridge, Jr. & Philip P. Frickey, eds., 1994). The Hart and Sacks quote is still accurate even though it is more than forty years old. Contrary to Justice Scalia's lament, judges do not always agree on how to interpret statutes. And, perhaps more concerning, you should "not expect anybody's theory of statutory interpretation ... to be an accurate statement of what courts actually do with statutes." *Id.*

So then why study theory? Theory is relevant even if judges find it impossible to apply consistently. It is relevant because judges need a way to approach statutes to determine, among other things, whether to rely more heavily on the text and linguistic canons or on other, extra-textual evidence of meaning; whether to consider legislative history and if so, which history; whether to consider the unexpressed purpose of the bill; and how to determine the weight to give a source that a judge will consider.

Judges use a variety of methods to interpret statutes. These methods vary in their emphasis on the sources identified above. The methods are called the theories of statutory interpretation. Adherents of the different theories differ in what they believe best shows the intent of the enacting legislature and, thus, the meaning of the statute. They also differ about what role the courts and legislature should play in resolving statutory ambiguity. Simply put, adherents of the theories differ in their willingness to consider sources other than the statutory text. For example, one group of theorists, textualists, believe that the text of the statute is central, while purposivists believe that the purpose of the statute is equally, if not at times more, important. *See, e.g.*, *King v. Burwell*, 135 S. Ct. 2480 (2015) (in which the majority opinion focused in large part of the purpose of the Affordable Care Act, while the dissent focused exclusively on the text).

Judges can and do blend these theories for a variety of reasons. Being consistent is more difficult than it may seem. A judge may generally prefer one theory, but find that for a specific case or even a specific issue, the preferred theory does not work. Hence, that judge may adopt a different theory or meld a variety of theories. Additionally, because one judge, who may approach statutory interpretation in one way, writes an appellate opinion, and other judges, who may approach statutory interpretation differently, join the opinion, appellate opinions rarely exemplify consistency. The theories described below are neither exhaustive nor exclusive.

Importantly, none of the theories is perfect; each has its strengths and its weaknesses, its proponents and its critics. Perhaps because of the imperfections, the preferred theory has varied with time. A theory that dominated during one era often falls out of favor in the next. For example, early in American jurisprudence, judges preferred to look at the purpose of the statute; today, the text has gained currency. Debate over the appropriate theory has raged; indeed, the battle over the appropriate way to interpret statutes has left the pages of academic law journals and become center stage in judicial opinions and in legislative debates. *See, e.g., State v. Courchesne*, 816 A.2d 562, 587 (Conn. 2003) (rejecting textualism in favor of purposivism only to be legislatively overruled Conn. Gen. Stat. Ann. § 1-2z (West 2003)).

Below, the strengths and weaknesses of the more prevalent theories are explained in some detail, beginning with textualism.

1. Textualism

Textualism is a theory of statutory interpretation that prioritizes the text of the statute at issue. Textualists look for the ordinary, public meaning of the words and phrases in the statute as of the time it was enacted. Textualists (unlike literalists) do not hone in on isolated words or sections in the statute, but rather look to the "whole law" in statutory context. *King v. Burwell*, 135 S. Ct. 2480 (2015) (Scalia, J., dissenting). Textualists do not look for the legislature's intent *per se*, but believe that the text best shows what the legislature was trying to accomplish. Textualists approach statutory interpretation in a relatively linear fashion, turning from one source to the next source in hierarchical order until an interpretation is found. Of all the theorists, textualists examine the fewest sources, because they focus primarily on intrinsic sources, especially the text and its relationship to the law as a whole.

As we saw earlier in *Yates v. United States*, 135 S. Ct. 1074 (2015), and in *King v. Burwell*, 135 S. Ct. 2480 (2015), a judge's understanding of separation of powers affects that judge's approach to statutory interpretation. Textualists believe that a judge's role is to be faithful to the Constitution by protecting the power distribution identified within that document: The legislature has the power to enact laws, while the judiciary has the power to interpret laws. And the Constitution requires a specific process for enacting statutes: bicameral passage and executive approval. U.S. CONST. art. I, § 7, Cls. 2 & 3. Pursuant to this constitutionally prescribed process, only the text of the bill is actually enacted; thus, textualists believe that looking beyond the enacted text raises constitutional concerns. Textualists "would hold Congress to the words it used.... [T]o do otherwise would permit Congress to legislate without completing the required process for enactment of legislation." Carol Chomsky, *Unlocking the Mysteries of Holy Trinity: Spirit, Letter, and History in Statutory Interpretation*, 100 COLUM. L. REV. 901, 951 (2000). Moreover, textualists believe that the text best shows the compromises reached during the legislative process. John F. Manning, *Federalism and the Generality Problem in Constitutional Interpretation*, 122 Harv. L. Rev. 2004, 2016 (2009) ("[R]eliance on purpose threatens to upset necessary legislative compromises because it arbitrarily shifts the level of generality at which the lawmakers have expressed their policy."); *see* Frank H. Easterbrook, *Statutes' Domains*, 50 U. Chi. L. Rev. 533, 540 (1983) (discussing legislative compromises).

Textualism is sometimes called the plain meaning *theory* of interpretation because textualism is based on the plain meaning *canon* of interpretation. The plain meaning canon of interpretation instructs that the ordinary, or plain, meaning of the words of a statute should control interpretation. The plain meaning canon nicely matches textualists' interpretative goal of finding the ordinary, public meaning of the words of the statute. Textualists presume that the legislature used words, grammar, and punctuation to communicate this meaning. Thus, textualists will start by looking at the text of the statute as it fits within the entire act (the statute in its textual context). If the meaning is still elusive, textualists will next consult other intrinsic sources, including the statute's grammar and punctuation, the linguistic canons, textual components such as title and purpose clauses, and the text of other statutes (the statute in its legal context). If meaning remains elusive, textualists will turn next to the extrinsic sources and, lastly, to the policy-based sources. Textualists are not completely text focused, but they generally refuse to look at non-intrinsic sources unless the language of the statute is ambiguous or absurd (*See* Chapter 6 for a discussion of both ambiguity and absurdity). In other words, only if intrinsic sources fail to resolve the meaning of the language at issue will textualists then look beyond intrinsic sources for meaning.

Textualism comes in gradations. While all textualists, indeed all theorists, start with and rely foremost on the text, textualists differ regarding when they will consider *non-text* intrinsic sources and what *non-intrinsic* sources they will consider. Some textualists require the text to be ambiguous or absurd before they will consult other non-text intrinsic sources such as the linguistic canons and grammar. *See, e.g., State ex rel. Kalal v. Circuit Court of Dane Cty*, 681 N.W.2d 110, 125 (Wis. 2004) (stating that "Wisconsin courts ordinarily do not consult extrinsic sources of statutory interpretation unless the language of the statute is ambiguous."). In addition, some textualists refuse to consider certain non-extrinsic sources altogether, such as legislative history. *See* Antonin Scalia, A Matter of Interpretation: Federal Courts and the Law 29–37 (1987) (explaining why he believes that legislative history is unreliable and irrelevant).

There are three types of textualists. First, there are the "soft plain meaning" theorists — those who view the text as the primary, but never the exclusive, evidence of meaning. The soft plain meaning approach is the oldest form of textualism. These theorists do not need to find the language to be ambiguous or absurd to consider either non-text intrinsic sources or non-intrinsic sources.

> If the words chosen for the statute exhibit a plain, clear statutory meaning, without ambiguity, the statute is applied according to the plain meaning of the statutory terms. However, if a statute is capable of being understood by reasonably well-informed persons in two or more senses[,] then the statute is ambiguous, and we may consult extrinsic sources to discern its meaning.

> While extrinsic sources are usually not consulted if the statutory language
> bears a plain meaning, we nevertheless may consult extrinsic sources to con-
> firm or verify a plain-meaning interpretation.

State v. Grunke, 752 N.W.2d 769, 775 (Wis. 2008) (internal quotations omitted).
Moreover, unlike strict textualists, soft plain meaning theorists are willing to consider
legislative history and legislative acquiescence.

Second, there are the moderate textualists for whom the plain meaning canon
controls. When the ordinary meaning of the text is plain, or clear, from the text in
context, interpretation is complete; no other sources are consulted, whether they be
non-text intrinsic sources or non-intrinsic sources. When, however, the meaning of
the text is ambiguous or absurd, moderate textualists will consider non-text intrinsic
sources (such as the linguistic canons, grammar, and components) and non-intrinsic
sources, including legislative history.

> When the statute is clear and unambiguous, courts will not look behind the
> statute's plain language for legislative intent or resort to rules of statutory con-
> struction to ascertain intent. In such instance, the statute's plain and ordinary
> meaning must control, unless this leads to an unreasonable result or a result
> clearly contrary to legislative intent. However, if the statutory intent is unclear
> from the plain language of the statute, then we apply rules of statutory con-
> struction and explore legislative history to determine legislative intent.

Florida Dep't of Highway Safety & Motor Vehicles v. Hernandez, 74 So. 3d 1070, 1074–
75 (Fla. 2011) (internal quotations omitted). Most textualists today are moderate
textualists.

Third, and finishing our textualist continuum, are the strict, or new, textualists.
Professor William Eskridge coined the term "new textualist" to show that this "new"
form of textualism differed from prior versions of textualism in that it was based on
a strict view of separation of powers, ideological conservatism, and public choice
theory. William Eskridge, *The New Textualism*, 37 UCLA L. Rev. 621 (1990). These
theorists, like moderate textualists, also require ambiguity or absurdity to look at
non-text intrinsic sources and non-intrinsic sources; but new textualists, unlike moderate textualists, refuse to look at some types of non-intrinsic sources altogether, such
as legislative history, legislative acquiescence, and unexpressed purpose. *See, e.g., INS
v. Cardoza-Fonseca*, 480 U.S. 421, 452 (1987) (Scalia, J., concurring) (criticizing the
Supreme Court's use of legislative history). Within the textualists' camps, new textualists are unique in their refusal to consider legislative history, legislative
acquiescence, and unexpressed purpose at all. New textualists believe that it is unconstitutional to consider anything that was not subject to the enactment process
outlined in the Constitution: namely, bicameralism and presentment. None of these
sources went through that process.

New textualists refusal to consider legislative history is multifaceted. Remember
that textualists are searching for the ordinary, public meaning of the words; hence,
discerning legislative intent is not their goal.

The meaning of terms on the statute books ought to be determined, not on the basis of which meaning can be shown to have been understood by a larger handful of the Members of Congress; but rather on the basis of which meaning is (1) most in accord with context and ordinary usage, and thus most likely to have been understood by the *whole* Congress which voted on the words of the statute (not to mention the citizens subject to it), and (2) most compatible with the surrounding body of law into which the provision must be integrated—a compatibility which, by a benign fiction, we assume Congress always has in mind....

Green v. Bock Laundry Mach. Co., 490 U.S. 504, 529 (1989) (Scalia, J., concurring). For this reason, new textualists do not believe that legislative history is helpful to the interpretive process. *See, e.g., Conroy v. Anskoff*, 507 U.S. 511, 519 (1993) (Scalia, J., concurring) ("If one were to search for an interpretive technique that, *on the whole*, was more likely to confuse than to clarify, one could hardly find a more promising candidate than legislative history."). Second, even if legislative intent were relevant to the interpretive process, it is not clear that legislators read committee reports, which staff often write; thus, the reports do not articulate the intent of a body that did not read or write them. Third, when legislative history cannot be considered as relevant to meaning, the cost of discerning meaning lessens and certainty increases. Because meaning becomes more assured, litigation decreases. Finally, when legislatures are held to the words they use, they are more likely to choose those words with care.

The most famous proponent of new textualism was former Justice Antonin Scalia, who was appointed to the Supreme Court in 1986. He first outlined his approach in 1985–86 during a series of speeches in which he urged judges to ignore legislative history, especially committee reports. When he was appointed to the Supreme Court, he brought his criticism of the Court's use of legislative history into the Court's jurisprudence. *INS v. Cardoza-Fonseca*, 480 U.S. 421, 452 (1987) (Scalia, J., concurring). At that time, many members of the Supreme Court regularly reviewed legislative history to look for evidence of legislative intent. Justice Scalia both brought life back to textualism, which had largely disappeared, and simultaneously narrowed the sources that could be considered. Justice Scalia initially gained a following for his new textualist approach and his criticism of the use of legislative history. Indeed, Judge Easterbrook of the Seventh Circuit promoted a similar agenda. Frank Easterbrook, *Statutes' Domains*, 50 U. CHI. L. REV. 533, 544–51 (1983). Justice Thomas is also a fan. While many of the other Justices have explicitly rejected Justice Scalia's suggestion that legislative history can never be relevant to statutory interpretation, Justice Scalia can be credited with returning the judicial focus to the statutory text as the starting point for interpretation. *See Wisconsin Public Intervenor v. Mortier*, 501 U.S. 597, 610 n.4 (1991) (rejecting Justice Scalia's disdain of legislative history).

Textualism, especially moderate textualism, is appealing, in part, because of its inherent simplicity—examine the text with dictionary in hand, and then be done. Turn to other sources in serial fashion if required. But textualism may favor simplicity over accuracy. One problem with the plain meaning canon is that language that seems clear to one person can be ambiguous or even mean something completely different to another person. For example, is a "buck" a male deer or a dollar? Is a "pig" an animal or a policeman? Is "dust" a verb or a noun? Is "bay" a body of water, a horse, or a noise? Is a mosquito an animal? While textual context may resolve which of multiple meanings was intended, litigation arises precisely because litigants and their lawyers disagree about the text's meaning. Theoretically, the plain meaning canon should never resolve an issue in any litigated case involving statutory interpretation unless one party is simply being unreasonable. If the meaning were that clear, the litigants would not be in court, paying large sums of money to attorneys to litigate the meaning of these clear words.

Notably dictionaries are not the nirvana that textualists claim. Sometimes a dictionary definition of a word differs from the ordinary meaning of a word, yet some judges rigidly adhere to the dictionary definition. For example, if a statute increases the sentence of anyone who "uses or carries a firearm" in relation to a drug offense, an ordinary reading of this language would suggest that a defendant must use the gun as a weapon to incur the additional penalty, not as an item of value to barter. But a dictionary definition of "use" is sufficiently broad to include bartering a gun for drugs. In *Smith v. United States*, 508 U.S. 223, 229 (1993), the majority used the dictionary definition to find that the statute included bartering a gun for drugs, while the dissent strongly objected, noting that "[t]he Court does not appear to grasp the distinction between how a word *can be* used and how it *ordinarily is* used." *Id.* at 242 (Scalia, J., dissenting). Justice O'Connor, who was an intentionalist, wrote the majority opinion in *Smith*, while Justice Scalia, who was a textualist, wrote the dissent.

Moreover, the meaning of words can vary with context. For example, the word "assault" might mean one thing in a criminal statute and something completely different in a tort statute. Or the word "tomato" may mean one thing to someone making a salad and another thing to a botanist. Further, the linguistic capability of the readers (including judges) can affect meaning. For example, some readers thoroughly understand the grammar rules, while others do not. For example, how many writers know when to use "which" and when to use "that"? For this reason, non-textualists argue that all sources of meaning are essential to interpretation. The New Mexico Supreme Court put it this way:

> [Textualism's] beguiling simplicity may mask a host of reasons why a statute, apparently clear and unambiguous on its face, may for one reason or another give rise to legitimate (*i.e.*, nonfrivolous) difference of opinion concerning the statute's meaning.... [T]his rule is deceptive in that it implies that words have intrinsic meanings. A word is merely a symbol which can be used to refer to different things. Difficult questions of statutory interpretation ought not to be decided by the bland invocation of abstract jurisprudential maxims.... The assertion in a judicial opinion that a statute needs no interpretation because it is "clear and unambiguous" is in reality evidence that the court has already considered and construed the act.

State ex rel. Helman v. Gallegos, 871 P.2d 1352, 1359 (N.M. 1994). Thus, despite its intuitive appeal, the plain meaning canon (the very essence of moderate textualism) is imperfect. We will study more of its limitations in Chapter 5.

New textualism can be faulted for other reasons. First, it can be faulted for the unwillingness of its adherents to ever consider some sources of meaning, namely legislative history and unexpressed purpose. It makes little sense to prohibit all evidence generated during the legislative process simply because that evidence was not enacted. Non-textualists do not claim that legislative history is part of the statute, or even that, in any sense, it is law. While the text is authoritative and has the force of law, legislative history and purpose provide evidence of what that law means. In other words, legislative history and purpose can help illuminate the meaning of the words that do make up the law. In short, new textualists' refusal to consider legislative history or unarticulated purpose in any case seems unreasonable.

Second, it is not clear why new textualists are willing to consult dictionaries and the linguistic canons, which similarly do not go through the legislative process, but are not willing to consult legislative history and unexpressed purpose. While it might be a good idea for legislators to use dictionaries and the canons when drafting, there is no proof that they do so. *See generally*, Abbe R. Gluck & Lisa Schultz Bressman, *Statutory Interpretation from the Inside — An Empirical Study of Congressional Drafting, Delegation, and the Canons: Part I.* 65 Stan. L. Rev. 901 (2013) (discussing the important role that legislative history plays in legislative drafting). If the Constitution allows judges to consider some non-textual sources, then why does it not allow consideration of all non-textual sources? Why is legislative history so untrustworthy?

In any event, Justice Scalia properly returned judicial focus to the text of the statute as the starting point for interpretation. As a result of his and others' influence, the text of the statute has gained primacy in recent years, which it will retain in the years to come. But support for new textualism itself seems to be waning. Thus, in the remainder of this text, when the word "textualism" is used, moderate, rather than new, textualism is intended.

To summarize, textualism examines the fewest sources. Textualists will look first at the text of the statute in its context. If ambiguity and absurdity remain, textualists turn next to the other non-text intrinsic sources, such as grammar and punctuation, the linguistic canons, and the components. If the ambiguity or absurdity still remains, textualists turn to extrinsic sources and, finally, policy-based sources.

In the case below, see if you can identify the distinction the majority makes between searching for legislative intent and for the meaning of the statute. Which approach is more similar to textualism? See also if you can identify the approach the concurrence prefers.

State *ex rel.* Kalal v. Circuit Court of Dane County

Supreme Court of Wisconsin
681 N.W.2d 110 (Wis. 2004)

modern Textualist

◆ DIANE S. SYKES, J. *2 Approaches*

In Wisconsin, the district attorney is primarily responsible for the decision whether to charge a person with a crime....

stat.

There are exceptions to this rule, however, and this case arises from one of them. Subsection (3) of Wis. Stat. § 968.02 provides that "[i]f a district attorney *refuses or is unavailable* to issue a complaint, a circuit judge may permit the filing of a complaint, if the judge finds there is probable cause to believe that the person to be charged has committed an offense." Wis. Stat. § 968.02(3)(2001–02)(emphasis added.).

Facts:
Complaint

This case involves an effort by a Madison attorney to invoke this procedure against her former employer and his wife for allegedly stealing funds earmarked for her retirement account. The attorney, Michele Tjader, first complained to the Madison Police Department and the Dane County District Attorney about the alleged theft by Ralph and Jackie Kalal. Several months later, after receiving word from the district attorney that she "was free to proceed legally in whatever manner she believed necessary," Tjader filed a motion pursuant to Wis. Stat. § 968.02(3) for the issuance of a criminal complaint against the Kalals....

Issue

We are confronted only with a question about the meaning of the term "refuses" in the statute....

[The lower court] held a hearing on Tjader's motion on March 13, 2002. [At the hearing, Deputy District Attorney Hanson] ... acknowledged that Tjader had contacted the district attorney's office "some months ago," and that the office had not filed a complaint in the matter. Hanson advised Judge Finn that he thought the district attorney's response to Tjader qualified as a refusal to prosecute under the statute:

> I don't think our office has ever affirmatively stated we would not prosecute. What we have done is fail to do so, so I think a fair reading of refusal in the statute encompasses both of the situations. We haven't told Ms. Tjader that we're not going to seek charges. We simply haven't done it yet.

... [The lower court held that the district attorney had refused to file.] We accepted review....

4 arg.

The Kalals ... argue ... that the statutory term "refuses" must be accorded a strict and literal interpretation, to require a direct and explicit statement of refusal from the district attorney, in order to avoid conflict between the branches in this area of shared power. While we recognize the constitutional tension inherent in this statute, we see no reason to depart from a straightforward, plain-meaning interpretation of the statutory term "refuses."

More than 25 years ago this court made the following observation about statutory interpretation:

There are two accepted methods for interpretation of statutes. The first, determining legislative intent, looks to extrinsic factors for construction of the statute. The second, determining what the statute means, looks to intrinsic factors such as punctuation or common meaning of words for construction of the statute. Whichever of these methods is used, the cardinal rule in interpreting statutes is that the purpose of the whole act is to be sought and is favored over a construction which will defeat the manifest object of the act.

[There is a difference] between the "statutory meaning" and "legislative intent" approaches to statutory interpretation … :

> Generally when legislative intent is employed as the criterion for interpretation, the primary emphasis is on what the statute meant to members of the legislature which enacted it. On the other hand, inquiry into the meaning of the statute generally manifests greater concern for what members of the public to whom it is addressed, understand.

… And finally, "resource materials for statutory construction are commonly classified into two fundamentally different categories, called 'intrinsic' and 'extrinsic' aids…." As a general matter, "[e]xtrinsic aids … are useful to decisions based on the intent of the legislature, while intrinsic aids have greater significance for decisions based on the 'meaning of the statute' as understood by people in general."

Viewed against these background general principles, Wisconsin's statutory interpretation case law has evolved in something of a combination fashion, generating some analytical confusion. The typical statutory interpretation case will declare that the purpose of statutory interpretation is to discern and give effect to the intent of the legislature, but will proceed to recite principles of interpretation that are more readily associated with a determination of statutory meaning rather than legislative intent—most notably, the plain-meaning rule. Although ascertainment of legislative intent is the frequently-stated goal of statutory interpretation, our cases generally adhere to a methodology that relies primarily on intrinsic sources of statutory meaning and confines resort to extrinsic sources of legislative intent to cases in which the statutory language is ambiguous.

Accordingly, we now conclude that the general framework for statutory interpretation in Wisconsin requires some clarification. It is, of course, a solemn obligation of the judiciary to faithfully give effect to the laws enacted by the legislature, and to do so requires a determination of statutory meaning. Judicial deference to the policy choices enacted into law by the legislature requires that statutory interpretation focus primarily on the language of the statute. We assume that the legislature's intent is expressed in the statutory language. Extrinsic evidence of legislative intent may become relevant to statutory interpretation in some circumstances, but is not the primary focus of inquiry. It is the enacted law, not the unenacted intent, that is binding on the public. Therefore, the purpose of statutory interpretation is to determine what the statute means so that it may be given its full, proper, and intended effect.

Thus, we have repeatedly held that statutory interpretation "begins with the language of the statute. If the meaning of the statute is plain, we ordinarily stop the inquiry." Statutory language is given its common, ordinary, and accepted meaning, except that technical or specially-defined words or phrases are given their technical or special definitional meaning....

Not ambiguous no need for further inquiry

... Where statutory language is unambiguous, there is no need to consult extrinsic sources of interpretation, such as legislative history. "In construing or interpreting a statute the court is not at liberty to disregard the plain, clear words of the statute."

The test for ambiguity generally keeps the focus on the statutory language: a statute is ambiguous if it is capable of being understood by reasonably well-informed persons in two or more senses. It is not enough that there is a disagreement about the statutory meaning; the test for ambiguity examines the language of the statute "to determine whether 'well-informed persons *should have* become confused,' that is, whether the statutory ... language *reasonably* gives rise to different meanings." "Statutory interpretation involves the ascertainment of meaning, not a search for ambiguity."

If ambiguous

At this point in the interpretive analysis the cases will often recite the following: "If a statute is ambiguous, the reviewing court turns to the scope, history, context, and purpose of the statute." ... [T]his common formulation is somewhat misleading: scope, context, and purpose are perfectly relevant to a plain-meaning interpretation of an unambiguous statute as long as the scope, context, and purpose are ascertainable from the text and structure of the statute itself, rather than extrinsic sources, such as legislative history.

Some statutes contain explicit statements of legislative purpose or scope. A statute's purpose or scope may be readily apparent from its plain language or its relationship to surrounding or closely-related statutes — that is, from its context or the structure of the statute as a coherent whole. Many words have multiple dictionary definitions; the applicable definition depends upon the context in which the word is used. Accordingly, it cannot be correct to suggest, for example, that an examination of a statute's purpose or scope or context is completely off-limits unless there is ambiguity. It is certainly not inconsistent with the plain-meaning rule to consider the intrinsic context in which statutory language is used; a plain-meaning interpretation cannot contravene a textually or contextually manifest statutory purpose.[8]

What is clear, however, is that Wisconsin courts ordinarily do not consult extrinsic sources of statutory interpretation unless the language of the statute is ambiguous.

---

8. In her concurrence the chief justice represents that "[t]his opinion correctly concludes that a court resorts to the scope, context, and purpose of the statute without having to declare an ambiguity in the statute." This somewhat overstates our holding. We have noted that a statute's scope, context, and purpose are often apparent from the statutory text itself. A plain meaning, text-based approach to statutory interpretation certainly does not prohibit the interpretation of a statute in light of its textually manifest scope, context, or purpose. We do not by this conclusion endorse the methodology advanced by the chief justice in her concurrence that calls for consultation of extrinsic, non-textual sources of interpretation in every case, regardless of whether the language of the statute is clear. Such an approach subordinates the statutory text and renders the analysis more vulnerable to subjectivity....

By "extrinsic sources" we mean interpretive resources outside the statutory text—typically items of legislative history....

... [A]s a general matter, legislative history need not be and is not consulted except to resolve an ambiguity in the statutory language, although legislative history is sometimes consulted to confirm or verify a plain-meaning interpretation.

Properly stated and understood, this approach to statutory interpretation is not literalistic, nor is it "conclusory" or "result-oriented" in application, as suggested by the chief justice's concurrence. An interpretive method that focuses on textual, intrinsic sources of statutory meaning and cabins the use of extrinsic sources of legislative intent is grounded in more than a mistrust of legislative history or cynicism about the capacity of the legislative or judicial processes to be manipulated. The principles of statutory interpretation that we have restated here are rooted in and fundamental to the rule of law....

Applying these principles here, we conclude that the language of Wis. Stat. § 968.02(3) is clear and unambiguous. More particularly, the term "refuse" (as in "the district attorney refuses") has a common and accepted meaning, ascertainable by reference to the dictionary definition.

To refuse is "[t]o indicate unwillingness to do, accept, give, or allow." *The American Heritage Dictionary of the English Language* 1519 (3d ed.1992). As the term is ordinarily understood, a "refusal" involves a decision to reject a certain choice or course of action. This definition is reasonable in the statutory context and consistent with the manifest statutory purpose. Accordingly, the statute's meaning is plain, there is no ambiguity to clarify, and no need to consult extrinsic sources such as legislative history....

♦ SHIRLEY S. ABRAHAMSON, C.J., (concurring).

I join the mandate, but I return once again to this court's approach(es) to statutory interpretation. It is important, as I have written before, that litigants, lawyers, legislators, courts, and the people of Wisconsin know and understand our approach to legislative interpretation.

This opinion makes what I consider a significant advance in explaining what the court is actually doing in statutory interpretation. I think, however, it will be difficult to understand and apply parts of this opinion because it works at cross purposes in several respects. For example, the opinion strongly emphasizes textualism but broadens textualism to include many matters the plain meaning folk (including those on this court) have rejected. It recognizes that the purposes of the legislation should be considered in interpretation but refuses to consider the consequences of different interpretations as an aid to interpretation (but does consider the consequences right in this opinion).

The most significant advance is that the court at long last abandons its too-oft quoted but erroneous aphorism that to determine the intent of the legislature[3] "if a

---

3. As I have written previously, this court has consistently and resolutely held that the purpose of statutory interpretation is to determine and give effect to the intent of the legislature in enacting

statute is ambiguous, the reviewing court turns to the scope, history, context, and purpose of the statute."

This opinion correctly concludes that a court resorts to the scope, context, and purpose of the statute without having to declare an ambiguity in the statute. The majority opinion states: "[S]cope, context, and purpose are perfectly relevant to a plain-meaning interpretation of an unambiguous statute as long as the scope, context, and purpose are ascertainable from the text and structure of the statute itself, rather than extrinsic sources, such as legislative history."

The trick in understanding and applying this sentence is to give meaning to the phrase "ascertainable from the text and structure of the statute itself." "Ascertainable," "text," and "structure of the statute itself" have elasticity. From my perspective that is a saving grace.

Our cases have been inconsistent in stating whether an ambiguity must be declared before a court examines the terms of a statute in relation to the scope, history, context, and subject matter of the legislation, the spirit or nature of the act, the evil intended to be remedied, the general object sought to be accomplished, and the consequences. The majority opinion now separates "history" from the other listed sources of legislative intent, without defining history, and discusses only legislative history. Before a court uses legislative history, a court must declare the statute ambiguous, according to the majority opinion.

I part company with the majority opinion when it declares that extrinsic sources (not defined) such as legislative history may be used only when the statutory language is ambiguous or when the legislative history supports (but does not contradict) the plain meaning of the statute....[11] Language is often ambiguous; the distinction between "plain" and "ambiguous" is in the eye of the beholder; and both words too often are conclusory labels a court pins on a statute, making its decision appear result-oriented....

Legislative history, especially legislative committee reports and the congressional record, has gotten a bad reputation in recent years in federal circles because legislative

---

a particular statute. It is, of course, a legal fiction to assert that there is an actual legislative "intent." "It is impossible to argue that a legislative body actually has a collective, corporate intent that is somehow the sum of the individual, and often conflicting, intents of its members."

Rather, discerning and giving effect to the "intent" of the legislature is an exercise in logic in which a court determines what a reasonable person in the position of a legislator enacting the statute would have said about the legal issue presented in a given case.

11. Justice Scalia, a textualist and an opponent of the use of federal legislative history, nevertheless allows the use of legislative history to avoid an absurd result. *Green v. Bock Laundry Mach. Co.*, 490 U.S. 504, 527 (1989) (Scalia, J., concurring). When a student at the University of Washington Law School challenged Justice Scalia to tell the audience how he would interpret a particular constitutional provision whose plain meaning was obviously unacceptable, the Justice is reported to have said, "I'm a strict constructionist but I'm not a kook." The New York Times reported that Justice Scalia was quick to assure an audience that he might not be prepared to follow all of his criticisms of constitutional interpretation to their logical conclusion. The justice commented, "I am a textualist. I am an originalist. I am not a nut." Adam Liptak, *In Re Scalia the Outspoken v. Scalia the Reserved*, The New York Times, May 2, 2004, at 27.

history may be manufactured by both proponents and opponents of the legislation, and often every position can be buttressed by something in the federal legislative history. Nevertheless, legislative history that is well understood and carefully weighed can help a court understand a statute.

Legislative history at the state level differs from federal legislative history. For one thing, there is a lot less legislative history in Wisconsin than at the federal level, and manufacturing of legislative history is a less well-known and less perfected skill here....

I agree with the approach the Canadian courts take. In *Ontario (Ministry of Labour) v. Hamilton,* [2002] 58 O.R.3d 37, the court of appeal for Ontario wrote as follows:

> The modern approach to statutory interpretation calls on the court to interpret a legislative provision in its total context. The court should consider and take into account all relevant and admissible indicators of legislative meaning. The court's interpretation should comply with the legislative text, promote the legislative purpose, reflect the legislature's intent, and produce a reasonable and just meaning.... The Supreme Court has repeatedly affirmed this approach to statutory interpretation....

... Without this comprehensive approach, this court risks usurping the legislative role and substituting its judgment for the legislature's intent. It is only through complete analysis and weighing of available materials that we can ascertain the meaning of a statute and effectuate legislative intent.

◆ ANN WALSH BRADLEY, J. (concurring).

... I also agree that the district attorney's actions constituted a "refusal" under Wis. Stat. § 968.02(3). However, I write separately because of the competing discussions of statutory interpretation. Although I commend both the majority and concurrence for their endeavors, I ultimately join neither.

* * *

Points for Discussion

1. *Statutory Language*: What was the language at issue? What did each party want that language to mean? What meaning did the majority and concurrences adopt and why?

2. *Theories*: From this case forward, you should begin to identify the theories of statutory interpretation that are used in each opinion. While judges can and do mix the approaches, typically one approach pervades the opinion. Which of the opinions best exemplifies textualism? Which form of textualism?

3. *Using Other Sources When Text Is Clear*: Pursuant to the majority's approach, can a judge look to a statute's unexpressed purpose or legislative history when the statute is clear? What about the concurrences?

4. *Concurrences*: Why does Judge Abrahamson concur? Judge Bradley?

5. *Constitutional Interpretation Distinguished*: Like statutory interpretation, there are many ways to approach constitutional interpretation including textualism, originalism, strict constructionism, functionalism, doctrinalism, developmentalism, contextualism, and structuralism. For now, let's explore just two of these theories: originalism and textualism. Originalist theorists focus on finding the subjective intentions of the drafters of particular constitutional provisions. Originalists look for the meaning or understanding of the constitutional provision at the time the provision was ratified or amended. In contrast, textualists or strict constructionalists focus on the literal meaning of a constitutional provision and reject claims that the text can mean more or less than what it expressly says. For example, former Supreme Court Justice Hugo Black claimed that the First Amendment's language that "Congress shall make no law ... abridging the freedom of speech" was clear: "No law" meant absolutely no law, not even laws imposing time, place, or manner restrictions. Strict constructionism appeals to those who wish for simplicity and determinacy. Today, the most fundamental disagreement among constitutional theorists is whether the U.S. Constitution is a living document, which is to some degree dynamic and able to change with a changing society, or whether it is a document fixed as of a certain point in time, its origination. Justice Breyer and former Justice Scalia disagreed about this issue. You can see their debate here: http://www.c-span.org/video/?289637-1/principles-constitutional-statutory-interpretation.

6. *Follow-up*: Shortly after *Kalal* was decided, indeed in the same term, the Wisconsin Supreme Court decided *Keup v. Wisconsin Dept. of Health & Family Services*, 675 N.W. 2d 755 (Wis. 2004). In that case, the court used the language the *Kalal* majority had expressly rejected:

> If the statute is unambiguous, we must give effect to the words within the statute according to their common meanings. As a general rule, we do not review extrinsic sources unless there is an ambiguity. If the statutory language is ambiguous, however, we then may *use the scope, history, context, and subject matter* of the statute in order to ascertain legislative intent.

Id. at 763 (emphasis added). The *Kalal* majority had worked so hard to make its approach clear in *Kalal*, then simply returns to the earlier formulation. Why? While it is difficult to know for certain, the *Keup* majority opinion was written by a different judge from the one who wrote the *Kalal* majority opinion. The *Keup* judge (Judge Crooks) may be more willing to approach interpretation in the way the *Kalal* concurrence does. Judges Abrahamson and Bradley dissented for reasons unrelated to the approach used. None of the opinions mentioned *Kalal*.

7. *Legislating Methodology*: Although the Justices of the Supreme Court have wrestled with the appropriate approach to statutory interpretation, Congress has chosen not to provide direct guidance, though some scholars have suggested that it should. *Compare* Nicholas Quinn Rosenkranz, *Federal Rules of Statutory Interpretation*, 115 Harv. L. Rev. 2085, 2103–10 (2002) (arguing that Congress can constitutionally enact statutes telling federal courts which theory to use

when interpreting statutes); *with* Linda D. Jellum, *"Which is to be Master," the Judiciary or the Legislature? When Statutory Directives Violate Separation of Powers*, 56 UCLA L. Rev. 837, 847 (2009) (arguing that Congress cannot enact such statutes without violating separation of powers); Antonin Scalia & Bryan A. Garner, Reading Law: The Interpretation of Legal Texts 245 (2012) (saying that any attempt by Congress to direct statutory interpretation would likely be unconstitutional).

8. *Textualism in the States*: In contrast, many state legislatures have adopted statutes telling their judges how to interpret statutes. Not surprisingly, textualism is the most common choice. For example, Connecticut has a textualist directive that reads as follows:

> The meaning of a statute shall, in the first instance, be ascertained from the text of the statute itself and its relationship to other statutes. If, after examining such text and considering such relationship, the meaning of such text is plain and unambiguous and does not yield absurd or unworkable results, extratextual evidence of the meaning of the statute shall not be considered.

Conn. Gen. Stat. Ann. § 1-2z (West 2015). Colorado, Hawaii, Iowa, North Dakota, Ohio, and Pennsylvania also have textualist directives. Colo. Rev. Stat. § 2-4-203 (2015); Haw. Rev. Stat. Ann. § 1-15 (LexisNexis 2015); Iowa Code Ann. § 4.6 (West 2015); N.D. Cent. Code § 1-02-39 (2015); Ohio Rev. Code Ann. § 1.49 (West 2015); 1 Pa. Cons. Stat. § 1921(b) (2015).

* * *

2. Intentionalist-Based Theories

Intentionalist-based theorists reject textualism for the reasons identified in the last section. Intentionalist-based theories are rooted in the belief that an elected, representative body should choose the policies that govern society. For intentionalist-based theorists, the court's duty is to discern the intent of that representative body and interpret statutes to further that intent. Thus, intentionalist-based theorists attempt to understand the meaning of statutes by looking for the enacting legislature's intent.

There are two kinds of intent: specific intent and general intent. Specific intent can be defined as the intent of the enacting legislature on a specific issue. For example, if a court had to determine whether affirmative action programs were allowable under a statute providing that "no person shall be discriminated against on the basis of race," a judge looking for specific intent would search the sources of meaning to determine whether the enacting legislature intended the word "discriminate" to apply to affirmative action programs that promote the hiring of racial minorities. If the legislative history for this statute showed that the legislators actually discussed affirmative action programs positively or negatively during, for example, the House or Senate floor debates, then a judge looking for specific intent would conclude that the legislature intended the word "discriminate" to include or to not include affirmative action programs, depending on the tenor of the debate. Thus, a judge seeking specific intent is looking to see whether the enacting legislature had a specific intent as to the language in dispute, in this case "discriminate."

In contrast, general intent refers to the overall goal or purpose of the legislature as a whole and is generally much easier to find. For example, if we return to the discrimination statute in the last paragraph, a judge looking for general intent would search the sources of meaning to determine whether the enacting legislature's purpose was to make society color-blind or was to improve the plight of racial minorities. If the legislative history for this statute showed that the legislators wanted to improve the plight of minorities, then a judge looking for general intent would likely conclude that the word "discriminate" should not include affirmative action programs. Whether the legislators actually thought about whether the word "discriminate" included affirmative action programs would not be the central question for a judge seeking general intent (though it may still be relevant). A judge seeking general intent is looking to see what the legislators' goal, or purpose, for enacting the statute was.

The two, prominent intentionalist-based theories are ① intentionalism, which focuses on specific intent, and ② purposivism, which focuses on general intent. Each of these theories is explored in detail below. A few of the less common, but related theories are also addressed.

a. Intentionalism → specific intent, "originalists"

Intentionalists, sometimes referred to as originalists, seek out the *specific intent* of the legislature that enacted the statute: What did that legislature have in mind in regard to the specific issue before the court when the legislature enacted the statute? To find specific intent, intentionalists start with the statutory text. But intentionalists do not stop with the text even if the text is clear, as a textualist would do; rather, intentionalists move on and examine the other sources of meaning. Unlike a textualist, an intentionalist does not need a reason, such as ambiguity or absurdity, to consider sources beyond the text. In perusing other sources, intentionalists are looking for help in discerning the specific intent of the enacting legislature. Thus, intentionalists often find statements made during the enactment process and early draft versions of the bill relevant, though intentionalists are willing to consider all sources of meaning. If these sources demonstrate that the legislature did not intend for the text to have its ordinary meaning, intentionalists will reject the ordinary meaning for a meaning that furthers the specific intent, as discovered in these other sources.

As mentioned, a judge's understanding of separation of powers affects that judge's approach to statutory interpretation. Intentionalists believe that the judicial role is to be faithful agents of the legislature, working to ensure that the legislature's policy choices are implemented. They believe that examining sources other than the text helps constrain the judiciary and helps maintain its separate function — that of interpreting — by providing more information for a fully informed decision. Further, intentionalists believe that their approach furthers separation of powers, because it protects the legislature's power to legislate from judicial interference: Judges must implement the *enacting* legislature's intent not impose their own policy preferences.

Intentionalism is not without weaknesses. For example, consider whether the Senate, a group of 100 individuals, all with different constituencies, can have one, unified intent. Some say not. Each legislator may have a unique reason for voting for a bill. For example, Title VII of the Civil Rights Act, which prohibits discrimination in the workplace, was a compromise of various competing interests: The liberal, Northern and Eastern legislators (who sponsored the bill) wanted to help African-American workers; the conservative Southern legislators wanted to ensure that African-American workers were not helped at the expense of white workers; and finally the conservative Midwestern legislators, the pivotal voters, wanted to limit government interference in business. With so many different legislators with so many different intentions, it is unlikely that each of these legislators would agree about whether affirmative action programs should be allowed. The liberal Northern and Eastern legislators would likely have said "yes," while the more conservative Southern and Midwestern legislators would likely have said "no."

Additionally, one might ask, whose intent matters: "the 51st senator, needed to pass the bill, or the 67th, needed to break the southern filibuster"? William N. Eskridge, Jr. *et al.*, Legislation and Statutory Interpretation 219 (2d 2006). In *United Steelworkers v. Weber,* 443 U.S. 193 (1979) (Burger, C.J., Rehnquist, J. dissenting), the case in which this issue was addressed, the Supreme Court's majority and dissent disagreed on whose intent was central. The majority focused on the liberal, Northern and Eastern legislators, while the dissent focused on the conservative, Southern and Midwestern legislators.

Of course, intentionalists respond to that criticism by arguing that a group can have intent. While the individual members may have different, private *motives* for their own actions, the existence of private motives does not necessarily eliminate the possibility that the group has a common goal or agenda. For example, consider a sports team as it takes the field, a political party as it enters an election, or the board of a company preparing annual strategy. The group's agenda and the members' motives might not be identical, but each group has one, overarching intent: to win. Intentionalism is thus less about the reality of always finding a unified intent and more about the *possibility* of finding one.

Intentionalists' use of legislative history takes us to a second criticism of intentionalism. Because legislative history is often contradictory (as it was in the *Weber* case), some argue that legislative history can be manipulated to support any result a judge or a legislator wants. Judges may choose which legislative history might be relevant and reject contradictory history. As Judge Harold Leventhal used to say, "[T]he trick is to look over the heads of the crowd and pick out your friends." Antonin Scalia, A Matter Of Interpretation: Federal Courts and the Law 36 (1997). Additionally, legislators may manipulate legislative history; they may decide to add information to the legislative record to influence future litigation, although relatively recent procedural rules have abated this practice. *See, e.g., Harrisburg v. Franklin,* 806

F. Supp 1181, 1184 (M.D. Pa. 1992) (refusing to consider a legislator's written statements, which were made after the bill passed and were "*never actually spoken on the floor of the legislature.*"). Finally, legislative history is not subject to bicameral passage and presentment, the constitutionally proscribed process for enactment. Thus, even if a single, unified intent exists, the criticism continues, that intent should not be ascertained from anything other than the language of the statute, for it is only that language that goes through the enactment process. *King v. Burwell*, 135 S. Ct. 2480, 2505 (2015) (Scalia, J., dissenting).

why legislative history is not all bad

While these criticisms are valid, they suggest caution, not wholesale rejection, of the use of legislative history. True, legislative history is not enacted law; intentionalists do not claim it is. Rather, the legislative history can offer insight into what some or all of the legislators may have been thinking when the law, which did go through the constitutionally prescribed process, was enacted. Because intentionalists wish to know what legislators were thinking, legislative history can be useful; legislative history simply offers a fuller picture of the legislative process for a particular bill.

summary of intentionalists

To summarize, intentionalists focus on finding the specific intent of the enacting legislature in regard to the specific question before the court. Judges using this approach focus first on text (do not forget this!), but also find legislative history and draft versions of the bill very relevant. Importantly, these theorists will examine all of the sources of meaning regardless of whether the text is ambiguous or absurd.

In the case that follows, see if you can identify the intentionalist reasoning.

Kosak v. United States

majority-intentionalist

Supreme Court of the United States
465 U.S. 848 (1984)

◆ MARSHALL, J., delivered the opinion of the Court [with whom BURGER, BRENNAN, WHITE, BLACKMUN, POWELL, REHNQUIST, JJ., concur].

… While a serviceman stationed in Guam, petitioner assembled a large collection of oriental art. When he was transferred from Guam to Philadelphia, petitioner brought his art collection with him. In his customs declaration, petitioner stated that he intended to keep the contents of the collection for himself. Subsequently, acting upon information that, contrary to his representations, petitioner planned to resell portions of his collection, agents of the United States Customs Service obtained a valid warrant to search petitioner's house. In executing that warrant, the agents seized various antiques and other objects of art.

[Ultimately, the petitioner was acquitted, and the goods were returned].

Alleging that some of the objects returned to him had been injured while in the custody of the Customs Service, petitioner filed an administrative complaint with the Service requesting compensation for the damage. The Customs Service denied relief. Relying on the Federal Tort Claims Act, petitioner then filed suit…, seeking approximately $12,000 in damages for the alleged injury to his property. The Government moved for a dismissal of the complaint or for summary judgment on the ground that petitioner's claim was barred by § 2680(c). The District Court granted the Government's motion.

The Court of Appeals, with one judge dissenting, affirmed, ... [observing that] the "clear language" of § 2680(c) shields the United States from "all claims arising out of detention of goods by customs officers and does not purport to distinguish among types of harm." ...

We granted certiorari [and] affirm.

The Federal Tort Claims Act, enacted in 1946, provides generally that the United States shall be liable, to the same extent as a private party, "for injury or loss of property, or personal injury or death caused by the negligent or wrongful act or omission of any employee of the Government while acting within the scope of his office or employment." 28 U.S.C. § 1346(b). The Act's broad waiver of sovereign immunity is, however, subject to 13 enumerated exceptions. One of those exceptions, § 2680(c), exempts from the coverage of the statute "[a]ny claim arising in respect of ... the detention of any goods or merchandise by any officer of customs...."[6] Petitioner asks us to construe the foregoing language to cover only claims "for damage caused by the detention itself and not for the negligent ... destruction of property while it is in the possession of the customs service." By "damage caused by the detention itself," petitioner appears to mean harms attributable to an illegal detention, such as a decline in the economic value of detained goods (either because of depreciation or because of a drop in the price the goods will fetch), injury resulting from deprivation of the ability to make use of the goods during the period of detention, or consequential damages resulting from lack of access to the goods. The Government asks us to read the exception to cover all injuries to property sustained during its detention by customs officials.

The starting point of our analysis of these competing interpretations must, of course, be the language of § 2680(c). "[W]e assume 'that the legislative purpose is expressed by the ordinary meaning of the words used.'" At first blush, the statutory language certainly appears expansive enough to support the Government's construction; the encompassing phrase, "arising in respect of," seems to sweep within the exception all injuries associated in any way with the "detention" of goods. It must be admitted that this initial reading is not ineluctable; as Judge Weis, dissenting in the Court of Appeals, pointed out, it is possible (with some effort) to read the phrase, "in respect of" as the equivalent of "as regards" and thereby to infer that "the statutory exception is directed to the fact of detention itself, and that alone." But we think that the fairest interpretation of the crucial portion of the provision is the one that first springs to mind: "any claim arising in respect of" the detention of goods means any

---

6. The full text of § 2680(c) provides:

"The provisions of [28 U.S.C. §§ 2671–2680] and of § 1346(b) shall not apply to—

(c) Any claim arising in respect of the assessment or collection of any tax or customs duty, or the detention of any goods or merchandise by any officer of customs or excise or any other law-enforcement officer." ....

claim "arising out of" the detention of goods, and includes a claim resulting from negligent handling or storage of detained property. . . .

The legislative history of § 2680(c), though meager, supports the interpretation of the provision that we have derived from its language. . . . Two specific aspects of the evolution of the provision are telling. First, the person who almost certainly drafted the language under consideration clearly thought that it covered injury to detained property caused by the negligence of customs officials. It appears that the portion of § 2680(c) pertaining to the detention of goods was first written by Judge Alexander Holtzoff, one of the major figures in the development of the Tort Claims Act. In his Report explicating his proposals, Judge Holtzoff explained:

> "[The proposed provision would exempt from the coverage of the Act] [c]laims arising in respect of the assessment or collection of any tax or customs duty. This exception appears in all previous drafts. It is expanded, however, so as to include immunity from liability in respect of *loss in connection with the detention of goods or merchandise* by any officer of customs or excise. The additional proviso has special reference to the detention of imported goods in appraisers' warehouses or customs houses, as well as seizures by law enforcement officials, internal revenue officers, and the like." A. Holtzoff, Report on Proposed Federal Tort Claims Bill 16 (1931) (Holtzoff Report) (emphasis added).

Though it cannot be definitively established that Congress relied upon Judge Holtzoff's report, it is significant that the apparent draftsman of the crucial portion of § 2680(c) believed that it would bar a suit of the sort brought by petitioner.[13]

Second, the Congressional committees that submitted reports on the various bills that ultimately became the Tort Claims Act suggested that the provision that was to become § 2680(c), like the other exceptions from the waiver of sovereign immunity, covered claims "arising out of" the designated conduct. Thus, for example, the House Judiciary Committee described the proposed exceptions as follows:

> "These exemptions cover claims arising out of the loss or miscarriage of postal matter; the assessment or collection of taxes or assessments; the detention of goods by customs officers; admiralty and maritime torts; deliberate torts such as assault and battery; and others." H.R.Rep. No. 1287, 79th Cong., 1st Sess., 6 (1945).

---

13. Mr. Holtzoff wrote his report while serving as Special Assistant to the Attorney General. He had been "assigned by Attorney General Mitchell to the special task of co-ordinating the views of the Government departments" regarding the proper scope of a tort claims statute. Holtzoff submitted his report, in which his draft bill was contained, to Assistant Attorney General Rugg, who in turn transmitted it to the General Accounting Office of the Comptroller General. Insofar as Holtzoff's report embodied the views of the Executive Department at that stage of the debates over the tort claims bill, it is likely that, at some point, the report was brought to the attention of the Congressmen considering the bill. We agree with the dissent that, because the report was never introduced into the public record, the ideas expressed therein should not be given great weight in determining the intent of the legislature. But, in the absence of any direct evidence regarding how members of Congress understood the provision that became § 2680(c), it seems to us senseless to ignore entirely the views of its draftsman.

The Committees' casual use of the words, "arising out of," with reference to the exemption of claims pertaining to the detention of goods substantially undermines petitioner's contention that the phrase, "in respect of," was designed to limit the sorts of suits covered by the provision. . . .

[The majority explains why the purposes for the statute's exceptions will be furthered by this interpretation.]

Petitioner and some commentators argue that § 2680(c) should not be construed in a fashion that denies an effectual remedy to many persons whose property is damaged through the tortious conduct of customs officials. That contention has force, but it is properly addressed to Congress, not to this Court. . . .

◆ JUSTICE STEVENS, dissenting.

The Government's construction of 28 U.S.C. § 2680(c) is not the one that "first springs" to my mind. Rather, I read the exception for claims arising "in respect of . . . the detention of goods" as expressing Congress's intent to preclude liability attributable to the temporary interference with the owner's possession of his goods, as opposed to liability for physical damage to his goods. That seems to me to be the normal reading of the statutory language that Congress employed, and the one that most Members of Congress voting on the proposal would have given it. Moreover, my reading, unlike the Court's, is supported by an examination of the language used in other exceptions. Congress did not use the words "arising out of" in § 2680(c) but did use those words in three other subsections of the same section of the Act. See § 2680(b), (e) and (h). Absent persuasive evidence to the contrary, we should assume that when Congress uses different language in a series of similar provisions, it intends to express a different intention.

The language of the statute itself is thus clear enough to persuade me that Congress did not intend to exempt this property damage claim from the broad coverage of the Act. I would, of course, agree that if there were legislative history plainly identifying a contrary congressional intent, that history should be given effect. I do not believe, however, that it is proper for the Court to attach any weight at all to the kind of "clues" to legislative intent that it discusses, or to its concept of the "general purposes" that motivated various exceptions to the statute. Because the Court has done so, however, I shall respond to both parts of its rather creative approach to statutory construction.

In the entire 15 year history preceding the enactment of the Tort Claims Act in 1946, the Court finds only two "clues" that it believes shed any light on the meaning of § 2680(c). The first — the so-called "Holtzoff Report" — is nothing but an internal Justice Department working paper prepared in 1931 and never even mentioned in the legislative history of the 1946 Act. There is no indication that any Congressman ever heard of the document or knew that it even existed. The position of the majority — that it is "significant" that the "apparent draftsman" of the relevant language himself "believed that it would bar a suit of the sort brought by petitioner," is manifestly ill-advised. The intent of a lobbyist — no matter how public spirited he may have been — should not be attributed to the Congress without positive evidence that elected legislators were aware of and shared the lobbyist's intent.

Unless we know more about the collective legislative purpose than can be gleaned from an internal document prepared by a person who was seeking legislative action, we should be guided by the sensible statement that "in construing a statute ... the worst person to construe it is the person who is responsible for its drafting. He is very much disposed to confuse what he intended to do with the effect of the language which in fact has been employed." If the draftsman of the language in question intended it to cover such cases as this one, he failed.

The second "clue" relied upon by the majority consists of a brief summary in the House Committee Report which casually uses the prepositional phrase "arising out of" to introduce a truncated list of the exceptions. But the "casual" use of the latter phrase in the committee report is as understandable as it is insignificant. It is nothing more than an introduction. In such an introduction, precision of meaning is naturally and knowingly sacrificed in the interest of brevity....

[The dissent explains why the purposes of the statute as a whole will be furthered by his interpretation.]

In the final analysis, one must conclude that the legislative history provides only the most general guidance on resolving the issue in this case....

Therefore, this is "a case for applying the canon of construction of the wag who said, when the legislative history is doubtful, go to the statute." *Greenwood v. United States,* 350 U.S. 366, 374 (1956). I would acknowledge — indeed I do acknowledge — that the Court's reading of the statutory language is entirely plausible. I would, however, tilt the scales in favor of recovery by attaching some weight to the particular language used in § 2680(c). And I must disagree with the Court's reliance on the general purposes underlying exceptions when no consideration is given to the general purpose of the statute itself. But most importantly, I would eschew any reliance on the intent of the lobbyist whose opinion on the question before us was not on the public record.

I therefore respectfully dissent.

* * *

Points for Discussion

1. *Statutory Language*: What was the language at issue? What did Kosak argue that language meant? The Government? What meaning did the majority and dissent adopt?

2. *Theories*: Which theory did the majority use? The dissent?

3. *Legislative History*: What two items within the legislative history did the majority find helpful and why did the dissent reject both items?

4. *Identical Words Presumption*: The dissent noted that Congress used "arising out of" in other subsections of the act — (b), (e), and (h) — but not in (c). Why did this matter to the dissent?

5. *Purpose*: The majority focused on the purposes of the exception, while the dissent focused on the purposes of the waiver. Which purpose should the court focus on? In this case, is there a way to reconcile both purposes?

6. *Exceptions*: Generally, exceptions are to be construed narrowly. (*See* Chapter 9.) Which opinion more narrowly construed the exception?

7. *Waiver of Sovereign Immunity*: Generally, courts will not assume that the government waived its immunity absent a clear statement from the legislature that waiver was intended (*See* Chapter 14). The Federal Tort Claims Act itself is a pretty clear statement that the legislature waived immunity, but such waivers are generally construed narrowly. Again, which opinion more narrowly construed the waiver?

8. *Imaginative Reconstructionism*: As noted above, discerning the specific intent of the enacting legislature is often a difficult, if not impossible task. And limiting interpretation to a static point in time, enactment, creates its own issues. For these reasons, in 1907, Dean Roscoe Pound urged courts to use "imaginative reconstructionism" to discern the intent of the enacting legislature. Using Dean Pound's approach, a judge would try to imagine what the enacting legislature would have intended had the precise factual problem before the court been raised during the enactment process. As described by Judge Learned Hand:

> As nearly as we can, we must put ourselves in the place of those who uttered the words, and try to divine how they would have dealt with the unforeseen situations; and, although their words are by far the most decisive evidence of what they would have done, they are by no means final.

Guiseppi v. Walling, 144 F.2d 608, 624 (2d Cir. 1944).

Dean Pound proposed that judges *re*-create intent by examining the available historical evidence, including the statute, with a sense of morality and justice, to determine what the enacting legislature likely intended given the realities of today. Roscoe Pound, *Spurious Interpretation*, 7 COLUM. L. REV. 379, 381 (1907). This approach borrows from common law analysis and civil law practice in that the statute guides but often does not answer the question; rather, by using reason and analogy, a judge can apply the statute to situations the language does not explicitly cover to arrive at a just result. Imaginative reconstructionism is normative (meaning it establishes norms) for it allows the judiciary to consider public policy when making interpretive choices. Using "practical reasoning," judges can adopt interpretations that are flexible enough to change based on current public norms. Justice Learned Hand was a proponent of this theory.

Two cases that show this form of reasoning include *Leo Sheep Co. v. Unites States*, 440 U.S. 668 (1979), and *Church of the Holy Trinity v. United States*, 143 U.S. 457 (1892). In *Leo Sheep Co.*, Justice Rehnquist started his opinion as follows:

> This is one of those rare cases evoking episodes in this country's history that, if not forgotten, are remembered as dry facts and not as adventure. Admittedly the issue is mundane: Whether the Government has an implied easement to build a road across land that was originally granted to the

Union Pacific Railroad under the Union Pacific Act of 1862.... But that issue is posed against the backdrop of a fascinating chapter in our history.... "[C]ourts, in construing a statute, may with propriety recur to the history of the times when it was passed; and this is frequently necessary, in order to ascertain the reason as well as the meaning of particular provisions in it."

Id. at 670. And in *Holy Trinity*, Justice Brewer famously wrote in some detail about "our Christian Nation" to explain why it is unlikely that Congress intended to draft a statute that would prevent ministers from immigrating to this Country.

Not surprisingly, imaginative reconstructionism suffers from some of the same criticisms as intentionalism: Whose intent is reconstructed? Should unenacted information play any role in interpretation? While Dean Pound's approach has had some followers in academic circles, it garners little support among the judiciary. However, see how Justice Rehnquist explores the role of western development in the case below to resolve a "mundane issue."

9. *Intentionalism in the States*: Only New York has adopted intentionalism by statute. That state's statute provides as follows:

    • Generally

    The primary consideration of the courts in the construction of statutes is to ascertain and give effect to the intention of the Legislature.

    • Ascertainment of intention

    The intention of the Legislature is first to be sought from a literal reading of the act itself, but if the meaning is still not clear, the intent may be ascertained from such facts and through such rules as may, in connection with the language, legitimately reveal it.

    N.Y. STAT. LAW §§ 92(a) & (b) (McKinney 2012). The official comment explains New York's choice:

    Since the intention of the Legislature, embodied in a statute, is the law, in the construction of statutes the basic rule of procedure and the primary consideration of the courts are to ascertain and give effect to the intention of the Legislature.... So it is the duty of courts to adopt a construction of a statute that will bring it into harmony with the Constitution and with legislative intent....

    The intent of the Legislature is controlling and must be given force and effect, regardless of the circumstance that inconvenience, hardship, or injustice may result. Indeed the Legislature's intent must be ascertained and effectuated whatever may be the opinion of the judiciary as to the wisdom, expediency, or policy of the statute, and whatever excesses or omissions may be found in the statute. The courts do not sit in review of the discretion of the Legislature and may not substitute their judgment for that of the lawmaking body.

Id. cmt. a.

* * *

b. Purposivism → General intent or Purpose, "legal Process theory"

Purposivists try to identify the *general intent*, or purpose of the legislature that enacted the statute. Purposivists believe that law, both as a whole and specifically, is designed to solve identifiable problems; thus, every statute has a purpose or reason for its enactment. Purposivists strive to discern and then implement this purpose. To do so, they will look broadly, but enacted text is the starting point. Purposivists and intentionalists differ in what they seek when examining the sources of meaning. As we just saw, intentionalists seek specific intent: What did the enacting legislature intend regarding the precise issue presented to the court. In contrast, purposivists seek the legislature's general intent or purpose: What problem was the legislature trying to remedy, and how did it redress that problem? Once the purpose and remedy have been identified, purposivists interpret the statute to further that purpose subject to two caveats: purposivists believe that judges should not give words (1) a meaning those words cannot bear, nor (2) a meaning that would violate generally prevailing policies of law.

[margin note: intentionalists v. Purposivists]

Purposivism, also known as legal process theory, is perhaps the oldest form of interpretation. In the middle ages, detailed statutes were difficult to produce, so it was hard to develop and circulate multiple drafts. Copiers did not exist. Thus, early English legislators voted based on the general goal, or purpose, of the statute, not on the precise text. To interpret statutes enacted in this way, judges focused on the spirit of the legislation rather than on the exact wording. Purposivism permitted this focus.

Like early English statutes, early American statutes were also very general. For example, the Sherman (Antitrust) Act, which was enacted in 1890, fits on only one page, while the Patient Protection and Affordable Care Act, which was enacted in 2010, is 907 pages long. In the past, the legislature drafted broad statutes to allow reasoned judicial development of a particular area of law. Because there was so little textual guidance, judges needed something other than the text to guide and to unify interpretation. Purpose provided that guiding and unifying factor. Judges could easily test their decisions by discerning which interpretation best furthered the statutory purpose. Thus, by focusing on the purpose of the statute, judges were better able to fit the statute into the legal system as a whole and make public policy coherent.

In the United States, purposivism made an early appearance in 1892 in *Church of the Holy Trinity v. United States*, 143 U.S. 457 (1892). In that case, a statute made it unlawful for anyone to import any alien into the United States to "perform labor or service of any kind." *Id.* at 458. Holy Trinity Church had hired a rector from England. *Id.* Despite the clarity of the text—rectoring is "labor or service"—the Court held that the statute did not apply because the purpose of the Act was to "stay the influx of … cheap unskilled labor…." *Id.* at 465. Rectoring was not unskilled labor. Famously stating that "[i]t is a familiar rule that a thing may be within the letter of the statute and yet not within the statute, because not within its spirit nor within the intention of its makers," the Court rejected the definitional interpretation. *Id.* at 45.

Purposivism came into vogue shortly after World War II, during a time of "relative consensus ... sustained economic growth, and burgeoning optimism about government's ability to foster economic growth by solving market failures and creating opportunities." ESKRIDGE *ET AL.*, LEGISLATION AND STATUTORY INTERPRETATION, *supra*, at 727. Many Justices on the Supreme Court used this approach, for the most part, throughout the 1950s and 1960s. By the 1970s, however, America was changing. Economic growth had faltered and issues relating to war, family, and government were much more controversial. Government became the enemy rather than the savior. Additionally, statutes became more complex and comprehensive. With those changes came a change in the judicial approach to statutory interpretation. Intentionalism garnered favor with justices such as former Chief Justices Burger and Rehnquist. Justice Breyer and former Justice Stevens are proponents of purposivism. More recently, Justice Roberts' majority opinion in *King v. Burwell*, 135 S. Ct. 2480 (2015), and Justice Ginsburg's majority opinion in *Yates v. United States*, 135 S. Ct. 1074 (2015), are purposivist.

Like intentionalists, purposivists begin with the text but do not end the analysis there:

> There is, of course, no more persuasive evidence of the purpose of a statute than the words by which the legislature undertook to give expression to its wishes. Often these words are sufficient in and of themselves to determine the purpose of the legislation. In such cases we have followed their plain meaning. When that meaning has led to absurd or futile results, however, this Court has looked beyond the words to the purpose of the act. Frequently, however, even when the plain meaning did not produce absurd results but merely an unreasonable one plainly at variance with the policy of the legislation as a whole this Court has followed that purpose, rather than the literal words. When aid to construction of the meaning of words as used in the statute is available, there certainly can be no rule of law which forbids its use, however clear the words may appear on superficial examination.

United States v. Am. Trucking Ass'ns, Inc., 310 U.S. 534, 543–44 (1940) (internal citations omitted).

While textualists view themselves as faithful agents of the Constitution, and intentionalists view themselves as faithful agents of the legislature, purposivists view themselves as "faithful agent[s] of a well-functioning regulatory regime." ESKRIDGE *ET AL.*, LEGISLATION AND STATUTORY INTERPRETATION, *supra*, at 7 (emphasis omitted). For this reason, purposivists attempt to discern the evil or mischief the legislature meant to address when enacting the statute. To do so, purposivists are willing to examine text and legislative history, as well as other relevant sources, such as social and legal context. To a purposivist, a statute makes sense only when understood in light of its purpose: a rule without purpose is meaningless. For example, consider our hypothetical city ordinance prohibiting "vehicles" in the park. Is a non-motorized scooter a vehicle? To decide this question, a purposivist might ask why the city council enacted the ordinance in the first place. If the council's purpose was to limit air and noise pollution, then "vehicle" should not be interpreted to include scooters. If, instead, the city's purpose was to increase pedestrian safety, then, perhaps, "vehicle" should be so interpreted. Thus, purposivists believe that knowing the evil, or mischief, at which the statute was aimed aids interpretation.

One benefit of purposivism is that it permits flexibility that the other theories may not. While purposivism and intentionalism are somewhat similar, purposivism has one advantage over intentionalism: Purposivists can interpret statutes in situations the enacting legislature never contemplated. "Purposivism … renders statutory interpretation adaptable to new circumstances." ESKRIDGE *ET AL.*, LEGISLATION AND STATUTORY INTERPRETATION, *supra*, at 221. For example, in the hypothetical city ordinance prohibiting "vehicles" in the park, a purposivist judge could determine that the ordinance applied to drones even though these "vehicles" may not have been around when the ordinance was adopted. But an intentionalist judge might have more difficulty with this issue because the city council could not have intended to regulate something not in existence when the ordinance was adopted. Therefore, purposivism allows for laws to change with technological, social, legal, and other advances—something true intentionalism is incapable of doing.

Purposivism is not without weaknesses. The most troublesome aspect of purposivism is, of course, how to legitimately discern a statute's purpose. Ideally, legislatures would include a findings or purpose provision in the enacted text of every statute. More commonly, they do not. Older statutes, in particular, often do not have such clauses. And even when a bill includes a purpose clause, its wording may have been subject to controversy and political compromise during the enactment process. Thus, even when included, purpose clauses may be so general as to be unhelpful.

For these reasons, judges often look for *unexpressed* purpose. To find unexpressed purpose, purposivists consider the text, the legislative history, the legal history, the social context, and other sources. But these sources may not be conclusive. What then? Some legal theorists have suggested that to figure out a statute's primary purpose, a judge should posit various situations. In other words, a judge should start with the situations clearly covered and radiate outward. While doing so, judges should presume that legislatures are "made of reasonable persons pursuing reasonable purposes, reasonably." HENRY HART & ALBERT SACHS, THE LEGAL PROCESS 1378 (William N. Eskridge, Jr. & Philip P. Frickey eds., 1994). You can see why this approach might concern some.

Purposivism has other flaws as well. For example, even if a statutory purpose is discernible, there may be competing ideas of how to further that purpose: is affirmative action the best way to achieve racial parity or is color-blindness better? A related criticism of purposivism is that statutes often have more than one purpose, and these purposes can conflict. For example, one purpose of Title VII of the Civil Rights Act—which prohibits discrimination in the workplace—was to increase the number of African Americans in the workforce. Another purpose was to make hiring and other work related decisions race neutral. Voluntary affirmative action programs further the first purpose but not the second. Is the fact that one purpose is furthered enough to sustain an interpretation? Purposivism does not answer the question of whether an interpretation is appropriate when one, but not another, purpose is furthered.

Similarly, a statute may have one purpose, while an exception to that statute may have a conflicting purpose. For example, the purpose of the Freedom of Information Act (FOIA) (5 U.S.C. §552 (2012)), is to encourage open government. But some of the exceptions within the Act, such as prohibiting the disclosure of personnel files, exist to protect individual privacy. If a judge interprets an exception, which purpose should control: the purpose of the Act or the purpose of the exception? In other words, should the judge interpret the exception in FOIA narrowly to better further the purpose of the Act as a whole or broadly to better further the purpose of the exception? *See, e.g., Church of Scientology v. Department of Justice*, 612 F.2d 417, 425 (9th Cir. 1979) (broadly interpreting an exemption in FOIA to further the exception's purpose despite the dissent's argument that the exemption should be narrowly construed to further the Act's purpose). Again, purposivism does not answer this question.

Finally, judges are constitutionally required to interpret statutory language not make law. When judges make decisions based on their own policy choices, disguised as purpose, they aggrandize their own power at the expense of the legislature.

To summarize, purposivists focus on finding the general intent, or purpose, of the enacting legislature in regard to the issue before the court. Judges using this approach focus first on text (do not forget this!), but also find legislative history and social context very relevant. Importantly, like intentionalists, these theorists will examine all of the sources of meaning regardless of whether the text is ambiguous or absurd.

In the opinion below, try to identify which theory of interpretation the majority and dissent adopt and their reasons for doing so.

State v. Courchesne

Supreme Court of Connecticut
816 A.2d 562 (Conn. 2003)

◆ Borden, J.

Under our statutory scheme, a defendant becomes eligible for the death penalty if he is convicted of a capital felony for the "murder of two or more persons at the same time or in the course of a single transaction...." General Statutes (Rev. to 1997) §53a–54b (8), as amended by No. 98–126, §1, of the 1998 Public Acts (P.A. 98–126). One of the aggravating factors that permits the imposition of the death penalty is that "the defendant committed the offense in an especially heinous, cruel or depraved manner...." [§53a–46 (i)(4)]....

Thus, the sole issue of this appeal is whether ... the state, in order to establish the aggravating factor defined by §53a–46 (i)(4), must prove that the defendant murdered both victims in an especially heinous, cruel or depraved manner. We conclude that proof that the defendant committed at least one of the murders in the specified aggravated manner is sufficient....

In the late evening hours of December 15, 1998, the defendant stabbed Demetris Rodgers to death [over a $410 drug debt]. At the time she was stabbed, she was pregnant with Antonia Rodgers. Although Demetris Rodgers was dead on arrival at the hospital, the physicians at the hospital performed an emergency cesarean section and delivered Antonia Rodgers, who lived for forty-two days before dying....

Facts

[The majority acknowledges that the defendant's textual argument "probably carries more weight than that of the state" because it would be "linguistically appealing" to say that: (1) §53a–46a (i)(4) requires that "the offense" be committed in the aggravated manner; (2) the likely referent of "the offense" is the capital felony of which the defendant has been convicted; (3) that capital felony at issue in the present case is the "murder of two or more persons," as defined in §53a–54b (8); and (4) therefore, the murder of *two* persons must be committed in the aggravated manner. The majority nevertheless rejects this interpretation, claiming the statutes context and history suggest "the offense," as applied in the circumstances of the present case, meant the murder of either of the "two" persons referred to in §53a–54b (8), and does not mean both murders.].

We take this opportunity to clarify the approach of this court to the process of statutory interpretation....

[There is] a dichotomy in our case law regarding whether resort to extratextual sources [is] appropriate even in those instances where the text's meaning appeared to be plain and unambiguous. In [one case] we stated: "It is true that, in construing statutes, we have often relied upon the canon of statutory construction that we need not, and indeed ought not, look beyond the statutory language to other interpretive aids unless the statute's language is not absolutely clear and unambiguous. That maxim requires some slight but plausible degree of linguistic ambiguity as a kind of analytical threshold that must be surmounted before a court may resort to aids to the determination of the meaning of the language as applied to the facts of the case. It is also true, however, that we have often eschewed such an analytical threshold, and have stated that, in interpreting statutes, we look at all the available evidence, such as the statutory language, the legislative history, the circumstances surrounding its enactment, the purpose and policy of the statute, and its relationship to existing legislation and common law principles. This analytical model posits that the legislative process is purposive, and that the meaning of legislative language (indeed, of any particular use of our language) is best understood by viewing not only the language at issue, but by its context and by the purpose or purposes behind its use."

Only look beyond if not clear & ambiguous

but we also look at other evidence ↓ Purposive

[W]e have not been consistent in our formulation of the appropriate method of interpreting statutory language. At times, we have adhered to the formulation that requires identification of some degree of ambiguity in that language before consulting any sources of its meaning beyond the statutory. We refer herein to that formulation as the "plain meaning rule," which we discuss in further detail later in this opinion. At other times, we have, as in the present case ... adhered to a more encompassing formulation that does not require passing any threshold of ambiguity as a precondition of consulting extratextual sources of the meaning of legislative language.

'Plain meaning' Rule

We now make explicit … our approach…. [T]the fundamental task of the court in engaging in the process of statutory interpretation [is] engaging in a "reasoned search for the intention of the legislature," which we further defined as a reasoned search for "the meaning of the statutory language as applied to the facts of [the] case, including the question of whether the language actually does apply." [As for] the range of sources that we will examine in order to determine that meaning … the court [should] consider all relevant sources of meaning of the language at issue—namely, the words of the statute, its legislative history and the circumstances surrounding its enactment, the legislative policy it was designed to implement, and its relationship to existing legislation and to common-law principles governing the same general subject matter. We also now make explicit that we ordinarily will consider all of those sources beyond the language itself, without first having to cross any threshold of ambiguity of the language.

We emphasize, moreover, that the language of the statute is the most important factor to be considered, for three very fundamental reasons. First, the language of the statute is what the legislature enacted and the governor signed. It is, therefore, the law. Second, the process of interpretation is, in essence, the search for the meaning *of that language* as applied to the facts of the case, including the question of whether it does apply to those facts. Third, all language has limits, in the sense that we are not free to attribute to legislative language a meaning that it simply will not bear in the usage of the English language.

Therefore—and we make this explicit as well—we always *begin* the process of interpretation with a searching examination of that language, attempting to determine the range of plausible meanings that it may have in the context in which it appears and, if possible, narrowing that range down to those that appear most plausible. Thus, the statutory language is always the starting point of the interpretive inquiry. A significant point of [our] formulation, however, is that we do not end the process with the language.

The reason for this … is that "the legislative process is purposive, and … the meaning of legislative language (indeed, of any particular use of our language) is best understood by viewing not only the language at issue, but by its context and by the purpose or purposes behind its use."

Thus, the purpose or purposes of the legislation, and the context of that legislative language, which includes the other sources noted [above], are directly relevant to its meaning as applied to the facts of the case before us. *See* L. Fuller, "Positivism and Fidelity to Law—A Reply to Professor Hart," 71 Harv. L.Rev. 630, 664 (1958) (it is not "possible to interpret a word in a statute without knowing the aim of the statute").

Indeed, in our view, the concept of the context of statutory language should be broadly understood. That is, the context of statutory language necessarily includes the other language used in the statute or statutory scheme at issue, the language used in other relevant statutes, the general subject matter of the legislation at issue, the history or genealogy of the statute, as well as the other, extratextual sources identified [above]. All of these sources, textual as well as contextual, are to be considered, along with the purpose or purposes of the legislation, in determining the meaning of the language of the statute as applied to the facts of the case.

This brings us to a discussion of what is commonly known as the "plain meaning rule." ... [T]he fundamental premise, stated generally, that, where the statutory language is plain and unambiguous, the court must stop its interpretive process with that language; there is in such a case no room for interpretation; and, therefore, in such a case, the court must not go beyond that language.

Plain Meaning Rule

It is useful to note that both the plain meaning rule and [our new] formulation have, as a general matter, their starting points in common: both begin by acknowledging that the task of the court is to ascertain the intent of the legislature in using the language that it chose to use, so as to determine its meaning in the context of the case. Where these approaches differ, however, is on how to go about that task.

Plain Meaning & Purposivists have same starting points

Unlike [our new] formulation, under the plain meaning rule, there are certain cases in which that task must, as a matter of law, end with the statutory language. Thus, it is necessary to state precisely what the plain meaning rule means.

The plain meaning rule means that in a certain category of cases—namely, those in which the court first determines that the language at issue is plain and unambiguous—the court is *precluded as a matter of law* from going beyond the text of that language to consider any extratextual evidence of the meaning of that language, no matter how persuasive that evidence might be. Indeed, the rule even precludes reference to that evidence where that evidence, if consulted, would *support or confirm* that plain meaning. Furthermore, inherent in the plain meaning rule is the admonition that the courts are to seek the objective meaning of the language used by the legislature "not in what (the legislature) meant to say, but in (the meaning of) what it did say." Another inherent part of the plain meaning rule is the exception that the plain and unambiguous meaning is *not* to be applied if it would produce an unworkable or absurd result.

Plain Meaning described

Thus, the plain meaning rule, at least as most commonly articulated in our jurisprudence, may be restated as follows: If the language of the statute is plain and unambiguous, and if the result yielded by that plain and unambiguous meaning is not absurd or unworkable, the court must not *interpret* the language (i.e., there is no room for construction); instead, the court's sole task is to apply that language literally to the facts of the case, and it is precluded as a matter of law from consulting any extratextual sources regarding the meaning of the language at issue. Furthermore, in deciding whether the language is plain and unambiguous, the court is confined to what may be regarded as the objective meaning of the language used by the legislature, and may not inquire into what the legislature may have intended the language to mean—that is, it may not inquire into the purpose or purposes for which the legislature used the language. Finally, the plain meaning rule sets forth a set of thresholds of ambiguity or uncertainty, and the court must surmount each of those thresholds in order to consult additional sources of meaning of the language of the statute. Thus, whatever may lie beyond any of those thresholds may in any given case be barred from consideration by the court, irrespective of its ultimate usefulness in ascertaining the meaning of the statutory language at issue....

We disagree with the plain meaning rule as a useful rubric for the process of statutory interpretation for several reasons.

First, the rule is fundamentally inconsistent with the purposive and contextual nature of legislative language. Legislative language *is* purposive and contextual, and its meaning simply cannot be divorced from the purpose or purposes for which it was used and from its context. Put another way, it *does* matter, in determining that meaning, what purpose or purposes the legislature had in employing the language; it *does* matter what meaning the legislature intended the language to have.

Second, the plain meaning rule is inherently self-contradictory. It is a misnomer to say, as the plain meaning rule says, that, if the language is plain and unambiguous, there is no room for interpretation, because application of the statutory language to the facts of the case *is interpretation* of that language. In such a case, the task of interpretation may be a simple matter, but that does not mean that no interpretation is required....

Third, application of the plain meaning rule necessarily requires the court to engage in a threshold determination of whether the language is ambiguous. This requirement, in turn, has led this court into a number of declarations that are, in our view, intellectually and linguistically dubious, and risk leaving the court open to the criticism of being result-oriented in interpreting statutes.[28] Thus, for example, we have stated that statutory language does not become ambiguous "merely because the parties contend for different meanings." Yet, if parties contend for different meanings, and each meaning is plausible, that is essentially what "ambiguity" ordinarily means in such a context in our language. For example, in Merriam Webster's Collegiate Dictionary, the most apt definition of "ambiguous" for this context is: "[C]apable of being understood in two or more possible senses or ways." ...

Eschewing the plain meaning rule does not mean, however, that we will not in any given case follow what may be regarded as the plain meaning of the language. Indeed, in most cases, that meaning will, once the extratextual sources of meaning contained in [our new] formulation *are* considered, prove to be the legislatively intended meaning of the language.

There are cases, however, in which the extratextual sources will indicate a different meaning strongly enough to lead the court to conclude that the legislature intended the language to have that different meaning. Importantly, and consistent with our

---

28. ... "Justice Aharon Barak of the Supreme Court of Israel ... has perceptively noted that the 'minimalist' judge 'who holds that the purpose of the statute may be learned only from its language' has more discretion than the judge 'who will seek guidance from every reliable source.' A method of statutory interpretation that is deliberately uninformed, and hence unconstrained, may produce a result that is consistent with a court's own views of how things should be, but it may also defeat the very purpose for which a provision was enacted." *Circuit City Stores, Inc. v. Adams,* 532 U.S. 105 (2001) (Stevens, J., dissenting).

admonition that the statutory language is the most important factor in this analysis, in applying [our new] formulation, we necessarily employ a kind of sliding scale: the more strongly the bare text of the language suggests a particular meaning, the more persuasive the extratextual sources will have to be in order for us to conclude that the legislature intended a different meaning.[31] Such a sliding scale, however, is easier to state than to apply. In any given case, it necessarily will come down to a judgmental weighing of all of the evidence bearing on the question.

The point of [our] formulation, however, is that it requires the court, in *all* cases, to consider *all* of the relevant evidence bearing on the meaning of the language at issue. Thus, [our new] underlying premise is that, the more such evidence the court considers, the more likely it is that the court will arrive at a proper conclusion regarding that meaning.

Moreover, despite the fact that, as we noted at the outset of this discussion, no other jurisdiction specifically has adopted the particular formulation for statutory interpretation that we now adopt, there is really nothing startlingly new about its core, namely, the idea that the court may look for the meaning of otherwise clear statutory language beyond its literal meaning, even when that meaning would not yield an absurd or unworkable result. It stretches back to the sixteenth century; *see, e.g., Heydon's Case*, 3 Co. Rep. 7a, Eng. Rep. (1584); to the early days of the last century; and forward to the present....

Before concluding this discussion, we respond to several of the main points of the dissent. The dissent takes issue with both the appropriateness and the reliability of ascertaining the purpose or purposes of the statute under consideration in determining its meaning. This point demonstrates a fundamental difference between our view and the dissent's view of the nature of legislation. We think that legislation is inherently purposive and that, therefore, it is not only appropriate, but necessary to consider the purpose or purposes of legislation in order to determine its meaning....

The dissent also suggests that judges, by employing a purposive approach to statutory interpretation rather than the plain meaning rule, will substitute our own notions of wise and intelligent policy for the policy of the legislature. We agree that this may happen; any court *may* be intellectually dishonest in performing *any* judicial task, whether it be interpreting a statute or adjudicating a dispute involving only the common law. We suggest, however, that the risk of intellectual dishonesty is just as great, or as minimal, in employing the plain meaning rule as in employing the method of interpretation that we articulate. If a court is determined to be intellectually dishonest and reach the result that it *wants* the statute to mandate, rather than the result that an honest and objective appraisal of its meaning would yield, it will find a way to do so under any articulated rubric of statutory interpretation. Furthermore, by insisting that *all* evidence of meaning be considered and explained before the court arrives at the meaning of a statute, we think that the risk of intellectual dishonesty in performing

---

31. Alaska has adopted a similar sliding scale approach.

that task will be minimized. Indeed, resort to and explanation of extratextual sources may provide a certain transparency to the court's analytical and interpretive process that could be lacking under the employment of the plain meaning rule. In sum, we have confidence in the ability of this court to ascertain, explain and apply the purpose or purposes of a statute in an intellectually honest manner.

The dissent also contends that the plain meaning rule is based on the constitutional doctrine of the separation of powers. Our only response to this assertion is that there is simply no basis for it.... Simply put, the task of the legislative branch is to draft and enact statutes, and the task of the judicial branch is to interpret and apply them in the context of specific cases. The constitution says nothing about ... what method or methods the judiciary must employ in ascertaining the meaning of that language.[32]

The dissent also makes the points that legislative history should be considered only if "the other tools of interpretation fail to produce a single, reasonable meaning," and that, in any event, it is an unreliable method of ascertaining legislative intent and facilitates "'decisions that are based upon the courts' policy preferences, rather than neutral principles of law.'" Thus, the dissent regards the use of legislative history as unreliable evidence of legislative intent, and as insidious in the sense that it permits the court to interpret a statute to reach a meaning that the court *wants* it to have, based on the court's own policy preference, rather than that of the legislature. As a result, in the dissent's five step formulation of the plain meaning rule, consideration of legislative history is relegated to the fourth, or penultimate, step.

In response, we note first that it is difficult to understand why the dissent would consider the use of legislative history at all in its formulation, given that it regards such use as both unreliable and insidious. More importantly, it appears to us that, under the dissent's formulation, only the most difficult cases of statutory interpretation would reach the fourth step of its analysis. Thus, the dissent reserves what it regards as an unreliable and insidious source of statutory meaning to act as the tiebreaker in the most difficult cases of interpretation. This strikes us as a curiously important role for what the dissent regards so negatively as a source of the meaning of legislative language....

[The case is reversed and remanded]. *What happened?*

♦ [The concurring opinion of JUDGE NORCOTT, and the concurring and dissenting opinion of JUDGE KATZ are omitted].

♦ ZARELLA, J., with whom SULLIVAN, C.J., joins, dissenting.

The majority's opinion is nothing short of breathtaking. The majority expressly abandons the plain meaning rule and fails to apply the rule of lenity in a death penalty

in favor of Δ

---

32. In this connection, we also reject the dissent's suggestion that, by employing the plain meaning rule, we will give the legislature an incentive to write clear statutes and, presumably, therefore, also give it a disincentive to write poorly drafted statutes. We do not regard it as appropriate for the judiciary, by creating incentives or disincentives, to instruct the legislature on how to write statutes, any more than it would be appropriate for the legislature, directly or indirectly, to instruct the judiciary on how to write opinions....

case in which the majority states that the text of the statutory provision at issue favors the defendant's interpretation. [The dissent finds the language ambiguous and applies the rule of lenity to adopt the defendant's interpretation.]. [I]n my view, the majority's abandonment of the plain meaning rule in favor of an alternative and novel method of statutory interpretation represents an incorrect deviation from our traditional mode of statutory interpretation and an impermissible usurpation of the legislative function. Accordingly, I dissent....

I ... strongly disagree with the majority's approach to statutory interpretation and its abandonment of the plain meaning rule.... I propose an alternative approach that builds upon the plain meaning rule and describes the manner in which I apply the various tools of statutory interpretation....

Abandoning is wrong

As the majority acknowledges, its approach to statutory interpretation "has not been adopted in the same specific formulation by *any* other court in the nation." (Emphasis added.) I think for good reason.

My most fundamental disagreement with the majority's approach to statutory interpretation is its heavy reliance upon unexpressed statutory purposes. Such reliance is particularly inappropriate when a statute's text is plain and unambiguous. Indeed, even proponents of the purposive approach to statutory interpretation that the majority embraces acknowledge that nontextual sources should be resorted to only when a statute is *unclear*. See, e.g., S. Breyer, "On the Uses of Legislative History in Interpreting Statutes," 65 S. Cal. L.Rev. 845, 848 (1992) (legislative history is useful in interpreting *unclear* statutes). Thus, the majority's contention that a statute's unenumerated purpose can trump statutory language that is plain and unambiguous is truly beyond the pale. I am particularly troubled by such an approach because ... "[A legislative] purpose, whether derived from legislative history, the entirety of the statute, the mischief at which the statute is aimed, or the judge's imagination, is normally of such generality as to be useless as an interpretative tool, unless, of course, it is being used as a cover for the judge to 'do justice' as he sees fit."

When its clear why go further

Indeed, I think that it is highly questionable whether it is epistemologically possible for legislation to reflect any single underlying purpose. In my view, notions of extratextual legislative intent or purpose are devoid of meaning because a "group may act (for example, by enacting a statute), but it is a mistake to attribute a collective intention to its action." In other words, "[i]ndividuals may have mental states, but groups do not."

Moreover, ... public choice theory presents a "substantial" critique of such a method. Such a theory teaches that legislation is the product of bargaining between various interest groups rather than an underlying common will or purpose among legislators. Thus, the theory suggests, as an empirical matter, that statutes will rarely have a single purpose that can guide interpretation.

Public choice theory

Finally, beyond properly stating that "the language of the statute is the most important factor to be considered," the majority, in introducing its new approach to statutory interpretation, fails to provide any guidance as to the significance that should be attached to the other interpretative tools that its approach encompasses. Instead, the majority's approach envisions the interpretation of statutes on a case-by-case basis, whereby the judicial authority can pick and choose from among various tools of interpretation to construct a meaning that might reflect a reasoned judgment. In contrast, I believe that an explanation of the relative usefulness of the various tools of statutory interpretation is of vital importance in providing litigants, judges, legislators and the public with clear guidance and notice as to how the statutes of this state will be interpreted in future cases.

As problematic as the majority's approach to statutory interpretation is in a case in which a statute is ambiguous, the majority's representation that it will apply such an approach even when a statute's text is clear is even more problematic....

As a preliminary matter, it is important to note that, in stating that when the plain meaning rule is applied, a court is "*precluded as a matter of law*" from inquiring beyond the text of a statute; the majority suggests that the plain meaning rule is a rule of law. It is well established, however, that "the plain-meaning rule is rather an axiom of experience than a rule of law...." Thus, the rule, as well as the majority's rejection of the rule, is one of judicial *philosophy,* not one of *substantive law.* Accordingly, it follows that ... the majority['s] opinion, in which the majority expresses the judicial philosophy of five members of this court, does not describe the manner in which I will interpret statutes.

The majority essentially outlines the plain meaning rule in a manner that is consistent with the way in which I view the rule. There is, however, one important statement that the majority makes in describing the rule with which I take issue. The majority maintains that, under the plain meaning rule, as well as the majority's own approach to statutory interpretation, "the task of the court is to ascertain *the intent of the legislature* in using the language that it chose to use, so as to determine [the] meaning [of that language] in the context of the case." (Emphasis added.) The plain meaning rule, however, is premised on the idea that we are governed by what the legislature actually said as opposed to that which it intended to say. Thus, while the majority's approach strives to uncover *subjective legislative intent,* the plain meaning rule searches for a statute's *objective textual meaning.*

With that clarification, I agree with the majority that the plain meaning rule dictates that, if the language of a statute is plain and unambiguous, and if a construction based on the plain and unambiguous language of the statute does not yield an absurd result, then the court should end its inquiry there. In my view, the majority's disavowal of this rule is unwarranted and problematic for several reasons.

First, ... The rule's doctrinal pedigree is, indeed, impressive.... The United States Supreme Court continues to rely on the rule in construing federal statutes. Indeed, an *overwhelming* majority of federal and state courts adhere to the plain meaning rule.

... [N]otwithstanding the majority's suggestion that there is "really nothing startlingly new about" its approach to statutory interpretation, the majority's rejection of the plain meaning rule renders this court an outlier among nearly all other federal and state courts in this country and, indeed, with respect to this court's jurisprudence for the last 100 years, on an issue of great importance....

The majority's abandonment of the plain meaning rule is unjustified for three related reasons. [First and m]ost importantly, the plain meaning rule is premised on the fact that only the text of a statute formally has been approved by the legislature and signed into law by the executive. The aspirations of legislators as expressed in the legislative history or this court's notions concerning the rationality of various legislative schemes have not.... Accordingly, it is the objective meaning of a statute's text that should govern rather than the legislature's subjective intent in choosing that text.

... I agree with United States Supreme Court Justice Antonin Scalia's eloquent expression regarding the essential unfairness of such a system: "I think ... that it is simply incompatible with democratic government, or indeed, even with fair government, to have the meaning of a law determined by what the lawgiver meant, rather than by what the lawgiver promulgated. That seems to me one step worse than the trick the emperor Nero was said to engage in: posting edicts high up on the pillars, so that they could not easily be read. Government by unexpressed intent is similarly tyrannical." ...

[Second, t]he plain meaning rule encourages both judicial restraint and predictability in interpretation. Indeed, a court's disregard of the plain meaning of a legislature's enactments amounts to little more than judicial lawmaking. Such judicial lawmaking constitutes an arrogation of the legislature's constitutional responsibility to enact laws.

Moreover, the majority's abandonment of the plain meaning rule and its adoption of the alternative purposive approach to statutory interpretation pays little heed to this fundamental principle of the separation of powers. In applying the majority's approach, a judge will ask himself for what purpose was the statute enacted. In answering this question, a judge likely will ask what purpose a wise and intelligent lawmaker would have attached to the statute. The judge then will ask himself what he, who, after all, also is wise and intelligent, believes the law's purpose is. In so doing, the judge will assume the role of law giver and substitute judicially ascribed notions of the statute's purpose for the plain meaning of the text that the legislature has chosen....

[Third, and c]onversely, the incentive for legislators to write clear statutes and for interest groups to prevail in getting their views enacted into law takes on a diminished importance if it is made known to them that this court will not limit itself to the plain meaning of the law but, rather, will decide cases on the basis of the unenacted purposes behind a law. By contrast, the plain meaning rule encourages legislators to "fulfill their constitutional responsibility to legislate by disabusing them of the expectation that the courts will do it for them."

The majority offers three criticisms of the plain meaning rule, which, according to the majority, provide justification for its rejection of the rule. I find the majority's criticisms unpersuasive. First, the majority states that "the rule is fundamentally inconsistent with the purposive and contextual nature of legislative language." Therefore, the majority states, "it *does* matter what meaning the legislature intended [statutory] language to have." Yet, the mere fact that the legislature *may* have had a purpose in enacting a statute does not mean that we should give *effect* to such an unenumerated purpose. In construing statutes, I believe that a court should not be governed by such *unstated purposes* but, rather, by what the legislature actually enacted into *law*. Thus, I disagree with the majority's proposition that, simply because legislation may have a purpose, that purpose is relevant to a court's construction of that legislation.

Second, the majority asserts that "the plain meaning rule is inherently self-contradictory." In support of its assertion, the majority questions the validity of the frequently heard refrain that, "if the language is plain and unambiguous, there is no room for interpretation...." The majority states that, in such a case, there is interpretation and that, even though interpretation may be a "simple matter" under such circumstances, interpretation still exists. Without disagreeing with the majority, I do not see what difference this makes. Whether we label it "interpretation," "application of the plain meaning rule," or "a merry dance," I simply do not see this as a reason to reject the plain meaning rule....

Third, the majority contends that the rule has spawned a body of inconsistent law regarding whether a plain meaning can be found and that such inconsistencies leave this court vulnerable to criticism for what may be perceived as a result oriented work product. Yet, it seems entirely unfair to cite to misguided *deviations* from the plain meaning rule as a reason not to *follow* the rule. In my view, many of the "intellectually and linguistically dubious" decisions to which the majority cites are examples of why this court should follow the plain meaning rule more closely, not why this court should abandon the rule....

Moreover, even if one accepts the premise that it is difficult to craft a plain meaning rule that fosters consistency in statutory interpretation, the debate the rule engenders with respect to the validity of textual arguments is one of the most important reasons justifying adherence to the rule. In other words, I believe that the plain meaning rule's ubiquity in our legal landscape is due in no small measure to the fact that it emphasizes the primacy of the text by advising litigants, legislators and judges that the best textual argument is likely to be the argument that prevails.

I also strongly disagree with the majority's proposition that adherence to the plain meaning rule leaves this court vulnerable to criticism of being "result-oriented." On the contrary, it is the majority's case-by-case approach to statutory interpretation that is subject to such criticism inasmuch as it encourages as a virtue unfettered discretion in utilizing the various tools of statutory construction. Such an approach expands the judiciary's power to the detriment of the legislature by allowing courts to depart from the plain meaning of the law under the guise of interpretation. Indeed, the majority's nebulous relativistic approach, under which all factors are considered, and under which no factor aside from the text is taken as a priori more informative than any other, virtually guarantees that there will be *some* evidence for nearly *any* interpretation that a court may wish to advance. As Justice Scalia has noted in paraphrasing Judge Harold Leventhal's statements about the expanded use of just one of the many tools that the majority embraces today: "[T]he trick is to look over the heads of the crowd and pick out your friends. The variety and specificity of result that [the majority's approach] can achieve is unparalleled." ...

... [T]he majority contends that the dissent's embrace of the plain meaning rule causes it to ignore statutory purpose. Yet, the plain meaning rule simply embodies the commonsense notion that when the text of a statute is plain and unambiguous, the statute's purpose will be reflected in the text....

As I noted previously, [because] I believe that the majority's approach to statutory interpretation is misguided I offer.... the following alternative method of interpreting statutes.

The process of statutory interpretation involves a reasoned and ordered search for the meaning of the legislation at issue. In other words, we seek to determine the meaning of statutory language as would be understood by a reasonable person reading the text of the statute.

[First, i]n determining this objective meaning, we look first and foremost to the words of the statute itself. If the language of a statute is plain and unambiguous, we need look no further than the words themselves, unless such an interpretation produces an absurd result. In seeking the plain meaning of a statute, we generally construe words and phrases "according to the commonly approved usage of the language"; in the context of the entire statute and employ ordinary rules of grammar. In addition, we may apply the ordinary canons of judicial construction in seeking the plain meaning, recognizing that such canons are not infallible in aiding the search for plain meaning.

[Second, w]hen, and only when, the meaning of a statute cannot be ascertained in this fashion, we next eliminate all possible interpretations that render the statutory scheme incoherent or inconsistent. [Third, i]f more than one reasonable interpretation of the statute remains, we next consider the statute's relationship to other existing legislation and to common-law principles governing the same general subject matter and eliminate any interpretations incompatible with this legal landscape.

[Fourth, i]f ambiguity still remains, we seek to uncover the meaning of the statute by way of review of the statute's legislative history and the circumstances surrounding its enactment. [Fifth and f]inally, if we are still left with an ambiguous statute after resort to all the foregoing tools of statutory interpretation, we apply any applicable presumptions in reaching a final interpretation.

This approach is premised on the notion that statutory text should be the polestar of a court's search for the meaning of a statute. This approach reflects the foregoing philosophy by attributing primary importance to statutory text and reaffirming this court's continued adherence to the plain meaning rule....

In addition, my approach to statutory interpretation permits the statutory interpreter to consider legislative history only when the utilization of other enumerated tools of construction has not produced a single, reasonable interpretation....

... [L]egislative history is an unreliable source for the discovery of such intent. For example, it is unrealistic to think that such history sufficiently can reveal the mental states of a majority of the legislators as well as the executive who signs the particular legislation into law. Yet, it is only this intent, and not that of a committee or of an individual legislator, that is arguably even relevant to the construction of a statute. In addition, other commentators [such as Justice Scalia] properly have questioned the reliability of legislative history because of concerns over the manipulation by legislators or interest groups seeking to influence judicial interpretation after having failed to have their views adopted in the text of the legislation.[23] …

* * *

Points for Discussion

1. *Statutory Language*: What was the language at issue? What did each party want that language to mean? What meaning did the majority and dissent adopt?

2. *Theories*: How did the majority describe its new approach? What reasons did the majority provide to support its new approach? How did the dissent describe his five-step approach? What reasons did the dissent give to support his approach?

3. *The Goal of Statutory Interpretation*: The majority's approach seeks to find the intent of the legislature. The dissent's approach seeks to find the statute's objective textual meaning. Do these goals really differ that fundamentally?

4. *Plain Meaning Rule*: What three reasons did the majority give for rejecting the plain meaning rule? What three responses to these reasons did the dissent offer?

5. *Legislative History*: Does it make sense that the least trustworthy material in the dissent's view, legislative history, is used to resolve only the hardest cases? Did the dissent adequately respond to this criticism in footnote 23?

6. *Only Connecticut*: The majority and dissent states that no other state had a similar approach to statutory interpretation. Both did acknowledge that Alaska's sliding scale approach is very similar. We will explore this approach in the next section.

7. *Legislative Response*: In direct response to the holding in *Courchesne* and just three months later, the state legislature rejected the court's adoption of contextual purposivism and enacted a statute directing the Connecticut courts to use a plain meaning approach to interpretation. The statute provided:

> The meaning of a statute shall, in the first instance, be ascertained from the text of the statute itself and its relationship to other statutes. If, after examining such text and considering such relationship, the meaning of such text is plain and unambiguous and does not yield absurd or unworkable results, extratextual evidence of the meaning of the statute shall not be considered.

---

23. The majority rhetorically asks why, if I believe that there are so many problems with legislative history, should legislative history have *any* place in my approach to statutory construction. My answer is simple. I believe that this court should attach the most weight to the most reliable indicators of a statute's meaning and the least weight to the least reliable indicators. Legislative history, in my view, is less reliable than other tools, but may have some usefulness under circumstances in which the other tools of interpretation fail to produce a single, reasonable meaning.

Conn. Gen. Stat. Ann. § 1-2z (West 2003). In a subsequent case, Justice Borden, the author of *Courchesne*, pointed out:

> It is ironic that the legislative debate surrounding [this statute] specifically indicated that its purpose was to overrule that part of Courchesne. If we were to read [this statute] literally, and assume that it is not ambiguous in any way, we would be barred by it from consulting that very legislative history in order to determine that its purpose was to overrule Courchesne.

Carmel Hollow Assocs. Ltd. P'ship v. Bethlehem, 848 A.2d 451, 470 n.1 (Conn. 2004) (Borden, J., concurring).

8. *Rule of Law or Judicial Philosophy*: The dissent noted that the majority's new approach was not a substantive rule of law, but rather a rule of judicial philosophy such that he would not be bound by it. What did he mean? As you just saw, the legislature subsequently overruled this case. Is the plain meaning rule now a rule of law that all the judges in the state of Connecticut are bound to follow?

9. *Dynamic Statutory Interpretation*: An academic theory related to purposivism is dynamic statutory interpretation. Professor William Eskridge created dynamic statutory interpretation in 1987. William Eskridge, *Dynamic Statutory Interpretation*, 135 U. Pa. L. Rev. 1479 (1987). It is not an approach that you will find referenced in an opinion or statute. Rather, it is one academic's ideal of what should happen in interpretation. Remember that intentionalist judges typically attempt to discern legislative intent as of the time the statute was enacted and that purposivist judges typically attempt to discern statutory purpose as of the time the statute was enacted. The dynamic approach encourages judges to be more flexible and consider what the enacting legislature would have wanted when social moral values change. For example, let's return to the Civil Rights Act of 1964, which was enacted to prohibit discrimination based on race. It is highly unlikely that the Congress of 1964 would have approved of affirmative action programs; the statute was enacted to encourage a race-blind society. Yet, years after the Act had been in effect, discrimination was still the norm. In other words, the Act was not having the intended effect. Should the Supreme Court consider this fact when interpreting the statute? The standard theories would say no; dynamic statutory interpretation would say yes. Even though no linguistic change had occurred since the Act's passage, the societal values of the interpreters (and society) had changed. Affirmative action programs were thought to be necessary to combat continued racism.

In general, dynamic statutory interpretation allows judges to work in concert with the legislature to accomplish its goals as times and values change. Consider statutes enacted in the 1800s that criminalize sodomy. We would define this term very differently today.

Note that a judge using this interpretive theory must identify the goals, or purposes, of the legislation. Thus, this theory is really a close cousin to purposivism. Because it is so similar to purposivism, dynamic interpretation shares some of the same weaknesses. Most notably, critics view this approach as judicial power-grabbing, which violates the Constitution's separation of powers. What is your reaction?

10. *Purposivism Down Under*: The Australian Parliament adopted purposivism and rejected textualism: (These provisions come from: Acts Interpretation Act 1901 (Cth)). Although the Act is dated 1901, section 15AA was added in 1982 (and amended in 2011). Section 15AB was added in 1984. Do you notice anything relevant about those dates regarding what was happening in the United States at that time? Notice the breadth of sources a judge must consider.

S 15AA Interpretation best achieving Act's purpose or object

In interpreting a provision of an Act, the interpretation that would best achieve the purpose or object of the Act (whether or not that purpose or object is expressly stated in the Act) is to be preferred to each other interpretation.

S 15AB Use of extrinsic material in the interpretation of an Act

(1) Subject to subsection (3), in the interpretation of a provision of an Act, if any material not forming part of the Act is capable of assisting in the ascertainment of the meaning of the provision, consideration may be given to that material:

(a) to confirm that the meaning of the provision is the ordinary meaning conveyed by the text of the provision taking into account its context in the Act and the purpose or object underlying the Act; or

(b) to determine the meaning of the provision when:

(i) the provision is ambiguous or obscure; or

(ii) the ordinary meaning conveyed by the text of the provision taking into account its context in the Act and the purpose or object underlying the Act leads to a result that is manifestly absurd or is unreasonable.

(2) Without limiting the generality of subsection (1), the material that may be considered in accordance with that subsection in the interpretation of a provision of an Act includes:

(a) all matters not forming part of the Act that are set out in the document containing the text of the Act as printed by the Government Printer;

(b) any relevant report of a Royal Commission, Law Reform Commission, committee of inquiry or other similar body that was laid before either House of the Parliament before the time when the provision was enacted;

(c) any relevant report of a committee of the Parliament or of either House of the Parliament that was made to the Parliament or that House of the Parliament before the time when the provision was enacted;

(d) any treaty or other international agreement that is referred to in the Act;

(e) any explanatory memorandum relating to the Bill containing the provision, or any other relevant document, that was laid before, or furnished to the members of, either House of the Parliament by a Minister before the time when the provision was enacted;

(f) the speech made to a House of the Parliament by a Minister on the occasion of the moving by that Minister of a motion that the Bill containing the provision be read a second time in that House;

(g) any document (whether or not a document to which a preceding paragraph applies) that is declared by the Act to be a relevant document for the purposes of this section; and (h) any relevant material in the Journals of the Senate, in the Votes and Proceedings of the House of Representatives or in any official record of debates in the Parliament or either House of the Parliament.

(3) In determining whether consideration should be given to any material in accordance with subsection (1), or in considering the weight to be given to any such material, regard shall be had, in addition to any other relevant matters, to:

(a) the desirability of persons being able to rely on the ordinary meaning conveyed by the text of the provision taking into account its context in the Act and the purpose or object underlying the Act; and

(b) the need to avoid prolonging legal or other proceedings without compensating advantage.

Is this approach clearer? Do you find it surprising that a legislature would prefer a non-textualist approach?

11. *Purposivism in the States*: Of the states that have enacted statutory directives, most legislatures have chosen textualism. It is unclear why this is so, but perhaps it is due to the lack of legislative history available in many states and the fact that states judges are often more restrained in their approach to interpretation than federal judges. Perhaps, as state legislative materials become increasingly available, this preference may be altered.

One state, Texas, does have a purposivist statute that provides as follows:

In construing a statute, *whether or not the statute is considered ambiguous on its face*, a court may consider among other matters the:

(1) object sought to be attained;

(2) circumstances under which the statute was enacted;

(3) legislative history;

(4) common law or former statutory provisions, including laws on the same or similar subjects;

(5) consequences of a particular construction;

(6) administrative construction of the statute; and

(7) title (caption), preamble, and emergency provision.

TEX. GOV'T CODE ANN. §311.023 (Vernon 2015) (emphasis added). But despite this clear legislative directive to look at all relevant information regardless of whether a statute is ambiguous, some members of the Texas judiciary refuse to follow it. For example, in *State v. Muller*, 829 S.W.2d 805 (Tex. Ct. Crim. App. 1992), the court said, "[W]e look to a statute's legislative history *only* if the plain meaning of the literal text of that statute is ambiguous or leads to highly improbable results." *Id.* at 811 n.7.

Similarly, a Georgia statute specifically directs courts to consider intent, purpose, and text when interpreting statutes:

(a) In all interpretations of statutes, the courts shall look diligently for the intention of the General Assembly, keeping in view at all times the old law, the evil, and the remedy....

(b) In all interpretations of statutes, the ordinary signification shall be applied to all words....

GA. CODE ANN. §§ 1-3-1(a) & (b) (2015). Though acknowledging the existence of this directive, Georgia courts generally ignore it, preferring instead to apply textualism. For example, in *Busch v. State*, 523 S.E.2d 21 (Ga. 1999), the court said, "If the words of a statute, however, are plain and capable of having but one meaning, and do not produce any absurd, impractical, or contradictory results, then this Court is bound to follow the meaning of those words." *Id.* at 23. In a later case, the Georgia Court of Appeals tried, but failed, to reconcile the court's use of textualism with the more purposivist directive of the statute:

In construing a statute, our goal is to determine its legislative purpose. In this regard, a court must first focus on the statute's text. In order to discern the meaning of the words of a statute, the reader must look at the context in which the statute was written, remembering at all times that "the meaning of a sentence may be more than that of the separate words, as a melody is more than the notes." *If the words of a statute, however, are plain and capable of having but one meaning, and do not produce any absurd, impractical, or contradictory results, then this Court is bound to follow the meaning of those words.* If, on the other hand, the words of the statute are ambiguous, then this Court must construe the statute, keeping in mind the purpose of the statute and "the old law, the evil, and the remedy."

State v. Brown, 551 S.E.2d 773, 775 (Ga. Ct. App. 2001) (emphasis added) (citing GA. CODE APP. § 1-3-1(a)).

* * *

3. A Compromise: Alaska's Sliding Scale Method

As we saw above, all of the theories have weaknesses. For this reason, the Alaska judiciary rejected all of them and created a hybridized approach. This approach, the "sliding scale method," blends textualism, intentionalism, and purposivism. It allows judges to consider a statute's meaning without first finding ambiguity or absurdity by applying a sliding scale of clarity. The sliding scale method states simply that all evidence of meaning is relevant; however, the clearer the statutory language, the more convincing the evidence of a contrary legislative purpose or intent must be. *LeFever v. State*, 877 P.2d 1298, 1299–1300 (Alaska Ct. App. 1994). In other words, Alaska adopted textualism with a twist. Much like a sliding door that can be opened a little or a lot to control the airflow, the sliding scale approach allows a little or a lot of contrary evidence of meaning to flow into the analysis. The size of the opening depends on the clarity of the text: the clearer the text, the smaller the opening.

The Alaska judiciary considered moderate textualism but rejected it because that approach overly restricted the inquiry. Because words are necessarily inexact and ambiguity is inherent in language, other sources of meaning often prove helpful in construing a statute. Thus, even if the statute under consideration is facially clear, the legislative history can be considered, because it might reveal an ambiguity not apparent on the face of the statute. *Anchorage v. Sisters of Providence in Wash., Inc.,* 628 P.2d 22, 27 n.6 (Alaska 1981).

Alaska's sliding scale approach has inherent appeal. The approach is a kissing cousin to the soft plain meaning approach; under the sliding scale approach, the plainer the text, the more convincing the contrary indications of meaning must be to trump the text. This soft version of textualism turns the plain meaning canon into a rebuttable presumption: the plain meaning will control absent convincing evidence that the legislature intended a different meaning. In many ways, this approach blends the best of the theories above, while avoiding the difficulties; the text is the primary, but not the exclusive, source of meaning. But this approach shares many of the problems of textualism and, thus, is not the perfect compromise it may appear to be. While, no other jurisdiction has expressly adopted this approach (although the Connecticut Supreme Court cited this approach with approval in *State v. Courchesne,* 816 A.2d 562, 574 (Conn. 2003)), judicial rhetoric is moving this direction. *See, e.g., King v. Burwell,* 135 S. Ct. 2480, 2491 (2015) (considering all evidence of meaning despite clear text to conclude that the statute was not clear in context).

In the case that follows, note why the court adopted its sliding scale approach.

LeFever v. State

Court of Appeals of Alaska
877 P.2d 1298 (Alaska Ct. App. 1994)

♦ COATS, Judge [BRYNER, C.J., and COATS and MANNHEIMER, JJ. concur].

The district court, sitting without a jury, convicted Jason P. LeFever of unlawful evasion in the first degree, a class A misdemeanor. AS 11.56.340. LeFever appealed his conviction..., contending ... that AS 11.56.340 does not apply to evasion of detention for an adjudication of juvenile delinquency.... [W]e now affirm.

P.H.

On June 16, 1992, ... the primary youth counselor for LeFever during his treatment at the Fairbanks Youth Facility, sent LeFever onto the grounds of the facility to work with the maintenance staff under minimal supervision.... LeFever did not return until his juvenile probation officer went to Seattle to retrieve him the following month. Defense counsel stipulated at trial that LeFever had been "in official detention at the time of these alleged incidents and that he was there based on children's proceedings and adjudications for what would have been felonies had he been an adult." Defense counsel did not stipulate that LeFever had been convicted of any felonies. LeFever had turned 18 years old before June 16, 1992; the state therefore charged him as an adult with unlawful evasion.

At the close of this evidence at trial, LeFever moved for a judgment of acquittal on the ground that the state had not proved one of the elements of first-degree unlawful evasion: that LeFever had left the facility "while charged with or convicted of a felony." AS 11.56.340(a). LeFever argued that his adjudication as a delinquent minor had not constituted a conviction of any crime, whether felony or misdemeanor. [The motion was denied].

LeFever appealed his conviction to the superior court. [T]he Superior Court ... affirmed the conviction, commenting: "Certainly LeFever's arguments are academically appealing; however, they would effectively eliminate any remedy there might be for juveniles who depart the Youth Facility without permission." LeFever petitioned this court for a hearing of the superior court's decision.

Alaska Statute 11.56.340(a) provides as follows:

> A person commits the crime of unlawful evasion in the first degree if, *while charged with or convicted of a felony,*
>
> (1) the person fails to return to official detention within the time authorized following temporary leave granted for a specific purpose or limited period ... ; (Emphasis added.)

LeFever's position is that a person who has been adjudicated as a juvenile cannot commit first-degree unlawful evasion because such a person is not "charged with or convicted of a felony." LeFever relies on the fact that proceedings for juvenile delinquency are distinct from adult criminal proceedings. LeFever particularly relies on AS 47.10.080(g), which provides:

> No adjudication under this chapter upon the status of a child may operate to impose any of the civil disabilities ordinarily imposed by *conviction* upon a criminal charge, nor may a minor afterward be considered a criminal by the adjudication, *nor may the adjudication be afterward deemed a conviction, nor may a minor be charged with or convicted of a crime in a court, except as provided in this chapter....* (Emphasis added.)

Alaska Statute 47.10.080, which deals with judgments and orders of the juvenile court upon finding that a minor is delinquent, nowhere uses the terms "conviction" or "convicted" except in the language emphasized above. Other than as quoted above, and in the statutes providing for waiver of juvenile jurisdiction and prosecution of minors as adults, the terms "charged" and "convicted" do not appear anywhere in the chapter devoted to delinquent minors. Therefore, LeFever contends, under the plain language of AS 11.56.340(a) (and AS 11.56.350(a)), a person who is in official detention as a result of an adjudication of delinquency cannot commit unlawful evasion in any degree because such a person has not been "charged with or convicted of" either a felony or a misdemeanor.

Textualist

However, Alaska does not adhere to a "plain meaning rule" of statutory interpretation that disregards any consideration of legislative purpose or intent. Instead, we consider a statute's meaning by applying a "sliding scale" such that, the plainer the statutory language, the more convincing the evidence of a contrary legislative purpose or intent must be. Even though we generally construe ambiguous criminal statutes in favor of the defendant, we must avoid construing a statute so as to yield patently absurd results or to defeat the obvious legislative purpose of the statute. In this case, we conclude that the legislature intended adjudicated delinquents to be subject to the unlawful evasion statutes. The evidence of this intent outweighs LeFever's "plain meaning" construction, which would result in the unlawful evasion statutes being inapplicable to adjudicated delinquents....

[I]t appears that the language "for a felony" and "for a misdemeanor" as used in the escape and unlawful evasion statutes alike is meant to divide the universe of persons who are in "official detention" into two categories, by seriousness of their underlying conduct, and is not meant to exclude adjudicated delinquents from the statutes. A contrary interpretation could lead to particularly anomalous results if applied to AS 11.81.410. Alaska Statute 11.81.410(b) generally authorizes guards or peace officers to use deadly force when necessary to prevent an escape of a prisoner from a correctional facility. However, AS 11.81.410(c) limits the use of deadly force by providing that a guard may not use deadly force against an escaping prisoner if the guard knows that the prisoner was "under official detention ... on a charge of a misdemeanor" and does not believe the prisoner has a firearm. If the phrase "on a charge of a misdemeanor" excluded juveniles who had been adjudicated delinquent, it would follow that guards could use deadly force against adjudicated delinquents escaping official detention regardless of the seriousness of their underlying conduct....

We recognize that the language of the unlawful evasion statutes, "while charged with or convicted of" a felony or misdemeanor, is different from and arguably narrower than the language of the escape statutes, "for" a felony or misdemeanor. However, we are not convinced that the legislature intended the different language to have any different meaning in this context. In particular, we note that the original unlawful evasion statutes had language identical to that of the corresponding escape statutes and that the subsequent divergence in language appears unintended to establish a difference in meaning.[5] We conclude that the unlawful evasion statutes, AS 11.56.340

---

5. The original unlawful evasion statute was passed in 1976. Former AS 11.30.093 (1976) provided as follows:

(a) A person commits an unlawful evasion if he wilfully fails to return to official detention ... following temporary leave granted for a specific purpose or limited period including but not limited to privileges granted under [identified statutes].

(b) An offense charged under (a) of this section is punishable as an unlawful evasion in the first degree *if the official detention is on a charge of a felony....*

(d) *Any other offense under this section is punishable as an unlawful evasion in the second degree.*

(Emphasis added.) Former AS 11.30.100(2) (1976) provided:

"official detention" means arrest, custody following surrender in lieu of arrest, detention and AS 11.56.350, are together intended to cover all people who fail to return to official detention, and that the statutes' introductory language is intended simply to

------

in any facility for custody of persons *under charge or conviction of crime or alleged to be delinquent*, detention for extradition or deportation *or any other detention for law-enforcement purposes*....

(Emphasis added.)

Under these original statutes, any evasion from official detention would be at least second-degree unlawful evasion under the catchall clause in former AS 11.30.093(d) without regard to "felony" or "misdemeanor" or "charge" or "conviction" requirements.... The original unlawful evasion law therefore offers no support for LeFever's position that adjudicated juvenile delinquents could not commit that offense in any degree.

In 1978, the legislature repealed the above statutes and enacted new definitions of unlawful evasion and official detention. Former AS 11.56.340(a) (1978) provided: "A person commits the crime of un- lawful evasion in the first degree if he fails to return to *official detention on a charge of a felony* following temporary leave granted for a specific purpose or limited period...." (emphasis added). Former AS 11.56.350(a) (1978) was identical except that it replaced the words "first" and "felony" with "second" and "misdemeanor." It appears that the 1978 division of unlawful evasion into two statutes was not meant to exclude anything from the definition of the unlawful evasion offense but instead served the same purpose as the division in the 1976 statute: to classify all unlawful evasions in terms of degrees of appropriate punishment. Again, the 1978 unlawful evasion language "on a charge of a felony" was identical to the 1978 escape language.

In 1980, the language of the escape statutes was changed to read "for a felony" instead of "on a charge of a felony." This court in [another case] held that this amendment was meant to clarify rather than change the scope of the escape offenses. The corresponding language of the unlawful evasion statutes was not changed at that time, nor was it changed in 1985 when the legislature made unrelated minor changes to the unlawful evasion statutes (replacing "he" with "the person" ...). This divergence of the escape statutes' language from the unlawful evasion statutes' language appears insignificant, however, because the legislature stated and this court has held that the two phrases ("for a felony" and "on a charge of a felony") have the same meaning in this context.

Finally, in 1986, the legislature rewrote the unlawful evasion statutes into their current form. The reason for this revision seems clear. The earlier unlawful evasion statutes had referred to a number of prison statutes [which] were all repealed in 1986, when the legislature rewrote that chapter of the Alaska Statutes. It was necessary for the new unlawful evasion statutes to refer to the new prison statutes. In order to accomplish this, the legislature for the first time split AS 11.56.340(a) into sub- sections:

A person commits the crime of unlawful evasion in the first degree if, while charged with or convicted of a felony,

(1) the person fails to return to official detention within the time authorized following temporary leave granted for a specific purpose or limited period, including leave granted under AS 33.30.181; or

(2) while on furlough under AS 33.30.101—33.30.131 the person fails to return to the place of confinement or residence within the time authorized by those having direct super- vision.

This change apparently recognizes that furloughs ... do not necessarily involve "official detention" but may be furloughs from a "residence" rather than a "place of confinement." It was therefore no longer an option for the legislature to refer to unlawful evasion from "official detention on a charge of a felony" (or "for a felony"). Instead, in order to apply the introductory language of the unlawful evasion statutes to both new subsections, one of which did not necessarily involve official detention, the legislature had to expand the language into a full modifying clause: "while charged with or convicted of a felony" (or "misdemeanor"). The 1986 amendments, if anything, expanded the definition of un- lawful evasion (by clarifying that evasion from furloughs not involving official detention was unlawful) rather than narrowed it.

classify unlawful evasion by seriousness of the evader's original conduct, not to exclude adjudicated delinquents from the definition of unlawful evasion.

We affirm the conviction.

* * *

Points for Discussion

1. *Statutory Language*: What was the language at issue, which is contained within AS § 11.56.340(a)? Why is AS § 47.10.080(g) relevant to the court's interpretation of the language in AS § 11.56.340(a)? What interpretation did the defendant want? The State? Which meaning did the court adopt?

2. *Theories*: Which theory did the court use? According to this court, what does such an approach require of the court? What result if the court had applied textualism? Intentionalism? Purposivism?

3. *How Clear Is Clear*: The court said it will always look at all the sources of information; however, the clearer the statutory language, the stronger the evidence of a contrary legislative intent must be. How clear was the language here? What contrary legislative evidence did the court consider? How persuasive was that contrary legislative evidence? Does your answer to that question show that this approach is closer to textualism, intentionalism, or purposivism?

4. *Legislative Amendment History*: In footnote 5, the court explained why the evolution of the statutory language showed that the legislature did not intend to change the meaning of AS § 11.56.340(a) when the legislature amended the statute. Do you find this evidence of intent overwhelming enough to reject the clear text? Would a textualist judge agree with you?

5. *In Pari Materia*: The court considered another statute, AS § 11.81.410, and noted that there would be "anomalous results" if the statute at issue, AS § 11.56.340(a), were interpreted as the defendant argued. A linguistic canon—*in pari materia*, the whole code aspect—directs judges to read and construe related statutes together. The court applied *in pari materia* in this case. Do you find the argument convincing? Note that just because different statutes include the same language does not mean that the identical language in the statutes has to have the same meaning, but there is a presumption that identical words in statutes with similar purposes do have identical meanings. This presumption is known as the identical words presumption. (*See* Chapter 8 for a discussion of both of these linguistic canons.)

6. *Rule of Lenity*: Why did the court not apply the rule of lenity? Would the court have reached a different result had it done so? Would that result have been consistent with the plain meaning of the statute? Pg. 133

* * * court doesn't apply → cannon or policy
court could have applied

E. Does Theory Matter?

Perhaps. But there is no empirical way to tell whether one theory more consistently leads to the "correct interpretation" of a statute. Only if we knew what the "right" interpretation was without applying a theory could we determine which theory most often leads to that "right" interpretation. But of course, we do not know which interpretation is right, nor do we even know what sources we are supposed to use to evaluate the correctness of any interpretation. Hence, no one theory is better at discerning the "right" meaning than any other. This is an important point, for you will want to believe that your theory is right and that the others are wrong.

While academics will continue rigorously to argue the correctness of the various approaches, few judges remain so dogmatic. Judges regularly mix approaches, fail to identify their approach, and even change approaches. Ultimately, judges want to further justice, not be dogmatically rigid. Professors Eskridge and Frickey call this *pragmatic theory*. "In deciding a question of statutory interpretation in the real, as opposed to the theoretical, world, few judges approach the interpretive task armed with a fixed set of rigid rules." John M. Walker, *Judicial Tendencies in Statutory Construction: Differing Views on the Role of the Judge*, 58 N.Y.U. Ann. Surv. Am. L. 203, 232 (2001). Hence, the reality is that few judges rigidly adhere to just one theory. Even former Justice Scalia admitted, "I play the game like everybody else.... I'm in a system which has accepted rules and legislative history is used.... You read my opinions, I sin with the rest of them." Frank H. Easterbrook, *What Does Legislative History Tell Us?*, 66 Chi.-Kent L. Rev. 441, 442 n.4 (1990) (quoting Judges and Legislators: Toward Institutional Comity 174–75 (R. Katzmann ed. 1988)).

Perhaps, as legal realists suggest, none of this theory stuff matters. The reality is that judges decide cases based on their own personal notions of justice and the underlying equities of the case. For this reason, you should not expect to win your case simply because you select a particular theory. To win your case, you must prove to your judge that a ruling for your client would be the just and right result. But knowing a judge's preferred theory can make your job easier. For example, if you are arguing before a purposivist, you would not talk about ambiguity and absurdity before discussing legislative history or context, as you must do if you are arguing before a textualist. Thus, the theories provide legal language, an outline for your analytical arguments, and seemingly impartial reasoning to help you win your case. In this world, the Ancient Greek aphorism "Know thyself" could be "Know thy judge's theory."

Professors Eskridge, Frickey, and Garrett best summed up the reality of today's doctrine:

> We do not think the Supreme Court has entirely returned to the pre-Scalia days and suggest the following generalities about where it is today. First, the text is now, more than it was 20 or 30 years ago, the central inquiry at the Supreme Court level and in other courts that are now following the Supreme Court's lead. A brief that starts off with, "The statute means thus-and-so because it says so in the committee report," is asking for trouble. Both advice

and advocacy should start with the statutory text. Because the Court frequently uses the dictionary to provide meaning to key statutory terms, the advocate should incorporate this methodology as well.... Second, the "contextual" evidence the Court is interested in is now statutory as much as or more than just historical context. Arguments that your position is more consistent with other parts of the same statute are typically winning arguments. Similarly, as [one case] indicates, the Court today goes beyond the "whole act" rule to something like a "whole code" rule, searching the United States Code for guidance on the usage of key statutory terms and phrases.*

Third, the Court will still look at contextual evidence and is very interested in the public law background of the statute. If a statute seems to require an odd result..., the Court will interrogate the background materials to find out why.... It remains important to research and brief the legislative history thoroughly. The effective advocate will appreciate that the presence of such materials in the briefs may influence the outcome more than the opinion in the case will indicate.

WILLIAM ESKRIDGE, JR. *ET AL.*, CASES AND MATERIALS ON LEGISLATION: STATUTES AND THE CREATION OF PUBLIC POLICY 770–71 (3d ed. 2001).

Problem 4

As you read the hypothetical case below, think about which judge's opinion you would join and why. Which theory do you think each judge prefers? Are any sources of information missing? Are any of the theories of interpretation missing? Identify the language being interpreted and the clarity of that language. How would you rule and why?

The Case of the Speluncean Explorers**

In The Supreme Court of New Garth, 4300

The defendants, having been indicted for the crime of murder, were convicted and sentenced to be hanged by the Court of General Instances of the County of Stowfield. They bring a petition of error before this Court. The facts sufficiently appear in the opinion of the Chief Justice.

◆   TRUEPENNY, C. J. The four defendants are members of the Speluncean Society, an organization of amateurs interested in the exploration of caves. Early in May of 4299 they, in the company of Roger Whetmore, then also a member of the Society, penetrated into the interior of a limestone cavern of the type found in the Central

---

* Notice that the court in *LeFever*, excerpted above, used this "whole code" approach to find the statute could not mean what it said. *LeFever v. State*, 877 P. 2d. 1298, 1301–02 (Alaska Ct. App. 1994) (noting the defendant's interpretation would lead to an absurd interpretation of another, related statute).

** Lon L. Fuller, *The Case of the Speluncean Explorers*, 62 HARV. L. REV. 616–45 (1949). Copyright Lon L. Fuller, Professor. Used with permission from Lynn Fuller and the Harvard Law Review.

Plateau of this Commonwealth. While they were in a position remote from the entrance to the cave, a landslide occurred. Heavy boulders fell in such a manner as to block completely the only known opening to the cave. When the men discovered their predicament they settled themselves near the obstructed entrance to wait until a rescue party should remove the detritus that prevented them from leaving their underground prison. On the failure of Whetmore and the defendants to return to their homes, the Secretary of the Society was notified by their families. It appears that the explorers had left indications at the headquarters of the Society concerning the location of the cave they proposed to visit. A rescue party was promptly dispatched to the spot.

The task of rescue proved one of overwhelming difficulty. It was necessary to supplement the forces of the original party by repeated increments of men and machines, which had to be conveyed at great expense to the remote and isolated region in which the cave was located. A huge temporary camp of workmen, engineers, geologists, and other experts was established. The work of removing the obstruction was several times frustrated by fresh landslides. In one of these, ten of the workmen engaged in clearing the entrance were killed. The treasury of the Speluncean Society was soon exhausted in the rescue effort, and the sum of eight hundred thousand frelars, raised partly by popular subscription and partly by legislative grant, was expended before the imprisoned men were rescued. Success was finally achieved on the thirty-second day after the men entered the cave.

Since it was known that the explorers had carried with them only scant provisions, and since it was also known that there was no animal or vegetable matter within the cave on which they might subsist, anxiety was early felt that they might meet death by starvation before access to them could be obtained. On the twentieth day of their imprisonment it was learned for the first time that they had taken with them into the cave a portable wireless machine capable of both sending and receiving messages. A similar machine was promptly installed in the rescue camp and oral communication established with the unfortunate men within the mountain. They asked to be informed how long a time would be required to release them. The engineers in charge of the project answered that at least ten days would be required even if no new landslides occurred. The explorers then asked if any physicians were present, and were placed in communication with a committee of medical experts. The imprisoned men described their condition and the rations they had taken with them, and asked for a medical opinion whether they would be likely to live without food for ten days longer. The chairman of the committee of physicians told them that there was little possibility of this. The wireless machine within the cave then remained silent for eight hours. When communication was re-established the men asked to speak again with the physicians. The chairman of the physicians' committee was placed before the apparatus, and Whetmore, speaking on behalf of himself and the defendants, asked whether they would be able to survive for ten days longer if they consumed the flesh of one of their number. The physicians' chairman reluctantly answered this question in the affirmative. Whetmore asked whether it would be advisable for them to cast lots to determine which of them should be eaten. None of the physicians present was willing to answer the question. Whetmore then asked if there were among the party a judge or other official of the government who would answer this question. None of those attached to the rescue camp was willing to assume the role of advisor in this matter. He then asked if any minister or priest would answer their question, and none was found who would do so. Thereafter no further messages were received from within the cave, and it was assumed (erroneously, it later appeared) that the electric batteries of the explorers' wireless machine had become exhausted. When the imprisoned men were finally released it was learned that on the twenty-third day after their entrance into the cave Whetmore had been killed and eaten by his companions.

From the testimony of the defendants, which was accepted by the jury, it appears that it was Whetmore who first proposed that they might find the nutriment without which survival was impossible in the flesh of one of their own number. It was also Whetmore who first proposed the use of some method of casting lots, calling the attention of the defendants to a pair of dice he happened to have with him. The defendants were at first reluctant to adopt so desperate a procedure, but after the conversations by wireless related above, they finally agreed on the plan proposed by Whetmore. After much discussion of the mathematical problems involved, agreement was finally reached on a method of determining the issue by the use of the dice.

Before the dice were cast, however, Whetmore declared that he withdrew from the arrangement, as he had decided on reflection to wait for another week before embracing an expedient so frightful and odious. The others charged him with a breach of faith and proceeded to cast the dice. When it came Whetmore's turn, the dice were cast for him by one of the defendants, and he was asked to declare any objections he might have to the fairness of the throw. He stated that he had no such objections. The throw went against him, and he was then put to death and eaten by his companions.

withdrew from consent

After the rescue of the defendants, and after they had completed a stay in a hospital where they underwent a course of treatment for malnutrition and shock, they were indicted for the murder of Roger Whetmore. At the trial, after the testimony had been concluded, the foreman of the jury (a lawyer by profession) inquired of the court whether the jury might not find a special verdict, leaving it to the court to say whether on the facts as found the defendants were guilty. After some discussion, both the Prosecutor and counsel for the defendants indicated their acceptance of this procedure, and it was adopted by the court. In a lengthy special verdict the jury found the facts as I have related them above, and found further that if on these facts the defendants were guilty of the crime charged against them, then they found the defendants guilty. On the basis of this verdict, the trial judge ruled that the defendants were guilty of murdering Roger Whetmore. The judge then sentenced them to be hanged, the law of our Commonwealth permitting him no discretion with respect to the penalty to be imposed. After the release of the jury, its members joined in a communication to the Chief Executive asking that the sentence be commuted to an imprisonment of six months. The trial judge addressed a similar communication to the Chief Executive. As yet no action with respect to these pleas has been taken, as the Chief Executive is apparently awaiting our disposition of this petition of error.

The language
is clear but
there should
be a clemency
here

It seems to me that in dealing with this extraordinary case the jury and the trial judge followed a course that was not only fair and wise, but the only course that was open to them under the law. The language of our statute is well known: "Whoever shall willfully take the life of another shall be punished by death." N.C.S.A. (N. S.) § 12-A. This statute permits of no exception applicable to this case, however our sympathies may incline us to make allowance for the tragic situation in which these men found themselves.

In a case like this the principle of executive clemency seems admirably suited to mitigate the rigors of the law, and I propose to my colleagues that we follow the example of the jury and the trial judge by joining in the communications they have addressed to the Chief Executive. There is every reason to believe that these requests for clemency will be heeded, coming as they do from those who have studied the case and had an opportunity to become thoroughly acquainted with all its circumstances. It is highly improbable that the Chief Executive would deny these requests unless he were himself to hold hearings at least as extensive as those involved in the trial below, which lasted for three months. The holding of such hearings (which would virtually amount to a retrial of the case) would scarcely be compatible with the function of the Executive as it is usually conceived. I think we may therefore assume that some form of clemency will be extended to these defendants. If this is done, then justice will be accomplished without impairing either the letter or spirit of our statutes and without offering any encouragement for the disregard of law.

◆   FOSTER, J. I am shocked that the Chief Justice, in an effort to escape the embarrassments of this tragic case, should have adopted, and should have proposed to his colleagues, an expedient at once so sordid and so obvious. I believe something more is on trial in this case than the fate of these unfortunate explorers; that is the law of our Commonwealth. If this Court declares that under our law these men have committed a crime, then our law is itself convicted in the tribunal of common sense, no matter what happens to the individuals involved in this petition of error. For us to assert that the law we uphold and expound compels us to a conclusion we are ashamed of, and from which we can only escape by appealing to a dispensation resting within the personal whim of the Executive, seems to me to amount to an admission that the law of this Commonwealth no longer pretends to incorporate justice.

For myself, I do not believe that our law compels the monstrous conclusion that these men are murderers. I believe, on the contrary, that it declares them to be innocent of any crime....

Now it is, of course, perfectly clear that these men did an act that violates the literal wording of the statute which declares that he who "shall willfully take the life of another" is a murderer. But one of the most ancient bits of legal wisdom is the saying that a man may break the letter of the law without breaking the law itself. Every proposition of positive law, whether contained in a statute or a judicial precedent, is to be interpreted reasonably, in the light of its evident purpose. This is a truth so elementary that it is hardly necessary to expatiate on it. Illustrations of its application are numberless and are to be found in every branch of the law. In *Commonwealth v. Staymore* the defendant was convicted under a statute making it a crime to leave one's car parked in certain areas for a period longer than two hours. The defendant had attempted to remove his car, but was prevented from doing so because the streets were obstructed by a political demonstration in which he took no part and which he had no reason to anticipate. His conviction was set aside by this Court, although his case fell squarely within the wording of the statute. Again, in *Fehler v. Neegas* there was before this Court for construction a statute in which the word "not" had plainly been transposed from its intended position in the final and most crucial section of the act. This transposition was contained in all the successive drafts of the act, where it was apparently overlooked by the draftsmen and sponsors of the legislation. No one was able to prove how the error came about, yet it was apparent that, taking account of the contents of the statute as a whole, an error had been made, since a literal reading of the final clause rendered it inconsistent with everything that had gone before and with the object of the enactment as stated in its preamble. This Court refused to accept a literal interpretation of the statute, and in effect rectified its language by reading the word "not" into the place where it was evidently intended to go.

The statute before us for interpretation has never been applied literally. Centuries ago it was established that a killing in self-defense is excused. There is nothing in the wording of the statute that suggests this exception. Various attempts have been made to reconcile the legal treatment of self-defense with the words of the statute, but in my opinion these are all merely ingenious sophistries. The truth is that the exception in favor of self-defense cannot be reconciled with the *words* of the statute, but only with its *purpose.*

The true reconciliation of the excuse of self-defense with the statute making it a crime to kill another is to be found in the following line of reasoning. One of the principal objects underlying any criminal legislation is that of deterring men from crime. Now it is apparent that if it were declared to be the law that a killing in self-defense is murder such a rule could not operate in a deterrent manner. A man whose life is threatened will repel his aggressor, whatever the law may say. Looking therefore to the broad purposes of criminal legislation, we may safely declare that this statute was not intended to apply to cases of self-defense.

When the rationale of the excuse of self-defense is thus explained, it becomes apparent that precisely the same reasoning is applicable to the case at bar. If in the future any group of men ever find themselves in the tragic predicament of these defendants, we may be sure that their decision whether to live or die will not be controlled by the contents of our criminal code. Accordingly, if we read this statute intelligently it is apparent that it does not apply to this case. The withdrawal of this situation from the effect of the statute is justified by precisely the same considerations that were applied by our predecessors in office centuries ago to the case of self-defense.

There are those who raise the cry of judicial usurpation whenever a court, after analyzing the purpose of a statute, gives to its words a meaning that is not at once apparent to the casual reader who has not studied the statute closely or examined the objectives it seeks to attain. Let me say emphatically that I accept without reservation the proposition that this Court is bound by the statutes of our Commonwealth and that it exercises its powers in subservience to the duly expressed will of the Chamber of Representatives. The line of reasoning I have applied above raises no question of fidelity to enacted law, though it may possibly raise a question of the distinction between intelligent and unintelligent fidelity. No superior wants a servant who lacks the capacity to read between the lines. The stupidest housemaid knows that when she is told "to peel the soup and skim the potatoes" her mistress does not mean what she says. She also knows that when her master tells her to "drop everything and come running" he has overlooked the possibility that she is at the moment in the act of rescuing the baby from the rain barrel. Surely we have a right to expect the same modicum of intelligence from the judiciary. The correction of obvious legislative errors or oversights is not to supplant the legislative will, but to make that will effective.

I therefore conclude that on any aspect under which this case may be viewed these defendants are innocent of the crime of murdering Roger Whetmore, and that the conviction should be set aside.

♦   TATTING, J. In the discharge of my duties as a justice of this Court, I am usually able to dissociate the emotional and intellectual sides of my reactions, and to decide the case before me entirely on the basis of the latter. In passing on this tragic case I find that my usual resources fail me. On the emotional side I find myself torn between sympathy for these men and a feeling of abhorrence and disgust at the monstrous act they committed. I had hoped that I would be able to put these contradictory emotions to one side as irrelevant, and to decide the case on the basis of a convincing and logical demonstration of the result demanded by our law. Unfortunately, this deliverance has not been vouchsafed me.

As I analyze the opinion just rendered by my brother Foster, I find that it is shot through with contradictions and fallacies.... The gist of my brother's argument may be stated in the following terms: No statute, whatever its language, should be applied in a way that contradicts its purpose. One of the purposes of any criminal statute is to deter. The application of the statute making it a crime to kill another to the peculiar facts of this case would contradict this purpose, for it is impossible to believe that the contents of the criminal code could operate in a deterrent manner on men faced with the alternative of life or death. The reasoning by which this exception is read into the statute is, my brother observes, the same as that which is applied in order to provide the excuse of self-defense.

On the face of things this demonstration seems very convincing indeed. My brother's interpretation of the rationale of the excuse of self-defense is in fact supported by a decision of this court, *Commonwealth v. Parry*.... Now let me outline briefly, however, the perplexities that assail me when I examine my brother's demonstration more closely. It is true that a statute should be applied in the light of its purpose, and that *one* of the purposes of criminal legislation is recognized to be deterrence. The difficulty is that other purposes are also ascribed to the law of crimes. It has also been said that its object is the rehabilitation of the wrongdoer. *Commonwealth v. Makeover*. Other theories have been propounded. Assuming that we must interpret a statute in the light of its purpose, what are we to do when it has many purposes or when its purposes are disputed?

A similar difficulty is presented by the fact that although there is authority for my brother's interpretation of the excuse of self-defense, there is other authority which assigns to that excuse a different rationale. Indeed, until I happened on *Commonwealth v. Parry* I had never heard of the explanation given by my brother. The taught doctrine of our law schools, memorized by generations of law students, runs in the following terms: The statute concerning murder requires a "willful" act. The man who acts to repel an aggressive threat to his own life does not act "willfully," but in response to an impulse deeply ingrained in human nature....

[margin note: Self-Defense is not a good analogy]

Now the familiar explanation for the excuse of self-defense just expounded obviously cannot be applied by analogy to the facts of this case. These men acted not only "willfully" but with great deliberation and after hours of discussing what they should do....

I recognize the relevance of the precedents cited by my brother concerning the displaced "not" and the defendant who parked overtime. But what are we to do with one of the landmarks of our jurisprudence, which again my brother passes over in silence? This is *Commonwealth v. Valjean.* Though the case is somewhat obscurely reported, it appears that the defendant was indicted for the larceny of a loaf of bread, and offered as a defense that he was in a condition approaching starvation. The court refused to accept this defense. If hunger cannot justify the theft of wholesome and natural food, how can it justify the killing and eating of a man? Again, if we look at the thing in terms of deterrence, is it likely that a man will starve to death to avoid a jail sentence for the theft of a loaf of bread? ...

There is still a further difficulty in my brother Foster's proposal to read an exception into the statute to favor this case, though again a difficulty not even intimated in his opinion. What shall be the scope of this exception? Here the men cast lots and the victim was himself originally a party to the agreement. What would we have to decide if Whetmore had refused from the beginning to participate in the plan? Would a majority be permitted to overrule him? Or, suppose that no plan were adopted at all and the others simply conspired to bring about Whetmore's death, justifying their act by saying that he was in the weakest condition. Or again, that a plan of selection was followed but one based on a different justification than the one adopted here, as if the others were atheists and insisted that Whetmore should die because he was the only one who believed in an afterlife. These illustrations could be multiplied, but enough have been suggested to reveal what a quagmire of hidden difficulties my brother's reasoning contains....

[margin note: Conditions - consent of agreement]

The more I examine this case and think about it, the more deeply I become involved. My mind becomes entangled in the meshes of the very nets I throw out for my own rescue. I find that almost every consideration that bears on the decision of the case is counterbalanced by an opposing consideration leading in the opposite direction. My brother Foster has not furnished to me, nor can I discover for myself, any formula capable of resolving the equivocations that beset me on all sides.

I have given this case the best thought of which I am capable. I have scarcely slept since it was argued before us. When I feel myself inclined to accept the view of my brother Foster, I am repelled by a feeling that his arguments are intellectually unsound and approach mere rationalization. On the other hand, when I incline toward upholding the conviction, I am struck by the absurdity of directing that these men be put to death when their lives have been saved at the cost of the lives of ten heroic workmen. It is to me a matter of regret that the Prosecutor saw fit to ask for an indictment for murder. If we had a provision in our statutes making it a crime to eat human flesh, that would have been a more appropriate charge. If no other charge suited to the facts of this case could be brought against the defendants, it would have been wiser, I think, not to have indicted them at all. Unfortunately, however, the men have been indicted and tried, and we have therefore been drawn into this unfortunate affair.

Since I have been wholly unable to resolve the doubts that beset me about the law of this case, I am with regret announcing a step that is, I believe, unprecedented in the history of this tribunal. I declare my withdrawal from the decision of this case.

Textualist   ◆   KEEN, J. I should like to begin by setting to one side two questions which are not before this Court.

The first of these is whether executive clemency should be extended to these defendants if the conviction is affirmed. Under our system of government, that is a question for the Chief Executive, not for us. I therefore disapprove of that passage in the opinion of the Chief Justice in which he in effect gives instructions to the Chief Executive as to what he should do in this case and suggests that some impropriety will attach if these instructions are not heeded. This is a confusion of governmental functions—a confusion of which the judiciary should be the last to be guilty. I wish to state that if I were the Chief Executive I would go farther in the direction of clemency than the pleas addressed to him propose. I would pardon these men altogether, since I believe that they have already suffered enough to pay for any offense they may have committed. I want it to be understood that this remark is made in my capacity as a private citizen who by the accident of his office happens to have acquired an intimate acquaintance with the facts of this case. In the discharge of my duties as judge, it is neither my function to address directions to the Chief Executive, nor to take into account what he may or may not do, in reaching my own decision, which must be controlled entirely by the law of this Commonwealth.

The second question that I wish to put to one side is that of deciding whether what these men did was "right" or "wrong," "wicked" or "good." That is also a question that is irrelevant to the discharge of my office as a judge sworn to apply, not my conceptions of morality, but the law of the land....

The sole question before us for decision is whether these defendants did, within the meaning of N. C. S. A. (N. S.) § 12-A, willfully take the life of Roger Whetmore. The exact language of the statute is as follows: "Whoever shall willfully take the life of another shall be punished by death." Now I should suppose that any candid observer, content to extract from these words their natural meaning, would concede at once that these defendants did "willfully take the life" of Roger Whetmore.

Whence arise all the difficulties of the case, then, and the necessity for so many pages of discussion about what ought to be so obvious? The difficulties, in whatever tortured form they may present themselves, all trace back to a single source, and that is a failure to distinguish the legal from the moral aspects of this case. To put it bluntly, my brothers do not like the fact that the written law requires the conviction of these defendants. . . .

Now, of course, my brother Foster does not admit that he is actuated by a personal dislike of the written law. Instead he develops a familiar line of argument according to which the court may disregard the express language of a statute when something not contained in the statute itself, called its "purpose," can be employed to justify the result the court considers proper. . . .

[We] have a clear-cut principle, which is the supremacy of the legislative branch of our government. From that principle flows the obligation of the judiciary to enforce faithfully the written law, and to interpret that law in accordance with its plain meaning without reference to our personal desires or our individual conceptions of justice. . . .

We are all familiar with the process by which the judicial reform of disfavored legislative enactments is accomplished. . . . The process of judicial reform requires three steps. The first of these is to divine some single "purpose" which the statute serves. This is done although not one statute in a hundred has any such single purpose, and although the objectives of nearly every statute are differently interpreted by the different classes of its sponsors. The second step is to discover that a mythical being called "the legislator," in the pursuit of this imagined "purpose," overlooked something or left some gap or imperfection in his work. Then comes the final and most refreshing part of the task, which is, of course, to fill in the blank thus created. *Quod erat faciendum.* . . .

One could not wish for a better case to illustrate the specious nature of this gap-filling process than the one before us. My brother thinks he knows exactly what was sought when men made murder a crime, and that was something he calls "deterrence." My brother Tatting has already shown how much is passed over in that interpretation. But I think the trouble goes deeper. I doubt very much whether our statute making murder a crime really has a "purpose" in any ordinary sense of the term. Primarily, such a statute reflects a deeply-felt human conviction that murder is wrong and that something should be done to the man who commits it. . . .

If we do not know the purpose of § 12-A, how can we possibly say there is a "gap" in it? How can we know what its draftsmen thought about the question of killing men in order to eat them? . . . [I]t remains abundantly clear that neither I nor my brother Foster knows what the "purpose" of § 12-A is.

Considerations similar to those I have just outlined are also applicable to the exception in favor of self-defense, which plays so large a role in the reasoning of my brothers Foster and Tatting. It is of course true that in *Commonwealth v. Parry* an obiter dictum justified this exception on the assumption that the purpose of criminal legislation is to deter. It may well also be true that . . . the true explanation of the exception lies in the fact that a man who acts in self-defense does not act "willfully." . . . But again the real trouble lies deeper. As in dealing with the statute, so in dealing with the exception, the question is not the conjectural *purpose* of the rule, but its *scope*. Now the scope of the exception in favor of self-defense as it has been applied by this Court is plain: it applies to cases of resisting an aggressive threat to the party's own life. It is therefore too clear for argument that this case does not fall within the scope of the exception, since it is plain that Whetmore made no threat against the lives of these defendants....

Now I know that the line of reasoning I have developed in this opinion will not be acceptable to those who look only to the immediate effects of a decision and ignore the long-run implications of an assumption by the judiciary of a power of dispensation. A hard decision is never a popular decision. Judges have been celebrated in literature for their sly prowess in devising some quibble by which a litigant could be deprived of his rights where the public thought it was wrong for him to assert those rights. But I believe that judicial dispensation does more harm in the long run than hard decisions. Hard cases may even have a certain moral value by bringing home to the people their own responsibilities toward the law that is ultimately their creation, and by reminding them that there is no principle of personal grace that can relieve the mistakes of their representatives.

Indeed, I will go farther and say that not only are the principles I have been expounding those which are soundest for our present conditions, but that we would have inherited a better legal system from our forefathers if those principles had been observed from the beginning. For example, with respect to the excuse of self-defense, if our courts had stood steadfast on the language of the statute the result would undoubtedly have been a legislative revision of it.... and the resulting regulation of the matter would have had an understandable and rational basis, instead of the hodge-podge of verbalisms and metaphysical distinctions that have emerged from the judicial and professorial treatment....

I conclude that the conviction should be affirmed.

•   HANDY, J. I have listened with amazement to the tortured ratiocinations to which this simple case has given rise. I never cease to wonder at my colleagues' ability to throw an obscuring curtain of legalisms about every issue presented to them for decision. We have heard this afternoon learned disquisitions on the distinction between ... the language of the statute and the purpose of the statute, judicial functions and executive functions, judicial legislation and legislative legislation. My only disappointment was that someone did not raise the question of the legal nature of the bargain struck in the cave — whether it was unilateral or bilateral, and whether Whetmore could not be considered as having revoked an offer prior to action taken thereunder.

What have all these things to do with the case? The problem before us is what we, as officers of the government, ought to do with these defendants. That is a question of practical wisdom, to be exercised in a context, not of abstract theory, but of human realities. When the case is approached in this light, it becomes, I think, one of the easiest to decide that has ever been argued before this Court....

I have never been able to make my brothers see that government is a human affair, and that men are ruled, not by words on paper or by abstract theories, but by other men. They are ruled well when their rulers understand the feelings and conceptions of the masses. They are ruled badly when that understanding is lacking....

[T]his case has aroused an enormous public interest, both here and abroad. Almost every newspaper and magazine has carried articles about it; columnists have shared with their readers confidential information as to the next governmental move; hundreds of letters-to-the-editor have been printed. One of the great newspaper chains made a poll of public opinion on the question, "What do you think the Supreme Court should do with the Speluncean explorers?" About ninety per cent expressed a belief that the defendants should be pardoned or let off with a kind of token punishment. It is perfectly clear, then, how the public feels about the case. We could have known this without the poll, of course, on the basis of common sense, or even by observing that on this Court there are apparently four-and-a-half men, or ninety per cent, who share the common opinion.

This makes it obvious, not only what we should do, but what we must do if we are to preserve between ourselves and public opinion a reasonable and decent accord. Declaring these men innocent need not involve us in any undignified quibble or trick. No principle of statutory construction is required that is not consistent with the past practices of this Court. Certainly no layman would think that in letting these men off we had stretched the statute any more than our ancestors did when they created the excuse of self-defense. If a more detailed demonstration of the method of reconciling our decision with the statute is required, I should be content to rest on the arguments developed in the second and less visionary part of my brother Foster's opinion.

Now I know that my brothers will be horrified by my suggestion that this Court should take account of public opinion....

But let us look candidly at some of the realities of the administration of our criminal law. When a man is accused of crime, there are, speaking generally, four ways in which he may escape punishment. One of these is a determination by a judge that under the applicable law he has committed no crime. This is, of course, a determination that takes place in a rather formal and abstract atmosphere. But look at the other three ways in which he may escape punishment. These are: (1) a decision by the Prosecutor not to ask for an indictment; (2) an acquittal by the jury; (3) a pardon or commutation of sentence by the executive. Can anyone pretend that these decisions are held within a rigid and formal framework of rules that prevents factual error, excludes emotional and personal factors, and guarantees that all the forms of the law will be observed?

In the case of the jury we do, to be sure, attempt to cabin their deliberations within the area of the legally relevant, but there is no need to deceive ourselves into believing that this attempt is really successful. In the normal course of events the case now before us would have gone on all of its issues directly to the jury. Had this occurred we can be confident that there would have been an acquittal or at least a division that would have prevented a conviction. If the jury had been instructed that the men's hunger and their agreement were no defense to the charge of murder, their verdict would in all likelihood have ignored this instruction and would have involved a good deal more twisting of the letter of the law than any that is likely to tempt us. Of course the only reason that didn't occur in this case was the fortuitous circumstance that the foreman of the jury happened to be a lawyer. His learning enabled him to devise a form of words that would allow the jury to dodge its usual responsibilities.

My brother Tatting expresses annoyance that the Prosecutor did not, in effect, decide the case for him by not asking for an indictment. Strict as he is himself in complying with the demands of legal theory, he is quite content to have the fate of these men decided out of court by the Prosecutor on the basis of common sense. The Chief Justice, on the other hand, wants the application of common sense postponed to the very end, though like Tatting, he wants no personal part in it....

I come now to the most crucial fact in this case, a fact known to all of us on this Court, though one that my brothers have seen fit to keep under the cover of their judicial robes. This is the frightening likelihood that if the issue is left to him, the Chief Executive will refuse to pardon these men or commute their sentence. As we all know, our Chief Executive is a man now well advanced in years, of very stiff notions. Public clamor usually operates on him with the reverse of the effect intended. As I have told my brothers, it happens that my wife's niece is an intimate friend of his secretary. I have learned in this indirect, but, I think, wholly reliable way, that he is firmly determined not to commute the sentence if these men are found to have violated the law....

I must confess that as I grow older I become more and more perplexed at men's refusal to apply their common sense to problems of law and government, and this truly tragic case has deepened my sense of discouragement and dismay....

Now, ... thanks to an ambitious Prosecutor and a legalistic jury foreman, I am faced with a case that raises issues ... of the life or death of four men who have already suffered more torment and humiliation than most of us would endure in a thousand years. I conclude that the defendants are innocent of the crime charged, and that the conviction and sentence should be set aside.

The Supreme Court being evenly divided, the conviction and sentence of the Court of General Instances is *affirmed*. It is ordered that the execution of the sentence shall occur at 6 a.m., Friday, April 2, 4300, at which time the Public Executioner is directed to proceed with all convenient dispatch to hang each of the defendants by the neck until he is dead....

* * *

Chapter 5

Canons Based on Intrinsic Sources: The Words

A. Introduction to This Chapter

Finally, we begin the interpretation process. To do so, we start where all interpretation should start: with the text of the statute. In this chapter, you will learn that generally, judges assume that legislatures meant to use words in their ordinary, or plain, sense. Occasionally, but much less commonly, the legislature meant to use a word in its technical sense. For example, statutes are often written for lawyers, who have a technical understanding of the word "assault," and not for lay persons, who have an ordinary understanding of that word. This chapter describes the plain and technical meaning rules. In the next chapter, you will learn the four situations when judges reject ordinary meaning.

B. The Intrinsic Sources

In Chapter 4, you learned that there are three sources of evidence judges use to glean the meaning of statutory language: intrinsic, extrinsic, and policy based. In the next few chapters, we will explore the relevance each of these sources has on interpretation. We begin with intrinsic sources, those sources that are part of the statute being interpreted. At this point, you know that the words of the statute are of central importance to all judges regardless of theory. But the words are not the only intrinsic source. Grammar, punctuation, and the linguistic canons of statutory construction are also intrinsic sources. We will explore the words now, and we will explore other intrinsic sources in later chapters.

C. The Textual Canons: Words and Syntax

"We do not inquire what the legislature meant; we ask only what the statute means." Oliver W. Holmes, *The Theory of Legal Interpretation*, 12 Harv. L. Rev. 417, 419 (1899). The language of the statute, including its words, grammar, and punctuation, is the starting point for all interpreters trying to find this meaning. "Unless a word or phrase is defined in the statute..., its meaning is determined by its context, the rules of grammar, and common usage." Unif. Statute & Rule Constr. Act, § 2

(1995). Thus, your job as an advocate is to identify the statutory language at issue and then explain why that language means what your client wants it to mean. To help you do so, let's examine the plain meaning rule.

1. The Plain Meaning Rule

The first place to start in interpreting a statute is with the words. "The text of a statute or rule is the primary, essential source of its meaning." UNIF. STATUTE & RULE CONSTR. ACT, § 19 (1995). You must first identify which words are at issue. Identifying the relevant language is not always easy, especially when you do not have a court identifying the language for you. Yet, which language you identify may be outcome determinative. For example, two cases out of Florida interpreted the same statute under almost identical facts but reached opposite results because each court focused on different words in the statute. The statute provided that traffic citations "shall not be admissible evidence in any trial." *Dixon v. Florida*, 812 So.2d 595, 596 (Fla. Dist. Ct. App. 2002) (quoting Fla. Stat. § 316.650(9) (2001)). In both cases, the defendants gave false information to an arresting officer. The officer entered the information on a traffic citation, which the defendants then signed using false names. Both defendants were arrested for forgery. At trial, the prosecutors offered the citations as evidence of the defendants' forgery (not of their traffic violations); the defendants objected, citing § 316.650(9).

Despite the factual similarities, the appellate courts reached different conclusions because they focused on different language in the statute. In *Dixon*, the court held that the traffic citation was inadmissible because the language of the statute was clear: "*any trial*" meant every trial without exception. *Id.* But in *Maddox v. Florida*, 862 So. 2d 783 (Fla. Dist. Ct. App. 2003), the court held that the statute did not apply because the ticket was not a "*traffic citation.*" Instead, it was "documentary evidence of Maddox's criminal conduct." *Id.* at 784. On appeal, the Florida Supreme Court agreed with the *Maddox* court, rejecting the interpretation in *Dixon*. *Maddox v. State*, 923 So.2d 442 (2006) (supporting its holding by identifying the purpose of the statute, reviewing other sections of the statute, and showing the absurdity of *Dixon's* plain meaning holding). As the appeal was pending, the Florida legislature amended the statute to allow citations to be admitted into evidence in subsequent forgery-related cases. 2005 Fla. Laws, c. 2005-164, § 42. (You will learn about the relevance of post-enactment legislative acts in Chapter 13.). These two cases show that identifying the appropriate language can be outcome-determinative.

Typically, courts presume that words in a statute have their "plain," or "ordinary," meaning. This presumption is known as the *Plain Meaning Rule*. In this book, we use the term "plain meaning rule" refers to the canon and "ordinary meaning" refers to the meaning of the word that most people would think of upon hearing the word. Be aware that judges use these terms interchangeably.

The plain meaning rule presumes, wrongly, that native listeners and readers of language understand words to mean the same thing the speakers intended. This presumption is inaccurate because words have multiple meanings. "[W]ords do not possess intrinsic meanings and cannot be given them; to make matters worse, speakers do not even have determinative intents about the meanings of their own words." Frank H. Easterbrook, *Statutes' Domains*, 50 U. Chi. L. Rev. 533, 536 (1983). Consider the word "blue." Blue is both a color and a feeling. If I say that I am "blue" today, likely I am saying that I am sad. But I may instead be pointing out that I am wearing blue clothing. Indeed, singers and poets take advantage of language's indeterminacy regularly; consider the song title, "Don't it Make My Brown Eyes Blue." Does the author mean blue in color, blue in feeling (sad), or both? While context often identifies which meaning is intended, context does not always resolve ambiguity.

How does a judge find the ordinary meaning of words? In the past, judges might have perused legislative history to understand what the legislators believed the words meant. More commonly today judges turn to their own understanding of a word's meaning and to dictionaries. Dictionary definitions are offered "not as evidence, but only as aids to the memory and understanding of the court." *Nix v. Heddon*, 149 U.S. 304, 307 (1893).

When a judge refers to his or her own understanding of a word to ascertain its meaning, the judge's choice appears subjective. In contrast, dictionaries lend an air of objectivity to the process. On the contrary, a judge's use of dictionaries is not objective; for example, which dictionary should a judge choose? There is no consensus about which dictionary to use, not even which era dictionary to use. As for era, former Justice Scalia, in his dissent in *Chisom v. Roemer*, 501 U.S. 380 (1991) (Scalia J., dissenting), indicated that a dictionary in effect at the time legislation was drafted would be appropriate. *Id.* at 410; *see, e.g., Free Enterprise Fund. v. Public Co. Accounting Oversight Bd.*, 561 U.S. 477, 511 (2010) (examining a dictionary from 1828 to understand the meaning of the word "department."). But not all judges agree. Earlier editions of dictionaries do not account for changes in meaning over time. If the point of interpretation is to find the intent of the enacting legislature, this latter concern may not matter. But if the point is to find the ordinary meaning the audience would give the words today, it may be essential.

As for which dictionary, there is no consensus on one specific choice. Apparently, not all dictionaries are equal. In *MCI Telecommunications Corp. v. American Telephone & Telegraph Co.*, 512 U.S. 218 (1994), Justice Scalia, for the majority, identified a number of different dictionaries with similar definitions of the word at issue: "modify." While the majority of dictionaries suggested that "modify" meant a modest change, one dictionary, *Webster's Third New International Dictionary*, suggested that "modify" could mean either a modest or substantial change. *Id.* at 225–26. The Court rejected the latter definition and the appropriateness of that dictionary. *Id.* at 227. "Virtually every dictionary we are aware of says that 'to modify' means to change moderately or in minor fashion." *Id.* at 225. Justice Scalia noted that there was widespread criticism of this dictionary when it was published for its "portrayal of common error as proper usage." *Id.* at 228 n.3. Apparently, Webster's Third was too colloquial to be considered authoritative for this Court. But if the point of statutory interpretation is to find the

ordinary meaning an audience member would likely ascribe to the language as textualists argue, why is colloquialism not a good thing? This fight is about the difference
between definitional meaning and ordinary meaning. The ordinary meaning of "modify" is a modest change; while a definitional meaning of "modify" includes substantial
change.

The use of dictionaries masks subjectiveness in another way. Dictionaries generally
have multiple meanings for each word. Yet, the presence of multiple dictionary definitions is not alone enough to show that a word is ambiguous. The Supreme Court
started down this road in one case when it accepted the argument that the presence
of multiple dictionary definitions meant that the word was inherently ambiguous.
National R.R. Passenger Corp., v. Boston & Maine Corp., 503 U.S. 407, 418 (1992)
(stating that "[t]he existence of alternative dictionary definitions of the word "required,"
each making some sense under the statute, itself indicates that the statute is open to
interpretation."). The Court quickly and correctly retreated from this unworkable
definition of ambiguity in a later case when it rejected an argument, based on *Nat'l
R.R. Passenger Corp.*, that the existence of multiple dictionary definitions established
ambiguity. *MCI Telecomms. Corp.*, 512 U.S. at 226. Had the Court adopted this definition every statutory word challenged in any future case would likely have been ambiguous, for it is rare, if not unheard of, for a word to have only one dictionary
definition.

A second concern relating to the fact that words have more than one dictionary
meaning is that there is no canon that says that the first dictionary meaning is *the
ordinary meaning*. While the primacy of the definition may carry weight, it is not
dispositive. "I cannot imagine that the majority favors interpreting statutes by choosing
the first definition that appears in a dictionary." *Mississippi Poultry Ass'n, Inc. v. Madigan*, 992 F.2d 1359, 1369 (5th Cir. 1993) (Reavley, J., dissenting)), *aff'd on reh'g*, 31
F.3d 293 (5th Cir. 1994) (en banc). Without guidance as to which meaning to pick,
how do judges know which of many meanings was intended? The choice of one meaning over another may be subjective.

Context helps to limit judicial discretion. Words often have different meanings in
different contexts. Consider an example: The defendant "assaulted" the plaintiff. Is
"assault" meant in its tortious sense, its criminal sense, or simply in its non-legal
sense, meaning a violent attack? To determine which of these possible meanings
should prevail, judges look to the statute's audience. For example, a Connecticut
state statute required state boards of education to indemnify personnel who were
harmed "as a result of an *assault*" while working. *Patrie v. Area Coop. Educ. Serv.*, 37
Conn. L. Rptr. 470 (Conn. Super. Ct. 2004) (citing Conn. Gen. Stat. § 10-236a) (emphasis added). The plaintiff had been injured when a student, without intending to
hurt the plaintiff, jumped playfully on the plaintiff's back. *Id.* at 470. Under the
statute, the plaintiff could only recover if the playful jump was "an assault." The
plaintiff argued that the legislature would have wanted "assault" interpreted broadly
to further the purpose of reimbursing school personnel for injuries that were no fault
of their own. *Id.* Thus, plaintiff suggested that the term meant either an assault as

defined in tort—freedom from the apprehension of a harmful or offensive contact—or as defined in that state's criminal law—an attempted but unsuccessful battery. Under either the tort definition or the criminal definition, any intent requirement would have been satisfied on these facts, for intent to harm is unnecessary under either legal theory. *Id.* at 473. But the court rejected both interpretations of the term. Instead, the court said, "The definition of 'assault' the plaintiff advocates forgets the audience the statute was aimed at—school administrators trying to meet budgets and run their schools and teachers concerned with their rights above and beyond workers' compensation." *Id.* Because administrators and teachers would more commonly think of an assault as being an intentionally violent attack (its non-legal meaning), the court held that in this statute "assault" meant an *intentionally* violent act. *Id.* Pursuant to this interpretation, the plaintiff could not recover for his injuries. Notice how textual context and audience were central to the court's textualist holding in *Patrie*.

In another case interpreting the same word in a different statute, a different court interpreted the term "assault" to have its legal, tortious meaning: specifically freedom from the apprehension of a harmful or offensive contact. *Dickens v. Puryear*, 276 S.E.2d 325 (N.C. 1981). In this case, the word was contained in a statute of limitations regarding intentional torts. Using the non-legal definition in this context would have made no sense because the audience for statutes of limitations is lawyers and judges, both of whom would have a different understanding of the word "assault" than would laypersons. *Id.*

Thus, dictionaries can be useful guides to determining ordinary meaning, but they have limitations as well. First, their use can mask the subjectiveness of the choice of meaning; choosing a dictionary and then choosing one meaning over another are both subjective choices. Moreover, dictionaries may at times be ill-suited for determining the meaning of particular language in a statute because context is so essential to meaning. Despite these limitations, judges increasingly rely on both the plain meaning rule and dictionaries to determine meaning. But they do not always understand that there is a difference between the definitional, or dictionary, meaning of a word and the ordinary meaning of a word. The definitional meaning is the many ways a word might be used, which dictionaries show, while the ordinary meaning is how a word is ordinarily used, which some dictionaries also note. Judges do not always distinguish between definitional meaning and ordinary meaning. In the case below, see if you can determine which justice used the dictionary meaning? The ordinary meaning? Before you begin, assume I asked you, "Did you use a firearm today?" How would you respond and what image comes to your mind?

[handwritten margin note: Summary]

Smith v. United States

Supreme Court of the United States
508 U.S. 223 (1993)

◆ JUSTICE O'CONNOR delivered the opinion of the Court [in which REHNQUIST, C.J., and WHITE, BLACKMUN, KENNEDY, and THOMAS, JJ., concur].

We decide today whether the exchange of a gun for narcotics constitutes "use" of a firearm "during and in relation to* ... [a] drug trafficking crime" within the meaning of 18 U.S.C. §924(c)(1).** We hold that it does.

Petitioner ... and his companion went from Tennessee to Florida to buy cocaine; they hoped to resell it at a profit.... The MAC–10 apparently is a favorite among criminals. It is small and compact, lightweight, and can be equipped with a silencer. Most important of all, it can be devastating: A fully automatic MAC–10 can fire more than 1,000 rounds per minute....

Upon arriving at [Petitioner's] motel room, [an] undercover officer presented himself to petitioner as a pawnshop dealer. Petitioner, in turn, presented the officer with a proposition: He had an automatic MAC–10 and silencer with which he might be willing to part.... Rather than asking for money, however, petitioner asked for drugs. He was willing to trade his MAC–10, he said, for two ounces of cocaine. The officer told petitioner ... that he wanted the MAC–10 and would try to get the cocaine. The officer then left, promising to return within an hour....

---

* Editor's footnote: The Petitioner did not deny that the alleged use occurred "during" a drug trafficking crime. He did dispute whether his use was "in relation to" the drug trafficking crime. The majority responded to this argument as follows: "We need not determine the precise contours of the 'in relation to' requirement here, however, as petitioner's use of his MAC-10 meets any reasonable construction of it."

** Editor's footnote: At the time of his arrest, 18 U.S.C. §924(c)(1) (1997) provided:

Whoever, during and in relation to any crime of violence or drug trafficking crime (including a crime of violence or drug trafficking crime which provides for an enhanced punishment if committed by the use of a deadly or dangerous weapon or device) for which he may be prosecuted in a court of the United States, uses or carries a firearm, shall, in addition to the punishment provided for such crime of violence or drug trafficking crime, be sentenced to imprisonment for five years, and if the firearm is a short-barreled rifle, short-barreled shotgun to imprisonment for ten years, and if the firearm is a machinegun, or a destructive device, or is equipped with a firearm silencer or firearm muffler, to imprisonment for thirty years. In the case of his second or subsequent conviction under this subsection, such person shall be sentenced to imprisonment for twenty years, and if the firearm is a machinegun, or a destructive device, or is equipped with a firearm silencer or firearm muffler, to life imprisonment without release. Notwithstanding any other provision of law, the court shall not place on probation or suspend the sentence of any person convicted of a violation of this subsection, nor shall the term of imprisonment imposed under this subsection run concurrently with any other term of imprisonment including that imposed for the crime of violence or drug trafficking crime in which the firearm was used or carried. No person sentenced under this subsection shall be eligible for parole during the term of imprisonment imposed herein.

But petitioner was not content to wait.... When law enforcement authorities tried to stop petitioner, he led them on a high-speed chase. Petitioner eventually was apprehended....

Under 18 U.S.C. § 924(c)(1), a defendant who ... uses a firearm must be sentenced to five years' incarceration. And where, as here, the firearm is a "machinegun" or is fitted with a silencer, the sentence is 30 years.... The jury convicted petitioner [of two drug-trafficking offenses and using a gun while committing them. In addition to the penalty for the underlying offenses, Petitioner received an additional 30 years for using a gun.].

On appeal, petitioner argued that § 924(c)(1)'s penalty for using a firearm during and in relation to a drug trafficking offense covers only situations in which the firearm is used as a weapon. According to petitioner, the provision does not extend to defendants who use a firearm solely as a medium of exchange or for barter....

Section 924(c)(1) requires the imposition of specified penalties if the defendant, "during and in relation to any crime of violence or drug trafficking crime[,] uses or carries a firearm." By its terms, the statute requires the prosecution to make two showings. First, the prosecution must demonstrate that the defendant "use[d] or carrie[d] a firearm." Second, it must prove that the use or carrying was "during and in relation to" a "crime of violence or drug trafficking crime."

Petitioner argues that exchanging a firearm for drugs does not constitute "use" of the firearm within the meaning of the statute. He points out that nothing in the record indicates that he fired the MAC–10, threatened anyone with it, or employed it for self-protection. In essence, petitioner argues that he cannot be said to have "use[d]" a firearm unless he used it as a weapon, since that is how firearms most often are used.... Of course, § 924(c)(1) is not limited to those cases in which a gun is used; it applies with equal force whenever a gun is "carrie[d]." In this case, however, the indictment alleged only that petitioner "use[d]" the MAC–10. Accordingly, we do not consider whether the evidence might support the conclusion that petitioner carried the MAC–10 within the meaning of § 924(c)(1)....

When a word is not defined by statute, we normally construe it in accord with its ordinary or natural meaning. Surely petitioner's treatment of his MAC–10 can be described as "use" within the everyday meaning of that term. Petitioner "used" his MAC–10 in an attempt to obtain drugs by offering to trade it for cocaine. Webster's defines "to use" as "[t]o convert to one's service" or "to employ." *Webster's New International Dictionary* 2806 (2d ed. 1939). *Black's Law Dictionary* contains a similar definition: "[t]o make use of; to convert to one's service; to employ; to avail oneself of; to utilize; to carry out a purpose or action by means of." *Black's Law Dictionary* 1541 (6th ed. 1990).... Petitioner's handling of the MAC–10 in this case falls squarely within those definitions. By attempting to trade his MAC–10 for the drugs, he "used" or "employed" it as an item of barter to obtain cocaine; he "derived service" from it because it was going to bring him the very drugs he sought.

Δ arg.

In petitioner's view, §924(c)(1) should require proof not only that the defendant used the firearm, but also that he used it *as a weapon*. But the words "as a weapon" appear nowhere in the statute. Rather, §924(c)(1)'s language sweeps broadly, punishing any "us[e]" of a firearm, so long as the use is "during and in relation to" a drug trafficking offense. Had Congress intended the narrow construction petitioner urges, it could have so indicated. It did not, and we decline to introduce that additional requirement on our own.

Language, of course, cannot be interpreted apart from context. The meaning of a word that appears ambiguous if viewed in isolation may become clear when the word is analyzed in light of the terms that surround it. Recognizing this, petitioner and the dissent argue that the word "uses" has a somewhat reduced scope in §924(c)(1) because it appears alongside the word "firearm." Specifically, they contend that the average person on the street would not think immediately of a guns-for-drugs trade as an example of "us[ing] a firearm." Rather, that phrase normally evokes an image of the most familiar use to which a firearm is put—use as a weapon. Petitioner and the dissent therefore argue that the statute excludes uses where the weapon is not fired or otherwise employed for its destructive capacity. Indeed, relying on that argument—and without citation to authority—the dissent announces its own, restrictive definition of "use." "To use an instrumentality," the dissent argues, "ordinarily means to use it for its intended purpose."

dissent

There is a significant flaw to this argument. It is one thing to say that the ordinary meaning of "uses a firearm" *includes* using a firearm as a weapon, since that is the intended purpose of a firearm and the example of "use" that most immediately comes to mind. But it is quite another to conclude that, as a result, the phrase also *excludes* any other use. Certainly that conclusion does not follow from the phrase "uses … a firearm" itself. As the dictionary definitions and experience make clear, one can use a firearm in a number of ways. That one example of "use" is the first to come to mind when the phrase "uses … a firearm" is uttered does not preclude us from recognizing that there are other "uses" that qualify as well. In this case, it is both reasonable and normal to say that petitioner "used" his MAC–10 in his drug trafficking offense by trading it for cocaine; the dissent does not contend otherwise.

Cane argument

The dissent's example of how one might "use" a cane suffers from a similar flaw. To be sure, "use" as an adornment in a hallway is not the first "use" of a cane that comes to mind. But certainly it does not follow that the *only* "use" to which a cane might be put is assisting one's grandfather in walking. Quite the opposite: The most infamous use of a cane in American history had nothing to do with walking at all [the caning of Senator Sumner in the United States Senate in 1856]; and the use of a cane as an instrument of punishment was once so common that "to cane" has become a verb meaning "[t]o beat with a cane." *Webster's New International Dictionary, supra,* at 390. In any event, the only question in this case is whether the phrase "uses … a firearm" in §924(c)(1) is most reasonably read as *excluding* the use of a firearm in a gun-for-drugs trade. The fact that the phrase clearly *includes* using a firearm to shoot someone, as the dissent contends, does not answer it. …

The dissent suggests that our interpretation produces a "strange dichotomy" between "using" a firearm and "carrying" one. We do not see why that is so. Just as a defendant may "use" a firearm within the meaning of § 924(c)(1) by trading it for drugs *or* using it to shoot someone, so too would a defendant "carry" the firearm by keeping it on his person whether he intends to exchange it for cocaine or fire it in self-defense. The dichotomy arises, if at all, only when one tries to extend the phrase " 'uses ... a firearm' " to any use " 'for any purpose whatever.' " ...

Finally, the dissent and petitioner invoke the rule of lenity. The mere possibility of articulating a narrower construction, however, does not by itself make the rule of lenity applicable.... Instead, that venerable rule is reserved for cases where, "[a]fter 'seiz[ing] everything from which aid can be derived,' " the Court is "left with an ambiguous statute." This is not such a case....

Imposing a more restrictive reading of the phrase "uses ... a firearm" does violence not only to the structure and language of the statute, but to its purpose as well. When Congress enacted the current version of § 924(c)(1), it was no doubt aware that drugs and guns are a dangerous combination. In 1989, 56 percent of all murders in New York City were drug related; during the same period, the figure for the Nation's Capital was as high as 80 percent. *The American Enterprise* 100 (Jan.–Feb. 1991).*** The fact that a gun is treated momentarily as an item of commerce does not render it inert or deprive it of destructive capacity. Rather, as experience demonstrates, it can be converted instantaneously from currency to cannon. We therefore see no reason why Congress would have intended courts and juries applying § 924(c)(1) to draw a fine metaphysical distinction between a gun's role in a drug offense as a weapon and its role as an item of barter; it creates a grave possibility of violence and death in either capacity....

The judgment of the Court of Appeals, accordingly, is affirmed.

◆ [Concurring opinion of JUSTICE BLACKMUN omitted.]

◆ JUSTICE SCALIA, with whom STEVENS and SOUTER, JJ., join, dissenting.

Section 924(c)(1) mandates a sentence enhancement for any defendant who "during and in relation to any crime of violence or drug trafficking crime ... uses ... a firearm." 18 U.S.C. § 924(c)(1). The Court begins its analysis by focusing upon the word "use" in this passage, and explaining that the dictionary definitions of that word are very broad. It is, however, a "fundamental principle of statutory construction (and, indeed, of language itself) that the meaning of a word cannot be determined in isolation, but must be drawn from the context in which it is used." That is particularly true of a word as elastic as "use," whose meanings range all the way from "to partake of" (as in "he uses tobacco") to "to be wont or accustomed" (as in "he used to smoke tobacco"). See *Webster's New International Dictionary* 2806 (2d ed. 1939).

In the search for statutory meaning, we give nontechnical words and phrases their ordinary meaning. To use an instrumentality ordinarily means to use it for its intended

---

*** Editor's footnote: *The American Enterprise* was a public policy magazine that the American Enterprise Institute in Washington, D.C. published.

purpose. When someone asks, "Do you use a cane?," he is not inquiring whether you have your grandfather's silver-handled walking stick on display in the hall; he wants to know whether you *walk* with a cane. Similarly, to speak of "using a firearm" is to speak of using it for its distinctive purpose, *i.e.*, as a weapon. To be sure, "one can use a firearm in a number of ways," including as an article of exchange, just as one can "use" a cane as a hall decoration—but that is not the ordinary meaning of "using" the one or the other. The Court does not appear to grasp the distinction between how a word *can be* used and how it *ordinarily is* used. It would, indeed, be "both reasonable and normal to say that petitioner 'used' his MAC–10 in his drug trafficking offense by trading it for cocaine." It would also be reasonable and normal to say that he "used" it to scratch his head. When one wishes to describe the action of employing the instrument of a firearm for such unusual purposes, "use" is assuredly a verb one could select. But that says nothing about whether the *ordinary* meaning of the phrase "uses a firearm" embraces such extraordinary employments. It is unquestionably *not* reasonable and normal, I think, to say simply "do not use firearms" when one means to prohibit selling or scratching with them. . . .

Given our rule that ordinary meaning governs, and given the ordinary meaning of "uses a firearm," it seems to me inconsequential that "the words 'as a weapon' appear nowhere in the statute," they are reasonably implicit. Petitioner is not, I think, seeking to introduce an "additional requirement" into the text, but is simply construing the text according to its normal import. . . .

Another consideration leads to the same conclusion: § 924(c)(1) provides increased penalties not only for one who "uses" a firearm during and in relation to any crime of violence or drug trafficking crime, but also for one who "carries" a firearm in those circumstances. The interpretation I would give the language produces an eminently reasonable dichotomy between "using a firearm" (as a weapon) and "carrying a firearm" (which in the context "uses or carries a firearm" means carrying it in such manner as to be ready for use as a weapon). The Court's interpretation, by contrast, produces a strange dichotomy between "using a firearm for any purpose whatever, including barter," and "carrying a firearm." . . .

Even if the reader does not consider the issue to be as clear as I do, he must at least acknowledge, I think, that it is eminently debatable—and that is enough, under the rule of lenity, to require finding for the petitioner here. "At the very least, it may be said that the issue is subject to some doubt. Under these circumstances, we adhere to the familiar rule that, 'where there is ambiguity in a criminal statute, doubts are resolved in favor of the defendant.'"[4]

For the foregoing reasons, I respectfully dissent.

---

4. The Court contends that giving the language its ordinary meaning would frustrate the purpose of the statute, since a gun "can be converted instantaneously from currency to cannon." Stretching language in order to write a more effective statute than Congress devised is not an exercise we should indulge in. But in any case, the ready ability to use a gun that is at hand as a weapon is perhaps one of the reasons the statute sanctions not only *using* a firearm, but *carrying* one. Here, however, the Government chose not to indict under that provision.

* * *

Points for Discussion

1. *Statutory Language*: What was the language at issue? What did the defendant and government want that language to mean? What meaning did the majority and dissent adopt?

2. *Theories*: Which theory did the Justice O'Connor use? Justice Scalia?

3. *Penalty Statute*: Note that this statute was a penalty enhancing statute. The issue was not whether the defendant committed a crime; rather, the issue was whether the defendant should receive an enhanced sentence for using a gun during the commission of that crime.

4. *Dictionary Meaning*: Which Justice used the definitional meaning? Which Justice used the ordinary meaning? Which meaning do you think the legislature intended?

5. *Dictionaries*: Justice O'Connor examined two dictionaries to determine the meaning of the language at issue: Webster's and Blacks. Ordinary dictionaries like Webster's are designed to include all possible definitions of a non-technical word. BLACK'S LAW DICTIONARY is designed to interpret legal terms. Is the language at issue here technical (legal) or ordinary? Assuming the latter, how relevant should Black's dictionary definition be? Is one dictionary more authoritative than another? Justice O'Connor and Justice Scalia both looked at an edition of Webster's Dictionary from 1939 and Black's Dictionary from 1990. Yet this case was decided in 1993, and the statute was enacted in 1968 and amended in 1984. Does the time the dictionary was published make any difference?

6. *Textual Context*: Should the word "firearm" narrow the word "use"? The plain meaning rule, though appealing in its simplicity, does not always answer the question, especially when dictionaries are consulted. Dictionaries define words broadly; thus, definitional meanings will always be broader than ordinary meanings, which textual and other context limit.

7. *Rule of Lenity*: The rule of lenity, which you will study in Chapter 14, is a policy-based source that directs judges to adopt the least penal interpretation when there are two or more reasonable interpretations of an ambiguous penal statute. Did Justice O'Connor address this issue? Justice Scalia?

8. *Hypothetical*: What if, instead of trading a gun for drugs, a defendant took a gun in exchange for drugs. Same result? *See Watson v. United States*, 552 U.S. 74 (2007) (resolving this issue).

* * *

The case that follows came just two years after *Smith*. Notice that Justice O'Connor again authors the majority opinion, but this time for a unanimous court.

Bailey v. United States

Supreme Court of the United States
516 U.S. 137 (1995)

◆ Justice O'Connor delivered the opinion for a unanimous Court [including Rehnquist, Stevens, Scalia, Kennedy, Souter, Thomas, Ginsburg, and Breyer, JJ.].

[This petition challenges petitioner's] conviction under 18 U.S.C. §924(c)(1). In relevant part, that section imposes a 5–year minimum term of imprisonment upon a person who "during and in relation to any crime of violence or drug trafficking crime ... uses or carries a firearm." We are asked to decide whether evidence of the proximity and accessibility of a firearm to drugs or drug proceeds is alone sufficient to support a conviction for "use" of a firearm during and in relation to a drug trafficking offense under 18 U.S.C. §924(c)(1).

In May 1989, petitioner Roland Bailey was stopped by police officers after they noticed that his car lacked a front license plate and an inspection sticker. When Bailey failed to produce a driver's license, the officers ordered him out of the car. As he stepped out, the officers saw Bailey push something between the seat and the front console. A search of the passenger compartment revealed one round of ammunition and 27 plastic bags containing a total of 30 grams of cocaine. After arresting Bailey, the officers searched the trunk of his car where they found, among a number of items, a large amount of cash and a bag containing a loaded 9–mm. pistol.

Bailey was charged on several counts, including using and carrying a firearm in violation of 18 U.S.C. §924(c)(1)....

We granted certiorari to clarify the meaning of "use" under §924(c)(1).

Section 924(c)(1) requires the imposition of specified penalties if the defendant, "during and in relation to any crime of violence or drug trafficking crime..., uses or carries a firearm." Petitioners argue that "use" signifies active employment of a firearm. The Government opposes that definition and [argues that it is enough that the gun is accessible]....

This action is not the first one in which the Court has grappled with the proper understanding of "use" in §924(c)(1). In *Smith*, we faced the question whether the barter of a gun for drugs was a "use," and concluded that it was. As the debate in *Smith* illustrated, the word "use" poses some interpretational difficulties because of the different meanings attributable to it. Consider the paradoxical statement: "I *use* a gun to protect my house, but I've never had to *use* it." "Use" draws meaning from its context, and we will look not only to the word itself, but also to the statute and the sentencing scheme, to determine the meaning Congress intended.

We agree ... that "use" must connote more than mere possession of a firearm by a person who commits a drug offense. Had Congress intended possession alone to trigger liability under §924(c)(1), it easily could have so provided....

This conclusion—that a conviction for "use" of a firearm under §924(c)(1) requires more than a showing of mere possession—requires us to answer a more difficult question. What must the Government show, beyond mere possession, to establish "use" for the purposes of the statute? We conclude that the language, context, and history of §924(c)(1) indicate that the Government must show active employment of the firearm.

1554

We start, as we must, with the language of the statute. The word "use" in the statute must be given its "ordinary or natural" meaning, a meaning variously defined as "[t]o convert to one's service," "to employ," "to avail oneself of," and "to carry out a purpose or action by means of." *Smith, supra*, at 228–229 (internal quotation marks omitted) (citing Webster's New International Dictionary of English Language 2806 (2d ed. 1949) and Black's Law Dictionary 1541 (6th ed. 1990)). These various definitions of "use" imply action and implementation.

We consider not only the bare meaning of the word but also its placement and purpose in the statutory scheme. "'[T]he meaning of statutory language, plain or not, depends on context.'" Looking past the word "use" itself, we read §924(c)(1) with the assumption that Congress intended each of its terms to have meaning. "Judges should hesitate ... to treat (as surplusage) statutory terms in any setting, and resistance should be heightened when the words describe an element of a criminal offense." Here, Congress has specified two types of conduct with a firearm: "uses" or "carries."

Under the Government's reading of §924(c)(1), "use" includes even the action of a defendant who puts a gun into place to protect drugs or to embolden himself. This reading is of such breadth that no role remains for "carry." The Government admits that the meanings of "use" and "carry" converge under its interpretation, but maintains that this overlap is a product of the particular history of §924(c)(1). Therefore, the Government argues, the canon of construction that instructs that "a legislature is presumed to have used no superfluous words" is inapplicable. We disagree. Nothing here indicates that Congress, when it provided these two terms, intended that they be understood to be redundant.

We assume that Congress used two terms because it intended each term to have a particular, nonsuperfluous meaning. While a broad reading of "use" undermines virtually any function for "carry," a more limited, active interpretation of "use" preserves a meaningful role for "carries" as an alternative basis for a charge. Under the interpretation we enunciate today, a firearm can be used without being carried, *e.g.*, when an offender has a gun on display during a transaction, or barters with a firearm without handling it; and a firearm can be carried without being used, *e.g.*, when an offender keeps a gun hidden in his clothing throughout a drug transaction....

The amendment history of §924(c) casts further light on Congress' intended meaning. *The original version, passed in 1968, read:* ← *leg. History*

"(c) Whoever—

"(1) uses a firearm to commit any felony which may be prosecuted in a court of the United States, or

"(2) carries a firearm unlawfully during the commission of any felony which may be prosecuted in a court of the United States,

"shall be sentenced to a term of imprisonment for not less than one year nor more than 10 years." § 102, 82 Stat. 1224.

The phrase "uses a firearm to commit" indicates that Congress originally intended to reach the situation where the firearm was actively employed during commission of the crime. This original language would not have stretched so far as to cover a firearm that played no detectable role in the crime's commission. For example, a defendant who stored a gun in a nearby closet for retrieval in case the deal went sour would not have "use[d] a firearm to commit" a crime. This version also shows that "use" and "carry" were employed with distinctly different meanings.

Congress' 1984 amendment to § 924(c) altered the scope of predicate offenses from "any felony" to "any crime of violence," removed the "unlawfully" requirement, merged the "uses" and "carries" prongs, substituted "during and in relation to" the predicate crimes for the earlier provisions linking the firearm to the predicate crimes, and raised the minimum sentence to five years. § 1005(a), 98 Stat. 2138–2139. The Government argues that this amendment stripped "uses" and "carries" of the qualifications ("to commit" and "unlawfully during") that originally gave them distinct meanings, so that the terms should now be understood to overlap. Of course, in *Smith* we recognized that Congress' subsequent amendments to § 924(c) employed "use" expansively, to cover both use as a weapon and use as an item of barter. But there is no evidence to indicate that Congress intended to expand the meaning of "use" so far as to swallow up any significance for "carry." If Congress had intended to deprive "use" of its active connotations, it could have simply substituted a more appropriate term—"possession"—to cover the conduct it wished to reach....

[O]ur decision today is not inconsistent with *Smith*. Although there we declined to limit "use" to the meaning "use as a weapon," our interpretation of § 924(c)(1) nonetheless adhered to an active meaning of the term. In *Smith*, it was clear that the defendant had "used" the gun; the question was whether that particular use (bartering) came within the meaning of § 924(c)(1). *Smith* did not address the question we face today of what evidence is required to permit a jury to find that a firearm had been used at all....

We reverse.... Because the Court of Appeals did not consider liability under the "carry" prong of § 924(c)(1) for Bailey [although he was charged with it], we remand for consideration of that basis for upholding the conviction[].

* * *

Points for Discussion

1. *Statutory Language*: What was the language at issue? What did the defendant and government want that language to mean? What meaning did the Court adopt?

2. *Theories*: Which theory did the Justice O'Connor use?

3. *Dictionaries*: What role did dictionaries play in *Bailey* compared to *Smith*? Why the difference? Where else might judges find evidence of the ordinary meaning of words? See *Muscarello v. United States*, 524 U.S. 125 (1998) excerpted later, for examples of other places courts might find evidence of a word's ordinary meaning.

4. *Legislative Amendment History*: Justice O'Connor explored the amendment history of § 924(c). How did she respond to the government's argument that the 1984 amendment stripped "uses" and "carries" of independent meaning?

5. *"Rule" Against Surplusage*: According to the rule against surplusage, the proper interpretation of a statute is one in which every word and phrase has a meaning and nothing is redundant or meaningless. This "rule" is no more than a presumption, which can be rebutted. Here, Justice O'Connor rejected the government's interpretation of "use," in part, because it would strip the word "carry" of any independent meaning.

6. *Smith*: How did the Court reconcile its holding in *Smith*?

7. *Backwards*: The provision's chief legislative sponsor said that the penalty enhancing statute seeks "to persuade the man who is tempted to commit a Federal felony to leave his gun at home." 114 Cong. Rec. 22231 (1968) (Rep. Poff). Would bringing a gun in car trunk be more or less likely to lead to violence than trading a gun for drugs? In other words, did not the Court get *Smith* and *Bailey* exactly backwards?

8. *"Carry"*: The Court remanded on the issue of whether the defendant carried the gun. How do you think the Court would have ruled on that issue? Justice Scalia in *Smith* provided a definition for carry: ("'carry a firearm' in the context 'uses or carries a firearm' means carrying it in such manner as to be ready for use as a weapon."). Assuming this definition to be correct, did either Bailey or Smith "carry" a firearm?

* * *

After *Smith*, you were asked a hypothetical: "What if, instead of trading a gun for drugs, a defendant took a gun in exchange for drugs. Same result?" Surprisingly, the answer is no. The question is: Why not?

Watson v. United States

Supreme Court of the United States
552 U.S. 74 (2007)

♦ JUSTICE SOUTER delivered the opinion of the Court [in which ROBERTS, C.J., and STEVENS, SCALIA, KENNEDY, THOMAS, BREYER, and ALITO, JJ., concur].

The question is whether a person who trades his drugs for a gun "uses" a firearm "during and in relation to ... [a] drug trafficking crime" within the meaning of 18 U.S.C. § 924(c)(1)(A). We hold that he does not.

Section 924(c)(1)(A) sets a mandatory minimum sentence, depending on the facts, for a defendant who, "during and in relation to any crime of violence or drug trafficking crime[,] ... uses or carries a firearm." The statute leaves the term "uses" undefined, though we have spoken to it twice before.

Smith v. United States, 508 U.S. 223 (1993) raised the converse of today's question, and held that "a criminal who trades his firearm for drugs 'uses' it during and in relation to a drug trafficking offense within the meaning of § 924(c)(1)." We rested primarily on the "ordinary or natural meaning" of the verb in context and understood its common range as going beyond employment as a weapon....

Two years later, the issue in *Bailey v. United States*, 516 U.S. 137 (1995) was whether possessing a firearm kept near the scene of drug trafficking is "use" under § 924(c)(1). We looked again to "ordinary or natural" meaning and decided that mere possession does not amount to "use."[3] ...

This third case on the reach of § 924(c)(1)(A) began to take shape when petitioner, Michael A. Watson, told a Government informant that he wanted to acquire a gun. On the matter of price, the informant quoted no dollar figure but suggested that Watson could pay in narcotics. Next, Watson met with the informant and an undercover law enforcement agent posing as a firearms dealer, to whom he gave 24 doses of oxycodone hydrochloride (commonly, OxyContin) for a .50-caliber semiautomatic pistol. When law enforcement officers arrested Watson, they found the pistol in his car, and a later search of his house turned up a cache of prescription medicines, guns, and ammunition. Watson said he got the pistol "to protect his other firearms and drugs."....

We granted certiorari to resolve a conflict among the Circuits on whether a person "uses" a firearm within the meaning of 18 U.S.C. § 924(c) (1)(A) when he trades narcotics to obtain a gun....

The Government's position that Watson "used" the pistol under § 924(c)(1)(A) by receiving it for narcotics lacks authority in either precedent or regular English. To begin with, neither *Smith* nor *Bailey* implicitly decides this case. While *Smith* held that firearms may be "used" in a barter transaction, even with no violent employment, the case addressed only the trader who swaps his gun for drugs, not the trading partner who ends up with the gun. *Bailey*, too, is unhelpful, with its rule that a gun must be made use of actively to satisfy § 924(c)(1)(A), as "an operative factor in relation to the predicate offense." The question here is whether it makes sense to say that Watson employed the gun at all; *Bailey* does not answer it.

With no statutory definition or definitive clue, the meaning of the verb "uses" has to turn on the language as we normally speak it; there is no other source of a reasonable inference about what Congress understood when writing or what its words will bring to the mind of a careful reader. So, in *Smith* we looked for "everyday meaning" revealed in phraseology that strikes the ear as "both reasonable and normal." This appeal to the ordinary leaves the Government without much of a case.

---

3. In 1998, Congress responded to *Bailey* by amending § 924(c)(1). The amendment broadened the provision to cover a defendant who "in furtherance of any (crime of violence or drug trafficking) crime, possesses a firearm." 18 U.S.C. § 924(c)(1)(A). The amendment did not touch the "use" prong of § 924(c)(1).

The Government may say that a person "uses" a firearm simply by receiving it in a barter transaction, but no one else would. A boy who trades an apple to get a granola bar is sensibly said to use the apple, but one would never guess which way this commerce actually flowed from hearing that the boy used the granola. So, when Watson handed over the drugs for the pistol, the informant or the agent "used" the pistol to get the drugs, just as *Smith* held, but regular speech would not say that Watson himself used the pistol in the trade. "A seller does not 'use' a buyer's consideration." ...

The [Government's] second effort to trump regular English is the claim that failing to treat receipt in trade as "use" would create unacceptable asymmetry with *Smith*. At bottom, this atextual policy critique says it would be strange to penalize one side of a gun-for-drugs exchange but not the other: "[t]he danger to society is created not only by the person who brings the firearm to the drug transaction, but also by the drug dealer who takes the weapon in exchange for his drugs during the transaction."

The position assumes that *Smith* must be respected, and we join the Government at least on this starting point. A difference of opinion within the Court (as in *Smith*) does not keep the door open for another try at statutory construction, where *stare decisis* has "special force [since] the legislative power is implicated, and Congress remains free to alter what we have done." What is more, in 14 years Congress has taken no step to modify *Smith's* holding, and this long congressional acquiescence "has enhanced even the usual precedential force" we accord to our interpretations of statutes.

... Whatever the tension between [*Smith*] and the outcome here, law depends on respect for language and would be served better by statutory amendment (if Congress sees asymmetry) than by racking statutory language to cover a policy it fails to reach. ...

♦ JUSTICE GINSBURG, concurring in the judgment.

It is better to receive than to give, the Court holds today, at least when the subject is guns. Distinguishing, as the Court does, between trading a gun for drugs and trading drugs for a gun, for purposes of the 18 U.S.C. §924(c)(1) enhancement, makes scant sense to me. I join the Court's judgment, however, because I am persuaded that the Court took a wrong turn in *Smith v. United States*, 508 U.S. 223 (1993), when it held that trading a gun for drugs fits within §924(c)(1)'s compass as "us[e]" of a firearm "during and in relation to any ... drug trafficking crime." For reasons well stated by Justice Scalia in his dissenting opinion in *Smith*, I would read the word "use" in §924(c)(1) to mean use as a weapon, not use in a bartering transaction. Accordingly, I would overrule *Smith*, and thereby render our precedent both coherent and consistent with normal usage.

* * *

Points for Discussion

1. *Statutory Language*: What was the language at issue? What did the defendant and government want that language to mean? What meaning did the Court adopt?

2. *Theories*: Which theory did the Justice Souter use? Justice Ginsburg?

3. *Stare Decisis*: After *Smith*, would you have expected the Court to have found Watson guilty of "using" the gun when he received it for the drugs? Assuming so, why did the Court reach a different result?

4. *Equal Protection*: The Equal Protection Clause of the U.S. Constitution requires equal protection of the laws such that those who are similarly situated should be treated similarly. Does the Court's result violate this clause? In a part of the opinion that was excised, the majority essentially dismisses this concern.

5. *Justice Ginsburg*: What was the point of her concurrence?

6. *Legislative Acquiescence*: Why did Justice Souter choose not to overrule *Smith* despite his apparent belief that it was wrongly decided? Some judges reason that a legislature's silence to a judicial interpretation means legislative acquiescence, or agreement, with that interpretation. Justice Souter noted that "in 14 years Congress has taken no step to modify *Smith's* holding, and this long congressional acquiescence 'has enhanced even the usual precedential force' we accord to our interpretations of statutes." We will address this issue in more detail in Chapter 13.

* * *

It was not long before the Court had to interpret the word "carry" in the same statute. As you read the Court's opinion, consider whether either Smith or Bailey "carried" a firearm under the majority or dissent's definition.

Muscarello v. United States

Supreme Court of the United States
524 U.S. 125 (1998)

♦ BREYER, J., delivered the opinion of the Court [in which STEVENS, O'CONNOR, KENNEDY, and THOMAS, JJ., concur].

A provision in the firearms chapter of the federal criminal code imposes a 5–year mandatory prison term upon a person who "uses or carries a firearm" "during and in relation to" a "drug trafficking crime." 18 U.S.C. § 924(c)(1). The question before us is whether the phrase "carries a firearm" is limited to the carrying of firearms on the person. We hold that it is not so limited. Rather, it also applies to a person who knowingly possesses and conveys firearms in a vehicle, including in the locked glove compartment or trunk of a car, which the person accompanies....

Petitioner ..., Frank J. Muscarello, unlawfully sold marijuana, which he carried in his truck to the place of sale. Police officers found a handgun locked in the truck's glove compartment. During plea proceedings, Muscarello admitted that he had "carried" the gun "for protection in relation" to the drug offense, though he later claimed to the contrary, and added that, in any event, his "carr[ying]" of the gun in the glove compartment did not fall within the scope of the statutory word "carries." ...

We begin with the statute's language. The parties vigorously contest the ordinary English meaning of the phrase "carries a firearm." Because they essentially agree that

Congress intended the phrase to convey its ordinary, and not some special legal, meaning, and because they argue the linguistic point at length, we too have looked into the matter in more than usual depth. Although the word "carry" has many different meanings, only two are relevant here. When one uses the word in the first, or primary, meaning, one can, as a matter of ordinary English, "carry firearms" in a wagon, car, truck, or other vehicle that one accompanies. When one uses the word in a different, rather special, way, to mean, for example, "bearing" or (in slang) "packing" (as in "packing a gun"), the matter is less clear. But, for reasons we shall set out below, we believe Congress intended to use the word in its primary sense and not in this latter, special way.

Consider first the word's primary meaning. The Oxford English Dictionary gives as its *first* definition "convey, originally by cart or wagon, hence in any vehicle, by ship, on horseback, etc." 2 *Oxford English Dictionary* 919 (2d ed. 1989); see also *Webster's Third New International Dictionary* 343 (1986) (*first* definition: "move while supporting (*as in a vehicle* or in one's hands or arms)"); *Random House Dictionary of the English Language Unabridged* 319 (2d ed. 1987) (*first* definition: "to take or support from one place to another; convey; transport").

The origin of the word "carries" explains why the first, or basic, meaning of the word "carry" includes conveyance in a vehicle. See *Barnhart Dictionary of Etymology* 146 (1988) (tracing the word from Latin "carum," which means "car" or "cart"); 2 *Oxford English Dictionary*, *supra*, at 919 (tracing the word from Old French "carier" and the late Latin "carricare," which meant to "convey in a car"); *Oxford Dictionary of English Etymology* 148 (C. Onions ed. 1966) (same); *Barnhart Dictionary of Etymology*, *supra*, at 143 (explaining that the term "car" has been used to refer to the automobile since 1896).

The greatest of writers have used the word with this meaning. See, *e.g.*, The King James Bible, 2 Kings 9:28 ("[H]is servants carried him in a chariot to Jerusalem"); *id.*, Isaiah 30:6 ("[T]hey will carry their riches upon the shoulders of young asses"). Robinson Crusoe says, "[w]ith my boat, I carry'd away every Thing." D. Defoe, Robinson Crusoe 174 (J. Crowley ed. 1972). And the owners of Queequeg's ship, Melville writes, "had lent him a [wheelbarrow], in which to carry his heavy chest to his boarding-house." H. Melville, Moby Dick 43 (U. Chicago 1952). This Court, too, has spoken of the "carrying" of drugs in a car or in its "trunk."

These examples do not speak directly about carrying guns.... And, to make certain that there is no special ordinary English restriction (unmentioned in dictionaries) upon the use of "carry" in respect to guns, we have surveyed modern press usage, albeit crudely, by searching computerized newspaper databases—both the New York Times data base in Lexis/Nexis, and the "US News" data base in Westlaw. We looked for sentences in which the words "carry," "vehicle," and "weapon" (or variations thereof) all appear. We found thousands of such sentences, and random sampling suggests that many, perhaps more than one-third, are sentences used to convey the meaning at issue here, *i.e.*, the carrying of guns in a car.

The New York Times, for example, writes about "an ex-con" who "arrives home driving a stolen car and carrying a load of handguns," and an "official peace officer who carries a shotgun in his boat." The Boston Globe refers to the arrest of a professional baseball player "for carrying a semiloaded automatic weapon in his car." The Colorado Springs Gazette Telegraph speaks of one "Russell" who "carries a gun hidden in his car." The Arkansas Gazette refers to a "house" that was "searched" in an effort to find "items that could be carried in a car, such as . . . guns. The San Diego Union–Tribune asks, "What, do they carry guns aboard these boats now?"

Now consider a different, somewhat special meaning of the word "carry"—a meaning upon which the linguistic arguments of petitioners and the dissent must rest. The Oxford English Dictionary's *twenty-sixth* definition of "carry" is "bear, wear, hold up, or sustain, as one moves about; habitually to bear about with one." 2 *Oxford English Dictionary*, at 921. Webster's defines "carry" as "to move while supporting," not just in a vehicle, but also "in one's hands or arms." *Webster's Third New International Dictionary, supra,* at 343. And Black's Law Dictionary defines the entire phrase "carry arms or weapons" as

> "To wear, bear or carry them upon the person or in the clothing or in a pocket, for the purpose of use, or for the purpose of being armed and ready for offensive or defensive action in case of a conflict with another person." Black's Law Dictionary 214 (6th ed. 1990).

These special definitions, however, do not purport to *limit* the "carrying of arms" to the circumstances they describe. No one doubts that one who bears arms on his person "carries a weapon." But to say that is not to deny that one may *also* "carry a weapon" tied to the saddle of a horse or placed in a bag in a car. . . .

We now explore more deeply the purely legal question of whether Congress intended to use the word "carry" in its ordinary sense, or whether it intended to limit the scope of the phrase to instances in which a gun is carried "on the person." We conclude that neither the statute's basic purpose nor its legislative history support circumscribing the scope of the word "carry" by applying an "on the person" limitation.

Leg. Purpose

This Court has described the statute's basic purpose broadly, as an effort to combat the "dangerous combination" of "drugs and guns." *Smith v. United States,* 508 U.S. 223, 240 (1993). And the provision's chief legislative sponsor has said that the provision seeks "to persuade the man who is tempted to commit a Federal felony to leave his gun at home." 114 Cong.Rec. 22231 (1968) (Rep. Poff); see also 114 Cong.Rec. 22243–22244 (statutes would apply to "the man who goes out taking a gun to commit a crime") (Rep. Hunt); *id.,* at 22244 ("Of course, what we are trying to do by these penalties is to persuade the criminal to leave his gun at home") (Rep. Randall); *id.,* at 22236 ("We are concerned . . . with having the criminal leave his gun at home") (Rep. Meskill).

From the perspective of any such purpose (persuading a criminal "to leave his gun at home"), what sense would it make for this statute to penalize one who walks with a gun in a bag to the site of a drug sale, but to ignore a similar individual who, like defendant..., travels to a similar site with a similar gun in a similar bag, but instead of walking, drives there with the gun in his car? How persuasive is a punishment that is without effect until a drug dealer who has brought his gun to a sale (indeed has it available for use) actually takes it from the trunk (or unlocks the glove compartment) of his car? It is difficult to say that, considered as a class, those who prepare, say, to sell drugs by placing guns in their cars are less dangerous, or less deserving of punishment, than those who carry handguns on their person....

Finally, petitioners and the dissent invoke the "rule of lenity." The simple existence of some statutory ambiguity, however, is not sufficient to warrant application of that rule, for most statutes are ambiguous to some degree. "'The rule of lenity applies only if, 'after seizing everything from which aid can be derived,' ... we can make 'no more than a guess as to what Congress intended.'" *Smith.* To invoke the rule, we must conclude that there is a "'grievous ambiguity or uncertainty in the statute.'" Certainly, our decision today is based on much more than a "guess as to what Congress intended," and there is no "grievous ambiguity" here. The problem of statutory interpretation in these cases is indeed no different from that in many of the criminal cases that confront us. Yet, this Court has never held that the rule of lenity automatically permits a defendant to win....

For these reasons, we conclude that petitioners' conduct falls within the scope of the phrase "carries a firearm." The judgments of the Courts of Appeals are affirmed.

◆ GINSBURG, J., filed a dissenting opinion, in which REHNQUIST, C.J., and SCALIA and SOUTER, JJ., joined.

... Without doubt, "carries" is a word of many meanings, definable to mean or include carting about in a vehicle. But that encompassing definition is not a ubiquitously necessary one. Nor, in my judgment, is it a proper construction of "carries" as the term appears in §924(c)(1). In line with *Bailey* and the principle of lenity the Court has long followed, I would confine "carries a firearm," for §924(c)(1) purposes, to the undoubted meaning of that expression in the relevant context. I would read the words to indicate not merely keeping arms on one's premises or in one's vehicle, but bearing them in such manner as to be ready for use as a weapon....

Unlike the Court, I do not think dictionaries, surveys of press reports, or the Bible tell us, dispositively, what "carries" means embedded in §924(c)(1). On definitions, "carry" in legal formulations could mean, *inter alia*, transport, possess, have in stock, prolong (carry over), be infectious, or wear or bear on one's person. At issue here is not "carries" at large but "carries a firearm." The Court's computer search of newspapers is revealing in this light. Carrying guns in a car showed up as the meaning "perhaps more than one-third" of the time. One is left to wonder what meaning showed up some two-thirds of the time. Surely a most familiar meaning is, as the Constitution's Second Amendment ("keep and *bear* Arms") (emphasis added) and Black's Law Dictionary, at 214, indicate: "wear, bear, or carry ... upon the person or in the clothing or in a pocket, for the purpose ... of being armed and ready for offensive or defensive action in a case of conflict with another person."

On lessons from literature, a scan of Bartlett's and other quotation collections shows how highly selective the Court's choices are. If "[t]he greatest of writers" have used "carry" to mean convey or transport in a vehicle, so have they used the hydra-headed word to mean, *inter alia,* carry in one's hand, arms, head, heart, or soul, sans vehicle. Consider, among countless examples:

Dictionaries, literature, movies, Popular Culture, news paper

"[H]e shall gather the lambs with his arm, and carry them in his bosom." The King James Bible, Isaiah 40:11.

"And still they gaz'd, and still the wonder grew, That one small head could carry all he knew." O. Goldsmith, The Deserted Village, ll. 215–216, in The Poetical Works of Oliver Goldsmith 30 (A. Dobson ed. 1949).

"There's a Legion that never was 'listed, That carries no colours or crest." R. Kipling, The Lost Legion, st. 1, in Rudyard Kipling's Verse, 1885–1918, p. 222 (1920).

"There is a homely adage which runs, 'Speak softly and carry a big stick; you will go far.'" T. Roosevelt, Speech at Minnesota State Fair, Sept. 2, 1901, in J. Bartlett, Familiar Quotations 575:16 (J. Kaplan ed. 1992).[6]

These and the Court's lexicological sources demonstrate vividly that "carry" is a word commonly used to convey various messages. Such references, given their variety, are not reliable indicators of what Congress meant, in § 924(c)(1), by "carries a firearm."...

Section 924(c)(1), as the foregoing discussion details, is not decisively clear one way or another. The sharp division in the Court on the proper reading of the measure confirms, "[a]t the very least, ... that the issue is subject to some doubt. Under these circumstances, we adhere to the familiar rule that, 'where there is ambiguity in a criminal statute, doubts are resolved in favor of the defendant.'"...

The Court, in my view, should leave it to Congress to speak "'in language that is clear and definite'" if the Legislature wishes to impose the sterner penalty.

* * *

Points for Discussion

1. *Statutory Language*: What was the language at issue? What did the defendant and government want that language to mean? What meaning did the majority and dissent adopt?

2. *Theories*: Which theory did the Justice Breyer use? Justice Ginsburg?

3. *Dictionaries*: What role did dictionaries play in this opinion? What other things did the Justices consider in identifying the ordinary meaning of the word "carry"?

---

6. Popular films and television productions provide corroborative illustrations. In "The Magnificent Seven," for example, O'Reilly (played by Charles Bronson) says: "You think I am brave because I carry a gun; well, your fathers are much braver because they carry responsibility, for you, your brothers, your sisters, and your mothers." And in the television series "M*A*S*H," Hawkeye Pierce (played by Alan Alda) presciently proclaims: "I will not carry a gun.... I'll carry your books, I'll carry a torch, I'll carry a tune, I'll carry on, carry over, carry forward, Cary Grant, cash and carry, carry me back to Old Virginia, I'll even 'hari-kari' if you show me how, but I will not carry a gun!"

4. *Gun's Purpose*: The defendant admitted that he brought the gun to the drug trans-action for protection. Should this admissions matter?

5. *Consistency*: In *Smith*, the Court held that a defendant who exchanges a gun for drugs *uses* that gun. In *Watson*, the Court held that a defendant who exchanges drugs for a gun does not *use* that gun. In *Bailey*, the Court held that a defendant who brings a gun in a trunk does not *use* that gun. In *Muscarello*, the Court held that a defendant who brings a gun in a locked glove compartment *carries* that gun. Are the Courts interpretations sufficiently consistent to show that "use" and "carry" have their ordinary meanings? Or do the opinions show that ordinary meaning is a very subjective determination?

* * *

2. The Technical Meaning Rule

A word in a statute may have both an ordinary and a technical meaning. As we saw earlier, "assault" can mean an intentionally violent attack—its ordinary mean-ing—or it can mean freedom from the apprehension of a harmful or offensive con-tact—a technical (in this case legal) meaning. While legislatures generally use words in their ordinary sense, occasionally, the ordinary meaning is not the one intended. Courts presume that legislatures intended words to have their ordinary meaning be-cause legislatures draft generally applicable statutes; however, sometimes legislatures intend words to be used in their technical sense. The technical and plain meaning rules work harmoniously to direct that "[u]nless a word or phrase is defined in the statute or rule being construed, its meaning is determined by its context, the rules of grammar, and common usage. A word or phrase that has acquired a technical or particular meaning in a particular context has that meaning *if it is used in that context*." UNIF. STATUTE & RULE CONSTR. ACT, § 2 (1995) (emphasis added).

The technical meaning rule reflects the reality that most often the ordinary meaning was intended. Additionally, the rule allows for those few times when the ordinary meaning was not intended. Thus, the ordinary meaning will generally prevail when both a technical and ordinary meaning co-exist, absent any indication that the word was used in its technical sense. For example, is a tomato a vegetable—its ordinary meaning—or a fruit—its technical meaning—to a botanist and linguist? Believe it or not, this issue was litigated before the Supreme Court!

Nix v. Hedden

Supreme Court for the United States
149 U.S. 304 (1893)

♦ JUSTICE GRAY ... delivered the opinion for a unanimous court.

[The Tariff Act of March 3, 1883, required businesses to pay a tax on imported vegetables, but not fruit. John Nix, John W. Nix, George W. Nix, and Frank W. Nix filed the case against the government, naming Edward L. Hedden, who was the Collector of the Port of New York, to recover back taxes paid under protest.] The single question in this case is whether tomatoes, considered as provisions, are to be classed as 'vegetables' or as 'fruit,' within the meaning of the tariff act of 1883.

The only witnesses called at the trial testified that neither 'vegetables' nor 'fruit' had any special meaning in trade or commerce different from that given in the dictionaries, and that they had the same meaning in trade to-day that they had in March, 1883.

The passages cited from the dictionaries define the word 'fruit' as the seed of plaints, or that part of plaints which contains the seed, and especially the juicy, pulpy products of certain plants, covering and containing the seed. These definitions have no tendency to show that tomatoes are 'fruit,' as distinguished from 'vegetables,' in common speech, or within the meaning of the tariff act.

There being no evidence that the words 'fruit' and 'vegetables' have acquired any special meaning in trade or commerce, they must receive their ordinary meaning. Of that meaning the court is bound to take judicial notice, as it does in regard to all words in our own tongue; and upon such a question dictionaries are admitted, not as evidence, but only as aids to the memory and understanding of the court.

Botanically speaking, tomatoes are the fruit of a vine, just as are cucumbers, squashes, beans, and peas. But in the common language of the people, whether sellers or consumers of provisions, all these are vegetables which are grown in kitchen gardens, and which, whether eaten cooked or raw, are, like potatoes, carrots, parsnips, turnips, beets, cauliflower, cabbage, celery, and lettuce, usually served at dinner in, with, or after the soup, fish, or meats which constitute the principal part of the repast, and not, like fruits generally, as dessert.

The attempt to class tomatoes as fruit is not unlike a recent attempt to class beans as seeds, of which Mr. Justice Bradley, speaking for this court, said: 'We do not see why they should be classified as seeds, any more than walnuts should be so classified. Both are seeds, in the language of botany or natural history, but not in commerce nor in common parlance. On the other hand in speaking generally of provisions, beans may well be included under the term 'vegetables.' As an article of food on our tables, whether baked or boiled, or forming the basis of soup, they are used as a vegetable, as well when ripe as when green. This is the principal use to which they are put. Beyond the common knowledge which we have on this subject, very little evidence is necessary, or can be produced.'

* * *

Points for Discussion

1. *Statutory Language*: What was the language at issue? What meaning did each party want that language to have? What meaning did the court adopt?

2. *Theories*: Which theory of interpretation did the court use?

3. *Expert Witnesses*: Why did a witness testify as to the meaning of the language at issue in this case? Which side do you think paid for the expert to testify? If the

court were only considering the ordinary meaning of the language, would an expert ever be relevant?

4. *Audience*: For whom was this statute written? Does that audience understand the words "vegetable" and "fruit" to mean something different than the general public? Does your answer to these questions help explain why the court rejected the technical meaning of this statute?

5. *Implications*: Vegetables were taxed at a higher rate than fruit. Does that difference help explain the Court's decision?

6. *Rhubarb*: Given the court's reasoning in *Nix*, is rhubarb a fruit or a vegetable for purposes of this Act? *See C.J. Tower & Sons*, 1947 WL 6081 (Cust. Ct.) (holding that rhubarb was a fruit because it is eaten in desserts).

7. *Statutory Definitions*: Often, a legislature will include definitions for words and phrases within a specific act in either a separate definitions sections or in the relevant subsection of the act. The legislature is free to define words in any way it wishes. *See, e.g.*, *Kentucky v. Plowman*, 86 S.W.3d 47 (Ky. 2002) (citing a state statute defining "building" to include "any dwelling, hotel, commercial structure, automobile, truck, watercraft, aircraft, trailer, sleeping car, railroad car, or other structure or vehicle...."). A statutory definition is not a technical definition. ·

8. *Interesting Fact*: In 2005, supporters in the New Jersey legislature cited *Nix* as a basis for a bill designating the tomato as the official state vegetable. *See* Lisa Anderson, *The political adventures of New Jersey's 'highly partisan' tomato* (April 30, 2005), http://articles.chicagotribune.com/2005-04-30/news/0504300163_1_fruit-vegetable-la-tomatina.

* * *

To determine which meaning was intended — technical or ordinary — a judge will look at two things: (1) whether the surrounding words are technical, and (2) whether the statute was directed to a technical audience. Illustrative of the first point, that surrounding textual context matters, is *Dickens v. Puryear*, 276 S.E.2d 325, (N.C. 1981). In that case, the court interpreted the word "assault" in its technical legal sense (specifically, as an intentional tort) because the list in the statute included only intentional torts: "libel, slander, assault, battery, or false imprisonment." *Id.* at 444 n.8. Illustrative of the second point (that audience matters) is *O'Hara v. Luchenbach Steamship Co.*, 269 U.S. 364 (1926). The statute at issue in that case involved the safety and welfare of those at sea. Because the statute was directed solely to individuals and companies in the maritime trade, the Court construed the statutory language in its technical way, as it would be understood by those in the maritime trade. *Id.* at 370–71. However, judges are not limited to audience and textual context in determining whether the technical meaning was intended. Other indicia of meaning, such as titles, purpose, and legislative history, may also inform the court. We will cover these other sources in later chapters.

In the case that follows, there are two interpretation issues, one relates to the timing of the defendant's convictions and the other relates to the finality of the defendant's convictions. See if you can identify whether the majority and dissenting opinions adopt the ordinary or technical meaning for either issue.

St. Clair v. Commonwealth

Supreme Court of Kentucky

140 S.W.3d 510 (Ky. 2004)

◆ THOMAS L. WALLER, J. [with whom LAMBERT, C.J., JOHNSTONE, JJ., concur. WINTERSHEIMER, J., concurred in the result only].

A Bullitt Circuit Court jury found Appellant, Michael D. St. Clair, guilty of murdering Frances C. Brady. At the subsequent capital sentencing proceeding, the jury found the presence of an aggravating circumstance and fixed Appellant's punishment at death....

In September 1991, while he was awaiting final sentencing for two (2) Oklahoma state Murder convictions, Appellant escaped from a jail ... accompanied by another inmate, Dennis Gene Reese ("Reese"). The two men fled from the facility in a vehicle—a pickup truck—stolen from a jail employee and, when that truck soon ran out of gas, stole another pickup truck, a handgun, and some ammunition from the nearby home ... and fled Oklahoma for the suburbs of Dallas, Texas. Appellant's then-wife, Bylynn, met the men in Texas and brought them money, clothing, and other items. When Reese was subsequently arrested several months later in Las Vegas, Nevada, he confessed to his involvement in an ensuing crime spree.

According to Reese, after hiding out in Dallas for a few days, the men: (1) boarded a Greyhound bus [and] disembarked in Colorado, where Appellant kidnapped a man, Timothy Keeling ("Keeling"), and took his vehicle—again, a pickup truck—and Appellant and Reese began driving back towards Texas; (2) while driving through New Mexico, ... Appellant used the stolen handgun to execute Keeling in the desert; (3) the men then drove Keeling's pickup truck to ... Kentucky, where Appellant kidnapped another man, Frances C. Brady ("Brady") and took his vehicle—another pickup truck; (4) the men then set fire to Keeling's pickup truck in order to destroy any incriminating evidence and Appellant used his handgun to execute Brady in a secluded area [in October 1991] ... ; (5) shortly thereafter, when Kentucky State Trooper Herbert Bennett ("Trooper Bennett") initiated a traffic stop of Brady's vehicle, which Appellant and Reese were then driving, Appellant fired shots from his handgun that struck Trooper Bennett's cruiser; and (6) during an ensuing flight—initially in Brady's pickup and subsequently on foot—Reese was able to split away from Appellant and had no further contact with him prior to his arrest....

[Final judgment and sentence were issued on November 22, 1991, for the two Oklahoma murders. In September 1998, t]he jury found Appellant guilty of murder[ing Brady.* On appeal, Appellant raised three issues related to the jury's finding of aggravating circumstances.] ...

---

* Editor's footnote: Keeling was killed in a different state.

KRS 532.025(2)(a)(1) [provides]:

> In all cases of offenses for which the death penalty may be authorized, the judge shall consider, or he shall include in his instructions to the jury for it to consider ... any of the following statutory aggravating ... circumstances which may be supported by the evidence:
>
> (a) Aggravating circumstances:
>
> (1) The offense of murder or kidnapping was committed by a person with a prior record of conviction for a capital offense....

... Appellant argues ... that he was entitled to a directed verdict of acquittal as to the aggravating circumstance because KRS 532.025(2)(a)(1) required that his "conviction for a capital offense" exist prior to the time of Brady's murder. Appellant argues that, although he had four (4) capital convictions for murders committed in Oklahoma by the time he came to trial in Kentucky, he did not have a "prior record of conviction for a capital offense" at the time he murdered Brady because final judgment and sentence had not yet been entered in two (2) of his Oklahoma murder cases and he had yet to stand trial in the others....

The parties' positions on this interpretive question are in clear opposition as to whether KRS 532.025(2)(a)(1) requires that the "prior record of conviction for a capital offense" exist at the time of the present capital offense [the killing of Bailey]. Appellant emphasizes the past tense of "was committed" and cites *Thompson* [*v. Commonwealth*, 862 S.W. 2d 871 (1993)] in support of its claim that the Commonwealth can demonstrate the applicability of the KRS 532.025(2)(a)(1) aggravating circumstance only by proving that, *at the time that a defendant committed the present offense of Murder or Capital Kidnapping,* the defendant had exhausted all of his or her appeals under a preexisting final judgment of conviction for a capital offense. In contrast, ... [relying on another case,] the Commonwealth argues that, to satisfy its burden of proof as to the KRS 532.025(2)(a)(1) aggravating circumstance, it need only demonstrate that, *at the time a capital sentencing proceeding is conducted,* the defendant's criminal record contains a conviction for a capital offense.

Without question, the specific language utilized in an aggravating circumstance is critical to interpreting its scope....

"The specification of aggravating circumstances is the legislature's prerogative, not ours." Thus, as is the case in any issue of statutory construction, our responsibility is "to ascertain and give effect to the intention of the legislature." In so doing, we are required by KRS 446.080(4) to construe words and phrases "according to the common and approved use of language." ...

> The best way in most cases to ascertain such intent or to determine the meaning of the statute is to look to the language used, but no intention must be read into the statute not justified by the language. The primary rule is to ascertain the intention from the words employed in enacting the statute and not to guess what the Legislature may have intended but did not express. Resort must be had first to the words, which are decisive if they are clear.

[The first issue the court must address is whether the statute requires the defendant to have a capital conviction before he commits the murder or kidnapping, as defendant argues, or before he is sentenced for the murder or kidnapping, as the state argues. W]e find the verb tense and phraseology utilized by the General Assembly in KRS 532.025(2)(a)(1) to be unequivocal, *i.e.*, "[t]he offense of murder or kidnapping *was committed by a person with* a prior record of conviction for a capital offense[.]" (emphasis added). We find KRS 532.025(2)(a)(1) susceptible to but one natural and reasonable construction: the aggravating circumstance is implicated only when the defendant has already been convicted of a capital offense prior to the commission of the present capital offense. The word "with" is self-explanatory; in the context used in KRS 532.025(2)(a)(1) it means "[h]aving as a possession, attribute, or characteristic," *American Heritage Dictionary of the English Language* (4th ed.2000). Accordingly, if an unarmed person uses his bare hands to strangle a victim to death, it is an objective fact that the offense was not committed by a person with a handgun. Similarly, in a case where a defendant with no prior criminal record kills Victim A, the murder of Victim A was not committed by a person with a prior record of conviction for a capital offense. The defendant's status *at the time of the offense* does not change if the defendant is subsequently convicted of murdering Victim B.... It is clear from the language of KRS 532.025(2)(a)(1), however, that a subsequently-obtained capital conviction, standing alone, will not make the defendant "death eligible."

A second interpretative question remains, however, as to what level of finality is contemplated by "a prior record of conviction for a capital offense." We recognize that we stated in *Thompson* that "a 'conviction, which of course means the final judgment' cannot be relied upon as a conviction if an appeal is taken because 'an appeal in a criminal case suspends the judgment, and this [sic] does not become final until a termination of the appeal.'" In doing so, however, it appears that we quoted out-of-context the authority upon which we relied ... and overlooked nearly a century of jurisprudence from this Court which recognizes that "[t]he word 'conviction' has a twofold meaning. One is the determination of the fact of guilt, as by the verdict of a jury. The other ... denotes the final judgment in the prosecution." ...

This Court has observed its different interpretations of "conviction" in different statutes are a function of "an attempt by the courts to determine legislative intent in each case." Turning to that inquiry, we again find guidance in KRS 446.080(4): "[a]ll words and phrases shall be construed according to the common and approved use of language." ... [T]he "ordinary or popular meaning" of conviction "refers to a finding of guilt by plea or verdict[.]" ... We ... find it significant that the General Assembly chose the phrase "prior record of conviction" in KRS 532.025(2)(a)(1) — a phrase that invokes the vernacular notion of a person's "criminal record" — instead of "judgment of conviction," [which has] a defined legal meaning.... Accordingly, we conclude that, for purposes of KRS 532.025(2)(a)(1), "prior record of conviction for a capital offense" includes a plea of guilty accepted by the trial court or a jury's or judge's verdict of guilty. To the extent that *Thompson* reaches a contrary holding, it is overruled....

Although the final judgments were not entered in Appellant's first two Oklahoma Murder convictions until November 22, 1991, or approximately six (6) weeks after Brady's murder, Appellant [was] convicted of those two (2) counts of Murder following a trial [before the day of Brady's murder]....

♦ [JUSTICE COOPER's opinion concurring in Part and dissenting in Part is omitted.]

♦ KELLER, JUSTICE, Concurring in Part and Dissenting in Part with whom STUMBO, J., joined.

... In my view, the trial court ... erred when it denied Appellant's motion for a directed verdict as to the KRS 532.025(2)(a)(1) aggravating circumstance.... In *Thompson v. Commonwealth,* this Court *correctly* interpreted KRS 532.025(2)(a)(1)'s "prior record of conviction for a capital offense" to mean a *final judgment* of conviction for a capital offense. By overruling *Thompson* and adopting a contrary and novel interpretation of the same language, today's opinion not only is inconsistent with Appellant's rights of due process but also turns its back on common sense and its own rules of statutory construction. The Opinion of the Court concedes that the term "conviction" is inherently ambiguous and is susceptible to different interpretations, but then fails to apply the "rule of lenity" that "require[s] us to give it the more lenient interpretation" when faced with such ambiguity. The opinion correctly observes that KRS 446.080(4) states that "[a]ll words and phrases shall be construed according to the common and approved usage of language[.]" However, the statute continues further, "but technical words and phrases, and such others as may have acquired a peculiar and appropriate meaning in the law shall be construed according to such meaning." And, although the popular meaning of "conviction" may apply where rights of persons other than the "convict" are involved, in situations "where legal disabilities, disqualifications, and forfeitures are to follow, the strict legal meaning is to be applied, absent some indication of contrary intent." ... Today's Opinion of the Court interprets KRS 532.025(2)(a)(1)'s "prior record of conviction for a capital offense" language in a manner inconsistent with the technical meaning of "conviction" ... "The death penalty cannot be imposed simply because we or the jury believe the actions or motives of a particular defendant are deserving of capital punishment[,]"and this Court must interpret the scope of KRS 532.025(2)(a)'s aggravating circumstance in the same manner that it interprets any legislative enactment—*i.e.,* by applying the rules of statutory construction. A proper application of those rules demonstrates that the Commonwealth was unable to prove that Brady's murder "was committed by a person with a prior record of conviction for a capital offense." Accordingly, the trial court should have directed a verdict in Appellant's favor and instructed the jury to fix Appellant's punishment at a sentence of imprisonment....

* * *

Points for Discussion

1. *Statutory Language*: What was the language at issue? What did the defendant and government want that language to mean? What meaning did the majority and dissent adopt?

2. *Theories*: Which theory did the majority use? The dissent?

3. *Two Interpretive Questions*: The court had to address two interpretive questions. First, the court had to determine timing: must a defendant have been convicted of the prior offense before the subsequent criminal act (the defendant's meaning) or before the penalty hearing for that crime (the government's meaning). Second, the court had to determine finality: whether the ordinary meaning (the government's meaning) or technical meaning (the defendant's meaning) of the word "conviction" applied. The dissent disagreed with the majority's resolution of only one of these two questions. Which one?

4. *Ordinary or Technical*: To determine which meaning was intended — technical or ordinary — a judge will look at two things: (1) whether the surrounding words are technical, and (2) whether the statute was directed to a technical audience. Which was relevant here for the majority in adopting the ordinary meaning? What about the dissent? To whom was this statute written?

5. *Grammar*: We will address grammar in a later chapter, but what role does grammar play in resolving the first question the court had to address in this case?

6. *Rule of Lenity*: What role, if any, should the rule of lenity have played in this case? Is a penalty enhancing statute penal?

7. *Implications*: If the majority was correct, what happens to a defendant's death penalty sentence if that defendant's underlying conviction is ultimately overturned? Would the defendant have the ability to ask a court to reduce his death sentence and resentence him at that time? Does not the answer to this question demonstrate that the majority was simply wrong?

8. *Technical Meaning*: Ordinary meaning is presumed. Technical meaning is rarely intended, as these two cases show. To argue that the legislature intended the technical meaning, you must show either that the context is technical or that the intended audience understands the word in a technical way, or both.

* * *

Problem 5

You work for the Department of Justice. The following case has come across your desk. Don and Lee Glover placed an old High Standard autoloading shotgun into a zippered gym bag, then put the bag in the trunk of their car. The gun is inoperable because a piece of steel was welded in the chamber so that the gun cannot hold ammunition or fire.

They drove the car to a proposed drug-sale point (across state lines), where they intended to steal drugs from drug dealers. Before they could get out of the car, federal agents at the scene stopped them, searched their car and the dealers' car, found the guns and drugs, and arrested them. The issue is whether to charge the Glovers with the enhanced penalty statute, 18 U.S.C. §924(c)(1)(A). The statute provides:

> Except to the extent that a greater minimum sentence is otherwise provided by this subsection or by any other provision of law, any person who, during

and in relation to any crime of violence or drug trafficking crime (including a crime of violence or drug trafficking crime that provides for an enhanced punishment if committed by the use of a deadly or dangerous weapon or device) for which the person may be prosecuted in a court of the United States, uses or carries a firearm, shall, in addition to the punishment provided for such crime of violence or drug trafficking crime—

(i) be sentenced to a term of imprisonment of not less than 5 years;

(ii) if the firearm is brandished, be sentenced to a term of imprisonment of not less than 7 years; and

(iii) if the firearm is discharged, be sentenced to a term of imprisonment of not less than 10 years.

Definition: As used in this section, the term "firearm" means (A) any weapon that will or is designed to or may readily be converted to expel a projectile by the action of an explosive; or (B) any destructive device. Such term does not include an antique firearm.

Assume the defendants are willing to plead guilty to criminal charges for carrying guns across state lines illegally and for conspiracy to comment robbery. They claim that they did not violate the penalty enhancing statute because the gun was inoperable. You need to decide whether you will charge the defendants with the enhanced penalty statute.

Problem Materials

Statutory Purpose: From case law:

"Imposing a more restrictive reading of the phrase "uses ... a firearm" does violence not only to the structure and language of the statute, but to its purpose as well. When Congress enacted the current version of §924(c)(1), it was no doubt aware that drugs and guns are a dangerous combination. In 1989, 56 percent of all murders in New York City were drug related; during the same period, the figure for the Nation's Capital was as high as 80 percent. *The American Enterprise* 100 (Jan.–Feb. 1991). The fact that a gun is treated momentarily as an item of commerce does not render it inert or deprive it of destructive capacity. Rather, as experience demonstrates, it can be converted instantaneously from currency to cannon. We therefore see no reason why Congress would have intended courts and juries applying §924(c)(1) to draw a fine metaphysical distinction between a gun's role in a drug offense as a weapon and its role as an item of barter; it creates a grave possibility of violence and death in either capacity...."

Smith v. United States, 508 U.S. 223, 240 (1993).

Legislative History: From case law:

The provision's chief sponsor in the House said that the provision seeks "to persuade the man who is tempted to commit a Federal felony to leave his gun at home." 114 Cong. Rec. 22231 (1968) (Rep. Poff); *see also* 114 Cong.Rec. 22243–22244 (provision would apply to "the man who goes out taking a gun to commit a crime") (Rep. Hunt); *id.*, at 22244 ("Of course, what we are trying to do by these penalties is to persuade the criminal to leave his gun at home") (Rep. Randall); *id.*, at 22236 ("We are concerned . . . with having the criminal leave his gun at home") (Rep. Meskill).

Muscarello v. United States, 524 U.S. 125, 132 (1998).

Chapter 6

Canons Based on Intrinsic Sources: Moving Beyond the Words

A. Introduction to This Chapter

As we saw in the last chapter, ordinary meaning generally controls, unless the words were used in their technical sense. Sometimes, however, there may be a reason to look beyond that ordinary meaning. For example, when language is ambiguous, judges look extra-textually to determine which of two or more equally plausible meanings was intended. Additionally, there are three other situations when judges may avoid the ordinary meaning of words: (1) if the ordinary meaning of the words causes the interpretation to be absurd, judges may adopt an alternative interpretation; (2) if there is an obvious scrivener's error, judges may adopt an alternative interpretation; or (3) if the ordinary meaning would raise constitutional issues, judges may adopt an alternative interpretation. However, in each situation, the alternative interpretation must be fair and reasonable.

Let's look at each of these four ways to reject the ordinary meaning in more detail.

B. Looking beyond the Ordinary Meaning of Words

While some judges are willing to look at all the sources of meaning even when the text is clear, more commonly, judges prefer to have a reason to look beyond allegedly clear text. Indeed, textualist judges refuse to look beyond the ordinary meaning of the statute unless one of four reasons is present. *See, e.g., Goswami v. American Collections Enters., Inc.,* 377 F.3d 488, 492 (5th Cir. 2004) ("In interpreting statutes we do not look beyond the plain meaning of the statute unless the statute is absurd or ambiguous."). The most common reason judges look beyond the ordinary meaning of the text is that the words are ambiguous, so let's start there.

1. Ambiguity

When is statutory language ambiguous? That question is actually more complex than it might seem. "Ambiguous" means "open to or having several possible meanings or interpretations; equivocal." Dictionary.com. http://dictionary.reference.com/browse/ambiguous. Ambiguous words may be likened to optical illusions in that both parties legitimately claim to see—or in the case of words, understand—the same thing in a different way. Consider the famous optical illusion in the text box below. Do you

see a young or old woman? Many people see the young woman first, but if you look at the picture long enough, you should be able to make out the old woman as well. The young woman's necklace is the old woman's mouth. The young woman's chin is the old woman's nose. The young woman's ear is the old woman's eye. They share the hair, fur, and feather. Anyone viewing the picture can legitimately say it is a picture of either a young or old woman. Both "interpretations" are legitimate because the picture is unclear, or "ambiguous," intentionally so in this case. Ambiguous words are similar to optical illusions; they have more than one legitimate meaning. Children love to joke using ambiguous words: For example, how did the baker get rich? She made a lot of dough! Or what kind of bagel can fly? A plane bagel. (I did not say they were good jokes!).

Judges do not consistently define ambiguity. A judge's theory of interpretation might affect that judge's willingness to define "ambiguity" narrowly ("equally plausible alternative meanings") or broadly ("reasonable people disagree about the meaning"). Possibly, a judge's desire to look beyond the text could affect this choice. A broader definition of ambiguity allows judges to review extra-textual evidence of meaning more readily, while a narrower definition constrains judicial review of such evidence. Hence, we might expect textualist judges to define ambiguity narrowly while non-textualist judges, if they define it at all, might choose a broader definition. Here are some real "ambiguity" definitions. Can you guess which theory the judge uses? Which, if any, seems right to you?

- "When a statute is as clear as a glass slipper and fits without strain, courts should not approve an interpretation that requires a shoehorn." *Demko v. United States*, 216 F.3d 1049, 1053 (Fed. Cir. 2000). Text.

- "While both sides present credible interpretations, Florida's is the better one. Congress could have used more precise language and thus removed all ambiguity, but the two readings are not equally plausible." *Florida Dep't of Revenue v. Piccadilly Cafeterias, Inc.*, 554 U.S. 33, 41 (2008). int.

- For statutory language to be ambiguous, however, it must be susceptible to more than one reasonable interpretation or more than one accepted meaning. *In re Amy Unknows*, 701 F.3d 749, 760 (5th Cir. 2012), *cert. granted in part*, 133 S. Ct. 2886 (2013).

- Only ambiguous statutes require judicial construction; statutes are "'not ambiguous simply because different interpretations are conceivable.'" *Department of Revenue v. Bi-More, Inc.*, 286 P.3d 417, 420 (Wash. 2012).

- "Language is ambiguous when it may be understood in more than one way, or simultaneously refers to two or more things. If the language is difficult to comprehend, is of doubtful import, or lacks clearness and definiteness, an ambiguity exists." *Williams v. Commonwealth*, 733 S.E.2d 124, 127–28 (Va. 2012).

- To determine whether there is an ambiguity, we must assess whether there is "an uncertainty of meaning or intention.'" *Republic of Ecuador v. Mackay*, 12-15572, 2014 WL 341060 (9th Cir. Jan. 31, 2014).

- "It may be that here, as in other cases, the strict dichotomy between clarity and ambiguity is artificial, that what we have is a continuum, a probability of meaning." *PDK Labs. Inc. v. DEA*, 362 F.3d 786, 797 (D.C. Cir. 2004).

Which gives you the best guidance in determining whether a statutory language is ambiguous? The most common articulation of ambiguity is that statutory language is "ambiguous if it is capable of being understood by reasonably well-informed persons in two or more senses." *State ex rel Kalal*, 681 N.W.2d 110, 124 (Wis. 2004). In other words, a statute is ambiguous when it has more than one meaning when applied to the facts of a particular case. For example, in *Church of the Holy Trinity v. United States*, 143 U.S. 457, 459 (1892), the Court had to interpret the word "labor." The statute could have included all types of labor or it could have included only unskilled, physical labor. The text of the statute alone (the word "labor" and its surrounding words) did not resolve the ambiguity, at least to the Court. Thus, the word "labor," in this context, was ambiguous. To resolve the ambiguity, the Court turned to other sources, namely the title and purpose of the act, to choose between the two possible meanings. *Id.*

In contrast, simply because a word has more than one meaning does not mean that the language is ambiguous. You may remember that in the *Kalal* case an employer allegedly stole retirement funds from an employee. 681 N.W.2d at 115. A statute allowed the district court to bring a criminal action directly if the district attorney "refuse[d]" to issue the complaint. *Id.* at 114 (quoting Wis. Stat. § 968.02(3) (2001–

02)). The district attorney told the employee that she "was free to proceed legally in whatever manner she believed necessary." *Id.* After being told this, the employee filed a motion for a criminal complaint, which the court granted. *Id.* The issue in the case was whether the word "refuse" required an explicit refusal or merely an indication of unwillingness to do something. *Id.* at 115. The court concluded that the language was not ambiguous, despite the two, possible interpretations, because the second interpretation better furthered the purpose of the statute. *Id.*

Thus, although the "reasonable people disagree" standard is often articulated, it cannot be correct because if it were, every case involving a statutory interpretation issue would involve ambiguity. Litigants always disagree as to the meaning of the statutory language, and judges often disagree as well. If the "reasonable people disagree" definition were correct, then most litigants, their lawyers, and many judges would be unreasonable people. An alternative definition is that one or more interpretations are *equally plausible. Florida Dep't of Revenue v. Piccadilly Cafeterias, Inc.,* 554 U.S. 33, 41 (2008). The case below explains why this stricter standard may make more sense.

Mayor of Lansing v. Michigan Public Service Commission

Supreme Court of Michigan
680 N.W.2d 840 (Mich. 2004)

♦ Taylor, J.

In this case, we are called on to determine if defendant Wolverine Pipe Line Company (Wolverine) must obtain the permission of the city of Lansing before constructing a gas pipeline longitudinally in the right-of-way adjacent to an interstate highway when part of the pipeline would be constructed within city limits. We [hold] that Wolverine must obtain local consent but that such consent need not be obtained before the application is submitted to the Michigan Public Service Commission (PSC)....

We review de novo a question of statutory construction. In construing a statute, we are required to give effect to the Legislature's intent. That intent is clear if the statutory language is unambiguous, and the statute must then be enforced as written....

The statute that controls this case is M.C.L. § 247.183, which reads:

(1) Telegraph, telephone, power, and other public utility companies, cable television companies, and municipalities may enter upon, construct, and maintain telegraph, telephone, or power lines, pipe lines, wires, cables, poles, conduits, sewers or similar structures upon, over, across, or under any public road, bridge, street, or public place, including subject to subsection (2), longitudinally within limited access highway rights of way, and across or under any of the waters in this state, with all necessary erections and fixtures for that purpose. A telegraph, telephone, power, and other public utility company, cable television company, and municipality, before any of this work is commenced, shall first obtain the consent of the governing body of

the city, village, or township through or along which these lines and poles are to be constructed and maintained.

(2) A utility as defined in 23 C.F.R. §645.105(m) may enter upon, construct, and maintain utility lines and structures longitudinally within limited access highway rights of way in accordance with standards approved by the state transportation commission that conform to governing federal laws and regulations. The standards shall require that the lines and structures be underground and be placed in a manner that will not increase highway maintenance costs for the state transportation department. The standards may provide for the imposition of a reasonable charge for longitudinal use of limited access highway rights of way....

Wolverine does not here dispute that it is both a "public utility," as that phrase is used in subsection 1 of the statute, as well as a subsection 2 "utility as defined in 23 C.F.R 645.105[.]" Definitionally, both subsections are applicable to Wolverine unless something in the statute excludes Wolverine from the reach of one subsection or the other. Wolverine argues that such exclusionary language is found in subsection 1, which, paraphrased, states that any covered utility, including those subject to subsection 2, may use a public road longitudinally within the limited access highway right-of-way if it has local permission before work commences. The company's construction of this passage is that the quoted phrase serves to remove subsection 2 utilities from subsection 1 rules and thus such utilities must only comply with the requirements of subsection 2. In support of this, Wolverine primarily contends that this reading is the only proper construction because otherwise the language "subject to subsection (2)" would be left without meaning. Because such constructions are to be avoided, and because Wolverine believes its reading gives the phrase meaning, it urges us to adopt that reading. We decline to do so, as did the Court of Appeals before us, because we think the reading urged by the city also gives meaning to and more accurately reflects the statute.

We note that *Random House Webster's College Dictionary* (2001 ed.), defines "subject" when used as an adjective in six ways. The most applicable is the fourth definition, "dependent upon something (usu. fol. by *to*): *His consent is subject to your approval.*" This definition, in essence, gives to the word "subject" the meaning, "dependent upon." When used as it is here and in other places in the Legislature's work, it is clear that the subsections work together. That is, both subsections are applicable because the relevant words in subsection 1, the "subject to" words, do not mean that the requirements of subsection 1 do not apply to those utilities that are covered also by subsection 2. Further, because the Legislature expressly (and uniquely) used the word "including" before the "subject to" phrase, the implication is even stronger that the two subsections are to be read in combination. Thus, subsection 1 means the project cannot go forward without local approval and, not at all incompatibly, subsection 2 means it cannot go forward unless it meets certain construction standards.

We are aware, and, indeed, Wolverine forcefully argues, that this reading of the statute may facilitate frivolous and potentially crippling resistance from local governments along the route of a utility project. Such an argument, however, misunderstands *which approach seperation of-powers?*

the role of the courts. Our task, under the Constitution, is the important, but yet limited, duty to read into and interpret what the Legislature has actually made the law. We have observed many times in the past that our Legislature is free to make policy choices that, especially in controversial matters, some observers will inevitably think unwise. This dispute over the wisdom of a law, however, cannot give warrant to a court to overrule the people's Legislature....

Concerning the dissent, we offer the following observations:

Absurd?

The justices in this majority do not necessarily disagree with the dissent that M.C.L. § 247.183, as we construe it here, may be "cumbersome." Nor, by this opinion, does any justice in this majority suggest that, had they been in the Legislature, they would have cast a vote in support of M.C.L. § 247.183 as it is interpreted here. Nor are the justices in this majority oblivious to the practical difficulties that our interpretation of the law may impose upon utilities such as Wolverine Pipe Line Company. Rather, what we decide today is merely that the language of M.C.L. § 247.183 compels a particular result, and the justices of this majority do not believe themselves empowered to reach a different result by substituting their own policy preferences for those of the Legislature.

Rather than interpreting the language of M.C.L. § 247.183, the dissent prefers to divine what it characterizes as the Legislature's "true intent." This "true intent" is not one to be gleaned from the words actually enacted into law by the Legislature, but through reliance on various random facts and circumstances that the dissent selectively picks out from the universe of potentially available facts and circumstances. In contrast, rather than engaging in legislative mind-reading to discern the "true intent" of the law, we believe that the best measure of the Legislature's intent is simply the words that it has chosen to enact into law. Among other salutary consequences, this approach to reading the law allows a court to assess not merely the intentions of one or two highlighted members of the Legislature, but the intentions of the *entire* Legislature.

only can find ambiguity after all means of interpretation have been applied

The dissent avoids the difficult task of having to read the actual language of the law and determine its best interpretation by peremptorily concluding that M.C.L. § 247.183 is "ambiguous." A finding of ambiguity, of course, enables an appellate judge to bypass traditional approaches to interpretation and either substitute presumptive "rule[s] of policy," or else to engage in a largely subjective and perambulatory reading of "legislative history." However, ... a finding of ambiguity is to be reached only after "all other conventional means of [ ] interpretation" have been applied and found wanting. Where the majority applies these conventional rules and concludes that the language of M.C.L. § 247.183 can be reasonably understood, the dissent, without demonstrating the flaws of the majority's analysis except to assert that its opinion is not in accord with the "true intent" of the Legislature, opines that an "ambiguity" exists. An analysis, such as that of the dissent, that is in conflict with the actual language of the law and predicated on some supposed "true intent" is necessarily a result-oriented analysis. In other words, it is not a legal analysis at all.

In peremptorily reaching its conclusion that M.C.L. § 247.183 is "ambiguous," the dissent entirely misstates the standard for discerning ambiguity. The dissent would hasten findings of "ambiguity" by courts by predicating these findings on the basis of whether "reasonable minds can differ regarding" the meaning of a statute. Especially in the context of the types of cases and controversies considered by this Court— those in which the parties have been the most determined and persistent, the most persuaded by the merits of their own respective arguments—it is extraordinarily difficult to conclude that reasonable minds cannot differ on the correct outcome. That is not, and has never been, the standard either for resolving cases or for ascertaining the existence of an ambiguity in the law. The law is not ambiguous whenever a dissenting (and presumably reasonable) justice would interpret such law in a manner contrary to a majority. Where a majority finds the law to mean one thing and a dissenter finds it to mean another, neither may have concluded that the law is "ambiguous," and their disagreement by itself does not transform that which is unambiguous into that which is ambiguous. Rather, a provision of the law is ambiguous only if it "irreconcilably conflict[s]" with another provision, or when it is *equally* susceptible to more than a single meaning. In lieu of the traditional approach to discerning "ambiguity"—one in which only a few provisions are truly ambiguous and in which a diligent application of the rules of interpretation will normally yield a "better," albeit perhaps imperfect, interpretation of the law—the dissent would create a judicial regime in which courts would be quick to declare ambiguity and quick therefore to resolve cases and controversies on the basis of something other than the words of the law.[7] . . .

The dissent wrongly asserts that "the majority fails to construe subsection 1 in light of subsection 2. . . ." Rather, we assert that "subsection 1 means the project cannot go forward without local approval and, not at all incompatibly, subsection 2 means it cannot go forward unless it meets certain construction standards," and further assert that the "including, subject to subsection (2)" language in subsection 1 makes "the implication . . . even stronger that the two subsections are to be read in combination." It is the dissent that misapprehends the relationship between subsections 1 and 2 by attempting to read these provisions in isolation and concluding that when read in this manner they compel different results and thus are "ambiguous." However, the subsections of M.C.L. § 247.183, as with all other provisions of law, are not to be read discretely, but as part of a whole. The dissent errs in first reading these subsections "alone" and then asserting that it is reading these subsections "together" when it merely combines its "alone" interpretations. Rather, to read the law as a whole, it must, in fact, be read as a whole. The interpretative process does not, as the dissent does, remove words and provisions from their context, infuse these words and provisions with meanings that are independent of such context, and then reimport these context-free meanings back into the law. The law is not properly read as a whole

---

7. The dissent also confusingly conflates unambiguousness and clarity. Instead, a great many unambiguous provisions of the law are far from clear. . . . A provision of law that is unambiguous may well be one that merely has a better meaning, as opposed to a clear meaning.

when its words and provisions are isolated and given meanings that are independent of the rest of its provisions. This is especially true when, as here, one of these provisions *expressly cross-references* the other.

Therefore, even if the existence of a reasonable disagreement *were* the standard for identifying ambiguity — which it is not — the dissent's interpretation of M.C.L. § 247.183 is simply not a reasonable one when subsections 1 and 2 are read together, as opposed to being read discretely....

Moreover, even if M.C.L. § 247.183 were truly ambiguous, the dissent's analysis of what it views as the relevant legislative history is altogether unpersuasive....

In the end, the essence of the dissent's analysis is its (perhaps understandable) frustrated assertion that "I cannot believe that the Legislature intended to subject federally defined public utilities to local consent requirements." This constitutes less a legal conclusion than a statement of discontent with the fact that the Legislature either had a different perspective on pipeline approval than the dissent or it failed effectively to communicate what the dissent alone knows to be its "true intent." In either case, there is no warrant for this Court replacing the words of the Legislature with those of its own.

We conclude that the plain language of M.C.L. § 247.183 requires Wolverine to obtain local consent before beginning construction of its project....

◆ Michael F. Cavanagh, J. (dissenting) [Marilyn J. Kelly, J., joins the dissent.]

Today, the majority finds no ambiguity in the statutory provision at issue and, in so doing, ignores the true intent of the Legislature. Because I believe the true intent of the Legislature must be given effect, I respectfully dissent. The majority, apparently frustrated with my refusal to follow its lead and use a dictionary while turning a blind eye to reality, has issued a lengthy response to this dissent. While the majority asserts that I substitute my own policy preferences for those of the Legislature, I think it is necessary to note the following in regard to the majority's approach: "A method of statutory interpretation that is deliberately uninformed, and hence unconstrained, increases the risk that the judge's own policy preferences will affect the decisional process." *BedRoc Ltd, LLC v. United States*, 541 U.S. 176 (2004) (Stevens, J., *dissenting*).

This case requires us to examine M.C.L. § 247.183 to determine whether defendant Wolverine Pipe Line Company (Wolverine) must obtain permission from plaintiff city of Lansing to construct a gas pipeline longitudinally in the right-of-way of an interstate highway within the city limits. The majority finds no ambiguity in the statute and, thus, holds that Wolverine must obtain local consent before constructing the pipeline. I, on the other hand, believe that the statute is ambiguous and turn to the legislative history accompanying the statute to discern the Legislature's true intent. A review of the legislative history indicates that the Legislature's intent was to create a streamlined permit system that would not require consent from each municipality a pipeline crosses. On the bases of the history of the statute itself and of the legislative history recorded when the statute was enacted, I would hold that Wolverine is not obligated to obtain local consent.

I agree with the majority that this case involves principles of statutory construction and that in construing a statute, we are required to give effect to the Legislature's intent. I also agree that legislative intent must be gleaned from the statutory text if the language is unambiguous. However, when a statute is ambiguous, judicial construction is necessary to determine its meaning.

A statute is ambiguous when reasonable minds can differ regarding its meaning....

> [W]hen there can be reasonable disagreement over a statute's meaning or, as others have put it, when a statute is capable of being understood by reasonably well-informed persons in two or more different senses, that statute is ambiguous.

... In this case, application of the statute to the facts has rendered the correct application of the statute uncertain.

M.C.L. § 247.183, in pertinent part, reads:

> (1) ... public utility companies ... may enter upon, construct, and maintain ... pipe lines ... upon, over, across, or under any public road, bridge, street or public place, including, subject to subsection (2), longitudinally within limited access highway rights of way, and across or under any of the waters of this state, with all necessary erections and fixtures for that purpose. A ... public utility company ..., before any of this work is commenced, shall first obtain the consent of the governing body of the city ... through or along which these lines and poles are to be constructed and maintained.

> (2) A utility as defined in 23 C.F.R. 645.105[ ] may enter upon, construct, and maintain utility lines and structures longitudinally within limited access highway rights of way in accordance with standards approved by the state transportation commission that conform to governing federal laws and regulations.

The majority's statutory analysis begins and ends with the dictionary definition of "subject to." The majority concludes that "subject to" does "not mean that the requirements of subsection 1 do not apply to those utilities that are covered also by subsection 2." While the majority uses a double negative to hedge, I think the more direct statement to be gleaned from the inclusion of "subject to" in subsection 1 and its conspicuous absence from subsection 2 is that subsection 2 utilities may not be "subject to" the requirements of subsection 1. Because subsection 2 utilities are a specific group of federally defined utilities that are subject to regulations beyond those imposed on the broad general utilities in subsection 1, I think it is fair to say that the Legislature may have intended to create a regulatory scheme specific to the more-regulated entities.

Thus, it is unclear whether the requirement in subsection 1, that public utility companies must obtain local consent, applies to a utility, as defined in subsection 2. When reading subsection 1 alone it appears that all public utilities must obtain local consent before constructing pipelines in any public place. When reading subsection 2 alone, however, it appears that federally defined utilities may construct pipelines longitudinally within limited access highway rights-of-way as long as they comply with the applicable state standards. When the two sections are read together, it is unclear whether subsection 2 utilities must comply with the local consent requirement in subsection 1.

"It is a well-established rule of statutory construction that provisions of a statute must be construed in light of the other provisions of the statute to carry out the apparent purpose of the Legislature." Here, the majority fails to construe subsection 1 in light of subsection 2 and, thus, concludes that the statute is not ambiguous.

I cannot agree that the meaning of M.C.L. § 247.183 is clear and unambiguous. A statute is ambiguous if there can be reasonable disagreement over the statute's meaning. The meaning of this statute is subject to reasonable disagreement. There is a reasonable argument that subsection 2 imposes requirements, in addition to those imposed by subsection 1, on utilities that meet the definition of utility in 23 C.F.R. § 645.105, and that are looking to construct lines longitudinally within limited access highway rights-of-way. Under this reading of the statute, subsection 2 utilities would be required to obtain local consent.

However, there is also a reasonable argument that subsections 1 and 2 apply to different entities and that subsection 2 entities are excepted from the requirements of subsection 1. Because there are at least two reasonable interpretations of M.C.L. § 247.183, the statute is ambiguous.

When a statute is ambiguous, judicial construction is appropriate. As previously stated, it is a maxim of statutory construction that "provisions of a statute must be construed in light of the other provisions of the statute...." In construing subsection 1 in light of subsection 2, I find that the Legislature intended to create a special process for federally defined utilities that wish to construct pipelines longitudinally within limited access highway rights-of-way.

The statutory and legislative history further supports the conclusion that the Legislature did not intend for federally defined utilities ... to have to obtain local consent before constructing pipelines longitudinally in limited access highway rights-of-way.... [The dissent's lengthy analysis of the amendment and legislative history is omitted.].

... After reviewing the language used in the statute and the legislative history, I cannot believe that the Legislature intended to subject federally defined public utilities to local consent requirements.

Because I believe that the statute is ambiguous and the true legislative intent was not to require local consent when federally defined utilities wish to construct pipelines longitudinally within limited access highway rights-of-way, I must respectfully dissent.

* * *

Points for Discussion

1. *Statutory Language*: What was the language at issue? What did each party want that language to mean? What meaning did the majority and dissent adopt? This

is a difficult case. Be sure you understand the two interpretations. One interpretation means all utilities must get local permission. The other means only non-federal utilities must get local permission.

2. *Theories*: Which theory did the majority use? The dissent? Did they use different theories or the same one? If their theories are the same, why did they reach different results?

3. *Making the Statute Easier to Read*: The majority included the entire statute, while the dissent eliminated irrelevant material using ellipses. Which do you find easier to read?

4. *Ambiguity*: When a judge determines that language in a statute is ambiguous, that judge opens the door to extra-textual sources. Just which sources a judge will consider continues to be influenced by that judge's theory of interpretation. What definition of "ambiguity" did the majority use? The dissent? Which definition is narrower, meaning that the court is less likely to find ambiguity?

5. *Removing the Language at Issue*: The language "subject to subjection (2)" is separated by commas, meaning it can stand alone. Is the issue any clearer when this language is removed:

    (1) ... public utility companies ... may ... construct ... pipe lines ... under any public road including ... longitudinally within limited access highway rights of way.... A ... utility company, ... before any of this work is commenced, shall first obtain the consent ... of the city....

    (2) A utility as defined in 23 C.F.R. § 645.105(m) may ... construct ... utility lines ... longitudinally within limited access highway rights of way in accordance with standards approved by the state transportation commission....

6. *"Combines its 'alone' interpretations"*: What did the majority mean by this statement? Which opinion better examined the two sections of the statute *in pari materia*, meaning as a whole?

7. *Absurdity*: The dissent said, "I cannot believe that the Legislature intended to subject federally defined public utilities to local consent requirements." In other words, the dissent found the majority's interpretation absurd. In response, the majority acknowledged that its interpretation was "cumbersome." Are these the same? We will cover absurdity in the next section.

8. *Legislative Response*: In response to the holding in this case, the legislature immediately amended the statute to remove the consent requirement. The statute as amended provides: "A utility as defined in 23 CFR 645.105(m) ... is not required to obtain the consent of the governing body of the city, village, or township as required under subsection (1)." Does this subsequent legislation action show that the dissent was correct after all?

9. *Ambiguous and Unclear*: Do these words mean the same thing? The majority said they mean different things, while the dissent seemed to conflate them. Regardless

of whether it was correct, the dissent's approach to this issue is consistent with the way most judges think about and discuss ambiguity and clarity.

10. *Types of Ambiguity*: There are two types of ambiguity: lexical ambiguity and structural ambiguity. *Lexical ambiguity* is far more common and occurs when a word or phrase has multiple meanings. Everyday examples include nouns like "bay," "pen" and "suit"; verbs like "dust," "draw," and "run"; and adjectives like "hard" and "blue." According to the Oxford English Dictionary, the 500 words used most in the English language each have an average of twenty-three different meanings.

Structural ambiguity, which is less common, occurs when a phrase or sentence has more than one underlying structure. Some examples include "the Tibetan history teacher," "short men and women," "the girl hit the boy with a book," and "visiting relatives can be boring." These ambiguities are said to be structural because each such phrase can be represented in two structurally different ways, e.g., "[Tibetan history] teacher" and "Tibetan [history teacher]." Also, is it relatives who come to visit that are boring or is it going to visit relatives that is boring?

Which type of ambiguity was at issue in this case?

11. *Vague, Broad, and General*: "Ambiguous" means something different from vague, broad, and general, although judges use the term "ambiguous" to mean all three.

First, ambiguity is not the same as vagueness. Vague means "not clearly or explicitly stated or expressed." Dictionary.com. http://dictionary.reference.com/browse/vague. Vagueness means that the boundaries of meaning are indistinct. For example, if I say I want the report next week sometime, "next week sometime" is vague, not ambiguous.

Second, ambiguity is not the same as broadness. "Broad" means "not limited or narrow; of extensive range or scope." Dictionary.com. http://dictionary.reference.com/browse/broad. If I say that I want a ten to fifty page report, that range may be broad; but it is not ambiguous.

Third, ambiguity is not the same as generalness. "General" means "not specific or definite." Dictionary.com. http://dictionary.reference.com/browse/general. If I say I want a report on birds, the topic "birds" may be general, but it is not ambiguous. Despite these differences, however, judges routinely say that language is ambiguous when it is merely vague, broad, or general.

* * *

Regina v. Ojibway

1965–1966 8 *Criminal Law Quarterly* 137
137 Judicial Humour—Construction of a Statute
Kent W. Roach, Henry S. Brown, Martha Shaffer, Gilles Renaud

◆ BLUE, J.

This is an appeal by the Crown by way of a stated case from a decision of the magistrate acquitting the accused of a charge under the Small Birds Act, R.S.O., 1960, c. 724, s. 2. The facts are not in dispute. Fred Ojibway … was riding his pony through Queen's Park on January 2, 1965. Being impoverished and having been forced to pledge his saddle, he substituted a downy pillow in lieu of the said saddle. On this particular day, the accused's misfortune was further heightened by the circumstance of his pony breaking its foreleg. In accord with Indian custom, the accused then shot the pony to relieve it of its awkwardness.

The accused was then charged with having breached the Small Birds Act, s. 2 of which states:

> "2. Anyone maiming, injuring or killing small birds is guilty of an offence ← statute
> and subject to a fine not in excess of two hundred dollars."] what?

The learned magistrate acquitted the accused holding, in fact, that he had killed his horse and not a small bird. With respect, I cannot agree.

In light of the definition section my course is quite clear. Section 1 defines "bird" as "a two legged animal covered with feathers." There can be no doubt that this case is covered by this section.

Counsel for the accused made several ingenious arguments to which, in fairness, I must address myself. He submitted that the evidence of the expert clearly concluded that the animal in question was a pony and not a bird, but this is not the issue. We are not interested in whether the animal in question is a bird or not in fact, but whether it is one in law. Statutory interpretation has forced many a horse to eat birdseed for the rest of its life.

Counsel also contended that the neighing noise emitted by the animal could not possibly be produced by a bird. With respect, the sounds emitted by an animal are irrelevant to its nature, for a bird is no less a bird because it is silent.

Counsel for the accused also argued that since there was evidence to show the accused had ridden the animal, this pointed to the fact that it could not be a bird but was actually a pony. Obviously, this avoids the issue. The issue is not whether the animal was ridden or not, but whether it was shot or not, for to ride a pony or a bird is of no offence at all. I believe counsel now sees his mistake.

Counsel contends that the iron shoes found on the animal decisively disqualify it from being a bird. I must inform counsel, however, that how an animal dresses is of no consequence to this court.

Counsel relied on the decision in *Re Chickadee*, where he contends that in similar circumstances the accused was acquitted. However, this is a horse of a different colour. A close reading of that case indicates that the animal in question there was not a small bird, but, in fact, a midget of a much larger species. Therefore, that case is inapplicable to our facts.

Counsel finally submits that the word "small" in the title Small Birds Act refers not to "Birds" but to "Act", making it The Small Act relating to Birds. With respect, counsel did not do his homework very well, for the Large Birds Act, R.S.O. 1960, c. 725 is just as small. If pressed, I need only refer to the Small Loans Act, R.S.O. 1960, c. 727 which is twice as large as the Large Birds Act.

It remains then to state my reason for judgment which, simply, is as follows: Different things may take on the same meaning for different purposes. For the purpose of the Small Birds Act, all two-legged, feather-covered animals are birds. This, of course, does not imply that only two-legged animals qualify, for the legislative intent is to make two legs merely the minimum requirement. The statute therefore contemplated multi-legged animals with feathers as well. Counsel submits that having regard to the purpose of the statute only small animals "naturally covered" with feathers could have been contemplated. However, had this been the intention of the legislature, I am certain that the phrase "naturally covered" would have been expressly inserted just as "Long" was inserted in the Longshoreman's Act.

Therefore, a horse with feathers on its back must be deemed for the purposes of this Act to be a bird, and a fortiori, a pony with feathers on its back is a small bird.

Counsel posed the following rhetorical question: If the pillow had been removed prior to the shooting, would the animal still be a bird? To this let me answer rhetorically: Is a bird any less of a bird without its feathers?

Appeal allowed.

Reported by: H. Pomerantz

S. Breslin

* * *

Points for Discussion

1. *Statutory Language*: What was the language at issue? What did each party want that language to mean? What meaning did the court adopt?

2. *Theories*: Which theory did the court (Blue, J. or "Blue jay") use?

3. *A Horse is a Horse of Course, of Course*: What did the court mean when it said, "We are not interested in whether the animal in question is a bird or not in fact, but whether it is one in law"?

4. *Do Your Homework*: This faux Canadian appellate case was written by a law professor to poke fun of legal reasoning. However, two authors failed to research its background before including a reference to the case in a footnote:

> To illustrate the bizarre results that can sometimes happen when courts consider such questions, see the Canadian case of *Regina v. Ojibwa*, 8 Criminal Law Quarterly, 137 (1965–66), (Op. Blue, J.), described in *United States v. Byrnes*, 644 F.2d 107, 112, n. 9 (2d Cir 1981). The Canadian court concluded that a pony saddled with a down pillow was a "bird" within the meaning of a statute defining the term as a "two legged animal covered with feathers." The court reasoned that the two legs were the statutory minimum, and that the feather covering need not be natural.

Michael J. Bean & Melanie J. Rowland, The Evolution of National Wildlife Law 5 n.5 (1997). Let's hope you do not make the same mistake.

* * *

2. Absurdity (The Golden Rule)

Absurdity is another reason judges will reject an interpretation based on the ordinary meaning of the language. Sometimes, the ordinary meaning is not what the legislature intended. This was the dissent's position in *Mayor of Lansing v. Michigan Public Service Commission*. When a statute would be absurd if implemented according to the ordinary meaning, can a judge refuse to follow that meaning? The answer to that question is sometimes yes, pursuant to *the absurdity doctrine* (with emphasis on the word "sometimes").

The absurdity doctrine was first adopted in this country in 1868. *See generally,* Linda D. Jellum, *But that is Absurd! Why Specific Absurdity Undermines Textualism,* 76 Brooklyn L. Rev. 917 (2011) (describing the doctrine's evolution). In *United States v. Kirby,* 74 U.S. (7 Wall.) 482 (1868), the Supreme Court dismissed an indictment charging members of the local sheriff's office with violating a statute that prohibited anyone from "knowingly and willfully obstruct[ing] or retard[ing] the passage of the mail, or of any driver or carrier." *Id.* at 483–84. The defendants had arrested a mail carrier who was wanted for murder while that mail carrier was delivering mail. Although the defendants had violated the clear terms of the statute, the Court dismissed the indictment. In doing so, the Court adopted the absurdity doctrine, explaining:

> All laws should receive a sensible construction. General terms should be so limited in their application as not to lead to injustice, oppression, or an absurd consequence. It will always, therefore, be presumed that the legislature intended exceptions to its language, which would avoid results of this character. The reason of the law in such cases should prevail over its letter.

Id. at 486–87. In support of its decision to reject the clear text, the Court referenced two early decisions from Europe, both of which had rejected the ordinary meaning of a statute. First, a medieval Italian court had refused to punish a surgeon "who opened the vein of a person that fell down in the street in a fit" for violating a law punishing anyone "who[] drew blood in the streets." *Id.* at 487. Second, an English court had refused to punish a prisoner who had escaped from a prison that was on fire under a statute prohibiting prison escapes. In these two cases, the courts deviated from the ordinary meaning of the statutes because application of the statute to the particular facts of each case led to a result not intended by the legislature. "[T]he absurdity doctrine therefore rests on the premise that if legislators had foreseen the problems raised by a specific statutory application, 'they could and would have revised the legislation to avoid such absurd results.'" Glen Staszewski, *Avoiding Absurdity*, 81 Ind. L.J. 1001, 1007 (2006) (quoting John F. Manning, *The Absurdity Doctrine*, 116 Harv. L. Rev. 2394 (2003)). Relying on the rationale in these prior cases, the Supreme Court in *Kirby* rejected the clear statutory text and adopted the absurdity doctrine. In all three cases, the courts' decisions to reject the clear text led to a result that seems just and fair.

In 1892, in its "most influential absurdity decision"—*Holy Trinity Church v. United States*, 143 U.S. 457 (1892)—the Supreme Court suggested that the rationale for absurdity was to avoid a result that was contrary to legislative intent. The statute at issue, the Alien Contract Labor Act, prohibited businesses from bringing anyone into the country "to perform labor or service of any kind." *Id.* at 458. The defendant contracted with an individual from England to immigrate to the United States to serve as a pastor in its church. In response and pursuant to the ordinary meaning of the Act, the federal government sued the church to recover a statutory penalty. The Supreme Court rejected the government's argument that "labor ... of any kind" covered pastoral services. Stating that "[i]t is a familiar rule, that a thing may be within the letter of the statute and yet not within the statute, because not within its spirit, nor within the intention of its makers," the Court found the statute to be absurd and looked to the legislative history of the Act. *Id.* at 459. According to the Court, the legislative history was relatively clear that the legislature intended the word labor to mean *manual* labor. Thus, the Court in *Holy Trinity* expanded *Kirby's* narrow absurdity doctrine such that the ordinary meaning of statutory text could henceforth be ignored whenever that meaning contradicted the intent of the legislature, as gleaned from nontextual sources.

The absurdity doctrine was commonly used up until the 1940s as a way to temper the sometimes harsh effects of the plain meaning canon in its literalist formulation. It was a useful doctrine in the early years of textualism, the late 1800s and early 1900s. In 1940, *United States v. American Trucking Ass'ns, Inc.*, 310 U.S. 534 (1940), launched purposivism back into the forefront. With the fall of textualism and the rise of purposivism, the absurdity exception proved less necessary, because purposivists (and intentionalists) do not need a reason, such as absurdity and ambiguity, to examine extra-textual sources of meaning. Thus, the absurdity doctrine faded briefly into obscurity.

More recently, however, the absurdity doctrine has made a comeback. In 1986, Justice Scalia was appointed to the Supreme Court. Part of his mission was to return the Court to a text-first analysis. With his more text-focused approach, the absurdity doctrine has been revived. Yet, the revival has been limited. In recent years, the Supreme Court has explicitly relied on the absurdity doctrine only six times.* Recall my emphasis on the word "sometimes" earlier.

Moreover, the Court has suggested that the doctrine is one of last resort, "rarely invoke[d] ... to override unambiguous legislation." *Barnhart v. Sigmon Coal Co.*, 534 U.S. 438, 441 (2002). As Justice Kennedy noted, "the potential of this doctrine to allow judges to substitute their personal predilections for the will of the Congress is so self-evident from the case which spawned it (*Holy Trinity Church*) as to require no further discussion of its susceptibility to abuse." *Public Citizen v. DOJ*, 491 U.S. 440, 474 (1989) (Kennedy, J., concurring). While the Justices of the Supreme Court turn to the doctrine increasingly rarely, to date, they have never rejected the doctrine outright. Indeed, in rejecting the application of the doctrine in particular cases, the Justices have reaffirmed the doctrine's continued vitality. Furthermore, the doctrine, despite its flaws, is alive and well in the lower federal and state courts. *See, e.g., Robbins v. Chronister*, 402 F.3d 1047 (10th Cir. 2005), *rev'd* 435 F.3d 1238 (10th Cir. 2006).

One flaw is that, absurdity, like ambiguity, is not consistently defined in the jurisprudence. For example, in *Holy Trinity*, the Supreme Court never explicitly defined absurdity. Instead, the Court merely suggested that a meaning that conflicts with congressional intent would be absurd. In another case, the Court equated absurd with "odd" and "likely unconstitutional." *Green v. Bock Laundry Machine Co.*, 490 U.S. 504, 509 (1989). More recently, in *King v. Burwell*, Justice Scalia defined an absurd result as "a consequence 'so monstrous, that all mankind would without hesitation, unite in rejecting the application.'" 135 S. Ct. 2480, 2497 (2015) (Scalia, J., dissenting) (quoting *Sturges v. Crowninshield*, 4 Wheat. 122, 203 (1819)). And in *Robbins v. Chronister*, 402 F.3d 1047 (10th Cir. 2005), *rev'd* 435 F.3d 1238 (10th Cir. 2006), the majority adopted *Holy Trinity's* broad definition of absurdity — contrary to congressional intent — while the dissent used a narrower definition — shocking to one's conscience.

---

* *Burwell v. Hobby Lobby Stores, Inc.*, 134 S. Ct. 2751, 2773 (2014) (invoking doctrine as an additional justification for its holding that for-profit corporations engage in the exercise of religion within the meaning of the Religious Freedom Restoration Act); *Clinton v. City of New York*, 524 U.S. 417, 428–29 (1998) (invoking doctrine to expand the meaning of "individuals" to include corporations as those who could seek expedited review under Line Item Veto Act); *United States v. X-Citement Video, Inc.*, 513 U.S. 64, 69 (1994) (holding it would be absurd to apply the term "knowingly" only to relevant verbs in criminal statute and not to elements of the crime concerning minor age of participant and sexually explicit nature of material); *Burns v. United States*, 501 U.S. 129, 135–37 (1991) (relying on absurdity to hold that district courts may not depart upward from sentencing range established by Sentencing Guidelines without first notifying parties of court's intent to depart); *Pub. Citizen v. U.S. Dep't of Justice*, 491 U.S. 440, 451, 454–55 (1989) (relying on absurdity, in part, to narrowly interpret "advisory committee" in the Federal Advisory Committee Act); *Green v. Bock Laundry Mach. Co.*, 490 U.S. 504, 509–11 (1989) (some justices reasoned that it would be absurd not to apply Federal Rule of Evidence 609(a)(1) to civil as well as criminal defendants). *See also, Utility Air Regulatory Group v. EPA*, 134 S. Ct. 2427, 2451 (2014) (Breyer, J., dissenting) (accusing the majority of using absurdity to reject an interpretation required by the Clean Air Act's text).

Which case has a more accurate definition of absurdity? Perhaps none. The majority's definition of absurdity in *Green* was so broad that it would essentially open the door for consideration of extra-textual evidence in almost every case. This broad definition might be appealing to non-textualist judges willing to look to extra-textual sources relatively readily, but less appealing to other judges. Yet Justice Scalia's definition of absurdity from *King* is little improved. It sets a standard that will rarely, if ever, be met. The correct definition of absurdity must lie between these two extremes. Just where is not clear, and the jurisprudence is of little help. Most commonly, instead of defining absurdity, judges simply list other cases that have found absurdity, thereby suggesting that the instant case is like or unlike those in the list.

In the cases below, identify the majority and dissent's definition of absurdity. Does each definition sets a high threshold (meaning hard to meet) or low threshold (meaning easy to meet)? Finally, if a judge finds absurdity, how does that judge then resolve the statute's meaning given that the ordinary meaning cannot control? This case and the case that follow address these issues.

Public Citizen v. Department Of Justice

Supreme Court of the United States
491 U.S. 440 (1989)

♦ Justice Brennen delivered the opinion of the Court [in which White, Marshall, Blackmun, and Stevens, JJ., joined. Justice Scalia took no part in the consideration or decision of the cases.]

[The issue for the Court was whether the American Bar Association's (ABA) Standing Committee on Federal Judiciary, which provides advice regarding judicial nominees to the Department of Justice and, thus, the president, is covered under the Federal Advisory Committee Act (FACA).* FACA applies to any "advisory committee" "utilized" by the president and requires such a committee to file a charter; afford notice

---

* Editor's footnote: The relevant sections of FACA provided:
Advisory Committee Procedures
Sec. 10(a)(1): Each Advisory Committee meeting shall be open to the public.....
Definitions
Sec. 3: For Purposes of this Act:
(2) The term "advisory committee" means any committee, board, commission, council, conference, panel, task force, or other similar group, ... which is—
(B) established or utilized by the President, or
(C) Established or utilized by one or more agencies
In the interest of obtaining advice or recommendations for the President or one or more agencies.... except that such term excludes (i) the Advisory Commission on Intergovernmental Relations, (ii) the Commission on Government Procurement, and (iii) any committee which is composed wholly of full-time officers of employees of the Federal Government.

of its meetings; open those meetings to the public; and make its minutes, records, and reports available to the public.].

... There is no doubt that the Executive makes use of the ABA Committee, and thus "utilizes" it in one common sense of the term. As the District Court recognized, however, "reliance on the plain language of FACA alone is not entirely satisfactory." "Utilize" is a woolly verb, its contours left undefined by the statute itself. Read unqualifiedly, it would extend FACA's requirements to any group of two or more persons, or at least any formal organization, from which the President or an Executive agency seeks advice. We are convinced that Congress did not intend that result....

FACA was enacted to cure specific ills, above all the wasteful expenditure of public funds for worthless committee meetings and biased proposals; although its reach is extensive, we cannot believe that it was intended to cover every formal and informal consultation between the President or an Executive agency and a group rendering advice.[9] As we said in *Church of the Holy Trinity v. United States*, 143 U.S. 457, 459 (1892): "[F]requently words of general meaning are used in a statute, words broad enough to include an act in question, and yet a consideration of the whole legislation, or of the circumstances surrounding its enactment, or of the absurd results which follow from giving such broad meaning to the words, makes it unreasonable to believe that the legislator intended to include the particular act."

Where the literal reading of a statutory term would "compel an odd result," *Green v. Bock Laundry Machine Co.*, 490 U.S. 504, 509 (1989), we must search for other evidence of congressional intent to lend the term its proper scope.... [The majority finds this evidence in the circumstances leading to enactment, the statutory purpose, and in the legislative history].

Weighing the deliberately inclusive statutory language against other evidence of congressional intent, it seems to us a close question whether FACA should be construed to apply to the ABA Committee, although on the whole we are fairly confident it should not....

---

9. ... Justice Kennedy refuses to consult FACA's legislative history—which he later denounces, with surprising hyperbole, as "unauthoritative materials," although countless opinions of this Court, including many written by the concurring Justices, have rested on just such materials—because this result would not, in his estimation, be "absurd." Although this Court has never adopted so strict a standard for reviewing committee reports, floor debates, and other nonstatutory indications of congressional intent, *and we explicitly reject that standard today*, even if "absurdity" were the test, one would think it was met here. The idea that Members of Congress would vote for a bill subjecting their own political parties to bureaucratic intrusion and public oversight when a President or Cabinet officer consults with party committees concerning political appointments is outlandish. Nor does it strike us as in any way "unhealthy" or undemocratic to use all available materials in ascertaining the intent of our elected representatives, rather than read their enactments as requiring what may seem a disturbingly unlikely result, provided only that the result is not "absurd." Indeed, the sounder and more democratic course, the course that strives for allegiance to Congress' desires in all cases, not just those where Congress' statutory directive is plainly sensible or borders on the lunatic, is the traditional approach we reaffirm today.

◆ JUSTICE KENNEDY filed an opinion concurring in the judgment [in which REHN-QUIST, C.J., and O'CONNOR, J., joined].

... [T]his suit presents [an issue regarding] separation of powers. The [issue] concerns the rules this Court must follow in interpreting a statute passed by Congress and signed by the President. On this subject, I cannot join the Court's conclusion that the Federal Advisory Committee Act (FACA) does not cover the activities of the American Bar Association's Standing Committee on Federal Judiciary in advising the Department of Justice regarding potential nominees for federal judgeships. The result seems sensible in the abstract; but I cannot accept the method by which the Court arrives at its interpretation of FACA, which does not accord proper respect to the finality and binding effect of legislative enactments....

The statutory question in this suit is simple enough to formulate. FACA applies to "any committee" that is "established or utilized" by the President or one or more agencies, and which furnishes "advice or recommendations" to the President or one or more agencies. All concede that the ABA Committee furnishes advice and recommendations to the Department of Justice and through it to the President. The only question we face, therefore, is whether the ABA Committee is "utilized" by the Department of Justice or the President. *language at issue*

There is a ready starting point, which ought to serve also as a sufficient stopping point, for this kind of analysis: the plain language of the statute. Yet the Court is unwilling to rest on this foundation, for several reasons. One is an evident unwillingness to define the application of the statute in terms of the ordinary meaning of its language. We are told that "utilize" is "a woolly verb," and therefore we cannot be content to rely on what is described, with varying levels of animus, as a "literal reading," a "literalistic reading," and "a dictionary reading" of this word. We also are told in no uncertain terms that we cannot rely on (what I happen to regard as a more accurate description) "a straightforward reading of 'utilize.'" Reluctance to working with the basic meaning of words in a normal manner undermines the legal process. These cases demonstrate that reluctance of this sort leads instead to woolly judicial construction that mars the plain face of legislative enactments.

The Court concedes that the Executive Branch "utilizes" the ABA Committee in the common sense of that word.... This should end the matter. The Court nevertheless goes through several more steps to conclude that, although "it seems to us a close question," Congress did not intend that FACA would apply to the ABA Committee.

Although I believe the Court's result is quite sensible, I cannot go along with the unhealthy process of amending the statute by judicial interpretation. Where the language of a statute is clear in its application, the normal rule is that we are bound by it. There is, of course, a legitimate exception to this rule, which the Court invokes, and with which I have no quarrel. Where the plain language of the statute would lead to "patently absurd consequences," that "Congress could not *possibly* have intended," we need not apply the language in such a fashion. When used in a proper manner, this narrow exception to our normal rule of statutory construction does not intrude upon the lawmaking powers of Congress, but rather demonstrates a respect for the coequal Legislative Branch, which we assume would not act in an absurd way.

This exception remains a legitimate tool of the Judiciary, however, only as long as the Court acts with self-discipline by limiting the exception to situations where the result of applying the plain language would be, in a genuine sense, absurd, where it is quite impossible that Congress could have intended the result and where the alleged absurdity is so clear as to be obvious to most anyone. . . .

A few examples of true absurdity are given in the *Holy Trinity* decision cited by the Court, such as where a sheriff was prosecuted for obstructing the mails even though he was executing a warrant to arrest the mail carrier for murder, or where a medieval law against drawing blood in the streets was to be applied against a physician who came to the aid of a man who had fallen down in a fit. In today's opinion, however, the Court disregards the plain language of the statute not because its application would be patently absurd, but rather because, on the basis of its view of the legislative history, the Court is "fairly confident" that "FACA should [not] be construed to apply to the ABA Committee." I believe the Court's loose invocation of the "absurd result" canon of statutory construction creates too great a risk that the Court is exercising its own "WILL instead of JUDGMENT," with the consequence of "substituti[ng] [its own] pleasure to that of the legislative body." The Federalist No. 78, p. 469 (C. Rossiter ed. 1961) (A. Hamilton).

The Court makes only a passing effort to show that it would be absurd to apply the term "utilize" to the ABA Committee according to its commonsense meaning. . . .

Although I disagree with the Court's conclusion that FACA does not cover the Justice Department's use of the ABA Committee, I concur in the judgment of the Court because, in my view, the application of FACA in this context would be a plain violation of the Appointments Clause of the Constitution [because application of FACA would interfere with the President's exclusive responsibility to select and nominate federal judges]. . . .

* * *

Points for Discussion

1. *Statutory Language*: Look at the editor's footnote. There are two steps to identifying the relevant language in this case. First, the operative section of the Act defines the obligations of an "advisory committee." Then, the definitions section defines "advisory committee." Finally, we come to the language the Court describes in the opinion. What was that language? Did the parties disagree about the meaning of that language or about the boundaries of that language? In other words, did the parties argue that language was ambiguous or did they argue something else?

2. *Theories*: Which theory did the Justice Brennen use? Justice Kennedy? Did Justice Kennedy disagree with the majority's approach to interpreting statutes, the majority's finding of absurdity, the majority's definition of absurdity, or some combination of these three?

3. *Absurdity*: Note that when judges apply the absurdity doctrine, they look not to whether an interpretation is absurd in the abstract, but whether the statute as interpreted produces an absurd outcome in the particular case or in future cases. How did Justice Brennen define absurdity? Justice Kennedy? Which definition provides a lower threshold, or easier to meet standard? In footnote nine, Justice Brennen explicitly rejected Justice Kennedy's strict absurdity standard and Justice Kennedy's refusal to consider legislative history, in favor of "the traditional approach." What did Justice Brennen mean?

4. *Woolly Verbs & Woolly Judicial Constructions*: What did Justice Brennen mean when he said "[u]tilize is a woolly verb"? Is "utilize" ambiguous, or is it broad and general? How did Justice Kennedy respond to that characterization?

5. *Resolving Absurdity*: How did Justice Brennen resolve the absurdity? How did Justice Kennedy resolve it? The constitutional avoidance doctrine is a doctrine that we will cover shortly. That doctrine directs judges to avoid an interpretation that will raise constitutional questions when another, reasonable interpretation is possible. Justice Kennedy relied on this canon.

6. *Concurrence*: If Justices Brennen and Kennedy ultimately reached the same outcome, why did Justice Kennedy write separately? What was Justice Brennen's response to that reason, which can be found in footnote 9?

7. *The Absurdity of the Absurdity Doctrine*: The absurdity doctrine allows judges to avoid the results of the plain meaning canon in those cases where it would be absurd to believe the legislature intended the statute to apply as written. Yet, if textualists eschew looking for legislative intent, does not their use of this exception seem odd? While Justice Kennedy might well have preferred to have eliminated this doctrine altogether, he faced an insurmountable hurdle given the breadth of prior precedent relying on it. Despite that fact, he tried to limit the doctrine's reach by defining absurdity very narrowly. Justice Scalia's dissent in *King v. Burwell* similarly tries to rein in this doctrine.

* * *

Once absurdity is found, how should it be resolved? In the next case, notice that Justice Scalia looks at legislative history. What exactly is he looking for? Why is he willing to examine legislative history in this situation but not in others?

Green v. Bock Laundry Machine Co.

Supreme Court of the United States
490 U.S. 504 (1989)

[While in custody at a county prison, petitioner Paul Green obtained work-release employment at a car wash. On his sixth day at work, Green reached inside a large dryer to try to stop it. A heavy rotating drum caught and tore off his right arm. Green brought this product liability action against respondent Bock Laundry Co. (Bock), manufacturer of the machine. At trial Green testified that he had been instructed inadequately concerning the machine's operation and dangerous character. Pursuant to Federal Rule of Evidence 609(a), the trial court admitted evidence of Green's prior felonies for impeachment. At that time, Federal Rule of Evidence 609(a) provided:

> *General Rule.* For the purpose of attacking the credibility of a witness, evidence that the witness has been convicted of a crime shall be admitted ... only if ... the court determines that the probative value of admitting this evidence outweighs its prejudicial effect to the defendant....

Bock Laundry impeached Green's testimony by eliciting admissions that he had been convicted of conspiracy to commit burglary and burglary, both felonies. The jury returned a verdict for Bock Laundry, likely because of Green's criminal history rather than his fault. On appeal Green argued that the trial court should have excluded the impeaching evidence. The Court of Appeals disagreed and affirmed.

On appeal to the Supreme Court, the majority concluded that the language was ambiguous, examined the legislative history, and determined that "the defendant" in the rule should be interpreted to mean "the *criminal* defendant." Thus, the majority held that rule 609(a) does not apply in civil litigation. As such, the decision was affirmed and Green received no compensation. The dissent would have interpreted "the defendant" to mean "any party."].

♦ [Both the majority opinion of Justice Stevens, in which Rehnquist, C.J., and White, O'Connor, and Kennedy, JJ., joined, and the dissenting opinion of Justice Blackmun, with whom Brennen and Marshall, JJ., join, have been omitted.]

♦ Justice Scalia, concurring in the judgment.

We are confronted here with a statute which, if interpreted literally, produces an absurd, and perhaps unconstitutional, result. Our task is to give some alternative meaning to the word "defendant" in Federal Rule of Evidence 609(a)(1) that avoids this consequence....

I think it entirely appropriate to consult all public materials, including the background of Rule 609(a)(1) and the legislative history of its adoption, to verify that what seems to us an unthinkable disposition (civil defendants but not civil plaintiffs receive the benefit of weighing prejudice) was indeed unthought of, and thus to justify a departure from the ordinary meaning of the word "defendant" in the Rule. For that purpose, however, it would suffice to observe that counsel have not provided, nor have we discovered, a shred of evidence that anyone has ever proposed or assumed such a bizarre disposition. The Court's opinion, however, goes well beyond this. Approximately four-fifths of its substantive analysis is devoted to examining the evolution of Federal Rule of Evidence 609 ... all with the evident purpose, not merely of confirming that the word "defendant" cannot have been meant literally, but of determining what, precisely, the Rule does mean.

I find no reason to believe that any more than a handful of the Members of Congress who enacted Rule 609 were aware of its interesting evolution ... ; or that any more than a handful of them (if any) voted, with respect to their understanding of the word "defendant" ... on the basis of the referenced statements in the Subcommittee, Committee, or Conference Committee Reports, or floor debates—statements so marginally relevant, to such minute details, in such relatively inconsequential legislation. The meaning of terms on the statute books ought to be determined, not on the basis of which meaning can be shown to have been understood by a larger handful of the Members of Congress; but rather on the basis of which meaning is (1) most in accord with context and ordinary usage, and thus most likely to have been understood by the *whole* Congress which voted on the words of the statute (not to mention the citizens subject to it), and (2) most compatible with the surrounding body of law into which the provision must be integrated — a compatibility which, by a benign fiction, we assume Congress always has in mind. I would not permit any of the historical and legislative material discussed by the Court, or all of it combined, to lead me to a result different from the one that these factors suggest.

I would analyze this case, in brief, as follows:

(1) The word "defendant" in Rule 609(a)(1) cannot rationally (or perhaps even constitutionally) mean to provide the benefit of prejudice-weighing to civil defendants and not civil plaintiffs. Since petitioner has not produced, and we have not ourselves discovered, even a snippet of support for this absurd result, we may confidently assume that the word was not used (as it normally would be) to refer to all defendants and only all defendants.

(2) The available alternatives are to interpret "defendant" to mean (a) "civil plaintiff, civil defendant, prosecutor, and criminal defendant," (b) "civil plaintiff and defendant and criminal defendant," or (c) "criminal defendant." Quite obviously, the last does least violence to the text. It adds a qualification that the word "defendant" does not contain but, unlike the others, does not give the word a meaning ("plaintiff" or "prosecutor") it simply will not bear. The qualification it adds, moreover, is one that could understandably have been omitted by inadvertence — and sometimes is omitted in normal conversation ("I believe strongly in defendants' rights"). Finally, this last interpretation is consistent with the policy of the law in general and the Rules of Evidence in particular of providing special protection to defendants in criminal cases....

I am frankly not sure that, despite its lengthy discussion of ideological evolution and legislative history, the Court's reasons for both aspects of its decision are much different from mine. I respectfully decline to join that discussion, however, because it is natural for the bar to believe that the juridical importance of such material matches its prominence in our opinions — thus producing a legal culture in which, when counsel arguing before us assert that "Congress has said" something, they now frequently mean, by "Congress," a committee report; and in which it was not beyond the pale for a recent brief to say the following: "Unfortunately, the legislative debates are not helpful. Thus, we turn to the other guidepost in this difficult area, statutory language." ...

* * *

Points for Discussion

1. *Statutory Language*: What was the language at issue? What did each party want that language to mean? What meaning did the Justice Scalia adopt and why?

2. *Theories*: Which theory did Justice Scalia use?

3. *Absurdity*: How did Justice Scalia define absurdity? Is this an easy definition to meet? How does this definition differ from Justices Brennen and Kennedy's definitions in the prior case (*Public Citizen v. DOJ*)?

4. *Legislative History*: Generally, Justice Scalia rejects legislative history as a source for discerning statutory meaning, but in this case, he conceded its relevance. Why was he willing to use legislative history in this case? Is his use of legislative history here consistent with his strong criticisms of using legislative history more generally?

5. *Resolving Absurdity*: How does Justice Scalia resolve the absurdity? In other words, because the word "defendant" cannot have its ordinary meaning, what meaning should it have and why?

6. *Statutory Guidepost-Legislative History*: Why, if Scalia agreed with the majority, did he concur? Justice Scalia was appointed to the Supreme Court in 1986. One of his goals was to rid the bar of its reliance on legislative history and non-textualist elements. Notice his final, descriptive paragraph.

* * *

Are all cases of absurdity equally in need of judicial correction? The excerpt below identifies two types of absurdity, general and specific, and explains why judges should not apply statutory text literally in cases of specific absurdity. Further, the author argues that absurdity undermines textualism. Do you agree? Keep in mind that this is just one scholar's criticism of this doctrine and that the specific-general distinction is not one that judges are yet making.

But That Is Absurd!
Why Specific Absurdity Undermines Textualism

Linda D. Jellum

76 Brooklyn L. Rev. 917 (2011)*

[I] TYPES OF ABSURDITY

[There are two types of absurdity.] Specific absurdity refers to a statute that is absurd *only* in the particular situation. General absurdity refers to a statute that is absurd *regardless* of the particular situation. [Statutes that are specifically absurd are those statutes that are absurd as applied to the facts of a particular case, but not absurd as applied generally. For example, a statute that penalizes individuals from escaping from prison is absurd as applied to an individual who escaped from a prison that was on fire, but

---

* Used with permission.

is not absurd in general. In contrast, statutes that are generally absurd are those statutes that are patently absurd as written and, thus, as applied generally, to a group of individuals. For example, a statute that creates a waiting period rather than a deadline for a litigant to file an appeal is absurd in all cases, not just one isolated case.]

To be sure, the difference between general and specific absurdity is not bright lined. One could ask: At what point do the specific facts become relevant to an absurdity finding? It is easy in some cases to see that the absurdity is apparent only when the facts of the case are considered. For instance, a statute that prohibits individuals from interfering with the delivery of mail only becomes absurd when it is applied to a sheriff arresting a mail carrier wanted for murder. A statute that prohibits anyone from drawing blood in the street only becomes absurd when applied to a doctor offering medical treatment. A statute that prohibits anyone from owning a fur-bearing animal only becomes absurd when applied to a person who rescued a squirrel that would otherwise die. A statute that prohibits prisoners from escaping from prison only becomes absurd when applied to a prisoner who escaped from a prison that was on fire. In each of these cases, the applicable statutes are perfectly logical in the abstract, but when the statute is applied to the specific facts of the case before the court, the "results [are] 'so gross as to shock the general moral or common sense.'" In other words, as applied to the specific situation before the court, a situation unlikely to repeat itself, the statute is absurd. In these cases, the absurdity is downright shocking.

In contrast, statutes that are generally absurd are absurd not because they are shocking, but because they are simply contrary to congressional intent. Thus, a statute that prohibits the importation of brain toilers is not shocking, just unintended. A statute that imposes a waiting period for filing an appeal rather than a deadline is not shocking, just sloppy. A statute that purports to treat civil defendants and civil plaintiffs differently is not shocking, just poorly considered.

Another important distinction between general and specific absurdity is that general absurdity is often readily apparent from the text of the statute itself. The specific facts of the case will play little, if any, role. While the facts of the case may bring the absurdity to light—a cap on attorney's fees for prisoner-filed litigation does not seem absurd until that cap limits recovery of fees to $1.50—the facts are not essential to either the absurdity finding or a court's interpretation. In other words, the [Prison Litigation Reform Act] was not absurd because it limited fees to $1.50, rather the statute was absurd because it limited fees in all cases in which the person filing a claim was a prisoner, regardless of whether the claim related to prison-condition litigation. Also, a statute that prohibits the importation of anyone performing labor or service of any kind is absurd, if at all, only when applied to all brain toilers, not just pastors. A statute that allows a judge to weigh the probative versus prejudicial effect of a witness's prior conviction is absurd when applied to all civil plaintiffs, not just a plaintiff who has lost his arm. A statute that imposes a waiting period for filing an appeal rather than a time limit in which to file is absurd in all cases. In each of these examples, the applicable statute is illogical as written *and* as generally applied. It is not absurd as applied to just the specific individual before the court. You might think of the difference in this way: when a statute is generally absurd, Congress did not intend to draft the statute as written and likely, if given a chance, would redraft. The facts of the case merely bring this point to light. In contrast, when a statute is specifically absurd, Congress intended to draft the statute as written and likely, if given a chance, would not redraft, other than to except the isolated situation before the court. In short, in one case, Congress did its job poorly, while in the other case, Congress did its job well.

With statutes that are generally absurd, the absurdity is often caused by drafting error or the hubbub of the legislative process. For this reason, cases of general absurdity are rarer than cases of specific absurdity precisely because it is unusual for Congress to get it so wrong. Importantly, even when Congress does err in its drafting, judges have other doctrines they can rely on to avoid the absurd result. For example, a judge could apply the constitutional avoidance doctrine, as the majority should have done in *Green* [*v. Bock Laundry Machine Co.*], or could apply the scrivener's error exception, as the majority should have done in *Amalgamated Transit* [the case addressing a statute that had a seven day waiting period rather than a deadline]. Like the absurdity doctrine, both of these doctrines allow textualists to avoid the ordinary meaning of a clear statute.

... [G]eneral absurdity is often apparent and resolvable with intrinsic sources, including the textual context. Illustratively, when I misspeak, my listener often knows what I meant from the rest of the words. Similarly, when a statute provides that litigants have a seven day waiting period to appeal, the absurdity and fix are both readily apparent from the textual context. Because general absurdity can be resolved using intrinsic sources, turning to absurdity to avoid clear language in cases of general absurdity does not undermine textualism, at least not to the same extent that specific absurdity does.

In contrast, specific absurdity is neither facially apparent nor resolvable with intrinsic sources. Again illustratively, when I speak more broadly or narrowly than I intended, my listener is unlikely to know my boundaries, and my other words are less likely to make those boundaries clear. Similarly, when a statute provides that prisoners should not escape from prison, there is no apparent absurdity. Yet when the statute is applied to a specific case in which a prisoner escaped to save his life, the boundaries become uncertain, and the application clearly absurd. Thus, specific absurdity comes to light only when the facts of a specific case come into play. Resolving specific absurdity often requires a judge to determine whether excepting the situation before the court will further the purpose of the statute or otherwise be consistent with the legislature's intent. For example, a statute that prohibits individuals from drawing blood in the streets is not absurd until applied to a doctor offering medical care. But in deciding whether to except the doctor from the statute's reach, a judge should consider the purpose of the statute. If the purpose of the statute was to prohibit individuals from fighting in the streets, then excepting the doctor would be consistent with that purpose. If the purpose of the statute was to protect public health by keeping blood—which is unsanitary—off the street, then excepting the doctor would be inconsistent with that purpose. Hence, specific absurdity often must be resolved through nontextual sources such as legislative history and unexpressed purpose. Because specific absurdity requires judges to resort to nontextual sources to determine statutory meaning, specific absurdity undermines textualism.

[II] WHY SPECIFIC ABSURDITY UNDERMINES TEXTUALISM

Assuming this analysis to be correct, it results in an oddity: textualist judges can intervene only when judicial intervention is less necessary. Let me explain. When a statute is specifically absurd, Congress is unlikely to amend that statute to correct the absurdity because it is unlikely to recur. Although the absurdity did manifest in one isolated case, the exact circumstances are unlikely to ever occur again; hence, Congress has little incentive to act. Moreover, Congress has a good reason not to act; the statute as generally applied does exactly what Congress intended the statute to do. Why mess with a perfectly good statute? No statutory language can ever be perfect. Thus, there will always be cases that may fit within the ordinary meaning of the text of a statute and to which the statute should not apply. Consequently, it is precisely in these cases that a court should step in and correct the resulting injustice even though stepping in to resolve cases of specific absurdity violates textualist principles....

In contrast, when a statute is generally absurd, Congress is more likely to amend that statute to correct the absurdity because it is almost certain to recur. The absurdity will manifest in every case, or at least in a large number of cases, because Congress crafted a statute it never intended to draft. The statute, as generally applied, does not do what Congress intended the statute to do. The language is not just imperfect or imprecise, it is wrong; thus, Congress has a good reason to act. Hence, it is less important that a court intervene in cases of general absurdity because Congress has more incentive to fix such a statute.... [W]hen Congress crafts a generally absurd statute, Congress can and does correct its mistake.

In light of the distinction between specific and general absurdity, textualists should rethink the absurdity safety valve. As demonstrated, they should be especially loath to apply the doctrine in cases of specific, as opposed to general, absurdity because specific absurdity is neither apparent nor resolvable from the text. Yet it is precisely in cases of specific absurdity that judicial intervention is needed most. Textualists neither recognize this distinction, nor appreciate how it undermines textualism's underpinnings.

* * *

Points for Discussion

1. *Type of Absurdity*: What type of absurdity was at issue in *Public Citizen v. Department of Justice*? What about in *Green v. Bock Laundry Machine, Co.*? Does this difference help explain the outcomes in anyway? Do you agree with the author that the absurdity doctrine would be more necessary in *Public Citizen* than in *Bock Laundry*?

Problem 6A

You are a prosecutor for the East Carolina District Attorney's office. The following case has just crossed your desk. Analyze whether you will bring child abandonment charges against Mr. Wells for abandoning any of his nine children. In doing so, determine whether the statute is ambiguous or absurd.

Claiming he could no longer care for them, Lee Wells dropped off his nine children at the emergency room in East Carolina University Medical Center Wednesday night at 8 p.m. His wife, and the mother of the nine kids, died from a brain aneurysm seventeen months earlier, just days after delivering the youngest child. The oldest child was fifteen, the youngest was seventeen months. When he dropped the children off, Mr. Wells said, "I was with her for seventeen years, and then she was gone. What was I going to do with nine kids? We raised them together. I don't think I can do it alone. I can't take care of them."

Wells said he was overwhelmed by his family responsibilities and had to quit his job. He said he couldn't pay the rent or utilities. "I was able to get the kids to a safe place before they were homeless," he said. He handed the nurse the children's birth certificates and said he was there to surrender his kids. "I hope they know I love them," he said. "I hope their future is better without me around them."

Three years ago, Wells and his wife were cited for child neglect, according to police records.

Materials for Problem 6A

East Carolina Rev. Stat. § 157.010:

A BILL FOR AN ACT relating to children; to prohibit prosecution for leaving a child at a hospital; and to provide a duty for the hospital.

Be it enacted by the people of the State of East Carolina,

Section 1. Findings & Purpose: The legislature finds that many parents of newborns and infant children are overwhelmed with the responsibilities of parenting children and have limited financial and social means to care for these children. For these reasons, some parents choose to abandon their children in unsafe ways. The purpose of this act is to protect the children of this state by allowing parents to give up their children in safe ways.

Section 2: No person shall be prosecuted for abandonment based solely upon the act of leaving a child or children in the custody of an employee on duty at a hospital licensed by the State of East Carolina. The hospital shall promptly contact appropriate authorities to take custody of the child.

Governor's signing statement:

I am delighted to sign this bill entitled "East Carolina's Save Haven Law." This Act will protect newborns, infants, and toddlers from the danger of unsafe abandonment. While it's important to recognize the potential trauma abandonment can cause for children of any age, infants and newborns are at particular risk. This bill is designed to encourage parents to act promptly and safely in choosing to give up their children.

Problem Questions

1. What is the language at issue?

2. According to Wells, what does that language mean?

3. According to the State, what does that language mean?

4. Is the language absurd, ambiguous, or both?

5. Which side should argue that the language is not ambiguous/absurd?

6. If you represent Wells, what definition of ambiguity/absurdity would you use and why?

7. If you represent the State, what definition of ambiguity/absurdity would you use and why?

8. If you were the judge deciding the case, how would you rule and why?

* * *

3. Scrivener's Error

A third reason judges reject the ordinary meaning of the text is because the statute contains an obvious scrivener's error, or drafting mistake. The *scrivener's error exception* to the plain meaning rule permits judges to correct obvious clerical or typographical errors. For example, in *U.S. National Bank of Oregon v. Independent Insurance Agents of America, Inc.*, 508 U.S. 439, 462 (1993), the Court corrected punctuation that had been misplaced in a statute. Similarly, in *United States v. Coatoam*, 245 F.3d 553, 557 (6th Cir. 2001), the Sixth Circuit corrected a cross-reference to the wrong subsection of an act. And in *United States v. Scheer*, 729 F.2d 164 (2nd Cir. 1984), the Second Circuit changed the word "request" in a statute to "receipt" where the statute had erroneously provided that a certificate be furnished "upon *request* of the ... request." *Id.* at 169. The scrivener's error doctrine is a subset of general absurdity; Congress made a simple mistake, and so the court fixes it.

The scrivener's error exception is a narrow one and is not used simply because the court believes an error might have been made. Rather, "[i]t is beyond [a court's] province to rescue Congress from its drafting errors, and to provide for what we might think ... is the preferred result." *United States v. Granderson*, 511 U.S. 39, 68 (1994). In the case below, why is the dissent so convinced that Congress made a drafting error while the majority is equally unwilling to correct that perceived error?

United States v. Locke

Supreme Court of the United States
471 U.S. 84 (1985)

♦ Justice Marshall [in which Burger, CJ., and White, Blackmun, and Rehnquist, JJ., concur].

[The Federal Land Policy and Management Act of 1976 (FLPMA) establishes a recording system to rid federal lands of mining claims that have become stale. Section

314(a) requires that those extracting and selling minerals to record "prior to December 31" of every year a notice of their intention to hold their claim. The statute further provides that failure to comply with this requirement "shall be deemed conclusively to constitute an abandonment" of the claim. Appellees failed to meet the annual filing requirement,[7] because they filed on December 31.]

... Before the District Court, appellees asserted that the § 314(a) requirement of a filing "prior to December 31 of each year" should be construed to require a filing "on or before December 31." Thus, appellees argued, their December 31 filing had in fact complied with the statute, and the BLM had acted ultra vires in voiding their claims.... It is clear to us that the plain language of the statute simply cannot sustain the gloss appellees would put on it.... While we will not allow a literal reading of a statute to produce a result "demonstrably at odds with the intentions of its drafters," with respect to filing deadlines a literal reading of Congress' words is generally the only proper reading of those words. To attempt to decide whether some date other than the one set out in the statute is the date actually "intended" by Congress is to set sail on an aimless journey, for the purpose of a filing deadline would be just as well served by nearly any date a court might choose as by the date Congress has in fact set out in the statute. "Actual purpose is sometimes unknown," and such is the case with filing deadlines; as might be expected, nothing in the legislative history suggests why Congress chose December 30 over December 31, or over September 1 ..., as the last day on which the required filings could be made. But "[d]eadlines are inherently arbitrary," while fixed dates "are often essential to accomplish necessary results." Faced with the inherent arbitrariness of filing deadlines, we must, at least in a civil case, apply by its terms the date fixed by the statute....

In so saying, we are not insensitive to the problems posed by congressional reliance on the words "prior to December 31." But the fact that Congress might have acted with greater clarity or foresight does not give courts a *carte blanche* to redraft statutes in an effort to achieve that which Congress is perceived to have failed to do. "There is a basic difference between filling a gap left by Congress' silence and rewriting rules that Congress has affirmatively and specifically enacted." Nor is the Judiciary licensed to attempt to soften the clear import of Congress' chosen words whenever a court believes those words lead to a harsh result. On the contrary, deference to the supremacy of the Legislature, as well as recognition that Congressmen typically vote on the language of a bill, generally requires us to assume that "the legislative purpose is expressed by the ordinary meaning of the words used." "Going behind the plain language of a statute in search of a possibly contrary congressional intent is 'a step to be taken cau-

---

7. An affidavit submitted to the District Court by one of appellees' employees stated that BLM officials ... had told the employee that the filing could be made at the BLM Reno office "on or before December 31, 1980." The 1978 version of a BLM question and answer pamphlet erroneously stated that the annual filings had to be made "on or before December 31" of each year. Later versions have corrected this error to bring the pamphlet into accord with the BLM regulations that require the filings to be made "on or before December 30." ...

tiously' even under the best of circumstances." When even after taking this step nothing in the legislative history remotely suggests a congressional intent contrary to Congress' chosen words, and neither appellees nor the dissenters have pointed to anything that so suggests, any further steps take the courts out of the realm of interpretation and place them in the domain of legislation. The phrase "prior to" may be clumsy, but its meaning is clear. Under these circumstances, we are obligated to apply the "prior to December 31" language by its terms. . . .

The judgment below is reversed, and the case is remanded for further proceedings consistent with this opinion.

- ◆ [JUSTICE O'CONNOR's concurring and JUSTICE POWELL's dissenting opinions are omitted.]
- ◆ JUSTICE STEVENS, with whom JUSTICE BRENNEN joins, dissenting.

Purposivist

. . . [T]he choice of the language "prior to December 31" when read in context in 43 U.S.C. § 1744(a) is, at least, ambiguous, and, at best, "the consequence of a legislative *accident,* perhaps caused by nothing more than the unfortunate fact that Congress is too busy to do all of its work as carefully as it should." In my view, Congress actually intended to authorize an annual filing at any time prior to the close of business on December 31st, that is, prior to the end of the calendar year to which the filing pertains. [It is unlikely that] Congress irrationally intended that the applicable deadline for a calendar year should end *one day before* the end of the calendar year that has been recognized since the amendment of the Julian Calendar in 8 B.C. . . .

Absurdity Arg.

ambiguous or sc. error

Absurdity

A careful reading of § 314 discloses at least [two] respects in which its text cannot possibly reflect the actual intent of Congress. First, the description of what must be filed in the initial filing and subsequent annual filings is quite obviously garbled. Read literally, § 314(a)(2) seems to require that a notice of intent to hold the claim and an affidavit of assessment work performed on the claim must be filed "on a detailed report provided by § 28–1 of Title 30." One must substitute the word "or" for the word "on" to make any sense at all out of this provision. This error should cause us to pause before concluding that Congress commanded blind allegiance to the remainder of the literal text of § 314.

Second, the express language of the statute is unambiguous in describing the place where the second annual filing shall be made. If the statute is read inflexibly, the owner must "file in the office of the Bureau" the required documents. Yet the regulations that the Bureau itself has drafted, quite reasonably, construe the statute to allow filing in a mailbox, provided that the document is actually received by the Bureau prior to the close of business on January 19 of the year following the year in which the statute requires the filing to be made. A notice mailed on December 30, 1982, and received by the Bureau on January 19, 1983, was filed "in the office of the Bureau" during 1982 within the meaning of the statute, but one that is hand-delivered to the office on December 31, 1982, cannot be accepted as a 1982 "filing." . . .

I cannot believe that Congress intended the words "prior to December 31 of each year" to be given the literal reading the Court adopts today. The statutory scheme requires periodic filings on a calendar-year basis. The end of the calendar year is, of course, correctly described either as "prior to the close of business on December 31," or "on or before December 31," but it is surely understandable that the author of § 314 might inadvertently use the words "prior to December 31" when he meant to refer to the end of the calendar year. As the facts of this case demonstrate, the scrivener's error is one that can be made in good faith. The risk of such an error is, of course, the greatest when the reference is to the end of the calendar year. That it was in fact an error seems rather clear to me because no one has suggested any rational basis for omitting just one day from the period in which an annual filing may be made, and I would not presume that Congress deliberately created a trap for the unwary by such an omission....

I respectfully dissent.

* * *

Points for Discussion

1. *Statutory Language*: What was the language at issue? What did each party want that language to mean? What meaning did the majority and dissent adopt?

2. *Theories*: Which theory did the majority use? The dissent?

3. *Scrivener's Error*: What reasons does Justice Stevens give to show that Congress simply drafted inartfully here? Do you find that argument persuasive? Justice Marshall is not generally known as a stickler for text. Why did he refuse to consider the deadline to be a scrivener's error?

4. *Estoppel*: Should it matter if the BLM misinformed the Lockes? The Lockes might have argued that the United States was equitably estopped from forfeiting their claims because they provided inaccurate advice. *See Heckler v. Community Health Services, Inc.*, 467 U. S. 51 (1984). However, estoppel claims made against the federal government are rarely successful. *Office of Personnel Management v. Richmond*, 496 U.S. 414, 426 (1990) (refusing to recognize a blanket rule against such estoppel claims, but suggesting that success would be rare). Luckily for the Lockes, after the Court remanded, the Lockes were ultimately able to keep their mineral rights.

5. *Other Examples*: As the majority notes, the scrivener's error canon does not give courts *carte blanch* to redraft poorly written statutes to correct legislative "mistakes"; rather, it is a canon that allows courts limited authority to fix obvious drafting errors. For an example of a case in which a court corrected what it perceived to be a drafting error, see *Shine v. Shine*, 802 F.2d 583 (1st Cir. 1986) ("While the wording of the statute may have given rise to some confusion, '(t)he result of an obvious mistake should not be enforced, particularly when it overrides common sense and evident statutory purpose.'") (quoting *In re Adamo*, 619 F.2d 216, 222 (2d Cir. 1980), *cert denied*, 449 U.S. 843 (1980)) (internal quotations omitted). This result is surprising because, unlike *Locke*, there was no obvious drafting error, yet the court used the scrivener's doctrine to "correct" the statute anyway. Few courts, especially today, are willing to redraft legislation so freely.

For example, in *King v. Burwell*, 135 S. Ct. 2480 (2015), the Supreme Court had to decide whether the phrase "an Exchange established by the State" included only those exchanges established by states or whether it also included those exchanges established by the federal government on behalf of a state that refused to provide its own health care exchanges. Likely, Congress simply missed this point when it was drafting. Indeed, the majority specifically noted that the Affordable Care Act "contains more than a few examples of inartful drafting. (To cite just one, the Act creates three separate Section 1563s. See 124 Stat. 270, 911, 912.)" *Id.* at 2492. Yet, the majority did not turn to the scrivener's error doctrine to resolve the meaning of the phrase. Instead, the majority turned to the purpose of the statute to find that the phrase included both exchanges established by states and the federal government.

This dissent agreed that the scrivener's error doctrine was not applicable:

> Perhaps sensing the dismal failure of its efforts to show that "established by the State" means "established by the State or the Federal Government," the Court tries to palm off the pertinent statutory phrase as "inartful drafting." This Court, however, has no free-floating power "to rescue Congress from its drafting errors." Only when it is patently obvious to a reasonable reader that a drafting mistake has occurred may a court correct the mistake. The occurrence of a misprint may be apparent from the face of the law, as it is where the Affordable Care Act "creates three separate Section 1563s." But the Court does not pretend that there is any such indication of a drafting error on the face of § 36B. The occurrence of a misprint may also be apparent because a provision decrees an absurd result — a consequence "so monstrous, that all mankind would, without hesitation, unite in rejecting the application." But § 36B does not come remotely close to satisfying that demanding standard.... We therefore have no authority to dismiss the terms of the law as a drafting fumble.

King v. Burwell, 135 S. Ct. 2480, 2504–05 (2015) (Scalia, J., dissenting).

* * *

4. The Constitutional Avoidance Doctrine

A fourth reason that courts reject the ordinary meaning of the text is that the ordinary meaning raises a constitutional issue. The *Constitutional Avoidance Doctrine* directs that, when there are two reasonable interpretations of statutory language, one which raises constitutional issues and one which does not, the statute should be interpreted in a way that does not raise the constitutional issue. *Murray v. The Charming Betsy*, 6 U.S. (2 Cranch) 64, 118 (1804). When the court faces a question about the constitutionality of a statute, even if serious constitutional doubt is raised, the court should first ascertain whether another interpretation of the statute is *fairly possible* so that the constitutional question can be avoided.

In theory, the avoidance canon should apply only if there are two *reasonable* and *fair* interpretations of a statute. Limiting the choice to interpretations that are fair and reasonable prevents the judiciary from rewriting a statute to mean something the legislature did not intend. This limit confines the judiciary to its proper constitutional role of interpreting statutes so as to give effect to congressional intent and words. In reality, however, some judges may adopt an interpretation that is not reasonable and fair simply to avoid the constitutional issue.

For example, in *NLRB v. Catholic Bishop*, 440 U.S. 490 (1979), the majority refused to adopt an interpretation of the National Labor Relations Act that might violate the First Amendment of the Constitution. In that case, the Court was asked to determine whether the National Labor Relations Board, an agency, had jurisdiction over lay teachers who taught at church-operated schools. By its terms, the Act applied to all "employer[s]," defined as "any person acting as an agent of an employer, directly or indirectly...." *Id.* at 510 (Brennen, J., dissenting) (quoting 29 U.S.C. §152(2)). Citing the avoidance doctrine, the Court said it could reject the ordinary meaning "if any other *possible construction* remain[ed] available." *Id.* at 500 (majority opinion) (emphasis added). The majority then looked for "a clear expression of Congress' intent to [raise Constitutional questions involving] the First Amendment Religion Clauses." *Id.* at 507. Not finding any such expression, the majority refused to use the ordinary meaning of "employer" and instead concluded that "employer" must mean all employers *except* church-operated schools. *Id.* at 499. In sum, the majority misquoted the doctrine and rewrote the statute to include an implied exception all to avoid reaching the constitutional issue.

The avoidance canon serves two purposes: first, it protects separation of powers. A court avoids declaring an act of Congress unconstitutional unless the court has no other choice. The rationale here is simple and reflects judicial respect for the legislature. Judges presume that legislatures intend to enact a statute that is constitutional. Judges further presume that legislatures do not intend to enact a statute that would raise questions about constitutional boundaries. Hence, the legislature would have intended an interpretation that does not raise these questions or would have made its intent to challenge the boundaries clear. The Oklahoma legislature did just that recently when it passed a law making it a felony to perform an abortion. The sponsor specifically said he wanted to challenge *Roe v. Wade*, 410 U.S. 113 (1973).

Second, this canon furthers judicial economy. If the court need not determine whether a statute is constitutional, why should the court bother? It is important to note that this canon does not require a court to first find that an interpretation violates the constitution before adopting another interpretation; rather, this canon requires a court to find only that one interpretation would require the court to *consider* the constitutionality of the statute in question before adopting another interpretation.

> [W]here a statute is susceptible of two constructions, by one of which grave and doubtful constitutional questions arise and by the other of which such questions are avoided, our duty is to adopt the later. This "cardinal principle,"

which "has for so long been applied by the Court that it is beyond debate," requires merely a determination of serious constitutional *doubt*, and not a determination of *unconstitutionality*. That must be so, of course, for otherwise the rule would "mea[n] that our duty is to first decide that a statute is unconstitutional and then proceed to hold that such ruling was unnecessary because the statute is susceptible of a meaning, which causes it not to be repugnant to the Constitution."

Almendarez-Torres v. United States, 523 U.S. 224, 250 (1998) (citations omitted). Thus, a judge need not first, indeed must not first, reach the constitutional issue. Rather, the constitutional issue need simply appear before the ordinary meaning can be rejected. This distinction is fundamental and often confuses judges.

Let's see how this canon works in practice.

United States v. Marshall

United States Court of Appeals for the Seventh Circuit.
908 F.2d 1312 (7th Cir. 1990) (en banc)
aff'd sub nom, Chapman v. United States, 500 U.S. 453 (1991)

◆ EASTERBROOK, CIRCUIT JUDGE [with whom COFFEY, FLAUM, RIPPLE, MANION, and KANE, CIRCUIT JUDGES concur].

… Stanley J. Marshall was convicted after a bench trial and sentenced to 20 years' imprisonment for conspiring to distribute, and distributing, more than ten grams of LSD, enough for 11,751 doses. Patrick Brumm, Richard L. Chapman, and John M. Schoenecker were convicted by a jury of selling ten sheets (1,000 doses) of paper containing LSD. Because the total weight of the paper and LSD was 5.7 grams, a five-year mandatory minimum applied. The district court sentenced Brumm to 60 months (the minimum), Schoenecker to 63 months, and Chapman to 96 months' imprisonment. All four defendants confine their arguments on appeal to questions concerning their sentences.

The … questions we must resolve are these: (1) Whether 21 U.S.C. §841(b)(1)(A)(v) and (B)(v),* which set mandatory minimum terms of imprison-

---

* Editor's footnote: 21 U.S.C. §841(b)(1)(B) at the time provided:
"any person who violates subsection (a) of this section [making it unlawful to knowingly or intentionally manufacture, distribute, dispense, or possess with intent to manufacture, distribute, or dispense, a controlled substance] shall be sentenced as follows:
"(1)(B) In the case of a violation of subsection (a) of this section involving—….
"(v) 1 gram or more of a mixture or substance containing a detectable amount of lysergic acid diethylamide (LSD);…. such person shall be sentenced to a term of imprisonment which may not be less than 5 years…."
In addition, U.S.C. §841(b)(1)(A)(v) at the time provided "for a mandatory minimum of 10 years' imprisonment for a violation of subsection (a) involving "10 grams or more of a mixture or substance containing a detectable amount of [LSD]."

ment—five years for selling more than one gram of a "mixture or substance containing a detectable amount" of LSD, ten years for more than ten grams—exclude the weight of a carrier medium. (2) ... Whether the statute [is] unconstitutional to the extent [its] computations [are] based on anything other than the weight of the pure drug....

According to the Sentencing Commission, the LSD in an average dose weighs 0.05 milligrams. Twenty thousand pure doses are a gram. But 0.05 mg is almost invisible, so LSD is distributed to retail customers in a carrier. Pure LSD is dissolved in a solvent such as alcohol and sprayed on paper or gelatin; alternatively the paper may be dipped in the solution. After the solvent evaporates, the paper or gel is cut into one-dose squares and sold by the square. Users swallow the squares or may drop them into a beverage, releasing the drug. Although the gelatin and paper are light, they weigh much more than the drug. Marshall's 11,751 doses weighed 113.32 grams; the LSD accounted for only 670.72 mg of this, not enough to activate the five-year mandatory minimum sentence, let alone the ten-year minimum. The ten sheets of blotter paper carrying the 1,000 doses Chapman and confederates sold weighed 5.7 grams; the LSD in the paper did not approach the one-gram threshold for a mandatory minimum sentence. This disparity between the weight of the pure LSD and the weight of LSD-plus-carrier underlies the defendants' arguments.

Fun Facts about LSD → *enhanced for selling paper not the drug*

If the carrier counts in the weight of the "mixture or substance containing a detectable amount" of LSD, some odd things may happen. Weight in the hands of distributors may exceed that of manufacturers and wholesalers. Big fish then could receive paltry sentences or small fish draconian ones. Someone who sold 19,999 doses of pure LSD (at 0.05 mg per dose) would escape the five-year mandatory minimum of § 841(b)(1)(B)(v) and be covered by § 841(b)(1)(C), which lacks a minimum term and has a maximum of "only" 20 years. Someone who sold a single hit of LSD dissolved in a tumbler of orange juice could be exposed to a ten-year mandatory minimum. Retailers could fall in or out of the mandatory terms depending not on the number of doses but on the medium: sugar cubes weigh more than paper, which weighs more than gelatin. One way to eliminate the possibility of such consequences is to say that the carrier is not a "mixture or substance containing a detectable amount" of the drug. Defendants ask us to do this....

It is not possible to construe the words of § 841 to make the penalty turn on the net weight of the drug rather than the gross weight of carrier and drug. The statute speaks of "mixture or substance containing a detectable amount" of a drug. "Detectable amount" is the opposite of "pure"; the point of the statute is that the "mixture" is not ✱ to be converted to an equivalent amount of pure drug.

The structure of the statute reinforces this conclusion. The 10–year minimum applies to any person who possesses, with intent to distribute, "100 grams or more of phencyclidine (PCP) or 1 kilogram or more of a mixture or substance containing a detectable amount of phencyclidine (PCP)", § 841(b)(1)(A)(iv). Congress distinguished the pure drug from a "mixture or substance containing a detectable amount of" it. All drugs other than PCP are governed exclusively by the "mixture or substance" language. Even brute force cannot turn that language into a reference to

PCP

pure LSD. Congress used the same "mixture or substance" language to describe heroin, cocaine, amphetamines, and many other drugs that are sold after being cut—sometimes as much as LSD. There is no sound basis on which to treat the words "substance or mixture containing a detectable amount of", repeated verbatim for every drug mentioned in §841 except PCP, as *different* things for LSD and cocaine although the language is identical, while treating the "mixture or substance" language as meaning the *same* as the reference to pure PCP in 21 U.S.C. §841(b)(1)(A)(iv) and (B)(iv).

Although the "mixture or substance" language shows that the statute cannot be limited to pure LSD, it does not necessarily follow that blotter paper *is* a "mixture or substance containing" LSD. That phrase cannot include all "carriers". One gram of crystalline LSD in a heavy glass bottle is still only one gram of "statutory LSD". So is a gram of LSD being "carried" in a Boeing 747. How much mingling of the drug with something else is essential to form a "mixture or substance"? The legislative history is silent, but ordinary usage is indicative.

"Substance" may well refer to a chemical compound, or perhaps to a drug in a solvent. LSD does not react chemically with sugar, blotter paper, or gelatin, and none of these is a solvent. "Mixture" is more inclusive. Cocaine often is mixed with mannitol, quinine, or lactose. These white powders do not react, but it is common ground that a cocaine-mannitol mixture is a statutory "mixture".

LSD and blotter paper are not commingled in the same way as cocaine and lactose. What is the nature of their association? ... LSD is applied to paper in a solvent; after the solvent evaporates, a tiny quantity of LSD remains. Because the fibers absorb the alcohol, the LSD solidifies inside the paper rather than on it. You cannot pick a grain of LSD off the surface of the paper. Ordinary parlance calls the paper containing tiny crystals of LSD a mixture.

... [W]e [conclude] that blotter paper treated with LSD is a "mixture or substance containing a detectable quantity of" LSD.

[Defendants have suggested] that statutes should be construed to avoid constitutional problems ...

A preference for giving statutes a constitutional meaning is a reason to construe, not to rewrite or "improve". Canons are doubt-resolvers, useful when the language is ambiguous and "a construction of the statute is *fairly possible* by which the question may be avoided". "[S]ubstance or mixture containing a detectable quantity" is not ambiguous, avoidance not "fairly possible". Neither the rule of lenity nor the preference for avoiding constitutional adjudication justifies disregarding unambiguous language.

The canon about avoiding constitutional decisions, in particular, must be used with care, for it is a closer cousin to invalidation than to interpretation. It is a way to enforce the constitutional penumbra, and therefore an aspect of constitutional law proper. Constitutional decisions breed penumbras, which multiply questions. Treating each as justification to construe laws out of existence too greatly enlarges the judicial power....

A constitutional question remains, given our construction of the statute and guidelines.... [The majority rejected the defendants' constitutional arguments based on the Fifth and Eighth Amendments and affirmed.].

♦ CUMMINGS, CIRCUIT JUDGE, with whom BAUER, CHIEF JUDGE, and WOOD, JR., CUDAHY, and POSNER, CIRCUIT JUDGES, join, dissenting.

... The words "mixture or substance" are ambiguous, and a construction of those words that can avoid invalidation on constitutional grounds is therefore appropriate....

The majority has decided that ambiguous language is clear and that rational basis review is toothless. I therefore respectfully dissent.

♦ POSNER, CIRCUIT JUDGE, with whom BAUER, CHIEF JUDGE, and WOOD, JR., CUDAHY, and CUMMINGS, CIRCUIT JUDGES, join, dissenting:

In each of these cases consolidated for decision en banc ... the district court sentenced sellers of LSD in accordance with an interpretation of 21 U.S.C. §841 that is plausible but that makes the punishment scheme for LSD irrational. It has been assumed that an irrational federal sentencing scheme denies the equal protection of the laws and therefore violates the due process clause of the Fifth Amendment. The assumption is proper, and in order to avoid having to strike down the statute we are entitled to adopt a reasonable interpretation that cures the constitutional infirmity, even if that interpretation might not be our first choice were there no such infirmity.

The statute fixes the minimum and maximum punishments with respect to each illegal drug on the basis of the weight of the "mixture or substance containing a detectable amount of" the drug.... The quoted words are critical. Drugs are usually consumed, and therefore often sold, in a diluted form, and the adoption by Congress of the "mixture or substance" method of grading punishment reflected a conscious decision to mete out heavy punishment to large retail dealers, who are likely to possess "substantial street quantities," which is to say quantities of the diluted drug ready for sale. H.R.Rep. No. 845, 99th Cong., 2d Sess. 11–12 (1986). That decision is well within Congress's constitutional authority even though it may sometimes result in less severe punishment for possessing a purer, and therefore a lighter, form of the illegal drug than a heavier but much less potent form....

[This system] works well for drugs that are sold by weight....

LSD, however, is sold to the consumer by the dose; it is not cut, diluted, or mixed with something else. Moreover, it is incredibly light. An average dose of LSD weighs .05 milligrams, which is less than two millionths of an ounce. To ingest something that small requires swallowing something much larger. Pure LSD in granular form is first diluted by being dissolved, usually in alcohol, and then a quantity of the solution containing one dose of LSD is sprayed or eyedropped on a sugar cube, or on a cube of gelatin, or, as in the cases before us, on an inch-square section of "blotter" paper.... The consumer drops the cube or the piece of paper into a glass of water, or orange juice, or some other beverage, causing the LSD to dissolve in the beverage, which is then drunk. This is not dilution. It is still one dose that is being imbibed....

[handwritten margin notes: Absurd; Con. Avoidance is Proper ↓ wrong resolving the con. issue]

[A] quart of orange juice containing one dose of LSD is not more, in any relevant sense, than a pint of juice containing the same one dose, and it would be loony to punish the purveyor of the quart more heavily than the purveyor of the pint. It would be like basing the punishment for selling cocaine on the combined weight of the cocaine and of the vehicle (plane, boat, automobile, or whatever) used to transport it or the syringe used to inject it or the pipe used to smoke it. The blotter paper, sugar cubes, etc. are the vehicles for conveying LSD to the consumer....

... [W]e must consider whether Congress might have had a reason for wanting to key the severity of punishment for selling LSD to the weight of the carrier rather than to the number of doses or to some reasonable proxy for dosage (as weight is, for many drugs)....

A person who sells LSD on blotter paper is not a worse criminal than one who sells the same number of doses on gelatin cubes, but he is subject to a heavier punishment. A person who sells five doses of LSD on sugar cubes is not a worse person than a manufacturer of LSD who is caught with 19,999 doses in pure form, but the former is subject to a ten-year mandatory minimum no-parole sentence while the latter is not even subject to the five-year minimum. If defendant Chapman, who received five years for selling a thousand doses of LSD on blotter paper, had sold the same number of doses in pure form, his Guidelines sentence would have been fourteen months. And defendant Marshall's sentence for selling almost 12,000 doses would have been four years rather than twenty.... Congress might as well have said: if there is a carrier, weigh the carrier and forget the LSD.

This is a quilt the pattern whereof no one has been able to discern. The legislative history is silent, and since even the Justice Department cannot explain the why of the punishment scheme that it is defending, the most plausible inference is that Congress simply did not realize how LSD is sold....

Well, what if anything can we judges do about this mess? The answer lies in the shadow of a jurisprudential disagreement that is not less important by virtue of being unavowed by most judges. It is the disagreement between the severely positivistic view that the content of law is exhausted in clear, explicit, and definite enactments by or under express delegation from legislatures, and the natural lawyer's or legal pragmatist's view that the practice of interpretation and the general terms of the Constitution (such as "equal protection of the laws") authorize judges to enrich positive law with the moral values and practical concerns of civilized society. Judges who in other respects have seemed quite similar, such as Holmes and Cardozo, have taken opposite sides of this issue. Neither approach is entirely satisfactory. The first buys political neutrality and a type of objectivity at the price of substantive injustice, while the second buys justice in the individual case at the price of considerable uncertainty and, not infrequently, judicial willfulness. It is no wonder that our legal system oscillates between the approaches. The positivist view, applied unflinchingly to this case, commands the affirmance of prison sentences that are exceptionally harsh by the standards of the modern Western world, dictated by an accidental, unintended scheme of punishment nevertheless implied by the words (taken one by one) of the relevant enactments. The natural law or pragmatist view leads to a freer interpretation, one influenced by norms of equal treatment; and let us explore the interpretive possibilities here. One is to interpret "mixture or substance containing a detectable amount of [LSD]" to exclude the carrier medium—the blotter paper, sugar or gelatin cubes, and orange juice or other beverage....

The flexible interpretation that I am proposing is decisively strengthened by the constitutional objection to basing punishment of LSD offenders on the weight of the carrier medium rather than on the weight of the LSD. Courts often do interpretive handsprings to avoid having even to *decide* a constitutional question. In doing so they expand, very questionably in my view, the effective scope of the Constitution, creating a constitutional penumbra in which statutes wither, shrink, are deformed. A better case for flexible interpretation is presented when the alternative is to nullify Congress's action: when in other words there is not merely a constitutional question about, but a constitutional barrier to, the statute when interpreted literally. This is such a case....

Our choice is between ruling that the provisions of section 841 regarding LSD are irrational, hence unconstitutional, and therefore there is no punishment for dealing in LSD—Congress must go back to the drawing boards, and all LSD cases in the pipeline must be dismissed—and ruling that, to preserve so much of the statute as can constitutionally be preserved, the statutory expression "substance or mixture containing a detectable amount of [LSD]" excludes the carrier medium. Given *this* choice, we can be reasonably certain that Congress would have preferred the second course; and this consideration carries the argument for a flexible interpretation over the top....

The literal interpretation adopted by the majority is not inevitable. All interpretation is contextual. The words of the statute—interpreted against a background that includes a constitutional norm of equal treatment, a (closely related) constitutional commitment to rationality, an evident failure by both Congress and the Sentencing Commission to consider how LSD is actually produced, distributed, and sold, and an equally evident failure by the same two bodies to consider the interaction between heavy mandatory minimum sentences and the Sentencing Guidelines—will bear an interpretation that distinguishes between the carrier vehicle of the illegal drug and the substance or mixture containing a detectable amount of the drug. The punishment of the crack dealer is not determined by the weight of the glass tube in which he sells the crack; we should not lightly attribute to Congress a purpose of punishing the dealer in LSD according to the weight of the LSD carrier. We should not make Congress's handiwork an embarrassment to the members of Congress and to us.

* * *

Points for Discussion

1. *Statutory Language*: What was the language at issue? What did each party want that language to mean? What meaning did Judges Easterbrook and Posner adopt?

2. *Theories*: Which theory did Judge Easterbrook use? Judge Posner? Posner talked about positivism and pragmatism. What is the difference? Do either sound familiar to you?

3. *Two Steps*: The majority concluded first that Congress did not intend to refer to LSD in its pure form and that "mixture or substance" includes the blotter paper. The majority then concluded that Congress's decision to include the blotter paper weight is constitutional. Why were both steps necessary to the analysis? In contrast, the Judge Posner agreed that Congress did not intend to refer to LSD in its pure form, but that "mixture or substance" does not include the blotter paper. Notice that the second step (examining the constitutionality of the statute) should have been unnecessary.

4. *Ambiguity & Absurdity*: Did any of the judges conclude that the language was ambiguous or absurd? Note that in *Green v. Bock Laundry Machine Co.*, 490 U.S. 504 (1989), which you read earlier, the Court could have turned to this canon as well. Justice Scalia did note that the ordinary meaning of the statute at issue in that case could not "rationally (or perhaps even constitutionally) mean" what it said. *Id.* at 528. Alternatively, would absurdity have worked better in this case (*Marshall*)? After all, the penalty disproportionally affected defendants who sold one type of drug in a heavier carrier. As the dissent noted:

> That irrationality is magnified when we compare the sentences for people who sell other drugs prohibited by 21 U.S.C. §841. Marshall, remember, sold fewer than 12,000 doses and was sentenced to twenty years. Twelve thousand doses sounds like a lot, but to receive a comparable sentence for selling heroin Marshall would have had to sell ten kilograms, which would yield between one and two million doses. To receive a comparable sentence for selling cocaine he would have had to sell fifty kilograms, which would yield anywhere from 325,000 to five million doses. While the corresponding weight is lower for crack—half a kilogram— this still translates into 50,000 doses....

Why is not the statute absurd as interpreted in this way?

5. *Defining the Doctrine*: According to Judge Easterbrook, judges should use the constitutional avoidance doctrine only "when the language is ambiguous and a construction of the statute is *fairly possible* by which the question may be avoided." Did he conflate ambiguity and the constitutional avoidance doctrine? Under his articulation, does the constitutional avoidance doctrine serve as a way to avoid ordinary meaning or as a way to resolve ambiguity (and presumably absurdity)? (Notice that Judge Easterbrook similarly relegates the rule of lenity into this same, tie-breaking role).

In contrast, Judge Posner said that judges should use the constitutional avoidance doctrine when "there is not merely a constitutional question about, but a constitutional barrier to, the statute when interpreted literally." Did he misunderstand the doctrine as well? Under his articulation, must judges first conclude that a statute is likely unconstitutional, but because an alternative interpretation can be found, that alternative interpretation should control?

6. *Resolving Statutes Raising Constitutional Issues*: Judge Easterbrook did not apply the canon. Regardless, how did he resolve the statute's meaning? Judge Posner did apply the canon. How did he resolve the statute's meaning?

7. *Alternative Interpretations*: The avoidance canon should apply only if there are two *reasonable* and *fair* interpretations of a statute. When judges fail to adopt fair and reasonable interpretations, judges can be accused of rewriting the statute rather than interpreting it. Notice that Judge Easterbrook calls the avoidance canon "a closer cousin to invalidation than to interpretation." Why? What did Judge Posner mean when he said that "[c]ourts do interpretive handsprings to avoid having even to *decide* a constitutional question."

8. *Uniform Statute & Rule Construction Act*: Uniform Acts are covered in Chapter 10. Simply put, Uniform Acts are proposed state laws that the National Conference of Commissioners on Uniform State Laws ("Conference") or another institutional actor drafts. The Conference has no legislative power; rather, a proposed uniform act becomes law only when it is adopted in a particular state. There is a Uniform Statute & Rule Construction Act. It provides: "A statute or rule is construed, if possible, to: ... avoid an unconstitutional ... result." UNIF. STATUTE & RULE CONSTR. ACT, §18(a3) (1995). Did the Commissioners accurately describe this doctrine?

9. *Subsequent Activity*. In *Chapman v. United States*, 500 U.S. 453 (1991), the Supreme Court affirmed, similarly disagreeing on what "mixture" meant. Writing for the majority, Chief Justice Rehnquist turned to the dictionary definition of "mixture" and concluded it was broad enough to include the weight of the blotter paper. Two years later, the Sentencing Commission revised the Sentencing Guidelines. Abandoning its former approach of including the weight of the blotter paper, the Commission amended the Guidelines such that each dose of LSD on a carrier has a presumed weight of 0.4 mg. U.S. Sentencing Comm'n, U.S. Sentencing Guidelines Manual §2D1.1I, n.* (H).

* * *

In sum, the avoidance doctrine allows a court to avoid the ordinary meaning of text when that meaning would raise questions about the constitutionality of the statute. The doctrine directs that to avoid having to declare the statute unconstitutional, a court should adopt an interpretation that can be fairly discerned from the text and that does not raise constitutional issues.

Problem 6B

You are a new law clerk for Justice Clifton, the newest Supreme Court Justice. Justice Clifton has asked you to draft a memo indicating whether the Court should recognize the "exculpatory no" doctrine. The exculpatory no doctrine provides that the government may not prosecute an individual for making false or fraudulent denials in response to questioning initiated by the government when a truthful statement would incriminate the defendant. The doctrine is based on the Fifth Amendment right to remain silent. The Fifth Amendment provides: "No person shall be ... compelled in any criminal case to be a witness against himself, nor be deprived of life, liberty, or property, without due process of law...."

A case is pending before the Supreme Court due to a circuit split. *Compare United States v. Taylor*, 907 F.2d 801 (8th Cir. 1990) (holding that the exculpatory no doctrine applied where a defendant had denied to the bankruptcy court that he signed his wife's name on bankruptcy pleadings), *with United States v. Rodriguez-Rios*, 14 F.3d 1040 (5th Cir. 1994) (holding that the exculpatory no doctrine did not apply where a defendant entered the Country and claimed he was carrying "only about $1,000" when he was actually carrying $598,000).

The relevant statute, 18 U.S.C. § 1001(a) provides: "Whoever, in any matter within the jurisdiction of any department or agency of the United States knowingly and willfully ... makes any false, fictitious or fraudulent statements or representations.... shall be fined under this title or imprisoned not more than 5 years, or both."

The legislative enactment history shows that Congress originally enacted this statute in 1863 in response to a spate of frauds by military personnel upon the Government. Congress progressively expanded the statute to cover a wider range of fraudulent practices. Relevantly, in 1996, Congress amended the statute in response the Supreme Court's decision in *Hubbard v. United*, 514 U.S. 695 (1995). The Court in *Hubbard* held that § 1001 did not apply when individuals made false statements in judicial proceedings. The 1996 amendment changed the language of the statute by explicitly providing that § 1001 applied to false statements made "in any matter within the jurisdiction of the executive, legislative, or judicial branch of the Government." Act of Oct. 11, 1996, Pub. L. No. 104292, 110 Stat. 3459 (codified as amended at 18 U.S.C. § 1001). Congress did not address the exculpatory no doctrine when it enacted the 1996 amendment.

During the legislative debates on earlier amendments, a member of the House of Representatives stated, "It is an unheard-of proposition to try to convict a man for a mere statement unless he has testified under oath." 78 Cong. Rec. 3724 (1934). Likewise, a member of the Senate expressed concern with the more affirmative types of false statements and "understood that the purpose of the legislation was to deter those individuals "hovering over every department of the Government like obscene harpies, like foul buzzards." 78 Cong. Rec. 2858 (1934). There is no other relevant legislative history.

Lower courts developed the exculpatory no doctrine prior to the 1996 Amendments. Specifically, in *United States v. Levin*, 133 F. Supp. 88 (D. Colo. 1953), the District Court of Colorado held that a defendant's unsworn false statement to an F.B.I. agent that he did not have information concerning the identity of a lady's dinner ring did not violate § 1001. The court noted that such an interpretation would subject defendants to greater criminal liability under § 1001 than defendants who perjured themselves in court and, thus, would be just.

Two years later, the District Court of Maryland followed suit. In *United States v. Stark*, 131 F. Supp. 190 (D. Md. 1955), the court distinguished between affirmative representations and mere exculpatory denials, and held that the mere denials were not "statements" within the language of section 1001. The court reasoned that the statute's purpose was to protect the government from the affirmative or aggressive and voluntary actions of individuals who take the initiative to lie. In other words, the purpose was to protect the government from being the victim of some positive statement, whether written or oral, which had the tendency and effect of misleading the government.

The Fifth Circuit was the first circuit to officially adopt the doctrine. *United States v. Paternostro*, 311 F.2d 298, 309 (5th Cir. 1962). A majority of the jurisdictions soon followed suit. *Moser v. United States*, 18 F.3d 469, 473–74 (7th Cir. 1994); *United States v. Taylor*, 907 F.2d 801, 805 (8th Cir. 1990); *United States v. Cogdell*, F.2d 179, 183 (4th Cir. 1988); *United States v. Tabor*, 788 F.2d 714, 717–19 (11th Cir. 1986); *United States v. Fitzgibbon*, 619 F.2d 874, 880–81 (10th Cir. 1980); *United States v. Rose*, 570 F.2d 1358, 1364 (9th Cir. 1978); *United States v. Chevoor*, 526 F.2d 178, 183–84 (1st Cir. 1975). Because silence is an unnatural response to an accusation, courts reasoned that a literal application of § 1001 conflicted with the spirit of the Fifth Amendment.

Ironically, it was also the Fifth Circuit that first rejected the doctrine. *United States v. Rodriguez-Rios*, 14 F.3d 1040 (5th Cir. 1994). Rejecting its earlier case, the Fifth Circuit reasoned that the language of § 1001 was clear and that neither the legislative history of the statute nor the Fifth Amendment warranted departing from that clear language. The Second Circuit agreed. *United States v. Wiener*, 96 F.3d 35 (2d Cir. 1996), *aff'd sub nom. Brogan v. United States*, 522 U.S. 398 (1998). An appeal from *Wiener* is before the Supreme Court.

The facts in *Wiener* are as follows: the defendant was a union officer who received cash payments from a real estate company whose employees were represented by the union. Federal agents of the Department of Labor and the Internal Revenue Service came to the defendant's home to question him. During the visit to his home, the agents told the defendant that they were seeking his cooperation in the investigation and if he chose to cooperate, he should retain an attorney. He declined. After eliciting background information, the agents asked him whether he had received any cash or gifts from the real estate company, and the defendant responded, "no." After this answer, the agents informed the defendant that lying to federal agents in the course of an investigation was a crime and that they had obtained records of the real estate company indicating that his answer was false. The interview ended then because the defendant asked to speak to an attorney. The defendant was convicted of making false statements within the jurisdiction of a federal agency in violation of 18 U.S.C. 8 1001.

On appeal, the defendant argued that his false statements fell within the exculpatory no exception to § 1001. The Second Circuit rejected this argument and held that the exculpatory no doctrine was not a viable defense under § 1001. The court also declared with little discussion, that "the Fifth Amendment ha[d] no application to circumstances in which a person lies instead of remaining silent."

On appeal, the defendant has argued that a literal application of § 1001 places "a cornered suspect" in "a cruel trilemma" of incriminating himself, being charged with a § 1001 felony, or remaining silent when his silence would be considered a tacit admission of guilt and later used against him at trial. The defendant also stated that the silence option was often "illusory" because a citizen may not even know that he has the right to remain silent.

Justice Clifton would like to find for the defendant, but the language of the statute seems to be clear. Justice Clifton believes an exculpatory no is far removed from the type of behavior § 1001 originally sought to prohibit. Further, she is concerned about the extraordinary authority this statute confers on prosecutors to manufacture crimes, either by questioning a defendant on an issue to which the agents already know the answer, as occurred here, or by eliciting a false denial of guilt after the statute of limitations has run on the underlying conduct. As for this case, she notes that the Government was in no way injured by the defendant's conduct; rather, the agents seemed to merely set a trap for the unwary and unsophisticated defendant. What do you advise? Please consider whether any of the four ways of avoiding ordinary meaning apply here. Assuming one or more applies, what other sources of meaning are relevant and how should she interpret the statute?

1. sc. error
2. rm
3. Ab
4. constitution

Chapter 7

Canons Based on Intrinsic Sources: Grammar and Punctuation

A. Introduction to This Chapter

We continue looking at intrinsic sources in this chapter. To do so, we move from the most important source, the words, to a relatively unimportant source, grammar and punctuation. You will likely be surprised to learn of the surprisingly small role that grammar and punctuation play in interpretation. Hence, this is a relatively short chapter. Because of the small role they play, this chapter might have appeared near the end of the text; however, because grammar and punctuation are intrinsic sources, they are included early with the other intrinsic sources.

B. The General Punctuation and Grammar Rule

In England, "until 1849 statutes were enrolled upon parchment and enacted without punctuation. No punctuation appearing upon the rolls of Parliament such as was found in the printed statutes simply expressed the understanding of the printer." *Taylor v. Inhabitants of Town of Caribou*, 67 A. 2 (Me. 1907). Because the "printer" or clerk added punctuation after the statute was enacted, English judges refused to consider punctuation when interpreting a statute.

In contrast, in the United States, Congress passes bills with the punctuation included; hence, "[t]here is no reason why punctuation, which is intended to and does assist in making clear and plain the meaning of all things else in the English language, should be rejected in the case of the interpretation of [American] statutes." *Id.* at 2. American legislators are presumed to know and apply common rules of grammar and punctuation (syntactic rules). Because the plain meaning canon presumes that legislators use grammar and punctuation appropriately, the general rule provides that punctuation and grammar matter unless the ordinary meaning suggests that they should be ignored. 2A Jabez Gridley Sutherland Statutes and Statutory Construction §47.15 at 346 (7th ed. 2007 Norman Singer ed.) ("[A]n act should be read as punctuated unless there is some reason to do otherwise....").

Sometimes, there is a reason for ignoring grammar. For example, in *U.S. National Bank of Oregon v. Independent Insurance Agents of America, Inc.*, 508 U.S. 439 (1993), the Court ignored the placement of quotation marks to conclude that a specific section of a statute had not been repealed. In so doing, the Court said,

A statute's plain meaning must be enforced, of course, and the meaning of a statute will typically heed the commands of its punctuation. But a purported plain-meaning analysis based only on punctuation is necessarily incomplete and runs the risk of distorting a statute's true meaning.... No more than isolated words or sentences are punctuation alone a reliable guide for discovery of a statute's meaning. Statutory construction is a holistic endeavor and, at a minimum, must account for a statute's full text, language[,] as well as punctuation, structure, and subject matter.

Id. at 455.

When grammar and punctuation are used correctly and consistently, a reader's understanding of written material is enhanced. However, not everyone uses grammar and punctuation correctly or consistently, not even legislators. Indeed, some grammar rules are optional. Let's look at one example: the serial comma rule (also known as the Oxford or Harvard comma rule). Pursuant to the serial comma rule, a writer should separate each item in a series of items with a comma to make clear that each item is separate from the others. This is the rule, but not every English writer follows it. Indeed, while the Chicago Manual of Style insists on its use, the Associated Press considers this comma superfluous.

Lawyers should always use the serial comma. Let's see why. Serial comma adherents use a comma to separate each item in a list (yellow, blue, red, and white), while non-serial comma adherents use a comma to separate all but the final two items in a list (yellow, blue, red and white). Someone who uses a serial comma might interpret the second list to include only three types of items: (1) those that are yellow, (2) those that are blue, and (3) those that are red and white. Yet the writer may have intended four types of items: (1) those that are yellow, (2) those that are blue, (3) those that are red, and (4) those that are white. Without knowing whether the writer is a serial comma user, the reader cannot know which meaning the writer intended. But when the comma is included, ambiguity disappears. Thus, because the serial comma aids clarity, legal writers should always use serial commas when writing.

As noted, when used correctly and consistently, grammar and punctuation aid understanding. Used incorrectly or inconsistently, grammar and punctuation can easily confuse a reader. For example, one familiar and fun example is the following: "With gratitude to my parents, the Pope and Mother Teresa." Without the serial comma after the word "Pope," the sentence suggests that the writer's parents are the Pope and Mother Teresa, rather than additional recipients of the writer's gratitude. Thus, punctuation is a fallible standard of meaning and is used only as a last resort in construing doubtful statutes. "Punctuation is a minor, and not a controlling, element in interpretation, and courts will disregard the punctuation of a statute, or re-punctuate it, if need be, to give effect to what otherwise appears to be its purpose and true meaning." *United States v. Ron Pair Enter., Inc.*, 489 U.S. 235, 250 (1989) (O'Connor, J., concurring) (quotations omitted). Hence, punctuation and grammar matter but only when viewed within their textual context.

The case below explains the general punctuation rule.

Manager v. Board of State Medical Examiners

Court of Appeals of Maryland
45 A. 891 (Md. Ct. App. 1900)

[handwritten: — good example of Scrivenor's errors]

◆ J. Upshur Dennis, Judge.

The difficulty presented by [the statute at issue] arises out of its punctuation. As printed, the section contains two sentences. The second sentence, separated by a period from the first, is utterly unintelligible. Obviously, it was not intended to read as it does read. The period after the word "registered," and the capital letter "I" following, break into two sentences what was evidently designed to be but one sentence. If the period be changed to a comma, and the capital "I" to a small "i," some meaning is given to the last clause of the section, and the whole section is made to harmonize with the general scheme of the legislation of which it forms a part. Can such a change be made? Neither bad grammar nor inaccurate punctuation can alter the obvious sense of a legislative enactment. This is necessarily so. The statutes in England are not punctuated in the original rolls, but more or less marks of punctuation appear in them as printed by authority. With us, the punctuation is the work of the draftsman, the engrosser, or the printer. In the legislative body the bill is read, so that the ear, not the eye, takes cognizance of it. Therefore the punctuation is not, in either country, of controlling effect in the interpretation...." Punctuation is a most fallible standard by which to interpret a writing. It may be resorted to when all other means fail.... In *Kinkele v. Wilson*, 45 N. E. 869, where the punctuation accorded with common sense, the use of a capital letter in the middle of a sentence was regarded as accidental.... And in *Weatherly v. Mister*, 39 Md. 629, this court said: "Punctuation may perhaps be resorted to when no other means can be found of solving an ambiguity, but not in cases where no real ambiguity exists, except what the punctuation itself creates. In such cases it will not be allowed to confuse a construction otherwise clear." "Punctuation may aid in ascertaining the true reading of a production, but the production may be read and interpreted without such aid." "Punctuation is no part of the statute."

* * *

Points for Discussion

1. *Statutory Language*: While it's hard to tell with this opinion, can you tell what the punctuation issue was?

2. *Theories*: Can you discern any specific approach in this opinion?

3. *General Rule*: What is the general rule regarding punctuation? What is the rationale for that rule? Does it surprise you that punctuation and grammar are relatively unimportant for discerning meaning?

4. *Scrivener's Error*: In this case, the court essentially refused to read the statute as written because it had a scrivener error. Additionally, the examples the court of-

fered similarly appear to have been scrivener's errors. Why didn't the court simply apply that doctrine?

* * *

C. Special Punctuation Rules

1. Commas: The General Rule

Commas are particularly troubling in the English language—their use is "exceedingly arbitrary and indefinite." *United States v. Palmer*, 3 Wheat. 610, 638 (1818) (separate opinion of Johnson, J.) Commas are troubling, in part, because comma rules are not consistently followed, yet their placement can be critical to meaning. Lynne Truss famously pointed out: "[A] panda eats shoots and leaves" means something very different from "a panda eats, shoots, and leaves." LYNNE TRUSS, EATS, SHOOTS & LEAVES THE ZERO TOLERANCE APPROACH TO PUNCTUATION (2003). The two sentences vary by only two commas. But their meanings are entirely different. The phrase "the panda eats shoots and leaves" tells us what the panda has for dinner. The phrase "the panda eats, shoots, and leaves" tells us in what order the panda had his dinner, shot his companions, and left the party. Note that the second sentence again illustrates the importance of the serial comma rule that we saw earlier: When a comma separates a series of items, each item that is distinct from the others should be set off by a comma.

In statutes, comma placement can be critical. For example, in *Peterson v. Midwest Security Insurance Co.*, 636 N.W.2d 727 (Wis. 2001), a statute provided that owners of "real property and buildings, structures and improvements thereon...." were immune from certain lawsuits. *Id.* at 728. The plaintiff had fallen from a tree stand owned by the defendant. The defendant did not own the land beneath the tree stand. Despite the absence of a comma between "real property" and "buildings," the majority ignored the missing punctuation and interpreted the language to provide immunity to (1) real property, and (2) buildings, structures, and improvements on *any* real property. *Id.* at 578 & n.7. The dissent disagreed, applied the serial comma rule, and argued that the statute meant (1) real property, and (2) any buildings, structures, and improvements *on that* real property. *Id.* at 588 (Bradley, J., dissenting). Thus, the dissent found the absence of a comma critical, while the majority ignored its absence. *See also Plymouth Mut. Life Ins. v. Illinois Mid-Continent Life Ins., Co.*, 378 F.2d 389, 390 (3d Cir. 1967) (holding that language set off by commas in a contract was intended to describe not limit the words preceding it).

In the next case, notice that the legislature did not use the serial comma. Had it done so, resolution of this issue would have been easier. Do you see why?

People v. Walsh

Criminal Court, City of New York
859 N.Y.S.2d 906, 19 Misc. 3d 1105(A) (Crim. Ct. 2008)

◆ SHAWNDYA L. SIMPSON, J.

The defendant is charged with one count of Overdriving, Torturing and Injuring Animals; Failure to Provide Proper Sustenance under Agriculture and Markets Law (hereinafter A.M.L.) §353....

New York Agriculture and Markets Law [A.M.L.] §353 states, in pertinent part that: A person who overdrives, overloads, tortures or cruelly beats or unjustifiably injures, maims, mutilates or kills any animal, whether wild or tame, and whether belonging to himself or to another, or deprives any animal of necessary sustenance, food or drink, or neglects or refuses to furnish it such sustenance or drink, or causes, procures or permits any animal to be overdriven, overloaded, tortured, cruelly beaten, or unjustifiably injured, maimed, mutilated or killed, or to be deprived of necessary food or drink, or who willfully sets on foot, instigates, engages in, or in any way furthers any act of cruelty to any animal, or any act tending to produce such cruelty, is guilty of a class A misdemeanor....

The accusatory instrument upon which the defendant is arraigned reads as follows:

Deponent is informed by Dr. Robert Reisman, of the Bergh Memorial Animal Hospital, that at the above stated date and time informant observed one feline suffering from: (i) dehydration; (ii) emaciation/underweight; (iii) a swollen and bleeding front right paw and said paw has a tumor; (iv) bone loss in the digits of said paw due to said tumor that was left untreated; (v) a polyp in the nasal cavity which caused said feline to have breathing difficulty; (vi) an ingrown nail that grew back into said feline's front left paw; (vii) chronic liver and kidney disease; and (viii) advanced periodontal disease. Informant further informs deponent that said feline has been medically neglected.

Deponent states that she asked the defendant if the defendant owned the feline and whether the feline had any medical conditions to which the defendant stated in sum and substance: I NEVER TOOK THE CAT TO THE VET. I OWNED HIM FOR FIFTEEN YEARS AND NEVER TOOK HIM TO THE VET. I NOTICED THE PAW WAS LIKE THAT. IT HAS BEEN LIKE THAT FOR A YEAR....

In its motion, the defense argues that the failure to provide medical care to an animal does not violate A.M.L. §353 because medical care is not "necessary sustenance".... In response, the People assert that ... the term "sustenance" covers more than food and drink....

That part of A.M.L. §353 that deals with acts by omission imposes criminal liability where a defendant deprives an animal of necessary sustenance or neglects or refuses to furnish such sustenance to an animal or where the animal is permitted to be tortured or subjected to cruelty. Although it is alleged that the animal was under weight and dehydrated, this allegation does not establish that the defendant deprived the animal of necessary sustenance, that is food or water, given the additional facts alleged herein. To this extent, the defense is correct in its assertions.

A plain reading of the statute reveals that "necessary sustenance" is described within that clause as "food or drink." The grammatical construction of the clause "or deprives any animal of necessary sustenance, food or drink, or neglects or refuses to furnish it such sustenance or drink" indicates that "necessary sustenance" is "food or drink." " '[W]here phrases were meant to be separated, the statute delineates such separation by placement of a comma before the disjunctive or' ". Was the statute intended to list three separate types of deprivation it would have read " … sustenance, food, or drink …". For example, in an author's dedication "to my parents, the Pope and Mother Theresa", the absence of a comma between "Pope" and "and" indicates that the author's parents are the Pope and Mother Theresa and not that a separate dedication was being made to each of the three. "Three or more items in a series should be separated by commas". Evidently, the clause " … necessary sustenance, food or drink, or …" is not a series or a list. Further, "[w]here a statute describes a particular situation to which it applies, an inference must be drawn that what is omitted or not included was intended to be omitted or excluded". The plain language of the law must be relied upon and in this instance, the meaning of "necessary sustenance" is reiterated in the statute as food or drink.[2]

The statute also states that the law applies where the defendant " … refuses to furnish it such sustenance or drink, or causes, …", omitting or replacing the term sustenance for food. The terms "sustenance" and "food" are used interchangeably in the statute and are consequently one in the same. "A central rule of statutory construction is that when the statutory language is clear and unambiguous, the court should construe the language so as to give effect to the plain, ordinary meaning of the words used."[3] Under the statute, "necessary sustenance" is defined by its ordinary meaning as essential alimentations. Therefore, the failure to provide an animal with medical care is not encompassed in the phrase "necessary sustenance." …

A charge under A. M. L. 353 for failure to provide medical care cannot be based solely on the term "necessary sustenance" since such care is not included in the ordinary meaning of the phrase. However, the failure to provide medical care alone may be chargeable based on [another section of the act] since torture and cruelty are defined therein as every act, omission, or neglect, that causes or permits an animal to suffer unjustifiable physical pain or death (A.M.L. 350 (2)). The instant allegations suffi-

---

2. The words "food or drink" in this instance are what is known as Appositives since they serve to give additional information about the immediately preceding word, in this case "sustenance," and are set off from the rest of the clause with commas.

3. "[G]enerally, penal laws must be construed so as to give effect to their most natural and obvious meaning. A court is obligated to construe an unambiguous statute according to its plain meaning, even if the plain meaning seems unintended or inadvisable. Moreover, it is basic that a criminal statute is to be narrowly construed against the State and in favor of the accused. A strained or unnatural interpretation of a penal statute could potentially expand criminal liability and therefore courts must be scrupulous in insuring that penal responsibility is not extended beyond the fair scope of the statutory mandate."

ciently show that the defendant neglected the animal and permitted it to suffer unjustifiable physical pain. Consequently, the allegations are sufficient for [that] charge.

Accordingly, the defendant's motion to dismiss is denied....

* * *

Points for Discussion

1. *Statutory Language*: What was the language at issue? What did each party want that language to mean? What meaning did the court adopt?

2. *Theories*: Which theory did the court use?

3. *Punctuation*: Why did the court conclude that the defendant had not violated the statute by failing to provide medical care? How was the punctuation relevant to the court's decision? Would the outcome have been different if the statute had been written as follows: "a person who deprives any animal of necessary sustenance, food, or drink ... is guilty of a class A misdemeanor"?

4. *Appositives*: An appositive is a noun or noun phrase that renames another noun, which is next to it. Appositive can be short or long combination of words. Appositives are set apart from the first noun by commas or other punctuation. Here are some examples; the appositives are written in italics: The insect, *an ant*, is crawling across the dog's food bowl. The insects, *hundreds or more angry red ants*, are swarming around the dog's food bowl. What language in A.M.L. 353 did the court conclude was an appositive?

5. *Rule of Lenity*: Did the court consider the rule of lenity? See footnote 3.

6. *Guilty*: Although the court agreed with the defendant on his punctuation or grammar argument, the court still found him guilty. Why?

* * *

2. Commas: Special Rules

a. Reddendo Singula Singulis

Reddendo singula singulis is Latin meaning "rendering each to his own." This canon is appropriate when a complex sentence has multiple subjects and either multiple verbs or objects that are incorrectly placed. "Under the canon *reddendo singula singulis*, where a sentence contains several antecedents and several consequents they are to be read distributively. In other words, the words are to be applied to the subjects that seem most properly related by context and applicability." *In re Macke Intern. Trade, Inc.*, 370 B.R. 236, 251–52 (9th Cir. 2007) (internal quotations omitted).

By "rendering," or associating, each object or verb to its appropriate subject, the sentence is correctly understood. To illustrate, assume that a will provides, "I devise and bequeath my real property and personal property to State University." The term "devise" is more appropriate for real property, while the term "bequeath" is more appropriate for personal property. The sentence would have been clearer if written as follows: "I devise my real property and bequeath my personal property to State University." Notice that this second sentence is much longer, even while being clearer and more accurate. *Reddendo singula singulis* allows a reader to interpret the first sentence as if it were written like the second. In other words, the canon allows readers to ignore grammar and interpret the language as intended. To illustrate again, a contract might say "for money or other good consideration paid or given." *Reddendo singula singulis* tells us that the phrase really means "for money paid or other good consideration given."

b. The Doctrine of Last Antecedent

The *Doctrine (or Rule) of Last Antecedent,* is a subset of *reddendo singular singulis.* Jabez Sutherland, a lawyer, created the doctrine of last antecedent in 1891, when he wrote his famous treatise on interpreting contracts and statutes. He created the doctrine to help legal interpreters derive the meaning of contract clauses that contained multiple obligations or conditions. To understand the doctrine, you must first understand what an antecedent is. In grammar parlance, an "antecedent" is a word, phrase, or clause that is replaced by a pronoun or other substitute later (sometimes earlier) in the same or in a subsequent sentence. For example, in the sentence "*The professor asked the students whether they liked him,*" the phrase "the students" is the antecedent of "they," and the "professor" is the antecedent of "him." Pronouns are generally understood to replace their closest antecedent. Thus, in the following sentence, "*The professor asked the student whether he liked the reading,*" the pronoun "he" is ambiguous because "he" could refer either to "the student" or "the professor." Most readers will assume that "he" refers to the last antecedent in the sentence: "the student." If the writer did not intend that meaning, the writer should repeat the noun "professor" rather than use the pronoun "he."

The doctrine of last antecedent builds on this grammatical assumption. Assume that rather than using a pronoun to replace an antecedent, the writer included a list of items with a modifying, or qualifying, phrase. For example, assume a regulation provides as follows: "holders of commercial vehicular licenses may operate cars, boats, tractors, and trucks under three tons." When a modifying word or phrase is used with a group of obligations or conditions, the modifying phrase is presumed to modify only the condition or obligation that immediately precedes that modifying phrase. Hence, in our example, the modifying phrase "under three tons" would be understood to apply only to trucks and not to cars, boats, or tractors. This first step is relatively intuitive and mirrors regular grammar use.

Conversely, the second step is less intuitive and is Sutherland's addition: if there is a comma between the modifying phrase and the list, then the modifying phrase applies to all of the antecedents. Hence, if we modify our example by adding a comma after the word "trucks" — "holders of commercial vehicular licenses may operate cars, boats, tractors, and trucks, under three tons" — then the modifying phrase "under three tons" would be understood to apply to cars, boats, tractors, and trucks. Notice how one, simple comma can significantly affect meaning under this doctrine.

Importantly, this doctrine is not absolute (which is why the term "doctrine" is used here, rather than "rule"); it is meant to be an aid to interpretation, especially because the doctrine conflicts with general comma rules. *Lessee v. Irvine*, 3 U.S. (3 Dall.) 425, 444 (1799). The choice to put a comma between the qualifying phrase and the preceding list of antecedents is grammatically optional. *United States v. Bass*, 404 U.S. 336, 340 n.6. (1971). For this reason, judges will ignore the doctrine when applying it would result in an absurd result or would make no sense. *See, e.g., State v. One 1990 Chevrolet Pickup*, 857 P.2d 44, 48 (N.M. Ct. App. 1993) (stating it was applying "a less technical version of the 'last antecedent rule'").

Here is a well-known case that shows a court's application of this doctrine to resolve the meaning of a statute.

Commonwealth v. Kelly
Supreme Judicial Court of Massachusetts
58 N.E. 691 (Mass. 1900)

◆ Knowlton, J.

Pub. St. c. 100, § 9, provides, as one of the conditions of licenses, "that no sale of spirituous or intoxicating liquor shall be made between the hours of twelve at night and six in the morning; nor during the Lord's day, except that if the licensee is also licensed as an innholder, he may supply such liquor to guests who have resorted to his house for food or lodgings." By St.1885, c. 90, the word "twelve" is changed to "eleven." The only question in this case is whether the exception permitting innholders to supply guests extends to the hours between 11 at night and 6 in the morning. The ordinary rule of construction in a case like this confines the exception to the last antecedent. The purpose of the legislature seems to have been absolutely to prohibit sales of intoxicating liquor during the late hours of the night, except by apothecaries, and on Sundays to permit the supply of liquor by innholders only to guests who have resorted to the house for food or lodging. Following this interpretation of the law, we believe it generally has been understood that all places where liquor is sold to be drunk on the premises are to be closed at 11 o'clock in the evening, and are to remain closed until 6 the next morning. If rooms in inns were to remain open for the supply of liquor to guests of the house, it would be easy for licensees to evade the law by keeping their rooms open for sales to others, and thus to promote disorder. As the act is printed ... there is a semicolon after the word "morning," although when the original act was first published the point used was a comma. If this punctuation is given full effect as an indication of the meaning to be expressed in reading the act, the case is free from question. Although it has been held that punctuation may be disregarded, it may be resorted to as an aid in construction when it tends to throw light on the meaning. In the present case the repeated re-enactments by the legislature with the same punctuation, and the absolute form of the title of the latest act, tend to support the claim of the commonwealth. This latest statute is called "An act to prohibit the sale of spirituous and intoxicating liquors between the hours of eleven at night and six in the morning." St.1885, c. 90. We are of opinion that the exception does not apply to sales made between the hours of 11 at night and 6 in the morning. Exceptions overruled.

* * *

Points for Discussion

1. *Statutory Language*: What was the language at issue? What did each party want that language to mean? What meaning did the court adopt?

2. *Theories*: Which theory did the court use?

3. *Doctrine of Last Antecedent*: What role did this doctrine play in the court's reasoning?

4. *Exceptions and Provisos*: The language at issue in this case was contained in an exception to the general rule contained in the statute. The general rule provided that "no sale of ... liquor shall be made between the hours of twelve at night and six in the morning; nor during the Lord's day." The exception allowed innkeepers to supply liquor to its guests. As you will learn in Chapter 9, exceptions and provisos are generally narrowly construed. Would this canon have aided the court in resolving this issue?

5. *Amend the Statute*: If the legislature intended that hotels could sell alcohol both on Sundays and between 11:00PM and 6:00AM: how should the statute be amended pursuant to the doctrine of last antecedent?

* * *

In the case that follows, the doctrine is being used to resolve the meaning of language in an insurance contract. This case demonstrates that many of the canons that you are learning are relevant to more than just interpreting statutes; they are relevant to interpreting all written, legal language. In addition to the rule of last antecedent, notice that both the majority and concurrence resort to substantive canons relevant specifically to insurance law and contract law. Can you identify these canons?

Phoenix Control Systems, Inc. v. Insurance Co. of North America

Supreme Court of Arizona
769 P.2d 463 (Az. 1990)

◆ CAMERON, JUSTICE.

... PCS and Johnson are both engaged in the business of designing and selling industrial automated control systems, including computer programs and devices for the control of water and waste water treatment plants.

Each module of Johnson's software contains a proprietary statement that the computer program is Johnson's property, and that use without their [sic] written consent is prohibited. Johnson used its software to develop a computer program for process control at a waste water treatment plant on 91st Avenue in Phoenix. The JC–5000S water treatment program is a registered copyright of Johnson's, under the title "JC–5000 Process Control System".

John Schratz was an employee of Johnson's from April 1974 through December 1982 when he was fired. He then formed PCS and engaged in competition with Johnson.

Rodney Larsen was the project manager of the 91st Avenue project. He was a Johnson employee from 13 September 1976, through 4 January 1984. According to Johnson, Larsen was discharged because of his involvement in the preparation of the PCS Union Hills bid. Larsen then joined PCS.

Schratz allegedly intended to market the JC–5000S, or its functional equivalent, as a PCS product. Johnson sued PCS, Schratz, and Larsen in federal district court based on this and other actions PCS took allegedly to interfere with Johnson's business ... [The interference related to a bid for work].

During this time, PCS held a comprehensive property damage and liability insurance policy with INA. The policy provided that INA would defend PCS "in any lawsuits brought against you as the result of any activity covered by YOUR LIABILITY COVERAGE ..."

PCS requested that INA defend it in the federal court and INA refused. INA maintained that it had no duty to defend PCS in the Johnson action because the alleged copyright infringement did not occur in connection with advertising activity....

APPLICATION OF THE LAST ANTECEDENT RULE

Liability claims covered under the INA insurance policy included "*bodily injury, personal injury,* or *property damage,* resulting from an *occurrence....*" (Emphasis in original). Personal injury was defined in eight separate categories:

- Mental suffering caused by the fact that someone was killed or suffered *bodily injury,* if the original injury or death was covered by this policy....

- *Any infringement of copyright or improper or unlawful use of slogans in your advertising.*

INA contends that the phrase "any infringement of copyright or improper or unlawful use of slogans in your advertising" means that PCS would be covered only if the "infringement of copyright" or "unlawful use of slogans" occurred in connection with advertising activity. In other words, INA believes that "in your advertising" modifies *both* infringement of copyright and the unlawful use of slogans. Thus, from INA's perspective there is no coverage for infringement of copyright because PCS's actions were not in connection with advertising activity....

PCS contends that the last antecedent doctrine should be applied to interpret "infringement of copyright" to include all forms of copyright infringement and not just that in connection with advertising.

The last antecedent rule is recognized in Arizona and requires that a qualifying phrase be applied to the word or phrase immediately preceding as long as there is no contrary intent indicated. *Town of Florence v. Webb*, 40 Ariz. 60, 9 P.2d 413 (1932) (rule will not apply where its application would render the rest of the statute at issue merely surplusage, and where more important rules of construction, such as giving effect to every part of a statute, are applicable). The last antecedent rule is not inflexible and it will not be applied where the context or clear meaning of a word or phrase requires otherwise. As stated by Appleman in his treatise on insurance:

> Qualifying words and phrases in an insurance contract ordinarily refer only to their immediately preceding antecedent. When a sentence contains several antecedents and several consequents, the words are applied to the subjects to which they seem most properly related by context and applicability.
>
> An insurance policy is not to be interpreted in a factual vacuum.

13 Appleman, Insurance Law and Practice § 7383 at 8 (1989 Supp.).

By applying the last antecedent rule, PCS asserts that "in your advertising" modifies only the words "improper or unlawful use of slogans", and does not modify "infringement of copyright." Thus, any form of copyright infringement would be covered and INA would have a duty to defend the federal district court action instituted by Johnson. We agree.

We will construe insurance contracts to protect the reasonable expectations of the insured. We believe that PCS, from reading the policy, could reasonably expect that all forms of copyright infringement would be covered, while coverage for the improper or unlawful use of slogans would be limited to that in connection with advertising activity. We believe that the context and clear meaning of the insurance policy does not require us to construe copyright infringement as limited to that in connection with advertising activity. Accordingly, we hold that infringement of copyright is covered by the policy....

♦ FELDMAN, VICE CHIEF JUSTICE, specially concurring.

I concur in the court's opinion and in its conclusions. I write separately only because I believe the use of the doctrine of the last antecedent gives us no aid in interpreting the policy. We have recognized the limitations of this canon of construction when interpreting legislative acts. *See Town of S. Tucson v. Board of Supervisors*, 84 P.2d 581, 585 (1938) (clear intent of the legislature takes precedence as a canon of construction over all grammatical rules, particularly the doctrine of the last antecedent). I see no benefit and much harm in using the doctrine of the last antecedent in construing contracts. Reliance on such arcane, judicially adopted grammatical rules does not help us reach the intentions of the parties. Surely, even if the parties had bargained for the boilerplate language in this policy—something the record does not establish at all— it would be a fiction to pretend they drafted the language mindful that its meaning would be ascertained through use of the doctrine of the last antecedent.

The meaning of the policy is to be determined by the intent of the parties. Where, as here, we deal with a standardized policy and its boilerplate language, the parties had no meeting of the minds and their intentions are not evident. Therefore, [another case] requires us to follow the plain meaning of the words of the boilerplate provision, unless we would have reason to believe the party assenting would not have done so if he knew the policy contained the term in question.

In this case, however, the words have no plain meaning. The clause in question can be reasonably interpreted to have either the meaning advanced by the insured or that advanced by the insurer.... It is, in short, ambiguous. If ever the rule of ambiguity should apply, it is here, and the clause should be interpreted against the drafter.

I therefore concur in the court's interpretation of the clause but not in the reasoning of that portion of the opinion dealing with the last antecedent doctrine.

* * *

Points for Discussion

1. *Statutory Language*: What was the language at issue? What did each party want that language to mean? What meaning did the majority and concurrence adopt?

2. *Theories*: Which theory did the majority use? The concurrence?

3. *Substantive Law*: Insurance law, in this case a form of contract law, has its own unique, interpretive rules. First, insurance contracts should be interpreted to protect the reasonable expectation of the parties. Second, ambiguities in contracts should be construed against the drafter. Can you guess why we do not construe ambiguous statutes against the drafter? Other substantive areas, such as tax law, have their own interpretive canons as well.

4. *Amend the Contract*: Can you amend the contract to achieve the resulted urged by INA?

5. *Current Relevance*: As textualism has gained currency and the linguistic canons have gained favor, this doctrine has become more of a hard-and-fast rule than a rule of thumb. In 2003, Justice Scalia brought the doctrine to the forefront of judicial attention in *Barnhart v. Thomas*, 540 U.S. 20 (2003). In applying the doctrine, Justice Scalia acknowledged that "this rule is not an absolute and can assuredly be overcome by other indicia of meaning," but that "construing a statute in accord with the rule is quite sensible as a matter of grammar." *Id.* at 26. He supported his approach to the doctrine with the following example:

> Consider, for example, the case of parents who, before leaving their teenage son alone in the house for the weekend, warn him, — "You will be punished if you throw a party or engage in any other activity that damages the house." If the son nevertheless throws a party and is caught, he should hardly be able to avoid punishment by arguing that the house was not damaged. The parents proscribed (1) a party, and (2) any other activity that damages the house. As far as appears from what they said, their reasons for prohibiting the home-alone party may have had nothing to do with damage to the house — for instance, the risk that underage drinking

or sexual activity would occur. And even if their only concern was to prevent damage, it does not follow from the fact that the same interest underlay both the specific and the general prohibition that proof of impairment of that interest is required for both. The parents, foreseeing that assessment of whether an activity had in fact—"damaged" the house could be disputed by their son, might have wished to preclude all argument by specifying and categorically prohibiting the one activity—hosting a party—that was most likely to cause damage and most likely to occur. *Id.* at 27–28.

Consider the following response to Justice Scalia.

> [A] law firm partner instructs her associate to review a client's file—"for emails or documents written by the CEO." Although [the sentence is] ambiguous, an astute associate would not apply the Rule, but would read the modifying clause,—"written by the CEO," as modifying both the first and last antecedent and search for both emails written by the CEO and documents written by the CEO.

Jeremy L. Ross, *A Rule of Last Resort: A History of the Doctrine of the Last Antecedent in the United State Supreme Court*, 39 SOUTHWESTERN L.R. 325 (2010). Do these word battles suggest that the doctrine should have a significant or minor role in interpretation? Were you aware of this doctrine before you studied this topic? Do you anticipate most legislators are aware of it?

* * *

Thus, as with all the canons but even more so with this canon, the doctrine of last antecedent must be used, not robotically, but with common sense and an understanding of context. Indeed, one might say that to call it a "rule" as many judges do is, at best, "oxymoronic." Ross, *supra*, at 336.

D. Special Grammar Rules

We turn now from the general punctuation rule and its exceptions to the general grammar rule and its exceptions. The general grammar rule is the same as the general punctuation rule: (1) grammar matters, unless the ordinary meaning suggests that grammar should be ignored, and (2) courts presume that legislatures use grammar accurately and consistently. For example, in *Robinson v. City of Lansing*, 782 N.W.2d 171 (2010), the plaintiff tripped on a sidewalk, fracturing her wrist and requiring surgery. Both parties agreed that the portion of the sidewalk where she tripped was less than two inches above a depressed portion. The Michigan legislature had codified a common law rule, known as the two-inch rule, which relieved municipalities of liability when the difference in a sidewalk was less than two inches. The statute provided:

> (1) Except as otherwise provided by this section, a municipal corporation has no duty to repair or maintain, and is not liable for injuries arising from,

a portion of *a county highway* outside of the improved portion of the highway designed for vehicular travel, including a sidewalk, trailway, crosswalk, or other installation....

(2) A discontinuity defect of less than 2 inches creates a rebuttable inference that the municipal corporation maintained the sidewalk, trailway, crosswalk, or other installation outside of the improved portion of *the highway* designed for vehicular travel in reasonable repair....

Id. at 178 (quoting MCL 691.1402a) (emphasis added). The plaintiff sued, claiming that the City had failed to maintain the sidewalk in reasonable repair. In response, the City raised the two inch rule as an affirmative defense. The issue for the court was whether subsection 2 of the statute — which created a rebuttable inference that a discontinuity defect of less than two inches in a sidewalk meant that the municipality maintained the sidewalk in reasonable repair — applied to sidewalks adjacent to state highways or only to sidewalks adjacent to county highways. The court focused on the definite article "the" preceding the word "highway" in subsection 2 to conclude that the highways referred to in subsection 2 were the "county highways" identified in subsection 1 and were not highways in general. *Id.* at 179–80. Had the legislature used the indefinite article "a" before the word "highway" in subsection 2 the result may well have been different.

We turn next to some specific grammar rules.

1. The Meaning of "And" and "Or"

Two simple words that are typically used to connect items and phrases in sentences can be critical. These words are "and" and "or." Generally, they mean different things. The word "or" means either. In contrast, the word "and" means all. But sometimes the word "and" is used to mean either and the word "or" is used to mean all. For example, consider the phrase: "Would you like cream *or* sugar?" Surely, you could choose both cream and sugar, or you could choose neither cream or sugar. In the last sentence, the writer used the word "or" to mean none, one, the other, or both. Similarly, sometimes the word "and" is used to mean either: consider the phrase, "She was forced to choose between getting gas *and* making it to class on time." In this sentence, "and" does not mean both; it means one or the other; either she would have time to get gas and be late for class, or she could chose not to get gas and arrive at class on time. When drafting, it can be difficult to know whether to use "and" or "or." To counteract this conundrum, many legal drafters have resorted to using the imprecise wording "and/or," a practice that should be discouraged as imprecise, and one that results in ambiguity.

When legislators draft statutes, they typically use the conjunctive "and" when two or more requirements must be fulfilled to comply with a statute. Where failure to comply with any one requirement would not be fatal, legislatures use the disjunctive "or." 1A JABEZ GRIDLEY SUTHERLAND STATUTES AND STATUTORY CONSTRUCTION (7th ed. 2009 Norman Singer ed.). Ordinarily, "and" and "or" are not interchangeable.

But because the use of these two terms baffles legislators as much as other legal writers, judges will construe the word "and" to mean "or" whenever such interpretation will better effectuate the obvious intention of the legislature. Often, just as in both examples above, textual or other context can help determine which meaning was intended.

In summary, generally "and" and "or" are understood as grammar intended; however, occasionally, they are not.

2. Singular and Plural

Unlike the and/or canon, which follows the general grammar rule, the canon relating to number usage does not follow the general grammar rule; just the opposite is true. For ease of drafting, statutes are typically written in the singular. But for statutory interpretation, a legislature's use of the singular is presumed to include the plural, and the legislature's use of the plural is presumed to include the singular. The *United States Code* provides, "In determining the meaning of any act or resolution of Congress, unless the context otherwise indicates, words importing the singular include and apply to several persons, parties, or things; words importing the plural include the singular...." 1 U.S.C. § 1 (2015). Many states have similar statutes, for example, Minnesota and Pennsylvania. Minn. Stat. § 645.08(2) (2015); 1 Pa. Cons. Stat. §§ 1921–28 (2015).

Judges ignore grammar in this instance because "[t]he historical purpose of construing plural and singular nouns and verbs interchangeably is to avoid requiring the legislature to use such expressions as 'person or persons,' 'he, she, or they,' and 'himself or themselves.' Under this principle, the plural has often been held to apply to the singular in a statute, absent evidence of contrary legislative intent." *Homebuilders Ass'n v. Scottsdale*, 925 P.2d 1359, 1366 (Ariz. Ct. App. 1996) (interpreting the words "council men" in Ariz. Rev. Stat. § 19-142(a) to include the singular "council man"). As with the other canons of interpretation, a judge will ignore this canon when the court finds a contrary legislative intent. *See, e.g., Van Horn v. William Blanchard Co.*, 438 A.2d 552, 554 (N.J. 1981) *overruled by* N.J. Stat. Ann. § 2A:15-5.3 (holding that New Jersey's Comparative Negligence Act's use of the singular "person" did not include the plural "persons," because textual context showed that the legislature had intended the singular to be used).

Does the court apply the singular/plural exception or the general grammar canon in the case that follows?

Sursely v. Peake

United States Court of Appeals, Federal Circuit.
551 F.3d 1351 (Fed. Cir. 2009)

GARJARSA, C.J. [with whom NEWMAN, and PLAGER, JJ. concur].

Claimant–Appellant James E. Sursely appeals a decision of the Court of Appeals for Veterans Claims ("Veterans Court") affirming a decision of the Board of Veterans'

Appeals ("Board") that denied his claim for two separate clothing allowances pursuant to 38 U.S.C. § 1162. The central issue in this case is whether proper interpretation of the statute requires the Secretary of Veterans Affairs ("Secretary") to award more than one clothing allowance to a veteran suffering from multiple service-connected disabilities requiring multiple orthopedic appliances. Because the Board and the Veterans Court incorrectly read the statute to preclude the Secretary from making more than one award, we reverse.

Mr. Sursely served on active duty from December 1966 to November 1969 in the Republic of Vietnam. On January 11, 1969, he "was hit by a land mine," which (among other injuries) required a left-hip disarticulation, an above-the knee amputation of his right leg, and an above-the-elbow amputation of his left arm. Mr. Sursely was retired from active duty due to permanent disability. On January 8, 1970, the Department of Veterans Affairs ("VA") awarded Mr. Sursely a 100% disability rating, found service connection, and awarded special monthly compensation pursuant to 38 U.S.C. § 314 (now 38 U.S.C. § 1114 (2006)).

The VA received Mr. Sursely's claim for two separate clothing allowances in March 2003. Mr. Sursely explained in his application that he "is entitled to an annual clothing allowance for [his] artificial arm, which is a prosthetic appliance that tends to wear and/or tear shirts.... In addition, Mr. Sursely qualifies for a separate clothing allowance based upon loss of both legs that requires the use of a wheelchair that tends to wear and/or tear pants."

The VA Regional Office ("RO") requested the Director of the Compensation and Pension Service ("Director") to provide an advisory opinion on whether § 1162, which authorizes annual payment to veterans whose disabilities require clothing-damaging orthopedic appliances, permitted more than one annual clothing allowance. The Director interpreted the statute to permit only a single allowance based primarily on § 1162's use of the phrase "*a* (emphasis added) clothing allowance." The Director also found support for this interpretation in the implementing regulation, 38 C.F.R. § 3.810, which "mirrored" the statutory language. Based on that interpretation, the RO denied Mr. Sursely's request for a second clothing allowance.

After Mr. Sursely appealed this determination, the Board stated

> The Board is sympathetic to the veteran's argument that he has separate and distinct service connected disabilities which require separate and distinct clothing allowances; however, the plain language of the statute and implementing regulation is that a single annual clothing allowance is payable. Accordingly, the veteran's claim must be denied for lack of legal merit.

Mr. Sursely appealed ... to the Veterans Court, which ... upheld the denial of benefits, on the grounds that "the statutory language in section 1162 clearly provides only one clothing allowance per eligible veteran." Mr. Sursely now appeals to this court....

... We review the Veterans Court's interpretation of a statute de novo.... The statute at issue in this appeal, § 1162, states that:

The Secretary under regulations which the Secretary shall prescribe, shall pay a clothing allowance of $588 per year to each veteran who—

(1) because of a service-connected disability, wears or uses a prosthetic or orthopedic appliance (including a wheelchair) which the Secretary determines tends to wear out or tear the clothing of the veteran.... 38 U.S.C. § 1162 (2003)....

[T]he sole question presented for our review is one of statutory interpretation.... "[T]he starting point in every case involving construction of a statute is the language itself." We interpret statutes "in accordance with [their] ordinary or natural meaning." "We must not be guided by a single sentence or member of a sentence, but look to the provisions of the whole law." "If the statutory language is clear and unambiguous, the inquiry ends with the plain meaning." In veterans benefits cases, "interpretive doubt is to be resolved in the veteran's favor." *Brown v. Gardner,* 513 U.S. 115, 118 (1994).

The Director, the Board, and the Veterans Court all emphasized that the statute authorizes "a clothing allowance," in the singular. Based on this phrasing, the VA determined that it was not statutorily authorized to pay more than one clothing allowance to Mr. Sursely and denied Mr. Sursely's request for a second clothing allowance for his independently qualifying orthopedic appliances affecting different articles of clothing. We disagree with this interpretation.

The *United States Code* provides very few intrinsic rules of construction. However, 1 U.S.C. § 1 (2006) provides that "unless the context indicates otherwise—words importing the singular include and apply to several persons, parties, or things; words importing the plural include the singular." As a result, it is impossible to determine the proper boundaries of the Secretary's authority pursuant to § 1162 with reference only to the singular nature of the indefinite article "a." Instead, a more thorough consideration of the statutory provision as a whole is required to provide the appropriate context.

In relevant part, the statute provides for "a clothing allowance" for "each veteran" who, "because of a service-connected disability, wears or uses a prosthetic or orthopedic appliance (including a wheelchair) which the Secretary determines tends to wear out or tear the clothing of the veteran." The key to clearly understanding the statute is the connection between the phrases "a clothing allowance" (setting out the benefit) and "a prosthetic or orthopedic appliance" (setting out the qualification for the benefit). This language is not a limitation, and does not expressly limit the veteran to a single clothing allowance. Instead, by linking receipt of the benefit to a single qualifying appliance, Congress recognized that multiple appliances might allow the award of multiple benefits.

To the extent that the Veterans Court's contrary interpretation suggests ambiguity in the statute, two factors require us to resolve that ambiguity in Mr. Sursely's favor. First, the link between a single clothing allowance and a single qualifying appliance is supported by Congress's decision to amend the statute in 1989. ["When Congress acts to amend a statute, we presume it intends its amendment to have real and substantial effect."]. As originally passed in 1972, the statute provided for a clothing allowance based on a disability necessitating the use of "a prosthetic or orthopedic appliance *or appliances*." The reference to a single clothing allowance for veterans using multiple appliances in the 1972 version demonstrates that the original version did not permit a veteran to receive multiple allowances for multiple prosthetic appliances. The language of the 1972 statute would have supported the Secretary's position and the denial of Mr. Sursely's claim would have been proper.

In 1989, however, Congress amended the statute to *delete* the reference to multiple appliances. The present statute now provides for a clothing allowance based on a disability necessitating the use of "a prosthetic or orthopedic appliance." The amended language indicates that the statute no longer contemplates the payment of a single clothing allowance for the use of multiple appliances. By changing the qualification for a clothing allowance from single or multiple orthopedic appliances to only a single qualifying appliance, Congress evidenced a clear intent to provide additional benefits for those veterans such as Mr. Sursely who use multiple orthopedic appliances.

Second, in the face of statutory ambiguity, we must apply the rule that "interpretive doubt is to be resolved in the veteran's favor."[5] *Brown*, 513 U.S. at 118. Clearly it is more favorable to veterans if the clothing allowance may be awarded on a per-appliance, rather than a per-veteran basis. Thus, even if the government's asserted interpretation of § 1162 is plausible, it would be appropriate under *Brown* only if the statutory language unambiguously permitted only one clothing allowance per veteran. As discussed above, the language at a minimum permits the reading whereby the benefit is linked to each qualifying appliance. The rule in *Brown* therefore requires that expansive reading of the applicable statute....

Because the Veterans Court erroneously concluded that the statute prohibited the award of multiple clothing allowances to a veteran, we reverse and remand for a determination of whether Mr. Sursely qualifies for multiple clothing allowances under the statute as we have interpreted it.

* * *

Points for Discussion

1. *Statutory Language*: What was the language at issue? What did each party want that language to mean? What meaning did the court of appeals adopt?

2. *Theories*: Which theory did the appeals court use? The Veterans Court? Did either court find the statute ambiguous? If so, how did it resolve that ambiguity?

3. *Singular/Plural Canon*: Which court applied the traditional grammar rule? Which applied the singular/plural exception canon?

---

5. Because the Secretary has not provided an interpretation of the statute eligible for *Chevron* deference, we need not consider the applicability of *Sears v. Principi*, 349 F.3d 1326 (Fed.Cir.2003), which properly urges caution when considering the meaning of a statute in light of both *Brown* and *Chevron*.

4. *United States Court of Appeals for Veterans Claims*: The Veterans Court, as it is commonly known, was established in 1988 as part of the Judicial Review Act. (Pub. L. No. 100-687). The Court has exclusive jurisdiction over decisions of the Board of Veterans' Appeals (Board or BVA). The Court reviews Board decisions appealed by claimants who believe the Board erred in its decision. The Court's review of Board decisions is based on the record before the agency and arguments of the parties, which are presented in a written brief, with oral argument generally held only in cases presenting new legal issues.

   The court is part of the United States judiciary. It is not part of the Department of Veterans Affairs. It is an Article I court, not an Article III court. Article I courts differ from Article III courts regarding their jurisdiction and authority. Congress delegates powers granted to it in Article I, namely the payment of money owed by the United States, taxation, regulation of the armed forces, and the governance of the District of Columbia and the territories. In addition to the Veterans Court, Congress has established others Article I courts, including the U.S. Court of Military Appeals, territorial courts like Guam, the U.S. Court of Federal Claims, and the U.S. Tax Court.

5. *Substantive Interpretive Rules*: In veterans' law, courts apply a presumption known as *Gardner's* Presumption, which directs that interpretive doubt, or ambiguity, is to be resolved in the veteran's favor. This canon was developed in *Brown v. Gardner*, 513 U.S. 115, 118 (1994). For a discussion of how this canon developed and why it conflicts with the *Chevron* doctrine, see Linda D. Jellum, *Heads I Win, Tails You Lose: Reconciling* Brown v. Gardner's *Presumption That Interpretive Doubt Be Resolved In Veterans' Favor With* Chevron, 61 Am. U. L. Rev. 59 (2011).

6. *Deference Standard*: Note that the appellate court applies a *de novo* standard of review to statutory interpretations made by the Veterans Court rather than a deference standard known as *Chevron* deference. *Chevron* deference is inapplicable to interpretations of statutes made by the Veterans Court because it is not the agency charged with administering veterans' laws. The Veteran's Administration is the agency in charge of administering these statutes and would generally receive *Chevron* deference for any reasonable interpretations of these laws. In Chapter 19, you will learn why the court said in footnote 5 that the Secretary's interpretation was not entitled to *Chevron* deference.

* * *

3. Words with Masculine, Feminine, and Neuter Meaning

The third specific grammar canon relates to masculine, feminine, and non-gendered words; it too defies typical grammar expectations. Until the 1980s or so, statutes were generally written using the masculine gender, because the masculine pronoun was used as a "generic" pronoun reference. Legislators did not intend to refer only to men when using the masculine pronoun; rather, this grammatical practice was just accepted as a language norm of the time. Although this historical practice has largely changed, for statutory interpretation purposes, the masculine pronoun is still generally interpreted to include the feminine. For example, the U.S. Code provides, "words importing the masculine gender include the feminine as well." 1 U.S.C. §2 (Lexis 2015). Most states have similar provisions. "Words used in the masculine gender may include the feminine and the neuter." Or. Rev. Stat. 174.110(2) (West 2015). Increasingly, legislatures are drafting in gender-neutral terms. *See, e.g.,* Or. Rev. Stat. Ann. §174.129 (West 2015) ("It shall be the policy of the State of Oregon that all statutes, rules and orders enacted, adopted or amended after October 3, 1979, be written in sex-neutral terms unless it is necessary for the purpose of the statute, rule or order that it be expressed in terms of a particular gender.").

A simple application of this canon can be seen in *Commonwealth. v. Henninger,* 25 Pa. D. & C.3d 625 (Pa. Ct. Com. Pl. 1981). The statute at issue in that case provided, "A person who is 18 years of age or older commits statutory rape, a felony of the second degree, when *he* engages in sexual intercourse with another person not his spouse who is less than 14 years of age." *Id.* at 626 (citing 18 Pa. Cons. Stat. §3122) (emphasis added). The female defendant argued that the gender-based language "he" demonstrated an "intent on the part of the legislators to protect only women" from statutory rape. *Id.* Citing the gender canon, the court rejected the defendant's argument. *Id.*

Notice that the statutes above only allow the masculine to include the feminine and neuter. None provide that the feminine includes the masculine and neuter. Why might this be so? The canon exists because the masculine pronoun was used as a gender-neutral pronoun. The feminine pronoun has not typically been used this way, although that use is increasing. Should the feminine pronoun be understood to include the masculine? Perhaps, but in *In Re Compensation of Williams,* the court refused to interpret the word "woman" to include men claiming that Or. Rev. Stat. 174.110(2) (quoted above) did not allow it to do so. 635 P.2d 384, 386 (Or. Ct. App. 1981) (holding that the word "woman" was not a word of gender), *aff'd,* 653 P.2d 970 (Or. 1982). As statutes are increasingly written in gender-neutral terms, this issue will become less relevant.

4. Mandatory and Discretionary

While the preceding canons did not follow the general grammar rule (that grammar matters), this last canon does. One issue that may arise when a court interprets a statute is whether the action at issue is required or is allowed, in other words, are the statutory requirements mandatory or discretionary. To resolve this question, courts will most commonly examine the verb used in a statute. For example, a court will look to see whether something "may," "shall," "must," or "should" be done. The legislature's verb choice is the most important consideration in determining whether a statute is mandatory. Ordinarily, "may" is considered discretionary, "shall" is considered mandatory, "must" is considered mandatory when a condition precedent is present, and "should" is considered discretionary. *Daniel v. United Nat'l Bank,* 505 S.E.2d 711 (W. Va. 1998).

When the legislature uses "shall" or "must," judges generally interpret those words as excluding judicial or executive discretion to take into account equity or policy. *Escondido Mut. Water Co. v. LaJolla Indians*, 466 U.S. 765, 772 (1984) ("The mandatory nature of the language chosen by Congress [—shall—] appears to require that the Commission include the Secretary's conditions in the license even if it disagrees with them."). Sometimes, though, "shall" can mean may:

> Ordinarily, the use of the word 'shall' in a statute carries with it the presumption that it is used in the imperative rather than in the directory sense. But this is not a conclusive presumption. Both the character and context of the legislation are controlling.... The mandatory sense to the word 'shall' should not be given, if by so doing the door to miscarriages of justice should be opened.

Jersey City v. State Bd. of Tax Appeals, 43 A.2d 799, 803–04 (N.J. Sup. Ct. 1945) (refusing to interpret "shall" in a statute to be mandatory); *Cobb Cnty. v. Robertson*, 724 S.E.2d 478, 479 (Ga. App. 2012) ("Even though the word "shall" is generally construed as mandatory, it need not always be construed in that fashion").

Conversely, "may" sometimes means shall or must:

> The word "may" generally denotes a discretionary provision while the use of the word "shall" suggests that the provision is mandatory. However, when the context indicates otherwise, "may" can have the effect of "must" or "shall".

Fink v. City of Detroit, 333 N.W.2d 376, 379 (Mich. Ct. App. 1983) (holding that "may" was mandatory) (internal citations omitted). In sum, generally a legislature's use of "shall" means statutory obligations are required, while its use of "may" means they are mandatory; however, occasionally, courts will ignore the usual meaning of these words to further legislative intent.

In the case that follows, does the court find that the word "shall" means may or did the court conclude that the two obligations were independent of each other?

Christian Disposal, Inc. v. Village Of Eolia

Missouri Court of Appeals
895 S.W.2d 632 (Mo. Ct. App. 1995)

WHITE, J. [CRANDALL, P.J., and CRAHAN, J., concur],

Christian Disposal, Inc. (Christian) appeals from a declaratory judgment in favor of the Village of Eolia (Village). The trial court found Christian was estopped from claiming the protection of the two year notice provision contained in § 260.247 RSMo Supp. 1992 because it failed to comply with Village's statutory request for information. We reverse.

The record reveals Christian has provided waste collection services to both residents and businesses within the corporate limits of Village since 1987. In 1993, Village advertised for waste collection bids in three local newspapers.

Christian, upon learning of Village's actions, notified Village it was required under § 260.247[1] to provide Christian with two years notice before terminating Christian's services in the area. Subsequently, in a letter dated March 9, 1993, Village gave Christian the required two years notice. Village also requested in the letter information regarding all contracts Christian had with residents and commercial establishments within Village for the collection of solid waste and other information including the names and addresses of all customers, collection sites, charges and length of time such services had been provided. This request for information was made pursuant to § 260.247(4). Christian did not provide the requested information within the thirty day period mandated by the statute.

Thereafter, Village informed Christian [that] its failure to comply with the statutory request for information removed Christian from the protection of the two year notice requirement contained in § 260.247(2) and, consequently, its solid waste collection services in Village would be terminated as of August 1, 1993. Village granted the exclusive waste collecting franchise to Sutton & Sons Refuse Disposal Service, Inc.

Christian filed a petition seeking a declaration Village's actions violated § 260.247 ... The trial court found Christian was estopped from claiming the protection of the statute's notice provision because it had failed to provide the information requested by Village. This appeal followed....

Resolution of this appeal centers around the interpretation of § 260.247. Namely, we must determine whether the legislature intended noncompliance with paragraph 4 of the statute to estop a party from claiming the statute's two year notice provision.

In matters of statutory construction, the intent of the legislature controls. This court should use rules of construction which subserve rather than subvert the legislative intent. Similarly, this court should not construe a statute so as to work an unreasonable, oppressive, or absurd result. We also assume the legislature's intent in enacting a statute is to serve the best interests and welfare of the citizenry at large. To determine the legislature's intent, we look to the language of the statute and the plain and ordinary meaning of the words employed.

The fundamental purpose of § 260.247 is to provide an entity engaged in waste collecting with sufficient notice to make necessary business adjustments prior to

---

1. The relevant provisions of § 260.247 are as follows:
   1. Any city which annexes an area or enters into or expands solid waste collection services into an area where the collection of solid waste is presently being provided by one or more private entities shall notify the private entity or entities of its intent to provide solid waste collection services in the area by certified mail.
   2. A city shall not commence solid waste collection in such area for at least two years from ... the effective date of the notice that the city intends to enter into the business of solid waste collection or to expand existing solid waste collection services into the area ....
   4. Any private entity or entities which provide collection service in the area which the city has decided to annex or enter into or expand its solid waste collection services into shall make available upon written request by the city not later than thirty days following such request, all information in its possession or control which pertains to its activity in the area necessary for the city to determine the nature and scope of the potential contract....

having its services terminated in a given area. If estoppel applied in this situation then the purpose of the statute would be circumvented. We also recognize the statute itself does not state a waste collector's failure to provide information requested pursuant to § 260.247(4) relieves the respective city, town, or village of the obligation to provide the waste collector with two years notice as mandated by the statute. If the legislature had intended to relieve governmental entities, like Village, of their obligation to provide two years notice under these circumstances, it could have incorporated such a provision in § 260.247. The fact such a provision was not incorporated into the statute indicates the legislature did not intend such a result.

Village emphasizes § 260.247(4) states a trash collector shall make available upon written request all information in its possession and control necessary to determine the nature and scope of potential contracts. However, this terminology is not necessarily determinative of the legislature's intention regarding whether a statute is mandatory or directive. Although "shall" when used in a statute will usually be interpreted to command the doing of what is specified, the term is "frequently used indiscriminately and courts have not hesitated to hold that legislative intent will prevail over common meaning." To determine whether a statute is mandatory or directory, the general rule is when a statute provides what results shall follow a failure to comply with its terms, it is mandatory and must be obeyed. However, if the statute merely requires certain things to be done and, yet, does not prescribe what results will follow if those requirements are not met, such a statute is merely directory.

Section 260.247(4) does not prescribe penalties for failure of a trash collector to provide the requested statutory information. Therefore, we conclude "shall," as contained in § 260.247(4), was intended to be directory and the legislative intent of protecting waste collectors from having their businesses dismantled unexpectedly controls....

* * *

Points for Discussion

1. *Statutory Language*: What was the language at issue? What did each party want that language to mean? What meaning did the court adopt?

2. *Theories*: Which theory did the court use?

3. *Mandatory v. Directory Statutes*: The parties did not argue that the word "shall" in this statute meant "may." What did they argue? Why did the court conclude that this statute was discretionary and not mandatory? What is the difference between the two? What if any sources helped the court resolve the issue of whether "shall" was meant in its mandatory sense?

4. *Legislative Drafting*: Legislatures often draft statutes in the passive voice, failing to identify the duties under the statute. For example, one section of the Age Discrimination in Employment Act of 1967 provides, "It *shall be* unlawful for an employer to limit, segregate, or classify his employees in any way which would deprive or tend to deprive any individual of employment opportunities or oth-

erwise adversely affect his status as an employee, because of such individual's age...." 29 U.S.C. §623(a)(2) (emphasis added). This statute would be much clearer if written as follows: "An employer *shall not* limit, segregate, or classify his employees in any way which would deprive or tend to deprive any individual of employment opportunities or otherwise adversely affect his status as an employee, because of such individual's age...." As rewritten, the statute more clearly identifies who has the obligation to act or not act. When drafting statutory language, a drafter should always identify who is "shalling."

* * *

Problem 7

On November 8, 1996, defendant pleaded guilty to one count of manslaughter and one count of carrying a pistol without a license. He was sentenced to thirty years for the manslaughter count, with fifteen years to serve and the balance suspended, with probation, and a consecutive ten-year term, suspended, with probation, for the firearms conviction. While on probation after his release from incarceration, defendant was arrested. The circumstances of that arrest follow.

On December 30, 2012, Police Patrolmen Ludwig Castro (Castro) and Eugene Chin (Chin) observed defendant make a right turn without using a turn signal and then stop in the roadway, obstructing the flow of traffic, to speak to a pedestrian. Chin activated the overhead lights of his police cruiser, and Castro exited the cruiser and approached the driver's side door of the car. Patrolman Castro instructed defendant to pull the vehicle over; defendant responded by fleeing the scene. Castro testified that he and Chin pursued defendant at speeds in excess of forty miles per hour until the car was cut off by another police cruiser, bringing the chase to an abrupt end.

Castro further testified that, when he approached the vehicle after the stop, he observed the defendant hunched over with his hands between his legs. Castro then spotted the "shiny barrel of a revolver" on the floor of the car. Defendant was taken into custody, and the officers retrieved a 1858 Remington 1858 .44-caliber black powder revolver from the floor of the vehicle. The weapon was damaged and unable to be fired in the condition in which it was found. The defendant claimed he kept the gun for sentimental reasons because it belonged to his great grandfather. The gun was incapable of being fixed to become operable.

It is illegal for individuals on probation to carry a firearm. East Carolina statute section 11-47-1 provides:

A person on probation commits the crime of unlawful use of weapons if he knowingly carries ... a firearm ... upon his person.

East Carolina statute section 11-47-2(3) defines firearm as follows:

'Firearm' includes any handgun, machine gun, pistol, rifle, or other instrument from which steel or metal projectiles are propelled ... except crossbows, longbows, and instruments propelling projectiles which are designed or used for a primary purpose other than as a weapon.

The statute defining "firearms" was first enacted in 1927 and the term "firearm" was defined to "include any machine gun or pistol." The language of the earlier statute made clear that the machine gun and pistol had to be "capable of being shot." Inoperable machine guns and pistols were not covered. The statute was amended in 1950 to include the catchall phrase and the exception, as written above.

Problem Questions

1. What is the language at issue? There are two separate arguments the defendant could make that he is not guilty of violating this statute. Do you see both?

2. How does the defendant want that language interpreted?

3. How does the state want that language interpreted?

4. Is the language structurally or lexically ambiguous, if so, why?

5. Is the ordinary meaning specifically or generally absurd, if so, why?

6. Does the ordinary meaning of the language raise a constitutional question that the court should try to avoid?

7. Assuming you answered yes to question 4, 5, or 6, what intrinsic sources are relevant? What arguments would the defendant make regarding this source(s)? The state?

8. Assuming you answered yes to question 4, 5, or 6, what extrinsic sources are relevant? What arguments would the defendant make regarding this source(s)? The state?

9. Assuming you answered yes to question 4, 5, or 6, are there any policy-based sources that are relevant? What arguments would the defendant make regarding this source(s)? The state?

Chapter 8

Canons Based on Intrinsic Sources: The Linguistic Canons

A. Introduction to This Chapter

In this chapter, we continue our exploration of the text and turn to another intrinsic source. Here, you will learn that one source judges commonly turn to after finding ambiguity or absurdity is the linguistic canons. These canons reflect commonly understood rules about the use of language. Because many of the canons have Latin names, they may seem erudite. In reality, these canons reflect common rules native to all English speakers and are, for the most part, quite simple, despite their intimidating names.

B. The Linguistic Canons: An Introduction

The linguistic canons are rules of thumb that help judges draw inferences from the words of a statute. These canons are not hard and fast rules, but rather guides and presumptions to which judges turn to discern the legislative intent from the words used, or if textualists, to determine the public meaning of the words used. The linguistic canons simply reflect shared assumptions about the way native-English speakers and writers use language and grammar.

These canons were the bedrock of early Anglo-American statutory interpretation, and many early treatises were organized around them. Although the canons fell out of favor with federal judges when purposivism edged out textualism as the preferred statutory interpretation approach, the linguistic canons remained important to state court judges. Indeed, many states have codified these canons. For example, both Minnesota and Pennsylvania have statutory construction acts that codify some of these various canons. Minn. Stat. Ann. §§ 645.001–645.510 (Lexis 2015); 1 Pa. Cons. Stat. Ann. §§ 1921–28 (Lexis 2015). Today, the linguistic canons have enjoyed a comeback with the reemergence of textualism.

Most commonly, the linguistic canons are applied either to help identify ordinary meaning or to resolve ambiguity. *State v. Peters*, 263 Wis.2d 475, 491 (2003) (Abrahamson, C.J., concurring) ("The canon [*ejusdem generis*] is an 'intrinsic aid' that is germane to a textualist approach to statutory interpretation; that is, it is both compatible with and necessary to the plain meaning rule...."). In particular, textualists like these canons because, like dictionaries, the canons appear to be neutral. Moreover, textualists believe that turning to the linguistic canons early in the interpretive process will help further the drafting process. If judges apply the canons predictably and if legislators know how judges will apply the canons, then legislators can more easily enact text that will be interpreted as intended. The linguistic canons thus serve a communication function, if you will, one that aids predictability.

These canons presume common understandings regarding how people understand written words. Some of the canons are merely weak presumptions that act as tie-breakers (e.g., *expressio unius*). Others are stronger presumptions that regularly inform meaning (e.g., *in pari materia*). While rigid application of these canons can make interpretation somewhat mechanical and simplistic, judges regularly use them anyway. However, these canons should be used cautiously. First, and most importantly, using the linguistic canons makes sense only when both the drafter and the interpreter are aware of them, understand them, and correctly use them. If a drafter is unaware of a particular canon and did not use it while drafting, then it makes little sense to apply that canon to that drafter's final product. In truth, legislatures rarely consciously think about these canons while drafting; thus, it makes little sense to apply them religiously.

Second, the canons are presumptions based on how *ordinary* English writers use language. The canons may be unsuitable in legal drafting because *legal* writers are trained to write differently than ordinary English writers. Legal writing is replete with redundancy and wordiness. Legal writers are less concerned with repeating themselves than with covering all their bases (think of "cease and desist" and "will and testament"). For example, legal writers learn to include a comprehensive list of items with a general catch-all phrase to ensure that no circumstance is omitted or overlooked. Yet, one of the linguistic canons—the rule against surplusage—directs that every word in a list should have independent meaning. Another—*ejusdem generis*—directs that catch-all phrases should be narrowly construed. Yet, the writers' legal training and the linguistic canons directly conflict. Legal writers expect that their drafting may have overlap; indeed, legal drafters prefer such overlap to inadvertent omission.

Third, the canons presume that the legislature carefully considered every word in the statute and included each word for a reason. Hence, the presumption is that the linguistic canons should apply because the legislature chose its words carefully. The reality: Legislatures are far more concerned with the big picture than with the small details. Moreover, legislation is the result of compromise. Fighting over one word could halt the enactment process entirely. Thus, legislators cannot be concerned with the exact wording of a statute, or a statute would never be drafted. Rather, legislators must choose their battles.

Fourth, the linguistic canons mask subjectivity. The canons are appealing, in part, because, like dictionaries, they appear to offer a neutral way of resolving the meaning of language. In other words, these canons provide the appearance of neutrality for decision-making. They "do not, on their face at least, express any policy preference, but simply purport to be helpful ways of divining the nature and limits of what the drafters of the legislation were trying to achieve." David L. Shapiro, *Continuity and Change in Statutory Interpretation*, 67 N.Y.U. L. Rev. 921, 927 (1992).

But this apparent objectivity simply masks subjectivity. The linguistic canons, like every method of interpretation, are merely rebuttable presumptions. As such, they can be manipulated to produce a desired result. Liberal justices may use the canons to further liberal agendas, while conservative justices may use the canons to further conservative agendas. "[T]he canons [do not have] an independent, constraining effect on the Justices' decisionsmaking—in particular, they are not functioning as a set of overarching 'neutral principles' in the hands of either liberal or conservative Justices." James J. Brudney & Corey Ditsler, *Canons of Construction and the Elusive Search for Neutral Reasoning*, 58 Vand. L. Rev. 1, 55–56 (2005). In 1949, Professor Karl Llewellyn demonstrated that for every canon of construction (the "thrust") there is an equal, but opposing canon (the "parry"). Karl N. Llewellyn, *Remarks on the Theory of Appellate Decision and the Rules of Cannon about How Statutes are to be Construed*, 3 Vand. L. Rev. 395 (1949). His point was to debunk the myth that application of the canons was an unbiased method of interpretation; judges can easily use the canons to mask the real reason for deciding a case in a particular way.

Perhaps Llewellyn's critique was overstated. The linguistic canons merely set forth *presumptions* about statutory meaning. The very nature of a presumption is that it can always be overcome by other evidence; presumptions are rebuttable. The rebuttable nature of the canons allows judges to use discretion when applying them, which, of course makes their application somewhat unpredictable. Llewellyn's "parries" identify the circumstances when the "thrusts," or presumptions, should fail.

There is another subjectivity issue. Often, more than one canon may apply. When that happens, which canon controls? There is no hierarchy within the linguistic canons; thus, selecting which canon to argue may simply depend on which better leads you to your client's preferred outcome. While there is no hierarchy, the choice of one canon can be outcome determinative. Often, the canon that furthers the interpreter's choice of meaning is the one selected. One famous example of judges using multiple, conflicting canons is the case of *Babbitt v. Sweet Home Chapter of Communities*, 515 U.S. 687 (1995). In that case, the majority and dissenting justices used many of the linguistic canons, including *in pari materia*; *noscitur a sociis*; *ejusdem generis*; *expressio unius*; the rule against surplusage; and the presumption of consistent usage. The majority and dissent focused on different canons to reach their desired outcome. The majority turned to *in pari materia* (which allows a court to look at the statute in its entirety) and the rule against surplusage (which suggests that every word in a statute must have independent meaning); while the dissent turned to *noscitur a sociis* (which allows a court to narrow words in a list) and *expressio unius* (which suggests that if something is not expressly included in a statute, the legislature intentionally excluded it). *Id.* at 701–02 (majority opinion), 720–21 (Scalia, J., dissenting). Interestingly, both the majority and dissent specifically rejected the other side's argument that the identified canon was controlling. *Id.* at 688 (majority opinion), 721 (Scalia, J., dissenting).

For all these reasons, the linguistic canons should be used with common sense and a realization that lawyers often draft differently than the canons presume. The canons are, for the most part, presumptions, gap-fillers, and tie-breakers. When there is better evidence of legislative intent, the canons should take a back seat. Also, because the canons counter each other, it is important to remember that, as a litigant, you will win your case based on the underlying equities, not based on a canon. Like the theories in Chapter 4, the linguistic canons simply give you language to *help* a judge rule in your client's favor once the judge has made up his or her mind. In other words, it is still up to you to make a judge *want* to rule in your client's favor.

Below are the contemporary linguistic canons. While other linguistic canons may have been used in the past, they are less commonly used today and have not been included for that reason.

C. The Linguistic Canons: Explained

1. In Pari Materia

The most popular and least controversially used linguistic canon is *in pari materia*. Unlike the linguistic canons we will cover next, *in pari materia* is not a canon about how words are used, but because it has a Latin name, it is generally included with the other linguistic canons. *In pari materia* is a canon that identifies the statutory material that judges may legitimately look at to discern meaning or fill gaps. *See, e.g., Florida Dep't of Highway Safety & Motor Vehicles v. Hernandez*, 74 So. 3d 1070, 1076 (Fla. 2011) (noting that a statute that allowed the state to suspend the driver's license of any person who refused to submit to a "lawful" breath test must be read *in pari materia* with a different statute that defined the parameters of a lawful breath-alcohol test).

Practice Pointer

Many judges (and academics) incorrectly equate *in pari materia* and the presumption of consistent usage. It is true, they work in harmony and are often referenced together; however, they are different. *In pari materia* identifies the material to be considered, while the presumption of consistent usage explains what to do with that material.

In pari materia answers the question of which parts of a bill, an act, or the entire code are relevant to the meaning of language in a particular statute. As such, the canon works in tandem with the other linguistic canons. So, for example, a judge might very well apply the canon of consistent usage (that identical words should have identical meanings) to interpret a word that appears in more than one section of an act, even though only the one section of the act is applicable to the facts before the court. *See, e.g., Mohasco Corp. v. Silver,* 447 U.S. 807, 809 (1980) (holding that Congress meant the word "filed" in subsection (e) in the Civil Rights Act of 1964 to have the same meaning as the word "filed" in subsection (c)). As you can see from this example, *in pari materia* is the canon that allowed the court to look for meaning in language beyond the narrow language being interpreted. Judges often say, "We do not construe statutes in isolation, but rather read each statute with reference to the entire scheme of law of which it is part so that the whole may be harmonized and retain its effectiveness...." *Azusa Land Partners v. Department of Indus. Relations,* 191 Cal. App. 4th 1, 21 (2010).

In Latin, "*in pari materia*" means "part of the same material." This canon has two aspects — the whole act aspect and the whole code aspect. First, the *whole act* aspect directs that a section of a legislative act should not be interpreted in isolation. Rather, the entire act is relevant. Second, the *whole code* (or related acts) aspect directs that statutes should be interpreted harmoniously with other statutes concerning the same subject. *In pari materia* promotes coherence. Both aspects of *in pari materia* together attempt to ensure internal consistency across acts, related statutes, and even the code as a whole. Let's look at each aspect in turn, starting with the less controversial aspect: the whole act aspect.

a. The Whole Act Aspect of In Pari Materia

When a bill is enacted, the ensuing act is not simply placed *in serum* (in order) in the code; rather, sections of the act are codified (placed into the code) where appropriate. For example, sections of the U.S. Patriot Act can be found throughout the *United States Code*. The U.S. Patriot Act created nine new sections of the Code and amended more than 100 others. It addressed things from foreign intelligence, to money laundering, to immigration, to library usage. When the Act was codified, those sections that addressed foreign intelligence surveillance were placed in one part of the Code, while those sections that addressed immigration law were placed in another section of the Code. Yet, the U.S. Patriot Act was one bill, enacted as a package. Hence, all of the U.S. Patriot Act's sections should be interpreted to work together. If the word "terrorist" is used in more than one section of the Act, then "terrorist" should have the same meaning throughout the Act (pursuant to the presumption of consistent usage), unless the legislature clearly indicated that it had a different intent. The *whole act rule* presumes that although the sections of an act are not codified together, the act's sections should be interpreted harmoniously. *See, e.g., Rhyne v. K-Mart Corp.,* 594 S.E.2d 1, 20 (N.C. 1994) (using the whole aspect of *in pari materia* to interpret the words "[P]unitive damages awarded against *a defendant*" to mean punitive damages awarded to each plaintiff).

The whole act aspect of *in pari materia* is based on the idea that there was a single drafter for the bill, whether that drafter was an individual legislator or a committee. Yet, the single-drafter assumption does not reflect the political reality. Legislation comes about from the compromises of many legislators from different political parties, having different constituencies, and with different agendas. Even the president has a role. To suggest that one drafter (whether it be a unified group or an individual) wrote the bill with internal consistency simply ignores the reality of the legislation process. "'No man should see how laws or sausages are made.'" *Community Nutrition Institute v. Block*, 749 F.2d 50, 51 (1984) (quoting Otto Van Bismarck).

b. The Whole Code Aspect of In Pari Materia

Judges will also consider the relevance of other statutes within the whole code. This aspect of *in pari materia* is known as the *whole code aspect*. The whole code aspect of *in pari materia* directs that statutes should be interpreted harmoniously with other statutes in the code *concerning the same subject*. This aspect of *in pari materia* presumes that the legislature was aware of all related, existing statutes when it enacted the one in question; thus, the new statute should be interpreted harmoniously with all related, existing statutes. Thus, if a statute criminalizes certain behavior, that statute should be interpreted consistently with other statutes criminalizing the same or similar behavior. Practically speaking, it is highly unlikely that the legislature was aware of every statute, yet the presumption persists and actually makes some sense. Legislatures should be aware of the limits of existing law when they enact new law.

One challenge with this aspect of the canon is defining what statutes concern the same or similar subject matter. Do rape statutes concern the same subject as incest statutes? While many of us would think they do, the Massachusetts Supreme Court disagreed. In *Massachusetts v. Smith*, 728 N.E.2d 272, 278–79 (Mass. 2000), the court held that the definition of sexual intercourse used in a rape statute did not apply to an incest statute, because the statutes did not concern sufficiently similar subject matters and were located in separate chapters in the code. Do punitive damages statutes concern the same subject as aggravating factors statutes? While many of us would think they do not, in *Rhyne v. K-Mart Corp.*, 594 S.E.2d 1, 7 (N.C. 1994), the majority concluded that the punitive damages statute concerned the same subject matter as an aggravating factors statute, because both statutes were located in the same chapter of the code.

The courts' test in both of these cases, location within the same code chapter, should not be determinative of whether two statutes relate to the same subject and are thus *in pari materia*. "The mere fact that the statutes appear in the same chapter [does not show the statutes relate to a common subject matter.] The Legislature may choose to employ a term differently in two different statutes. In each statute, the term should be construed to effectuate the purposes of that particular statute." *Smith*, 728 N.E.2d. at 280 (Ireland, J., dissenting). A court should look to see whether the related statutes share similar purposes such that the legislature was likely aware of the existing statute when it drafted the newer statute and, thus, intended harmony. *Id.*; *Smith v. Jackson*, 544 U.S. 228, 233–34 (2005).

In the case below, identify why the majority concludes that the two acts are *in pari materia*, while the concurrence rejects that conclusion.

Smith v. Jackson

Supreme Court of the United States
544 U.S. 228 (2005)

◆ Justice Stevens delivered the opinion of the Court [in which Souter, Ginsburg, and Breyer, JJ., concur].

… On October 1, 1998, the City [of Jackson, Mississippi] adopted a pay plan granting raises to all City employees. The stated <u>purpose</u> of the plan was to "attract and retain qualified people, provide incentive for performance, maintain competitiveness with other public sector agencies and ensure equitable compensation to all employees regardless of age, sex, race and/or disability." [The plan] granted raises to all police officers and police dispatchers[; however, t]hose who had less than five years of tenure received proportionately greater raises when compared to their former pay than those with more seniority.… Petitioners are a group of older officers who filed suit under the ADEA [Age Discrimination in Employment Act of 1967] claiming both that the City deliberately discriminated against them because of their age (the "disparate-treatment" claim) and that they were "adversely affected" by the plan because of their age (the "disparate impact" claim).* The District Court granted summary judgment to the City.… The Court of Appeals … affirmed [and] concluded that disparate-impact claims are categorically unavailable under the ADEA.…

We granted the officers' petition for certiorari, and now hold that the ADEA does authorize recovery in "disparate-impact" cases.… Because, however, we conclude that petitioners have not set forth a valid disparate-impact claim, we affirm.

During the deliberations that preceded the enactment of the Civil Rights Act of 1964, Congress considered and rejected proposed amendments that would have included older workers among the classes protected from employment discrimination. Congress did, however, request the Secretary of Labor to "make a full and complete study of the factors which might tend to result in discrimination in employment because of age and of the consequences of such discrimination on the economy and individuals affected." The Secretary's report, submitted in response to Congress' request, noted that there was little discrimination arising from dislike or intolerance of older people, but that "arbitrary" discrimination did result from certain age limits. (hereinafter Wirtz Report). Moreover, the report observed that discriminatory effects resulted from "[i]nstitutional arrangements that indirectly restrict the employment of older workers."

In response to that report Congress … enacted in 1967, § 4(a)(2) of the ADEA, now codified as 29 U.S.C. § 623(a)(2),** [which provides] that it shall be unlawful

---

* Editor's footnote: Disparate treatment claims require proof that the employer discriminated intentionally against the suspect class. They are more difficult to prove. In contrast, disparate impact claims do not require proof that the employer discriminated intentionally; they require only that the effect of an employment practice disparately impacts the protected class. They are easier to prove.

** Editor's footnote: The statute provided: "It shall be unlawful for an employer—

(2) to limit, segregate, or classify his employees in any way which would deprive or tend to

for an employer "to limit, segregate, or classify his employees in any way which would deprive or tend to deprive any individual of employment opportunities or otherwise adversely affect his status as an employee, because of such individual's age...." Except for substitution of the word "age" for the words "race, color, religion, sex, or national origin," the language of that provision in the ADEA is identical to that found in §703(a)(2) of the Civil Rights Act of 1964 (Title VII).... Unlike Title VII, however, §4(f)(1) of the ADEA, contains language that significantly narrows its coverage by permitting any "otherwise prohibited" action "where the differentiation is based on reasonable factors other than age (hereinafter RFOA provision)."

In determining whether the ADEA authorizes disparate-impact claims, we begin with the premise that when Congress uses the same language in two statutes having similar purposes, particularly when one is enacted shortly after the other, it is appropriate to presume that Congress intended that text to have the same meaning in both statutes. We have consistently applied that presumption to language in the ADEA that was "derived *in haec verba* from Title VII." Our unanimous interpretation of ... Title VII ... is therefore a precedent of compelling importance. [*Griggs v. Duke Power Co.*]

In *Griggs*, ... we held that good faith "does not redeem employment procedures or testing mechanisms that operate as 'built-in headwinds' for minority groups and are unrelated to measuring job capability. We explained that Congress had "directed the thrust of the Act to the *consequences* of employment practices, not simply the motivation." We relied on the fact that history is "filled with examples of men and women who rendered highly effective performance without the conventional badges of accomplishment in terms of certificates, diplomas, or degrees....

We thus squarely held that ... Title VII did not require a showing of discriminatory intent.[5] While our opinion in *Griggs* relied primarily on the purposes of the Act, ... we have subsequently noted that our holding represented the better reading of the statutory text as well. Neither [Title VII] nor the comparable language in the ADEA simply prohibits actions that "limit, segregate, or classify" persons; rather the language prohibits such actions that "deprive any individual of employment opportunities or *otherwise adversely affect* his status as an employee, because of such individual's" race or age. Thus the text focuses on the *effects* of the action on the employee rather than the motivation for the action of the employer. *Griggs*, which interpreted the identical text at issue here, thus strongly suggests that a disparate impact theory should be cognizable under the ADEA....

---

deprive any individual of employment opportunities or otherwise adversely affect his status as an employee, because of such individual's age...."

5. The congressional purposes on which we relied in *Griggs* have a striking parallel to two important points made in the Wirtz Report. Just as the *Griggs* opinion ruled out discrimination based on racial animus as a problem in that case, the Wirtz Report concluded that there was no significant discrimination of that kind so far as older workers are concerned. And just as *Griggs* recognized that the high school diploma requirement, which was unrelated to job performance, had an unfair impact on African-Americans who had received inferior educational opportunities in segregated schools, the Wirtz Report identified the identical obstacle to the employment of older workers....

The Court of Appeals' categorical rejection of disparate-impact liability, like Justice O'Connor's, rested primarily on the RFOA provision and the majority's analysis of legislative history....

The RFOA provision provides that it shall not be unlawful for an employer "to take any action otherwise prohibited under subsectio[n] (a) ... where the differentiation is based on reasonable factors other than age discrimination...." In most disparate-treatment cases, if an employer in fact acted on a factor other than age, the action would not be prohibited under subsection (a) in the first place. In those disparate-treatment cases, ... the RFOA provision is simply unnecessary to avoid liability under the ADEA, since there was no prohibited action in the first place. The RFOA provision is not, as Justice O'Connor suggests, a "safe harbor from liability," since there would be no liability under § 4(a). In disparate-impact cases, however, the allegedly "otherwise prohibited" activity is not based on age. It is, accordingly, in cases involving disparate-impact claims that the RFOA provision plays its principal role by precluding liability if the adverse impact was attributable to a nonage factor that was "reasonable." Rather than support an argument that disparate impact is unavailable under the ADEA, the RFOA provision actually supports the contrary conclusion....

The text of the statute, as interpreted in Griggs, the RFOA provision, and the EEOC regulations all support petitioners' view. We therefore conclude that it was error for the Court of Appeals to hold that the disparate impact theory of liability is categorically unavailable under the ADEA....

[Although the plurality held that a lawsuit could be brought under the ADEA based on disparate impact, it concluded that the petitioners in this case did not meet the requirements for bringing that cause of action, so the plurality affirmed the judgment of the Court of Appeals.]

♦ JUSTICE O'CONNOR, with whom KENNEDY and THOMAS, JJ. join, concurring in the judgment.

Disparate treatment ... captures the essence of what Congress sought to prohibit in the [ADEA]. It is the very essence of age discrimination for an older employee to be fired because the employer believes that productivity and competence decline with old age." In the nearly four decades since the ADEA's enactment, however, we have never read the statute to impose liability upon an employer without proof of discriminatory intent. I decline to join the Court in doing so today.

I would instead affirm the judgment below on the ground that disparate impact claims are not cognizable under the ADEA. The ADEA's text, legislative history, and purposes together make clear that Congress did not intend the statute to authorize such claims. Moreover, the significant differences between the ADEA and Title VII of the Civil Rights Act of 1964 counsel against transposing to the former our construction of the latter in *Griggs v. Duke Power Co*....

Our starting point is the statute's text.... [N]either petitioners nor the plurality contend that the first paragraph, § 4(a)(1), authorizes disparate impact claims, and

arg against dissent

I think it obvious that it does not. That provision plainly requires discriminatory intent ... petitioners look instead to the second paragraph, § 4(a)(2), as the basis for their disparate impact claim. But the petitioners' argument founders on the plain language of the statute, the natural reading of which requires proof of discriminatory intent. Section 4(a)(2) uses the phrase "because of ... age" in precisely the same manner as does the preceding paragraph — to make plain that an employer is liable only if its adverse action against an individual is motivated *by the individual's age*. ...

The legislative history of the ADEA confirms what the text plainly indicates — that Congress never intended the statute to authorize disparate impact claims. ...

The plurality and Justice Scalia [argue] that the relevant provision of the ADEA should be read *in pari materia* with the parallel provision of Title VII. ... The language of the ADEA's prohibitory provisions was modeled on, and is nearly identical to, parallel provisions in Title VII. Because *Griggs* held that Title VII's § 703(a)(2) permits disparate impact claims, the plurality concludes that we should read § 4(a)(2) of the ADEA similarly. ...

To be sure, where two statutes use similar language we generally take this as "a strong indication that [they] should be interpreted [similarly]." But this is not a rigid or absolute rule, and it " 'readily yields' " to other indicia of congressional intent. Indeed, " 'the meaning [of the same words] well may vary to meet the purposes of the law.' " Accordingly, we have not hesitated to give a different reading to the same language — whether appearing in separate statutes or in separate provisions of the same statute — if there is strong evidence that Congress did not intend the language to be used uniformly. Such is the case here.

First, there are significant textual differences between Title VII and the ADEA that indicate differences in congressional intent. Most importantly, whereas the ADEA's RFOA provision protects employers from liability for any actions not motivated by age, Title VII lacks any similar provision. In addition, the ADEA's structure demonstrates Congress' intent to combat intentional discrimination through § 4's prohibitions while addressing employment practices having a disparate impact on older workers through independent noncoercive mechanisms. There is no analogy in the structure of Title VII. Furthermore, as the Congresses that adopted *both* Title VII *and* the ADEA clearly recognized, the two statutes were intended to address qualitatively different kinds of discrimination Disparate impact liability may have a legitimate role in combating the types of discrimination addressed by Title VII,* but the nature of aging and of age discrimination makes such liability inappropriate for the ADEA. ...

Even venerable canons of construction must bow, in an appropriate case, to compelling evidence of congressional intent. In my judgment, the significant differences between Title VII and the ADEA are more than sufficient to overcome the default presumption that similar language is to be read similarly.

---

* Editor's footnote: *Griggs* was a unanimous decision. Justice O'Connor was not on the bench at that time.

* * *

Points for Discussion

1. *Statutory Language*: Did the justices dispute the meaning of any specific words (like age) or was the issue something different? What did each party argue the statute required?

2. *Theories*: Which theory did the plurality use? What was the first source that Justice Stevens turned to? Which theory did the concurrence use? What was the first source Justice O'Connor turned to?

3. *Civil Rights Act*: Why did the plurality look to the Civil Rights Act to interpret the ADEA?

4. *In Pari Materia*: Which aspect of *in pari materia* was relevant here, the whole act aspect or the whole code aspect? Why did the plurality conclude that the two acts, ADEA and the Civil Rights Act, should be read *in pari materia*? Why did Justice O'Connor disagree? Did Justice O'Connor disagree that related statutes in a code should be interpreted *in pari materia* or that these specific statutes should not be interpreted *in pari materia*?

5. *Legislative History*: What is the Wirtz Report? Is it legislative history or something else? Where does it fit within our sources? How persuasive should it be?

6. *Ambiguity Threshold*: Textualist judges often require a finding of ambiguity before they will consider the linguistic canons, including *in pari materia*. *Compare City of Columbiana v. J & J Car Wash, Inc.*, 2005 WL 678750, at *6 (Ohio Ct. App. 2005) (stating, "we cannot use the doctrine of in pari materia at this point because this rule of construction is to be used only after ... ambiguity exists"), *with Chatham v. Sanamon*, 814 N.E.2d 216, 230 (Myerscough, J., dissenting) (Ill. Ct. App. 2004) (rejecting this approach). Consider whether it makes sense to impose an ambiguity hurdle.

* * *

2. The Presumption of Consistent Usage and Meaningful Variation

After *in pari materia*, the next most commonly used and least controversial linguistic canon is *the presumption of consistent usage and meaningful variation* (also known as the identical words presumption). This canon presumes that when the legislature uses the same word in different parts of the same act or a related act, the legislature intended those words to have the same meaning (consistent usage). And, contrariwise, if the legislature uses a word in one part of an act or a related act, then changes to a different word in another part of the same or related act, the legislature intended to change the meaning (meaningful variation). The purpose of this canon is, like the purpose of *in pari materia*, to promote internal consistency; lawyers are taught that a change in word usage signifies a new meaning. In English class, variety of word usage is commended. However, monotony in statutory drafting is a good thing. *See, e.g., Robinson v. City of Lansing*, 782 N.W.2d 171, 182 (2010) ("[U]nless the Legislature indicates otherwise, when it repeatedly uses the same phrase in a statute, that phrase should be given the same meaning throughout the statute.").

Like all the linguistic canons, this canon can be rebutted with evidence that the same or a different meaning was intended. *See, e.g., Jensen v. Elgin, Joliet & Eastern Railway Co.*, 182 N.E.2d 211 (Ill. 1962) (holding that the cannon was not applicable to the word "children," which was included in both sections 1 and 9 of the Federal Employers' Liability Act, because the two sections allowed recovery for different types of injuries: *injuries the deceased employee sustained* and *losses the dependents of the deceased employee suffered directly*).

Practice Pointer

While variety of language is highly praised in some disciplines, lawyers should avoid it. For a lawyer, a change in language signals a change in meaning. For example, "shall" and "will" mean very different things in law, although a thesaurus identifies these words as synonyms. Legal concepts are difficult enough to understand; do not make your reader work harder by changing words unnecessarily.

In the next case, try to determine whether the judges below disagree about whether to apply the presumption of consistent usage or how to apply it.

Travelscape, LLC v. South Carolina Department Of Revenue

Supreme Court of South Carolina

705 S.E.2d 28 (2011)

◆ Hearn, J. [Toal, C.J., Kittredge, J., and Moore, A.J., concur].

The Administrative Law Court ("ALC") found Travelscape, LLC was required to remit sales tax on the gross proceeds it received from providing hotel reservations in South Carolina.... We agree with the ALC's findings and affirm.

Travelscape is an online travel company offering hotel reservations at locations across the country through the website Expedia.com ("Expedia"). Although Travelscape neither owns nor operates hotels, it enters into contracts with hotels whereby the hotels agree to accept a discounted rate from those offered to the general public ("net rate") for reservations made on Expedia. Travelscape then adds a facilitation fee, service fee, and tax recovery charge to the net rate of the room. The facilitation and service fees are retained by Travelscape as compensation for its role in the transaction. The tax recovery charge, which is based on the net room rate, corresponds with the sales tax owed by the hotel. The sum of the net room rate, facilitation fee, service fee, and tax recovery charge is the actual price listed for the room on Expedia.

If a customer books a hotel reservation on Expedia, Travelscape charges the customer's credit card for the transaction. Unless the customer purchases additional guests services while staying at the hotel (i.e. room service, movie rentals, or valet parking), the customer pays no money to the hotel for her stay. After the customer checks out of the hotel, the hotel invoices Travelscape for the net room rate as well as sales tax owed by the hotel. Travelscape then remits the net room rate and tax recovery charge to the hotel. Travelscape retains the facilitation and service fees and does not pay sales tax on these fees.

The [State] Department of Revenue ("Department") conducted an audit of Travelscape's records for the period of July 1, 2001 through June 30, 2006. The Department determined Travelscape was required to pay a sales tax of seven percent on the gross proceeds received from furnishing hotel accommodations in South Carolina. Thereafter, the Department issued Travelscape an assessment and penalty in the amount of $6,376,454.71.... Following a two-day hearing, the ALC issued a final order, finding Travelscape was required to pay the tax.... This appeal followed....

We begin our analysis in this case by focusing on the statutory scheme of section 12–36–920. Both parties agree, and the ALC found, that section 12–36–920 is divided into two relevant parts. Section 12–36–920(A) sets forth what is subject to the tax — "the gross proceeds derived from the rental or charges for any rooms ... or sleeping accommodations *furnished* to transients by any hotel ... or any place in which rooms, lodgings, or sleeping accommodations are *furnished* to transients for a consideration." (emphasis added). In turn, section 12–36–920(E) establishes who is subject to the tax — "every person engaged ... *in the business of furnishing accommodations* to transients for consideration." (emphasis added). Therefore, the task before us is to harmonize these two provisions and determine whether the service and facilitation fees are gross proceeds derived from the furnishing of sleeping accommodations and, if so, whether Travelscape is engaged in the business of furnishing these accommodations.

Travelscape contends it is not required to pay sales tax on the service and facilitation fees it retains because such fees are "derived from" the services it provides, not from the rental charge for the hotel room. We disagree....

← arg. *Expedia's*

"The cardinal rule of statutory construction is to ascertain and effectuate the intent of the legislature." Where the statute's language is plain, unambiguous, and conveys a clear, definite meaning, the rules of statutory interpretation are not needed and the court has no right to impose another meaning.

[*What is taxed*] [The majority concludes that the fees Travelscape retained for its services are taxable as gross proceeds. The majority then turns to whether Travelscape can be taxed].

[*Who is taxed*] Section 12–36–920(E) imposes the Accommodations Tax "on every person engaged or continuing within this State in the business of furnishing accommodations to transients for consideration." Travelscape argues it is not subject to the Accommodations Tax because it ... is not engaged in the business of furnishing accommodations....

Travelscape ... asserts it is not engaged in the business of furnishing accommodations because it neither owns nor operates hotels. According to Travelscape, the ordinary and commonplace understanding of the term "furnish," as well as the manner that the term is used throughout section 12–36–920, demonstrates that the term carries with it the connotation of physically providing sleeping accommodations to customers. Because Travelscape is only an intermediary providing hotel reservations to transients and does not physically provide sleeping accommodations, Travelscape contends it is not subject to the Accommodations Tax. We disagree....

As a general rule, "identical words and phrases within the same statute should normally be given the same meaning." The South Carolina Court of Appeals has long recognized a similar rule[:] "Where the same word is used more than once in a statute it is presumed to have the same meaning throughout unless a different meaning is necessary to avoid an absurd result." This Court has held that words in a statute must be construed in context, and their meaning may be ascertained by reference to words associated with them in the statute.

Travelscape is correct in pointing out that "furnish" as used in subsection (A) invokes the connotation of physically providing sleeping accommodations to customers. Indeed, the American Heritage Dictionary defines "furnish" as "[t]o equip with what is needed" and to "supply" or "give." *Am. Heritage Dictionary* 540 (2d College Ed.1982).... Travelscape argues the term "furnish" as used in subsection (E) should be read consonant with its use in subsection (A). We agree. As used in subsection (E), "furnish" does mean to physically provide sleeping accommodations. However, Travelscape's argument ignores the antecedent language in (E) that it applies to all persons "engaged ... in the business of" furnishing accommodations. "Business" includes "all activities, with the object of gain, profit, benefit, or advantage, either direct or indirect." S.C.Code Ann. § 12–36–20 (2000). Accordingly, we find the context of "furnish" as it appears in subsection (E) demonstrates that it encompasses the activities of entities such as Travelscape who, whether directly or indirectly, provide hotel reservations to transients for consideration. Contrary to the dissent's view, we do not read the term "furnish" differently in subsection (E) than we do in (A). Instead, we interpret subsection (E) in such a manner as to give effect to all the language contained therein—particularly that the entity be "engaged ... in the business of" furnishing accommodations—rather than focusing on the term "furnish" in isolation. While Travelscape does not physically provide accommodations, it is in the business of doing so.

The legislative purpose of section 12–36–920 supports such a finding.... In our view, the legislative purpose of section 12–36–920 is [to "levy a tax on the amount of money visitors to the municipality spend on their hotel rooms or other accommodations."] The application of the tax to "every person engaged ... in the business of furnishing accommodations" also reveals that the legislature intended to levy the tax not merely on those physically providing sleeping accommodations, but on those entities who were accepting money in exchange for supplying hotel rooms. Additionally, section 12–36–920(C) specifically dispels the notion that the tax is imposed only on those entities physically providing the sleeping accommodations. Subsection (C) establishes that the tax is also assessed against real estate agents, brokers, corporations, and listing services. Therefore, we find the legislative purpose of subsection (E) and the context of the term "furnish" in that subsection demonstrates that Travelscape is subject to the Accommodations Tax because it is "engaged ... in the business of furnishing accommodations to transients for consideration." S.C.Code Ann. § 12–36–920(E)....

◆ PLEICONES, J., dissenting.

I respectfully dissent. I am not persuaded that the legislature intended S.C.Code Ann. § 12–36–920 to include the separate fee charged by intermediaries, such as Travelscape, in the seven percent sales tax "imposed on the gross proceeds derived from the rental or charges for any rooms ... or sleeping accommodations furnished to transients by any hotel...." Accordingly, I would reverse the administrative law court.

Travelscape is an international company which operates primarily as an internet facilitator of hotel reservations. Travelscape does not provide accommodations to the customer. Instead, Travelscape negotiates favorable rates with hotel chains. A Travelscape customer receives the benefit of the reduced rate and pays a fee to Travelscape for handling the transaction, all of which is spelled out in the agreement between Travelscape and the customer.

For hotel reservations in South Carolina, a seven percent sales tax is collected on that portion of proceeds derived from the rental of the hotel room. The question before us is whether the legislature intended the statutory seven percent sales tax to reach the separate fee charged by Travelscape for the service it provides. I do not believe the statute unambiguously answers this question. Because it is not clear as to whether Travelscape is subject to § 12–36–920, we must resort to the rules of statutory construction.

S.C.Code Ann. § 12–36–920 (Supp.2009) provides in relevant part:

> (A) A sales tax equal to seven percent is imposed on the gross proceeds derived from the rental or charges for any rooms, campground spaces, lodgings, or sleeping accommodations furnished to transients by any hotel, inn, tourist court, tourist camp, motel, campground, residence, or any place in which rooms, lodgings, or sleeping accommodations are furnished to transients for consideration....

Statute

> (E) The taxes imposed by this section are imposed on every person engaged or continuing within this State in the business of furnishing accommodations to transients for consideration.

I begin with the word "furnish" as it is used in § 12–36–920. Section 12–36–920(A) describes what fees are subject to the tax, while § 12–36–920(E) describes who is subject to the tax. As the majority acknowledges, the word "furnished" as used in subsection (A) connotes physically providing accommodations to customers, which Travelscape does not do. Thus, in order to find Travelscape to be in the business of "furnishing accommodations," the majority imposes a different meaning of the word "furnish" in subsection (E). Under the majority's view, "furnish" in subsection (A) is used narrowly and "invokes the connotation of physically providing sleeping accommodations to customers," while in subsection (E), the phrase "business of furnishing" includes not only those who furnish but also those who provide a service to "furnishers" and "transients."

"A standard principle of statutory construction provides that identical words and phrases within the same statute should normally be given the same meaning." Where the same word is used more than once in a statute, it is presumed to have the same meaning throughout unless a different meaning is necessary to avoid an absurd result. In my opinion, giving the term "furnish" a different meaning in subsection (A) than is given in subsection (E), is in contravention to the rule of statutory construction that the same terms or words in a statute should be given the same meaning.

I see no reason to deviate from the general rule of statutory construction that the same words within the same statute should be given the same meaning. I believe this is especially so in light of the additional and well-recognized rule of statutory construction, that in the enforcement of tax statutes, the taxpayer should receive the benefit in cases of doubt. The majority's construction of the tax statute violates this rule.

Applying the language of § 12–36–920 and utilizing our rules of statutory construction, I am forced to conclude that Travelscape is not subject to the tax. To conclude otherwise would require a clearer expression of legislative intent. I would reverse.

* * *

Points for Discussion

1. *Statutory Language*: What was the language at issue? What did each party want that language to mean? What meaning did the majority and dissent adopt?

2. *Theories*: Which theory did the majority use? The dissent? What sources were most relevant to the majority? The dissent? Did the majority and dissent find the language ambiguous, absurd, to have a scrivener's error, or to raise a constitutional question?

3. *In Pari Materia*: Notice that two separate sections of the statute are being interpreted to work in harmony. Which aspect of *in pari materia* is this? This aspect is so intuitive you likely missed it. Bottom line, we do not interpret statutory language in isolation.

4. *Identical Words Presumption*: Did the majority and dissent disagree about the applicability of this linguistic canon or about its application? What does the word "furnish" mean according to the majority's interpretation of subsection (A)? Did the majority change that meaning for the word "furnish" in subsection (E) as the dissent claimed? Or, did the majority explain why, even though the word "furnish" has the same meaning in both subsections, additional language in subsection (E) broadens the meaning of "furnish" in that subsection?

5. *Policy Source*: What tax policy (interpretive presumption) did the dissent use to resolve the ambiguity? Does this rule sound familiar to any other policy presumptions we have seen, such as in criminal cases? Why do we have similar interpretive presumptions in both the criminal and tax law areas?

related ⟨ 1. In Pari materia
2. Identical words assum
3. Surplusage
related ⟨ 4. Noscitur a sociis
5. ejusdem generis
6. expressio unius

* * *

3. Noscitur a Sociis

The next four canons are more controversial and interrelated: the rule against surplusage, *noscitur a sociis*, *ejusdem generis*, and *expressio unius*. These canons often conflict with one another and, like the other canons, do not always reflect the reality of legal drafting. Let's take a closer look at each, starting with two related canons: *noscitur a sociis* and *ejusdem generis*.

Most words have multiple meanings. *Noscitur a sociis* and *ejusdem generis* are fancy, Latin terms for a common sense notion: that words can best be understood in their textual context. In Latin, n*oscitur a sociis* means "it is known from its associates." This canon is based on the simple presumption that when a word has more than one meaning, the appropriate meaning should be gleaned from the words surrounding the word being interpreted, in other words, from the textual context. 2A JABEZ GRIDLEY SUTHERLAND STATUTES AND STATUTORY CONSTRUCTION § 47.16, at 352 (Norman Singer ed. 7th ed. 2007). In practice, we use this canon all the time when we communicate. For example, Justice Scalia has famously said: "If you tell me, 'I took the boat out on the bay,' I understand 'bay' to mean one thing; if you tell me, 'I put the saddle on the bay,' I understand it to mean something else." ANTONIN SCALIA, A MATTER OF INTERPRETATION: FEDERAL COURTS AND THE LAW 26 (1987). And as one of my students suggested, if you tell me that "Fido bays at the moon," I might understand "bay" to mean a third thing altogether. Similarly, the word "answer" might mean a legal document that responds to a complaint or it might mean a response to a question. *Noscitur a sociis* helps identify which meaning was intended. Without *noscitur a sociis*, we would need a new word for each situation identified above. The English language is wordy enough already!

While *noscitur a sociis* has force when any word is being interpreted (as we saw with "bay" above), judges explicitly use the canon most commonly when they are interpreting words in a list. When applying *noscitur a sociis*, judges try to find the shared trait, called the unifier, in the list of items. Thus, in the following list of items: "yellow, blue, red, chartreuse, and white," all of the items are colors; color is the unifier. Even if you did not know what chartreuse was, you would likely surmise that it was a color.

Notice that when judges identify a unifier and then interpret the word in light of that unifier, judges narrowly interpret the language in dispute. Hence, *noscitur a sociis* narrows a statute's application. Yet, legislators as legal drafters are trained to draft broadly, to include every possibility. Thus, the presumption behind the canon and the reality of legislative drafting conflict. For example, in *People v. Vasquez*, 631 N.W.2d 711 (Mich. 2001), the majority applied *noscitur a sociis* to determine whether a defendant who lied to a police officer about his age "obstruct[ed], resist[ed], oppose[d], assault[ed], beat, or wound[ed]" that officer. *Id.* at 714 (quoting Mich. Comp. Laws § 750.479). Applying *noscitur a sociis*, the majority concluded that the words shared the common trait of threatened or actual *physical* interference. *Id.* at

[margin annotations:] noscitur a sociis ← Definition · ← Purpose · How judge's use → · Narrows applications → · Issue →

716. Because lying was not *physical* interference, the majority concluded that the defendant had not violated the statute when he lied to the police about his age. *Id.*

The dissent disagreed for two reasons. First, the dissent thought the term "obstruct" was clear, obstructing an officer includes lying to the officer. Because it was inappropriate to turn to the linguistic canon absent ambiguity, the dissent said that the majority unnecessarily narrowed the term "obstruct" by resorting to *noscitur a sociis. Id.* at 731 (Corrigan, C.J., dissenting). Second, the dissent argued that even if the canon were appropriate, the majority incorrectly identified the unifier. The dissent suggested that the unifier was simply *interference*, not *physical* interference. *Id.* And lying was interference.

This case nicely illustrates one problem with this canon — how similar must items in a list be? At times, *noscitur a sociis* and the rule against surplusage may conflict. *Noscitur a sociis* directs that words share meaning, while the rule against surplusage directs that each word should have a different meaning. Arguably, the majority in *Vasquez* violated the rule against surplusage by interpreting the terms in the statute so similarly they lost independent meaning. What, under the majority's interpretation, is the difference between "obstruct" and "resist" if physical interference is required? The dissent's interpretation preserved the distinction better than the majority's interpretation.

Judges also disagree about when to apply *noscitur a sociis*. Should the canon be used only when ambiguity remains after applying the plain meaning canon, or should the canon be used in conjunction with the plain meaning canon? *Compare Stryker Corp. v. Director, Division of Taxation*, 773 A.2d 674, 684 (N.J. 2001) (refusing to apply the canon because the text was clear), *with G.C. Timmis & Co. v. Guardian Alarm, Co.*, 662 N.W. 710, 718 n.12 (Mich. 2003) (applying the canon without first finding ambiguity). The canon *noscitur a sociis* should not only apply when a court first finds ambiguity. The basic notion that textual context aids interpretation is unarguable. Any language in which words have multiple meanings, like English, requires such a rule; in fact, you could not understand either the written or spoken word without using this canon. For this reason, *noscitur a sociis* should apply regardless of ambiguity. Indeed, it is likely that judges intuitively apply the canon whether they say they are applying it or not. Yet the rhetoric continues.

The case below is a little complicated, but the discussion between the majority and dissent regarding whether a pig can fly is priceless. Be sure to read the majority's footnote 12.

G.C. Timmis & Co. v. Guardian Alarm Co.

Supreme Court of Michigan
662 N.W.2d 710 (Mich. 2003)

◆ MARKMAN, J. [CORRIGAN, CAVANAGH, KELLY, and TAYLOR, JJ., concur].

This case concerns whether plaintiff acted as a real estate broker under § 2501(d) of the real estate brokers act (REBA), [Michigan Compiled Laws] M.C.L. § 339.2501 *et seq.*... We ... remand this case to the trial court for a determination [of] whether defendant's transaction here constituted a "real estate" transaction for purposes of REBA.

Plaintiff is a registered investment advisor, but it is not a licensed real estate broker. Plaintiff introduced itself to defendant, a security-systems company, in order to discuss how it might assist defendant in acquiring other security-systems companies. According to plaintiff, the parties entered into an oral contract, which specified that plaintiff would receive a "success fee" for any company plaintiff contacted on defendant's behalf that defendant subsequently purchased. Plaintiff eventually introduced defendant to a company, MetroCell.... Subsequently, defendant purchased the alarm contracts of MetroCell and its customers, and plaintiff sought the "success fee." However, defendant refused to pay, claiming that REBA precluded plaintiff from bringing suit because plaintiff had acted as an unlicensed real estate broker.... *

This Court must determine whether plaintiff's conduct fell within the scope of Michigan's real estate brokers licensing act. To determine whether plaintiff acted as a "real estate broker," this Court must first determine: ... whether the Legislature intended the definition of "real estate broker" to encompass the brokerage of non-"real estate" transactions....

MCL 339.2501(d) provides:

> "Real estate broker" means an individual ... [or entity] who with the intent to collect or receive a fee, compensation, or valuable consideration, sells or offers for sale, buys or offers to buy, provides or offers to provide market analysis, lists or offers or attempts to list, or negotiates the purchase or sale or exchange or mortgage of real estate, or negotiates for the construction of a building on real estate; who leases or offers or rents or offers for rent real estate or the improvements on the real estate for others, as a whole or partial vocation; who engages in property management as a whole or partial vocation; *who sells or offers for sale, buys or offers to buy, leases or offers to lease, or negotiates the purchase or sale or exchange of a business, business opportunity, or the goodwill of an existing business for others;* or who, as owner or otherwise, engages in the sale of real estate as a principal vocation. [Emphasis added.]

When construing a statute, the Court's primary obligation is to ascertain the legislative intent that may be reasonably inferred from the words expressed in the statute. If the language of the statute is unambiguous, the Legislature is presumed to have intended the meaning expressed.

---

* Editor's footnote. The relevant section of REBA prohibited anyone from "shar[ing] or pay[ing] a fee, commission, or other valuable consideration to a person not licensed under this article including payment to any person providing the names of, or any other information regarding, a potential seller or purchaser of *real estate* but excluding payment for the purchase of commercially prepared lists of names." Mich. Comp. Laws Ann. §339.2512 (emphasis added). Hence, plaintiff, who was not a licensed real estate broker, could recover the "success fee" only if the transaction did not involve real estate. Section 2501(d) was part of the definitions section of REBA.

Real estate brokering is not the only profession regulated by the Legislature under the Occupational Code. Rather, the Code regulates a number of other professions, including public accounting, barbering, hearing-aid dealing, and residential building. A common theme prevails throughout each of these articles—namely, that each article deals with a single or discrete group of identified professions. For example, article 11 deals only with barbering and does not contain language that would suggest that it applies to any other professions, such as dog grooming.

The doctrine of *noscitur a sociis,* i.e., that "a word or phrase is given meaning by its context or setting," affords us assistance in interpreting § 2501(d). Thus, we utilize this doctrine, and apply this theme of a "single or discrete group of identified professions" in the Occupational Code to REBA. Because there is no reason to believe that in drafting REBA, the Legislature chose not to employ this "single or discrete group of identified professions" theme, we find this to be the first indication that REBA applies only to the brokering of real estate.

However, our inquiry does not stop there. Next, we apply *noscitur a sociis* to the individual phrases of § 2501(d), as well as to the other provisions of REBA because the emphasized language does not stand alone, and thus it cannot be read in a vacuum. Instead, "[i]t exists and must be read in context with the entire act, and the words and phrases used there must be assigned such meanings as are in harmony with the whole of the statute...." "[W]ords in a statute should not be construed in the void, but should be read together to harmonize the meaning, giving effect to the act as a whole." Although a phrase or a statement may mean one thing when read in isolation, it may mean something substantially different when read in context. "In seeking meaning, words and clauses will not be divorced from those which precede and those which follow." "It is a familiar principle of statutory construction that words grouped in a list should be given related meaning."

The emphasized language of REBA's definition of "real estate broker," part III(A) above, includes the phrase, one "who ... negotiates the purchase or sale ... of a business, business opportunity, or the goodwill of an existing business for others...." M.C.L. § 339.2501(d). In interpreting this language, we examine its context and must give it a meaning that is not only logically related to the type of broker specifically defined in § 2501(d), but also a meaning logically related to the other five phrases used in § 2501(d) to define a "real estate broker," and the other provisions of REBA.

Section 2501(d) defines not merely a broker, but specifically a "real estate" broker, and thus provides the first indication that the Legislature intended that REBA apply only to persons brokering real estate. Further, immediately following REBA's definition of "real estate" broker, the Legislature defines "real estate" salesperson [the next statutory definition], in terms that expressly cross-reference the definition of "real estate" broker, i.e., a "real estate salesperson" is one who is employed by a "real estate broker." The Legislature also defines five other terms in § 2501, all of which are defined by express reference to "real estate" or "real property." The Legislature then employs six definitional phrases in § 2501(d) to give meaning to the term "real estate broker," and each of those phrases, with the exception of the one at issue, either expressly uses or references the term "real estate." The Legislature proceeds to employ these same definitional phrases in giving meaning to "real estate salesperson."

Moreover, ... there is nothing within REBA that suggests any legislative intent that it apply to non-"real estate" transactions. Thus, application of the "single or discrete group of identified professions" theme, along with an examination of the text of § 2501(d), as well as the text of REBA's surrounding provisions, together suggest that REBA's licensing requirement only applies to "the purchase or sale ... of a business, business opportunity, or the goodwill of an existing business"[8] when that purchase or sale involves a real estate transaction.

The purpose of REBA, which is to protect the integrity of real estate transactions by ensuring that they are brokered by persons expert in that realm, requires the interpretation that REBA applies only to real estate transactions. The conclusion that the emphasized language of § 2501(d) applies only to real estate transactions affords reasonable meaning to this language within the context of the provisions that surround it, while maintaining the focus of REBA on transactions involving the purchase or sale of business real estate....

The dissent criticizes [our] interpretation of § 2501(d) by asserting that we "ignore[ ] the clear language of the REBA" and "sidestep [ ] the plain meaning of the words...." We respectfully, but strongly, disagree. Although we may reach a different conclusion than the dissent, we do not "ignore" the language of the statute. Rather, our conclusion that the real estate brokers act is limited to transactions involving real estate is predicated on the following analysis: (1) that § 2501(d) defines a specific type of broker, a "real estate" broker; (2) that the Legislature defines other occupations in this provision, all of which expressly cross-reference "real estate" broker; (3) that the Legislature defines five other terms in § 2501, all of which are defined by express reference to "real estate" and "real property"; (4) that five of the six definitional phrases used by the Legislature in § 2501(d) either expressly use or reference the term "real estate"; (5) that the Legislature then proceeds to employ these same definitional phrases in giving meaning to "real estate salesperson"; (6) that all the courses that a person is required by the statute to complete to become a "real estate broker" concern real estate; and (7) that other sections of REBA *only* discuss "real estate" and "real estate brokers." Thus, it is only on the basis of its language that we reach our conclusions concerning the meaning of REBA....[12]

---

8. ... In our judgment, because goodwill can be acquired merely through a business's premises, i.e., real estate, and because the surrounding text and provisions of REBA relate only to real estate, we find that the "goodwill" language of § 2501(d) applies only to situations in which the purchase or sale of an existing business's goodwill is made in conjunction with the purchase or sale of the premises in which that goodwill was acquired....

12. Moreover, we disagree with the dissent that the interpretative doctrine of *noscitur a sociis* cannot "properly" be applied in the instant context because the language being defined in § 2501(d) has only a single "customary meaning." We disagree, and we believe that the dissent's "pig" hypothetical example makes our point. Concerning this hypothetical example, *noscitur a sociis* can not only be "accurately" applied, but must necessarily be applied. Contrary to the dissent's assertion, the term "pig" does not have a single, invariable meaning. Rather, it has several separate and distinct meanings,

[Handwritten margin note: Holding]

For these reasons, we cannot join the dissent in concluding that the Legislature intended that "real estate broker" within REBA be understood to mean "broker," or "a broker of all things, real estate or otherwise." ... [We conclude that] REBA applies only to real estate transactions. Further, under § 2501(d), one must only be a licensed real estate broker when, for a fee, one "sells or buys" real estate or "negotiates" a real estate transaction for another. → *Narrow Interpretation*

♦ YOUNG, J., dissenting.

The majority ignores the clear language of the REBA, M.C.L. § 339.2501 *et seq.*, favoring instead an interpretation whose result the majority deems more palatable. The majority also ignores the historical evolution of the statute, which is not dispositive but is entirely consistent with the unambiguous language of the statute. I believe that the statute encompasses the brokerage of business opportunities that do not involve real estate transactions. Accordingly, I would affirm the decision of the Court of Appeals. Because the majority concludes otherwise, I respectfully dissent.

[Handwritten margin note: 1. yes 2. Brokers of Real Estate & Non Real Estate]

[Handwritten margin note: π arg.]

Plaintiff maintains that the transaction it allegedly contracted to perform, which did not involve real estate, is not covered by the REBA and thus plaintiff was not required to be licensed under that act as a precondition of bringing suit for breach of the alleged agreement. The majority contends that the issue in this case is whether the Legislature "intended" the definition of real estate broker to encompass the brokerage of non-real estate transactions. However, rather than seeking to divine a free floating legislative intent, I believe that the Court's task in this case is to determine whether the words *actually used* by the Legislature encompass the brokerage of business opportunities that do not involve real estate.

Our obligation of giving effect to the intent of the Legislature begins by examining the language of a statute. The words of a statute provide the most reliable evidence

---

including: (1) a swine; (2) a person who is gluttonous, greedy, or slovenly; or (3) an oblong mass of metal that has been run into a mold of sand while still molten. *Random House Webster's College Dictionary* (2d ed.). Further, "pig" may also be defined as: (4) a segment of a citrus fruit or an apple; (5) a device that fits within an oil or gas pipeline to clean or inspect its insides; or (6) an earthenware pitcher, jar or other vessel. *New Shorter Oxford English Dictionary* (4th ed.). That the first of these definitions would suggest itself to a "native speaker of English as the common, most likely meaning of the term," is surely a correct, but an irrelevant, observation on the part of the dissent. We do not accord words "default" definitions on the basis of their order of appearance in the dictionary. Rather, because the term "pig" has several different meanings, we initially apply *noscitur a sociis* (whether or not in an explicit fashion) to accord it one of these meanings—that which is contextually related to the language that surrounds "pig." Such a meaning, we assume, is that which is most likely intended by the lawmaker. In the dissent's hypothetical example, after examining the immediately surrounding terms, all of which have in common that they relate to animals, we accord "pig" its only meaning possessed in common with these other terms, i.e., "a swine." Moreover, our analysis would not necessarily stop there. Instead, depending on the matter in controversy, *noscitur a sociis* might have to be further applied to determine an even narrower common characteristic between "a swine" and the other listed terms, for example, that each of these terms can be characterized as an animal that is a mammal. Similarly, we believe that the instant phrase is susceptible to different meanings, at least until *noscitur a sociis* refocuses our interpretative gaze from the phrase itself to the words and phrases that surround it.

of legislative intent. If the language of the statute is clear, the Legislature must have intended the meaning expressed, and the statute is enforced as written. It is only in the face of an ambiguity that a court may properly look outside the words utilized in the statute to ascertain legislative intent. Finally, in construing a statute, we must give the words used by the Legislature their common, ordinary meaning. MCL 8.3a....

The statute at issue is contained in the Occupational Code. M.C.L. § 339.2501(d) defines "real estate broker" as follows:

> "Real estate broker" means an individual, sole proprietorship, partnership, association, corporation, common law trust, or a combination of those entities who with intent to collect or receive a fee, compensation, or valuable consideration, sells or offers for sale, buys or offers to buy, provides or offers to provide market analyses, lists or offers or attempts to list, or negotiates the purchase or sale or exchange or mortgage of real estate, or negotiates for the construction of a building on real estate; who leases or offers or rents or offers for rent real estate or the improvements on the real estate for others, as a whole or partial vocation; who engages in property management as a whole or partial vocation; *who sells or offers for sale, buys or offers to buy, leases or offers to lease, or negotiates the purchase or sale or exchange of a business, business opportunity, or the goodwill of an existing business for others;* or who, as owner or otherwise, engages in the sale of real estate as a principal vocation. (Emphasis added.)

The plain language of the statute defines a real estate broker as, among other things, one who "negotiates the purchase ... of a business, business opportunity, or the goodwill of an existing business for others...." There is no textual indication in the statute that brokering a "business," "business opportunity," or the "goodwill of an existing business" is limited to only those transactions involving real estate. To the contrary, the clear language of "business, business opportunity, or the goodwill of an existing business" encompasses the brokerage of transactions without regard to real estate. The majority does not discuss the plain meaning of the statutory language; rather, the majority's analysis sidesteps the plain meaning of the words and proceeds directly to the use of a canon of statutory construction and other contextual tools to explain why the plain language *could not possibly* mean what it so obviously says.

In fact, by its very definition, the term "goodwill" refutes any notion that real estate is the factor common to all the actions assigned to real estate brokers by the Legislature. Goodwill is an intangible asset defined as "[t]he favor which the management of a business wins from the public" and "[t]he fixed and favorable consideration of customers arising from established and well-conducted business." Black's Law Dictionary (5th ed.). Thus, contrary to the majority's assertions, goodwill has *nothing to do* with real estate; rather, it attaches *only* to an ongoing business concern. The irreducible problem faced by the majority is that it cannot fit this round peg into its square hole. That is, the majority cannot declare the term "goodwill" to mean "real estate" without completely emasculating the definition of "goodwill." The majority makes a conscientious effort to ignore the fact that the word "goodwill" is a legal term of art that is distinct from real estate or any other physical asset.

Of importance, I believe that the majority misuses canons of statutory construction to actually *deprive* the words of the statute their customary meaning. This is contrary to the well-understood principle that statutory construction aids should not be utilized to *create* an ambiguity where one does not otherwise exist. Under the doctrine of *noscitur a sociis*, "the meaning of *questionable* words and phrases in a statute may be ascertained by reference to the meaning of words or phrases associated with it." Black's Law Dictionary (5th ed.) (emphasis added). United States Supreme Court Justice Antonin Scalia discussed the meaning of this rule by illustration: "If you tell me, 'I took the boat out on the bay,' I understand 'bay' to mean one thing; if you tell me, 'I put the saddle on the bay,' I understand it to mean something else." Using Justice Scalia's example as a guide, it is clear that the common meaning of the terms "business, business opportunity, or the goodwill of an existing business" are not contextually altered by the rest of the language in the REBA.

I offer the following as an example to illustrate the majority's abuse and misapplication of this canon of statutory construction. Suppose that a hypothetical statute were to preclude ownership of the following animals without a license:

Duck, Goose, Bittern, Swan, Heron

Presume that the word "bittern" had no commonly understood meaning that could be discerned by resort to a dictionary. In order to determine the meaning of the word, the doctrine of *noscitur a sociis* could be utilized to reasonably come to the conclusion that a bittern is a type of waterfowl. That is, where the meaning of the word is not apparent, the meaning could be ascertained by reference to the meaning of words associated with it.

Now suppose that the hypothetical example were altered slightly, and the statute listed these animals:

Duck, Goose, Pig, Swan, Heron

Unlike bittern, the word "pig" does have a fixed, commonly understood meaning, and it is *not* "waterfowl."[5] However, under the majority's analysis, the doctrine of *noscitur a sociis* could properly be used to come to the conclusion that a pig is a waterfowl (despite the clear, unambiguous meaning of pig), because all the surrounding terms were waterfowls.

Similarly, despite the clear and unambiguous meaning of "business, business opportunity, or the goodwill of an existing business," the majority concludes that these words are limited to those involving "a real estate transaction." By misuse of the rules of construction, I believe the majority is amending the statute in order to avoid giving

---

5. We agree with the majority that "pig" does have many meanings beyond swine. However, none of the alternatives cited in the majority opinion, such as an "oblong mass of metal," would suggest themselves to a native speaker of English as the common, most likely meaning of the term as used in our hypothetical statute.

meaning to the words the Legislature has employed because to do so would result in the enforcement of a *policy* the majority rejects as unsound. The doctrinal difference separating me from the majority is that I am satisfied with applying the plain meaning of the statutory words, whereas the majority is uncomfortable with a construction that results in licensed real estate brokers being the only persons in Michigan authorized to buy and sell businesses for others for a fee. This is an admittedly odd result, but one of the Legislature's making. As my colleague Justice Taylor has observed elsewhere, I "take comfort in the fact that the Legislature is free to amend" this statute if it now considers that the statute no longer reflects a sound policy choice. I fully agree with the proposition that "the Legislature should not have to suffer judicial interference with the choice made in its legislative product." Thus, in my view, it remains the duty of the Legislature, not this Court, to change the state's licensing policy....

Under the clear language of the statute, ... I believe that the statute encompasses the brokerage of business opportunities that do not involve real estate transactions. Therefore, the plaintiff was required to be a licensed real estate broker as a precondition to entering into the alleged contract and is now precluded by M.C.L. §339.2512a from suing to enforce any such contract.

Accordingly, I respectfully dissent from the majority opinion and would affirm the decision of the Court of Appeals.

* * *

Points for Discussion

1. *Statutory Language*: What was the language at issue? What did each party want that language to mean? What meaning did the majority and dissent adopt?

2. *Theories*: Which theory did the majority use? The dissent? Did the majority or dissent find the language ambiguous, absurd, to have a scrivener's error, or to raise a constitutional question?

3. *When Pigs Fly*: What is the point of the dissent's example list: "Duck, Goose, Bittern, Swan, and Heron"? If we replace the word "bittern" (which is a type of waterfowl) with the word "pig" (which is not), does this mean that the word "pig" has to be understood as a type of waterfowl? In other words, is the dissent correct that application of *noscitur a sociis* is inappropriate here because the canon would require us to understand a pig to be a type of waterfowl? Or is the majority correct that application of *noscitur a sociis* is appropriate and narrows the possible meanings to one that the word "pig" will bear, namely an animal? Does "pig" have only one commonly understood meaning or does it have multiple possible meanings, which textual context then identifies? If a word has only one commonly understood meaning, then applying this canon only when there is ambiguity would make sense. Can you think of a word that has only one, commonly understood meaning? Could an English reader ever understand language without considering its textual context?

4. *In Pari Materia*: Using both aspects of *in pari materia*, the majority looked at the textual context of the language in the definition section. Specifically, using the

whole code aspect, the majority examined all the professions within the Occupational Code and concluded that each section addresses a single or discrete group of identified professions. Hence, the relevant section must do so as well. Second, using the whole act aspect, the majority looked at the language within the specific section at issue (2501(d)), applied *noscitur a sociis*, and concluded that the term "business" means real estate business. Remember, *in pari materia* tells the court what material to consider to discern meaning; *noscitur a sociis* tells the court what to do with that material.

5. *Assault*: What does the word "assault" mean? Does it have more than one meaning? Does it have both a technical and ordinary meaning? Does it have more than one technical meaning? Which meaning did I intend with my heading? Look at the three lists below. Does the meaning of the word assault change in each? Assuming so, what accounts for this difference?

    1. Hit, *assault*, beat, wound, maim, kill....

    2. *Assault*, battery, intentional infliction of emotional distress, libel, slander....

    3. *Assault*, robbery, kidnapping, rape, murder....

6. *Goodwill*: The dissent argued that the majority should not apply *noscitur a sociis* because the language "business and business opportunity" is clear. Next, the dissent argued that the word "goodwill" in the list—"business, business opportunity, or the goodwill of an existing business"—"refutes any notion that real estate is the factor common to all." If the legislature had intended the words "business and business opportunity" to apply only to real estate businesses, then why did the legislature include "goodwill," which is an intangible asset and is not a business, the dissent asked. By understanding the meaning of the words "business and business opportunity" in light of the neighboring words "goodwill of an existing business," has not the dissent applied *noscitur a sociis*?

* * *

4. Ejusdem Generis

In Latin, *ejusdem generis* means "of the same kind, class, or nature." The canon directs that when general words are near specific words, the general words should be limited to include only things similar in nature to the specific words. 2A Jabez Gridley Sutherland Statutes and Statutory Construction § 47.17 at 359–60 (Norman Singer 7th ed. 2007). When used to interpret a general catch-all phrase, *ejusdem generis* adds by implication the phrase "everything else of the same type as those in the list."

Ejusdem generis is a subset, or type of, *noscitur a sociis*. *Ejusdem generis* is similar to *noscitur a sociis* in that it is used most commonly when there is a list of items in a statute (e.g., lemons, limes, grapefruits, and others); however, unlike *noscitur a sociis*, *ejusdem generis* is primarily used when the statute ends with a general term, or a catch-all phrase, such as "and others." "Whereas *ejusdem generis* tells us how to find items outside the list expressed in the statute, *noscitur a sociis* tells us how the list gives meaning to the items within it." *Stebbens v. Wells*, 2001 WL 1255079 (R.I. Super. Ct. 2001). Thus, in the example, "lemons, limes, grapefruits, and others," most readers would assume that "others" would likely include other citrus fruits like oranges but would not include vegetables like broccoli. Note how *ejusdem generis* narrows the general catch-all — "and others" — from being interpreted broadly to include anything (and others) to including only certain items (and other citrus fruit). The canon presumes that if the legislative body had intended the general words to be used in their unrestricted sense, the specific words would have not have been included. *Cf., Begay v. United States*, 553 U.S. 137, 153 (2008) (using the rule against surplusage for the point that Congress would not have included the items in the list if Congress had intended the catch-all to have its broadest possible meaning). As Justice Breyer has explained, legislatures use catch-alls for fear "that they would not be able to imagine, in advance, every possible kind of [activity] that should be included. [But this approach] is a common cause of generality, or lack of precision, in statutes." Stephen Breyer, *On the Uses of Legislative History in Interpreting Statutes*, 65 S. Cal. L. Rev. 845, 854 (1992).

Are you wondering why we need two canons for one similar concept? Lawyers do occasionally confuse these two canons. *See, e.g., Babbitt v. Sweet Home Chapter Communities*, 515 U.S. 687, 720 (1995) (Scalia, J., dissenting) (noting that the Solicitor of the Fish and Wildlife Service incorrectly identified the relevant canon as *ejusdem generis* rather than *noscitur a sociis*). The confusion is understandable. Both canons share the same principle — when there are several items in a list that share a common attribute, the relevant item (*noscitur a sociis*) or the catch-all phrase (*ejusdem generis*) should be interpreted as possessing that same attribute. To avoid confusing the two, remember these rules: *Ejusdem generis* should be applied only when there is a general term or catch-all that is being interpreted. "The *ejusdem generis* rule is generally applied to general and specific words clearly associated in the same sentence in a pattern such as '[specific], [specific], or [general]' or '[general], including [specific] and [specific].'" *State v. Van Woerden*, 967 P.2d 14, 18 (Wash. Ct. App. 1998). In contrast, *noscitur a sociis* is applied when an item in the list is being interpreted rather than the catchall.

Of course, there are numerous difficulties with this canon, including determining (1) what the unifier between the listed items is, and (2) how narrowly to limit the general term. In other words, in the list above ("lemons, limes, grapefruits, and others"), is the unifier "fruit," "citrus fruit," or "sour citrus fruit"? Moreover, application of *ejusdem generis* can lead to an interpretation at odds with the ordinary meaning of words. *See, e.g., Commonwealth v. Plowman*, 86 S.W.3d 47, 49 (Ky. 2002) (finding a defendant guilty of committee arson of a "building" after he set fire to a bulldozer); *McKinney v. Robbins*, 892 S.W.2d 502, 599 (Ark. 1995) (refusing to interpret the phrase "domesticated animals" to include kittens).

Like the other the linguistic canons, this canon does not reflect the reality of legal drafting, at least as it relates to catch-alls. If a legislature wishes to ensure that a statute applies only to the items listed or very similar items, then the legislature should not include a catch-all. More commonly, legislatures include catch-alls because they cannot identify, in advance, everything they would want included within a statute's coverage. Legislatures use catch-alls to broaden statutes, not narrow them. Thus, legislatures would likely prefer that catch-alls and general terms be interpreted broadly, not narrowly, to cover all possible, but similar, contingencies.

Ejusdem generis, like all the linguistic canons of construction, is not an iron-clad rule, but rather is a guide to meaning. When the list of things is not sufficiently similar, *ejusdem generis* should not apply. Moreover, some judges refuse to apply the canon absent ambiguity. *See, e.g., People v. Fields*, 105 Cal. App. 3d 341 (1980) (refusing to apply the canon to limit a general catch-all in a statute prohibiting "the knowing destruction ... of any book, paper, record, instrument in writing, or *other matter or thing*" because the statute was not ambiguous and reasoning that the statute applied to "an unending variety of physical objects" including the marijuana the defendant flushed down the toilet). More appropriately and like application of *noscitur a sociis*, *ejusdem generis* applies as part of the determination of ordinary meaning.

The case below addresses the sovereign immunity doctrine. Pursuant to this doctrine, the government cannot be sued absent its consent. In the Federal Tort Claims Act, Congress waived sovereign immunity for certain types of tort claims. Generally, courts require a clear statement from Congress before sovereign immunity is waived. Here, there is no question that Congress waived immunity; the question was how broad or narrow was that waiver. As you read the case, consider how the majority and dissents disagree about the applicability and usefulness of *ejusdem generis* and *noscitur a sociis*.

Ali v. Federal Bureau of Prisons

Supreme Court of the United States
552 U.S. 214 (2008)

◆ Justice Thomas delivered the opinion of the Court [in which Roberts, C. J., and Scalia, Ginsburg, and Alito, JJ., concur].

... Petitioner Abdus-Shahid M.S. Ali was a federal prisoner at the United States Penitentiary.... In December 2003, petitioner was scheduled to be transferred to [another penitentiary]. Before being transferred, he left two duffle bags containing his personal property [to be shipped]. Petitioner was transferred, and his bags arrived some days later. Upon inspecting his property, he noticed that several items were missing.... Many of the purportedly missing items were of religious and nostalgic significance, including two copies of the Qur'an, a prayer rug, and religious magazines. Petitioner estimated that the items were worth $177....

In the FTCA [Federal Torts Claims Act], Congress waived the United States' sovereign immunity for claims arising out of torts committed by federal employees. As relevant here, the FTCA authorizes "claims against the United States, for money damages ... for injury or loss of property ... caused by the negligent or wrongful act or omission of any employee of the Government while acting within the scope of his office or employment." 28 U.S.C. § 1346(b)(1). The FTCA exempts from this waiver certain categories of claims. Relevant here is the exception in subsection (c), which provides that § 1346(b) shall not apply to "[a]ny claim arising in respect of the assessment or collection of any tax or customs duty, or the detention of any goods, merchandise, or other property by any officer of customs or excise or any other law enforcement officer." § 2680(c).

This case turns on whether the BOP officers who allegedly lost petitioner's property qualify as "other law enforcement officer[s]" within the meaning of § 2680(c). Petitioner argues that they do not because "any other law enforcement officer" includes only law enforcement officers acting in a customs or excise capacity. Noting that Congress referenced customs and excise activities in both the language at issue and the preceding clause in § 2680(c), petitioner argues that the entire subsection is focused on preserving the United States' sovereign immunity only as to officers enforcing those laws.

Petitioner's argument is inconsistent with the statute's language. The phrase "*any other law enforcement officer*" suggests a broad meaning. We have previously noted that "[r]ead naturally, the word 'any' has an expansive meaning, that is, 'one or some indiscriminately of whatever kind.'" *United States v. Gonzales*, 520 U.S. 1, 5 (1997) (quoting Webster's Third New International Dictionary 97 (1976))....

... Congress' use of "any" to modify "other law enforcement officer" is most naturally read to mean law enforcement officers of whatever kind. The word "any" is repeated four times in the relevant portion of § 2680(c), and two of those instances appear in the particular phrase at issue: "*any* officer of customs or excise or *any* other law enforcement officer." (Emphasis added.) Congress inserted the word "any" immediately before "other law enforcement officer," leaving no doubt that it modifies that phrase. To be sure, the text's references to "tax or customs duty" and "officer[s] of customs or excise" indicate that Congress intended to preserve immunity for claims arising from an officer's enforcement of tax and customs laws. The text also indicates, however, that Congress intended to preserve immunity for claims arising from the detention of property, and there is no indication that Congress intended immunity for those claims to turn on the type of law being enforced.

Petitioner would require Congress to clarify its intent to cover all law enforcement officers by adding phrases such as "performing any official law enforcement function," or "without limitation." But Congress could not have chosen a more all-encompassing phrase than "any other law enforcement officer" to express that intent. We have no reason to demand that Congress write less economically and more repetitiously....

[P]etitioner invokes numerous canons of statutory construction. He relies primarily on *ejusdem generis,* or the principle that "when a general term follows a specific one, the general term should be understood as a reference to subjects akin to the one with specific enumeration." In petitioner's view, "any officer of customs or excise or any other law enforcement officer" should be read as a three-item list, and the final, catchall phrase "any other law enforcement officer" should be limited to officers of the same nature as the preceding specific phrases.

Petitioner asserts that § 2680(c) … "'presents a textbook *ejusdem generis* scenario.'" We disagree. The structure of the phrase "any officer of customs or excise or any other law enforcement officer" does not lend itself to application of the canon. The phrase is disjunctive, with one specific and one general category, not … a list of specific items separated by commas and followed by a general or collective term. The absence of a list of specific items undercuts the inference embodied in *ejusdem generis* that Congress remained focused on the common attribute when it used the catchall phrase.

Moreover, it is not apparent what common attribute connects the specific items in § 2680(c). Were we to use the canon to limit the meaning of "any other law enforcement officer," we would be required to determine the relevant limiting characteristic of "officer of customs or excise." … [N]o relevant common attribute immediately appears from the phrase "officer of customs or excise." Petitioner suggests that the common attribute is that both types of officers are charged with enforcing the customs and excise laws. But we see no reason why that should be the relevant characteristic as opposed to, for example, that officers of that type are commonly involved in the activities enumerated in the statute: the assessment and collection of taxes and customs duties and the detention of property.

Petitioner's appeals to other interpretive principles are also unconvincing. Petitioner contends that his reading is supported by the canon *noscitur a sociis,* according to which "a word is known by the company it keeps." … [A]lthough customs and excise are mentioned twice in § 2680(c), nothing in the overall statutory context suggests that customs and excise officers were the exclusive focus of the provision. The emphasis in subsection (c) on customs and excise is not inconsistent with the conclusion that "any other law enforcement officer" sweeps as broadly as its language suggests.

Similarly, the rule against superfluities lends petitioner sparse support. The construction we adopt today does not necessarily render "any officer of customs or excise" superfluous; Congress may have simply intended to remove any doubt that officers of customs or excise were included in "law enforcement officers." Moreover, petitioner's construction threatens to render "any other law enforcement officer" superfluous because it is not clear when, if ever, "other law enforcement officer[s]" act in a customs or excise capacity. In any event, we do not woodenly apply limiting principles every time Congress includes a specific example along with a general phrase.

In the end, we are unpersuaded by petitioner's attempt to create ambiguity where the statute's text and structure suggest none. Had Congress intended to limit § 2680(c)'s reach as petitioner contends, it easily could have written "any other law enforcement officer *acting in a customs or excise capacity.*" Instead, it used the unmodified, all-encompassing phrase "any other law enforcement officer." Nothing in the statutory context requires a narrowing construction…. We are not at liberty to rewrite the statute to reflect a meaning we deem more desirable. Instead, we must give effect to the text congress enacted: Section 2680(c) forecloses lawsuits against the United States for the unlawful detention of property by "any," not just "some," law enforcement officers….

◆ JUSTICE KENNEDY, with whom STEVENS, SOUTER, and BREYER, JJ., join, dissenting.

Statutory interpretation, from beginning to end, requires respect for the text. The respect is not enhanced, however, by decisions that foreclose consideration of the text within the whole context of the statute as a guide to determining a legislature's intent. To prevent textual analysis from becoming so rarefied that it departs from how a legislator most likely understood the words when he or she voted for the law, courts use certain interpretative rules to consider text within the statutory design. These canons do not demand wooden reliance and are not by themselves dispositive, but they do function as helpful guides in construing ambiguous statutory provisions. Two of these accepted rules are *ejusdem generis* and *noscitur a sociis*, which together instruct that words in a series should be interpreted in relation to one another....

As the Court states, at issue here is the extent of the exception for suits arising from the detention of goods in defined circumstances. The relevant provision excepts from the general waiver

"claim[s] arising in respect of the assessment or collection of any tax or customs duty, or the detention of any goods, merchandise, or other property by any officer of customs or excise or any other law enforcement officer." 28 U.S.C. §2680(c).

Both on first reading and upon further, close consideration, the plain words of the statute indicate that the exception is concerned only with customs and taxes. The provision begins with a clause dealing exclusively with customs and tax duties. And the provision as a whole contains four express references to customs and tax, making revenue duties and customs and excise officers its most salient features.

This is not to suggest that the Court's reading is wholly impermissible or without some grammatical support.... Still, this ought not be the preferred reading; for between the beginning of the second clause and its closing reference to "any other law enforcement officer" appears another reference to "officer[s] of customs or excise," this time in the context of property detention. This is quite sufficient, in my view, to continue the limited scope of the exception. At the very least, the Court errs by adopting a rule which simply bars all consideration of the canons of *ejusdem generis* and *noscitur a sociis*. And when those canons are consulted, together with other common principles of interpretation, the case for limiting the exception to customs and tax more than overcomes the position maintained by the Government and adopted by the Court.

The *ejusdem generis* canon provides that, where a seemingly broad clause constitutes a residual phrase, it must be controlled by, and defined with reference to, the "enumerated categories ... which are recited just before it," so that the clause encompasses only objects similar in nature. The words "any other law enforcement officer" immediately follow the statute's reference to "officer[s] of customs or excise," as well as the first clause's reference to the assessment of tax and customs duties.

The Court counters that §2680(c) "is disjunctive, with one specific and one general category," rendering *ejusdem generis* inapplicable. The canon's applicability, however, is not limited to those statutes that include a laundry list of items. In addition, *ejusdem generis* is often invoked in conjunction with the interpretative canon *noscitur a sociis,* which provides that words are to be "'known by their companions.'" The general rule is that the "meaning of a word, and, consequently, the intention of the legislature," should be "ascertained by reference to the context, and by considering whether the word in question and the surrounding words are, in fact, *ejusdem generis,* and referable to the same subject-matter."

A proper reading of § 2680(c) thus attributes to the last phrase ("any other law enforcement officer") the discrete characteristic shared by the preceding phrases ("officer[s] of customs or excise" and "assessment or collection of any tax or customs duty"). Had Congress intended otherwise, in all likelihood it would have drafted the section to apply to "any law enforcement officer, including officers of customs and excise," rather than tacking "any other law enforcement officer" on the end of the enumerated categories as it did here.

The common attribute of officers of customs and excise and other law enforcement officers is the performance of functions most often assigned to revenue officers, including, *inter alia,* the enforcement of the United States' revenue laws and the conduct of border searches. Although officers of customs and officers of excise are in most instances the only full-time staff charged with this duty, officers of other federal agencies and general law enforcement officers often will be called upon to act in the traditional capacity of a revenue officer. [Justice Kennedy identifies examples.].

The Court reaches its contrary conclusion by concentrating on the word "any" before the phrase "other law enforcement officer." It takes this single last phrase to extend the statute so that it covers all detentions of property by any law enforcement officer in whatever capacity he or she acts. There are fundamental problems with this approach, in addition to the ones already mentioned.

First, the Court's analysis cannot be squared with the longstanding recognition that a single word must not be read in isolation but instead defined by reference to its statutory context. This is true even of facially broad modifiers. The word "any" can mean "different things depending upon the setting," and must be limited in its application "to those objects to which the legislature intended to apply them." ...

Second, the Court's construction of the phrase "any other law enforcement officer" runs contrary to "'our duty "to give effect, if possible, to every clause and word of a statute."'" The Court's reading renders "officer[s] of customs or excise" mere surplusage, as there would have been no need for Congress to have specified that officers of customs and officers of excise were immune if they indeed were subsumed within the allegedly all-encompassing "any" officer clause.

Third, though the final reference to "any other law enforcement officer" does result in some ambiguity, the legislative history, by virtue of its exclusive reference to customs and excise, confirms that Congress did not shift its attention from the context of revenue enforcement when it used these words at the end of the statute. See, *e.g.,* S.Rep. No. 1400, 79th Cong., 2d Sess., 33 (1946) (in discussing 28 U.S.C. § 2680(c) referring only to "the detention of goods by customs officers"); A. Holtzoff, Report on Proposed Federal Tort Claims Bill 16 (1931) (noting that the property-detention exception was added to the legislation to "include immunity from liability in respect of loss in connection with the detention of goods or merchandise by any officer of customs or excise").

Indeed, the Court's construction reads the exception to defeat the central purpose of the statute, an interpretative danger the Court has warned against in explicit terms. It is difficult to conceive that the FTCA, which was enacted by Congress to make the tort liability of the United States "the same as that of a private person under like circumstance[s]," S.Rep. No. 1400, at 32, would allow any officer under any circumstance to detain property without being accountable under the Act to those injured by his or her tortious conduct. If Congress wanted to say that all law enforcement officers may detain property without liability in tort, including when they perform general law enforcement tasks, it would have done so in more express terms; one would expect at least a reference to law enforcement officers outside the customs or excise context either in the text of the statute or in the legislative history. In the absence of that reference, the Court ought not presume that the liberties of the person who owns the property would be so lightly dismissed and disregarded.

If Congress had intended to give sweeping immunity to all federal law enforcement officials from liability for the detention of property, it would not have dropped this phrase onto the end of the statutory clause so as to appear there as something of an afterthought....

◆ JUSTICE BREYER, with whom JUSTICE STEVENS joins, dissenting.

... I write separately to emphasize, as Justice Kennedy's dissent itself makes clear, that the relevant context extends well beyond Latin canons and other such purely textual devices.

As with many questions of statutory interpretation, the issue here is not the *meaning* of the words. The dictionary meaning of each word is well known. Rather, the issue is the statute's *scope*. What boundaries did Congress intend to set? To what circumstances did Congress intend the phrase, as used in *this* statutory provision, to apply? The majority answers this question by ... emphasizing the statutory word "any." ... [I]n my view, the word "any" provides no help whatsoever.

The word "any" is of no help because all speakers (including writers and legislators) who use general words such as "all," "any," "never," and "none" normally rely upon context to indicate the limits of time and place within which they intend those words to do their linguistic work.... When I call out to my wife, "There isn't any butter," I do not mean, "There isn't any butter in town." The context makes clear to her that I am talking about the contents of our refrigerator. That is to say, it is context, not a dictionary, that sets the boundaries of time, place, and circumstance within which words such as "any" will apply.

Context, of course, includes the words immediately surrounding the phrase in question. And canons such as *ejusdem generis* and *noscitur a sociis* offer help in evaluating the significance of those surrounding words. Yet that help is limited. That is because other contextual features can show that Congress intended a phrase to apply more broadly than the immediately surrounding words by themselves suggest. It is because canons of construction are not "conclusive" and "are often countered ... by some maxim pointing in a different direction." And it is because these particular canons simply crystallize what English speakers already know, namely, that lists often (but not always) group together items with similar characteristics. (That is why we cannot, without comic effect, yoke radically different nouns to a single verb, *e.g.*, "He caught three salmon, two trout, and a cold.")

In this case, not only the immediately surrounding words but also every other contextual feature supports Justice Kennedy's conclusion. The textual context includes the location of the phrase within a provision that otherwise exclusively concerns customs and revenue duties. And the nontextual context includes several features that, taken together, indicate that Congress intended a narrow tort-liability exception related to customs and excise.

First, drafting history shows that the relevant portion of the bill that became the Federal Tort Claims Act concerned only customs and excise. Initially, the relevant provision of the bill exempted only claims "arising in respect of the assessment or collection of any tax or customs duty." In 1931, a Special Assistant to the Attorney General, Alexander Holtzoff, wrote additional draft language, namely, "or the detention of any goods or merchandise by any officer of customs or excise or *any other law enforcement officer.*" Holtzoff, in a report to a congressional agency, said that the expanded language sought "to include immunity from liability in respect of loss in connection with the detention of goods or merchandise by any officer of customs or excise." Holtzoff explained that the language was suggested by a similar British bill that mentioned only customs and excise officials. And Members of Congress repeatedly referred to the exception as encompassing claims involving customs and excise functions.

Second, insofar as Congress sought, through the Act's exceptions, to preclude tort suits against the Government where "adequate remedies were already available," a limited exception makes sense; a broad exception does not. Other statutes already provided recovery for plaintiffs harmed by federal officers enforcing customs and tax laws but not for plaintiffs harmed by all other federal officers enforcing most other laws.

Third, the practical difference between a limited and a broad interpretation is considerable, magnifying the importance of the congressional silence to which Justice Kennedy points. A limited interpretation of the phrase "any other law enforcement officer" would likely encompass only those law enforcement officers working, say, at borders and helping to enforce customs and excise laws. The majority instead interprets this provision to include the tens of thousands of officers performing unrelated tasks. The Justice Department estimates that there are more than 100,000 law enforcement officers, not including members of the armed services. And although the law's history contains much that indicates the provision's scope is limited to customs and excise, it contains *nothing at all* suggesting an intent to apply the provision more broadly, indeed, to multiply the number of officers to whom it applies by what is likely one or more orders of magnitude. It is thus not the Latin canons, *ejusdem generis* and *noscitur a sociis,* that shed light on the application of the statutory phrase but Justice Scalia's more pertinent and easily remembered English-language observation that Congress "does not ... hide elephants in mouseholes." ...

* * *

Points for Discussion

1. *Statutory Language*: What was the language at issue? What did each party want that language to mean? What meaning did the majority and dissents adopt?

2. *Theories*: Which theory did the majority use? The dissents? Did the majority or dissents find the language ambiguous, absurd, to raise a constitutional question, or to have a scrivener's error?

3. *Ambiguity*: If any opinion found ambiguity, did the author require a threshold finding of ambiguity before applying *ejusdem generis* and *noscitur a sociis*? Is the word "any" ambiguous or broad? Assuming the latter, how should broad language be narrowed? Does the addition of the word "any" before a catch-all negate any possibility that the legislature intended to limit the catch-all to the types of items included within a specified list?

4. *Ejusdem Generis*: Why did the majority refuse to apply this canon in this case? Is there a catch-all or, alternatively, a general word that should be limited? Assuming there was neither a general word nor a catch-all, would *noscitur a sociis* have been more appropriate? Assuming so, what result? In other words, if the result of applying either of these two canons is the same, then does it matter which you apply; is the difference merely semantic?

5. *Ejusdem Generis's Role*: Typically and appropriately, courts apply *ejusdem generis* to narrow broadly worded catch-alls and other general language. For example, in *McKinney v. Robbins*, 892 S.W.2d 502 (Ark. 1995), the relevant statute allowed individuals to kill a dog that has killed or is about to catch, injure, or kill "any domesticated animal." *Id.* at 503 (citing Ark. Code Ann. § 20-19-102). The statute further provided that "'[d]omesticated animals' includes, but is not limited to, sheep, goats, cattle, swine, and poultry...." The defendant in the case shot the plaintiff's dog after the dog killed the defendant's kitten. Hence, the issue before the court was whether a kitten was a domesticated animal, for purposes of this statute. The majority concluded no. Despite the ordinary meaning of "domesticated animal" and despite the non-limiting language included within the definition — "not limited to," the court used *ejusdem generis* to narrow the general term "domesticated animals" to include livestock only. Because a kitten is not livestock, the defendant had no right to kill the plaintiff's dog.

In contrast, in *People v. Fields*, 105 Cal. App. 3d 341 (1980), the court refused to apply the canon to narrow a broad catch-all. The statute at issue in that case prohibited inmates from "destroying or concealing documentary evidence." Documentary evidence was defined to include, "book, paper, record, instrument in writing, or other matter or thing." *Id.* at 343 (citing Cal. Penal Code § 135 (West 2015)). The defendant flushed marijuana down the prison toilet. The issue for the court was whether marijuana was "documentary evidence," specifically, whether it was covered by the broad catch-all: "other matter or thing." Finding the language clear, the court refused to apply *ejusdem generis* to limit the catch-all to paper-like items. *Id.* at 344.

Which of these two cases was similar to the majority's approach in *Ali*? The dissents'?

6. *Rule against Surplusage*: What role did this canon play, if any, in the majority and dissents' opinions? In a case we will study in our next section (*Begay v. Unites States*, 553 U.S. 137 (2008)), the majority used listed items to limit a similarly broad catch-all. The majority suggested that the listed items must have been included to limit the broad catch-all or they would have been surplusage. Are these cases consistent?

7. *Drafting & Legislative History*: According to the dissents, what did the drafting and legislative history show about the meaning of the language at issue? Why did the majority not consider that history?

8. *Elephants in Mouseholes*: In *Whitman v. American Trucking Ass'ns., Inc.*, 531 U.S. 457, 468 (2001), Justice Scalia wrote, "Congress ... does not alter the fundamental details of a regulatory scheme in vague terms or ancillary provisions—it does not, one might say, hide elephants in mouseholes." Why did Justice Breyer include this quote? Essentially, if Congress intended to enact such a sweeping change, Congress would have made that intent clearer.

* * *

Ejusdem generis and *noscitur a sociis* are often discussed together. Let's return to *Yates v. United States*, 135 S. Ct. 1074 (2015). In the case excerpted below, the justices dispute the role and application of *noscitur a sociis* and *ejusdem generis*. Notice how both Justice Ginsburg and Kagan begin with the plain meaning, then discuss the canons, among other things. Why did Justice Alito concur rather than sign the majority opinion? How does the dissent respond to the majority and concurrence's discussion of these two canons?

→ Yates v. United States Fish
Supreme Court of the United States
135 S. Ct. 1074 (2015)

♦ JUSTICE GINSBURG delivered the opinion of the Court [in which ROBERTS, C.J., and BREYER, and SOTOMAYOR, JJ., concur].

John Yates, a commercial fisherman, caught undersized red grouper in federal waters in the Gulf of Mexico. To prevent federal authorities from confirming that he had harvested undersized fish, Yates ordered a crew member to toss the suspect catch into the sea. For this offense, he was charged with, and convicted of, violating 18 U.S.C. § 1519, which provides:

"Whoever knowingly alters, destroys, mutilates, conceals, covers up, falsifies, or makes a false entry in any record, document, or tangible object with the intent to impede, obstruct, or influence the investigation or proper administration of any matter within the jurisdiction of any department or agency of the United States or any case filed under title 11, or in relation to or contemplation of any such matter or case, shall be fined under this title, imprisoned not more than 20 years, or both." ...

... At the end of the Government's case in chief, [Yates] moved for a judgment of acquittal on the § 1519 charge. Pointing to § 1519's title and its origin as a provision of the Sarbanes-Oxley Act, Yates argued that the section sets forth "a documents offense" and that its reference to "tangible object[s]" subsumes "computer hard drives, logbooks, [and] things of that nature," not fish. ...

The Government countered that a "tangible object" within § 1519's compass is "simply something other than a document or record." The trial judge expressed misgivings about reading "tangible object" as broadly as the Government urged: "Isn't there a Latin phrase [about] construction of a statute.... The gist of it is ... you take a look at [a] line of words, and you interpret the words consistently. So if you're talking about documents, and records, tangible objects are tangible objects in the nature of a document or a record, as opposed to a fish." The first-instance judge nonetheless followed controlling Eleventh Circuit precedent. While recognizing that § 1519 was passed as part of legislation targeting corporate fraud, the Court of Appeals had instructed that "the broad language of § 1519 is not limited to corporate fraud cases, and 'Congress is free to pass laws with language covering areas well beyond the particular crisis *du jour* that initially prompted legislative action.'" Accordingly, the trial court read "tangible object" as a term "independent" of "record" or "document." ...

On appeal, the Eleventh Circuit found the text of § 1519 "plain." Because "tangible object" was "undefined" in the statute, the Court of Appeals gave the term its "ordinary or natural meaning," *i.e.*, its dictionary definition, "[h]aving or possessing physical form." (quoting Black's Law Dictionary 1592 (9th ed. 2009)). We granted certiorari and now reverse the Eleventh Circuit's judgment....

The ordinary meaning of an "object" that is "tangible," as stated in dictionary definitions, is "a discrete ... thing," Webster's Third New International Dictionary 1555 (2002), that "possess[es] physical form," Black's Law Dictionary 1683 (10th ed. 2014). From this premise, the Government concludes that "tangible object," as that term appears in § 1519, covers the waterfront, including fish from the sea. Whether a statutory term is unambiguous, however, does not turn solely on dictionary definitions of its component words. Rather, "[t]he plainness or ambiguity of statutory language is determined [not only] by reference to the language itself, [but as well by] the specific context in which that language is used, and the broader context of the statute as a whole." Ordinarily, a word's usage accords with its dictionary definition. In law as in life, however, the same words, placed in different contexts, sometimes mean different things....

... [A]lthough dictionary definitions of the words "tangible" and "object" bear consideration, they are not dispositive of the meaning of "tangible object" in § 1519....

The words immediately surrounding "tangible object" in § 1519—"falsifies, or makes a false entry in any record [or] document"—also cabin the contextual meaning of that term.... [W]e rely on the principle of *noscitur a sociis*—a word is known by the company it keeps—to "avoid ascribing to one word a meaning so broad that it is inconsistent with its accompanying words, thus giving unintended breadth to the Acts of Congress....

The *noscitur a sociis* canon operates in a similar manner here. "Tangible object" is the last in a list of terms that begins "any record [or] document." The term is therefore appropriately read to refer, not to any tangible object, but specifically to the subset of tangible objects involving records and documents, *i.e.,* objects used to record or preserve information.

This moderate interpretation of "tangible object" accords with the list of actions § 1519 proscribes. The section applies to anyone who "alters, destroys, mutilates, conceals, covers up, *falsifies,* or *makes a false entry in* any record, document, or tangible object" with the requisite obstructive intent. (Emphasis added.) The last two verbs, "falsif[y]" and "mak[e] a false entry in," typically take as grammatical objects records, documents, or things used to record or preserve information, such as logbooks or hard drives. See, *e.g.,* Black's Law Dictionary 720 (10th ed. 2014) (defining "falsify" as "[t]o make deceptive; to counterfeit, forge, or misrepresent; esp., to tamper with (a document, record, etc.)"). It would be unnatural, for example, to describe a killer's act of wiping his fingerprints from a gun as "falsifying" the murder weapon. But it would not be strange to refer to "falsifying" data stored on a hard drive as simply "falsifying" a hard drive. Furthermore, Congress did not include on § 1512(c)(1)'s list of prohibited actions "falsifies" or "makes a false entry in." See § 1512(c)(1) (making it unlawful to "alte[r], destro[y], mutilat[e], or concea[l] a record, document, or other object" with the requisite obstructive intent)....

A canon related to *noscitur a sociis, ejusdem generis,* counsels: "Where general words follow specific words in a statutory enumeration, the general words are [usually] construed to embrace only objects similar in nature to those objects enumerated by the preceding specific words." In *Begay v. United States,* 553 U.S. 137, 142–143 (2008), for example, we relied on this principle to determine what crimes were covered by the statutory phrase "any crime ... that ... is burglary, arson, or extortion, involves use of explosives, or otherwise involves conduct that presents a serious potential risk of physical injury to another," [citation omitted]. The enumeration of specific crimes, we explained, indicates that the "otherwise involves" provision covers "only *similar* crimes, rather than *every* crime that 'presents a serious potential risk of physical injury to another.'" Had Congress intended "tangible object" in § 1519 to be interpreted so generically as to capture physical objects as dissimilar as documents and fish, Congress would have had no reason to refer specifically to "record" or "document." The Gov-

ernment's unbounded reading of "tangible object" would render those words misleading surplusage.

Having used traditional tools of statutory interpretation to examine markers of congressional intent within the Sarbanes-Oxley Act and § 1519 itself, we are persuaded that an aggressive interpretation of "tangible object" must be rejected. It is highly improbable that Congress would have buried a general spoliation statute covering objects of any and every kind in a provision targeting fraud in financial record-keeping....

◆ JUSTICE ALITO, concurring in the judgment.

This case can and should be resolved on narrow grounds. And though the question is close, traditional tools of statutory construction confirm that John Yates has the better of the argument. Three features of 18 U.S.C. § 1519 stand out to me: the statute's list of nouns, its list of verbs, and its title. Although perhaps none of these features by itself would tip the case in favor of Yates, the three combined do so.

Start with the nouns. Section 1519 refers to "any record, document, or tangible object." The *noscitur a sociis* canon instructs that when a statute contains a list, each word in that list presumptively has a "similar" meaning. A related canon, *ejusdem generis* teaches that general words following a list of specific words should usually be read in light of those specific words to mean something "similar." Applying these canons to § 1519's list of nouns, the term "tangible object" should refer to something similar to records or documents. A fish does not spring to mind—nor does an antelope, a colonial farmhouse, a hydrofoil, or an oil derrick. All are "objects" that are "tangible." But who wouldn't raise an eyebrow if a neighbor, when asked to identify something similar to a "record" or "document," said "crocodile"?

This reading, of course, has its shortcomings. For instance, this is an imperfect *ejusdem generis* case because "record" and "document" are themselves quite general. And there is a risk that "tangible object" may be made superfluous—what is similar to a "record" or "document" but yet is not one? An e-mail, however, could be such a thing. An e-mail, after all, might not be a "document" if, as was "traditionally" so, a document was a "piece of paper with information on it," not "information stored on a computer, electronic storage device, or any other medium." Black's Law Dictionary 587–588 (10th ed. 2014). E-mails might also not be "records" if records are limited to "minutes" or other formal writings "designed to memorialize [past] events." *Id.*, at 1465. A hard drive, however, is tangible and can contain files that are precisely akin to even these narrow definitions. Both "record" and "document" can be read more expansively, but adding "tangible object" to § 1519 would ensure beyond question that electronic files are included. To be sure, "tangible object" presumably can capture more than just e-mails; Congress enacts "catchall[s]" for "known unknowns." But where *noscitur a sociis* and *ejusdem generis* apply, "known unknowns" should be similar to known knowns, *i.e.*, here, records and documents. This is especially true because reading "tangible object" too broadly could render "record" and "document" superfluous.

Next, consider § 1519's list of verbs: "alters, destroys, mutilates, conceals, covers up, falsifies, or makes a false entry in." Although many of those verbs could apply to nouns as far-flung as salamanders, satellites, or sand dunes, the last phrase in the list — "makes a false entry in" — makes no sense outside of filekeeping. How does one make a false entry in a fish? "Alters" and especially "falsifies" are also closely associated with filekeeping. Not one of the verbs, moreover, *cannot* be applied to filekeeping — certainly not in the way that "makes a false entry in" is always inconsistent with the aquatic.

... One can imagine Congress trying to write a law so broadly that not every verb lines up with every noun. But failure to "line up" may suggest that something has gone awry in one's interpretation of a text. Where, as here, each of a statute's verbs applies to a certain category of nouns, there is some reason to think that Congress had that category in mind. Categories, of course, are often underinclusive or overinclusive.... But this does not mean that categories are not useful or that Congress does not enact them. Here, focusing on the verbs, the category of nouns appears to be filekeeping. This observation is not dispositive, but neither is it nothing....

◆ JUSTICE KAGAN with whom SCALIA, KENNEDY, and THOMAS, JJ., join, dissenting.

... I ... begin with § 1519's text. When Congress has not supplied a definition, we generally give a statutory term its ordinary meaning. As the plurality must acknowledge, the ordinary meaning of "tangible object" is "a discrete thing that possesses physical form." A fish is, of course, a discrete thing that possesses physical form. *See generally* Dr. Seuss, One Fish Two Fish Red Fish Blue Fish (1960). So the ordinary meaning of the term "tangible object" in § 1519, as no one here disputes, covers fish (including too-small red grouper)....

That is not necessarily the end of the matter; I agree with the plurality (really, who does not?) that context matters in interpreting statutes. We do not "construe the meaning of statutory terms in a vacuum." Rather, we interpret particular words "in their context and with a view to their place in the overall statutory scheme." And sometimes that means, as the plurality says, that the dictionary definition of a disputed term cannot control. But this is not such an occasion, for here the text and its context point the same way. Stepping back from the words "tangible object" provides only further evidence that Congress said what it meant and meant what it said.

Begin with the way the surrounding words in § 1519 reinforce the breadth of the term at issue. Section 1519 refers to "any" tangible object, thus indicating (in line with *that* word's plain meaning) a tangible object "of whatever kind." Webster's Third New International Dictionary 97 (2002). This Court has time and again recognized that "any" has "an expansive meaning," bringing within a statute's reach *all* types of the item (here, "tangible object") to which the law refers. [S]ee, *e.g.*, *Ali* v. *Federal Bureau of Prisons*, 552 U. S. 214, 219–220 (2008). And the adjacent laundry list of verbs in § 1519 ("alters, destroys, mutilates, conceals, covers up, falsifies, or makes a false entry") further shows that Congress wrote a statute with a wide scope. Those words are supposed to ensure — just as "tangible object" is meant to — that § 1519 covers the whole world of evidence-tampering, in all its prodigious variety....

[The plurality turns to] *noscitur a sociis* and *ejusdem generis*. The first of those related canons advises that words grouped in a list be given similar meanings. The second counsels that a general term following specific words embraces only things of a similar kind. According to the plurality, those Latin maxims change the English meaning of "tangible object" to only things, like records and documents, "used to record or preserve information." But understood as this Court always has, the canons have no such transformative effect on the workaday language Congress chose.

As an initial matter, this Court uses *noscitur a sociis* and *ejusdem generis* to resolve ambiguity, not create it. Those principles are "useful rule[s] of construction where words are of obscure or doubtful meaning." But when words have a clear definition, and all other contextual clues support that meaning, the canons cannot properly defeat Congress's decision to draft broad legislation. See, *e.g.*, *Ali*, 552 U. S., at 227 (rejecting the invocation of these canons as an "attempt to create ambiguity where the statute's text and structure suggest none").

Anyway, assigning "tangible object" its ordinary meaning comports with *noscitur a sociis* and *ejusdem generis* when applied, as they should be, with attention to § 1519's subject and purpose. Those canons require identifying a common trait that links all the words in a statutory phrase. In responding to that demand, the plurality characterizes records and documents as things that preserve information—and so they are. But just as much, they are things that provide information, and thus potentially serve as evidence relevant to matters under review. And in a statute pertaining to obstruction of federal investigations, that evidentiary function comes to the fore. The destruction of records and documents prevents law enforcement agents from gathering facts relevant to official inquiries. And so too does the destruction of tangible objects—of whatever kind. Whether the item is a fisherman's ledger or an undersized fish, throwing it overboard has the identical effect on the administration of justice. For purposes of § 1519, records, documents, and (all) tangible objects are therefore alike....

And the plurality's invocation of § 1519's verbs does nothing to buttress its canon-based argument. The plurality observes that § 1519 prohibits "falsif[ying]" or "mak[ing] a false entry in" a tangible object, and no one can do those things to, say, a murder weapon (or a fish). But of course someone can alter, destroy, mutilate, conceal, or cover up such a tangible object, and § 1519 prohibits those actions too. The Court has never before suggested that all the verbs in a statute need to match up with all the nouns. And for good reason. It is exactly when Congress sets out to draft a statute broadly—to include every imaginable variation on a theme—that such mismatches will arise. To respond by narrowing the law, as the plurality does, is thus to flout both what Congress wrote and what Congress wanted....

The concurring opinion is a shorter, vaguer version of the plurality's. It relies primarily on the *noscitur a sociis* and *ejusdem generis* canons, tries to bolster them with 1519 s list of verbs, and concludes with the section s title.... From those familiar materials, the concurrence arrives at the following definition: tangible object should mean something similar to records or documents. In amplifying that purported guidance, the concurrence suggests applying the term tangible object in keeping with what a neighbor, when asked to identify something similar to record or document, might answer. [W]ho wouldn't raise an eyebrow, the concurrence wonders, if the neighbor said crocodile? Courts sometimes say, when explaining the Latin maxims, that the words of a statute should be interpreted consistent with their neighbors. The concurrence takes that expression literally.

But 1519's meaning should not hinge on the odd game of Mad Libs the concurrence proposes. No one reading 1519 needs to fill in a blank after the words records and documents. That is because Congress, quite helpfully, already did so adding the term tangible object. The issue in this case is what that term means. So if the concurrence wishes to ask its neighbor a question, I'd recommend a more pertinent one: Do you think a fish (or, if the concurrence prefers, a crocodile) is a tangible object? As to that query, who wouldn't raise an eyebrow if the neighbor said no?

In insisting on its different question, the concurrence neglects the proper function of catchall phrases like "or tangible object." The reason Congress uses such terms is precisely to reach things that, in the concurrence's words, do[ ] not spring to mind to my mind, to my neighbor's, or (most important) to Congress's. As this Court recently explained: [T]he whole value of a generally phrased residual [term] is that it serves as a catchall for matters not specifically contemplated known unknowns. Congress realizes that in a game of free association with record and document, it will never think of all the other things including crocodiles and fish whose destruction or alteration can (less frequently but just as effectively) thwart law enforcement. And so Congress adds the general term or tangible object again, exactly because such things do[ ] not spring to mind.[7]

The concurrence suggests that the term tangible object serves not as a catchall for physical evidence but to ensure beyond question that e-mails and other electronic files fall within 1519's compass. But that claim is eyebrow-raising in its own right. Would a Congress wishing to make certain that 1519 applies to e-mails add the phrase tangible object (as opposed, say, to electronic communications)? Would a judge or jury member predictably find that tangible object encompasses something as virtual as e-mail (as compared, say, with something as real as a fish)? If not (and the answer is not), then that term cannot function as a failsafe for e-mails....

* * *

Points for Discussion

1. *Statutory Language*: What was the language at issue? What did each party want that language to mean? What meaning did the plurality, concurrence, and dissent adopt?

---

7. The concurrence contends that when the *noscitur* and *ejusdem* canons are in play, known unknowns should be similar to known knowns, *i.e.*, here, records and documents. But as noted above, records and documents *are* similar to crocodiles and fish as far as 1519 is concerned: All are potentially useful as evidence in an investigation. The concurrence never explains why *that* similarity isn't the relevant one in a statute aimed at evidence-tampering.

2.   *Theories*: Which theory did the plurality use? The concurrence and dissent? Judges typically turn to dictionaries to find the ordinary meaning of words. What did Justice Kagan cite to prove that a fish is a tangible object?

3.   *Ambiguity*: Which, if any, of the justices required a threshold finding of ambiguity or absurdity before applying *noscitur a sociis* and *ejusdem generis*? Is "tangible object" actually ambiguous or is it broad and general?

4.   *Noscitur a Sociis*: According to the plurality, what was the role of the canon *noscitur a sociis*? When judges apply the canon, they seek a unifier. What was the unifier the plurality and concurrence found that narrowed the words "tangible object"? The concurrence divided his *noscitur a sociis* arguments in two: one based on the nouns used, and one based on the verbs used. How did each subset of words narrow the word "tangible object"? Although the dissent disagreed that this canon was appropriate, what unifier did she suggest if one were to be used?

5.   *Ejusdem Generis*: Is the term "other tangible object" a general word or a catch-all? If so, is not the appropriate canon *ejusdem generis*? Are both canons relevant in this case or should only one apply?

6.   *Rule against Surplusage*: The plurality referred to the rule, or doctrine, against surplusage, a canon that you will learn about in the next section of this text (indeed, Justice Ginsburg cited *Begay*, the case excerpted below). That canon directs that every word and phrase in a statute must have meaning. Congress does not add superfluous words. You might consider whether lawyers are trained to eliminate or add superfluous words. Did the plurality and concurrence eliminate the distinction between document, record, and tangible object? How did Justice Alito identify a difference?

* * *

5. The Rule against Surplusage (or Redundancy)

According to the *rule against surplusage*, the proper interpretation of a statute is one in which every word has meaning; nothing is redundant or meaningless. There are two separate aspects to this canon: (1) every word must have independent meaning; and (2) two different words cannot have the same meaning. If different words had the same meaning, then the second word would be surplusage, or unnecessary. Note that this canon compliments the identical words presumption in that both canons direct that the same words in a statute should mean the same thing and that different words in a statute should mean different things, absent contrary legislative intent. *See, e.g., Feld v. Robert & Charles Beauty Salon*, 459 N.W.2d 279, 284 (Mich. 1990) (applying the canon to conclude that a workers' compensation claimant could not bring an attorney to a medical exam where the statute explicitly allowed claimants to bring "a physician," because the word "physician" would be redundant if anyone was allowed to attend).

Like many of the other linguistic canons, this canon is a tie-breaking presumption and yields to contrary legislative intent. Thus, courts can reject words "as surplusage" when they are "inadvertently inserted or if repugnant to the rest of the statute...." *Chickasaw Nation v. United States*, 534 U.S. 84, 94 (2001) (quoting K. LLEWELLYN, THE COMMON LAW TRADITION 525 (1960)). In *Chickasaw Nation*, the Court held that the rule against surplusage did not apply when the rule produced an interpretation that conflicted with the intent of Congress. The canon was particularly inappropriate in the Court's view because the surplus words were simply a numerical cross-reference in a parenthetical. *Id.* Such minor surplusage should not overcome the ordinary meaning of the rest of the text.

 The rule against surplusage presumes three things: (1) that the statute was drafted with care, (2) that each word was the result of thoughtful deliberation, and (3) that if the legislature had found extra words, it would have removed them during the deliberation process. In other words, the canon presumes that the legislature would not include surplus language to communicate its meaning. But these presumptions are flawed. Statutes are not always carefully drafted. Legal drafters often intend to include redundant language to cover any unforeseen gaps, and legislatures simply fail to identify the redundancy timely. Legislators are not likely to waste time or energy arguing to remove redundancy when there are more important issues to address. Thus, the presumptions simply do not match drafting reality. "[A] statute that is the product of compromise may contain redundant language as a by-product of the strains of the negotiating process." Richard A. Posner, *Statutory Interpretation—In the Classroom and the Courtroom,* 50 U. CHI. L. REV. 800, 812 (1983). For these reasons, not all judges use this canon. *Mayer v. Spanel Int'l Ltd.*, 51 F.3d 670, 674 (7th Cir. 1995) ("Redundancy is common in statutes; we do not subscribe to the view that every enacted word must carry independent force.").

In the case that follows, the majority turns to the rule against surplusage to narrow the broad meaning of the catch-all. Why do the concurrence and dissent disagree?

Begay v. United States

Supreme Court of the United States
553 U.S. 137 (2008)

◆ JUSTICE BREYER delivered the opinion of the Court [in which ROBERTS, C. J., and STEVENS, GINSBURG, and KENNEDY, JJ., concur].

... Federal law prohibits a previously convicted felon from possessing a firearm. A related provision provides for a prison term of up to 10 years for an ordinary offender. §924(a)(2). The Armed Career Criminal Act imposes a more stringent 15–year mandatory minimum sentence on an offender who has three prior convictions "for a violent felony or a serious drug offense." §924(e)(1).

The Act defines a "violent felony" as "any crime punishable by imprisonment for a term exceeding one year" that

"(i) has as an element the use, attempted use, or threatened use of physical force against the person of another; or "(ii) is burglary, arson, or extortion, involves use of explosives, or otherwise involves conduct that presents a serious potential risk of physical injury to another." § 924(e)(2)(B). *[Definition]*

We here consider whether driving under the influence of alcohol (DUI), as set forth in New Mexico's criminal statutes, falls within the scope of the second clause [(ii)].

... In September 2004, New Mexico police officers received a report that Larry Begay, the petitioner here, had threatened his sister and aunt with a rifle. The police arrested him. Begay subsequently conceded he was a felon and pleaded guilty to a federal charge of unlawful possession of a firearm.... Begay's presentence report said that he had been convicted a dozen times for DUI, which under New Mexico's law becomes a felony ... the fourth (or subsequent) time an individual commits it.... The judge consequently concluded that Begay had three or more prior convictions for a "violent felony" and should receive a sentence that reflected a mandatory minimum prison term of 15 years.

Begay, claiming that DUI is not a "violent felony" within the terms of the statute, appealed. The Court of Appeals ... rejected that claim. Begay sought certiorari, and we agreed to decide the question.

... In determining whether [DUI] is a violent felony, we consider the offense generically, that is to say, we examine it in terms of how the law defines the offense and not in terms of how an individual offender might have committed it on a particular occasion.... *[He actually pulled trigger → Objectively not subjectively]* *[Language]*

... DUI involves conduct that "presents a serious potential risk of physical injury to another." § 924(e)(2)(B)(ii).... Even so, we find that DUI falls outside the scope of clause (ii). It is simply too unlike the provision's listed examples for us to believe that Congress intended the provision to cover it.

In our view, the provision's listed examples—burglary, arson, extortion, or crimes involving the use of explosives—illustrate the kinds of crimes that fall within the statute's scope. Their presence indicates that the statute covers only *similar* crimes, rather than *every* crime that "presents a serious potential risk of physical injury to another." If Congress meant the latter, *i.e.,* if it meant the statute to be all encompassing, it is hard to see why it would have needed to include the examples at all. Without them, clause (ii) would cover *all* crimes that present a "serious potential risk of physical injury." Additionally, if Congress meant clause (ii) to include *all* risky crimes, why would it have included clause (i)? A crime which has as an element the "use, attempted use, or threatened use of physical force" against the person (as clause (i) specifies) is likely to create "a serious potential risk of physical injury" and would seem to fall within the scope of clause (ii)....

These considerations taken together convince us that, "'to give effect ... to every clause and word'" of this statute, we should read the examples as limiting the crimes that clause (ii) covers to crimes that are roughly similar, in kind as well as in degree of risk posed, to the examples themselves....

The statute's history offers further support for our conclusion that the examples in clause (ii) limit the scope of the clause to crimes that are similar to the examples *[History]* themselves. Prior to the enactment of the current language, the Act applied its enhanced sentence to offenders with "three previous convictions for robbery or burglary." Congress sought to expand that definition to include both crimes against the person (clause (i)) and certain physically risky crimes against property (clause (ii)). See H.R.Rep. No. 99–849, p. 3 (1986). When doing so, Congress rejected a broad proposal that would have covered *every* offense that involved a substantial risk of the use of " 'physical force against the person or property of another.' " *Taylor,* 495 U.S., at 583 (quoting S. 2312, 99th Cong., 2d Sess. (1986); H.R. 4639, 99th Cong., 2d Sess. (1986)). Instead, it added the present examples. And in the relevant House Report, it described clause (ii) as including "State and Federal felonies against property such as burglary, arson, extortion, use of explosives and *similar* crimes as predicate offenses where the conduct involved presents a serious risk of injury to a person." H.R. Rep., at 5 (emphasis added)....

When viewed in terms of the Act's basic purposes, this distinction matters considerably. As suggested by its title, the Armed Career Criminal Act focuses upon the special danger created when a particular type of offender—a violent criminal or drug trafficker—possesses a gun. In order to determine which offenders fall into this category, the Act looks to past crimes. This is because an offender's criminal history is relevant to the question whether he is a career criminal, or, more precisely, to the kind or degree of danger the offender would pose were he to possess a gun.

In this respect—namely, a prior crime's relevance to the possibility of future danger with a gun—crimes involving intentional or purposeful conduct (as in burglary and arson) are different from DUI, a strict-liability crime. In both instances, the offender's prior crimes reveal a degree of callousness toward risk, but in the former instance they also show an increased likelihood that the offender is the kind of person who might deliberately point the gun and pull the trigger. We have no reason to believe that Congress intended a 15–year mandatory prison term where that increased likelihood does not exist....

The dissent's approach, on the other hand, would likely include these crimes within the statutory definition of "violent felony," along with any other crime that can be said to present a " 'potential risk of physical injury.' " And it would do so because it believes such a result is compelled by the statute's text. But the dissent's explanation does not account for a key feature of that text—namely, the four example crimes intended to illustrate what kind of "violent felony" the statute covers. The dissent at most believes that these examples are relevant only to define the requisite serious risk associated with a "crime of violence." But the dissent does not explain how to identify the requisite level of risk, nor does it describe how these various examples might help determine what other offenses involve conduct presenting the same level of risk. If they were in fact helpful on that score, we might expect more predictable results from a purely risk-based approach. Thus, the dissent's reliance on these examples for a function they appear incapable of performing reads them out of the statute and, in so doing, fails to effectuate Congress' purpose to punish only a particular subset of offender, namely, career criminals.

The distinction we make does not minimize the seriousness of the risks attached to driving under the influence. Nor does our argument deny that an individual with a criminal history of DUI might later pull the trigger of a gun. (Indeed, we may have such an instance before us)....

We consequently conclude that New Mexico's crime of "driving under the influence" falls outside the scope of the Armed Career Criminal Act's clause (ii) "violent felony" definition....

♦ JUSTICE SCALIA concurring in the judgment.

... Contrary to the Court, I conclude that the residual clause unambiguously encompasses *all* crimes that present a serious risk of injury to another. But because I cannot say that drunk driving clearly poses such a risk (within the meaning of the statute), the rule of lenity brings me to concur in the judgment of the Court....

In my view..., the best way to interpret § 924(e) is first to determine which of the enumerated offenses poses the least serious risk of physical injury, and then to set that level of risk as the "serious potential risk" required by the statute. Crimes that pose at least that serious a risk of injury are encompassed by the residual clause; crimes that do not are excluded.

Today the Court ... engrafts a requirement onto the residual clause that a predicate crime involve "purposeful, 'violent,' and 'aggressive' conduct.".... ..[T]he problem with the Court's holding today is that it is not remotely faithful to the statute that Congress wrote....

The Court is correct that the clause "otherwise involves conduct that presents a serious potential risk of physical injury to another" signifies a similarity between the enumerated and unenumerated crimes. It is not, however, *any* old similarity, such as (to take a random example) "purposeful, 'violent,' and 'aggressive' conduct." Rather, it is the *particular* similarity specified after the "otherwise" — *i.e.*, that they all pose a serious potential risk of physical injury to another. They need not be similar in any other way. As the Court correctly notes, the word "otherwise" in this context means "'in a different way or manner.'" Webster's New International Dictionary 1729 (2d ed.1957) ("in another way, or in other ways"). Therefore, by using the word "otherwise" the writer draws a substantive connection between two sets only on one specific dimension — *i.e.*, whatever follows "otherwise." What that means here is that "committing one of the enumerated crimes ... is *one way* to commit a crime 'involv[ing] a serious potential risk of physical injury to another'; and that *other ways* of committing a crime of that character similarly constitute 'violent felon[ies].'" ...

... The phrase "otherwise involves conduct that presents a serious potential risk of physical injury to another" limits inclusion in the statute only by a crime's degree of risk. The use of the adjective "serious" seems to me to signify a purely quantitative measure of risk. If both an intentional and a negligent crime pose a 50% risk of death, could one be characterized as involving a "serious risk" and the other not? Surely not....

The Court says that an interpretation of the residual clause that includes all crimes posing a serious risk of injury would render superfluous §924(e)(2)(B)(i), which provides that a "violent felony" is any crime that "has as an element the use, attempted use, or threatened use of physical force against the person" of another. But the canon against surplusage has substantially less force when it comes to interpreting a broad residual clause like the one at issue here. Though the second clause renders the first superfluous, it would raise no eyebrows to refer to "crimes that entail the use of force and crimes that, while not entailing the use of force, nonetheless present a serious risk of injury to another person." In any event, the canon against surplusage merely helps decide between competing permissible interpretations of an ambiguous statute; it does not sanction writing in a requirement that Congress neglected to think of. And finally, come to think of it, the Court's solution does nothing whatever to solve the supposed surplusage problem. Crimes that include as an element "the use ... of physical force against the person of another" are all embraced (and the reference to them thus rendered superfluous) by the requirement of "purposeful, 'violent,' and 'aggressive' conduct" that the Court invents.

Under my interpretation of §924(e), I must answer one question: Does drunk driving pose at least as serious a risk of physical injury to another as burglary? From the evidence presented by the Government, I cannot conclude so. Because of that, the rule of lenity requires that I resolve this case in favor of the defendant.... Applying the rule of lenity to a statute that demands it, I would reverse the decision of the Court of Appeals.

♦ JUSTICE ALITO, with whom SOUTER and THOMAS, JJ., join, dissenting.

The statutory provision at issue in this case — the so-called "residual clause" of 18 U.S.C. §924(e)(2)(B)(ii) — calls out for legislative clarification, and I am sympathetic to the result produced by the Court's attempt to craft a narrowing construction of this provision. Unfortunately, the Court's interpretation simply cannot be reconciled with the statutory text, and I therefore respectfully dissent.

In September 2004, after a night of heavy drinking, petitioner pointed a rifle at his aunt and threatened to shoot if she did not give him money. When she replied that she did not have any money, petitioner repeatedly pulled the trigger, but the rifle was unloaded and did not fire. Petitioner then threatened his sister in a similar fashion.

At the time of this incident, petitioner was a convicted felon. He had 12 prior convictions in New Mexico for driving under the influence of alcohol (DUI). While DUI is generally a misdemeanor under New Mexico law, the offense of DUI after at least three prior DUI convictions is a felony requiring a sentence of 18 months' imprisonment....

The only ... question, therefore, is whether the risk presented by petitioner's qualifying DUI felony convictions was "serious," *i.e.,* "significant" or "important." See, *e.g.,* Webster's Third New International Dictionary 2073 (2002) (hereinafter Webster's); 15 Oxford English Dictionary 15 (def. 6(a)) (2d ed.1989) (hereinafter OED). In my view, it was.

Statistics dramatically show that driving under the influence of alcohol is very dangerous....

Petitioner's qualifying offenses, moreover, fell within the statute only because he had been convicted of DUI on at least three prior occasions. As noted, petitioner had *a dozen* prior DUI convictions. Persons who repeatedly drive drunk present a greatly enhanced danger that they and others will be injured as a result. In addition, it has been estimated that the ratio of DUI incidents to DUI arrests is between 250 to 1 and 2,000 to 1. Accordingly, the risk presented by a 10th, 11th, and 12th DUI conviction may be viewed as the risk created by literally thousands of drunk-driving events. That risk was surely "serious," and therefore petitioner's offenses fell squarely within the language of the statute....

The Court holds that an offense does not fall within the residual clause unless it is "roughly similar, in kind as well as in degree of risked posed," to the crimes specifically listed in 18 U.S.C. §924(e)(2)(B), *i.e.*, burglary, extortion, arson, and crimes involving the use of explosives. These crimes, according to the Court, "all typically involve purposeful, 'violent,' and 'aggressive' conduct."

This interpretation cannot be squared with the text of the statute, which simply does not provide that an offense must be "purposeful," "violent," or "aggressive" in order to fall within the residual clause. Rather, after listing burglary, arson, extortion, and explosives offenses, the statute provides (in the residual clause) that an offense qualifies if it "otherwise involves conduct that presents a serious potential risk of physical injury to another." Therefore, offenses falling within the residual clause must be similar to the named offenses in one respect only: They must "otherwise"—which is to say, "in a different manner," 10 OED 984 (def. B(1)); see also Webster's 1598—"involv[e] conduct that presents a serious potential risk of physical injury to another." Requiring that an offense must also be "purposeful," "violent," or "aggressive" amounts to adding new elements to the statute, but we "ordinarily resist reading words or elements into a statute that do not appear on its face." ...

For all these reasons, I would affirm the decision of the Tenth Circuit.

* * *

Points for Discussion

1. *Statutory Language*: What was the language at issue? What did each party want that language to mean? What meaning did the majority, concurrence, and dissent adopt?

2. *Theories*: Which theory did the majority use? The concurrence? The dissent? Did any of the three find the language ambiguous, absurd, to have a scrivener's error, or to present a constitutional question?

3. *Rule against Surplusage*: Why was this canon determinative for the majority, but irrelevant to both the concurrence and dissent? In answering this question, consider whether any of the justices found the phrase ambiguous? Are the linguistic canons only appropriate when there is ambiguity?

4. *Ejusdem Generis*: Because the language being interpreted was included within a catch-all phrase—"or otherwise involves conduct that presents a serious potential

risk of physical injury to another"—why was not *ejusdem generis* relevant? Did not the majority use the listed items—burglary, arson, extortion, and the use of explosives—to find the unifier? If the rule against surplusage applies to every list with a catch all, then is there any difference between these two canons? In other words, did the majority conflate these two canons?

5. *Rule of Lenity:* Typically, the rule of lenity applies when there are two possible interpretations of an ambiguous penal statute, which we have here. Justice Scalia turned to this canon to resolve the potential ambiguity. Yet, notice that he did not actually find the language ambiguous. Rather, he found application of the clear language to the facts in the case to be ambiguous: "Does drunk driving pose at least as serious a risk of physical injury to another as burglary? From the evidence presented by the Government, I cannot conclude so." This use of the rule of lenity is atypical.

6. *Twelve DUIs:* The dissent went to great lengths to explain the horrific nature of the facts in this case and the tremendous number of DUIs the defendant had. In response, the majority said, "In determining whether [DUI] is a violent felony, we consider the offense generically, that is to say, we examine it in terms of how the law defines the offense and not in terms of how an individual offender might have committed it on a particular occasion." Why is the majority right on this point?

7. *Last Antecedent Doctrine:* Why is this doctrine not relevant here even though the language at issue is contained in a modifying phrase?

* * *

6. Expressio Unius Est Exclusio Alterius

The next canon, *expressio unius*, is a rule of negative implication: it literally means "the inclusion of one thing means the exclusion of the other." Young children (and as I'm learning, teenagers) use *expressio unius* all the time. For a simple example, let's assume that a mother tells her child not to "hit or push" any of the other children. When that child then kicks another child on the playground and gets in trouble, the child argues, "But you didn't tell me I couldn't *kick* anyone!" Parents learn early to try to anticipate every contingency in their communications. Judges presume that legislatures do the same.

Expressio unius is implicated when a statute has a gap. The existence of the gap permits two very different inferences: either the legislature intended to omit the circumstance or the legislature never considered the circumstance. *Expressio unius* presumes the former: that when the legislature includes some circumstances explicitly, then the legislature intentionally omitted other similar circumstances that would logically have been included. In other words, the canon presumes that the legislature considered and rejected every related possibility. It further presumes that if the legislature had intended to cover every circumstance, then the legislature would have included a general catch-all. If we return to a modified version of our hypothetical statute from the last section "lemons, limes, and grapefruits," *expressio unius* would tell us that oranges, which are not specifically included, are specifically omitted because (1) they are not specifically included, although they are sufficiently similar to the other items that a drafter likely would have thought about including them; and (2) there is no general word or catch-all following the list. While the presumption is that the legislature intentionally left out anything omitted, the reality is that the legislature may never have considered the omitted circumstance at all.

This canon, like so many others, presumes something about legislative drafting that may not reflect reality. *Silvers v. Sony Pictures Entertainment, Inc.*, 402 F.3d 881, 899 (9th Cir. 2005) (stating that the canon is best "[u]nderstood as a descriptive generalization about language rather than a prescriptive rule of construction;" explaining that "'My children are Jonathan, Rebecca and Seth' means 'none of my children are Samuel'" but that "'get milk, bread, peanut butter and eggs at the grocery' probably does not mean 'do not get ice cream.'"). This canon presumes that the legislature actually considered all the possible options and included those options it wanted. Nonsense! "[*Expressio unius*] is increasingly considered unreliable, for it stands on the faulty premise that all possible alternative or supplemental provisions were necessarily considered and rejected by the legislative draftsmen." *Nat'l Petroleum Refiners Ass'n v. FTC*, 482 F.2d 672, 676 (D.C. Cir. 1973). In reality, legislatures omit things for a variety of reasons, some intentional, some not. Despite the canon's limitations, some judges still use this canon. Hence, you need to be aware that it exists and know how it is used. What follows is a relatively simple case based on extraordinary facts. Be sure to read the footnote.

Dickens v. Puryear

Supreme Court of North Carolina
276 S.E.2d 325 (N.C. 1981)

◆ Exum, J.,

Plaintiff's complaint is cast as a claim for intentional infliction of mental distress....

[The question on appeal is] whether plaintiff's claim is barred by the one-year statute of limitations applicable to assault and battery.... We hold that defendants properly raised the limitations defense but that on its merits plaintiff's claim is not altogether barred by the one-year statute because plaintiff's factual showing indicates plaintiff may be able to prove a claim for intentional infliction of mental distress a claim which is governed by the three-year statute of limitations. G.S. 1-52(5)....

The facts brought out at the hearing on summary judgment may be briefly summarized: For a time preceding the incidents in question plaintiff Dickens, a thirty-one year old man, shared sex, alcohol and marijuana with defendants' daughter, a seventeen year old high school student. On 2 April 1975 defendants, husband and wife, lured plaintiff into [a rural area]. Upon plaintiff's arrival defendant Earl Puryear, after identifying himself, called out to defendant Ann Puryear who emerged from beside a nearby building and, crying, stated that she "didn't want to see that SOB." Ann Puryear then left the scene. Thereafter Earl Puryear pointed a pistol between plaintiff's eyes and shouted "Y'all come on out." Four men wearing ski masks and armed with nightsticks then approached from behind plaintiff and beat him into semi-consciousness. They handcuffed plaintiff to a piece of farm machinery and resumed striking him with night-sticks. Defendant Earl Puryear, while brandishing a knife and cutting plaintiff's hair, threatened plaintiff with castration. During four or five interruptions of the beatings defendant Earl Puryear and the others, within plaintiff's hearing, discussed and took votes on whether plaintiff should be killed or castrated. Finally, after some two hours and the conclusion of a final conference, the beatings ceased. Defendant Earl Puryear told plaintiff to go home, pull his telephone off the wall, pack his clothes, and leave the state of North Carolina; otherwise he would be killed. Plaintiff was then set free.

Plaintiff filed his complaint on 31 March 1978. It alleges that defendants on the occasion just described intentionally inflicted mental distress upon him. He further alleges that as a result of defendants' acts plaintiff has suffered "severe and permanent mental and emotional distress, and physical injury to his nerves and nervous system." He alleges that he is unable to sleep, afraid to go out in the dark, afraid to meet strangers, afraid he may be killed, suffering from chronic diarrhea and a gum disorder, unable effectively to perform his job, and that he has lost $1000 per month income.

... Defendants contend ... that this is an action grounded in assault and battery. Although plaintiff pleads the tort of intentional infliction of mental distress, the Court of Appeals concluded that the complaint's factual allegations and the factual showing at the hearing on summary judgment support only a claim for assault and battery. The claim was, therefore, barred by the one-year period of limitations applicable to assault and battery. Plaintiff, on the other hand, argues that the factual showing on the motion supports a claim for intentional infliction of mental distress a claim which is governed by the three-year period of limitations.[8] At least, plaintiff argues, his factual showing is such that it cannot be said as a matter of law that he will be unable to prove such a claim at trial. We agree with plaintiff's position....

[T]hreats for the future are actionable, if at all, not as assaults but as intentional inflictions of mental distress....

Although plaintiff labels his claim one for intentional infliction of mental distress, ... much of the factual showing at the hearing related to assaults and batteries committed by defendants against plaintiff. The physical beatings and the cutting of plaintiff's hair constituted batteries. The threats of castration and death, being threats

---

8. Defendants argue that even the tort of intentional infliction of mental distress is governed by the one-year statute of limitations, we are satisfied that it is not. The one-year statute applies to "libel, slander, assault, battery, or false imprisonment." [T]he tort of intentional infliction of mental distress is none of these things. Thus the rule of statutory construction embodied in the maxim, *expressio unius est exclusio alterius*, meaning the expression of one thing is the exclusion of another, applies. No statute of limitations addresses the tort of intentional infliction of mental distress by name. It must, therefore, be governed by the more general three-year statute of limitations which applies to "any other injury to the person or rights of another, not arising on contract and not hereafter enumerated." ...

which created apprehension of immediate harmful or offensive contact, were assaults. Plaintiff's recovery for injuries, mental or physical, caused by these actions would be barred by the one-year statute of limitations.

The evidentiary showing on the summary judgment motion does, however, indicate that defendant Earl Puryear threatened plaintiff with death in the future unless plaintiff went home, pulled his telephone off the wall, packed his clothes, and left the state. The Court of Appeals characterized this threat ... also an assault barred by the one-year statute of limitations.

We disagree with the Court of Appeals' characterization of this threat. The threat was not one of imminent, or immediate, harm. It was a threat for the future apparently intended to and which allegedly did inflict serious mental distress; therefore it is actionable, if at all, as an intentional infliction of mental distress....

[W]e hold that summary judgment for defendants based upon the one-year statute of limitations was error and we remand the matter for further proceedings against defendant Earl Puryear not inconsistent with this opinion. Reversed....

* * *

Points for Discussion

1. *Statutory Language*: What is the language at issue? What did each party want that language to mean? What meaning did the court adopt?

2. *Theories*: Which theory did the court use? Did the court find the language ambiguous, absurd, to have a scrivener's error, or to raise a constitutional question?

3. *Technical Meaning*: The court used the technical meaning of the words in the statute. What technical meaning was used and why is that choice appropriate?

4. *Noscitur a sociis*: The court did not mention this canon by name. Did it play any role in the court's holding?

5. *Intentional Omission or Oversight*: Do you think the legislature intended that claims alleging intentional infliction of emotional distress would have a longer statute of limitations than the other tort claims that were included? Or do you think the tort's omission was a likely oversight? If so, could the court have "fixed" the statute using the scrivener's error doctrine?

6. *Catch-All*: Remember that *expressio unius* should not be applied when the legislature includes a general catch-all. Did the relevant statute in this case include a catch-all? Had one been included, would the result have been different? How would you draft the statute so that claims for intentional infliction of emotional distress would be included within the one year statute of limitations? Clearly omitted? Would you include a catch-all?

7. *Criminal Conviction*: Earl Puryear was charged with committing simple assault and conspiring to commit an assault with a deadly weapon inflicting serious injury. He offered no evidence at trial. He was convicted of simple assault and sentenced to two years in prison, of which all but 180 days were suspended. He

was acquitted of conspiring to commit assault with a deadly weapon. *State v. Puryear*, 228 S.E.2d 536, *appeal dismissed*, 230 S.E.2d 678 (N.C. 1976).

* * *

In conclusion, the linguistic canons provide common sense rules for understanding how English speakers and writers use words. As such, these canons are merely presumptions and should yield when there is either evidence that the drafter did not follow the canons or evidence that the drafter did not intend for a particular canon to apply to a specific situation. Because these canons help us understand how English writers ordinarily use words, the canons may not accurately reflect how legal (technical) writers use words and should be used with some caution. Finally, it is simply illogical, as some judges argue, to apply the canons only after ambiguity or absurdity are found. The point of the canons is to help a reader understand the ordinary meaning of the words used; hence, the canons should be used in the search for ordinary meaning. Despite the limitations of using these canons, they have come back into vogue with the renewed emphasis on the text.

Problem 8

The defendants, logging companies, sued the US government arguing that the language in the statute below should not apply to habitat modification or destruction that could kill or injure endangered animals. Logging companies clear cut forests, which destroys the habitat where endangered animals live. Assume logging companies would be considered a person for purposes of this statute.

The Endangered Species Act of 1973:

16 § 1538(a)(1)(B): "[I]t is unlawful for any person subject to the jurisdiction of the United States to ... take any [endangered or threatened] species within the United States...."

16 § 1532(19): Definitions: "The term 'take' means to harass, harm, pursue, hunt, shoot, wound, kill, trap, capture, or collect, or to engage in any similar conduct."

Agency Regulation:

50 C.F.R. § 17.3: Harm in the definition of 'take' in the Act means an act that actually kills or injures wildlife. Such act may include significant habitat modification or degradation where it actually kills or injures wildlife by significantly impairing essential behavior patterns, including breading, feeding, or sheltering.

Problem Questions

1. Identify the language you need to interpret from each section of the statute. How has the agency interpreted this language? Ignore the agency's interpretation for now; you are interpreting the language *de novo*. We will return to it in a later problem.

2. Using a *de novo* standard of review, a court should apply the canon *noscitur a sociis/ejusdem generis*/the rule against surplusage (circle one or more) to this language because:

3. What is the unifier among the list of words?

4. The canon *expressio unius* is/is not (circle one) appropriate to apply to this statute because:

5. Applying the canon you selected above, how would you expect a court to rule on the issue of whether habitat destruction is unlawful and why?

Chapter 9

Canons Based on Intrinsic Sources: The Components

A. Introduction to This Chapter

In this chapter, we survey our final, intrinsic source: the remaining components of a bill or act. Some components of an act are critical to interpretation, such as definition sections. Some components of an act may be relevant to interpretation, such as titles and purpose clauses. Some components of an act play less no role in interpretation, such as enacting clauses. This chapter follows the chapter on linguistic canons although the two are intimately connected. The canon *in pari materia*, the whole act aspect, makes clear that the entire act is relevant to interpretation. Now that you understand that point, we can talk about the various parts of the act, known as the components. In addition, you know what to do with the language you find in these components. For example, you might apply the identical words presumption or the rule against surplusage.

Using a simple bill that was never enacted, this chapter will identify the various bill components and explore the canons surrounding their relevance to the interpretation of the ensuing statute. The House bill and the Senate's companion bill are reproduced in full in Appendices B and C. For ease of reference, however, each section in this chapter includes the relevant component from the sample bill or another bill so that you can see actual bill language.

B. Codification

To understand the role components play in interpretation, you must first understand what codification is. Let's begin with some history: In early America, acts were not codified. Rather, they were simply placed in books sequentially. Ronald B. Brown & Sharon J. Brown, The Search for Legislative Intent 163 (2d ed. 2011). During these days there were far fewer statutes; hence, codification was less necessary. Eventually, smart entrepreneurs figured out that codifying statutes—placing statutes with similar subject matters together—would be profitable. *Id.* Today, all federal and state acts are codified.

Codification is simple. When Congress passes a bill, it becomes an enrolled bill and is presented to the president for approval. If the president signs (or fails to effectively veto the bill), it becomes an act. The act is delivered to the Archivist of the

United States; duplicates of the act are published chronologically in official pamphlets called "slip laws," which the Government Printing Office publishes. Ultimately, slip laws are bound chronologically into "session laws" and placed into the U.S. STATUTES AT LARGE. Acts may be only one page long or thousands of pages in length. They may cover just one topic or a variety of topics.

As you might imagine, researching the U.S. STATUTES AT LARGE would be time consuming and frustrating because the acts are arranged chronologically, not topically. Moreover, statutes are regularly amended and repealed; thus, extensive cross-referencing would be essential. For this reason, most acts are rearranged and published in a topical code. The process of inserting sections of an act into a code is called *codification*. The official code for federal statutes is the *United States Code*, which is divided into more than fifty different "titles" based on subject matter. Title 18, for example, contains many of the federal criminal statutes. Title 26 contains the tax statutes. The code is much simpler to search than the U.S. STATUTES AT LARGE. But you cannot search the code for a named act, such as the Patriot Act. Sections of the Patriot Act are scattered throughout the code. But you can find the Patriot Act in the U.S. STATUTES AT LARGE.

The Office of the Law Revision Counsel of the U.S. House of Representatives ("LRC") maintains the *United States Code*. LRC determines which acts in the U.S. STATUTES AT LARGE should be codified. It also determines whether a new statute amends or repeals any existing statutes and whether any existing statutes have lapsed.

Because the legislature originally had nothing to do with the placement of a statute in a particular section of the code, placement itself was considered irrelevant to meaning. Even when the states and federal government began officially codifying statutes, the legislature continued to have no role in this process; hence, where a statute was located in a code continued to be irrelevant to meaning. Today, however, the legislature may specifically indicate where sections or parts of an act should be placed in the code. When the legislature does so, placement may affect meaning. *See, e.g., Commonwealth v. Smith*, 728 N.E.2d 272, 275 (Mass. 2000) (holding that the term "sexual intercourse" in an incest statute did not mean the same thing as the term "sexual intercourse" in a rape statute because the two statutes were located in different sections of the code).

Codification is imperfect. Many statutes cover more than one subject. For example, tax evasion is a felony. But the relevant statute criminalizing tax evasion can be found in the tax chapter of the code, not the criminal chapter. The statute cannot be placed in both (consider how enormous the code would become), yet arguably tax evasion relates to both subjects.

Regardless of the relevancy of placement in the code, relying solely on the code and ignoring the U.S. STATUTES AT LARGE can be foolhardy. First, codification is imperfect. For the most part, the code is accurate; but occasionally, there have been transpositions or other errors. While the code is *prima facie* evidence of the law, the text of the U.S. STATUTES AT LARGE is "legal evidence" of the law as enacted. *Stephan v. United States*, 319 U.S. 423, 426 (1943). Thus, on the rare occasion when there is conflict, the U.S. STATUTES AT LARGE control. "[T]he very meaning of 'prima facie' is that the Code cannot prevail over the Statutes at Large when the two are inconsistent." *Id.* For example, 12 U.S.C. § 92 was omitted from the *United States Code* for decades. Despite that fact, Congress amended § 92 in 1982. In *U.S. National Bank of Oregon v. Independent Insurance Agents of America, Inc.*, 508 U.S. 439 (1993), the parties disputed whether § 92 had remained valid law. Despite omission from the code, the Supreme Court held that the section was still valid law because the U.S. STATUTES AT LARGE so dictated. *Id.* at 440.

Importantly, not every section (or component) of an act is codified. Acts have a variety of components. Some components are required, such as enacting clauses and titles; many are optional, such as findings clauses and short titles. Generally, only those components that follow the enacting clause, which we will address in a moment, are codified. The enacting clause itself is not codified, only the language following it. Moreover, "[w]hile the enacting clause is required for the act to become law, it does not itself become law...." *State v. Phillips*, 560 S.E.2d 852, 856 (N.C. Ct. App. 2002). Long titles and preambles, which precede the enacting clause, are not codified. Similarly, provisions for the effective date of amendments to existing laws may not be codified. When not codified, these titles, preambles, and effective date provisions can only be found by looking at the full act in the U.S. STATUTES AT LARGE or the state equivalent. Perhaps surprisingly, codification does not affect the relevance components have on meaning. Components that are not codified can affect interpretation, while components that are codified may have little to no effect. Let's explore this dichotomy more closely.

C. The Components and Their Canons

1. Heading

In the box on the next page, you will see the heading of a sample bill (it was not passed, so technically, it is not an act; the term "act" should be used to refer to an enacted bill only). You can find the entire bill in Appendix C. This heading identifies the Congress responsible for enacting the bill (the 110th), the session in which the bill was debated (the first), the bill designation number (H.R. 916), the Chamber from which the bill came (H.R. identifies it as House bill, S. would be a Senate bill), the primary sponsor (Representative Scott of Georgia) and the other sponsors of the bill, what happened to the bill, and when it happened (the bill was referred to the Committee on the Judiciary on February 8, then sent to the Committee of the Whole on May 14, 2007). Note that a sponsor signs a bill before introducing it; a bill number is assigned when the bill is introduced.

[handwritten note in right margin: - when a bill is not passed its not an act, only enacted bills should be called Acts]

[handwritten note at bottom: Components → Heading, title]

Component: Bill Heading

[handwritten: Congress Responsible for Bill →]

[handwritten: Session the Bill was debated →]

Union Calendar No. 88
110TH CONGRESS
1ST SESSION   *[handwritten: Chamber Bill came from →]* H.R. 916 *[handwritten: ← Bill designation number]*

[Report No. 110–148]

To provide for loan repayment for prosecutors and public defenders.

_____

IN THE HOUSE OF REPRESENTATIVES

FEBRUARY 8, 2007

[handwritten: Primary sponsor & other sponsors →] Mr. SCOTT of Georgia (for himself, Mr. GORDON of Tennessee, Mr. LEWIS of Georgia, Mr. PAYNE....) introduced the following bill; which was referred to the Committee on the Judiciary

MAY 14, 2007

Additional sponsors: Mr. LINCOLN DAVIS of Tennessee, Mr. COOPER, Mr. CHANDLER, Mr. UDALL of Colorado....

MAY 14, 2007

Reported with an amendment, committed to the Committee of the Whole House on the State of the Union, and ordered to be printed

[handwritten: when & what happen with the Bill]

_____

A BILL

None of the information in this heading is codified, but some of the information can be useful for further research. For the most part, none of this information is relevant to statutory interpretation. Following the heading are the components relevant to interpretation, beginning with titles: long titles, short titles, and section titles.

2. Titles

There are three types of titles in a bill: (1) long titles, (2) short titles, and (3) section titles. The canon for using any one of the three in interpretation is identical and simple: titles are not controlling. But the rationale differs depending on which title is relevant, so let's look at each in more detail. We will start with the long title because it precedes the other two.

a. Long Titles and Enacting Clauses   *[handwritten: Not Codified]*

Every bill has a long title. Look in the box below. The long title immediately follows the words "A Bill." Generally, all long titles begin with the words "to" or "relating to"; they then identify the purpose of the bill and where the bill will fit within existing law. Does the bill contain new statutes? Does this bill amend, repeal, or replace existing statutes? One purpose of the long title is to answer these questions. Another purpose of the long title is to provide the reader, including legislators, with a convenient way to determine what topics the bill addresses without having to read the whole bill. Both federal and state law requires titles, in part, to prevent a legislator from including extraneous provisions in a bill while attempting to avoid legislative or public notice.

Component: Long Title and Enacting Clause

> **A BILL**
>
> To provide for loan repayment for prosecutors and public defenders. ← *Long Titles*
>
> *Be it enacted by the Senate and House of Representatives of the United States of America in Congress assembled,*

The long title of our bill is "To provide for loan repayment for prosecutors and public defenders." This long title is actually very short! A more illustrative long title follows:

A BILL ... To amend Chapter 12 of Title 16 of the Official Code of Georgia Annotated, relating to offenses against health and morals, ... to provide for definitions; to require that a female give her informed consent prior to an abortion; to require that certain information be provided to or made available to a female prior to an abortion; to require a written acknowledgment of receipt of such information; to provide for the preparation and availability of certain information; to provide for procedures in a medical emergency; to provide for reporting; ... and for other purposes.

H.B. 364, 144th Cong. (1997).

To understand the limited role that long titles have in statutory interpretation, we must turn to our English heritage. In England, the clerks in parliament historically added long titles to bills; thus, the early English rule prohibited judges from considering the long title during interpretation. For the most part in England, that rule still holds true.

In contrast, in the United States, the legislature writes long titles as part of the drafting process; therefore, a different rule developed. Can you identify the American rule from the very famous case below? This case is one of the most famous cases in statutory interpretation, despite its relatively uninteresting subject matter.

HOLY TRINITY CHURCH v. UNITED STATES

Supreme Court of the United States

143 U.S. 457 (1892)

♦ JUSTICE BREWER delivered the opinion of the Court [in which all concur].

Plaintiff in error is a corporation duly organized and incorporated as a religious society under the laws of the state of New York. E. Walpole Warren was, prior to Sep-

any kind → catch-all?

tember, 1887, an alien residing in England. In that month the plaintiff in error made a contract with him, by which he was to remove to the city of New York, and enter into its service as rector and pastor; and, in pursuance of such contract, Warren did so remove and enter upon such service. It is claimed by the United States that this contract on the part of the plaintiff in error was forbidden by chapter 164, 23 St. p. 332; and an action was commenced to recover the penalty prescribed by that act.

P. H. The circuit court held that the contract was within the prohibition of the statute, and rendered judgment accordingly, and the single question presented for our determination is whether it erred in that conclusion.

The first section describes the act forbidden, and is in these words:

Act →

'Be it enacted by the senate and house of representatives of the United States of America, in congress assembled, that from and after the passage of this act it shall be unlawful for any person, company, partnership, or corporation, in any manner whatsoever, to prepay the transportation, or in any way assist or encourage the importation or migration, of any alien or aliens, any foreigner or foreigners, into the United States, its territories, or the District of Columbia, under contract or agreement, parol or special, express or implied, made previous to the importation or migration of such alien or aliens, foreigner or foreigners, to perform labor or service of any kind in the United States, its territories, or the District of Columbia.'

It must be conceded that the act of the corporation is within the letter of this section, for the relation of rector to his church is one of service, and implies labor on the one side with compensation on the other. Not only are the general words 'labor' and 'service' both used, but also, as it were to guard against any narrow interpretation and emphasize a breadth of meaning, to them is added 'of any kind;' and, further, as noticed by the circuit judge in his opinion, the fifth section, which makes specific exceptions, among them professional actors, artists, lecturers, singers, and domestic servants, strengthens the idea that every other kind of labor and service was intended to be reached by the first section. While there is great force to this reasoning, we cannot think congress intended to denounce with penalties a transaction like that in the present case. It is a familiar rule that a thing may be within the letter of the statute and yet not within the statute, because not within its spirit nor within the intention of its makers. This has been often asserted, and the Reports are full of cases illustrating its application. This is not the substitution of the will of the judge for that of the legislator; for frequently words of general meaning are used in a statute, words broad enough to include an act in question, and yet a consideration of the whole legislation, or of the circumstances surrounding its enactment, or of the absurd results which follow from giving such broad meaning to the words, makes it unreasonable to believe that the legislator [sic] intended to include the particular act....

Purpose = spirit of the law

Among other things which may be considered in determining the intent of the legislature is the title of the act. We do not mean that it may be used to add to or take from the body of the statute, but it may help to interpret its meaning. In the case of *U. S. v. Fisher*, 2 Cranch, 358, 386, Chief Justice Marshall said: 'On the influence which the title ought to have in construing the enacting clauses, much has been said, and yet it is not easy to discern the point of difference between the opposing counsel in this respect. Neither party contends that the title of an act can control plain words in the body of the statute; and neither denies that, taken with other parts, it may assist in removing ambiguities. Where the intent is plain, nothing is left to construction. Where the mind labors to discover the design of the legislature, it seizes everything from which aid can be derived; and in such case the title claims a degree of notice, and will have its due share of consideration.' And in the case of *U. S. v. Palmer*, 3 Wheat. 610, 631, the same judge applied the doctrine in this way: "The words of the section are in terms of unlimited extent. The words 'any person or persons' are broad enough to comprehend every human being. But general words must not only be limited to cases within the jurisdiction of the state, but also to those objects to which the legislature intended to apply them.... The title of an act cannot control its words, but may furnish some aid in showing what was in the mind of the legislature...."

... Now, the title of this act is, 'An act to prohibit the importation and migration of foreigners and aliens under contract or agreement to perform labor in the United States, its territories, and the District of Columbia.' Obviously the thought expressed in this reaches only to the work of the manual laborer, as distinguished from that of the professional man. No one reading such a title would suppose that congress had in its mind any purpose of staying the coming into this country of ministers of the gospel, or, indeed, of any class whose toil is that of the brain. The common understanding of the terms 'labor' and 'laborers' does not include preaching and preachers, and it is to be assumed that words and phrases are used in their ordinary meaning. So whatever of light is thrown upon the statute by the language of the title indicates an exclusion from its penal provisions of all contracts for the employment of ministers, rectors, and pastors....

[The Court then reviews the Act's legislative history and concludes that the purpose of the Act was to stem the influx of cheap unskilled labor from China.].

We find, therefore, that the title of the act, the evil which was intended to be remedied, the circumstances surrounding the appeal to congress, the reports of the committee of each house, all concur in affirming that the intent of congress was simply to stay the influx of this cheap, unskilled labor.

But, beyond all these matters, no purpose of action against religion can be imputed to any legislation, state or national, because this is a religious people. [Justice Brewer describes in detail some of the many ways that the United States embraces Christianity and why, given that fact, Congress could not have intended to prohibit ministers from coming into the United States.].

The judgment will be reversed, and the case remanded for further proceedings in accordance with this opinion.

* * *

Points for Discussion

1. *Statutory Language*: What was the language at issue? What did each party want that language to mean? What meaning did the Court adopt?

2. *Theories*: What theory of interpretation did Justice Brewer adopt? Look for the following sentence: "It is a familiar rule that a thing may be within the letter of the statute and yet not within the statute, because not within its spirit nor within the intention of its makers." Why do you think this statement is often cited in briefs to support interpretations that contradict the text of the statute?

3. *Ambiguity*: Did Justice Brewer concede too quickly that the statute was not ambiguous — "It must be conceded that the act of the corporation is within the letter of this section, for the relation of rector to his church is one of service, and implies labor on the one side with compensation on the other...."? A current dictionary definition of labor is "work, especially hard physical work." "Service" means "the action of helping or doing work for someone." Could the term "service" be narrowed to include only service that involves physical work, pursuant to *noscitur a sociis*?

4. *U.S. Title Canon*: "The title of an act cannot control its words, but may furnish some aid in showing what was in the mind of the legislature." *Church of the Holy Trinity v. United States*, 143 U.S. 457, 462 (1892). In other words, a judge may consider a long title, but it cannot overcome clear text. Is not that what occurred here? What was the long title? Why did that long title "*obviously* ... reach only to the work of the manual laborer"? The short title of the Act was "the Alien Contract Labor Act." Does the short title provide any more guidance than the long title?

5. *Expressio Unius*: The statute specifically excepted actors, artists, lecturers, singers, and domestic servants, but not ministers. Further, exceptions are to be construed narrowly (*See* this Chapter, section C4f). Should these arguments matter? The legislative history showed that the legislators excepted "personal or domestic servants, personal friends or members of an individual family, [and] artists." Carol Chomsky, *Unlocking the Mysteries of Holy Trinity: Spirit, Letter, and History in Statutory Interpretation*, 100 COLUM. L. REV. 901, 930–31 (2000).

6. *Legislative History*: This was the first time the Court used legislative history, specifically two committee reports, to support an interpretation so at odds with the text. As you can imagine, legislative history was not easily researched in the late 1800s. Brewer's inclusion of the two reports that supported the Court's interpretation has been criticized because he neglected to mention that some supporters of the bill wanted it to be broadly applied. Chomsky, *supra* at 947 (explaining that *Holy Trinity* was "so often cited as creating a revolution in statutory interpretation ... [because] the Court used [legislative history] ... to ignore the literal language").

7. *Legislative Response*: After the district court held that the statute applied to Warren, Congress amended the statute to exempt ministers and other professionals. Act of March 3, 1891, § 12.26 stat 1084, 1086. The amendment came too late to apply

in this case; however, judges do, at times, consider the relevance of subsequent legislative action. (*See* Chapter 13). In *United States v. Laws*, 163 U.S. 258, 265 (1896), the Supreme Court held that the Alien Contract Labor Act did not apply to a chemist. In reaching this result, the Court referenced the 1891 amendment even though the amendment was enacted after the chemist entered the Country.

8. *Imaginative Reconstruction*: Justice Brewer was the son of Christian missionaries. Owen Fiss, *David J. Brewer: The Judge as Missionary*, in THE FIELDS AND THE LAW, 53–71 (1986) (explaining that Justice Brewer looked at government regulation warily and proclaimed at every possible opportunity "this is a Christian nation"). Justice Brewer explains in detail, in a portion of the case that has been omitted, why Congress could not possibly have intended to exclude ministers because of our Christian heritage. This reasoning is similar to the theory of imaginative reconstruction, which was explained in Chapter 4.

* * *

If a legislature writes the long title, why would such a title be less controlling than the words of the statute? One reason might be that long titles are not codified because they precede the enacting clause. But this reason alone is not sufficient because short titles, which follow the enacting clause and are codified, similarly do not carry as much weight as the text. Hence, codification alone cannot be the answer. More likely, the reluctance to give weight to titles stems from our English heritage, where titles are not considered in interpretation.

Following the long title in a bill is the enacting or resolving clause. Enacting clauses are used for bills, both at the federal and state levels, while resolving clauses are used for joint resolutions. In the United States, enacting clauses are required, and their language is prescribed. 1 U.S.C. §§ 101, 102 (2015). Enacting clauses are so foundational that in Texas, a "bill" without an enacting clause cannot be amended by adding an enacting clause, nor may "such a bill" be referred to committee under that state's house and senate rules. Texas legislators must get it right the first time.

For a federal bill, the required language of the enacting clause is "*Be it enacted by the Senate and House of Representatives of the United States of America in Congress assembled....*" 1 U.S.C. § 101 (2015). Notice that the enacting clause in the text box above has this magic language. For a joint resolution, the language differs slightly: "*Resolved by the Senate and House of Representatives of the United States of America in Congress assembled....*" 1 U.S.C. § 102 (2015). There are no interpretation issues surrounding enacting clauses because the language is required and never varies.

All components following the enacting clause are codified; all components preceding the clause are not. *See* 1 U.S.C. § 103 (2015). Thus, the components we have studied up to this point are not codified. The ones we are about to study are codified.

b. Short Titles → codified

For some bills, a short title may also be included, even if the long title is not all that long. The short title is located in a separate section of the statute, usually the first section. The short title typically is written as follows: "This act may be cited as the ____ Act of ____." The short title of our sample bill is the "John R. Justice Prosecutors and Defenders Incentive Act of 2007."

Component: Short Title

SECTION 1. SHORT TITLE.

This Act may be cited as the "John R. Justice Prosecutors and Defenders Incentive Act of 2007".

In this case, the short title is almost as long as the long title! So why would a legislature include one? Legislatures include short titles for a variety of reasons. One obvious reason is that, when a title is truly long, a short title eases reference. However, short titles are used for other reasons as well. Short titles are often used to persuade either legislators or the public to support the bill. For example, consider the following two short titles: "The No Child Left Behind Act" and "The Patriot Act." A legislator would be hard-pressed to vote against children and patriotism!

In addition to persuasion, a short title can be used, as in this case, to honor someone involved in either the bill process or the subject. In this case, John R. Justice was the Solicitor (the highest state prosecutor) of South Carolina; the bill's title was chosen to honor his public service work. Some acts earn their short name (not a true short title) only after enactment, e.g. the Sherman Act, which was originally called the "Act of july 2, 1890." For an excellent discussion of short names, see Mary Whisner, *What's in a Statute Name?*, 97 Law Libr. J. 169 (2005).

One Hundred Eleventh Congress of the United States of America

AT THE SECOND SESSION

Begun and held at the City of Washington on Tuesday, the fifth day of January, two thousand and ten

AN ACT

To modernize the air traffic control system, improve the safety, reliability, and availability of transportation by air in the United States, provide for modernization of the air traffic control system, reauthorize the Federal Aviation Administration, and for other purposes.

Be it enacted by the Senate and House of Representatives of the United States of America in Congress assembled,

SHORT TITLE

Section 1. This Act may be cited as the "____ Act of ____."

Interestingly, sometimes during the drafting process, errors can occur. In 2010, Congress enacted and President Obama signed into law the "The __[blank]__ Act of __[blank]__." See the text box on the prior page, and note the short title. To date, the error has not been corrected!

Unlike the long title, the short title follows the enacting clause, and is, thus, codified. But the canon for short titles remains the same: "the name given to an act by way of designation or description ... cannot change the plain import of its words." *Caminetti v. United States*, 242 U.S. 470, 490 (1917). See whether the majority or dissent better adheres to the title canon in the case below.

Caminetti v. United States
Supreme Court of the United States
242 U.S. 470 (1917)

♦ Justice Day delivered the opinion of the Court [in which Holmes, Van Devanter, Pitney, and Brandis, JJ. concur; McReynolds, J. took no part in the decision].

... [In this case], the petitioner [and two others were] indicted ... for alleged violations of [the so-called White Slave Traffic Act of June 25, 1910].* The indictment was in four counts, the first of which charged him with transporting and causing to be transported, and aiding and assisting in obtaining transportation for a certain woman from Sacramento, California, to Reno, Nevada, in interstate commerce, for the purpose of debauchery, and for an immoral purpose, to wit, that the aforesaid woman should be and become his mistress and concubine. A verdict of not guilty was returned as to the other three counts of this indictment. As to the first count, defendant was found guilty and sentenced to imprisonment for eighteen months and to pay a fine of $1,500. Upon writ of error to the United States circuit court of appeals for the ninth circuit, that judgment was affirmed....

It is contended that the act of Congress is intended to reach only 'commercialized vice,' or the traffic in women for gain, and that the conduct for which the several petitioners were indicted and convicted, however reprehensible in morals, is not within the purview of the statute when properly construed in the light of its history and the purposes intended to be accomplished by its enactment. In none of the cases was it charged or proved that the transportation was for gain or for the purpose of furnishing women for prostitution for hire, and it is insisted that, such being the case, the acts charged and proved, upon which conviction was had, do not come within the statute.

It is elementary that the meaning of a statute must, in the first instance, be sought in the language in which the act is framed, and if that is plain, and if the law is within the constitutional authority of the lawmaking body which passed it, the sole function of the courts is to enforce it according to its terms.

---

* Editor's footnote: The statute prohibited anyone from transporting a woman or girl across state lines "to become a prostitute or to give herself up to debauchery, or to engage in any other immoral practice."

Where the language is plain and admits of no more than one meaning, the duty of interpretation does not arise, and the rules which are to aid doubtful meanings need no discussion. There is no ambiguity in the terms of this act. It is specifically made an offense to knowingly transport or cause to be transported, etc., in interstate commerce, any woman or girl for the purpose of prostitution or debauchery, or for 'any other immoral purpose,' or with the intent and purpose to induce any such woman or girl to become a prostitute or to give herself up to debauchery, or to engage in any other immoral practice.

Statutory words are uniformly presumed, unless the contrary appears, to be used in their ordinary and usual sense, and with the meaning commonly attributed to them. To cause a woman or girl to be transported for the purposes of debauchery, and for an immoral purpose, to wit, becoming a concubine or mistress, for which Caminetti and Diggs were convicted; or to transport an unmarried woman, under eighteen years of age, with the intent to induce her to engage in prostitution, debauchery, and other immoral practices, for which Hays was convicted, would seem by the very statement of the facts to embrace transportation for purposes denounced by the act, and therefore fairly within its meaning.

While such immoral purpose would be more culpable in morals and attributed to baser motives if accompanied with the expectation of pecuniary gain, such considerations do not prevent the lesser offense against morals of furnishing transportation in order that a woman may be debauched, or become a mistress or a concubine, from being the execution of purposes within the meaning of this law. To say the contrary would shock the common understanding of what constitutes an immoral purpose when those terms are applied, as here, to sexual relations. . . .

But it is contended that though the words are so plain that they cannot be misapprehended when given their usual and ordinary interpretation, and although the sections in which they appear do not in terms limit the offense defined and punished to acts of 'commercialized vice,' or the furnishing or procuring of transportation of women for debauchery, prostitution, or immoral practices for hire, such limited purpose is to be attributed to Congress and engrafted upon the act in view of the language of §8 [the short title] and the report which accompanied the law upon its introduction into and subsequent passage by the House of Representatives.

In this connection, it may be observed that while the title of an act cannot overcome the meaning of plain and unambiguous words used in its body, the [long] title of this act embraces the regulation of interstate commerce 'by prohibiting the transportation therein for immoral purposes of women and girls, and for other purposes.' It is true that §8 of the act provides that it shall be known and referred to as the 'White Slave Traffic Act,' and the report accompanying the introduction of the same into the House of Representatives set forth the fact that a material portion of the legislation suggested was to meet conditions which had arisen in the past few years, and that the legislation was needed to put a stop to a villainous interstate and international traffic in women and girls. Still, the name given to an act by way of designation or description, or the report which accompanies it, cannot change the plain import of its words. If the words are plain, they give meaning to the act, and it is neither the duty nor the privilege of the courts to enter speculative fields in search of a different meaning.

Reports to Congress accompanying the introduction of proposed laws may aid the courts in reaching the true meaning of the legislature in cases of doubtful interpretation. But, as we have already said, and it has been so often affirmed as to become a recognized rule, when words are free from doubt they must be taken as the final expression of the legislative intent, and are not to be added to or subtracted from by considerations drawn from titles or designating names or reports accompanying their introduction, or from any extraneous source. In other words, the language being plain, and not leading to absurd or wholly impracticable consequences, it is the sole evidence of the ultimate legislative intent. . . .

◆ Justice McKenna, dissenting, with whom the White, C.J., and Clarke, J. concur.

Undoubtedly, in the investigation of the meaning of a statute we resort first to its words, and, when clear, they are decisive. The principle has attractive and seemingly disposing simplicity, but that it is not easy of application, or, at least, encounters other principles, many cases demonstrate. The words of a statute may be uncertain in their signification or in their application. If the words be ambiguous, the problem they present is to be resolved by their definition; the subject matter and the lexicons become our guides. But here, even, we are not exempt from putting ourselves in the place of the legislators. If the words be clear in meaning, but the objects to which they are addressed be uncertain, the problem then is to determine the uncertainty. And for this a realization of conditions that provoked the statute must inform our judgment. Let us apply these observations to the present case.

The transportation which is made unlawful is of a woman or girl 'to become a prostitute or to give herself up to debauchery, or to engage in any other immoral practice.' Our present concern is with the words 'any other immoral practice,' which, it is asserted, have a special office. The words are clear enough as general descriptions; they fail in particular designation; they are class words, not specifications. Are they controlled by those which precede them? If not, they are broader in generalization and include those that precede them, making them unnecessary and confusing. To what conclusion would this lead us? 'Immoral' is a very comprehensive word. It means a dereliction of morals. In such sense it covers every form of vice, every form of conduct that is contrary to good order. It will hardly be contended that in this sweeping sense it is used in the statute. But, if not used in such sense, to what is it limited and by what limited? If it be admitted that it is limited at all, that ends the imperative effect assigned to it in the opinion of the court. But not insisting quite on that, we ask again, By what is it limited? By its context, necessarily, and the purpose of the statute.

For the context I must refer to the statute; of the purpose of the statute Congress itself has given us illumination. It devotes a section to the declaration that the 'act shall be known and referred to as the "White Slave Traffic Act."' And its prominence gives it prevalence in the construction of the statute. It cannot be pushed aside or subordinated by indefinite words in other sentences, limited even there by the context. It is a peremptory rule of construction that all parts of a statute must be taken into account in ascertaining its meaning, and it cannot be said that § 8 has no object. Even if it gives only a title to the act, it has especial weight. But it gives more than a title; it makes distinctive the purpose of the statute. The designation 'white slave traffic' has the sufficiency of an axiom. If apprehended, there is no uncertainty as to the conduct it describes. It is commercialized vice, immoralities having a mercenary purpose, and this is confirmed by other circumstances.

[The House Committee on Interstate Commerce Report stated:]

> 'The White Slave Trade. — A material portion of the legislation suggested and proposed is necessary to meet conditions which have arisen within the past few years. The legislation is needed to put a stop to a villainous interstate and international traffic in women and girls. The legislation is not needed or intended as an aid to the states in the exercise of their police powers in the suppression or regulation of immorality in general. It does not attempt to regulate the practice of voluntary prostitution, but aims solely to prevent panderers and procurers from compelling thousands of women and girls against their will and desire to enter and continue in a life of prostitution.' Cong. Rec. vol. 50, pp. 3368, 3370.

In other words, it is vice as a business at which the law is directed, using interstate commerce as a facility to procure or distribute its victims....

Of course, ... the declarations of the report of the committee on interstate commerce of the House ... [is not] conclusive of the meaning of the law, but [it is] highly persuasive....

This being the purpose, the words of the statute should be construed to execute it, and they may be so construed even if their literal meaning be otherwise. In *Church of the Holy Trinity v. United States*, 143 U. S. 457, there came to this court for construction an act of Congress which made it unlawful for anyone in any of the United States 'to prepay the transportation, or in any way assist or encourage the importation or migration of any alien or aliens, any foreigner or foreigners, into the United States ... under contract or agreement ... to perform labor or *service of any kind* [italics mine] in the United States, its territories or the District of Columbia.' The Trinity Church made a contract with one E. W. Warren, a resident of England, to remove to the city of New York and enter its service as rector and pastor. The church was proceeded against under the act and the circuit court held that it applied, and rendered judgment accordingly.

It will be observed that the language of the statute is very comprehensive, — fully as much so as the language of the act under review, — having no limitation whatever from the context; and the circuit court, in submission to what the court considered its imperative quality, rendered judgment against the church. This court reversed the judgment, and, in an elaborate opinion by Mr. Justice Brewer, declared that 'it is a familiar rule that a thing may be within the letter of the statute and yet not within the statute, because not within its spirit, nor within the intention of its makers.' ...

There is danger in extending a statute beyond its purpose, even if justified by a strict adherence to its words....

For these reasons I dissent from the opinion and judgment of the court....

* * *

Points for Discussion

1. *Statutory Language*: What was the language at issue? What did each party want that language to mean? What meaning did the majority and dissent adopt?

2. *Theories*: Which theory did the majority use? The dissent? Did the majority or dissent find the language ambiguous, absurd, to have a scrivener's error, or to raise a constitutional question?

3. *Plain Meaning Rule*: This case was one of the first cases in which the court applied the Plain Meaning Rule in a new stricter form, which we call moderate textualism today. In this strict form, judges do not look outside of the statutory text at any additional sources to find the legislative intent if the statute is "plain," or clear, from the text alone.

4. *Short title*: The canon for titles provides that title is relevant, but cannot overcome clear text. Was this text clear? Assuming there was ambiguity, does the short title—The White Slave Trade—remove the ambiguity? For what purpose did the dissent use the short title? Does the long title—"prohibiting the transportation therein for immoral purposes of women and girls, and for other purposes"—suggest the same or a different interpretation as the short title?

5. *Holy Trinity*: Are *Holy Trinity* and *Caminetti* consistent? In *Holy Trinity*, the Court used the long title to overcome allegedly clear text. In *Caminetti*, the majority refused to consider the short title to narrow a broad catch-all. Can you reconcile these different outcomes?

6. *Other Indicia of Meaning*: Is *ejusdem generis* useful? What is the meaning of the words prostitution and debauchery? Did the legislative history support the dissent's point that the purpose of bill and the intent of the legislature was to curtail commercialized prostitution? What about the rule of lenity, should that have been relevant here?

7. *Legislative Response*: In 1986, Congress amended the statute to prohibit individuals from "knowingly transport[ing] an individual in interstate or foreign commerce ... with intent that such individual engage in prostitution, *or in any sexual activity for which any person can be charged with a criminal offense....*" 18 U.S.C. §2412. Does this amendment show that the majority or dissent was correct or neither?

* * *

c. Section and Code Titles

Almost all bills have section titles or headings to aid the reader in determining the content of a particular section of a bill. A section title is merely a short-hand reference to the general subject matter in the section. Earlier, you might have noticed that a section title preceded the short title of the John R. Jones Prosecutor and Defenders Incentive Act. The section title reads: *Section 1: Short Title*. If not, go back and find this section title; while it is not hugely helpful to a reader, it does provide some focus. Generally, section titles do no more than indicate the content of the section in a general manner, especially when text is complicated and prolific. It would be impossible for the legislature to attempt to capture everything contained within a section with one short section title. Thus, section titles were never meant to take the place of the detailed provisions of the text; hence, they offer little to judges who are interpreting statutory language.

The canon for section titles is identical to that of the other titles: the section title cannot limit the ordinary meaning of the text. For interpretative purposes, section titles are relevant when the text is ambiguous or absurd. In other words, section titles "are but tools available for the resolution of a doubt. But they cannot undo or limit that which the text makes plain." *Brotherhood of R. R. Trainmen v. Baltimore & O. R. Co.*, 331 U.S. 519, 529 (1947); *accord, Yates v. United States*, 135 S. Ct. 1074, 1083 (2015) ("While [section] headings are not commanding, they supply cues...."); *Almendarez-Torres v. United States*, 523 U.S. 224, 234 (1998) ("[T]he title of a statute and the heading of a section are tools available for the resolution of a doubt about the meaning of a statute.") (internal quotation marks omitted)).

In state courts, some legislatures do not write section titles in bills; instead, a publisher of a code may do so. Such was the case in *Michigan Ave. National Bank v. County of Cook*, 191 Ill. 2d 493 (2000). In that case, the plaintiff relied on a caption, or section title, that was not in the official version of the statute, but rather was added by West when it published the statute. Not surprisingly, the court rejected the argument that this caption should carry any interpretative weight. *Id.* at 506.

In addition to section titles, codes have titles identifying the general subject matter. For example, the title of 17 U.S.C. is "Copyright." The laws related to copyright are generally found within this section of the code. The Office of the Law Revision Council ("OLRC") prepares and publishes the *United States Code*. When Congress specifies amendments and repeals of statutes, OLRC makes the changes. Sometimes, bills create new statutes and OLRC must decide where to place these new laws. It is the job of the OLRC's classifying attorneys to determine whether and how to classify new sections of the code. Hence, code titles are generally irrelevant to meaning.

State law is similar. For example, in *State v. Bussey*, 463 So. 2d 1141 (Fla. 1985), the court found that a statute penalizing the sale of drugs was a criminal statute despite being located in the "Fraudulent Practices" section of the code. The court reasoned, "The arrangement and classification of laws for purposes of codification in the Florida Statutes is an administrative function of the Joint Legislative Management Committee of the Florida Legislature. The classification of a law or a part of a law in a particular title or chapter of Florida Statutes is not determinative on the issue of legislative intent...." *Id.* at 1143 (internal citation omitted).

3. Preambles, Purpose Clauses, and Legislative Findings

After either the short title, if there is one, or the enacting/resolving clause if there is no short title, there may be a section called legislative findings or purpose. These clauses are called preambles, findings clauses, or purpose clauses. These clauses are generally called preambles when they precede the enacting clause and findings, purpose, or policy clauses (or some combination) when they follow the enacting clause. Findings clauses and purpose clauses differ somewhat from each other. Findings clauses identify the legislative facts that lead the legislature to enact the new law, while purpose clauses identify the purpose of the act. While findings and purpose clauses can be separate sections of a bill, or one can be included and the other not included, the common practice is to include both clauses together in one section.

While preambles, legislative findings, and purpose clauses are not required, they can be informative. The sample bill has a simple purpose clause, which is in the box below. While the language of the clause would suggest it applies only to one section of the bill (it says "[t]he purpose of this section"), there is really only one relevant section in the bill; thus, the purpose clause applies to all the important provisions in this bill.

[handwritten margin note: Findings Clause v. Purpose Clause]

Component: Purpose Clause

> "SEC. 3111. GRANT AUTHORIZATION.
>
> "(a) PURPOSE.—The purpose of this section is to encourage qualified individuals to enter and continue employment as prosecutors and public defenders."

Commonly, findings and purpose clauses are much longer and more detailed. A highly edited sample findings and purpose clause from The Rehabilitation Act appears in the box on the next page. Notice that this example clause contains findings, purposes, and policy.

Component: Finding & Purpose Clause

(a) **Findings**

Congress finds that— ...

   (3) disability is a natural part of the human experience and in no way diminishes the right of individuals to—

     (A) live independently;

     (B) enjoy self-determination;

     (C) make choices;

     (D) contribute to society;

     (E) pursue meaningful careers; and

     (F) enjoy full inclusion and integration in the economic, political, social, cultural, and educational mainstream of American society; ...

(b) **Purpose**

The purposes of this Act are— ...

   (2) to ensure that the Federal Government plays a leadership role in promoting the employment of individuals with disabilities....

(c) **Policy**

It is the policy of the United States that all programs, projects, and activities receiving assistance under this Act shall be carried out in a manner consistent with the principles of—

   (1) respect for individual dignity ...

In England, judges gave preambles great weight because preambles were considered the best source for determining the statutory purpose. You might remember that purpose played an important and early role in interpretation when society was less technologically advanced, and carbon paper (let alone Xerox machines!) was not available.

In contrast, the United States' rule is more modest; generally, the preamble and findings and purpose clauses cannot control clear, enacted text. In other words, the canon for preambles and findings and purpose clauses is identical to the titles' canon. Like titles, preambles and findings and purpose clauses can help resolve ambiguity, if a judge is willing to consider them. *See, e.g., Commonwealth v. Besch*, 674 A.2d 655, 659 (Pa. 1996) (looking to the purpose clause to conclude that defendants who sold marijuana and cocaine to each other did not violate a statute aimed at protecting legitimate businesses from money laundering). Whether a judge is willing to consider such clauses depends largely on that judge's approach to interpretation. Some judges are willing to

Some

consider findings and purpose clauses only when the statute is ambiguous. *See, e.g., Knebel v. Hein*, 429 U.S. 288, 292 n.9 (1977).

Increasingly, Congress is including findings and purposes to increase the likelihood that a judge will use the findings or purpose to interpret it. Findings and purpose clauses can play an important role in interpretation. What role did the preamble play in the case that follows?

Sutton v. United Air Lines, Inc.

Supreme Court of the United States
527 U.S. 471 (1999)

◆ Justice O'Connor delivered the opinion of the Court [in which Rehnquist, C.J., and Scalia, Kennedy, Souter, Thomas, and Ginsburg, JJ., concur].

[Petitioners are twin sisters with severe myopia. Without corrective lenses, they cannot see well enough to drive, watch television, or shop. With glasses or contacts, their vision is fine].

... In 1992, petitioners applied to respondent for employment as commercial airline pilots. Petitioners did not meet respondent's minimum vision requirement.... Due to their failure to meet this requirement, petitioners' interviews were terminated, and neither was offered a pilot position....

[P]etitioners filed suit ... alleging that respondent had discriminated against them "on the basis of their disability ... in violation of the [Americans with Disabilities Act ("ADA")].... Specifically, petitioners alleged that due to their severe myopia they actually have a substantially limiting impairment ... and are thus disabled under the Act.

The District Court dismissed petitioners' complaint.... [T]he Court of Appeals ... affirmed....

The ADA prohibits discrimination by covered entities, including private employers, against qualified individuals with a disability. Specifically, it provides that no covered employer "shall discriminate against a qualified individual with a disability because of the disability of such individual in regard to job application procedures, the hiring, advancement, or discharge of employees, employee compensation, job training, and other terms, conditions, and privileges of employment." 42 U.S.C. § 12112(a). A "qualified individual with a disability" is identified as "an individual with a disability who, with or without reasonable accommodation, can perform the essential functions of the employment position that such individual holds or desires." § 12111(8). In turn, a "disability" is defined as:

"(A) a physical or mental impairment that substantially limits one or more of the major life activities of such individual;

"(B) a record of such an impairment; or

"(C) being regarded as having such an impairment." § 12102(2).

Accordingly, to fall within this definition one must have an actual disability (subsection (A)), have a record of a disability (subsection (B)), or be regarded as having one (subsection (C))....

With this statutory and regulatory framework in mind, we turn first to the question whether petitioners have stated a claim under subsection (A) of the disability definition, that is, whether they have alleged that they possess a physical impairment that substantially limits them in one or more major life activities. See 42 U.S.C. § 12102(2)(A). Because petitioners allege that with corrective measures their vision "is 20/20 or better," they are not actually disabled within the meaning of the Act if the "disability" determination is made with reference to these measures. Consequently, with respect to subsection (A) of the disability definition, our decision turns on whether disability is to be determined with or without reference to corrective measures.

Petitioners maintain that whether an impairment is substantially limiting should be determined without regard to corrective measures. Respondent, in turn, maintains that an impairment does not substantially limit a major life activity if it is corrected....

Justice Stevens relies on the legislative history of the ADA for the contrary proposition that individuals should be examined in their uncorrected state. Because we decide that, by its terms, the ADA cannot be read in this manner, we have no reason to consider the ADA's legislative history....

... The Act defines a "disability" as "a physical or mental impairment that *substantially limits* one or more of the major life activities" of an individual. § 12102(2)(A) (emphasis added). Because the phrase "substantially limits" appears in the Act in the present indicative verb form, we think the language is properly read as requiring that a person be presently — not potentially or hypothetically — substantially limited in order to demonstrate a disability. A "disability" exists only where an impairment "substantially limits" a major life activity, not where it "might," "could," or "would" be substantially limiting if mitigating measures were not taken. A person whose physical or mental impairment is corrected by medication or other measures does not have an impairment that presently "substantially limits" a major life activity. To be sure, a person whose physical or mental impairment is corrected by mitigating measures still has an impairment, but if the impairment is corrected it does not "substantially limi[t]" a major life activity....

Finally, and critically, findings enacted as part of the ADA require the conclusion that Congress did not intend to bring under the statute's protection all those whose uncorrected conditions amount to disabilities. Congress found that "some 43,000,000 Americans have one or more physical or mental disabilities, and this number is increasing as the population as a whole is growing older." § 12101(a)(1).* This figure is inconsistent with the definition of disability pressed by petitioners.

---

* Editor's footnote: At the time, the ADA provided:
SEC. 2. FINDINGS AND PURPOSES.
(a) FINDINGS.—The Congress finds that—
    (1) some 43,000,000 Americans have one or more physical or mental disabilities, and this

Although the exact source of the 43 million figure is not clear, the corresponding finding in the 1988 precursor to the ADA was drawn directly from a report prepared by the National Council on Disability. See Burgdorf, *The Americans with Disabilities Act: Analysis and Implications of a Second–Generation Civil Rights Statute*, 26 Harv. Civ. Rights Civ. Lib. L.Rev. 413, 434, n. 117 (1991) (reporting, in an article authored by the drafter of the original ADA bill introduced in Congress in 1988, that the report was the source for a figure of 36 million disabled persons quoted in the versions of the bill introduced in 1988). That report detailed the difficulty of estimating the number of disabled persons due to varying operational definitions of disability. National Council on Disability, Toward Independence 10 (1986). It explained that the estimates of the number of disabled Americans ranged from an overinclusive 160 million under a "health conditions approach," which looks at all conditions that impair the health or normal functional abilities of an individual, to an underinclusive 22.7 million under a "work disability approach," which focuses on individuals' reported ability to work. It noted that "a figure of 35 or 36 million [was] the most commonly quoted estimate." *Id.* at 10. The 36 million number included in the 1988 bill's findings thus clearly reflects an approach to defining disabilities that is closer to the work disabilities approach than the health conditions approach.

This background also provides some clues to the likely source of the figure in the findings of the 1990 Act. Roughly two years after issuing its 1986 report, the National Council on Disability issued an updated report. See On the Threshold of Independence (1988). This 1988 report settled on a more concrete definition of disability. It stated that 37.3 million individuals have "difficulty performing one or more basic physical activities," including "seeing, hearing, speaking, walking, using stairs, lifting or carrying, getting around outside, getting around inside, and getting into or out of bed." The study from which it drew this data took an explicitly functional approach to evaluating disabilities. See U.S. Dept. of Commerce, Bureau of Census, Disability, Functional Limitation, and Health Insurance Coverage: 1984/85, p. 2 (1986). It measured 37.3 million persons with a "functional limitation" on performing certain basic activities when using, as the questionnaire put it, "special aids," such as glasses or hearing aids, if the person usually used such aids. The number of disabled provided by the study and adopted in the 1988 report, however, includes only noninstitutionalized persons with physical disabilities who are over age 15. The 5.7 million gap between the 43 million figure in the ADA's findings and the 37.3 million figure in the

---

number is increasing as the population as a whole is growing older …

(7) individuals with disabilities are a discrete and insular minority who have been faced with restrictions and limitations, subjected to a history of purposeful unequal treatment, and relegated to a position of political powerlessness in our society, based on characteristics that are beyond the control of such individuals and resulting from stereotypic assumptions not truly indicative of the individual ability of such individuals to participate in, and contribute to, society …

(b) PURPOSE.—It is the purpose of this Act—

(1) to provide a clear and comprehensive national mandate for the elimination of discrimination against individuals with disabilities …

report can thus probably be explained as an effort to include in the findings those who were excluded from the National Council figure....

Regardless of its exact source, however, the 43 million figure reflects an understanding that those whose impairments are largely corrected by medication or other devices are not "disabled" within the meaning of the ADA....

Because it is included in the ADA's text, the finding that 43 million individuals are disabled gives content to the ADA's terms, specifically the term "disability." Had Congress intended to include all persons with corrected physical limitations among those covered by the Act, it undoubtedly would have cited a much higher number of disabled persons in the findings. That it did not is evidence that the ADA's coverage is restricted to only those whose impairments are not mitigated by corrective measures....

◆ JUSTICE GINSBURG concurring.

I agree that 42 U.S.C. § 12102(2)(A) does not reach the legions of people with correctable disabilities. The strongest clues to Congress' perception of the domain of the Americans with Disabilities Act of 1990 (ADA), as I see it, are legislative findings that "some 43,000,000 Americans have one or more physical or mental disabilities," § 12101(a)(1), and that "individuals with disabilities are a discrete and insular minority," persons "subjected to a history of purposeful unequal treatment, and relegated to a position of political powerlessness in our society," § 12101(a)(7). These declarations are inconsistent with the enormously embracing definition of disability petitioners urge. As the Court demonstrates, the inclusion of correctable disabilities within the ADA's domain would extend the Act's coverage to far more than 43 million people. And persons whose uncorrected eyesight is poor, or who rely on daily medication for their well-being, can be found in every social and economic class; they do not cluster among the politically powerless, nor do they coalesce as historical victims of discrimination. In short, in no sensible way can one rank the large numbers of diverse individuals with corrected disabilities as a "discrete and insular minority." ... Congress' use of the phrase ... is a telling indication of its intent to restrict the ADA's coverage to a confined, and historically disadvantaged, class.

◆ [The dissenting opinion of JUSTICE BREYER is omitted].

◆ JUSTICE STEVENS, with whom JUSTICE BREYER joins, dissenting.

When it enacted the Americans with Disabilities Act of 1990 (ADA or Act), Congress certainly did not intend to require United Air Lines to hire unsafe or unqualified pilots. Nor, in all likelihood, did it view every person who wears glasses as a member of a "discrete and insular minority." [42 U.S.C. § 12101(a)(7).] Indeed, by reason of legislative myopia it may not have foreseen that its definition of "disability" might theoretically encompass, not just "some 43,000,000 Americans," 42 U.S.C. § 12101(a)(1), but perhaps two or three times that number. Nevertheless, if we apply customary tools of statutory construction, it is quite clear that the threshold question whether an individual is "disabled" within the meaning of the Act—and, therefore, is entitled to the basic assurances that the Act affords—focuses on her past or present physical condition without regard to mitigation that has resulted from rehabilitation, self-improvement, prosthetic devices, or medication. One might reasonably argue that the general rule should not apply to an impairment that merely requires a near-sighted person to wear glasses. But I believe that, in order to be faithful to the remedial purpose of the Act, we should give it a generous, rather than a miserly, construction....

"As in all cases of statutory construction, our task is to interpret the words of [the statute] in light of the purposes Congress sought to serve." Congress expressly provided that the "purpose of (the ADA is) to provide a clear and comprehensive national mandate for the elimination of discrimination against individuals with disabilities." 42 U.S.C. § 12101(b)(1). To that end, the ADA prohibits covered employers from "discriminat[ing] against a qualified individual *with a disability* because of the disability" in regard to the terms, conditions, and privileges of employment. 42 U.S.C. § 12112(a) (emphasis added)....

[Justice Stevens then compares the definition of "disability" in the Rehabilitation Act of 1973 because ADA's definition is drawn "almost verbatim" from that statute. He concludes that the text of both statutes is broadly inclusive and not meant to provide three discrete categories. "On the contrary, [the definitions] furnish three overlapping formulas aimed at ensuring that individuals who now have, or ever had, a substantially limiting impairment are covered by the Act."]

To the extent that there may be doubt concerning the meaning of the statutory text, ambiguity is easily removed by looking at the legislative history. The Committee Reports on the bill that became the ADA make it abundantly clear that Congress intended the ADA to cover individuals who could perform all of their major life activities only with the help of ameliorative measures.

The ADA originated in the Senate. The Senate Report states that "whether a person has a disability should be assessed without regard to the availability of mitigating measures, such as reasonable accommodations or auxiliary aids." S.Rep. No. 101–116, p. 23 (1989)....

When the legislation was considered in the House of Representatives, its Committees reiterated the Senate's basic understanding of the Act's coverage, with one minor modification: They clarified that "correctable" or "controllable" disabilities were covered in the first definitional prong as well. The Report of the House Committee on the Judiciary states, in discussing the first prong, that, when determining whether an individual's impairment substantially limits a major life activity, "[t]he impairment should be assessed without considering whether mitigating measures, such as auxiliary aids or reasonable accommodations, would result in a less-than-substantial limitation." H.R.Rep. No. 101–485, pt. III, p. 28 (1990). The Report continues that "a person with epilepsy, an impairment which substantially limits a major life activity, is covered under this test," as is a person with poor hearing, "even if the hearing loss is corrected by the use of a hearing aid".

The Report of the House Committee on Education and Labor likewise states that "[w]hether a person has a disability should be assessed without regard to the availability of mitigating measures, such as reasonable accommodations or auxiliary aids." *Id.,* pt. II, at 52. To make matters perfectly plain, the Report adds:

> "For example, a person who is hard of hearing is substantially limited in the major life activity of hearing, *even though the loss may be corrected through the use of a hearing aid.* Likewise, persons with impairments, such as epilepsy or diabetes, which substantially limit a major life activity are covered under the first prong of the definition of disability, *even if the effects of the impairment are controlled by medication." Ibid.*(emphasis added).

All of the Reports, indeed, are replete with references to the understanding that the Act's protected class includes individuals with various medical conditions that ordinarily are perfectly "correctable" with medication or treatment....

In my judgment, the Committee Reports ... merely confirm the message conveyed by the text of the Act—at least insofar as it applies to impairments such as the loss of a limb, the inability to hear, or any condition such as diabetes that is substantially limiting without medication. The Act generally protects individuals who have "correctable" substantially limiting impairments from unjustified employment discrimination on the basis of those impairments....

... I suspect[] the Court has been cowed by respondent's persistent argument that viewing all individuals in their unmitigated state will lead to a tidal wave of lawsuits. None of the Court's reasoning, however, justifies a construction of the Act that will obviously deprive many of Congress' intended beneficiaries of the legal protection it affords....

In the end, the Court is left only with its tenacious grip on Congress' finding that "some 43,000,000 Americans have one or more physical or mental disabilities,"— and that figure's legislative history extrapolated from a law review "article authored by the drafter of the original ADA bill introduced in Congress in 1988." We previously have observed that a "statement of congressional findings is a rather thin reed upon which to base" a statutory construction. "43 million" is not a fixed cap on the Act's protected class: By including the "record of" and "regarded as" categories, Congress fully expected the Act to protect individuals who lack, in the Court's words, "actual" disabilities, and therefore are not counted in that number.

What is more, in mining the depths of the history of the 43 million figure—surveying even agency reports that predate the drafting of any of this case's controlling legislation—the Court fails to acknowledge that its narrow approach may have the perverse effect of denying coverage for a sizeable portion of the core group of 43 million. The Court appears to exclude from the Act's protected class individuals with controllable conditions such as diabetes and severe hypertension that were expressly understood as substantially limiting impairments in the Act's Committee Reports, and even ... in the studies that produced the 43 million figure. Given the inability to make the 43 million figure fit any consistent method of interpreting the word "disabled," it would be far wiser for the Court to follow—or at least to mention—the documents reflecting Congress' contemporaneous understanding of the term: the Committee Reports on the actual legislation....

I therefore respectfully dissent.

* * *

Points for Discussion

1. *Statutory Language*: What was the language at issue? What did each party want that language to mean? What meaning did the majority and concurrence adopt? The dissent?

2. *Theories*: Which theory did the majority use? The dissent? Did the majority or dissent find the language ambiguous, absurd, to have a scrivener's error, or to raise a constitutional question?

3. *Grammar*: Why did the majority find the grammar dispositive?

4. *Findings & Purpose Clauses*: Often, purpose and findings (and sometimes policies) are combined in one or more sections of a bill, as was done in the ADA. In this case, the majority cited one findings subsection (the "43 million Americans" section), the concurrence cited the same findings subsection and another findings subsection (the "discrete and insular minority" section), and the dissent cited these same findings subsections and a purpose subsection (the "clear and comprehensive national mandate" section). Note that Congress amended the findings section of the ADA in 2008, removing the "43 million" language and the "discrete and insular" language. The "clear and comprehensive national mandate" language remained unchanged. *See* ADA Amendments Act of 2008, Pub.L. 110–325, 122 Stat. 3553 (2008).

   Remember that the general canon directs that findings and purpose clauses cannot contradict clear text, but can be used as aids to meaning. Was the text clear? Assuming not, did any of these findings and purposes subsections resolve the ambiguity or did they add to the ambiguity by pointing in different directions?

   The dissent said, "We previously have observed that a 'statement of congressional findings is a rather thin reed upon which to base' a statutory construction." Why is the majority willing to place such great emphasis on such a thin reed here?

5. *Legislative History*: As the dissent noted, the legislative history was very clear that the committees considered the exact issue before the Court and addressed it: disabilities under section (A) included correctable disabilities. Yet the majority refused to consider this legislative history, because the majority concluded that the text was clear. One reason the majority found the language clear was the findings subsection. In the findings subsection, Congress indicated that there were "43 million Americans" who have one or more disabilities. Acknowledging that the source of this number was unclear, the majority pointed to a law review article written by one of the bill's sponsors as proof that Congress intended the "work

disability approach" to apply rather than the "health conditions approach." Under the "work disability approach" correctable disabilities are not disabilities. Is a law review article written by a sponsor regarding how this number was computed the equivalent of legislative history? Why was the majority willing to look at a law review article written by the sponsor but not at committee reports authored by legislators?

6. *Remedial Statute*: The dissent noted that the ADA is a remedial statute, thus it should be broadly construed. We will learn in Chapter 15 that remedial statutes are typically broadly construed to further their remedial purpose. Remedial statutes are typically defined as statutes that provide a new remedy that was unavailable at common law.

* * *

4. The Purview: The Substantive Provisions

After the introductory clauses identified above, the substantive provisions begin. By law, each section of a bill must be separately numbered. 1 U.S.C. § 104 (2015). The sample bill began numbering with the short title. Additionally, "as nearly as may be" each section must contain only a single proposition of enactment. *Id.*

The order of the substantive provisions is predictable: definitions first, principal operative provisions second, enforcement provisions third, and severability provisions last. Intermingled within these provisions are many other provisions, including effective date provisions, savings provisions, and provisos. When this expected order is not followed, ambiguity may result. For example, in *Bank One v. Midwest Bank & Trust Co.*, 516 U.S. 264 (1996), the Supreme Court had to determine whether it had jurisdiction under the Expedited Funds Availability Act to hear a case one bank brought against another. The Act was poorly drafted because the section authorizing interbank litigation—an enforcement provision—was placed in the wrong section of the Act. As Justice Stevens noted, "When Congress creates a cause of action, the provisions describing the new substantive rights and liabilities typically precede the provisions describing enforcement procedures; [this statute] does not conform to that pattern." *Id.* at 276 (Stevens, J., concurring).

Let's look at the substantive sections in more detail.

a. Definitions

Codes may have definitions that apply globally. For example, 1 U.S.C. § 1 (2015) defines a number of words—including signature, oath, and writing—for all federal statutes. "In determining the meaning of any Act of Congress, [these definitions control] unless the context indicates otherwise." *Id.* States also have global definitional statutes.

However, most statutory definitions are contained within the relevant act in a separate section of that act, known as the definitions section. Not every statute includes a definitions section; but if there is such a section, then the definitions typically precede the substantive provisions. Only definitions that are applicable to the bill as a whole are included within a definitions section. Definitions that apply to only one particular section of a bill are usually placed within that specific section.

Sometimes, legislatures do not follow this rule, so a competent attorney will search the entire act for definitions. The sample bill has a definition section contained within section 3. (See below.) Because this bill only has three sections, this definition section likely applies to all of the relevant provisions of the bill despite its limiting language: "In this section." But it would have been clearer had Congress placed the definition section in its own separate section. As drafted, section 3 of the bill is unwieldy. In a different, longer act, misplacement might create interpretation issues: Does the definition apply to all sections of the bill or just the section in which it is located?

Component: Definitions Section

> "SEC. 3111. GRANT AUTHORIZATION....
>
> "(b) DEFINITIONS.—In this section:
>
> "(1) PROSECUTOR.—The term 'prosecutor' means a full-time employee of a State or local agency who—
>
> "(A) is continually licensed to practice law; and
>
> "(B) prosecutes criminal or juvenile delinquency cases (or both) at the State or local level, including an employee who supervises, educates, or trains other persons prosecuting such cases...."

Including definitions for every word might seem to be the perfect answer to avoiding ambiguity. If the legislature simply defined every word it used, would not ambiguity disappear? Actually, no. It is not possible, nor even desirable, for the legislature to define every word used in a bill, for a number of reasons. First, bills would become unwieldy to say the least! Also, defining words can be challenging. Legislatures may not know in advance every circumstance they would want covered. Hence, the ambiguity would simply move from the operative section of the act to the definitions section. Finally, where would drafters draw the line? Should they define common words like "the"? Less common words like "any"? Only very uncommon words? For all these reasons, legislators should only define those words and phrases (1) that have a unique, technical meaning (e.g., "summary judgment"), (2) that they wish to have a meaning broader, narrower, or different from the ordinary or dictionary definition (e.g., "discrimination"), or (3) that have been created to refer to a complex or wordy idea in a simpler way (e.g., "Department" for "Department of Health and Human Services").

Definitions are critical and controlling. Often, the interpretation of a statute depends on the words in the statute. If the legislature has defined those words, then that definition trumps all other interpretations, *even if the legislature's definition makes no sense.* And occasionally, a legislature's definitions defy common sense. For example, in the next case, does the majority hold that a bulldozer is a building, or does the majority hold that a bulldozer is a vehicle? How do the definitions help the majority reach its odd outcome?

Kentucky v. Plowman

Supreme Court of Kentucky
86 S.W.3d 47 (Ky. 2002)

◆ WINTERSHEIMER, Justice [LAMBERT, C.J., GRAVES and JOHNSTONE, JJ., concur.].

[The defendant was charged with] second-degree arson.

The sole question is whether a bulldozer is a vehicle for purposes of the arson statutes.

Plowman was indicted for second-degree arson. The indictment charged that he started a fire with the intent to destroy or damage a bulldozer owned by another. After hearing oral arguments, the circuit judge granted the pre-trial motion by Plowman to dismiss the indictment. The circuit judge examined the plain meaning of the words "bulldozer" and "vehicle," and held that the bulldozer involved in the charge was not a vehicle covered by the arson statute. The Court of Appeals affirmed for the same reason but also found that the policy and purpose of the statutes as well as the doctrine of *ejusdem generis* supported the conclusion of the circuit judge. This Court granted discretionary review.

It is well settled that the interpretation of a statute is a matter of law. Accordingly, a reviewing court is not required to adopt the decisions of the trial court as to a matter of law, but must interpret the statute according to the plain meaning of the act and in accordance with the legislative intent. The seminal duty of a court in construing a statute is to effectuate the intent of the legislature.

KRS 513.030 defines second-degree arson as follows:

(1) A person is guilty of arson in the second degree when he starts a fire or causes an explosion with intent to destroy or damage a building:

(a) Of another; or

(b) Of his own or of another, to collect or facilitate the collection of insurance proceeds for such loss. . . .

KRS 513.010 provides for the following definition of building:

"Building," in addition to its ordinary meaning, specifically includes any dwelling, hotel, commercial structure, automobile, truck, watercraft, aircraft, trailer, sleeping car, railroad car, or other structure or vehicle, or any structure with a valid certificate of occupancy.

An unambiguous statute is to be applied without resort to any outside aids. This Court has repeatedly held that statutes must be given a literal interpretation unless they are ambiguous and if the words are not ambiguous, no statutory construction is required. KRS 446.080* provides for a liberal construction of statutes with the view to promote their objects and to carry out the intent of the legislature. All words and phrases shall be construed according to the common and approved usage of language. Here, the language of KRS 513.010 is clear and unambiguous when considered in its expansive content and no further interpretation is required. Although dictionary definitions can sometimes offer guidance as to statutory construction, they are not conclusive. The predominant element is the legislative intent....

KRS 513.010, as originally enacted in 1974, defined a "building" for purposes of the arson statutes as including, in addition to the ordinary meaning, the following property:

... structure, vehicle, watercraft or aircraft:

(a) Where any person lives; or

(b) Where people assemble for purposes of business, government, education, religion, entertainment or public transportation; or

(c) Which is used for overnight accommodation of persons.

In 1982, the legislature amended this definitional statute to provide for the current definition as set out previously in this opinion. The amended statute expanded the types of vehicles qualifying as "buildings" for purposes of the arson statutes by deleting the requirement that any such vehicle be used as a residence, meeting place or for overnight accommodation. Clearly, the legislature intended for the word building to be interpreted with an expansive view.

It is also clear that the 1982 amendment by the legislature has almost completely changed the arson statutes. For that reason, it was improper in this case for the Court of Appeals to rely on the 1974 commentary to the arson statutes to interpret its policy and purpose. The definitional statute does not place a limitation on the

---

* Editor's footnote: KRS 446.080 provides in full:

(1) All statutes of this state shall be liberally construed with a view to promote their objects and carry out the intent of the legislature, and the rule that statutes in derogation of the common law are to be strictly construed shall not apply to the statutes of this state....

(4) All words and phrases shall be construed according to the common and approved usage of language, but technical words and phrases, and such others as may have acquired a peculiar and appropriate meaning in the law, shall be construed according to such meaning.

purpose for which the vehicle is used in order to determine if the conveyance is a vehicle.

The defining statute of the 1974 law considered arson as more of an offense against person than property. In the 1982 version of the arson law, there is not even a reference to "places where people live or assemble" as contrasted with the 1974 law.

It is totally unnecessary to employ the doctrine of *ejusdem generis,* which is a Latin phrase indicating the same kind or class. The phrase is used as a tool of construction when a general word or phrase follows a list of specific persons or things. The general word or phrase will be interpreted to include only persons or things of the same type of those listed. Here, the statute in question has been legislatively expanded to include "or other structure or vehicle." The intent of the General Assembly is clear.

After considering both the plain meaning of the words and the legislative intent, we must conclude that the interpretations of the Court of Appeals and the circuit judge were in error. As a matter of law, we hold that a bulldozer is a "vehicle" within the definition of a "building" under KRS 513.010 for purposes of the arson statutes.

◆ Justice Keller dissenting [opinion joined by Cooper and Stumbo, JJ.].

I respectfully dissent from the majority opinion and would affirm the Court of Appeals because I subscribe to the less-than-radical notion that a bulldozer is not a "building" — certainly not in common everyday parlance, but, for the purposes of this appeal, not even under the KRS 513.010 definition of "building" that some observers have aptly characterized as "frighteningly expansive." ... I disagree with the majority's conclusion that a bulldozer constitutes a "vehicle" under KRS 513.010 and, thus, a "building" for the purposes of Kentucky's arson statutes.... [A] "vehicle" is commonly defined as a means of transporting persons or property and ... bulldozers do not fall within the KRS 513.010 "or other ... vehicle" language because bulldozers perform functions distinct from transportation.

In the outset, I observe that I find it exceedingly difficult to track the reasoning supporting the majority's conclusion. Although the majority holds that KRS 513.010's "or other ... vehicle" language includes bulldozers, the majority gives little indication of how it reached this conclusion and even less indication of what the majority believes the General Assembly intended by its use of the word "vehicle." Specifically, I observe that the majority neither defines "vehicle" or makes any effort to illuminate the meaning of that term. In fact, other than a passing reference to some undefined "plain meaning of the words" and four (4) uses of the term "expansive" or some derivation thereof, the majority opinion offers no explanation of how the language of KRS 513.010 displays legislative intent that supports the majority's conclusion that the General Assembly intended to provide a ten (10) to twenty (20) year prison sentence for a person who sets a bulldozer ablaze with the intent to destroy it. Rather than attempt to "shadow box" with a majority interpretation no more concrete than "whatever 'vehicle' means, it includes bulldozers," I will attempt to demonstrate that: (1) the majority's ambiguous interpretation of "vehicle" is inconsistent with that word's common and ordinary meaning; and (2) the definition of "vehicle" that excludes bulldozers … is more consistent with the word's ordinary and contextual meaning.

While I do not question the premise that the General Assembly's 1982 amendments reflect an expansion of the scope of the Kentucky Penal Code's arson provisions, the result in this case turns on whether *through the language in KRS 513.010*—specifically, the word "vehicle"—the General Assembly intended to define "building" in a manner inclusive of bulldozers. And, unless bulldozers fall within the scope of the KRS 513.010 "or other … vehicle" language, no amount of "expansive intent" will permit the conclusion that the indictment at issue alleges facts that would constitute Second–Degree Arson. Taking note of the presumption that statutes are written "using words with common and everyday meanings" and the legislature's direction to construe its enactments "according to the common and approved usage of language," I believe an examination of the ordinary meaning of "vehicle" leaves a gaping hole in the majority's suggestion that its conclusion is supported by the language of KRS 513.010.

The word "vehicle" stems from the Latin noun "vehiculum" and the Latin verb "vehere," meaning "to carry." Thus "vehicle" is defined denotatively as "a device or structure for *transporting persons or things;* a conveyance"[5] or "[t]hat in or on which any person is, or may be carried … ; a means of conveyance; specifically, a means of conveyance upon land"[6] or "[s]omething used as an instrument of conveyance; any conveyance *used in transporting passengers or merchandise* by land, water, or air."[7] In statutes addressing subjects such as the transportation of hazardous materials,[8] motor vehicle licensing,[9] traffic regulations,[10] emissions control,[11] and the transportation of alcoholic beverages,[12] the Kentucky General Assembly has defined "vehicle" in accordance with its denotative meaning. And, significantly, the General Assembly also has excluded construction equipment from the scope of some of its definitions of "vehicle." While I do not suggest that it would be appropriate to apply definitions from other statutes to KRS 513.010's use of the term "vehicle," I believe the General

---

5. AMERICAN HERITAGE DICTIONARY OF THE ENGLISH LANGUAGE (4th ed.2000) (emphasis added).

6. WEBSTER'S REVISED UNABRIDGED DICTIONARY (1988).

7. BLACK'S LAW DICTIONARY (7th ed.1999) (emphasis added).

8. KRS 174.405(6) ("'Vehicle' means any device or contrivance for carrying or conveying persons, property, or substances, including conveyance by highways or by airway.").

9. KRS 186.010(8)(b) ("'[V]ehicle' means every device in, upon or by which any person or property is or may be transported or drawn upon a public highway, excepting devices moved by human and animal power or used exclusively upon stationary rails or tracks, or which derives its power from overhead rails.").

10. KRS 189.010(19)(a) ("'Vehicle' includes: 1. All agencies for the transportation of persons or property over or upon the public highways of the Commonwealth; and 2. All vehicles passing over or upon the highways.").

11. KRS 224.20–710(7) ("'Vehicle' means any automobile or truck registered in this Commonwealth … and used upon the public highways of the Commonwealth for the purpose of transporting persons or property.").

12. KRS 241.010(45) ("'Vehicle' means any device or animal used to carry, convey, transport, or otherwise move alcoholic beverages or any products, equipment or appurtenances used to manufacture, bottle, or sell these beverages.").

Assembly's consistent use of the common and ordinary definition of "vehicle" creates a presumption that it intended the ordinary meaning when it used "vehicle" in KRS 513.010.

In contrast to a "vehicle" used to transport persons or goods, a bulldozer is "[a] heavy, driver-operated machine for clearing and grading land, usually having continuous treads and a broad hydraulic blade in front."[14] Other than pushing dirt, brush, and other debris around, bulldozers serve no meaningful transportation function. Thus, in the two (2) Kentucky statutory provisions specifically referencing bulldozers, the word "vehicle" does not appear, and bulldozers are instead mentioned alongside graders and earth movers in the context of capital construction projects and grouped with backhoes and draglines as "heavy equipment." Thus, ... "[b]ased on the plain meaning of the word, it does not appear that 'bulldozer' falls within the definition of 'vehicle' when given its ordinary meaning." The majority opinion offers no justification for its undefined, but apparently other-than-its-common-usage, interpretation of "vehicle." In any event, however, the denotative meaning of "vehicle" compels not the result reached by the majority, but instead the opposite conclusion reached by the courts below.

Although the majority finds no need to apply the rules of statutory interpretation to KRS 513.010 because it believes that "the language of KRS 513.010 is clear and unambiguous when considered in its expansive content," KRS 513.010 may not be as "unambiguous" as advertised. First, and foremost, ambiguity is inherent when people can reach different reasonable interpretations regarding the meaning of language, and the litigants in this case and the Kentucky judiciary clearly do not agree on the meaning of "vehicle" in this statute. Second, KRS Chapter 513 itself contains no definition of "vehicle," and thus, in order to determine what the General Assembly intended by its use of that term, this Court necessarily must perform an interpretive function. Third, patent redundancies in the KRS 513.010 definition—e.g., "dwelling, hotel, commercial structure ... or other structure ... or any structure with a valid certificate of occupancy"—belie the majority's attempt to label the statute unambiguous and suggest that the definition was cobbled together without substantial attention to internal coherence....

In the face of such ambiguity, courts commonly turn to principles of statutory construction. Because the majority opinion fails to disclose its operational definition of "vehicle," however, I find it difficult to apply accepted standards of statutory interpretation to distinguish between the competing alternative interpretations. However, I would make two (2) observations: (1) the majority goes to great lengths—and by "great lengths" I mean repeated assertions that the statute is "unambiguous" and claims that "[t]he intent of the General Assembly is clear"—to suggest that the doctrine of *ejusdem generis* has no relevance to the issues at hand; and, unsurprisingly, (2) an application of *ejusdem generis*—a principle of statutory interpretation that preferences contextual or connotative meaning—supports the definition of the term

---

14. AMERICAN HERITAGE DICTIONARY OF THE ENGLISH LANGUAGE (4th ed. 2000).

"vehicle" utilized by the courts below and urged in this dissenting opinion. Under the doctrine of *ejusdem generis*, "broad and comprehensive expressions in an act such as, 'and all others,' or 'any others,' are usually to be restricted to persons or things of the same kind or class with those specifically named in the *preceding* words." Thus, in KRS 513.010, all of the non-structural items defined as "buildings"—i.e. automobiles, trucks, watercraft, aircraft, trailers, sleeping cars, and railroad cars—illustrate the context of "or other ... vehicle." Significantly, each of the specifically-named items is a "vehicle" in the ordinary meaning of that term—i.e., an instrument for transporting persons or property. Accordingly, I believe that the more reasonable interpretation of KRS 513.010's "any other ... vehicle" language is that the language refers to "vehicle" in its plain meaning—i.e., a means of transporting persons or goods—rather than some nebulous (but other-than-ordinary) definition of "vehicle" that would include construction equipment not used to transport persons or goods. This interpretation of "vehicle" places bulldozers outside the scope of Chapter 513.

* * *

Points for Discussion

1. *Statutory Language*: What was the language at issue? What did each party want that language to mean? What meaning did the majority and dissent adopt? The language in the operative section of the statute is the word "building." The ordinary meaning of a "building" does not include a bulldozer; however, the ordinary meaning does not apply here. Why not? The statute defines building to include "automobile ... or other ... vehicle." Hence, the issue is whether a bulldozer is a "vehicle." Be sure you understand both steps in identifying the language at issue in this case and in any case in which language in a definitions section is being interpreted.

2. *Theories*: Which theory did the majority use? The dissent? Did the majority or dissent find the language ambiguous, absurd, to have a scrivener's error, or to raise a constitutional question?

3. *How a Bulldozer became a Building*: The majority concluded that a bulldozer is a building. How did it reach that conclusion? What role did the statutory definition play in the majority's analysis?

4. *Legislative Amendment*: Why did the majority find the amendment history relevant to the meaning?

5. *Dissent*: According to the dissent, why was a bulldozer not a building? What sources did the dissent use to discern the meaning of the word?

6. *Ejusdem Generis & Noscitur a Sociis*: Were either of these canons relevant according to the majority or dissent? Why or why not? Is one canon more appropriate to apply in this case than the other?

7. *Distinguishing Technical Meaning*: Even though the legislature defined "building," that definition is not a technical definition. Can you explain why? Can you think of any time when "building" would have a technical meaning? Recall that, with the exception of legal words, technical meaning rarely applies.

8.   *Another Example*: Return to *Regina v. Ojibway* in Chapter 6. You will recall that the defendant shot a horse and was found to have violated the Small Birds Act. The statutory definition was critical to the decision. It defined "bird" as "a two legged animal covered with feathers." As the court noted, the legislature can define words any way it wishes: "We are not interested in whether the animal in question is a bird or not in fact, but whether it is one in law. Statutory interpretation has forced many a horse to eat birdseed for the rest of its life...." You will recall that this "case" is one scholar's legal parody of literalism.

* * *

b. Operating and Enforcement Provisions

Following the definitions section are the principal operative provisions. There are two types of provisions within this category: (1) *substantive provisions*, which provide the rights, duties, powers, and privileges being created, and (2) *administrative provisions*, which address the creation, organization, powers, and procedures of the governmental organization that will enforce or adjudicate the law. If the law is drafted well, substantive provisions with general applicability will precede provisions with specific applicability, and general rules will precede any exceptions to those rules. The substantive provisions, along with the administrative and enforcement provisions, are the essence of the bill. Indeed, it is likely that the language that is being interpreted comes from one of these sections. For the most part, there are no unique canons that apply to these sections. Rather, the canons throughout this text help resolve the meaning of text in these subsections.

The administrative provisions identify how government will implement the law. In these provisions, the legislature will create or identify the governmental organization or organizations that will be responsible for administering and enforcing the law and explain how the government will administer and enforce the law. In the example bill, the Department of Justice would have been in charge of administering the bill had it passed. An excerpt is in the box below.

Component: Administrative Provision

"SEC. 3111. GRANT AUTHORIZATION.

"(c) PROGRAM AUTHORIZED. — The Attorney General shall ... establish a program by which the Department of Justice shall assume the obligation to repay a student loan ...

(d), for any borrower who —

"(1) is employed as a prosecutor or public defender; and

"(2) is not in default on a loan for which the borrower seeks forgiveness."

The final substantive sections of an act are enforcement provisions. Generally, the purpose for enacting a bill is to affect conduct. The legislature can best affect conduct by prescribing either a punishment for noncompliance or a reward for compliance with an enacted rule. The rule is included within the substantive provisions, while the consequence (reward or punishment) is included within the enforcement provisions. The more common enforcement provisions include (1) the potential for criminal, civil, and administrative penalties, and (2) the availability of injunctive relief. Notice that in the enforcement provision excerpted below, the federal government has the power to recover funds owed to it by any legal means.

Component: Enforcement Provision

"SEC. 3111. GRANT AUTHORIZATION.

"(d) TERMS OF LOAN REPAYMENT. —

"(1) BORROWER AGREEMENT. —

"(C) if the borrower is required to repay an amount to the Attorney General under subparagraph (B) and fails to repay such amount, a sum equal to that amount shall be recoverable by the Federal Government from the employee (or such employee's estate, if applicable) by such methods as are provided by law for the recovery of amounts owed to the Federal Government."

---

c. Severability and Inseverability Provisions

Sometimes courts find acts to be unconstitutional. Does that mean the entire act is invalid or only a section of that act? If the unconstitutional section of an act is "severable" from the rest of the act, then only that section is invalid. But if the unconstitutional section cannot be severed, meaning it is "inseverable," then the entire act is invalid.

Provisions may be included in a bill to address issues relating to the severability of various sections of an act. Severability and inseverability (also known as non-severability) provisions address the validity of the bill should any section of it be found invalid. Severability provisions allow for the remaining sections of the act to remain valid, while inseverability provisions require that the act as a whole be held invalid if any one section is invalid. Inseverability provisions come in two types: "general" and "specific." *General inseverability provisions* provide that *none* of the provisions of an act are severable; in contrast, *specific inseverability provisions* provide that *specific* provisions of an act are not severable from one another. Early acts had neither severability nor inseverability provisions; however, in response to judicial interpretations of acts not having these provisions, severability clauses began to appear in bills in the early 1900s. Inseverability provisions are a more modern, less utilized creature.

If a severability or inseverability provision is included in a bill, it generally is placed at the end of the act. The John R. Justice Prosecutor and Defenders Incentive Act contains neither a severability nor an inseverability provision. Instead, two sample provisions are provided in the box below.

Component: Severability & Inseverability Clauses

SEC. 10A. SEVERABILITY.

If any provision of this Act or its application to any person or circumstance is held invalid, the invalidity does not affect other provisions or applications of this Act that can be given effect without the invalid provision or application, and to this end the provisions of this Act are declared to be severable.

SEC. 10B. INSEVERABILITY.

Section 1 of this Act, prohibiting the sale of alcohol without a license, and Section 2 of this Act, imposing a tax on the sale of alcohol, are not severable, and neither section would have been enacted without the other. If either provision is held invalid, both provisions are invalid.

---

i. Severability Provisions

Severability provisions raise many issues including constitutional issues, relevance issues, and effectiveness issues. Constitutional issues arise when a court strikes one part of an act, but not another. By altering the law as written, some argue that the court has effectively rewritten the act in violation of the Constitution. Under the Constitution, it is the legislature's job to write laws. By striking some sections of the act and not others, the court has effectively redrafted the law. Would the legislature have wanted the act to become law as redrafted? Possibly not. Thus, separation of powers concerns arise when the judiciary alters the law as written. Effectiveness and relevance issues arise because, despite the clear text of these clauses, their ordinary meaning often does not control.

The *doctrine of severability* is simple: statutes are presumed to be severable. The Supreme Court has said repeatedly that severability provisions are merely presumptions about what the legislature intended. In other words, it matters little whether or not Congress includes a severability clause. When Congress includes a clause indicating that sections in the act are severable, this severability clause provides a rebuttable presumption that provisions in the act are severable, and that presumption can be overcome "by strong evidence that Congress intended otherwise." *Alaska Airlines, Inc. v. Brock*, 480 U.S. 678, 686 (1987).

Perhaps surprisingly, Congress's inclusion of a severability clause does not resolve the question of what Congress intended. Rather, a severability clause merely preserves the general severability presumption just explained. Why? Commonly, and much like boilerplate language in contracts, legislatures include severability provisions with little thought about their true impact, partly because their true impact can be unknowable. Rather than carefully consider whether some provisions in a bill should survive if others do not, legislatures, without thought, simply include a severability clause directing that all provisions remain valid regardless of what the act might actually look like after litigation has excised some provisions. Thus, the doctrine that severability provisions are rebuttable presumptions makes sense; if the legislature does not think about what it is doing, then courts should not rubber-stamp the decision to include such a provision.

Severability provisions are actually unnecessary because courts today uniformly construe statutes as severable regardless of whether there is a severability provision in them (this was not always true). Some states provide as much by statute. For example, a Texas statute provides that all statutes are severable unless the statute specifically indicates that it is not. Tex. Gov't Code Ann. §§ 311.032 & 312.013 (West 2015). Thus, if the Texas legislature wishes for an entire act or specific sections of an act to be held invalid, the legislature must so provide. In the case that follows, the Court applies the general presumption that unconstitutional provisions are severable, even though it is uncertain whether the act at issue actually included a severability provision.

Alaska Airlines v. Brock

Supreme Court of the United States
480 U.S. 678 (1987)

◆ JUSTICE BLACKMUN delivered the opinion for a unanimous Court [REHNQUIST, C.J., BRENNAN, WHITE, MARSHALL, POWELL, STEVENS, O'CONNOR, SCALIA, JJ., concur]

[In *INS v. Chadha*, 462 U.S. 919 (1983), the Supreme Court held congressional-veto provisions to be unconstitutional.]

Petitioners, 14 commercial airlines, in the present case contend that provisions protecting employees in the Airline Deregulation Act of 1978 (Act) are ineffective because § 43(f)(3) of the Act ... subjects to a legislative veto implementing regulations issued by the Department of Labor (DOL). We granted certiorari to consider whether that legislative-veto provision is severable from the remainder of the Act.

After 40 years of extensive regulation of the commercial-airline industry by the Civil Aeronautics Board (CAB), Congress in 1978 decided to make "a major change and fundamental redirection as to the manner of regulation of interstate and overseas air transportation so as to place primary emphasis on competition." Congress abandoned the industrywide fare structure gradually, altered the procedures by which airlines could enter new markets, and phased out the regulatory power of the CAB, eliminating the agency altogether in 1984.

Congress sought to ensure that the benefits to the public flowing from this deregulation would not be "paid for" by airline employees who had relied on the heavily regulated nature of the industry in deciding to accept and to retain positions with commercial air carriers. In order to assist employees dislocated as a result of deregulation, Congress enacted an Employee Protection Program (EPP). The EPP [imposed a "first right of hire" for protected employees. But the EPP also contained a legislative veto]....

Petitioners ... challenged the EPP's ... legislative-veto provision ... [as] unconstitutional under *Chadha,* and [argued] that the entire program must be invalidated because the veto provision is nonseverable from the rest of the EPP.... The District Court granted summary judgment for petitioners, striking down the entire EPP.... The United States Court of Appeals for the District of Columbia Circuit reversed, holding that the legislative-veto clause is severable from the remainder of the EPP program. We agree and affirm.

"[A] court should refrain from invalidating more of the statute than is necessary.... '[W]henever an act of Congress contains unobjectionable provisions separable from those found to be unconstitutional, it is the duty of this court to so declare, and to maintain the act in so far as it is valid.'" The standard for determining the severability of an unconstitutional provision is well established: "'Unless it is evident that the Legislature would not have enacted those provisions which are within its power, independently of that which is not, the invalid part may be dropped if what is left is fully operative as a law.'"

Congress could not have intended a constitutionally flawed provision to be severed from the remainder of the statute if the balance of the legislation is incapable of functioning independently....

The ... relevant inquiry in evaluating severability is whether the statute will function in a *manner* consistent with the intent of Congress.... The final test ... is the traditional one: the unconstitutional provision must be severed unless the statute created in its absence is legislation that Congress would not have enacted.[7]

The inquiry is eased when Congress has explicitly provided for severance by including a severability clause in the statute. This Court has held that the inclusion of such a clause creates a presumption that Congress did not intend the validity of the statute in question to depend on the validity of the constitutionally offensive provision. In such a case, unless there is strong evidence that Congress intended otherwise, the objectionable provision can be excised from the remainder of the statute. In the ab-

---

7. Petitioners argue that the Court of Appeals formulated a completely new standard for severability. They rest this argument on the court's statement that an invalid portion of a statute may be severed unless, ... it is proved "that Congress would have preferred no airline employee protection provision at all to the existing provision *sans* the veto provision." Petitioners interpret this statement as a signal that the court asked whether Congress would have enacted *some* form of protection for airline employees, rather than whether Congress would have enacted the same protections currently found in the Act. Any such inquiry, of course, would be tautological, as Congress' intent to enact a statute on the subject is apparent from the existence of the EPP in the Act. We find the Court of Appeals' language to be completely consistent with the established severability standard. Even if one had doubts, when the court's analysis is viewed in its entirety, it is plain that the correct standard was applied in this case.

sence of a severability clause, however, Congress' silence is just that—silence—and does not raise a presumption against severability.

In this case, the parties disagree as to whether there is a severability clause applicable to the EPP.[8] We need not resolve this question, for there is no need to resort to a presumption in order to find the legislative-veto provision severable in this case. There is abundant indication of a clear congressional intent of severability both in the language and structure of the Act and in its legislative history.

Congress' intent that the EPP's ... [first hire] provisions should survive in the absence of the legislative-veto provision is suggested strongly by the affirmative duty the statute places directly on air carriers. The first-hire portion of the EPP establishes in detail an obligation to hire protected employees that scarcely needs the adoption of regulations by the Secretary, and thus leaves little of substance to be subject to a veto....

The Act simply provides that the Secretary "may" issue such regulations as are necessary to the administration of the program. §43(f)(1). A duty to hire that is not dependent upon the issuance of regulations is unlikely to be dependent upon an opportunity for Congress to veto those regulations....

In arguing that the legislative veto is nonseverable, petitioners place great significance on the fact that the EPP is the only section of the Act to delegate authority to the DOL and only rules issued pursuant to that section are subject to the veto. We find this emphasis misplaced. The EPP is the only aspect of the Act concerned with labor protection and thus naturally is the only provision to involve the DOL. The fact that this is the only veto in the Act is unremarkable given the nature of the rest of the statute. Although it did not remove completely the need for regulation, the Act is primarily a "deregulatory" statute and, aside from the EPP, did not create any new programs requiring congressional oversight. Moreover, the absence of a veto clause in *other* provisions of the Act indicates nothing about whether Congress regarded the clause as essential to the duty-to-hire provisions of §43.

The legislative history of the EPP supports the conclusion that Congress would have enacted the duty-to-hire provisions even without a legislative-veto provision by revealing that Congress regarded labor protection as an important feature of the Act, while it paid scant attention to the legislative-veto provision. [The Court quotes from various forms of legislative history to show congressional concern with employee job protection.].

In contrast to this extensive discussion of employee protection, the Committee paid scant attention to legislative oversight. When it did show concern with retaining control over the form the program would take, it was in the context of the compensation program, not the duty to hire....

The bill that emerged from the Conference Committee contained a version of the EPP "basically the same as the Senate bill." The debate on the final bill again illustrates

---

8. The Airline Deregulation Act of 1978 does not contain a severability clause, but it amends the Federal Aviation Act of 1958, 72 Stat. 731, which does contain such a clause....

the relative unimportance of the legislative-veto provision in this legislation. The only discussion of the EPP reflected wholesale approval of the program, with many Members stressing their support for the provisions, or regrets that the EPP provisions were not even stronger. One comment alone — in fact, the only such comment made during the entire deliberation on the Act — concerned the legislative veto.[24] This was an endorsement of the provision by Representative Levitas, which is best understood as an expression of his general support for legislative-veto provisions rather than a judgment that oversight was particularly important to the EPP.

The language and structure of the EPP and its legislative history provide an uncontradicted view of congressional intent with regard to severance of the legislative-veto provisions from the duty-to-hire program. This evidence leads to the conclusion that any concerns about the operation of the EPP related principally to the financial-assistance program. Even this concern was minimal. The emphasis during deliberations on the Act was placed overwhelmingly on the substantive provisions of the statute, with scant attention paid to any need for congressional oversight. In the almost total absence of any contrary refrain, we cannot conclude that Congress would have failed to enact the Airline Deregulation Act, including the EPP's first-hire program, if the legislative veto had not been included. Accordingly, we affirm the judgment of the Court of Appeals....

* * *

Points for Discussion

1. *Statutory Language*: What was the issue for the Court? Note here that because there was no severability provision, there was not really language at issue.

2. *Theories*: Which theory did the Court use?

3. *Was There a Provision?*: Did this Act even contain a severability provision? Why did the Court conclude that whether the act contained such a provision was irrelevant to its analysis?

4. *Statutes without Severability Provisions*: For an act without a severability provision, the severability canon provides that a statute is severable if (1) the legislature would have enacted the remaining provisions of the statute without the invalid provisions, and (2) the remaining provisions of the statute can function independently of the invalid provision. Both elements are required for a statute to be severable from the remainder of the act. The first element is predictive; the second element is objective.

---

24. Representative Levitas stated:

"Finally, Mr. Speaker, I cannot let this moment go by without making this observation. While there have been several bills sent to the President this year and signed by him which contained a provision for a congressional veto, I am happy to say that this piece of legislation contains a one-House veto over the regulations which may be issued by the Secretary of Labor on the labor protection provisions, so that the Congress and not an unelected bureaucrat will have the final word on the regulations that will have the effect of law." *Id.*, at 38524.

5. *Statutes with Severability Provisions*: The severability, or separability, clause is a comparatively modern legislative device, which responds to the judicial "practice of holding statutes separable long before the innovation of separability clauses." Norman J. Singer, Statutes and Statutory Construction § 44:8, at 585 (2001). It is increasingly common for legislatures to include a severability, or saving, clause providing that if any part of the act be found invalid, the remainder of the act shall nevertheless be upheld. Courts consider such clauses in deciding the separability of an enactment, but oddly, perhaps, they are not controlling.

Statutes are presumed to be severable if they contain a severability clause. This presumption can be rebutted in two situations. First, the presumption is rebutted if the act, without its unconstitutional provisions, cannot function. *See, e.g., Warren v. Mayor & Aldermen of Charlestown*, 68 Mass. (2 Gray) 84, 100 (1854) (finding that "various provisions of the act … are so connected with each other" that the legislature could not have intended the remaining, constitutional statutory remnants to remain in force). *Warren* was the first case to hold that an unconstitutional statutory provision rendered an entire statute unconstitutional. Prior to *Warren*, severability was simply assumed. *See, e.g., Marbury v. Madison*, 5 U.S. (1 Cranch) 137 (1803) (finding section 13 of the Judiciary Act of 1789 unconstitutional).

Second, the severability presumption is rebutted if Congress "intended otherwise," meaning that Congress would have preferred no act at all to the act without its unconstitutional provisions. In situations where there is evidence that Congress actually thought about this issue and wanted the legislation to be severable or inseverable that intent should control. For example, the Bipartisan Campaign Finance Reform Act (the "McCain-Feingold Act") resulted from a legislative bargain: Members of Congress agreed that in exchange for a ban on soft-money contributions, then-existing hard-money contribution limits would be increased. Without this compromise, the Act would have failed. But the compromise raised a potential conflict: If a court found the soft money ban to be unconstitutional, should the increase in allowable hard-money contributions remain in effect?

In anticipation of this issue, Congress specifically included a severability provision. Pub. L. No. 107-155, § 401 (2012). First, two Republican senators attempted to include an inseverability provision. In response, the bill's sponsors and the Democratic leadership effectively inserted a severability provision. Michael D. Shumsky, *Severability, Inseverability, and the Rule of Law*, 41 Harv. J. on Legis. 227, 229–30 (2004). The debate over whether to include the severability provision was long and arduous.

Given that Congress actually considered and fought over including a severability provision in the McCain-Feingold Act, that unambiguously expressed intent of Congress should control (in other words, the presumption of severability would not be rebutted). Parenthetically, in *Citizens United v. FEC*, 558 U.S. 310 (2010), the Supreme Court held that the First Amendment of the Federal Constitution prohibits the government from restricting independent political expenditures by corporations and unions.

6. *One State's Approach*: Virginia's history with severability provisions is interesting. In that state, the legislature changed the presumption by statute in 1986. Before 1986, courts presumed that statutes were not severable. In 1986, the legislature changed that presumption. "The provisions of all statutes are severable unless (i) the statute specifically provides that its provisions are not severable, or (ii) it is apparent that two or more statutes or provisions must operate in accord with one another." Va. Code. Ann § 1-17.1 Now, all statutes, not just those enacted after 1986, without severability provisions are presumed to be severable in Virginia. *Elliott v. Virginia*, 593 S.E.2d 263, 267 (Va. 2004). You should identify the presumption in your own state.

* * *

ii. Inseverability Clauses

In contrast to the commonness and, thus, thoughtlessness of including severability provisions, inseverability (or non-severability) provisions are included much less frequently. Arguably, these provisions demonstrate more clearly a legislature's intent. "A non-severability [provision] is almost unheard of and constitutes a legislative finding that every section [of an act] is so important to the single subject that no part of the act can be removed without destruction of the legislative purpose." *Farrior v. Sodexho, U.S.A.*, 953 F. Supp. 1301, 1302 (N.D. Ala. 1997).

Inseverability clauses are different from severability clauses for another reason as well. If an inseverability clause is included in a bill, its very presence likely represents proof that the bill was a compromise of competing interests:

> When Congress includes an inseverability clause in constitutionally questionable legislation, it does so in order to insulate a key legislative deal from judicial interference. Such clauses are iron-clad guarantees—clear statements by Congress that it would not have enacted one part of a statute without the others. Legislation containing an inseverability clause can thus be conceived of as a contract among competing political interests containing a structural enforcement mechanism designed to alleviate the concerns of those legislators who were willing to vote for ... a particular statutory scheme only if credibly assured that certain limiting provisions would be secure in the enacted legislation.

Shumsky, *Severability, Inseverability, and the Rule of Law, supra* at 267–68.

Congress rarely uses inseverability provisions; thus, the Supreme Court has not yet addressed their validity. *Id.* at 243–44. Because there is no guidance from the Supreme Court, lower courts have tended to treat inseverability clauses in the same way that the Court has treated severability clauses; "a non-severability clause cannot ultimately bind a court, it establishes [only] a presumption of non-severability." *Biszko v. RIHT Fin. Corp.*, 758 F.2d 769, 773 (1st Cir. 1985). Thus, again, "[d]espite the unambiguous command of … inseverability clauses … [they] create only a rebuttable presumption that guides—but does not control—a reviewing court's severability determination." Shumsky, *Severability, Inseverability, and the Rule of Law, supra* at 230. So, for example, in *Stiens v. Fire & Police Pension Ass'n*, 684 P.2d 180, 184 (Colo. 1984), the court held that the legislature intended the benefit provisions of a pension act to be severable from the act's unconstitutional funding provisions despite the existence of an inseverability provision.

Louk v. Cormier

Supreme Court of West Virginia
622 S.E.2d 788 (W. Va. 2005)

◆ DAVIS, JUSTICE:

On May 20, 2002, Ms. Louk filed a medical malpractice action against Dr. Cormier. The central allegation in the complaint was that Dr. Cormier perforated Ms. Louk's cecum when he performed the hysterectomy and salpingo-oophorectomy. Dr. Cormier defended the action on a theory that the cecum spontaneously ruptured.

The case proceeded to trial on December 2, 2003, before a twelve person jury. After both parties presented their case-in-chief, the trial court gave its jury charge. Among the instructions given was an instruction that informed the jury that it was not necessary to reach a unanimous verdict. The jury returned a verdict in which ten jurors found in favor of Dr. Cormier. Two jurors found in favor of Ms. Louk.

Thereafter, Ms. Louk filed a post-trial motion seeking a new trial arguing that the non-unanimous verdict instruction authorized by W. Va.Code § 55–7B–6d was unconstitutional. [The majority concluded that the statute was unconstitutional and turned to the severability issue.]…

D. The MPLA's Severability Statute

Because of an amendment to the MPLA's Severability statute in 2001, our determination that the non-unanimous verdict provision in W. Va.Code § 55–7B–6d is invalid impacts other provisions of the MPLA.… The MPLA's Severability statute, W. Va.Code § 55–7B–11 (2001) (Supp.2004), reads as follows:

> (b) *If any provision of the amendments to [certain, identified sections], is held invalid, or the application thereof to any person is held invalid, then, notwithstanding any other provision of law, every other provision of said House Bill 601 shall be deemed invalid and of no further force and effect.*

> (c) If any provision of the amendments to [other identified sections] is held invalid, such invalidity shall not affect other provisions or applications of this article, and to this end, such provisions are deemed severable.

(Emphasis added).

A fair reading of the Severability statute indicates that it is a hybrid, *i.e.,* it contains both [a] *severability* provision[] and a *non-severability* provision. It is the non-severability provision, W. Va.Code § 55–7B–11(b), that is relevant to our decision in this case. Under the non-severability provision, the Legislature has determined that, if this Court invalidates [certain provisions], then all of said provisions are invalid. In other words, the non-severability provision has presumptively invalidated the remaining twelve juror provision in [the other specific statutes], as a result of our determination that the non-unanimous verdict provision in W. Va.Code § 55–7B–6d is unconstitutional. The issue of the deference to be accorded a non-severability provision appears to be one of first impression for this Court.

It has been observed that "[a] non-severability clause is almost unheard of and constitutes a legislative finding that every section is so important to the single subject that no part of the act can be removed without destruction of the legislative purpose." Our research indicates that only a few courts have addressed the issue of non-severability provisions. A majority of those courts have enforced non-severability provisions without comment.

A few courts, however, have commented on the degree of deference to be accorded to non-severability provisions. These courts have held that "a non-severability clause cannot ultimately bind a court, it establishes [only] a presumption of non-severability." That is, "[d]espite the unambiguous command of … [non]severability clauses, … they create only a rebuttable presumption that guides—but does not control—a reviewing court's severability determination."

We have discerned from courts and commentators that statutory construction principles that apply to "severability" provisions are equally applicable to "non-severability" provisions. Consequently, we now hold that a non-severability provision contained in a legislative enactment is construed as merely a presumption that the Legislature intended the entire enactment to be invalid if one of the statutes in the legislation is found unconstitutional. When a non-severability provision is appended to a legislative enactment and this Court invalidates a statute contained in the enactment, we will apply severability principles of statutory construction to determine whether the non-severability provision will be given full force and effect.

1. Severability principles of statutory construction. Under this Court's severability principles of statutory construction we do not defer, as a matter of course, to severability provisions contained in statutes. Instead, we engage in an independent analysis to "determine legislative intent and the effect of the severability section of the statute." The reason for this procedure is that a severability provision "provides a rule of construction which may aid in determining legislative intent, 'but it is an aid merely; not an inexorable command.'"

This Court has adopted the following statutory construction principle that is applied in determining the issue of severability:

> A statute may contain constitutional and unconstitutional provisions which may be perfectly distinct and separable so that some may stand and the others will fall; and if, when the unconstitutional portion of the statute is rejected, the remaining portion reflects the legislative will, is complete in itself, is ca-

pable of being executed independently of the rejected portion, and in all other respects is valid, such remaining portion will be upheld and sustained.

The most critical aspect of severability analysis involves the degree of dependency of statutes. Thus, "[w]here the valid and the invalid provisions of a statute are so connected and interdependent in subject matter, meaning, or purpose as to preclude the belief, presumption or conclusion that the Legislature would have passed the one without the other, the whole statute will be declared invalid." ... [the majority then applies this approach to find each of the remaining provisions severable or inseverable.]

♦ MAYNARD, JUSTICE, dissenting:

[T]he majority ... strikes a non-severability provision. The reader should understand that the Legislature passed, as part of its reform package, what I call a "poison pill" non-severability provision. Simply put, it says that if this Court strikes down any part of specified articles in House Bill 601, which makes up part of the Medical Professional Liability Act, then every other provision of House Bill 601 shall be deemed invalid and of no further force and effect. The majority now says the Legislature cannot do that. This I find astonishing. The majority actually says the Legislature cannot reverse a statute *it* passed. It seems to me if the Legislature has the power to enact a law, it certainly has the power to repeal the same law....

♦ BENJAMIN, JUSTICE, concurring, in part, and dissenting, in part:

... I dissent from ... the majority's analysis of the non-severability clause contained in W. Va.Code § 55–7B–11(b). Instead of invalidating the clause in question as unconstitutional, the majority utilizes a statutory interpretation approach to the clause. The result is that the majority premises its invalidity finding on the statutory interpretation of a clause which is clear and unambiguous. Principles of statutory interpretation should only be invoked where the statutory language is ambiguous. The language contained within W. Va.Code § 55–7B–11(b) is not ambiguous and is as clear as any that this Court has been called upon to consider. By its terms, the clause is either a valid exercise of power or it is an invalid attempt to appropriate power. The middle ground of invoking statutory interpretation principles to determine validity is simply not a [sic] option, in my opinion, for deciding the validity of W. Va.Code § 55–7B–11.

I conclude that a legislative body may not, years after it has dissolved and been replaced by a new legislative body, reach out from the grave to invalidate an otherwise valid law of this state in the manner intended by this clause. The insertion of a "poison pill" clause into otherwise valid legislation constitutes a usurpation of this Court's role in determining the validity of lawfully enacted statutes. Our system of governance does not envision legislative "dares" to this Court to not invalidate unconstitutional legislative enactments. A non-severability clause, such as here, improperly seeks to protect an unconstitutional enactment from legitimate scrutiny by the judicial branch by linking it to viability of valid law (law which has been followed and properly relied upon in this State for years). By such "poison pills", the message to this Court is clear—either we permit unconstitutional legislation to stand, or otherwise valid statutes which have been relied upon and used for years by citizens of West Virginia become collateral damage. The Judiciary must resist such an injection of politics into this Court's decisions. This Court's duty to determine the constitutionality of legislation must not be impeded, constrained, threatened or cajoled. Separation of Powers, a foundation of our constitutional system of governance, proscribes any such legislative posturing which would cause us indirectly to do that which we would not do directly.

The non-severability provision of W. Va.Code § 55–7B–11(b) violates the Separation of Powers Clause of our Constitution. It constitutes an improper attempt by the Legislature to usurp this Court's independent consideration of the constitutionality of individual statutes. Any attempt to improperly influence this Court's duty of constitutional scrutiny by hinging the validity of otherwise constitutional legislation upon the requirement that this Court uphold otherwise unconstitutional legislation is intolerable and, therefore, invalid. The 2001 Legislature cannot now act to repeal otherwise valid legislation in 2005. Should the current Legislature seek to do so, it may.

* * *

Points for Discussion

1. *Statutory Language*: What was the language at issue? What did each party want that language to mean? What meaning did the various opinions adopt?

2. *Theories*: Which theory did the majority use? The dissents? Did the majority or dissents find the language ambiguous, absurd, to have a scrivener's error, or to raise a constitutional question?

3. *Presumption of Severability*: If a statute contains neither a severability clause nor an inseverablity clause, the statute is presumably severable. Here, the statute included both a severability clause and an inseverability clause. The majority held that both provisions were presumptive only. Why?

4. *Poison Pills*: The majority rejected the clear language of the inseverability clause, even though the legislature thought about this issue and intended that if certain sections were held to be unconstitutional, the entire act should be struck down. Why was not the clear language in the inseverability clause controlling? Given that this inseverability clause was meant to be a poison pill, did the majority reject the legislative compromise that lead to the statute's enactment?

5. *Purpose of Inseverability Clauses*: "[C]ontroversial legislation sometimes includes an inseverability clause, a clause declaring that, if any one provision of the statute is held invalid, the remainder of the statute shall not have effect." Mark L. Movsesian, *Severability in Statutes and Contracts,* 30 Ga. L. Rev. 41, 77 (1995). Legislatures often include an inseverability provision "in an effort to prevent the courts from sustaining a piece of controversial legislation in the event that they invalidate one central provision." Lars Noah, *The Executive Line Item Veto and the Judicial Power to Sever: What's The Difference?,* 56 Wash. & Lee L. Rev. 235, 237–38 (1999); *see also* Michael D. Shumsky, *Severability, Inseverability, and the Rule of Law,* 41 Harv. J. on Legis. 227, 267–68 (2004) ("When [a legislature] includes an inseverability clause in constitutionally questionable legislation, it

does so in order to insulate a key legislative deal from judicial interference. Such clauses are iron-clad guarantees—clear statements by [the legislature] that it would not have enacted one part of a statute without the others. Legislation containing [a non-]severability clause can thus be conceived of as a contract among competing political interests containing a structural enforcement mechanism designed to alleviate the concerns of those legislators who were willing to vote for ... a particular statutory scheme only if credibly assured that certain limiting provisions would be secure in the enacted legislation."); Fred Kameny, *Are Inseverability Clauses Constitutional?*, 68 Alb. L. Rev. 997, 1001-2 (2005) (claiming that inseverability clauses represent an attempt by the legislature to prevent the judiciary from exercising judicial review altogether).

6. *Interpretation or Invalidation*: The majority interpreted the inseverability provision, then applied that interpretation to each of the sections of the statute that were identified by the legislature as being non-severable. In contrast, one of the dissents stated that the only judicial role was to evaluate the constitutionality or non-constitutionality of the provision. If constitutional, it should be enforced as written. The other dissent said that inseverability provisions are always unconstitutional because they usurp both judicial and legislative power. Which approach is correct? Did the majority rewrite a statute that as rewritten the legislature did not want to be enforced? Here, we have no doubt that the legislature thought about this issue and tried to address it. Is not the issue then whether the legislature had the power to do so?

7. *Separation of Powers*: Which theory of separation of powers do each of these opinions demonstrate?

* * *

d. Effective Date and Saving Provisions

Often, a bill expressly provides a starting date, known as the *effective date*. If it does not, a federal statute is effective on the date the president signs the bill or on the date that Congress overrides a veto. Because of this default rule, many federal bills, like the John R. Justice Prosecutor and Defenders Incentive Act, do not include an effective date provision. But if an act is to be effective on a date other than the signing date, Congress must provide that effective date in the bill.

States take a variety of approaches to this issue. Most commonly, a state's constitution or a statute will provide a default date for any statute not containing an effective date provision. For example, in Alaska, a bill takes effect at 12:01 a.m. on the ninetieth day after the governor signs it, unless the legislature specifies a different date. Alaska Const. art. II, § 18; Alaska Stat. Ann. § 01.10.070 (West 2015). The Texas Constitution states that a bill becomes effective 91 days from the date of the legislature's final adjournment. Texas Const. art III, § 39 (West 2015).

Generally, effective date provisions raise few interpretation issues. *But see Fowler v. State*, 70 P.3d 1106, 1109 (Alaska 2003) (holding that an act with an effective date provision that preceded the governor's signature was effective the day after the governor actually signed the bill, even though that day was a state holiday). In the case below, a child's future hinges on an effective date provision. As you read this case, determine whether the issue is the effective date of the statute or the statute's retroactivity.

Sims v. Adoption Alliance
Court of Appeals of Texas
922 S.W.2d 213 (Tx. Ct. App. 1996)

◆ JUSTICE HARDBERGER [with whom CHAPA, C.J., and GREEN, J. join].

This heart-rending case, which ultimately may have no winners, pits the clear language of a statute against equity. Judges on the campaign trail always promise they will uphold the law as written, and not what they wish was written. The separation of powers doctrine requires such obedience. Having so promised, and being so bound by law, we follow the statute.

At the heart of the case is a little baby girl, whom in the quaint way of the law, is referred to as Baby Girl Sims: born into this world in San Antonio on August 17, 1995. Her biological mother is Rena Sims. Long before Baby Girl Sims was born, Rena had decided she did not want to keep the child. She responded to an advertisement that had been placed in the *TV Guide* by the future adoptive parents, Michael and Sherry Hollander. She visited them in their Long Island home in New York. Michael owns a diesel repair business; Sherry is a former teacher. They have no children. All indications are they would be, and are, suitable loving parents. Arrangements were lawfully made between the parties through the Adoption Alliance and the adoption plans were finalized. The Hollanders were to take the baby at birth.

There is little to recommend the biological father that is developed in the record. He beat Rena, never married her, abandoned her while she was pregnant, and sent her no money even though he knew she was pregnant. She was very much on her own, and this, no doubt influenced her to give the child up for adoption when she was born.

Rena signed the affidavit of voluntary relinquishment twenty-six (26) hours after the birth. There were no allegations of coercion or lack of understanding. There is no evidence that Rena was suffering from the effects of any medication she may have been given during the birth. The Adoption Alliance filed suit for termination of parental rights on August 22, 1995. Some time after she signed the affidavit, Rena changed her mind. The record reveals that the change of heart was, at least in part, prompted by a phone conversation with the biological father who promised Rena some sort of financial help. Rena Sims filed her answer opposing the termination on August 30, 1995.

The trial court held a hearing on the merits on September 8, 1995. At the hearing, the court ordered that Rena Sims' parental rights be terminated and that the Adoption Alliance be appointed managing conservator. The trial judge signed the order on September 12, 1995. Rena Sims also filed a motion for writ of habeas corpus which was denied on September 29, 1995. The trial court made an express finding of fact that termination of Rena Sims' parental rights was in the best interest of Baby Girl

Sims. That finding has not been challenged on appeal. The Hollanders have had Baby Girl Sims since she was released from the hospital.

In the past this would have been the end of the matter. But the Texas legislature in 1995 had just passed legislation that required that a biological mother must wait forty-eight (48) hours after the birth of the child before signing an affidavit of relinquishment. The law didn't go into effect until September 1, 1995, so when Rena signed the relinquishment affidavit on August 18 there was no such requirement. But, the legislature had added that this new law, while it didn't take effect until September 1, would apply to pending suits even if they had been filed before September 1st. Thus, this lawsuit.

... Rena Sims argues that the trial court erred in concluding that the forty-eight (48) hour waiting period for voluntary relinquishment of parental rights did not apply to the affidavit she signed. Rena Sims contends that if the forty-eight (48) hour waiting period applies to her then the affidavit she signed is ineffective and no grounds for termination exist under Texas Family Code § 161.001.

In 1995, the Texas Legislature amended several provisions of the Family Code. Among the changes, the legislature provided that a biological mother must wait forty-eight (48) hours after the birth of her child before signing an affidavit of relinquishment. Specifically, the new law states: "An affidavit for voluntary relinquishment of parental rights must be: (1) signed after the birth of the child, but not before 48 hours after the birth of the child, by the parent, whether or not a minor, whose parental rights are to be relinquished...." Act of June 16, 1995, 74th Leg., R.S., ch. 751, 1995 Tex.Sess.Law Serv. 214 (codified at Tex.Fam.Code § 161.103). The effective date of the enacted legislation provides as follows: "This Act takes effect September 1, 1995 and applies to a pending suit affecting the parent-child relationship without regard to whether the suit was commenced before, on, or after the effective date of this Act." *Id.* Baby Girl Sims was born on August 17, 1995 and the affidavit of relinquishment was signed on August 18, 1995. The lawsuit to terminate Rena Sims' parental rights was filed on August 22, 1995. Rena Sims filed a motion for habeas corpus relief on September 1, 1995. The hearing on the merits was held on September 8, 1995. Sims contends that the forty-eight (48) hour waiting period applies to her because the suit was pending on September 1, 1995.

When a disputed statute is clear and unambiguous, rules of statutory construction are inappropriate and the statute should be given its plain meaning. *Cail v. Service Motors, Inc.,* 660 S.W.2d 814, 815 (Tex.1983); *Ex Parte Roloff,* 510 S.W.2d 913, 915 (Tex.1974). In this case, the unambiguous language of the statute provides that the new law, which includes the forty-eight (48) hour waiting period, applies to any cases "pending" on September 1, 1995. An action or suit is pending from the time of its inception until the rendition of final judgment. The statute in question specifically provides that it "takes effect September 1, 1995 and applies to a pending suit affecting the parent-child relationship without regard to whether the suit was commenced before, on, or after the effective date of this Act." This language unambiguously covers the present situation. The affidavit of relinquishment was signed on August 18, 1995 some twenty-six hours after the child was born. It really cannot be argued that this lawsuit was not "pending" on September 1, 1995, and we so hold. The termination was not completed until September 8, 1995. These facts are undisputed. The plain meaning of the statute controls. The forty-eight (48) hour waiting period was applicable to the suit to terminate Rena Sims' parental rights.

The Adoption Alliance argues that the legislature never intended the effective date language of this bill to apply to the forty-eight (48) hour waiting period. In support of this argument, The Adoption Alliance points out that the effective date provision in the bill does not specifically refer to the forty-eight (48) hour waiting period. Furthermore, the effective date provision and the forty-eight (48) hour provision are twenty-one (21) pages apart in the bill itself. Finally, the forty-eight (48) hour provision was added as an amendment to a much larger bill. For these reasons, The Adoption Alliance argues that the legislature never intended for the forty-eight (48) hour waiting period to apply retroactively. We are not persuaded by these arguments.

Statutes are presumed to be prospective unless expressly made retroactive. Tex.Gov't Code § 311.022 (Vernon 1990). As previously discussed, the language of the effective date provision makes the forty-eight (48) hour waiting period retroactive. The effective date of the bill applies to the entire bill, including the forty-eight (48) hour waiting period. The Adoption Alliance has failed to cite any authority for the proposition that an effective date provision applies only to some parts of a bill but not others. Furthermore, we know of no law that says an effective date provision does not apply to a particular part of a bill just because they are separated by twenty-one (21) pages or however many pages. This court is not free to ignore the plain meaning of the statute. We conclude that the effective date provision applies to the forty-eight (48) waiting period. . . .

We . . . hold that Texas Family Code § 161.103(a)(1), which provides for a forty-eight (48) hour waiting period between the birth of a child and the signing of an affidavit of relinquishment, is applicable to the present case because it was pending on September 1, 1995. We further hold that the affidavit in this case was invalid because it was signed twenty-six (26) hours after the birth. We can understand a caring trial court, focused on the best interest of the infant, ruling as she did. But the affidavit of relinquishment was invalid and the trial court erred in terminating the parental rights of Rena Sims on that basis.

♦ JUSTICE GREEN, concurring.

The outcome in this case is tragic, and it is with great reluctance that I concur in the result.

The result is wrong when judged on the basis of whether it is in the best interest of the child. The result is wrong when judged on the basis of whether it is fair and just. And the result is wrong when judged on the basis of sympathy and emotion. Indeed, one has only to read the anguished testimony of Mr. and Mrs. Hollander at the habeas corpus hearing to gain an understanding of the horror they were experiencing at the prospect of losing their adopted child. But this case cannot be decided on the basis of such standards. Unhappily, we are instead compelled by our oaths of office to apply the pertinent law to the facts, and we have no discretion in this instance. Under these facts, however, the faceless, unemotional objectivity of the law does not seem well-suited.

Ironically, the result in this case occurs despite the good intentions of those acting to protect against just this result. In adding the 48-hour waiting period to the voluntary relinquishment provision of the termination statute, I am sure the legislature intended to strengthen the finality of the procedure for terminating parental rights. As applied to these facts, however, the legislation instead provides appellant with a legal loophole to escape the consequences of her "irrevocable" affidavit relinquishing her rights to Baby Girl Sims. This is a nightmare scenario for any adoptive family; to the Hollander's, it is now a terrible reality.

The affidavit of relinquishment signed by appellant was valid and enforceable when it was signed on August 18, 1995. Had the termination suit based on the affidavit been disposed of prior to September 1, 1995, appellant would have had no recourse. If the affidavit had been signed twenty-two (22) hours later than it was, Baby Girl Sims would remain the adopted daughter of her new and obviously very devoted and loving parents. It cannot be right that a legal technicality—the difference of a mere twenty-two hours, or even a delay of thirteen days—should have such an enormous impact when speaking of the life of a child. The effect on either the Hollander's or Baby Girl Sims is not at all assuaged by the trite explanation that it is what the law requires.

Justice Hardberger was correct in noting that this is a heart-rending case. The law has failed in this instance to protect the child in whose best interests we purportedly act.

* * *

Points for Discussion

1. *Statutory Language*: What was the language at issue? What did each party want that language to mean? What meaning did the majority adopt?

2. *Theories*: Which theory did the majority use? Did the majority find the language ambiguous, absurd, to have a scrivener's error, or to raise a constitutional question?

3. *Statutory Directive*: You may recall that Texas has a statutory directive that is purposive in nature. (*See* Chapter 4). Yet the majority did not cite the statute, citing two cases instead. The court then adopted a different approach. Why do you think the majority ignored the statute?

4. *Effective Date Provision*: What were the adoption agency's arguments as to why the effective date provision did not apply to the 48 hour waiting period? How did the court respond to those arguments? Do you agree with the court or the agency?

5. *Retroactivity*: In many ways, the issue is this case was not about the statute's effective date. All parties agreed on the effective date. The disagreement centered

around whether that date applied to all parts of the statute, thus making the statute retroactive in some situations. While statutes are presumptively prospective, that presumption can be overcome. Why was that presumption overcome here?

6. *Separation of Powers*: What role did the judge's view of separation of powers play in the outcome of this case? All the judges seemed to agree that the result was contrary to the statutory purpose. Given that Texas has a purposivist directive, is the outcome wrong?

* * *

Related to effective date provisions are *saving provisions*. Such provisions "save," or exempt, behavior or legal relationships that existed before or on the effective date of a new law. Our sample bill does not have a savings provision. Another example has been provided in the box below. These provisions are commonly used when a penal statute is amended or repealed. For example, when many states raised the drinking age in the 1980s from eighteen to twenty-one, those individuals who were between eighteen and twenty on the date the law took effect were "grandfathered," meaning they could legally continue to drink alcohol despite being underage.

Component: Savings Provision

SECTION 9. SAVING PROVISION

(a) The change in law made by this Act applies only to an offense committed on or after the effective date of this Act. For purposes of this section, an offense is committed before the effective date of this Act if any element of the offense occurs before that date.

(b) An offense committed before the effective date of this Act is covered by the law in effect when the offense was committed, and the former law is continued in effect for that purpose.

---

* * *

e. Sunset Provisions

A sunset provision terminates, or repeals, all or portions of an act after a specific date, unless further legislative action is taken to extend the act. *Acree v. Republic of Iraq*, 370 F.3d 41, 62 (D.C. Ct. App. 2004) (Roberts, J., concurring) ("'[s]unsetting laws does not mean repealing them. Laws would only expire if Congress failed to meet its responsibility to reexamine and renew these statutes within a specified period of time.'") (quoting S.REP. NO. 104-85, at 64 (1995) (statement of Sen. Grams)).

Most laws do not have sunset provisions; in such cases, the law goes on indefinitely. The John R. Justice Prosecutor and Defenders Incentive Act does not have a sunset provision.

Perhaps the most famous act that includes a sunset provision is the U.S. Patriot Act. Under the sunset provision in that Act, many of the surveillance sections were set to expire in December of 2005. Congress has temporarily extended these sections repeatedly. Tax statutes often have sunset provisions as well. *See, e.g.,* Economic Growth and Tax Relief Reconciliation Act of 2001 (Pub.L. 107–16, 115 Stat. 38, June 7, 2001); *cf.* Violent Crime Control and Law Enforcement Act of 1994 (Pub.L. 103-322, 108 Stat. 1796, September 13, 1994); V.T.C.A., Water Code § 5.014 (West 2015).

f. Exceptions and Provisos

Exceptions, also known as *provisos*, are provisions or clauses that limit the effect of a statutory provision. In other words, provisos create an exception or limit a general rule. They typically begin with the words "except for," "provided however," and "provided that." Hence, they are also called provisos. Because provisos exempt something from an act's reach or qualify something within the act, provisos are generally narrowly construed. Narrow interpretation makes sense because the statute provides a general rule while the proviso limits that general rule or provides an exception to it. Thus, any limit or exception should be confined to its express and clear terms. Otherwise, the proviso's exception could swallow the general rule.

The proviso canon is somewhat similar to *expressio unius* in that both are canons of negative implication. However, application of the proviso canon leads to a result that is opposite to that of the application of *expressio unius*. With *expressio unius*, that which is omitted in the statute is *omitted* in the statute's application; in contrast, with exceptions and provisos, that which is omitted in the exception or proviso is *included* in statute's application. *See, e.g., Gay & Lesbian Law Students Ass'n v. Board of Trustees*, 673 A.2d 484, 473–74 (Conn. 1996).

The case below is not an easy case to read because it involves three acts that must be read together. First, the Foreign Sovereign Immunities Act, (FISA), 28 U.S.C. § 1605(a)(7), specifically prohibited federal courts from hearing claims against foreign states except when "money damages are sought" for acts of torture from a state that sponsored terrorism. The plaintiffs filed an action against the Republic of Iraq because sponsored terrorism had caused their injuries. Second, section 1503 of the Emergency Wartime Supplemental Appropriations Act ("EWSAA"), allowed the president to suspend any provision in a third act, the Iraq Sanctions Act (ISA). Section 1503 of EWSAA, which allowed the president to suspend ISA, included eight provisos. One of those eight provisos, which was at issue in the case, allowed the president to "make inapplicable with respect to Iraq [a specific section of the ISA] *or any other provision of law that applies to countries that have supported terrorism.*" (emphasis added).

The issue for the Court was whether the catch-all in the proviso—"any other provision of law"—gave the president (1) the power to suspend any law involving Iraq (including the FISA), or (2) the power to suspend only laws relating to the ISA. As you read the case, see if you can identify the canon regarding provisos that the majority applies. How does the dissent's proviso canon differ?

Acree v. Republic Of Iraq

United States Court of Appeals District of Columbia Circuit
370 F.3d 41 (D.C. Cir. 2004)

♦ CIRCUIT JUDGE EDWARDS [with whom TATEL, J. concurs.]

The facts in this case are undisputed. While serving in the Gulf War..., Colonel Clifford Acree and 16 other American soldiers ... were captured and held as prisoners of war in Kuwait and the Republic of Iraq between January and March 1991. On April 4, 2002, these POWs and their close family members filed a complaint in the District Court against the Republic of Iraq, the Iraqi Intelligence Service, and Saddam Hussein, in his official capacity as President of Iraq, for personal injuries caused to them and their family members as a result of their treatment by Iraq. In their complaint, the POW plaintiffs described brutal and inhumane acts of physical and psychological torture suffered during their captivity, including severe beatings, starvation, mock executions, dark and unsanitary living conditions, and other violent and shocking acts....

Jurisdiction in the plaintiffs' lawsuit was based on the terrorism exception to the Foreign Sovereign Immunities Act, 28 U.S.C. § 1605(a)(7) [FSIA]. Under the FSIA, foreign states enjoy immunity from suit in American courts.... Section 1605(a)(7) ... creates an exception to foreign sovereign immunity in civil suits "in which money damages are sought against a foreign state for personal injury or death that was caused by an act of torture" or other terrorist acts. 28 U.S.C. § 1605(a)(7). This exception applies only if the defendant foreign state was designated as a state sponsor of terrorism at the time the alleged acts of torture occurred.... [T]he Republic of Iraq was designated as a state sponsor of terrorism on September 13, 1990.... Iraq was therefore amenable to suit in federal court under the FSIA at the time the plaintiffs commenced their lawsuit....

... [T]he District Court entered final judgment in favor of appellees ... [and] awarded compensatory and punitive damages ... totaling over $959 million....

In April 2003, Congress enacted the Emergency Wartime Supplemental Appropriations Act ("EWSAA" or "Act"), ... Of particular relevance to this appeal, § 1503 of the EWSAA ... "[p]rovided further, [t]hat the President may make inapplicable with respect to Iraq section 620A of the Foreign Assistance Act of 1961 or any other provision of law that applies to countries that have supported terrorism." [EWSAA § 1503.]....

On May 7, 2003, President Bush ... issu[ed a] Presidential Determination, ... which "ma(d)e inapplicable with respect to Iraq [a specific statute] and any other provision of law that applies to countries that have supported terrorism." In a message to Congress delivered on May 22, 2003, President Bush explained the need to protect Iraqi assets from attachment, judgment, or other judicial process, and stated his view that the May 7 Determination applied to, *inter alia*, the terrorism exception to the FSIA, 28 U.S.C. § 1605(a)(7)....

This case requires us to consider whether § 1503 of the EWSAA, as implemented by the May 7 Presidential Determination, makes the terrorism exception to the FSIA inapplicable with respect to Iraq. While it is a close question, we agree with appellees that 28 U.S.C. § 1605(a)(7) is not a provision of law that falls within the scope of § 1503....

... It is uncontested that at the time appellees commenced their lawsuit in April 2002, the District Court had jurisdiction over the case under § 1605(a)(7), because appellees sought damages for injuries arising from alleged acts of torture that occurred while Iraq was designated as a state sponsor of terrorism. The United States now argues that § 1503 of the EWSAA, as implemented by the May 7 Presidential Determination, made § 1605(a)(7) inapplicable to Iraq and thereby divested the District Court of its jurisdiction in appellees' case. Appellees respond that § 1605(a)(7) is not a provision of law that falls within the scope of § 1503 of the EWSAA....

This issue presents us with a basic question of statutory interpretation. We therefore begin with the language of the EWSAA. Section 1503 provides, in its entirety:

> The President may suspend the application of any provision of the Iraq Sanctions Act of 1990: *Provided,* That nothing in this section shall affect the applicability of the Iran–Iraq Arms Non–Proliferation Act of 1992, except that such Act shall not apply to humanitarian assistance and supplies: ***Provided further, That the President may make inapplicable with respect to Iraq section 620A of the Foreign Assistance Act of 1961 or any other provision of law that applies to countries that have supported terrorism:**** *Provided further,* That military equipment, as defined by title XVI, section 1608(1)(A) of Public Law 102–484, shall not be exported under the authority of this section: *Provided further,* That section 307 of the Foreign Assistance Act of 1961 shall not apply with respect to programs of international organizations for Iraq: *Provided further,* That provisions of law that direct the United States Government to vote against or oppose loans or other uses of funds, including for financial or technical assistance, in international financial institutions for Iraq shall not be construed as applying to Iraq: *Provided further,* That the President shall submit a notification 5 days prior to exercising any of the authorities described in this section to the Committee on Appropriations of each House of the Congress, the Committee on Foreign Relations of the Senate, and the Committee on International Relations of the House of Representatives: *Provided further,* That not more than 60 days after enactment of this Act and every 90 days thereafter the President shall submit a report to the Committee on Appropriations of each House of the Congress, the Com-

---

* Editor's footnote: bolding has been added to help the reader identify the proviso at issue.

mittee on Foreign Relations of the Senate, and the Committee on International Relations of the House of Representatives containing a summary of all licenses approved for export to Iraq of any item on the Commerce Control List contained in the Export Administration Regulations, including identification of end users of such items: *Provided further,* That the authorities contained in this section shall expire on September 30, 2004, or on the date of enactment of a subsequent Act authorizing assistance for Iraq and that specifically amends, repeals or otherwise makes inapplicable the authorities of this section, whichever occurs first.

The controversy in this case concerns the second proviso of § 1503, authorizing the President to "make inapplicable with respect to Iraq section 620A of the Foreign Assistance Act of 1961 or *any other provision of law that applies to countries that have supported terrorism." Id.* (emphasis added). The United States argues that this language embraces the authority to make § 1605(a)(7) inapplicable to Iraq, and that the President carried out that authority in the May 7 Presidential Determination.

The logic of this interpretation is straightforward: Section 1605(a)(7) creates an exception to the sovereign immunity normally enjoyed by foreign states in American courts for suits based on acts of torture or other terrorist acts. This exception applies only if the defendant foreign state was designated as a sponsor of terrorism at the time the acts took place. Section 1605(a)(7) is thus a "provision of law that applies to countries that have supported terrorism." The EWSAA authorizes the President to make such provisions inapplicable to Iraq, which authority the President exercised in the May 7 Determination. Section 1605(a)(7) therefore no longer applies to Iraq and cannot provide a basis for jurisdiction in appellees' case....

The difficulty with this view is that it focuses exclusively on the meaning of one clause of § 1503, divorced from all that surrounds it. This approach violates "the cardinal rule that a statute is to be read as a whole, since the meaning of statutory language, plain or not, depends on context." In interpreting any statute, we must "'consider not only the bare meaning' of the critical word or phrase 'but also its placement and purpose in the statutory scheme.'"

Traditional interpretive canons ... counsel against a reading of the second proviso of § 1503 that ignores the context of § 1503 and the EWSAA as a whole. In particular, the canons of *noscitur a sociis* and *ejusdem generis* remind us that "[w]here general words follow specific words in a statutory enumeration, the general words are construed to embrace only objects similar in nature to those objects enumerated by the preceding specific words." In addition, where statutory language is phrased as a proviso, the presumption is that its scope is confined to that of the principal clause to which it is attached.

Applying the foregoing principles, we conclude that the scope of § 1503 is narrower than the Government suggests....

Section 1503 ... authorizes the President to suspend the application of any provision of the Iraq Sanctions Act of 1990 [ISA], subject to eight provisos. Three of the provisos impose notification or reporting requirements and provide for expiration of the suspension authority granted in § 1503. The remaining provisos are each responsive to a specific aspect of the ISA or other statutes that are implicated by the suspension authority granted in § 1503, thereby resolving potential ambiguities that may arise in the statutory landscape as a result of the suspension of the ISA. Thus, the first proviso, stating that nothing in § 1503 shall affect the applicability of the Iran–Iraq Arms Non–Proliferation Act of 1992, reflects the fact that portions of the Non–Proliferation Act incorporate the ISA by reference and are to remain in effect despite suspension of the ISA. Similarly, the fifth proviso states that "provisions of law that direct the United States Government to vote against or oppose loans or other uses of funds, including for financial or technical assistance, in international financial institutions for Iraq shall not be construed as applying to Iraq." This language responds in part to § 586G(a)(5) of the ISA, which requires the United States to oppose any loan or financial or technical assistance to Iraq by international financial institutions, pursuant to other provisions of law incorporated into the ISA. *See* ISA § 586G(a)(5), 104 Stat.1979, 2052. This fifth proviso thus makes clear that the President may suspend not only the ISA, but also those provisions of law that are incorporated by reference into the ISA's prohibition on American support for assistance to Iraq from international financial institutions. The remaining provisos are similarly tied to specific features of the ISA and the other statutes with which the ISA interacts.

The second proviso of § 1503 — which lies at the heart of the controversy in the instant case — provides that "the President may make inapplicable with respect to Iraq section 620A of the Foreign Assistance Act of 1961 or any other provision of law that applies to countries that have supported terrorism." Just like the other provisos in § 1503, this language is responsive to a particular section of the ISA. As we have seen, the ISA required that certain enumerated provisions of law, including § 620A of the Foreign Assistance Act of 1961, and "all other provisions of law that impose sanctions against a country which has repeatedly provided support for acts of international terrorism" be fully enforced against Iraq. The second proviso in § 1503 thus makes clear that the authority in § 1503 to suspend the ISA includes the authority to make inapplicable to Iraq § 620A of the FAA and those additional provisions of law incorporated into § 586F(c) of the ISA. . . .

To recapitulate, the meaning of the disputed language in § 1503, like each of the other substantive provisos in that section, is thus illuminated by consideration of the corresponding provisions of the ISA. *See Morrow,* 266 U.S. at 534–35, ("The general office of a proviso is to except something from the enacting clause, or to qualify and restrain its generality and prevent misinterpretation. Its grammatical and logical scope is confined to the subject-matter of the principal clause.") (citations omitted). The reference in § 586F(c) of the ISA to § 620A of the FAA and "all other provisions of law" that impose sanctions on state sponsors of terrorism appears clearly to encompass laws which, like the FAA and the other enumerated provisions, impose obstacles to assistance to designated countries. None of these provisions remotely suggests any relation to the jurisdiction of the federal courts. Thus, when read in juxtaposition with this portion of the ISA, the second proviso of § 1503 is more persuasively interpreted as sharing a similar scope. That is, it authorizes the President to make inapplicable with respect to Iraq those provisions of law that impose economic sanctions on Iraq or that present legal obstacles to the provision of assistance to the Iraqi Government. This interpretation reflects a central function of Chapter 5 of the EWSAA, which is to provide for relief and reconstruction in post-war Iraq.

Although sparse, the legislative history of § 1503 of the EWSAA likewise supports our interpretation of the disputed language in § 1503....

Having concluded that jurisdiction in this case properly lies in the District Court, we ... conclude that appellees have failed to state a cause of action....

◆ CIRCUIT JUDGE ROBERTS, concurring in part and concurring in the judgment:

... I ... concur in the court's judgment of dismissal, but I reach that result by a different path than the majority has taken. In my view, Section 1503 of the EWSAA includes the authority to make Section 1605(a)(7) of the FSIA—on its face a "provision of law that applies to countries that have supported terrorism"—inapplicable to Iraq, and the Presidential Determination of May 7, 2003 therefore ousted the federal courts of jurisdiction in cases that relied on that exception to Iraq's sovereign immunity. I also conclude that this ouster of jurisdiction is properly applied to pending cases, and that the district court's judgment should thus be vacated and the case dismissed for want of jurisdiction.

The pertinent language of Section 1503 is straightforward, authorizing the President to make inapplicable to Iraq Section 620A of the Foreign Assistance Act of 1961 and "*any* other provision of law that applies to countries that have supported terrorism" (emphasis added). As this court recently observed, "the Supreme Court has consistently instructed that statutes written in broad, sweeping language should be given broad, sweeping application." "Any other provision" should be read to mean "any other provision," not, as the majority would have it, "provisions that present obstacles to assistance and funding for the new Iraqi Government."

This is particularly true given that Congress knows how to use more limited language along the lines of the majority's construction when it wants to. Congress did just that in another ... statute enacted just two months prior to the EWSAA. In that statute, Congress declared that certain restrictions on funding to foreign countries should not be construed to restrict assistance to nongovernmental organizations in those countries, but provided that this easing of restrictions would not apply "with respect to section 620A of the Foreign Assistance Act of 1961 or any *comparable* provision of law *prohibiting assistance* to countries that support international terrorism." Consolidated Appropriations Resolution, 2003, Pub. L. No. 108-7, Div. E, § 537(c)(1), 117 Stat. 11, 196 (Feb. 20, 2003) (emphases added). The EWSAA, of course, refers to the very same section of the Foreign Assistance Act but includes substantially broader language in its subsequent catchall phrase. This use of different language in two statutes so analogous in their form and content, enacted so close in time, suggests that the statutes differ in their meaning, and that the facially broader language was in fact intended to have the broader scope....

I agree with the majority that this question of statutory interpretation is close, and I do not suggest that the EWSAA is entirely unambiguous. But the plaintiffs err in their assumption that the government must somehow prove that Congress intended the statute's broad terms to be construed broadly. The burden is precisely the opposite: the party seeking to narrow the application of the statute must demonstrate that Congress intended something less than what the law on its face says. And as this court has stated, "the plainer the language, the more convincing contrary legislative history must be." ...

... The majority can cite *United States v. Morrow*, 266 U.S. 531 (1925), for a presumption that supports its construction of the pertinent proviso, but I can respond with a case of similar vintage for the opposite proposition that "a frequent use of the proviso in Federal legislation [is] to introduce ... new matter extending rather than limiting or explaining that which has gone before." *Interstate Commerce Comm'n v. Baird*, 194 U.S. 25, 37 (1904).

In such circumstances I prefer to rest on the firmer foundation of the statutory language itself. Give me English words over Latin maxims. The words here — "any other provision of law that applies to countries that have supported terrorism" — are, even if not entirely unambiguous, plain enough to impose a heavy burden on those who would rely on canons, or structure, or assumed purposes to conclude the words do not reach a law that applies, by its terms, to a foreign state "designated as a state sponsor of terrorism." 28 U.S.C. § 1605(a)(7)(A). The majority ably marshals the arguments on the other side, but at the end of the day I find greater solace in the words themselves. *See Connecticut Nat'l Bank v. Germain*, 503 U.S. 249, 253–54 (1992) ("canons of construction are no more than rules of thumb that help courts determine the meaning of legislation, and in interpreting a statute a court should always turn first to one, cardinal canon before all others. We have stated time and again that courts must presume that a legislature says in a statute what it means and means in a statute what it says there.")....

* * *

Points for Discussion

1. *Statutory Language*: What was the language at issue? What did each party want that language to mean? What meaning did the majority and concurrence adopt?

2. *Theories*: Which theory did the majority use? The concurrence? Did the majority or concurrence find the language ambiguous, absurd, to have a scrivener's error, or to raise a constitutional question?

3. *Provisos*: Both the majority and concurrence noted that the proviso canon should apply, but they described the canon differently. How did they describe the proviso canon? The majority's approach narrowed the broad language in the catch-all, while the concurrence left the language broad. Which approach do you find more persuasive and why?

4. *Intrinsic Sources*: Other than the proviso canon, what other linguistic canons did the majority use to limit the broad reach of this proviso? Are these arguments

convincing? The concurrence seemed to stop at the first step of interpretation, finding the language clear and very broad. Despite criticizing the linguistic canons, does not the concurrence rely on *in pari materia* and either the identical words presumption or *noscitur a sociis*? He reasoned that Congress used narrower language in the Consolidated Appropriates Resolution and that the "use of different language in two statutes so analogous in their form and content, enacted so close in time, suggests that the statutes differ in their meaning, and that the facially broader language was in fact intended to have the broader scope."

5. *Wilmot Proviso*: Representative David Wilmot introduced this famous proviso in the House of Representatives in 1846 as a rider to a $2 million appropriations bill, which President Polk had introduced to facilitate negotiations with Mexico over the settlement of the Mexican-American War. The proposed language read:

> Provided, That, as an express and fundamental condition to the acquisition of any territory from the Republic of Mexico by the United States by virtue of any treaty which may be negotiated between them, and to the use by the Executive of the money herein appropriated, neither slavery nor involuntary servitude shall ever exist in any part of said territory except for crime, whereof the party shall first be duly convicted.

Louise Weinberg, *Dred Scott and the Crisis of 1860*, 82 Chi.-Kent L. Rev. 97, 99 (2007) (quoting Chaplain W. Morrison, Democratic Politics and Sectionalism: The Wilmot Proviso Controversy 18 (1967)). Wilmot's purpose in submitting the proviso was to prevent slavery from being introduced into any territory the United States acquired from Mexico. While the House approved the bill with the proviso included, Congress adjourned before the Senate could vote on it; thus, the bill and its proviso failed. Yet, some commentators have suggested that this proviso may have been one cause of the Civil War.

* * *

This chapter, components, was our last on intrinsic sources. It might have surprised you that some components are less relevant to interpretation than are the linguistic canons and other intrinsic sources; however, England's influence in this area continues to have an impact. After the problem, we turn to the first of our extrinsic sources, those sources related to conflicting and related statutes.

Problem 9

Read the two cases below. Then answer the questions that follow.

Dixon v. Florida

Florida District Court of Appeals
812 So. 2d 595 (Fla. Dist. Ct. App. 2002)

◆ Per Curiam.

Richard L. Dixon appeals his convictions for forgery of a written instrument and driving without a valid driver's license. He argues that the trial court erred in denying his motion *in limine* by which he sought to exclude, on the authority of section 316.650(9), Florida Statutes (2000), the admission into evidence of a traffic citation issued to him. Because the language of section 316.650(9) unambiguously provides that traffic citations are not admissible in any trial, we must reverse.

Upon being stopped by a police officer following the commission of several traffic infractions, appellant provided a false name to the officer. That name was placed on the traffic citation, which appellant signed using the false name. When it was learned that appellant gave a false name, he was charged with forgery under section 831.01 and driving without a valid driver's license. By his motion *in limine*, appellant sought to preclude the admission of the traffic citation into evidence. The trial court denied the motion....

Florida courts have recognized that signing another person's name to a traffic citation constitutes a forgery. Nevertheless, section 316.650(9) provides that a traffic citation "shall not be admissible evidence in any trial." The statute contains no exceptions to this clear and unambiguous prohibition. It is a well-established principle of statutory interpretation that an unambiguous statute is not subject to judicial construction, no matter how wise it may seem to alter the plain language of the statute. "Moreover, '[e]ven where a court is convinced that the legislature really meant and intended something not expressed in the phraseology of the act, it will not deem itself authorized to depart from the plain meaning of the language which is free from ambiguity.'" Further, although courts may interpret a statute to give effect to discernable legislative intent even though such intent may contradict the strict language of the statute, here we have been presented with no basis to discern a legislative intent contrary to the unambiguous language of section 315.650(9).

Courts should go behind the unambiguous meaning of the words in a statute only when "an unreasonable or ridiculous conclusion" would result from failure to do so. While following the unambiguous mandate of section 315.650(9) will make convictions for forgery of a traffic citation more difficult, the application of the plain and ordinary meaning of the words of the statute do not lead to either an unreasonable or ridiculous result. As the Florida Supreme Court stated in [another case]:

> We trust that if the legislature did not intend the result mandated by the statute's plain language, the legislature itself will amend the statute at the next opportunity.

Accordingly, in view of the absolute mandatory terms of section 316.650(9), we conclude that the trial court erred in denying appellant's motion....

* * *

Maddox v. Florida

Florida District Court of Appeals
862 So.2d 783 (Fla. Dist. Ct. App. 2003)

◆ Davis, Judge.

Robert E. Maddox challenges his convictions and sentences.... We affirm Maddox's convictions and sentences without comment but write to address the issue of the admissibility of the forged traffic citations at his trial.

A Polk County Deputy Sheriff stopped Maddox for an improper lane change. Upon being asked for his driver's license and proof of insurance, Maddox advised the deputy that he did not have his license or proof of insurance with him. The deputy then asked for his name and date of birth, in response to which Maddox said his name was Nathaniel Lewis Maddox and his date of birth was November 1, 1980. Based on this information, the deputy issued two citations in the name of Nathaniel Lewis Maddox—one for improper lane change and the other for failure to produce proof of insurance. When Maddox was hesitant to sign the citations, the deputy advised that failure to sign was a criminal offense. Maddox then signed the citations.

During the traffic stop, a second deputy arrived on the scene. The owner of the car, who had been riding in the front passenger seat, gave permission for the deputies to search the vehicle. During the search, the second deputy found an identification card that identified Maddox as Robert Edwin Maddox. A license check for Robert Edwin Maddox showed that his driver's license was suspended. The deputy retained possession of the two traffic citations issued to Nathaniel Maddox and issued a citation to Maddox charging him with driving while his licensed was suspended. Maddox initially refused to sign this citation but agreed to after the deputy issued him a subsequent citation for refusing to sign a citation. Later, while in custody, Maddox volunteered that Nathaniel Maddox was his brother. Accordingly, Maddox was charged with two counts of forgery for signing the citations issued in the name of Nathaniel and two counts of uttering a forged instrument.

Maddox went to trial on the forgery and uttering counts, as well as on one count of giving false information to a police officer and one count of driving while license suspended. He was found guilty as charged.

On appeal, Maddox argues that, pursuant to section 316.650(9), Florida Statutes (2001), the trial court erred by admitting these traffic citations into evidence. In making this assertion, Maddox relies on the First District's opinion in *Dixon v. State*, 812 So.2d 595, 595 (Fla. 1st DCA 2002) ("Because the language of section 316.650(9) unambiguously provides that traffic citations are not admissible in any trial, we must reverse [appellant's forgery conviction]."). We, however, do not agree with the reasoning in *Dixon*....

[W]e do not believe the trial court erred in admitting the citations as evidence of the forgeries. Although section 316.650(9) does provide that traffic citations "shall not be admissible evidence in any trial," that statutory proscription does not apply to the facts of this case. Based on our reading of the statute, we conclude that the purpose of the statute is to protect the person to whom the citation is issued. Here, the citation was issued to a person the deputy believed to be Nathaniel Maddox; the deputy charged Nathaniel Maddox with two civil infractions. When the deputy learned that Maddox was, in fact, not Nathaniel Maddox, but rather Robert Maddox, he withdrew the charges against Nathaniel Maddox and retained the documents as evidence of the criminal offenses of forgery. Maddox misrepresented himself to be Nathaniel and signed the ticket to carry out the misrepresentation. Maddox was not on trial for either of the civil infractions, nor was Nathaniel Maddox. In fact, after the withdrawal of the citations, the charges of improper lane change and failure to show proof of insurance were no longer pending against anyone. Thus, the documents were not "citations" as contemplated by the statute, but rather were documentary evidence of Maddox's criminal conduct. Thus, the statute does not apply....

* * *

Problem Questions

Assume you are a justice on the Florida Supreme Court and have to draft the opinion for an appeal in *Maddox*. Explain whether any of the information below would be relevant to your decision. Which way would you rule?

(1) the statute at issue is located within the code titled: Florida Uniform Traffic Control Laws;

(2) the codified purpose of the act provides, "It is the legislative intent in the adoption of this chapter to make uniform traffic laws to apply throughout the state and its several counties and uniform traffic ordinances to apply in all municipalities";

(3) the long title of the act is an act *"relating to the regulation of traffic on highway"*;

(4) section 316.066(4) of the Florida Statutes (2001), located in the same chapter of the code as the statutory provision at issue in this case, mandates that neither a crash report nor a statement made in connection with such a report "shall be used as evidence in any trial, civil or criminal."

(5) after the Supreme Court granted review in *Maddox*, the Legislature amended the statute to read as follows: "Such citations shall not be admissible evidence in any trial, *except when used as evidence of falsification, forgery, uttering, fraud, or perjury, or when used as physical evidence resulting from a forensic examination of the citation.*"

Chapter 10

Canons Based on Extrinsic Sources and Legislative Process: Harmonizing Statutes

A. Introduction to This Chapter

In this chapter, we turn from the intrinsic sources to the first of the extrinsic sources: canons regarding conflicting and related statutes. This chapter explains how judges resolve conflicts among statutes, determine when one statute impliedly repeals another, and look to related statutes for guidance. In resolving these issues, judges presume that the legislature intended to act "normally," unless there is evidence that the legislature intended to act otherwise. For example, if two or more statutes address an issue, the statute that was enacted last controls unless there is evidence that the legislature would have wanted one of the earlier statutes to control. Similarly, if one state copies another state's statute, the copying, or borrowing, state also presumptively borrows the judicial interpretations of that statute from the lending state *up to the date of enactment*. But if the borrowing legislature is clear that it did not intend to adopt the judicial interpretations of the other state, then the judicial interpretations do not accompany the borrowed statute.

The topics covered in this chapter highlight the importance of uniformity and harmony when there are multiple statutes across one or more jurisdictions. Let's start with conflicting statutes: What happens when multiple statutes within the same jurisdiction address the same issue?

B. Extrinsic Sources

Before we begin this discussion, a brief reminder might be in order; extrinsic sources are those sources outside of the official act but within the legislative process that created the act. In other words, these are sources intimately related to the enactment process, such as legislative history, purpose, administrative regulations, and the like; but they are separate from the text of the statute at issue.

C. Conflicting Statutes

Sometimes, two sections of one statute or, more commonly, two or more different statutes within one jurisdiction conflict. For example, assume that statute A provides that all criminal defendants are entitled to parole, while statute B provides that only non-violent criminal defendants are entitled to parole. These hypothetical statutes conflict. When a judge is faced with two conflicting statutes or sections of a statute, the judge will first see if the conflict between the two can be reconciled, because the judge will assume that the legislature, when it passed the second statute, did not intend to interfere with or abrogate any existing statutes relating to the same topic. This policy of reconciling first is based on the assumptions that the enacting legislature (1) was aware of all relevant statutes when it enacted the new one, (2) would have expressly repealed or amended an existing statute had the legislature wanted the new statute to replace the existing one, and (3) failed to repeal the existing statute because the legislature intended for both statutes to exist in harmony. These assumptions fail to reflect reality: A legislature cannot possibly know every law that exists when it enacts legislation. And even if the legislature were aware of every existing statute, the conflict between an existing statute and the new statute may not have been apparent when the second statute was enacted. At times, conflicts only appear after a statute has been applied to a particular set of facts. Finally, as we have seen, it is difficult to pass legislation. There are many reasons why the legislature might have chosen not to amend or repeal a conflicting, existing statute. Yet, despite the reality, the assumptions remain.

When conflict cannot be reconciled, judges apply three canons to reconcile the conflict: (1) specific statutory language controls general statutory language, (2) later enacted statutes control earlier enacted statutes, and (3) unless the earlier statute is more specific, repeal by implication is disfavored. Stated simply:

> [i]f statutes appear to conflict, they must be construed, if possible, to give effect to each. If the conflict is irreconcilable, the later enacted statute governs. However, an earlier enacted specific, special, or local statute prevails over a later enacted general statute unless the context of the later enacted statute indicates otherwise.

UNIF. STATUTE & RULE CONSTR. ACT, § 10a (1995). Let's explore each of these canons in more detail, starting with implied repeal. If two statutes so conflict that, despite a judge's best attempts to reconcile them, they are irreconcilable, what should a judge do? How does a judge know whether a statute was meant to be repealed, wholly or partially, and which of two conflicting statutes was meant to apply? These next sections resolve these questions.

1. Specific Statutes

When two statutes conflict and cannot be reconciled, the starting point for the court should be to determine whether one of the two statutes is more specific, because a specific statute should control rather than a general statute. This canon has special force when Congress has enacted a comprehensive statutory scheme, deliberately targeting specific problems with specific solutions. The general-specific canon is often applied to statutes in which a specific prohibition or permission contradicts a general permission or prohibition. To eliminate the contradiction, the specific provision is construed as an exception to the general one. RONALD B. BROWN & SHARON J. BROWN, STATUTORY INTERPRETATION: THE SEARCH FOR LEGISLATIVE INTENT 111 (2d ed. 2011). But the canon applies equally as well to statutes in which a general authorization and a more limited, specific authorization exist side-by-side. "There the canon avoids not contradiction but the superfluity of a specific provision that is swallowed by the general one, 'violat[ing] the cardinal rule that, if possible, effect shall be given to every clause and part of a statute.'" *RadLAX Gateway Hotel, LLC v. Amalgamated Bank*, 132 S. Ct. 2065, 2070–71 (2012). The general-specific canon is not absolute; it is merely a strong indication of statutory meaning and can be overcome.

What is the difference between a general and specific statute? General statutes apply universally, while specific statutes apply in certain situations. Thus, a statute regulating domesticated animals would be general, while one regulating swine would be specific. But determining whether a statute is general or specific can be more difficult than it might seem. *See, e.g., Palm Beach Cty. Canvassing Bd. v. Harris*, 772 So. 2d 1220 (Fla. 2000) (finding one statute more specific because its text and title identified deadlines and penalties for filing late election returns, while the more general statute "only tangentially addresses the penalty for returns filed after the statutory date."). While determining whether one statute is more specific can be challenging, generally, where one statute has a broader application, it is the more general statute. When the general-specific inquiry fails, however, courts apply a second canon: the last-in-time, or later enacted, canon.

2. Later Enacted Statutes

If both statutes are specific or both are general, then judges apply a different tie-breaking canon. The newer statute (or provision) generally trumps the older one (the last-in-time canon). The more recently enacted statute is viewed as the clearest and most recent expression of legislative intent. This last-in-time canon respects the power of each legislature. A legislature has the power to enact laws only while its members are in office. One legislature cannot bind the ability of a future legislature to enact statutes; thus, subsequent legislatures can always amend, repeal, modify, or leave alone a statute. Hence, the latter enacted statute controls to the extent of any inconsistency between it and an existing statute, unless the legislature intended otherwise. Often these two canons—specific versus general and last-in-time—are examined serially in judicial opinions. First, a court should try to reconcile the statutes. If harmony is impossible, then the court should ask whether one statute is more specific. If not, then a court should determine which statute was enacted last. Did either the majority or dissent properly analyze the statutes in the case below? In other words, did they first try to harmonize the statutes, then determine which was more specific, and only as a last resort determine which was enacted last?

Williams v. Kentucky

Court of Appeals of Kentucky

829 S.W.2d 942 (Ky. Ct. App. 1992)

+ HOWERTON, J. [MCDONALD, J., concurs].

P.H.

Robert Williams appeals from his conviction ... for manslaughter, second degree, for which he received a five-year prison sentence. He now argues that the trial court erred ... by refusing to consider alternative sentencing as required by KRS 500.095. Considering all of the particular facts in this case, we find no reversible error and affirm.

Facts

On March 30, 1990, Williams killed Albert Combs with a shotgun.... Williams claims to have acted in self-defense; however, the specific details of the shooting are not necessary to a resolution of the three issues raised by Williams....

Δ arg. →

Williams' ... argument is that the court erred by refusing to consider the alternative sentencing provisions of KRS 500.095. Subsection (1) of that statute, which was enacted in 1990, provides:

most recent statute

> *In every case in which a person* pleads guilty to or *is convicted of a crime punishable by imprisonment, the judge shall* consider whether the person should be sentenced to a term of *community service as an alternative to the prison term....* (Emphasis added.)

The trial court declined to consider alternative sentencing, however, because of KRS 533.060(1), which was enacted in 1976. That statute reads:

old statute

court finds controlling

> *When a person has been convicted of* an offense or has entered a plea of guilty to an offense classified as *a Class A, B, or C felony and the commission* of such offense *involved the use of a weapon from which a shot or projectile may be discharged that is readily capable of producing death* or other serious physical injury, *such person shall not be eligible for probation, shock probation or conditional discharge.* (Emphasis added.)

Williams argues that KRS 500.095 is more specific, and that it was enacted subsequent to KRS 533.060(1), and it is therefore controlling.

Step 3:
Later v. earlier

Several principles of statutory construction come in for consideration in resolving this problem. Where a conflict exists between two statutes, the later statute enacted is generally controlling. This principle standing alone would favor KRS 500.095, which was enacted in 1990. KRS 533.060(1) was enacted in 1976. We also note, however, that where there is conflict between statutes or sections thereof, it is the duty of the court to attempt to harmonize the interpretation so as to give effect to both sections or statutes, if possible. The court must not interpret a statute so as to bring about an absurd or unreasonable result. If we agreed with Williams and concluded that KRS 500.095 were controlling, we would make a nullity of KRS 533.060(1).

Step 1:
Harmonize

Another rule of statutory construction is that specific provisions of a statute take precedence over general provisions. The language in KRS 500.095(1) is very specific when it directs that *in every case* the judge *shall consider* alternatives to prison, but we also note that KRS 533.060(1) is very specific when it directs that anyone convicted of using a firearm in the commission of a Class A, B, or C felony must be sentenced to a term in prison....

... [T]he General Assembly clearly intended to provide severe penalties for convicted and paroled felons who commit subsequent felonies. It is also clear that the General Assembly specifically intended to provide a prison sentence for anyone convicted of using a firearm in the commission of a serious crime.

On the other hand, it is just as clear that the legislature has recognized the need and value for giving the courts some options and alternatives to incarceration when imposing just sentences.... Having to resolve the conflict, we determine that KRS 533.060(1) is controlling over KRS 500.095. If the legislature intends otherwise, it must rewrite several conflicting statutes. Using the principles we have discussed, we could have decided this case either way. However, while digging deeper to find the true legislative intent, we took note of ... additional statutes not otherwise presented and argued in this appeal....

KRS 533.010 was originally enacted in 1974. It authorized probation or conditional discharge in any case except where the death penalty was imposed.... [In 1990,] the General Assembly added an allowance for "probation with an alternative sentencing plan." ... This amendment essentially changed nothing.

[Second, in 1990, the legislature] created KRS 533.070, which ... reads in pertinent part as follows: "In any case where imprisonment is an authorized penalty and *where imprisonment is not required* by the statute relating to the crime committed, a court may, as a form of conditional discharge, sentence the defendant to work at community service related projects...." (Emphasis added.) This enactment clearly indicates that the legislature was aware of some mandatory prison requirements which it did not wish to repeal.

Because KRS 533.070 was enacted in 1990, just as was KRS 500.095, we determine that the legislature intended to continue mandatory imprisonment in the specific situations set out in KRS 533.060(1). The trial court properly declined to consider alternatives to incarceration for Williams.

The judgment of conviction ... is affirmed.

♦ HUDDLESTON, JUDGE, concurring in part and dissenting in part.

I dissent from that portion of the Court's opinion which rejects Williams' argument that the trial court erred by refusing to consider the alternative sentencing provisions of KRS 500.095(1). That statute, enacted in 1990, provides that:

> In *every case* in which a person pleads guilty to or is convicted of a crime punishable by imprisonment, *the judge shall consider* whether the person should be sentenced to a term of community service as an alternative to the prison term.... (Emphasis supplied.)

At the 1990 session of the general assembly, KRS 533.010 was amended and reenacted. It now provides that

> (1) *Any person* who has been convicted of a crime and who has not been sentenced to death may be sentenced to probation, probation with an alternative sentencing plan, or conditional discharge as provided in this chapter.
>
> (2) Before imposition of a sentence of imprisonment, *the court shall consider the possibility of probation, probation with an alternative sentencing plan, or conditional discharge*.... (Emphasis supplied.)

The trial court's refusal to consider probation was based on the prohibitive language contained in KRS 533.060(1):

> When a person has been convicted of an offense or has entered a plea of guilty to an offense classified as a Class A, B, or C felony and the commission of such offense involved the use of a weapon from which a shot or projectile may be discharged that is readily capable of producing death or other serious physical injury, such person shall not be eligible for probation, shock probation or conditional discharge.

The statutes clearly contain conflicting language. Where a conflict exists, the latter statute controls. The Legislature, in enacting KRS 500.095(1) and in reenacting KRS 533.010 in 1990, is presumed to have been aware of KRS 533.060(1), which has been in effect since 1976, and which was amended as recently as 1986.

As used in KRS 500.095(1) and KRS 533.010(2), the word "shall" is mandatory. KRS 446.010(29). And as used in KRS 533.010(1), the phrase "any person" means everyone (except, according to the statute, those sentenced to death). The trial court was thus obliged, when sentencing Williams to consider the possibility of probation, probation with an alternative sentencing plan, or conditional discharge, despite the language of the earlier statute, KRS 533.060(1), prohibiting such consideration.

I would set aside the sentencing in this case and remand this case to Fayette Circuit Court with directions to consider the sentencing alternative set forth in KRS 533.010 and KRS 500.095(1).

Points for Discussion

1. *Statutory Language*: There are two (or three according to the dissent) relevant statutes in this case. Language in each statute applied to this situation. What was that language in each statute? How did the parties reconcile that language, if at all? How did the majority and dissent reconcile that language?

2. *Theories*: Which theory did the majority use? The dissent? Did either the majority or dissent find the language ambiguous, absurd, to have a scrivener's error, or to raise a constitutional question?

3. *Conflict*: Be sure you understand how the two statutes conflicted. Ky. Rev. Stat. Ann. § 500.095 directed the trial judge to consider whether a criminal defendant

was entitled to community service as an alternative to prison in every case. Ky. Rev. Stat. Ann. § 533.060(1) prohibited a judge from sentencing defendants who used a gun to "probation ... or conditional discharge." Because these two statutes conflicted, it was unclear whether the judge should have considered community service for a defendant who used a gun in the commission of a crime.

4. *Step One: Reconciliation*: The first step for a court when it has to resolve conflicting statutes is to attempt to harmonize those statutes. Can these statutes be reconciled? If KRS § 500.095 applies, is KRS § 533.060(1) a nullity? Or can KRS § 533.060(1) be read as a narrow exception to KRS § 500.095? If it is meant to be an exception, should not the legislature have made that clear when it enacted KRS § 500.095?

5. *Step Two*: *Specific v. General Canon*: The second step, assuming the statutes cannot be harmonized, is to determine whether one of the statutes is more specific than the other. Is a statute that prohibits judges from sentencing defendants to non-prison sentences for crimes involving guns more specific than a statute that requires judges to consider whether to sentence all defendants to non-prison sentences? The majority thought not, but why not? Is that reasoning convincing? Did the dissent address this canon?

6. *Step Three*: *Later v. Earlier Canon*: The third step, assuming the neither statute is more specific, is to determine which statute was enacted later. The later statute should control over the earlier statute. This canon was critical to the dissent. How did the majority deal with the fact that the statute requiring community service was enacted later and, therefore, should have been controlling?

7. *Implied Repeal*: If the conflict between two statutes cannot be harmonized, and neither is more specific, then the later-enacted statute controls. When this happens, the later-enacted statute necessarily impliedly repeals part of all of the earlier-enacted statute. We will see, however, that implied repeals are disfavored. We address that issue next.

* * *

3. Repeal by Implication Is Disfavored

New statutes should be interpreted harmoniously with existing statutes whenever possible. But, sometimes, harmony is simply not possible. When two statutes cannot be reconciled, one way to address the conflict is to conclude that the later statute repealed the earlier statute if not explicitly then implicitly. Judges presume that a legislature would not go through the legislative process without intending to change existing law in some way. Thus, every new act should change the status quo, by adding to, modifying, or repealing existing law. But while modification is to be expected, outright repeal is not. Normally, when a legislature wants to repeal a statute or a section of a statute, it does so expressly. Thus, in the absence of an express repeal, it is likely the legislature did not intend any repeal at all. When a legislature intends to repeal a statute, the legislature should say so clearly; repeals should not be implied. Thus, courts apply a canon of negative presumption: repeals by implication—full or partial—are disfavored.

However, by requiring the equivalent of a clear statement to overcome the presumption against repeals, the court essentially rejects the possibility of ever finding an implied repeal. Hence, the later-enacted canon and the implied repeal canon conflict; the former directs courts to apply the later-enacted statute, while the latter directs courts not to find an implied repeal absent strong evidence that the legislature intended that outcome.

This tension rests on the potentially flawed presumption that the legislature was aware of the conflict with the existing statute and specifically opted not to repeal it. This presumption yields when there is evidence that the legislature intended for the second statute to repeal the first. For example, if the new statute comprehensively covers the entire subject matter of the existing statute and is itself complete, then the legislature likely intended the new statute to supersede any existing statutes on the subject. Also, if the new statute is completely incompatible with an existing statute, repeal may be appropriate.

In statutory interpretation cases, this issue arises when a judge finds that a statute conflicts with an existing statute, that the conflict is irreconcilable, and that the legislature did not explain how the conflict should be resolved. If there are two reasonable interpretations, the judge should choose the interpretation that does not repeal an existing statute or any part of it. If repeal is unavoidable, then the second statute is only repealed to the extent of the irreconcilability; if any part of the earlier statute can exist in harmony with the later statute, that part of the earlier statute is not repealed. In the case below, can the two statutes be reconciled?

Morton v. Mancari

Supreme Court of the United States
417 U.S. 535 (1974)

◆ JUSTICE BLACKMAN delivered the opinion for a unanimous Court [including BRENNAN, BURGER, DOUGLAS, MARSHALL, POWELL, REHNQUIST, STEWART, & WHITE].

The Indian Reorganization Act of 1934 ... accords an employment preference for qualified Indians in the Bureau of Indian Affairs (BIA or Bureau). Appellees, non-Indian BIA employees, challenged this preference as contrary to the anti-discrimination provisions of the Equal Employment Opportunity Act of 1972....

Section 12 of the Indian Reorganization Act, provides:

"The Secretary of the Interior is directed to establish standards of health, age, character, experience, knowledge, and ability for Indians who may be appointed, without regard to civil-service laws, to the various positions maintained, now or hereafter, by the Indian Office, in the administration of functions or services affecting any Indian tribe. Such qualified Indians shall hereafter have the preference to appointment to vacancies in any such positions."

In June 1972, pursuant to this provision, the Commissioner of Indian Affairs, with the approval of the Secretary of the Interior, issued a directive ... stating that the

BIA's policy would be to grant a preference to qualified Indians ... in the situation where an Indian and a non-Indian, both already employed by the BIA, were competing for a promotion within the Bureau. The record indicates that this policy was implemented immediately.... [Petitioners, a group of non-Indian employees of the BIA, challenge this policy.]

complaint

[T]he District Court concluded that the Indian preference was implicitly repealed by §11 of the Equal Employment Opportunity Act of 1972, proscribing discrimination in most federal employment on the basis of race.[6] ...

P. H.

The federal policy of according some hiring preference to Indians in the Indian service dates at least as far back as 1834. Since that time, Congress repeatedly has enacted various preferences of the general type here at issue. The purpose of these preferences, as variously expressed in the legislative history, has been to give Indians a greater participation in their own self-government; to further the Government's trust obligation toward the Indian tribes; and to reduce the negative effect of having non-Indians administer matters that affect Indian tribal life.

Purpose for Statutes

The preference directly at issue here was enacted as an important part of the sweeping Indian Reorganization Act of 1934. The overriding purpose of that particular Act was to establish machinery whereby Indian tribes would be able to assume a greater degree of self-government, both politically and economically. Congress was seeking to modify the then-existing situation whereby the primarily non-Indian-staffed BIA had plenary control, for all practical purposes, over the lives and destinies of the federally recognized Indian tribes. Initial congressional proposals would have diminished substantially the role of the BIA by turning over to federally chartered self-governing Indian communities many of the functions normally performed by the Bureau. Committee sentiment, however, ran against such a radical change in the role of the BIA. The solution ultimately adopted was to strengthen tribal government while continuing the active role of the BIA, with the understanding that the Bureau would be more responsive to the interests of the people it was created to serve.

Purpose of IRA

One of the primary means by which self-government would be fostered and the Bureau made more responsive was to increase the participation of tribal Indians in the BIA operations. In order to achieve this end, it was recognized that some kind of preference and exemption from otherwise prevailing civil service requirements was necessary. Congressman Howard, the House sponsor, expressed the need for the preference:

> 'The Indians have not only been thus deprived of civic rights and powers, but they have been largely deprived of the opportunity to enter the more important positions in the service of the very bureau which manages their

---

6. Section 2000e-16(a) reads:

"All personnel actions affecting employees or applicants for employment..., and in those units of the legislative and judicial branches of the Federal Government having positions in the competitive service, ... shall be made free from any discrimination based on race, color, religion, sex, or national origin."

affairs. Theoretically, the Indians have the right to qualify for the Federal civil service. In actual practice there has been no adequate program of training to qualify Indians to compete in these examinations, especially for technical and higher positions; and even if there were such training, the Indians would have to compete under existing law, on equal terms with multitudes of white applicants.... The various services on the Indian reservations are actually local rather than Federal services and are comparable to local municipal and county services, since they are dealing with purely local Indian problems. It should be possible for Indians with the requisite vocational and professional training to enter the service of their own people without the necessity of competing with white applicants for these positions. This bill permits them to do so.' 78 Cong.Rec. 11729 (1934).

Congress was well aware that the proposed preference would result in employment disadvantages within the BIA for non-Indians. Not only was this displacement un-avoidable if room were to be made for Indians, but it was explicitly determined that gradual replacement of non-Indians with Indians within the Bureau was a desirable feature of the entire program for self-government. Since 1934, the BIA has imple-mented the preference with a fair degree of success. The percentage of Indians em-ployed in the Bureau rose from 34% in 1934 to 57% in 1972. This reversed the former downward trend and was due, clearly, to the presence of the 1934 Act. The Commis-sioner's extension of the preference in 1972 to promotions within the BIA was designed to bring more Indians into positions of responsibility and, in that regard, appears to be a logical extension of the congressional intent.

It is against this background that we encounter the first issue in the present case: whether the Indian preference was repealed by the Equal Employment Opportunity Act of 1972. Title VII of the Civil Rights Act of 1964, was the first major piece of federal legislation prohibiting discrimination in private employment on the basis of "race, color, religion, sex, or national origin." 42 U.S.C. § 2000e-2(a). Significantly, §§ 701(b) and 703(i) of that Act explicitly exempted from its coverage the preferential employment of Indians by Indian tribes or by industries located on or near Indian reservations. 42 U.S.C. §§ 2000e(b) and 2000e-2(i).[19] This exemption reveals a clear congressional recognition, within the framework of Title VII, of the unique legal status of tribal and reservation-based activities. The Senate sponsor, Senator Humphrey, stated on the floor by way of explanation:

'Thus exemption is consistent with the Federal Government's policy of encouraging Indian employment and with the special legal position of In-dians.' 110 Cong.Rec. 12723 (1964).

---

19. Section 701(b) excludes "an Indian Tribe" from the Act's definition of "employer." Section 703(i) states:

"Nothing contained in this subchapter shall apply to any business or enterprise on or near an Indian reservation with respect to any publicly announced employment practice of such business or enterprise under which a preferential treatment is given to any individual because he is an Indian living on or near a reservation."

The 1964 Act did not specifically outlaw employment discrimination by the Federal Government. Yet the mechanism for enforcing longstanding Executive Orders forbidding Government discrimination had proved ineffective for the most part. In order to remedy this, Congress, by the 1972 Act, amended the 1964 Act and proscribed discrimination in most areas of federal employment. In general, it may be said that the substantive anti-discrimination law embraced in Title VII was carried over and applied to the Federal Government. As stated in the House Report:

> 'To correct this entrenched discrimination in the Federal service, it is necessary to insure the effective application of uniform, fair and strongly enforced policies. The present law and the proposed statute do not permit industry and labor organizations to be the judges of their own conduct in the area of employment discrimination. There is no reason why government agencies should not be treated similarly....' H.R.Rep. No. 92-238, on H.R. 1746, pp. 24–25 (1971).

Nowhere in the legislative history of the 1972 Act, however, is there any mention of Indian preference.

Appellees assert, and the District Court held, that since the 1972 Act proscribed racial discrimination in Government employment, the Act necessarily, albeit *sub silentio*, repealed the provision of the 1934 Act that called for the preference in the BIA of one racial group, Indians, over non-Indians:

> 'When a conflict such as in this case, is present, the most recent law or Act should apply and the conflicting Preferences passed some 39 years earlier should be impliedly repealed.' Brief for Appellees 7.

We disagree.... [W]e conclude that Congress did not intend to repeal the Indian preference and that the District Court erred in holding that it was repealed....

Appellees encounter head-on the "cardinal rule ... that repeals by implication are not favored." They and the District Court read the congressional silence as effectuating a repeal by implication. There is nothing in the legislative history, however, that indicates affirmatively any congressional intent to repeal the 1934 preference. Indeed, there is ample independent evidence that the legislative intent was to the contrary.

This is a prototypical case where an adjudication of repeal by implication is not appropriate. The preference is a longstanding, important component of the Government's Indian program. The anti-discrimination provision, aimed at alleviating minority discrimination in employment, obviously is designed to deal with an entirely different and, indeed, opposite problem. Any perceived conflict is thus more apparent than real.

In the absence of some affirmative showing of an intention to repeal, the only permissible justification for a repeal by implication is when the earlier and later statutes are irreconcilable. Clearly, this is not the case here. A provision aimed at furthering Indian self-government by according an employment preference within the BIA for qualified members of the governed group can readily co-exist with a general rule prohibiting employment discrimination on the basis of race. Any other conclusion can be reached only by formalistic reasoning that ignores both the history and purposes of the preference and the unique legal relationship between the Federal Government and tribal Indians.

Furthermore, the Indian preference statute is a specific provision applying to a very specific situation. The 1972 Act, on the other hand, is of general application. Where there is no clear intention otherwise, a specific statute will not be controlled or nullified by a general one, regardless of the priority of enactment.

The courts are not at liberty to pick and choose among congressional enactments, and when two statutes are capable of co-existence, it is the duty of the courts, absent a clearly expressed congressional intention to the contrary, to regard each as effective. When there are two acts upon the same subject, the rule is to give effect to both if possible.... The intention of the legislature to repeal must be clear and manifest. In light of the factors indicating no repeal, we simply cannot conclude that Congress consciously abandoned its policy of furthering Indian self-government when it passed the 1972 amendments....

holding

* * *

Points for Discussion

1. *Statutory Language*: There are two relevant statutes in *Morton v. Mancari*. Language in each statute applied to this situation. What was that language in each statute? Which statute did the employees want to apply? The government?

2. *Theories*: Which theory did the Court use? Did the Court find the language ambiguous, absurd, to have a scrivener's error, or to raise a constitutional question?

3. *Harmonize*: Step one requires courts to harmonize conflicting statutes before finding that one statute impliedly repeals another. Can a statute that prohibits the federal government from making any hiring decisions based on race co-exist with a statute that allows a federal agency to make promotion decisions based on race? The Court said "yes" and explained:

   > In the absence of some affirmative showing of an intention to repeal, the only permissible justification for a repeal by implication is when the earlier and later statutes are irreconcilable. Clearly, this is not the case here. A provision aimed at furthering Indian self-government by according an employment preference within the BIA for qualified members of the governed group can readily co-exist with a general rule prohibiting employment discrimination on the basis of race.

   How persuasive do you find the Court's reasoning?

4. *Rebuttal Presumption*: The canon that repeal by implication is disfavored can be overcome by evidence that the legislature intended to repeal part or all of an existing statute. The question then is how clear must that other evidence be and where should a court look for it? Where does this Court look for that evidence in this case?

5. *Legislative History*: What was the relevance of the legislative history of the two statutes? Did the Court look for specific intent that the legislature intended to

retain or reject the BIA Indian preference or did the Court look for the purpose of the two statutes, or both?

6. *Specific v. General Canon*: Was one of these two statutes more specific than the other? Did the specific statute control? If not, why not? Which statute was the later enacted statute? Did the later enacted statute control? If not, why not?

7. *Appropriations Bill*: There is a related aspect to the implied repeal canon: The presumption against repeal is especially strong when the later bill is an appropriations (or budget) bill. The presumption is stronger because appropriations bills have a limited and specific purpose: providing funds for authorized programs. These types of bills are supposed to be purely fiscal in nature and not make substantive changes to the law; hence, courts consider it highly unlikely that a legislature would repeal existing law through an appropriations bill. But, as with all canons, this presumption can be overcome with specific evidence that the legislature did intend to repeal the existing law impliedly through the later appropriations bill.

The quintessential case rejecting such an argument is *Tennessee Valley Authority v. Hill*, 437 U.S. 153 (1978). *Tennessee Valley* is well-known in the environmental arena because the Court permanently enjoined construction of the Tellico Dam, which was virtually complete, to protect the snail darter, a very small and nondescript species of fish (*see* picture below). Construction on the dam started in 1967. In 1973, Congress passed the Endangered Species Act, which authorized the Secretary of the Interior to declare animal species "endangered" and to identify any "critical habitat" of that species. 16 U.S.C. § 1531 et seq. (1976). The Secretary was further authorized to take "such action necessary to insure that *actions* authorized, funded, or carried out by [the federal government] do not jeopardize the continued existence of [an] endangered species ... or result in the destruction or modification of habitat of such species...." *Id.* at 160 (quoting 16 U.S.C. § 1536 (1976) (emphasis added).

In 1975, the Secretary identified the snail darter as endangered and declared that the area that the Tellico Dam would affect was the snail darter's "critical habitat." The Secretary then directed the Tennessee Valley Authority, which was building the dam, to stop construction. *Id*. at 161–62. Litigation ensued. The issue in the case was whether the word "actions" in the Act included almost completed projects.

While the litigation was pending and with full knowledge of the Secretary's order, Congress continued to appropriate funds for the dam's completion: "The [House Committee on Appropriations] directs that the project ... should be completed as promptly as possible...." *Id*. at 164 (citing H.R. Rep. No. 94-319, at 76 (1975)). Meanwhile, the litigation was winding its way through the courts. Because the dam was so close to completion, the district court refused to stop the dam construction, despite agreeing with the Secretary that completion of the dam would completely destroy the fish's habitat. *Id*. at 165–66. But the Court of Appeals disagreed. On appeal, the Supreme Court held that the language of the Endangered Species Act contained no exceptions, even for projects near completion. *Id*. at 169. Citing *Morton v. Mancari*, 417 U.S. 535 (1974), for the cardinal rule that repeals by implication are disfavored, the majority explained that "the [canon] applies with even *greater* force when the claimed repeal rests solely on an Appropriations Act." *Id*.

The canon has greater force, the majority explained, because when voting to approve appropriations bills, legislators should be able to assume that the funds earmarked in such a bill will be devoted to projects that are lawful. Without this assumption, every appropriations measure might alter substantive legislation, repealing by implication any prior statute that conflicted with the expenditure. Thus, members of Congress would need to exhaustively review every appropriation in excruciating detail before voting on it. *Id*. Ultimately Congress legislatively overruled the Court's decision to halt construction of the dam.

8. *No Revival*: Sometimes, Congress repeals an existing statute with a later statute and then later repeals the second statute. In the past, courts had held that when this happened, the earlier statute was revived, or became effective, again. But Congress and many state legislatures have abolished this old common law canon. Hence, today, an express or implied repeal of one statute does not revive an earlier statute. The original statute remains repealed. 1 U.S.C. § 108 (2012).

9. *No Automatic Repeal*: Just because a statute is no longer necessary does not mean it is automatically repealed. For example, state sodomy laws were not repealed as society's mores changed. Rather, state legislatures would have to repeal any existing statutes. For this reason, sodomy laws remain on the books in many states, even though they are unconstitutional under *Lawrence v. Texas*, 539 U.S. 558 (2003).

* * *

In summary, when two statutes conflict and the conflict cannot be reconciled, courts ask first whether one statute is specific and the other general. If that distinction does not resolve the dispute, courts look next to whether one statute was enacted later than the other because the last in time should control. Finally, if neither of these tie-breakers resolves the issue, the court will determine whether one statute expressly or impliedly repealed the other statute. Generally, implied repeals are disfavored, especially when the later, conflicting statute is an appropriations act.

4. Federal Preemption

In the last section, we examined conflicts within a jurisdiction. In this section, we turn to conflicts across jurisdictions, specifically Federal and state. Pursuant to the U.S. Constitution's Supremacy Clause, federal law "shall be the supreme Law of the Land: and the Judges in every State shall be bound thereby...." U.S. CONST. art. VI, cl 2. Thus, federal law of any kind trumps, or preempts, state law. Whether a federal statute preempts state law turns on the enacting Congress's intent. "[T]he purpose of Congress is the ultimate touchstone in every preemption case." *Wyeth v. Levine,* 555 U.S. 555, 565 (2009) (quoting *Medtronic, Inc. v. Lohr,* 518 U.S. 470, 485 (1996)).

Some federal statutes expressly preempt state law; in such cases, preemption should be easy to find. *English v. General Elec. Co.,* 496 U.S. 72, 78 (1990) (citing *Shaw v. Delta Air Lines, Inc.,* 463 U.S. 85, 95–98 (1983)). However, even when Congress includes such a provision, courts require that Congress be clear. *See, e.g., Medtronic, Inc. v. Lohr,* 518 U.S. 470 (1996) (refusing to find preemption even though the statute provided that "no state ... may establish ... any requirement ... which is different from, or in addition to any [federal] requirement....").

But preemption may also be implied in two circumstances. First, preemption may be implied when Congress legislates so comprehensively that federal law occupies an entire field of law and leaves no room for state law. This type of preemption is known as field preemption. It happens rarely. *See Rogers v. Yonce,* 2008 WL 2853207, * 10 (N.D. Okla, July 21, 2008) (identifying the three times the Supreme Court has found field preemption: (1) the Labor Management Relations Act; (2) the Employee Retirement Income Security Act, and (3) the National Bank Act).

Second, preemption may be implied when federal law conflicts with state law. This type of preemption is known as conflict preemption and occurs more often. To determine whether conflict preemption exists, courts look to see whether the conflict between federal and state law is such that it is impossible for an individual to comply with both laws, or whether the state law stands as an obstacle to the accomplishment of the federal objective. Either is sufficient to find preemption.

The case below involves a conflict between federal law (the Full Faith and Credit for Child Support Orders Act) and state law (the Uniform Interstate Family Support Act, as adopted in Florida). The lower court had held that the federal law preempted the state law. See if you can understand why the appellate court disagrees. As you read the case, it will be helpful to remember the difference between personal jurisdiction (jurisdiction over an individual) and subject matter jurisdiction (jurisdiction over the controversy).

Pulkkinen v. Pulkkinen

District Court of Appeal of Florida
127 So. 3d 738 (Fl. Ct. App. 2013)

◆ RAY, J. [LEWIS, C.J., and CLARK, J., concur].

We have before us a petition ... to restrain a circuit court's exercise of jurisdiction on a petition to modify a Michigan child support order.... The father ... contends that the Uniform Interstate Family Support Act ("UIFSA"), chapter 88, Florida Statutes [a state statute], excludes the instant case from the jurisdiction of Florida's courts and binds the circuit court to dismiss the case. The mother ... argues that Florida has jurisdiction under the federal Full Faith and Credit for Child Support Orders Act ("FFCCSOA"), 28 U.S.C. § 1738B [a federal statute], and therefore must entertain the modification action. We agree with the father. Section 88.6111(1), Florida Statutes (2010) ... precludes jurisdiction over the modification proceeding in this case, and federal law does not conflict with this state law. Accordingly, we grant the petition.

FACTS AND PROCEDURAL HISTORY

... In 2007, a Michigan court dissolved the parties' marriage and ordered the father to pay the mother child support. In March 2010, after having moved to Florida with the parties' two minor children, the mother petitioned the Florida circuit court to domesticate and modify the Michigan child support order. The father, who now lives in California, requested that the order be registered in Florida under the UIFSA....

Thereafter, the mother filed ... to [m]odify [the] [f]inal [j]udgment, and the father moved to dismiss the modification proceeding for lack of subject matter jurisdiction.... The father relied on the UIFSA, which grants jurisdiction to modify a foreign child support order only when the moving party is not a Florida resident.... The mother argued that modification in Florida is proper because the FFCCSOA removes the continuing, exclusive jurisdiction of a state that has issued a child support order when neither the child nor any of the parties continue to reside in the issuing state, as is the case here. The circuit court agreed with the mother, concluding that the FFCCSOA provides jurisdiction and preempts the UIFSA on this subject. The father requests a writ of prohibition to prevent the exercise of jurisdiction over this modification action....

LAW AND ANALYSIS

To decide the question presented in this case, we must determine whether the UIFSA [the state law] conflicts with the FFCCSOA [the federal law] concerning a state's jurisdiction to modify a foreign child support order ... This issue implicates federal preemption doctrine....

B. *Preemption Doctrine*

Under federal preemption doctrine, which derives from the Supremacy Clause of the United States Constitution, a state law is void to the extent it conflicts with a valid federal law. The United States Supreme Court has instructed that "the purpose of Congress is the ultimate touchstone in every preemption case."

Congress can manifest intent to preempt state law in three ways. First, Congress can overtly displace state authority with explicit preemption guidelines. Second, when no explicit guidelines exist, Congress can engage in implied field preemption. Such preemption occurs where the federal regulatory scheme is "so pervasive as to make reasonable the inference that Congress left no room for the States to supplement it," or because the federal interest in regulating the field is so dominant as to preclude the enforcement of state laws in the same field. Third, even in circumstances where a federal scheme does not occupy an entire regulatory field, Congress has the power to supersede state law that actually conflicts with federal law.

This case is the 3rd type — conflict preemption

The federal statute at issue in the instant case, the FFCCSOA, does not contain explicit preemption guidance, nor does it exhibit the preclusive effect of field preemption. Therefore, we must consider the third category of preemption: implied conflict preemption. Conflict preemption occurs when it is impossible to comply with both state and federal requirements or where state law "stands as an obstacle to the accomplishment and execution of the full purposes and objectives of Congress."

conflict preemption

C. *Application of Preemption Doctrine to the FFCCSOA and the UIFSA*

To apply these concepts, we begin with the plain language of the two acts, which is the best evidence of legislative intent. To understand the meaning of any particular provision of either statute, we consider the provisions of the whole law and do not interpret words or sentences in isolation. If the language of a statute reveals an unambiguous meaning, we need not resort to any other sources to understand it.

Plain language

The FFCCSOA provides a framework for each state to give full faith and credit to child support orders issued by other states. Its first provision announces that each state "shall enforce according to its terms a child support order made consistently with this section by a court of another State." The FFCCSOA then provides plainly that states "shall not" modify other states' child support orders "except in accordance with subsections (e), (f), and (i)." ...

Federal

The mother claims that the exception identified in subsection (e) applies to this case. The FFCCSOA's subsection (e) permits a court of another state to modify a child support order only if:

(1) the court has jurisdiction to make such a child support order pursuant to subsection (i); and

(2) (A) the court of the other State no longer has continuing, exclusive jurisdiction of the child support order because that State no longer is the child's State or the residence of any individual contestant; or

(B) each individual contestant has filed written consent with the State of continuing, exclusive jurisdiction for a court of another State to modify the order and assume continuing, exclusive jurisdiction over the order.

Under these provisions, in order for State B to modify a child support order issued by State A, State A must have lost continuing, exclusive jurisdiction of the child support order, either because the child and the parents are no longer residents of State A or the parents consent in writing to State B's assumption of continuing, exclusive jurisdiction over the order. Additionally, State B must have jurisdiction to make such a child support order under subsection (i), which provides:

> If there is no individual contestant or child residing in the issuing State, the party ... seeking to modify ... a child support order issued in another State shall register that order in a State with *jurisdiction over the nonmovant for the purpose of modification.*

§ 1738B(i) (emphasis added).

State

The UIFSA, as codified in Florida, contains similar provisions. Under the UIFSA, even when a support order of another state is properly registered in Florida for enforcement, a Florida court cannot modify a foreign support order ... unless it finds after notice and a hearing that:

(a) The following requirements are met:

1. The child, the individual obligee, and the obligor do not reside in the issuing state;

2. A petitioner who is a nonresident of this state seeks modification; *and*

3. The respondent is subject to the personal jurisdiction of the tribunal of this state; or

(b) The child, or a party who is an individual, is subject to the personal jurisdiction of the tribunal of this state and all of the parties who are individuals have filed written consents in the issuing tribunal for a tribunal of this state to modify the support order and assume continuing exclusive jurisdiction over the order....

§ 88.6111(1) (emphasis added). Here, neither the parents nor the children still live in Michigan, the trial court found that the father consented to personal jurisdiction, and the father has not filed a written consent to the circuit court's jurisdiction to modify. Therefore, for the purposes of this case, the relevant distinction between the federal FFCCSOA and Florida's UIFSA is the nonresident requirement of section 88.6111(1)(a) 2.

The mother contends that Florida must exercise jurisdiction despite the UIFSA's nonresident requirement because Michigan has lost continuing, exclusive jurisdiction under the terms of the FFCCSOA. Michigan's loss of continuing, exclusive jurisdiction, however, does not automatically confer jurisdiction on a Florida court to modify Michigan's child support order. Under the plain language of the FFCCSOA, modification may occur only *"in a State with jurisdiction over the nonmovant for the purpose of modification."* § 1738B(i) (emphasis added).

Some courts have declined to apply the UIFSA's nonresident requirement because they view it as a hurdle to modification not contemplated by the FFCCSOA. *Draper v. Burke*, 450 Mass. 676 (2008); *Bowman v. Bowman*, 82 A.D.3d 144, 148 (N.Y.App.Div.2011). Those courts interpret section 1738B(i)'s jurisdictional language as requiring only that the modification court have personal jurisdiction over the nonmovant. Other courts, which have found no conflict between the federal and state law, have interpreted this same language as conditioning modification upon finding both personal and subject matter jurisdiction. *See, e.g., LeTellier v. LeTellier,* 40 S.W.3d 490, 498–99 (Tenn. 2001); *Gentzel v. Williams,* 25 Kan.App.2d 552, 965 P.2d 855, 860–61 (1998). We are persuaded by the latter interpretation.

To the extent there is any ambiguity in the language, we have resolved it by reference to the rule that a statute should not be construed so as to render any of its words meaningless. In *Draper v. Burke,* the court reasoned that the language "over the non-movant" indicates personal jurisdiction to the exclusion of subject matter jurisdiction. If we were to construe the jurisdiction referenced in section 1738B(i) as solely pertaining to personal jurisdiction, we would render the phrase "for the purpose of modification" superfluous. Furthermore, we must acknowledge that if Congress had intended the language to characterize only personal jurisdiction, it could have used the words "personal jurisdiction," just as it did in [another] section ... Thus, to give full effect to the plain meaning of subsection (i), we hold that the text "jurisdiction over the nonmovant for the purpose of modification" properly refers to both personal jurisdiction and subject matter jurisdiction.

[handwritten margin note: Ambiguity]

The federal FFCCSOA does not attempt to define the subject matter jurisdiction of state courts. Instead, that task is left to the states, which have embraced the UIFSA's requirements governing when any court in a state may modify another state's child support order. The UIFSA establishes those requirements as defining a jurisdictional concept by references to a state's "jurisdiction to modify." Those requirements include the petitioner's nonresidency as a distinct component from personal jurisdiction, and they are not procedural. § 88.611(1)(a). Therefore, they are best understood as limiting the subject matter jurisdiction of all the courts in a particular state over proceedings to modify a foreign child support order. Because the federal law allows modification only when a state has both personal and subject matter jurisdiction, the latter of which is defined in the uniform state law, compliance with both federal and state law is not only possible, but required.

We also find nothing in a state's limitations on its own modification jurisdiction through the UIFSA that stands as "an obstacle to the accomplishment and execution of the full purposes and objectives of Congress." In fact, a contrary holding would be difficult to justify because Congress essentially implemented both acts.

Congress enacted the FFCCSOA in 1994, and two years later passed the Personal Responsibility and Work Opportunity Reconciliation Act, which required all states to adopt the UIFSA in order to receive federal funding for aid to families with dependent children. In conjunction with this mandate, Congress made "improvements" to section 1738B, including the addition of the language requiring that modification of a child support order occur "in a State with jurisdiction over the nonmovant for the purpose of modification." Congressional reports contemporaneous with the 1996 revisions of the FFCCSOA explain that their purpose was to promote consistency with the UIFSA. *See* H.R. Conf. Rep. No. 104-725, at 351 (1996) (revisions to FFCC-SOA proposed "to ensure that full faith and credit laws can be applied consistently with UIFSA"); H.R. Rep. 104-651, at 1413 (1996) (same); Because Congress induced the states to adopt the UIFSA in an effort to create interstate consistency and simultaneously modified the FFCCSOA to comport with the UIFSA's substance, the two acts are generally considered "complementary or duplicative and not contradictory."

Indeed, ... the two acts are "virtually identical ... both in terms of structure and intent." The express policy of the FFCCSOA is "to establish national standards under which the courts of the various States shall determine their jurisdiction to issue a child support order and the effect to be given by each State to child support orders issued by the courts of other States." The FFCCSOA identifies three specific purposes: to facilitate enforcement of support orders among the states, to discourage continuing interstate controversies over child support, and to avoid jurisdictional competition and conflict in the establishment of child support orders. The UIFSA accomplishes these same goals by providing uniform and consistent jurisdictional rules relating to the establishment, enforcement, and modification of child support orders by virtue of its adoption in all fifty states. *See* Nat'l Conference of Comm'rs on Uniform State Laws, *Unif. Interstate Family Support Act* ("UIFSA"), Prefatory Note (amended 1996). Both the UIFSA and the FFCCSOA "create a national regime in which only a single support order is effective at any given time."

The UIFSA's nonresident provision does not run afoul of the FFCCSOA's goals. It minimizes jurisdictional competition and interstate controversies by restricting the circumstances under which a state can modify another state's order. Further, it promotes certainty concerning the proper venue for a modification action by limiting the moving party's venue choices. Finally, by restraining the exercise of jurisdiction, it promotes the goal embodied in the FFCCSOA's title, to preserve the full faith and credit to which each state order is entitled.

Before concluding, we pause to note that binding precedent recognizes a presumption against preemption, particularly in areas that have traditionally been regulated by the states. *E.g., Wyeth v. Levine*, 555 U.S. 555, 565 (2009) (quoting *Lohr*, 518 U.S. at 485). Family law is such an area. Recent Supreme Court case law, however, suggests a shift away from the presumption. *See, e.g., Mut. Pharm. Co., Inc. v. Bartlett*, 133 S.Ct. 2466 (2013) (omitting discussion of the presumption in the majority opinion and stating that, without an explicit expression of congressional intent to preempt or not preempt, courts are "left to divine Congress' will from the duties the statute imposes"); *PLIVA, Inc. v. Mensing*, 131 S.Ct. 2567, 2580 (2011) (plurality opinion) (suggesting "that courts should not strain to find ways to reconcile federal law with seemingly conflicting state law"). Whatever the continuing vitality of the presumption doctrine may be, it does not affect our decision today, because we readily conclude from the language used in the two statutes that there is no conflict, express or implied. Consequently, we need not invoke the presumption to tip the scales.

CONCLUSION

In conclusion, having thoroughly considered the text of the two acts, we hold that the FFCCSOA does not preempt section 88.6111(1) of the Florida UIFSA. Neither the language nor the purposes of either statute create any conflict that requires displacing state provisions. Therefore, the circuit court is required to give full effect to section 88.6111(1) and refrain from exercising modification jurisdiction in this matter.

Points for Discussion

1. *Statutory Language*: What was the language at issue? What did each party want that language to mean? What meaning did the court adopt?

2. *Theories*: Which theory did the court use? Did the court find the language ambiguous, absurd, to have a scrivener's error, or to raise a constitutional question?

3. *Conflict Preemption*: As noted above, there are three types of preemption. The relevant one here, conflict preemption, occurs when either (1) it is impossible for an individual to comply with both state and federal requirements, or (2) the state law impedes the accomplishment of the federal objective. If either factor is present, then preemption exists.

4. *Factor One*: Do you understand why the court concluded that it was possible (in fact required) for an individual to comply with both federal and state law? The court concluded that the federal statute's, FFCCSOA, jurisdictional requirement ("in a State with jurisdiction *over the nonmovant* for the purpose of modification") required a Florida court to have both personal jurisdiction over the nonmovant *and* subject matter jurisdiction. Which linguistic canons did the court use to reach this conclusion?

   In this case, the father had consented to personal jurisdiction. However, according to the court, UIFSA (the state law) defined subject matter jurisdiction to require the petitioner, in this case the mother, to be a nonresident. Because the mother was a resident, the Florida court did not have subject matter jurisdiction; hence, the court concluded that it had no authority to modify the Michigan Support Order.

5. *Factor Two*: Do you understand why the court concluded that Florida's subject matter requirement of non-residence was not "an obstacle to the accomplishment and execution of the full purposes and objectives of Congress"? Who, according to the court, implemented both acts? What sources did the court review to consider whether the state law and federal law can coexist?

6. *Uniform Law*: Note that the Florida law at issue in this case is a uniform law. One purpose of uniform laws is to have uniformity among the states. In this case, however, the federal law has introduced a potential conflict: namely, which law applies: the uniform state law or the federal law. Some states have concluded that the federal law preempts the state law, while others, like this one, have concluded that the state law and federal law both apply. Ultimately, federal courts will have to resolve the controversy created by the uniform act.

* * *

Problem 10A

You represent Tom Marshall ("Marshall" or "Tom"). On July 26, 2010, he pled guilty to the felony offense of possession of heroin. The trial court sentenced him to five years imprisonment, suspended the imposition of the sentence, and then placed him on community supervision for five years. On September 1, 2012, the trial court, after finding that appellant satisfactorily fulfilled the conditions of community supervision and pursuant to East Carolina Criminal Code §42-12-20(a), entered the following order:

> It is the order of the Court that the judgment of conviction entered in said cause be and is hereby set aside and the indictment against said defendant be and the same is hereby dismissed.

On November 6, 2013, Tom was a passenger in a car that was pulled over for a routine traffic violation. Tom and his friend were on their way hunting. The officer asked the driver and Tom whether they possessed any weapons. Tom informed the officer that he had a hunting rifle behind the seat. The officer then processed his license to check for prior criminal history and outstanding warrants and learned of the 2010 conviction. Tom was subsequently arrested and indicted for the offense of unlawful possession of a firearm by a felon under East Carolina Penal Code §2-46-04.

RELEVANT MATERIALS

East Carolina Code Crim. Procedure §42-12-20 (enacted 1975):

(a) At any time, after the defendant has satisfactorily completed one-third of the original community supervision period or two years of community supervision, whichever is less, the period of community supervision may be reduced or terminated by the judge. Upon the satisfactory fulfillment of the conditions of community supervision, and the expiration of the period of community supervision, the judge, by order duly entered, shall amend or modify the original sentence imposed, if necessary, to conform to the community supervision period and shall discharge the defendant.

If the judge discharges the defendant under this section, the judge may set aside the verdict or permit the defendant to withdraw his plea, and shall dismiss the conviction against the defendant, who shall thereafter be released from all penalties and disabilities resulting from the offense or crime of which he had been convicted or to which he had pleaded guilty.

(b) **Findings and Purpose:**

The underlying purpose of community supervision is to provide criminal defendants with a chance to "mend their ways." If a defendant accepts the challenge and successfully completes the terms and conditions of community supervision, he or she should not be stigmatized for life. Such persons have demonstrated that they are ready to rejoin the community as law-abiding citizens.

East Carolina Penal Code §2-46-04 (enacted 2004):

(a) Unlawful Possession of a Firearm by a Felon

(1) A person who has been convicted of a felony commits an offense if he or she possesses a firearm following conviction of a felony and before the fifth an-

niversary of the person's release from confinement or the fifth anniversary of the person's release from supervision under community supervision, parole, or mandatory supervision, whichever date is later.

(2) Violation of this section is a Class C felony.

(b) **Findings and Purpose:**

The legislature finds that the State of East Carolina has an interest in protecting its citizens from violent felons. Hence, for a period of five years following their release from confinement and community supervision, convicted felons may not possess weapons, even in their homes.

Legislative History of § 2-46-04

Statements by Representative Longan, the sponsor of the bill, contained in the House Report:

The prohibition against a felon possessing firearms has been part of our jurisprudence, in one form or another, since 1949. The legislature has changed the substance of this offense several times with the addition or deletion of just a few words. At times, the offense has only applied to people after their release from the penitentiary, but not to those who never went to prison. At times, the statute has applied specifically only to people who have committed crimes of violence. And at times, the statute has prohibited weapon possession only for certain kinds of guns or only if possessed away from home.

With this amendment, the statute will take on the broadest possible meaning it has ever had in order to best protect the citizens of East Carolina from violent felons. For the first time, the prohibition against possessing a weapon will apply to all felons, regardless of whether the underlying offense involved an act of violence. And for the first time, a felon will be prohibited from possessing a gun, even at home, for five years after supervision ended.

This amendment makes the statute broader than all its previous versions. It applies regardless of the nature of the prior offense. And, it applies to a person whether or not he ever spent time in prison.

* * *

Assume that you represent Tom and are appearing before Judge Scalitia, a moderate textualist. Draft a trial brief (*argument section only*), arguing your client's case.

D. Statutes Shared Among Jurisdictions

What relevance should judicial interpretations from other jurisdictions, generally state, have on the interpretation of a statute in a particular jurisdiction? You likely know by now that the judicial interpretations of other jurisdictions are merely persuasive authority, never mandatory. But when statutory interpretation is involved, judicial interpretations from other jurisdictions are more influential in two situations:

when one state borrows a statute from another jurisdiction and when one state enacts a uniform or model act. In addition, a legislature may model a statute after an existing statute within its own jurisdiction. Let's begin with modeled and borrowed statutes.

1. Modeled and Borrowed Statutes

a. Modeled Statutes

Modeling happens intra-jurisdictionally (within a jurisdiction). Sometimes, a legislature will use an existing statute or statutes to serve as a model for a new statute. For example, the Age Discrimination in Employment Act ("ADEA") was modeled after three acts: the National Labor Relations Act, the Fair Labor Standards Act ("FLSA"), and Title VII of the Civil Rights Act.

When a legislature models a statute, courts will look to the modeling statute and its settled judicial interpretations for guidance for interpreting the new statute. Following this canon, the Supreme Court in *Lorrillard v. Pons*, 434 U.S. 575 (1978), looked at the FLSA to determine whether the ADEA provided a right to jury trials because the ADEA specifically provided that it should be interpreted in accordance with the "powers, remedies, and *procedures*" of the FLSA. *Id.* at 579 n.5 (quoting 29 U.S.C. §626(b)). Because the FLSA provided such a right, the Court held that ADEA did as well. *Id.* at 579.

When a statute is modeled after another statute or shares similar language, courts often apply the identical words presumption to resolve interpretation issues. *See, e.g., Smith v. Jackson*, 544 U.S. 228, 234 (2005) (holding that the ADEA authorized disparate-impact claims because it that was "derived in *haec verba* from Title VII" of the Civil Rights Act, which the Court had interpreted to authorize such claims); *Sutton v. United Air Lines, Inc.*, 527 U.S. 471, 497 (1999) (Stevens, J., dissenting) (interpreting the word "disability" in the Americans with Disabilities Act (ADA) consistently with the word "disability" in the Rehabilitation Act because the ADA's definition was drawn "almost verbatim" from the Rehabilitation Act).

b. Borrowed Statutes

Borrowing happens inter-jurisdictionally (among jurisdictions). Sometimes, a legislature will use a statute, in whole or in part, from another jurisdiction. States borrow statutory language because it is simpler to borrow than to create a statute anew.

When a state legislature borrows a statute from another jurisdiction—whether state or federal—courts assume that the borrowing legislature took not only the statutory language but also any judicial opinions interpreting that statute from the highest court in the patterning jurisdiction at the time of the adoption. *Zerbe v. State*, 583 P.2d 845, 846 (Alaska 1978) (refusing to adopt the judicial opinion of a lower court from the patterning state). This canon is based on the presumptions that the borrowing legislature (1) was aware of the judicial interpretations in the patterning jurisdiction, and (2) intended those interpretations to guide its own judiciary. Note that after the borrowing occurs, any subsequent judicial opinions in the patterning jurisdiction are simply informative; the borrowing state's judiciary remains free to reject the later interpretations.

Van Horn v. William Blanchard Co.

Supreme Court of New Jersey

438 A.2d 552 (N.J. 1981)

◆ CLIFFORD, J. [WILENTZ, C.J., and CLIFFORD, SCHREIBER, POLLOCK, JJ. concur].

After a bifurcated trial in this negligence action the jury returned a verdict finding plaintiff fifty percent negligent, one defendant thirty percent negligent and a second defendant twenty percent negligent. The trial court molded the verdict and entered judgment in favor of defendants, and thereafter denied plaintiff's motion ... to amend the judgment. The Appellate Division affirmed, ... concluding that despite the fact that plaintiff's negligence was not greater than the combined negligence of defendants, recovery was barred under the Comparative Negligence Act, N.J.S.A. 2A:15-5.1 to -5.3. Plaintiff appeals.... We affirm.

On September 25, 1975 plaintiff, Lloyd K. Van Horn, was employed by Beach Electric Company.... The general contractor was defendant William Blanchard Company (Blanchard). Defendant Epic Construction Company (Epic) was another subcontractor.... On the date in question plaintiff sustained injuries giving rise to this suit when he slipped and fell on the job site while running into a building to avoid a rain storm. The cause of action was predicated on defendants' failure to have maintained the building entrance in a safe condition....

... [T]he jury ... found the negligence of Van Horn, Blanchard and Epic jointly to have produced the accident.... [T]he jury apportioned the negligence as follows: plaintiff, fifty percent; Blanchard, thirty percent; and Epic, twenty percent. Because the plaintiff's negligence exceeded the individual negligence of either of the joint tortfeasors, the trial court entered judgment for defendants.

On appeal plaintiff argued that "(i)n multiple defendant cases, in order to avoid harsh and unfair results, the negligence of an individual plaintiff must be compared to the combined negligence of the several tortfeasors." According to plaintiff he was entitled to a judgment on liability inasmuch as his negligence (fifty percent) was not greater than the aggregated negligence (fifty percent) of the two tort feasors.

A majority of the Appellate Division rejected this contention....

The Comparative Negligence Act, L.1973, C. 146, was the Legislature's response to the harshness of the complete bar to recovery imposed by the rule of contributory negligence. New Jersey has a "modified" comparative negligence system, as distinguished from a "pure" system under which "a plaintiff may recover even if his negligence is greater than the negligence of the adverse tortfeasor," with the recovery "diminished by his degree of contributory negligence."

Section 1 of the Act reads as follows:

Contributory negligence shall not bar recovery in an action by any person or his legal representative to recover damages for negligence resulting in death or injury to person or property, if such negligence was not greater than the negligence of the person against whom recovery is sought, but any damages sustained shall be diminished by the percentage sustained of negligence attributable to the person recovering. (N.J.S.A. 2A:15-5.1).

The Legislature's use of the singular "the person" rather than the plural form strongly suggests that a plaintiff's negligence should be compared to the negligence of only one person at a time. Plaintiff would have us reject that sensible construction by resort to N.J.S.A. 1:1-2, which provides that "(w)herever, in describing or referring to any person * * * any word imparting the singular number * * * is used, the same shall be understood to include and to apply to several persons or parties as well * * *." The argument is that "in its use of the phrase 'the person against whom recovery is sought' the Legislature intended to refer to the tortfeasor concept in its collective and adjectival sense * * *."

Whatever persuasive appeal is inherent in that approach is overcome when section 1 of the Act is read in conjunction with section 3. The latter section reads:

The party so recovering, may recover the full amount of the molded verdict from any party against whom such recovering party is not barred from recovery. Any party who is so compelled to pay more than such party's percentage share may seek contribution from the other joint tortfeasors. (N.J.S.A. 2A:15-5.3).

This statute obviously addresses a multi-defendant situation, as in the case before us. Equally obvious is that it contemplates a fact pattern in which the plaintiff is entitled to recover from at least one defendant, while at the same time there are other negligent defendants from whom he is not entitled to recover — the antithesis of aggregating all the defendants' negligence. No other meaning can reasonably be ascribed to the descriptive phrase "any party against whom such recovering party is not barred from recovery." And if there are defendants from whom plaintiff is entitled to recover and others from whom recovery is barred, then it is clear that aggregation of defendants' percentages of fault is not contemplated; for if it were, and if a plaintiff were entitled to recover against any negligent defendant, he would be entitled to recover against all under the minority's theory....

The Comparative Negligence Act was taken nearly verbatim from the Wisconsin comparative negligence statute. A legislative enactment patterned after a statute of another state is ordinarily adopted with the prior constructions placed on it by the highest court of the parent jurisdiction. Hence it is significant that at the time New Jersey adopted the Wisconsin "modified" form of comparative negligence, the individual approach rather than the aggregate system was a fixture in Wisconsin law. In cases decided after New Jersey had embraced comparative negligence Wisconsin continued to adhere to the principle that the comparison of negligence in multiple defendant cases must be between the plaintiff and each defendant individually [citing Wisconsin cases]. Whereas it is true that Wisconsin flirted with the notion of em-

Borrowing statutes ←

bracing the aggregate approach, the departure was but a momentary aberration, as disclosed by *Reiter v. Dyken*, 290 N.W.2d 510 (1980)[:]

> To change from the present rule to one in which a plaintiff would be allowed to recover against a person less negligent than himself would have significant ramifications throughout the tort system of allocating losses as it now exists in this state. Specifically, such a change would raise important questions about the extent of a less negligent defendant's liability and the operation of the rules of joint and several liability, contribution, set-off and release. Indeed, unless accompanying changes are made in these related areas of law, the change requested by plaintiff may very well create far more serious problems that it is intended to resolve. For this reason we think plaintiffs' request would be better addressed to the legislature.

Demonstrating that it meant what it said, the Wisconsin Supreme Court made the following observation within a month of the *Reiter* decision:

> On a number of occasions this court has considered the question of whether or not it should modify or change our comparative negligence rule of law (requiring individual comparison) and this court has consistently held that the decision of whether to change the comparative negligence rule of law is a legislative matter.

It is therefore apparent that Wisconsin has put to rest any question of changing its judicial interpretation of that state's comparative negligence law....

◆ HANDLER, J., dissenting with whom SULLIVAN and PASHMAN, JJ., join.

The Court in this case has ruled that New Jersey's Comparative Negligence Act, N.J.S.A. 2A:15-5.1 et seq., prevents a plaintiff injured in an accident from recovering damages from defendants whose combined fault for the accident equaled or exceeded that of the plaintiff. It does so notwithstanding the statute's intent to permit recovery by a plaintiff whose own fault for accidental injury constitutes no more than half of the total fault. The Court apparently feels bound to this result for two reasons-because the language of the statute admits of no other interpretation and because this particular interpretation was reached by the courts of another jurisdiction whose decisions are said to be binding upon us. In my view, these reasons, singly or together, do not justify the inequitable result embodied in the majority's interpretation of the Comparative Negligence Act. I therefore dissent....

The majority concludes that the plain language of the New Jersey Comparative Negligence Act dictates the individual approach. The statutory language upon which the majority relies provides that "(c)ontributory negligence shall not bar recovery" in a negligence action if the claimant's contributory "negligence was not greater than the negligence of the person against whom recovery is sought ..." N.J.S.A. 2A:15-5.1. Further reference is made to another provision of the Act that states that a successful claimant "may recover the full amount" of the verdict to which he is entitled "from any party against whom (he) is not barred from recovery." N.J.S.A. 2A:15-5.3.

In reasoning that the emphasized words* in these passages dictate the individual approach, the majority has succumbed to a common judicial temptation in the interpretation of statutes. In effect, the Court has already interpreted the statute to require the singular significance of the term "person" and then declares that the "plain language" admits of only one interpretation—the one it has selected.

The essential judicial task, of course, is to ascertain the statutory meaning intended by the Legislature. Where the plain meaning of a statute is revealed by its language, given its ordinary significance and understanding, that meaning, and no other, must be ascribed to the enactment. What constitutes "plain" language, however, is not always obvious. The meaning of language that is seemingly clear and unequivocal may become doubtful and elusive when considered in a wider context. In my estimation, the statutory language at issue does not simply or plainly reveal the intentions of the Legislature....

While the facial or literal terms in question permit the construction chosen by the Court, neither the intrinsic nor contextual meaning of the words of the statute requires this interpretation. The Legislature has provided its own guidelines for the interpretation of statutes, which in this case counsel a different construction from that imposed by the majority. N.J.S.A. 1:1-2 defines certain words and phrases for interpretive purposes and specifically states ... that "any word importing the singular number ... shall be understood to include and apply to several persons or parties as well as to one person or party." Thus, the word "person" as used in the Act does not necessarily or plainly denote "one person." [As the dissent below noted,] "the person against whom recovery is sought" is a legislative reference "to the tortfeasor concept in its collective and adjectival sense."

The majority's reliance on N.J.S.A. 2A:15-5.3 to extract a contextual meaning from the words "the person" or "any person" as denoting the singular usage does not advance its "plain language" thesis. That provision has to do with the allocation of the recovery of a successful plaintiff. It simply states that such a plaintiff may recover the entire or full amount of the verdict from any defendant "against whom (the plaintiff) is not barred from recovery." This class of defendants, of course, encompasses all, and means any of the defendants who are liable to the plaintiff....

The second reason for the Court's conclusion that the New Jersey comparative negligence scheme embraces the individual approach is its belief that determinative weight must be given to the construction placed on the comparative negligence statute of Wisconsin by the courts of that state. It is true that New Jersey's Comparative Negligence Act mirrors Wisconsin's. The majority opinion assumes that in adopting a comparative negligence statute similar to Wisconsin's, our Legislature intended to embrace that state's judicial interpretation of its statute as well.

As a general rule, courts give a legislative enactment patterned after the statute of another state the same construction placed upon it by the highest court of that jurisdiction. New Jersey follows this approach. This rule, of course, is merely a tool for ascertaining the true intention of the Legislature. The judicial decisions of another state are not conclusive evidence of legislative intent. Thus, where the legislature of

---

* Editor's footnote: No words are emphasized in the dissent's opinion.

one state chooses to adopt as part of its laws the statute of another state, the judiciary of the adopting state may, if appropriate, choose to interpret its statute differently from the judicial interpretations of the source state. If there is some doubt that the adopting legislature fully intended to embrace the particular interpretations or applications by the courts of the source state, the courts of the adopting jurisdiction do not have to give greater weight to the originating state's judicial decisions than their intrinsic persuasiveness demands; and this is especially so where the public policies of the adopting state elicit different concerns and invoke priorities that are important or unique to that jurisdiction.

[Margin note: Permissible to interpret differently]

The assumption that the New Jersey Legislature intended to embrace not only Wisconsin's statute but also its judicial interpretations of that statute is questionable. The majority seemingly takes the view that the New Jersey law does not merely follow but is actually cloned from the Wisconsin statute. While references to the Wisconsin statute are present in the legislative history, there is nothing in that history to indicate that the Legislature, in adopting this statute, considered the central issue presented by this case — whether to employ the aggregate or the individual approach.

[Margin note: Leg. History]

[Margin note: ISSUE]

In addition, the sponsors' statement accompanying the bill introduced in the Assembly did not refer exclusively to the Wisconsin approach. Rather, it read, in pertinent part: "This State will not be unique if it adopts the law of comparative negligence. Other jurisdictions such as Wisconsin, Arkansas, Georgia, Maine, Florida, Iowa, Mississippi, Nebraska, South Dakota, Puerto Rico, the Canal Zone, the Canadian provinces, etc., have a form of comparative negligence." Therefore, it seems clear that the sponsors of the bill considered not only the law of Wisconsin but also that of a variety of jurisdictions, some of which adhere to the aggregate approach.

[Margin note: all these other states]

One such state, specifically mentioned by the sponsors, is Arkansas. Though its comparative negligence statute was couched in terms of singular usage, that state adopted the aggregate approach through judicial construction as early as 1962. . . .

[Margin note: Arkansas]

In 1978, the Oklahoma Supreme Court held that the state's comparative negligence statute, then phrased in the singular, should be interpreted to apply an aggregate approach. The court reasoned that its statute was based on the statutory scheme of both Wisconsin and Arkansas and that Arkansas' "aggregate" approach was preferable.

[Margin note: OK referring to Arkansas]

In opting to follow exactly or literally the Wisconsin judicial interpretation of the Comparative Negligence Act, this Court has abandoned any genuine interpretation of the Act and has walled off its analysis from any considerations of public policy. Yet no compelling argument is made why the decisions of the Wisconsin Supreme Court should be clamped around this State's comparative negligence law like an iron girdle, yielding no breathing room for our own tort law jurisprudence and public policy. In light of a legislative history that does not dictate such a course, our deliberations should be aired fully with reflections of our own public policy and legal traditions. . . .

[Margin note: very strong language]

[The dissent then explains why public policy reasons support the aggregate approach.]

[Margin note: Reason to interpret differently]

Plain lang.
→ doesn't
support individual

In sum, I find no forceful argument in favor of construing the Comparative Negligence Act, as has the majority, to require the comparison of the negligence of a plaintiff with those of defendants on an individual basis. The language of the Act itself does not demand this. The decisions of the Wisconsin Courts do not constitute persuasive evidence of the intent of the New Jersey Legislature on this facet of the Act. Those decisions betray serious misgivings as to the soundness and wisdom of the interpretation of that state's law and are entitled to neither dispositive nor great weight by us in interpreting our law. Most importantly, our own public policy considerations strongly impel the aggregate approach to our Comparative Negligence Act.

* * *

Points for Discussion

1. *Statutory Language*: What was the language at issue? What did each party want that language to mean? What meaning did the majority and dissent adopt?

2. *Theories*: Which theory did the majority use? The dissent? Did the majority or dissent find the language ambiguous, absurd, to have a scrivener's error, or to raise a constitutional question?

3. *Singular & Plural*: The majority refused to apply N.J.S.A. 1:1-2, which provides that "(w)herever, in describing or referring to any person … any word imparting the singular number … is used, the same shall be understood to include and to apply to several persons or parties as well…." Why did the majority refuse to apply this statutory directive?

4. *Borrowed Statutes Canon*: Generally, judicial interpretations from other jurisdictions are merely persuasive and are followed when their reasoning is persuasive. Does the canon for borrowed statutes change the level of deference afforded sister opinions (are they more than persuasive) or change the rationale for deference?

5. *Wisconsin, Arkansas, and Oklahoma*: Which, if any of these states, was the state from which the New Jersey legislature borrowed its statutory language? Should not the court be certain that its own legislature intended to borrow the specific jurisdiction's statute before the court adopts that state's judicial interpretations?

6. *Role of the Borrowed State's Jurisprudence*: Did the majority or dissent better follow the borrowing statute canon, which directs that courts should presume that the legislature intended to adopt the patterning state's judicial interpretations when it borrows a statute?

7. *N.J.S.A. §2A:15-5.3*: The majority found this second statute dispositive. Why? Why did the dissent disagree?

8. *Legislative Correction*: A year after this case, the legislature overturned it. *Buckley v. Estate of Pirolo*, 500 A.2d 703, 710 (N.J. 1985) ("To remedy the perceived inequity in that result the legislature adopted the 'aggregate' approach: plaintiff in a negligence action may recover damages in any case in which his negligence is less than or equal to the combined negligence of multiple defendants."). Does this subsequent legislative action show that the dissent was right—that the ag-

gregate approach better furthers New Jersey's public policy—or that the majority was right to let the legislature make the decision?

* * *

2. Uniform and Model Acts

Uniform and model acts are similar to borrowed statutes, but these acts are borrowed from another source altogether. The National Conference of Commissioners on Uniform State Laws, the American Law Institute, and other institutional drafters develop model and uniform acts. Both types of acts are created to address multijurisdictional issues, such as interstate commerce and child custody. Some familiar examples of these acts include the Uniform Commercial Code, the Model Business Corporation Act, the Uniform Child Custody Jurisdiction and Enforcement Act, and the Model Penal Code. For some reason, Nevada appears to have adopted the most model and uniform acts with the least number of changes. American Law Sources On-Line, *Uniform Law and Model Acts*, (last accessed January 17, 2016) http://www.lawsource.com/also/usa.cgi?usm. In addition to the web, model and uniform acts can be found in the Uniform Laws Annotated, which is a set of books that includes the laws and annotations showing where the laws have been adopted, interpreted, and cited.

The principle difference between model acts and uniform acts is the importance of wide adoption and uniform interpretation to each. Let's start with uniform acts.

a. Uniform Acts

Uniform Acts are proposed state laws that the National Conference of Commissioners on Uniform State Laws ("Conference") or another institutional actor drafts. The Conference was established in 1892 and is made up of lawyers, judges, and law professors. Members of the Conference draft laws on a variety of subjects and propose them for enactment within the states, the District of Columbia, the U.S. Virgin Islands, and Puerto Rico. The Conference has no legislative power; rather, the proposed uniform acts become law only when they are adopted in a particular state. Thus, proposed uniform acts serve as guidelines, or samples, for the state legislatures. The United States is a country with one federal system of laws and fifty or more state systems of laws. The purpose of the Conference is to help encourage uniformity across state lines, particularly in areas where state boundaries are essentially irrelevant. For example, the Uniform Commercial Code, which has been widely adopted among the states, unifies the law regarding the sale of goods. There are currently more than 100 different uniform acts.

For *uniform acts*, uniformity is essential. *Pileri Indus., Inc. v. Consolidated Indus., Inc.*, 740 So. 2d 1108, 1114 (Ala. Civ. App. 1999) (Crawley, J., dissenting). The Commissioners draft a uniform act in two situations: (1) when they anticipate enactment in a large number of jurisdictions, and (2) when they have uniformity among the various jurisdictions as a principal objective. NATIONAL CONFERENCE OF COMMISSIONERS ON UNIFORM STATE LAWS, STATEMENT OF POLICY ESTABLISHING CRITERIA AND PRO-

CEDURES FOR DESIGNATION AND CONSIDERATION OF ACTS (2001). Thus, the Commissioners encourage state legislatures to adopt a uniform act in its entirety with as few changes as possible. The Commissioners' principle goal when drafting a uniform act is to obtain immediate uniformity, not uniqueness, among the states on a particular legal subject. This goal affects interpretation in that the judicial interpretations from other states are always strongly persuasive, regardless of when they occur.

> While opinions by courts of sister states construing a uniform act are not binding upon this court, we are mindful that the objective of uniformity cannot be achieved by ignoring utterances of other jurisdictions.... This does not mean that this court will blindly follow decisions of other states interpreting uniform acts but, this court will seriously consider the constructions given to comparable statutes in other jurisdictions and will espouse them to maintain conformity when they are in harmony with the spirit of the statute and do not antagonize public policy of this state.

Holiday Inns, Inc. v. Olsen, 692 S.W.2d 850, 853 (Tenn. 1985) (rejecting the state tax department's interpretation of "business earnings" in the Uniform Division of Income for Tax Purposes Act because others states had interpreted the term differently).

When courts from one jurisdiction follow the interpretations of uniform acts in other states, courts help ensure that the construction of such acts remains standard and uniform. *Blitz v. Beth Isaac Adas Israel Congregation*, 720 A.2d 912, 918 (Md. 1998) (interpreting the word "disbursements" in the Uniform Arbitration Act to include attorney's fees, in part, because other states had done so even though the text of the Act suggested that attorney's fees should not be included). As noted, for uniform acts, uniformity is central.

Believe it or not, there is a Uniform Statute and Rule Construction Act ("the Act"). The National Conference of Commissioners on Uniform State Laws approved the Act in 1993 and recommended enactment in the states. The Act represents a compromise among the various conflicting preferences in the field of statutory construction. For example, in Chapter 4, this text describes various theories, or approaches, of statutory interpretation, including textualism—which focuses on the text—and purposivism—which focuses on the text together with the purpose of the statute. The drafters of the Act refused to adopt any theory; however, the Act does emphasize the primacy of the text. But the Act also recognizes the relevance of non-textual sources, such as legislative history, from which purpose may be discerned. The Act thus takes a middle ground approach to the philosophical and academic debate. Additionally, the Act makes clear that its "rules" are not rules in the typical legal sense, but rather are simply a hierarchy of values for the interpreter to follow as the circumstances allow. UNIF. STATUTE & RULE CONSTR. ACT, § 18 cmt. (1995). To date, only the state of New Mexico has adopted the Act.

b. Model Acts

In contrast to uniform acts, uniformity and wide adoption are less important for model acts. The Commissioners choose to draft a model act in two situations: (1)

when uniformity is desirable but not primary, and (2) when the purposes of an act can be substantially achieved even if the act is not adopted in its entirety by every state. NATIONAL CONFERENCE OF COMMISSIONERS ON UNIFORM STATE LAWS, STATEMENT OF POLICY ESTABLISHING CRITERIA AND PROCEDURES FOR DESIGNATION AND CONSIDERATION OF ACTS (2001). A model act may develop new or unusual approaches to particular legal problems; the effectiveness of these approaches will likely become clearer with time. Model acts are intended as guidelines that states may adapt to best address their unique circumstances. Hence, uniformity of interpretation and application, which is so important for uniform acts, is less critical for model acts. While uniformity is less critical, it is still a guiding principle when the model act has been widely adopted. *Brown v. Arp & Hammond Hardware Co.*, 141 P.3d 673, 680 (Wyo. 2006) ("When the words of a statute are materially the same and where the reasoning of another court interpreting the statute is sound, we do not sacrifice sovereign independence, nor undermine the unique character of Wyoming law, by relying upon the precedent of a foreign jurisdiction.") (internal quotations omitted).

Sometimes a *uniform* act is adopted in fewer states than was originally expected. When this happens, the Commissioners may either formally or informally relegate the uniform act to *model-act* status; the Uniform Construction Lien Act was one such act. Such a change illustrates simply that the act was less popular than originally expected. Importantly, state legislatures do not always make it clear that they are adopting a model or uniform act. Hence, it may be necessary to check the legislative history to determine whether a model or uniform act adoption was intended.

The canons in this chapter all relate to the timing of legislative enactments. Courts make certain assumptions about how legislatures would expect legislation to be interpreted based on the legislative process. Hence, specific statues generally control general ones, later statutes generally control earlier ones, and implied repeals are generally disfavored. Additionally statutes in different jurisdictions may also impact interpretation.

* * *

Problem 10B

Students at West Carolina State Law School are required to take Constitutional Law in their second year. The course is typically taught in two different sections in the same semester. Students chose their section subject to a lottery; no more than 60% of the class can enroll in any one section.

This past year, the law school offered three sections to accommodate a new professor's teaching package: Professor Logan. The rule was adjusted so no more than 45% of the class could enroll in any one section. The students selected their second year courses in the spring of their first year and were place into one of the constitutional law sections. Professor Logan ended up with the smallest group of students (35), likely because she taught the course on Wednesday and Friday afternoons and required attendance.

In the fall, after an unusually large number of first year students transferred out of West Carolina, some of the students in Professor Logan's section transferred into one of the other two sections as there were openings. For some reason, the registrar did not adjust the section limits to reflect the smaller class size. At the end of the add-drop period, Professor Logan had only 13 students.

You are Professor Logan's research assistant. Professor Logan knows that you are taking statutory interpretation and has asked for your advice regarding what grade average she may impose. Constitutional Law is a second year required, sectionalized course, which suggests that section 2 should apply. However, Professor Logan has only 13 students, which suggests that section 4 should apply. Professor Logan would like to have an average of 87.5, plus or minus one-half point. Professor Logan has no interest in seeking special dispensation from the Dean.

West Carolina Grading Policy

In 2004, the West Carolina Law School faculty adopted a policy calling for more uniform grading. This policy was adopted from a similar policy in use at the University of North Virginia School of Law, which is adopted in full. The policy mandates that the average grade awarded in each course fall within a predetermined narrow range. The purpose of the policy is to ensure equity in grading across courses and course sections, both in fact and in the perception of the students. The specific ranges adopted reflect the traditional overall grading patterns at West Carolina.

1. All first year courses shall have an average grade of 84.5, plus or minus one-half point.

2. Except as otherwise authorized by the Dean under subsection (5), all sectionalized upper division courses shall have an average grade of 85.5, plus or minus one-half point.

3. Except as otherwise authorized by the Dean under subsection (5), all other courses not specifically exempt from this policy shall have an average grade ranging from 84.5 to 86.5.

4. Seminars, advanced skills courses, and all other courses in which 15 or fewer students are enrolled are specifically exempted from this policy.

5. Any instructor wishing to deviate from subsections (2) or (3) must obtain prior approval from the Dean. Factors that the Dean may be asked to consider as appropriate bases for deviation from the approved average or range include: an unusual average GPA of the students enrolled in the course; grading of the course on the basis of a paper rather than an examination; and a class that as a whole performs on the examination in a manner justifying deviation.

* * *

In addition to the policy, you have learned that in the North Virginia School of law, two sectionalized courses are exempt from the mandatory average in section 2 because the sections always have fewer than 15 students. The two courses are Advanced Legal Research and Advanced Legal Writing. Neither course is required. Both have multiple sections. Advanced Legal Research is capped at 15 students. Advanced Legal

Writing is capped at 6 students. North Virginia School of Law decided to exempt these courses from section 2 because (1) they are non-required; (2) all sections are entitled to the exemption, so no students are penalized by being in a one or another section; (3) they always have 15 or fewer students. There are no other exceptions.

What advice do you provide to Professor Logan? Does your answer differ depending on when North Virginia made its decision to exempt the two classes (i.e., before or after 2004)?

[handwritten margin note: why N.V. has exemptions]

[handwritten notes:]

ISSUE: Whether the 13 student class fall into the exemption in Provision 4.

Operative language — Provision 4
language at issue "all other courses"

Support →

Chapter 11

Canons Based on Extrinsic Sources and Legislative Process: Enactment Context

A. Introduction to This Chapter

We continue with our examination of extrinsic sources and turn to enactment context. Legislative intent can often be found by understanding what motivated the legislature to act, by knowing what information the legislature considered when it acted, and by knowing what was said during the enactment process. This chapter will explore the canons related to using legislative context, including legislative history, to discern meaning.

B. Using What Occurred Prior to and During Enactment

1. Context

Knowing why a legislature chose to act may help a judge interpret a statute. *Contextualism* is the process of using context to determine why a legislature enacted a law to better understand what that law means. There are different types of context, including social and historical events (social or historical context), legal and political climate (legal or political context), economic or market factors (economic context), and even textual and linguistic patterns (textual context). We already looked at textual and linguistic context in preceding chapters (*See* Chapters 5–9).

In this chapter, we move to other types of context. A judge's interpretative theory determines which, if any, of these contexts are relevant. (*See* Chapter 4). For example, textualists will look at textual and linguistic context to understand the way that a particular legislature may have used words and phrases. In contrast, purposivists will look at social, historical, legal, economic, and political context; any one of which may help identify the statutory purpose. These types of context can help reveal the purpose of an act by showing how events of the time might have impacted a legislature's choices. For example, consider how the contexts of the following statutes would be germane to their meaning:

- *Social and historical context*—the Patriot Act, which enacted in response to the terrorist attacks of 9-11,
- *Political context*—the McCain-Feingold Act, which was enacted in response to perceived, illegal political spending,
- *Legal context*—an appropriation provision that was included in a budget bill to continue building the Tellico Dam and which was enacted during the pendency of litigation to shut down construction of the dam,
- *Economic context*—statutes enacted during the New Deal, which were enacted in response to the Great Depression.

Intentionalists will look at social, historical, legal, political, economic, and political context, which may help them identify the specific legislative intent. But most relevant to intentionalists is the enactment process itself. As we have seen, a statute is often the result of political compromise; contextualism allows intentionalist judges to interpret the statute so as to promote that compromise, thereby furthering legislative intent. *Mohasco Corp. v. Silver*, 447 U.S. 807, 819–20 (1980).

For some judges, context can trump ordinary meaning. For example, a federal statute prohibited individuals bringing into the United States "*any* false, forged, or counterfeit coin or bar." *United States v. Falvey*, 676 F.2d 871, 872 (1st Cir. 1982) (quoting 18 U.S.C. §§ 485, 486) (emphasis added). The three defendants owned counterfeit Krugerrands, which are coins from South Africa and which are not in circulation in the United States. Arguably, the ordinary meaning of the statute was clear. The defendants were guilty because they brought counterfeit coins into the United States. However, the court did not find the defendants guilty because early drafts of the bill and its legislative history demonstrated that "the only foreign coins covered by the [statute were] those 'current … or in actual use and circulation as money within the United States.'" *Id.* at 873 (quoting the lower court opinion). Thus, the history of the statute's enactment trumped ordinary meaning in this case.

In the case that follows, notice how the legal background plays a role in the court's interpretation of clear language.

D.C. Federation v. Volpe

United States District Court, District of Columbia

308 F. Supp. 423 (D.D.C. 1970) *rev'd* 434 F.2d 436 (D.C. Cir. 1970)

- SIRICA, DISTRICT JUDGE.

… The subject of this litigation, the Three Sisters Bridge between Virginia and the District of Columbia, has been a matter of controversy for several years in the courts, the Congress and the various agencies of the District of Columbia government. In February, 1968, the Court of Appeals for the District of Columbia Circuit in the case of *D.C. Federation of Civic Associations, Inc. v. Airis*, 391 F.2d 478, reversed the decision … of this court, and enjoined the construction of the Bridge and several other freeway projects until the District of Columbia had complied with the planning provisions of Title 7 of the D.C. Code.

In response to this decision, the Congress enacted Section 23 of the Federal-Aid Highway Act of 1968 ... the pertinent part of which provides

(a) Notwithstanding any other provisions of law or any court decision or administrative action to the contrary, the Secretary of Transportation and the government of the District of Columbia shall * * * construct all routes on the Interstate System * * *. Such construction shall be undertaken as soon as possible after the date of enactment of this Act, except as otherwise provided in this section and shall be carried out in accordance with all applicable provisions of title 23 of the United States Code. (b) Not later than 30 days after the date of enactment * * * the government of the District of Columbia shall commence work on the following projects: (1) Three Sisters Bridge * * *.

The plaintiffs here contend that the District of Columbia and Federal government should be enjoined from going forward with the construction of the Bridge until they have complied with the various planning and public hearing requirements of Title 23 of the United States Code. They base this argument on a broad reading of the language of Section 23 of the 1968 Act "in accordance with all applicable provisions of title 23 of the United States Code."

Both the Federal and the District of Columbia defendants argue that the intent of Congress in the 1968 Act was that the construction of the Bridge should proceed forthwith, with no further planning procedures necessary. They read the "in accordance with all applicable provisions of title 23" language to mean that only the provisions of Title 23 which deal with actual construction, rather than the planning and public hearing requirements, are to be applied in connection with the Bridge project.

The resolution of this suit thus comes down to a question of statutory interpretation. The court is of the opinion that the interpretation of Section 23 of the 1968 Highway Act proposed by the defendants is the most reasonable. The court has taken into consideration the fact that the Act was passed soon after the *Airis* decision which had held up the construction of the Bridge pending compliance with the planning provisions of the D.C. Code. That this was a factor motivating the passage of this legislation is shown by the opening language of Section 23(a) "[n]otwithstanding * * * any court decision * * * to the contrary." The intent of Congress is most clearly shown by the provision that work shall commence on the Bridge "[not] later than 30 days after the date of enactment." The Court believes that in passing this legislation, Congress intended that the District of Columbia commence construction on the Bridge project as soon as possible, and that no further planning or hearing requirements of Title 23 need be complied with....

* * *

Points for Discussion

1. *Statutory Language*: What was the language at issue? What did each party want that language to mean? What meaning did the court adopt?

2. *Theories*: Which theory did the court use? Did the court find the language ambiguous, absurd, to have a scrivener's error, or to raise a constitutional question? Where did the court look for evidence of meaning?

3. *Legal Context*: The language of the statute was clear that "all applicable provisions of title 23 of the United States Code" applied. Yet, despite that clear language, the court held that only some of the provisions in title 23 applied. Why? What impact did the court's holding in *D.C. Federation of Civic Associations, Inc. v. Airis*, 391 F.2d 478 (D.C. Cir. 1968), and the legislative response to that holding have on the court's interpretation in this case? This case shows the importance prior judicial and legislative activities can play in interpretation. Note that in Chapter 13, we will learn about the role of *subsequent* legislative and judicial activities. *See, e.g., Flood v. Kuhn*, 407 U.S. 258 (1972) (discussing legislative acquiescence and super strong *stare decisis*).

4. *An Example of Historical Context*: In *Leo Sheep Co. v. United States*, 440 U.S. 668 (1979), the Supreme Court had to determine whether the government had implicitly reserved easements in the Union Pacific Act in May 1862. The Act granted public land to the Union Pacific Railroad for each mile of track that it built to encourage the development of a transcontinental railroad. Union Pacific Railroad sold this land to private parties, including Leo Sheep Company. Leo Sheep Company then fenced its land, keeping the public from accessing the Seminoe Reservoir. The statute did not include an express reservation, although the Act did specifically include other reservations. To determine whether easements were impliedly reserved, the Court detailed the country's development of a transcontinental railroad. In doing so, the Court explained, "[C]ourts, in construing a statute, may with propriety recur to the history of the times when it was passed; and this is frequently necessary, in order to ascertain the reason as well as the meaning of particular provisions in it." Ultimately, the government lost; it had no easements, implied or express.

* * *

2. Legislative History

Historical, legal, economic, and social context can be found in many places, such as newspapers that were current at the time. However, most commonly, judges turn to the legislative history of the bill at issue, including draft versions of the bill. Judges vary in their willingness to consider a bill's legislative history and even in their willingness to consider all forms of legislative history. Some forms of legislative history are believed to be more trustworthy than others. Also, some forms of legislative history are believed to be more relevant than other forms; let's explore these issues in more detail.

Legislative history can be defined as the written record of deliberations accompanying a bill's enactment. Legislative history includes all the documentation that was generated during the enactment process, including bill drafts, committee reports and hearing transcripts, floor debates, recorded votes, conference committee reports, presidential signing statements, veto messages, and more. Most legislative history is generated at the chokeholds, or vetogates, within the legislative process. (*See* Chapter 3 for a discussion of vetogates.).

Perhaps more than any other area in statutory interpretation jurisprudence, the use of legislative history to discern meaning is highly controversial. As a litigant, you need to be aware of what legislative history is relevant, how relevant it is, how to find it, how to use it, and how to criticize its use. This next section will explore the relevance of legislative history to interpretation.

a. The Legislative History Hierarchy

As mentioned above, legislative history includes everything developed during the legislative process including bill drafts and amendments, committee reports, floor debates, conference committee reports, executive signing and veto statements, override memos, hearing transcripts, and even statements from sponsors. A search through all of the available documentation for the gold nugget of meaning can be burdensome, expensive, and time-consuming. Because not all legislative history has the same relevance, a savvy litigant should focus the search, especially when time and cost matter. Some types of legislative history are more relevant than other types; in other words, there is a legislative history hierarchy, and smart litigants know where to focus their search.

At the top of that hierarchy is the conference committee report. This report is, perhaps, "the most persuasive evidence of congressional intent, next to the statute itself." *United States v. Salim*, 287 F. Supp. 2d 250, 340 (S.D.N.Y. 2003). Remember from Chapter 3 that commonly the House and Senate pass different versions of a bill and that the conference committee—an ad hoc committee of select senators and representatives—meets, discusses the differences in the bill, resolves those differences, recommends action, and writes a report analyzing its work. This report is considered very good evidence of what the legislature wanted as a whole, because it is the only report members from both chambers generate. It truly identifies the compromises that lead to the bill's passage. But even a conference committee report may not trump clear text. In *In the Matter of Sinclair*, 870 F.2d 1340 (7th Cir. 1989), the plaintiffs pointed to a conference committee report that contradicted the plain language of the statute. Writing for the majority, Judge Easterbrook, a textualist judge, refused to consider the report because the language of the statute was so clear. *Id.* at 1344.

Next on the hierarchy are House and Senate committee reports. Committee reports are also considered reliable evidence of meaning because the committee primarily responsible for drafting, amending, considering, and reporting the bill to the full chamber generates them. Committee reports are written by the committee or committees (or its staff) that had jurisdiction over the bill. Generally, a committee report summarizes the bill and identifies the committee's recommendations and actions. Theoretically, all members of the committee read the report (or at least a summary of it) and vote based on the content of the report. The report follows the bill to the floor of the House or Senate, where it is expected that all members of the chamber will read the report. For these reasons, judges often rely on committee reports. *See, e.g., Church of the Holy Trinity v. United States*, 143 U.S. 457, 464 (1892) (relying on a committee report to hold that the legislature intended the word "labor" to include manual labor only).

If you would like to see what a simple report looks like, you will find a section of the Senate Report for the sample bill we explored in Chapter 9 in Appendix D. You may recall that the sample bill established a loan forgiveness program for lawyers who become public defenders and prosecutors. The Senate Report identifies a concern of at least two members of the Senate: the high cost of law school. Had the bill become law, this report may have aided a court with any subsequent interpretation issues.

Strict textualists refuse to consider legislative history at all. In the case that follows, then Judge Scalia initiated his assault on legislative history, particularly committee reports. In this case, Judge Scalia was particularly concerned about the majority's use of a house committee report of a subsequent congress. In other words, one legislature enacted the statute, while another congress wrote a committee report explaining what the statute meant. Be sure to read the footnote about whether Senator Dole had even read the committee report, let alone written it.

Hirschey v. FERC

United States Court of Appeals, District of Columbia Circuit
777 F.2d 1 (D.C. Cir. 1985)

♦ [The majority opinion, determining the appropriate amount of attorneys' fees under the Equal Access to Justice Act ("EAJA"), has been omitted.].

♦ SCALIA, CIRCUIT JUDGE, concurring:

Although I dissented in *Hirschey II*, believing that the EAJA did not apply to the present case, since the court held otherwise I have participated in this subsequent consideration of what the amount of the EAJA award should be. I join the court's opinion with the exception of the dictum discussed below. I write separately principally to clarify several points in the current opinion related to my earlier dissent....

While not contesting that *Hirschey II* is now the law of this circuit, I must nonetheless dissociate myself from the dictum of the court — which may be given effect in other circuits — that the legislative history of the 1985 EAJA amendments "ratifies the holding of the majority opinion in *Hirschey II*."... The entire case for the majority's asserted "ratification" of *Hirschey II* rests upon the following statement in the House Committee Report:

> The language of section 2412(d)(1)(A) expresses the view that prevailing parties shall be awarded attorney's fees and, when available, costs as well. This interpretation ratifies the approach taken by four circuits. [Citing, *inter alia, Hirschey II*.] ... Thus, the Committee rejects the interpretations of the statute by the 9th Circuit....

H.R. REP. No. 120, 99th Cong., 1st Sess. 17 (1985), 1985 U.S. Code Cong. & AD.News 132, 145. It is most interesting that the House Committee rejected the interpretation of the Ninth Circuit, and perhaps that datum should be accorded the weight of an equivalently unreasoned law review article. But the authoritative, as opposed to the persuasive, weight of the report depends entirely upon how reasonable it is to assume that the rejection was reflected in the law which *Congress* adopted. I frankly doubt that it is ever reasonable to assume that the details, as opposed to the broad outlines of purpose, set forth in a committee report come to the attention of, much less are approved by, the House which enacts the committee's bill.[1] And I think it time for courts to become concerned about the fact that routine deference to the detail of committee reports, and the predictable expansion in that detail which routine deference has produced, are converting a system of judicial construction into a system

---

1. Several years ago, the following illuminating exchange occurred between members of the Senate, in the course of floor debate on a tax bill:

> Mr. ARMSTRONG.... My question, which may take [the chairman of the Committee on Finance] by surprise, is this: Is it the intention of the chairman that the Internal Revenue Service and the Tax Court and other courts take guidance as to the intention of Congress from the committee report which accompanies this bill?
>
> Mr. **DOLE.** I would certainly hope so....
>
> Mr. ARMSTRONG. Mr. President, will the Senator tell me whether or not he wrote the committee report?
>
> Mr. **DOLE.** Did I write the committee report?
>
> Mr. ARMSTRONG. Yes.
>
> Mr. **DOLE.** No; the Senator from Kansas did not write the committee report.
>
> Mr. ARMSTRONG. Did any Senator write the committee report?
>
> Mr. **DOLE.** I have to check.
>
> Mr. ARMSTRONG. Does the Senator know of any Senator who wrote the committee report?
>
> Mr. **DOLE.** I might be able to identify one, but I would have to search. I was here all during the time it was written, I might say, and worked carefully with the staff as they worked....
>
> Mr. ARMSTRONG. Mr. President, has the Senator from Kansas, the chairman of the Finance Committee, read the committee report in its entirety?
>
> Mr. **DOLE.** I am working on it. It is not a bestseller, but I am working on it.
>
> Mr. ARMSTRONG. Mr. President, did members of the Finance Committee vote on the committee report?
>
> Mr. **DOLE.** No.
>
> Mr. ARMSTRONG. Mr. President, the reason I raise the issue is not perhaps apparent on the surface, and let me just state it:.... The report itself is not considered by the Committee on Finance. It was not subject to amendment by the Committee on Finance. It is not subject to amendment now by the Senate..... .
>
> ... If there were matter within this report which was disagreed to by the Senator from Colorado or even by a majority of all Senators, there would be no way for us to change the report. I could not offer an amendment tonight to amend the committee report.
>
> ... [F]or any jurist, administrator, bureaucrat, tax practitioner, or others who might chance upon the written record of this proceeding, let me just make the point that this is not the law, it was not voted on, it is not subject to amendment, and we should discipline ourselves to the task of expressing congressional intent in the statute.

128 CONG.REC. S8659 (daily ed. July 19, 1982).

of committee-staff prescription. But the authority of the committee report in the present case is even more suspect than usual. Where a committee-generated report deals with the meaning of a committee-generated text, one can at least surmise that someone selected these statutory words to convey this intended meaning. The portion of the report at issue here, however, comments upon language drafted in an earlier congress, and reenacted, *unamended*, so far as is relevant to the present point, in the 1985 law. We are supposed to believe that the legislative action recommended by the committee and adopted by the congress, in order to resolve a difficult question of interpretation that had produced a conflict in the circuits and internal disagreement within three of the five courts that had considered it, was reenactment of the same language unchanged? Such a supposition is absurd on its face; and doubly absurd since the precise section was amended in 1985 on such a point of minute detail as changing an "and" to "or."

In sum, even if the 1985 EAJA amendments had been relevant to our determination in *Hirschey II*, I think the question should still have been resolved, as it was, not on the basis of what the committee report said, but on the basis of what we judged to be the most rational reconciliation of the relevant provisions of law Congress had adopted. I was disappointed that the court did not reconcile them as I would have, but I at least had the comfort, which implementation of the dictum here under discussion would deny me, of thinking that the court was wrong for the right reason.

* * *

Points for Discussion

1. *Statutory Language*: Given the short excerpt, you cannot identify the relevant language.

2. *Theories*: Which theory did the dissent use?

3. *Point*: Why did Justice Scalia dissent in this case? What was his goal? Was he more concerned about the judicial use of legislative history (especially committee reports) in general or the use in this case where the committee report came from a subsequent Congress?

4. *Footnote One*: Why did Justice Scalia include footnote one in this opinion? What was your reaction upon reading it?

* * *

There is another form of legislative history that should be distinguished from committee reports called "committee prints." Committee prints are documents created for a congressional committee about topics related to that committee's legislative or investigatory responsibilities. Studies by committee staff members or experts on the subject matter of a proposed bill, committee rules, and summaries of the legislative history of earlier failed bills are all examples. Committee prints are drafted for the committee's internal use and are not always available publically. *See* U.S. Government Publishing Office, *About Congressional Committee Prints* https://www.gpo.gov/help/about_congressional_committee_prints.htm. Arguably, because committee prints vary significantly in content, are not always forwarded to the full chambers, and may not reflect the intent of the legislature as a whole, they should play less, if any, role in interpretation.

Another potentially relevant source of legislative history is earlier drafts, or versions, of the bill and rejected amendments to it. The enactment process frequently involves numerous drafts as the bill's language is refined with time. It can be instructive to see what the committee, subcommittee, or full chamber changed. Thus, earlier versions and rejected amendments might help explain what a legislature intended when it adopted the language it enacted. *See, e.g., NLRB v. Catholic Bishop*, 440 U.S. 490, 515 (1979) (Brennan, J., dissenting) (finding rejected amendments informative).

It is less clear whether bills that were never enacted are relevant at all. If a prior legislature refused to enact a bill, that fact should have no relevance for interpreting bills that are subsequently enacted. But if a legislature rejects one bill and instead adopts a compromise bill, the rejected bill might help a judge discern legislative intent for the compromise bill. Ronald Benton Brown & Sharon Jacobs Brown, Statutory Interpretation: The Search for Legislative Intent 146–47 (2d ed. 2011). Moreover, judges might consider the rejected bill to be evidence that the legislature acquiesced in, or agreed with, an earlier judicial interpretation of an act. (*See* Chapter 13).

Some argue that the most relevant statements are the drafter's, or drafters', commentary because that commentary is prepared before the bill is subject to legislative manipulation by either those in favor or those opposed to the bill's passage. For example, the comments on the Uniform Commercial Code (UCC) were prepared jointly by the National Conference of Commissioners on Uniform State Laws, the American Bar Association, and the American Law Institute. These comments are generally found to be very relevant to that Act's meaning. These drafters are considered experts in the area; they had tremendous knowledge of the bill and its purpose. Given that they are academics and practicing attorneys, their comments were deliberate and thoughtful, rather than political. Additionally, the legislature that voted to enact the UCC likely considered their comments and intended that the UCC be interpreted as the comments recommended. Had the legislature wanted a different interpretation, the legislature would likely have changed the language of the bill, which the legislature was free to do. Thus, in certain circumstances, drafters' commentary can aid interpretation. *See, e.g., United Steelworkers v. Weber*, 443 U.S. 193, 231–44 (1979) (Rehnquist, J., dissenting) (considering statements from both the Senate and House sponsors to argue that Title VII of the Civil Rights Act was color-blind).

Others, however, argue that statements from a drafter or sponsor (the legislator proposing the bill to Congress) are not relevant to meaning because the critical intent is not that of the individual or individuals. The critical intent is that of the legislature that enacted the bill. Additionally, staff members or lobbyists often provide the initial drafts for bills, and their intent is irrelevant. Regardless of these criticisms, some judges will still consider drafter and sponsor statements. "[N]o one can gainsay the overwhelming judicial support for the proposition that explanations by sponsors of legislation during floor discussion are entitled to weight when they cast light on the construction properly to be placed upon statutory language." *Overseas Educ. Ass'n, Inc., v. Federal Labor Relations Auth.*, 876 F.2d 960, 967 n.41 (D.C. Cir. 1989) (citing more than ten cases relying on sponsor statements). In contrast, lobbyist materials are usually not relevant to interpretation.

Statements, remarks, and debates that take place in either the Committee of the Whole or on the floor of either chamber are relatively low on the legislative hierarchy. Even lower are floor debate comments made by those opposed to the legislation, which carry even less weight than statements from those in agreement. "[S]peeches by opponents of legislation are entitled to relatively little weight in determining the meaning of the Act in question." *United States v. Pabon-Cruz*, 391 F.3d 86, 101 (2d Cir. 2004).

There are a few problems with relying on floor statements of either type. One problem is that they reflect only one legislator's intent, not the intent of the legislature as a whole. Because each legislator may have a unique reason for voting for a particular bill, one person's intent shows little. "The floor statements of individual legislators are larded with remarks which reflect a political ('sales talk') rather than a legislative purpose." *In re Virtual Network Serv. Corp.*, 98 B.R. 343, 349 (Bankr. N.D. Ill. 1989).

A second problem is that in the past remarks could be added to the debate record without ever having been spoken on the floor for other legislators to hear. For example, in *Harrisburg v. Franklin*, 806 F. Supp. 1181 (M.D. Pa. 1992), the court refused to consider a legislator's written statements, which were made after the bill was passed and were "*never actually spoken on the floor of the legislature.*" *Id.* at 1184. Importantly, a relatively recent rule has required that these statements be clearly marked in the extension of remarks section of the legislative history; thus, this concern has lessened, but it should be kept in mind for statutes enacted less recently. Moreover, some have suggested that this rule is not well enforced.

Another potential problem with relying on floor remarks is that legislators do not always attend or hear all debates; sometimes, speeches are made to empty chambers for political or other reasons. And even if the remarks are heard, it is not always clear whether the remarks influenced the vote. If not influential, should these remarks matter? Would not this rule set up a requirement that legislators respond to all floor comments with which they disagree? Would such a rule be efficient?

For all these reasons, floor debate statements, both pro and con, are generally not considered as reliable as the other forms of legislative history. Despite these concerns, judges still rely on these statements when interpreting statutes. *See, e.g., United Steelworkers v. Weber*, 443 U.S. 193 (1979) (in which the majority and dissent both relied on different parts of the floor debates to prove that their interpretation of the word "discriminate" in Title VII of the Civil Rights Act was accurate).

Finally, we reach the tail end of the hierarchy: executive signing statements and veto messages. Signing statements are actually *subsequent* history for they generally follow a bill's enactment (presidents typically sign a bill and then issue a signing statement). Moreover, neither is *legislative* history in the sense that neither comes from the legislature, but instead both come from the executive; hence, they are subsequent executive history. But they are similar enough to the other forms of legislative history to be discussed here.

As noted in Chapter 3, signing statements may indicate how an executive intends to implement a law. The relevance (if any) these statements should have on interpretation is unclear. Those advocating for their use argue that signing statements illustrate the executive's position in negotiating with the legislature. Supporters further argue that, because the executive has a constitutional role to play in enactment, the statements are germane to meaning. Those opposed to the use of these statements argue that the legislature, and only the legislature, has the constitutional power to enact law. Only the enacting legislature's intent is relevant; the executive's understanding and misunderstanding are irrelevant. Further, those opposed to the use of these statements fear that the executive has an incentive to alter meaning when writing signing statements, a fear which recent presidents have proved to be well founded. Thus, opponents argue that signing statements should be irrelevant, even though the executive has to sign the bill before it becomes law. The majority took this approach in *Hamdan v. Rumsfeld*, 548 U.S. 557 (2006), when it gave no weight to President Bush's memorandum regarding his understanding of the Detainee Treatment Act of 2005.

Regardless of whether they play any role in interpretation, increasingly presidents include such statements. For example, former President George W. Bush regularly used signing statements to limit the reach of some laws. In July 2006, a task force of the American Bar Association challenged his use of the statements in this way as "contrary to the rule of law and our constitutional system of separation of powers." American Bar Association, *Blue-Ribbon Task Force Finds President Bush's Signing Statement Undermine Separation of Powers*, July 24, 2006 Press release. President Obama has also issued signing statements regularly to indicate his disagreement with portions of a bill. The ABA has been similarly critical. Letter from William Robinson to President Barak Obama, (December 30, 2011) http://www.americanbar.org/content/dam/aba/administrative/litigation/materials/sac_2012/52-5_agr_2011_12_30_aba_letter_to_obama_re_signing_statements.authcheckdam.pdf.

b. Using Legislative History

Once you find legislative history, what do you do with it? Typically, judges use legislative history for one of two reasons: (1) to shed light on the specific intent of the enacting legislature, or (2) to identify the unexpressed statutory purpose. This section will focus on the first reason, finding specific intent; we will look at the second reason, finding statutory purpose, in the next chapter. Generally, when judges use legislative history to discern specific intent, they are looking to discover whether the legislature had a specific idea about the precise issue before the court.

If the text of your statute is clear, you face a threshold issue: whether a judge will look at legislative history at all. Generally, textualist judges refuse to look at legislative history unless the language is ambiguous or absurd. But other judges are willing to use legislative history to confirm the ordinary meaning of a clear language. And a few are willing to use legislative history to defeat the ordinary meaning of a statute. One could say that there is a legislative continuum regarding the willingness of a judge to use legislative history. Some judges are always willing to use legislative history (Justices Breyer and Stevens, for example); other judges are almost never willing to use legislative history (former Justice Scalia and Justice Thomas, for example). Most judges today are willing to use legislative history when the language is ambiguous, absurd, raises a constitutional question, or has a scrivener's error. And many judges are willing to use legislative history to confirm the meaning of clear text. Less common today are judges willing to use legislative history to overcome the clear text. Here is a graphic that depicts this continuum:

The Continuum of Judicial Willingness to Use Legislative History

Never willing	To determine the meaning of ambiguous & absurd text	To confirm the meaning of clear text	To defeat the meaning of clear text	*Always* willing

The judicial approach to using legislative history has not been consistent. *Compare In the Matter of Sinclair*, 870 F.2d 1340, 1344 (7th Cir. 1989) (refusing to consider a contrary conference committee report because the statute was clear) *with In Re Idalski*, 123 B.R. 222 (Bankr. E.D. Mich. 1991) (considering the legislative history of a statute despite first noting that the text of the statute was clear). This inconsistency is even more apparent in the Supreme Court. As the Court's membership and preferred statutory theory have changed over time, the willingness of the justices to consider legislative history has also changed. While the justices routinely looked at legislative history before Justice Scalia joined the Court, that practice has modified slightly with his textualist influence. Lower courts have followed suit.

c. Criticizing Your Opponent's Use of Legislative History

As noted, depending on a judge's theory, legislative history may be used to try to confirm the meaning of clear text, to discern the meaning of ambiguous or absurd text, or to defeat the meaning of clear text. While many judges are willing to review legislative history when faced with ambiguous or absurd text; today, fewer judges are willing to review legislative history to confirm clear text. And even fewer judges are willing to review legislative history to defeat plain text, although this use may have occurred in the past. Let's explore that history now as we discuss ways that you can critique your opponent's use of legislative history.

i. Understanding the Supreme Court's Use of Legislative History

In early England, judges refused to consider the legislative history of a statute for any reason. This rule is known as the exclusionary rule. The rigidity of this rule relaxed slightly in the case below, but was later reinvigorated. See if you can determine which forms of legislative history this court is willing to consider and when.

Pepper v. Hart*

House of Lords for the United Kingdom
[1992] 3 W.L.R. 1032, [1993] 1 All E.R. 42 (1993)

◆ LORD BROWNE-WILKINSON [delivered the opinion of the House of Lords, in which LORDS KEITH, BRIDGE, GRIFFITHS, ACKNER, and OLIVER concur].

[This taxpayer appeal raises an important question:] whether in construing ambiguous or obscure statutory provisions your Lordships should relax the historic rule that the courts must not look at the Parliamentary history of legislation or Hansard** for the purpose of construing such legislation.

[Hart and nine others were employees at Malvern College. They took advantage of a "concessionary fee" scheme, which allowed their children to be educated at rates one fifth of those paid by other students. There was no issue that the benefit, called an emolument, was taxable. The issue was the value of the emolument. The taxpayers argued that the value of the emolument was the marginable cost to the school of a few more students. The tax authority (Island Revenue) argued that the value of the emolument was essentially the market value of admission. Section 61, 63(1) and (2) of the 1976 Finance Act provided: The cash equivalent of any benefit chargeable to tax under section 61 above is an amount equal to the cost of the benefit..., the cost of a benefit is the amount of any expense incurred in or in connection with its provision...."]

The taxpayers contend that the only expense incurred by the school "in or in connection" with the education of their children is the additional, or marginal, cost to the school.... Therefore "the cash equivalent of the benefit" is nil.

The [Government] on the other hand contend[s] that the "expense incurred in or in connection with" the provision of education for the children of the taxpayers was exactly the same as the expense incurred in or in connection with the education of all other pupils at the school and accordingly the expense of educating any one child is a proportionate part of the cost of running the whole school.

The special commissioner held in favour of the taxpayers. That decision was reversed.... The taxpayers appeal....

The case was originally argued ... without reference to any Parliamentary proceedings.... Your Lordships then invited the parties to consider whether they wished to present further argument on the question whether it was appropriate for the House

---

* Editor's footnote: This case has been edited to read like a case from the United States. For example, dissents and concurrences follow the majority opinion rather than precede it.

** Editor's footnote: Hansard is the traditional name of the transcripts from the Parliamentary Debates in Britain and other Commonwealth countries. Thomas Curson Hansard (1776–1833) was the first official printer to the parliament at Westminster.

to depart from previous authority of this House which forbids reference to such material in construing statutory provisions and, if so, what guidance such material provided in deciding the present appeal....

In the result, the following issues arise. (1.) Should the existing rule prohibiting any reference to Hansard in construing legislation be relaxed and, if so, to what extent? (2.) If so, does this case fall within the category of cases where reference to Parliamentary proceedings should be permitted? (3.) If reference to Parliamentary proceedings is permissible, what is the true construction of the statutory provisions? (4.) If reference to the Parliamentary proceedings is not permissible, what is the true construction of the statutory provisions?...

I will consider these issues in turn....

1. Should the rule prohibiting references to Parliamentary material be relaxed?

Under present law, there is a general rule that references to Parliamentary material as an aid to statutory construction is not permissible ("the exclusionary rule")....

... This rule has now been relaxed so as to permit [committee reports] to be looked at for the purpose solely of ascertaining the mischief which the statute is intended to cure but not for the purpose of discovering the meaning of the words used by Parliament to effect such cure....

[The attorney] for the taxpayers did not urge us to abandon the exclusionary rule completely. His submission was that where the words of a statute were ambiguous or obscure or were capable of giving rise to an absurd conclusion it should be legitimate to look at the Parliamentary history, including the debates in Parliament, for the purpose of identifying the intention of Parliament in using the words it did use. He accepted that the function of the court was to construe the actual words enacted by Parliament so that in no circumstances could the court attach to words a meaning that they were incapable of bearing. He further accepted that the court should only attach importance to clear statements showing the intention of the promoter of the Bill, whether a Minister or private member: there could be no dredging through conflicting statements of intention with a view to discovering the true intention of Parliament in using the statutory words.

In *Beswick v. Beswick* [1968] A.C. 58, 74 Lord Reid said:

> "For purely practical reasons we do not permit debates in either House to be cited: it would add greatly to the time and expense involved in preparing cases involving the construction of a statute if counsel were expected to read all the debates in Hansard, and it would often be impracticable for counsel to get access to at least the older reports of debates in Select Committees of the House of Commons; moreover, in a very large proportion of cases such a search, even if practicable, would throw no light on the question before the court."

In *Black-Clawson International Ltd. v. Papierwerke Waldhof-Aschaffenburg A.G.* [1975] A.C. 591 Lord Reid said, at pp. 613–615:

"We often say that we are looking for the intention of Parliament, but that is not quite accurate. We are seeking the meaning of the words which Parliament used. We are seeking not what Parliament meant but the true meaning of what they said...."

In the same case Lord Wilberforce said, at p. 629:

"The second [reason] is one of constitutional principle. Legislation in England is passed by Parliament, and put in the form of written words. This legislation is given legal effect upon subjects by virtue of judicial decision, and it is the function of the courts to say what the application of the words used to particular cases or individuals is to be.... [I]t would be a degradation of that process if the courts were to be merely a reflecting mirror of what some other interpretation agency might say."

In *Fothergill v. Monarch Airlines Ltd.* [1981] A.C. 251, 279, Lord Diplock said:

"The constitutional function performed by courts of justice as interpreters of the written law laid down in Acts of Parliament is often described as ascertaining 'the intention of Parliament;' but what this metaphor, though convenient, omits to take into account is that the court, when acting in its interpretative role, as well as when it is engaged in reviewing the legality of administrative action, is doing so as mediator between the state in the exercise of its legislative power and the private citizen for whom the law made by Parliament constitutes a rule binding upon him and enforceable by the executive power of the state. Elementary justice or ... the need for legal certainty demands that the rules by which the citizen is to be bound should be ascertainable by him (or, more realistically, by a competent lawyer advising him) by reference to identifiable sources that are publicly accessible."

In *Davis v. Johnson* [1979] A.C. 264, 350, Lord Scarman said:

"such material is an unreliable guide to the meaning of what is enacted...."

Thus the reasons put forward for the present rule are first, that it preserves the constitutional proprieties leaving Parliament to legislate in words and the courts (not Parliamentary speakers), to construe the meaning of the words finally enacted; second, the practical difficulty of the expense of researching Parliamentary material which would arise if the material could be looked at; third, the need for the citizen to have access to a known defined text which regulates his legal rights; fourth, the improbability of finding helpful guidance from Hansard....

[Counsel for the taxpayers] submitted that the time has come to relax the rule to the extent which I have mentioned. He points out that the courts have departed from the old literal approach of statutory construction and now adopt a purposive approach, seeking to discover the Parliamentary intention lying behind the words used and construing the legislation so as to give effect to, rather than thwart, the intentions of Parliament. Where the words used by Parliament are obscure or ambiguous, the Parliamentary material may throw considerable light not only on the mischief which the Act was designed to remedy but also on the purpose of the legislation and its anticipated effect ... Other common law jurisdictions have abandoned the rule without adverse consequences.... [E]xperience in Commonwealth countries which have abandoned the rule does not suggest that the drawbacks are substantial, provided that the court keeps a tight control on the circumstances in which references to Parliamentary material are allowed.

On the other side, the Attorney-General submitted that the existing rule had a sound constitutional and practical basis. If statements by Ministers as to the intent or effect of an Act were allowed to prevail, this would contravene the constitutional rule that Parliament is "sovereign only in respect of what it expresses by the words used in the legislation it has passed." It is for the courts alone to construe such legislation. It may be unwise to attach importance to ministerial explanations which are made to satisfy the political requirements of persuasion and debate, often under pressure of time and business. Moreover, in order to establish the significance to be attached to any particular statement, it is necessary both to consider and to understand the context in which it was made. For the courts to have regard to Parliamentary material might necessitate changes in Parliamentary procedures to ensure that ministerial statements are sufficiently detailed to be taken into account. In addition, there are all the practical difficulties as to the accessibility of Parliamentary material, the cost of researching it and the use of court time in analysing it, which are good reasons for maintaining the rule....

My Lords ... In my judgment, ... reference to Parliamentary material should be permitted as an aid to the construction of legislation which is ambiguous or obscure or the literal meaning of which leads to an absurdity....

I accept [the attorney for the taxpayer's] submissions, but my main reason for reaching this conclusion is based on principle. Statute law consists of the words that Parliament has enacted. It is for the courts to construe those words and it is the court's duty in so doing to give effect to the intention of Parliament in using those words. It is an inescapable fact that, despite all the care taken in passing legislation, some statutory provisions when applied to the circumstances under consideration in any specific case are found to be ambiguous.... Parliament never intends to enact an ambiguity.... The courts are faced simply with a set of words which are in fact capable of bearing two meanings. The courts are ignorant of the underlying Parliamentary purpose. Unless something in other parts of the legislation discloses such purpose, the courts are forced to adopt one of the two possible meanings using highly technical rules of construction. In many, I suspect most, cases references to Parliamentary materials will not throw any light on the matter. But in a few cases it may emerge that the very question was considered by Parliament in passing the legislation. Why in such a case should the courts blind themselves to a clear indication of what Parliament intended in using those words? The court cannot attach a meaning to words which they cannot bear, but if the words are capable of bearing more than one meaning why should not Parliament's true intention be enforced rather than thwarted? ...

It is said that Parliamentary materials are not readily available to, and understandable by, the citizen and his lawyers who should be entitled to rely on the words of

Parliament alone to discover his position. It is undoubtedly true that Hansard and particularly records of Committee debates are not widely held by libraries outside London and that the lack of satisfactory indexing of Committee stages makes it difficult to trace the passage of a clause after it is redrafted or renumbered. But such practical difficulties can easily be overstated. It is possible to obtain Parliamentary materials and it is possible to trace the history. The problem is one of expense and effort in doing so, not the availability of the material....

... Experience in the United States of America, where legislative history has for many years been much more generally admissible than I am now suggesting, shows how important it is to maintain strict control over the use of such material....

I therefore reach the conclusion ... that the exclusionary rule should be relaxed so as to permit reference to Parliamentary materials where (a) legislation is ambiguous or obscure, or leads to an absurdity; (b) the material relied upon consists of one or more statements by a Minister or other promoter of the Bill together if necessary with such other Parliamentary material as is necessary to understand such statements and their effect; (c) the statements relied upon are clear.

Further than this, I would not at present go.

2. Does this case fall within the relaxed rule?

(a) Is section 63 ambiguous?

I have no hesitation in holding that it is. The "expense incurred in or in connection with" the provision of in-house benefits may be either the marginal cost caused by the provision of the benefit in question or a proportion of the total cost incurred in providing the service both for the public and for the employee ("the average cost")....

The statutory words are capable of bearing either meaning. There is an ambiguity or obscurity.

3. If reference to Hansard is permissible, what is the true construction of clause 63?

... [T]he Parliamentary history shows that Parliament passed the legislation on the basis that the effect of sections 61 and 63 of the Act was to assess ... benefits, and particularly concessionary education for teachers' children, on the marginal cost to the employer and not on the average cost. Since the words of section 63 are perfectly capable of bearing that meaning, in my judgment that is the meaning they should be given....

♦ LORD BRIDGE, concurring.

... It should, in my opinion, only be in the rare cases where the very issue of interpretation which the courts are called on to resolve has been addressed in Parliamentary debate and where the promoter of the legislation has made a clear statement directed to that very issue, that reference to Hansard should be permitted. Indeed, it is only in such cases that reference to Hansard is likely to be of any assistance to the courts. Provided the relaxation of the previous exclusionary rule is so limited, I find it difficult to suppose that the additional cost of litigation or any other ground of objection can justify the court continuing to wear blinkers which, in such a case as this, conceal the vital clue to the intended meaning of an enactment. I recognise that practitioners will in some cases incur fruitless costs in the search for such a vital clue where none exists. But, on the other hand, where Hansard does provide the answer, it should be so clear to both parties that they will avoid the cost of litigation....

◆ LORD GRIFFITHS, concurring.

My Lords, I have long thought that the time had come to change the self-imposed judicial rule that forbade any reference to the legislative history of an enactment as an aid to its interpretation. The ever increasing volume of legislation must inevitably result in ambiguities of statutory language which are not perceived at the time the legislation is enacted. The object of the court in interpreting legislation is to give effect so far as the language permits to the intention of the legislature. If the language proves to be ambiguous I can see no sound reason not to consult Hansard to see if there is a clear statement of the meaning that the words were intended to carry. The days have long passed when the courts adopted a strict constructionist view of interpretation which required them to adopt the literal meaning of the language. The courts now adopt a purposive approach which seeks to give effect to the true purpose of legislation and are prepared to look at much extraneous material that bears upon the background against which the legislation was enacted. Why then cut ourselves off from the one source in which may be found an authoritative statement of the intention with which the legislation is placed before Parliament?....

◆ [LORD OLIVER's concurring opinion has been omitted]

◆ LORD MACKAY, dissenting.

... I believe that practically every question of *statutory* construction that comes before the courts will involve an argument that the case falls under one or more of these three heads. It follows that the parties' legal advisors will require to study Hansard in practically every such case to see whether or not there is any help to be gained from it.... Such an approach appears to me to involve the possibility at least of an immense increase in the cost of litigation in which statutory construction is involved. It is of course easy to overestimate such cost but it is I fear equally easy to underestimate it. Your Lordships have no machinery from which any estimate of such cost could be derived....

Your Lordships are well aware that the costs of litigation are a subject of general public concern and I personally would not wish to be a party to changing a well established rule which could have a substantial effect in increasing these costs ... unless and until a new inquiry demonstrated that that advice was no longer valid....

* * *

Points for Discussion

1. *Statutory Language*: What was the language at issue? What did each party want that language to mean? What meaning did the court adopt?

2. *Theories*: Which theory did the majority adopt and why?

3. *Changing the Existing Practice*: Prior to this case, what was the rule in England regarding legislative history? How did this court modify that practice? Why was

Lord Browne-Wilkinson willing to change the rule? Lord Bridge? Lord Griffiths? Why did the Lord Mackay disagree?

4. *Triple Locks*: Lord Browne-Wilkinson identified three situations when parliamentary material should be admissible. What are they?

5. *America's Experience*: Was Lord Browne-Wilkinson admiring or critical of the American approach?

6. *Shortlived*: Before *Pepper*, English judges followed a strict textual approach. Following a report from the Law Commission, issued in 1969, THE INTERPRETATION OF STATUTES, English judges began to use a more purposive approach to statutory interpretation. The purposivist approach expanded the amount of material judges could consider, including reports made by government bodies, the Law Commission (an independent body set up by English Parliament to propose changes to the law of England and Wales to make the law simpler, more accessible, fairer, modern and more cost-effective), and the Royal Commission (a body set up to gather information about the operation of existing laws or to investigate any social, educational, or other matter). *Pepper* allowed judges to include Hansard reports (similar to committee reports) in this list as well, but also broadened the uses judges could make of such material. After *Pepper*, this material was relevant not only to establish the overall purpose of an act but to define what was meant by a particular provision. Like the United States, the use of such history in England proved controversial.

Judicial acceptance of *Pepper* soon began to wane. Although the lower courts and the Lords initially applied the decision, allowing the use of Hansard, the courts soon began to whittle the holding down. For example, in *Massey v Boulden*, [2003] 2 All ER 87, the court held that *Hansard* could not be used in criminal law cases, because the rule of lenity precluded its use. And in *Robinson v Secretary of State for Northern Ireland*, [2002] UKHL 32, three of the Lords said that dissenting Lord Mackay had "turned out to be the better prophet" because of the inefficiency and expense associated with *Pepper*. Additional criticism and limitations followed. As a result of these criticisms and limitations, Professor Stefan Vogenauer, from Oxford, concluded that "the scope of *Pepper v Hart* has been reduced to such an extent that the ruling has almost become meaningless." Stefan Vogenauer, *A Retreat from* Pepper v Hart? *A Reply to Lord Steyn*, 25 OXFORD J. LEG. STUDIES 629–674 (2005).

Whatever the accuracy of the criticisms, references to *Hansard* increased since its debut. *See, e.g., Harding v Wealands*, [2006] UKHL 32 (acknowledging that *Pepper* had been "out of judicial favour in recent years," but responding that legislative history was "perhaps especially [useful] as a confirmatory aid").

* * *

The United States rejected the exclusionary rule relatively early in its jurisprudential history. In 1892, in *Church of the Holy Trinity v. United States*, 143 U.S. 457 (1892), the Court began expressly to look to legislative history. In that case, the Court had to decide whether a statute that prohibited the importation of foreigners to perform "labor or service of any kind" applied to ministers. Despite the relative clarity of the text (rectoring is labor and service), the Court examined the legislative history of the bill and concluded that the enacting legislature had intended to stem the influx of cheap, manual labor from China. Because the purpose of the bill was to stem cheap Chinese labor, "labor" included manual labor only. *Id.* at 464. Oddly, the Court did not address the additional category: service. Following *Holy Trinity's* approach, courts began regularly to turn to legislative history to discern legislative intent.

Over time, the Court's willingness to consider legislative history has waxed and waned. As the preferred statutory interpretation theory has changed, the use of legislative history has changed accordingly. When purposivism was popular, so was the Court's use of legislative history. At that time, the Court did not need a reason to look at legislative history, such as ambiguity or absurdity. Legislative history was considered regardless of the clarity of the text. "When aid to the construction of the meaning of words, as used in the statute, is available, there certainly can be no 'rule of law' which forbids its use, however clear the words may appear on 'superficial examination.'" *United States v. Am. Trucking Ass'ns, Inc.*, 310 U.S. 534, 543–44, 60 (1940) (footnotes omitted). Remember that in *Pepper v. Hart* Lords Browne-Wilkinson and Griffiths both reasoned that because English judges had become more purposivist, limited use of Hansard was appropriate.

Similarly, when members of the Supreme Court preferred intentionalism, legislative history was central to their analyses. *See, e.g., Chevron U.S.A. Inc. v. Natural Resources Defense Council, Inc.*, 467 U.S. 837 (1984) (examining legislative history among other sources)

All that changed, however, after Justice Scalia joined the Court in 1986 and refocused the statutory interpretation discourse (something he had started while on the D.C. Circuit Court). As a result of his efforts, text reemerged as primary to the inquiry. In refocusing the inquiry, Justice Scalia directly assaulted the other justices' use of legislative history. For example, in *Koons Buick Pontiac GMC, Inc. v. Nigh*, 543 U.S. 50 (2004), Justice Scalia said:

> Needless to say, I also disagree with the Court's reliance on things that the sponsors and floor managers of the 1995 amendment failed to say. I have often criticized the Court's use of legislative history because it lends itself to a kind of ventriloquism. The Congressional Record or committee reports are used to make words appear to come from Congress's mouth which were spoken or written by others (individual Members of Congress, congressional aides, or even enterprising lobbyists.)

Id. at 73 (Scalia, J., dissenting). While a few judges, such as former Justice Scalia, Justice Thomas, and Judge Easterbrook, are unwilling to consider legislative history at all, the majority of judges generally allow lawyers *some* opportunity to "prove" the correctness of their interpretation with evidence from the legislative history. For example, the remaining members of the Rehnquist Court did not agree that legislative history should always be out-of-bounds. In *Wisconsin Public Intervenor v. Mortier*, 501 U.S. 597 (1991), they rejected Justice Scalia's position on legislative history. "Our precedents demonstrate that the Court's practice of utilizing legislative history reaches well into its past. We suspect that the practice will likewise reach well into the future." *Id.* at 610 n.4 (internal citation omitted). Under the Roberts Court, most of the justices continue to consider legislative history; however, their use is more limited than in the past.

There can be no doubt that Justice Scalia's criticisms had an effect on the use of legislative history in judicial interpretation. Judges today are far less likely to rely significantly on legislative history than in the past. And for some judges, litigants must first show that the statute as written is absurd or ambiguous before suggesting that the legislative history is relevant. But not all members of the judiciary have embraced moderate textualism.

ii. The Criticisms of Using Legislative History

There are many criticisms of judicial use of legislative history, including the following: (1) constitutionality issues, (2) accessibility and cost considerations, and (3) reliability concerns.

First, critics argue that reliance on legislative history is unconstitutional for a few reasons. State and federal constitutions provide a process for enactment: passage by both chambers in identical form (bicameral passage) and presentment to the executive for approval or veto (presentment). Legislative history does not follow this constitutional process; only the text of the statute does. Hence, legislative history is not law and should not be consulted.

Moreover, critics reason that the Constitution delegates law-making power to the legislature as a whole, not to committees or individual legislators. For this reason, statements made in committee reports and floor debates, which are only the statements of individual legislators, should not be cited as evidence of the whole legislature's intent. Complicating the issue further is the fact that staff members or lobbyists and not legislators regularly draft committee reports and other legislative documents. Justice Scalia once said:

> As anyone familiar with modern-day drafting of congressional committee reports is well aware, the [language was] … inserted, at best by a committee staff member on his or her own initiative, and at worst by a committee staff member at the suggestion of a lawyer-lobbyist; and the purpose of [that language] was not primarily to inform Members of Congress about what the bill meant, … but rather to influence judicial construction.

Blanchard v. Bergeron, 489 U.S. 87, 98–99 (1989). Thus, strict textualists point out that the intent of staffers and lobbyists regarding the meaning of a law is simply irrelevant and, arguably, unconstitutional.

Finally, they note that due process requires that citizens have notice of the law. If judges cannot understand what a statute means without perusing the legislative history, how can an ordinary citizen, who is unlikely to have access to such history, know what a statute means?

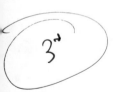

The second criticism of using legislative history is that it is not equally accessible and available to all. Legislative history is often voluminous (or non-existent), obscure, hard to find, and poorly indexed, especially at the state level. It can be expensive and time-consuming to examine all of it. The dissent in *Pepper v. Hart* made this same point. Lawyers are trained to search exhaustively for the "smoking gun." Doing so in this context may cost a client a lot of money. Many clients cannot afford to pay for such a search, putting them at a disadvantage.

A third criticism textualists make regarding the use of legislative history is that it may be unreliable. Legislators simply do not read every report or attend every debate (remember footnote 1 in *Hirschey*); thus, comments made within those documents and during those hearings may not reflect the understanding of every legislator. For example, in *Amalgamated Transit Union Local 1309 v. Laidlaw Transit Services, Inc.*, 435 F.3d 1140 (9th Cir. 2006), the court relied on a Senate report to discern the purpose of the Class Action Fairness Act. However, that particular report was not submitted until after the House and Senate had voted on the bill and the President had signed it into law. *Amalgamated Transit Union Local 1309 v. Laidlaw Transit Servs., Inc.*, 448 F.3d 1092, 1096 (9th Cir. 2006) (Bybee, J., dissenting) (order denying en banc rehearing). The report could have had no influence whatsoever on the legislators' decisions; yet it influenced the court's interpretation.

Similarly, in *Hamdan v. Rumsfeld*, 548 U.S. 557 (2006), Senators Jon Kyl and Lindsey Graham filed an amicus brief in which they offered a colloquy from *The Congressional Record* as evidence that Congress was aware that the Detainee Treatment Act would strip the Supreme Court of jurisdiction to hear cases the Guantanamo detainees filed. The Justice Department relied on this legislative history to argue that its interpretation of the Act was the correct one. Yet, the majority rejected this particular colloquy because it was inserted into *The Congressional Record* after the Senate debate. *Id.* at 734 n.10. In other words, members of Congress never considered the comments nor had an opportunity to disagree with them. The majority did consider floor debates and other legislative history that were a part of the enactment process, but not these after-the-fact insertions into the record.

As you might imagine, Justice Scalia was not happy with the majority's willingness to consider any of the legislative history:

> The Court immediately goes on to discount numerous floor statements by the [act's] sponsors that flatly contradict its view, because "those statements appear to have been inserted into the Congressional Record after the Senate debate." Of course this observation, even if true, makes no difference unless one indulges the fantasy that Senate floor speeches are attended (like the Philippics of Demosthenes) by throngs of eager listeners, instead of being delivered (like Demosthenes' practice sessions on the beach) alone into a vast emptiness. Whether the floor statements are spoken where no Senator hears, or written where no Senator reads, they represent at most the views of a single Senator.

Id. at 664–665.

Critics raise another criticism of the use of legislative history: it is often voluminous and includes contradictory statements. When contradictory legislative history exists, which history counts? *The case below* illustrates a problem with using legislative history; judges and litigants tend to rely on the history that supports their interpretation while ignoring or minimizing the history that contradicts that interpretation. Notice that the legislative history relevant to the majority and the dissent differs. Also, this case illustrates the difference between purposivism and intentionalism better than any case you have studied yet. As you read, try to identify which opinion is which.

United Steelworkers v. Weber

Supreme Court of the United States
443 U.S. 193 (1979)

♦ Justice Brennen delivered the opinion of the Court [with whom Stewart, White, Marshall, Blackmun JJ. concur]. [Powell and Stevens, JJ. took no part in the consideration or decision of these cases.].

... This case arose from the operation of [an affirmative action] plan at Kaiser's plant in Gramercy, La. Until 1974, Kaiser hired as craftworkers for that plant only persons who had had prior craft experience. Because blacks had long been excluded from craft unions, few were able to present such credentials. As a consequence, prior to 1974 only 1.83% (5 out of 273) of the skilled craftworkers at the Gramercy plant were black, even though the work force in the Gramercy area was approximately 39% black.

Pursuant to the national agreement Kaiser altered its craft-hiring practice in the Gramercy plant. Rather than hiring already trained outsiders, Kaiser established a training program to train its production workers to fill craft openings. Selection of craft trainees was made on the basis of seniority, with the proviso that at least 50% of the new trainees were to be black until the percentage of black skilled craftworkers in the Gramercy plant approximated the percentage of blacks in the local labor force.

During 1974, the first year of the operation of the Kaiser-USWA affirmative action plan, 13 craft trainees were selected from Gramercy's production work force. Of these, seven were black and six white. The most senior black selected into the program had less seniority than several white production workers whose bids for admission were rejected. Thereafter one of those white production workers, respondent Brian Weber (hereafter respondent), instituted this class action....

The complaint alleged that the filling of craft trainee positions at the Gramercy plant pursuant to the affirmative action program had resulted in junior black employees' receiving training in preference to senior white employees, thus discriminating against respondent and other similarly situated white employees in violation of §§ 703(a)[2] and (d)[3] of Title VII. The District Court held that the plan violated Title

---

2. Section 703(a), 78 Stat. 255, as amended, 86 Stat. 109, 42 U.S.C. § 2000e–2(a), provides:

VII.... A divided panel of the Court of Appeals for the Fifth Circuit affirmed.... We granted certiorari. We reverse.

We emphasize at the outset the narrowness of our inquiry.... The only question before us is the narrow statutory issue of whether Title VII *forbids* private employers and unions from voluntarily agreeing upon bona fide affirmative action plans that accord racial preferences in the manner and for the purpose provided in the Kaiser-USWA plan....

Respondent argues that Congress intended in Title VII to prohibit all race-conscious affirmative action plans. Respondent's argument rests upon a literal interpretation of §§ 703(a) and (d) of the Act. Those sections make it unlawful to "discriminate ... because of ... race" in hiring and in the selection of apprentices for training programs. Since, ... Title VII forbids discrimination against whites as well as blacks, and since the Kaiser-USWA affirmative action plan operates to discriminate against white employees solely because they are white, it follows that the Kaiser-USWA plan violates Title VII.

Respondent's argument is not without force. But it overlooks the significance of the fact that the Kaiser-USWA plan is an affirmative action plan voluntarily adopted by private parties to eliminate traditional patterns of racial segregation. In this context respondent's reliance upon a literal construction of §§ 703(a) and (d) ... is misplaced. It is a "familiar rule that a thing may be within the letter of the statute and yet not within the statute, because not within its spirit nor within the intention of its makers." *Holy Trinity Church v. United States*, 143 U.S. 457, 459 (1892). The prohibition against racial discrimination in §§ 703(a) and (d) of Title VII must therefore be read against the background of the legislative history of Title VII and the historical context from which the Act arose. Examination of those sources makes clear that an interpretation of the sections that forbade all race-conscious affirmative action would "bring about an end completely at variance with the purpose of the statute" and must be rejected.

Congress' primary concern in enacting the prohibition against racial discrimination in Title VII of the Civil Rights Act of 1964 was with "the plight of the Negro in our

---

"(a) ... It shall be an unlawful employment practice for an employer—

"(1) to fail or refuse to hire or to discharge any individual, or otherwise to discriminate against any individual with respect to his compensation, terms, conditions, or privileges of employment, because of such individual's race, color, religion, sex, or national origin; or

"(2) to limit, segregate, or classify his employees or applicants for employment in any way which would deprive or tend to deprive any individual of employment opportunities or otherwise adversely affect his status as an employee, because of such individual's race, color, religion, sex, or national origin."

3. Section 703(d), 78 Stat. 256, 42 U.S.C. § 2000e–2(d), provides:

"It shall be an unlawful employment practice for any employer, labor organization, or joint labor-management committee controlling apprenticeship or other training or retraining, including on-the-job training programs to discriminate against any individual because of his race, color, religion, sex, or national origin in admission to, or employment in, any program established to provide apprenticeship or other training."

economy." 110 Cong.Rec. 6548 (1964) (remarks of Sen. Humphrey). Before 1964, blacks were largely relegated to "unskilled and semi-skilled jobs." *Ibid.* (remarks of Sen. Humphrey); *id.*, at 7204 (remarks of Sen. Clark); *id.*, at 7379–7380 (remarks of Sen. Kennedy). Because of automation the number of such jobs was rapidly decreasing. See *id.*, at 6548 (remarks of Sen. Humphrey); *id.*, at 7204 (remarks of Sen. Clark). As a consequence, "the relative position of the Negro worker [was] steadily worsening. In 1947 the nonwhite unemployment rate was only 64 percent higher than the white rate; in 1962 it was 124 percent higher." *Id.*, at 6547 (remarks of Sen. Humphrey). See also *id.*, at 7204 (remarks of Sen. Clark). Congress considered this a serious social problem.....

Congress feared that the goals of the Civil Rights Act—the integration of blacks into the mainstream of American society—could not be achieved unless this trend were reversed. And Congress recognized that that would not be possible unless blacks were able to secure jobs "which have a future." *Id.*, at 7204 (remarks of Sen. Clark). As Senator Humphrey explained to the Senate:

> "What good does it do a Negro to be able to eat in a fine restaurant if he cannot afford to pay the bill? What good does it do him to be accepted in a hotel that is too expensive for his modest income? How can a Negro child be motivated to take full advantage of integrated educational facilities if he has no hope of getting a job where he can use that education?" *Id.*, at 6547....

Accordingly, it was clear to Congress that "[t]he crux of the problem [was] to open employment opportunities for Negroes in occupations which have been traditionally closed to them," 10 Cong.Rec. 6548 (1964) (remarks of Sen. Humphrey), and it was to this problem that Title VII's prohibition against racial discrimination in employment was primarily addressed.

It plainly appears from the House Report accompanying the Civil Rights Act that Congress did not intend wholly to prohibit private and voluntary affirmative action efforts as one method of solving this problem. The Report provides:

> "No bill can or should lay claim to eliminating all of the causes and consequences of racial and other types of discrimination against minorities. There is reason to believe, however, that national leadership provided by the enactment of Federal legislation dealing with the most troublesome problems *will create an atmosphere conducive to voluntary or local resolution of other forms of discrimination.*" H.R.Rep. No. 914, 88th Cong., 1st Sess., pt. 1, p. 18 (1963); U.S.Code Cong. & Admin.News 1964, pp. 2355, 2393. (Emphasis supplied.)

Given this legislative history, we cannot agree with respondent that Congress intended to prohibit the private sector from taking effective steps to accomplish the goal that Congress designed Title VII to achieve. The very statutory words intended as a spur or catalyst to cause "employers and unions to self-examine and to self-evaluate their employment practices and to endeavor to eliminate, so far as possible, the last vestiges of an unfortunate and ignominious page in this country's history," cannot be interpreted as an absolute prohibition against all private, voluntary, race-conscious affirmative action efforts to hasten the elimination of such vestiges.[4] It would be ironic indeed if a law triggered by a Nation's concern over centuries of racial injustice and intended to improve the lot of those who had "been excluded from the American dream for so long," 110 Cong.Rec. 6552 (1964) (remarks of Sen. Humphrey), constituted the first legislative prohibition of all voluntary, private, race-conscious efforts to abolish traditional patterns of racial segregation and hierarchy.

Our conclusion is further reinforced by examination of the language and legislative history of § 703(j) of Title VII.[5] Opponents of Title VII raised two related arguments against the bill. First, they argued that the Act would be interpreted to *require* employers with racially imbalanced work forces to grant preferential treatment to racial minorities in order to integrate. Second, they argued that employers with racially imbalanced work forces would grant preferential treatment to racial minorities, even if not required to do so by the Act. See 110 Cong.Rec. 8618–8619 (1964) (remarks of Sen. Sparkman). Had Congress meant to prohibit all race-conscious affirmative action, as respondent urges, it easily could have answered both objections by providing that Title VII would not require or *permit* racially preferential integration efforts. But Congress did not choose such a course. Rather, Congress added § 703(j) which addresses only the first objection. The section provides that nothing contained in Title VII "shall be interpreted to *require* any employer ... to grant preferential treatment ... to any group because of the race ... of such ... group on account of" a *de facto* racial imbalance in the employer's work force. The section does *not* state that "nothing in Title VII shall be interpreted to *permit*" voluntary affirmative efforts to correct racial imbalances. The natural inference is that Congress chose not to forbid all voluntary race-conscious affirmative action....

The reasons for this choice are evident from the legislative record. Title VII could not have been enacted into law without substantial support from legislators in both Houses who traditionally resisted federal regulation of private business. Those legislators demanded as a price for their support that "management prerogatives, and union freedoms ... be left undisturbed to the greatest extent possible." H.R.Rep. No. 914, 88th Cong., 1st Sess., pt. 2, p. 29 (1963), U.S.Code Cong. & Admin.News 1964, p. 2391. Section 703(j) was proposed by Senator Dirksen to allay any fears that the Act might be interpreted in such a way as to upset this compromise. The section was

---

4. The problem that Congress addressed in 1964 remains with us. In 1962, the nonwhite unemployment rate was 124% higher than the white rate.

5. Section 703(j) of Title VII, 78 Stat. 257, 42 U.S.C. § 2000e–2(j), provides:

"Nothing contained in this title shall be interpreted to require any employer ... to grant preferential treatment to any individual or to any group because of the race ... on account of an imbalance which may exist with respect to the total number or percentage of persons of any race ... employed by any employer ... or admitted to, or employed in, any apprenticeship or other training program, in comparison with the total number or percentage of persons of such race ... in ... in the available work force in any community, State, section, or other area."

designed to prevent § 703 of Title VII from being interpreted in such a way as to lead to undue "Federal Government interference with private businesses because of some Federal employee's ideas about racial balance or racial imbalance." 110 Cong.Rec. 14314 (1964) (remarks of Sen. Miller). See also *id.*, at 9881 (remarks of Sen. Allott); *id.*, at 10520 (remarks of Sen. Carlson); *id.*, at 11471 (remarks of Sen. Javits); *id.*, at 12817 (remarks of Sen. Dirksen). Clearly, a prohibition against all voluntary, race-conscious, affirmative action efforts would disserve these ends. Such a prohibition would augment the powers of the Federal Government and diminish traditional management prerogatives while at the same time impeding attainment of the ultimate statutory goals. In view of this legislative history and in view of Congress' desire to avoid undue federal regulation of private businesses, use of the word "require" rather than the phrase "require or permit" in § 703(j) fortifies the conclusion that Congress did not intend to limit traditional business freedom to such a degree as to prohibit all voluntary, race-conscious affirmative action.

We therefore hold that Title VII's prohibition in §§ 703(a) and (d) against racial discrimination does not condemn all private, voluntary, race-conscious affirmative action plans....

◆ JUSTICE BLACKMUN, concurring.

While I share some of the misgivings expressed in Mr. Justice Rehnquist's dissent concerning the extent to which the legislative history of Title VII clearly supports the result the Court reaches today, I believe that additional considerations, practical and equitable, only partially perceived, if perceived at all, by the 88th Congress, support the conclusion reached by the Court today, and I therefore join its opinion as well as its judgment.

... If Title VII is read literally, on the one hand [employers] face liability for past discrimination against blacks, and on the other they face liability to whites for any voluntary preferences adopted to mitigate the effects of prior discrimination against blacks....

[Kaiser conceded that its past hiring practices might have been discriminatory. After critical reviews from the Federal Government, Kaiser and the Steelworkers established the training program in question here.] ...

Respondent Weber's reading of Title VII endorsed by the Court of Appeals, places voluntary compliance with Title VII in profound jeopardy. The only way for the employer and the union to keep [from being sued would be to] eschew all forms of voluntary affirmative action. Even a whisper of emphasis on minority recruiting would be forbidden. Because Congress intended to encourage private efforts to come into compliance with Title VII, ... employers and unions who had committed "arguable violations" of Title VII should be free to make reasonable responses without fear of liability to whites. Preferential hiring along the lines of the Kaiser program is a reasonable response for the employer....

[I] if the Court has misperceived the political will, it has the assurance that because the question is statutory Congress may set a different course if it so chooses.

♦ [CHIEF JUSTICE BURGER's dissenting opinion is omitted].

♦ JUSTICE REHNQUIST, with whom the CHIEF JUSTICE [BURGER] joins, dissenting.

The operative sections of Title VII prohibit racial discrimination in employment *simpliciter*. Taken in its normal meaning ... this language prohibits a covered employer from considering race when making an employment decision, whether the race be black or white....

§ 703(d) of Title VII [provides]:

> "It shall be an unlawful employment practice for any employer, labor or-ganization, or joint labor-management committee controlling apprenticeship or other training or retraining, including on-the-job training programs to discriminate against any individual because of his race, color, religion, sex, or national origin in admission to, or employment in, any program estab-lished to provide apprenticeship or other training." 78 Stat. 256, 42 U.S.C. § 2000e–2(d).

Equally suited to the task would be § 703(a)(2)....

Quite simply, Kaiser's racially discriminatory admission quota is flatly prohibited by the plain language of Title VII. This normally dispositive fact, however, gives the Court only momentary pause. An "interpretation" of the statute upholding Weber's claim would, according to the Court, " 'bring about an end completely at variance with the purpose of the statute.' " To support this conclusion, the Court calls upon the "spirit" of the Act, which it divines from passages in Title VII's legislative history indicating that enactment of the statute was prompted by Congress' desire " 'to open employment opportunities for Negroes in occupations which [had] been traditionally closed to them.' " But the legislative history invoked by the Court to avoid the plain language of §§ 703(a) and (d) simply misses the point. To be sure, the reality of em-ployment discrimination against Negroes provided the primary impetus for passage of Title VII. But this fact by no means supports the proposition that Congress in-tended to leave employers free to discriminate against white persons. In most cases, "[l]egislative history ... is more vague than the statute we are called upon to interpret." Here, however, the legislative history of Title VII is as clear as the language of §§ 703(a) and (d), and it irrefutably demonstrates that Congress meant precisely what it said in §§ 703(a) and (d) — that *no* racial discrimination in employment is permissible under Title VII, not even preferential treatment of minorities to correct racial imbalance.

In undertaking to review the legislative history of Title VII, I am mindful that the topic hardly makes for light reading, but I am also fearful that nothing short of a thorough examination of the congressional debates will fully expose the magnitude of the Court's misinterpretation of Congress' intent.

[House Debate and Passage]

Introduced on the floor of the House of Representatives on June 20, 1963, the bill ... that ultimately became the Civil Rights Act of 1964 ... was promptly referred to the Committee on the Judiciary, where it was amended to include Title VII.... [which contained] §§ 703(a) and (d)....

... [T]he Judiciary Committee's Report simply paraphrased the provisions of Title VII without elaboration. In a separate Minority Report, however, opponents of the measure on the Committee advanced a line of attack which was reiterated throughout the debates in both the House and Senate and which ultimately led to passage of § 703(j). Noting that the word "discrimination" was nowhere defined in H.R.7152, the Minority Report charged that the absence from Title VII of any reference to "racial imbalance" was a "public relations" ruse and that "the administration intends to rely upon its own construction of 'discrimination' as including the lack of racial balance...." H.R.Rep., pt. 1, pp. 67–68. To demonstrate how the bill would operate in practice, the Minority Report posited a number of hypothetical employment situations, concluding in each example that the employer "*may be forced to hire according to race,* to 'racially balance' those who work for him *in every job classification* or be in violation of Federal law." *Id.,* at 69 (emphasis in original).

When [the bill] reached the House floor, the opening speech in support of its passage was delivered by Representative Celler, Chairman of the House Judiciary Committee and the Congressman responsible for introducing the legislation. A portion of that speech responded to criticism "seriously misrepresent[ing] what the bill would do and grossly distort[ing] its effects":

"[T]he charge has been made that the Equal Employment Opportunity Commission to be established by title VII of the bill would have the power to prevent a business from employing and promoting the people it wished, and that a 'Federal inspector' could then order the hiring and promotion only of employees of certain races or religious groups. This description of the bill is entirely wrong....

" ... The Bill would do no more than prevent ... employers from discriminating against *or in favor* of workers because of their race, religion, or national origin...." (emphasis added).

... Thus, the battle lines were drawn early in the legislative struggle over Title VII, with opponents of the measure charging that ... the Federal Government ... by interpreting the word "discrimination" to mean the existence of "racial imbalance," would "require" employers to grant preferential treatment to minorities, and supporters responding that the [government] would be granted no such power and that, indeed, Title VII prohibits discrimination "in favor of workers because of their race." Supporters of H.R. 7152 in the House ultimately prevailed by a vote of 290 to 130, and the measure was sent to the Senate to begin what became the longest debate in that body's history.

[Senate Debate and Passage]

The Senate debate was broken into three phases: the debate on sending the bill to Committee, the general debate on the bill prior to invocation of cloture, and the debate following cloture.

[Debate on Sending the Bill to Committee]

When debate on the motion to refer the bill to Committee opened, opponents of Title VII in the Senate immediately echoed the fears expressed by their counterparts in the House....

Senator Humphrey, ... stated: "[T]he meaning of racial or religious discrimination is perfectly clear.... [I]t means a distinction in treatment given to different individuals because of their different race, religion, or national origin." ... Senator Humphrey further stated that "nothing in the bill would permit any official or court to require any employer or labor union to give preferential treatment to any minority group."

After 17 days of debate, the Senate voted to take up the bill directly, without referring it to a committee. Consequently, there is no Committee Report in the Senate.

[General Debate Prior to Cloture]

Formal debate on the merits of [the bill] began....

In the opening speech of the formal Senate debate on the bill, Senator Humphrey [the majority whip] addressed the main concern of Title VII's opponents, advising that not only does Title VII not require use of racial quotas, *it does not permit* their use. "The truth," stated the floor leader of the bill, "is that this title forbids discriminating against anyone on account of race. This is the simple and complete truth about title VII." 110 Cong.Rec. 6549 (1964). Senator Humphrey continued:

> "Contrary to the allegations of some opponents of this title, there is nothing in it that will give any power to the Commission or to any court to require hiring, firing, or promotion of employees in order to meet a racial 'quota' or to achieve a certain racial balance.

> "That bugaboo has been brought up a dozen times; but it is nonexistent. In fact, *the very opposite is true. Title VII prohibits discrimination.* In effect, it says that race, religion and national origin are not to be used as the basis for hiring and firing. Title VII is designed to encourage hiring on the basis of ability and qualifications, not race or religion." *Ibid.* (emphasis added)....

Senator Kuchel [the minority whip] ... observed that ... "Employers and labor organizations could not discriminate *in favor of or against* a person because of his race, his religion, or his national origin. In such MATTERS ... THE BILL NOW BEFORE US ... Is color-blind." *id.*, at 6564 (emphasis added).

... In an interpretative memorandum submitted jointly to the Senate, Senators Clark and Case [bipartisan captains] took pains to refute the opposition's charge that Title VII would result in preferential treatment of minorities. Their words were clear and unequivocal:

> "There is no requirement in title VII that an employer maintain a racial balance in his work force. On the contrary, any deliberate attempt to maintain a racial balance, whatever such a balance may be, would involve a violation

of title VII because maintaining such a balance would require an employer to hire or to refuse to hire on the basis of race. It must be emphasized that discrimination is prohibited as to any individual."

Of particular relevance to the instant litigation were their observations regarding seniority rights. As if directing their comments at Brian Weber, the Senators said:

"Title VII would have no effect on established seniority rights. Its effect is prospective and not retrospective. Thus, for example, if a business has been discriminating in the past and as a result has an all-white working force, when the title comes into effect the employer's obligation would be simply to fill future vacancies on a nondiscriminatory basis. He would not be obliged—*or indeed permitted*—to fire whites in order to hire Negroes, *or to prefer Negroes for future vacancies, or, once Negroes are hired, to give them special seniority rights at the expense of the white workers hired earlier.*" *Ibid.* (emphasis added).

Thus, with virtual clairvoyance the Senate's leading supporters of Title VII anticipated precisely the circumstances of this case and advised their colleagues that the type of minority preference employed by Kaiser would violate Title VII's ban on racial discrimination....

Despite these clear statements from the bill's leading and most knowledgeable proponents, the fears of the opponents were not put to rest. Senator Robertson reiterated the view that "discrimination" could be interpreted by a federal "bureaucrat" to require hiring quotas. Senators Smathers and Sparkman, while conceding that Title VII does not in so many words require the use of hiring quotas, repeated the opposition's view that employers would be coerced to grant preferential hiring treatment to minorities by agencies of the Federal Government. Senator Williams was quick to respond:

"Those opposed to [the bill] should realize that to hire a Negro solely because he is a Negro is racial discrimination, just as much as a 'white only' employment policy. Both forms of discrimination are prohibited by title VII of this bill. The language of that title simply states that race is not a qualification for employment.... Some people charge that [the bill] favors the Negro, at the expense of the white majority. But how can the language of equality favor one race or one religion over another? Equality can have only one meaning, and that meaning is self-evident to reasonable men. Those who say that equality means favoritism do violence to common sense."

... While the debate in the Senate raged, a bipartisan coalition ... was working with House leaders and representatives of the Johnson administration on a number of amendments to [the bill] designed to enhance its prospects of passage. The so-called "Dirksen-Mansfield" amendment ... added ... §703(j), [which] was specifically directed at the opposition's concerns regarding racial balancing and preferential treatment of minorities, [and which provided] in pertinent part: "Nothing contained in

[Title VII] shall be interpreted to require any employer ... to grant preferential treatment to any individual or to any group because of the race ... of such individual or group on account of" a racial imbalance in the employer's work force.

The Court draws from the language of § 703(j) primary support for its conclusion that Title VII's blanket prohibition on racial discrimination in employment does not prohibit preferential treatment of blacks to correct racial imbalance. Alleging that opponents of Title VII had argued (1) that the Act would be interpreted to require employers with racially imbalanced work forces to grant preferential treatment to minorities and (2) that "employers with racially imbalanced work forces would grant preferential treatment to racial minorities even if not required to do so by the Act," the Court concludes that § 703(j) is responsive only to the opponents' first objection and that Congress therefore must have intended to permit voluntary, private discrimination against whites in order to correct racial imbalance.

Contrary to the Court's analysis, the language of § 703(j) is precisely tailored to the objection voiced time and again by Title VII's opponents. Not once during the 83 days of debate in the Senate did a speaker, proponent or opponent, suggest that the bill would allow employers *voluntarily* to prefer racial minorities over white persons. In light of Title VII's flat prohibition on discrimination "against any individual ... because of such individual's race," § 703(a), such a contention would have been, in any event, too preposterous to warrant response.... The complaint consistently voiced by the opponents was that Title VII, particularly the word "discrimination," would be *interpreted* by federal agencies ... to *require* the correction of racial imbalance through the granting of preferential treatment to minorities. Verbal assurances that Title VII would not require—indeed, would not permit—preferential treatment of blacks having failed, supporters of H.R. 7152 responded by proposing an amendment carefully worded to meet, and put to rest, the opposition's charge. Indeed, unlike §§ 703(a) and (d), which are by their terms directed at entities—*e. g.,* employers, labor unions—whose actions are restricted by Title VII's prohibitions, the language of § 703(j) is specifically directed at entities—federal agencies and courts—charged with the responsibility of interpreting Title VII's provisions....

Section 703(j) apparently calmed the fears of most of the opponents; after its introduction, complaints concerning racial balance and preferential treatment died down considerably....

[Debate Following Cloture]

On June 10, the Senate, for the second time in its history, imposed cloture on its Members....

As the civil rights bill approached its final vote, several supporters rose to urge its passage. Senator Muskie adverted briefly to the issue of preferential treatment: "It has been said that the bill discriminates in favor of the Negro at the expense of the rest of us. It seeks to do nothing more than to lift the Negro from the status of inequality to one of *equality* of treatment." ...

Later that day, June 19, the issue was put to a vote, and the Dirksen-Mansfield substitute bill was passed.

The Act's return engagement in the House was brief.... By a vote of 289 to 126, the House [agreed] to the Senate's amendments.... Later that same day, July 2, the President signed the bill and the Civil Rights Act of 1964 became law.

Reading the language of Title VII, as the Court purports to do, "against the background of [its] legislative history ... and the historical context from which the Act arose," one is led inescapably to the conclusion that Congress fully understood what it was saying and meant precisely what it said....

Our task in this case, like any other case involving the construction of a statute, is to give effect to the intent of Congress. To divine that intent, we traditionally look first to the words of the statute and, if they are unclear, then to the statute's legislative history. Finding the desired result hopelessly foreclosed by these conventional sources, the Court turns to a third source—the "spirit" of the Act. But close examination of what the Court proffers as the spirit of the Act reveals it as the spirit animating the present majority, not the 88th Congress....

* * *

Points for Discussion

1. *Statutory Language*: What was the language at issue? What did each party want that language to mean? What meaning did the majority and dissent adopt?

2. *Theories*: Which theory did the majority use? The dissent? Did the majority or dissent find the language ambiguous, absurd, to have a scrivener's error, or to raise a constitutional question? This case offers an excellent example of the differences between intentionalism and purposivism. Notice how the majority and dissent both use legislative history, but they use it for very different purposes.

3. *Defining Discrimination*: How does a dictionary define "discrimination"? Dictionary.com provides two definitions: (1) "to treat differently, unfairly favorably or unfavorably, on the basis of race, gender, or religious beliefs"; and (2) "to act on the basis of prejudice." Which interpretation do you think the legislature intended? The lack of a definition in the Act was raised during the debates. One fix would have been to define the term in the Act. The legislature specifically opted not to do so. Why? What alternative did it adopt instead?

4. *Section 703(j)*: Pursuant to *in pari materia*, the whole act aspect, all sections of an act are relevant to meaning. According to the dissent, section 703(j) was added to allay concerns that the government would force employers to hire individuals from specific races to remedy past racial discrimination. The majority agreed but added that section 703(j) specifically did not include language preventing employers from choosing to have voluntary affirmative action programs: "Had Congress meant to prohibit all race-conscious affirmative action, as respondent urges, it easily could have answered both objections by providing that Title VII would not require or *permit* racially preferential integration efforts. But Congress did

not choose such a course." Why does the dissent respond that it was simply unnecessary for section 703(j) to prohibit employers from permitting voluntarily racially preferential integration efforts?

5. *Selective Use of Legislative History*: What legislative history did the majority point to? What legislative history did the dissent point to? Why did they not use the same legislative history?

Those who criticize the use of legislative history point to cases like *Weber* to demonstrate that legislative history is malleable; it can be manipulated to support any result a judge or litigator wants. Judge Harold Leventhal has said quite famously, "the trick is to look over the heads of the crowd and pick out your friends." Antonin Scalia, A Matter Of Interpretation: Federal Courts and the Law 36 (1997). Some critics have even suggested that legislators may insert language into legislative history for the sole purpose of influencing later judicial interpretations. The facts of *Hamdan v. Rumsfeld* lend some weight to this argument. 548 U.S. 557, 734 n.10 (2006) (refusing to consider legislative colloquy that was inserted into The Congressional Record after the Senate debate).

6. *Dynamic Interpretation*: Critics of the *Weber* holding note that Justice Rehnquist's dissent more faithfully explored and characterized the legislative history. But Justice Rehnquist ignored the fact that this statute was enacted to remedy discrimination against African-Americans, which continued to exist ten years later. Consider this point from Justice Blackmun:

> The bargain struck in 1964 with the passage of Title VII guaranteed equal opportunity for white and black alike, but where Title VII provides no remedy for blacks, it should not be construed to foreclose private affirmative action from supplying relief. It seems unfair for respondent Weber to argue, as he does, that the asserted scarcity of black craftsmen in Louisiana, the product of historic discrimination, makes Kaiser's training program illegal because it ostensibly absolves Kaiser of all Title VII liability. Absent compelling evidence of legislative intent, I would not interpret Title VII itself as a means of "locking in" the effects of segregation for which Title VII provides no remedy.

Weber, 443 U.S. at 214–15 (Blackmun, J., concurring). In Dynamic Statutory Interpretation, 135 U. Pa. L. Rev. 1479 (1987), Professor William Eskridge agreed with Blackmun. Eskridge noted that the text of the Act was not clear and that the historical context supported Weber's position. Nonetheless, he suggested that the majority was right for the following reasons.

> I agree with the *Weber* Court's result because of the evolutive perspective. The separate concurring opinion of Justice Blackmun is the most sensible opinion in the *Weber* case. Justice Blackmun argued that the evolution of Title VII created a practical dilemma for unions and employers that justified voluntary affirmative action in many cases.... An assumption of most supporters of Title VII in 1964 was that equality of opportunity for mi-

norities would in due time yield equality of result in employment. . . . however, it became apparent that formally equal opportunities were not always leading to significantly greater representation of minorities in the workforce.[48] American society came to understand that the invidious effects of discrimination might last long after the discrimination itself ceased and that more affirmative measures were needed to afford any reasonable chance for a color-blind society in the future. Consequently, there was greater pressure on employers and unions to undertake voluntary efforts to re-evaluate their employment practices; the Supreme Court strongly encouraged such voluntary efforts in the 1970's. . . .

Given the Supreme Court's endorsement of voluntary programs, the natural response was voluntary affirmative action programs such as the one in *Weber.* . . .

[When the Civil Rights Act was enacted, p]eople thought that rooting out actual prejudice would create a color-blind society. The intellectual focus changed over the next fifteen years, as the legal community came to realize that discrimination could be just as invidious even when it could not be established that prejudice was at its root. . . .

To proclaim that the single purpose of Title VII was to provide jobs for minorities, as the Court did in *Weber*, is to misstate history. There were many purposes embodied in Title VII—some of them, such as the sex discrimination provision, added quite adventitiously—and if there were a single overriding purpose, it would be to create a color-blind society, a purpose invoked most persuasively by the dissenting opinion. . . .

My purpose . . . is to challenge the often-stated (but less often believed) assumption that statutory interpretation is nothing but an exercise in finding answers that were fixed when the legislature originally enacted the statute. Like other texts, statutes are dynamic things: they have different meanings to different people, at different times, and in different legal and societal contexts. It is a significant departure from current doctrine to assert, as I do, that federal courts should interpret statutes in light of their current as well as historical context. Dynamic interpretation is most appropriate when the statute is old yet still the source of litigation, is generally phrased, and faces significantly changed societal problems or legal contexts. Dynamic interpretation is least appropriate when the statute is recent and addresses the issue in a relatively determinate way. . . .

DYNAMIC STATUTORY INTERPRETATION, 135 U. PA. L. REV. 1479, 1492–55 (1987). What do you think of what Professor Eskridge calls "dynamic interpretation"?

---

48. The facts of *Weber* illustrate this problem. Even though the employer claimed it did not discriminate against blacks, the craft workforce remained only 1.83% black into the 1970's, in large part because one qualification for becoming a craft worker was prior experience, which blacks did not have, arguably due to past discrimination.

Does his analysis help make sense of why the majority reached a result apparently at odds with the text?

* * *

In sum, all of the concerns are valid and are ones that you or your opponent should be aware of and be able to articulate. But rather than prohibit the use of legislative history entirely, these concerns merely show that legislative history should be relegated to a non-leading role in interpretation. Legislative history is certainly not law, but legislative history can offer insight into what some or all of the legislators may have been thinking when the act, which did go through the constitutional process, was enacted. Legislative history offers context for the enactment process of a particular act. A skilled litigant will know where to find legislative history, how to use it, and how to criticize an opponent's use of it. But what if the legislative history is deadly silent? Should legislative silence ever be relevant to statutory interpretation?

iii. The "Dog Does Not Bark" Canon: When Congress Is Silent

What if the legislative history is silent on a particular issue? Ordinarily, "[s]ilence in the legislative history about a particular provision ... is not a good guide to statutory interpretation and certainly is not more persuasive than the words of a statute." *America Online, Inc. v. United States*, 64 Fed. Cl. 571, 578 (Fed. Cl. 2005). However, silence can sometimes be illuminating. Suppose, for example, that a statute on its face makes a radical and controversial change in the law—one that you would expect Congress would have discussed and debated. Yet, the legislative history is silent; Congress did not mention the change at all. Under these circumstances, would not silence speak volumes? Generally, the answer is no; occasionally, the answer is yes.

To illustrate, in *Harrison v. PPG Industries, Inc.*, 446 U.S. 578 (1980), the issue for the Court was whether a general catch-all term, "any other final action," in the Clean Air Act meant *any* final agency action or just acts similar in nature to the specific actions preceding the general catch-all. *Id.* at 587, 592. In other words, the question was whether the other surrounding, listed actions narrow the general catch-all, as *ejusdem generis* would suggest. A broad interpretation would dramatically shift responsibility for reviewing the Environmental Protection Agency's actions under this Act from the district courts to the courts of appeals. *Id.* at 585. For this reason, the Fifth Circuit found it unlikely that Congress would have intended such a major jurisdictional shift without expressly addressing this change during the enactment process. For the court, "[t]he 'most revealing' aspect of the legislative history of [the subsection at issue] ... was the complete absence of any discussion of such a 'massive shift' in jurisdiction." *Id.* at 585 (citing *PPG Industries, Inc. v. Harrison*, 587 F.2d 237 (5th Cir. 1979)).

On appeal, the Supreme Court rejected this "silence speaks volumes" argument. "In ascertaining the meaning of a statute, a court cannot, in the manner of Sherlock Holmes, pursue the theory of the dog that did not bark." *Id.* at 592.*

---

* The Court was referring to A. Conan Doyle, Silver Blaze, in The Complete Sherlock Holmes 289 (1927), in which the following exchange took place:

Despite strong rhetoric in *PPG Industries* against the-dog-did-not-bark argument, this argument can, at times, be persuasive; hence, it should not be ignored. For example, in *Chisom v. Roemer*, 501 U.S. 380 (1991), the majority found legislative silence informative. In that case, the Court had to determine whether Section Two of the Voting Rights Act, which protected individuals' rights to elect "*representatives*," applied to the election of state judges. *Id.* at 384. The petitioners, African American voters, alleged that Louisiana's method of electing two justices to the State Supreme Court at-large from the New Orleans area impermissibly diluted the minority vote; the state responded that the Act did not apply to the election of state judges because judges were not representatives. *Id.* at 385, 390.

The legislative history was telling precisely because it was not telling. Congress had amended Section Two of this Act in 1982. Prior to the amendment, there was no question that judges were covered. *Id.* at 392. With the amendment, Congress had responded to a prior judicial interpretation of the statute that had required proof of intent to discriminate. Congress had eliminated this judicially imposed intent requirement. *Id.* at 393. The majority concluded that had Congress intended, by using the word "representatives," to exclude vote dilution claims involving judges, "Congress would have made it explicit in the statute, or at least some of the Members would have identified or mentioned it at some point in the unusually extensive legislative history of the 1982 amendment." *Id.* at 396. Thus, because no legislator had ever suggested that judges would no longer be covered, Congress must have meant to maintain the status quo in this regard despite its choice of the term "representatives." Thus, silence spoke volumes.

Justice Scalia, in dissent, chastised the majority's dog-does-not-bark analysis:

> Finding nothing in the legislative history affirming that judges were excluded from the coverage of § 2, the Court gives the phrase "to elect representatives" the quite extraordinary meaning that covers the election of judges.
>
> As method, this is just backwards, and however much we may be attracted by the result it produces in a particular case, we should in every case resist it. Our job begins with a text that Congress has passed and the President has signed. We are to read the words of that text as any ordinary Member of Congress would have read them ... and apply the meaning so determined. In my view, that reading reveals that § 2 extends to vote dilution claims for the elections of representatives only, and judges are not representatives.... Apart from the questionable wisdom of assuming that dogs will bark when something important is happening, we have forcefully and explicitly rejected the Conan Doyle approach to statutory construction in the past.

"Is there any point to which you would wish to draw my attention?" Asked the Scotland Yard Detective.
  To which Holmes responded, "To the curious incident of the dog in the night-time."
  Detective: "The dog did nothing in the night-time."
  "That was the curious incident," replied Sherlock Holmes.

Id. at 405, 406 (Scalia, J., dissenting) (citations omitted). For another example, see *Mississippi Poultry Association, Inc. v. Madigan*, 992 F.2d 1359–78 (5th Cir. 1993) (Reavley, C.J., dissenting) (arguing that it was inconceivable that Congress would enact a statute that effectively created a trade barrier without talking about "why a barrier was justified, what it was supposed to accomplish, or how its effectiveness would be monitored.") *aff'd on reh'g*, 31 F.3d 293 (5th Cir. 1994) (en banc) *overruled by*, 21 U.S.C. section 466(d)(1) (1994) amended through Pub. L. 103-465, §431 (k)(1) (1994).

Despite the reality that Congress is unlikely to make a radical shift in law or policy without some discussion, the presumption remains that legislative silence during enactment is not relevant to meaning. If the legislature did not mean what it wrote, then the legislature, not the court, should fix the error, as it did after the *Mississippi Poultry Association* case.

We have now surveyed the various types of legislative history, identified the many criticisms of using legislative history, and explored the relevance of silence during the enactment process. In our next chapter, we turn to another way to use legislative history: to identify unexpressed statutory purpose.

Problem 11

About 7 billion chickens and turkeys are processed annually in the United States. Proper handling during processing is important because about 40 percent of raw poultry is contaminated with salmonella, a bacterium that causes various diseases in humans and animals. Although the government inspects poultry processors, at least 40,000 salmonella infections are reported each year to the Centers for Disease Control and Prevention (CDC), a federal agency that tracks infectious diseases. The CDC estimates that each year between 40,000 and 4 million people become ill from salmonella and about 500 of these persons die of salmonellosis, an illness that causes fever and intentional disorders. Foreign poultry and poultry products have been responsible for approximately 50% of recent illnesses. In response, Congress enacted the Poultry Products Inspection Act (PPIA). The PPIA amends existing law by requiring foreign countries to implement testing programs at the point of slaughter for poultry and poultry products offered for importation into the United States.

The Food Safety and Inspection Service (FSIS) is a federal agency located within the Department of Agriculture (USDA). The FSIS has primary responsibility for determining that countries producing poultry or poultry products for export to the United States have inspection programs that are designed to assure that all such exports are safe, wholesome, unadulterated, and comply with the PPIA and regulations established thereunder.

The process works as follows. The foreign country applies to the FSIS for certification that its country's inspection systems meets PPIA's standards. Once the FSIS certifies that the poultry inspection system of a foreign country meets the PPIA standards, individual businesses operating within that country may export poultry and poultry products to the U.S. so long as the individual business obtains a certification from its national inspection authority that the individual business meets that country's standards. The individual business must also agree to allow FSIS to inspect its systems on site.

The National Poultry Association (NPA) is a non-profit trade association of domestic poultry producers. NPA files suit, alleging that the USDA's regulation unreasonably interprets 21 U.S.C. § 466. The USDA responds on behalf of itself and FSIS, defending its regulation. Both sides cross move for summary judgment, given that there are no disputed facts, only a disputed legal issue. The judge assigned to the case has set oral argument on the motions for two weeks from now and has requested briefs be filed by Monday.

You are a staff attorney for the USDA. You have been assigned the task of writing the draft argument section, which your supervisor will revise and edit. Draft the argument section of a brief addressing whether the USDA's regulation is a valid interpretation of the statute (*do not address the law's application to the facts at this time*). In making your argument, assume the standard of review is *de novo*, meaning that a court will employ all the traditional tools of interpretation we have covered to date. You will learn later that this standard is modified when an agency interprets a statute, but ignore that issue for now. Be sure to respond to the arguments the NPA's counsel is likely to make regarding the regulation's validity. You do not need to include argument headings or citations.

Problem Materials

21 U.S.C. § 452. Congressional declaration of policy.

It is hereby declared to be the policy of the Congress to provide for the inspection of poultry and poultry products to prevent the movement or sale in interstate or foreign commerce of poultry products that are contaminated or otherwise dangerous to consume. It is the purpose of the act to encourage those countries that wish to export to the United States, to develop and implement safe and effective inspection and testing procedures that are as safe as or safer than domestic procedures. It is the intent of Congress that when poultry and poultry products are condemned because of disease, the reason for condemnation in such instances shall be supported by scientific fact.

21 U.S.C. § 460(e): Domestic States and Territories subject to regulation

Whenever the Secretary determines that a U.S. State or territory does not have inspection requirements that are at least equal to those imposed under this Act, such state shall be "designated" for federal oversight....

21 U.S.C. § 466: Import Standards

(a) Compliance with standards and regulations; status after importation

No slaughtered poultry or poultry products shall be imported into the United States unless they are healthful, wholesome, fit for human food, not adulterated, and contain no dye, chemical, preservative, or ingredient that renders them unhealthful, unwholesome, adulterated, or unfit for human food. All such products must comply with the rules and regulations made by the Secretary of Agriculture to assure that imported poultry or poultry products comply with the standards provided for in this chapter.

(b) Authority ⟶ Agency?

The Secretary of Agriculture is authorized to make rules and regulations to carry out the purposes of this section, relating to the importation of poultry.

(d) Applicable standards

(1) Notwithstanding any other provision of law, all poultry, or parts or products of poultry, capable for use as human food offered for importation into the United States shall—

  (A) be subject to the same standards applied to products produced in the United States; and

  (B) be processed in facilities and under conditions that are the same as those under which similar products are processed in the United States.

(2) Any such imported poultry or poultry products that do not meet such standards shall not be permitted entry into the United States.

S. Rep. No. 99-145: (Report of the Senate Committee on Agriculture, Nutrition, and Forestry) ⟶ leg. History

This Act will amend existing law to require all poultry and poultry products, capable of use as human food that are imported into the Unites States, be subject to the inspection, sanitary, and quality standards applied to poultry in the United States. The Act would also require that such products be produced in facilities and under conditions at least equal to those under which similar products are processed in the United States. Any imported poultry product that does not meet the standards would not be permitted entry into the Unites States.

Congressional Record: Senate Debate.

Mr. Floyd: As chair of the Agriculture Committee, I offer a purely technical amendment to the Agriculture Committee's draft. In sections 466(d)(1)(A)&(B), strike out "at least equal to" and insert in lieu thereof "the same as."

I offer this amendment to change the provision relating to inspection of imported poultry products to provide that imported poultry must have been processed in facilities and under conditions that are the same as those under which similar products are processed in the United States. This change clarifies the provision to reflect the original intent of the committee.

Presiding officer: Is there further debate? Hearing none, the question is on agreeing to the amendment. All in favor? [The amendment was overwhelming approved without discussion.].

H. Rep. No. 99-147: (Report of the House Committee on Agriculture)

This Act will amend existing law to require foreign exporters of poultry and poultry products to have inspection systems and safety provisions that are at least as safe as those employed in the United States. Because it is highly unlikely that foreign systems can be identical to those systems in the United States (for example, the United States producers do not use the metric system), the Committee recommends that such procedures be at least as safe as the United States systems. For example, Australian poultry producers use radiation to kill bacteria on poultry. Radiation is used widely throughout the European Union and Australia because radiation is the most effective process for eliminating bacteria thereby making poultry safer. Radiation is not used in the United States currently because consumers have indicated a reluctance to purchase radiated foods. For this reason, the USDA does not require either U.S. or foreign poultry producers to use radiation, but the agency acknowledges on its website that the process, radiating poultry, is at least as good as, if not better than, the U.S. system of using antimicrobial washes.

Hence, a standard that protects the public while not simultaneously imposing a trade barrier is appropriate.

Conference Committee Report: [The House bill required that both inspection processes and conditions be "at least equal" to U.S. processes. The Senate bill required that the inspection processes and conditions be "the same as" U.S. processes. Without discussing this specific issue, the Conference Committee recommended adoption of the Senate bill without any discussion of this particular issue.]

9 C.F.R. Part 381 (USDA Regulation)

The inspection systems for all those entities offering poultry and poultry products for importation must maintain an inspection program and processing facilities that are at least equal to those of the United States.

Merriam-Webster Dictionary Definitions:

Equal: adjective

1   a: of the same measure, quantity, amount, or number as another

     b: identical in mathematical value or logical denotation: equivalent

     c: like in quality, nature, or status

2   : regarding or affecting all objects in the same way: impartial

3   : free from extremes: as in tranquil in mind or mood, not showing variation in appearance, structure, or proportion

Identical: adjective

1   : being the same

2   : having such close resemblance as to be essentially the same

Same: adjective

1   a: resembling in every relevant respect

      b: conforming in every respect—used with as

2   a: being one without addition, change, or discontinuance: identical

      b: being the one under discussion or already referred to

3   : corresponding so closely as to be indistinguishable

4   : equal in size, shape, value, or importance—usually used with *the* or a demonstrative (as *that, those*)

Chapter 12

Canons Based on Extrinsic Sources and Legislative Process: Purpose

A. Introduction to This Chapter

We continue with our examination of enactment context and turn to the relevance of unexpressed purpose. In Chapter 9, you learned that purpose clauses may or may not be relevant to statutory interpretation. Purpose clauses are express statements of statutory purpose. Here, we look at unexpressed purpose. What is its relevance, if any?

While statutory interpretation centers on the language in the text, finding statutory meaning is more than simply discovering the ordinary meaning of that language by using dictionaries. Some argue that statutes have a body and soul: "[T]he letter of the law is the body of the law, and the sense and reason of the law is the soul of the law." William N. Eskridge, Jr., *All About Words: Early Understandings of the "Judicial Power" in Statutory Interpretation, 1776–1806,* 101 Colum. L. Rev. 990, 1001 (quoting *Eyston v. Studd,* 75 Eng. Rep. 688, 695–700). In other words:

> Legislation has an aim; it seeks to obviate some mischief, to supply an in-adequacy.... That aim ... is not drawn, like nitrogen, out of the air; it is evinced in the language of the statute, as read in the light of other external manifestations of purpose.

Felix Frankfurter, *Some Reflections on the Reading of Statutes,* 47 Colum. L. Rev. 527, 538–39 (1947). We turn now to the soul of the law: purpose. Below, you will learn first how to find it, then how to use it.

B. Finding and Using Purpose

a. Finding Purpose from Text

In Chapter 9, we examined preambles, findings, and purpose clauses. When Congress includes one of these, finding purpose appears easier. Whether purpose can be used if it is located in one of these clauses was explored in Chapter 9. But many statutes, particularly older statutes, do not have preambles, explanatory findings, or other indicia of purpose. And because of the political nature of the legislative process, even when bills contain these clauses, the clauses may be incomplete or unhelpful. When acts have no such clause or have incomplete clauses, one area from which you can derive purpose is from the language of the act. Discerning an act's purpose from text alone can be challenging, but it is the first place to start.

> There is, of course, no more persuasive evidence of the purpose of a statute than the words by which the legislature undertook to give expression to its wishes. Often these words are sufficient in and of themselves to determine the purpose of the legislation.

United States v. American Trucking Ass'ns, Inc., 310 U.S. 534, 543 (1940).

In 1584, the quintessential purpose case was decided in England: *Heydon's Case,* 76 Eng. Rep. 637 (Ex. 1584). The facts were few. King Henry VIII adopted a statute that specified which property interests would be invalidated if used to avoid his ability to seize property. In the case, the property owner used copyhold interests (an ancient form of landownership), which were not expressly identified in the statute. The court, thus, had to decide whether to expand the statute to include these types of property interests to give the King more property, even though they were not explicitly included within the text or whether to limit the statute to its words, even though the King had likely omitted this interest inadvertently. I doubt that you will be surprised to learn that the court expanded the statute. To resolve the case, the court developed a four-step test. See if you can identify each step.

Heydon's Case
Court of Exchequer
76 Eng. Rep. 637 (Eng. 1584)

... And it was resolved by them, that for the sure and true (*a*) interpretation of all statutes in general (be they penal (B) or beneficial, restrictive or enlarging of the common law,) four things are to be discerned and considered:

(*b*) 1st. What was the common law before the making of the Act.

(*c*) 2nd. What was the mischief and defect for which the common law did not provide.

3rd. What remedy the Parliament hath resolved and appointed to cure the disease of the commonwealth.

And, 4th. The true reason of the remedy; and then the office of all the Judges is always to make such (*d*) construction as shall suppress the mischief, and advance the remedy, and to suppress subtle inventions and evasions for continuance of the mischief, and *pro private commodo,* and to add force and life to the cure and remedy, according to the true intent of the makers of the Act, *pro bono publico.*

* * *

Points for Discussion

1. *Statutory Language*: In this case, we do not even know exactly what the statute said. But we do know that it included a list of specific property types and that the issue for the court was whether to add another property type that was not

already included. How would you have approached this issue if you represented the copyright holder? Likely, you would have looked at the language in the general catch-all, then interpreted that language using *ejusdem generis*. If there were no catch-all, which seems likely here, then you likely would have turned to *expressio unius*. Did the court use either?

2. *Theories*: Which theory did the court use?

3. *Four Steps*: Identify the four steps the court identified for finding unexpressed purpose from text. How does one identify the mischief and the remedy?

4. *Another Articulation*: Professors Henry Hart and Albert Sachs simplified the steps in *Heydon's Case* as follows:

> In interpreting a statute a court should:
>
> (1) Decide what purpose ought to be attributed to the statute.... ; and then
>
> (2) Interpret the words ... to carry out the purpose as best it can, making sure, however, that it does not give the words ...
>
>   (a) a meaning they will not bear....

WILLIAM N. ESKRIDGE, JR. & PHILIP P. FRICKEY, INTRODUCTION TO HENRY M. HART, JR. & ALBERT M. SACKS, THE LEGAL PROCESS (1994) 1374 (William N. Eskridge, Jr. & Philip P. Frickey, eds., 1994). If you look back to *Pepper v. Hart*, [1992] 3 W.L.R. 1032, [1993] 1 All E.R. 42 (1993), you may recognize this articulation.

* * *

b. Finding Purpose from Legislative History

In our modern era, judges often turn to legislative history to identify purpose, especially when the text is unclear. Knowing why a bill was enacted can help a judge understand the purpose for the legislation. You have already studied the next case, *Holy Trinity Church* in Chapter 9 when you learned about titles. Here, we see it again. Many statutory interpretation cases address more than one issue. This time, see if you can identify the source the Court uses to discern the purpose of the statute at issue.

Church of The Holy Trinity v. United States
Supreme Court of the United States
143 U.S. 457 (1892)

♦ JUSTICE BREWER delivered the opinion of the Court.

Plaintiff in error is a corporation duly organized and incorporated as a religious society under the laws of the state of New York. E. Walpole Warren was, prior to September, 1887, an alien residing in England. In that month the plaintiff in error made a contract with him, by which he was to remove to the city of New York, and enter into its service as rector and pastor; and, in pursuance of such contract, Warren did so remove and enter upon such service. It is claimed by the United States that this contract on the part of the plaintiff in error was forbidden by chapter 164, 23 St. p.

contracts case

332; and an action was commenced to recover the penalty prescribed by that act. The circuit court held that the contract was within the prohibition of the statute, and rendered judgment accordingly, and the single question presented for our determination is whether it erred in that conclusion.

The first section describes the act forbidden, and is in these words:

> 'Be it enacted by the senate and house of representatives of the United States of America, in congress assembled, that from and after the passage of this act it shall be unlawful for any person, company, partnership, or corporation, in any manner whatsoever, to prepay the transportation, or in any way assist or encourage the importation or migration, of any alien or aliens, any foreigner or foreigners, into the United States, its territories, or the District of Columbia, under contract or agreement, parol or special, express or implied, made previous to the importation or migration of such alien or aliens, foreigner or foreigners, to perform labor or service of any kind in the United States, its territories, or the District of Columbia.'

It must be conceded that the act of the corporation is within the letter of this section, for the relation of rector to his church is one of service, and implies labor on the one side with compensation on the other. Not only are the general words 'labor' and 'service' both used, but also, as it were to guard against any narrow interpretation and emphasize a breadth of meaning, to them is added 'of any kind;' and, further, as noticed by the circuit judge in his opinion, the fifth section, which makes specific exceptions, among them professional actors, artists, lecturers, singers, and domestic servants, strengthens the idea that every other kind of labor and service was intended to be reached by the first section. While there is great force to this reasoning, we cannot think congress intended to denounce with penalties a transaction like that in the present case. It is a familiar rule that a thing may be within the letter of the statute and yet not within the statute, because not within its spirit nor within the intention of its makers. This has been often asserted, and the Reports are full of cases illustrating its application. This is not the substitution of the will of the judge for that of the legislator; for frequently words of general meaning are used in a statute, words broad enough to include an act in question, and yet a consideration of the whole legislation, or of the circumstances surrounding its enactment, or of the absurd results which follow from giving such broad meaning to the words, makes it unreasonable to believe that the legislator [sic] intended to include the particular act....

[The Court examines the long title of the act and concludes that Congress meant for "labor" to mean manual labor.]

Again, another guide to the meaning of a statute is found in the evil which it is designed to remedy; and for this the court properly looks at contemporaneous events, the situation as it existed, and as it was pressed upon the attention of the legislative body. The situation which called for this statute was briefly but fully stated [in] the case of *U. S. v. Craig*, 28 Fed. Rep. 795, 798: 'The motives and history of the act are matters of common knowledge. It had become the practice for large capitalists in this country to contract with their agents abroad for the shipment of great numbers of an ignorant and servile class of foreign laborers, under contracts by which the employer agreed, upon the one hand, to prepay their passage, while, upon the other hand, the laborers agreed to work after their arrival for a certain time at a low rate of wages. The effect of this was to break down the labor market, and to reduce other laborers engaged in like occupations to the level of the assisted immigrant. The evil finally became so flagrant that an appeal was made to congress for relief by the passage of the act in question, the design of which was to raise the standard of foreign immigrants, and to discountenance the migration of those who had not sufficient means in their own hands, or those of their friends, to pay their passage.'

It appears, also, from the petitions, and in the testimony presented before the committees of congress, that it was this cheap, unskilled labor which was making the trouble, and the influx of which congress sought to prevent. It was never suggested that we had in this country a surplus of brain toilers, and, least of all, that the market for the services of Christian ministers was depressed by foreign competition. Those were matters to which the attention of congress, or of the people, was not directed. So far, then, as the evil which was sought to be remedied interprets the statute, it also guides to an exclusion of this contract from the penalties of the act.

A singular circumstance, throwing light upon the intent of congress, is found in this extract from the report of the senate committee on education and labor, recommending the passage of the bill: 'The general facts and considerations which induce the committee to recommend the passage of this bill are set forth in the report of the committee of the house. The committee report the bill back without amendment, although there are certain features thereof which might well be changed or modified, in the hope that the bill may not fail of passage during the present session. Especially would the committee have otherwise recommended amendments, substituting for the expression, 'labor and service,' whenever it occurs in the body of the bill, the words 'manual labor' or 'manual service,' as sufficiently broad to accomplish the purposes of the bill, and that such amendments would remove objections which a sharp and perhaps unfriendly criticism may urge to the proposed legislation. The committee, however, believing that the bill in its present form will be construed as including only those whose labor or service is manual in character, and being very desirous that the bill become a law before the adjournment, have reported the bill without change.' Page 6059, Congressional Record, 48th Cong. And, referring back to the report of the committee of the house, there appears this language: 'It seeks to restrain and prohibit the immigration or importation of laborers who would have never seen our shores but for the inducements and allurements of men whose only object is to obtain labor at the lowest possible rate, regardless of the social and material well-being of our own citizens, and regardless of the evil consequences which result to American laborers from such immigration. This class of immigrants care nothing about our institutions, and in many instances never even heard of them. They are men whose passage is paid by the importers. They come here under contract to labor for a certain number of years. They are ignorant of our social condition, and, that they may remain so, they are isolated and prevented from coming into contact with Americans. They are generally from the lowest social stratum, and live upon the coarsest food, and in hovels of a character before unknown to American workmen. They, as a rule, do not become citizens, and are certainly not a desirable acquisition to the body politic. The inevitable tendency of their presence among us is to degrade American labor, and to reduce it to the level of the imported pauper labor.' Page 5359, Congressional Record, 48th Cong.

We find, therefore, that the title of the act, the evil which was intended to be remedied, the circumstances surrounding the appeal to congress, the reports of the committee of each house, all concur in affirming that the intent of congress was simply to stay the influx of this cheap, unskilled labor.

Finding

But, beyond all these matters, no purpose of action against religion can be imputed to any legislation, state or national, because this is a religious people. [Justice Brewer describes in detail some of the many ways that the United States embraces Christianity and why, given that fact, Congress could not have intended to prohibit ministers from coming into the United States.]

* * *

Points for Discussion

1. *Statutory Language*: What was the language at issue? What did each party want that language to mean? What meaning did the Court adopt?

2. *Theories*: What theory of interpretation did Justice Brewer adopt? Did the Court find the language ambiguous, absurd, to have a scrivener's error, or to raise a constitutional question? Look for the following sentence: "It is a familiar rule that a thing may be within the letter of the statute and yet not within the statute, because not within its spirit nor within the intention of its makers." Why do you think this statement is often cited in briefs to support interpretations that contradict the text of the statute?

3. *Clear Text*: The Court stated that the text of the statute is clear: "It must be conceded that the act of the corporation is within the letter of this section, for the relation of rector to his church is one of service, and implies labor on the one side with compensation on the other." Yet one definition of labor is manual labor. Why might Justice Brewer have been willing to concede this point so quickly? Assuming that the text was clear, was the evidence of purpose strong enough to overcome the text?

4. *Legislative History*: How did the Court use legislative history to find the statutory purpose? Which legislative history was relevant? Do you find the legislative history helpful, regardless of whether you are willing to consider legislative history in light of clear text?

5. *Imaginative Reconstruction*: Justice Brewer was the son of Christian missionaries. Owen Fiss, *David J. Brewer: The Judge as Missionary*, in THE FIELDS AND THE LAW, 53–71 (1986) (explaining that Justice Brewer looked at government regu-

lation warily and proclaimed at every possible opportunity "this is a Christian nation"). Brewer explains in detail, in a portion of the case that has been omitted, why Congress could not possibly have intended to exclude ministers because of the Nation's Christian heritage. This reasoning is similar to the theory of imaginative reconstruction, identified in Chapter 4.

6. *Last Laugh*: As a side note, Pastor Warren did not stay in the United States for long. Shortly after this decision, he left New York claiming that it was an "immoral place to be."

* * *

c. Using Purpose

As you just saw, when a statute does not include a purpose clause and the included clause is unhelpful, purpose may be found in the text of the statute, in its legislative history, or even in the social and historical context surrounding a bill's enactment. Once you identify purpose, how do you use it?

[handwritten margin note: where to find Purpose]

Judges use purpose in many ways. Judges use purpose to confirm ordinary meaning, to resolve ambiguity, and to provide guidance in the case of absurdity. In addition, some judges may use purpose to trump ordinary meaning. As you just saw, in *Holy Trinity*, the Supreme Court stated first that the language at issue was not ambiguous and included rectoring. The Court then used purpose, which it found in the legislative history, to trump the text's ordinary meaning.

[handwritten margin note: How judges use Purpose]

Similarly, in a more modern case, the Ninth Circuit used purpose to hold that "less" actually meant "more." In *Amalgamated Transit Union Local 1309 v. Laidlaw Transit Services, Inc.*, 435 F.3d 1140 (2006), the court rejected the ordinary meaning of the text of the Class Action Fairness Act. That Act provided that "a court of appeals may accept an appeal ... denying a motion to remand a class action to the State court from which it was removed if application is made to the court of appeals *not less than 7 days* after entry of the order." *Id.* at 1142 (quoting 28 U.S.C. § 1543(c)(1)) (emphasis added). The ordinary meaning of the text of the statute imposed a seven day waiting period and contained no upper time limit for appealing. The Ninth Circuit found this ordinary meaning "illogical" but not absurd. *Id.* The court then turned to the legislative history of the Act (specifically a Senate committee report) to discern the purpose of the Act and concluded that Congress had intended the Act to impose a *time limit* for appealing rather than a waiting period to appeal. *Id.* at 1146.

One member of the Ninth Circuit, Judge Bybee, was so upset with the majority's decision that he *sua sponte* called for an en banc rehearing, which was denied. *Amalgamated Transit Union Local 1309 v. Laidlaw Transit Servs., Inc.*, 448 F.3d 1092 (2006). Judge Bybee then dissented from the order denying the rehearing, which is very unusual. *Id.* at 1094 (Bybee, J., dissenting). In his dissent, Judge Bybee chastised the majority for rejecting the ordinary meaning of the statute when the text was so clear. According to Judge Bybee, none of the reasons for avoiding the plain meaning canon applied. The statute was not absurd or ambiguous, there was no scrivener's error, and there was no constitutional question. (*See* Chapter 6). Hence, if there was an error, then Congress, not the courts, should correct it. *Id.* at 1096–98. Judge Bybee was particularly concerned that the majority relied on a Senate committee report that "was not submitted until eighteen days after the Senate had passed the bill, eleven days after the House had passed the bill, and ten days after the President signed the bill into law." *Id.* at 1096. In Judge Bybee's opinion, the majority relied on legislative history that no member of Congress or the President considered to interpret the statute to mean the exact opposite of what the statute actually said. *Id.*

Was Judge Bybee correct? Regardless of the relevance of the committee report, consider just the text. Could Congress truly have meant to enact a statute identifying an appeal timeline that created a waiting period rather than a time limit? And, assuming not, who should fix the error? Consider the implications of waiting for Congress to fix its mistake. Textualists would say the legislature must correct its own errors, while purposivist and intentionalists would say the courts should fix the error when a mistake is so clear. Would the scrivener's error doctrine have been appropriate here?

The debate between the majority and dissent in this case illustrates nicely the impact that a judge's theory of interpretation can have on meaning. In *Amalgamated Transit Union* and in *Holy Trinity*, the judges were willing to look beyond clear text to statutory purpose, as found in the legislative history, to interpret the relevant statute as Congress likely intended but certainly did not say. In contrast, the dissent in *Amalgamated Transit Union* was unwilling to look beyond the text because no exceptions applied, even though it was likely that Congress never intended the statute to mean what it actually said. When text is clear, purpose generally plays a supporting, not leading, role. "To let general words draw nourishment from their purpose is one thing. To draw on some unexpressed spirit outside the bounds of the normal meaning of words is quite another." *Addison v. HollyHill Fruit Prods., Inc.*, 322 U.S. 607, 617 (1944).

In the case below, how does the court use purpose, to confirm ordinary meaning or to defeat it?

Ohio Division of Wildlife v. Clifton

Circleville Municipal Court Ohio
692 N.E.2d 253 (Ohio Mun. Ct. 1997)

♦ JOHN R. ADKINS, JUDGE.

This matter began October 20, 1997, when Officer Kenneth Bebout filed a misdemeanor complaint against the defendant alleging that she did "unlawfully have a game quadruped to wit; a squirrel in captivity without applying for or possessing a game propagating license from the Ohio Division of Wildlife, a violation of 1533.71 of the Ohio Revised Code." ... The subject of the controversy is a certain grey squirrel, which was apparently dislodged from its nest shortly after birth. It was discovered by the defendant in this obviously imperiled state. The defendant exercised control over the squirrel, providing nutrition and hydration in such a way that notwithstanding the low potential for survival, the squirrel, in fact, was habilitated and survived. Nearly a year and a half passed, during which time the squirrel remained in the residence of Clifton and became habituated to that environment. Enthralled with the creature, Clifton carried it through the 1997 Pumpkin Show parade and won first prize in the most unusual pet category, thereby garnering the attention of Wildlife Officer Bebout. He and another officer drove to the residence of the alleged offender and attempted to take into custody this squirrel. Custody was refused by Clifton and she was cited into Circleville Municipal Court, the maximum possible penalty being $500 and sixty days in jail. The section under which she was cited states as follows:

[handwritten: Came to attention b/c in parade]

> "Any person desiring to engage in the business of raising and selling game birds, game quadrupeds, or fur-bearing animals in a wholly enclosed preserve of which he is the owner or lessee, or *to have game birds, quadrupeds, or fur-bearing animals in captivity, may apply in writing to the Division of Wildlife for a license to do so.*

[handwritten: statute 1533.7]

> "The Division when it appears that the application is made in good faith, *shall, upon the payment of the fee for each license, issue to the applicant* such of the following licenses as may be applied for:

> "(A) 'Commercial propagating license' permitting the licensee to propagate game birds, game quadrupeds, or fur-bearing animals ... to sell ... and ship them from the state alive at any time and to kill such propagated game bird, game quadrupeds, or fur-bearing animals and sell the carcasses for food subject to sections 1533.10 to 1533.80 of the Revised Code. The fee for such a license is twenty-five dollars per annum.

[handwritten: sell & ship]

> "(B) 'Noncommercial propagating license' permitting the licensee to propagate game birds, game quadrupeds, or fur-bearing animals and to hold such animals in captivity.... for the licensee's own use and shall not be sold. The fee for such a license is ten dollars per annum.

[handwritten: Pet]

> "(C) A free 'raise to release license' permitting duly organized clubs, associations, or individuals approved by the division to engage in the raising of game birds, game quadruped, or fur-bearing animals for release only and not for sale or personal use.

[handwritten: rehabilitation]

> "Except as provided by law no person shall possess game birds, game quadrupeds, or fur-bearing animals in closed season, provided that municipal or governmental zoological parks shall not be required to obtain the licenses provided for in this section." (Emphasis added.)

[Ohio Rev. Code § 1533.71].

In response to the issuance of the citation, on November 4, 1997, Clifton made an application for a game propagation permit, which was refused with an annotation at the bottom noting, "squirrel was taken from wild—no permit can be issued for this animal—must be released to the wild."

[handwritten: Δ applied for permit & denied]

The court ordered the Division of Wildlife to set forth all written rules, regulations or other documents published by the Division of Wildlife setting out the criteria for the allowance or rejection of applications for licenses contemplated in R.C. 1533.71(A) and 1533.71(B) in addition to other information sought. The Division has no such rules or regulations, but provided copies of Ohio Adm. Code 1501:31-15-09 "Hunting and trapping regulations for fur-bearing animals," the essence of which, according to Officer Lehman, is that an animal listed may be hunted, trapped, taken, or possessed, if immediately thereafter it is put to death by any reasonable means. Further, the department in R.C. 1533.16 has set forth that game birds and wild quadrupeds shall be taken only by hunting with a gun, a gun and dog, a bow and arrow, or a bow, arrow and dog. The implication, of course, is that utilizing such weaponry or hunting dogs, the animal shall be killed forthwith if taken only during the appropriate season as set forth in Ohio Adm.Code 1501:31-15-17 It is clear from Officer Lehman's testimony that had Clifton captured this grey squirrel during the appropriate season and subsequently killed it, she would have committed no wrong, assuming that she had acquired the proper license from the state to engage in such activity. The state's position, therefore, is clear: A person may take any such listed game animal during the appropriate season, having paid the appropriate licensing fee, and kill such animal. That is the only way a person may possess a listed animal, unless pursuant to R.C. 1533.71 a license is issued. However, the state has no criteria by which a person may reasonably be adjudged worthy of or not worthy of possession of a wild animal having been acquired by other means. Therefore, there is no lawful method, according to the Division of Wildlife officers, for a person to (a) properly take a game animal during season, merely wounding the animal, and then resuscitating or rehabilitating that animal; (b) be given an animal by some other person who may have acquired it by a recognized process or otherwise; (c) find an injured, distressed, abandoned or animal otherwise selected through the Darwinian process for death and provide that animal shelter, nutrition and hydration and, hence, life....

The court finds that there are no appropriate rules setting forth clearly and distinctly the standards for a person in good faith to satisfy the obvious legislative intent, which includes the preservation of animal life. No one could be so myopic as to believe that the legislature was so ambivalent toward the protection of wild animals as to have legislated an Act that requires, manifestly, that all animals found in whatever location defined under the statute must be thereafter killed.... The legislature of the state of Ohio expressly set forth that "[a]ny person" "may apply" for a license "to have game birds, game quadrupeds, or fur-bearing animals in captivity." R.C. 1533.71. That language is clear, it is uncontroverted, and it is constitutional....

The court also notes that no one disputes that Clifton, upon coming into possession of the infant squirrel, contacted the Division of Wildlife and inquired whether there were provisions for her to follow.... Upon such inquiry, she was reportedly advised that she need follow no special procedures. Obviously, she relied upon that to her detriment. A citizen should be able to obtain competent advice from a state agency.

... In common law, "justice" was a title given to judicial officers of the King's Bench. It has come to be a term used in the United States to denote not only the individual empowered by the electorate to ensure appropriate checks and balances, but also the constant and perpetual disposition to place all men in equality. In the most expansive sense of the word, "justice" differs little from "virtue," which includes a gamut of Judeo-Christian values. Yet the common distinction between the terms "justice" and "virtue" is that virtue is wholly positive, while justice includes the imposition of punishment to ensure that people live within the law of their jurisdiction. "Justice" is not an abstract thought or concept, but sometimes the essence of justice, which is the common experience of man yielded from common sense, logic and decency, is lost in our society. Even though we charge jurors to apply the test of common sense that we use in our everyday lives, judges and lawyers often become lost in abstract thought and concepts, believing that they should apply statutes blindly. This court takes its obligation and its oath of office much more seriously. "No right of the victim is advanced, and no interest of the state served, by incarcerating the innocent." The Supreme Court of Ohio has stated ... that "a trial before a judicial tribunal is primarily a truth-determining process, and if it in any sense loses its character as such, it becomes the veriest sort of a mockery." The ultimate aim of the criminal justice system, then, is not the balancing of rights, but the uncovering of truth.

The court finds that the truth of this case is that a citizen of the state of Ohio attempted to extend humanitarian aid to an otherwise helpless animal. The Wildlife Officer in this case would choose to reward her with a potential fine and incarceration and, obviously, death for the squirrel. Officer Lehman himself testified that the average life expectancy of a squirrel in the wild, due to Darwinian effects of predation and so forth, is eleven months. The court notes that the squirrel has so far survived seventeen. Officer Lehman further testified that the anticipated life expectancy of this squirrel in Clifton's residence is five to seven years. And yet, the state insists on regaining possession of this squirrel to return it to the wild, even though it knows that the animal would not survive. This makes no sense. Even a child could see that there is no justice or right in the position of the state.

Is there a rationale for the underlying statute? Of course! It must be learned from this case that citizens may not arbitrarily take animals from the wild to habituate, tame and otherwise domesticate them, for the obvious reason that the animals may be infected with various serious diseases, and they may pose a potential public safety risk to children and others. Therefore, the statute is logical and its general enforcement may be appropriate. As applied in this case, it is inappropriate....

This court sees all manner of lamentable activities of mankind against other people and property. Day after day there is an endless parade of people demonstrating incredible acts of culpability against others, even defenseless children. When a person appears before the court having demonstrated only affection for an orphaned animal and an incredible regard for life, that person should be rewarded....

The French philosopher Chamfort said, "Intelligent people make many blunders, because they never believe the world to be as stupid as it is." This court does not wish to be stupid and perpetuate the waste of time and resources of this court and the state of Ohio in pursuing this matter. At a time when the state is struggling to find resources to educate our children and to make them intelligent, compassionate people involved in honest, life-enhancing pursuits, it is more than ironic that the state, as well as the Director of Law of Circleville, would choose to allocate the resources of two uniformed officers to pursue a woman who demonstrates no moral culpability whatsoever. This court is not so foolhardy. Therefore, for all the reasons set forth above, the court finds the defendant's motion to be well taken and the case is dismissed forthwith. Further, this grey squirrel shall be permitted to be retained in and about the property of Mary Jane Clifton without further interference, although the court cautions Clifton that it does not expect to view this squirrel being bandied about in public in strange wearing apparel of any kind.

So ordered.

This opinion could have been reduced to a simple poem:

> The court hereby announces a pearl,
> It's sometimes OK to have a squirrel.
> The legislature did a statute create,
> The Wildlife Division obviously did not equate.
> The necessity to be kind, thorough and specific,
> The lack of these is legally terrific.
> The result is this very short epistle,
> The defendant/squirrel is granted a dismissal.

* * *

Points for Discussion

1. *Statutory Language*: What was the language at issue? What did each party want that language to mean? What meaning did the court adopt?

2. *Theories*: Which theory did the court use? Did the court find the language ambiguous, absurd, to have a scrivener's error, or to raise a constitutional question?

3. *Trumping Text*: How did the court use purpose here (and what purposes did it use)? Using purpose to trump clear text is not common. Purpose is more commonly used when a statute is unclear, absurd, or when purpose confirms the ordinary meaning of the text. *See, e.g., Church of Scientology v. Department of Justice*, 612 F.2d 417, 424–25 (9th Cir. 1979) (turning to the purpose as found in the legislative history to confirm the statute's clear text).

4. *Multiple Purposes*: Sometimes a statute has more than one purpose. What should a court do when these purposes conflict? When multiple purposes of a statute conflict and are impossible to reconcile, which purpose should control? There is no easy answer to this question. One approach is to further more of the purposes. By furthering as many purposes as possible, the court does not elevate one purpose at the expense of others. *See, e.g., Office Planning Group, Inc. v. Baraga-Houghton-Keweenaw Child Development Bd.*, 697 N.W.2d 871, 894 (Mich. 2005) (Kelley, J. dissenting) (arguing that implying a private right of action would better further a second purpose while not adversely affecting the statute's primary purpose).

5. *Statutes with Exceptions*: Sometimes the purpose of an exception in a statute conflicts with the statute's general purpose. When this occurs, which purpose should matter: the purpose of the statute as a whole or the purpose of the statute's exception? Currently, there is no agreed answer to this question. Generally, a court will try first to find an interpretation that furthers more of the purposes, but when the court cannot reconcile the purposes, the court should read the exception's purpose narrowly, much like a proviso. (*See* Chapter 9). *See, e.g., Church of Scientology v. Department of Justice*, 612 F.2d 417, 431 (9th Cir. 1979).

6. *Related Statutes*: What if two, related statutes have purposes that conflict? Which should control? Generally, courts try to reconcile both of the statutes' purposes, but when that is not possible, the purpose of the applicable statute controls. This approach mirrors the courts' approach to conflicting statutes: reconcile if at all possible. *See, e.g., Kentucky Off-Track Betting, Inc. v. McBurney*, 993 S.W.2d 946 (Ky. 1999) (comparing the purposes of an earlier existing statute and later enacted amendments).

* * *

In conclusion, as statutes have become more complex and detailed, purpose seems to have become less valuable to many judges than in years past. Perhaps the days in which purpose can overcome clear text have ended. But wholesale rejection of purpose is not appropriate either. Like legislative history, purpose has a role in interpretation, albeit only a supporting role.

In these last two chapters, we explored the role in interpretation of the context that precedes and accompanies the enactment process. In the next chapter, we turn to the role in interpretation of the context following enactment.

Problem 12

You are a law clerk for Judge Wasson, a trial judge in New Mexico. The following case has been filed. The judge has asked you for your reaction to the two issues identified below.

The Placitas horses are a group of ownerless, unbranded horses that have lived and roamed on public land near Placitas, New Mexico, since at least 1965. The Placitas horses do not now have nor have ever had owners, and no private landowner, rancher, horse rescue, or Indian tribe currently claims the horses. At the time this issue arose, approximately forty Placitas horses still roamed the Placitas area. The New Mexico Livestock Board took the horses directly from public land, impounded them, and plans to auction them in a matter of days. The Board did not DNA-test the horses and has no plans to relocate them. No owner has claimed the horses to date.

The Wild Horse Observers Association has filed suit, claiming that the Board has unlawfully treated the Placitas horses as "livestock" and "estray" rather than as "wild horses" under the Livestock Code. The Association asks for declaratory order declaring that the Placitas horses are wild as opposed to estray and declaring that the Board must DNA-test and relocate the wild horses, rather than auction them. The Association further seeks an injunction to prevent the auction.

The Board maintains that the horses are estray livestock and, therefore, subject to its control. Under the Livestock Code, the Board is required to search for the owner of estray livestock, publish notice of the impoundment of estray livestock, and eventually sell estray livestock for the benefit of the legal owner. NMSA §77–13–1. The Board claims to have complied with these steps. Alternatively, if the horses are not estray livestock, then the Board argues that it has no power to DNA test and relocate the horses because the statute does not give the Board this specific power.

There are two issues for you to address. The first issue is whether the Placitas horses, which have never been owned, are estray livestock or wild horses. The second issue is, assuming the horses are wild, does the Board have the power and responsibility to test and relocate the horses.

Problem Materials

NMSA §77–2–1: Short title; purpose

Chapter 77, Articles 2 through 18 may be cited as "The Livestock Code." The Livestock Code shall be liberally construed to carry out its purposes, which are to promote greater economy, service and efficiency in the administration of the laws relating to the livestock industry of New Mexico, to control disease, to prevent the theft or illegal movement of livestock, and to oversee the New Mexico meat inspection program.

NMSA §77-2-1.1: Definitions

As used in The Livestock Code:

1. "animals" or "livestock" means all domestic or domesticated animals that are used or raised on a farm or ranch, including the carcasses thereof, and exotic animals in captivity and includes horses, asses, mules, cattle, sheep, goats, swine, bison, poultry, ostriches, emus, rheas, camelids, and farmed cervidae upon any land in New Mexico;

2. "estray" means livestock found running at large upon public or private lands, either fenced or unfenced, whose owner is unknown, or that is branded with a brand that is not on record in the office of the board, or is a freshly branded or marked offspring not with its branded or marked mother, unless other proof of ownership is produced.

§77-2-2: New Mexico livestock board created; transfer of powers; transfer of property

"In order to achieve the purposes set forth in Section 77-2-1, including the administration of laws relating to the livestock industry of New Mexico, there is hereby created a board to be known as the 'New Mexico livestock board.'"

NMSA §77-18-1: Sale, purchase, trade and possession of certain animals regulated

The sale, purchase, trade and possession with intent to keep as a pet of any subhuman primate, skunk, raccoon, fox, or other sylvatic carnivore may be regulated by regulation of the Department of Health for the protection of public health and safety.

NMSA § 77-18-5: Wild horses; conformation, history and deoxyribonucleic acid testing; Spanish colonial horses

1. As used in this section:

(A) "Spanish colonial horse" means a wild horse that is descended from horses of the Spanish colonial period; and

(B) "wild horse" means an unclaimed horse on public land that is not an estray.

2. A wild horse that is captured on public land shall have its conformation, history and deoxyribonucleic acid tested to determine if it is a Spanish colonial horse. If it is a Spanish colonial horse, the wild horse shall be relocated to a state or private wild horse preserve created and maintained for the purpose of protecting Spanish colonial horses. If it is not a Spanish colonial horse, it shall be returned to the public land, relocated to a public or private wild horse preserve or put up for adoption by the agency on whose land the wild horse was captured.

3. If the Mammal Division of the Museum of Southwestern Biology at the University of New Mexico determines that a wild horse herd exceeds the number of horses that is necessary for preserving the genetic stock of the herd and for preserving and maintaining the range, it may cause control of the wild horse population through the use of birth control and may cause excess horses to be:

(A) humanely captured and relocated to other public land or to a public or private wild horse preserve;

(B) adopted by a qualified person for private maintenance; or

(C) euthanized, provided that this option applies only to wild horses that are determined by a veterinarian to be crippled or otherwise unhealthy.

Chapter 13

Canons Based on Extrinsic Sources and Legislative Process: Post-Enactment Legislative Context

A. Introduction to This Chapter

In this chapter, we continue with our examination of extrinsic sources and context. We move from an exploration of what happens before and during the legislative process to an examination of what occurs afterward. Subsequent events may shed light on what a statute means. This chapter will explore the canons related to subsequent actions and inactions of the legislature, including legislative acquiescence, subsequent enactments, subsequent legislative history, and legislator affidavits. In a later chapter, we will take a look at the subsequent actions of the executive.

B. Using What Occurred After Enactment

If using what occurred prior to and during enactment can be controversial, using what occurred after enactment is even more so. If the goal of interpretation is discerning the intent of the enacting legislature, regardless of whether that is accomplished by finding purpose or intent, then anything that happens after passage should be irrelevant. Similarly, if the goal of interpretation is discerning the common understanding of words when the text was originally adopted, then subsequent events should be irrelevant. Yet, complete irrelevancy is not the presumption. While some subsequent acts are generally considered irrelevant (*e.g.*, affidavits of legislators and subsequent legislative history), most are relevant at times (*e.g.*, legislative acquiescence and subsequent enactments), others (*e.g.*, executive subsequent acts, such as agency interpretations) are not only relevant, they may well be conclusive.

1. Subsequent Legislative Inaction

a. Super Strong Stare Decisis

In Latin, *stare decisis* means to stand by things decided. In law, it means that courts are reluctant to overturn prior judicial decisions absent a good reason to do so. *Stare decisis* furthers certainty in the law and faith in the judicial system. It also gives the appearance of objectivity; judges decide cases based on legal principles rather than based on political leanings and personal preferences.

There are two aspects to *stare decisis*. First, the decisions of higher courts bind lower courts within the same jurisdiction. This aspect is not controversial. Second, a court should not overturn its own precedents without good reason. This aspect is neither controversial nor absolute: when their existing judicial opinion is clearly wrong, courts will overturn it. The most famous example of this latter aspect is the Supreme Court's decision in *Brown v. Board of Education*, 347 U.S. 483 (1954). In *Brown*, the Supreme Court overturned *Plessy v. Ferguson*, 163 U.S. 537 (1896), in which the Court had held that racial segregation in public accommodations was constitutional.

For cases involving the interpretation of statutes, the Supreme Court (and some lower courts) applies a heightened form of *stare decisis* known as super strong *stare decisis*. Super strong *stare decisis* refers to the heightened *stare decisis* effect given to supreme court (state and federal) opinions interpreting statutes. Pursuant to super strong *stare decisis*, the Supreme Court presumes that its statutory precedents are correct. Once it has authoritatively construed a federal statute, the Court believes that pursuant to separation of powers Congress is the more appropriate body to change the interpretation if there is any error. If Congress disagrees with the Court's interpretation, then Congress should change the interpretation. "When a court says to a legislature: 'You (or your predecessor) meant X,' it almost invites the legislature to answer: 'We did not.'" Guido Calabresi, A Common Law for the Age of Statutes 31–32 (1985). The fact that Congress did not change the interpretation suggests that Congress agreed with the decision.

Under super strong *stare decisis*, judicial decisions interpreting statutes should be overruled less easily than decisions refining the common law because the legislature is the more appropriate body to correct erroneous interpretations of statutes. Thus, under super strong *stare decisis*, even when a prior decision is inarguably wrong, the justices should be reluctant to overrule it. *See, e.g., Faragher v. Boca Raton*, 524 U.S. 775 (1998) (applying the super strong *stare decisis* doctrine, because Congress had relied on statements from an earlier case when fashioning later-enacted legislation).

While this heightened form of *stare decisis* may make sense in situations like *Faragher*—where Congress bases later legislative action on an existing Supreme Court interpretation—sometimes a court's unwillingness to overturn an erroneous prior decision for this reason alone makes little sense. We will look at one example in the next section after we talk about legislative acquiescence, because heightened stare decisis and legislative acquiescence are tightly intertwined.

b. Legislative Acquiescence

The most common legislative response to a judicial interpretation of a statute is silence. What, if anything, does silence mean? Some judges reason that a legislature's silence to an interpretation means acquiescence, or agreement, with that interpretation.

One reason for concluding that silence means acquiescence is super strong *stare decisis*. As you just learned, courts presume the correctness of the federal or a state supreme court's* statutory interpretation. If a legislature disagrees with a particular interpretation, then the legislature should change the interpretation, not remain silent. The fact that a legislature remained silent shows that it agreed with, or legislatively acquiesced in, the decision.

Does legislative acquiescence reflect reality? At times, the legislature probably does acquiesce to an interpretation by not acting in response. But more often, the reality is that such silence means little. There are a multitude of reasons the legislature could have failed to amend the statute. The legislature could be unaware of the judicial opinion; the legislature might be unable to act in response to the interpretation; the legislature might have more pressing business; or the legislature might, indeed, agree with the decision.

A criticism of legislative acquiescence is that when interpreting statutes, courts generally focus on finding the intent or purpose of the *enacting* legislature, not of a subsequent legislature. The legislature that silently approves the interpretation is most likely a different legislature than the legislature that enacted the statute. Silence from a subsequent legislature should have absolutely no relevance in the discussion regarding the meaning the *enacting* legislature intended.

Also, legislative acquiescence by-passes the constitutional process for enacting legislation; silence is neither passed bicamerally nor presented to the president. If silence is accepted as a legislative action, then Congress can effectively legislate in a way the Constitution does not contemplate. For this reason, textualists are particularly loathe to rest an interpretation on legislative acquiescence. At bottom, "legislative acquiescence [is] focused on the wrong legislature and it may be unreliable. On close analysis, it may even be unconstitutional. But, it is frequently invoked...." RONALD BENTON BROWN & SHARON JACOBS BROWN, STATUTORY INTERPRETATION: THE SEARCH FOR LEGISLATIVE INTENT 172 (2d 2011).

Below is one of the more famous cases exploring legislative acquiescence and super strong *stare decisis*. In *Flood v. Kuhn*, 407 U.S. 258 (1972), the issue was whether baseball should continue to be exempt from federal anti-trust laws. Curtis Flood had been the center fielder for the St. Louis Cardinals. He missed a fly ball in the 7th inning of the 1968 World Series with Detroit. His error cost his team the series. Not surprisingly, the following year St. Louis traded him, along with six other players, to the Philadelphia Phillies. Flood did not want to go to Philadelphia, for a variety of reasons. He wrote to the Commissioner of Baseball and asked the Commissioner to

---

* Legislative acquiescence may be appropriate when the deciding court is the highest court within a jurisdiction. But it is never appropriate when a lower court issues the decision, because there is still a chance that a higher court will correct the lower court's error. Despite this reality, in fact, lower courts sometimes apply the canon anyway.

let other teams know of his availability. The Commissioner refused. Flood sued, claiming the Commissioner's action violated federal anti-trust laws. *Id.* at 265. He would never play baseball again.

A little background is in order. In two earlier cases, *Federal Baseball Club v. National League*, 259 U.S. 200 (1922) and *Toolson v. New York Yankees, Inc.*, 346 U.S. 356 (1953), the Court had held that baseball was not an interstate trade or commerce, which is an element of the anti-trust law. The Court faced the same issue again in 1953 and reached the same result. In 1922, when *Federal Baseball* was decided, baseball may not have affected interstate commerce, but by 1972, it was clear that baseball did have such an effect. Should the Court change its interpretation and reverse the earlier opinions?

Flood v. Kuhn

Supreme Court of the United States
407 U.S. 258 (1972)

◆ JUSTICE BLACKMUN delivered the opinion of the Court [in which STEWART and REHNQUIST, JJ., joined and in all but part I of which BURGER, C.J., and WHITE, J. joined].

The petitioner, Curtis Charles Flood, born in 1938, began his major league career in 1956 when he signed a contract with the Cincinnati Reds for a salary of $4,000 for the season. He had no attorney or agent to advise him on that occasion. He was traded to the St. Louis Cardinals before the 1958 season. Flood rose to fame as a center fielder with the Cardinals during the years 1958–1969....

But at the age of 31, in October 1969, Flood was traded to the Philadelphia Phillies of the National League in a multi-player transaction. He was not consulted about the trade. He was informed by telephone and received formal notice only after the deal had been consummated. In December he complained to the Commissioner of Baseball and asked that he be made a free agent and be placed at liberty to strike his own bargain with any other major league team. His request was denied.

Flood then instituted this antitrust suit in January 1970 in federal court ... [Flood claimed that the reserve clause in his contract violated the antitrust laws, because it prevented him from contracting with the team of his choice. Lower courts denied relief based on Supreme Court precedents holding baseball immune from the antitrust laws.]

The Legal Background

[In] *Federal Baseball Club v. National League*, 259 U.S. 200 (1922), ... Mr. Justice Holmes, in speaking succinctly for a unanimous Court, said:

> "The business is giving exhibitions of baseball, which are purely state affairs.... But the fact that in order to give the exhibitions the Leagues must induce free persons to cross state lines and must arrange and pay for their doing so is not enough to change the character of the business.... The trans-

port is a mere incident, not the essential thing. That to which it is incident, the exhibition, although made for money would not be called trade or commerce in the commonly accepted use of those words. As it is put by the defendants, personal effort, not related to production, is not a subject of commerce. That which in its consummation is not commerce does not become commerce among the States because the transportation that we have mentioned takes place. To repeat the illustrations given by the Court below, a firm of lawyers sending out a member to argue a case, or the Chautauqua lecture bureau sending out lecturers, does not engage in such commerce because the lawyer or lecturer goes to another State.

In the years that followed, baseball continued to be subject to intermittent antitrust attack. The courts, however, rejected these challenges on the authority of *Federal Baseball*. In some cases stress was laid, although unsuccessfully, on new factors such as the development of radio and television with their substantial additional revenues to baseball. For the most part, however, the Holmes opinion was generally and necessarily accepted as controlling authority....

The Court granted certiorari, in the *Toolson* [*v. New York Yankees, Inc.*, 346 U.S. 356 (1953)], *Kowalski*, and *Corbett* cases, and, by a short *per curiam* ... affirmed the judgments of the respective courts of appeals in those three cases. *Federal Baseball* was cited as holding "that the business of providing public baseball games for profit between clubs of professional baseball players was not within the scope of the federal antitrust laws," and:

"Congress has had the ruling under consideration but has not seen fit to bring such business under these laws by legislation having prospective effect. The business has thus been left for thirty years to develop, on the understanding that it was not subject to existing antitrust legislation. The present cases ask us to overrule the prior decision and, with retrospective effect, hold the legislation applicable. We think that if there are evils in this field which now warrant application to it of the antitrust laws it should be by legislation. Without reexamination of the underlying issues, the judgments below are affirmed on the authority of *Federal Baseball*..., so far as that decision determines that Congress had no intention of including the business of baseball within the scope of the federal antitrust laws."

This quotation reveals four reasons for the Court's affirmance of *Toolson* and its companion cases: (a) Congressional awareness for three decades of the Court's ruling in *Federal Baseball*, coupled with congressional inaction. (b) The fact that baseball was left alone to develop for that period upon the understanding that the reserve system was not subject to existing federal antitrust laws. (c) A reluctance to overrule *Federal Baseball* with consequent retroactive effect. (d) A professed desire that any needed remedy be provided by legislation rather than by court decree. The emphasis in *Toolson* was on the determination, attributed even to *Federal Baseball*, that Congress had no intention to include baseball within the reach of the federal antitrust laws....

[Also, in *United States v. International Boxing Club,* 348 U.S. 236 (1955), the Court reversed a district court for dismissing the antitrust complaint; the Court denied that *Federal Baseball* gave sports other than baseball an exemption from the antitrust laws. And, in *Radovich v. National Football League,* 352 U.S. 445 (1957), the Supreme Court reversed the lower courts for dismissing another antitrust complaint against a football league. Justice Clark's opinion for the Court noted that *Toolson* upheld baseball's immunity, "because it was concluded that more harm would be done in overruling *Federal Baseball* than in upholding a ruling which at best was of dubious validity." In *Radovich,* the Court said:]

> "Since *Toolson* and *Federal Baseball* are still cited as controlling authority in antitrust actions involving other fields of business, we now specifically limit the rule there established to the facts there involved, *i.e.*, the business of organized professional baseball. As long as the Congress continues to acquiesce we should adhere to—but not extend—the interpretation of the Act made in those cases....

> "If this ruling is unrealistic, inconsistent, or illogical, it is sufficient to answer, aside from the distinctions between the businesses, that were we considering the question of baseball for the first time upon a clean slate we would have no doubts. But *Federal Baseball* held the business of baseball outside the scope of the Act. No other business claiming the coverage of those cases has such an adjudication. We, therefore, conclude that the orderly way to eliminate error or discrimination, if any there be, is by legislation and not by court decision. Congressional processes are more accommodative, affording the whole industry hearings and an opportunity to assist in the formulation of new legislation. The resulting product is therefore more likely to protect the industry and the public alike. The whole scope of congressional action would be known long in advance and effective dates for the legislation could be set in the future without the injustices of retroactivity and surprise which might follow court action."...

Finally, in *Haywood v. National Basketball Assn.,* 401 U.S. 1204 (1971), [the Court] said, "Basketball ... does not enjoy exemption from the antitrust laws."...

Legislative proposals have been numerous and persistent. Since *Toolson* more than 50 bills have been introduced in Congress relative to the applicability or nonapplicability of the antitrust laws to baseball. A few of these passed one house or the other. Those that did would have expanded, not restricted, the reserve system's exemption to other professional league sports....

In view of all this, it seems appropriate now to say that:

1. Professional baseball is a business and it is engaged in interstate commerce.

2. With its reserve system enjoying exemption from the federal antitrust laws, baseball is, in a very distinct sense, an exception and an anomaly. *Federal Baseball* and *Toolson* have become an aberration confined to baseball.

3. Even though others might regard this as "unrealistic, inconsistent, or illogical," the aberration is an established one, and one that has been recognized not only in *Federal Baseball* and *Toolson*, but in *Shubert, International Boxing,* and *Radovich*, as well, a total of five consecutive cases in this Court. It is an aberration that has been with us now for half a century, one heretofore deemed fully entitled to the benefit of *stare decisis*, and one that has survived the Court's expanding concept of interstate commerce. It rests on a recognition and an acceptance of baseball's unique characteristics and needs.

4. Other professional sports operating interstate — football, boxing, basketball, and, presumably, hockey and golf are not so exempt....

5. The Court has emphasized that since 1922 baseball, with full and continuing congressional awareness, has been allowed to develop and to expand unhindered by federal legislative action. Remedial legislation has been introduced repeatedly in Congress but none has ever been enacted. The Court, accordingly, has concluded that Congress as yet has had no intention to subject baseball's reserve system to the reach of the antitrust statutes. This, obviously, has been deemed to be something other than mere congressional silence and passivity.

6. The Court has ... voiced a preference that if any change is to be made, it come by legislative action that, by its nature, is only prospective in operation....

... We continue to be loath, 50 years after *Federal Baseball* and almost two decades after *Toolson*, to overturn those cases judicially when Congress, by its positive inaction, has allowed those decisions to stand for so long and, far beyond mere inference and implication, has clearly evinced a desire not to disapprove them legislatively.

Accordingly, we adhere once again to *Federal Baseball* and *Toolson* and to their application to professional baseball.... Under these circumstances, there is merit in consistency even though some might claim that beneath that consistency is a layer of inconsistency....

[W]hat the Court said in *Federal Baseball* in 1922 and what it said in *Toolson* in 1953, we say again here in 1972: the remedy, if any is indicated, is for congressional, and not judicial, action.

♦ CHIEF JUSTICE BURGER, concurring.

... I have grave reservations as to the correctness of *Toolson*; as [Justice Douglas] notes in his dissent, he joined that holding but has "lived to regret it." The error, if such it be, is one on which the affairs of a great many people have rested for a long time. Courts are not the forum in which this tangled web ought to be unsnarled. I agree with Mr. Justice Douglas that congressional inaction is not a solid base, but the least undesirable course now is to let the matter rest with Congress; it is time the Congress acted to solve this problem.

♦ JUSTICE DOUGLAS, with whom JUSTICE BRENNEN concurs, dissenting.

... In 1922 the Court had a narrow, parochial view of commerce. With the demise of the old landmarks of that era, the whole concept of commerce has changed. Under the modern [commerce clause] decisions, the power of Congress was recognized as broad enough to reach all phases of the vast operations of our national industrial system. An industry so dependent on radio and television as is baseball and gleaning vast interstate revenues would be hard put today to say with the Court in the *Federal Baseball* case that baseball was only a local exhibition, not trade or commerce....

If congressional inaction is our guide, we should rely upon the fact that Congress has refused to enact bills broadly exempting professional sports from antitrust regulation. The only statutory exemption granted by Congress to professional sports concerns broadcasting rights. I would not ascribe a broader exemption through inaction than Congress has seen fit to grant explicitly.

There can be no doubt "that were we considering the question of baseball for the first time upon a clean slate" we would hold it to be subject to federal antitrust regulation. The unbroken silence of Congress should not prevent us from correcting our own mistakes.

 ◆ JUSTICE MARSHALL, with whom JUSTICE BRENNEN joins, dissenting.

This is a difficult case because we are torn between the principle of *stare decisis* and the knowledge that the decisions in *Federal Baseball Club* and *Toolson* are totally at odds with more recent and better reasoned cases....

Has Congress acquiesced in our decisions in *Federal Baseball Club* and *Toolson*? I think not. Had the Court been consistent and treated all sports in the same way baseball was treated, Congress might have become concerned enough to take action. But, the Court was inconsistent, and baseball was isolated and distinguished from all other sports. In *Toolson*, the Court refused to act because Congress had been silent. But the Court may have read too much into this legislative inaction....

We do not lightly overrule our prior constructions of federal statutes, but when our errors deny substantial federal rights, like the right to compete freely and effectively to the best of one's ability as guaranteed by the antitrust laws, we must admit our error and correct it. We have done so before and we should do so again here.

To the extent that there is concern over any reliance interests that club owners may assert, they can be satisfied by making our decision prospective only. Baseball should be covered by the antitrust laws beginning with this case and henceforth, unless Congress decides otherwise.

* * *

Points for Discussion

1. *Statutory Language*: What was the language at issue? What did each party want that language to mean? What meaning did the majority and dissents adopt?

2. *Theories*: Which theory did the majority use? Concurrence? Dissents? Did any of them find ambiguity, absurdity, a constitutional question to avoid, or a scrivener's error?

3. *Is Actual Legislative Awareness Necessary*: In *Flood*, Congress indicated its awareness of the judicial holdings and tried, but failed, to expand those holdings. Legislative awareness was demonstratively present. In contrast, in *Bocchino v. Nationwide Mutual Fire Insurance, Co.*, 716 A.2d 883 (Conn. 1998), there was evidence that the state legislature likely had no awareness of its supreme court's decision. Yet, the majority presumed legislative acquiesce in its earlier decisions from the legislative silence. If *Flood* is a case in which legislative acquiescence could reasonably have been found, *Bocchino* is a case in which legislative acquiescence should not have been found.

4. *Soundness of the Doctrine*: If *Flood* presents one situation where Congress may have acquiesced, it is perhaps the only such situation. Judges should find legislative acquiescence rarely. It is, perhaps, legitimate to say that Congress acquiesced when it tried, but failed, more than fifty times to overturn a prior precedent. It is quite another thing to say that silence *in all cases* means that the legislature agreed with the opinion:

> It is perhaps too late now to deny that, legislatively speaking as in ordinary life, silence in some instances may give consent. But it would be going even farther beyond reason and common experience to maintain, as there are signs we may be by way of doing, that in legislation any more than in other affairs silence or nonaction always is acquiescence equivalent to action.

Cleveland v. United States, 329 U.S. 14, 22–24 (1946) (Rutledge, J., concurring). Silence can mean any number of things; judges should not presume silence always means agreement.

5. *Congressional Response*: In the next section, we discuss the relevance of subsequent legislative acts. For now, you might be interested to know that Congress's response to *Flood* was to enact The Curt Flood Act of 1998, 15 U.S.C. § 26b. You can find it here: http://roadsidephotos.sabr.org/baseball/curtflood.htm. Did anything change? Perhaps. The Act did not alter the bargaining relationship between players and management in Major League Baseball. However, the socio-economic and political concerns surrounding the Curt Flood Act did impact that bargaining relationship. *See* J. Gordon Hylton, *The Curt Flood Act: Why Baseball's Antitrust Exemption Still Survives*, 9 MARQ. SPORTS L.J. 391 (1999).

6. *Flood Lives On*: The Ninth Circuit recently rejected an invitation to reconsider *Flood*. In *San Jose v. Office of the Commissioner of Baseball*, 776 F.3d 686 (9th Cir. 2015), the court held that Major League Baseball's franchise relocation policies were exempt from anti-trust laws under *Flood*. Although San Jose had argued that *Flood* applied only to baseball's reserve system, which had now been legislatively overrule, the court disagreed: "Antitrust claims against MLB's franchise relocation policies are in the heartland of those precluded by *Flood*'s rational...." The Supreme Court denied cert. *Id.* at 691.

* * *

2. Subsequent Legislative Action

The last section explored subsequent legislative inaction. This section explores subsequent legislative action. After a statute is enacted, legislatures and legislators act in ways that could be relevant to an existing statute's meaning. For example, legislatures may enact subsequent legislation or discuss existing statutes during the legislative enactment of a new bill. In addition, legislators may testify or offer affidavits to "prove" a statute's meaning. This section explores the relevance of each of these in turn.

a. Subsequent Acts

Enactment of a subsequent act may affect the meaning of an existing statute. *Franklin v. Gwinnett Cty Pub. Schools,* 503 U.S. 60 (1992). For example, in *Franklin,* the Court had to decide whether, under Title IX's implied causes of action, a plaintiff could recover money damages in addition to injunctive relief. The plaintiff in the case, a student at the public high school, was the subject of inappropriate and unwanted sexual advances by one of her teachers. *Id.* at 64. By the time the case was heard, both the student and teacher had left the school. Hence, injunctive relief would not have benefitted the student-plaintiff. As for the remedy, the legislative history was silent, which makes sense given that the cause of action was not express but was implied. The silence did not trouble the Supreme Court. "Since the Court ... [had already] concluded that this statute supported no express right of action, it is hardly surprising that Congress also said nothing about the applicable remedies for an implied right of action." *Id.* at 71.

Because the legislative history of the statute at issue did not resolve the ambiguity, the Court turned to another source to resolve the ambiguity: subsequent legislative acts. In two related acts (the Rehabilitation Act Amendments of 1986 and the Rehabilitation Act of 1973), Congress broadly defined the express remedies available under those acts to include all forms of damages. *Id.* at 73. The Court found Congress's subsequent legislation to be "a validation of [its earlier] holding" and "an implicit acknowledgment that damages [were] available." *Id.* at 78 (Scalia, J., concurring).

As this example shows, subsequent acts may provide insight into the contours of an existing act. More famously, the Court explored subsequent acts in *FDA v. Brown & Williamson Tobacco Corp.,* 529 U.S. 120 (2000), to hold that the Food and Drug Administration could not regulate tobacco, even though the language of the statute alone appeared clear. As you read this opinion, notice that there are six separate pieces of legislation the majority points to as proof that Congress did not intend the FDA to regulate in this economically and politically significant area. How does Justice Breyer respond to the majority's overwhelming proof?

Food & Drug Administration v.
Brown & Williamson Tobacco Corp.

Supreme Court of the United States
529 U.S. 120 (2000)

◆ O'CONNOR, J., delivered the opinion of the Court [in which REHNQUIST, C.J., and SCALIA, KENNEDY, and THOMAS, JJ., concur].

... The [Food, Drug, and Cosmetic Act (FDCA or Act)] grants the [Food and Drug Administration ("FDA")], as the designee of the Secretary of Health and Human Services (HHS), the authority to regulate, among other items, "drugs" and "devices." The Act defines "drug" to include "articles (other than food) intended to affect the structure or any function of the body." 21 U.S.C. § 321(g)(1)(C). It defines "device," in part, as "an instrument, apparatus, implement, machine, contrivance, ... or other similar or related article, including any component, part, or accessory, which is ... intended to affect the structure or any function of the body." § 321(h). The Act also grants the FDA the authority to regulate so-called "combination products," which "constitute a combination of a drug, device, or biological product." § 353(g)(1). The FDA has construed this provision as giving it the discretion to regulate combination products as drugs, as devices, or as both....

On August 28, 1996, the FDA ... determined that nicotine is a "drug" and that cigarettes and smokeless tobacco are "drug delivery devices," and therefore it had jurisdiction under the FDCA to regulate tobacco products.... [The FCA promulgated regulations addressing tobacco products' promotion, labeling, and accessibility to children and adolescents.].

Respondents, a group of tobacco manufacturers, retailers, and advertisers, filed suit ... challenging the regulations. They moved for summary judgment on the grounds that the FDA lacked jurisdiction to regulate tobacco products.... The District Court ... held that the FDCA authorizes the FDA to regulate tobacco products.... The Court of Appeals for the Fourth Circuit reversed....

We granted the federal parties' petition for certiorari to determine whether the FDA has authority under the FDCA to regulate tobacco products....

... Because this case involves an administrative agency's construction of a statute that it administers, our analysis is governed by *Chevron U.S.A. Inc. v. Natural Resources Defense Council, Inc.*, 467 U.S. 837 (1984). Under *Chevron*, a reviewing court must first ask "whether Congress has directly spoken to the precise question at issue." If Congress has done so, the inquiry is at an end; the court "must give effect to the unambiguously expressed intent of Congress." But if Congress has not specifically addressed the question, a reviewing court must respect the agency's construction of the statute so long as it is permissible. Such deference is justified because "[t]he responsibilities for assessing the wisdom of such policy choices and resolving the struggle between competing views of the public interest are not judicial ones," and because of the agency's greater familiarity with the ever-changing facts and circumstances surrounding the subjects regulated.

whole code aspects

In determining whether Congress has specifically addressed the question at issue, a reviewing court should not confine itself to examining a particular statutory provision in isolation. The meaning—or ambiguity—of certain words or phrases may only become evident when placed in context. It is a "fundamental canon of statutory construction that the words of a statute must be read in their context and with a view to their place in the overall statutory scheme." A court must therefore interpret the statute "as a symmetrical and coherent regulatory scheme," and "fit, if possible, all parts into an harmonious whole," Similarly, the meaning of one statute may be affected by other Acts, particularly where Congress has spoken subsequently and more specifically to the topic at hand. In addition, we must be guided to a degree by common sense as to the manner in which Congress is likely to delegate a policy decision of such economic and political magnitude to an administrative agency.

With these principles in mind, we find that Congress has directly spoken to the issue here and precluded the FDA's jurisdiction to regulate tobacco products....

In determining whether Congress has spoken directly to the FDA's authority to regulate tobacco, we must ... consider in greater detail the tobacco-specific legislation that Congress has enacted over the past 35 years. At the time a statute is enacted, it may have a range of plausible meanings. Over time, however, subsequent acts can shape or focus those meanings. The "classic judicial task of reconciling many laws enacted over time, and getting them to 'make sense' in combination, necessarily assumes that the implications of a statute may be altered by the implications of a later statute." This is particularly so where the scope of the earlier statute is broad but the subsequent statutes more specifically address the topic at hand. As we recognized recently "a specific policy embodied in a later federal statute should control our construction of the [earlier] statute, even though it ha[s] not been expressly amended."

Congress has enacted six separate pieces of legislation since 1965 addressing the problem of tobacco use and human health....

In adopting each statute, Congress has acted against the backdrop of the FDA's consistent and repeated statements that it lacked authority under the FDCA to regulate tobacco absent claims of therapeutic benefit by the manufacturer. In fact, on several occasions over this period, and after the health consequences of tobacco use and nicotine's pharmacological effects had become well known, Congress considered and rejected bills that would have granted the FDA such jurisdiction. Under these circumstances, it is evident that Congress' tobacco-specific statutes have effectively ratified the FDA's long-held position that it lacks jurisdiction under the FDCA to regulate tobacco products. Congress has created a distinct regulatory scheme to address the problem of tobacco and health, and that scheme, as presently constructed, precludes any role for the FDA.

[Subsequent Legislation]

[In June 1964], the Federal Trade Commission (FTC) ... promulgated a ... rule requiring cigarette manufacturers "to disclose, clearly and prominently, in all advertising and on every pack, box, carton or other container ... that cigarette smoking is dangerous to health and may cause death from cancer and other diseases.".…

In response to ... the FTC's proposed rule, Congress convened hearings to consider legislation addressing "the tobacco problem." During those deliberations, FDA representatives testified before Congress that the agency lacked jurisdiction under the FDCA to regulate tobacco products.…

The FDA's disavowal of jurisdiction was consistent with the position that it had taken since the agency's inception. As the FDA concedes, it never asserted authority to regulate tobacco products as customarily marketed until it promulgated the regulations at issue here.…

Moreover, before ... 1965, Congress considered and rejected several proposals to give the FDA the authority to regulate tobacco. In April 1963, Representative Udall introduced a bill "[t]o amend the Federal Food, Drug, and Cosmetic Act so as to make that Act applicable to smoking products." H.R. 5973, 88th Cong., 1st Sess., 1. Two months later, Senator Moss introduced an identical bill in the Senate. S. 1682, 88th Cong., 1st Sess. (1963). In discussing his proposal on the Senate floor, Senator Moss explained that "this amendment simply places smoking products under FDA jurisdiction, along with foods, drugs, and cosmetics." 109 Cong. Rec. 10322 (1963). In December 1963, Representative Rhodes introduced another bill that would have amended the FDCA "by striking out 'food, drug, device, or cosmetic,' each place where it appears therein and inserting in lieu thereof 'food, drug, device, cosmetic, or smoking product.'" H.R. 9512, 88th Cong., 1st Sess., § 3 (1963). And in January 1965, five months before passage of the FCLAA, Representative Udall again introduced a bill to amend the FDCA "to make that Act applicable to smoking products." H.R. 2248, 89th Cong., 1st Sess., 1. None of these proposals became law.

[In response to the FTC's proposed rule,] Congress ultimately decided in 1965 to subject tobacco products to the less extensive regulatory scheme [by] enacting the [Federal Cigarette Labeling and Advertising Act ("FCLAA")], which created a "comprehensive Federal program to deal with cigarette labeling and advertising with respect to any relationship between smoking and health." The FCLAA rejected any regulation of advertising, but it required the warning, "Caution: Cigarette Smoking May Be Hazardous to Your Health," to appear on all cigarette packages.…

[With this Act n]ot only did Congress reject the proposals to grant the FDA jurisdiction, but it explicitly pre-empted any other regulation of cigarette labeling.…

Subsequent tobacco-specific legislation followed a similar pattern. By the FCLAA's own terms, the prohibition on any additional cigarette labeling or advertising regulations relating to smoking and health was to expire July 1, 1969. In anticipation of the provision's expiration, both the FCC and the FTC proposed rules governing the advertisement of cigarettes. After debating the proper role for administrative agencies in the regulation of tobacco, Congress amended the FCLAA by banning cigarette advertisements "on any medium of electronic communication subject to the jurisdiction of the Federal Communications Commission" and strengthening the warning required to appear on cigarette packages. Public Health Cigarette Smoking Act of 1969.... Moreover, it expressly forbade the FTC from taking any action on its pending rule until July 1, 1971, and it required the FTC, if it decided to proceed with its rule thereafter, to notify Congress at least six months in advance of the rule's becoming effective. As the chairman of the House committee in which the bill originated stated, "the Congress—the body elected by the people—must make the policy determinations involved in this legislation—and not some agency made up of appointed officials." 116 Cong. Rec. 7920 (1970) (remarks of Rep. Staggers).

Four years later, after Congress had transferred the authority to regulate substances covered by the Hazardous Substances Act (HSA) from the FDA to the Consumer Products Safety Commission (CPSC), [an association] petitioned the CPSC to regulate cigarettes.... After the CPSC determined that it lacked authority under the HSA to regulate cigarettes, a District Court held that the HSA did ... and ordered it to reexamine the petition. Before the CPSC could take any action, however, Congress mooted the issue by adopting legislation that eliminated the agency's authority to regulate "tobacco and tobacco products." ... A separate statement in the Senate Report underscored that the legislation's purpose was to "unmistakably reaffirm the clear mandate of the Congress that the basic regulation of tobacco and tobacco products is governed by the legislation dealing with the subject, ... and that any further regulation in this sensitive and complex area must be reserved for specific Congressional action." S.Rep. No. 94–251, p. 43 (1975)....

In 1983, Congress again considered legislation on the subject of smoking and health. HHS Assistant Secretary Brandt testified [about the dangers of smoking and] that "the issue of regulation of tobacco ... is something that Congress has reserved to itself, and we do not within the Department have the authority to regulate nor are we seeking such authority." He also testified before the Senate, stating that, despite the evidence of tobacco's health effects and addictiveness, the Department's view was that "Congress has assumed the responsibility of regulating ... cigarettes."

Against this backdrop, Congress enacted three additional tobacco-specific statutes over the next four years that incrementally expanded its regulatory scheme for tobacco products. In 1983, Congress adopted the Alcohol and Drug Abuse Amendments, which require the Secretary of HHS to report to Congress every three years on the "addictive property of tobacco" and to include recommendations for action that the Secretary may deem appropriate. A year later, Congress enacted the Comprehensive Smoking Education Act, which amended the FCLAA by again modifying the prescribed warning. Notably, during debate on the Senate floor, Senator Hawkins argued that the FCLAA was necessary in part because "[u]nder the Food, Drug and Cosmetic Act, the Congress exempted tobacco products." And in 1986, Congress enacted the Comprehensive Smokeless Tobacco Health Education Act of 1986 (CSTHEA), which essentially extended the regulatory provisions of the FCLAA to smokeless tobacco products. Like the FCLAA, the CSTHEA provided that "[n]o statement relating to the use of smokeless tobacco products and health, other than the statements required by [the Act], shall be required by any Federal agency to appear on any package ... of a smokeless tobacco product."....

Between 1987 and 1989, Congress considered [and rejected] three more bills that would have amended the FDCA to grant the FDA jurisdiction to regulate tobacco products....

Taken together, these actions by Congress over the past 35 years preclude an interpretation of the FDCA that grants the FDA jurisdiction to regulate tobacco products. We do not rely on Congress' failure to act — its consideration and rejection of bills that would have given the FDA this authority — in reaching this conclusion. Indeed, this is not a case of simple inaction by Congress that purportedly represents its acquiescence in an agency's position. To the contrary, Congress has enacted several statutes addressing the particular subject of tobacco and health, creating a distinct regulatory scheme for cigarettes and smokeless tobacco. In doing so, Congress has been aware of tobacco's health hazards and its pharmacological effects. It has also enacted this legislation against the background of the FDA repeatedly and consistently asserting that it lacks jurisdiction under the FDCA to regulate tobacco products.... Further, Congress has persistently acted to preclude a meaningful role for *any* administrative agency in making policy on the subject of tobacco and health....

Under these circumstances, it is clear that Congress' tobacco-specific legislation has effectively ratified the FDA's previous position that it lacks jurisdiction to regulate tobacco.... Congress has affirmatively acted to address the issue of tobacco and health, relying on the representations of the FDA that it had no authority to regulate tobacco. It has created a distinct scheme to regulate the sale of tobacco products, focused on labeling and advertising, and premised on the belief that the FDA lacks such jurisdiction under the FDCA. As a result, Congress' tobacco-specific statutes preclude the FDA from regulating tobacco products as customarily marketed.

The dissent ... argues that the proper inference to be drawn from Congress' tobacco-specific legislation is "critically ambivalent." We disagree. In that series of statutes, Congress crafted a specific legislative response to the problem of tobacco and health, and it did so with the understanding, based on repeated assertions by the FDA, that the agency has no authority under the FDCA to regulate tobacco products....

... [W]e are confident that Congress could not have intended to delegate a decision of such economic and political significance to an agency in so cryptic a fashion. To find that the FDA has the authority to regulate tobacco products, one must ... ignore the plain implication of Congress' subsequent tobacco-specific legislation. It is therefore clear, based on the FDCA's overall regulatory scheme and the subsequent tobacco legislation, that Congress has directly spoken to the question at issue and precluded the FDA from regulating tobacco products....

♦ BREYER, J., filed a dissenting opinion, in which STEVENS, SOUTER, and GINSBURG, JJ., joined.

The Food and Drug Administration (FDA) has the authority to regulate "articles (other than food) intended to affect the structure or any function of the body...."

Federal Food, Drug, and Cosmetic Act (FDCA), 21 U.S.C. §321(g)(1)(C). Unlike the majority, I believe that tobacco products fit within this statutory language.... [N]icotine is a "drug"; the cigarette that delivers nicotine to the body is a "device"; and the FDCA's language, read in light of its basic purpose, permits the FDA to assert the disease-preventing jurisdiction that the agency now claims.]

In its own interpretation, the majority nowhere denies the following two salient points. First, tobacco products (including cigarettes) fall within the scope of this statutory definition, read literally. Cigarettes achieve their mood-stabilizing effects through the interaction of the chemical nicotine and the cells of the central nervous system. Both cigarette manufacturers and smokers alike know of, and desire, that chemically induced result. Hence, cigarettes are "intended to affect" the body's "structure" and "function," in the literal sense of these words.

Second, the statute's basic purpose—the protection of public health—supports the inclusion of cigarettes within its scope....

Despite the FDCA's literal language and general purpose (both of which support the FDA's finding that cigarettes come within its statutory authority), the majority nonetheless reads the statute as *excluding* tobacco products [because]: ...

> Congress has enacted other statutes, which, when viewed in light of the FDA's long history of denying tobacco-related jurisdiction and considered together with Congress' failure explicitly to grant the agency tobacco-specific authority, demonstrate that Congress did not intend for the FDA to exercise jurisdiction over tobacco.

In my view, [this] proposition[] is [in]valid....

... I believe that the most important indicia of statutory meaning—language and purpose—along with the FDCA's legislative history are sufficient to establish that the FDA has authority to regulate tobacco....

In the majority's view, laws enacted since 1965 require us to deny jurisdiction, whatever the FDCA might mean in their absence. But why? Do those laws contain language barring FDA jurisdiction? The majority must concede that they do not. Do they contain provisions that are inconsistent with the FDA's exercise of jurisdiction? With one exception, the majority points to no such provision. Do they somehow repeal the principles of law that otherwise would lead to the conclusion that the FDA has jurisdiction in this area? ... Perhaps the later laws "shape" and "focus" what the 1938 Congress meant a generation earlier. But this Court has warned against using the views of a later Congress to construe a statute enacted many years before. *Sullivan v. Finkelstein,* 496 U.S. 617, 632 (1990) (Scalia, J., concurring) ("Arguments based on subsequent legislative history ... should not be taken seriously, not even in a footnote").

Regardless, the later statutes do not support the majority's conclusion. That is because, whatever individual Members of Congress after 1964 may have assumed about the FDA's jurisdiction, the laws they enacted did not embody any such "no jurisdiction" assumption. And one cannot automatically *infer* an antijurisdiction intent, as the majority does, for the later statutes are both (and similarly) consistent with quite a different congressional desire, namely, the intent to proceed without interfering with whatever authority the FDA otherwise may have possessed. As I demonstrate below, the subsequent legislative history is critically ambivalent, for it can be read *either* as (a) "ratif[ying]" a no-jurisdiction assumption, *or* as (b) leaving the jurisdictional question just where Congress found it. And the fact that both inferences are "equally tenable," prevents the majority from drawing from the later statutes the firm, anti-jurisdiction implication that it needs.

Consider, for example, Congress' failure to provide the FDA with express authority to regulate tobacco—a circumstance that the majority finds significant. In fact, Congress *both* failed to grant express authority to the FDA when the FDA denied it had jurisdiction over tobacco *and* failed to take that authority expressly away when the agency later asserted jurisdiction. Consequently, the defeat of various different proposed jurisdictional changes proves nothing. This history shows only that Congress could not muster the votes necessary either to grant or to deny the FDA the relevant authority. It neither favors nor disfavors the majority's position.

The majority also mentions the speed with which Congress acted to take jurisdiction away from other agencies once they tried to assert it. But such a congressional response again proves nothing. On the one hand, the speedy reply might suggest that Congress somehow resented agency assertions of jurisdiction in an area it desired to reserve for itself—a consideration that supports the majority. On the other hand, Congress' quick reaction with respect to *other* agencies' regulatory efforts contrasts dramatically with its failure to enact any responsive law (at any speed) after the FDA asserted jurisdiction over tobacco more than three years ago. And that contrast supports the opposite conclusion.

The majority's historical perspective also appears to be shaped by language in the Federal Cigarette Labeling and Advertising Act (FCLAA). The FCLAA requires manufacturers to place on cigarette packages, etc., health warnings such as the following:

> "SURGEON GENERAL'S WARNING: Smoking Causes Lung Cancer, Heart Disease, Emphysema, And May Complicate Pregnancy."

The FCLAA has an express pre-emption provision which says that "[n]o statement relating to smoking and health, other than the statement required by [this Act], shall be required on any cigarette package." § 1334(a). This pre-emption clause plainly prohibits the FDA from requiring on "any cigarette package" any other "statement relating to smoking and health," but no one contends that the FDA has failed to abide by this prohibition. Rather, the question is whether the FCLAA's pre-emption provision does *more*. Does it forbid the FDA to regulate at all?

This Court has already answered that question expressly and in the negative. See *Cipollone v. Liggett Group, Inc.*, 505 U.S. 504 (1992). *Cipollone* held that the FCLAA's pre-emption provision does not bar state or federal regulation outside the provision's literal scope. And it described the pre-emption provision as "merely prohibit[ing] state and federal rulemaking bodies from mandating particular cautionary statements on cigarette labels...."

This negative answer is fully consistent with Congress' intentions in regard to the pre-emption language. When Congress enacted the FCLAA, it focused upon the regulatory efforts of the Federal Trade Commission (FTC), not the FDA.... Why would one read the FCLAA's pre-emption clause — a provision that Congress intended to limit even in respect to the agency directly at issue — so broadly that it would bar a different agency from engaging in any other cigarette regulation at all? The answer is that the Court need not, and should not, do so. And, inasmuch as the Court already has declined to view the FCLAA as pre-empting the entire field of tobacco regulation, I cannot accept that that same law bars the FDA's regulatory efforts here.

When the FCLAA's narrow pre-emption provision is set aside, the majority's conclusion that Congress clearly intended for its tobacco-related statutes to be the exclusive "response" to "the problem of tobacco and health" is based on legislative silence....

I now turn to the final historical fact that the majority views as a factor in its interpretation of the subsequent legislative history: the FDA's former denials of its tobacco-related authority.

Until the early 1990's, the FDA expressly maintained that the 1938 statute did not give it the power that it now seeks to assert [because the intent requirement was missing]. It then changed its mind. The majority agrees with me that the FDA's change of positions does not make a significant legal difference. *Chevron*, 467 U.S., at 863 ("An initial agency interpretation is not instantly carved in stone"). Nevertheless, it labels those denials "important context" for drawing an inference about Congress' intent. In my view, the FDA's change of policy, like the subsequent statutes themselves, does nothing to advance the majority's position....

Nothing in the law prevents the FDA from changing its policy [based on new evidence that tobacco companies knew about chemical changes its products caused in the body]. By the mid–1990's, the evidence needed to prove objective intent ... had been found. The emerging scientific consensus about tobacco's adverse, chemically induced, health effects may have convinced the agency that it should spend its resources on this important regulatory effort....

The upshot is that the Court today holds that a regulatory statute aimed at unsafe drugs and devices does not authorize regulation of a drug (nicotine) and a device (a cigarette) that the Court itself finds unsafe. Far more than most, this particular drug and device risks the life-threatening harms that administrative regulation seeks to rectify. The majority's conclusion is counterintuitive. And, for the reasons set forth, I believe that the law does not require it....

* * *

Points for Discussion

1. *Statutory Language*: What was the language at issue? What did each party want that language to mean? What meaning did the majority and dissent adopt?

2. *Theories*: Which theory did the majority use? The dissent? Did the justices stay true to their typical approaches? In other words, why did Justices Scalia and Thomas sign onto an opinion that rejected the clear text? Why did Justices Breyer and Stevens highlight the "literal" meaning of the words? Did politics trump ideology in this case?

3. *Six Acts*: According to the majority, Congress enacted six different laws to demonstrate that "that the basic regulation of tobacco and tobacco products ... must be reserved for specific Congressional action." See if you can identify each of those six laws and what those laws actually did. Why did Justice Breyer find each of the subsequent legislative acts ambiguous regarding Congress's intent to retain control over regulating tobacco?

4. *Legislative Silence*: Justice Breyer criticized the majority's analysis of the relevance of the six acts, then concluded that the majority's decision rested exclusively "on legislative silence." Is that fair? Did not Congress act to regulate tobacco in some ways, even if Congress did not act specifically to curtail FDA action?

5. *Executive Rejections*: The majority said repeatedly that Congress acted in the shadow of the FDA's longstanding claims that it had no authority to regulate. Bear in mind that agencies can and do change their minds about their ability to regulate. See, e.g., *FCC v. Fox Television Stations, Inc.*, 556 U.S. 502, 530 (2009) (upholding a regulation that reversed the FCC's approach to penalizing "fleeting expletives"). Prior to the 1990s, the FDA claimed it had no evidence that the tobacco companies *intended* to used tobacco "to affect any structure or any function of the body." However, "[b]y the mid-1990s.... [t]he scientific consensus about tobacco's adverse, chemically induced, health effects may have convinced the agency that it should spend it resources on this important regulatory effort...." Hence, are the FTC's jurisdictional denials relevant?

6. *Chevron*: In *Brown & Williams*, the Court examines the validity of an agency interpretation contained in a regulation. In determining whether to defer to an agency's interpretation, courts apply the test from *Chevron U.S.A. Inc. v. Natural Resources Defense Council, Inc.*, 467 U.S. 837 (1984). Pursuant to the first step in this test, a court must determine whether Congress has spoken to the precise issue before the court. This step involves a typical statutory interpretation analysis.

   Why did the majority conclude that Congress had spoken under step one? Why did the dissent disagree? Under *Chevron*, if Congress has not spoken, a court should adopt any reasonable agency interpretation. Assuming Congress had not spoken, was the FDA's interpretation reasonable? Likely yes. So, if the majority had not found that Congress had spoken at step one, the majority would have had to defer to the FDA's interpretation.

7. *"So Significant" & Clear Statements*: As we will learn more fully in Chapter 14, *Brown & Williamson* is well-known for creating an exception to *Chevron*'s application. Prior to *Brown & Williamson*, *Chevron* applied when an agency interpreted

ambiguous statutory language. Explicit delegation was unnecessary, because ambiguity was equivalent to an implicit delegation.

As a result of *Brown & Williamson*, a court applies *Chevron*'s two steps when an agency interprets ambiguous statutory language unless the issue is one "of such economic and political significance" that Congress would not have intended to delegate. Explicit delegation is now necessary in these cases. In 2015, the Supreme Court confirmed that a clear statement was required in such cases. In *King v. Burwell*, 135 S. Ct. 2480, 2483 (2015), the Court refused to apply *Chevron* at all because the issue of health care involved such "deep 'economic and political significance'" that if Congress wished to assign resolution of that question to the agency, "[Congress] *surely would have done so expressly.*" The majority opinion specifically relied on *Brown & Williamson*.

* * *

b. "Subsequent Legislative History"

Sometimes, while enacting a new law, the legislature will comment on an existing statute during the floor debate or as part of a committee report. This *subsequent legislative history* should be irrelevant. (Note the irony in the title: How can subsequent events ever be historical?) While the legislature's comments might be relevant to the interpretation of the new act, those comments are generally not relevant to the interpretation of an existing act. "[S]ubsequent legislative history will rarely override a reasonable interpretation of a statute that can be gleaned from its language and legislative history prior to its enactment." *Consumer Product Safety Comm'n v. GTE Sylvania*, 447 U.S. 102, 117–18 n.13 (1980). Use of these comments for interpreting a statute is extremely controversial, but done, for the reasons Justice Scalia identifies below:

> The legislative history of a statute is the history of its consideration and enactment. "Subsequent legislative history"—which presumably means the *post*-enactment history of a statute's consideration and enactment—is a contradiction in terms. The phrase is used to smuggle into judicial consideration legislators' expressions *not* of what a bill currently under consideration means (which, the theory goes, reflects what their colleagues understood they were voting for), but of what a law *previously enacted* means....
>
> In my opinion, the views of a legislator concerning a statute already enacted are entitled to no more weight than the views of a judge concerning a statute not yet passed. In some situations, of course, the expression of a legislator relating to a previously enacted statute may bear upon the meaning of a provision in a bill under consideration—which provision, if passed, may in turn affect judicial interpretation of the previously enacted statute, since statutes *in pari materia* should be interpreted harmoniously. Such an expression would be useful, if at all, not because it was subsequent legislative history of the earlier statute, but because it was plain old legislative history of the later one.

Arguments based on subsequent legislative history, like arguments based on antecedent futurity, should not be taken seriously, not even in a footnote.

Sullivan v. Finkelstein, 496 U.S. 617, 631 (1990) (Scalia, J., concurring). (Notice that Justice Breyer threw these words back at the majority in his dissent in *Brown & Williamson*). In other words, comments made during the enactment of a new bill do not reflect what the enacting legislature intended or what the words meant when the existing statute was drafted. Thus, any such comments would show no more than what a latter legislature believed an earlier legislature thought. Any other balance would elevate the intent of the second legislature above that of the enacting legislature. But comments by a legislator about an enacted statute during debate on a pending bill may become relevant regarding the enacted statute because of the doctrine of *in pari materia*, under which statutes should be interpreted to work together.

Despite this canon, however, a court may find subsequent legislative history relevant in some situations. Let's look at an example. In the case below, there are two acts discussed: the Alaska Lands Act and the Colorado Wilderness Act. The Colorado Wilderness Act was passed shortly after the Alaska Lands Act. The court found information in the conference committee report from the subsequent act conclusive and sufficient to overcome the ordinary meaning of the statute at issue.

Montana Wilderness Ass'n v. United States Forest Service

United States Court of Appeals for the Ninth Circuit
655 F.2d 951 (1981), *cert. denied*, 455 U.S. 989

♦ Norris, Circuit Judge [Anderson, C.J., and Schwarzer, D.J. concur]:

… Defendant-Appellee Burlington Northern, Inc. owns timberland located within the Gallatin National Forest southwest of Bozeman, Montana….

To harvest its timber, Burlington Northern in 1979 acquired a permit from defendant-appellee United States Forest Service, allowing it to construct an access road across national forest land. The proposed roads would cross the Buck Creek and Yellow Mules drainages, which are protected by the Montana Wilderness Study Act of 1977, as potential wilderness areas. The proposed logging and road-building will arguably disqualify the areas as wilderness under the Act.

The plaintiffs, Montana Wilderness Association, The Wilderness Society, and Nine Quarter Circle Ranch … filed suit after [the permit] was granted, seeking declaratory and injunctive relief…. The parties … filed cross-motions for summary judgment…. The district court denied the plaintiffs' motion and granted the defendants' partial summary judgment motion….

The sole issue on appeal is whether Burlington Northern has a right of access across federal land to its inholdings of timberland. Appellees contend that the recently enacted Alaska National Interest Lands Conservation Act (Alaska Lands Act), …

[specifically § 1323(a) of the Act,] requires that the Secretary of Agriculture provide access to Burlington Northern for its enclosed land.

Section 1323 is a part of the administrative provisions ... of the Alaska Lands Act. Appellees argue that it is the only section of the Act which applies to the entire country; appellants argue that, like the rest of the Act, it applies only to Alaska. Section 1323 reads as follows:

> Sec. 1323. (a) Notwithstanding any other provision of law, and subject to such terms and conditions as the Secretary of Agriculture may prescribe, the Secretary shall provide such access to nonfederally owned land within the boundaries of the National Forest System as the Secretary deems adequate to secure to the owner the reasonable use and enjoyment thereof: Provided, That such owner comply with rules and regulations applicable to ingress and egress to or from the National Forest System.
>
> (b) Notwithstanding any other provision of law, and subject to such terms and conditions as the Secretary of the Interior may prescribe, the Secretary . shall provide such access to nonfederally owned land surrounded by public lands managed by the Secretary under the Federal Land Policy and Management Act of 1976 as the Secretary deems adequate to secure to the owner the responsible use and enjoyment thereof: Provided, That such owner comply with rules and regulations applicable to access across public lands.

This section provides for access to nonfederally-owned lands surrounded by certain kinds of federal lands. Subsection (b) deals with access to nonfederal lands "surrounded by public lands managed by the Secretary (of the Interior)." Section 102(3) of the Act defines "public lands" as certain lands "situated in Alaska." Subsection (b), therefore, is arguably limited by its terms to Alaska, though we do not find it necessary to settle that issue here. Our consideration of the scope of § 1323(a) proceeds under the assumption that § 1323(b) is limited to Alaska.

Subsection (a) deals with access to nonfederally-owned lands "within the boundaries of the National Forest System." The term "National Forest System" is not specifically defined in the Act.

The question before the court is whether the term "National Forest System" as used in § 1323(a) is to be interpreted as being limited to national forests in Alaska or as including the entire United States. We note at the outset that the bare language of § 1323(a) does not, when considered by itself, limit the provision of access to Alaskan land. We must look, however, to the context of the section to determine its meaning. ...

Congress did, however, supply us with a general definition of the term in another statute. Pub. Law 93-378, 88 Stat. 480 (1974). 16 U.S.C. s 1609(a) states inter alia that:

> Congress declares that the National Forest System consists of units of federally owned forest, range, and related lands throughout the United States and its territories, united into a nationally significant system dedicated to the long-term benefit for present and future generations, and that it is the purpose

of their section to include all such areas into one integral system. The 'National Forest System' shall include all national forest lands reserved or withdrawn from the public domain of the United States....

Application of this definition to § 1323(a) would necessarily yield the conclusion that the section was intended to have nation-wide effect. This seems especially so when Congress uses the term "National Forest System" in § 1323(a) without limitation or qualification.

As the parties agreed at oral argument, however, § 1323(b) is *in pari materia* with § 1323(a). The two subsections are placed together in the same section, and use not only a parallel structure but many of the same words and phrases. The natural interpretation is that they were meant to have the same effect, one on lands controlled by the Secretary of Agriculture, the other on lands controlled by the Secretary of the Interior. Since we assume that § 1323(b), by definition of public lands in s 102(3), applies only to Alaskan land, we face a presumption that § 1323(a) was meant to apply to Alaska as well.

That interpretation is supported by a review of the entire Act which discloses no other provision having nation-wide application. We therefore conclude that the language of the Act provides tentative support for the view that § 1323(a) applies only to national forests in Alaska. Bearing in mind that "(a)bsent a clearly expressed legislative intent to the contrary, (the statutory) language must ordinarily be regarded as conclusive," we turn to the legislative history.

The legislative history concerning § 1323 is surprisingly sparse. The report of the Senate committee which drafted the section is ambiguous. At times when the Senate could have been expected to comment on its intention to make a major change in current law, it did not.[7] The only expression of intent that § 1323 apply nation-wide came from a single senator eight days after the Alaska Lands Act was passed by Congress.[8] In the House debates, three representatives suggested that § 1323 did apply nation-wide, but the chairman of one of the responsible committees said it did not.... All this gives only slight support at best to the appellees' interpretation that § 1323 applies nation-wide.

The appellees, however, have uncovered subsequent legislative history that, given the closeness of the issue, is decisive. Three weeks after Congress passed the Alaska Lands Act, a House-Senate Conference Committee considering the Colorado Wilderness Act interpreted § 1323 of the Alaska Lands Act as applying nation-wide:

---

7. The Alaska Lands bill was discussed endlessly on the Senate floor. There are numerous occasions when one would expect a change in current laws of access of the magnitude of the appellees' proposed interpretation of § 1323 to be discussed, mentioned or at least alluded to....

8. Senator Melcher, the author of the section, discussed it on the floor of the Senate, 126 Cong.Rec. S14770-71 (daily ed. Nov. 20, 1980). The remarks of Senator Melcher, however, were made on November 20th, eight days after Congress passed H.R. 39. His remarks clearly demonstrate that his personal understanding of the section is that it applies nationwide, but because they are the remarks of but one senator made subsequent to the passage of the bill they do not provide a reliable indication of the understanding of the Senate as a whole.

Section 7 of the Senate amendment contains a provision pertaining to access to non-Federally owned lands within national forest wilderness areas in Colorado. The House bill has no such provision.

The conferees agreed to delete the section because similar language has already passed Congress in Section 1323 of the Alaska National Interest Lands Conservation Act.

This action was explained to both Houses during discussion of the Conference Report. Both houses then passed the Colorado Wilderness bill as it was reported by the Conference Committee.

Although a subsequent conference report is not entitled to the great weight given subsequent legislation, it is still entitled to significant weight, particularly where it is clear that the conferees had carefully considered the issue. The conferees, including Representatives Udall and Sieberling and Senator Melcher, had an intimate knowledge of the Alaska Lands Act.[11] Moreover, the Conference Committee's interpretation of § 1323 was the basis for their decision to leave out an access provision passed by one house. In these circumstances, the Conference Committee's interpretation is very persuasive. We conclude that it tips the balance decidedly in favor of the broader interpretation of § 1323. We therefore hold that Burlington Northern has an assured right of access to its land pursuant to the nation-wide grant of access in § 1323....

* * *

Points for Discussion

1. *Statutory Language*: What was the language at issue? What did each party want that language to mean? What meaning did the court adopt?

2. *Theories*: Which theory did the court use? Did the court find ambiguity, absurdity, a constitutional question to avoid, or a scrivener's error?

3. *Section 1323(a) & (b)*: The court explains that subsection (b) applies only to public lands in Alaska because the Act defines "public lands" as lands "situated in Alaska." There is no similar definition for the language in subsection (a): "National Forest System." Hence, while subsection (b) applies only to Alaska because of the definition, it is less clear whether subsection (a) applies nationally or just to Alaska. On the one hand, the language suggests that subsection (a) is *not* so limited; on the other hand, *in pari materia* would suggest that is so limited. Specifically, subsection (a) applies to lands within Alaska that the Secretary of Agriculture has control over, while subsection (b) applies to lands within Alaska that the Secretary of the Interior has control over. Moreover, and not mentioned by the court, the title of the Act similarly suggests that subsection (a) is limited to Alaska National Forests. The title is "the Alaska Lands Act." What other intrinsic sources did the court consider?

---

11. The participation of Representative Udall is particularly noteworthy since he was the one congressman to proclaim in the legislative history of the Alaska Lands Act that § 1323 applied only to Alaska.

4. *Legislative History*: What legislative history of the Alaska Lands Act did the court consider? Why did the court find that legislative history unhelpful? Is it ironic that the court gives little weight to the legislative history of the Alaska Act, but relies on the legislative history of the subsequent act, the Colorado Wilderness Act?

5. *Subsequent Legislative History*: *Montana Wilderness* represents the exception to the rule that subsequent legislative history is irrelevant to interpretation. What subsequent legislative history did the court use, and why did it find that history particularly relevant in this situation even though the court acknowledged that "a subsequent conference report is not entitled to the great weight"? Why is reliance on subsequent legislative history disfavored?

6. *Absurd*: The court concluded that this one section of the Act applies nationally while every other provision in the Act applies only in Alaska. Given that the Act's title is the Alaska Lands Act, does it makes sense to reject the presumption that subsequent legislative history is generally irrelevant? Do you agree with the majority that the subsequent legislative history here was overwhelming?

7. *Udall*: Why did the court find Representative Udall's comments specifically relevant?

* * *

c. The Reenactment Canon

You will remember that codification refers to the insertion of sections of an act into the relevant section of the code, whether state or federal. Codification was covered in detail in Chapter 9. Recodification simply means to codify again. Reenactment means, essentially, the same thing.

Occasionally, legislatures recodify or reenact the whole or portions of a code. Legislatures recodify for many reasons, including to simplify and to consolidate statutes, to eliminate defects in the original enactment, to remove inconsistencies and obsolete provisions, to expand titles to permit past or future growth, and to reorganize to make provisions easier to find. For example, Congress re-codified the criminal code in 1948. When it did so, Congress changed some statutory language, but left other language intact. When a legislature recodifies a code, the presumption is that the recodification clarified the law, but did not make substantive changes, unless the new language unmistakably indicates the legislature's intent to make substantive changes. *Fourco Glass Co. v. Transmirra Products Corp.*, 353 U.S. 222, 227 (1957).

When the text is changed during recodification, new interpretations will likely follow. But when a statute is reenacted in identical or similar form (for example, when statutes are simply renumbered), there is a presumption that the legislature knew of any existing judicial or administrative interpretations of that statute and intended to continue those interpretations. *Lorillard v. Pons*, 434 U.S. 575, 580–81 (1978). Otherwise, the presumption continues, the legislature would have amended the text. The reenactment canon is stated simply as follows: When Congress reenacts or recodifies a statute that a court or an agency had previously interpreted, judges presume that

Congress intended to continue that interpretation. This canon is similar to the super strong *stare decisis* canon discussed above. Yet, the reenactment canon is also broader because it applies not only to Supreme Court decisions but also to existing agency and lower court interpretations.

This presumption is bolstered when there is evidence that the reenacting Congress was aware of the specific interpretation. For example, Congress reenacted the Voting Rights Act on two separate occasions. Both times it was clear from the legislative history that Congress agreed with earlier interpretations of the Act. Thus, those interpretations survived reenactment. "When a Congress that re-enacts a statute voices its approval of an administrative or other interpretation thereof, Congress is treated as having adopted that interpretation, and this Court is bound thereby." *United States v. Board of Comm'r of Sheiffeld*, 435 U.S. 110, 134 (1978). This presumption can be overcome with evidence that the legislature was unaware of the existing interpretation or did not intend for it to continue.

d. Testimony by and Affidavits from Legislators and Staff Members

Least relevant of all to interpretation are testimony and affidavits from legislators or staff members. Sometimes, during litigation, one party will introduce the testimony or affidavit of a legislator or staff member who was present when the statute was enacted. This "evidence" of intent is generally considered irrelevant to the meaning of the statute, even when the affidavit comes from the drafter of the bill. "[E]vidence of a … draftsman of a statute is not a competent aid to a court in construing a statute." *S.D. Educ. Ass'n v. Barnett*, 582 N.W.2d 386, 400 (S.D. 1998) (Zinter, J., concurring in part and dissenting in part) (quoting *Cummings v. Mickelson*, 495 N.W.2d 493, 499 n. 7 (S.D. 1993)).

There are three reasons why such evidence is ignored. First, these affidavits indicate only one specific legislator's or, even worse a lobbyist or staffer's, understanding of the meaning and not the intent of the legislature as a whole. "Views of individuals involved with the legislative process as to intent [are of] no assistance … [for] it is the intent of the legislative body that is sought, not the intent of the individual members who may have diverse reasons for or against a proposition…." *American Meat Instit. v. Barnett*, 64 F. Supp. 2d 906, 916 (D.S.D. 1999).

Second, such affidavits are created to support one party's position in litigation after the legislative process has concluded. Memories may be inaccurate, incomplete, or intentionally wrong. Giving these statements weight could encourage gamesmanship. Finally, allowing such evidence of meaning would set legislators as rivals against one another and might give an individual legislator too much power to determine the meaning of a statute a legislature enacts. Despite these concerns, affidavits may be useful in limited situations. When the affidavit is "provided as background as to the nature of the problem and why and how the Legislature sought to address it," these concerns disappear. *S.D. Education Ass'n*, 582 N.W.2d at 397 (Gilbert, J., concurring).

In this chapter, we have discussed the role of subsequent legislative inaction and actions in interpretation. We did not, however, discuss subsequent actions of the *executive* branch, including presidential signing statements and agency interpretations. We are going to delay this discussion until Chapters 16–19. For you to understand the role that these sources play in interpretation, you must learn about administrative agencies. Instead, we will turn in the next two chapters to the canons based on policy-considerations.

Problem 13

Federal law criminalizes knowing or intentional possession of controlled substances in certain circumstances: 21 U.S.C. §841(a)(1) provides:

(a) Unlawful acts

Except as authorized by this subchapter, it shall be unlawful for any person knowingly or intentionally

(1) to manufacture, distribute, or dispense, or possess with intent to manufacture, distribute, or dispense, a controlled substance....

In *United States v. Jewell*, 532 F.2d 697 (9th Cir. 1976), the Ninth Circuit developed the "deliberate ignorance standard." In *Jewell*, a man offered to sell marijuana to the defendant and his friend in a Tijuana bar, and then to pay them $100 to drive a car across the border. The friend refused, but the defendant accepted the offer, even though he "thought there was probably something illegal in the vehicle." The defendant determined that there was no contraband in the glove compartment, under the front seat, or in the trunk, so he concluded that "the people at the border wouldn't find anything either." He admitted to seeing a secret compartment in the trunk (where 110 pounds of marijuana was later found), but did not attempt to open it.

The Ninth Circuit held that the knowledge element in section 841(a) could be satisfied without positive, confirmed personal knowledge that the marijuana was in the trunk. In other words, when Congress makes it a crime to "knowingly ... possess with intent to manufacture, distribute, or dispense, a controlled substance," 21 U.S.C. §841(a)(1), Congress meant to punish not only those who know they possess a controlled substance but also those who do not know they possess a controlled substance because they do not want to know.

Since *Jewell* was decided in 1976, those circuits that have addressed the issue—with the exception of the D.C. Circuit—have adopted this "deliberate ignorance" holding. *United States v. Flores*, 454 F.3d 149, 156 (3d Cir. 2006); *United States v. Ruhe*, 191 F.3d 376, 384 (4th Cir. 1999); *United States v. Fuchs*, 467 F.3d 889, 902 (5th Cir. 2006); *United States v. Beaty*, 245 F.3d 617, 621 (6th Cir. 2001); *United States v. McClellan*, 165 F.3d 535, 549 (7th Cir. 1999); *United States v. King*, 351 F.3d 859, 866 (8th Cir. 2003); *United States v. Puche*, 350 F.3d 1137, 1148 (11th Cir. 2003); *United States v. Aina-Marshall*, 336 F.3d 167, 171 (2d Cir. 2003). Two other circuits have recognized conflicts in their caselaw regarding the appropriate standard of review, but have declined, thus far, to resolve them. *See United States v. Lizardo*, 445 F.3d 73, 85 (1st Cir. 2006); *United States v. McConnel*, 464 F.3d 1152, 1158 n.3 (10th Cir. 2006). The D.C. Circuit has yet to fully endorse the deliberate ignorance instruction. *United States v. Alston-Graves*, 435 F.3d 331, 339–41 (D.C. Cir. 2006).

Section § 841 was initially enacted in 1970. Congress has amended this statute many times. Pub. L. 95–633, title II, § 201, Nov. 10, 1978, 92 Stat. 3774; Pub. L. 96–359, § 8(c), Sept. 26, 1980, 94 Stat. 1194; Pub. L. 98–473, title II, §§ 224(a), 502, 503(b)(1), (2), Oct. 12, 1984, 98 Stat. 2030, 2068, 2070; Pub. L. 99–570, title I, §§ 1002, 1003(a), 1004(a), 1005(a), 1103, title XV, § 15005, Oct. 27, 1986, 100 Stat. 3207–2, 3207–5, 3207–6, 3207–11, 3207–192; Pub. L. 100–690, title VI, §§ 6055, 6254(h), 6452(a), 6470(g), (h), 6479, Nov. 18, 1988, 102 Stat. 4318, 4367, 4371, 4378, 4381; Pub. L. 101–647, title X, § 1002(e), title XII, § 1202, title XXXV, § 3599K, Nov. 29, 1990, 104 Stat. 4828, 4830, 4932; Pub. L. 103–322, title IX, § 90105(a), (c), title XVIII, § 180201(b)(2)(A), Sept. 13, 1994, 108 Stat. 1987, 1988, 2047; Pub. L. 104–237, title II, § 206(a), title III, § 302(a), Oct. 3, 1996, 110 Stat. 3103, 3105; Pub. L. 104–305, § 2(a), (b)(1), Oct. 13, 1996, 110 Stat. 3807; Pub. L. 105–277, div. E, § 2(a), Oct. 21, 1998, 112 Stat. 2681–759; Pub. L. 106–172, §§ 3(b)(1), 5(b), 9, Feb. 18, 2000, 114 Stat. 9, 10, 13; Pub. L. 107–273, div. B, title III, § 3005(a), title IV, § 4002(d)(2)(A), Nov. 2, 2002, 116 Stat. 1805, 1809; Pub. L. 109–177, title VII, §§ 711(f)(1)(B), 732, Mar. 9, 2006, 120 Stat. 262, 270; Pub. L. 109–248, title II, § 201, July 27, 2006, 120 Stat. 611; Pub. L. 110–425, § 3(e), (f), Oct. 15, 2008, 122 Stat. 4828, 4829; Pub. L. 111–220, §§ 2(a), 4(a), Aug. 3, 2010, 124 Stat. 2372.). Not one of these amendments addressed the scienter requirement in section 841(a). Rather, Congress changed sentencing requirements, changed the controlled substances included within specific schedules, or altered penalties.

You are a federal prosecutor in the case of *United States v. Heremia*. The facts are as follows. Carmen Heremia was stopped at an inland Border Patrol checkpoint while driving from Nogales to Tucson, Arizona. Heremia was at the wheel and her two children, mother, and one of her aunts were passengers. The border agent at the scene noticed what he described as a "very strong perfume odor" emanating from the car. A second agent searched the trunk and found 349.2 pounds of marijuana surrounded by dryer sheets, apparently used to mask the odor. Heredia was arrested and charged with possessing a controlled substance with intent to distribute under 21 U.S.C. § 841(a)(1).

At trial, Heremia testified that on the day of her arrest she had accompanied her mother on a bus trip from Tucson to Nogales, where her mother had a dentist's appointment. After the appointment, she borrowed her Aunt's car to transport her mother back to Tucson. Heremia told the DEA Agent at the time of her arrest that, while still in Nogales, she had noticed a "detergent" smell in the car as she prepared for the trip and asked her Aunt to explain. The Aunt told Heremia that she had spilled Downey fabric softener in the car a few days earlier, but Heremia found this explanation incredible.

Heremia admitted on the stand that she suspected there might be drugs in the car, based on the fact that her Aunt was visibly nervous during the trip and carried a large amount of cash, even though she wasn't working at the time. However, Heremia claimed that her suspicions were not aroused until she had passed the last freeway exit before the checkpoint, by which time it was too dangerous to pull over and investigate.

At trial, the government requested a deliberate ignorance instruction, and the judge obliged, overruling Heremia's objection. The instruction read as follows:

> You may find that the defendant acted knowingly if you find, beyond a reasonable doubt, that the defendant was aware of a high probability that drugs were in the vehicle driven by the defendant and deliberately avoided learning the truth. You may not find such knowledge, however, if you find that the defendant actually believed that no drugs were in the vehicle driven by the defendant, or if you find that the defendant was simply careless.

Heremia was convicted. She appeals to the Ninth Circuit. How will Hermia argue that *Jewell* should be overruled such that section 841(a)(1) extends liability only to individuals who act with actual knowledge? How would you respond to her counsel's arguments?

"Knowingly"

State

- Constructive Knowledge
- Absurdity
    - Purpose
- Leg. acq.
    - expect DC an accepted
- Super strong decisis
    - 9th
- Congress amended many times but never changed it

Δ

- Dictionary definition "actual"
arg.
    - Plain meaning
    - Textual context   "OR"
    - Rule of lenity

Chapter 14

Canons Based on Policy-Based Considerations: Constitutional

A. Introduction to This Chapter

We have finished examining the intrinsic and extrinsic sources with the exception of subsequent executive actions. We will cover this in Chapters 16–19. In this chapter and the next, we turn to the third and final source of meaning: policy-based sources. You will remember from Chapter 4 that policy-based sources are sources that are extrinsic both to the statute and to the legislative process. They reflect important social and legal choices derived from the Constitution, social policy, and prudential ideals. These canons protect fundamental constitutional rights, such as due process, and advance particular policy objectives, such as requiring Congress to be clear when it impacts states' rights. There are two types of policy based sources: those based on constitutional considerations and those based on prudential considerations. This chapter will explain the former, while the next chapter will explain the latter.

B. Introduction to Policy-Based Sources

Policy-based sources can play a fundamental role in interpretation. Your education in statutory interpretation would be incomplete without a discussion of these sources and the canons developed to further them. While you will gain an overview of these canons in this chapter, it is critical for you as a lawyer to research the role these canons play within your particular jurisdiction, for jurisdictions vary in their willingness to embrace or reject these sources.

Unlike the canons we have looked at so far, these canons do not claim to be neutral; rather, they value one consideration at the expense of another. For example, the rule of lenity directs judges to adopt the least penal interpretation of an ambiguous criminal statute or civil statute with a penal component. In this example, fair notice trumps penalizing bad behavior.

Because these canons are non-neutral, their use may seem activist. Consider, for example, the 2000 Bush versus Gore election debacle. A Florida canon, derived from that state's constitution, directed Florida judges to construe election statutes so that the right of Florida voters to participate fully in the federal electoral process would be protected. *Palm Beach Cty. Canvassing Bd. v. Harris*, 772 So. 2d 1220, 1237 (Fla. 2000). Hence, the court ordered the Florida Secretary of State to accept some amended returns. *Id.* at 1240. To some, this outcome appeared activist because it favored Democrat Al Gore over Republican George Bush.

Judges' willingness to use a particular policy-based source changes over time and across jurisdictions. For example, the rule of lenity, which arises from constitutional due process concerns about providing adequate notice of penal conduct, has been relegated to a rule of last resort in many states as a result of society's current focus on penalizing criminals. *See, e.g., United States v. Sanchez*, 2008 WL 1926701 at *6– 7 (E.D.N.Y. Apr. 30, 2008) (stating that "the court may resort to the rule of lenity as a last resort") (internal quotations omitted). Indeed, some state legislatures, such as California's, have attempted to abolish the rule of lenity entirely. *See* Cal. Pen. Code § 4. However, because the rule of lenity flows from procedural due process, the California courts have had difficulty discarding it, even though there is a statute directing them to do so. *See, e.g. Wooten v. Superior Court*, 93 Cal. App. 4th 422, 432 (Cal. App. 4th Dist. 2001) (applying the rule of lenity to determine that a customer's observation of sexual contact between two exotic dancers was not a "lewd act" for purposes of a prostitution statute and failing to mention Cal. Pen. Code § 4).

C. Law's Hierarchy

Some of the policy-based canons respect the United States' legal structure. There is a hierarchy of laws in the United States. As you are no doubt aware, the U.S. Constitution is the highest source of law. No statute passed by Congress or any state legislature can conflict with the U.S. Constitution. Statutes that do so are unconstitutional. Thus, to avoid declaring statutes unconstitutional, courts avoid interpreting statutes when possible in a way that would raise a constitutional issue.

The historical development of judicial review is informative. In early England, parliament (the legislature) enjoyed almost unlimited power. In 1610, a "physician" was jailed for practicing medicine without a license. *The Case of the College of Physicians*, 8 Co. Rep. 107a, 77 Eng. Rep. 638 (C.P. 1610) (known as *Bonham's Case*). He sued for false imprisonment. In its defense, the Royal College of Physicians argued that a statute allowed the doctor to be imprisoned and fined. The Chief Justice, Sir Edward Coke, held for the doctor and said in dicta, "[W]hen an Act of Parliament is against common right or reason, or repugnant, or impossible to be performed, the common law will controul it and adjudge such Act to be void." *Id.* at 118a, 77 Eng. Rep. at 652. Despite what some thought at the time, *Bonham's Case* did not actually make English common law supreme over statutory law. *Hurtado v. California*, 110 U.S. 516, 531 (1884) ("[N]otwithstanding what was attributed to Lord Coke in *Bonham's Case* ... the omnipotence of parliament over the common law was absolute ... for English liberty against legislative tyranny was the power of a free public opinion represented by the commons.").

But Coke's dictum set the stage for the acceptance of judicial review of legislation in America by "providing an early foundation for the idea that courts might invalidate legislation that they found inconsistent with a *written* constitution." *Seminole Tribe v. Florida*, 517 U.S. 44, 162 n.56 (1996) (Souter, J., dissenting). Judicial review was, of course, adopted in this country in *Marbury v. Madison*, 5 U.S. (1 Cranch) 137 (1803). As a result, our judiciary has the power to determine whether statutes are constitutional.

The second highest source of law is federal law, first statutes then federal common law. While you may have heard that there is no federal common law, this statement is not quite accurate. It is true that there is no federal common law in areas traditionally reserved to state courts, such as torts and contracts. But, there are two basic areas where federal common law exists. The first area of federal common law includes those areas in which Congress has given federal courts the power to develop substantive law (for example, in admiralty, antitrust, bankruptcy, interstate commerce, and civil rights). The second area of federal common law includes those areas in which a federal rule of decision is necessary to protect interests that are uniquely federal. *Clearfield Trust Co. v. United States*, 318 U.S. 363 (1943) (identifying a three-step test for determining whether a federal common law rule is necessary to protect a significantly important federal interest). Thus, federal common law does exist, but it exists only so long as Congress allows it to exist.

Next on the hierarchy are federal regulations. Federal regulations are legislative-like rules that federal administrative agencies promulgate. First, Congress enacts a statute granting an agency the power to regulate, called the enabling statute. This enabling statute defines the boundaries of the administrative agency's regulatory power. Second, the agency promulgates a regulation to exercise its delegated power. So long as the agency stays within the boundaries of the delegated power, the regulations are generally valid. When an agency steps outside of its parameters, however, any regulations are *ultra vires,* or invalid. Linda D. Jellum, *Dodging the Taxman: Why Treasury's Anti-Abuse Regulation is Unconstitutional*, 70 Miami L. Rev. 152, 204 (2015) (describing the difference between unconstitutional and *ultra vires*). For example, the Environmental Protection Agency (EPA) has the power to regulate environmental issues. However, the EPA has no power to regulate international trade or taxes.

Federal law of any kind trumps state law. The U.S. Constitution explicitly places federal law above state law, even state constitutions. Under the Supremacy Clause of the Constitution, federal law "preempts" state laws that conflict with it. U.S. Const., art. 6, Cl. 2. Thus, for example, if a federal statute required gasoline to be lead-free, a state law that permitted the sale of leaded gasoline would conflict with federal law, would be preempted, and would be unconstitutional. *But see Oxygenated Fuels Ass'n, Inc. v. Davis,* 331 F.3d 665 (9th Cir. 2003) (rejecting preemption claim when California banned a chemical used to reduce gasoline emissions).

Although it occupies a lower tier of our legal hierarchy, state law is the overwhelming source of most rights and obligations. Virtually all tort law, contract law, and property law comes from state statutes and cases. State law comes in four forms: constitutions, statutes, common law, and regulations. Each state has its own constitution. Many of them differ in important respects from the U.S. Constitution, often by providing for greater protection than the federal one. State constitutions can legitimately provide more protection to state citizens than the U.S. Constitution; however, state constitutions cannot provide less protection.

Just as all federal statutes must be constitutional under the U.S. Constitution, each state statute must be constitutional under that state's constitution. A state statute that conflicts with its state's constitution is unconstitutional. Accordingly, state courts endeavor to interpret state statutes to be constitutional, just as federal courts do the same with respect to the federal Constitution. And, similar to federal agencies, state agencies have the power to enact rules. State law creates one additional issue that seldom arises in connection with construing federal statutes: State statutes can conflict with state common law. Thus, courts must determine how to interpret state statutes that conflict with state common law. The next sections explore how courts interpret statutes in light of these hierarchies, starting with the constitutional avoidance doctrine.

D. Policy-Based Canons Based on the Constitution

1. The Constitutional Avoidance Doctrine

The constitutional avoidance doctrine is a statutory canon that respects this hierarchy. We studied it in Chapter 6, because it is one doctrine that allows judges to reject the ordinary meaning of clear text. You should reread that section if you have forgotten the doctrine's relevance. In this section, we explore the role that this doctrine plays in respecting separation of powers and the Constitution. In the case below, was the doctrine appropriate, meaning were there two fair and reasonable interpretations? Or did the Court "do interpretive handsprings to avoid having even to *decide* a constitutional question"? *United States v. Marshall*, 908 F.2d 1312, 1335 (7th Cir. 1990) (en banc) (Cummings, Posner JJ., dissenting), *aff'd sub nom, Chapman v. United States*, 500 U.S. 453 (1991).

NLRB v. Catholic Bishop of Chicago
Supreme Court of the United States
440 U.S. 490 (1979)

◆ Chief Justice Burger delivered the opinion of the Court [in which Steward, Powell, Rehnquist, and Stevens, JJ. concur].

This case arises out of the National Labor Relations Board's exercise of jurisdiction over lay faculty members at two groups of Catholic high schools. We granted certiorari to consider two questions: (a) Whether teachers in schools operated by a church to teach both religious and secular subjects are within the jurisdiction granted by the

National Labor Relations Act; and (b) if the Act authorizes such jurisdiction, does its exercise violate the guarantees of the Religion Clauses of the First Amendment?

[The National Labor Relations Act, 29 U.S.C. § 152 et seq. (2006) gives employees the right to organize, form, or join a labor organization to bargain collectively, and to participate in concerted activity for the purpose of collective bargaining. There is no express exception in the statute for educational or other charitable institutions or their employees.

For many years, the NLRB declined to exercise jurisdiction over the employees of nonprofit educational institutions, both secular and religious. In 1970, the NLRB changed its policy, deciding that nonprofit educational institutions whose operations had a substantial effect on interstate commerce were within the scope of the Act. With respect to religious schools specifically, the NLRB would henceforth exercise jurisdiction when a school was "merely religiously associated," but not when the school was "completely religious." Two church operated high schools challenged the NLRB's finding that they had violated the Act by refusing to recognize or to bargain with unions representing the lay faculty members at the schools. The issue for the Court was whether the schools were "employers" within the meaning of the Act. Section 152(2) defines that term as explained by the dissenting opinion.]

... That there are constitutional limitations on the Board's actions has been repeatedly recognized by this Court even while acknowledging the broad scope of the grant of jurisdiction. The First Amendment, of course, is a limitation on the power of Congress. Thus, if we were to conclude that the Act granted the challenged jurisdiction over these teachers we would be required to decide whether that was constitutionally permissible under the Religion Clauses of the First Amendment.

Although the respondents press their claims under the Religion Clauses, the question we consider first is whether Congress intended the Board to have jurisdiction over teachers in church-operated schools. In a number of cases the Court has heeded the essence of Mr. Chief Justice Marshall's admonition in *Murray v. The Charming Betsy*, 2 Cranch 64, 118 (1804), by holding that an Act of Congress ought not be construed to violate the Constitution if any other possible construction remains available....

In *Machinists v. Street*, 367 U.S. 740 (1961), for example, the Court considered claims that serious First Amendment questions would arise if the Railway Labor Act were construed to allow compulsory union dues to be used to support political candidates or causes not approved by some members. The Court looked to the language of the Act and the legislative history and concluded that they did not permit union dues to be used for such political purposes, thus avoiding "serious doubt of [the Act's] constitutionality."

Similarly in *McCulloch v. Sociedad Nacional de Marineros de Honduras*, 372 U.S. 10 (1963), a case involving the Board's assertion of jurisdiction over foreign seamen, the Court declined to read the National Labor Relations Act so as to give rise to a serious question of separation of powers which in turn would have implicated sensitive issues of the authority of the Executive over relations with foreign nations. The international implications of the case led the Court to describe it as involving "public questions particularly high in the scale of our national interest." *Id.* Because of those questions the Court held that before sanctioning the Board's exercise of jurisdiction "'there must be present the affirmative intention of the Congress clearly expressed.'"

The values enshrined in the First Amendment plainly rank high "in the scale of our national values." In keeping with the Court's prudential policy it is incumbent on us to determine whether the Board's exercise of its jurisdiction here would give rise to serious constitutional questions. If so, we must first identify "the affirmative intention of the Congress clearly expressed" before concluding that the Act grants jurisdiction....

There is no clear expression of an affirmative intention of Congress that teachers in church-operated schools should be covered by the Act. Admittedly, Congress defined the Board's jurisdiction in very broad terms; we must therefore examine the legislative history of the Act to determine whether Congress contemplated that the grant of jurisdiction would include teachers in such schools.

In enacting the National Labor Relations Act in 1935, Congress sought to protect the right of American workers to bargain collectively. The concern that was repeated throughout the debates was the need to assure workers the right to organize to counterbalance the collective activities of employers which had been authorized by the National Industrial Recovery Act. But congressional attention focused on employment in private industry and on industrial recovery.

Our examination of the statute and its legislative history indicates that Congress simply gave no consideration to church-operated schools. It is not without significance, however, that the Senate Committee on Education and Labor chose a college professor's dispute with the college as an example of employer-employee relations *not* covered by the Act....

The absence of an "affirmative intention of the Congress clearly expressed" fortifies our conclusion that Congress did not contemplate that the Board would require church-operated schools to grant recognition to unions as bargaining agents for their teachers....

Accordingly, in the absence of a clear expression of Congress' intent to bring teachers in church-operated schools within the jurisdiction of the Board, we decline to construe the Act in a manner that could in turn call upon the Court to resolve difficult and sensitive questions arising out of the guarantees of the First Amendment Religion Clauses....

◆ JUSTICE BRENNAN, with whom WHITE, MARSHALL, and BLACKMUN, JJ. join, dissenting.

The Court today holds that coverage of the National Labor Relations Act does not extend to lay teachers employed by church-operated schools. That construction is plainly wrong in light of the Act's language, its legislative history, and this Court's precedents. It is justified solely on the basis of a canon of statutory construction seemingly invented by the Court for the purpose of deciding this case. I dissent.

The general principle of construing statutes to avoid unnecessary constitutional decisions is a well-settled and salutary one. The governing canon, however, is *not* that expressed by the Court today. The Court requires that there be a "clear expression of an affirmative intention of Congress" before it will bring within the coverage of a broadly worded regulatory statute certain persons whose coverage might raise constitutional questions. But those familiar with the legislative process know that explicit expressions of congressional intent in such broadly inclusive statutes are not commonplace. Thus, by strictly or loosely applying its requirement, the Court can virtually remake congressional enactments. This flouts Mr. Chief Justice Taft's admonition "that amendment may not be substituted for construction, and that a court may not exercise legislative functions to save [a] law from conflict with constitutional limitation."[1]

The settled canon for construing statutes wherein constitutional questions may lurk was stated in *Machinists v. Street*, 367 U. S. 740 (1961):

> When the validity of an act of the Congress is drawn in question, and even if a serious doubt of constitutionality is raised, it is a cardinal principle that this Court will first ascertain whether a construction of the statute is *fairly possible* by which the question may be avoided.

This limitation to constructions that are "fairly possible," and "reasonable," acts as a brake against wholesale judicial dismemberment of congressional enactments. It confines the judiciary to its proper role in construing statutes, which is to interpret them so as to give effect to congressional intention. The Court's new "affirmative expression" rule releases that brake.

The interpretation of the National Labor Relations Act announced by the Court today is not "fairly possible." The Act's wording, its legislative history, and the Court's own precedents leave "the intention of the Congress ... revealed too distinctly to permit us to ignore it because of mere misgivings as to power."

Section 2(2) of the Act, 29 U.S.C. § 152(2), defines "employer" as

> " ... any person acting as an agent of an employer, directly or indirectly, *but shall not include* the United States or any wholly owned Government corpo-

---

1. The Court's new canon derives from the statement, "'there must be present the affirmative intention of the Congress clearly expressed,'" in *McCulloch v. Sociedad Nacional de Marineros de Honduras*, 372 U.S. 10, 21–22 (1963). Reliance upon that case here is clearly misplaced. The question in *McCulloch* was whether the National Labor Relations Act extended to foreign seamen working aboard foreign-flag vessels. No question as to the constitutional power of Congress to cover foreign crews was presented. Indeed, all parties agreed that Congress was constitutionally empowered to reach the foreign seamen involved while they were in American waters. The only question was whether Congress had intended to do so.

The *McCulloch* Court [relied] upon the fact ... that the legislative history "'inescapably describe[d] the boundaries of the Act as including only the workingmen of our own country and its possessions.'" ... In light of that contrary legislative history..., it is not at all surprising that *McCulloch* balked at holding foreign seamen covered without a strong affirmative showing of congressional intent. As the Court today admits, there is no such contrary legislative history or precedent with respect to jurisdiction over church-operated schools. The *McCulloch* statement, therefore, has no role to play in this case.

ration, or any Federal Reserve Bank, or any State or political subdivision thereof, or any person subject to the Railway Labor Act, as amended from time to time, or any labor organization (other than when acting as an employer), or anyone acting in the capacity of officer or agent of such labor organization." (Emphasis added.)

Thus, the Act covers all employers not within the eight express exceptions. The Court today substitutes amendment for construction to insert one more exception—for church-operated schools. This is a particularly transparent violation of the judicial role: The legislative history reveals that Congress itself considered and rejected a very similar amendment....

The Hartley bill, which passed the House of Representatives in 1947..., would have provided the exception the Court today writes into the statute:

> "The term 'employer'... shall not include ... any corporation, community chest, fund, or foundation organized and operated exclusively for *religious*, charitable, scientific, literary, or *educational* purposes, ... no part of the net earnings of which inures to the benefit of any private shareholder or individual...."

(Emphasis added.)

In construing the Board's jurisdiction to exclude church-operated schools, therefore, the Court today is faithful to neither the statute's language nor its history....

Under my view that the NLRA includes within its coverage lay teachers employed by church-operated schools, the constitutional questions presented would have to be reached. I do not now do so only because the Court does not. I repeat for emphasis, however, that while the resolution of the constitutional question is not without difficulty, it is irresponsible to avoid it by a cavalier exercise in statutory interpretation which succeeds only in defying congressional intent. A statute is not "a nose OF WAX TO BE CHANGED FROM THAT WHICH THE PLAIN LANGUAGE IMPORTS...."

* * *

Points for Discussion

1. *Statutory Language*: What was the language at issue? What did each party want that language to mean? What meaning did the majority and dissent adopt?

2. *Theories*: Which theory did the majority use? The dissent? Did either find ambiguity, absurdity, a constitutional issue to avoid, or scrivener's error?

3. *Separation of Powers*: How does the constitutional avoidance doctrine further separation of powers? Why did the dissent criticize the majority for "exercise[ing] legislative functions"? What theory of separation of powers did each opinion follow?

4. *Applying the Constitutional Avoidance Doctrine*: According to the majority, when should the constitutional avoidance doctrine be applied? Is this an easy or hard threshold to meet? According to the dissent, when should the doctrine be applied? Is this an easy or hard to reach threshold to meet? The dissent charged the majority

with inventing "a canon of statutory construction seemingly ... for the purpose of deciding this case." How did the majority reformulate the constitutional avoidance doctrine?

5. *Clear Statement Rules*: The majority cited the following language from *McCulloch v. Sociedad Nacional de Marineros de Honduras*: "there must be present the affirmative intention of the Congress clearly expressed." Why, according to the dissent was the majority's reliance misplaced? This language is known as a clear statement rule. We will learn about clear statement rules at the end of this chapter. Notice here, however, that the majority refused to interpret the statute in a way that would raise a constitutional question without a clear statement from Congress that it intended the constitutional question to be raised. The majority then concluded that Congress never considered this issue at all and, thus, did not provide the required clear statement.

6. *Expressio Unius*: The statute included eight types of employers that were expressly exempt from the statute's coverage. The statute did not include a general catch-all. Did either the majority or dissent discuss this canon?

7. *Legislative History*: A bill was introduced that would have added religious organizations to the eight excluded employers. The bill was rejected. Does the failed bill support either side?

8. *Constitutional Question*: The constitutional avoidance is a doctrine by which a court avoids having to resolve a constitutional issue. When applying the doctrine, a court must ask two questions. First, a court must ask whether a fair interpretation exists that would avoid the constitutional question; if so, then the court will adopt that interpretation. Second, if there is no such alterative interpretation, then the court must address the constitutional issue.

    In this case, the majority phrased the first question as whether Congress clearly expressed its intent to include teachers in church operated schools within the jurisdiction the National Labor Relations Act grants to the NLRB. Because the majority answered this question in the negative, it did not reach the second question. In contrast, the dissent answered the first question in the affirmative; hence, the dissent would have reached the constitutional question, namely, does the Act violate the Religion Clauses of the First Amendment. The dissent chose to skip this step.

* * *

2. The Rule of Lenity and Penal Statutes

The next canon, the rule of lenity, is based on concerns about the Fifth (and Fourteenth) Amendment's guarantee of procedural due process—specifically, the right to fair notice. Pursuant to the *rule of lenity*, judges should strictly interpret penal statutes, which are statutes that impose a fine or imprisonment to punish citizens. Why? Historically, the rule of lenity flourished in seventeenth and eighteenth century

England as a result of statutory proliferation. Citizens grew nervous about the expansion of parliamentary power. English judges took on the role of guardian of individual liberty against legislative intrusions. One way judges could limit this expansion was by narrowly construing criminal statutes.

In this country, the U.S. Constitution (and all state constitutions for that matter) requires notice before the government can deprive a person of a protected interest involving life, liberty, or property. If a statute does not clearly and unambiguously target specific conduct, an individual should not be penalized, because that individual would not have had notice prior to the deprivation. Thus, the rule of lenity furthers the Constitution's promise that people should have fair warning of crimes before they are penalized. "[I]ndividuals should not languish in prison unless the legislature has clearly articulated precisely what conduct constitutes a crime." *United States v. Gonzalez*, 407 F.3d 118, 125 (2d Cir. 2005). "When language which is susceptible of two constructions is used in a penal law, the policy of this state is to construe the statute as favorably to the defendant as its language and the circumstance of its application reasonably permit. The defendant is entitled to the benefit of every reasonable doubt as to the true interpretation of words or the construction of a statute." *Wooten v. Superior Court*, 93 Cal. App. 4th 422, 429 (2001). Although ignorance of the law is no defense, in this country, those accused of crimes should be able to know what the law is should they bother to check.

The rule of lenity also furthers a second consideration; one that relates to the power distribution between the judiciary and the legislature. Congress defines crimes in statutes; judges have no power to determine that an activity not clearly criminalized by a statute should be penalized. In other words, if judges included activity not explicitly covered in the statutory language, they would be expanding the statute's reach. *United States v. Bass*, 404 U.S. 336, 347–48 (1971) ("[L]egislatures and not courts should define criminal activity."). In this quote, the California appellate court identified both points:

> Application of the rule of lenity ensures that criminal statutes will provide fair warning concerning conduct rendered illegal and strikes the appropriate balance between the legislature, the prosecutor, and the court in defining criminal liability. (Citation omitted in original.) ("[B]ecause of the seriousness of criminal penalties, and because criminal punishment usually represents the moral condemnation of the community, legislatures and not courts should define criminal activity"). (Citation omitted in original.) [C]riminal penalties, because they are particularly serious and opprobrious, merit heightened due process protections for those in jeopardy of being subject to them, including the strict construction of criminal statutes.

Wooten, 93 Cal. App. 4th at 429.

Thus, the rule of lenity furthers separation of powers and respects the constitutional power distribution. You will see this concern in the case excerpted below.

Keeler v. Superior Court

Supreme Court of California
470 P.2d 617 (Cal. 1970)

◆ Mosk, Justice [with whom McComb, Peters, Tobriner, Peek, JJ. concur].

In this proceeding for writ of prohibition we are called upon to decide whether an unborn but viable fetus is a 'human being' within the meaning of the California statute defining murder (Pen.Code, s 187). We conclude that the Legislature did not intend such a meaning, and that for us to construe the statute to the contrary and apply it to this petitioner would exceed our judicial power and deny petitioner due process of law.

[The Keeler's divorced after 16 years of marriage. Unknown to Mr. Keeler, Ms. Keeler was pregnant with another man's child. When Mr. Keeler learned of her pregnancy, he was extremely upset. He confronted her and said, "I'm going to stomp it out of you." He pushed her, shoved his knee into her abdomen, and struck her in the face with several blows.... The fetus did not survive the attack. After the autopsy, a physician found that the fetus's head was severely fractured. Cause of death was the skull fracture and consequent cerebral hemorrhaging. The fetus would have had a 75 percent to 96 percent chance of survival had it be born prematurely on the day of the assault.]

… An information was filed charging petitioner, in Count I, with committing the crime of murder in that he did 'unlawfully kill a human being, to wit Baby Girl Vogt, with malice aforethought.'....

Penal Code section 187 provides: 'Murder is the unlawful killing of a human being, with malice aforethought.' The dispositive question is whether the fetus which petitioner is accused of killing was, on February 23, 1969, a 'human being' within the meaning of this statute. If it was not, petitioner cannot be charged with its 'murder'...

Section 187 was enacted as part of the Penal Code of 1872.... [T]he Legislature ... intended that term ["human being'] to have the settled common law meaning of a person who had been born alive, and did not intend the act of feticide—as distinguished from abortion—to be an offense under the laws of California....

It is the policy of this state to construe a penal statute as favorably to the defendant as its language and the circumstances of its application may reasonably permit; just as in the case of a question of fact, the defendant is entitled to the benefit of every reasonable doubt as to the true interpretation of words or the construction of language used in a statute. We hold that in adopting the definition of murder in Penal Code section 187 [in 1872] the Legislature intended to exclude from its reach the act of killing an unborn fetus.

The People urge, however, that the sciences of obstetrics and pediatrics have greatly progressed since 1872, to the point where with proper medical care a normally developed fetus prematurely born at 28 weeks or more has an excellent chance of survival, i.e., is 'viable'; that the common law requirement of live birth to prove the fetus had become a 'human being' who may be the victim of murder is no longer in accord with scientific fact, since an unborn but viable fetus is now fully capable of independent life; and that one who unlawfully and maliciously terminates such a life should therefore be liable to prosecution for murder under section 187. We may grant the premises of this argument; indeed, we neither deny nor denigrate the vast progress of medicine in the century since the enactment of the Penal Code. But we cannot join in the conclusion sought to be deduced: we cannot hold this petitioner to answer for murder by reason of his alleged act of killing an unborn — even though viable — fetus. To such a charge there are two insuperable obstacles, one 'jurisdictional' and the other constitutional.

Penal Code section 6 declares in relevant part that 'No act or omission' accomplished after the code has taken effect 'is criminal or punishable, except as prescribed or authorized by this Code, or by some of the statutes which it specifies as continuing in force and as not affected by its provisions, or by some ordinance, municipal, county, or township regulation * * *. This section embodies a fundamental principle of our tripartite form of government, i.e., that subject to the constitutional prohibition against cruel and unusual punishment, the power to define crimes and fix penalties is vested exclusively in the legislative branch. Stated differently, there are no common law crimes in California. 'In this state the common law is of no effect so far as the specification of what acts or conduct shall constitute a crime is concerned. In order that a public offense be committed, some statute, ordinance or regulation prior in time to the commission of the act must denounce it; likewise with excuses or justifications — if no statutory excuse or justification apply as to the commission of the particular offense, neither the common law nor the so-called 'unwritten law' may legally supply it.'

Settled rules of construction implement this principle. Although the Penal Code commands us to construe its provisions 'according to the fair import of their terms, with a view to effect its objects and to promote justice' (Pen. Code, § 4), it is clear the courts cannot go so far as to create an offense by enlarging a statute, by inserting or deleting words, or by giving the terms used false or unusual meanings. Penal statutes will not be made to reach beyond their plain intent; they include only those offenses coming clearly within the import of their language. Indeed, 'Constructive crimes — crimes built up by courts with the aid of inference, implication, and strained interpretation — are repugnant to the spirit and letter of English and American criminal law.'

Applying these rules to the case at bar, we would undoubtedly act in excess of the judicial power if we were to adopt the People's proposed construction of section 187. As we have shown, the Legislature has defined the crime of murder in California to apply only to the unlawful and malicious killing of one who has been born alive. We recognize that the killing of an unborn but viable fetus may be deemed by some to be an offense of similar nature and gravity; but as Chief Justice Marshall warned long ago, 'It would be dangerous, indeed, to carry the principle, that a case which is within the reason or mischief of a statute, is within its provisions, so far as to punish a crime not enumerated in the statute, because it is of equal atrocity, or of kindred character, with those which are enumerated.' Whether to thus extend liability for murder in California is a determination solely within the province of the Legislature. For a court to simply declare, by judicial fiat, that the time has now come to prosecute under section 187 one who kills an unborn but viable fetus would indeed be to rewrite the statute under the guise of construing it. Nor does a need to fill an asserted 'gap' in the law between abortion and homicide ... justify judicial legislation of this nature: to make it 'a judicial function 'to explore such new fields of crime as they may appear from time to time' is wholly foreign to the American concept of criminal justice' and 'raises very serious questions concerning the principle of separation of powers.'

The second obstacle to the proposed judicial enlargement of section 187 is the guarantee of due process of law. Assuming Arguendo that we have the power to adopt the new construction of this statute as the law of California, such a ruling, by constitutional command, could operate only prospectively, and thus could not in any event reach the conduct of petitioner on February 23, 1969.... [The court refuses this interpretation, reasoning that such an interpretation would be an unconstitutional ex post facto law.]

We conclude that the judicial enlargement of section 187 now urged upon us by the People would not have been foreseeable to this petitioner, and hence that its adoption at this time would deny him due process of law.

* * *

Points for Discussion

1. *Statutory Language*: What was the language at issue? What did each party want that language to mean? What meaning did the court adopt?

2. *Theories*: Which theory did the court use? Did the court find ambiguity, absurdity, a constitutional issue to avoid, or a scrivener's error?

3. *Separation of Powers*: The rule of lenity furthers separation of powers. As the Supreme Court explained in *United States v. Santos*, 553 U.S. 507, 514 (2008):

   This venerable rule not only vindicates the fundamental principle that no citizen should be held accountable for a violation of a statute whose commands are uncertain, or subjected to punishment that is not clearly prescribed. It also places the weight of inertia upon the party that can best induce Congress to speak more clearly and keeps courts from making criminal law in Congress's stead.

4. *The Rule of Lenity*: The court did not refer to the rule of lenity by name. Can you find the reference to it anyway?

5. *Two Insuperable Obstacles*: The state argued that because of scientific advances, the court should reject the legislature's 1872 intent. The court identified two obstacles to doing so, one "jurisdictional" and the other constitutional. The first concern related to separation of powers while the second related to retroactivity of a criminal statute. Both of these concerns are constitutional. What were the

court's concerns? We will cover retroactive statutes, both civil and criminal in the next two sections.

6. *The Anti-Rule of Lenity Statute*: California Penal Code § 4 impliedly directed the court not to apply the rule of lenity, but rather "to construe [penal] provisions according to the fair import of their terms, with a view to effect its objects and to promote justice." Why did the court refuse to follow the anti-rule of lenity statute and chose to interpret broadly the penal statute at issue?

7. *Trump Card or Rule of Last Resort*: The question of exactly when to apply the rule of lenity is subject to some controversy. Should a defendant "win" from the start if ambiguity appears on the face of the statute or should all sources of meaning be explored first? Alternatively, should the government "win" from the start if the statute is mostly clear? In other words, should the canon be a rule of first or last resort: a trump card or a tie breaker? Some courts suggest that the rule "applies only if, after seizing everything from which aid can be derived, … we can make no more than a guess as to what Congress intended." *United States* v. *Wells*, 519 U.S. 482, 499 (1997) (internal citations omitted). With this interpretation, the rule of lenity is not the starting point for analysis, but it is effectively the end.

However, the Supreme Court has said that the rule of lenity is premised on the idea that "fair warning should be given to the world in language that the common world will understand, of what the law intends to do if a certain line is passed." *Babbitt v. Sweet Home Chapter of Communities for a Great Or.*, 515 U.S. 687, 704 n.18 (1995). This language suggests the rule of lenity should come earlier in the analysis. *Accord State v. Courchesne*, 816 A.2d 562, 618 n.24 (Zarella, J., dissenting) ("I would leave for another day the question of whether, because of the constitutional underpinnings embodied in its fair warning rationale, the rule of lenity should be employed immediately upon determining that the text of a criminal statute is ambiguous, or whether it should, along with other substantive presumptions, be employed only as a last resort after all of the relevant tools of construction have been employed."). But the Supreme Court subsequently cautioned, "this Court has never held that the rule of lenity automatically permits a defendant to win." *Muscarello v. United States*, 524 U.S. 125, 139 (1998). *Muscarello* suggests that the rule of lenity should be applied only when the other sources have failed to resolve the ambiguity. *Accord Reno v. Koray*, 515 U.S. 50, 65 (1995); *Moskal v. United States*, 498 U.S. 103, 108 (1990).

While the canon may have been applied as a rule of first resort in the past, today other sources of meaning are usually explored before the canon is applied. *United States v. Gonzalez*, 407 F.3d 118, 125 (2005) (stating that the canon "is not a catch-all maxim that resolves all disputes in the defendant's favor — a sort of juristical 'tie goes to the runner.'"). Commonly courts do not apply the canon when the statutory text is ambiguous, rather they apply the canon only when the ambiguity remains after the court has examined most other sources of meaning, including legislative history and statutory purpose. *Reno*, 515 U.S. at 65; *Moskal*, 498 U.S. at 108 (stating that the canon is reserved "for those situations in which a reasonable doubt persists about a statute's intended scope even *after* resort to the language and structure, legislative history, and motivating policies of the statute."); *McNally v. United States*, 483 U.S. 350, 375 (1987) (Stevens, J., dissenting) (arguing that because the mail fraud statute was clear, the rule of lenity was inapplicable); *Modern Muzzleloading, Inc. v. Magaw*, 18 F. Supp. 2d 29, 33 (D.D.C. 1998) (refusing to apply the rule of lenity because the statute was not "*grievously ambiguous*").

8. *The Alternate Interpretation*: Regardless of when it is applied and like the constitutional avoidance doctrine, this canon also requires that the alternate interpretation be a *fair* or *reasonable* interpretation of the statute. "[A]n appellate court should not strain to interpret a penal statute in defendant's favor if it can fairly discern a contrary legislative intent." *People v. Avery*, 38 P.3d 1, 6 (Cal. 2002).

9. *Civil v. Criminal Use*: While the rule of lenity applies to both criminal statutes and civil statutes that have a penal component, judges are reluctant to rely too heavily on the canon when interpreting civil statutes. *See, e.g., Babbitt v. Sweet Home Chapter*, 515 U.S. 687, 704 n.18 (1995) (refusing to apply the rule of lenity to create ambiguity in the word "harm" in the Endangered Species Act because "the rule of lenity should [not] provide the standard for reviewing facial challenges to administrative regulations whenever the governing statute authorizes criminal enforcement."). But that is not to say that the courts will not consider this canon in civil cases. *See, e.g., United States v. Thompson/Center Arms Co.*, 504 U.S. 505 (1992); *Modern Muzzleloading, Inc. v. Magaw*, 18 F. Supp. 2d 29 (D.D.C. 1998).

10. *Rejecting the Rule of Lenity*: In the past, the rule of lenity was applied relatively often in criminal cases. *See, e.g., McNally v. United States*, 483 U.S. 350, 360 (1987) (stating "when there are two rational readings of a criminal statute, one harsher than the other, we are to choose the harsher only when Congress has spoken in clear and definite language."). Judges and legislatures are less enthusiastic about the rule of lenity today than was true in the past. The South Carolina Supreme Court refused to apply the rule of lenity to the word "child" in a child abuse and endangerment statute. *Whittner v. State*, 492 S.E.2d 777 (S.C. 1977). The mother had been convicted for smoking crack in her third trimester. The statute criminalized neglect of a "child," which was defined as "a person under the age of eighteen." The issue for the court was whether a fetus was a child. The majority claimed to find the term "child" to be clear and unambiguous after a thorough analysis and, therefore, refused to apply the rule of lenity. *Id.* at 784. Disagreeing by saying that the language was ambiguous, the dissent noted that the majority should have applied the rule of lenity: "I cannot accept the majority's assertion that the child abuse and neglect statute unambiguously includes a 'viable fetus.' If that is the case, then why is the majority compelled to go to such great lengths to ascertain that a 'viable fetus' is a 'child?'" *Id.* at 787–88 (Fine, C.J., dissenting).

11. *State Courts*: The rule of lenity applies in many state courts. *E.g., People v. Powell*, 839 N.E.2d 1008, 1018 (Ill. 2005). However, some state legislatures, such as those in New York and California, have attempted to abrogate it by statute. For example, a California statute provides, "The rule of the common law, that penal statutes

are to be strictly construed, has no application to this Code." Cal. Penal Code § 4 (2015). But because the rule of lenity rests on constitutional concerns, courts are understandably reluctant to eliminate it entirely. Thus, in New York, the Court of Appeals cautioned that "[a]lthough [the anti-lenity statute] obviously does not justify the imposition of criminal sanctions for conduct that falls beyond the scope of the Penal Law, it does authorize a court to dispense with hypertechnical or strained interpretations...." *People v. Ditta*, 422 N.E.2d 515, 517 (N.Y. 1981). Similarly, the California courts have explained that "while ... the rule of [lenity] ... has been abrogated ... it is also true that the defendant is entitled to the benefit of every reasonable doubt, whether it arises out of a question of fact, or as to the true interpretation of words or the construction of language used in a statute." *People v. Superior Court*, 926 P.2d 1042, 1056 (Cal. 1996) (citations omitted).

12. *Federal Approach*: The rule of lenity generally remains viable in the federal arena although Congress attempted in at least one instance to limit its reach. The federal Racketeer Influenced and Corrupt Organization Act specifically directs that its "provisions ... be liberally construed to effectuate [the bill's] remedial purposes...." Pub. L. No. 91-452, § 904(a), 84 Stat. 922 (1970). Like the state courts, the federal courts have refused to apply this "anti-lenity" provision broadly, instead limiting its application to the civil aspects of the Act. *Keystone Ins. Co. v. Houghton*, 863 F.2d 1125, 1128 (3d Cir. 1988) ("[A]pplicability of the liberal construction standard has been questioned in *criminal* RICO cases in view of the general canon of interpretation that ambiguities in criminal statutes are to be construed in favor of leniency....") (emphasis added). Thus, at least in the criminal context, the rule of lenity can provide some powerful arguments for a criminal defendant. But a good prosecutor will be aware of the rule's limitations and current use as a canon of last resort.

* * *

3. Retroactive Civil Statutes

As you saw in the last case, sometimes judges must determine whether a particular statute was meant to apply to past behavior. Legislatures have the power to amend statutes and to decide that the amended statute applies to events occurring before the statute's effective date, meaning it has retroactive effect. Legislatures normally enact statutes with prospective effect. For a variety of reasons—most notably that statutes that apply retroactively may violate due process—statutes generally apply to future conduct. Less commonly legislatures enact statutes with retroactive effect as well. Hence, the retroactivity canon presumes that statutes are not retroactive.

For example, in *Landgraf*, an employee sued her former employer for a co-worker's sexual harassment and retaliation. *Landgraf v. USI Film Prods.*, 511 U.S. 244, 248 (1994). At the time she sued, Title VII did not authorize any recovery of damages even though the plaintiff had been injured. *Id.* at 250. While the action was pending, however, the Civil Rights Act of 1991 was enacted, which created a right to recover compensatory and punitive damages for violations of Title VII and provided for a jury trial when such damages were claimed. *Id.* at 249. Plaintiff argued that the Act applied retroactively to her case. Applying the presumption against retroactivity, the Court disagreed and held that the Act did not apply to cases pending on appeal when it was enacted. *Id.* at 286.

The canon against retroactivity is only a presumption, because retroactivity provisions can serve legitimate purposes. For example, such provisions allow a legislature to respond to emergencies, to correct mistakes, to prevent circumvention of a new statute in the interval immediately preceding its passage, and to give comprehensive effect to a new law. The requirement that a legislature clearly state its intention to make a statute retroactive helps ensure that the legislature actually thought about this issue and concluded that the benefits of retroactivity outweighed the potential for disruption or unfairness.

The applicable canon thus states that civil statutes are applied prospectively rather than retroactively absent a retroactivity provision or clear legislative intent to the contrary. In other words, prospective application is the default. *Landgraf*, 511 U.S. at 286 (Scalia, J., concurring) ("a legislative enactment affecting substantive rights does not apply retroactively absent [a] *clear statement* to the contrary.") Prospective application is the default because "[e]lementary considerations of fairness dictate that individuals should have an opportunity to know what the law is and to conform their conduct accordingly; settled expectations should not be lightly disrupted." *Id.* at 265. Additionally, the *Ex Post Facto Clause* of the U.S. Constitution flatly prohibits retroactive application of *penal* legislation; thus, retroactivity issues should arise primarily in civil actions. We will explore the retroactive effect of penal statutes in more detail in the next section; this section is limited to the application of this canon in civil cases.

Before deciding whether a statute is *impermissibly* retroactive, a court must ask first whether the effect of a statute is retroactive. A statute has retroactive effect when the statute defines the legal significance of actions or events that occurred prior to the statute's enactment. *See, e.g., State Ethics Comm'n v. Evans*, 855 A.2d 364 (Md. 2004). Simply because a statute is retroactive does not make it *impermissibly* retroactive. Retroactive statutes are allowable in certain situations. A statute may apply retroactively when (1) there is clear evidence that the legislature intended retroactive effect, and (2) no vested right is impaired. *Id.* at 374. The first caveat is a statutory interpretation caveat, while the latter caveat is a constitutional one. *Id.* Hence, we will explore only the first caveat.

As noted, evidence that the legislature intended retroactive effect can rebut the presumption against retroactivity, but such evidence is not found easily. For example, in *McClung v. Employment Development Department*, 99 P.3d 1015 (Cal. 2004), the Supreme Court of California rejected an argument that a statute that had been amended was retroactive despite language in the amended statute that it was meant to clarify the unamended version. *Id.* at 1021.

The facts of *McClung* are largely irrelevant, but the procedural history is central. In an earlier case, *Carrisales v. Department of Corrections*, 988 P.2d 1083 (1999), the court had interpreted a California statute prohibiting employment discrimination to impose liability on employers, but not on nonsupervisory employees. The state legislature did not agree with the *Carrisales* decision. Thus, following *Carrisales*, the state legislature amended the statute to impose personal liability on nonsupervisory employees who committed harassment. Importantly, the legislature added language to the amendment that said it was "declaratory of existing law" to make it clear that the court in *Carrisales* had been wrong. *McClung*, 99 P.3d at 1017 (citing Cal. Gov't Code § 12940(j)(2)). The issue for the court was whether the amendment should have retroactive effect (1) when the amendment stated that it simply declared existing law, and (2) when the amendment conflicted with an existing judicial interpretation of that statute.

The court noted that if the amendment merely stated existing law, then the issue of retroactivity would not be presented because a statute that merely clarifies existing law and does not change existing law would have no retroactive effect even if applied to circumstances predating its enactment. *Id.* at 1019. In other words, liability would have attached at the time the act became law; the later amendment would not have changed liability. In contrast, when an amendment changes the law, then issues related to retroactivity do arise. So, the court then asked two questions: First, did the amendment merely clarify the law or did it change existing? And second, if the amendment changed existing law, did that change apply retroactively? *Id.* Holding that the *Carrisales* case had stated the existing law because the judiciary is charged with interpreting statutes, the court held that the legislative amendment changed rather than clarified existing law because the amendment conflicted with *Carrisales*'s holding. *Id.* at 1021.

The court then turned to the question of whether the legislative amendment applied retroactively. The court noted that prospective application is the presumption, but this presumption can be overcome with a showing that the legislature intended otherwise. *Id.* Finding nothing in the statute or legislative history to overcome the presumption, the court held that the presumption was not rebutted and, thus, the amendment applied prospectively only. *Id.*

As a side point, the plaintiff had argued that because *Carrisales* postdated the actions in the lawsuit in question, even the court's interpretation should pose retroactivity issues. But the court disagreed and explained that judicial interpretations may always apply retroactively because "a judicial construction of a statute is an authoritative statement of what the statute meant before as well as after the decision of the case giving rise to that construction." *McClung*, 99 P.3d at 1021. In other words, courts interpret statutes as of the enactment date forward; hence, there is no retroactivity when courts interpret statutes.

In summary, courts presume that statutes apply prospectively. For civil statutes, the presumption can be rebutted with clear evidence that the legislature intended the statute to apply retroactively if retroactive application will not impair a vested right. And, a statute has retroactive effect when that statute defines the legal significance of acts or events that occurred prior to the statute's enactment.

* * *

4. Retroactive Criminal Statutes and the *Ex Post Facto* Clause

We turn now to another policy-based constitutional consideration, the prohibition against *ex post facto*, or retroactive, criminal laws. The U.S. Constitution provides that Congress shall pass "[no] ... ex post facto law." U.S. Const. art. I, § 9, cl. 3. This section addresses retroactivity in regard to criminal, not civil, cases.

Ex post facto is Latin for something done afterwards. Under the Constitution, an *ex post facto* law is impermissible if it is *both* retroactive and disadvantageous to a criminal defendant. An *ex post facto* statute is a statute that changes the legal consequences of an action after the action has occurred, specifically, by redefining criminal conduct or by increasing the penalty for criminal conduct. There are four types of *ex post facto* statutes: (1) those criminalizing actions that were legal when committed; (2) those altering the nature of a crime so that it is categorized more severely than it was when committed; (3) those increasing the punishment for a crime; and (4) those altering the rules of evidence to make conviction easier. *Calder v. Bull*, 3 U.S. (3 Dall.) 386 (1798). The Constitution prohibits *ex post facto* laws to prevent legislatures from enacting vindictive laws to punish individuals and to ensure that statutes give fair notice of their legal effect. The canon shares this latter purpose with the rule of lenity.

Retroactive effect alone is not enough to make a law unconstitutional. A law may have *retroactive* effect and still not be an impermissible *ex post facto* law. To be an impermissible *ex post facto* law, the statute must punish individuals for prior actions. For example, the Adam Walsh Child Protection and Safety Act of 2006, Pub. L. 109-248, 120 Stat. 587 (2006), requires convicted sex offenders to register in a sex offender database. When enacted, the law applied retroactively, to all those individuals already convicted of a sex offense. Yet in *Smith v. Doe*, 538 U.S. 84, 105 (2003), the Supreme Court held that the Act did not violate the *ex post facto* clause, because compulsory registration was not a punishment. Hence, the law was retroactive, but not an *ex post facto* law.

Similarly, the Domestic Violence Offender Gun Ban of 1996, 18 U.S.C. § 922(g)(9), prohibits persons who are convicted of misdemeanor domestic violence and who are subject to a restraining order from owning guns or ammunition. When enacted, this Act also applied retroactively. Persons convicted of violating the Act could be sentenced to up to ten years for possessing a firearm, regardless of whether they legally possessed the weapon at the time the law was passed. In *United States v. Brady*, 26 F.3d 282 (2d Cir. 1994), *cert. denied*, 513 U.S. 894 (1994), the court denied an *ex post facto* challenge because the Act was considered regulatory, not punitive — in other words, violation of the Act was a status offense, not a punishment.

Hence, the legislature cannot enact statutes that have retroactive punitive effects without violating the *ex post facto* clause of the U.S. Constitution. The challenge, of course, is determining exactly when a statute has a punitive, rather than regulatory, effect. Determining whether a statute has punitive effect is challenging. Even judges do not always agree. For example, in *People v. Leroy*, 828 N.E.2d 786 (Ill. App. Ct. 2005), the Illinois Court of Appeals addressed this issue in determining whether a statute that limited where convicted sex offenders could live was an *ex post facto* law. As a child, the defendant had been convicted of a sexual offense. He later pled guilty for failing to register as a sex offender and was sentenced to one year's probation. While on probation, he lived in his mother's house, which was located near an elementary school. A statute, which was enacted after his underlying criminal conviction, prohibited him from "knowingly resid[ing] within 500 feet of a playground or a facility providing programs or services exclusively directed toward persons under 18 years of age." *Id.* at 533 (quoting 720 Ill. Comp. Stat. 5/11-9.4(b-5)). The state sought to revoke the defendant's probation because he violated this statute.

The defendant admitted violating the statute but argued that the statute was an unconstitutional *ex post facto* law because the statute increased the penalty he received for his underlying conviction. The appellate court disagreed, holding instead that (1) the legislature intended to enact a regulatory scheme, not to punish individuals, and (2) the effect of the law was not so punitive that it prevented the state from creating civil restrictions. Therefore, the statute was not an impermissible *ex post facto* law. *Id.* at 469. Disagreeing, the dissent claimed that "a punitive effect unquestionably flow[ed] from this enactment [and violated the] constitutional guarantee against the imposition of *ex post facto* punishment." *Id.* at 475 (Kuehn, J., dissenting).

While legislatures cannot enact *ex post facto* laws, court interpretations of statutes apply retroactively (because a statute is presumed to have that meaning from its enactment). Can a judicial interpretation of a criminal statute ever violate the *ex post facto* clause? The next case addresses that question.

Bouie v. Columbia

Supreme Court of the United States
378 U.S. 347 (1964)

◆ Justice Brennen delivered the opinion of the Court [with whom Warren, C.J., Douglas, Clark, Stewart, and Goldberg, JJ., concur].

This case arose out of a 'sit-in' demonstration at Eckerd's Drug Store in Columbia, South Carolina. In addition to a lunch counter, Eckerd's maintained several other departments, including those for retail drugs, cosmetics, and prescriptions. Negroes and whites were invited to purchase and were served alike in all departments of the store with the exception of the restaurant department, which was reserved for whites. There was no evidence that any signs or notices were posted indicating that Negroes would not be served in that department.

On March 14, 1960, the petitioners, two Negro college students, took seats in a booth in the restaurant department at Eckerd's and waited to be served. No one spoke to them or approached them to take their orders for food. After they were seated, an employee of the store put up a chain with a 'no trespassing' sign attached. Petitioners continued to sit quietly in the booth. The store manager then called the city police department and asked the police to come and remove petitioners. After the police arrived at the store the manager twice asked petitioners to leave. They did not do so. The Assistant Chief of Police then asked them to leave. When petitioner Bouie asked 'For what?' the Assistant Chief replied: 'Because it's a breach of the peace * * *.' Petitioners still refused to leave, and were then arrested. They were charged with breach of the peace ... [and] resisting arrest [but these charges were dismissed or reversed on appeal]. Both petitioners were also charged with criminal trespass in violation of § 16—386 of the South Carolina Code of 1952;[1] on this charge they were convicted, and their convictions were affirmed by the State Supreme Court over objections based upon the Due Process.... We granted certiorari....

We ... find merit in petitioners' contention under the Due Process Clause and reverse the judgments on that ground.

Petitioners claim that they were denied due process of law ... because ... the statute failed to afford fair warning that the conduct for which they have now been convicted had been made a crime. The terms of the statute define the prohibited conduct as 'entry upon the lands of another * * * after notice from the owner or tenant prohibiting such entry * * *.' Petitioners emphasize the conceded fact that they did not commit such conduct; they received no 'notice * * * prohibiting such entry' either before they entered Eckerd's Drug Store (where in fact they were invited to enter) or before they entered the restaurant department of the store and seated themselves in the booth. Petitioners thus argue that, under the statute as written, their convictions would have to be reversed.... The argument is persuasive but beside the point, for the case in its present posture does not involve the statute 'as written.' The South Carolina Supreme Court, in affirming petitioners' convictions, construed the statute to cover not only the act of entry on the premises of another after receiving notice not to enter, but also the act of remaining on the premises of another after receiving notice to leave.[2] Under the statute as so construed, it is clear that there was evidence to support petitioners' convictions, for they concededly remained in the lunch counter booth after being asked to leave. Petitioners contend, however, that by applying such a construction of the statute to affirm their convictions in this case, the State has punished them for conduct that was not criminal at the time they committed it, and hence has

---

1. That section provides: 'Entry on lands of another after notice prohibiting same. Every entry upon the lands of another where any horse, mule, cow, hog or any other livestock is pastured, or any other lands of another, after notice from the owner or tenant prohibiting such entry, shall be a misdemeanor and be punished by a fine not to exceed one hundred dollars, or by imprisonment with hard labor on the public works of the county for not exceeding thirty days. When any owner or tenant of any lands shall post a notice in four conspicuous places on the borders of such land prohibiting entry thereon, a proof of the posting shall be deemed and taken as notice conclusive against the person making entry as aforesaid for the purpose of trespassing.'

2. This construction of the statute was first announced by the South Carolina Supreme in *City of Charleston v. Mitchell*, 239 S.C. 376, decided on December 13, 1961, certiorari granted and judgment reversed, 378 U.S. 551, 84 S.Ct. 1901. In the instant case, ... the South Carolina Supreme Court simply relied on its ruling in *Mitchell*.

violated the requirement of the Due Process Clause that a criminal statute give fair warning of the conduct which it prohibits. We agree with this contention.

The basic principle that a criminal statute must give fair warning of the conduct that it makes a crime has often been recognized by this Court....

'The constitutional requirement of definiteness is violated by a criminal statute that fails to give a person of ordinary intelligence fair notice that his contemplated conduct is forbidden by the statute. The underlying principle is that no man shall be held criminally responsible for conduct which he could not reasonably understand to be proscribed.'

Thus we have struck down a state criminal statute under the Due Process Clause where it was not 'sufficiently explicit to inform those who are subject to it what conduct on their part will render them liable to its penalties.' We have recognized in such cases that 'a statute which either forbids or requires the doing of an act in terms so vague that men of common intelligence must necessarily guess at its meaning and differ as to its application violates the first essential of due process of law,' and that 'No one may be required at peril of life, liberty or property to speculate as to the meaning of penal statutes. All are entitled to be informed as to what the State commands or forbids.'

... [T]he language of § 16—386 of the South Carolina Code was admirably narrow and precise; the statute applied only to 'entry upon the lands of another * * * after notice * * * prohibiting such entry * * *'.... When a statute on its face is vague or overbroad, it at least gives a potential defendant some notice, by virtue of this very characteristic, that a question may arise as to its coverage, and that it may be held to cover his contemplated conduct. When a statute on its face is narrow and precise, however, it lulls the potential defendant into a false sense of security, giving him no reason even to suspect that conduct clearly outside the scope of the statute as written will be retroactively brought within it by an act of judicial construction. If the Fourteenth Amendment is violated when a person is required 'to speculate as to the meaning of penal statutes,' or to 'guess at (the statute's) meaning and differ as to its application,' the violation is that much greater when, because the uncertainty as to the statute's meaning is itself not revealed until the court's decision, a person is not even afforded an opportunity to engage in such speculation before committing the act in question.

There can be no doubt that a deprivation of the right of fair warning can result not only from vague statutory language but also from an unforeseeable and retroactive judicial expansion of narrow and precise statutory language.... '[J]udicial enlargement of a criminal act by interpretation is at war with a fundamental concept of the common law that crimes must be defined with appropriate definiteness'....

Indeed, an unforeseeable judicial enlargement of a criminal statute, applied retroactively, operates precisely like an ex post facto law, such as Art. I, § 10, of the Constitution forbids. An ex post facto law has been defined by this Court as one 'that makes an action done before the passing of the law, and which was innocent when done, criminal; and punishes such action,' or 'that aggravates a crime, or makes it greater than it was, when committed.' If a state legislature is barred by the Ex Post Facto Clause from passing such a law, it must follow that a State Supreme Court is barred by the Due Process Clause from achieving precisely the same result by judicial construction. The fundamental principle that 'the required criminal law must have existed when the conduct in issue occurred,' must apply to bar retroactive criminal prohibitions emanating from courts as well as from legislatures. If a judicial construction of a criminal statute is 'unexpected and indefensible by reference to the law which had been expressed prior to the conduct in issue,' it must not be given retroactive effect....

Applying those principles to this case, we agree with petitioners that § 16—386 of the South Carolina Code did not give them fair warning, at the time of their conduct in Eckerd's Drug Store in 1960, that the act for which they now stand convicted was rendered criminal by the statute. By its terms, the statute prohibited only 'entry upon the lands of another * * * after notice from the owner * * * prohibiting such entry * * *.' There was nothing in the statute to indicate that it also prohibited the different act of remaining on the premises after being asked to leave. Petitioners did not violate the statute as it was written; they received no notice before entering either the drugstore or the restaurant department. Indeed, they knew they would not receive any such notice before entering the store, for they were invited to purchase everything except food there. So far as the words of the statute were concerned, petitioners were given not only no "fair warning," but no warning whatever, that their conduct in Eckerd's Drug Store would violate the statute....

We think it clear that the South Carolina Supreme Court, in applying its new construction of the statute to affirm these convictions, has deprived petitioners of rights guaranteed to them by the Due Process Clause. If South Carolina had applied to this case its new statute prohibiting the act of remaining on the premises of another after being asked to leave, the constitutional proscription of ex post facto laws would clearly invalidate the convictions. The Due Process Clause compels the same result here, where the State has sought to achieve precisely the same effect by judicial construction of the statute.... Application of this rule is particularly compelling where, as here, the petitioners' conduct cannot be deemed improper or immoral....

The crime for which these petitioners stand convicted was 'not enumerated in the statute' at the time of their conduct. It follows that they have been deprived of liberty and property without due process of law in contravention of the Fourteenth Amendment....

♦ JUSTICE BLACK, with whom HARLAN and WHITE, JJ., join, dissenting.

Petitioners ... contend that they were denied due process of law ... because that statute as applied was so vague and indefinite that it failed to furnish fair warning that it prohibited a person who entered the property of another without notice not to do so from remaining after being asked to leave.... We cannot believe that either the petitioners or anyone else could have been misled by the language of this statute into believing that it would permit them to stay on the property of another over the owner's protest without being guilty of trespass. . . .

* * *

Points for Discussion

1. *Statutory Language*: What was the language at issue? What did each party want that language to mean? What meaning did the majority and dissent adopt?

2. *Theories*: Which theory did the majority use? The dissent? Did either find ambiguity, absurdity, a constitutional question to avoid, or a scrivener's error?

3. *Due Process or Ex Post Facto Clause*: In this case did the Court hold that South Carolina had violated the Due Process Clause by failing to provide fair notice, the Ex Post Facto clause by retroactively altering the statute, or both?

4. *Vague Statutes*: The majority argued that subsequent judicial interpretation of vague statutes is less concerning than clear statutes that are broadened by subsequent judicial interpretation. Do you see why?

5. *The Dissent's Point*: Statutes presumptively apply prospectively, while judicial interpretations apply retroactively (but only because the statute when enacted meant what the court says it meant). Did the majority follow these presumptions? Why was the majority convinced that it would be unfair to find the defendants guilty of criminal trespass? What was the dissent's point? Would you think that remaining in another's property, whether home or business, after you had been asked to leave was trespass? Do you think the defendants thought they were committing trespass? Does it matter whether the defendants thought what they were doing was criminal? Or does it only matter what the statute said?

6. *Another Example*: In *Michigan v. Schaeffer*, 703 N.W.2d 774 (Mich. 2005), the defendant struck and killed an eleven-year-old girl while he was driving drunk. He was charged with driving while intoxicated *"by the operation of that motor vehicle caus[ing] the death of another person." Id.* at 781 (quoting Mich. Comp. Laws § 257.625(4)). In an earlier case, the Michigan Supreme Court had held that "the people must establish that the particular defendant's decision to drive while intoxicated produced a change in that driver's operation of the vehicle that caused the death of the victim." *Id.* at 781–82 (quoting *People v. Lardie*, 551 N.W.2d 656, 668 (Mich. 1996)). At the preliminary hearing in *Schaeffer*, the prosecutor's expert testified that it was irrelevant that the defendant was drunk because the accident was unavoidable. *Id.* at 779. Thus, the defendant moved to dismiss the charges against him. In response, the state argued that *Lardie* should be overruled. The majority agreed, finding that the language of the statute clearly stated that "the defendant's *operation* of the motor vehicle [] must cause the victim's death, not the defendant's 'intoxication.'" *Id.* at 783. Despite changing the interpretation, the majority did not find an *ex post facto* concern because the court concluded that it was merely correcting its prior, erroneous interpretation. The corrected interpretation should have been clear from the statute's face. "[I]t is not 'inde-

fensible or unexpected' that a court would . . . overrule a case that failed to abide by the express terms of a statute." *Id.* at 790 n.80.

The concurring judge disagreed. He argued that the court had already interpreted the statute in such a way that the majority's new interpretation criminalized behavior that was not criminal when performed. *Id.* at 793 (Cavanagh, J., concurring in part and dissenting in part). Thus, the new interpretation violated the *ex post facto* clause. The concurrence argued that if the legislature had responded to *Lardie* by enacting a statute that mirrored the majority's interpretation and had done so after the defendant hit the child, the statute would be an impermissible *ex post facto* law. Thus, because the legislature could not change the law without violating the *ex post facto* clause, the court should similarly not be able to do so. *Id.* at 794. The concurrence's reasoning is similar to the majority's reasoning in *Bouie.*

7. *Bouie Dicta Rejected*: In *Rogers v. Tennessee,* 378 U.S. 347 (2001), the Supreme Court held that the *Ex Post Facto* Clause applies to retroactive legislation only, not to retroactive judicial opinions. The Court explicitly rejected *Bouie*'s dicta that the *Ex Post Facto* Clause principles can be incorporated into the Due Process Clause to limit judicial interpretation. In *Rogers,* the Supreme Court held that the *Ex Post Facto* Clause was not violated when the Tennessee Supreme Court retroactively abandoned the common-law rule that a person could not be convicted of first degree murder when the victim died more than "a year and a day" after the injury. The Court was concerned that its application to common law decision-making would unduly impair the incremental and reasoned development of precedent that is the foundation of the common law system. *Id.* at 362. The Court distinguished *Bouie,* saying that the principal concern in that case was of fair notice and warning.

5. Clear Statement Rules

In the last sections, we were introduced to the concept that, for some situations, courts require legislatures to express clearly their intent. In this section, we explore this concept in four specific areas.

Where a statute can be interpreted to abridge long-held individual or states' rights, or when it appears that a legislature has made a large policy change, courts will generally not interpret the statute to abridge those rights or make that change unless the legislature was clear about its intention. The requirement of a clear, or plain, statement is based on the simple assumption that a legislature would not make major policy changes without being absolutely clear about doing so. Thus, courts require clear statements to encourage the legislature to explicitly indicate that it wants a change in the status quo.

Courts tend to require clear statements to maintain under-enforced constitutional traditions. Above, we saw two examples of when courts require clear statement rules: the constitutional avoidance doctrine and the rule of lenity. Below, we turn to four additional areas of important concern: federalism, preemption, American Indian rights, and sovereign immunity. We will look at each in turn. You should be aware, however, that clear statement rules have a role in many areas of statutory interpretation. We are looking at just a few of those areas so that you understand what a court means when the court requires the legislature to be clear about what it intends.

a. Federalism

Our nation is made up of one federal government and fifty state governments. At times, the laws of the two sovereigns conflict. The principle of federalism respects the sovereignty of states from federal intrusion. Judges will not interpret federal statutes to burden state sovereignty unless Congress clearly expresses its intent to do so. The requirement of a clear statement respects federalism because Congress must be clear when it wishes to impact areas of traditional state power, such as land management and taxation.

> Federal statutes impinging upon important state interests "cannot … be construed without regard to the implications of our dual system of government…. (W)hen the Federal Government takes over … local radiations in the vast network of our national economic enterprise and thereby radically readjusts the balance of state and national authority, those charged with the duty of legislating (must be) reasonably explicit."

BFP v. Resolution Trust Corp., 511 U.S. 531, 544 (1994) (quoting Felix Frankfurter, *Some Reflections on the Reading of Statutes*, 47 COLUM. L. REV. 527, 539–540 (1947)).

For example, "[r]egulation of land [and water] use … is a quintessential state and local power." *Rapanos v. United States*, 547 U.S. 715, 738 (2006). If Congress wants to encroach on this traditional and primary state power, then Congress should say so very clearly. In 1972, Congress enacted the Clean Water Act, which made it illegal to discharge dredged or fill material into "navigable waters" without a permit. Congress defined "navigable waters" in the Act as "the waters of the United States, including the territorial seas." *Id.* at 760 (quoting 33 U.S.C. §§ 1362(7) & (12)). The Army Corps of Engineers by regulation interpreted "the waters of the United States" very broadly to include not only waters that were navigable but also "[t]ributaries of such waters" and "'wetlands' adjacent to such waters and tributaries." *Id.* at 724 (quoting 33 CFR §§ 328.3(a)(5) & (7)). In essence, the Corps interpreted the language broadly to include any waters that might ultimately enter navigable waters. In *Rapanos*, the Court had to consider whether four Michigan wetlands, which lay near ditches and man-made drains that would eventually empty into traditional navigable waters constituted "waters of the United States" within the meaning of the Act. Rejecting the Corps's interpretation as unreasonable, the Court noted that it ordinarily requires a "'clear and manifest' statement from Congress to authorize an unprecedented intrusion into traditional state authority. [And t]he phrase 'the waters of the United States' hardly qualifies." *Id.* at 738.

The case below involves a federal bankruptcy and its effects on state taxes. As you read the case, notice all of the different canons the majority and dissent examine to resolve the issue.

Florida Department of Revenue v. Piccadilly Cafeterias, Inc.

Supreme Court of the United States
554 U.S. 33 (2008)

◆ JUSTICE THOMAS delivered the opinion of the Court, [in which ROBERTS, C.J., and SCALIA, KENNEDY, SOUTER, GINSBURG, and ALITO, JJ., concur].

The Bankruptcy Code provides a stamp-tax exemption for any asset transfer "under a plan confirmed under [Chapter 11]" of the Code. 11 U.S.C. § 1146(a) (2000 ed., Supp. V). Respondent Piccadilly Cafeterias, Inc., was granted an exemption for assets transferred after it had filed for bankruptcy but before its Chapter 11 plan was submitted to, and confirmed by, the Bankruptcy Court. Petitioner, the Florida Department of Revenue, seeks reversal of the decision of the Court of Appeals upholding the exemption for Piccadilly's asset transfer. Because we hold that § 1146(a)'s stamp-tax exemption does not apply to transfers made before a plan is confirmed under Chapter 11, we reverse the judgment below.

Piccadilly was founded in 1944 and was one of the Nation's most successful cafeteria chains until it began experiencing financial difficulties in the last decade. On October 29, 2003, Piccadilly declared bankruptcy under Chapter 11 of the Bankruptcy Code, § 1101 *et seq.* (2000 ed. and Supp. V), and requested court authorization to sell substantially all its assets outside the ordinary course of business pursuant to § 363(b)(1) (2000 ed., Supp. V). Piccadilly prepared to sell its assets as a going concern and sought an exemption from any stamp taxes* on the eventual transfer under § 1146(a) of the Code. The Bankruptcy Court conducted an auction in which the winning bidder agreed to purchase Piccadilly's assets for $80 million....

On February 13, 2004, the Bankruptcy Court approved the proposed sale and settlement agreement. The court also ruled that the transfer of assets was exempt from stamp taxes under § 1146(a). The sale closed on March 16, 2004.

Piccadilly filed its initial Chapter 11 plan in the Bankruptcy Court on March 26, 2004, and filed an amended plan on July 31, 2004.... Before the Bankruptcy Court confirmed the plan, Florida filed an objection, seeking a declaration that the $39,200 in stamp taxes it had assessed on certain of Piccadilly's transferred assets fell outside § 1146(a)'s exemption because the transfer had not been "under a plan confirmed" under Chapter 11. On October 21, 2004, the bankruptcy court confirmed the plan. On cross-motions for summary judgment on the stamp-tax issue, the Bankruptcy Court granted summary judgment in favor of Piccadilly, reasoning that the sale of substantially all Piccadilly's assets was a transfer "under" its confirmed plan because

---

* Editor's footnote: Stamp taxes are taxes derived from the sale of stamps that the state requires to be affixed to certain legal documents, generally involving the transfer of assets or property.

the sale was necessary to consummate the plan. The District Court upheld the decision....

The Court of Appeals for the Eleventh Circuit affirmed ... Finding the statutory text ambiguous, the Court of Appeals concluded that § 1146(a) should be interpreted consistent with "the principle that a remedial statute such as the Bankruptcy Code should be liberally construed." ...

We granted certiorari....

Section 1146(a), entitled "Special tax provisions," provides: "The issuance, transfer, or exchange of a security, or the making or delivery of an instrument of transfer *under a plan confirmed under section 1129 of this title,* may not be taxed under any law imposing a stamp tax or similar tax." (Emphasis added.) Florida asserts that § 1146(a) applies only to postconfirmation sales; Piccadilly contends that it extends to preconfirmation transfers as long as they are made in accordance with a plan that is eventually confirmed. Florida and Piccadilly base their competing readings of § 1146(a) on the provision's text, on inferences drawn from other Code provisions, and on substantive canons of statutory construction. We consider each of their arguments in turn.

Florida contends that § 1146(a)'s text unambiguously limits stamp-tax exemptions to postconfirmation transfers made under the authority of a confirmed plan. It observes that the word "confirmed" modifies the word "plan" and is a past participle, *i.e.,* "[a] verb form indicating past or completed action or time that is used as a verbal adjective in phrases such as *baked beans* and *finished work.*" American Heritage Dictionary 1287 (4th ed.2000). Florida maintains that a past participle indicates past or completed action even when it is placed after the noun it modifies, as in "beans baked in the oven," or "work finished after midnight." Thus, it argues, the phrase "plan confirmed" denotes a "confirmed plan" — meaning one that has been confirmed in the past.

Florida further contends that the word "under" in "under a plan confirmed" should be read to mean "with the authorization of" or "inferior or subordinate" to its referent, here the confirmed plan. Florida points out that, in the other two appearances of "under" in § 1146(a), it clearly means "subject to." Invoking the textual canon that " 'identical words used in different parts of the same act are intended to have the same meaning,' " Florida asserts the term must also have its core meaning of "subject to" in the phrase "under a plan confirmed." Florida thus reasons that to be eligible for § 1146(a)'s exemption, a transfer must be subject to a plan that has been confirmed subject to § 1129.... Florida concludes that a transfer made prior to the date of plan confirmation cannot be subject to, or under the authority of, something that did not exist at the time of the transfer — a confirmed plan.

Piccadilly counters that the statutory language does not unambiguously impose a temporal requirement. It contends that "plan confirmed" is not necessarily the equivalent of "confirmed plan," and that had Congress intended the latter, it would have used that language, as it did in a related Code provision. See § 1142(b) (referring to "any instrument required to effect a transfer of property dealt with by a confirmed plan"). Piccadilly also argues that "under" is just as easily read to mean "in accordance with." It observes that the variability of the term "under" is well documented, noting that the American Heritage Dictionary 1395 (1976) provides 15 definitions, including "[i]n view of," "because of," "by virtue of," as well as "[s]ubject to the restraint ... of." Although "under" appears several times in § 1146(a), Piccadilly maintains there is no reason why a term of such common usage and variable meaning must have the same meaning each time it is used, even in the same sentence.... Piccadilly contends that this provision is best read as: "The commencement of a joint case *subject to the provisions of* a chapter of this title constitutes an order for relief *in* such chapter." Piccadilly thus concludes that the statutory text — standing alone — is susceptible of more than one interpretation.

While both sides present credible interpretations of § 1146(a), Florida has the better one. To be sure, Congress could have used more precise language — *i.e.,* "under a plan *that has been* confirmed" — and thus removed all ambiguity. But the two readings of the language that Congress chose are not equally plausible: Of the two, Florida's is clearly the more natural. The interpretation advanced by Piccadilly....

Although we agree with Florida that the more natural reading of § 1146(a) is that the exemption applies only to postconfirmation transfers, ultimately we need not decide whether the statute is unambiguous on its face. Even assuming, *arguendo,* that the language of § 1146(a) is facially ambiguous, the ambiguity must be resolved in Florida's favor. We reach this conclusion after considering the parties' other arguments, to which we now turn.

Piccadilly insists that, whatever the degree of ambiguity on its face, § 1146(a) becomes even more ambiguous when read in context with other Bankruptcy Code provisions. Piccadilly asserts that if Congress had intended § 1146(a) to apply exclusively to transfers occurring after confirmation, it would have made its intent plain with an express temporal limitation similar to those appearing elsewhere in the Code. For example, § 1127 governs modifications to a Chapter 11 plan, providing that the proponent of a plan may modify the plan "at any time before confirmation," or, subject to certain restrictions, "at any time after confirmation of such plan." §§ 1127(a)–(b). Similar examples abound. See, *e.g.,* § 1104(a) ("[a]t any time after the commencement of the case but before confirmation of a plan ..."); § 1104 (c) ("at any time before the confirmation of a plan ..."). Piccadilly emphasizes that, "where Congress includes particular language in one section of a statute but omits it in another section of the same Act, it is generally presumed that Congress acts intentionally and purposely in the disparate inclusion or exclusion." Because Congress did not impose a clear and commonly used temporal limitation in § 1146(a), Piccadilly concludes that Congress did not intend one to exist. Piccadilly buttresses its conclusion by pointing out that § 1146 (b) — the subsection immediately following § 1146(a) — includes an express temporal limitation. But Congress included no such limitation in subsection (a)....

For its part, Florida argues that the statutory context of § 1146(a) supports its position that the stamp-tax exemption applies exclusively to postconfirmation transfers. It observes that the subchapter in which § 1146(a) appears is entitled, "POSTCON-

FIRMATION MATTERS." Florida contends that, while not dispositive, the placement of a provision in a particular subchapter suggests that its terms should be interpreted consistent with that subchapter. In addition, Florida dismisses Piccadilly's references to the temporal limitations in other Code provisions on the ground that it would have been superfluous for Congress to add any further limitations to § 1146(a)'s already unambiguous temporal element.

Even on the assumption that the text of § 1146(a) is ambiguous, we are not persuaded by Piccadilly's contextual arguments. As noted above, Congress could have used language that made § 1146(a)'s temporal element clear beyond question. Unlike § 1146(a), however, the temporal language examples quoted by Piccadilly are indispensable to the operative meaning of the provisions in which they appear.... It was unnecessary for Congress to include in § 1146(a) a phrase such as "at any time after confirmation of such plan" because the phrase "under a plan confirmed" is most naturally read to require that there be a confirmed plan at the time of the transfer....

If the statutory context suggests anything, it is that § 1146(a) is inapplicable to preconfirmation transfers. We find it informative that Congress placed § 1146(a) in a subchapter entitled, "POSTCONFIRMATION MATTERS." To be sure, a subchapter heading cannot substitute for the operative text of the statute. Nonetheless, statutory titles and section headings "'are tools available for the resolution of a doubt about the meaning of a statute.'" The placement of § 1146(a) within a subchapter expressly limited to postconfirmation matters undermines Piccadilly's view that § 1146(a) covers preconfirmation transfers.

But even if we were fully to accept Piccadilly's textual and contextual arguments, they would establish at most that the statutory language is ambiguous. They do not— and largely are not intended to—demonstrate that § 1146(a)'s purported ambiguity should be resolved in Piccadilly's favor. Florida argues that various nontextual canons of construction require us to resolve any ambiguity in its favor. Piccadilly responds with substantive canons of its own. It is to these dueling canons of construction that we now turn....

Florida ... invokes the substantive canon ... that courts should "'proceed carefully when asked to recognize an exemption from state taxation that Congress has not clearly expressed.'" In light of this directive, Florida contends that § 1146(a)'s language must be construed strictly in favor of the States to prevent unwarranted displacement of their tax laws....

In response, Piccadilly contends that [this] federalism principle ... does not apply where there is a "clear expression of an exemption from state taxation" overriding a State's authority to tax. In Piccadilly's view, that is precisely the case with regard to § 1146(a), which proscribes the imposition of stamp taxes and demonstrates Congress' intent to exempt a category of state taxation....

[Also], Piccadilly urges us to adopt the ... maxim that "a remedial statute such as the Bankruptcy Code should be liberally construed." In Piccadilly's view, any ambiguity in the statutory text is overshadowed by § 1146(a)'s obvious purpose: to facilitate the Chapter 11 process "through giving tax relief." Piccadilly characterizes the tax on asset transfers at issue here as tantamount to a levy on the bankruptcy process itself. A stamp tax like Florida's makes the sale of a debtor's property more expensive and reduces the total proceeds available to satisfy the creditors' claims....

What is unclear, Piccadilly argues, is why "Congress would have intended the anomaly that a transfer essential to a plan that occurs two minutes before confirmation may be taxed, but the same transfer occurring two seconds after may not." After all, interpreting § 1146(a) in the manner Florida proposes would lead precisely to that result. And that, Piccadilly asserts, is "absurd" in light of § 1146(a)'s policy aim — evidenced by the provision's text and legislative history — of reducing the cost of asset transfers. In that vein, Piccadilly contends that interpreting § 1146(a) to apply solely to postconfirmation transfers would undermine Chapter 11's twin objectives of "preserving going concerns and maximizing property available to satisfy creditors." In order to obtain the maximum value for its assets — especially assets rapidly declining in value — Piccadilly claims that a debtor often must close the sale before formal confirmation of the Chapter 11 plan.

We agree with Florida that the federalism canon ... obliges us to construe § 1146(a)'s exemption narrowly. Piccadilly's effort to evade the canon falls well short of the mark because reading § 1146(a) in the manner Piccadilly proposes would require us to do exactly what the canon counsels against. If we recognized an exemption for preconfirmation transfers, we would in effect be "'recogniz[ing] an exemption from state taxation that *Congress has not clearly expressed*'" — namely, an exemption for preconfirmation transfers. Indeed, Piccadilly proves precisely this point by resting its entire case on the premise that Congress has expressed its stamp-tax exemption in ambiguous language. Therefore, far from being inapposite, the canon is decisive in this case....

Nor are we persuaded that in this case we should construe § 1146(a) "liberally" to serve its ostensibly "remedial" purpose.... [T]his Court has rejected the notion that "Congress had a single purpose in enacting Chapter 11." Rather, Chapter 11 strikes a balance between a debtor's interest in reorganizing and restructuring its debts and the creditors' interest in maximizing the value of the bankruptcy estate. The Code also accommodates the interests of the States in regulating property transfers by "'generally [leaving] the determination of property rights in the assets of a bankrupt's estate to state law.'" Such interests often do not coincide, and in this case, they clearly do not. We therefore decline to construe the exemption granted by § 1146(a) to the detriment of the State.

As for Piccadilly's assertion that reading § 1146(a) to allow preconfirmation transfers to be taxed while exempting others moments later would amount to an "absurd" policy, we reiterate that "'it is not for us to substitute our view of ... policy for the legislation which has been passed by Congress.'" That said, we see no absurdity in reading § 1146(a) as setting forth a simple, bright-line rule instead of the complex, after-the-fact inquiry Piccadilly envisions....

The most natural reading of § 1146(a)'s text, the provision's placement within the Code, and applicable substantive canons all lead to the same conclusion: Section 1146(a) affords a stamp-tax exemption only to transfers made pursuant to a Chapter 11 plan that has been confirmed. Because Piccadilly transferred its assets before its Chapter 11 plan was confirmed by the Bankruptcy Court, it may not rely on § 1146(a) to avoid Florida's stamp taxes. Accordingly, we reverse the judgment below and remand the case for further proceedings consistent with this opinion....

◆ Justice Breyer, with whom Justice Stevens joins, dissenting.

Dissent

The Bankruptcy Code provides that the "transfer" of an asset "*under a plan confirmed under section 1129 of this title,* may not be taxed under any law imposing a stamp tax or similar tax." 11 U.S.C. § 1146(a) (2000 ed., Supp. V) (previously § 1146(c)) (emphasis added). In this case, the debtor's reorganization "plan" provides for the "transfer" of assets. But the "plan" itself was not "confirmed under section 1129 of this title" (*i.e.,* the Bankruptcy Judge did not formally approve the plan) until *after* the "transfer" of assets took place.

Hence we must ask whether the time of transfer matters. Do the statutory words "under a plan confirmed under section 1129 of this title" apply only where a transfer takes place "under a plan" that at the time of the transfer *already has been* "confirmed under section 1129 of this title"? Or, do they also apply where a transfer takes place "under a plan" that *subsequently is* "confirmed under section 1129 of this title"? The Court concludes that the statutory phrase applies only where a transfer takes place "under a plan" that at the time of transfer *already has been* "confirmed under section 1129 of this title." In my view, however, the statutory phrase applies "under a plan" that at the time of transfer either *already has been* or *subsequently is* "confirmed." In a word, the majority believes that the time (pre- or post- transfer) at which the bankruptcy judge confirms the reorganization plan matters. I believe that it does not. (And construing the provision to refer to a plan that simply "is" confirmed would require us to read fewer words into the statute than the Court's construction, which reads the provision to refer only to a plan "that has been" confirmed.

The statutory language itself is perfectly ambiguous on the point. Linguistically speaking, it is no more difficult to apply the words "plan confirmed" to instances in which the "plan" *subsequently is* "confirmed" than to restrict their application to instances in which the "plan" *already has been* "confirmed."

Nor can I find any text-based argument that points clearly in one direction rather than the other. Indeed, the majority, after methodically combing the textualist beaches, finds that a comparison with other somewhat similar phrases in the Bankruptcy Code sheds little light. For example, on the one hand, if Congress thought the time of confirmation mattered, why did it not say so expressly as it has done elsewhere in the Code? On the other hand, if Congress thought the time of confirmation did *not* matter, why did it place this provision in a subchapter entitled "POSTCONFIRMA-TION MATTERS"? And yet one could also argue that the tax-exemption provision appears under the "postconfirmation matters" title because the trigger for the exemption is plan confirmation. Thus, the exemption is a "postconfirmation matter," regardless of when the transfer occurs.

The canons of interpretation offer little help. And the majority, for the most part, seems to agree. It ultimately rests its interpretive conclusion upon this Court's statement that courts "must proceed carefully when asked to recognize an exemption from state taxation that Congress has not clearly expressed." But when, as here, we interpret a provision the *express point of which* is to exempt some category of state taxation, how can [that] statement ... prove determinative? See § 1146(a) ("The issuance, transfer, or exchange of a security, or the making or delivery of an instrument of transfer under a plan confirmed under section 1129 of this title, *may not be taxed* under any law imposing a stamp tax or similar tax" (emphasis added))....

The absence of a clear answer in text or canons, however, should not lead us to judicial despair. Consistent with Court precedent, we can and should ask a further question: *Why* would Congress have insisted upon temporal limits? What reasonable *purpose* might such limits serve? In fact, the majority's reading of temporal limits in § 1146(a) serves *no reasonable congressional purpose at all.*

The statute's purpose is apparent on its face. It seeks to further Chapter 11's basic objectives: (1) "preserving going concerns" and (2) "maximizing property available to satisfy creditors." *Bank of America Nat. Trust and Sav. Assn. v. 203 North LaSalle Street Partnership*, 526 U.S. 434, 453 (1999). As an important bankruptcy treatise notes, "[i]n addition to tax relief, the purpose of the exemption of [§ 1146(a)] is to encourage and facilitate bankruptcy asset sales." It furthers these objectives where, *e.g.*, asset transfers are at issue, by turning over to the estate (for the use of creditors or to facilitate reorganization) funds that otherwise would go to pay state stamp taxes on plan-related transferred assets. The requirement that the transfers take place pursuant to a reorganization "plan" that is "confirmed" provides the bankruptcy judge's assurance that the transfer meets with creditor approval and the requirements laid out in § 1129.

How would the majority's temporal limitation further these statutory objectives? It would not do so in any way. From the perspective of these purposes, it makes no difference whether a transfer takes place before or after the plan is confirmed. In both instances the exemption puts in the hands of the creditors or the estate money that would otherwise go to the State in the form of a stamp tax. In both instances the confirmation of the related plan ensures the legitimacy (from bankruptcy law's perspective) of the plan that provides for the assets transfer ...

Moreover, one major reason why a transfer may take place *before* rather than *after* a plan is confirmed is that the preconfirmation bankruptcy ... may continue for many years." And a firm (or its assets) may have more value (say, as a going concern) where sale takes place quickly. Thus, an immediate sale can often make more revenue available to creditors or for reorganization of the remaining assets. Stamp taxes on related transfers simply reduce the funds available for any such legitimate purposes. And insofar as the Court's interpretation of the statute reduces the funds made available, that interpretation inhibits the statute's efforts to achieve its basic objectives....

What conceivable reason could Congress have had for silently writing into the statute's language a temporal distinction with such consequences? The majority can find none. It simply says that the result is not "'absurd'" and notes the advantages of a "bright-line rule." I agree that the majority's interpretation is not absurd and do not dispute the advantages of a clear rule. But I think the statute supplies a clear enough rule — transfers are exempt when there is confirmation and are not exempt when there is no confirmation. And I see no reason to adopt the majority's preferred construction (that only transfers completed after plan confirmation are exempt), where it conflicts with the statute's purpose.

Of course, we should not substitute *"our view* of ... policy" for the statute that Congress enacted. But we certainly should consider *Congress'* view of the policy for the statute it created, and that view inheres in the statute's purpose. "Statutory interpretation is not a game of blind man's bluff. Judges are free to consider statutory language in light of a statute's basic purposes." It is the majority's failure to work with this important tool of statutory interpretation that has led it to construe the present statute in a way that, in my view, runs contrary to what Congress would have hoped for and expected.

* * *

Points for Discussion

1. *Statutory Language*: What was the language at issue? What did each party want that language to mean? What meaning did the majority and dissent adopt?

2. *Theories*: Which theory did the majority use? The dissent? Did either find ambiguity, absurdity, a constitutional question to avoid, or a scrivener's error? Why do you think Justice Thomas, typically a strict textualist, stated "we need not decide whether the statute is unambiguous on its face" before turning to the other sources of meaning?

3. *Clear Statements*: The majority and dissent disagreed that Congress clearly express its intent to exempt something from state taxation. In the bankruptcy statute, Congress expressly provided, "The ... transfer ... *may not be taxed* under *any* law imposing a stamp tax or similar tax." (Emphasis added). Why, according to the majority, was this prohibition not clear enough? How could Congress be any clearer? Given that this language is clear, what then was not clear, according to the majority?

4. *Remedial Statutes*: Piccadilly argues that because the bankruptcy statute is a remedial statute, the Court should construe the statute liberally in its favor. We will explore this canon in Chapter 15. For now, why did the majority refuse to apply this policy-based canon?

5. *Review*: This case serves as an excellent review of the linear approach we have been learning. Notice that the majority and dissent start with the ordinary meaning of the language at issue, discuss whether that language is ambiguous or absurd, and finally discuss the intrinsic, extrinsic, and policy-based sources. Which sources did the majority find most compelling? The dissent?

* * *

b. Preemption

Preemption is the displacing effect that federal law has on conflicting or inconsistent state law. Preemption occurs because the Supremacy Clause in the Constitution states that "[t]he Laws of the United States, (which shall be made in Pursuance to the Constitution), shall be the supreme Law of the land." U.S. CONST. art. VI, § 2. Thus, if there is a conflict between state and federal law, federal law preempts state law. Courts require clear statements in the area of preemption. We discussed the conflict aspect of preemption in Chapter 10. Here we examine the role of clear statements and preemption.

Preemption is an enormously complicated area of law, which we need not delve into too deeply here. It is sufficient for you to know that there is a presumption in favor of the applicability of state law and against preemption. Courts presume that Congress generally does not intend to preempt state law when enacting a federal law; thus, Congress must provide a clear statement that it intended to preempt state law:

> In all pre-emption cases, and particularly in those in which Congress has "legislated ... in a field which the States have traditionally occupied," ... we "start with the assumption that the historic police powers of the States were not to be superseded by the Federal Act unless that was the clear and manifest purpose of Congress."

Medtronic, Inc. v. Lohr, 518 U.S. 470, 485 (1996) (quoting *Rice* v. *Santa Fe Elevator Corp.*, 331 U.S. 218, 230 (1947)).

Sometimes, Congress includes a specific preemption clause in the act at issue, which makes the preemption question relatively easy. For example, the Supreme Court held that the Medical Device Amendments Act of 1976 preempted state common-law claims challenging the safety and effectiveness of any medical device approved by the Federal Drug Administration. *Riegel v. Medtronic, Inc.*, 552 U.S. 312 (2008). The Act contained a clause that expressly preempted state requirements that differed from federal law. *Id.* at 330 (citing 21 U.S.C. § 360k(a)(1)). These are the easy cases.

But Congress is not always so clear about its intent. What happens when Congress is not clear? When possible, courts generally try to reconcile seemingly inconsistent state and federal laws (Remember our discussion of conflicting statutes from Chapter 10). But reconciliation is not always possible. For example, in *Wyeth v. Levine*, 555 U.S. 555 (2009), the Supreme Court had to determine whether the federal Food, Drug, and Cosmetic Act ("FDCA"), which did not include a preemption provision, impliedly preempted state tort law. *Id.* at 560–61. The plaintiff in the case had lost her arm after she was injected with an anti-nausea drug manufactured by the defendant. Although the label warned of this risk, the plaintiff argued that under state tort law the defendant should not have allowed the drug to be used intravenously, even with the labeling. The FDCA outlined a comprehensive process for approving drug labels. The drug manufacturer-defendant argued that the FDCA's labeling process preempted state tort law for two reasons. First, the defendant raised the issue of "impossibility preemption" and argued that a manufacturer could not comply with both the federal labeling requirements and state tort law. The Court rejected this argument, noting that the defendant "failed to demonstrate that it was impossible for it to comply with both federal and state requirements." *Id.* at 574–75.

Second, the defendant argued that the state tort claims were preempted because allowing state tort claims to apply would interfere with "Congress's purpose to entrust an expert agency to make drug labeling decisions that strike a balance between competing objectives." *Id.* at 574. The Court similarly rejected this argument, in part, because Congress had enacted a preemption provision in a related act, the Medical Device Amendments Act but not here:

> "The case for federal pre-emption is particularly weak where Congress has indicated its awareness of the operation of state law in a field of federal interest, and has nonetheless decided to stand by both concepts and to tolerate whatever tension there [is] between them."

Id. at 575 (quoting *Bonito Boats, Inc.* v. *Thunder Craft Boats, Inc.*, 489 U.S. 141, 166–67 (1989) (internal quotation marks omitted). In sum, the Court held that the FDCA's regulatory approval process did not preempt state tort law.

Justice Thomas wrote separately to criticize the majority for routinely invalidating state laws based on perceived conflicts with broad federal policy objectives, legislative history, and statutory purposes that were not contained within the text of federal law. *Id.* at 582 (Thomas, J., concurring). For Justice Thomas, preemption can be implied only through a textual analysis. Consider the illogicality of that position.

Lastly, even in the absence of any clear statement that Congress intended to "occupy the field" of a particular area, courts will be more likely to find that federal law preempts state law if the state law touches upon an area where there has historically been a strong federal interest, such as banking, interstate commerce, or foreign affairs.

c. American Indian Treaty Rights

Clear statements are also required when Congress impacts American Indian treaty rights by diminishing native lands. Not only are we a nation with various sovereigns, we are a nation within a nation. American Indian lands should be protected from unnecessary federal intrusion and diminishment. The *diminishment doctrine* was established to distinguish those statutes that removed lands from a reservation and those statutes that merely made surplus lands available for settlement within a reservation. Courts require a clear statement when Congress "diminishes" reservation boundaries. *Hagen v. Utah*, 510 U.S. 399, 411 (1993).

When a statute has two possible interpretations that implicate native lands, the non-diminishment interpretation should govern. Courts presume that Congress would not have wanted to diminish the reservation boundaries without being explicit. Thus, in *Solem v. Bartlett*, 465 U.S. 463 (1984), the Supreme Court held that there was no such clear statement to reduce the Cheyenne River Sioux Reservation in the Cheyenne River Act, despite language describing opened areas as being in "the public domain" and describing unopened areas as comprising "the reservation thus diminished." *Id.* at 475–76. This language simply was not clear enough to imply diminishment. Additionally, the Court noted that the Act had been enacted at a time when the word "diminished" was not yet a term of art in American Indian law. *Id.* at 476 n.17. Finally, the Court found that there was no clear congressional purpose to reduce the reservation. *Id.* at 476.

d. Sovereign Immunity

Clear statement rules are also used to protect sovereign immunity. Sovereign immunity is a judge-made doctrine that dates from the beginning of our nation's birth. The doctrine is fairly straightforward: the federal government, or sovereign, may not be sued without its consent. To further this doctrine, federal courts developed two statutory interpretation principles to help judges determine when a statute waives immunity. The first principle is that a statutory waiver of sovereign immunity must be definitely and unequivocally expressed. In other words, Congress must provide a clear statement that it intended to waive sovereign immunity. The second principle is that when a waiver is found, a court must construe that waiver narrowly in favor of the government.

In the case below, notice how the presumption against waiving sovereign immunity is so strong that the court concludes that it trumps all the other canons. The Court of Federal Claims, which decided this case, is an Article I Court, which is explained in more detail in the notes. As you read this case, try to identify the two competing policy-based canons and why they conflict.

Burch v. Secretary of Health & Human Services
2001 WL 180129 (Fed. Cl. 2001)

◆ Hastings, Special Master.

This is an action seeking an award under the National Vaccine Injury Compensation Program (hereafter "the Program")....

Shon S. Burch and Jonathan Burch are the mother and father, respectively, of Sabian E. Burch, who was born on November 21, 1996. While Shon Burch was pregnant with Sabian, she received an "MMR" (measles, mumps, rubella) vaccination on March 25, 1996. After Sabian was born, the infant was determined to be suffering from a serious neurologic abnormality known as Aicardi's Syndrome. Sabian has suffered from a seizure disorder, brain malformation, and significant developmental delay.

The instant petition, filed on November 19, 1999, alleged that Sabian's severe neurologic abnormality was a result of the MMR vaccination that her mother received on March 25, 1996, while pregnant with Sabian. [Respondent disagrees.]....

The legal question ... at issue is whether, *assuming* that petitioners could prove as a factual matter that their daughter Sabian's neurologic abnormality resulted from the MMR vaccine that was administered to her mother on March 25, 1996, they would be eligible for a Program award on her behalf. For the reasons set forth below, I conclude, as a matter of law, that they would not.

Under the Program, compensation is available, under certain circumstances, to a person who has suffered an injury after having "received" a vaccine of the type set forth in the statute. The relevant statutory provision reads, in pertinent part, as follows:

stat.

> A petition for compensation under the Program for a vaccine-related injury or death shall contain—
>
> (1) * * * an affidavit, and supporting documentation, demonstrating that the person who suffered such injury or who died—
>
> (A) received a vaccine set forth in the Vaccine Injury Table or, if such person did not receive such a vaccine, contracted polio, directly or indirectly, from another person who received an oral polio vaccine * * *.

Before I move to my analysis of the particular statutory provision here in question, I note that respondent has argued that in reaching an interpretation of that statutory provision, I am bound by the "sovereign immunity" principles of statutory construction, which would mean that I should "strictly" and "narrowly" construe the statute. On the other hand, there also exists a principle of statutory construction that states that a "remedial" statute is generally to be construed in a "liberal" fashion so as to give broad effect to the "remedial" purpose behind the statute. Accordingly, in the following subsections of this Ruling, I will examine each of these principles of statutory construction.

The starting point of the doctrine of "sovereign immunity," a judge-made doctrine which dates from the early days of our country, is that the federal government, as this nation's "sovereign," may not be sued without its consent. From that initial principle, the federal courts have derived certain principles of *statutory construction* that have been applied in interpreting legislation which is said to have *waived* that immunity with respect to a particular type of suit against the United States. One principle is that a statutory waiver of sovereign immunity must be "definitely and unequivocally expressed." The second is that the statutory language setting forth such a waiver is to be "construed strictly" or "construed narrowly" in favor of the government.

… Respondent argues that because this particular provision is *part* of the Vaccine Act, which *as a whole* constitutes a waiver of sovereign immunity, in reaching an interpretation I must "narrowly and strictly" construe the statutory language.

After reviewing a great number of the cases that have discussed these principles of statutory construction, to which I will sometimes refer collectively as the "sovereign immunity doctrine," I note that over the years the federal courts, including the Supreme Court, appear to have waxed and waned in their level of devotion to the doctrine. In fact, there have been opinions, especially in the middle of the last century, in which the courts have indicated that the doctrine was falling into "disfavor." Several Supreme Court opinions, indeed, suggested that waivers of sovereign immunity in some circumstances could be construed "liberally" rather than "strictly." …

More recently, however, the Supreme Court has vigorously *reaffirmed and reemphasized* the principles of requiring "unequivocal" expression of an immunity waiver and of "strictly and narrowly construing" such waivers. Specifically, the Supreme Court decisions of the 1990's have resoundingly endorsed these principles....

Moreover, the ... Supreme Court decisions [have] done more than to merely reaffirm the sovereign immunity doctrine in the face of prior indications that the doctrine might have been falling into "disfavor;" those decisions seem clearly to have actually *strengthened and reinforced* the doctrine, making it more rigorous than ever before. As one commentator has put it, those recent decisions have given the sovereign immunity doctrine "some extra teeth." For example, those decisions have specified that the fact and extent of the waiver must be unequivocally indicated in the language of the *statutory text itself.* In other words, if the waiver is not apparent in the statutory text itself, the Court will *not utilize the legislative history* to interpret the text. Further, in one case where the text itself did not contain an unequivocal waiver, the Court declined to find a waiver even though such an interpretation admittedly would have fostered the general purpose behind the statute. The commentators, as well as at least one Supreme Court justice, have referred to these pronouncements as creating a "clear statement rule" with regard to sovereign immunity waivers. Some commentators have even dubbed it a "super strong clear statement rule." At the least, these recent decisions firmly entrench the rule that statutory waivers of sovereign immunity must be unequivocally expressed, and that the statutory language of such waivers must be strictly and narrowly construed in favor of the government....

Another principle of statutory construction, however, must also be considered. That is, a number of federal courts have stated that "remedial" or "welfare" legislation should be given a "broad construction" or a "liberal interpretation" in order to further the "remedial," "beneficent," or "humanitarian" purposes behind the statute.

Thus, the question arises whether the Vaccine Act should be viewed as legislation that is "remedial" in nature, and therefore should be "liberally" construed so as to give a wider application to the remedial purposes behind the statute.[3] The cases that I have identified mentioning this "remedial legislation" rule do not provide any precise definition of what legislation should be considered to be "remedial" in nature. However, the cases all seem to refer to statutes that are designed to benefit or protect classes of persons who have been harmed or disadvantaged in some fashion. In that light, it seems reasonable to conclude that the Vaccine Act, which is designed to benefit persons injured by vaccinations, does constitute a "remedial" statute. Does it follow, therefore, that the provisions of that Act are to be "liberally" or "broadly" interpreted? I conclude that it does not. Rather, my analysis of the case law is that with respect to statutes which are *both* "remedial" in nature *and* also waive the federal government's immunity from suit, it is the sovereign immunity doctrine which "trumps" the competing principle of statutory construction, so that *strict and narrow construction* remains the controlling principle with respect to such statutes.

---

3. The petitioners in this case have not cited these cases, nor have they cited this principle of liberal construction of remedial statutes. Nevertheless, I have found it appropriate to consider on my own this potentially-applicable theory of statutory construction.

The most straightforward reason for this conclusion, with respect to the Vaccine Act, is simply that binding precedent mandates it. [T]he Federal Circuit has clearly stated that the doctrine of sovereign immunity *does* apply in interpreting Vaccine Act provisions....

For the reasons set forth above, I have concluded that the sovereign immunity statutory construction principles *are* properly applicable to the statutory interpretation question at issue here. This means that I must "constru[e] ambiguities in favor of immunity." It means that if there exist more than one "plausible" reading of the statutory provision at issue or two possible interpretations of "equal likelihood", then I must choose the interpretation that produces the more limited award.

The question of whether an unborn child *in utero* "receives" a vaccine that is administered to his mother, under the meaning of the word "received" as used in § 300aa–11(c)(1)(A), presents a difficult issue of statutory interpretation. Petitioners argue that Sabian "received" the MMR vaccine administered to her mother while Sabian was *in utero,* contending as a matter of fact that the vaccine injected into the mother's body would automatically pass into the unborn child's system, "just as that fetus receives the nutrients that the mother ingests." Petitioners argue that since the vaccine passes into the unborn child's system, that child has "received" the vaccine. Respondent argues, on the other hand, that the term "received" applies only to situations in which a person was *directly administered* the vaccine by the vaccine administrator—*i.e.,* was injected with a vaccine or ingested it (took it orally). Respondent argues that Sabian did not "receive" the vaccine within the statutory meaning; only her mother did....

I find this statutory interpretation question to be a difficult one, with reasonable arguments on both sides. However, I ultimately must conclude that the sovereign immunity doctrine dictates the outcome of this issue. I conclude that the statutory language of § 300aa–11(c)(1)(A) is ambiguous in its application to this situation, and that both competing interpretations are at least "plausible." Therefore, as explained above, I must choose the interpretation that produces the most narrow and restricted waiver of sovereign immunity. In other words, I must adopt respondent's interpretation, since that produces the more narrow waiver.

In reaching this conclusion, I acknowledge that I find much that is persuasive [for the parents' position].... First, I find considerable merit in the argument ... that an unborn child can be said to have "received" a vaccine under the ordinary meaning and usage of the term "received." That is, assuming that it is true as a factual matter that the MMR vaccine would have naturally flowed through the mother's system into Sabian's system at that stage of the pregnancy, then it does seem logical to conclude that Sabian "received" the vaccine. Although Sabian did not receive it *directly* from the vaccine administrator, it is reasonable to say that she did "receive" it through her mother's system. [T]here seems to be no particular reason to restrict the word "received" in the statute to receipt by *injection* or *ingestion,* as respondent argues. Certainly, under the ordinary usage of the word "receive," a person can "receive" things by means other than injection or ingestion. I see no inherent reason why a person could not be said to "receive" a vaccine in this third fashion—that is, by transfer from a pregnant woman's system into the system of the unborn child.

Second, ... petitioners' interpretation of the term "received" would be more in keeping with the general spirit and the remedial nature of the Program, which was intended to "generously" assist injured persons whose injuries may have been vaccine-caused.

However, on the other hand, I can also see merit in respondent's argument. Although a person can "receive" other things by means other than injection or ingestion, it is true that when one thinks of "receiving" a vaccine, one would normally think of having the vaccine administered by injection or ingestion. So, there is some appeal to respondent's argument that when Congress used the phrase "received a vaccine" in § 300aa–11(c)(1)(A), Congress likely had in mind only receipt by injection or ingestion.[9] ...

In short, ... the statutory language is "ambiguous" as to its application here, and that both statutory interpretations advanced in this case are "plausible." Therefore, as dictated by the recent Supreme Court sovereign immunity decisions cited above, I am bound to choose the interpretation that produces the more narrow waiver of immunity. Here, that is the respondent's interpretation of the statute....

As a final point, I note that I reach my decision on this case even though I am well aware of the statement in the legislative history indicating that Vaccine Act awards are to be made with "generosity." .... [I]t seems clear that the *general spirit* behind enactment of the Act was one of generosity to persons who have suffered very unfortunate injuries. Therefore, I candidly acknowledge that my own initial intuitive inclination was to resist the idea that the sovereign immunity doctrine should apply to questions of statutory interpretation in Vaccine Act cases, requiring use of the most narrow interpretation as to close questions. It seems counter-intuitive to apply this doctrine to a statute with such a generous, remedial purpose....

* * *

Points for Discussion

1. *Statutory Language*: What was the language at issue? What did each party want that language to mean? What meaning did the special master adopt?

2. *Theories*: Which theory did the special master use? Did she find ambiguity, absurdity, a constitutional question to avoid, or a scrivener's error?

3. *Article I Court*: This case comes from the United States Court of Federal Claims, which Congress established pursuant to Article 1 of the United States Constitution. Article I courts are courts of limited jurisdiction. The Court of Federal Claims is authorized primarily to hear claims seeking monetary damages against the

---

9. I note that I have not found any legislative history that relates specifically to the statutory provision at issue here. Further, as explained above, the recent Supreme Court "sovereign immunity" rulings indicate that a court should *not* look to the legislative history to interpret a statutory provision subject to the sovereign immunity doctrine.

United States. Article I Courts are administrative agencies, which we will learn more about in Chapter 16.

4. *Sources*: According to the special master, the purpose of the statute, the remedial statute canon, and the legislative history all suggested that Congress intended the Vaccine Act to be broadly interpreted. Yet the special master interpreted the statute narrowly. Why?

5. *Sovereign Immunity Canon*: According to the Supreme Court's most recent jurisprudence in this area, the sovereign immunity canon requires two things. First, the government must expressly waive immunity, in other words, the court must find a clear statement of waiver. The special master notes in footnote 9 that such waivers cannot be found in the legislative history alone. Here, the Vaccine Act provides that clear waiver. Second, any such waiver should be narrowly construed. Unfortunately, for the Burchs, this second half of the canon decided this case.

* * *

In summary, when a statute can be interpreted to abridge federalism, to preempt state law, to diminish American Indian lands, or to waive sovereign immunity, the statute must express clearly the legislature's intention to impact these rights. Additionally, courts require clear statements in other situations not explored here, such as when Congress intends to enforce its laws beyond the territorial boundaries of the United States.

Clear statement rules place the burden on Congress to be clear when drafting. In doing so, the clear statement rules can frustrate Congress's intent by requiring meticulousness. Importantly, nothing in the Federal Constitution requires Congress to identify its intent to legislate in these areas clearly. Hence, one could question whether the court has the power to demand clear statements at all. *See generally*, John F. Manning, *Clear Statement Rules and the Constitution*, 100 COLUM. L. REV. 101 (2010).

Problem 14

Rania Akbar, a naturalized Citizen of the United States, who was born in Lebanon and is Muslim, was dismissed from her job as an engineer with Americo Oil, Inc. (Americo) an American Oil company whose principal place of business is in Saudi Arabia. Americo is licensed to do business in the State of Delaware.

Claiming that she was discharged because of her race, religion, and national origin in violation of Title VII of the Civil Rights Act of 1964, Rania brought an action in the United States District Court for the Southern District of Kent against Americo, seeking damages and reinstatement. Americo filed a motion for summary judgment, arguing that the District Court lacked subject matter jurisdiction, because the protections of Title VII do not apply to United States citizens employed abroad by American employers. The District Court agreed and dismissed the claim. The Appellate Court affirmed. The Supreme Court has granted certiorari.

Both parties concede that Congress has the authority to enforce its laws beyond the territorial boundaries of the United States. However, "[i]t is a longstanding principle of American law that legislation of Congress, unless a contrary intent appears, is meant to apply only within the territorial jurisdiction of the United States. This canon of construction is a valid approach whereby unexpressed congressional intent may be ascertained." *Foley Bros., Inc. v. Filardo,* 336 U. S. 281, 284–85 (1949). Requiring a clear statement protects against unintended clashes between our laws and those of other nations which could result in international discord.

You represent Rania. The issue is whether Title VII applies extraterritorially to regulate the employment practices of U.S. employers who employ U.S. citizens abroad. What arguments can you make on your client's behalf that Title VII of the Civil Rights Act applies to U.S. citizens working overseas? What would Americo likely argue in response? Assume the Act is as provided below (not what it currently provides).

Problem Materials

Civil Rights Act of 1964
Title VII

701: DEFINITIONS

For the purposes of this subchapter-

(a) The term "alien" means an individual who is not a naturalized or other citizen of the United States....

(f) The term "employer" means a person engaged in industry affecting commerce who has fifteen or more employees.

(g) The term "commerce," means trade, traffic, commerce, transportation, transmission, or communication among the several States; or between a State and any place outside thereof; ...

(i) The term "State" includes a State of the United States, the District of Columbia, Puerto Rico, the Virgin Islands, American Samoa, Guam, Wake Island, and the Canal Zone."

702: APPLICABILITY TO FOREIGN AND RELIGIOUS EMPLOYMENT

(a) Inapplicability to certain aliens and employees of religious entities

This subchapter shall not apply to an employer with respect to the employment of aliens outside any State, or to a religious corporation, association, educational institution, or society with respect to the employment of individuals of a particular religion to perform work connected with the carrying on by such corporation, association, educational institution, or society of its activities.

703: UNLAWFUL EMPLOYMENT PRACTICES

(a) Employer practices

It shall be an unlawful employment practice for an employer -

(1) to fail or refuse to hire or to discharge any individual, or otherwise to discriminate against any individual with respect to his compensation, terms, conditions, or privileges of employment, because of such individual's race, color, religion, sex, or national origin....

Legislative History

In hearings before the House Committee on the Judiciary regarding the Civil Rights Act, Representative Cruz explained that the alien exemption provision of Sec. 702 was to be "a limited exemption intended to remove conflicts of law that might otherwise exist between the U.S. and a foreign nation in the employment of aliens outside the U.S. by an American enterprise." In other words, the legislature did not intend for American companies to have to violate foreign law, to the extent there was a conflict. The phrase was to be very narrowly construed to further the remedial purposes of the Act.

During debate in the Senate, Senator Sheppard questioned whether the definition of commerce should include the terms "foreign commerce" or "foreign nations," but the sponsor of the bill, Senator Durskie, responded that such an amendment was unnecessary for "places outside thereof" was already clear enough to show that the scope of the statute was broad enough to include foreign states. There was no further relevant legislative history.

Chapter 15

Canons Based on Policy-Based Considerations: Prudential

A. Introduction to This Chapter

In the last chapter, we explored policy-based canons, specifically those related to the Constitution. We move now away from the constitutional-based policy considerations and into the prudential-based policy considerations. Here, the constitution is not the star; rather, concerns about the interplay between the common law and statutes are center-front. This chapter comes late in this text, in part, because these canons are the least relevant to interpretation today. However, in the past, they played an important role. Hence, you will often see them referenced.

We will begin with two related, but opposing canons: (1) courts should strictly construe statutes in derogation of the common law, and (2) courts should broadly construe remedial statutes. (We saw this second canon in the two last cases we studied: *Florida Department of Revenue v. Piccadilly Cafeterias, Inc.* and *Burch v. Secretary of Health & Human Services.*) These rules sound easy in theory, but it can be difficult to tell whether a statute is remedial or in derogation of the common law and to determine just how broadly or narrowly to interpret the relevant statute. These two canons are generally relevant in state interpretation cases because there is limited federal common law.

B. Statutes v. Common Law

1. Statutes in Derogation

An oft-stated canon provides: Courts should strictly construe statutes in derogation of the common law. A statute is in derogation of common law when the statute partially repeals or abolishes existing common law rights or otherwise limits the scope, utility, or force of that common law right. BLACK'S LAW DICTIONARY 476 (8th ed. 2004).

For example, statutes that alter existing property rights are in derogation of the common law. Wrongful death statutes are also in derogation of the common law. Before wrongful death statutes existed, the common law did not recognize the existence of a wrongful death claim. Instead, any claim died with the victim, because there was no way to compensate a dead victim. Thus, under the common law, no surviving family members could seek damages from the person who caused the victim's death.

But this common law rule led to odd results—a tortfeasor would be off the hook if the victim died, but not if the victim lived. For this reason, England enacted Lord Campbell's Act in 1846: the first "wrongful death statute" that allowed relatives who were damaged by the death of the victim to sue the tortfeasor despite the victim's death. American states quickly followed suit. Because these wrongful death statutes were in derogation of the common law, the early thought was that they should be strictly construed.

To illustrate: in *Boroughs v. Oliver*, 64 So. 2d 338 (Miss. 1953), the Mississippi Supreme Court narrowly construed the word "parent" in its wrongful death statute to prevent adoptive parents from suing for the negligent death of their son. *Id.* at 314. Shortly after that case, the Mississippi legislature corrected this absurdly narrow reading. Miss. Code Ann. § 11-7-13 (2004) ("Any rights which a blood parent or parents may have under this section are hereby conferred upon and vested in an adopting parent or adopting parents surviving their deceased adopted child, just as if the child were theirs by the full blood and had been born to the adopting parents in lawful wedlock.").

But, you may ask, why should statutes in derogation of the common law be strictly construed? Basically, the short answer to this question is power. Before the 1900s, common law was more prevalent than statutory law. Hence, judges viewed statutes with suspicion:

> Statutes then were not created from common law methodology. Indeed, 18th century judges felt them rather subject to tyrannical majorities and shifting whims. England had suffered through the civil wars of the Seventeenth Century and the abuses of unchecked majorities in Parliament. The beheading of Charles I was followed by the post-restoration instability leading to the Glorious Revolution in 1685. [Judges] viewed the common law as a source of social stability, cast from the wisdom of the ages and forged in cases evolving over the long sweep of history. Statutes often emerged from ephemeral, narrow and parochial interests, but the common law was eternal and universal.

Blankfeld v. Richmond Health Care, Inc., 902 So. 2d 296, 305 (Fla. Dist. Ct. App. 2005) (Farmer, J., concurring).

Not only were statutes viewed with suspicion, but those statutes that did exist were either very narrow, were limited exceptions to existing common law, or were narrow corrections of common law. Hence, judges developed the canon that statutes in derogation of the common law should be strictly construed. A common articulation of the canon from that time is as follows: "No statute is to be construed as altering the common law, farther than its words import." *Shaw v. Merchants' Nat. Bank*, 101 U.S. (11 Otto) 557, 565 (1879). Thus, the derogation canon is best understood as reflecting the early reluctance of American courts to allow legislatures to restrict common law rights.

In the twentieth century, a power struggle ensued. Wishing to increase its law-making power, legislatures enacted more statutes. Wishing to maintain the power it had, the judiciary limited the breadth of these statutes with the derogation canon. If the legislature failed to clearly address an issue, then that issue fell into the judiciary's jurisdiction. Eventually, the legislature won this battle; today, statutes create most rights and responsibilities, while common law acts as a gap filler. As a consequence, the usefulness of derogation canon has waned.

Today, many states have abolished the derogation canon. For example, a Kentucky statute provides: "All statutes of this state shall be liberally construed with a view to promote their objects and carry out the intent of the legislature, and the rule that statutes in derogation of the common law are to be strictly construed shall not apply to the statutes of this state." Ky. Rev. Stat. Ann. §446.080(1) (West 2016). In sum, the derogation canon is less useful to litigants than it once was. In contrast, the remedial canon, which we will address next, remains more firmly relevant.

2. Remedial Statutes

One purpose of the derogation canon was to prevent a legislature from unintentionally abrogating rights the common law granted. Prior to the twentieth century, legislatures focused on running the government, not making law. So, when a legislature did enact statutes, many of those statutes were designed to remedy errors in the common law. These statutes were specific, narrow, and limited in application. A statute passed to repair the common law was not *in derogation* of the common law, but rather was *in aid* of the common law. Hence, courts did not view such statutes with suspicion because common law remained supreme. Courts interpreted these "remedial statutes," as they were known, liberally, not narrowly, to achieve the statutory purpose. *Chrisom v. Roemer,* 501 U.S. 380, 403 (1991); *Smith v. Brown,* 35 F.3d 1516, 1525 (Fed. Cir. 1994).

In addition to those statutes that corrected common law, remedial statutes also created new rights or expanded remedies that were otherwise unavailable at common law. To illustrate, a tax statute would not be remedial, while a statute intended to protect civil rights would be. While the definition of a remedial statute seems clear, in reality the distinction between remedial and non-remedial is elusive. "[I]t is not at all apparent just what is and what is not remedial legislation; indeed all legislation might be thought remedial in some sense—even massive codifications." *Ober United Travel Agency, Inc. v. U.S. Dep't of Labor,* 135 F.3d 822, 825 (D.C. Cir. 1998). In the case below, the majority finds this canon dispositive, while the concurrence finds it useless.

Blankfield v. Richmond Health Care, Inc.

Court of Appeals of Florida
902 So. 2d 296 (Fl. Ct. App. 2005)

◆ Per Curiam [Gunther, Stone, Warner, Polen, Klein, Stevenson, Shahood, Gross, Taylor, Hazouri and May, JJ., concur.].

… In 2001 Riva Blankfeld, who was senile, was readmitted to Sunrise Health and Rehabilitation Center, a nursing home facility, and the admission agreement, which was signed by her son, provided that all disputes "shall be resolved by binding arbitration administered by the National Health Lawyers Association." This suit against the nursing home was filed while Riva was still alive, and after her death, her son Melvin, as personal representative, maintained it, asserting that ... Sunrise had negligently cared for Riva. Sunrise moved to compel arbitration, but Melvin contended that the arbitration provisions were unenforceable.... [The trial] court granted Sunrise's motion to compel arbitration.

We first address Melvin's argument that the method of arbitration, which is by the National Health Lawyers Association, limits the remedies created by the legislature in the Nursing Home Residents Act and is therefore void as contrary to public policy.

The arbitration provision provides that "any action, dispute, claim, or controversy of any kind ... now existing or hereafter arising between the parties ... shall be resolved by binding arbitration administered by the National Health Lawyers Association." Section 606 of the NHLA Rules [now known as the American Health Lawyers Association Arbitration Rules of Procedure] provides in part:

> [T]he arbitrator may not award consequential, exemplary, incidental, punitive or special damages against a party unless the arbitrator determines, based on the record, that there is clear and convincing evidence that the party against whom such damages are awarded is guilty of conduct evincing an intentional or reckless disregard for the rights of another party or fraud, actual, or presumed.

Requiring clear and convincing evidence of intentional or reckless misconduct effectively eliminates recovery for negligence, and is contrary to the Nursing Home Residents Act, which provides ... :

> In any claim brought pursuant to this part alleging a violation of resident's rights or negligence causing injury to or the death of a resident, the claimant shall have the burden of proving, by a preponderance of the evidence, that:
>
> (a) The defendant owed a duty to the resident;
>
> (b) The defendant breached the duty to the resident;
>
> (c) The breach of the duty is a legal cause of loss, injury, death, or damage to the resident; and
>
> (d) The resident sustained loss, injury, death, or damage as a result of the breach.

Melvin argues that the [Nursing Home Residents'] statute is remedial, is declarative of public policy, and that the limitation on the statutory remedies is therefore void.

A remedial statute is one which confers or changes a remedy. The Nursing Home Resident's Act is remedial. The "Residents Rights" provisions in [it] were enacted in 1980 to respond to a Dade County Grand Jury investigation of nursing homes which revealed detailed evidence of substantial elder abuse occurring in nursing homes. In 1993, the Legislature amended the statute by enacting [a statute allowing civil causes of action against nursing homes]....

If nursing home residents had to arbitrate under the NHLA rules, some of the remedies provided in the legislation for negligence would be substantially affected and, for all intents and purposes, eliminated. The provision requiring arbitration under those rules is accordingly contrary to the public policy behind the statute and therefore void....

[Reversed on other grounds.]

♦ FARMER, C.J., concurs specially with opinion.

... I ... part company with the court's ... holding that the arbitration is against public policy. The public policy decision turns on the notion that the nursing home statute is remedial. *The decisions involving the remedial canon point in diverse interpretive directions. In my view, reading a statute as remedial has little real meaning....*

There are many instances in which the [Florida] supreme court has qualified the remedial canon. Sometimes the canon may mean an expansive interpretation, but it may not. Along with those decisions, there is another body of supreme court decisions referring to remedial statutes as procedural. In some the fact that the statute is both remedial and procedural may lead to special treatment, but it may not. There is yet a third body of opinions referring to remedial statutes, but this time only to distinguish them from penal statutes. The fact that a remedial statute is penal may mean something, but it may not.

All these variations on *remedial* rob the canon of any real interpretive weight. The fact that one statute is remedial never leads to annulling another. Because all civil statutes are remedial in one sense or another, the cases really suggest that reliance on the remedial canon is little more than a subjective rationalization for a particular outcome, a post hoc justification.

The canon's actual meaning is found in its origins. It was born when the common law was the primary source of social ordering. Most rule-making was by the common law. Statutes filled gaps or addressed conflicts untouched by the common law. Judges used statutes warily because they were few and judges were not accustomed to them.

Early interpretation was limited to these questions: "What was the mischief and defect for which the Common Law did not provide; [and] What remedy the Parliament hath resolved and appointed to cure the disease of the commonwealth ..." *Heydon's Case*, 76 Eng. Rep. 637 (Ex. 1584). The function of judges was "to make such construction as shall suppress the mischief and advance the remedy ..." *Id.* These two guides emerged: the remedial canon, and the derogation canon against implied repeals of the common law. The derogation canon would be used for a statute changing the common law, while the remedial canon carried out the holding in *Heydon's Case....*

[Today] statutes have displaced the common law in most areas of American life. Nevertheless our rules for reading them are filled with relics of the English monarchy, and the remedial canon is one of them.

Some in the Academy think the remedial canon was effectively killed by the legal realists. Karl Llewellyn prominently demonstrated that each canon was offset by a contrary canon, that the derogation canon nullified the remedial canon. If the substantive canons feed on one another, how is the judge to use them sensibly? Some judges have thus been critical of the use of the substantive canons. In Florida perhaps the only sense of being remedial is suggested in one early case:

> "The sole authority of the Legislature to make laws is the foundation of the principle that courts of justice are bound to give effect to its intention. When that is plain and palpable they must follow it implicitly. The rules of construction with which the books abound apply only where the words used are of doubtful import; they are only so many lights to assist the courts in arriving with more accuracy at the true interpretation of the intention. This is true whether the statute be public or private, general or special, remedial *or penal*."

Interpretive guides are really only tools to find meaning and purpose in statutory texts. With multiple statutory schemes a broad construction of one at the expense of the other may defeat legislative goals for both.

The issue of arbitration is the heart of our case, and this alternative method of dispute resolution is itself the subject of an entire chapter of the Florida Statutes. [One statute in this chapter] provides that arbitration provisions are "valid, enforceable, and irrevocable without regard to the justiciable character of the controversy." ...

... [H]ere the two statutory schemes are in direct conflict. The nursing home code creates rights and remedies; the arbitration code creates rights and remedies. Neither mentions the other. We have only the rule that we must harmonize them if possible. It is not easy to harmonize conflicting statutes if one is not even acknowledged.

If the clash of statutes is to be solved by the remedial canon, then they are fighting each other with the same borrowed weapon. Both are remedial. The arbitration code because it creates new rights and remedies, a statutory right for the enforcement of arbitration agreements, to which the courts had previously been hostile. Wielding the remedial canon to settle the conflict leaves us in hopeless stalemate.

Both codes start on equal footing; neither suggests one is superior.... We must give each effect. We must acknowledge the right to enforce valid arbitration agreements. We must work out how they coexist.

In the end, it seems to me that enforcing arbitration over the patient's rights under the nursing home code allows the former to displace the latter. Without a contrary statutory provision, these rights of the patients are supposed to be on the same footing as the right to arbitrate. How does the right to arbitrate end up canceling the nursing home code? Nothing textual supports this. The court offers the remedial canon, but it lacks any content or logic to make either the silent master of the other.

Yet there is a theory with which—for now—one might give slight way to the other. Nursing homes are now inevitable in people's lives.... We can deduce that a form arbitration provision is now becoming routine throughout Florida. Indeed, the testimony below is that it was prepared for that very purpose. The effect of such usage may be the utter displacement of the nursing home code by private agreement. Most

Florida patients intended to be safeguarded by the code will not receive any of these prescribed protections.

If the attempt at harmony yields only the utter negation of one, maybe the result is absurd. Another ancient canon, the "golden rule" of statutory construction, has been used in Florida.... The absurdity principle must be applied with restraint. It serves only to prevent truly absurd results unwittingly generated by a given application of a statute.

When a statute is found to lead to absurd results, its provisions being annulled by another statute, preferably the court applies a "clear statement" holding. As one court explained: "[i]n traditionally sensitive areas ... the requirement of clear statement assures that the legislature has in fact faced, and intended to bring into issue, the critical matters involved in the judicial decision." ... I believe the restrained course for judges is to require a clear legislative statement as to which is dominant.

I would hold that a construction of the statutes allowing the arbitration provision to be given effect leads to the absurd result of eviscerating the nursing home code for nearly every patient intended to be protected by it. Such a construction could lead to the failure of the nursing home code to protect a single person. I would hold that the arbitration code will not be so interpreted without a clear statement by the Legislature making that result indubitable. Because the current statutes do not make that intent clear, I would simply hold in every case presenting this result that this arbitration provision is not enforceable unless the legislature clarifies the statutes to say so.

* * *

Points for Discussion

1. *Statutory Language*: What was the language at issue? What did each party want that language to mean? What meaning did the majority and concurrence adopt?

2. *Theories*: Which theory did the majority use? The concurrence? Did either find ambiguity, absurdity, a constitutional question to avoid, or a scrivener's error?

3. *Definition of Remedial*: How does the majority identify statutes as remedial? What is the concurrence's response? Many statutes today could be characterized as remedial in nature, enacted to solve a problem the legislature identified. Yet, as the concurrence notes, interpreting remedial statutes broadly may conflict with the plain meaning canon or other canons. In *Burch v. Secretary of Health & Human Services*, 2001 WL 180129 (Fed. Cl. 2001), the court rejected the ordinary meaning of the word "received" and refused to interpret the statute broadly despite the statute's remedial nature because the statute implicated sovereign immunity.

4. *Resolving the Issue*: Why did the concurrence conclude that the remedial canon was not determinative in this case? If the concurrence was unwilling to apply the canon, what sources did he turn to instead?

5. *Conflicting Statutes*. Is one statute more specific than the other? If not, one statute was enacted later than the other, but the opinion does not tell us which. Assuming

the nursing home statute was the later enacted statute, what result? Is the arbitration statute impliedly repealed, at least in part? Assuming the arbitration statute was the later enacted statute, what result?

6. *Clear Statement Rule*: The concurrence would require a clear statement whenever one statute nullifies another. Is this clear statement requirement a correct formulation of the presumption against implied repeals?

7. *Heydon's Case*: Why did the concurrence suggest that remedial canon furthers the holding in *Heydon's Case*? Why, in contrast, does the derogation canon not further this holding?

8. *Another Example*: Are wrongful death statutes remedial or in derogation of the common law? They are remedial as to a plaintiff because they add a cause of action or new type of damages otherwise unavailable. But for the defendant, who would have been exempt from liability under common law, these statutes are non-remedial. Thus, some states consider wrongful death statutes to be remedial, such as Wyoming and Rhode Island. *See, e.g., Corkill v. Knowles*, 955 P.2d 438, 442 (Wyo. 1998); *O'Sullivan v. Rhode Island Hosp.*, 874 A.2d 179, 183 (R.I. 2005). Other states, such as Arkansas and Maryland, consider wrongful death statutes to be in derogation of the common law. *See, e.g., Cockrum v. Fox*, 199 S.W.3d 69, 73 (Ark. 2004) (Thornton, J., dissenting); *Cohen v. Rubin*, 460 A.2d 1046, 1056 (Md. Ct. Spec. App. 1983).

9. *Canards of Statutory Interpretation*: Does the remedial canon have any force today? The concurrence would say not. According to former Justice Scalia, the remedial canon "is surely among the prime examples of lego-babble. We lawyers have all heard it and read it since our first year in law school. Yet I am not sure that anybody knows—and, worse yet, that anybody really *cares*—what in the world it means."

    He explains that there are a number of problems with the canon:

    > Foremost among them, I suppose, is the unstated assumption that it is perfectly all right for judges to pick and choose among statutes, interpreting some "liberally" and some "'strictly"—or perhaps "conservatively," if you think that is the appropriate antonym of "liberally.'" As an original matter, that seems to me quite wrong. I should think that the effort, with respect to *any* statute, should be neither liberally to expand nor strictly to constrict its meaning, but rather to get the meaning precisely right. Now that may often be difficult, but I see no reason, *a priori*, to compound the difficulty, and render it even more unlikely that the precise meaning will be discerned, by laying a judicial thumb on one or the other side of the scales. And that is particularly so when the thumb is of indeterminate weight. How "liberal'" is liberal, and how "strict" is strict? ...
    >
    > ... What makes this rule unique is that there is not the slightest agreement on what its subject—the phrase "remedial statutes"—consists of. Webster's Dictionary defines "remedial" as "intended for a remedy or for the removal or abatement ... of an evil." On this assumption, of course,

all statutes would be remedial, since one can hardly conceive of a law that is not meant to solve some problem. Presumably this normal meaning must be rejected, if only because if *all* statutes were liberally construed *none* would be — the norm having been gobbled up by the exception....

And I could go on. The fact is that there does not exist, and does not seem to have existed since at least the eighteenth century, even a rough consensus as to what the term "remedial statute'" might mean — except that it clearly does not mean a penal statute, and clearly does mean (I suppose) a statute that provides a new remedy for violation of a preexisting private right.

Of what value, one might reasonably ask, is a rule that is both of indeterminate coverage (since no one knows what a "remedial statute" is) and of indeterminate effect (since no one knows how liberal is a liberal construction). Surely the rule must have *some* virtue, or it would not have grown so venerable and remained so popular. The answer, of course, is that its virtue is precisely its vice. It is so wonderfully indeterminate, as to both when it applies and what it achieves, that it can be used, or not used, or half-used, almost *ad libitum,* depending mostly upon whether its use, or nonuse, or half-use, will assist in reaching the result the court wishes to achieve.

Antonin Scalia, *Assorted Canards of Contemporary Legal Analysis*, 40 CASE W. RES. L. REV. 581 (1990).

* * *

C. Implied Causes of Action and Remedies

Our next topic is, in many ways, at the cutting edge of the academic and judicial debate about statutory interpretation. Implied causes of action and remedies are, as their name suggests, implied. Because neither is explicitly set forth in the text of a statute, their existence confounds textualists. As such, the current trend is to deny the existence of new implied actions and remedies and restrict the reach of those already in existence, as we will see below.

An implied cause of action exists when a court determines that even though a statute does not expressly grant private parties the right to sue, the statute does so implicitly. In early English common law, private lawsuits were the primary method of enforcing common law and statutes. WILLIAM ESKRIDGE, JR. ET AL., CASES AND MATERIALS ON LEGISLATION: STATUTES AND THE CREATION OF PUBLIC POLICY 1110 (3d ed. 2001). Early American courts adopted this presumption. Thus, when Congress drafted a statute protecting important interests, courts readily assumed private individuals had the ability to enforce those rights in court, regardless of whether Congress said so.

But after the New Deal, agencies were delegated the responsibility of enforcing many of these rights; thus, private rights of action became less necessary and, over time, courts rejected implied rights claims more easily. Over the past half century, the Supreme Court has taken three different approaches to implied causes of action; each approach has more severely limited the availability of implied causes of action.

J.I. Case Co. v. Borak, 377 U.S. 426 (1964) illustrates the first, and most liberal, approach. In that case, the Supreme Court had to decide whether the Securities Exchange Act of 1934 allowed a private right of action when none was expressly provided in the Act. Examining the Act's legislative history and purposes, the Court held that a private right of action should be implied. The Court believed that it was "the duty of the courts to be alert to provide such remedies as are necessary to make effective the congressional purpose." *Id.* at 433.

This case was decided in 1964, long before new textualism refocused attention on statutory text. The case also offered a somewhat simplistic rationale, "for it assume[d] that more enforcement is always better." ESKRIDGE *ET AL.*, CASES AND MATERIALS ON LEGISLATION, *supra,* at 1111. Beginning in 1975, the Court began its retreat from this simplistic approach. In *Cort v. Ash*, 422 U.S. 66 (1975), the Supreme Court retreated from the broad language of *Borak*. The issue in *Cort* was whether a civil cause of action existed under a criminal statute prohibiting corporations from making contributions to a presidential campaign. The Court held that a civil action should not be implied. In doing so, the Court identified four factors for courts to consider when deciding whether a statute implicitly included a private cause of action. *Id.* at 78. These factors included the following:

1. Whether the plaintiff was one of the class of persons "for whose especial benefit" the statute was enacted,

2. Whether the legislative history showed that Congress intended to create or deny a private cause of action,

3. Whether an implied cause of action would be consistent with the underlying purposes of the statute, and

4. Whether the issue would be one that is traditionally left to state law.

For several years after *Cort*, the Supreme Court applied this four-part test and generally refused to create implied causes of action. A notable exception was the case of *Cannon v. University of Chicago*, 441 U.S. 677 (1979), in which the Court recognized an implied cause of action for claims brought under Title IX of the Education Amendments of 1972. *Id.* at 695. Justice Powell, in dissent, criticized the majority's decision and the creation of implied causes of action in general. Powell believed that the Court's test for implied causes of action violated separation of powers. *Id.* at 730 (Powell, J., dissenting). Because Congress, not the judiciary, has the power to create causes of action, "[a]bsent the most compelling evidence of affirmative congressional intent, a federal court should not infer a private cause of action." *Id.* at 731. In essence, Justice Powell required a clear statement rule for implied causes of action.

Despite Powell's heartfelt dissent, *Cannon*'s four factor test was reaffirmed in *Jackson v. Birmingham Board of Education*, 544 U.S. 167 (2005), in which the Supreme Court allowed a private individual to sue for sex-based *retaliation* under Title IX, which prohibits discrimination based on "sex." One might question whether the Court created a new implied cause of action or simply expanded an existing one. In *Cannon*, the plaintiff was discriminated against because of her sex, or gender. In contrast, in *Jackson*, the male plaintiff was discriminated against because of *other people's* gender, namely the members of the women's basketball team. Apparently, the majority believed that it was merely determining the contours of an existing cause of action, for the majority never discussed *Cort* or *Alexander*.

Soon after *Cannon* was decided, the Supreme Court again modified its approach to implying causes of action in *Touche Ross & Co. v. Remington*, 442 U.S. 560 (1979). The issue before the Court was whether a provision in the Securities Exchange Act of 1934 had an implied cause of action. While the Court mentioned all of the *Cort* factors, it suggested that the first three were relevant only because they showed legislative intent. "The ultimate question is one of congressional intent, not one of whether this Court thinks that it can improve upon the statutory scheme that Congress enacted into law." *Id.* at 576. Thus, the *Cort* factors continued to be relevant, but only to the extent that they demonstrated congressional intent.

In 1986, Justice Scalia joined the Supreme Court. Needless to say, the Court's implied cause of action doctrine, which was based on congressional intent, was not immune from his textualist influence. How does the majority refine the *Cort* test in the case that follows?

Alexander v. Sandoval

Supreme Court of the United States
532 U.S. 275 (2001)

♦ JUSTICE SCALIA delivered the opinion of the Court, [in which REHNQUIST, C.J., and O'CONNOR, KENNEDY, and THOMAS, JJ., concur].

This case presents the question whether private individuals may sue to enforce disparate-impact regulations promulgated [by the Department of Justice (DOJ)] under Title VI of the Civil Rights Act of 1964....

The State of Alabama amended its Constitution in 1990 to declare English "the official language of the state of Alabama." Pursuant to this provision..., the [State Department of Licensing] decided to administer state driver's license examinations only in English. Respondent Sandoval ... brought suit ... to enjoin the English-only policy, arguing that it [was discriminatory under Title VI of the Civil Rights Act of 1964]. The District Court agreed. It enjoined the policy and ordered the Department to accommodate non-English speakers. Petitioners appealed to the Court of Appeals for the Eleventh Circuit, which affirmed. Both courts rejected petitioners' argument that Title VI did not provide respondents a cause of action....

[W]e agreed to review ... whether there is a private cause of action to enforce the regulation [promulgated by DOJ under the Act. The regulation prohibited agencies and programs receiving federal funding from taking actions that had a disparate impact on persons of a certain race, color, or nationality. The Department of Transportation (DOT) had a similar regulation.]....

[First, i]t is thus beyond dispute that private individuals may sue to enforce § 601 [of the Act].... Second, it is similarly beyond dispute—and no party disagrees—that § 601 prohibits only intentional discrimination.... [Third, because] petitioners have not challenged the regulations here[, w]e ... assume for the purposes of deciding this case that the DOJ and DOT regulations proscribing activities that have a disparate impact on the basis of race are valid.... [The only issue is whether petitioner has a right to sue to enforce the regulations.].

Like substantive federal law itself, private rights of action to enforce federal law must be created by Congress. *Touche Ross & Co. v. Redington*, 442 U.S. 560, 578 (1979) (remedies available are those "that Congress enacted into law"). The judicial task is to interpret the statute Congress has passed to determine whether it displays an intent to create not just a private right but also a private remedy. Statutory intent on this latter point is determinative. Without it, a cause of action does not exist and courts may not create one, no matter how desirable that might be as a policy matter, or how compatible with the statute. "Raising up causes of action where a statute has not created them may be a proper function for common-law courts, but not for federal tribunals."

Respondents would have us revert in this case to the understanding of private causes of action that held sway 40 years ago when Title VI was enacted. That understanding is captured by the Court's statement in *J.I. Case Co. v. Borak*, 377 U.S. 426, 433 (1964), that "it is the duty of the courts to be alert to provide such remedies as are necessary to make effective the congressional purpose" expressed by a statute. We abandoned that understanding in *Cort v. Ash*, 422 U.S. 66, 78 (1975)—which itself interpreted a statute enacted under the *ancien regime*—and have not returned to it since. Not even when interpreting the same Securities Exchange Act of 1934 that was at issue in *Borak* have we applied *Borak's* method for discerning and defining causes of action. Having sworn off the habit of venturing beyond Congress's intent, we will not accept respondents' invitation to have one last drink.

Nor do we agree with the Government that our cases interpreting statutes enacted prior to *Cort v. Ash* have given "dispositive weight" to the "expectations" that the enacting Congress had formed "in light of the 'contemporary legal context.'" ... We have never accorded dispositive weight to context shorn of text. In determining whether statutes create private rights of action, as in interpreting statutes generally, legal context matters only to the extent it clarifies text.

We therefore begin (and find that we can end) our search for Congress's intent with the text and structure of Title VI. Section 602 authorizes federal agencies "to effectuate the provisions of (§ 601) ... by issuing rules, regulations, or orders of general applicability." It is immediately clear that the "rights-creating" language so critical to the Court's analysis in *Cannon* of § 601 is completely absent from § 602. Whereas § 601 decrees that "(n)o person ... shall ... be subjected to discrimination," the text of § 602 provides that "(e)ach Federal department and agency ... is authorized and directed to effectuate the provisions of (§ 601)." Far from displaying congressional intent to create new rights, § 602 limits agencies to "effectuat(ing)" rights already created by § 601....

Nor do the methods that § 602 goes on to provide for enforcing its authorized regulations manifest an intent to create a private remedy; if anything, they suggest the opposite.... [T]hese elaborate restrictions on agency enforcement ... tend to contradict a congressional intent to create privately enforceable rights through § 602 itself. The express provision of one method of enforcing a substantive rule suggests that Congress intended to preclude others....

Both the Government and respondents argue that the *regulations* contain rights-creating language and so must be privately enforceable, but that argument skips an analytical step. Language in a regulation may invoke a private right of action that Congress through statutory text created, but it may not create a right that Congress has not....

Neither as originally enacted nor as later amended does Title VI display an intent to create a freestanding private right of action to enforce regulations promulgated under § 602. We therefore hold that no such right of action exists. Since we reach this conclusion applying our standard test for discerning private causes of action, we do not address petitioners' additional argument that implied causes of action against States ... are inconsistent with the clear statement rule....

♦ Justice STEVENS, with whom SOUTER, GINSBURG, and BREYER, JJ., join, dissenting.

In 1964, as part of a groundbreaking and comprehensive civil rights Act, Congress prohibited recipients of federal funds from discriminating on the basis of race, ethnicity, or national origin. Title VI of the Civil Rights Act of 1964. Pursuant to powers expressly delegated by that Act, the federal agencies and departments responsible for awarding and administering federal contracts immediately adopted regulations prohibiting federal contractees from adopting policies that have the "effect" of discriminating on those bases. At the time of the promulgation of these regulations, prevailing principles of statutory construction assumed that Congress intended a private right of action whenever such a cause of action was necessary to protect individual rights granted by valid federal law. Relying both on this presumption and on independent analysis of Title VI, this Court has repeatedly and consistently affirmed the right of private individuals to bring civil suits to enforce rights guaranteed by Title VI. A fair reading of those cases, and coherent implementation of the statutory scheme, requires the same result under Title VI's implementing regulations....

The majority is undoubtedly correct that this Court has never said in so many words that a private right of action exists to enforce the disparate-impact regulations promulgated under § 602. However, ... [t]his Court has already considered the question presented today and concluded that a private right of action exists.... I would answer the question presented in the affirmative and affirm the decision of the Court of Appeals as a matter of *stare decisis*....

The majority's statutory analysis does violence to both the text and the structure of Title VI. Section 601 does not stand in isolation, but rather as part of an integrated remedial scheme. Section 602 exists for the sole purpose of forwarding the antidiscrimination ideals laid out in § 601. The majority's persistent belief that the two sections somehow forward different agendas finds no support in the statute....

... For three decades, we have treated § 602 as granting the responsible agencies the power to issue broad prophylactic rules aimed at realizing the vision laid out in § 601, even if the conduct captured by these rules is at times broader than that which would otherwise be prohibited....

This understanding is firmly rooted in the text of Title VI. As § 602 explicitly states, the agencies are authorized to adopt regulations to "effectuate" § 601's antidiscrimination mandate. The plain meaning of the text reveals Congress' intent to provide the relevant agencies with sufficient authority to transform the statute's broad aspiration into social reality. So too does a lengthy, consistent, and impassioned legislative history.[12] ...

The majority couples its flawed analysis of the structure of Title VI with an uncharitable understanding of the substance of the divide between those on this Court who are reluctant to interpret statutes to allow for private rights of action and those who are willing to do so if the claim of right survives a rigorous application of the criteria set forth in *Cort v. Ash*, 422 U.S. 66 (1975). As the majority narrates our implied right of action jurisprudence, the Court's shift to a more skeptical approach represents the rejection of a common-law judicial activism in favor of a principled recognition of the limited role of a contemporary "federal tribuna[l]." According to its analysis, the recognition of an implied right of action when the text and structure of the statute do not absolutely compel such a conclusion is an act of judicial self-indulgence. As much as we would like to help those disadvantaged by discrimination, we must resist the temptation to pour ourselves "one last drink." To do otherwise would be to "ventur[e] beyond Congress's intent."

Overwrought imagery aside, it is the majority's approach that blinds itself to congressional intent. While it remains true that, if Congress intends a private right of action to support statutory rights, "the far better course is for it to specify as much when it creates those rights," *Cannon*, its failure to do so does not absolve us of the responsibility to endeavor to discern its intent. In a series of cases since *Cort v. Ash*, we have laid out rules and developed strategies for this task.

The very existence of these rules and strategies assumes that we will sometimes find manifestations of an implicit intent to create such a right. Our decision in *Cannon* represents one such occasion. As the *Cannon* opinion iterated and reiterated, the question whether the plaintiff had a right of action that could be asserted in federal court was a "question of statutory construction," 441 U.S., at 688 (Rehnquist, J., concurring), not a question of policy for the Court to decide. Applying the *Cort v. Ash* factors, we examined the nature of the rights at issue, the text and structure of the statute, and the relevant legislative history. Our conclusion was that Congress un-

---

12. See, *e.g.*, 110 Cong. Rec. 6543 (1964) (statement of Sen. Humphrey) ("Simple justice requires that public funds, to which all taxpayers of all races contribute, not be spent in any fashion which encourages, entrenches, subsidizes, or results in racial discrimination"); *id.*, at 1520 (statement of Rep. Celler) (describing § 602 as requiring federal agencies to "reexamine" their programs "to make sure that adequate action has been taken to preclude ... discrimination").

mistakably intended a private right of action to enforce both Title IX and Title VI. Our reasoning—and, as I have demonstrated, our holding—was equally applicable to intentional discrimination and disparate-impact claims.

Underlying today's opinion is the conviction that *Cannon* must be cabined because it exemplifies an "expansive rights-creating approach." But, as I have taken pains to explain, it was Congress, not the Court, that created the cause of action....

In order to impose its own preferences as to the availability of judicial remedies, the Court today adopts a methodology that blinds itself to important evidence of congressional intent....

... [I]f the majority is genuinely committed to deciphering congressional intent, its unwillingness to even consider evidence as to the context in which Congress legislated is perplexing. Congress does not legislate in a vacuum. As the respondents and the Government suggest, and as we have held several times, the objective manifestations of congressional intent to create a private right of action must be measured in light of the enacting Congress' expectations as to how the judiciary might evaluate the question.

At the time Congress was considering Title VI, it was normal practice for the courts to infer that Congress intended a private right of action whenever it passed a statute designed to protect a particular class that did not contain enforcement mechanisms which would be thwarted by a private remedy. Indeed, the very year Congress adopted Title VI, this Court specifically stated that "it is the duty of the courts to be alert to provide such remedies as are necessary to make effective the congressional purpose." *J.I. Case Co. v. Borak,* 377 U.S. 426, 433 (1964). Assuming, as we must, that Congress was fully informed as to the state of the law, the contemporary context presents important evidence as to Congress' intent—evidence the majority declines to consider....

The question the Court answers today was only an open question in the most technical sense. Given the prevailing consensus in the Courts of Appeals, the Court should have declined to take this case. Having granted certiorari, the Court should have answered the question differently by simply according respect to our prior decisions. But most importantly, even if it were to ignore all of our post–1964 writing, the Court should have answered the question differently on the merits.

* * *

Points for Discussion

1. *Statutory Language*: What was the language at issue? What did each party want that language to mean? What meaning did the majority and dissent adopt?

2. *Theories*: Which theory did the majority use? The dissent? Did either find ambiguity, absurdity, a constitutional question to avoid, or a scrivener's error?

3. *Finding Implied Actions*: The majority did not apply the *Cort* factors, nor cite the case as relevant to the analysis. (The majority did cite *Cort* to point out that *Cort*

marked the end of *Borak*.). What is the majority's test for finding implied causes of action? Does it make sense to find implied causes of action only from the text of the statute? Would not such causes of action be express? Yet the majority explained how the text of § 601 includes an implied cause of action. What language did the majoriy point to? According to the dissent, are the *Cort* factors still relevant? *See Correctional Servs. Corp. v. Malesko*, 534 U.S. 61, 67 n.3 (2001) (noting that the Supreme Court has "retreated from [its] previous willingness to imply a cause of action where Congress has not [explicitly] provided one."). With the justices renewed focus on the text of the statute, it is unlikely that implied actions will become more common.

4. *Legal Context*: The plaintiffs argued that because the Civil Rights Act was enacted during the timeframe when the Court more readily found implied causes of action, the statute should be interpreted to include one. The majority rejected this argument, while the dissent found it persuasive. *See* Bradford C. Mank, *Legal Context: Reading Statutes in Light of Prevailing Legal Precedent*, 34 Ariz. St. L.J. 815, 868 (2002) (criticizing Justice Scalia's rejection of legal context). Should not Congress's expectations of whether the judiciary would imply a cause of action be relevant to the analysis?

5. *Another Example*: In *CBOCS West, Inc. v. Humphries*, 533 U.S. 442 (2008), the plaintiff alleged that he was fired after he complained that another employee was fired because of race. Section 1981 of the Civil Rights Act provides that all persons "shall have the same right in every State and Territory to make and enforce contracts ... as is enjoyed by white citizens...." 42 U.S.C. § 1981(a). Employment is considered a contract, so the employee who was fired because of his race would have been covered under the Act. This case raised the question of whether an employee who was fired for whistleblowing could bring a claim for *retaliation* under Section 1981. Relevantly, the Court had held, in an earlier case, that a companion statute to section 1981, 42 U.S.C. § 1982 ("Section 1982"), included a prohibition against retaliation for advocating for the rights of those individuals Section 1982 protects. *Sullivan v. Little Hunting Park, Inc.*, 396 U.S. 229, 237 (1969). Because sections 1981 and 1982 were enacted together, the plaintiff argued that the statutes should be interpreted similarly. The majority agreed and held that Section 1981 did encompass retaliation claims.

Not surprisingly, Justices Thomas and Scalia dissented from the majority decision finding an implied cause of action. *CBOCS West*, 553 U.S. at 456–47. (Thomas, J., dissenting). Justice Scalia stated at oral argument: "We inferred that cause of action [for section 1982] in the bad old days, when we were inferring causes of action all over the place." Oral Argument at 45, *CBOCS West, Inc. v. Humphries*, 553 U.S. 442 (2008).

6. *Implied Remedies for Implied Actions*: "[A] right without a remedy is not a right at all." *Doe v. County of Centre*, 242 F.3d 437, 456 (3rd Cir. 2001). So once a cause of action has been implied, courts must determine which, if any, remedies are available. After *Cannon* was decided, the Supreme Court had to determine the

appropriate remedy for Title IX's implied claims. In *Franklin v. Gwinnett County Public Schools*, 503 U.S. 60, 66 (1992), the plaintiff was a student at the public high school and was the subject of inappropriate and unwanted sexual advances by one of her teachers. According to the student, the school failed to respond appropriately. *Id.* at 64. By the time the case was heard, both the student and the teacher had left the school. Hence, injunctive relief would not have benefited this particular student.

The Supreme Court held that both injunctive relief and monetary damages were recoverable. The Court indicated that it would "presume the availability of all appropriate remedies unless Congress has expressly indicated otherwise." *Id.* (internal citations omitted). Consider whether it will be easy to find that "Congress has expressly indicated otherwise" when Congress does not expressly grant a private cause of action.

In holding that all forms of relief were available unless Congress had indicated otherwise, the *Franklin* majority was quick to distinguish its evolving test for finding implied remedies. "[T]he question whether a litigant has a 'cause of action' is analytically distinct and prior to the question of what relief, if any, a litigant may be entitled to receive." *Id.* at 69 (quotations omitted). Because the Court had implied a cause of action in *Cannon*, the legislative silence surrounding available remedies did not trouble the *Franklin* majority. "Since the Court in *Cannon* concluded that this statute supported no express right of action, it is hardly surprising that Congress also said nothing about the applicable remedies for an implied right of action." *Id.* at 71.

The Court turned to another source to resolve the issue: subsequent legislative acts. In two subsequent, related acts (the Rehabilitation Act Amendments of 1986 and the Rehabilitation Act of 1973), Congress had eliminated the states' Eleventh Amendment immunity from suit. In doing so, Congress broadly defined the available remedies to include all forms of damages. *Id.* at 73. The *Franklin* majority and concurrence saw Congress's subsequent legislation as "a validation of *Cannon's* holding" and "as an implicit acknowledgment that damages are available." *Id.* at 78 (Scalia, J., concurring). Even Justice Scalia, a firm critic of implied causes of action, was willing to grant all available remedies once the cause of action was implied. Thus, if the Court is willing to imply a cause of action, it will likely be willing to award both equitable and legal remedies. *See, e.g., Pandazides v. Virginia Bd. of Educ.*, 13 F.3d 823, 830–32 (4th Cir. 1994) (relying on the *Franklin* presumption—that all remedies are available absent congressional intent to the contrary—to hold that a plaintiff could seek punitive damages under Section 504 of the Rehabilitation Act.).

7. *Implied Remedies for Express Action*: There is a different, but related, issue regarding implied remedies. When a statute expressly provides a private cause of action, are the explicitly identified remedies in the statute exclusive? If a statute does not specifically say that punitive damages, for example, are recoverable, should a court interpret the statute to allow them? What about equitable relief?

Should a statute that provides for monetary damages be interpreted to provide equitable relief as well?

As you might imagine, the decision of whether to expand a statute to include remedies not specifically identified in the statute turns on the judge's particular approach to statutory interpretation. Judges who follow a purposivist approach to this issue consider whether the identified remedy will further the purpose of the statute. *See, e.g., Orloff v. Los Angeles Turf Club, Inc.*, 180 P.2d 321, 325 (Cal. 1947) (holding that injunctive relief was necessary to effectuate the purpose of the statute: to prevent the exclusion of persons from certain places based on their race). However, with the emerging hostility towards implied remedies and the refocus on the text of the statute, it is unlikely that a court today would expand remedies beyond those explicitly provided in the statute. *See, e.g., Snapp v. Unlimited Concepts, Inc.*, 208 F.3d 928, 935 (11th Cir. 2000) (holding that the Fair Labor Standards Act's anti-retaliation provision for general damages did not include punitive damages based on the text of the statute).

* * *

These two areas of law—implied causes of action and implied remedies—are at the forefront of statutory interpretation. Over time, with changes in the composition of the Supreme Court, the doctrines have completely morphed in ways that make little sense. How will it ever be possible to find an implied cause of action using textualism? If Congress is to be clear and only the text can be consulted, then unless Congress expressly includes such a cause of action, one may not be implied. This tension between the power of the legislature to say what the law is, and the power of the judiciary to say what the law means, underscores every aspect of statutory interpretation, but it is most visible in this area. The two most recent additions to the Supreme Court, Justice Sotomayor and Justice Kagan, will likely play a huge role in shaping the Court's doctrine and approach to statutory interpretation. Sit back and relax. It should be an interesting show!

Problem 15

You represent Jim Thaler, an Iraq veteran. Jim was injured by an improvised explosive device (IED) in the Iraq War. His left arm was amputated above the elbow and his right leg was amputated above the knee. He wears an "artificial arm" and uses a wheelchair.

In March, Jim filed a claim for an annual clothing allowance for his artificial arm, because the prosthetic appliance tends to wear and/or tear his shirts. He also sought a separate clothing allowance based upon loss of his leg that requires the use of a wheelchair that tends to wear and/or tear pants. The Veterans Administration (VA) denied his claim for multiple clothing allowances, claiming that the plain language of the statute allows each veteran to receive only one clothing allowance. Write a letter to the VA appealing the interpretation. You may have read this case in Chapter 7. You may use some of those arguments; however, you should include arguments about whether the statute is remedial and should be broadly construed.

38 U.S.C. § 1162 provides:

> The Veteran's Administration shall pay a clothing allowance of $662 per year to each veteran who because of a service-connected disability, wears or uses a prosthetic or orthopedic appliance (including a wheelchair), which tends to wear out or tear the clothing of the veteran....

As originally passed in 1972, the statute provided for a clothing allowance based on a disability necessitating the use of "a prosthetic or orthopedic appliance *or appliances*." Veterans' Compensation and Relief Act of 1972, Pub. L. No. 92–328, § 103, 86 Stat. 393, 394 (emphasis added). In 1989, Congress amended the statute to delete the reference to multiple appliances. Veterans' Benefits Amendments of 1989, Pub.L. No. 101–237, § 112, 103 Stat. 2062, 2065. As noted above, the present statute now provides for a clothing allowance based on a disability necessitating the use of "a prosthetic or orthopedic appliance."

As part of the enactment of section 1162, Congress estimated the first-year cost for implementation to be $6.6 million. S. Rep. No. 92-845, at 10 (1972), U.S. Code Cong. & Admin. News 1972, p. 2081. Before estimating that sum, Congress sought from the VA an estimate of how many veterans would be eligible for the clothing allowance. According to the Senate report addressing the enactment of section 1162, the Senate Committee quoted the VA's estimate that 44,000 veterans would be eligible for the clothing allowance. *Id.* Upon this basis, Congress made the following calculation: $150 multiplied by 44,000 eligible veterans (receiving only one clothing allowance each) equals the $6.6 million estimated for the first year of the clothing allowance.

Chapter 16

The Regulatory Process: Introduction to Agencies

A. Introduction to This Chapter

In Chapter 13, we covered post-enactment context: what happens both before and after enactment. You may have noticed that we covered both subsequent *judicial* and subsequent *legislative* action but did not address subsequent *executive* action. In this chapter, we begin our journey into the world of regulation and the role of agencies in our government. Agencies are part of the executive branch. They exercise a variety of powers. This chapter explains what agencies are and how they fit within our constitutional structure. You may wish to reread the section on separation of powers. You are about to see that the modern administrative state challenges formalism and fits uncomfortably in our tripartite government.

This chapter proceeds as follows. First, you will learn *what* agencies are. What makes an authority of the government an agency? In anyone working for the government an agency? Next, you will learn *why* agencies regulate. Here, you might ask, do we need agency regulation at all? After learning why agencies regulate, we will turn to the question of *how* agencies regulate. Agencies can act in a variety of ways, from issuing rules, to adjudicating cases, to inspecting businesses. We will look at all of these ways in some detail, for the way that an agency acts plays a role in the deference a court will give an agency when it interprets a statute. Finally, you will conclude this chapter by learning *where* agencies fit within our constitutional structure. Agencies have executive, quasi-legislative, and quasi-adjudicatory powers. Yet, they are located within the executive branch. Under separation of powers, how can agencies legitimately exercise any power other than executive?

B. What Agencies Are

The Administrative Procedures Act (APA), 5 U.S.C. § 551 *et. seq.* (2015), governs agencies and identifies their procedural law, which lawyers call *Administrative Law*. You may wish to take a quick glance through the APA as we discuss this topic.

The APA defines an agency as "each authority of the Government of the United States … not includ[ing Congress, the courts, state governments, etc.]." APA §§ 551(1), 701(b)(1). For purposes of the APA, the term "agency" is defined to include all governmental authorities including administrations, commissions, corporations (*i.e.*, the Federal Deposit Insurance Corporation), boards, departments, divisions, and agencies. This definition is very broad. Most recently, the Supreme Court held that Amtrak is a governmental entity because of the government's oversight of and involvement with the corporation. *DOT v. Association of Am. R.&R.*, 135 S. Ct. 1225, 1231 (2015).

There are a couple of things to note about the APA's definition of an agency. First, it is very broad and, notably, does not define the term "authority." Second, the definition lists specific exclusions but does not exclude the president. Is the president an agency? *Expressio unius* would suggest so given that there is no catch-all. Surprisingly, the issue of whether the president is considered an agency subject to the APA did not come before the Supreme Court until 1992. As you will see in the excerpt below, despite the strong textual argument, the Supreme Court held that the president was not an agency because of separation of powers.

Franklin v. Massachusetts

Supreme Court of the United States

505 U.S. 788 (1992)

◆ O'Connor, Justice delivered the opinion of the Court [with respect to this issue in which Rehnquist, C.J., and White, Scalia, and Thomas, JJ., concur.].

… This decade, as a result of the 1990 census and reapportionment, Massachusetts lost a seat in the House of Representatives. Appellees Massachusetts and two of its registered voters brought this action against the President, [and others], challenging, among other things, the method used for counting federal employees serving overseas…. A three-judge panel of the United States District Court for the District of Massachusetts held that the decision to allocate military personnel serving overseas to their "homes of record" was arbitrary and capricious under the standards of the Administrative Procedure Act (APA). As a remedy, the District Court directed the Secretary to eliminate the overseas federal employees from the apportionment counts, directed the President to recalculate the number of Representatives per State…. The federal officials appealed…. We now reverse….

The APA provides for judicial review of "final agency action for which there is no other adequate remedy in a court." At issue in this case is whether the "final" action that appellees have challenged is that of an "agency" such that the federal courts may exercise their powers of review under the APA. We hold that the final action complained of is that of the President, and the President is not an agency within the meaning of the Act. Accordingly, there is no final agency action that may be reviewed under the APA standards….

The APA defines "agency" as "each authority of the Government of the United States, whether or not it is within or subject to review by another agency, but does not include—(A) the Congress; (B) the courts of the United States; (C) the governments of the territories or possessions of the United States; (D) the government of the District of Columbia." 5 U.S.C. §§ 701(b)(1), 551(1). The President is not explicitly excluded from the APA's purview, but he is not explicitly included, either. Out of respect for the separation of powers and the unique constitutional position of the President, we find that textual silence is not enough to subject the President to the provisions of the APA. We would require an express statement by Congress before assuming it intended the President's performance of his statutory duties to be reviewed for abuse of discretion. As the APA does not expressly allow review of the President's actions, we must presume that his actions are not subject to its requirements. Although the President's actions may still be reviewed for constitutionality, we hold that they are not reviewable for abuse of discretion under the APA. The District Court erred in proceeding to determine the merits of the APA claims....

violation of separations of powers

– not an agency

[The plurality then addresses the constitutional claim, finding it to be without merit.]

◆ [The concurring opinions of STEVENS, and SCALIA, JJ., have been omitted.]

* * *

Points for Discussion

1. *Statutory Language*: What was the language at issue? What did each party want that language to mean? What meaning did the plurality adopt?

2. *Theories*: Which theory did the plurality use? Did the plurality find ambiguity, absurdity, a constitutional question to avoid, or a scrivener's error?

3. *Agency Definition*: Section 702 of the APA permits "[a] person suffering legal wrong because of *agency* action ... to [seek] judicial review thereof. Additionally, section 704 of the APA provides for judicial review of 'final *agency* action for which there is no other adequate remedy in a court.'" The APA broadly defines "agency" as "each authority of the Government of the United States [except for] (A) the Congress; (B) the courts of the United States; (C) the governments of the territories or possessions of the United States; (D) the government of the District of Columbia." 5 U.S.C. §§701(b)(1), 551(1). Note that the president is not specifically excluded. Had the Court applied *expressio unius*, what result? What was Justice O'Connor's response to this argument?

4. *Separation of Powers*: While the justices split on their reasoning about finality and standing, they were mostly united in their understanding that they lacked power to order a sitting president to act (although Justice Stevens did not address this issue because he found the Secretary's report to be final agency action). Justice Scalia was the most outraged by the trial court's order: "It is a commentary upon the level to which judicial understanding—indeed, even judicial awareness—of the doctrine of separation of powers has fallen, that the District Court entered this order against the President without blinking an eye. I think it clear that no court has authority to direct the President to take an official act." *Franklin*, 505 U.S. at 826 (Scalia, J., concurring).

* * *

Before we leave the topic of what agencies are, there is one more topic we need to cover. There are two types of agencies: *independent agencies* and *executive agencies*.

Independent agencies are less subject to the president's influence because they are often headed by multimember groups from both political parties serving specific terms, and these multimember board members can only be removed for cause. Examples of independent agencies include the Securities and Exchange Commission, the Federal Trade Commission, the Federal Election Commission, the Equal Opportunity Commission, and the National Labor Relations Board.

Executive agencies, in contrast, are generally headed by individuals (usually called secretaries), whom the president appoints with the advice and consent of the Senate, and who serve at the discretion of the president. Examples include the Department of the Treasury, Department of Agriculture, and the Department of Labor. The largest and most influential executive agencies are called *departments*; departments contain a host of sub-agencies. A few examples of departments include the Commerce Department, the Justice Department, the Department of Energy, the Department of Education, and the Department of Homeland Security. Sub-entities within the Department of the Interior include the Fish and Wildlife Service, the National Park Services, the Bureau of Indian Affairs, the Bureau of Reclamation, and the Bureau of Land Management. The heads of the departments are known collectively as the Cabinet, and presidential succession flows to these important secretaries, staring with the Department of State. While presidents turned to the Cabinet for advice in the past, more recent presidents tended to turn to other entities.

* * *

C. Why Agencies Regulate: A Case Study

A government may regulate in numerous ways. The legislature regulates by enacting statutes. The courts incrementally regulate through judicial opinions. And the executive regulates by promulgating rules and issuing orders. Executive regulation, or agency regulation, has advantages over legislative and judicial regulation. Generally, agencies have the flexibility to act more quickly than either the legislature or courts, and agencies can act with more detail. In short, the legislature and courts simply cannot do it all quickly enough. *Mistretta v. United States*, 488 U.S. 361, 372 (1989) ("[The Court's] jurisprudence has been driven by a practical understanding that in our increasingly complex society ... Congress simply cannot do its job absent an ability to delegate power.").

Also, and critically important, agencies have specialized and relevant expertise. The modern administrative state is vastly complex. Agencies have expertise in their area of responsibility. Consider the U.S. Department of Veterans' Affairs (VA), the Environmental Protection Agency (EPA), and the Food and Drug Administration (FDA). Each of these agencies has experts and specialists trained in the relevant field. Judges are generalists with expertise in law, not in the environment or food safety. Hence, it simply makes more sense for medical personnel within the VA to determine disability benefits for veterans, for scientists within the EPA to determine acceptable levels of pollutants in the air, and for nutritionists within the FDA to determine the safety of food additives.

Moreover, agencies may be more responsive to the electorate than the judiciary would be, although perhaps less responsive than the legislature. National goals and policies change as society evolves. Agency administrators are accountable to the public via the Office of the President and, therefore, will be more likely to conform their policies to match populist expectations. Federal judges, in contrast, are elected for life and are, thus, more insulated from political backlash. They tend to protect minority interests, rather than represent the majority position.

Today, many of us take for granted that our world is safe. Would we be better off without agency regulation? Regulated entities (the general term for those entities that agencies regulate) and others argue that overregulation hurts the economy and business. Former President Reagan was elected, in part, because of his promises to deregulate. Some individuals argue that market forces can adequately and more efficiently protect the public. Is that true? Consider the following example.

Prior to 1938, drugs were largely unregulated in the United States. Then more than 100 people died from one drug. That drug, sulfanilamide, had been safely used to treat streptococcal infections for some time in both a tablet and powder form. But there was a growing demand for a liquid form. In response to this market demand, the chief chemist and pharmacist from S.E. Massengill Company* experimented and found that sulfanilamide dissolved in diethylene glycol. The chemist lab tested his new liquid mixture for flavor, appearance, and fragrance. He did not test for toxicity. Unfortunately, diethylene glycol is a chemical that is normally used as antifreeze; it is deadly.

After the liquid mixture passed the taste and smell test, Massengill immediately sent 633 shipments of its new drug to doctors and pharmacists throughout the country. The drug had a pleasant, raspberry flavor that was particularly appealing to children. More than 100 people died after taking the drug; many of those who died were children being treated for sore throats. The victims were sick for seven to ten days and experienced symptoms characteristic of kidney failure, including inability to urinate, severe abdominal pain, nausea, vomiting, stupor, and convulsions. They suffered intense and unrelenting pain.

One mother described the heartache she experienced at the loss of her daughter:

> The first time I ever had occasion to call in a doctor for [Joan] and she was given Elixir of Sulfanilamide. All that is left to us is the caring for her

---

* Massengill was a pharmaceutical company started in 1898 by Samuel Evans Massengill. Samuel graduated from the University of Nashville Medical School, but decided to manufacture drugs rather than practice medicine. It employed more than 200 people in Bristol, Tennessee, including six pharmaceutical chemists. The company operated as a family owned company until 1971, when it was acquired by another company. Most recently, it merged with Prestige Brands Holdings, Inc.

little grave. Even the memory of her is mixed with sorrow for we can see her little body tossing to and fro and hear that little voice screaming with pain and it seems as though it would drive me insane....

Carol Ballentine, *Taste of Raspberries, Taste of Death The 1937 Elixir Sulfanilamide Incident*, FDA Consumer Magazine, June 1981, http://www.fda.gov/aboutfda/ whatwedo/history/productregulation/sulfanilamidedisaster/default.htm.

A doctor described his distress:

Nobody but Almighty God and I can know what I have been through these past few days. I have been familiar with death in the years since I received my M.D. from Tulane University School of Medicine with the rest of my class of 1911. Covington County has been my home. I have practiced here for years. Any doctor who has practiced more than a quarter of a century has seen his share of death.

But to realize that six human beings, all of them my patients, one of them my best friend, are dead because they took medicine that I prescribed for them innocently, and to realize that that medicine which I had used for years in such cases suddenly had become a deadly poison in its newest and most modern form, as recommended by a great and reputable pharmaceutical firm in Tennessee: well, that realization has given me such days and nights of mental and spiritual agony as I did not believe a human being could undergo and survive. I have known hours when death for me would be a welcome relief from this agony.

Letter from Dr. A.S. Calhoun (October 22, 1937), available at http://www.fda.gov/ aboutfda/whatwedo/history/productregulation/sulfanilamidedisaster/default.htm.

Although Massengill quickly discovered that the drug was toxic, the company was in no hurry to recall it. Instead, Massengill merely sent telegrams to its salesmen, druggists, and doctors asking them to return the drug. The telegrams provided little explanation: they failed to mention the urgency of the situation or that the drug was lethal. Only after insistence from governmental officials, did the company finally send out a second set of telegrams warning of the danger. But Massengill admitted no responsibility: Dr. Samuel Evans Massengill, the company's owner, said: "My chemists and I deeply regret the fatal results, but there was no error in the manufacture of the product. We have been supplying a legitimate professional demand and not once could have foreseen the unlooked-for results. I do not feel that there was any responsibility on our part." He was wrong. A few simple tests on experimental animals would have demonstrated the lethal properties of the elixir. Even a review of the current existing scientific literature would have shown that diethylene glycol was toxic and could cause kidney damage or failure. Massengill's chemist, the person who created the formula, must have felt more culpable. He committed suicide.

Under the law in effect at the time, the U.S. Department of Agriculture (USDA) had almost no power to seize the drug or to prosecute Massengill. The agency focused its early efforts on convincing the company to help find and destroy the drug. Ultimately, the USDA charged Massengill for drug misbranding. The USDA argued that the company, by using the term "elixir" in its product description had implied that the product was an alcoholic solution. However, the product contained no alcohol. At that time, misbranding was only a fineable offense. Had Massengill called the product a "solution" instead of an "elixir," the USDA would have had no legal authority to penalize the company or even to seize the drug. Undoubtedly, many more people would have died.

Why did the USDA have no authority to act? The Pure Food and Drug Act of 1906 was obsolete. That Act together with the Meat Inspection Act were Congress's response to the public outcry from Upton Sinclair's 1905 book, THE JUNGLE—an exposé about the Chicago meat-packing industry—and from articles about the widespread adulteration of drugs and food. When it was enacted, the Pure Food and Drug Act of 1906 was the federal government's most significant intrusion into industry through the interstate commerce clause. Although other federal agencies could regulate prices and workplace safety, Congress gave the USDA the power to regulate the manufacture, sale, and advertising of food, drugs, and medicines.

The Act provided, in relevant part:

> An Act—for preventing the manufacture, sale, or transportation of adulterated or misbranded or poisonous or deleterious foods, drugs, medicines, and liquors, and for regulating traffic therein, and for other purposes....

> [Section 2] That the introduction into any State or Territory or the District of Columbia ... of any article of food or drugs which is adulterated or misbranded, within the meaning of this Act, is hereby prohibited.

> [Section 4] That the examinations of specimens of foods and drugs shall be made in the Bureau of Chemistry of the Department of Agriculture, or under the direction and supervision of such Bureau, for the purpose of determining from such examinations whether such articles are adulterated or misbranded within the meaning of this Act....

Federal Food and Drugs Act of 1906, 21 U.S.C. Sec 1-15 (1934), *repealed by* 21 U.S.C. Sec 329 (a) (1938).

While this Act was a significant first step, it actually provided little protection to the public. The Act did not prohibit the sale of dangerous, untested, or poisonous drugs, nor did it require that safety studies be done on new drugs before they entered the marketplace. While selling toxic drugs was, undoubtedly, bad for business, it was not illegal. By the 1930s it was widely recognized that this Act needed amendment; however, Congress was at an impasse to effect change until the "Elixir Sulfanilamide" incident. After that, Congress quickly enacted the Federal Food, Drug, and Cosmetic Act, giving authority to the Food and Drug Administration (FDA), which is within the USDA, to regulate food, cosmetic, and drug safety. The new Act required manufacturers to demonstrate to the FDA the safety of new drugs prior to making them available to the public. Twenty-five years after its enactment, this Act saved the United States from another potential drug tragedy—the thalidomide disaster. The FDA had prevented the drug from being approved in the United States, but it was used widely in Europe with devastating effects. Today, the Food and Drug Act continues to be the basis for FDA regulation of these products. While the Act is not perfect, few would argue that the market place can safely and adequately protect our nation.

D. How Agencies Regulate

Agencies regulate private conduct, administer entitlement programs, collect taxes, deport aliens, issue permits, run the space program, manage the national parks, and so on. Simply put, agencies run the functions we think of as government, whether state or federal. Of more interest to us is *how* agencies do what they do. Congress delegates power to agencies to regulate specific conduct or run programs. To regulate conduct and run programs, agencies act in three ways: by adjudicating, rulemaking, and investigating. Agencies act like courts when they adjudicate, like legislatures when they promulgate rules, and like the police when they investigate. In this next section, we will explore the three ways that agencies act. As we do so, keep in mind that these agency powers are defined in the APA. We will focus on federal agencies; state agencies may operate differently.

For a federal agency to have any power to act, Congress must enact a statute that both creates the agency (if it does not already exist) and identifies the agency's powers and regulatory agenda. This statute is known as the *enabling*, authorizing, or organic statute (all three names are used). In an enabling statute, Congress commonly authorizes an agency to use one or more of the powers identified above: rulemaking, adjudication, and investigation. This next section explores each power in more detail, beginning with rulemaking.

1. Rulemaking

The APA defines rulemaking as the "agency process for formulating, amending, or repealing a rule." APA § 551(5). A rule is "an agency statement of general ... applicability and future effect designed to implement, interpret, or prescribe law or policy." APA § 551(4). In sum, rules, like statutes, are laws that when *promulgated*, or enacted, apply prospectively to large numbers of regulated entities. In contrast, orders, which agencies make through adjudication, are like judicial opinions; generally, they apply just to the prior actions of the adjudicating parties.

There are two kinds of rules, legislative rules and non-legislative rules. Further, there are three kinds of legislative rulemaking procedures, (1) formal rulemaking procedures, (2) informal rulemaking procedures (more commonly called notice-and-comment rulemaking), and (3) publication rules, those that are exempt rulemaking procedures. The flowchart below shows the types of rulemaking available to agencies.

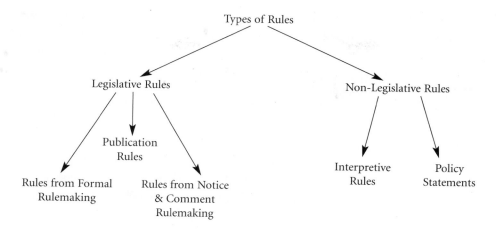

a. Legislative Rulemaking

Legislative rules are rules with legal (or binding) effect, meaning if a regulated entity violates the rule, the entity will be subject to penalty. Agencies promulgate legislative rules, known as regulations, through three different processes. These processes differ in their degree of procedural formality.

The most formal process is formal rulemaking. The procedures for formal rulemaking can be found in sections 556 and 557 of the APA. In short, formal rulemaking includes a hearing with civil, trial-like procedures. Entities and individuals who might be affected by the rule have a right to notice of the hearing, and they have a right to participate in the hearing in some fashion. APA §§ 554(b) & (c). The rules of evidence do not apply. *See* APA § 556(c)(3) (instructing ALJs to receive relevant evidence). A hearing officer, known as an administrative law judge (ALJ), compiles the record and makes either an initial decision or recommendation to the agency head. APA § 554(d). The agency head then either adopts the ALJ decision or issues a final decision. That decision is subject to judicial review. APA § 706(2).

The procedures used in formal rulemaking are better suited for resolving adjudicative facts (*e.g.,* who is telling the truth) rather than for resolving legislative facts (*e.g.,* what degree of arsenic in the soil is safe). For this reason, formal rulemaking is not common. Moreover, the APA requires agencies to use formal rulemaking only "[w]hen rules are required by statute to be made on the record after opportunity for an agency hearing...." APA § 553(c). While Congress may have intended formal rulemaking to apply often under this statute, the Supreme Court took a literal approach to interpreting this language in *United States v. Florida East Coast Railway,* 410 U.S. 224 (1973). In that case, the Court held that enabling statutes that merely require an agency to issue a rule "after a hearing" do not trigger formal rulemaking. *Id.* at 238. If Congress wants agencies to use formal rulemaking, Congress must be explicit (essentially, Congress must provide a clear statement). Thus, for formal rulemaking to be required, the enabling statute must require both a hearing *and* that the proceeding be on the record. As a result, formal rulemaking is quite rare at the federal level. It is, however, common in the states; for example, the Minnesota legislature frequently requires formal rulemaking.

The next most procedurally prescribed rulemaking process is notice-and-comment rulemaking (also known as informal rulemaking). Like its name suggests, notice-and-comment rulemaking requires an agency to publish notice of its proposed rule in the Federal Register (notice) and to solicit and respond to comments from the public and others about the proposed rule (comment). APA §§ 553(b) & (c). At the conclusion of this notice-and-comment process the agency typically promulgates a regulation.

While Congress likely intended notice-and-comment rulemaking to be a relatively quick process, it has become much more time consuming. Congress and the executive have added a number of procedures beyond those procedures the APA requires. For example, Executive Order 12866, which is discussed in detail below, requires agencies to conduct a cost-benefit analysis on all proposed rules that are "significant." E.O. 12,866, 58 Fed. Reg. 51735 (1993). Additionally, the Regulatory Flexibility Act requires agencies to create a Regulatory Flexibility Analysis for any proposed rule that will significantly impact a substantial number of small businesses, organizations, or governments. 5 U.S.C. § 601 *et seq.* (2015). And the Unfunded Mandates Reform Act requires agencies to prepare a statement assessing the effect of any proposed regulation that will cause state, local, or tribal governments to incur more than $100 million annually. 2 U.S.C. § 1501 *et seq.* (2015). Additionally, in the enabling statute, Congress may require an agency to use additional procedures to those the APA requires. In sum, Congress, the president, and even agencies can impose additional rulemaking procedures to those the APA requires.

The number and variety of these additional procedures has led commentators to lament the slowing-down, or "ossification," of the rulemaking process. Importantly, however, in a landmark case, the Supreme Court held that courts cannot require more procedure than that required by the APA, the Constitution, or a statute. *Vermont Yankee Nuclear Power Corp. v. Natural Resource Defense Council, Inc.,* 435 U.S. 519, 524 (1978). Today, agencies must follow time-consuming, detailed procedures to enact a regulation. Therefore, notice-and-comment rulemaking is informal in name only. And, the APA is only the starting point for procedural requirements. It is not the ending point.

Finally, the least procedurally prescribed process for legislative rulemaking allows agencies to avoid both formal rulemaking and notice-and-comment rulemaking procedures. The APA exempts the following rules from both formal and notice-and-comment procedures: (1) rules relating to military and foreign affairs; (2) rules relating to agency management and personnel; (3) rules relating to public property, loans, grants, benefits, and contracts; (4) rules for which the agency has "good cause" reason to avoid notice-and-comment rulemaking; and (5) rules of agency organization, procedure, and practice. 5 U.S.C. §§ 553(a), (b)(3)(A), & (b)(3)(B). Rules within these five categories together account for a tremendous number of rules. For example, if you have a federal student loan, the agency rules related to your loan need not be promulgated with notice-and-comment or formal rulemaking procedures. If you visit federal parks, the agency rules related to your use of the parks need not be promulgated with notice-and-comment or formal rulemaking procedures. Importantly, however, while the agency need not use notice-and-comment or formal rulemaking procedures, the APA does require that the agency publish these rules in the Federal Registrar or provide actual notice to anyone against whom the agency wishes to enforce a rule. APA § 552(1). Hence, these types of rules can be called "publication rules." Peter L. Strauss, An Introduction to Administrative Justice in the United States, 222–24 (2d. ed. 2002).

These three types of procedures—formal, notice-and-comment, and publication—are required for any legislative rule, meaning any rule that has independent legal effect.

b. Non-Legislative Rulemaking

Unlike legislative rules, non-legislative rules do not have independent legal effect. Rather, any legal effect they have comes from pre-existing legislative rules (whether from Congress or the agency). Non-legislative rules are often collectively called "guidance documents." Guidance documents are exempt from the formal and notice-and-comment procedures. 5 U.S.C. § 553(b)(3)(A). The APA identifies two types of guidance documents: (1) interpretative (or interpretive) rules, and (2) general statements of policy. *Id.* Interpretive rules are self-describing; they are rules interpreting language in an existing statute or regulation. In contrast, policy statements are statements from an agency that prospectively advise the public and agency personnel on the way in which the agency plans to exercise discretionary power in the future. Agencies may issue policy statements to announce new duties the agency plans to adopt by future adjudication or rulemaking. Note that there is no such thing as an "interpretive statement" or a "policy rule." Terminology is important.

Agencies use non-legislative rules for many reasons. For example, assume that after an agency has enacted a regulation, questions arise about how the agency will interpret that regulation. Lower level administrators may seek guidance from senior level administrators about how to implement the new regulation, or regulated entities may seek clarification about their responsibilities under the new rule. In response, agency administrators may develop a list of "frequently asked questions," update an agency manual, or provide guidance in some other form. To illustrate, the Corps of Engineers maintains Regulatory Guidance Letters, which are issued to field personnel to interpret or clarify existing regulatory policy. Similarly, the Internal Revenue Service issues letter rulings, which are written statements issued to taxpayers that interpret tax laws. There are many different ways that an agency might issue a non-legislative rule. Because agencies do not go through a procedurally prescribed process, such as formal or notice-and-comment rulemaking, when they issue these rules, the rules are easily modifiable and non-binding.

Non-legislative rules play a legitimate and important role in agency policy-making. They help agencies apply law consistently across field offices by affording guidance to both the public and lower level agency personnel. Non-legislative rules ensure greater and faster compliance than legislative rules alone, because legislative rules may lack specificity and clarity. Finally, non-legislative rules also help agencies develop a flexible policy quickly and easily, while still giving the regulated entities and the public advance notice of new policies. From an agency's perspective, non-legislative rules are "law" in a practical sense, because they influence the conduct of regulated entities and, thus, regulate behavior. But legally, non-legislative rules are not truly "law," because they are not legally binding. If an agency wants a rule to legally bind regulated entities, the agency must use formal, notice-and-comment, or, in limited cases, publication procedures.

You need not fully understand the differences in the various processes described above at this point. What should be clear, however, is that an agency can act with varying degrees of procedural formality. During any of these rulemaking processes, an agency may interpret a statute. Should courts defer to an agency's interpretation or decide the interpretation *de novo*? And if the courts defer, how much should they defer? As we will see in Chapter 19, judicial deference to an agency's interpretation of a statute depends, in large part, on the formality of the procedure the agency used to make its interpretation. While courts afford *some* deference to agency interpretations of statutes contained in non-legislative rules due to the agency's special knowledge and expertise in the area, such an interpretation is not afforded as much judicial deference as interpretations made after notice-and-comment or formal rulemaking. Hence, an agency might choose to use notice-and-comment rulemaking, even when the APA does not require it, simply to earn a higher level of judicial deference for its interpretation. Let's turn now to adjudication.

2. Adjudication

What is adjudication? The APA defines "adjudication" as the "agency process for the formulation of an order." APA § 551(7). An "order" is "the whole or a part of a final disposition ... of an agency in a matter other than rulemaking...." APA § 551(6). Combined, these definitions are so broad that any agency activity that is not rulemaking or investigating is adjudication (including the granting of a permit). In sum, agency orders, like court orders, are decisions that apply to the prior conduct of the adjudicating parties.

Like rulemaking, there are two kinds of adjudication: formal adjudication and informal adjudication. Congress may, in the enabling statute, impose additional requirements than those the APA requires; however, this discussion will focus only on the APA requirements.

The more formal process is formal adjudication. The procedures an agency must use for formal adjudication are the same procedures it must use for formal rulemaking. APA §§ 554, 556. Because formal adjudication is more common than formal rulemaking, we will look at the process in more detail here than we did earlier.

Formal administrative hearings resemble a civil trial with all the procedural accoutrements, including the right to notice, a hearing, a record, and a (mostly) neutral decision-maker. The primary differences between civil trials and formal administrative hearings are that (1) administrative hearings take place before an administrative law judge (ALJ) rather than a trial judge, and (2) the rules of evidence do not apply in administrative hearings. *See* APA §556(c)(3) (instructing ALJs to receive relevant evidence). Similar to trial court decisions, agency adjudications are subject to judicial review. APA §706(2).

ALJs generally preside over formal agency adjudications, although the person or persons in charge of the agency may choose to preside instead. APA §556(b). ALJs have the power to administer oaths, issue subpoenas, receive evidence, hold settlement conferences, dispose of procedural requests, take official notice of facts, and, most importantly, decide the case by either making an initial decision or by making a recommendation to the agency. APA §557(b). When the APA was first adopted, ALJs were known as "hearing examiners" and were expected only to assemble the record for the agency head; the term was changed to administrative law judges in 1978 to elevate their status.

The ALJ is an employee of the agency for which the ALJ works. 5 U.S.C §3105 (2015). To ensure that ALJs retain as much independence and neutrality as possible, agencies may not evaluate, discipline, reward, punish, or remove their ALJs; instead, the Merit Systems Protection Board makes these decisions, using a formal adjudication process. 5 U.S.C §7521 (2015). Also, the APA prohibits the agency investigator and prosecutor from interacting with the ALJ about a pending case, unless the investigator is a witness. APA §554(d). For these reasons, and as a practical matter, ALJs view and conduct themselves as independent, neutral decision-makers. Whether they are or not has been subject to considerable debate recently. A number of regulated entities have challenged the impartiality of the Securities and Exchange Commission's ALJs. *See, e.g. Bebo v. SEC*, 799 F.3d 765 (7th Cir. 2015); *Timbervest, LLC v. SEC*, 2015 U.S. Dist. LEXIS 132082 (N.D. Ga. Aug. 4, 2015); *Hill v. SEC*, 2015 U.S. Dist. LEXIS 74822 (N.D. Ga. June 8, 2015); *Duka v. SEC*, 2015 U.S. Dist. LEXIS 124444 (S.D.N.Y. Sept. 17, 2015); *Tilton v. SEC*, 2015 U.S. Dist. LEXIS 85015 (S.D.N.Y. June 30, 2015); *Gray Financial Group, Inc., v. SEC*, 2015 U.S. Dist. LEXIS 131792 (N.D. Ga. Aug. 4, 2015).

To appeal an ALJ's initial decision—which includes findings of fact, conclusions of law, the basis for the findings, and the order—a party must appeal first to the agency itself. Unlike appeals in a court of law, appeals to the agency are reviewed using a *de novo* standard of review: "the agency has all the powers which it would have in making the initial decision." APA §557(b). The process is similar to an appeal in court; the parties submit written briefs and argue orally. If the agency rules against itself, there is no further appeal. If, however, the agency rules in favor of itself, the losing party may appeal to a court of law, usually an appellate court. Judicial review concludes the formal adjudication process.

While formal adjudication resembles a civil trial, informal adjudication is altogether different. Often, the agency provides no hearing at all. Indeed, the APA requires few procedures; rather, an agency need only promptly decide an issue and notify the affected party. 5 U.S.C. §552 (2015). Informal adjudications can be as simple as an agency administrator approving an individual's application for a permit. If you have ever received a driving, hunting, fishing, or business license, you have been involved in an informal adjudication (albeit at the state level).

Although the APA requires few procedures for informal adjudication, the U.S. Constitution or the agency's enabling statute may require more. In cases involving the deprivation of life, liberty, or property rights, the Due Process Clause of the U.S. Constitution requires some form of a hearing. The hearing need not be elaborate; rather, the required procedures for that hearing vary in accordance with the competing interests. To determine whether an agency provided sufficient procedures to an individual who was deprived of a life, liberty, or property interest, a court will balance (1) the private interest being affected, (2) the risk of erroneous deprivation of this interest through the procedures the agency used, and (3) the administrative and fiscal burden to the agency of using of additional procedures (the government's interest). *Mathews v. Eldridge*, 424 U.S. 319, 335 (1976). Moreover, absent a really good reason, the government must offer a pre-deprivation hearing (rather than post-deprivation), although an abbreviated form is sufficient if the agency offers a post-deprivation hearing that comports with the *Mathews'* requirements. *Cleveland Bd. of Educ. v. Loudermill*, 470 U.S. 532, 542 (1985). In sum, compared to formal adjudication, informal adjudication procedures are generally minimal, and the process is much faster.

As in the case of rulemaking, agencies often prefer to act informally because the APA requires so few procedures for informal adjudication. Whether an agency must use formal instead of informal procedures is question of statutory interpretation. Simply put, to determine whether an agency should have used formal adjudication procedures when it adjudicated a case, a court will look at the language of the enabling statute and the agency's interpretation of that language. The court will apply a test known as the *Chevron* two-step (from *Chevron U.S.A., Inc. v. Natural Resources Defense Council, Inc.*, 467 U.S. 837 (1984)), which we will study in detail in the next chapter. In essence, a court will first determine whether Congress was clear as to which type of hearing was required, and if not, the court will determine second whether the agency's interpretation of the language was reasonable. *Dominion Energy v. Johnson*, 443 F.3d 12, 16 (1st Cir. 2006) (overruling an earlier case establishing a presumption in favor of formal adjudication); *Chemical Waste Management, Inc. v. EPA*, 873 F.2d 1477, 1482 (D.C. Cir. 1989) (applying *Chevron*). In general, unless Congress included the specific language from APA § 554(a) in the enabling statute—"on the record after opportunity for an agency hearing"—an agency's decision to use informal adjudication procedures will be upheld as reasonable.

During either type of adjudication—formal or informal—an agency may interpret a statute. As we will see in the next chapter, the appropriate level of deference a court will give that interpretation appears to depend on whether the agency used formal or informal procedures when doing so.

3. Investigation

Investigation is typically a function of the executive; thus, it should come as no surprise that Congress may grant agencies investigatory powers. Agencies conduct inspections, require the filing of reports, compel regulated entities to provide information, and issue subpoenas for a variety of reasons, including ensuring that regulated entities are complying with the law. Here are just a few examples. State health inspectors need the ability to enter and inspect restaurants to ensure that they are meeting applicable health standards. When a state welfare agency receives a complaint that a child is being abused or neglected by the child's parents, the welfare officials may need to enter and inspect the home to determine whether the complaint is valid. Federal Occupational Safety and Health Administration inspectors must visit worksites to ensure that the employers are providing safe working environments for their employees. The Federal Trade Commission may require corporations to submit information in a report.

Agencies conduct inspections, require the filing of reports, and issue subpoenas for a variety of reasons in addition to ensuring compliance with the law. Agencies may need (1) to obtain information to set policy through the promulgation of rules, (2) to keep Congress advised of their regulatory agenda, (3) to gain information needed to enforce their regulatory requirements, and (4) to obtain information needed to prosecute regulated entities for civil and criminal violations.

You likely know that the U.S. Constitution requires that the government obtain a warrant based on probable cause prior to searching citizens' property for evidence of criminal activity. U.S. CONST. amend. IV. It also requires the government obtain a warrant to search citizens' property for evidence of administrative violations. However, the probable cause standard for administrative searches is significantly less stringent. *Marshall v. Barlow's, Inc.* 436 U.S. 307, 320 (1978) (explaining that the "[p]robable cause justifying the issuance of a warrant [in the administrative context] may be based not only on specific evidence of an existing violation but also on a showing that reasonable legislative or administrative standards for conducting an ... inspection are satisfied."); *See v. Seattle*, 387 U.S. 541, 545–46 (1967); *Camara v. Municipal Court*, 387 U.S. 523, 538 (1967).

In *Camara*, the Court held that inspectors did have to get a warrant before they could search an apartment for violations of a city housing code. 387 U.S. at 538. The inspectors did not have to show cause that they would find violations at the particular apartment complex they wanted to inspect; rather, the inspectors had to show that "reasonable legislative or administrative standards for conducting an area inspection are satisfied with respect to a particular dwelling." *Id.* The Court explained that such standards, which will vary with the administrative program being enforced, may be based upon the passage of time, the nature of the building, or the condition of the entire area. Further, the standards will not necessarily depend upon specific knowledge of the condition of the particular dwelling. In other words, an inspection can occur without evidence of wrongdoing. The Court reached this conclusion because a search under these circumstances would be reasonable: the warrant procedure is designed to guarantee that a decision to search private property is justified by a reasonable governmental interest. "If a valid public interest justifies the intrusion contemplated, then there is probable cause to issue a suitably restricted search warrant." *Id.* at 538.

Note, however, that Congress cannot simply provide in a statute that an agency has the authority to conduct a warrantless search. *Marshall*, 436 U.S. at 316 (holding that the agency did not have power to conduct warrantless searches despite an explicit grant to do so in the statute). The Fourth Amendment limits Congress's authority to allow warrantless, administrative searches.

Although the Fourth Amendment requires an agency to obtain a warrant based on probable cause before the agency conducts an administrative inspection, few inspections are actually based on a warrant. Rather, individuals and businesses often give consent. Indeed, many trade and industry groups advise their members to consent to searches absent unusual circumstances that might justify refusal. For this reason, unless there is an emergency, an inspector may wish to seek consent prior to seeking a warrant. In addition, when an inspector has the businesses consent to search, the inspector can inspect more broadly than a warrant would have allowed. Searches based on a warrant are limited to areas and items identified in the warrant.

While administrative searches of ordinary businesses require a warrant, searches of businesses that are closely—the Court also uses the term pervasively—regulated do not require a warrant, because these businesses have lower expectations of privacy. *New York v. Burger*, 482 U.S. 691, 702–03 (1987). Such businesses have a long tradition of being closely supervised by the government. Hence, warrants are unnecessary. The closely regulated exception to the warrant requirement is essentially an outgrowth of the waiver/consent doctrine: by voluntarily engaging in a heavily regulated business, business owners voluntarily give up or waive their privacy expectations. While the Fourth Amendment applies, it does not require either a warrant or probable cause. *Id*. The standard for a valid warrantless search of a closely held business is threefold: (1) the regulatory scheme has to be justified by a substantial governmental interest, (2) warrantless inspections must be necessary to further that regulatory scheme, and (3) the terms of the inspection must provide a constitutionally adequate substitute for a warrant. *Id*. This third element requires that the scheme be detailed enough to put regulated entities on notice that they will be subject to periodic inspections, and the scheme must limit the inspector's discretion, requiring the inspector to act reasonably. *Id*.

To date, only a few businesses have been found to be closely regulated. *Colonade Catering Corp. v. United States*, 397 U.S. 72, 77 (1970) (liquor dealers); *United States v. Biswell*, 406 U.S. 311, 315 (1972) (weapon dealers); *Donovan v. Dewey*, 452 U.S. 594, 602–03 (1981) (mining companies); *New York v. Burger*, 482 U.S. at 707 (junkyards engaging in vehicle dismantling). Importantly, when an agency conducts an administrative search as a pretense to search for evidence of criminal activity, the agency must obtain a warrant and meet the criminal probable cause standard. *Burger*, 482 U.S. at 716–17 n.27 (saying that an administrative inspection cannot be used as a "pretext" for a traditional law enforcement search for evidence of a crime).

In sum, absent an exception to the warrant requirement (including consent), agencies must obtain a warrant prior to an administrative search, even when a statute provides authority to the agency to conduct searches. Indeed, if the statute did not provide the agency with authority to search, then even if the agency obtained a warrant, the search would be invalid because the agency would not have been delegated this authority.

E. Where Agencies Fit Constitutionally

As we saw in Chapter 2, the U.S. Constitution anticipates a legislature, an executive, and a judiciary, and it defines each of their powers. Agencies are not mentioned. Likely, the Framers did not foresee the expansive role of agencies (and certainly not their proliferation) and, as a result, did not address them. How then are they constitutional? In the next two sections, we examine how the Supreme Court has accepted agency power to quasi-legislate and quasi-adjudicate, beginning with quasi-legislative power.

1. Delegation of Legislative Power

Administrative agencies operate within the executive branch, either under the direction of the president of the United States or under the direction of the governor of a state. Although the executive is the branch that enforces the law, administrative agencies not only enforce law, they make law in areas that Congress or a state legislature delegates to them. Agencies promulgate legislative rules, called *regulations*, which are similar to statutes Congress or a state legislature enacts. Like statutes, these regulations make conduct illegal or require people and businesses to act in specific ways. For example, the Federal Aviation Administration (FAA) has the power to enact a regulation that would require all airlines to inspect airplanes for fuselage cracks at specific intervals. If the FAA required yearly inspections, then airlines that failed to comply could be subject to a fine or other penalty.

If agencies are in the executive branch, how are they able to enact regulations that have the force and effect of law? The short answer to this question is that the Supreme Court long ago held that Congress has the ability (indeed, for decades that ability has been a necessity) to delegate such power to agencies pursuant to the Necessary and Proper Clause, U.S. CONST. art. I, §8, so long as Congress provides *intelligible principles*, or standards, for agencies to use when exercising that power. *J.W. Hampton, Jr. & Co. v. United States*, 276 U.S. 394, 409 (1928).

a. Historical Doctrine

The 1930s represented a time of great turmoil for the United States because of the Great Depression, among other things. During this time, President Franklin Delano Roosevelt was elected into office after promising to improve the economy. Just five days after his election, Congress was called into session and enacted five major statutes after only forty hours of debate. This enactment speed and breadth was unprecedented. And the expansive delegation of power to agencies had never before been seen. The federal judiciary's reaction to the power grab was hostile, to say the least; lower federal courts soon found four major pieces of legislation unconstitutional and issued numerous injunctions. These cases made their way to the Supreme Court. The cases raised the question: when can Congress delegate to administrative agencies?

The Supreme Court decided three cases raising this delegation question. In the first, *Panama Refining Co. v. Ryan*, 293 U.S. 388 (1935) (known as the "Hot Oil Case"), the Court struck down a provision of the National Industrial Recovery Act ("NIRA") that allowed the president to prohibit the interstate transportation of oil in excess of that allowed by state law. *Id.* at 420–21. Under the NIRA, Congress wanted to prevent oil producers from evading state laws limiting the amount of oil they could sell. Striking down the statute, the Court held that Congress did not provide sufficient standards to limit the executive's exercise of power. The Court stated: "As to the transportation of oil production in excess of state permission, the Congress has declared no policy, has established no standard, has laid down no rule. There is no requirement, no definition of circumstances and conditions in which the transportation is to be allowed or prohibited." *Id.* at 430. In other words, Congress had not provided an intelligible principle to guide the executive's exercise of its delegated power.

In the second case, *A.L.A. Schechter Poultry Corp. v. United States*, 295 U.S. 495 (1935) (known as the "Sick Chicken Case"), the Court struck down another provision in the NIRA that allowed the president to approve codes for "fair competition" that were established jointly with the chicken industry so long as the following conditions were met: (1) the code was written by a representative group of businesses, (2) the code did not promote monopolies, and (3) the code served goals identified in another section of the NIRA. *Id.* at 538–39. The Court struck down the provision, stating that the President's authority was not sufficiently limited:

> [The provision] supplies no standards for any trade, industry or activity. It does not undertake to prescribe rules of conduct to be applied to particular states of fact determined by appropriate administrative procedure. Instead of prescribing rules of conduct, it authorizes the making of codes to prescribe them. For that legislative undertaking, section 3 sets up no standards, aside from [general aims]. In view of the scope of that broad declaration, and of the nature of the few restrictions that are imposed, the discretion of the President in approving or prescribing codes, and thus enacting laws for the government of trade and industry throughout the country, is virtually unfettered.

Id. at 541–42. Justice Cardozo, who dissented in the Hot Oil Case, agreed and eloquently stated that "[t]his [was] delegation running riot." *Id.* at 553 (Cardozo, J., concurring). In this case, the Court also expressed concern that the statute delegated legislative power to private entities (industry), not just federal agencies. *Id.* at 554.

The statute at issue in the third case, *Carter v. Carter Coal Co.* 298 U.S. 238 (1936), allowed certain mine owners and miners the authority to set maximum labor hours, which would be binding on other mine owners and miners. *Id.* at 279 (citing 15 U.S.C.A. § 801 to 827). The Court struck down this third party delegation and stated:

> The power conferred upon the majority is, in effect, the power to regulate the affairs of an unwilling minority. This is legislative delegation in its most

obnoxious form; for it is not even delegation to an official or an official body, presumptively disinterested, but to private persons whose interests may be and often are adverse to the interests of others in the same business.

Id. at 311. While we will see in a moment that the delegation doctrine of today has no teeth, the *Carter Coal* principle—that delegations to third parties are unconstitutional—remains vibrant. *Department of Transp. v. Association of Am. R.R*, 135 S. Ct. 1225, 1238 (2015) (stating that "handing off regulatory power to a private entity is 'legislative delegation in its most obnoxious form.' (quoting *Carter v. Carter Coal Co.*, 298 U.S. 238, 311 (1936)).

As you might imagine, President Roosevelt was less than thrilled with the Court's invalidation of his New Deal legislation. To change the Court's future decision-making, he proposed adding an additional justice to the Court for each justice over the age of 70 (known as the Court Packing Plan). Although the plan was never adopted (the supporting legislator died during the enactment process), the threat of adoption achieved the desired effect. For the next fifty years, the Court adopted a broad view of delegation and never again struck down a statute on those grounds.

b. Modern Doctrine

So, does the delegation doctrine have any teeth today? Not really. In the case below, notice that the majority rejects the lower court's suggestion that an agency can avoid the consequences of the delegation doctrine by narrowly interpreting its enabling statute. Note also the dispute between Justices Scalia and Stevens regarding what type of power the legislature is delegating. Their dispute exemplifies the functionalist-formalist divide we discussed in Chapter 2.

Whitman v. American Trucking Ass'n

Supreme Court of the United States
531 U.S. 457 (2001)

◆ Justice Scalia delivered the opinion of the Court [in which Rehnquist, C.J., O'Connor, Kennedy, Thomas, Ginsburg, and Breyer, JJ. concur].

These cases present the following question[]: (1) Whether § 109(b)(1) of the Clean Air Act (CAA) delegates legislative power to the Administrator of the Environmental Protection Agency (EPA).…

Section 109(a) of the CAA … requires the Administrator of the EPA to promulgate NAAQS for each air pollutant for which "air quality criteria" have been issued under § 108. Once a NAAQS has been promulgated, the Administrator must review the standard (and the criteria on which it is based) "at five-year intervals" and make "such revisions … as may be appropriate." These cases arose when, on July 18, 1997, the Administrator revised the NAAQS for particulate matter and ozone. American Trucking Associations, Inc., … challenged the new standards.…

The District of Columbia Circuit … agreed with … respondents that § 109(b)(1) delegated legislative power to the Administrator in contravention of the United States

Constitution, Art. I, § 1, because it found that the EPA had interpreted the statute to provide no "intelligible principle" to guide the agency's exercise of authority. The court thought, however, that the EPA could perhaps avoid the unconstitutional delegation by adopting a restrictive construction of § 109(b)(1), so instead of declaring the section unconstitutional the court remanded the NAAQS to the agency....

... We granted certiorari....

Section 109(b)(1) of the CAA instructs the EPA to set "ambient air quality standards the attainment and maintenance of which in the judgment of the Administrator, based on [the] criteria [documents of § 108] and allowing an adequate margin of safety, are requisite to protect the public health." 42 U.S.C. § 7409(b)(1). The Court of Appeals held that this section as interpreted by the Administrator did not provide an "intelligible principle" to guide the EPA's exercise of authority in setting NAAQS. "[The] EPA," it said, "lack[ed] any determinate criteria for drawing lines. It has failed to state intelligibly how much is too much." The court hence found that the EPA's interpretation (but not the statute itself) violated the nondelegation doctrine. We disagree.

In a delegation challenge, the constitutional question is whether the statute has delegated legislative power to the agency. Article I, § 1, of the Constitution vests "[a]ll legislative Powers herein granted ... in a Congress of the United States." This text permits no delegation of those powers, and so we repeatedly have said that when Congress confers decisionmaking authority upon agencies *Congress* must "lay down by legislative act an intelligible principle to which the person or body authorized to [act] is directed to conform." *J.W. Hampton, Jr., & Co. v. United States*, 276 U.S. 394, 409 (1928). We have never suggested that an agency can cure an unlawful delegation of legislative power by adopting in its discretion a limiting construction of the statute.... The idea that an agency can cure an unconstitutionally standardless delegation of power by declining to exercise some of that power seems to us internally contradictory. The very choice of which portion of the power to exercise — that is to say, the prescription of the standard that Congress had omitted — would *itself* be an exercise of the forbidden legislative authority. Whether the statute delegates legislative power is a question for the courts, and an agency's voluntary self-denial has no bearing upon the answer.

We agree with the Solicitor General that the text of § 109(b)(1) of the CAA at a minimum requires that "[f]or a discrete set of pollutants and based on published air quality criteria that reflect the latest scientific knowledge, [the] EPA must establish uniform national standards at a level that is requisite to protect public health from the adverse effects of the pollutant in the ambient air." Requisite, in turn, "mean[s] sufficient, but not more than necessary." These limits on the EPA's discretion are strikingly similar to the ones we approved in *Touby v. United States*, 500 U.S. 160 (1991), which permitted the Attorney General to designate a drug as a controlled substance for purposes of criminal drug enforcement if doing so was " 'necessary to avoid an imminent hazard to the public safety.' " They also resemble the Occupational Safety and Health Act of 1970 provision requiring the agency to " 'set the standard which most adequately assures, to the extent feasible, on the basis of the best available evidence, that no employee will suffer any impairment of health'"—which the Court upheld....

The scope of discretion § 109(b)(1) allows is in fact well within the outer limits of our nondelegation precedents. In the history of the Court we have found the requisite "intelligible principle" lacking in only two statutes, one of which provided literally no guidance for the exercise of discretion, and the other of which conferred authority to regulate the entire economy on the basis of no more precise a standard than stimulating the economy by assuring "fair competition." See *Panama Refining Co. v. Ryan,* 293 U.S. 388, (1935); *A.L.A. Schechter Poultry Corp. v. United States,* 295 U.S. 495 (1935). We have, on the other hand, upheld the validity of § 11(b)(2) of the Public Utility Holding Company Act of 1935, which gave the Securities and Exchange Commission authority to modify the structure of holding company systems so as to ensure that they are not "unduly or unnecessarily complicate[d]" and do not "unfairly or inequitably distribute voting power among security holders." We have approved the wartime conferral of agency power to fix the prices of commodities at a level that "'will be generally fair and equitable and will effectuate the [in some respects conflicting] purposes of th[e] Act.'" And we have found an "intelligible principle" in various statutes authorizing regulation in the "public interest." In short, we have "almost never felt qualified to second-guess Congress regarding the permissible degree of policy judgment that can be left to those executing or applying the law." ...

It is true enough that the degree of agency discretion that is acceptable varies according to the scope of the power congressionally conferred....

We therefore reverse the judgment of the Court of Appeals remanding for reinterpretation that would avoid a supposed delegation of legislative power....

... Section 109(b)(1) does not delegate legislative power to the EPA in contravention of Art. I, § 1, of the Constitution.

[Justice Breyer's concurring opinion has been omitted].

Justice Stevens, with whom Justice Souter joins, concurring in part and concurring in the judgment.

Section 109(b)(1) delegates to the Administrator of the Environmental Protection Agency (EPA) the authority to promulgate national ambient air quality standards (NAAQS). In ... its opinion, the Court convincingly explains why the Court of Appeals erred when it concluded that § 109 effected "an unconstitutional delegation of legislative power." I wholeheartedly endorse the Court's result and endorse its explanation of its reasons, albeit with the following caveat.

The Court has two choices. We could choose to articulate our ultimate disposition of this issue by frankly acknowledging that the power delegated to the EPA is "legislative" but nevertheless conclude that the delegation is constitutional because adequately limited by the terms of the authorizing statute. Alternatively, we could pretend, as the Court does, that the authority delegated to the EPA is somehow not "legislative power." Despite the fact that there is language in our opinions that supports the

Court's articulation of our holding, I am persuaded that it would be both wiser and more faithful to what we have actually done in delegation cases to admit that agency rulemaking authority is "legislative power."

The proper characterization of governmental power should generally depend on the nature of the power, not on the identity of the person exercising it. See Black's Law Dictionary 899 (6th ed.1990) (defining "legislation" as, *inter alia*, "[f]ormulation of rule[s] for the future"); 1 K. Davis & R. Pierce, Administrative Law Treatise § 2.3, p. 37 (3d ed. 1994) ("If legislative power means the power to make rules of conduct that bind everyone based on resolution of major policy issues, scores of agencies exercise legislative power routinely by promulgating what are candidly called 'legislative rules'"). If the NAAQS that the EPA promulgated had been prescribed by Congress, everyone would agree that those rules would be the product of an exercise of "legislative power." The same characterization is appropriate when an agency exercises rulemaking authority pursuant to a permissible delegation from Congress.

My view is not only more faithful to normal English usage, but is also fully consistent with the text of the Constitution. In Article I, the Framers vested "All legislative Powers" in the Congress, just as in Article II they vested the "executive Power" in the President. Those provisions do not purport to limit the authority of either recipient of power to delegate authority to others. See *Bowsher v. Synar*, 478 U.S. 714, 752 (1986) (Stevens, J., concurring in judgment) ("Despite the statement in Article I of the Constitution that 'All legislative powers herein granted shall be vested in a Congress of the United States,' it is far from novel to acknowledge that independent agencies do indeed exercise legislative powers"); *INS v. Chadha*, 462 U.S. 919 (1983) (White, J., dissenting) ("[L]egislative power can be exercised by independent agencies and Executive departments ..."); 1 Davis & Pierce, Administrative Law Treatise § 2.6, p. 66 ("The Court was probably mistaken from the outset in interpreting Article I's grant of power to Congress as an implicit limit on Congress' authority to delegate legislative power"). Surely the authority granted to members of the Cabinet and federal law enforcement agents is properly characterized as "Executive" even though not exercised by the President.

It seems clear that an executive agency's exercise of rulemaking authority pursuant to a valid delegation from Congress is "legislative." As long as the delegation provides a sufficiently intelligible principle, there is nothing inherently unconstitutional about it. Accordingly, while I ... agree with almost everything said [by the majority], I would hold that when Congress enacted § 109, it effected a constitutional delegation of legislative power to the EPA.

* * *

Points for Discussion

1. *Statutory Language*: What was the language at issue? How did the parties argue that that language satisfied or failed to satisfy the delegation doctrine? Why did the majority find that the language provided an intelligible principle?

2. *Constitutional Avoidance*: Note that this was a statutory interpretation case with a constitutional question. Justice Scalia, however, interpreted the statute first, then addressed the constitutional question. "[S]ince the first step in assessing whether a statute delegates legislative power is to determine what authority the statute confers, we address that issue of interpretation first and reach respondents' constitutional arguments [later]." He then notes that because the text of relevant statute in its context was clear, the constitutional avoidance canon was inapplicable: "It should be clear from what we have said that the canon requiring texts to be so construed as to avoid serious constitutional problems has no application here. No matter how severe the constitutional doubt, courts may choose only between reasonably available interpretations of a text." Hence, the majority had to address the constitutional question.

3. *Formalism v. Functionalism*: Which separation of powers theory did the majority use? The concurrence? According to the majority, which power is being delegated? Why did Justice Steven's disagree? Despite their disagreement on this issue, they reach the same result. Does that suggest that their disagreement is a distinction without a difference?

4. *Delegation*: How did the lower court resolve the nondelegation issue? Why did the majority disagree with that solution? Do you understand why an agency cannot resolve a delegation deficiency simply by adopting a narrow interpretation?

5. *Near Death*: Is it fair to say that as a result of the Supreme Court's jurisprudence the delegation doctrine is a doctrine that fails to limit delegation at all? Would you spend your time as a regulated entity's attorney arguing this issue in court?

* * *

Whether the legislature is delegating legislative power or constraining nondelegated executive power, there can be little doubt that agencies today have the power to enact regulations with the force and effect of law. The modern delegation doctrine focuses the judicial inquiry on whether the legislature has provided sufficient standards (in the form of intelligible principles) to limit the scope of the agency's authority. And the answer to that question seems always to be "yes." What about delegations of judicial power? Are the standards the same?

2. Delegation of Judicial Power

Article III, §1 of the U.S. Constitution provides that "all judicial power of the United states shall be vested in one Supreme Court and such inferior courts as the Congress may from time to time ordain and establish." Adjudication by non-Article III judges can violate this provision. Yet, agencies adjudicate disputes regularly. How can that be constitutional?

Early in its jurisprudence in this area, the Supreme Court distinguished between claims involving public and private rights. Private rights involve the liability of one individual to another, whereas public rights involve the liability of the government to its citizens. The Court reasoned that non-article III courts could adjudicate claims involving public rights. Because the government does not have to agree to be sued at all under the doctrine of sovereign immunity, if the government does agree to be sued, the government can set the parameters of being sued, including that such adjudication occur before a non-Article III tribunal. *Murray's Lessee v. Hoboken Land & Improvement Co.*, 59 U.S. (18 How.) 272 (1855); *See* Peter L. Strauss, *The Place of Agencies in Government: Separation of Powers and The Fourth Branch*, 84 COLUM L. REV. 573, 632 (1984) (saying that "the whole point of the 'public rights' analysis was that no judicial involvement at all was required—executive determination alone would suffice.").

In contrast, the Court has stated that adjudication involving private rights must be heard by an Article III court or at least be subject to Article III judicial review. *See Crowell v. Benson*, 285 U.S. 22 (1932) (holding that an agency could constitutionally adjudicate a case involving purely private rights because the agency made only factual findings, which were subject to judicial review by an Article III court).

Let's look at an example. Prior to 1978, federal district courts served as bankruptcy courts, appointing referees to conduct the hearings. In 1978, Congress enacted the Bankruptcy Act of 1978, which created bankruptcy courts and eliminated this referee system. Although called courts, bankruptcy courts are actually administrative agencies. They are known as Article I courts, because Congress created them pursuant to its powers under Article I of the Constitution. Other Article I courts include the United States Court of Appeals for Veterans Claims, the United States Court of Military Appeals, the United States Court of Federal Claims, and the United States Tax Court, to name just a few. These are agencies, not Article III courts. Do not let their names confuse you.

The Bankruptcy Act provided that the president, with the advice and consent of the Senate, would appoint bankruptcy judges for fourteen year terms. Northern Pipeline Construction Company filed for Chapter 11 bankruptcy. In its bankruptcy case, Northern included a number of purely state law claims against Marathon Pipe Line Company. Marathon moved to dismiss the claims, arguing that the Act unconstitutionally conferred Article III powers on administrative judges who lacked constitutional protections, including lifetime tenure and salary protections. The plurality agreed. *Northern Pipeline Construct. Co. v. Marathon Pipe Line Co.*, 458 U.S. 50, 87 (1982). The Court explained that an Article I court could not hear a purely private claim. *Id.* at 77.

But in 1986, the Court appeared to retreat from this private-public rights distinction in *Commodity Futures Trading Comm'n v. Schor*, 478 U.S. 833 (1986). *Schor* involved a statute that allowed customers of federal securities brokers to seek reparations from a broker who violated federal commodities law. The Commodity Futures Trading Commission, a federal agency, adjudicated the case. Schor, a customer, sued his broker for a debt balance; the broker counter-claimed for money it claimed Schor owed it. This second claim was a private state law claim. Although the broker had originally filed the claim in district court under diversity jurisdiction, Schor demanded that the broker bring the claim before the Commission. So the broker voluntarily dismissed the district court claim and brought the counter-claim before the Commission. When Schor lost, he argued, for the first time, that the Commission lacked jurisdiction to hear the counter-claim against him. *Id.* at 840. Given these facts, it should not be too surprising that the plurality ruled against Schor even though the counter-claim involved purely private rights.

The Court said, "Our precedents ... demonstrate ... that Article III does not confer on litigants an absolute right to the plenary consideration of every nature of claim by an Article III court." *Id.* at 847. Invoking functionalism, the Court explained that the inquiry regarding "the constitutionality of a given congressional delegation of adjudicative functions to a non-Article III body ... is guided by the principle that practical attention to substance rather than doctrinaire reliance on formal categories should inform application of Article III." *Id.* at 847–48 (internal quotations omitted). Because Schor had "expressly demanded" that the broker's counterclaim be brought in the administrative proceeding, he had "indisputably waived any right he may have possessed to [a] full trial ... before an Article III court." *Id* at 849. The Court distinguished *Northern Pipeline*, noting that the statute in *Schor* left "far more of the essential attributes of judicial power to Article III courts than did [the statute] found unconstitutional in *Northern Pipeline*." *Id.* at 852. In *Schor*, the Court reasoned that because "the decision to invoke this forum [was] left entirely to the parties and [because] the power of the federal judiciary to take jurisdiction of these matters [was] unaffected ... separation of powers concerns [were] diminished...." *Id.* at 855.

Shor's new functionalist test was short-lived. In this case that follows, the parties challenged the Bankruptcy Act, which Congress had amended after *Northern Pipeline*. Both the litigants in the case, one of whom was Anna Nicole Smith, died while this case was being litigated. Their estates continued the long fight. Does the Court return to its private-public rights distinction?

Stern v. Marshall

Supreme Court of the United States
131 S. Ct. 2594 (2011)

◆ JUSTICE ROBERTS delivered the opinion of the Court [in which SCALIA, KENNEDY, THOMAS, and ALITO, JJ. concur].

... [This case involves a] long-running dispute between Vickie Lynn Marshall and E. Pierce Marshall over the fortune of J. Howard Marshall II, a man believed to have been one of the richest people in Texas.... [A] Texas state probate court and the Bankruptcy Court for the Central District of California—have reached contrary decisions on its merits. The Court of Appeals below held ... [that] the Bankruptcy Court lacked the authority to enter final judgment on a counterclaim that Vickie brought against Pierce in her bankruptcy proceeding.... To determine whether the Court of Appeals was correct in that regard, we must resolve two issues: (1) whether the Bankruptcy Court had the statutory authority ... to issue a final judgment on

Vickie's counterclaim; and (2) if so, whether conferring that authority on the Bankruptcy Court is constitutional.

Although the history of this litigation is complicated, its resolution ultimately turns on very basic principles. Article III, § 1, of the Constitution commands that "[t]he judicial Power of the United States, shall be vested in one supreme Court, and in such inferior Courts as the Congress may from time to time ordain and establish." That Article further provides that the judges of those courts shall hold their offices during good behavior, without diminution of salary. Those requirements of Article III were not honored here. The Bankruptcy Court in this case exercised the judicial power of the United States by entering final judgment on a common law tort claim, even though the judges of such courts enjoy neither tenure during good behavior nor salary protection. We conclude that, although the Bankruptcy Court had the statutory authority to enter judgment on Vickie's counterclaim, it lacked the constitutional authority to do so....

Known to the public as Anna Nicole Smith, Vickie was J. Howard's third wife and married him about a year before his death. Although J. Howard bestowed on Vickie many monetary and other gifts during their courtship and marriage, he did not include her in his will. Before J. Howard passed away, Vickie filed suit in Texas state probate court, asserting that Pierce—J. Howard's younger son—fraudulently induced J. Howard to sign a living trust that did not include her, even though J. Howard meant to give her half his property. Pierce denied any fraudulent activity and defended the validity of J. Howard's trust and, eventually, his will.

After J. Howard's death, Vickie filed a petition for bankruptcy in the Central District of California. Pierce filed a complaint in that bankruptcy proceeding, contending that Vickie had defamed him by inducing her lawyers to tell members of the press that he had engaged in fraud to gain control of his father's assets.... Vickie responded to Pierce's initial complaint by asserting truth as a defense to the alleged defamation and by filing a counterclaim for tortious interference with the gift she expected from J. Howard.* As she had in state court, Vickie alleged that Pierce had wrongfully prevented J. Howard from taking the legal steps necessary to provide her with half his property.

... The [Bankruptcy] court later awarded Vickie over $400 million in compensatory damages and $25 million in punitive damages.... [The Court of Appeals held that the Bankruptcy court did not have authority to issue a final judgment on Vickie's claim.] ...

Vickie's counterclaim against Pierce for tortious interference is a "core proceeding" under the plain text of [the Bankruptcy Act, so the Bankruptcy court had statutory authority to issue a final judgment]....

---

* Editor's footnote: Smith claimed that J. Howard had orally promised to give her half of his estate if she married him.

Although we conclude that [the Act] permits the Bankruptcy Court to enter final judgment on Vickie's counterclaim, Article III of the Constitution does not.

Article III, §1, of the Constitution mandates that "[t]he judicial Power of the United States, shall be vested in one supreme Court, and in such inferior Courts as the Congress may from time to time ordain and establish." The same section provides that the judges of those constitutional courts "shall hold their Offices during good Behaviour" and "receive for their Services[ ] a Compensation[ ] [that] shall not be diminished" during their tenure.

As its text and our precedent confirm, Article III is "an inseparable element of the constitutional system of checks and balances" that "both defines the power and protects the independence of the Judicial Branch." *Northern Pipeline*, 458 U.S. [50], 58 [(1982) (plurality opinion)]. Under "the basic concept of separation of powers ... that flow[s] from the scheme of a tripartite government" adopted in the Constitution, "the 'judicial Power of the United States' ... can no more be shared" with another branch than "the Chief Executive, for example, can share with the Judiciary the veto power, or the Congress share with the Judiciary the power to override a Presidential veto."

In establishing the system of divided power in the Constitution, the Framers considered it essential that "the judiciary remain[ ] truly distinct from both the legislature and the executive." The Federalist No. 78, p. 466 (C. Rossiter ed. 1961) (A. Hamilton). As Hamilton put it, quoting Montesquieu, " 'there is no liberty if the power of judging be not separated from the legislative and executive powers.' "

We have recognized that the three branches are not hermetically sealed from one another, but it remains true that Article III imposes some basic limitations that the other branches may not transgress. Those limitations serve two related purposes. "Separation-of-powers principles are intended, in part, to protect each branch of government from incursion by the others. Yet the dynamic between and among the branches is not the only object of the Constitution's concern. The structural principles secured by the separation of powers protect the individual as well."

Article III protects liberty not only through its role in implementing the separation of powers, but also by specifying the defining characteristics of Article III judges. The colonists had been subjected to judicial abuses at the hand of the Crown, and the Framers knew the main reasons why: because the King of Great Britain "made Judges dependent on his Will alone, for the tenure of their offices, and the amount and payment of their salaries." The Framers undertook in Article III to protect citizens subject to the judicial power of the new Federal Government from a repeat of those abuses. By appointing judges to serve without term limits, and restricting the ability of the other branches to remove judges or diminish their salaries, the Framers sought to ensure that each judicial decision would be rendered, not with an eye toward currying favor with Congress or the Executive, but rather with the "[c]lear heads ... and honest hearts" deemed "essential to good judges."

Article III could neither serve its purpose in the system of checks and balances nor preserve the integrity of judicial decisionmaking if the other branches of the Federal

Government could confer the Government's "judicial Power" on entities outside Article III. That is why we have long recognized that, in general, Congress may not "withdraw from judicial cognizance any matter which, from its nature, is the subject of a suit at the common law, or in equity, or admiralty." When a suit is made of "the stuff of the traditional actions at common law tried by the courts at Westminster in 1789" and is brought within the bounds of federal jurisdiction, the responsibility for deciding that suit rests with Article III judges in Article III courts. The Constitution assigns that job — resolution of "the mundane as well as the glamorous, matters of common law and statute as well as constitutional law, issues of fact as well as issues of law" — to the Judiciary.

This is not the first time we have faced an Article III challenge to a bankruptcy court's resolution of a debtor's suit. In *Northern Pipeline*, we considered whether bankruptcy judges serving under the Bankruptcy Act of 1978 — appointed by the President and confirmed by the Senate, but lacking the tenure and salary guarantees of Article III — could "constitutionally be vested with jurisdiction to decide [a] state-law contract claim" against an entity that was not otherwise part of the bankruptcy proceedings. The Court concluded that assignment of such state law claims for resolution by those judges "violates Art. III of the Constitution."

The plurality in *Northern Pipeline* recognized that there was a category of cases involving "public rights" that Congress could constitutionally assign to "legislative" courts for resolution. That opinion concluded that this "public rights" exception extended "only to matters arising between" individuals and the Government "in connection with the performance of the constitutional functions of the executive or legislative departments ... that historically could have been determined exclusively by those" branches....

After our decision in *Northern Pipeline*, Congress revised the statutes [to provide] that the [bankruptcy] judges ... would be appointed by the courts of appeals for the circuits in which their districts are located. And, ... Congress permitted the newly constituted bankruptcy courts to enter final judgments only in "core" proceedings....

[T]he Bankruptcy Court in this case exercised the "judicial Power of the United States" in purporting to resolve and enter final judgment on a state common law claim, just as the court did in *Northern Pipeline*. No "public right" exception excuses the failure to comply with Article III in doing so.... Here Vickie's claim is a state law action independent of the federal bankruptcy law.... *Northern Pipeline* ... rejected the application of the "public rights" exception in such cases....

Vickie's counterclaim ... does not fall within any of the varied formulations of the public rights exception in this Court's cases. It is not a matter that can be pursued only by grace of the other branches, or one that "historically could have been determined exclusively by" those branches. The claim is instead one under state common law between two private parties. It does not "depend[ ] on the will of congress," Congress has nothing to do with it....

The dissent reads our cases differently, and in particular contends that more recent cases view *Northern Pipeline* as "'establish[ing] only that Congress may not vest in a non-Article III court the power to adjudicate, render final judgment, and issue binding orders in a traditional contract action arising under state law, without consent of the litigants, and subject only to ordinary appellate review.'" Just so: Substitute "tort" for "contract," and that statement directly covers this case.

We recognize that there may be instances in which the distinction between public and private rights … fails to provide concrete guidance as to whether, for example, a particular agency can adjudicate legal issues under a substantive regulatory scheme…. [But] this case involves the most prototypical exercise of judicial power: the entry of a final, binding judgment *by a court* with broad substantive jurisdiction, on a common law cause of action, when the action neither derives from nor depends upon any agency regulatory regime. If such an exercise of judicial power may nonetheless be taken from the Article III Judiciary simply by deeming it part of some amorphous "public right," then Article III would be transformed from the guardian of individual liberty and separation of powers we have long recognized into mere wishful thinking….

Finally, … [i]t goes without saying that "the fact that a given law or procedure is efficient, convenient, and useful in facilitating functions of government, standing alone, will not save it if it is contrary to the Constitution." …

Article III of the Constitution provides that the judicial power of the United States may be vested only in courts whose judges enjoy the protections set forth in that Article. We conclude today that Congress, in one isolated respect, exceeded that limitation in the Bankruptcy Act of 1984. The Bankruptcy Court below lacked the constitutional authority to enter a final judgment on a state law counterclaim….

◆ Justice Scalia, concurring.

[While] I agree with the Court…, I adhere to my view … that—our contrary precedents notwithstanding—"a matter of public rights … must at a minimum arise between the government and others."

◆ Justice Breyer, with whom Ginsburg, Sotomayor, and Kagan, JJ. join dissenting.

… [In precedent more recent than the plurality opinion from *Northern Pipeline*, a majority of this Court] sought to determine whether, in the particular instance, the challenged delegation of adjudicatory authority posed a genuine and serious threat that one branch of Government sought to aggrandize its own constitutionally delegated authority by encroaching upon a field of authority that the Constitution assigns exclusively to another branch….

[*Commodity Futures Trading Commission v. Schor*, 478 U.S. 833, 836 (1986)] … requires us to determine pragmatically whether a congressional delegation of adjudicatory authority to a non-Article III judge violates the separation-of-powers principles inherent in Article III. That is to say, we must determine through an examination of certain relevant factors whether that delegation constitutes a significant encroachment by the Legislative or Executive Branches of Government upon the realm of authority that Article III reserves for exercise by the Judicial Branch of Government. Those factors include (1) the nature of the claim to be adjudicated; (2) the nature of the non-Article III tribunal; (3) the extent to which Article III courts exercise control over the proceeding; (4) the presence or absence of the parties' consent; and (5) the nature and importance of the legislative purpose served by the grant of adjudicatory authority to a tribunal with judges who lack Article III's tenure and compensation protections. The presence of "private rights" does not automatically determine the outcome of the question but requires a more "searching" examination of the relevant factors.

Applying [that] approach here, I conclude that the delegation of adjudicatory authority before us is constitutional....

First, I concede that *the nature of the claim to be adjudicated* argues against my conclusion. Vickie Marshall's counterclaim — a kind of tort suit — resembles "a suit at the common law." ...

Second, *the nature of the non-Article III tribunal* argues in favor of constitutionality. That is because the tribunal is made up of judges who enjoy considerable protection from improper political influence. Unlike the 1978 Act which provided for the appointment of bankruptcy judges by the President with the advice and consent of the Senate, current law provides that the federal courts of appeals appoint federal bankruptcy judges. Bankruptcy judges are removable by the circuit judicial counsel (made up of federal court of appeals and district court judges) and only for cause. Their salaries are pegged to those of federal district court judges, and the cost of their courthouses and other work-related expenses are paid by the Judiciary. Thus, ... bankruptcy judges can be compared to magistrate judges, law clerks, and the Judiciary's administrative officials, whose lack of Article III tenure and compensation protections do not endanger the independence of the Judicial Branch.

Third, *the control exercised by Article III judges over bankruptcy proceedings* argues in favor of constitutionality. Article III judges control and supervise the bankruptcy court's determinations.... Any party may appeal those determinations to the federal district court, where the federal judge will review all determinations of fact for clear error and will review all determinations of law *de novo*.... Moreover, ... [t]he District Court here may "withdraw, in whole or in part, any case or proceeding referred (to the Bankruptcy Court) ... on its own motion or on timely motion of any party, for cause shown." ...

Fourth, the fact that *the parties have consented* to Bankruptcy Court jurisdiction argues in favor of constitutionality, and strongly so.... Pierce Marshall likely had "an alternative forum to the bankruptcy court in which to pursue [his] clai[m]." ...

Fifth, *the nature and importance of the legislative purpose served* by the grant of adjudicatory authority to bankruptcy tribunals argues strongly in favor of constitutionality.... [A] bankruptcy court's determination of [compulsory counterclaims] has more than "some bearing on a bankruptcy case." It plays a critical role in Congress' constitutionally based effort to create an efficient, effective federal bankruptcy system. At the least, that is what Congress concluded. We owe deference to that determination, which shows the absence of any legislative or executive motive, intent, purpose, or desire to encroach upon areas that Article III reserves to judges to whom it grants tenure and compensation protections.

Considering these factors together, I conclude that "the magnitude of any intrusion on the Judicial Branch can only be termed *de minimis*." ...

... [U]nder the majority's holding, the federal district judge, not the bankruptcy judge, would have to hear and resolve the[se] counterclaim[s].... Why is that a problem? Because these types of disputes arise in bankruptcy court with some frequency. Because the volume of bankruptcy cases is staggering, involving almost 1.6 million filings last year, compared to a federal district court docket of around 280,000 civil cases and 78,000 criminal cases. Because unlike the "related" non-core state law claims that bankruptcy courts must abstain from hearing, compulsory counterclaims involve the same factual disputes as the claims that may be finally adjudicated by the bankruptcy courts. Because under these circumstances, a constitutionally required game of jurisdictional ping-pong between courts would lead to inefficiency, increased cost, delay, and needless additional suffering among those faced with bankruptcy ... with respect, I dissent.

* * *

Points for Discussion

1. *Statutory Amendment*: In *Northern Pipeline*, the Court had held that the Bankruptcy Act of 1978 was unconstitutional because it granted Article I courts the power to hear private claims that Article III courts should hear. How did Congress amend the statute in response? Why, according to Justice Roberts, were these changes insufficient to fix correct the constitutional infirmity?

2. *Formalism v. Functionalism:* Which separation of powers theory did the majority use? The dissent? In this case, theory dictates outcome unlike in *Whitman*.

3. *Public v. Private Rights Distinction*: The Court had appeared to move away from public-private rights distinction in *Schor*. Did the majority revitalize the distinction in *Stern*? According to the majority, public rights "depend[ ] on the will of congress," meaning a federal statute creates the right. The majority acknowledges that this line will not always be bright. Why, according to the majority, was that line clear in this case? How would Justice Scalia describe the difference between public and private rights? Is that test clearer?

4. *Distinguishing* Schor: How did the majority characterize Vickie's counterclaim: as a private or public right? How then does this case differ from *Schor*? Did Pierce voluntarily agree to the bankruptcy court's jurisdiction? Does the agency have expertise in resolving this type of state law counter-claim?

5. *Dissent*: Why did the dissent disagree? Did the dissent dispute the private nature of the counter-claim or the impact of the intrusion into the judiciary? What factors would the dissent consider in deciding future claims and whether an administrative agency should have the power to resolve them? Does the dissent's approach offer a clear distinction for litigants who have to decide whether to file their state law counterclaims?

* * *

Problem 16

Lisa was convicted of violating a National Park Service (Service) rule regulating surfboarding and swimming at a national seashore park (park). The Service's enabling statute provides that the Service may take "such measures as it deems necessary to provide for the enjoyment and safety" of those using federal parks pursuant to either rule-making or adjudication. Further, the statute authorizes the Service to impose fines for violation of any law related to swimming in national parks.

The Service promulgated a regulation under this act using notice-and-comment rulemaking procedures, prohibiting swimming and surfboarding at Cape Lookout National Seashore when the regional park director determines that conditions are unsafe. The regulation also authorizes fines for willful violations. The park director had posted a warning for surfers and swimmers to stay out of the water on the day in question.

Lisa ignored the warning that the beach was considered unsafe on the day she was found surfboarding, and she was fined. Lisa appealed her fine to the agency. The secretary of the National Park Service upheld the fine. Lisa then appealed the decision to the appropriate federal district court for review. She admits she violated the regulation but contends that the statute violates separation of powers because it unconstitutionally delegates legislative power to the agency without providing intelligible standards. The Service counters that first, the statute includes an intelligible principle, and second, because the agency can narrowly interpret the enabling statute, there is no delegation concern even if there is no intelligible principle. Explain who is correct and why. In doing so, be sure to identify the type of agency action that Lisa challenges: (1) is it rulemaking or adjudication, and (2) is it formal or informal? Explain.

Chapter 17

The Regulatory Process: Legislative and Executive Oversight

A. Introduction to this Chapter

In the last chapter, we learned what agencies do and how they do it. In this chapter, we learn how agencies fit into our constitutional structure and how the legislature and executive control agency action. We will see that there are both direct and indirect methods of control that each branch can use.

After learning how the legislature and executive exert control in this chapter, in the next chapter, we will learn about the role agencies play in statutory interpretation.

B. Legislative Oversight

As you learned, agencies have only the power that Congress delegates to them. Broadly or narrowly delegating is one way that Congress controls agency activity. Additionally, Congress controls agency activity in ways other than through delegation. There are both direct and indirect methods of legislative oversight.

1. Direct Legislative Oversight

Direct methods of oversight include Congress's power to enact subsequent legislation and to fund agencies (the power of the purse). With subsequent legislative action, Congress can narrow or revoke the authority it gave to an agency or require an agency to follow new procedures. For example, after a tremendous public outcry regarding the Food and Drug Administration's decision to ban saccharin, the only alternative sweetener at the time, Congress suspended regulatory action in this area and required a warning label to replace the proposed ban. 91 Stat. 1451 (1977). Similarly, in 1969 with the National Environmental Policy Act, 42 U.S.C. §§ 4321–61 *et seq.*, Congress required all agencies to consider the environmental impact of major decisions. And in 1980, Congress enacted the Regulatory Flexibility Act, 5 U.S.C. §§ 601–12 *et seq.*, which requires agencies to consider and minimize the economic effects of regulations on small businesses. Further, with the Unfunded Mandates Reform Act of 1995, 2 U.S.C. §§ 1501–71 *et seq.*, Congress directed agencies to consider the impact of their regulations on state governmental agencies and adopt the least burdensome alternative that would further the agency's objectives or explain why another option was chosen.

Additionally, Congress controls the purse. Sometimes Congress withholds funding altogether. For example, Congress enacted the Administrative Conference Act of 1964. The Act established the Administrative Conference of the United States ("ACUS"), which is an independent federal agency dedicated to improving the administrative process and federal agency procedures. In 1995, rather than repeal the Administrative Conference Act, Congress simply refused to fund ACUS; it is not clear why. *See generally*, Jeffrey Lubbers, *"If It Didn't Exist, It Would Have to Be Invented"—Reviving the Administrative Conference*, 30 ARIZ. ST. L.J. 147 (1998). Oddly, Congress even reauthorized the Act in 2004 and 2008, expanding the agency's powers, all while still refusing to fund it. Congress finally restored funding in 2009, after President Obama took office. More recently, Congress has significantly underfunded the Treasury, specifically the IRS, after the agency revealed that it had selected political groups applying for tax-exempt status for intensive scrutiny based on their conservative names or political themes.

Agencies need funding to operate. Congressional approval of agency funding requires two things. First, the agency's enabling statute (or another statute) must provide authorization for legislative appropriations. Such authorizations may be limited by time or purpose, have a ceiling, or be unlimited. Second, each year Congress must approve an agency's budget request. To receive funding, agencies must submit annual budget requests to the Office of Management and Budget (OMB), which the president oversees. These budgets, after any adjustments by OMB, are forwarded to the House and Senate appropriations committees, which then hold hearings and allocate funding accordingly. As you will see in our next case, *Tennessee Valley Authority v. Hill*, 437 U.S. 153 (1978), appropriation bills can impact regulatory policy and statutory interpretation. There are two entities involved in this case: the Tennessee Valley Authority (TVA), which is a federally owned corporation, and the Secretary of the Interior (the Secretary), which is a federal agency. Their goals are at odds.

Tennessee Valley Authority v. Hill

Supreme Court of the United States
437 U.S. 153 (1978)

◆ CHIEF JUSTICE BURGER delivered the opinion of the Court [with whom BRENNAN, STEWART, WHITE, MARSHALL, STEVENS, JJ., concur].

[TVA decided to build the Tellico Dam on the Little Tennessee River. The dam would impound water covering some 16,500 acres—valuable and productive farmland—converting the river's shallow, fast-flowing waters into a deep reservoir over 30 miles in length. Local citizens and environmental groups sued to stop the project. As the litigation was pending, a University of Tennessee ichthyologist discovered a previously unknown species of perch: the snail darter. Four months after this discovery, Congress enacted the Endangered Species Act of 1973, authorizing the Secretary to declare a species endangered and to protect its critical habitat. Respondents petitioned to have the snail darter listed as endangered.

Meanwhile, Congress had also become involved. Appearing before a Subcommittee of the House Committee on Appropriations in April 1975 — some seven months before the snail darter would be listed as endangered — TVA representatives described the discovery of the fish and the relevance of the Endangered Species Act to the Tellico Project. TVA argued that the Act did not prohibit the completion of a project authorized, funded, and substantially constructed before the Act was passed. In response, the House Committee on Appropriations, in its June 20, 1975, Report, stated the following in the course of recommending that an additional $29 million be appropriated for Tellico: "The Committee directs that the project, for which an environmental impact statement has been completed and provided the Committee, should be completed as promptly as possible ...".

The Secretary then listed the snail darter as endangered and identified the portion of the Little Tennessee River to be damned as its "critical habitat." Further, the secretary declared that all Federal agencies must take such actions as will not destroy or modify this critical habitat area.

In February 1976, pursuant to the Endangered Species Act, the respondents filed suit, seeking to enjoin completion of the dam on the ground that those actions would violate the Act by directly causing the extinction of the snail darter. The District Court denied the injunction and the plaintiffs appealed. The Court of Appeals reversed. The Supreme Court granted certiorari. Although the dam was virtually complete, it had never opened because of the pending lawsuits.]

... We begin with the premise that operation of the Tellico Dam will either eradicate the known population of snail darters or destroy their critical habitat....

Starting from the above premise, two questions are presented: (a) Would TVA be in violation of the Act if it completed and operated the Tellico Dam as planned? (b) If TVA's actions would offend the Act, is an injunction the appropriate remedy for the violation? ... [W]e hold that both questions must be answered in the affirmative.

It may seem curious to some that the survival of a relatively small number of three-inch fish among all the countless millions of species extant would require the permanent halting of a virtually completed dam for which Congress has expended more than $100 million. The paradox is not minimized by the fact that Congress continued to appropriate large sums of public money for the project, even after congressional Appropriations Committees were apprised of its apparent impact upon the survival of the snail darter. We conclude, however, that the explicit provisions of the Endangered Species Act require precisely that result.

One would be hard pressed to find a statutory provision whose terms were any plainer than those in §7 of the Endangered Species Act. Its very words affirmatively command all federal agencies "to *insure* that actions *authorized, funded,* or *carried out* by them do not *jeopardize* the continued existence" of an endangered species or "*result* in the destruction or modification of habitat of such species...." 16 U.S.C. §1536 (1976 ed.). (Emphasis added.) This language admits of no exception. Nonetheless, petitioner urges, as do the dissenters, that the Act cannot reasonably be interpreted as applying to a federal project which was well under way when Congress passed the Endangered Species Act of 1973. To sustain that position, however, we would be forced to ignore the ordinary meaning of plain language. It has not been shown, for example, how TVA can close the gates of the Tellico Dam without "carrying out" an action that has been "authorized" and "funded" by a federal agency. Nor can we understand how such action will "*insure*" that the snail darter's habitat is not disrupted.[18] Accepting the Secretary's determinations, as we must, it is clear that TVA's proposed operation of the dam will have precisely the opposite effect, namely the *eradication* of an endangered species.

Concededly, this view of the Act will produce results requiring the sacrifice of the anticipated benefits of the project and of many millions of dollars in public funds. But examination of the language, history, and structure of the legislation under review here indicates beyond doubt that Congress intended endangered species to be afforded the highest of priorities.

When Congress passed the Act in 1973, it was not legislating on a clean slate. [Congress had already passed two Acts to address the problem.] Despite the fact that the 1966 and 1969 legislation represented "the most comprehensive of its type to be enacted by any nation" up to that time, Congress was soon persuaded that a more expansive approach was needed if the newly declared national policy of preserving endangered species was to be realized. By 1973, when Congress held hearings on what would later become the Endangered Species Act of 1973, it was informed that species were still being lost at the rate of about one per year and "the pace of disappearance of species" appeared to be "accelerating." Moreover, Congress was ... informed that the greatest [threat] was destruction of natural habitats....

As it was finally passed, the Endangered Species Act of 1973 represented the most comprehensive legislation for the preservation of endangered species ever enacted by any nation. Its stated purposes were "to provide a means whereby the ecosystems upon which endangered species and threatened species depend may be conserved," and "to provide a program for the conservation of such ... species...." 16 U.S.C. § 1531(b) (1976 ed.). In furtherance of these goals, Congress expressly stated in § 2(c)

---

18. In dissent, Mr. Justice Powell argues that the meaning of "actions" in § 7 is "far from 'plain,'" and that "it seems evident that the 'actions' referred to are not all actions that an agency can ever take, but rather actions that the agency is *deciding whether* to authorize, to fund, or to carry out." Aside from this bare assertion, however, no explanation is given to support the proffered interpretation. This recalls Lewis Carroll's class advice on the construction of language:

"'When *I* use a word,' Humpty Dumpty said, in rather a scornful tone, 'it means just what *I* choose it to mean—neither more nor less.'" Through the Looking Glass, in The Complete Works of Lewis Carroll 196 (1939).

Aside from being unexplicated, the dissent's reading of § 7 is flawed on several counts. First, under its view, the words "or carry out" in § 7 would be superfluous since all prospective actions of an agency remain to be "authorized" or "funded." Second, the dissent's position logically means that an agency would be obligated to comply with § 7 only when a project is in the planning stage. But if Congress had meant to so limit the Act, it surely would have used words to that effect, as it did in the National Environmental Policy Act.

that "all Federal departments and agencies *shall* seek *to conserve endangered species and threatened species....*" 16 U.S.C. §1531(c) (1976 ed.). (Emphasis added.) Lest there be any ambiguity as to the meaning of this statutory directive, the Act specifically defined "conserve" as meaning "to use and the use of *all methods and procedures which are necessary* to bring *any endangered species or threatened species* to the point at which the measures provided pursuant to this chapter are no longer necessary." §1532(2). (Emphasis added.) Aside from §7, other provisions indicated the seriousness with which Congress viewed this issue: Virtually all dealings with endangered species, including taking, possession, transportation, and sale, were prohibited, except in extremely narrow circumstances. The Secretary was also given extensive power to develop regulations and programs for the preservation of endangered and threatened species. Citizen involvement was encouraged by the Act, with provisions allowing interested persons to petition the Secretary to list a species as endangered or threatened and bring civil suits in United States district courts to force compliance with any provision of the Act....

It is against this legislative background[29] that we must measure TVA's claim that the Act was not intended to stop operation of a project which, like Tellico Dam, was near completion when an endangered species was discovered in its path. While there is no discussion in the legislative history of precisely this problem, the totality of congressional action makes it abundantly clear that the result we reach today is wholly in accord with both the words of the statute and the intent of Congress. The plain intent of Congress in enacting this statute was to halt and reverse the trend toward species extinction, whatever the cost. This is reflected not only in the stated policies of the Act, but in literally every section of the statute....

Notwithstanding Congress' expression of intent in 1973, we are urged to find that the continuing appropriations for Tellico Dam constitute an implied repeal of the 1973 Act, at least insofar as it applies to the Tellico Project. In support of this view, TVA points to the statements found in various House and Senate Appropriations Committees' Reports; as described [earlier], those Reports generally reflected the attitude of the *Committees* either that the Act did not apply to Tellico or that the dam should be completed regardless of the provisions of the Act. Since we are unwilling to assume that these latter Committee statements constituted advice to ignore the provisions of a duly enacted law, we assume that these Committees believed that the Act simply was not applicable in this situation. But even under this interpretation of the Committees' actions, we are unable to conclude that the Act has been in any respect amended or repealed.

There is nothing in the appropriations measures, as passed, which states that the Tellico Project was to be completed irrespective of the requirements of the Endangered

---

29. When confronted with a statute which is plain and unambiguous on its face, we ordinarily do not look to legislative history as a guide to its meaning. Here it is not *necessary* to look beyond the words of the statute. We have undertaken such an analysis only to meet Mr. Justice Powell's suggestion that the "absurd" result reached in this case is not in accord with congressional intent.

Species Act. These appropriations, in fact, represented relatively minor components of the lump-sum amounts for the *entire* TVA budget.[35] To find a repeal of the Endangered Species Act under these circumstances would surely do violence to the " 'cardinal rule ... that repeals by implication are not favored....' "

The doctrine disfavoring repeals by implication "applies with full vigor when ... the subsequent legislation is an *appropriations* measure." This is perhaps an understatement since it would be more accurate to say that the policy applies with even *greater* force when the claimed repeal rests solely on an Appropriations Act. We recognize that both substantive enactments and appropriations measures are "Acts of Congress," but the latter have the limited and specific purpose of providing funds for authorized programs. When voting on appropriations measures, legislators are entitled to operate under the assumption that the funds will be devoted to purposes which are lawful and not for any purpose forbidden. Without such an assurance, every appropriations measure would be pregnant with prospects of altering substantive legislation, repealing by implication any prior statute which might prohibit the expenditure. Not only would this lead to the absurd result of requiring Members to review exhaustively the background of every authorization before voting on an appropriation, but it would flout the very rules the Congress carefully adopted to avoid this need. House Rule XXI(2), for instance, specifically provides:

> "No appropriation shall be reported in any general appropriation bill, or be in order as an amendment thereto, for any expenditure not previously authorized by law, unless in continuation of appropriations for such public works as are already in progress. *Nor shall any provision in any such bill or amendment thereto changing existing law be in order.*" (Emphasis added.)

Thus, to sustain petitioner's position, we would be obliged to assume that Congress meant to repeal *pro tanto* § 7 of the Act by means of a procedure expressly prohibited under the rules of Congress....

... While "[i]t is emphatically the province and duty of the judicial department to say what the law is," *Marbury v. Madison*, 1 Cranch 137, 177 (1803), it is equally— and emphatically—the exclusive province of the Congress not only to formulate legislative policies and mandate programs and projects, but also to establish their relative priority for the Nation. Once Congress, exercising its delegated powers, has decided the order of priorities in a given area, it is for the Executive to administer the laws and for the courts to enforce them when enforcement is sought.

Our individual appraisal of the wisdom or unwisdom of a particular course consciously selected by the Congress is to be put aside in the process of interpreting a

---

35. The Appropriations Acts did not themselves identify the projects for which the sums had been appropriated; identification of these projects requires reference to the legislative history. Thus, unless a Member scrutinized in detail the Committee proceedings concerning the appropriations, he would have no knowledge of the possible conflict between the continued funding and the Endangered Species Act.

statute. Once the meaning of an enactment is discerned and its constitutionality determined, the judicial process comes to an end....

... [I]n our constitutional system the commitment to the separation of powers is too fundamental for us to pre-empt congressional action by judicially decreeing what accords with "common sense and the public weal." Our Constitution vests such responsibilities in the political branches.

♦ [The dissent of JUSTICE REHNQUIST is omitted].

♦ JUSTICE POWELL, with whom JUSTICE BLACKMUN joins, dissenting.

... In my view § 7 cannot reasonably be interpreted as applying to a project that is completed or substantially completed when its threat to an endangered species is discovered. Nor can I believe that Congress could have intended this Act to produce the "absurd result ..." of this case. If it were clear from the language of the Act and its legislative history that Congress intended to authorize this result, this Court would be compelled to enforce it. It is not our province to rectify policy or political judgments by the Legislative Branch, however egregiously they may disserve the public interest. But where the statutory language and legislative history, as in this case, need not be construed to reach such a result, I view it as the duty of this Court to adopt a permissible construction that accords with some modicum of common sense and the public weal....

In 1966, Congress authorized and appropriated initial funds for the construction by the Tennessee Valley Authority (TVA) of the Tellico Dam and Reservoir Project on the Little Tennessee River in eastern Tennessee....

Construction began in 1967, and Congress has voted funds for the project in every year since. In August 1973, when the Tellico Project was half completed, a new species of fish known as the snail darter was discovered in the portion of the Little Tennessee River that would be impounded behind Tellico Dam. The Endangered Species Act was passed the following December. More than a year later, in January 1975, respondents joined others in petitioning the Secretary of the Interior to list the snail darter as an endangered species. On November 10, 1975, when the Tellico Project was 75% completed, the Secretary placed the snail darter on the endangered list and concluded that the "proposed impoundment of water behind the proposed Tellico Dam would result in total destruction of the snail darter's habitat." In respondents' view, the Secretary's action meant that completion of the Tellico Project would violate § 7 of the Act:

> "All ... Federal departments and agencies shall, in consultation with and with the assistance of the Secretary, utilize their authorities in furtherance of the purposes of this chapter by carrying out programs for the conservation of endangered species ... listed pursuant to section 1533 of this title and by taking such action necessary to insure that actions authorized, funded, or carried out by them do not jeopardize the continued existence of such endangered species and threatened species or result in the destruction or modification of habitat of such species which is determined by the Secretary ... to be critical."

TVA nevertheless determined to continue with the Tellico Project in accordance with the prior authorization by Congress. In February 1976, respondents filed the instant suit to enjoin its completion. By that time the Project was 80% completed.

In March 1976, TVA informed the House and Senate Appropriations Committees about the Project's threat to the snail darter and about respondents' lawsuit....

In 1975, 1976, and 1977, Congress, with full knowledge of the Tellico Project's effect on the snail darter and the alleged violation of the Endangered Species Act, continued to appropriate money for the completion of the Project. In doing so, the Appropriations Committees expressly stated that the Act did not prohibit the Project's completion, a view that Congress presumably accepted in approving the appropriations each year. For example, in June 1976, the Senate Committee on Appropriations released a report noting the District Court decision and recommending approval of TVA's full budget request for the Tellico Project. The Committee observed further that it did "not view the Endangered Species Act as prohibiting the completion of the Tellico project at its advanced stage," and it directed "that this project be completed as promptly as possible in the public interest." The appropriations bill was passed by Congress and approved by the President....

In June 1977, and after being informed of the decision of the Court of Appeals (reversing the district court's denial of an injunction in this case), the Appropriations Committees in both Houses of Congress again recommended approval of TVA's full budget request for the Tellico Project. Both Committees again stated unequivocally that the Endangered Species Act was not intended to halt projects at an advanced stage of completion:

> "[The Senate] Committee has not viewed the Endangered Species Act as preventing the completion and use of these projects which were well under way at the time the affected species were listed as endangered. If the act has such an effect, which is contrary to the Committee's understanding of the intent of Congress in enacting the Endangered Species Act, funds should be appropriated to allow these projects to be completed and their benefits realized in the public interest, the Endangered Species Act notwithstanding." [Senate Report].

> "It is the [House] Committee's view that the Endangered Species Act was not intended to halt projects such as these in their advanced stage of completion, and [the Committee] strongly recommends that these projects not be stopped because of misuse of the Act." [House Report].

Once again, the appropriations bill was passed by both Houses and signed into law.

The starting point in statutory construction is, of course, the language of § 7 itself. I agree that it can be viewed as a textbook example of fuzzy language, which can be read according to the "eye of the beholder." The critical words direct all federal agencies to take "such action [as may be] necessary to insure that actions authorized, funded, or carried out by them do not jeopardize the continued existence of ... endangered species ... or result in the destruction or modification of [a critical] habitat of such species...." Respondents ... read these words as sweepingly as possible to include all "actions" that any federal agency ever may take with respect to any federal project, whether completed or not.

The Court today embraces this sweeping construction....

"[F]requently words of general meaning are used in a statute, words broad enough to include an act in question, and yet a consideration of the whole legislation, or of the circumstances surrounding its enactment, or of the absurd results which follow from giving such broad meaning to the words, makes it unreasonable to believe that the legislator intended to include the particular act." *Church of the Holy Trinity v. United States*, 143 U.S. 457, 459 (1892). The result that will follow in this case by virtue of the Court's reading of §7 makes it unreasonable to believe that Congress intended that reading. Moreover, §7 may be construed in a way that avoids an "absurd result" without doing violence to its language.

The critical word in §7 is "actions" and its meaning is far from "plain." It is part of the phrase: "actions authorized, funded or carried out." In terms of planning and executing various activities, it seems evident that the "actions" referred to are not all actions that an agency can ever take, but rather actions that the agency is *deciding whether* to authorize, to fund, or to carry out. In short, these words reasonably may be read as applying only to *prospective actions, i.e.,* actions with respect to which the agency has reasonable decisionmaking alternatives still available, actions *not yet* carried out. At the time respondents brought this lawsuit, the Tellico Project was 80% complete at a cost of more than $78 million....

This is a reasonable construction of the language and also is supported by the presumption against construing statutes to give them a retroactive effect....

The Court recognizes that the first purpose of statutory construction is to ascertain the intent of the legislature. The Court's opinion reviews at length the legislative history, with quotations from Committee Reports and statements by Members of Congress. The Court then ends this discussion with curiously conflicting conclusions.

It finds that the "totality of congressional action makes it abundantly clear that the result we reach today [justifying the termination or abandonment of any federal project] is wholly in accord with both the words of the statute and the intent of Congress." Yet, in the same paragraph, the Court acknowledges that "there is no discussion in the legislative history of precisely this problem." The opinion nowhere makes clear how the result it reaches can be "abundantly" self-evident from the legislative history when the result was never discussed. While the Court's review of the legislative history establishes that Congress intended to require governmental agencies to take endangered species into account in the planning and execution of their programs, there is not even a hint in the legislative history that Congress intended to compel the undoing or abandonment of any project or program later found to threaten a newly discovered species.

If the relevant Committees that considered the Act, and the Members of Congress who voted on it, had been aware that the Act could be used to terminate major federal projects authorized years earlier and nearly completed, or to require the abandonment of essential and long-completed federal installations and edifices, we can be certain that there would have been hearings, testimony, and debate concerning consequences so wasteful, so inimical to purposes previously deemed important, and so likely to arouse public outrage. The absence of any such consideration by the Committees or in the floor debates indicates quite clearly that no one participating in the legislative process considered these consequences as within the intendment of the Act.

As indicated above, this view of legislative intent at the time of enactment is abundantly confirmed by the subsequent congressional actions and expressions. We have held, properly, that post-enactment statements by individual Members of Congress as to the meaning of a statute are entitled to little or no weight. The Court also has recognized that subsequent Appropriations Acts themselves are not necessarily entitled to significant weight in determining whether a prior statute has been superseded. But these precedents are inapposite. There was no effort here to "bootstrap" a post-enactment view of prior legislation by isolated statements of individual Congressmen. Nor is this a case where Congress, without explanation or comment upon the statute in question, merely has voted apparently inconsistent financial support in subsequent Appropriations Acts. Testimony on this precise issue was presented before congressional committees, and the Committee Reports for three consecutive years addressed the problem and affirmed their understanding of the original congressional intent. We cannot assume—as the Court suggests—that Congress, when it continued each year to approve the recommended appropriations, was unaware of the contents of the supporting Committee Reports. All this amounts to strong corroborative evidence that the interpretation of §7 as not applying to completed or substantially completed projects reflects the initial legislative intent....

* * *

Points for Discussion

1. *Statutory Language*: What was the language at issue? What did each party want that language to mean? What meaning did the majority and dissent adopt?

2. *Theories*: Which statutory interpretation theory did the majority use? The dissent? Did either find ambiguity, absurdity, a constitutional question to avoid, or scrivener's error?

3. *Separation of Powers*: Which separation of powers theory did the majority use? The dissent?

4. *Two Questions*: What two issues were before the Court? Which of these issues was a statutory interpretation issue and which was a separation of powers issue? Justice Rehnquist's dissent was omitted. It addressed only the second issue, concluding that even if the majority were right in its interpretation of the Endangered Species Act, the Court should not enjoin the project at this point. Would that have been a better solution to this conflict?

5. *Legislative Control*: Is this a case of Congress attempting to control agency activities (here TVA's activities) using subsequent acts, the power of the purse, or both?

6. *Subsequent Acts & Implied Repeal*: The Endangered Species Act of 1973 and the 1975, 1976, and 1977 appropriations bills conflict. The respondents argued that the appropriations bills impliedly repealed part of the Endangered Species Act. Why did the majority reject this argument? How important was the fact that the subsequent acts were appropriations bills? Why did the dissent disagree?

7. *Absurdity*: The dissent argued that the majority's interpretation would lead to an absurd result. The majority disagreed. Did the majority and dissent define absurdity differently? Why is it not absurd to halt a virtually complete 100 million dollar project to save a tiny, non-descript fish?

    When an interpretation of a statute would lead to an absurd result however defined, judges consider the legislative history (1) to determine the meaning of the language, or (2) to determine whether Congress intended that absurd result. For which reason did the majority and dissent examine legislative history? According to the majority, what did the examination show? According to the dissent, what did the examination show?

8. *Dog Does Not Bark Canon*: The dissent also found it significant that when Congress considered the Endangered Species Act, no one discussed the potential "abandonment of essential and long-completed federal installations and edifices." The absence of any such discussion indicates that none of the members of Congress thought about this potential consequence. Do you find this argument persuasive?

9. *Subsequent Legislative Action*: In a part of his dissent that was excised, Justice Powell said, "I have little doubt that Congress will amend the Endangered Species Act to prevent the grave consequences made possible by today's decision." Justice Powell was correct. After a long fight, Congress added a rider to its 1980 appropriations bill, which explicitly excepted the Tellico Dam. *See* Energy and Water Appropriation Act of 1980, Pub. L. No. 96-69, tit. IV, 93 Stat. 449 (1979) (authorizing and directing the TVA "to complete construction, operate and maintain" the Dam, "notwithstanding the provisions of the" Endangered Species Act.) Why did this appropriations bill partially repeal the Endangered Species Act when the earlier bills did not? In answering the question, consider whether this later repeal was implied or explicit.

* * *

2. Indirect Legislative Oversight

In addition to direct methods of control, Congress has indirect methods of control. One indirect method of legislative oversight is Congress's power to *investigate* agencies. Any congressional committee that has jurisdiction over an aspect of an agency's program may hold hearings and investigate the agency's implementation of its authority. Often, these hearings are publicized to mobilize public and political pressure. For example, in 2012, the House Judiciary Committee held hearings regarding the Bureau of Alcohol, Tobacco, Firearms and Explosives' Fast and Furious Program, which was intended to track firearms that were transferred to higher-level drug traffickers in Mexican cartels, with the hope that tracking would lead to arrests and the dismantling of the cartels. The program was mostly unsuccessful. After a series of public hearings, Congress held Attorney General Eric Holder in criminal contempt for refusing to provide documents to the Committee. President Obama invoked executive privilege to prevent the disclosure.

There are other indirect methods as well. For example, Congress has established other organizations to help oversee agencies, including the Congressional Research Service and the Governmental Accountability Office (previously known as the General Accounting Office (GAO)). These agencies are both located within the Executive. For this reason, this method of oversight is indirect for Congress, while it is direct for the Executive. While the GAO was originally created to oversee the use of agency budgeting and funding, its authority to oversee agency program implementation has been expanding, as we will see below.

C. Executive Oversight

The legislature is not the only body that exerts control over agencies. The president also exerts control, albeit in different ways. As with legislative oversight, the executive has both direct and indirect methods of control. Let's begin with the direct methods.

1. Direct Executive Oversight

a. Appointment

Perhaps the president's strongest form of executive control is the power to appoint and remove agency personnel, such as the cabinet members. Although the president has the power to appoint government officials, the power is not absolute. U.S. CONST. art. II § 2 cl. 2. The Constitution gives the executive this power to appoint *principal* officers, subject to senate approval. Principal officers include all top level agency officials and many lower level officials, but the Court has never clearly defined the difference between a principal and inferior officer.

This difference between these two types of officers was litigated in *Morrison v. Olson*, 487 U.S. 654 (1988), in which the Supreme Court held that Congress could give the judiciary the power to appoint an executive officer. At issue in that case was the Ethics in Government Act. 28 U.S.C. §§ 49, 591 *et seq.*, which authorized a special division of the United States Court of Appeals for the District of Columbia to appoint an independent counsel to investigate and prosecute high-ranking executive officials. *Id.* at 661. The independent counsel would perform executive functions. *Id.* at 691. Although the Act empowered the judiciary to appoint and oversee an officer who would be performing executive functions, the Court did not invalidate the Act. Instead, using a functionalist approach, the Court concluded that the independent counsel performed only limited investigative and prosecutorial work for a set period of time; hence, the officer was an inferior officer, not a principal officer. *Id.* at 671–72. Because the Constitution allows Congress to delegate the appointment of inferior officers to the judiciary, the appointment provision in the Act was constitutional. *Id.* at 673–74. Justice Scalia dissented in *Morrison.*

Nine years later, in *Edmond v. United States,* 520 U.S. 651 (1997), Justice Scalia, writing for the majority, rejected *Morrison*'s multi-factor test for determining whether a government employee was an inferior officer. In *Edmond,* the issue was whether military trial judges were principal or inferior officers. Justice Scalia concluded that these judges were "inferior officers," because "[g]enerally speaking, the term 'inferior officer' connotes a relationship with some higher ranking officer or officers below the President: whether one is an 'inferior' officer depends on whether he has a superior." *Id.* at 662.

As just noted, the president does not have the sole power to appoint *inferior* officers. Rather, "Congress may by Law vest the Appointment of such inferior Officers, as they [sic] think proper, in the President alone, in the Court of Law, or in the Heads of Departments." U.S. CONST. art. II, § 2, cl. 2. As with principal officers, the Supreme Court has not yet defined the difference between an inferior officer and an employee. While there is no bright-line rule dividing inferior officers and employees, whether the employee exercises significant authority pursuant to the laws of the United States can be determinative, because employees do not exercise significant authority; officers do. *Freytag v. Commissioner,* 501 U.S. 868, 881 (1991) (quoting *Buckley v. Valeo,* 424 U.S. 1, 126 n.162 (1976)). When determining whether individuals exercise significant authority pursuant to the laws of the United States, courts consider a variety of factors, including the manner in which Congress created the employee's position, the appointment process, the responsibilities of the position, the tenure and duration of the position, the amount and manner of pay, the level of supervision, and the identity of the supervisor. No one factor is determinative.

The Supreme Court's most relevant case in this area is *Freytag v. Commissioner,* 501 U.S. 868 (1991). In *Freytag,* the Court determined that Tax Court special trial judges ("STJ") were inferior officers. *Id.* at 881–82. The Tax Court is an Article I court with judges who are appointed for limited terms. Congress authorized the Chief Judge of the Tax Court to appoint STJs to hear specific tax cases. For some of these cases the STJ could resolve the case directly, but for others the STJ could make a recommended decision only. A judge from the Tax Court would review the STJ's recommended decision and make the final decision. Freytag's case was one of the latter, requiring review and adoption by a Tax Court Judge.

Freytag challenged the validity of the judgment against him, arguing, in part, that the appointment of STJs by the Chief Judge of the Tax Court violated the Appointments Clause. The government argued that the STJs were merely employees, who did no more than assist the regular Tax Court Judges in taking evidence and preparing proposed findings and an opinion. The justices unanimously rejected this argument and held that the STJs were inferior officers. To find that STJs were inferior officers and not merely employees, the Court considered multiple factors. First, the Court noted that the office of special trial judge is "established by Law" and that the statute lays out the "duties, salary, and means of appointment for that office."

Second, the Court focused on the types of duties and level of discretion STJs had. STJs "perform more than ministerial task[s]"; they take testimony, conduct trials, rule on the admissibility of evidence, and can enforce compliance with discovery orders. *Id.* In the course of performing these tasks, STJs "exercise significant discretion." *Id.* at 882. Third, the Court added that "[e]ven if the duties of [STJs] were not as significant as ... we have found them to be," there are circumstances where "they exercise independent authority," and they cannot be "inferior Officers" for some purposes and not others. *Id.* Fourth, and almost as an aside, the Court pointed out that STJs were authorized to decide cases *in some instances,* even if in other instances STJs only proposed findings and orders, while the regular Tax Court judge rendered the final decision. Notably, the Court specifically rejected the argument that officials who "lack authority to enter into a final decision" must be employees and not inferior officers, because that argument "ignores the significance of the duties and discretion that special trial judges possess." *Id.* at 881. Even though the Court rejected this factor as determinative, the D.C. Circuit subsequently relied on this factor alone to conclude that ALJs working for the Federal Deposit Insurance Corporation were employees not inferior officers. *Landry v. FDIC*, 204 F.3d 1125, 1133–34 (D.C. Cir. 2000).

The distinctions between (1) principal officers and inferior officers and (2) inferior officers and employees are relevant not only to appointment issues but also to removal issues, as we will see next. Because the Supreme Court has not definitively established three distinct categories of agency personnel, appointment challenges and removal challenges often occur together.

b. Removal

While the Constitution explicitly provides for the appointment of principal and inferior officers, it does not explicitly provide for their removal. Rather, the Constitution contains only one removal provision, which provides that "all civil officers of the United States [may] be removed from office on impeachment for, and conviction of, treason, bribery, or other high crimes and misdemeanors." U.S. CONST. art. II, §4. The impeachment process is seldom used; yet, officers are removed regularly. How is that possible? The answer is that the Supreme Court has concluded that the Constitution vests removal power in the president *implicitly.* According to the Court, the president has the power to remove executive officers because that power was not "'expressly taken away'" from the president in the Constitution. *Free Enterprise Fund v. Public Co. Accounting Oversight Bd.*, 561 U.S. 477, 492 (2010) (citing Letter from James Madison to Thomas Jefferson (June 30, 1789), 16 Documentary History of the First Federal Congress 893 (2004)). Further, the Constitution provides that "[t]he executive Power shall be vested in a President of the United States of America." U.S. CONST. art. II, §1, cl. 1. As Madison stated on the floor of the First Congress, "if any power whatsoever is in its nature Executive, it is the power of appointing, overseeing, and controlling those who execute the laws." 1 Annals of Cong. 463 (1789).

In *Myers v. United States*, 272 U.S. 52 (1926), the Supreme Court struck down a statute that required the president to obtain the advice and consent of the Senate prior to removing the postmaster general. *Id.* at 106–18, 176. According to the Court, the power to remove a federal officer necessarily accompanies the constitutionally granted power to appoint that officer because the power to remove compliments the power to appoint. The Court rejected the argument that the power to remove flowed from the Senate's ability to advise on and consent to appointments. *Id.* at 126–27.

Like the appointment power, the president's removal power is not absolute. In some statutes, Congress chooses to limit the president's ability to remove an officer to protect that officer's independence. The Supreme Court has upheld such limitations. For example, in *Humphrey's Executor,* the Supreme Court upheld a removal provision limiting the president's ability to remove a commissioner of the Federal Trade Commission (FTC) for "inefficiency, neglect of duty, or malfeasance in office." The Court reached this result, in part, because the FTC was designed to be independent and free from domination and control of the president. 295 U.S. 602, 619 (1935); *see also Morrison v. Olson*, 487 U.S. 654, 693 (1988) (noting that "the congressional determination to limit the removal power of the Attorney General was essential ... to establish the necessary independence of the office"). You might wish to review the distinction between executive and independent agencies in Chapter 16.

Thus, there is little question that Congress can limit a president's power to remove officers, but the exact limits on the removal power are unclear. *Cf. Bowsher v. Synar*, 478 U.S. 714, 725–26 (1986) (holding that Congress cannot reserve for itself the power to remove executive officers). Early case law distinguished between officers who performed "purely executive" functions and officers who performed "quasi-legislative" and "quasi-judicial" functions. *See, e.g., Humphrey's Executor v. United States,* 295 U.S. 602 (1935); *Myers v. United States* 272 U.S. 52 (1926). Pursuant to this distinction, Congress could not limit a president's ability to remove principal officers whom he appointed and who performed "purely executive" powers. In contrast, Congress could limit a president's ability to remove principal officers he appointed who performed "quasi-legislative" or "quasi-judicial" functions. For example, in *Myers,* the Supreme Court struck down a federal statute that required the president to obtain Senate approval prior to removing the postmaster general, a principal officer. 272 U.S. at 106–18, 176. The Court reasoned that because executive officers, like the postmaster general, exercise executive authority, the legislature cannot retain the power to advise on and consent to their removal. The Court reasoned that if executive appointees were beholden to members of the legislature for their livelihood they would cease to be an independent executive officer. *Id.* at 131.

In contrast, in *Humphrey's Executor,* the Court upheld a provision in the Federal Trade Commission Act that permitted the president to dismiss a commissioner of the Federal Trade Commission (FTC), also a principal officer, only for "inefficiency, neglect of duty, or malfeasance in office." *Id.* at 620 (quoting The Federal Trade Commission Act, c. 311, 38 Stat. 717; 15 U.S.C. § 1). The Court distinguished its holding in *Myers* by noting that the postmaster general performed purely executive functions and had to be responsible to the president while the FTC member performed quasi-legislative or quasi-judicial powers and had to be independent from the president. *Id.* at 627–28. The Court expressly "disapproved" the statements in *Myers* suggesting that the president had an inherent constitutional power to remove members of quasi-judicial bodies. The Court limited the *Myers* holding to "all purely executive officers," noting that its holding did not apply to "an officer who occupies no place in the executive department, and who exercises no part of the executive power vested by the Constitution in the President." *Id.* at 628. The Court reasoned that Congress intended the FTC and its Commissioners to be independent from the president and provided that their tenure would be limited. *See also Weiner v. United States*, 357 U.S. 349, 350 (1958) (limiting the president's ability to remove a Commissioner of the War Claims Commission, which had only a three year existence, even though the relevant statute was silent regarding removal, because Congress intended to insulate the Commission from presidential interference).

Pursuant to this *Myers/Humphrey*'s distinction, a president has unlimited power to remove purely executive principal officers, but limited power to remove tenured quasi-legislative or quasi-judicial principal officers. Under this approach, the functions the officer performs dictate the validity of any restrictions on removal. Congress can limit the presidential removal power, a fundamental executive power, when officials have tenured, or limited, terms and when the officials must be free to act without presidential interference.

However, *Myers*, *Humphrey's Executor*, and *Weiner* all involved principal officers, who were appointed by a president with the advice and consent of the Senate. These cases did not address the removal of inferior officers, who may constitutionally be appointed by and, therefore, be removed by the heads of their department. *See Ex parte Hennen*, 38 U.S. 230 (13 Pet. 230), 259 (1839). The question that remains is whether Congress may impose greater or lesser limits on a president's removal power in the case of inferior officers.

In *Morrison v. Olson*, 487 U.S. 654 (1988), the Supreme Court addressed this issue and upheld a for-cause removal limitation on a "purely executive" inferior officer. In the relevant statute, the Ethics in Government Act, Congress created the position of an independent counsel, whose function was to "investigate and, if appropriate, prosecute certain high-ranking government officials" involved in criminal activity. The Act provided that the attorney general, a principal officer, could remove the independent counsel, an inferior officer, only "for good cause." The Court acknowledged that the independent counsel was purely an executive officer. *Id* at 671. Under *Humphrey's Executor* and *Myers*, the removal limitation should have been invalid.

Rejecting the *Myers/Humphrey*'s distinction as determinative in this case, the Court said, "the determination of whether the constitution allows Congress to impose a 'good cause'-type restriction on the President's power to remove an official cannot be made to turn on whether or not that official is classified as 'purely executive.'" *Id.*

at 689. Acknowledging that the type of functions an officer performs is relevant to the analysis, the Court reasoned that the more important question is whether the removal restriction "impedes the President's ability to perform his Constitutional duty" to ensure that the laws are faithfully executed. *Id.* The Court then reasoned that because the independent counsel (1) was an inferior officer, (2) had limited jurisdiction, (3) did not have tenure, (4) lacked policymaking power, and (5) did not have significant administrative authority, the for-cause removal provision was a reasonable restriction on the president's removal authority.

This case left open, however, the question of whether more than one level of for-cause removal would be constitutional. The Supreme Court answered that question in 2010 in the case below. See if you can identify which separation of powers theory each opinion used and why the majority concluded that more than one layer of for-cause removal is not constitutional.

Free Enterprise Fund v. Public Co. Accounting Oversight Board

Supreme Court of the United States
561 U.S. 477 (2010)

◆ Chief Justice Roberts delivered the opinion of the Court [in which Scalia, Kennedy, Thomas, and Alito, JJ., concur].

... Since 1789, the Constitution has been understood to empower the President to keep [executive] officers accountable — by removing them from office, if necessary. See generally *Myers v. United States,* 272 U.S. 52 (1926). This Court has determined, however, that this authority is not without limit. In *Humphrey's Executor v. United States,* 295 U.S. 602 (1935), we held that Congress can, under certain circumstances, create independent agencies run by principal officers appointed by the President, whom the President may not remove at will but only for good cause. Likewise, in ... *Morrison v. Olson,* 487 U.S. 654 (1988), the Court sustained similar restrictions on the power of principal executive officers — themselves responsible to the President — to remove their own inferiors....

We are asked ... to consider a new situation not yet encountered by the Court.... May the President be restricted in his ability to remove a principal officer, who is in turn restricted in his ability to remove an inferior officer, even though that inferior officer determines the policy and enforces the laws of the United States?

We hold that such multilevel protection from removal is contrary to Article II's vesting of the executive power in the President. The President cannot "take Care that the Laws be faithfully executed" if he cannot oversee the faithfulness of the officers who execute them. Here the President cannot remove an officer who enjoys more than one level of good-cause protection, even if the President determines that the officer is neglecting his duties or discharging them improperly. That judgment is instead committed to another officer, who may or may not agree with the President's determination, and whom the President cannot remove simply because that officer disagrees with him. This contravenes the President's "constitutional obligation to ensure the faithful execution of the laws."

After a series of celebrated accounting debacles, Congress enacted the Sarbanes–Oxley Act of 2002 (or Act).... [T]he Act introduced tighter regulation of the accounting industry under a new Public Company Accounting Oversight Board. The Board is composed of five members, appointed to staggered 5–year terms by the Securities and Exchange Commission....

... [T]he Board is a Government-created, Government-appointed entity, with expansive powers to govern an entire industry.... The Board is charged with enforcing the Sarbanes–Oxley Act, the securities laws, the Commission's rules, its own rules, and professional accounting standards. To this end, the Board may regulate every detail of an accounting firm's practice, including hiring and professional development, promotion, supervision of audit work, the acceptance of new business and the continuation of old, internal inspection procedures, professional ethics rules, and "such other requirements as the Board may prescribe."

The Board promulgates auditing and ethics standards, performs routine inspections of all accounting firms, demands documents and testimony, and initiates formal investigations and disciplinary proceedings. The willful violation of any Board rule is treated as a willful violation of the Securities Exchange Act of 1934 — a federal crime.... And the Board itself can issue severe sanctions in its disciplinary proceedings, up to and including the permanent revocation of a firm's registration, a permanent ban on a person's associating with any registered firm, and money penalties....

The Act places the Board under the SEC's oversight, particularly with respect to the issuance of rules or the imposition of sanctions (both of which are subject to Commission approval and alteration). But the individual members of the Board — like the officers and directors of the self-regulatory organizations — are substantially insulated from the Commission's control. The Commission cannot remove Board members at will, but only "for good cause shown," "in accordance with" certain procedures....

... The parties agree that the Commissioners cannot themselves be removed by the President except under the *Humphrey's Executor* standard of "inefficiency, neglect of duty, or malfeasance in office," and we decide the case with that understanding.

... [T]he Free Enterprise Fund, a nonprofit organization ... sued the Board and its members, seeking (among other things) a declaratory judgment that the Board is unconstitutional and an injunction preventing the Board from exercising its powers.

Before the District Court, petitioners argued that the Sarbanes–Oxley Act contravened the separation of powers by conferring wide-ranging executive power on Board members without subjecting them to Presidential control.... [T]he District Court granted summary judgment to respondents. A divided Court of Appeals affirmed.... We granted certiorari [and reverse]....

... [W]e have previously upheld limited restrictions on the President's removal power. In those cases, however, only one level of protected tenure separated the President from an officer exercising executive power. It was the President—or a subordinate he could remove at will—who decided whether the officer's conduct merited removal under the good-cause standard.

The Act before us does something quite different. It not only protects Board members from removal except for good cause, but withdraws from the President any decision on whether that good cause exists. That decision is vested instead in other tenured officers—the Commissioners—none of whom is subject to the President's direct control. The result is a Board that is not accountable to the President, and a President who is not responsible for the Board.

The added layer of tenure protection makes a difference. Without a layer of insulation between the Commission and the Board, the Commission could remove a Board member at any time, and therefore would be fully responsible for what the Board does. The President could then hold the Commission to account for its supervision of the Board, to the same extent that he may hold the Commission to account for everything else it does.

A second level of tenure protection changes the nature of the President's review. Now the Commission cannot remove a Board member at will. The President therefore cannot hold the Commission fully accountable for the Board's conduct, to the same extent that he may hold the Commission accountable for everything else that it does. The Commissioners are not responsible for the Board's actions. They are only responsible for their own determination of whether the Act's rigorous good-cause standard is met. And even if the President disagrees with their determination, he is powerless to intervene—unless that determination is so unreasonable as to constitute "inefficiency, neglect of duty, or malfeasance in office."

This novel structure does not merely add to the Board's independence, but transforms it. Neither the President, nor anyone directly responsible to him, nor even an officer whose conduct he may review only for good cause, has full control over the Board. The President is stripped of the power ... to execute the laws—by holding his subordinates accountable for their conduct—[his power] is impaired.

That arrangement is contrary to Article II's vesting of the executive power in the President. Without the ability to oversee the Board, or to attribute the Board's failings to those whom he *can* oversee, the President is no longer the judge of the Board's conduct. He is not the one who decides whether Board members are abusing their offices or neglecting their duties. He can neither ensure that the laws are faithfully executed, nor be held responsible for a Board member's breach of faith....

Indeed, if allowed to stand, this dispersion of responsibility could be multiplied. If Congress can shelter the bureaucracy behind two layers of good-cause tenure, why not a third? At oral argument, the Government was unwilling to concede that even *five* layers between the President and the Board would be too many. The officers of such an agency—safely encased within a Matryoshka doll of tenure protections—would be immune from Presidential oversight, even as they exercised power in the people's name....

By granting the Board executive power without the Executive's oversight, this Act subverts the President's ability to ensure that the laws are faithfully executed — as well as the public's ability to pass judgment on his efforts. The Act's restrictions are incompatible with the Constitution's separation of powers....

According to the dissent, Congress may impose multiple levels of for-cause tenure between the President and his subordinates when it "rests agency independence upon the need for technical expertise." The Board's mission is said to demand both "technical competence" and "apolitical expertise," and its powers may only be exercised by "technical experts." In this respect the statute creating the Board is, we are told, simply one example of the "vast numbers of statutes governing vast numbers of subjects, concerned with vast numbers of different problems, (that) provide for, or foresee, their execution or administration through the work of administrators organized within many different kinds of administrative structures, exercising different kinds of administrative authority, to achieve their legislatively mandated objectives."

No one doubts Congress's power to create a vast and varied federal bureaucracy. But where, in all this, is the role for oversight by an elected President? The Constitution requires that a President chosen by the entire Nation oversee the execution of the laws. And the "'fact that a given law or procedure is efficient, convenient, and useful in facilitating functions of government, standing alone, will not save it if it is contrary to the Constitution,'" for "'[c]onvenience and efficiency are not the primary objectives — or the hallmarks — of democratic government.'"

One can have a government that functions without being ruled by functionaries, and a government that benefits from expertise without being ruled by experts. Our Constitution was adopted to enable the people to govern themselves, through their elected leaders. The growth of the Executive Branch, which now wields vast power and touches almost every aspect of daily life, heightens the concern that it may slip from the Executive's control, and thus from that of the people. This concern is largely absent from the dissent's paean to the administrative state....

In fact, the multilevel protection that the dissent endorses "provides a blueprint for extensive expansion of the legislative power." In a system of checks and balances, "[p]ower abhors a vacuum," and one branch's handicap is another's strength. "Even when a branch does not arrogate power to itself," therefore, it must not "impair another in the performance of its constitutional duties." Congress has plenary control over the salary, duties, and even existence of executive offices. Only Presidential oversight can counter its influence. That is why the Constitution vests certain powers in the President that "the Legislature has no right to diminish or modify." ...

The parties here concede that Board members are executive "Officers," as that term is used in the Constitution. We do not decide the status of other Government employees.... [10]

---

10. [O]ur holding also does not address that subset of independent agency employees who serve as administrative law judges. Whether administrative law judges are necessarily "Officers of the United States" is disputed. See, *e.g., Landry v. FDIC,* 204 F.3d 1125 (C.A.D.C.2000). And unlike members of

As the judgment in this case demonstrates, restricting certain officers to a single level of insulation from the President affects the conditions under which those officers might someday be removed, and would have no effect, absent a congressional determination to the contrary, on the validity of any officer's continuance in office. The only issue in this case is whether Congress may deprive the President of adequate control over the Board, which is the regulator of first resort and the primary law enforcement authority for a vital sector of our economy. We hold that it cannot. [Although the majority found the for-cause removal provision for the Board to be unconstitutional, the majority concluded that the unconstitutional tenure provision was severable from the remainder of the statute.]

Petitioners raise three more challenges to the Board under the Appointments Clause. None has merit.

First, petitioners argue that Board members are principal officers requiring Presidential appointment with the Senate's advice and consent. We held in *Edmond v. United States*, 520 U.S. 651 (1997), that "[w]hether one is an 'inferior' officer depends on whether he has a superior," and that "'inferior officers' are officers whose work is directed and supervised at some level" by other officers appointed by the President with the Senate's consent. In particular, we noted that "[t]he power to remove officers" at will and without cause "is a powerful tool for control" of an inferior.... Given that the Commission is properly viewed, under the Constitution, as possessing the power to remove Board members at will, and given the Commission's other oversight authority, we have no hesitation in concluding that under *Edmond* the Board members are inferior officers whose appointment Congress may permissibly vest in a "Hea[d] of Departmen[t]."

But, petitioners argue, the Commission is not a "Departmen[t]" like the "Executive departments" (*e.g.*, State, Treasury, Defense) listed in 5 U.S.C. § 101. In *Freytag*, 501 U.S., at 887, n. 4, we specifically reserved the question whether a "principal agenc[y], such as ... the Securities and Exchange Commission," is a "Departmen[t]" under the Appointments Clause....

... [Our reading of the] Appointments Clause is consistent with the common, near-contemporary definition of a "department" as a "separate allotment or part of business; a distinct province, in which a class of duties are allotted to a particular person." 1 N. Webster, American Dictionary of the English Language (1828) (def.2) (1995 facsimile ed.).... And it is consistent with our prior cases, which have never invalidated an appointment made by the head of such an establishment. Because the Commission is a freestanding component of the Executive Branch, not subordinate to or contained within any other such component, it constitutes a "Departmen[t]" for the purposes of the Appointments Clause.

---

the Board, many administrative law judges of course perform adjudicative rather than enforcement or policymaking functions, or possess purely recommendatory powers. The Government below refused to identify either "civil service tenure-protected employees in independent agencies" or administrative law judges as "precedent for the PCAOB."

But petitioners are not done yet. They argue that the full Commission cannot constitutionally appoint Board members, because only the Chairman of the Commission is the Commission's "Hea[d]." The Commission's powers, however, are generally vested in the Commissioners jointly, not the Chairman alone....

◆ JUSTICE BREYER, with whom JUSTICE STEVENS, JUSTICE GINSBURG, and JUSTICE SOTOMAYOR join, dissenting.

The Court holds unconstitutional a statute providing that the Securities and Exchange Commission can remove members of the Public Company Accounting Oversight Board from office only for cause. It argues that granting the "inferior officer[s]" on the Accounting Board "more than one level of good-cause protection ... contravenes the President's 'constitutional obligation to ensure the faithful execution of the laws.'" I agree that the Accounting Board members are inferior officers. But in my view the statute does not significantly interfere with the President's "executive Power." It violates no separation-of-powers principle. And the Court's contrary holding threatens to disrupt severely the fair and efficient administration of the laws. I consequently dissent.

The legal question before us arises at the intersection of two general constitutional principles. On the one hand, Congress has broad power to enact statutes "necessary and proper" to the exercise of its specifically enumerated constitutional authority. Art. I, § 8, cl. 18....

On the other hand, the opening sections of Articles I, II, and III of the Constitution separately and respectively vest "all legislative Powers" in Congress, the "executive Power" in the President, and the "judicial Power" in the Supreme Court (and such "inferior Courts as Congress may from time to time ordain and establish"). In doing so, these provisions imply a structural separation-of-powers principle. And that principle, along with the instruction in Article II, § 3 that the President "shall take Care that the Laws be faithfully executed," limits Congress' power to structure the Federal Government. Indeed, this Court has held that the separation-of-powers principle guarantees the President the authority to dismiss certain Executive Branch officials at will. *Myers v. United States* 272 U.S. 52 (1926).

But neither of these two principles is absolute in its application to removal cases. The Necessary and Proper Clause does not grant Congress power to free *all* Executive Branch officials from dismissal at the will of the President. Nor does the separation-of-powers principle grant the President an absolute authority to remove *any and all* Executive Branch officials at will. Rather, depending on, say, the nature of the office, its function, or its subject matter, Congress sometimes may, consistent with the Constitution, limit the President's authority to remove an officer from his post. And we must here decide whether the circumstances surrounding the statute at issue justify such a limitation.

In answering the question presented, we cannot look to more specific constitutional text, such as the text of the Appointments Clause or the Presentment Clause, upon which the Court has relied in other separation-of-powers cases. That is because, with the exception of the general "vesting" and "take care" language, the Constitution is completely "silent with respect to the power of removal from office." ...

Nor does this Court's precedent fully answer the question presented. At least it does not clearly invalidate the provision in dispute. In *Myers, supra,* the Court invalidated—for the first and only time—a congressional statute on the ground that it unduly limited the President's authority to remove an Executive Branch official. But soon thereafter the Court expressly disapproved most of *Myers'* broad reasoning. See *Humphrey's Executor,* overruling in part *Myers; Wiener v. United States,* 357 U.S. 349, 352 (1958) (stating that *Humphrey's Executor* "explicitly 'disapproved'" of much of the reasoning in *Myers*). Moreover, the Court has since said that "the essence of the decision in *Myers* was the judgment that the Constitution prevents Congress from 'draw[ing] to itself*...* the power to remove or the right to participate in the exercise of that power.'" And that feature of the statute—a feature that would *aggrandize* the power of Congress—is not present here. Congress has not granted itself any role in removing the members of the Accounting Board.

In short, the question presented lies at the intersection of two sets of conflicting, broadly framed constitutional principles. And no text, no history, perhaps no precedent provides any clear answer....

Federal statutes now require or permit Government officials to provide, regulate, or otherwise administer, not only foreign affairs and defense, but also a wide variety of such subjects as taxes, welfare, social security, medicine, pharmaceutical drugs, education, highways, railroads, electricity, natural gas, nuclear power, financial instruments, banking, medical care, public health and safety, the environment, fair employment practices, consumer protection and much else besides. Those statutes create a host of different organizational structures.... Statutes similarly grant administrators a wide variety of powers.... The upshot is that today vast numbers of statutes governing vast numbers of subjects, concerned with vast numbers of different problems, provide for, or foresee, their execution or administration through the work of administrators organized within many different kinds of administrative structures, exercising different kinds of administrative authority, to achieve their legislatively mandated objectives. And, given the nature of the Government's work, it is not surprising that administrative units come in many different shapes and sizes.

The functional approach required by our precedents recognizes this administrative complexity and, more importantly, recognizes the various ways presidential power operates within this context—and the various ways in which a removal provision might affect that power....

... [H]ere, as in similar cases, we should decide the constitutional question in light of the provision's practical functioning in context. And our decision should take account of the Judiciary's comparative lack of institutional expertise.

To what extent then is the Act's "for cause" provision likely, as a practical matter, to limit the President's exercise of executive authority? In practical terms no "for cause" provision can, in isolation, define the full measure of executive power. This is because a legislative decision to place ultimate administrative authority in, say, the Secretary of Agriculture rather than the President, the way in which the statute defines the scope of the power the relevant administrator can exercise, the decision as to who controls the agency's budget requests and funding, the relationships between one agency or department and another, as well as more purely political factors (including Congress' ability to assert influence) are more likely to affect the President's power to get something done....

... [W]e should ... conclude that the "for cause" restriction before us will not restrict presidential power significantly. For one thing, the restriction directly limits, not the President's power, but the power of an already independent agency. The Court seems to have forgotten that fact when it identifies its central constitutional problem: According to the Court, the President "is powerless to intervene" if he has determined that the Board members' "conduct merit[s] removal" because "[t]hat decision is vested instead in other tenured officers—the Commissioners—none of whom is subject to the President's direct control." But so long as the President is *legitimately* foreclosed from removing the *Commissioners* except for cause (as the majority assumes), nullifying the Commission's power to remove Board members only for cause will not resolve the problem the Court has identified: The President will *still* be "powerless to intervene" by removing the Board members if the Commission reasonably decides not to do so.

In other words, the Court fails to show why *two* layers of "for cause" protection—Layer One insulating the Commissioners from the President, and Layer Two insulating the Board from the Commissioners—impose any more serious limitation upon the *President's* powers than *one* layer....

At the same time, Congress ... had good reason for enacting the challenged "for cause" provision. First and foremost, the Board adjudicates cases. This Court has long recognized the appropriateness of using "for cause" provisions to protect the personal independence of those who even only sometimes engage in adjudicatory functions....

Moreover, in addition to their adjudicative functions, the Accounting Board members supervise, and are themselves, technical professional experts....

Here, the justification for insulating the "technical experts" on the Board from fear of losing their jobs due to political influence is particularly strong. Congress deliberately sought to provide that kind of protection.... It did so for good reason.... [H]istorically, this regulatory subject matter—financial regulation—has been thought to exhibit a particular need for independence....

In sum, Congress and the President could reasonably have thought it prudent to insulate the adjudicative Board members from fear of purely politically based removal....

Where a "for cause" provision is so unlikely to restrict presidential power and so likely to further a legitimate institutional need, precedent strongly supports its constitutionality.... First, ... [h]ere, the removal restriction may somewhat diminish the *Commission's* ability to control the Board, but it will have little, if any, negative effect in respect to the President's ability to control the Board, let alone to coordinate the Executive Branch....

Second, ... this Court has repeatedly upheld "for cause" provisions where they restrict the President's power to remove an officer with adjudicatory responsibilities....

Third, consider ... *Perkins*, 116 U.S., at 483, 484 [in which] the Court upheld a removal restriction limiting the authority of the Secretary of the Navy to remove a "cadet-engineer," whom the Court explicitly defined as an "inferior officer." The Court said,

> We have no doubt that when Congress, by law, vests the appointment of inferior officers in the heads of Departments *it may limit and restrict the power of removal as it deems best for the public interest.* The constitutional authority in Congress to thus vest the appointment implies authority to limit, restrict, and regulate the removal by such laws as Congress may enact in relation to the officers so appointed....

And in *Freytag*, Justice Scalia stated in a concurring opinion written for four Justices, including Justice Kennedy, that "adjusting the remainder of the Constitution to compensate for *Humphrey's Executor* is a fruitless endeavor." In these Justices' view, the Court should not create a *separate* constitutional jurisprudence for the "independent agencies." That being so, the law should treat their heads as it treats other Executive Branch heads of departments. Consequently, as the Court held in *Perkins*, Congress may constitutionally "limit and restrict" the Commission's power to remove those whom they appoint (*e.g.,* the Accounting Board members).

Fourth, the Court has said that "[o]ur separation-of-powers jurisprudence generally focuses on the danger of one branch's *aggrandizing its power* at the expense of another branch." ... Congress here has "drawn" no power to itself to remove the Board members....

... [T]he Court's "double for-cause" rule applies to appointees who are "inferior officer[s]." And who are they? Courts and scholars have struggled for more than a century to define the constitutional term "inferior officers," without much success.... The Court does not clarify the concept. But without defining who is an inferior officer, to whom the majority's new rule applies, we cannot know the scope or the coherence of the legal rule that the Court creates....

The potential ... is [large].... [A]dministrative law judges (ALJs) "are all executive officers." And ALJs are each removable "only for good cause established and determined by the Merit Systems Protection Board." But the members of the Merit Systems Protection Board are themselves protected from removal by the President absent good cause.

... [T]he Federal Government relies on 1,584 ALJs to adjudicate administrative matters in over 25 agencies. These ALJs adjudicate Social Security benefits, employment disputes, and other matters highly important to individuals. Does every losing party before an ALJ now have grounds to appeal on the basis that the decision entered against him is unconstitutional? ...

One last question: How can the Court simply *assume* without deciding that the SEC Commissioners themselves are removable only "for cause"? Unless the Commissioners themselves are *in fact* protected by a "for cause" requirement, the Accounting Board statute, on the Court's own reasoning, is not constitutionally defective. I am not aware of any other instance in which the Court has similarly (on its own or through stipulation) *created* a constitutional defect in a statute and then relied on that defect to strike a statute down as unconstitutional....

The Court ... reads *into* the statute ... a "for cause removal" phrase that does not appear in the relevant statute and which Congress probably did not intend to write. And it does so in order to strike down, not to uphold, another statute. This is not a statutory construction that seeks to avoid a constitutional question, but its opposite.

I do not need to decide whether the Commissioners are in fact removable only "for cause" because I would uphold the Accounting Board's removal provision as constitutional regardless. But were that not so, a determination that the silent SEC statute means no more than it says would properly avoid the determination of unconstitutionality that the Court now makes....

* * *

Points for Discussion

1. *Issue*: In this case, the court was not interpreting the meaning of statutory language. The parties agreed on what the statute said. Instead, the parties were arguing that a section of the Sarbanes-Oxley Act was unconstitutional. What precisely were the issues?

2. *Theories*: Which separation of powers theory did the majority use? The dissent? Why did the majority conclude that the dual for-cause removal provisions violated the constitution? Why did the dissent disagree? Does this case make removal issues any clearer or merely muddy the waters?

3. *Aggrandizement*: Justice Breyer noted that because Congress had not assumed removal power for itself at the expense of the executive, there was no aggrandizement problem. Did the majority respond to this argument? Recall that functionalists are more concerned about legislative aggrandizement than about other forms of aggrandizement.

4. *Appointment*: This case addressed the constitutionality of the Board members' appointment as well as their removal. What three arguments did the petitioners make as to why the appointment procedure violated the constitution? How did the majority respond to those arguments?

5. *Removal*: Under the majority's analysis, does the distinction that *Myers* and *Humphrey's Executor* created (quasi-executive powers v. quasi-judicial and quasi-legislative) retain any force? What powers did the Board have? Might dual for-cause removal provisions be prudent for quasi-judicial officers (like ALJs), who should be more insulated from presidential influence? Perhaps single for-cause removal provisions are sufficient. But what if a quasi-executive officer is inves-

tigating executive misconduct, are dual layers appropriate then? Consider the case discussed in the note below regarding former President Nixon.

6. *President Nixon's Resignation*: Congress enacted the independent counsel statute at issue in the *Morrison* case in response to Watergate. Former Attorney General Elliot Richardson had hired attorney Archibald Cox to investigate the burglary at the Watergate complex. At some point during the investigation, President Nixon ordered Richardson to fire Cox. Rather than comply, Richardson resigned. The deputy attorney general under Richardson also resigned. The Solicitor General, Robert Bork, finally fired Cox. The debacle came to be known as the "Saturday Night Massacre." Ultimately, President Nixon resigned, in part, because of the adverse public response to Cox's firing. Do these facts suggest that some level of independence from presidential removal may be warranted in some cases?

7. *Clinton's Impeachment*: After Ken Starr's investigation of President Clinton, which cost more than $40 million and lead to President Clinton's impeachment, Congress refused to extend the Independent Counsel Act.

8. *Inferior Officers*: Both the majority and dissent concluded that the Board members were inferior officers and not principal officers. The majority reasoned that because the Board member were subject to the SEC Commissioners' oversight and were removable at will, they were inferior officers. The majority did not address why the Board members were inferior officers rather than mere employees. Justice Breyer noted this point in his dissent, yet he stated in his first paragraph that the Board members were inferior officers. Thus, the distinction between inferior officer and employee remains unclear. Should the Court have taken this opportunity to clarify the test?

9. *Impact on ALJs*: In his dissent, Justice Breyer notes the potential implications of the majority's decision that Congress cannot place dual-cause removal provisions on inferior officers. One example he cites are the 1,584 Administrative Law Judges (ALJ), who adjudicate formal adjudications for more than 25 agencies. Arguably, ALJs are inferior officers, although this issue is currently being litigated. *See, e.g., Gray Financial Group, Inc. v. SEC*, No. 1:15-cv-0492 (N.D. Ga. 2015) (concluding that SEC ALJs are inferior officers); *Tilton v. SEC*, No. 15-CV-2472(RA), 2015 WL 4006165 (S.D.N.Y. June 30, 2015) (remanded without deciding if ALJs are inferior officers); *Spring Hill Capital Partners, LLC, et al. v. SEC*, 1 :15-cv-04542, ECF No. 24 (S.D.N.Y June 29, 2015) (concluding that SEC ALJs are inferior officers); *Hill v. SEC*, No. 1:15–CV–1801–LMM, 2015 WL 4307088 (N.D. Ga. 2015) (concluding that SEC ALJs are inferior officers); *Duka*, No. 15 Civ. 357(RMB)(SN), 2015 WL 1943245, (S.D.N.Y. April 15, 2015) (concluding that SEC ALJs are inferior officers); *Stilwell v. SEC*, No. 1:14-cv-07931 (S.D.N.Y. Oct. 1, 2014) (dismissed); *but see Landry v. FDIC*, 204 F.3d 1125 (D.C. Cir. 2000) (holding that FDIC ALJs are employees); *see generally*, Kent Barnett, *Resolving the ALJ Quandary*, 66 VAND. L. REV. 797, 812 (2013). Further, ALJs are removable only for good cause. 5 U.S.C. § 7521(a).

To remove an ALJ, the agency must first bring a good cause proceeding before the Merit Service Protection Board (MSPB). Members of the MSPB, who determine whether sufficient good cause exists to remove an ALJ, are themselves protected from removal. They are removable by the President "only for inefficiency, neglect of duty, or malfeasance in office." 5 U.S.C. §1202(d). In addition, if the head of a particular agency trying to remove its ALJs is protected from removal, like the SEC Commissioners, then there may be a third layer of protection. For an SEC ALJ to be removed, first the SEC Commissioners must refer that ALJ to the MSPB and establish good cause, then the MSPB must conclude that good cause existed. Hence, presumably three levels of for-cause removal may be present. If SEC ALJs' appointment or removal process violates the constitution, then parties who lost in an administrative proceeding before an ALJ may now challenge the legality of the ALJ's decision. Does the potential for increased litigation and invalid decisions mean these provisions should be found to be constitutional? *Cf. NLRB v. Noel Canning*, 134 S. Ct. 2550 (2014) (finding President Obama's recess appointments to the NLRB invalid, which invalidated opinions issued by the NLRB).

10. *Constitutional Avoidance Canon*: In dissent, Justice Breyer notes that the majority simply accepted the parties' stipulation that the SEC Commissioners are removable only for cause. He further notes that the relevant statute actually is silent on this issue. Did the majority avoid its responsibility for deciding this case by accepting the parties' stipulation as to this legal conclusion? In other words, was not Justice Breyer correct that the majority made a critical legal finding based solely on the parties' failure to argue an issue and that this legal finding was essential to the majority's decision to find a provision of the Sarbanes-Oxley Act unconstitutional?

* * *

c. Executive Orders

An executive order is a directive issued by a president to implement or interpret federal law. Presidents have issued executive orders since 1789. Presidents have used executive orders to suspend habeas corpus, implement affirmative action requirements for government contractors, slow stem cell research, and authorize citizen surveillance. Executive orders are popular.

> In contrast to legislation or agency regulation, there are almost no legally enforceable procedural requirements that the president must satisfy before issuing (or repealing) an executive order.... That, no doubt, is central to their appeal to presidents. They rid the president of the need to assemble majorities in both houses of Congress, or to wait through administrative processes, such as notice-and-comment rulemaking, to initiate policy.

Kevin M. Stack, *The Statutory President*, 90 Iowa L. Rev. 539, 552–53 (2005).

Although there is no constitutional provision or statute that explicitly permits the president to issue executive orders, presidents assumed this power pursuant to their authority to "take Care that the Laws be faithfully executed." U.S. Const. art. II, §3, cl. 5. Presidents generally use executive orders to guide federal agencies and officials in their execution of statutory authority. However, presidents use executive orders in other ways as well. For example, presidents may use proclamations, a special type of executive order, for ceremonial or symbolic messages, such as when the president declares *National Take Your Child to Work Day*. Also, presidents issue National Security Directives, which concern national security or defense. Executive orders are printed in the Federal Register.

Executive orders are somewhat controversial because the Constitution gives Congress the power to make law, albeit with the executive's assistance. When a president issues an executive order, it might appear as if the president is making law unilaterally. Often, when a president from one party attempts to influence policy using an executive order, members of Congress who are in the other party accuse the president of exceeding constitutional authority. Most recently, the Republican Party has been highly critical of President Obama's executive orders addressing gun sales, deportation deferrals, and minimum wages. For example, former House Speaker John Boehner said, "President Obama has overstepped his constitutional authority — and it is the responsibility of the House of Representatives to defend the Constitution.... Congress makes the laws; the president executes them. That is the system the Founders gave us. This is not about executive orders. Every president issues executive orders. Most of them, though, do so within the law." John Boehner, *We're Defending the Constitution,* USA TODAY (July 27, 2014), http://www.usatoday.com/story/opinion/2014/07/27/president-obama-house-speaker-john-boehner-executive-orders-editorials-debates/13244117/ (explaining a congressional resolution to sue the president for extending a deadline in the Affordable Care Act).

Is President Obama unique? Simply put, no. All presidents issue executive orders. Former President Roosevelt issued the most (3,728) as the Country dealt with the Great Depression and World War II. Herbert Hoover issued 995. More recent presidents have issued fewer. Jimmy Carter issued 319 (in only four years); George W. Bush issued 291; Bill Clinton issued 364. In comparison, President Obama has issued 228 as of January 2016. *See generally*, John Woolley and Gerhard Peters, *Executive Orders: Washington — Obama* THE AMERICAN PRESIDENCY PROJECT (January 20, 2016), http://www.presidency.ucsb.edu/data/orders.php. Many important policy and legal changes have occurred through executive orders. For example, President Lincoln emancipated slaves; President Truman integrated the armed forces; President Eisenhower desegregated schools; Presidents Kennedy and Johnson barred racial discrimination in federal housing, hiring, and contracting; President Reagan barred the use of federal funds for abortion advocacy (which President Clinton reversed); President Clinton fought a war in Yugoslavia; and most recently, President Obama closed "the gun show loophole." All of these significant events occurred because of an executive order.

Executive orders are legitimate exercises of executive power. Congress gives agencies considerable leeway in implementing and administering federal statutes and programs. This leeway leaves gaps for the executive to fill and ambiguities for the executive to interpret. When Congress fails to spell out the details of how a law should be executed, the door is left open for a president to provide those details, and executive orders are one way to fill the gaps.

If a president deviates from "congressional intent" or exceeds the constitutional powers delegated to the executive, the executive order can be invalidated in court. For example, when President Truman seized control of the nation's steel mills in an effort to settle labor disputes that arose after World War II, the Supreme Court held that the seizure was unconstitutional and exceeded presidential powers, because neither the Constitution nor any statute authorized the President to seize private businesses to settle labor disputes. *Youngstown Sheet & Tube Co. v. Sawyer*, 343 U.S. 579 (1952). Notably, this outcome was unusual. Generally, the Court is fairly tolerant of executive orders. *See, e.g., Korematsu v. United States*, 323 U.S. 214 (1944) (upholding the constitutionality of E.O. 9066, which ordered Japanese Americans into internment camps during World War II); *see generally*, Erica Newland, Note, *Executive Orders in Court*, 124 YALE L.J. 2026 (examining 700 cases from the Supreme Court and D.C. Circuit Court addressing the validity of various executive orders).

Let's look more closely at a specific, executive order. In 1980, President Reagan campaigned on a platform of deregulation. Once elected, he issued Executive Order 12291. This executive order directed all executive agencies to perform a regulatory analysis assessing the costs and benefits of any "major" proposed regulations. E.O. 12291, 3 C.F.R. § 127 (1982). One of Reagan's purposes for issuing this executive order was to limit what he considered to be excessive regulation.

Although this executive order came from a Republican president, each president since Reagan has reissued this same order, albeit with slight changes. Former President Clinton issued Executive Order (E.O.) 12866, which mostly mirrored President Reagan's order; however, he changed the term "major rule" to "significant action." Next, former President George W. Bush adopted Clinton's order, but also issued two additional executive orders that slightly amended EO 12866; importantly, one of these orders added non-legislative rules to the order's coverage. E.O. 13422, 72 Fed. Reg. 2763 (2007). When President Obama took office, he repealed the two Bush orders, E.O. 13497, 74 Fed. Reg. 6113 (2009), and amended EO 12866 to allow agencies to consider not only monetary costs and benefits of "significant actions," but "human dignity" and "fairness" as well. Today, Executive Order 12866 is a fixture of executive agency rulemaking.

E.O. 12866 provides guiding principles that executive agencies (independent agencies are mostly exempt) must follow when developing regulations that will have an economic effect of at least a one-hundred million dollars. Pursuant to the order, agencies may promulgate regulations only when the regulations are "required by law," "necessary to interpret the law," or "are made necessary by compelling public need, such as material failures of private markets to protect or improve the health and safety of the public, the environment, or the well-being of the American people." E.O. 12866 § 1(a), 58 Fed. Reg. 51735 (October 4, 1993). Pursuant to Executive Order 12866, agencies must follow specific procedural steps when developing regulatory priorities, including the following: (1) identifying the problem the regulation was intended to address, including "the failures of private markets or public institutions that warrant new agency action"; (2) determining whether the problem could be addressed through modifications to existing regulations or laws; (3) assessing alternatives to regulation, such as economic incentives; (4) considering "the degree and nature of the risks posed by various substances or activities" within the agency's jurisdiction; (5) fashioning regulations "in the most cost-effective manner"; (6) assessing the costs and benefits, such that benefits justify the costs; (7) basing decisions "on the best reasonably obtainable scientific, technical, economic, and other information"; (8) recommending performance-based solutions rather than behavioral ones, when possible; (9) consulting with state, local, and tribal governments and assessing the impacts of regulations on these local governments; (10) avoiding duplications and inconsistencies among federal agencies; (11) minimizing the burdens; (12) considering the cumulative costs of regulation; and (13) writing all regulations in language that the general public can easily understand. E.O. 12866 §§ 1(b)(1)–(12), 58 Fed. Reg. 51735 (October 4, 1993).

Most importantly, in deciding whether regulation is necessary, agencies must assess the costs and benefits of the alternatives, "including the alternative of not regulating." E.O. 12866 § 1(a), 58 Fed. Reg. 51735 (October 4, 1993). "[U]nless [the] statute requires another regulatory approach," agencies must choose the regulatory path that maximizes net benefits. *Id.* Once an agency has completed its analysis, the agency submits the proposed regulation along with its analysis of that regulation to the Office of Information and Regulatory Affairs (OIRA). OIRA is responsible for overseeing the Federal Government's regulatory, paperwork, and information resource management activities and is located within the Office of Management and Budget (OMB). OMB is located within the executive office and is very closely aligned with the president and his or her policies. OIRA will review the agency's proposed rule and analysis to ensure compliance with E.O. 12866; in simple terms, OIRA acts as gatekeeper for the promulgation of all significant regulations.

Additionally, E.O. 12866 imposes regulatory planning measures. All agencies, including independent agencies, must produce a semi-annual *regulatory agenda* of all regulations under development or review. Pursuant to another executive order, E.O. 12291, the agencies provide their agenda in April and October of each year; a requirement that Congress partially codified in the Regulatory Flexibility Act. 5 U.S.C. § 602(a). Each regulatory agenda includes a summary of the action to be taken, the agency's legal authority for acting, legal deadlines if any, and an agency contact. E.O. 12866 § 1, 58 Fed. Reg. 51735 (October 4, 1993). An example of the 2012 Department of Health and Human Services regulatory agenda can be found at 77 Fed. Reg. 7946 (February 13, 2012), available at http://www.gpo.gov/fdsys/pkg/FR-2012-02-13/pdf/2012-1647.pdf.

In addition, pursuant to E.O. 12866, all agencies must produce a *regulatory plan*, which identifies the most significant regulatory activities the agency has planned for the upcoming year. E.O. 12866 § 1(c), 58 Fed. Reg. 51735 (October 4, 1993). While the regulatory *agenda* includes *all* proposed actions, the regulatory *plan* includes only the most important proposed actions. The agency must explain how the action relates to the president's priorities, determine anticipated costs and benefits, provide a summary of the legal basis for the action, and include a statement of why the action is needed. Regulatory plans are forwarded to OIRA on June 1st of every year. OIRA reviews the plans for consistency with the president's priorities, the requirements of E.O. 12866, and the regulatory agendas of other agencies.

OIRA publishes the regulatory agendas and plans together in the Unified Agenda, which is available to the public online: http://reginfo.gov. Each edition of the Agenda includes the regulatory agendas from all federal entities that currently have regulations under development or review. In addition, the fall edition of the Agenda includes the agencies' regulatory plans. The Agenda is an integral part of the federal regulatory process. Its semiannual publication enables regulated entities, the public, companies, and other interested persons to understand and prepare for new rules that are planned or under development. The Agenda provides important information to agency heads, centralized reviewers, and the public at large thereby serving the values of open government.

Finally, at the beginning of each planning period, the director of OMB convenes a meeting with the regulatory advisors and agency heads to coordinate regulatory priorities for the coming year. E.O. 12866 § 1(c)(1)(F)(2), 58 Fed. Reg. 51735 (October 4, 1993).

While E.O. 12866 is the most prominent executive order requiring regulatory analysis, it is by no means the only analysis requirement to come from the executive office. Over the years, presidents have required agencies to perform many different analyses. *See, e.g.,* E.O. 12630, 47 Fed. Reg. 30959 (1982) (requiring agencies to analyze the impact of proposed and final regulations on state and local governments); E.O. 13175, 65 Fed. Reg. 67249 (2000) (requiring agencies to analyze the impact of proposed and final regulations on tribal governments).

2. Indirect Executive Oversight

a. Presidential Signing Statements

In this section we turn to less direct methods of executive control. As mentioned in Chapter 3, when a president signs legislation that the president does not like but does not want to veto, the president may include a *signing statement* to try to limit the law's application in some way. Because these statements often indicate how the executive intends to implement the law, they are one way that the executive oversees agencies. The question is whether signing statements have any effect beyond oversight. As we noted, these statements have become controversial, in part, because presidents have begun to use them to influence statutory interpretation.

Below is the memo a young, deputy assistant attorney general wrote to identify a strategy for the Reagan administration to increase the relevance of these signing statements.

U.S. Department of Justice Office of Legal Counsel

Office of the Washington, D.C. 20S30*
Deputy Assistant Attorney General February 5, 1986

TO: The Litigation Strategy Working Group

FROM: Samuel A. Alito, Jr.
Deputy Assistant Attorney General
Office of Legal Counsel

SUBJ: Using Presidential Signing Statement to Make Fuller Use of the President's
Constitutionally Assigned Role in the Process of Enacting Law.

At our last meeting, I was asked to draft a preliminary proposal for implementing
the idea of making fuller use of Presidential signing statements. This memorandum
is a rough first effort in that direction.

A. Objectives

Our primary objective is to ensure that Presidential signing statements assume
their rightful place in the interpretation of legislation. In the past, Presidents have
issued signing statements when presented with bills raising constitutional problems.
OCL [Office of Legal Counsel] has played a role in this process, and the present proposal would not substantively alter that process.

The novelty of the proposal previously discussed by this Group is the suggestion
that Presidential signing statements be used to address questions of interpretation.
Under the Constitution, a bill becomes law only when passed by both houses of Congress and signed by the President (or enacted over his veto). Since the President's approval is just as important as that of the House or Senate, it seems to follow that the
President's understanding of the bill should be just as important as that of Congress.
Yet in interpreting statutes, both courts and litigants (including lawyers in the Executive
branch) invariably speak of "legislative" or "congressional" intent. Rarely if ever do
courts or litigants inquire into the President's intent. Why is this so?

Part of the reason undoubtedly is that Presidents, unlike Congress, do not customarily comment on their understanding of bills. Congress churns out great masses
of legislative history bearing on its intent—committee reports, floor debates, hearings.
Presidents have traditionally created nothing comparable. Presidents have seldom
explained in any depth or detail how they interpreted the bills they have signed. Presidential approval is usually accompanied by a statement that is often little more than
a press release.

---

* Editor's Footnote: Reproduced from the Holdings of the National Archives and Records Administration Record Group 60, Department of Justice Files of Stephen Galebach, 1985–1987 Accession
060-89-269, Box 6 Folder: SG/Litigation Strategy Working Group.

From the perspective of the Executive Branch, the issuance of interpretive signing statements would have two chief advantages. First, it would increase the power of the Executive to shape the law. Second, by forcing some rethinking by courts, scholars, and litigants, it may help to curb some of the prevalent abuses of legislative history.

B. Problems

I see five primary obstacles to the enhanced use of Presidential signing statements.

1. **Resources.** The most important problem is the manpower that will be required....

2. **Timing.** [It will be difficult to issue signing statements of any substance within the 10 day window provided in the Constitution. (Art. I, sec. 7)].

3. **Congressional Relations.** It seems likely that our new type of signing statement will not be warmly welcomed by Congress.... Congress is likely to resent the fact that the President will get in the last word on questions of interpretation....

4. **Acceptance by Executive Departments and Agencies....** [I]t seems likely that there will be friction [with] the various departments and agencies wishing to insert interpretive statements into presidential signing statements....

5. **Theoretical problems.** Because presidential intent has been all but ignored in interpreting the meaning of statutes, the theoretical problems have not been explored. For example:

> – In general, is presidential intent entitled to the same weight as legislative intent or is it of much less significance? As previously noted, presidential approval of legislation is generally just as important as congressional approval. Moreover, the President frequently proposes legislation. On the other hand, Congress has the opportunity to shape the bills that are presented to the President, and the President's role at that point is limited to approving or disapproving. For this reason, some may argue that only Congressional intent matters for purposes of interpretation. If our project is to succeed, we must be fully prepared to answer this argument.

> – What happens when there is a clear conflict between the congressional and presidential understanding? Whose intent controls? Is the law totally void? Is it inoperative only to the extent that there is disagreement?

> – If presidential intent is of little or no significance when inconsistent with congressional intent, what role is there for presidential intent? Is it entitled to the deference comparable to that customarily given to administrative interpretations?

C. A Proposal.

In view of the concerns noted above, I would make the following recommendation.

> – As an introductory step, the Department should seek to have interpretive signing statements issued for a reasonable number of bills that fall within its own field of responsibility....

– For use in this pilot project, we should try to identify bills that (a) are reasonably likely to pass, (b) are of some importance, and (c) are likely to present suitable problems of interpretation.

– Again, as an introductory step, our interpretive statements should be of moderate size and scope. Only relatively important questions should be addressed. We should concentrate on points of true ambiguity, rather than issuing interpretations that may seem to conflict with those of Congress. The first step will be to convince the courts that Presidential signing statements are valuable interpretive tools. . . .

– Because of the time problems previously noted, the drafting of our pilot signing statements should begin well before final passage of the bills. Moreover, if Presidential signing statements are ever to achieve much importance, I think it will be necessary to escape from the requirement of having to complete our work prior to the signing of the bill. Accordingly, after the first few efforts, the President could merely state when signing the bill that his signing is based on an interpretation to be set out in detail in a statement to be issued later. If this procedure is followed, it presumably would still be necessary to provide the President with an internal interpretive memorandum prior to signing, but the pressure to complete a formal statement for public release would be relieved. This procedure would mirror the procedure followed by congressional committees, which vote out proposed legislation long before the committee report is issued.

– The Department should continue and should intensify its internal consideration of the theoretical problems posed by the proposed expanded role for Presidential signing statements. Once a few of signing statements of this new type have been issued, discussion in legal journals may be, stimulated and should be encouraged.

* * *

Points for Discussion

1. *The Author*: Did you notice who wrote this memorandum? While acting under the direction of Attorney General Edwin Meese, Assistant Attorney General Samuel Alito, now Justice Alito, wrote this memo. As a result, President Reagan began to use signing statements to enhance the executive's influence over statutory interpretation. Meese then convinced West Publishing Company to include signing statements in the legislative histories section of the UNITED STATES CODE CONGRESSIONAL AND ADMINISTRATIVE NEWS (USCCAN), stating that inclusion would assist courts in the future to determine what the statute actually means. Since 1986, signing statements have been published in USCCAN.

2. *Presidential Role*: In the memo, Justice Alito argues that because bills require presidential approval in addition to approval by both houses to become law, "it seems to follow that the President's understanding of the bill should be just as important

as that of Congress." Are you persuaded? In answering this question, consider the role of the president in formulating social policy. Does your answer to this question differ if you consider which political party holds the presidency? In the memo, Justice Alito suggested that signing statements should be used to "increase the power of the Executive to shape the law" and, further, "help curb some of the prevalent abuses of legislative history." Would Justice Alito likely want a democratic president to have increased power to shape the law?

3. *Which President Issued the Most*: Ronald Reagan issued 250 signing statements. George H. W. Bush issued 228 signing statements (in only four years). Bill Clinton issued 381 statements. George W. Bush issued 152 signing statements. As of January 2016, Barak Obama had issued 31. Do you think the use of signing statements is on the rise? Does it surprise you to learn that Bill Clinton issued more signing statements than George W. Bush?

4. *Congress's Response*: The growing use of signing statements to influence interpretation has attracted the attention of Congress. A few bills have been introduced to stop this practice. For example, Senator Arlen Specter introduced the Presidential Signing Statements Act of 2006, which would have prohibited courts from considering signing statements. Presidential Signing Statements Act of 2006, S. 3731, 109th Cong. § 4 (2006) ("In determining the meaning of any Act of Congress, no State or Federal court shall rely on or defer to a presidential signing statement as a source of authority."). The bill died in committee. *See also* Congressional Lawmaking Authority Protection Act of 2007, H.R. 264, 110th Cong. § 4 (2007) ("For purposes of construing or applying any Act enacted by the Congress, a governmental entity shall not take into consideration any statement made by the President contemporaneously with the President's signing of the bill or joint resolution that becomes such Act."); H.R.3045, 110th Congress (2007–2008) (prohibiting any state or federal court from relying on or deferring to a presidential signing statement as a source of authority when determining the meaning of any Act of Congress). Likely, Congress will keep trying.

* * *

As noted above, President Reagan's administration persuaded West Publishing Company to include signing statements in the USCCAN specifically to influence statutory interpretation. Courts, however, do not appear to have turned to signing statements in the manner that the administration wished. The Constitution specifically identifies the role that presidents have in enacting legislation — presidents sign a bill into law or veto it. The Constitution allows a president to note objections when vetoing a bill, but the Constitution does not require a president to announce the reasons for approving a bill. Moreover, if a president vetoes a bill, Congress may constitutionally respond to the veto message during its attempt to override that veto. In contrast, there is no constitutional process for Congress to respond to presidential objections contained in signing statements. While this difference does not require courts to ignore signing statements, it suggests that presidential signing statements that conflict with congressional intent should be discounted, at a minimum.

Relatedly, a president has constitutional authority to approve or veto a bill only in its entirety. Signing statements, however, often contain objections to specific statutory provisions, making them akin to line item vetoes. The president does not possess line item veto authority, and Congress cannot grant the president such authority. *Clinton v. City of New York*, 524 U.S. 417, 447–49 (1998).

Below is an example of a very short signing statement. In it, former President George W. Bush attempted to limit the breadth of certain provisions in the Act. Specifically, he tried to reserve the power to interpret certain provisions within the Act in a way that would not impact his constitutional authority to be Commander-in-Chief. In other words, he noted an interpretation that raised a constitutional question he wanted to avoid. Is interpreting a statute in a way that will avoid a constitutional question an executive function or judicial function, or both?

**President Bush's signing statement for H.R. 4986,
the National Defense Authorization Act for Fiscal Year 2008**

Today, I have signed into law H.R. 4986, the National Defense Authorization Act for Fiscal Year 2008. The Act authorizes funding for the defense of the United States and its interests abroad, for military construction, and for national security-related energy programs.

Provisions of the Act, including sections 841, 846, 1079, and 1222, purport to impose requirements that could inhibit the President's ability to carry out his constitutional obligations to take care that the laws be faithfully executed, to protect national security, to supervise the executive branch, and to execute his authority as Commander in Chief. The executive branch shall construe such provisions in a manner consistent with the constitutional authority of the President.

GEORGE W. BUSH
THE WHITE HOUSE,
January 28, 2008.

It is unlikely that his statement would have much impact on the courts. For various reasons, courts give little to no weight to signing statements. For example, in *DaCosta v. Nixon*, 55 F.R.D. 145, 146 (E.D.N.Y. 1972), the court rejected a signing statement in which President Nixon claimed that a provision in a statute did not "represent the policies of this Administration" and was "without binding force or effect." The court explained that a signing statement "denying efficacy to the legislation could have [n]either validity or effect." *Id.*

And in *Hamdan v. Rumsfeld*, 548 U.S. 557 (2006), the majority completely ignored President Bush's signing statement in holding that the Detainee Treatment Act did not apply to pending habeas petitions of Guantanamo detainees. In a dissenting opinion (joined by Justice Alito), Justice Scalia criticized the majority for using legislative history while ignoring the President's signing statement. *Id.* at 666 (Scalia, J., dissenting) ("Of course in its discussion of legislative history the Court wholly ignores the President's signing statement, which explicitly set forth his understanding that the [statute] ousted jurisdiction over pending cases.").

Lastly, in *United States v Stevens*, 559 U.S. 460, 130 S. Ct. 1577, 1591 (2010), the Court noted that President Clinton's signing statement, which promised to limit prosecutions under an animal cruelty statute only to those cases of "wanton cruelty to animals designed to appeal to a prurient interest in sex," did not save an otherwise unconstitutionally overbroad statute. As these cases show, signing statements generally have little interpretive relevance in court.

There are times, however, when a signing statement might provide limited judicial guidance. When a president has worked closely with Congress in developing legislation and when the enacted version of the bill address the president's veto concerns, then a court might consider an ensuing signing statement as evidence of the political compromises that were reached. In such a situation, signing statements might help explain rather than negate congressional action. For example, former President Franklin Roosevelt issued a signing statement during World War II contesting the constitutionality of section 304 of the Urgent Deficiency Appropriations Act of 1943 (ch. 218, 57 Stat. 431, 450 (1943)). He indicated that he felt that he had no choice but to sign the bill "to avoid delaying our conduct of the war." *United States v. Lovett*, 328 U.S. 303, 313 (1946) (quoting H.Doc. 264, 78th Cong., 1st Sess). When the statute was challenged, the Court struck down the provision, citing the signing statement for support.

Although signing statements are not generally relevant in court, such statements nonetheless greatly affect the actions of administering agencies. The president oversees agencies and sets administrative policy. While the executive's interpretation of a statute does not bind judges, it binds agency personnel. Moreover, as we will see in the next chapter, courts generally defer to agency interpretations of statutes that are made during rulemaking or other formal processes. To the effect that a signing statement impacts an agency's interpretation of a statute, that signing statement will impact interpretation, albeit indirectly. Thus, while signing statements may not have had the interpretive impact former Attorney General Edwin Meese would have liked, there is no question that they are having at least some impact.

* * *

Problem 17

Because of recent changes to the Securities Exchange Act of 1934 (Exchange Act), the Securities and Exchange Commission (SEC) may choose whether to bring an enforcement action in an internal adjudication or whether to bring it in United States

District Court. When bringing an action in-house, the SEC uses a federal administrative law judge (ALJ) to hear the adjudication. According to at least one study, the SEC wins 61% of the time in District Court and 100% of the time before its own ALJs. As the SEC has begun using in-house adjudications more regularly, attorneys representing those on the receiving end of an SEC enforcement action ("respondents") have begun to file lawsuits in federal district courts, raising a variety of constitutional claims including unlawful delegation and unlawful removal and appointment of SEC ALJs.

The Administrative Procedure Act (APA), 5 U.S.C. § 551, *et seq.* (2015), authorizes agencies, including the SEC, to conduct formal, in-house administrative proceedings, or adjudications, before an ALJ. The Office of Personnel Management ("OPM") interviews and creates a list of eligible candidates for all federal ALJ positions. Agencies can appoint ALJs only from OPM's list of eligible candidates (or with prior approval of OPM). ALJs have career appointments; they are not term-limited. Their salary is set by statute.

ALJs are removable "only" for "good cause," which must be "established and determined" by the Merit Systems Protection Board ("MSPB") after a formal adjudication. Members of the MSPB, who determine whether "good cause" exists to remove an ALJ, are themselves protected; the president may remove them "only for inefficiency, neglect of duty, or malfeasance in office."

The SEC selects ALJs from OPM's list of eligible candidates. However, the Commissioners of the SEC are not involved in the selection. Rather, the SEC's Chief ALJ identifies and selects SEC ALJs.

By statute, the SEC may delegate any of its functions to its ALJs. Pursuant to that statutory authority, the SEC has delegated significant authority to its ALJs to conduct administrative proceedings. Specifically, during these hearing, ALJs may:

> (1) Administer oaths and affirmations; (2) Issue subpoenas; (3) Rule on offers of proof; (4) Examine witnesses; (5) Regulate the course of a hearing; (6) Hold pre-hearing conferences; (7) Rule upon motions; and (8) Unless waived by the parties, prepare an initial decision containing the conclusions as to the factual and legal issues presented, and issue an appropriate order.

SEC Rules provide that the ALJ for each hearing is selected by the Chief ALJ. The selected ALJ then presides over the hearing and issues an initial decision. That decision can be appealed by either the litigant or the SEC's Division of Enforcement. If neither party appeals, the ALJ's decision is "deemed the action of the Commission," and the SEC issues an order making the ALJ's initial order final.

If either party appeals, the SEC's review is essentially de novo. If a majority of the participating Commissioners do not agree with the ALJ's initial decision, the ALJ's initial decision "shall be of no effect, and an order will be issued in accordance with this result." If, instead, they agree with the ALJ, the SEC will adopt the ALJ's initial order as its final order. An appealed decision is not final until the SEC issues it.

If a respondent loses before the SEC, the respondent may petition the appropriate federal court of appeals to review the SEC's final order. Once an appeal is filed, the court of appeals has "exclusive" jurisdiction "to affirm or modify and enforce or to set aside the order in whole or in part." On judicial review, the SEC's findings of facts are "conclusive" "if supported by substantial evidence."

The respondents lawsuits raise two claims under Article II of the Federal Constitution: (1) that the SEC ALJs' appointment violates the Appointments Clause of Article II because SEC ALJs are not appointed by the president, a court of law, or a department head, and (2) the SEC ALJs' dual for-cause tenure protection violates Article II and the separation of powers, because the president is not able to exercise executive power over these inferior officers. Both of these claims depend on a court concluding first that the SEC ALJs are inferior officers entitled to these constitutional protections.

You are in-house counsel for the SEC. How do you respond to these claims? Assume that the SEC Commissioners are only removable for cause. Does your analysis to either issue change if the SEC Commissioners are removable at will?

Chapter 18

The Regulatory Process: Deference to Agency Interpretations

A. Introduction to This Chapter

In the last two chapters, you learned about agencies: what they are, what they do, and how the executive and legislature oversee them. When agencies regulate, they often interpret statutes. In this chapter and the next, we address the level of deference courts give to agency interpretations of statutes. This topic is exploding, as the appropriate role agencies should play in this area is debated in legal and academic circles. Agencies are playing a more important and ever-expanding part. Indeed, you might say that agencies play a leading role in statutory interpretation. Over the last forty years, the Supreme Court has struggled with the appropriate level of deference to give agency interpretations. The Court has vacillated from affording little to no deference, to affording high deference, and back again. This struggle reflects the Court's concern over ceding too much interpretive power and respecting the appropriate roles of the executive, legislative, and judicial branches of government. Although members of the executive and legislative branches are generally accountable to the public, members of the judiciary are not.

Agencies are entrusted to implement complicated regulatory schemes. Congress delegates the power to regulate to agencies. With delegation comes the power to make rules and adjudicate. Agencies have expertise that informs the policy choices they make. Agency expertise should not be ignored simply because the judiciary has the Constitutional authority to interpret laws. Moreover, to be able to respond to economic, technological, and political changes, agencies must maintain flexibility. Hence, rigid boundaries are inappropriate. However, when agencies exceed the power delegated to them, deference is no longer appropriate. Linda D. Jellum, *Dodging the Taxman: Why Treasury's Anti-Abuse Regulation is Unconstitutional*, 70 Miami L. Rev. 152, 204 (2015) (describing the difference between regulations that are unconstitutional and regulations that are *ultra vires*).

The tension between the judiciary's role of interpreting and the executive's role of executing permeates the jurisprudence in this area. To be an effective litigant, you must be aware of when and why agencies interpret statutes, must know the level of deference judges will give to agency interpretations, and must understand why agencies receive that level of deference. Because the appropriate level of deference has changed over time, the common-law history is extremely relevant here. We start, therefore, in the past.

B. The Interpretive Role Agencies Play

Agencies regulate almost all aspects of modern society. In doing so, they regularly interpret statutes and regulations. Do agency interpretations of these laws control? The short answer is no. The long answer is that simply because agency interpretations do not control does not mean that they are irrelevant. They are highly relevant; therefore, some level of deference is appropriate.

Article III of the Constitution grants the judiciary all "[j]udicial power." U.S. Const. art. III, § 1. According to *Marbury v. Madison*, "[i]t is emphatically the province and duty of the judicial department to say what the law is." 5 U.S. (1 Cranch) 137, 177 (1803). Because the Constitution delegates interpretive power to the judiciary, a formalist might argue that agencies should have no interpretive role, or, at the very least, not one that trumps the judicial role. Yet, the formalist view is extreme.

For many reasons, agency interpretation is necessary, making judicial deference appropriate. The modern administrative state is vastly complex. Agencies have expertise in their area of responsibility; consider the U.S. Department of Veterans' Affairs (VA), the Environmental Protection Agency (EPA), and the Food and Drug Administration (FDA). Each of these agencies has experts and specialists trained in the relevant field. Judges are generalists with expertise in law, not in the environment or food safety. Hence, it simply makes more sense for medical personnel within the VA to determine disability benefits for veterans, for scientists within the EPA to determine acceptable levels of pollutants in the air, and for nutritionists within the FDA to determine what food additives are safe.

Moreover, agencies may be more responsive to the electorate than the judiciary. National goals and policies change as society evolves. Agency administrators are accountable to the public via the Office of the President and, therefore, will be more likely to conform their policies to match populist expectations. Judges, in contrast, are elected for life and are more insulated from political backlash. As a result, they tend to protect minority interests. Thus, agencies should receive some deference when they interpret statutes within their area of expertise. Even *Marbury's* author, Chief Justice John Marshall, suggested that courts respect an agency's "uniform construction" of "doubtful" statutes. *United States v. Vowell*, 9 U.S. (5 Cranch) 368, 371 (1810).

In this chapter, we will explore the level of deference a court will give to an agency interpretation of a statute or regulation. This is a politically important question because the power to say what the law means shifts to the executive branch when courts defer to agency interpretations. *See generally* Linda D. Jellum, *The Impact of the Rise and Fall of* Chevron *on the Executive's Power to Make and Interpret Law*, 44 Loy. U. Chi. L.J. 141, 169–71 (2012) (arguing that when the Supreme Court decided *Chevron*, the Court dramatically, and likely unintentionally, shifted interpretive power from the judiciary to the executive). The appropriate level of deference has changed over time as the justices have been more or less comfortable with deferring to the executive. The question is what level of deference judges should give to an agency when, in the process of developing a rule or adjudicating a case, the agency interprets a statute or regulation. As the Supreme Court has addressed this issue over the last seventy years, it has oscillated among three deference standards: (1) complete deference, (2) limited deference, and (3) no deference. While the level of deference has changed, the rationale for affording deference has remained relatively consistent. Courts defer to agency interpretations because of agency expertise and implied congressional delegation. The next section will explore the Court's approach to deference prior to its landmark decision in *Chevron v. Natural Resources Defense Council, Inc.*, 467 U.S. 837 (1984). Before we get there, you need to understand the types of issues agencies resolve.

Agencies resolve three types of legal issues. First, they determine the boundaries of their delegated authority and the meaning of the laws within that authority. Questions related to these types of issues are questions of law. When an agency resolves a question of law, the facts of an individual case are largely irrelevant. What matters is what the statute or regulation says. In this chapter, we will focus on these questions: questions of law. But you need to be aware that agencies resolve other kinds of questions as well.

A second type of question that agencies resolve is questions of fact and policy. For example, are airbags safer enough than seatbelts to justify the higher cost to industry of installing them? How much pollutant can be in water before it is unsafe to drink? Should genetically modified produce be labeled as such? When an agency resolves a question of fact or policy, the law is not relevant (although there may also be a question of law implicated).

When an agency resolves a question of fact or policy, courts apply one of two different standards to determine the validity of that finding. APA § 706(2). For agency findings of fact made during informal rulemaking and informal adjudication, the relevant standard is whether the agency's findings are arbitrary and capricious. APA § 706(2)(A). Under the arbitrary and capricious standard, a court determines whether the agency's findings were based on a consideration of irrelevant factors or whether the agency made a clear error of judgment. *Citizens to Preserve Overton Park, Inc. v. Volpe*, 401 U.S. 402, 416 (1971). For agency findings of fact made during formal rulemaking and formal adjudication, the standard is whether the agency's findings were supported by substantial evidence. APA § 706(2)(E). Under the substantial evidence standard, a court determines whether the record contains "such evidence as a reasonable mind might accept as adequate to support a conclusion." *Consolidated Edison Co. v. NLRB*, 305 U.S. 197, 229 (1938). While these two standards originally differed, today, they tend to converge, and the distinction is "largely semantic." *Association of Data Processing Servs. Org. v. Board of Governors*, 745 F.2d 677, 684 (D.C. Cir. 1984) (citation omitted) (internal quotation marks omitted). You will explore these standards in more detail in a traditional administrative law course.

The third type of question that agencies resolve is a mixed question of law and fact. These questions require an agency to determine whether a particular law applies to a given set of the facts. For example, are newspaper delivery people employees or independent contractors? The appropriate standard applicable to mixed questions of law and fact is currently unclear. Some courts apply the test from *NLRB v. Hearst Publication, Inc.*, 322 U.S. 111 (1944): An agency's decision is to be accepted if it has "warrant in the record" and a reasonable basis in the law. *Id.* at 131. Other courts break the mixed question into its component parts of law and fact. To the extent part of the issue involves a question of law, the analysis that follows applies.

C. Deference Pre-*Chevron*

In the 1940s and early 1950s, the Supreme Court used two, different, deference standards: "no deference" (or a *de novo* standard) and "limited deference." While the deference world was never black and white, the standard the Court used seemed to depend on the type of question that was presented. When an agency interpretation involved a question of law, the Court used the "no deference" standard. *See, e.g., Gray v. Powell*, 314 U.S. 402, 414–17 (1941), (refusing to defer to the agency's determination that coal that was transported from one entity to another without a title transfer constituted coal that was "sold or otherwise disposed of" within the meaning of the Bituminous Coal Act of 1937); *Hearst Publication*, 322 U.S. at 124–29 (refusing to defer to the agency's determination that newsboys were "employees" under the National Labor Relations Act); *O'Leary v. Brown-Pacific-Maxon, Inc.*, 340 U.S. 504, 506 (1951) (refusing to defer to the agency's interpretation of the term "course of employment" in the Longshoremen's and Harbor Workers' Compensation Act).

In contrast, when an agency interpretation involved a mixed question of law and fact, the Supreme Court used the "limited deference" standard. *See, e.g., Gray*, 314 U.S. at 410–13 (deferring to the agency's finding that the specific plaintiff was a coal producer); *O'Leary*, 340 U.S. at 507–08 (deferring to the agency's factual finding that a particular rescue occurred during the course of employment). For mixed questions, the Court afforded the agency interpretations some deference because of agency expertise and express congressional delegation. *Hearst Publication*, 322 U.S. at 120; *Gray*, 314 U.S. at 412 ("Congress ... found it more efficient to delegate [these issues] to those whose experience in a particular field gave promise of a better informed, more equitable" resolution of the issues.").

In sum, when the issue involved law application, courts deferred because of the agency's expertise and the likelihood that Congress intended to delegate resolution of the issue to the agency. However, when the agency interpretation involved a pure question of law, the Court did not defer to the agency interpretation because judges were as competent, if not more so, than agencies to determine the intended meaning of ambiguous statutory language. Pursuant to this bifurcated deference approach, judges retained the primary responsibility for interpreting statutes. Judges generally reviewed questions of law *de novo*, giving the agency's interpretation no deference at all. Judges reviewed questions of law application more deferentially, giving the agency's interpretation some level of deference.

This bifurcated deference, or two-tracked, approach to judicial review of agency interpretations made sense and was consistent with the judicial review approach in civil litigation. In civil cases, appellate judges determine questions of law *de novo*. Because appellate judges are experts at interpreting law, no deference is due when trial courts are resolving conclusions of law. But questions of fact and law application are reviewed under a more deferential standard. There is another reason that this two-tracked approach made sense: leaving questions of law for judicial resolution was consistent with the APA, which provides that "the reviewing court shall decide all relevant questions of law, interpret constitutional and statutory provisions, and determine the meaning or applicability of the terms of an agency action." APA § 706.

While judges deferred to agency interpretations involving law application, the level of their deference was uncertain. In 1944, the Supreme Court decided two cases that addressed how much judges should defer. In the first case, *Hearst Publication*, the Court held that as long as an agency interpretation had a "warrant in the record and a reasonable basis in law," a court should not substitute its own interpretation for that of the agency entrusted with administering the statute. 322 U.S. at 130. The second case is below. See if you can identify the Court's deference test and rationale for affording deference. As you read this case, try to determine what type of agency action was at issue: a legislative or non-legislative rule.

Skidmore v. Swift & Co.
Supreme Court for the United States
323 U.S. 134 (1944)

◆ Justice Jackson delivered the opinion of the Court [with whom Stone, C.J., and Douglas, Black, Roberts, Murphy, Reed, Rutledge, and Frankfurter, JJ., concur].

Seven employees of the Swift and Company packing plant at Fort Worth, Texas, brought an action under the Fair Labor Standards Act, 29 U.S.C.A. § 201 et seq.,* to recover overtime, liquidated damages, and attorneys' fees, totaling approximately $77,000.... [Petitioners claim that the time they spent in the fire hall subject to call to answer fire alarms were periods of work. Combined with their daytime employment, petitioners were entitled to overtime pay.]

It is not denied that the daytime employment of these persons was working time within the Act. [And that t]hey were paid weekly salaries.

Under their oral agreement of employment, however, petitioners undertook to stay in the fire hall on the Company premises, or within hailing distance, three and

---

* Editor's Footnote. The overtime provisions of FLSA applied only to "employees" and to "employment" in excess of a specified number of hours. 29 U.S.C. § 207. The definitions section of FLSA provided that "employ includes to suffer or permit to work." 29 U.S.C. § 203(g).

a half to four nights a week. This involved no task except to answer alarms, either because of fire or because the sprinkler was set off for some other reason. No fires occurred during the period in issue, the alarms were rare, and the time required for their answer rarely exceeded an hour. For each alarm answered the employees were paid in addition to their fixed compensation an agreed amount, fifty cents at first, and later sixty-four cents. The Company provided a brick fire hall equipped with steam heat and air-conditioned rooms. It provided sleeping quarters, a pool table, a domino table, and a radio. The men used their time in sleep or amusement as they saw fit, except that they were required to stay in or close by the fire hall and be ready to respond to alarms. It is stipulated that 'they agreed to remain in the fire hall and stay in it or within hailing distance, subject to call, in event of fire or other casualty, but were not required to perform any specific tasks during these periods of time, except in answering alarms.' The trial court ... said, however, as a 'conclusion of law' that 'the time plaintiffs spent in the fire hall subject to call to answer fire alarms does not constitute hours worked, for which overtime compensation is due them under the Fair Labor Standards Act, as interpreted by the Administrator and the Courts,' and in its opinion observed, 'of course we know pursuing such pleasurable occupations or performing such personal chores does not constitute work.' The Circuit Court of Appeals affirmed.

No Congressional Intent

Analysis

... [W]e hold that no principle of law found either in the statute or in Court decisions precludes waiting time from also being working time. We have not attempted to, and we cannot, lay down a legal formula to resolve cases so varied in their facts as are the many situations in which employment involves waiting time....

Congress ... create[d] the office of Administrator, impose[d] upon him a variety of duties, endow[ed] him with powers to inform himself of conditions in industries and employments subject to the Act, and put on him the duties of bringing injunction actions to restrain violations. Pursuit of his duties has accumulated a considerable experience in the problems of ascertaining working time in employments involving periods of inactivity and a knowledge of the customs prevailing in reference to their solution. From these he is obliged to reach conclusions as to conduct without the law, so that he should seek injunctions to stop it, and that within the law, so that he has no call to interfere. He has set forth his views of the application of the Act under different circumstances in an interpretative bulletin and in informal rulings. They provide a practical guide to employers and employees as to how the office representing the public interest in its enforcement will seek to apply it. Wage and Hour Division, Interpretative Bulletin No. 13.

The Administrator thinks the problems presented by inactive duty require a flexible solution, rather than the all-in or all-out rules respectively urged by the parties in this case, and his Bulletin endeavors to suggest standards and examples to guide in particular situations.... In general, [whether it is work] depends 'upon the degree to which the employee is free to engage in personal activities during periods of idleness when he is subject to call and the number of consecutive hours that the employee is subject to call without being required to perform active work'....

The facts of this case do not fall within any of the specific examples given, but the conclusion of the Administrator, as expressed in the brief amicus curiae, is that the general tests which he has suggested point to the exclusion of sleeping and eating time of these employees from the work-week and the inclusion of all other on-call time: although the employees were required to remain on the premises during the entire time....

There is no statutory provision as to what, if any, deference courts should pay to the Administrator's conclusions. And, while we have given them notice, we have had no occasion to try to prescribe their influence. The rulings of this Administrator are not reached as a result of hearing adversary proceedings in which he finds facts from evidence and reaches conclusions of law from findings of fact. They are not, of course, conclusive, even in the cases with which they directly deal, much less in those to which they apply only by analogy. They do not constitute an interpretation of the Act or a standard for judging factual situations which binds a district court's processes, as an authoritative pronouncement of a higher court might do. But the Administrator's policies are made in pursuance of official duty, based upon more specialized experience and broader investigations and information than is likely to come to a judge in a particular case. They do determine the policy which will guide applications for enforcement by injunction on behalf of the Government. Good administration of the Act and good judicial administration alike require that the standards of public enforcement and those for determining private rights shall be at variance only where justified by very good reasons. The fact that the Administrator's policies and standards are not reached by trial in adversary form does not mean that they are not entitled to respect. This Court has long given considerable and in some cases decisive weight to Treasury Decisions and to interpretative regulations of the Treasury and of other bodies that were not of adversary origin.

We consider that the rulings, interpretations and opinions of the Administrator under this Act, while not controlling upon the courts by reason of their authority, do constitute a body of experience and informed judgment to which courts and litigants may properly resort for guidance. The weight of such a judgment in a particular case will depend upon the thoroughness evident in its consideration, the validity of its reasoning, its consistency with earlier and later pronouncements, and all those factors which give it power to persuade, if lacking power to control.

... [I]n this case, although the District Court referred to the Administrator's Bulletin, its evaluation and inquiry were apparently restricted by its notion that waiting time may not be work, an understanding of the law which we hold to be erroneous. Accordingly, the judgment is reversed and the cause remanded for further proceedings consistent herewith.

* * *

Points for Discussion

1. *Statutory Language*: What was the language at issue? What did each party want that language to mean? What meaning did the Court adopt?

2. *Theories*: The court was determining the correct deference standard and not determining the meaning of the language; hence, no theory of interpretation is apparent.

3. *Type of Agency Action*: Neither lower court considered an "interpretive bulletin" that the Administrator of the Wage and Hour division of the Department of Labor had issued. What type of agency action is an interpretive bulletin? The Supreme Court remanded the issue of whether the Act required overtime pay for "inactive duty" and directed the Court of Appeals to consider the interpretive bulletin in resolving this interpretive question. Why?

4. *Type of Question*: Was the issue before the Court a question of law or fact or application of law to fact?

5. *Skidmore Deference*: How does the Court describe the weight the courts should give to the interpretation in the bulletin? In other words, is the agency's interpretation controlling or persuasive? What factors make it persuasive? Why is the agency entitled to any deference al all for its interpretation; are not courts the appropriate branch to interpret statutes pursuant to *Marbury v. Madison*? Does *Skidmore* deference violate separation of powers? As you will see, *Skidmore* deference is understood to be a relatively weak form of deference.

* * *

D. *Chevron*

In 1984, the Court instituted a new deference approach. In one of the most cited Supreme Court cases of all time, *Chevron v. National Resources Defense Council, Inc.*, 467 U.S. 837 (1984), the Court flipped the deference standard it had been using, in which agencies earned deference because of their expertise and reasoned-decision-making, but courts were the final determiners of what an ambiguous statute meant. The interpretation at issue in *Skidmore* was contained in a non-legislative interpretive rule. In contrast, in *Chevron*, the Court addressed the level of deference appropriate for a legislative—specifically notice-and-comment—rule.

In the excerpt below, identify the two step process the Court develops. At which step does a court determine the meaning of a statute *de novo* and at which step does the court consider the agency's interpretation?

Chevron U.S.A., Inc. v.
Natural Resources Defense Council, Inc.

Supreme Court for the United States
467 U.S. 837 (1984)

◆   JUSTICE STEVENS delivered the opinion of the Court [in which BURGER, C.J., BRENNAN, WHITE, BLACKMUN, and POWELL, JJ. concur]. [JUSTICE MARSHALL and JUSTICE REHNQUIST took no part in the consideration or decision of these cases. JUSTICE O'CONNOR took no part in the decision of these cases.]

In the Clean Air Act Amendments of 1977, Congress enacted certain requirements applicable to States that had not achieved the national air quality standards established by the Environmental Protection Agency (EPA) pursuant to earlier legislation. The amended Clean Air Act required these "nonattainment" States to establish a permit program regulating "new or modified major stationary sources" of air pollution. Generally, a permit may not be issued for a new or modified major stationary source unless several stringent conditions are met.[1] The EPA regulation promulgated to implement this permit requirement allows a State to adopt a plantwide definition of the term "stationary source." Under [EPA's plantwide] definition, an existing plant that contains several pollution-emitting devices may install or modify one piece of equipment without meeting the permit conditions if the alteration will not increase the total emissions from the plant. The question presented by these cases is whether EPA's decision to allow States to treat all of the pollution-emitting devices within the same industrial grouping as though they were encased within a single "bubble" is based on a reasonable construction of the statutory term "stationary source." ... [Under the alternative interpretation, an increase in emissions at a single smokestack at a plant would trigger the requirement that the plant obtain a permit and install stringent control technology, regardless of whether the emissions from this single smokestack were offset by decreases in emissions from other smokestacks at the plant.].

The court [of appeals] observed that the relevant part of the amended Clean Air Act "does not explicitly define what Congress envisioned as a 'stationary source, to which the permit program ... should apply," and further stated that the precise issue was not "squarely addressed in the legislative history." In light of its conclusion that the legislative history bearing on the question was "at best contradictory," it reasoned that "the purposes of the nonattainment program should guide our decision here."

Based on two of its precedents concerning the applicability of the bubble concept to certain Clean Air Act programs, the court stated that the bubble concept was "mandatory" in programs designed merely to *maintain existing air quality*, but held that it was "inappropriate" in programs enacted to *improve air quality*. Since the purpose of the permit program [in nonattainment areas] ... was to improve air quality, the court held that the bubble concept was inapplicable in these cases under its prior precedents. It therefore set aside the regulations embodying the bubble concept as contrary to law. We granted certiorari, ... and we now reverse.

The basic legal error of the Court of Appeals was to adopt a static judicial definition of the term "stationary source" when it had decided that Congress itself had not commanded that definition....

When a court reviews an agency's construction of the statute which it administers, it is confronted with two questions. First, always, is the question whether Congress

Step 1

---

1. Section 172(b)(6), 42 U.S.C. §7502(b)(6), provides:
   "The plan provisions required by subsection (a) shall ... (6) require permits for the construction and operation of new or modified major *stationary sources* in accordance with section 173 (relating to permit requirements)" (emphasis added).

has directly spoken to the precise question at issue. If the intent of Congress is clear, that is the end of the matter; for the court, as well as the agency, must give effect to the unambiguously expressed intent of Congress.[9] If, however, the court determines Congress has not directly addressed the precise question at issue, the court does not simply impose its own construction on the statute, as would be necessary in the absence of an administrative interpretation. Rather, if the statute is silent or ambiguous with respect to the specific issue, the question for the court is whether the agency's answer is based on a permissible construction of the statute.

"The power of an administrative agency to administer a congressionally created ... program necessarily requires the formulation of policy and the making of rules to fill any gap left, implicitly or explicitly, by Congress." If Congress has explicitly left a gap for the agency to fill, there is an express delegation of authority to the agency to elucidate a specific provision of the statute by regulation. Such legislative regulations are given controlling weight unless they are arbitrary, capricious, or manifestly contrary to the statute. Sometimes the legislative delegation to an agency on a particular question is implicit rather than explicit. In such a case, a court may not substitute its own construction of a statutory provision for a reasonable interpretation made by the administrator of an agency.

We have long recognized that considerable weight should be accorded to an executive department's construction of a statutory scheme it is entrusted to administer, and the principle of deference to administrative interpretations "has been consistently followed by this Court whenever decision as to the meaning or reach of a statute has involved reconciling conflicting policies, and a full understanding of the force of the statutory policy in the given situation has depended upon more than ordinary knowledge respecting the matters subjected to agency regulations.

" ... If this choice represents a reasonable accommodation of conflicting policies that were committed to the agency's care by the statute, we should not disturb it unless it appears from the statute or its legislative history that the accommodation is not one that Congress would have sanctioned."

In light of these well-settled principles it is clear that the Court of Appeals misconceived the nature of its role in reviewing the regulations at issue. Once it determined, after its own examination of the legislation, that Congress did not actually have an intent regarding the applicability of the bubble concept to the permit program, the question before it was not whether in its view the concept is "inappropriate" in the general context of a program designed to improve air quality, but whether the Administrator's view that it is appropriate in the context of this particular program is a reasonable one. Based on the examination of the legislation and its history which follows, we agree with the Court of Appeals that Congress did not have a specific in-

---

9. The judiciary is the final authority on issues of statutory construction and must reject administrative constructions which are contrary to clear congressional intent. If a court, employing traditional tools of statutory construction, ascertains that congress had an intention on the precise question at issue, that intention is the law and must be given effect.

tention on the applicability of the bubble concept in these cases, and conclude that the EPA's use of that concept here is a reasonable policy choice for the agency to make....

The 1977 Amendments contain no specific reference to the "bubble concept." Nor do they contain a specific definition of the term "stationary source," though they did not disturb the definition of "stationary source" contained in [another section of the Act: § 111(a)(3)]*....

In August 1980, however, the EPA adopted a regulation that, in essence, applied the basic reasoning of the Court of Appeals in these cases. The EPA took particular note of the two then-recent Court of Appeals decisions, which had created the bright-line rule that the "bubble concept" should be employed in a program designed to maintain air quality but not in one designed to enhance air quality. Relying heavily on those cases, EPA adopted a dual definition of "source" for nonattainment areas that required a permit whenever a change in either the entire plant, or one of its components, would result in a significant increase in emissions even if the increase was completely offset by reductions elsewhere in the plant. The EPA expressed the opinion that this interpretation was "more consistent with congressional intent" than the plantwide definition because it "would bring in more sources or modifications for review," but its primary legal analysis was predicated on the two Court of Appeals decisions....

In 1981 a new administration took office and initiated a "Government-wide reexamination of regulatory burdens and complexities." In the context of that review, the EPA reevaluated the various arguments that had been advanced in connection with the proper definition of the term "source" and concluded that the term should be given the same definition in both nonattainment areas and [attainment, or clean air, areas] areas.

In explaining its conclusion, the EPA first noted that the definitional issue was not squarely addressed in either the statute or its legislative history and therefore that the issue involved an agency "judgment as how to best carry out the Act." It then set forth several reasons for concluding that the plantwide definition was more appropriate. It pointed out that the dual definition "can act as a disincentive to new investment and modernization by discouraging modifications to existing facilities" and "can actually retard progress in air pollution control by discouraging replacement of older, dirtier processes or pieces of equipment with new, cleaner ones." Moreover, the new definition "would simplify EPA's rules by using the same definition of 'source' for PSD [prevention of significant deterioration], nonattainment new source review and the construction moratorium. This reduces confusion and inconsistency." Finally, the agency explained that additional requirements that remained in place would accomplish the fundamental purposes of achieving attainment with NAAQS's as expe-

---

* Editor's footnote: Section 111(a)(3) provides: "For purposes of this section: ... [t]he term 'stationary source' means any building, structure, facility, or installation which emits or may emit any air pollutant."

ditiously as possible. These conclusions were expressed in a proposed rulemaking in August 1981 that was formally promulgated....

Statutory Language

... We are not persuaded that parsing of general terms in the text of the statute will reveal an actual intent of Congress. We know full well that this language is not dispositive; the terms are overlapping and the language is not precisely directed to the question of the applicability of a given term in the context of a larger operation. To the extent any congressional "intent" can be discerned from this language, it would appear that the listing of overlapping, illustrative terms was intended to enlarge, rather than to confine, the scope of the agency's power to regulate particular sources in order to effectuate the policies of the Act.

Legislative History

[*Specific Intent*] ... Based on our examination of the legislative history, we agree with the Court of Appeals that it is unilluminating.... We find that the legislative history as a whole is silent on the precise issue before us. It is, however, consistent with the view that the EPA should have broad discretion in implementing the policies of the 1977 Amendments....

[*Purpose*] More importantly, that history plainly identifies the policy concerns that motivated the enactment; the plantwide definition is fully consistent with one of those concerns — the allowance of reasonable economic growth — and, whether or not we believe it most effectively implements the other, we must recognize that the EPA has advanced a reasonable explanation for its conclusion that the regulations serve the environmental objectives as well ...

Policy

[*Reasonableness Analysis*]: The arguments over policy that are advanced in the parties' briefs create the impression that respondents are now waging in a judicial forum a specific policy battle which they ultimately lost in the agency and in the 32 jurisdictions opting for the "bubble concept," but one which was never waged in the Congress. Such policy arguments are more properly addressed to legislators or administrators, not to judges.

In these cases, the Administrator's interpretation represents a reasonable accommodation of manifestly competing interests and is entitled to deference: the regulatory scheme is technical and complex, the agency considered the matter in a detailed and reasoned fashion,[40] and the decision involves reconciling conflicting policies. Congress intended to accommodate both interests, but did not do so itself on the level of specificity presented by these cases. Perhaps that body consciously desired the Administrator to strike the balance at this level, thinking that those with great expertise and charged with responsibility for administering the provision would be in a better position to do so; perhaps it simply did not consider the question at this level; and perhaps Con-

---

40. *See SEC v. Sloan*, 436 U.S. at 117; *Adamo Wrecking Co. v. United States*, 434 U.S. 275, 287, n. 5 (1978); *Skidmore v. Swift & Co.*, 323 U.S. 134, 140 (1944).

gress was unable to forge a coalition on either side of the question, and those on each side decided to take their chances with the scheme devised by the agency. For judicial purposes, it matters not which of these things occurred.

Judges are not experts in the field, and are not part of either political branch of the Government. Courts must, in some cases, reconcile competing political interests, but not on the basis of the judges' personal policy preferences. In contrast, an agency to which Congress has delegated policy-making responsibilities may, within the limits of that delegation, properly rely upon the incumbent administration's views of wise policy to inform its judgments. While agencies are not directly accountable to the people, the Chief Executive is, and it is entirely appropriate for this political branch of the Government to make such policy choices-resolving the competing interests which Congress itself either inadvertently did not resolve, or intentionally left to be resolved by the agency charged with the administration of the statute in light of everyday realities.

When a challenge to an agency construction of a statutory provision, fairly conceptualized, really centers on the wisdom of the agency's policy, rather than whether it is a reasonable choice within a gap left open by Congress, the challenge must fail. In such a case, federal judges—who have no constituency—have a duty to respect legitimate policy choices made by those who do. The responsibilities for assessing the wisdom of such policy choices and resolving the struggle between competing views of the public interest are not judicial ones: "Our Constitution vests such responsibilities in the political branches."

We hold that the EPA's definition of the term "source" is a permissible construction of the statute which seeks to accommodate progress in reducing air pollution with economic growth....

The judgment of the Court of Appeals is reversed.

* * *

Points for Discussion

1. *Statutory Language*: What was the language at issue? What did each party want that language to mean? What meaning did the lower court and Supreme Court adopt?

2. *Theories*: Which theory did the Court use? The lower court? Did the Supreme Court find ambiguity, absurdity, a constitutional question to avoid, or a scrivener's error?

3. *Skidmore*: How did the Court alter, if at all, *Skidmore* deference? Understanding the difference between *Chevron* deference and *Skidmore* deference is not always so easy. Professor Gary Lawson has offered a way of thinking of the difference, which he defines as the difference between legal deference and epistemological deference. Gary Lawson, *Mostly Unconstitutional: The Case Against Precedent Revisited*, 5 Ave Maria L. Rev. 1, 2–10 (2007). Legal deference is deference earned solely based on the identity of the interpreter and the method of interpretation. *Id.* at 9. For example, lower courts must defer to interpretations of higher courts within the same jurisdiction, but need not defer to interpretations from courts

in other jurisdictions. The decision of whether to defer depends entirely on the identity of the interpreter. *Chevron* deference is a form of legal deference: agencies earn deference simply because they are agencies that interpreted statutes using a particular process. In contrast, epistemological deference is deference earned because of the persuasiveness of the reasoning. *Id.* at 10. Courts in neighboring jurisdictions need not follow each other's opinions but can choose to do so because the reasoning is persuasive. The decision of whether to defer depends entirely on the persuasiveness of the reasoning; the identity of the interpreter is irrelevant. *Skidmore* deference is a form of epistemological deference: agencies earn deference based on the soundness of their reasoning, not because they are agencies interpreting statutes.

4. *Flexibility*: Under *Skidmore*, you will recall that agency consistency was one factor earning an agency deference. Here, consistency was completely absent. Congress amended the Clean Air Act in 1977 to deal with those states that were failing to attain air quality standards. The EPA defined "stationary source" as any device in a manufacturing plant that produced pollution. In 1981, Ronald Reagan took office and the EPA adopted the new definition to further Reagan's deregulation agenda. Notice how the Court talked about agencies' need for flexibility in light of changing economic and political realities. Hence, the standard shifted from persuasiveness to reasonableness.

5. *Two Step*: *Chevron* has often been described as a two-step process. What are the two steps? At which step does the Court determine *de novo* what a statute means? At which step or steps does the court consider the agency's interpretation? Do the steps differ or is there overlap?

6. *Step One*: After *Chevron* was decided, there was some debate about the appropriate analysis for step one. Some, like Justice Scalia, argued that step one was a search for textual ambiguity, while others countered that it was a search for congressional intent involving all of the traditional tools of statutory interpretation. *See MCI Telecommuns. Corp. v. AT&T*, 518 U.S. 218 (1994) (applying a textual first step analysis to an agency's interpretation); *see generally,* Linda D. Jellum, *Chevron's Demise: A Survey of Chevron from Infancy to Senescence*, 59 ADMIN. L. REV. 725, 761 (2007) (exploring the Supreme Court's approach to step one). Look at footnote 9. Did not Justice Stevens answer this question in that footnote? Regardless, how did Justice Stevens apply step one in this case? Did he stop step one after finding the text ambiguous or continue examining the other sources of meaning? Professor William Eskridge and Lauren Baer analyzed the Court's practice in this area and concluded, "it is all but settled that relevant legislative history is admissible in the *Chevron* inquiry." William N. Eskridge, Jr. & Lauren E. Baer, *The Continuum of Deference: Supreme Court Treatment of Agency Statutory Interpretations from* Chevron *to* Hamdan, 96 GEO L.J. 1083, 1135 (2008).

7. *"Winning" at Step One*: While step one is not deferential to agencies at all, their interpretation will still be upheld as valid at this step if the interpretation is consistent with Congress's intent. Hence, agencies should consider arguing that the

statute is clear at step one and means what they have said it means. There is, however, one drawback to an agency "winning" at step one: unlike an interpretation that is upheld at step two, an agency cannot later change an interpretation that is upheld at step one because the court has found that Congress has directly spoken to the precise issue and, thus, the agency's interpretation must stay consistent with that intent. *National Cable & Telecommuns. Ass'n v. Brand X Internet Serv.*, 545 U.S. 967, 982 (2005) (holding that a court's "prior judicial [interpretation] of a statute trumps an agency [interpretation] otherwise entitled to *Chevron* deference only if the prior court decision holds that its [interpretation] follows from the unambiguous terms of the statute and thus leaves no room for agency discretion."). This issue is explored further in Chapter 19.

8. *Step Two*: While Justice Stevens used the word *permissible* at step two, courts today typically use the word *reasonable* instead. At step two, courts defer to agency interpretations that are reasonable, meaning they are within a range of possible statutory meanings. Deferring at step two is called *Chevron* deference, although sometimes court describe the entire *Chevron* two-step analysis as *Chevron* deference.

    Step two is supposed to be very differential to agencies, although it is becoming less so. *See* Orin S. Kerr, *Shedding Light on* Chevron: *An Empirical Study of the* Chevron *Doctrine in the United States Courts of Appeals*, 15 Yale J. Reg. 1, 31 (1998) (finding that agencies win forty-two percent of the time at step one and eighty-nine percent of the time at step two). Note also that because there is generally more than one reasonable interpretation, agencies may change their interpretation at a later time if they wish, which they can do so long as the new interpretation is reasonable. Why might agencies wish to change an existing interpretation?

9. *Understanding Reasonableness*: Professors John Manning and Mathew Stevenson described *Chevron*'s second step with a visual similar to the one below. Notice that an agency's interpretation will be reasonable so long as it stays within the range of reasonableness, even if the interpretation does not match the court's preferred interpretation. If, for example, the language being interpreted is "black" and the agency interprets black to include dark grey, that interpretation would likely be *reasonable*. But if the agency interprets "black" to include white or green, that interpretation would likely be *unreasonable*.

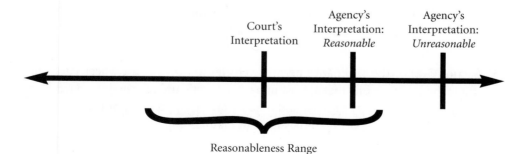

Reasonableness Range

10. *Arbitrary & Capricious Review:* While some law professors and even court opinions have suggested that *Chevron*'s second step is simply arbitrary and capricious review, others disagree. *See, e.g., Michigan v. EPA*, 135 S. Ct. 2699, 2707 (2015) (using a one-step, analysis that jumbled together *Chevron* and arbitrary and capricious review); Mark Seidenfeld, *A Syncopated* Chevron: *Emphasizing Reasoned Decision-Making in Reviewing Agency Interpretations of Statutes*, 73 Tex. L. Rev. 83, 129–30 (1994); Ronald M. Levin, *The Anatomy of* Chevron: *Step Two Reconsidered*, 72 Chi.-Kent L. Rev. 1253, 1254–55 (1997). Arbitrary and capricious review is the standard that courts apply to review agency findings of fact and policy in informal rulemakings and adjudications. While arbitrary and capricious review and reasonableness review are similar, what the court is reviewing differs. For arbitrary and capricious review, a court reviews the record to determine whether there is a "rational connection between the facts found and the choice made." *Motor Vehicles Manufs. Ass'n v. State Farm*, 463 U.S. 29, 43 (1983); *see also Citizens to Preserve Overton Park v. Volpe*, 401 U.S. 402, 416 (1971) (describing such review as whether the agency's findings were based on a consideration of irrelevant factors or whether the agency made a clear error of judgment).

* * *

Problem 18A

Return to Problem 1 (in Chapter 1) and the hypothetical local city ordinance prohibiting vehicles in the park. You were asked to determine whether you would charge different individuals of violating the ordinance.

Assume that before you resolve those cases, you learn that the Commission of Parks (an agency) promulgated a regulation (assume that notice and comment rulemaking procedures were used) to interpret the PPSO regarding whether certain vehicles are permitted in Pioneer Park. Does this regulation change any of your answers to any of the hypothetical cases? The regulation provides as follows:

33 C.F.R. § 2300

(1) "Motor vehicle" in the PPSO means a road vehicle driven by a motor or engine used or physically capable of being used upon any public highway in this state in the transportation of persons or property, except emergency vehicles.

(2) Section 2 of the Ordinance applies only to operable road vehicles (except that road vehicles may operate in Pioneer Park to the extent that they are necessary to transport boats to and from Crockett Lake).

(3) Section 3(a) of the Ordinance permits vehicles to operate in Pioneer Park only if: (1) the vehicle is one that at least in part is directly used for maintenance, such as lawnmowers, cherry pickers, and road surfacing equipment, or (2) the vehicle is necessary to transport materials used in maintaining Pioneer Park and is primarily used for that purpose.

(4) Section 3(b) of the Ordinance permits vehicles to operate in Pioneer Park only if the vehicle is operating in conjunction with erecting barricades or other traffic control devices for a parade, concert, or other event for which the event's promoters have a valid permit.

* * *

E. Applying *Chevron*

Shortly after *Chevron* was decided, debate arose regarding the nature of the inquiry at the first step. The debate centered around two questions. First, was step one a search for congressional intent or textual clarity? Second, was the search at step one to be broad and include a review of legislative history, statutory purpose, and other sources of statutory meaning, or was it to be narrow and focus primarily, if not exclusively, on the text? *Chevron* did not conclusively resolve this question. Justice Stevens described step one as a search for congressional intent that "employ[s] traditional tools of statutory construction," but he did not explain which tools of statutory construction were appropriate and "traditional." *Id.* at 843 n.9. Moreover, the opinion contained textualist language: "[If] the statute is silent or ambiguous with respect to the specific issue, the question for the court is whether the agency's answer is based on a permissible construction of the statute." *Id.* at 843. Finally, the Court approached the interpretive process in a decidedly non-textualist way, reviewing the text, legislative history, and purpose. *Id.* at 851.

As you should know by now, throughout history, the appropriate tools and approaches have changed as different theories of statutory interpretation have held favor. Because Justice Stevens used an intentionalist approach in *Chevron*, and because he referenced the traditional tools of statutory construction, it seemed that he anticipated step one to be intentionalist. Indeed, many of the justices on the bench when *Chevron* was decided were intentionalists or, at least, were willing to look at legislative history and purpose to find meaning.

In the years immediately following *Chevron*, the Court remained true to the intentionalist direction set forth by Justice Stevens. But with time and a change in the composition of the Court, *Chevron*'s first step changed: step one transformed from a search for congressional intent into a search to resolve textual ambiguity. This change started in 1986 when President Reagan appointed Justice Scalia to the Supreme Court. Coming from the D.C. Circuit Court, which handles many challenges to federal agency action, and having been a teacher of administrative law before his appointment to that court, Justice Scalia was particularly interested in agency issues. And, as a committed textualist, Justice Scalia must have felt compelled to "reformulate the two-step inquiry to purge it of these intentionalist elements." Thomas W. Merrill, *Textualism and the Future of the* Chevron *Doctrine*, 72 WASH. U. L.Q. 351, 353 (1994). By 2006, *Chevron*'s first step was routinely described and applied as a search to resolve ambiguity, using moderate textualist methods. Linda D. Jellum, *Chevron's*

Demise: A Survey of Chevron *from Infancy to Senescence*, 59 ADMIN. L. REV. 725, 761 (2007). A search to find and resolve ambiguity is not the same as a search to determine whether Congress has directly spoken to the precise issue before the court. While there is evidence that textualism has not completely won the battle (for many of the current justices will still consider legislative history and unexpressed purpose in some cases), there can be no doubt that Justice Scalia has, at a minimum, altered the discourse.

In the case below, the majority approaches its two step analysis in an unorthodox manner. Notice which step the majority considers first. The facts of the case are very complex. Do your best to understand the issue, but focus on the justices' application of *Chevron* for our subsequent discussion.

Zuni Public School District v. Department Of Education

Supreme Court of the United States
550 U.S. 81 (2007)

◆ JUSTICE BREYER delivered the opinion of the Court [in which STEVENS, KENNEDY, AND ALITO, JJ., concur].

A federal statute sets forth a method that the Secretary of Education is to use when determining whether a State's public school funding program "equalizes expenditures" throughout the State. The statute instructs the Secretary to calculate the disparity in per-pupil expenditures among local school districts in the State. But, when doing so, the Secretary is to "disregard" school districts "*with per-pupil expenditures ... above the 95th percentile or below the 5th percentile of such expenditures ... in the State.*" 20 U.S.C. §7709(b)(2)(B)(i) (emphasis added).

The question before us is whether the emphasized statutory language permits the Secretary to identify the school districts that should be "disregard[ed]" by looking to the *number of the district's pupils* as well as to the size of the district's expenditures per pupil. We conclude that it does....

This case requires us to decide whether the Secretary's present calculation method is consistent with the federal statute's "disregard" instruction. The method at issue is contained in a set of regulations that the Secretary first promulgated 30 years ago. Those regulations essentially state the following:

> When determining whether a state aid program "equalizes expenditures" (thereby permitting the State to reduce its own local funding on account of federal impact aid), the Secretary will first create a list of school districts ranked in order of per-pupil expenditure. The Secretary will then identify the relevant percentile cutoff point on that list on the basis of a specific (95th or 5th) percentile of *student population* — essentially identifying those districts whose students account for the 5 percent of the State's total student population that lies at both the high and low ends of the spending distribution. Finally the Secretary will compare the highest spending and lowest

spending school districts of those that remain to see whether they satisfy the statute's requirement that the disparity between them not exceed 25 percent....

Two of New Mexico's public school districts, Zuni Public School District and Gallup–McKinley County Public School District (whom we shall collectively call Zuni), sought [judicial review of the Department's interpretation]....

II A

Zuni's strongest argument rests upon the literal language of the statute. Zuni concedes, as it must, that if the language of the statute is open or ambiguous—that is, if Congress left a "gap" for the agency to fill—then we must uphold the Secretary's interpretation as long as it is reasonable. See *Chevron U.S.A. Inc. v. Natural Resources Defense Council, Inc.,* 467 U.S. 837, 842–843 (1984). For purposes of exposition, we depart from a normal order of discussion, namely, an order that first considers Zuni's statutory language argument. Instead, because of the technical nature of the language in question, we shall first examine the provision's background and basic purposes. That discussion will illuminate our subsequent analysis [of the text] in Part II–B. It will also reveal why Zuni concentrates its argument upon language alone.

Considerations other than language provide us with unusually strong indications that Congress intended to leave the Secretary free to use the calculation method before us and that the Secretary's chosen method is a reasonable one. For one thing, the matter at issue—*i.e.,* the calculation method for determining whether a state aid program "equalizes expenditures"—is the kind of highly technical, specialized interstitial matter that Congress often does not decide itself, but delegates to specialized agencies to decide.

For another thing, [this is a quintessential example of a case in which the statutory text was enacted to adopt the rule that the Secretary administered both before and after the enactment of the rather confusing language found in 20 U.S.C. §7709(b)(2)(B)(i).].

Finally, viewed in terms of the purpose of the statute's disregard instruction, the Secretary's calculation method is reasonable, while the reasonableness of a method based upon the number of districts alone (Zuni's proposed method) is more doubtful.... [The majority examines the legislative history and purpose of the statute to conclude that the secretary's interpretation is reasonable] and carries out Congress' likely intent in enacting the statutory provision before us.

II B

But what of the provision's literal language? The matter is important, for normally neither the legislative history nor the reasonableness of the Secretary's method would be determinative if the plain language of the statute unambiguously indicated that Congress sought to foreclose the Secretary's interpretation. And Zuni argues that the Secretary's formula could not possibly effectuate Congress' intent since the statute's language literally forbids the Secretary to use such a method. Under this Court's precedents, if the intent of Congress is clear and unambiguously expressed by the statutory language at issue, that would be the end of our analysis. A customs statute that imposes a tariff on "clothing" does not impose a tariff on automobiles, no matter how strong the policy arguments for treating the two kinds of goods alike. But we disagree with Zuni's conclusion, for we believe that the Secretary's method falls within the scope of the statute's plain language....

That language says that, when the Secretary compares (for a specified fiscal year) "the amount of per-pupil expenditures made by" (1) the highest-per-pupil-expenditure district and (2) the lowest-per-pupil-expenditure district, "the Secretary shall ... disregard" local school districts "with per-pupil expenditures ... above the 95th percentile or below the 5th percentile of such expenditures in the State." 20 U.S.C. §§ 7709(b)(2)(A)(B)(i). The word "such" refers to "per-pupil expenditures".... The question then is whether the phrase "*above the 95th percentile ... of ... [per pupil] expenditures*" permits the Secretary to calculate percentiles by (1) ranking local districts, (2) noting the student population of each district, and (3) determining the cutoff point on the basis of districts containing 95 percent (or 5 percent) of the State's students.

Our answer is that this phrase, taken with absolute literalness, limits the Secretary to calculation methods that involve "per-pupil expenditures." But it does not tell the Secretary which of several different possible methods the Department must use....

Here, the Secretary has distributed districts, ranked them according to per-pupil expenditure, but compared only those that account for 90 percent of the State's pupils. Thus, the Secretary has used—as her predecessors had done for a quarter century before her—the State's *students* as the relevant population for calculating the specified percentiles. Another Secretary might have distributed districts, ranked them by per-pupil expenditure, and made no reference to the number of pupils (a method that satisfies the statute's *language* but threatens the [purpose]). A third Secretary might have distributed districts, ranked them by per-pupil expenditure, but compared only those that account for 90 percent of total pupil expenditures in the State. A fourth Secretary might have distributed districts, ranked them by per-pupil expenditure, but calculated the 95th and 5th percentile cutoffs using the per-pupil expenditures of all the individual *schools* in the State. A fifth Secretary might have distributed districts, ranked them by per-pupil expenditure, but accounted in his disparity calculation for the sometimes significant differences in per-pupil spending at different grade levels.

Each of these methods amounts to a different way of determining which districts fall between the 5th and 95th "percentile of per-pupil expenditures." For purposes of that calculation, they each adopt different populations—students, districts, schools, and grade levels. Yet, linguistically speaking, one may attribute the characteristic of per-pupil expenditure to each member of any such population (though the values of that characteristic may be more or less readily available depending on the chosen population). Hence, the statute's literal language covers any or all of these methods. That language alone does not tell us (or the Secretary of Education), however, which method to use.

Justice Scalia's claim that this interpretation "defies any semblance of normal English" depends upon its own definition of the word "per." That word, according to the dissent, "connotes ... a single average figure assigned to a unit the composite members of which are individual pupils." In fact, the word "per" simply means "[f]or each" or "for every." Black's Law Dictionary 1171 (8th ed.1999); see Webster's Third 1674. Thus, nothing in the English language prohibits the Secretary from considering expenditures *for each* individual pupil in a district when instructed to look at a district's "per-pupil expenditures." The remainder of the dissent's argument, colorful language to the side, rests upon a reading of the statutory language that ignores its basic purpose and history....

We also find support for our view of the language in the more general circumstance that statutory "[a]mbiguity is a creature not [just] of definitional possibilities but [also] of statutory context." *FDA v. Brown & Williamson Tobacco Corp.*, 529 U.S. 120, 132–133 (2000) ("[m]eaning—*or ambiguity*—of certain words or phrases may only become evident when placed in context" (emphasis added)). That may be so even if statutory language is highly technical. After all, the scope of what seems a precise technical chess instruction, such as "you must place the queen next to the king," varies with context, depending, for example, upon whether the instructor is telling a beginner how to set up the board or telling an advanced player how to checkmate an opponent....

The upshot is that the language of the statute is broad enough to permit the Secretary's reading. That fact requires us to look beyond the language to determine whether the Secretary's interpretation is a reasonable, hence permissible, implementation of the statute. For the reasons set forth in Part II–A, we conclude that the Secretary's reading is a reasonable reading. We consequently find the Secretary's method of calculation lawful....

♦ JUSTICE STEVENS, concurring.

... In *Chevron*, we acknowledged that when "the intent of Congress is clear (from the statutory text), that is the end of the matter." But we also made quite clear that "administrative constructions which are contrary to clear congressional intent" must be rejected. *Id.*, at 843, n. 9. In that unanimous opinion, we explained:

> "If a court, employing traditional tools of statutory construction, ascertains that Congress had an intention on the precise question at issue, that intention is the law and must be given effect."

Analysis of legislative history is, of course, a traditional tool of statutory construction. There is no reason why we must confine ourselves to, or begin our analysis with, the statutory text if other tools of statutory construction provide better evidence of congressional intent with respect to the precise point at issue.

... [The] text is sufficiently ambiguous to justify the Court's exegesis, but my own vote is the product of a more direct route to the Court's patently correct conclusion. This happens to be a case in which the legislative history is pellucidly clear and the statutory text is difficult to fathom.[2] Moreover, it is a case in which I cannot imagine anyone accusing any Member of the Court of voting one way or the other because of that Justice's own policy preferences.

Given the clarity of the evidence of Congress' "intention on the precise question at issue," I would affirm the judgment of the Court of Appeals even if I thought that petitioners' literal reading of the statutory text was correct.[3] The only "policy" by which I have been driven is that which this Court has endorsed on repeated occasions regarding the importance of remaining faithful to Congress' intent....

◆ JUSTICE KENNEDY, with whom JUSTICE ALITO joins, concurring.

The district courts and courts of appeals, as well as this Court, should follow the framework set forth in *Chevron*, even when departure from that framework might serve purposes of exposition. When considering an administrative agency's interpretation of a statute, a court first determines "whether Congress has directly spoken to the precise question at issue." If so, "that is the end of the matter." Only if "Congress has not directly addressed the precise question at issue" should a court consider "whether the agency's answer is based on a permissible construction of the statute."

In this case, the Court is correct to find that the plain language of the statute is ambiguous. It is proper, therefore, to invoke *Chevron's* rule of deference. The opinion of the Court, however, inverts *Chevron's* logical progression. Were the inversion to become systemic, it would create the impression that agency policy concerns, rather than the traditional tools of statutory construction, are shaping the judicial interpretation of statutes. It is our obligation to set a good example; and so, in my view, it would have been preferable, and more faithful to *Chevron,* to arrange the opinion differently. Still, we must give deference to the author of an opinion in matters of exposition; and because the point does not affect the outcome, I join the Court's opinion.

◆ JUSTICE SCALIA, with whom CHIEF JUSTICE ROBERTS and JUSTICE THOMAS join, and with whom JUSTICE SOUTER joins as to Part I, dissenting.

In *Church of the Holy Trinity v. United States,* this Court conceded that a church's act of contracting with a prospective rector fell within the plain meaning of a federal labor statute, but nevertheless did not apply the statute to the church: "It is a familiar rule," the Court pronounced, "that a thing may be within the letter of the statute and yet not within the statute, because not within its spirit, nor within the intention of its makers." That is a judge-empowering proposition if there ever was one, and in the century since, the Court has wisely retreated from it, in words if not always in actions. But today *Church of the Holy Trinity* arises, Phoenix-like, from the ashes. The Court's con-

---

2. ... Moreover, I assume that, regardless of the statutory language's supposed clarity, any competent counsel challenging the validity of a presumptively valid federal regulation would examine the legislative history of its authorizing statute before filing suit.

3. See *Church of Holy Trinity v. United States,* 143 U.S. 457, 459 (1892) ("It is a familiar rule, that a thing may be within the letter of the statute and yet not within the statute, because not within its spirit, nor within the intention of its makers")

trary assertions aside, today's decision is nothing other than the elevation of judge-supposed legislative intent over clear statutory text. The plain language of the federal Impact Aid statute clearly and unambiguously forecloses the Secretary of Education's preferred methodology for determining whether a State's school-funding system is equalized. Her selection of that methodology is therefore entitled to zero deference under *Chevron*.

The very structure of the Court's opinion provides an obvious clue as to what is afoot. The opinion purports to place a premium on the plain text of the Impact Aid statute, but it first takes us instead on a roundabout tour of "[c]onsiderations *other* than language." Only after we are shown "why Zuni concentrates its argument upon language alone," (impliedly a shameful practice, or at least indication of a feeble case), are we informed how the statute's plain text does not unambiguously *preclude* the interpretation the Court thinks best. Part II–B (beginning "But what of the provision's literal language? The matter is important . . ."). This is a most suspicious order of proceeding, since our case law is full of statements such as "We begin, as always, with the language of the statute," and replete with the affirmation that, when "(g)iven (a) straightforward statutory command, there is no reason to resort to legislative history." Nor is this cart-before-the-horse approach justified by the Court's excuse that the statute before us is, after all, a technical one. This Court . . . confronts technical language all the time, but we never see fit to pronounce upon what we think Congress *meant* a statute to say, and what we think sound policy would *counsel* it to say, before considering what it *does* say. As [Justices Kennedy and Alito worry], "(we)re the inversion (of inquiry) to become systemic, it would create the impression that agency policy concerns, rather than the traditional tools of statutory construction, are shaping the judicial interpretation of statutes." True enough—except I see no reason to wait for the distortion to become systemic before concluding that that is precisely what is happening in the present case. For some, policy-driven interpretation is apparently just fine. But for everyone else, let us return to Statutory Interpretation 101.

We must begin, as we always do, with the text. . . .

There is no dispute that for purposes relevant here " 'percentile' refers to a division of a distribution of *some* population into 100 parts.' " And there is further no dispute that the statute concerns the percentile of "per-pupil expenditures or revenues," for that is what the word "such" refers to. The question is: Whose per-pupil expenditures or revenues? Or, in the Court's terminology, what "population" is assigned the "characteristic" "per-pupil expenditure" or revenue? At first blush, second blush, or twenty-second blush, the answer is abundantly clear: local educational agencies. The statute requires the Secretary to "disregard local educational agencies with" certain per-pupil figures above or below specified percentiles of those per-pupil figures. §7709(b)(2)(B)(i). The attribute "per-pupil expenditur[e] or revenu[e]" is assigned to [local school districts]—there is no mention of student population whatsoever. And thus under the statute, "per-pupil expenditures or revenues" are to be arrayed using a population consisting of [local school districts], so that percentiles are determined from a list of (in New Mexico) 89 per-pupil expenditures or revenues representing the 89 [local school districts] in the State. It is just that simple. . . .

In sum, the plain language of the ... statute compels the conclusion that the Secretary's method of calculation is ultra vires. Employing the formula that the statute requires, New Mexico is not equalized.

How then, if the text is so clear, are respondents managing to win this case? The answer can only be the return of that miraculous redeemer of lost causes, *Church of the Holy Trinity*.... [But] once one departs from "strict interpretation of the text" (by which Justice Stevens means the actual meaning of the text) fidelity to the intent of Congress is a chancy thing. The only thing we know for certain both Houses of Congress (and the President, if he signed the legislation) agreed upon is the text. Legislative history can never produce a "pellucidly clear" picture of what a law was "intended" to mean, for the simple reason that it is never voted upon — or ordinarily even seen or heard — by the "intending" lawgiving entity, which consists of both Houses of Congress and the President (if he did not veto the bill). Thus, what judges believe Congress "meant" (apart from the text) has a disturbing but entirely unsurprising tendency to be whatever judges think Congress *must* have meant, *i.e.*, *should* have meant. In *Church of the Holy Trinity*, every Justice on this Court disregarded the plain language of a statute that forbade the hiring of a clergyman from abroad because, after all (they thought), "this is a Christian nation," so Congress could not have meant what it said. Is there any reason to believe that those Justices were lacking that "intellectua[l] honest[y]" that Justice Stevens "presume[s]" all our judges possess? Intellectual honesty does not exclude a blinding intellectual bias. And even if it did, the system of judicial amendatory veto over texts duly adopted by Congress bears no resemblance to the system of lawmaking set forth in our Constitution....

Contrary to the Court and Justice Stevens, I do not believe that what we are sure the Legislature *meant* to say can trump what it *did* say. Citizens arrange their affairs not on the basis of their legislators' unexpressed intent, but on the basis of the law as it is written and promulgated.... By "depriving legislators of the assurance that ordinary terms, used in an ordinary context, will be given a predictable meaning," we deprive Congress of "a sure means by which it may work the people's will." ...

The only sure indication of what Congress intended is what Congress enacted; and even if there is a difference between the two, the rule of law demands that the latter prevail. This case will live with *Church of the Holy Trinity* as an exemplar of judicial disregard of crystal-clear text. We must interpret the law as Congress has written it, not as we would wish it to be. I would reverse the judgment of the Court of Appeals.

♦ [JUSTICE SOUTER's dissenting opinion is omitted.]

* * *

Points for Discussion

1. *Statutory Language*: What was the language at issue? What did each party want that language to mean? What meaning did the majority and dissent adopt?

2. *Theories*: Which theory did the majority use? The concurrences? Dissent? Did any of the justices find ambiguity, absurdity, a constitutional question to avoid, or a scrivener's error?

3. *Chevron's Two-Step Approach*: Did the majority follow the two step approach identified in *Chevron*? Assuming not, why not? If the text of a statute is clear and does not encompass an agency's interpretation, is that the end of the analysis under *Chevron*'s first step, or should a court examine the other tools of statutory interpretation?

4. *Concurrences*: Justices Kennedy and Alito concurred, but expressed concern about the majority's approach in this case. Why? Justice Stevens, who also concurred, has no concern about whether a court begins the analysis with the text or some other indication of legislative intent. So why did he concur?

5. *Clear Legislative History Trumping Not So Clear Text*: The legislative history was very clear that this statutory language was adopted at the Secretary's request and with the understanding that the Secretary interpreted the statute in this way. Should that drafting history matter at all? According to Justice Stevens, the legislative history is "pellucidly clear" and trumps "difficult to fathom" text. But Justice Scalia expressed concern both that legislative history is not law and that ordinary citizens typically do not consider legislative history when attempting to comply with a statute. Given that this interpretation had been in effect for many years, does Justice Scalia's criticism, at least in this case, have any merit?

6. *Textualizing Step One*: Why did the majority find the language ambiguous? Why did Justice Scalia disagree? Why did Justice Stevens say that whether the language alone was clear was irrelevant? Does the fact that the majority worked so hard to find textual ambiguity demonstrate that Justice Scalia and not Justice Stevens correctly applied *Chevron*'s first step? If not, why did not the majority simply say, "Even though the text says A, the legislative history and purpose suggest B; therefore, we accept the agency's reasonable interpretation: that the statute means B"?

7. *Ultra Vires*: If a court finds that Congress has spoken, an agency's interpretation may still be valid so long as that regulation is consistent with congressional intent. If the regulation is not consistent or if the regulation is unreasonable under *Chevron*'s second step, then the regulation is void as *ultra vires*, meaning that the agency has acted without legal authority.

* * *

Problem 18B

You represent the Secretary of the Department of the Interior (an agency). The agency is working on filing a brief in a pending case. The facts are not in dispute, so both parties have moved for summary judgment. Assume that *Chevron* applies. The Secretary would like you to draft the argument section of the brief. You need not include point headings, but do please begin with a conclusion.

The Plaintiffs in the case are a group of logging companies located in the Pacific Northwest that clear cut (a process by which every tree in a specific area is cut down and removed) old growth forests. Clear cutting impacts the habitat of some endangered species, specifically, the red-cockaded woodpecker and the northern spotted owl. When their habitat is modified or degraded, these animals stop breeding, further injuring their population by further reducing their numbers. However, there is no direct injury to an individual animal.

The parties disagree about whether the agency's interpretation of the Endangered Species Act (ESA) is valid. Please confine your arguments to that issue. For purposes of this motion only, *you need not apply the regulation to the facts* because the parties do not dispute that plaintiffs' activity is prohibited by the regulation if it applies.

ENDANGERED SPECIES ACT OF 1973

AN ACT To provide for the conservation of endangered and threatened species of fish, wildlife, and plants, and for other purposes.

Be it enacted by the Senate and House of Representatives of the United States of America in Congress assembled,

SECTION 1. SHORT TITLE; FINDINGS; PURPOSES; POLICY

(a) SHORT TITLE—this Act may be cited as the "Endangered Species Act of 1973."

(b) FINDINGS.—The Congress finds and declares that—

(1) various species of fish, wildlife, and plants in the United States have been rendered extinct as a consequence of economic growth and development untempered by adequate concern and conservation;...

(2) these species of fish, wildlife, and plants are of esthetic, ecological, educational, historical, recreational, and scientific value to the Nation and its people;...

(3) encouraging the States and other interested parties, through Federal financial assistance and a system of incentives, to develop and maintain conservation programs which meet national and international standards is a key to meeting the Nation's international commitments and to better safeguarding, for the benefit of all citizens, the Nation's heritage in fish, wildlife, and plants.

(c) PURPOSES.—

(1) The purposes of this Act are to provide a means whereby the ecosystems upon which endangered species and threatened species depend may be conserved, to provide a program for the conservation of such endangered species and threatened species, and to take such steps as may be appropriate to achieve the purposes of this section.

(d) POLICY.—

(1) It is further declared to be the policy of Congress that all Federal departments and agencies shall seek to conserve endangered species and threatened species and shall utilize their authorities in furtherance of the purposes of this Act....

SECTION 2. DEFINITIONS

(a) For the purposes of this Act—

(13) The term "person" means an individual, corporation, partnership, trust, association, or any other private entity; or any officer, employee, agent, department, or instrumentality of the Federal Government, of any State, municipality, or political subdivision of a State, or of any foreign government; any State, municipality, or political subdivision of a State; or any other entity subject to the jurisdiction of the United States....

(19) The term "take" means to harass, hunt, harm, trap, capture, shoot, wound, or kill, or to attempt to engage in any such conduct.

SECTION 3: AGENCY POWERS

(a) GENERAL—The Secretary of Department of the Interior ("Secretary") may issue such regulations as are necessary to interpret and implement this statute and conduct hearings as necessary to enforce this Act.

SECTION 9: PROHIBITED ACTS

(a) GENERAL.—

(1) Except as provided [elsewhere in this Act], it shall be unlawful for any person subject to the jurisdiction of the United States to—....

(B) take any such species within the United States or the territorial sea of the United States

(b) Any person who knowingly violates any provision of this Act may be imprisoned for up to six months and/or required to pay up to $10,000 for each violation.

Legislative History of the Endangered Species Act

Two bills, S. 1592 and S. 1983, were introduced in the Senate and referred to Commerce Committee. Neither bill included the word "harm" in its definition of "take," although the definitions otherwise closely resembled the one that appeared in the bill as ultimately enacted.

The definition of "take" that originally appeared in S. 1983 included "the destruction, modification, or curtailment of the habitat or range" of fish and wildlife. However, the Senate Commerce Committee's Subcommittee on Environment (Subcommittee) removed this phrase from the definition of "take" before S. 1983 went to the floor. During floor debates, Senator Tunney, the floor manager of the bill in the Senate, introduced a floor amendment to S. 1983 that added the word "harm" to the definition of "take," noting that this and accompanying amendments would "help to achieve the purposes of the bill." Senator Tunney stated:

> With this Act, we will be able to conserve habitats necessary to protect fish and wildlife from further destruction.

> Although most endangered species are threatened primarily by the destruction of their natural habitats, a significant portion of these animals

are subject to predation by man for commercial, sport, consumption, or other purposes. The provisions of this bill will prohibit the commerce in or the importation, exportation, or taking of endangered species.

After S. 1983 passed the Senate, it was sent to the House. Designated H.R. 1613, the bill passed out of committee unchanged and was sent to the full chamber for consideration. During debate in the House, floor manager, Representative Sullivan, stated:

The principal threat to animals stems from destruction of their habitat. This bill will meet this problem by providing funds for acquisition of critical habitat. It will also enable the Department of Agriculture to cooperate with willing landowners who desire to assist in the protection of endangered species, but who are understandably unwilling to do so at excessive cost to themselves. Another hazard to endangered species arises from those who would capture or kill them for pleasure or profit. There is no way that Congress can make it less pleasurable for a person to take an animal, but Congress can certainly make it less profitable for them to do so.

The Senate and House Committee Reports accompanying the bills that became the Endangered Species Act provide the following additional information. The Senate Report stated that " 'take' is defined ... in the broadest possible manner to include every conceivable way in which a person can 'take' or attempt to 'take' any fish or wildlife."

The House Report stated that "the broadest possible terms" were used to define restrictions on takings. The House Report noted that "take" included "harassment, whether intentional or not." The Report noted that the definition "would allow, for example, the Secretary to regulate or prohibit the activities of birdwatchers where the effect of those activities might disturb the birds and make it difficult for them to hatch or raise their young."

Agency Action

Using the appropriate procedures, the Secretary promulgated regulation 50 CFR § 17.3:

§ 17.3 Definitions

In addition to the definitions contained in [another part of the regulation], and unless the context otherwise requires:

Act means the Endangered Species Act of 1973;

Harass in the Act means an intentional or negligent act or omission, which creates the likelihood of injury to wildlife by annoying it to such an extent as to significantly disrupt normal behavioral patterns which include, but are not limited to, breeding, feeding, or sheltering;

Harm in the Act means an act which actually kills or injures individual wildlife or populations of wildlife. Such act may include significant habitat modification or degradation where it actually kills or injures a population by significantly impairing essential behavioral patterns, including breeding, feeding or sheltering.

* * *

Chapter 19

The Regulatory Process: Deference to Agency Interpretations Post-*Chevron*

A. Introduction to This Chapter

In the last chapter, you learned how courts balance the judicial role of interpreting statutes with the executive role of applying statutes. In that chapter, you learned that when agencies interpret statutes, the courts often apply *Chevron*'s two step analysis to determine whether to defer to the agency's interpretation.

In this chapter, you will learn that sometimes *Chevron* is not the appropriate standard. This chapter examines a very complex area of law: the intersection of statutory interpretation and administrative law. Here you will learn that *Chevron* may not apply in two situations: first, when an agency interprets a statute using a process that does not involve force of law procedures, and second, when an agency interprets a statute differently from a preexisting court interpretation. In addition, you will learn that some issues are simply too important to the national economy for agency resolution. This "too important" restriction on *Chevron*'s implicit delegation rational has recently gained importance.

B. *Chevron* Step Zero

When *Chevron* was decided, it appeared to streamline deference analysis into two straightforward steps: first, a court looked to see if Congress had an intent as to the specific issue before the court; if not, the court adopted the agency's interpretation so long as it was reasonable. But not long after *Chevron* was decided, the Court began to move away from a *Chevron* only world. *Chevron* addressed the degree of deference to be given to a legislative rule, specifically one promulgated via notice and comment rulemaking procedures. After *Chevron* was decided, the Court initially applied this two-step framework to all agency interpretations. In subsequent decisions, however, the Court resurrected *Skidmore*'s "power-to-persuade" test. *Skidmore* deference standard is thought to be less deferential than *Chevron*. Aaron-Andrew P. Bruhl, *Hierarchically Variable Deference to Agency Interpretations*, 89 Notre Dame L. Rev. 728, 729 (2013) (describing *Skidmore* deference as only deferring "a bit"). As a result of later cases, *Chevron* no longer applies in every case involving an agency interpretation.

See, e.g., Christensen v. Harris Cty., 529 U.S. 576 (2000); *United States v. Mead Corp.*, 533 U.S. 218 (2001). Hence, the question is when does *Chevron* apply?

Before a court can apply *Chevron*, the court must make sure that the interpretation is one deserving of *Chevron*. This step has become colloquially known as "*Chevron* Step Zero," and it is exceedingly complex. Cass R. Sunstein, Chevron *Step Zero*, 92 Va. L. Rev. 187, 207–09 (2006) (naming this "new" step). But if you break the analysis into its sub-questions, the analysis is at least approachable. Here are the sub-questions: (1) *What* did the agency interpret? (2) *Which* agency did the interpreting? (3) *How* did the agency do its interpreting? And (4) *Can* this agency interpret the statute? Below, each question is explored in more detail.

1. What Did the Agency Interpret?

Chevron analysis is applicable only when an agency interprets a specific type of legal text. To illustrate, *Chevron* does not apply when agencies interpret the Federal Constitution, court opinions, and legal instruments such as contracts. Similarly, *Chevron* does not apply when agencies interpret other agencies' regulations. Indeed, in these situations, courts do not defer at all.

When an agency interprets its own regulation, a different form of deference applies: *Auer* deference. While judicial deference to agency interpretations of statutes has varied widely through time, judicial deference to an agency's interpretation of its own regulations has remained relatively constant. Traditionally, courts defer almost completely to an agency's interpretation of its own regulation. This high level of deference should come as no surprise; after all, it was the agency that drafted the regulation in the first place. Thus, in 1945, the Supreme Court held that an agency's interpretation of its regulation has "controlling weight unless it is plainly erroneous or inconsistent with the regulation." *Bowles v. Seminole Rock & Sand Co.*, 325 U.S. 410, 414 (1945). The Supreme Court reasoned that when Congress delegates authority to promulgate regulations, it also delegates authority to interpret those regulations; such power is a necessary corollary to the former. This substantial level of deference is generally known as either *Seminole Rock* or *Auer* deference. The latter term refers to the Supreme Court case of *Auer v. Robbins*, 519 U.S. 452 (1997), which came after *Chevron* and confirmed that *Seminole Rock* deference had survived *Chevron*. *Id*. at 461–63

There is at least one limitation on when an agency will receive this high level of deference. When an agency does little more than parrot statutory language in its regulation and then claims that it is interpreting the regulation rather than the statute, the agency is not entitled to *Auer* deference. When an agency does no more than parrot a statute (meaning it simply replicates the language Congress used), the agency will not receive *Auer* deference because the agency is interpreting language from Congress, not from itself. *Gonzales v. Oregon*, 546 U.S. 243, 257 (2006).

In *Gonzales v. Oregon*, the Supreme Court refused to defer to the Attorney General's decision that physician-assisted suicide was not a legitimate medical purpose for prescribing medication. *Id.* at 281. The Attorney General had authority under the Federal Controlled Substances Act to identify the medical uses of controlled substances. *Id.* at 257. The Act allowed doctors to prescribe drugs that have a "currently accepted medical use" for a "medical purpose" *Id.* (quoting 21 U.S.C. §§ 812(b) & (c)). Further, the Act defined a "valid prescription" as one "issued for a legitimate medical purpose." *Id.* (quoting 21 U.S.C. § 830(b)(3)(A)(ii)).

In 1971, the Attorney General issued a regulation pursuant to this statute that required every prescription for a controlled substance "be issued for a legitimate medical purpose by an individual practitioner acting in the usual course of his professional practice." *Id.* at 250 (quoting 21 CFR § 1306.04(a)). After Oregon passed an assisted suicide law, the Attorney General issued an interpretive rule, without using notice and comment rulemaking, interpreting the language "legitimate medical purpose" in its own 1971 regulation. The interpretive rule provided that " 'assisting suicide [was] not a 'legitimate medical purpose' within the meaning of [the regulation].' " *Id.* at 254 (quoting 66 Fed. Reg. 56607, 56608 (Nov. 9, 2001)). Pursuant to the Attorney General's interpretive rule, if a physician prescribed medication for an assisted suicide, the physician would violate the Controlled Substances Act. *Id.* at 257–69.

When challenged, the United States Government argued that the Attorney General's interpretive rule was entitled to *Auer* deference because the Attorney General simply interpreted its own regulation. *Id.* at 257. The Court rejected the government's argument, stating that *Auer* deference is appropriate when agencies interpret regulations bringing "specificity" to the statutes they are enforcing. *Id.* When the agency interprets a regulation that simply repeats or paraphrases statutory text, the interpretation does not warrant *Auer* deference, because the agency is interpreting Congress's language, not its own.

In summary, *Chevron* applies only when an agency (1) *interprets a statute.*

2. Which Agency Interpreted the Statute

But it is not enough that an agency interprets the correct type of legal text, a statute. *Chevron* applies only when the agency that interprets the statute "administers" that statute. Agencies often interpret and apply statutes, including statutes that the agency does not administer. While the Court has never clearly articulated what it means to "administer" a statute, lower court cases that have addressed this issue suggest that agencies administer a statute when they have a special and unique responsibility for that statute. *See, e.g., Wagner Seed Co. v. Bush*, 946 F.2d 918, 925–26 (D.C. Cir. 1991) (Williams, J., dissenting) (arguing that the Environmental Protection Agency did not administer the reimbursement provisions of the Superfund Amendments and Reauthorization Act of 1986). Moreover, when more than one agency administers a statute, *Chevron* is generally inappropriate. *See Lawson v. FMR LLC*, 134 S. Ct. 1158, 1187 (2014) (Sotomayor, J., dissenting) (stating that "if any agency has the authority to resolve ambiguities in § 1514A with the force of law, it is the SEC, not the Department of Labor"); *Rapaport v. U.S. Dep't of the Treasury*, 59 F.3d 212, 216–17 (D.C. Cir. 1995) (declining to apply *Chevron* where the agency shared responsibility for the administration of the statute with another agency); *Illinois Nat'l Guard v. Fed. Labor Relations Auth.*, 854 F.2d 1396, 1400 (D.C. Cir. 1988) (declining to apply *Chevron* deference); *cf. CF Indus., Inc. v. Fed. Energy Regulatory Comm'n*, 925 F.2d 476, 478 n.1 (D.C. Cir. 1991) (stating in a footnote that there "might well be a compelling case to afford deference if it were necessary for decision [where] both agencies agree as to which of them has exclusive jurisdiction").

So, for example, although multiple agencies interpret the Internal Revenue Code, it is generally only the Department of Treasury that is authorized to administer those statutes; thus, only this agency should receive *Chevron* deference for interpretations of tax statutes in the federal tax code. *See, e.g., Mayo Found. for Med. Educ. & Research v. United States*, 562 U.S. 44, 55 (2011) (applying *Chevron* deference to review the Department of Treasury's interpretation of a tax statute). Note, however, that some statutes in the tax code are not just tax statutes. *See, e.g.*, the Affordable Care Act Patient Protection and Affordable Care Act, Pub. L. No. 111-148, 124 Stat. 119.

Agencies also must interpret generally applicable statutes, such as the Administrative Procedure Act (5 U.S.C. ch. 5, subch. I § 500 *et seq*), the Regulatory Flexibility Act (5 U.S.C. §§ 601–12), and the Freedom of Information Act. (5 U.S.C. § 552). For such generally applicable statutes, no agency's interpretation is entitled to *Chevron* deference. *See, e.g., Ass'n of Am. Physicians & Surgeons, Inc. v. Clinton*, 997 F.2d 898, 913 (D.C. Cir. 1993) (interpreting the Federal Advisory Committee Act); *FLRA. v. U.S. Dep't of Treasury*, 884 F.2d 1446, 1451 (D.C. Cir. 1989) (refusing to apply *Chevron* to the Federal Labor Relation Authority's (FLRA) interpretation of the Freedom of Information Act (FOIA) or the Privacy Act because "FLRA is not charged with a special duty to interpret [these statutes]"); *Reporters Comm. for Freedom of the Press v. U.S. Dep't of Justice*, 816 F.2d 730, 734 (D.C. Cir. 1987) (stating that no deference would be given to an agency's interpretation of the FOIA because "it applies to all government agencies, and thus no one executive branch entity is entrusted with its primary interpretation"), *rev'd on other grounds*, 489 U.S. 749 (1989).

In summary, *Chevron* applies only when an agency (1) interprets a statute (2) *that the agency administers*.

3. How Did the Agency Interpret the Statute: Force of Law

But it is not enough that an agency interpret a statute that it administers. Agencies act in a variety of ways. Some of these ways require more procedural formality and deliberation than others. For example, an agency might interpret a statute as part of a notice and comment rulemaking process, like the EPA did in *Chevron U.S.A. Inc. v. Natural Res. Def. Council, Inc.*, 467 U.S. 837, 855 (1984). Also, an agency might interpret a statute during a formal adjudication. Or, an agency might interpret a statute when drafting an internal policy manual or when writing a letter to a regulated entity. *See, e.g., Christensen v. Harris Cty.*, 529 U.S. 576, 580–81, 586–89 (2000) (interpreting a statute in response to a letter inquiry from the county); *see also United States v. Mead Corp.*, 533 U.S. 218, 221–27 (2001) (interpreting a tariff classification ruling). With the former processes (formal adjudication and notice and comment rulemaking), Congress has given the agency the authority to act with the force of law, and the agency has used that authority to implement change. With the latter processes (non-legislative rulemaking), Congress has not given the agency the authority to act with the force of law. For these reasons, the former processes are considered more formal, or procedurally prescribed, while the latter processes are thought to be less formal, or less procedurally prescribed. *See, e.g.,* Lisa Schultz Bressman, *How Mead Has Muddled Judicial Review of Agency Action*, 58 Vand. L. Rev. 1443, 1447 (2005) (questioning "whether *Chevron* deference applies to interpretations issued through informal procedures").

In *Chevron*, the Supreme Court did not indicate, expressly or implicitly, whether the deliberateness of the agency's procedures affected the applicability of the two step analysis. Linda D. Jellum, Chevron's *Demise: A Survey of* Chevron *from Infancy to Senescence*, 59 Admin. L. Rev. 725, 774 (2007). Before the Court decided *Chevron*, however, the Court factored the deliberative nature of the agency's interpretive process into the analysis. Under *Skidmore* deference, interpretations that are made through a more deliberative process, such as notice and comment rulemaking, are considered more persuasive than interpretations made through a less deliberative process, such as non-legislative rulemaking.

Immediately after the Court decided *Chevron*, the Court did not distinguish between deliberative agency decision-making and non-deliberative agency decision-making. Rather, the Court applied its two step analysis to all types of agency interpretations, regardless of the deliberative nature of the procedure involved. So, for example, in *Reno v. Koray*, 515 U.S. 50, 61 (1995), the Court held that *Chevron* should apply to an interpretation contained in an agency's internal guideline, a non-legislative rule. And in *NationsBank of North Carolina. v. Variable Annuity Life Insurance Co.*, 513 U.S. 251, 256–57, 263 (1995), the Court applied *Chevron* to an agency's decision to grant an entity's application to act as an agent and sell annuities, an informal adjudication. *See also Nat'l R.R. Passenger Corp. v. Boston & Me. Corp.*, 503 U.S. 407, 417 (1992) (applying *Chevron*'s framework to an agency's interpretation made informally); *Fed. Deposit Ins. Corp. v. Philadelphia Gear Corp.*, 476 U.S. 426, 439 (1986) (suggesting that *Chevron* should apply to an agency's longstanding "practice and belief"). But, with time, the formality of the procedure has gained importance.

Beginning in 2000, the Supreme Court decided a trilogy of cases that limited *Chevron*'s application based on the procedures the agency used to make the interpretation. In *Christensen v. Harris County*, 529 U.S. 576 (2000), *United States v. Mead Corp.*, 533 U.S. 218 (2001), and *Barnhart v. Walton*, 535 U.S. 212 (2002), the Court substantially checked *Chevron*'s applicability based, in part, upon the formality of the procedure the agency had used to reach the interpretation being challenged. Let's start with *Christensen*.

With *Christensen*, the Supreme Court began its retreat from a *Chevron* only deference world. At issue in *Christensen* was whether the United States Department of Labor's Wage and Hour Division (the Division) should receive *Chevron* deference for an interpretation the agency expressed in an opinion letter. The defendant in the case, Harris County, had been concerned about the fiscal consequences of having to pay its employees for accrued but unused compensatory time. For this reason, the County wrote to the Division and asked whether the County could require its employees to take, rather than continue to accrue, their unused compensatory time. Responding by letter, the Division told the County that absent an employment agreement to the contrary, the Fair Labor Standards Act of 1938 (FLSA) prohibited an employer from requiring employees to use accrued compensatory time. The County ignored the Division's letter and forbade its employees from accumulating more compensatory time than it deemed reasonable. The employees sued, arguing that the County's policy violated FLSA.

The issue for the Supreme Court was whether the agency's interpretation of FLSA, which was contained in an informal opinion letter, was entitled to *Chevron* deference. *Christensen*, 529 U.S. at 586–87. For the first time since *Chevron* had been decided, the Court directly addressed whether the agency process mattered in the deference analysis; in other words, did a different deference standard apply when an agency acted with less deliberation and process.

The majority found the level of process to be determinative. The majority reasoned that the agency's opinion letter was not entitled to *Chevron* deference because it lacked the "force of law." *Id.* at 587. Agency interpretations have the "force of law" when "Congress has delegated legislative power to the agency and … the agency … exercise[d] that power in promulgating the rule." *Am. Mining Cong. v. Mine Safety & Health Admin.*, 995 F.2d 1106, 1109 (D.C. Cir. 1993) (defining "force of law"). In other words:

> An interpretation will have the force of law when the agency has exercised delegated power, as to both subject matter and format, reflecting congressional intent that such an interpretation is to bind. "Force of law" … merely connotes the binding effect given the kinds of agency interpretations that Congress through its delegations *intends* to bind the courts. And that binding effect (force of law) means simply that the courts may not subject the interpretations to independent judicial review, but rather must accept them subject only to limited review for reasonableness and consistency with the statute. Thus, an interpretation carrying the force of law gets only limited review because by definition it is covered by delegation that contemplates only limited review.

Robert A. Anthony, *Which Agency Interpretations Should Bind Citizens and the Courts?*, 7 YALE J. ON REG. 1, 39 (1990) (footnotes omitted)

According to *Christensen*, procedurally prescribed actions, such as formal adjudication and notice and comment rulemaking, have the "force of law," while less procedurally prescribed actions, such as "opinion letters ... policy statements, agency manuals, and enforcement guidelines ... lack the force of law." *Christensen*, 529 U.S. at 587. The Court explained that "interpretations contained in [informal] formats such as opinion letters are 'entitled to respect' under our decision in *Skidmore*, but only to the extent that those interpretations have the 'power to persuade.'" Thus *Christensen* seemingly divided agency interpretations into two, well-defined categories: those subject to *Chevron* analysis—the "force of law" category—and those subject to *Skidmore* analysis—the no-"force of law" category.

Justice Scalia argued that *Chevron* had replaced *Skidmore*. *Id.* at 589–91 (Scalia, J., concurring in part and concurring in the judgment). Justice Scalia rejected the majority's "force of law" dichotomy, arguing instead that deference should be bestowed whenever an agency's interpretation was "authoritative" and reasonable; process was irrelevant. *Id.* at 589–90.

Justice Breyer dissented in *Christensen* and wrote separately to point out that in his view *Chevron* and *Skidmore* did not provide different deference *standards*. *Christensen*, 529 U.S. at 596–97 (Breyer, J., dissenting). Rather, these cases articulated different *reasons* for affording deference to agency interpretations: *Skidmore* directed courts to pay particular attention to an agency's interpretation of a statute when the agency had "'specialized experience,'" even though the agency's interpretation had not been formulated through an exercise of delegated lawmaking authority. *Id.* at 596 (quoting *Skidmore v. Swift & Co.*, 323 U.S. 134, 139 (1944)). The Court's opinion in *Skidmore* pointed out that the agency's views may possess the "power to persuade," even where those views lack the "power to control." *Skidmore*, 323 U.S. at 140. According to Justice Breyer, the Court in *Chevron* did not significantly change the level of deference due to an agency's interpretation; rather, the Court merely added a new reason for deferring to agency interpretations, namely, that by enacting gaps and ambiguities, Congress had implicitly delegated legal authority to the agency to make those interpretations. *Christensen*, 529 U.S. at 596–97 (Breyer, J., dissenting).

Christensen appeared to present a simple, albeit, formalistic test: courts should apply *Chevron* deference to an agency's interpretation of a statute when an agency used relatively formal procedures (including formal adjudication, formal rulemaking, and notice and comment rulemaking), and courts should apply *Skidmore* deference when an agency used non-legislative procedures (including issuing interpretive rules, policy statements, and ruling letters). This test would have been relatively simple for judges to apply: simply look to the agency action and apply the appropriate analysis, *Chevron* or *Skidmore*.

But alas, nothing remains so simple, and the Court refined *Christensen*'s force of law test a year later in *United States v. Mead Corp.*, 533 U.S. 218 (2001). As you read the case, try to identify how the Court refined *Christensen*'s force of law test.

United States v. Mead Corp.

Supreme Court of the United States
533 U.S. 218 (2001)

◆ JUSTICE SOUTER delivered the opinion of the Court [in which REHNQUIST, C.J., and STEVENS, O'CONNOR, KENNEDY, THOMAS, GINSBURG, and BREYER, JJ., concur].

The question is whether a tariff classification ruling by the United States Customs Service deserves judicial deference. The Federal Circuit rejected Customs's invocation of *Chevron U.S.A. Inc. v. Natural Resources Defense Council, Inc.,* 467 U.S. 837 (1984)....
We agree that a tariff classification has no claim to judicial deference under *Chevron,* there being no indication that Congress intended such a ruling to carry the force of law, but we hold that under *Skidmore v. Swift & Co.,* 323 U.S. 134 (1944), the ruling is eligible to claim respect according to its persuasiveness....

Imports are taxed under the Harmonized Tariff Schedule of the United States (HTSUS). Title 19 U.S.C. § 1500(b) provides that Customs "shall, under rules and regulations prescribed by the Secretary [of the Treasury,] ... fix the final classification and rate of duty applicable to ... merchandise" under the HTSUS. Section 1502(a) provides that

> "[t]he Secretary of the Treasury shall establish and promulgate such rules and regulations not inconsistent with the law (including regulations establishing procedures for the issuance of binding rulings prior to the entry of the merchandise concerned), and may disseminate such information as may be necessary to secure a just, impartial, and uniform appraisement of imported merchandise and the classification and assessment of duties thereon at the various ports of entry."

The Secretary provides for tariff rulings before the entry of goods by regulations authorizing "ruling letters" setting tariff classifications for particular imports. A ruling letter

> "represents the official position of the Customs Service with respect to the particular transaction or issue described therein and is binding on all Customs Service personnel in accordance with the provisions of this section until modified or revoked. In the absence of a change of practice or other modification or revocation which affects the principle of the ruling set forth in the ruling letter, that principle may be cited as authority in the disposition of transactions involving the same circumstances"....

Respondent, the Mead Corporation, imports "day planners," three-ring binders with pages having room for notes of daily schedules and phone numbers and addresses, together with a calendar and suchlike. The tariff schedule on point falls under the HTSUS heading for "[r]egisters, account books, notebooks, order books, receipt books, letter pads, memorandum pads, diaries and similar articles," HTSUS subheading 4820.10, which comprises two subcategories. Items in the first, "[d]iaries, notebooks and address books, bound; memorandum pads, letter pads and similar articles," were subject to a tariff of 4.0% at the time in controversy. Objects in the second, covering "[o]ther" items, were free of duty. HTSUS subheading 4820.10.40. Between 1989 and 1993, Customs repeatedly treated day planners under [one duty rate]. In January 1993, however, Customs changed its position, and issued a Headquarters ruling letter classifying Mead's day planners as "Diaries..., bound" subject to [a different, higher duty rate]. That letter was short on explanation, but after Mead's protest, Customs Headquarters issued a new letter, carefully reasoned but never published, reaching the same conclusion....

Mead [filed suit. T]he United States Court of Appeals for the Federal Circuit.... gave no deference at all to the ruling classifying the Mead day planners and rejected the agency's [interpretation].

We granted certiorari in order to consider the limits of *Chevron* deference owed to administrative practice in applying a statute. We hold that administrative implementation of a particular statutory provision qualifies for *Chevron* deference when it appears that Congress delegated authority to the agency generally to make rules carrying the force of law, and that the agency interpretation claiming deference was promulgated in the exercise of that authority. Delegation of such authority may be shown in a variety of ways, as by an agency's power to engage in adjudication or notice-and-comment rulemaking, or by some other indication of a comparable congressional intent. The Customs ruling at issue here fails to qualify, although the possibility that it deserves some deference under *Skidmore* leads us to vacate and remand.

When Congress has "explicitly left a gap for an agency to fill, there is an express delegation of authority to the agency to elucidate a specific provision of the statute by regulation," *Chevron*, and any ensuing regulation is binding in the courts unless procedurally defective, arbitrary or capricious in substance, or manifestly contrary to the statute. But whether or not they enjoy any express delegation of authority on a particular question, agencies charged with applying a statute necessarily make all sorts of interpretive choices, and while not all of those choices bind judges to follow them, they certainly may influence courts facing questions the agencies have already answered. "[T]he well-reasoned views of the agencies implementing a statute 'constitute a body of experience and informed judgment to which courts and litigants may properly resort for guidance,'" and "[w]e have long recognized that considerable weight should be accorded to an executive department's construction of a statutory scheme it is entrusted to administer...."

Since 1984, we have identified a category of interpretive choices distinguished by an additional reason for judicial deference. This Court in *Chevron* recognized that Congress not only engages in express delegation of specific interpretive authority, but that "[s]ometimes the legislative delegation to an agency on a particular question is implicit." Congress, that is, may not have expressly delegated authority or responsibility to implement a particular provision or fill a particular gap. Yet it can still be apparent from the agency's generally conferred authority and other statutory circumstances that Congress would expect the agency to be able to speak with the force of law when it addresses ambiguity in the statute or fills a space in the enacted law, even one about which "Congress did not actually have an intent" as to a particular result....

We have recognized a very good indicator of delegation meriting *Chevron* treatment in express congressional authorizations to engage in the process of rulemaking or adjudication that produces regulations or rulings for which deference is claimed. See, *e.g., EEOC v. Arabian American Oil Co.,* 499 U.S. 244, 257 (1991) (no *Chevron* deference to agency guideline where congressional delegation did not include the power to "'promulgate rules or regulations'"); see also *Christensen v. Harris County,* 529 U.S. 576, 596–597 (2000) (Breyer, J., dissenting) (where it is in doubt that Congress actually intended to delegate particular interpretive authority to an agency, *Chevron* is "inapplicable"). It is fair to assume generally that Congress contemplates administrative action with the effect of law when it provides for a relatively formal administrative procedure tending to foster the fairness and deliberation that should underlie a pronouncement of such force. Thus, the overwhelming number of our cases applying *Chevron* deference have reviewed the fruits of notice-and-comment rulemaking or formal adjudication. That said, and as significant as notice-and-comment is in pointing to *Chevron* authority, the want of that procedure here does not decide the case, for we have sometimes found reasons for *Chevron* deference even when no such administrative formality was required and none was afforded, see, *e.g., NationsBank of N.C., N.A. v. Variable Annuity Life Ins. Co.,* 513 U.S. 251, 256–257, 263, (1995). The fact that the tariff classification here was not a product of such formal process does not alone, therefore, bar the application of *Chevron.*

There are, nonetheless, ample reasons to deny *Chevron* deference here.... On the face of the statute, to begin with, the terms of the congressional delegation give no indication that Congress meant to delegate authority to Customs to issue classification rulings with the force of law....

It is difficult ... to see in the agency practice itself any indication that Customs ever set out with a lawmaking pretense in mind when it undertook to make classifications like these. Customs does not generally engage in notice-and-comment practice when issuing them, and their treatment by the agency makes it clear that a letter's binding character as a ruling stops short of third parties; Customs has regarded a classification as conclusive only as between itself and the importer to whom it was issued and even then only until Customs has given advance notice of intended change. Other importers are in fact warned against assuming any right of detrimental reliance.

Indeed, to claim that classifications have legal force is to ignore the reality that 46 different Customs offices issue 10,000 to 15,000 of them each year.... Any suggestion that rulings intended to have the force of law are being churned out at a rate of 10,000 a year at an agency's 46 scattered offices is simply self-refuting. Although the circumstances are less startling here, with a Headquarters letter in issue, none of the relevant statutes recognizes this category of rulings as separate or different from others; there is thus no indication that a more potent delegation might have been understood as going to Headquarters even when Headquarters provides developed reasoning, as it did in this instance....

In sum, classification rulings are best treated like "interpretations contained in policy statements, agency manuals, and enforcement guidelines." *Christensen*, 529 U.S., at 587. They are beyond the *Chevron* pale.

To agree with the Court of Appeals that Customs ruling letters do not fall within *Chevron* is not, however, to place them outside the pale of any deference whatever. *Chevron* did nothing to eliminate *Skidmore*'s holding that an agency's interpretation may merit some deference whatever its form, given the "specialized experience and broader investigations and information" available to the agency, and given the value of uniformity in its administrative and judicial understandings of what a national law requires.

Underlying the position we take here, like the position expressed by Justice Scalia in dissent, is a choice about the best way to deal with an inescapable feature of the body of congressional legislation authorizing administrative action. That feature is the great variety of ways in which the laws invest the Government's administrative arms with discretion, and with procedures for exercising it, in giving meaning to Acts of Congress. Implementation of a statute may occur in formal adjudication or the choice to defend against judicial challenge; it may occur in a central board or office or in dozens of enforcement agencies dotted across the country; its institutional lawmaking may be confined to the resolution of minute detail or extend to legislative rulemaking on matters intentionally left by Congress to be worked out at the agency level.

Although we all accept the position that the Judiciary should defer to at least some of this multifarious administrative action, we have to decide how to take account of the great range of its variety. If the primary objective is to simplify the judicial process of giving or withholding deference, then the diversity of statutes authorizing discretionary administrative action must be declared irrelevant or minimized. If, on the other hand, it is simply implausible that Congress intended such a broad range of statutory authority to produce only two varieties of administrative action, demanding either *Chevron* deference or none at all, then the breadth of the spectrum of possible agency action must be taken into account. Justice Scalia's first priority over the years has been to limit and simplify. The Court's choice has been to tailor deference to variety....

The Court ... said nothing in *Chevron* to eliminate *Skidmore*'s recognition of various justifications for deference depending on statutory circumstances and agency action; *Chevron* was simply a case recognizing that even without express authority to fill a specific statutory gap, circumstances pointing to implicit congressional delegation present a particularly insistent call for deference....

Since the *Skidmore* assessment called for here ought to be made in the first instance by the Court of Appeals..., we ... vacate the judgment and remand the case for further proceedings consistent with this opinion.

◆ JUSTICE SCALIA dissenting.

Today's opinion makes an avulsive change in judicial review of federal administrative action. Whereas previously a reasonable agency application of an ambiguous statutory provision had to be sustained so long as it represented the agency's authoritative interpretation, henceforth such an application can be set aside unless "it appears that Congress delegated authority to the agency generally to make rules carrying the force of law," as by giving an agency "power to engage in adjudication or notice-and-comment rulemaking, or ... some other (procedure) indicate(ng) comparable congressional intent," and "the agency interpretation claiming deference was promulgated in the exercise of that authority."[1] What was previously a general presumption of authority in agencies to resolve ambiguity in the statutes they have been authorized to enforce has been changed to a presumption of no such authority, which must be overcome by affirmative legislative intent to the contrary. And whereas previously, when agency authority to resolve ambiguity did not exist the court was free to give the statute what it considered the best interpretation, henceforth the court must supposedly give the agency view some indeterminate amount of so-called *Skidmore* deference. We will be sorting out the consequences of the *Mead* doctrine, which has today replaced the *Chevron* doctrine for years to come. I would adhere to our established jurisprudence, defer to the reasonable interpretation the Customs Service has given to the statute it is charged with enforcing, and reverse the judgment of the Court of Appeals....

While the Court disclaims any hard-and-fast rule for determining the existence of discretion-conferring intent, it asserts that "a very good indicator (is) express congressional authorizations to engage in the process of rulemaking or adjudication that produces regulations or rulings for which deference is claimed." Only when agencies act through "adjudication(,) notice-and-comment rulemaking, or ... some other (procedure) indicate(ng) comparable congressional intent (whatever that means)" is *Chevron* deference applicable — because these "relatively formal administrative procedure(s) (designed) to foster ... fairness and deliberation" bespeak (according to the Court) congressional willingness to have the agency, rather than the courts, resolve statutory ambiguities. Once it is determined that *Chevron* deference is not in order, the uncertainty is not at an end — and indeed is just beginning. Litigants cannot then assume that the statutory question is one for the courts to determine, according to traditional interpretive principles and by their own judicial lights. No, the Court now resurrects, in full force, the pre-*Chevron* doctrine of *Skidmore* deference, whereby "(t)he fair measure of deference to an agency administering its own statute ... var(ies) with circumstances," including "the degree of the agency's care, its consistency, formality, and relative expertise, and ... the persuasiveness of the agency's position." The Court has largely replaced *Chevron*, in other words, with that test most beloved by a court unwilling to be held to rules (and most feared by litigants who want to know what to expect): th' ol' "totality of the circumstances" test.

The doctrine of *Chevron* — that all *authoritative* agency interpretations of statutes they are charged with administering deserve deference — was rooted in a legal presumption of congressional intent, important to the division of powers between the

---

1. It is not entirely clear whether the formulation newly minted by the Court today extends to both formal and informal adjudication, or simply the former.

Second and Third Branches. When, *Chevron* said, Congress leaves an ambiguity in a statute that is to be administered by an executive agency, it is presumed that Congress meant to give the agency discretion, within the limits of reasonable interpretation, as to how the ambiguity is to be resolved. By committing enforcement of the statute to an agency rather than the courts, Congress committed its initial and primary interpretation to that branch as well....

The basis in principle for today's new doctrine can be described as follows: The background rule is that ambiguity in legislative instructions to agencies is to be resolved not by the agencies but by the judges. Specific congressional intent to depart from this rule must be found—and while there is no single touchstone for such intent it can generally be found when Congress has authorized the agency to act through (what the Court says is) relatively formal procedures such as informal rule-making and formal (and informal?) adjudication, and when the agency in fact employs such procedures.... But ... the Court's principal criterion of congressional intent to supplant its background rule seems to me quite implausible. There is no necessary connection between the formality of procedure and the power of the entity administering the procedure to resolve authoritatively questions of law. The most formal of the procedures the Court refers to—formal adjudication—is modeled after the process used in trial courts, which of course are not generally accorded deference on questions of law. The purpose of such a procedure is to produce a closed record for determination and review of the facts—which implies nothing about the power of the agency subjected to the procedure to resolve authoritatively questions of law....

The principal effect [of today's decision] will be protracted confusion.... [The majority] tells us, the absence of notice-and-comment rulemaking ... is not enough to decide the question of *Chevron* deference, "for we have sometimes found reasons for *Chevron* deference even when no such administrative formality was required and none was afforded." The opinion then goes on to consider a grab bag of other factors—including the factor that used to be the sole criterion for *Chevron* deference: whether the interpretation represented the *authoritative* position of the agency. It is hard to know what the lower courts are to make of today's guidance....

[F]inally, the majority's approach compounds the confusion it creates by breathing new life into the anachronism of *Skidmore*, which sets forth a sliding scale of deference owed an agency's interpretation of a statute that is dependent "upon the thoroughness evident in [the agency's] consideration, the validity of its reasoning, its consistency with earlier and later pronouncements, and all those factors which give it power to persuade, if lacking power to control"; in this way, the appropriate measure of deference will be accorded the "body of experience and informed judgment" that such interpretations often embody. Justice Jackson's eloquence notwithstanding, the rule of *Skidmore* deference is an empty truism and a trifling statement of the obvious: A judge should take into account the well-considered views of expert observers.

It was possible to live with the indeterminacy of *Skidmore* deference in earlier times. But in an era when federal statutory law administered by federal agencies is pervasive, and when the ambiguities (intended or unintended) that those statutes contain are innumerable, totality-of-the-circumstances *Skidmore* deference is a recipe for uncertainty, unpredictability, and endless litigation. To condemn a vast body of agency action to that regime ... is irresponsible....

To decide the present case, I would adhere to the original formulation of *Chevron*.... Any resolution of [statutory] ambiguity by the administering agency that is authoritative—that represents the official position of the agency—must be accepted by the courts if it is reasonable....

There is no doubt that the Customs Service's interpretation represents the authoritative view of the agency.... There is also no doubt that the Customs Service's interpretation is a reasonable one....

For the reasons stated, I respectfully dissent from the Court's judgment. I would uphold the Customs Service's [interpretation].... I dissent even more vigorously from the reasoning that produces the Court's judgment, and that makes today's decision one of the most significant opinions ever rendered by the Court dealing with the judicial review of administrative action. Its consequences will be enormous, and almost uniformly bad.

* * *

Points for Discussion

1. *Statutory Language*: What was the language at issue? What did each party want that language to mean? Ultimately this Court did not adopt a meaning in this case but instead remanded to the lower courts to determine whether to defer to Custom's interpretation.

2. *Theories*: The court was determining the correct deference standard and not determining the meaning of the language; hence, no theory of interpretation is apparent.

3. *Agency Action*: What kind of agency action was the Court examining: adjudication or rulemaking? Did the agency use formal or informal procedures to issue its interpretation? Why does the answer to that question matter now?

4. *Comparable Congressional Intent*: In *Christensen*, the Court held that an agency interpretation may be entitled to *Chevron* if the agency uses force of law procedures. According to the *Mead* majority, in addition to using force of law procedures, when might agency interpretations receive *Chevron* deference? If the interpretation is not deserving of *Chevron*, might another deference standard apply? What did *Mead* add to *Christensen*'s rule?

5. *Beyond Chevron's Pale*: Why were the tariff classifications in this case not entitled to *Chevron* analysis? Why were they entitled to *Skidmore* analysis?

6. *Authoritative Interpretations*: Justice Scalia described "the original formulation of *Chevron*" as follows: "Any resolution of [statutory] ambiguity by the administering agency that is authoritative—that represents the official position of the agency—must be accepted by the courts if it is reasonable." Is this an accurate articulation?

7. *Mead Doctrine*: Justice Scalia said, "We will be sorting out the consequences of the *Mead* doctrine, which today replaced the *Chevron* doctrine, for years to come." What did he mean? Justice Scalia disagreed with the majority that *Skidmore* survived *Chevron*. Hence, he would either apply *Chevron*'s analysis or review the issue *de novo*.

8. *Echoing Breyer*: In *Mead*, Justice Souter noted, "we have identified a category of interpretive choices distinguished by an additional reason for judicial deference." Notice how this statement echoes this language from Justice Breyer's dissent in *Christensen*: "*Chevron* made no relevant change [to *Skidmore*]. It simply focused upon an additional, separate legal reason for deferring to certain agency determinations, namely, that Congress had delegated to the agency the legal authority to make those determinations." *Christensen v. Harris Cty.*, 529 U.S. 576, 597 (2000).

9. *Comparable Indications of Congressional Intent*: Prior to *Mead*, the test was bright-lined: *Chevron* applied when the agency acted with more procedure, and *Skidmore* applied when the agency acted with less procedure. Now, the bright-line was blurring. The Court in *Mead* stated, without elaborating, that some agency actions might qualify for *Chevron* deference even though the agency used less formal procedures. Exactly what types of "other indications" would be sufficient to trigger *Chevron* was not readily apparent from *Mead* alone, in part, because the Court did not apply *Chevron*. However, in the following year, the Court decided *Barnhart v. Walton*, 535 U.S. 212 (2002), which addressed this question. In *Barnhart*, the Court said that the other indications sufficient to trigger *Chevron* analysis included the following: (1) the interstitial nature of the legal question, (2) the relevance of the agency's expertise, (3) the importance of the question to administration of the statute, (4) the complexity of the statutory scheme, and (5) the careful consideration the agency had given the question over a long period of time. You will recall that *Skidmore* deference is earned by agency thoroughness, reasoning validity, and interpretive consistency. The fifth *Barnhart* factor is identical to the third *Skidmore* factor.

* * *

In summary, *Chevron* applies only when an agency (1) interprets a statute (2) that the agency administers (3) *while using force of law procedures or while using non-force of law procedures if Congress otherwise indicates its intent that the agency interpret the statute.*

4. Can the Agency Interpret the Statute?

But it is not enough that an agency interpret a statute that the agency administers while using force of law procedures. In the midst of deciding the *Christensen/Mead/Barnhart* trilogy, the Supreme Court issued another trilogy of cases in this area that only added to the complexity. In *Chevron*, the Court rationalized deference to an agency's interpretation by suggesting that when Congress enacts gaps and creates ambiguities, Congress *implicitly* intends to delegate interpretive authority to the agency.

But in four cases, *Food and Drug Administration v. Brown & Williamson Tobacco Corp.*, 529 U.S. 120 (2000), *Gonzales v. Oregon*, 546 U.S. 243 (2006), *Hamdan v. Rumsfeld*, 548 U.S. 557 (2006), and, most recently, *King v. Burwell*, 135 S. Ct. 2480 (2015), the Court rejected, or at least narrowed, this rationale for some agency interpretations. In each of these cases, the Court reasoned that in some instances, despite ambiguity, Congress does not intend to delegate rulemaking authority to the agency at all. As the Court explained:

> Deference under *Chevron* to an agency's construction of a statute that it administers is premised on the theory that a statute's ambiguity constitutes an implicit delegation from Congress to the agency to fill in the statutory gaps. In extraordinary cases, however, there may be reason to hesitate before concluding that Congress has intended such an implicit delegation.

Brown & Williamson, 529 U.S. at 159 (internal citations omitted).

First, in *Brown & Williamson*, the majority rejected the Food and Drug Administration's (FDA) decision to regulate tobacco. *Brown & Williamson* is interesting historically. The FDA knew for years that tobacco was deadly. The FDA was authorized to regulate "drugs" and "devices," but chose not to regulate tobacco because it feared that Congress would reject its action. The tobacco companies had an extremely powerful lobby in Washington. Moreover, Presidents Reagan and Bush would not have supported the FDA's attempt to regulate tobacco. In 1993, Bill Clinton assumed the office of president. President Clinton was anti-tobacco. He appointed Dr. David Kessler to head the FDA and indicated a willingness to support the FDA's attempt to regulate tobacco. Armed with Clinton's support, the FDA interpreted cigarettes and tobacco products to be "drugs." In response, the tobacco companies sued.

Under the relevant statute, the FDA was authorized to regulate "drugs," "devices," and "combination products." *Brown & Williamson*, 529 U.S. at 126 (citing §§ 21 U.S.C. § 321(g)–(h) (1994 and Supp. III)). The statute defined these terms as "articles ... intended to affect the structure or any function of the body." *Id.* (quoting 21 U.S.C. § 321 (g)(1)(C)). The FDA interpreted this language as allowing it to regulate tobacco and cigarettes.

Despite the fact that the language of the statute alone was broad enough to support the agency's interpretation, the majority concluded, after applying *Chevron*'s first step "that Congress ha[d] directly spoken to the issue here and precluded the FDA's jurisdiction to regulate tobacco products." The majority supported its holding by noting that Congress had (1) created a distinct regulatory scheme for tobacco products in subsequent legislation, (2) squarely rejected proposals to give the FDA jurisdiction over tobacco, and (3) acted repeatedly to preclude other agencies from exercising authority in this area. The majority suggested that *Brown & Williamson* was "hardly an ordinary case," because of the importance of the tobacco industry to the American economy and Congress oversight of this area. Hence, while Congress may not have spoken to the precise issue when enacting the relevant statute, Congress had subsequently spoken broadly enough on related questions to prevent the agency from acting at all. Thus, the Court resolved *Brown & Williamson* at *Chevron* step one. Because the Court resolved the issue at step one, the Court never reached step two.

The Supreme Court would return to this "too important for the national economy" limitation on agency delegation fifteen years later in *King v. Burwell,* 135 S. Ct. 2480, 2489 (2015); however, before *King,* the Court refused to apply *Chevron* in two other cases.

Six years after *Brown & Williamson,* the Court in *Gonzales v. Oregon,* 546 U.S. 243 (2006), again held that Congress had not delegated interpretive authority to an agency despite an obvious gap in the statute. The issue before the Court in *Gonzales* was "whether the Controlled Substances Act allowed the United States Attorney General to prohibit doctors from prescribing regulated drugs for use in physician-assisted suicide, notwithstanding a state law permitting the procedure." *Id* at 248. The justices disagreed over which deference standard to apply to the Attorney General's interpretive rule, which interpreted a regulation enacted pursuant to notice and comment procedures. Typically, *Auer* deference would be appropriate; however, because the first regulation simply parroted the language in the statute, the majority refused to apply *Auer* deference.

Additionally, the majority refused to apply *Chevron* to the first regulation, promulgated through force of law procedures (notice and comment rulemaking). The majority reasoned that because Congress did not intend for the Attorney General to regulate in this area, Congress had not delegated interpretive power to the agency: "The idea that Congress gave the Attorney General such broad and unusual authority through an implicit delegation in the [Controlled Substances Act] registration provision is not sustainable." *Id.* at 267. However, the majority in *Gonzales* applied *Skidmore* analysis to the Attorney General's interpretation. Applying *Skidmore,* the majority reasoned that this issue was critically important to the nation. The majority was for this reason skeptical of what it viewed as the Attorney General's attempt to backdoor an overly broad interpretation into the statute. Ultimately, the majority rejected the Attorney General's interpretation under *Skidmore,* affording the Attorney General's interpretation no deference at all.

The next case refusing to apply *Chevron* to an executive interpretation was *Hamdan v. Rumsfeld.* 548 U.S. 557 (2006). In *Hamdan,* the Court rejected an interpretation contained in Executive Order 57,833, which former President George W. Bush issued to create military commissions to prosecute illegal "enemy combatants." 548 U.S. at 567. Executive Order 57,833: "Detention, Treatment, and Trial of Certain Non-Citizens in the War Against Terrorism" located at 66 Fed. Reg. 57,833 (Nov. 13, 2001). The facts are complex and not worth explaining here. The issue for the Court was whether the procedures in the military tribunals were "the same" as the procedures provided in traditional court martials. *See Hamdan,* 548 U.S. at 567 (citing 10 U.S.C. §§ 801 *et seq.*). The relevant statute explicitly provided that the procedures for the two proceedings should be the same, so far as "practicable." *Id.* at 620 (" 'The procedure, including modes of proof, in cases before courts-martial, courts of inquiry, military commissions, and other military tribunals may be prescribed by the President by regulations which shall, so far as he considers practicable, apply the principles of law and the rules of evidence generally recognized in the trial of criminal cases in the United States district courts, but which may not be contrary to or inconsistent with this chapter.'" *Id.* (quoting Article 36(a) of the Uniform Code of Military Justice, 10 U.S.C. §§ 801 *et seq.*)). Even though the statutory language provided the President with broad flexibility to determine what procedures were "practicable" and when uniformity was required, the majority applied neither *Chevron* nor *Skidmore* deference to resolve the issue. In a related case, *Hamdi v. Rumsfeld*, 542 U.S. 507 (2004), the Court similarly refused to apply either *Chevron* or *Skidmore* analysis to evaluate the correctness of the President's interpretation of another section of Congress's joint resolution.

Most recently, in the case below, the Supreme Court again refused to apply *Chevron* or *Skidmore* analysis. Instead, the majority returned to the "too important to the national economy" rationale from *Brown & Williamson*. Recall that in *Brown and Williamson*, the majority resolved the issue at *Chevron* step one: Congress had spoken precisely enough to preclude review. Does the majority resolve *King* in the same way?

King v. Burwell

Supreme Court of the United States
135 S. Ct. 2480 (2015)

◆ CHIEF JUSTICE ROBERTS, delivered the opinion of the Court [in which KENNEDY, GINSBURG, BREYER, SOTOMAYOR, and KAGAN, JJ., concur].

... The Patient Protection and Affordable Care Act ... grew out of a long history of failed health insurance reform. In the 1990s, several States began experimenting with ways to expand people's access to coverage. One common approach was to impose a pair of insurance market regulations — a "guaranteed issue" requirement, which barred insurers from denying coverage to any person because of his health, and a "community rating" requirement, which barred insurers from charging a person higher premiums for the same reason. Together, those requirements were designed to ensure that anyone who wanted to buy health insurance could do so.

The guaranteed issue and community rating requirements achieved that goal, but they had an unintended consequence: They encouraged people to wait until they got sick to buy insurance. Why buy insurance coverage when you are healthy, if you can buy the same coverage for the same price when you become ill? This consequence — known as "adverse selection" — led to a second: Insurers were forced to increase premiums to account for the fact that, more and more, it was the sick rather than the healthy who were buying insurance. And that consequence fed back into the first: As the cost of insurance rose, even more people waited until they became ill to buy it.

This led to an economic "death spiral." As premiums rose higher and higher, and the number of people buying insurance sank lower and lower, insurers began to leave the market entirely. As a result, the number of people without insurance increased dramatically.

This cycle happened repeatedly during the 1990s.... In 1996, Massachusetts adopted the guaranteed issue and community rating requirements and experienced similar results. But in 2006, Massachusetts added two more reforms: The Commonwealth required individuals to buy insurance or pay a penalty, and it gave tax credits to certain individuals to ensure that they could afford the insurance they were required to buy. The combination of these three reforms—insurance market regulations, a coverage mandate, and tax credits—reduced the uninsured rate in Massachusetts to 2.6 percent, by far the lowest in the Nation.

The Affordable Care Act adopts a version of the three key reforms that made the Massachusetts system successful. First, the Act adopts the guaranteed issue and community rating requirements.... Second, the Act generally requires individuals to maintain health insurance coverage or make a payment to the IRS.... Third, the Act seeks to make insurance more affordable by giving refundable tax credits to individuals with household incomes between 100 percent and 400 percent of the federal poverty line. Individuals who meet the Act's requirements may purchase insurance with the tax credits, which are provided in advance directly to the individual's insurer....

In addition to those three reforms, the Act requires the creation of an "Exchange" in each State where people can shop for insurance, usually online. An Exchange may be created in one of two ways. First, the Act provides that "[e]ach State shall ... establish an ... Exchange ... for the State." Second, if a State ... chooses not to establish its own Exchange, the Act provides that the Secretary of Health and Human Services "shall ... establish and operate such Exchange within the State." The issue in this case is whether the Act's tax credits are available in States that have a Federal Exchange rather than a State Exchange. The Act initially provides that tax credits "shall be allowed" for any "applicable taxpayer." The Act then provides that the amount of the tax credit depends in part on whether the taxpayer has enrolled in an insurance plan through "an Exchange *established by the State* under section 1311 of the Patient Protection and Affordable Care Act (hereinafter 42 U.S.C. § 18031)." (emphasis added).

The IRS addressed the availability of tax credits by promulgating a rule that made them available on both State and Federal Exchanges. As relevant here, the IRS Rule* provides that a taxpayer is eligible for a tax credit if he enrolled in an insurance plan through "an Exchange," which is defined as "an Exchange serving the individual market ... regardless of whether the Exchange is established and operated by a State ... or by HHS". At this point, 16 States and the District of Columbia have established their own Exchanges; the other 34 States have elected to have HHS do so.

---

  * Editor's footnote: Although Justice Roberts labels the regulation as an "IRS rule," he is mistaken. The Treasury actually promulgated it.

Petitioners are four individuals who live in Virginia, which has a Federal Exchange. They do not wish to purchase health insurance. In their view, Virginia's Exchange does not qualify as "an Exchange established by the State under (42 U.S.C. § 18031)," so they should not receive any tax credits. That would make the cost of buying insurance more than eight percent of their income, which would exempt them from the Act's coverage requirement. Under the IRS Rule, however, Virginia's Exchange *would* qualify as "an Exchange established by the State under (42 U.S.C. § 18031)," so petitioners would receive tax credits. That would make the cost of buying insurance *less* than eight percent of petitioners' income, which would subject them to the Act's coverage requirement. The IRS Rule therefore requires petitioners to either buy health insurance they do not want, or make a payment to the IRS. Petitioners challenged the IRS Rule in Federal District Court. The District Court dismissed the suit, holding that the Act unambiguously made tax credits available to individuals enrolled through a Federal Exchange.... The Fourth Circuit [affirmed]....

The Affordable Care Act ... Section 36B of the Internal Revenue Code ... provides: "In the case of an applicable taxpayer, there shall be allowed as a credit against the tax imposed by this subtitle ... an amount equal to the premium assistance credit amount." Section 36B then defines the term "premium assistance credit amount" as "the sum of the *premium assistance amounts* determined under paragraph (2) with respect to all *coverage months* of the taxpayer occurring during the taxable year." (emphasis added). Section 36B goes on to define the two italicized terms—"premium assistance amount" and "coverage month"—in part by referring to an insurance plan that is enrolled in through "an Exchange established by the State under (42 U.S.C. § 18031)."

The parties dispute whether Section 36B authorizes tax credits for individuals who enroll in an insurance plan through a Federal Exchange. Petitioners argue that a Federal Exchange is not "an Exchange established by the State under (42 U.S.C. § 18031)," and that the IRS Rule therefore contradicts Section 36B. The Government responds that the IRS Rule is lawful because the phrase "an Exchange established by the State under (42 U.S.C. § 18031)" should be read to include Federal Exchanges.

When analyzing an agency's interpretation of a statute, we often apply the two-step framework announced in *Chevron*. Under that framework, we ask whether the statute is ambiguous and, if so, whether the agency's interpretation is reasonable. This approach "is premised on the theory that a statute's ambiguity constitutes an implicit delegation from Congress to the agency to fill in the statutory gaps." *FDA v. Brown & Williamson Tobacco Corp.*, 529 U. S. 120, 159 (2000). "In extraordinary cases, however, there may be reason to hesitate before concluding that Congress has intended such an implicit delegation." *Ibid.*

This is one of those cases. The tax credits are among the Act's key reforms, involving billions of dollars in spending each year and affecting the price of health insurance for millions of people. Whether those credits are available on Federal Exchanges is thus a question of deep "economic and political significance" that is central to this statutory scheme; had Congress wished to assign that question to an agency, it surely would have done so expressly. It is especially unlikely that Congress would have delegated this decision to the IRS, which has no expertise in crafting health insurance policy of this sort. This is not a case for the IRS.

It is instead our task to determine the correct reading of Section 36B. If the statutory language is plain, we must enforce it according to its terms. But oftentimes the "meaning—or ambiguity—of certain words or phrases may only become evident when placed in context." So when deciding whether the language is plain, we must read the words "in their context and with a view to their place in the overall statutory scheme." Our duty, after all, is "to construe statutes, not isolated provisions."

We begin with the text of Section 36B. As relevant here, Section 36B allows an individual to receive tax credits only if the individual enrolls in an insurance plan through "an Exchange established by the State under (42 U.S.C. § 18031)." ...

[W]e must determine whether a Federal Exchange is "established by the State" for purposes of Section 36B. At the outset, it might seem that a Federal Exchange cannot fulfill this requirement. After all, the Act defines "State" to mean "each of the 50 States and the District of Columbia"—a definition that does not include the Federal Government. But when read in context, "with a view to [its] place in the overall statutory scheme," the meaning of the phrase "established by the State" is not so clear.

After telling each State to establish an Exchange, Section 18031 provides that all Exchanges "shall make available qualified health plans to qualified individuals." Section 18032 then defines the term "qualified individual" in part as an individual who "resides in the State that established the Exchange." And that's a problem: If we give the phrase "the State that established the Exchange" its most natural meaning, there would be *no* "qualified individuals" on Federal Exchanges. But the Act clearly contemplates that there will be qualified individuals on *every* Exchange....

[This and other] provisions suggest that the Act may not always use the phrase "established by the State" in its most natural sense. Thus, the meaning of that phrase may not be as clear as it appears when read out of context....

The upshot of all this is that the phrase "an Exchange established by the State under (42 U.S.C. § 18031)" is properly viewed as ambiguous. The phrase may be limited in its reach to State Exchanges. But it is also possible that the phrase refers to *all* Exchanges—both State and Federal—at least for purposes of the tax credits....

Petitioners and the dissent respond that the words "established by the State" would be unnecessary if Congress meant to extend tax credits to both State and Federal Exchanges. But "our preference for avoiding surplusage constructions is not absolute." And specifically with respect to this Act, rigorous application of the canon does not seem a particularly useful guide to a fair construction of the statute.

The Affordable Care Act contains more than a few examples of inartful drafting. (To cite just one, the Act creates three separate Section 1563s.) Several features of the

Act's passage contributed to that unfortunate reality. Congress wrote key parts of the Act behind closed doors, rather than through "the traditional legislative process." And Congress passed much of the Act using a complicated budgetary procedure known as "reconciliation," which limited opportunities for debate and amendment, and bypassed the Senate's normal 60-vote filibuster requirement. As a result, the Act does not reflect the type of care and deliberation that one might expect of such significant legislation. Cf. Frankfurter, *Some Reflections on the Reading of Statutes*, 47 Colum. L. Rev. 527, 545 (1947) (describing a cartoon "in which a senator tells his colleagues 'I admit this new bill is too complicated to understand. We'll just have to pass it to find out what it means.'").

Anyway, we "must do our best, bearing in mind the fundamental canon of statutory construction that the words of a statute must be read in their context and with a view to their place in the overall statutory scheme." After reading Section36B along with other related provisions in the Act, we cannot conclude that the phrase "an Exchange established by the State under (Section 18031)" is unambiguous.

Given that the text is ambiguous, we must turn to the broader structure of the Act to determine the meaning of Section 36B. "A provision that may seem ambiguous in isolation is often clarified by the remainder of the statutory scheme ... because only one of the permissible meanings produces a substantive effect that is compatible with the rest of the law." Here, the statutory scheme compels us to reject petitioners' interpretation because it would destabilize the individual insurance market in any State with a Federal Exchange, and likely create the very "death spirals" that Congress designed the Act to avoid.

As discussed above, Congress based the Affordable Care Act on three major reforms: first, the guaranteed issue and community rating requirements; second, a requirement that individuals maintain health insurance coverage or make a payment to the IRS; and third, the tax credits for individuals with household incomes between 100 percent and 400 percent of the federal poverty line. In a State that establishes its own Exchange, these three reforms work together to expand insurance coverage. The guaranteed issue and community rating requirements ensure that anyone can buy insurance; the coverage requirement creates an incentive for people to do so before they get sick; and the tax credits—it is hoped—make insurance more affordable. Together, those reforms "minimize ... adverse selection and broaden the health insurance risk pool to include healthy individuals, which will lower health insurance premiums."

Under petitioners' reading, however, the Act would operate quite differently in a State with a Federal Exchange. As they see it, one of the Act's three major reforms—the tax credits—would not apply. And a second major reform—the coverage requirement—would not apply in a meaningful way.... [T]he coverage requirement applies only when the cost of buying health insurance (minus the amount of the tax credits) is less than eight percent of an individual's income. So without the tax credits, the coverage requirement would apply to fewer individuals. And it would be a *lot* fewer....

The combination of no tax credits and an ineffective coverage requirement could well push a State's individual insurance market into a death spiral.... It is implausible that Congress meant the Act to operate in this manner. Congress made the guaranteed issue and community rating requirements applicable in every State in the Nation. But those requirements only work when combined with the coverage requirement and the tax credits. So it stands to reason that Congress meant for those provisions to apply in every State as well....

Petitioners' arguments about the plain meaning of Section 36B are strong. But while the meaning of the phrase "an Exchange established by the State under (42 U.S.C. § 18031)" may seem plain "when viewed in isolation," such a reading turns out to be "untenable in light of (the statute) as a whole." In this instance, the context and structure of the Act compel us to depart from what would otherwise be the most natural reading of the pertinent statutory phrase....

In a democracy, the power to make the law rests with those chosen by the people. Our role is more confined—"to say what the law is." *Marbury v. Madison*, 1 Cranch 137, 177 (1803). That is easier in some cases than in others. But in every case we must respect the role of the Legislature, and take care not to undo what it has done. A fair reading of legislation demands a fair understanding of the legislative plan. Congress passed the Affordable Care Act to improve health insurance markets, not to destroy them. If at all possible, we must interpret the Act in a way that is consistent with the former, and avoids the latter. Section 36B can fairly be read consistent with what we see as Congress's plan, and that is the reading we adopt....

♦ SCALIA, J., filed a dissenting opinion, in which THOMAS and ALITO, JJ., joined.

The Court holds that when the Patient Protection and Affordable Care Act says "Exchange established by the State" it means "Exchange established by the State or the Federal Government." That is of course quite absurd....

This case requires us to decide whether someone who buys insurance on an Exchange established by the Secretary gets tax credits. You would think the answer would be obvious—so obvious there would hardly be a need for the Supreme Court to hear a case about it. In order to receive any money under § 36B, an individual must enroll in an insurance plan through an "Exchange established by the State." The Secretary of Health and Human Services is not a State. So an Exchange established by the Secretary is not an Exchange established by the State—which means people who buy health insurance through such an Exchange get no money under § 36B.

Words no longer have meaning if an Exchange that is *not* established by a State is "established by the State." It is hard to come up with a clearer way to limit tax credits to state Exchanges than to use the words "established by the State." And it is hard to come up with a reason to include the words "by the State" other than the purpose of limiting credits to state Exchanges. "(T)he plain, obvious, and rational meaning of a statute is always to be preferred to any curious, narrow, hidden sense that nothing but the exigency of a hard case and the ingenuity and study of an acute and powerful intellect would discover." Under all the usual rules of interpretation, in short, the

Government should lose this case. But normal rules of interpretation seem always to yield to the overriding principle of the present Court: The Affordable Care Act must be saved.

... The Court claims that "the context and structure of the Act compel (it) to depart from what would otherwise be the most natural reading of the pertinent statutory phrase."

I wholeheartedly agree with the Court that sound interpretation requires paying attention to the whole law, not homing in on isolated words or even isolated sections. Context always matters. Let us not forget, however, *why* context matters: It is a tool for understanding the terms of the law, not an excuse for rewriting them....

... [T]here are *only* two ways to set up an Exchange in a State: establishment by a State and establishment by the Secretary. So saying that an Exchange established by the Federal Government is "established by the State" goes beyond giving words bizarre meanings; it leaves the limiting phrase "by the State" with no operative effect at all. That is a stark violation of the elementary principle that requires an interpreter "to give effect, if possible, to every clause and word of a statute." In weighing this argument, it is well to remember the difference between giving a term a meaning that duplicates another part of the law, and giving a term no meaning at all. Lawmakers sometimes repeat themselves—whether out of a desire to add emphasis, a sense of belt and suspenders caution, or a lawyerly penchant for doublets (aid and abet, cease and desist, null and void). Lawmakers do not, however, tend to use terms that "have no operation at all." So while the rule against treating a term as a redundancy is far from categorical, the rule against treating it as a nullity is as close to absolute as interpretive principles get. The Court's reading does not merely give "by the State" a duplicative effect; it causes the phrase to have no effect whatever....

For its next defense of the indefensible, the Court turns to the Affordable Care Act's design and purposes. As relevant here, the Act makes three major reforms. The guaranteed-issue and community-rating requirements prohibit insurers from considering a customer's health when deciding whether to sell insurance and how much to charge; its famous individual mandate requires everyone to maintain insurance coverage or to pay what the Act calls a "penalty"; and its tax credits help make insurance more affordable. The Court reasons that Congress intended these three reforms to "work together to expand insurance coverage"; and because the first two apply in every State, so must the third.

This reasoning suffers from no shortage of flaws. To begin with, "even the most formidable argument concerning the statute's purposes could not overcome the clarity (of) the statute's text." Statutory design and purpose matter only to the extent they help clarify an otherwise ambiguous provision. Could anyone maintain with a straight face that § 36B is unclear? ...

Having gone wrong in consulting statutory purpose at all, the Court goes wrong again in analyzing it....

The Court protests that without the tax credits, the number of people covered by the individual mandate shrinks, and without a broadly applicable individual mandate the guaranteed-issue and community-rating requirements "would destabilize the individual insurance market." If true, these projections would show only that the statutory scheme contains a flaw; they would not show that the statute means the opposite of what it says....

Perhaps sensing the dismal failure of its efforts to show that "established by the State" means "established by the State or the Federal Government," the Court tries to palm off the pertinent statutory phrase as "inartful drafting." This Court, however, has no free-floating power "to rescue Congress from its drafting errors." Only when it is patently obvious to a reasonable reader that a drafting mistake has occurred may a court correct the mistake. The occurrence of a misprint may be apparent from the face of the law, as it is where the Affordable Care Act "creates three separate Section 1563s." But the Court does not pretend that there is any such indication of a drafting error on the face of § 36B. The occurrence of a misprint may also be apparent because a provision decrees an absurd result—a consequence "so monstrous, that all mankind would, without hesitation, unite in rejecting the application." But § 36B does not come remotely close to satisfying that demanding standard. It is entirely plausible that tax credits were restricted to state Exchanges deliberately—for example, in order to encourage States to establish their own Exchanges. We therefore have no authority to dismiss the terms of the law as a drafting fumble. Let us not forget that the term "Exchange established by the State" appears twice in § 36B and five more times in other parts of the Act that mention tax credits. What are the odds, do you think, that the same slip of the pen occurred in seven separate places? No provision of the Act—none at all—contradicts the limitation of tax credits to state Exchanges. And as I have already explained, uses of the term "Exchange established by the State" beyond the context of tax credits look anything but accidental. If there was a mistake here, context suggests it was a substantive mistake in designing this part of the law, not a technical mistake in transcribing it....

Even less defensible, if possible, is the Court's claim that its interpretive approach is justified because this Act "does not reflect the type of care and deliberation that one might expect of such significant legislation." It is not our place to judge the quality of the care and deliberation that went into this or any other law. A law enacted by voice vote with no deliberation whatever is fully as binding upon us as one enacted after years of study, months of committee hearings, and weeks of debate. Much less is it our place to make everything come out right when Congress does not do its job properly. It is up to Congress to design its laws with care, and it is up to the people to hold them to account if they fail to carry out that responsibility.

Rather than rewriting the law under the pretense of interpreting it, the Court should have left it to Congress to decide what to do about the Act's limitation of tax credits to state Exchanges....

Today's opinion changes the usual rules of statutory interpretation for the sake of the Affordable Care Act.... The Act that Congress passed makes tax credits available only on an "Exchange established by the State." This Court, however, concludes that this limitation would prevent the rest of the Act from working as well as hoped. So it rewrites the law to make tax credits available everywhere. We should start calling this law SCOTUScare.

Perhaps the Patient Protection and Affordable Care Act will attain the enduring status of the Social Security Act or the Taft-Hartley Act; perhaps not. But this Court's two decisions on the Act will surely be remembered through the years. The somersaults of statutory interpretation they have performed ("penalty" means tax, "further (Medicaid) payments to the State" means only incremental Medicaid payments to the State, "established by the State" means not established by the State) will be cited by litigants endlessly, to the confusion of honest jurisprudence. And the cases will publish forever the discouraging truth that the Supreme Court of the United States favors some laws over others, and is prepared to do whatever it takes to uphold and assist its favorites.

* * *

Points for Discussion

1. *Statutory Language*: What was the language at issue? What did each party want that language to mean? What meaning did the majority and dissent adopt?

2. *Theories*: Which theory did the majority use? The dissent? Did either find ambiguity, absurdity, a constitutional question to avoid, or a scrivener's error?

3. *Key Reforms*: What three key reforms did Congress incorporate into the ACA to ensure that it would work? Which of these three reforms was at risk in this case?

4. *Treasury's Regulation*: Although Justice Roberts labels the regulation as an "IRS rule," the Treasury actually issued the regulation using notice and comment procedures. Because the Treasury used force of law procedures, then under *Christensen/Mead/Barnhart*, *Chevron* should apply. But the majority refused to apply *Chevron*. Why? What standard did the majority apply instead? Why did the Court not apply *Skidmore* analysis?

5. *The IRS*: The majority suggests that *Chevron* is not appropriate in part because the IRS interpreted statutory language in a health care statute, not a tax statute. Yet, the language relates to when tax credits are available. Would it make more sense for the Department of Health and Human Services to make the determination of when tax credits should be available? Or should no agency have interpretive authority, given that this statute addresses multiple areas of responsibility?

6. *Text*: According to the majority, why was the meaning of the phrase "established by the State" ambiguous? Why did Justice Scalia disagree? What linguistic canon did he use to bolster his interpretation?

7. *Statutory Scheme or Purpose*: According to the majority, why was the availability of tax credits essential for the ACA to function properly? What did the majority mean when it said, "It is implausible that Congress meant the Act to operate in this manner"?

8. *Applying Chevron*: Under *Chevron*, the Court should determine at step one whether Congress directly spoke to the precise issue before the court, and at step two, if

not, defer to the Treasury's interpretation if it is reasonable. If the majority had applied *Chevron*, how should they have resolved step one? Arguably, the majority should have found that the text pointed in one direction, while the statutory purpose pointed in another. Hence: Congress did not speak directly to the precise issue before the Court. Assuming the Court then reached step two, how should it have resolved this step? Arguably, the Court should have found the Treasury's interpretation was reasonable given the conflict between the text and the purpose.

Let's consider the implications of this case had the Court deferred at *Chevron*'s second step. If during the upcoming election a republican is elected president, the Treasury would likely have been instructed to change its interpretation. Pursuant to *Brand X*, the Treasury would have the power to change its interpretation, so long as the new interpretation was reasonable. Does this outcome suggest a possible reason why the majority refused to apply *Chevron* at all? We will examine *Brand X* in the next section.

9. *The Dissent*: Not surprisingly, the dissent relied almost entirely on the ordinary meaning of the text and a linguistic canon, while the majority relied on purpose. Assuming the dissent has the better argument as regards the text, how did the dissent respond to the majority's purpose argument?

10. *Rule Against Surplusage*: The majority's interpretation makes the words "established by a state" surplusage. The majority noted that the rule against surplusage is not categorical. The dissent agreed that the rule against surplusage is not categorical when words are duplicative. But, the dissent argued, here the words would not be duplicative; they would be null because they would have no effect whatsoever. According to the dissent, the rule against treating statutory language "as a nullity is as close to absolute as interpretive principles get."

11. *Inartful Drafting*: The majority noted that the ACA contains "more than a few examples of inartful drafting" and that it was not careful and deliberate legislation. Yet, the majority does not suggest that the language at issue contained a scrivener's error. Did it? Do you think that Congress considered the possibility that so many states would fail to establish their own exchanges? Is it likely then, that Congress did not consider the potential ramifications of this language? Assuming that Congress basically just wrote a bad law, then is not the dissent correct that the Congress should "fix" it? Or does it make more sense for the Court to work with Congress to help ensure that the statute works as Congress intended and does not destroy the very markets it was trying to establish? Does your answer to this question implicate your view of separation of powers? Do your political views impact your analysis of this case? Do you think the justices are immune from politics?

* * *

In these cases—*Brown & Williamson*, *Gonzales*, and *King*—the Supreme Court significantly limited the implied-delegation rationale. In all three cases, the Court held that Congress did not implicitly delegate interpretive power to the agency despite statutory ambiguity. The holdings in these cases are at odds with *Chevron*'s implicit-delegation rationale, which states that "[d]eference under *Chevron* to an agency's construction of a statute that it administers is premised on the theory that a statute's ambiguity constitutes an implicit delegation from Congress to the agency to fill in the statutory gaps." *Brown & Williamson*, 529 U.S. at 159. Notably, in none of the applicable statutes did Congress expressly say that it was not delegating to the agency. Rather, the Court inferred congressional intent not to delegate based on other factors, including the existence of other legislation (*Brown & Williamson*) and the importance of the issue to the national economy (*Brown & Williamson*, *Gonzales,* and *King*). Moreover, in *Brown & Williamson* and *King*, the Court reviewed the agency's interpretation *de novo*; while, in *Gonzales,* the Court applied *Skidmore* analysis, but ultimately rejected the agency's interpretation as unpersuasive. Is *Chevron*'s relevance fading?

To recap, when *Chevron* was decided, many thought it applied to all agency interpretations. *Christensen* limited *Chevron*'s reach by holding that *Chevron* applied only when the agency acted using force of law procedures. *Mead* and *Barnhart* then held that *Chevron* applies only when Congress intends that agencies decide the interpretive issue. *Brown & Williamson*, *Gonzales,* and *King* further limited *Chevron*'s reach. Now, for cases that involve questions that are too important to the national economy, the Court must find a clear statement from Congress that it intended to delegate interpretive power to the agency. In other words, courts must find that Congress expressly delegated interpretive power: gaps and ambiguities are no longer enough. Presumably, at this stage, the Court should apply arbitrary and capricious review. *Chevron, U.S.A. Inc. v. Natural Resources Defense Council, Inc*, 467 U.S. 837, 843 (1984).

In summary, *Chevron* applies only when an agency (1) interprets a statute (2) that the agency administers (3) while using force of law procedures, (4) *so long as Congress intended to delegate interpretive power to the agency.* You have now mastered the sub-steps of *Chevron* step zero.

Problem 19A

Assume that after *Chevron v. Natural Defense Resources*, the Environmental Protection Agency (EPA) interpreted the language in the statute, "statutory source," using a non-legislative interpretive rule to mean each individual, pollution emitting device, rather than the plant as a whole. In other words, the EPA changed its legislative rule and did so using a non-legislative interpretive rule. Assume that this choice in procedure was valid. There are no other relevant statutes or regulations. When industry challenges the agency's new interpretation of the statute, what standard of review would the court likely use and how would a court likely rule?

* * *

Problem 19B

The state of East Carolina authorized its Racing Commission to regulate the operation of auto tracks in the 1930s. Pursuant to statute, races involving formula racing, touring racing, motorcycle racing, together with wagering on the outcomes of these races, were legalized if conducted at facilities licensed by the Racing Commission. Racing generated increase tax revenue and boosted tourism. But as an increasing number of race track developers began to open more and more race tracks in East Carolina, the citizens began to complain about the negative effects of the race-car lifestyle on their towns and revenue began to decrease the race tracks failed.

In 2004, in response to these concerns, the East Carolina Racing Code was amended to add a provision designed (according to its purpose clause) "to prevent the over proliferation of auto race tracks to secure the competitiveness and profitability of such licensed race tracks." As introduced in the East Carolina legislature, the amendment to the Racing Code provided as follows:

A Bill

To amend the Racing Code to enhance auto race track facility profitability and productiveness.

Be it enacted by the Senate and the General Assembly of East Carolina assembled,

Section 1 Short title:

This Act may be cited as the East Carolina Location Amendment Act.

Section 2. Findings and Purpose.

The purpose of this amendment is to prevent the over proliferation of auto race tracks to secure the competitiveness and profitability of each such licensed race tracks in with the state. This statute should be broadly construed to further its remedial purpose.

Section 3: Licensing

Section 33 of the Racing Act of 1930 is amended by the following subsection 3: A racing permit may be issued by the Racing Commission to a motor racing facility only if such facility will not be located within two hundred miles by road travel of another location for which a permit has been issued and a racing track is located.

Section 33, subsection 4 of East Carolina's Racing Code authorizes the Racing Commission to promulgate rules and regulations, "which regulations shall have the force and effect of law, provided that no such regulation shall be valid if it is inconsistent with the Racing Code." (26 E.C. Rev. Statutes § 33(4)(a)).

The East Carolina Location Amendment bill passed the general assembly. The general assembly engrossing clerk, however, miscopied the text so that the engrossed bill read as follows:

A racing permit may be issued by the Racing Commission to a motor racing facility only if such facility will be located within two miles by road travel of another facility for which a permit has been issued and a racing track is located.

The clerk inadvertently deleted the "not" in the second line of the original bill and changed "two hundred miles" to "two miles."

This engrossed bill was introduced in the Senate, which modified the bill in other ways but made no change to the part of the bill mis-transcribed by the clerk. After voting to approve its version, the Senate returned the bill to the general assembly, which approved the Act with the errors. No conference was necessary. The amendment was then signed by East Carolina's governor.

Following enactment of the amendment, the Commission issued an interpretive rule, which provided in pertinent part:

> A racing permit may be granted for a racing facility only if the permit is for a racing facility more than two hundred miles by road travel from any other racing facility of the same type. A racing facility of one type (for example, motorcycle racing) may be located within two hundred miles of a facility of another type (drag car or stock car racing).

In its interpretive rule, the Commission said:

> "Taken literally the amendment would allow the commission to issue a license only if the auto facility seeking a license is located within two miles of another track. That result would be absurd and would not address the mischief the legislature was attempting to correct. The clear legislative intent was to prohibit the establishment of racing plants within two hundred miles of one another to further their likelihood of successful operation to generate revenue while not overpopulating any one part of the state with too many such facilities. This legislative purpose is adequately served by prohibiting the establishment of racing facilities of the same kind within two hundred miles of already licensed facilities."

Pursuant to its interpretive rule, the Commission recently approved an application by Mercer Downs to establish a small motorcycle track in Mercer, a city in East Carolina. Forsyth Downs is an existing licensed operator of a race car track in Forsyth, East Carolina, a city which is located just fifty miles away, by road, of the proposed cite.

Forsyth Downs has filed an action in state court seeking to enjoin the Racing Commission from issuing a license to Mercer Downs. Assume East Carolina follows federal law regarding the appropriate standard of review to apply to agency interpretations of statutes. You are general counsel to the Commission. What standard of review is the court most likely to apply and why? Assuming the court applies the standard you identified, how would you argue that the court should defer to the Commission's interpretation? How would Forsyth Downs respond, arguing that no deference is appropriate?

C. Agency Interpretations that Conflict with Judicial Interpretations

The cases in the last chapter identified what level of deference, if any, a court should give to an agency interpretation when there are no pre-existing judicial interpretations of the same statute. The next obvious question is: what if there is a prior judicial opinion? Should a court defer to an agency interpretation of a statute that varies from an existing judicial interpretation?

Prior judicial interpretations exist when a court defers to a prior agency interpretation or when a court interprets the meaning of a statutory provision that an agency has not yet interpreted. The question is whether, thereafter, an agency is bound to follow this judicial interpretation or whether the agency is free to interpret the statute differently. At issue is flexibility—the ability for an agency to adjust policy and statutory interpretations. On the one hand, flexibility is essential to the effective operation of administrative agencies as technology and economics advance and administrative priorities change with time and with a new administration. If agencies were unable to alter interpretations over time, flexibility would be significantly hindered and agencies would be less effective at responding to change. On the other hand, too much change can lead to unpredictability, uncertainty, and, potentially, unfairness. Similarly situated litigants expect the government to treat them similarly.

The Supreme Court addressed this issue in the case below. See if you can determine when agencies can reject an existing judicial interpretation and when agencies must accept the existing judicial interpretations. In other words, when does *Chevron* apply to agency interpretations that follow judicial interpretations?

National Cable & Telecommunications Association v. Brand X Internet Services

Supreme Court of the United States
545 U.S. 967 (2005)

◆ JUSTICE THOMAS delivered the opinion of the Court [in which REHNQUIST, STEVENS, O'CONNOR, KENNEDY, and BREYER, JJ., concur].

[During the era of dial-up internet service, the federal government ensured that small internet providers were given equal access to home telephone lines; the lines were regulated as common carriers. When cable television operators started to use coax cable to provide internet access, the small internet providers, like Brand X, wanted to use the cables in the same way that they had used the home telephone lines, to reach customers.

The Telecommunications Act identifies two categories of providers: (1) "information-service providers," and (2) "telecommunications carriers." The Act empowers the FCC to regulate telecommunications carriers, but not information-service providers. The Act requires telecommunications carriers (or service providers), but not information service providers, to sell access to their networks. The Federal Communications Commission (FCC) concluded that the cable companies did not provide "telecommunications servic[e]" and, therefore, did not have to share their lines. Brand X sued.]

Title II of the Communications Act of 1934, as amended, subjects all providers of "telecommunications servic[e]" to mandatory common-carrier regulation. In the order under review, the Federal Communications Commission concluded that cable companies that sell broadband Internet service do not provide "telecommunications servic[e]" as the Communications Act defines that term, and hence are exempt from mandatory common-carrier regulation under Title II. We must decide whether that conclusion is a lawful construction of the Communications Act under *Chevron, U.S.A., Inc. v. NRDC*, 467 U.S. 837 (1984), and the Administrative Procedure Act. We hold that it is.

The traditional means by which consumers in the United States access the network of interconnected computers that make up the Internet is through "dial-up" connections provided over local telephone facilities.... "Broadband" Internet service, by contrast, transmits data at much higher speeds. There are two principal kinds of broadband Internet service: cable modem service and Digital Subscriber Line (DSL) service. Cable modem service transmits data between the Internet and users' computers via the network of television cable lines owned by cable companies. DSL service provides high-speed access using the local telephone wires owned by local telephone companies....

At issue in these cases is the proper regulatory classification under the Communications Act of broadband cable Internet service. The Act, as amended by the Telecommunications Act of 1996, defines two categories of regulated entities relevant to these cases: telecommunications carriers and information-service providers....

The definitions of the terms "telecommunications service" and "information service" established by the 1996 Act are[:] "Telecommunications service ... is "the offering of telecommunications for a fee directly to the public.... regardless of the facilities used." 47 U.S.C. § 153(46). "Telecommunications" is "the transmission, between or among points specified by the user, of information of the user's choosing, without change in the form or content of the information as sent and received." § 153(43).... And "information service" ... is "the offering of a capability for generating, acquiring, storing, transforming, processing, retrieving, utilizing, or making available information via telecommunications...." § 153(20).

In September 2000, the Commission initiated a rulemaking proceeding ... that ... culminated in the *Declaratory Ruling* under review in these cases. In the *Declaratory Ruling*, the Commission concluded that broadband Internet service provided by cable companies is an "information service" but not a "telecommunications service" under the Act, and therefore not subject to ... regulation.... Its logic was that ... cable companies do not "offe[r] telecommunications service to the end user, but rather ... merely us[e] telecommunications to provide end users with cable modem service." ... Numerous parties petitioned for judicial review....

The [Ninth Circuit] Court of Appeals ... held that the Commission could not permissibly construe the Communications Act to exempt cable companies providing Internet service from ... regulation. Rather than analyzing the permissibility of that construction under the deferential framework of *Chevron*, however, the Court of Appeals grounded its holding in the *stare decisis* effect of *AT&T Corp. v. Portland*, 216 F.3d 871 (CA9 2000). *Portland* held that cable modem service was a "telecommunications service," though the court in that case was not reviewing an administrative proceeding and the Commission was not a party to the case.* Nevertheless, *Portland*'s holding, the Court of Appeals reasoned, overrode the contrary interpretation reached by the Commission in the *Declaratory Ruling....*

We first consider whether we should apply *Chevron*'s framework to the Commission's interpretation of the term "telecommunications service." We conclude that we should. We also conclude that the Court of Appeals should have done the same, instead of following the contrary construction it adopted in *Portland*.

In *Chevron*, this Court held that ambiguities in statutes within an agency's jurisdiction to administer are delegations of authority to the agency to fill the statutory gap in reasonable fashion. Filling these gaps, the Court explained, involves difficult policy choices that agencies are better equipped to make than courts. If a statute is ambiguous, and if the implementing agency's construction is reasonable, *Chevron* requires a federal court to accept the agency's construction of the statute, even if the agency's reading differs from what the court believes is the best statutory interpretation.

The *Chevron* framework governs our review of the Commission's construction. Congress has delegated to the Commission the authority to "execute and enforce" the Communications Act, § 151, and to "prescribe such rules and regulations as may be necessary in the public interest to carry out the provisions" of the Act, § 201(b). These provisions give the Commission the authority to promulgate binding legal rules; the Commission issued the order under review in the exercise of that authority; and no one questions that the order is within the Commission's jurisdiction. Hence, as we have in the past, we apply the *Chevron* framework to the Commission's interpretation of the Communications Act....

The Court of Appeals declined to apply *Chevron* because it thought the Commission's interpretation of the Communications Act foreclosed by the conflicting construction of the Act it had adopted in *Portland*. It based that holding on the assumption that *Portland*'s construction overrode the Commission's, regardless of whether *Portland* had held the statute to be unambiguous. That reasoning was incorrect.

A court's prior judicial construction of a statute trumps an agency construction otherwise entitled to *Chevron* deference only if the prior court decision holds that its construction follows from the unambiguous terms of the statute and thus leaves no room for agency discretion. This principle follows from *Chevron* itself. *Chevron* established a "presumption that Congress, when it left ambiguity in a statute meant for implementation by an agency, understood that the ambiguity would be resolved, first and foremost, by the agency, and desired the agency (rather than the courts) to possess whatever degree of discretion the ambiguity allows." Yet allowing a judicial precedent to foreclose an agency from interpreting an ambiguous statute, as the Court of Appeals assumed it could, would allow a court's interpretation to override an

---

* Editor's footnote: In *Portland*, AT&T sued the city of Portland to prevent the city from imposing "open-access" requirements on the company's cable broadband Internet service. The Ninth Circuit held that this service, unlike other cable services such as broadcasting of television shows, was a "telecommunications service" under federal law and, therefore, exempt from local regulation.

agency's. *Chevron*'s premise is that it is for agencies, not courts, to fill statutory gaps. The better rule is to hold judicial interpretations contained in precedents to the same demanding *Chevron* step one standard that applies if the court is reviewing the agency's construction on a blank slate: Only a judicial precedent holding that the statute unambiguously forecloses the agency's interpretation, and therefore contains no gap for the agency to fill, displaces a conflicting agency construction.

A contrary rule would produce anomalous results. It would mean that whether an agency's interpretation of an ambiguous statute is entitled to *Chevron* deference would turn on the order in which the interpretations issue: If the court's construction came first, its construction would prevail, whereas if the agency's came first, the agency's construction would command *Chevron* deference. Yet whether Congress has delegated to an agency the authority to interpret a statute does not depend on the order in which the judicial and administrative constructions occur. The Court of Appeals' rule, moreover, would "lead to the ossification of large portions of our statutory law," by precluding agencies from revising unwise judicial constructions of ambiguous statutes. Neither *Chevron* nor the doctrine of *stare decisis* requires these haphazard results.

The dissent answers that allowing an agency to override what a court believes to be the best interpretation of a statute makes "judicial decisions subject to reversal by Executive officers." It does not. Since *Chevron* teaches that a court's opinion as to the best reading of an ambiguous statute an agency is charged with administering is not authoritative, the agency's decision to construe that statute differently from a court does not say that the court's holding was legally wrong.... The precedent has not been "reversed" by the agency, any more than a federal court's interpretation of a State's law can be said to have been "reversed" by a state court that adopts a conflicting (yet authoritative) interpretation of state law....

Against this background, the Court of Appeals erred in refusing to apply *Chevron* to the Commission's interpretation of the definition of "telecommunications service." Its prior decision in *Portland* held only that the *best* reading of §153(46) was that cable modem service was a "telecommunications service," not that it was the *only permissible* reading of the statute. Nothing in *Portland* held that the Communications Act unambiguously required treating cable Internet providers as telecommunications carriers....

We next address whether the Commission's construction of the definition of "telecommunications service," is a permissible reading of the Communications Act under the *Chevron* framework.... [The majority applies *Chevron*'s two step test to conclude that under step one, Congress did not have a specific intent on the meaning of the word "offer" and that under step two, the Commission's construction was 'a reasonable policy choice for the (Commission) to make' at *Chevron*'s second step.]

♦ Justice Stevens, concurring.

While I join the Court's opinion in full, I add this caveat concerning [the section of the opinion that] correctly explains why a court of appeals' interpretation of an ambiguous provision in a regulatory statute does not foreclose a contrary reading by the agency. That explanation would not necessarily be applicable to a decision by this Court that would presumably remove any pre-existing ambiguity.

◆ [JUSTICE BREYER's concurring opinion is omitted].

◆ JUSTICE SCALIA, with whom JUSTICE SOUTER and JUSTICE GINSBURG join as to Part I, dissenting.

[The dissent applies *Chevron*'s first step and concludes that the statute is clear: cable companies "offer" high-speed access to the Internet.].

... In ... its opinion, the Court continues the administrative-law improvisation project it began four years ago in *United States v. Mead Corp.*, 533 U.S. 218 (2001). To the extent it set forth a comprehensible rule, *Mead* drastically limited the categories of agency action that would qualify for deference under *Chevron*. For example, the position taken by an agency before the Supreme Court, with full approval of the agency head, would not qualify. Rather, some unspecified degree of formal process was required—or was at least the only safe harbor.

As I pointed out in dissent, this in turn meant (under the law as it was understood until today) that many statutory ambiguities that might be resolved in varying fashions by successive agency administrations, would be resolved finally, conclusively, and forever, by federal judges—producing an "ossification of large portions of our statutory law." The Court today moves to solve this problem of its own creation by inventing yet another breathtaking novelty: judicial decisions subject to reversal by Executive officers.

Imagine the following sequence of events: FCC action is challenged as ultra vires under the governing statute; the litigation reaches all the way to the Supreme Court of the United States. The Solicitor General sets forth the FCC's official position (approved by the Commission) regarding interpretation of the statute. Applying *Mead*, however, the Court denies the agency position *Chevron* deference, finds that the *best* interpretation of the statute contradicts the agency's position, and holds the challenged agency action unlawful. The agency promptly conducts a rulemaking, and adopts a rule that comports with its earlier position—in effect disagreeing with the Supreme Court concerning the best interpretation of the statute. According to today's opinion, the agency is thereupon free to take the action that the Supreme Court found unlawful....

It is indeed a wonderful new world that the Court creates, one full of promise for administrative-law professors in need of tenure articles and, of course, for litigators. I would adhere to what has been the rule in the past: When a court interprets a statute without *Chevron* deference to agency views, its interpretation (whether or not asserted to rest upon an unambiguous text) is the law....

* * *

Points for Discussion

1. *Statutory Language*: What was the language at issue? What did each party want that language to mean? What meaning did the majority and dissent adopt?

2. *Theories*: The portion of the opinion determining the meaning of the language has been excised; hence, no theory of interpretation is apparent for either the majority or dissent, although both are typically textualist.

3. *Judicial v. Executive Interpretation*: According to *Brand X*, if a court and then an agency interpret a statute but interpret the language to mean different things, which interpretation controls and why? Pursuant to the majority, agencies can change an existing interpretation, even one affirmed in court, in certain situations. What are those situations? Additionally, there are situations when an agency has no power to change a prior interpretation. What are those situations? The majority said that any other result would lead to a race to the courthouse: whichever branch interprets the statute first wins, so to speak. Do you see why that is accurate?

4. *Executive Reversal*: Does the majority's distinction make sense and flow from *Chevron*'s two step process? Or is Justice Scalia correct that once a court interprets the meaning of a statute, interpretation is at an end?

5. *Justice Scalia's Dissent*: Why did Justice Scalia reject the majority's approach? What approach would he use instead?

6. *Deference to the Agency's New Interpretation*: *Brand X* answers the question of whether the agency has *the power* to interpret the statute differently from a preexisting judicial interpretation. Assuming the agency has that power, the new interpretation must still be *reasonable*. In sum, the court reviewing an agency's new interpretation must not only apply *Brand X* to determine whether the agency has the power to issue a different interpretation, but the court must then apply *Chevron* to determine whether the new interpretation is reasonable. The agency may have the power to change the interpretation, but the new interpretation must still be a reasonable interpretation of the statute. When a court applies *Chevron* to the new interpretation the only remaining issue is whether the new interpretation is reasonable under step two, because step one has already been resolved using the *Brand X* analysis. Assuming there are no relevant changes to the statute since the first judicial interpretation, Congress did not speak directly to the precise issue before the court. And, if this analysis is not complicated enough, there is a further wrinkle that we will cover in the next section: this analysis assumes that *Chevron* is the appropriate deference standard.

7. *Concurrence*: Why did Justice Steven concur? Does his conclusion—that a Supreme Court interpretation of a statute necessarily precludes an agency from subsequently issuing a different interpretation—follow from *Chevron*? Is not the whole point of the implied delegation rationale that agencies, not the courts (not even the Supreme Court), have authority to interpret a statute when there are multiple reasonable interpretations?

8. *Liberal & Conservative*: Notice the alignment in this case. Justices Breyer and Stevens joined Justice Thomas's majority opinion, while Justices Ginsburg and

Souter joined Justice Scalia's dissent. What does this alignment tell you about this issue?

9. *Pre & Post Chevron Application*: According to the majority, judicial interpretations of statutes are binding on agencies when the judicial "construction follows from the unambiguous terms of the statute." In other words, judicial interpretations are binding when they come from *Chevron* step one. The test seems easy in the abstract. However, cases that predate *Chevron* may not speak in step one and two terms. How does a subsequent court determine whether the prior judicial decision was decided at *Chevron* step one or step two? The next section addresses this issue.

* * *

Brand X's approach is intuitively appealing; however, judges have not always been so clear about whether an adopted interpretation rests on a finding that Congress was ambiguous at *Chevron*'s first step, especially for cases that predate *Brand X*.

The case below addresses this issue. The first case, *Colony, Inc. v. Commissioner*, 357 U.S. 28 (1958), held that an overstatement of basis* was not an omission from gross income. The Internal Revenue Service (IRS) sought a tax deficiency against a developer who understated its gross income by incorrectly adding certain expenses to its basis in real property. The Supreme Court held that the developer's overstatement of basis was not an "omission" from gross income, because the word "omits" means "[t]o leave out or unmentioned; not to insert, include, or name." Pursuant to this statutory language and the legislative history, the taxpayer had not omitted anything. *Id.* at 32–33.

The case below came more than fifty years later and arose out of the IRS's efforts to assess deficiencies against those who used a specific tax shelter (Son-of-BOSS) to create paper losses to offset real gains. These tax shelters cost the government $6 billion in lost revenue. Typically, the IRS did not learn about the taxpayer's use of a Son-of-BOSS shelter until after the three year statutory of limitations had run. For example, Home Concrete & Supply was a limited liability company formed in 1999 to facilitate a Son-of-BOSS tax scheme for two North Carolina oil and gas businessmen. As permitted, the two men filed their 1999 tax returns in 2000. The IRS audited them in 2006 and assessed a deficiency totaling $6 million. The men sued, arguing that the IRS violated the three-year statute of limitations. The IRS argued in response that the six-year limitations period applied. The case reached the Supreme Court, where the justices had to determine whether and how to apply *Chevron* analysis to a case that predated *Chevron*.

Notice how the majority appears to retreat from the approach it articulated in *Brand X*. As you read the case, see if you can determine why the majority refuses to defer to the agency's interpretation, even though the Court had said, in *Colony*, that the statutory language was "not unambiguous."

---

* The tax basis of an asset is generally the cost, or price paid, for an asset. Taxpayers may generally deduct their basis from any gain they realize when selling property.

United States v. Home Concrete & Supply, LLC

Supreme Court of the United States

132 S. Ct. 1836 (2012)

◆ Justice Breyer delivered the opinion of the Court, except as to Part IV-C. Roberts, C. J., and Thomas and Alito, JJ., joined that opinion in full, and Scalia, J., joined except for Part IV-C.

Ordinarily, the Government must assess a deficiency against a taxpayer within "3 years after the return was filed." 26 U.S.C. §6501(a) (2000 ed.). The 3-year period is extended to 6 years, however, when a taxpayer "*omits from gross income an amount properly includible therein* which is in excess of 25 percent of the amount of gross income stated in the return." §6501(e)(1)(A) (emphasis added). The question before us is whether this latter provision applies (and extends the ordinary 3-year limitations period) when the taxpayer *overstates his basis* in property that he has sold, thereby *understating the gain* that he received from its sale. Following *Colony, Inc. v. Commissioner,* 357 U.S. 28 (1958), we hold that the provision does not apply to an overstatement of basis. Hence the 6-year period does not apply.

For present purposes the relevant underlying circumstances are not in dispute. We consequently assume that (1) the respondent taxpayers filed their relevant tax returns in April 2000; (2) the returns overstated the basis of certain property that the taxpayers had sold; (3) as a result the returns understated the gross income that the taxpayers received from the sale of the property; and (4) the understatement exceeded the statute's 25% threshold. We also take as undisputed that the Commissioner asserted the relevant deficiency within the extended 6-year limitations period, but outside the default 3-year period. Thus, unless the 6-year statute of limitations applies, the Government's efforts to assert a tax deficiency came too late. Our conclusion—that the extended limitations period does not apply—follows directly from this Court's earlier decision in *Colony.*

In *Colony* this Court interpreted a provision of the Internal Revenue Code of 1939, the operative language of which is identical to the language now before us. The Commissioner there had determined

> "that the taxpayer had understated the gross profits on the sales of certain lots of land for residential purposes as a result of having overstated the 'basis' of such lots...."

The Commissioner's assessment came after the ordinary 3-year limitations period had run. And, it was consequently timely only if the taxpayer, in the words of the 1939 Code, had "omit[ted] from gross income an amount properly includible therein which is in excess of 25 per centum of the amount of gross income stated in the return...." 26 U.S.C. §275(c) (1940 ed.). The Code provision applicable to this case, adopted in 1954, contains materially indistinguishable language.

In *Colony* this Court held that taxpayer misstatements, overstating the basis in property, do not fall within the scope of the statute. But the Court recognized the

Commissioner's contrary argument for inclusion. Then as now, the Code itself defined "gross income" in this context as the difference between gross revenue (often the amount the taxpayer received upon selling the property) and basis (often the amount the taxpayer paid for the property). And, the Commissioner pointed out, an over-statement of basis can diminish the "amount" of the gain just as leaving the item entirely off the return might do. Either way, the error wrongly understates the taxpayer's income.

But, the Court added, the Commissioner's argument did not fully account for the provision's language, in particular the word "omit." The key phrase says "*omits . . . an amount.*" The word "omits" (unlike, say, "reduces" or "understates") means "'[t]o leave out or unmentioned; not to insert, include, or name.'" *Ibid.* (quoting Webster's New International Dictionary (2d ed. 1939)). Thus, taken literally, "omit" limits the statute's scope to situations in which specific receipts or accruals of income are *left out* of the computation of gross income; to inflate the basis, however, is not to "omit" a specific item, not even of profit.

While finding this latter interpretation of the language the "more plausibl[e]," the Court also noted that the language was not "unambiguous." *Colony,* 357 U.S., at 33. It then examined various congressional Reports discussing the relevant statutory language. . . .

This "history," the Court said, "shows . . . that the Congress intended an exception to the usual three-year statute of limitations only in the restricted type of situation already described," a situation that did not include overstatements of basis. . . .

Finally, the Court noted that Congress had recently enacted the Internal Revenue Code of 1954. And the Court observed that "the conclusion we reach is in harmony with the unambiguous language of § 6501(e)(1)(A)," *i.e.,* the provision relevant in this present case.

In our view, *Colony* determines the outcome in this case. The provision before us is a 1954 reenactment of the 1939 provision that *Colony* interpreted. The operative language is identical. It would be difficult, perhaps impossible, to give the same language here a different interpretation without effectively overruling *Colony,* a course of action that basic principles of *stare decisis* wisely counsel us not to take. . . .

. . . the Government points to Treasury Regulation § 301.6501(e)-1, which was promulgated in final form in December 2010. The regulation, as relevant here, departs from *Colony* and interprets the operative language of the statute in the Government's favor. The regulation says that "an understated amount of gross income resulting from an overstatement of unrecovered cost or other basis constitutes an omission from gross income." § 301.6501(e)-1(a)(1)(iii). In the Government's view this new regulation in effect overturns *Colony*'s interpretation of this statute.

The Government points out that the Treasury Regulation constitutes "an agency's construction of a statute which it administers." *Chevron, U.S.A. Inc. v. Natural Resources Defense Council, Inc.,* 467 U.S. 837, 842 (1984). The Court has written that a "court's prior judicial construction of a statute trumps an agency construction otherwise entitled to *Chevron* deference only if the prior court decision holds that its construction follows from the *unambiguous* terms of the statute...." *National Cable & Telecommunications Assn. v. Brand X Internet Services,* 545 U.S. 967, 982 (2005) (emphasis added). And, as the Government notes, in *Colony* itself the Court wrote that "it cannot be said that the language is unambiguous." 357 U.S., at 33. Hence, the Government concludes, *Colony* cannot govern the outcome in this case. The question, rather, is whether the agency's construction is a "permissible construction of the statute." *Chevron, supra,* at 843. And, since the Government argues that the regulation embodies a reasonable, hence permissible, construction of the statute, the Government believes it must win.

We do not accept this argument. In our view, *Colony* has already interpreted the statute, and there is no longer any different construction that is consistent with *Colony* and available for adoption by the agency.

IV

C

The fatal flaw in the Government's contrary argument is that it overlooks the *reason why Brand X* held that a "prior judicial construction," unless reflecting an "unambiguous" statute, does not trump a different agency construction of that statute. The Court reveals that reason when it points out that "it is for agencies, not courts, to fill statutory gaps." The fact that a statute is unambiguous means that there is "no gap for the agency to fill" and thus "no room for agency discretion." [quoting *Brand X*].

In so stating, the Court sought to encapsulate what earlier opinions, including *Chevron*, made clear. Those opinions identify the underlying interpretive problem as that of deciding whether, or when, a particular statute in effect delegates to an agency the power to fill a gap, thereby implicitly taking from a court the power to void a reasonable gap-filling interpretation. Thus, in *Chevron* the Court said that, when

> "Congress has explicitly left a gap for the agency to fill, there is an express delegation of authority to the agency to elucidate a specific provision of the statute by regulation.... Sometimes the legislative delegation to an agency on a particular question is implicit rather than explicit. [But in either instance], a court may not substitute its own construction of a statutory provision for a reasonable interpretation made by the administrator of an agency."

Chevron and later cases find in unambiguous language a clear sign that Congress did *not* delegate gap-filling authority to an agency; and they find in ambiguous language at least a presumptive indication that Congress did delegate that gap-filling authority. Thus, in *Chevron* the Court wrote that a statute's silence or ambiguity as to a particular issue means that Congress has not "directly addressed the precise question at issue" (thus likely delegating gap-filling power to the agency). 467 U.S., at 843. In *Mead* the Court, describing *Chevron*, explained:

> "Congress ... may not have expressly delegated authority or responsibility to implement a particular provision or fill a particular gap. Yet it can still be apparent from the agency's generally conferred authority and other statutory

circumstances that Congress would expect the agency to be able to speak with the force of law when it addresses ambiguity in the statute or fills a space in the enacted law, even one about which Congress did not actually have an intent as to a particular result."

Chevron added that "[i]f a court, *employing traditional tools of statutory construction,* ascertains that Congress had an intention on the precise question at issue, that intention is the law and must be given effect." 467 U.S., at 843, n. 9 (emphasis added).

As the Government points out, the Court in *Colony* stated that the statutory language at issue is not "unambiguous." But the Court decided that case nearly 30 years before it decided *Chevron.* There is no reason to believe that the linguistic ambiguity noted by *Colony* reflects a post-*Chevron* conclusion that Congress had delegated gap-filling power to the agency. At the same time, there is every reason to believe that the Court thought that Congress had "directly spoken to the question at hand," and thus left "[no] gap for the agency to fill."

For one thing, the Court said that the taxpayer had the better side of the textual argument. For another, its examination of legislative history led it to believe that Congress had decided the question definitively, leaving no room for the agency to reach a contrary result. It found in that history "persuasive indications" that Congress intended overstatements of basis to fall outside the statute's scope, and it said that it was satisfied that Congress "intended an exception ... only in the restricted type of situation" it had already described. Further, it thought that the Commissioner's interpretation (the interpretation once again advanced here) would "create a patent incongruity in the tax law." And it reached this conclusion despite the fact that, in the years leading up to *Colony,* the Commissioner had consistently advocated the opposite in the circuit courts. Thus, the Court was aware it was rejecting the expert opinion of the Commissioner of Internal Revenue. And finally, after completing its analysis, *Colony* found its interpretation of the 1939 Code "in harmony with the [now] unambiguous language" of the 1954 Code, which at a minimum suggests that the Court saw nothing in the 1954 Code as inconsistent with its conclusion.

It may be that judges today would use other methods to determine whether Congress left a gap to fill. But that is beside the point. The question is whether the Court in *Colony* concluded that the statute left such a gap. And, in our view, the opinion (written by Justice Harlan for the Court) makes clear that it did not.

Given principles of *stare decisis,* we must follow that interpretation. And there being no gap to fill, the Government's gap-filling regulation cannot change *Colony*'s interpretation of the statute. We agree with the taxpayer that overstatements of basis, and the resulting understatement of gross income, do not trigger the extended limitations period of §6501(e)(1)(A). The Court of Appeals['] ... judgment is affirmed....

◆ JUSTICE SCALIA, concurring in part and concurring in the judgment.

It would be reasonable, I think, to deny all precedential effect to *Colony*—to overrule its holding as obviously contrary to our later law that agency resolutions of ambiguities are to be accorded deference. Because of justifiable taxpayer reliance I would not take that course—and neither does the Court's opinion, which says that "*Colony* determines the outcome in this case." That should be the end of the matter.

The plurality, however, goes on to address the Government's argument that Treasury Regulation § 301.6501(e)-1 effectively overturned *Colony*. In my view, that cannot be: "Once a court has decided upon its *de novo* construction of the statute, there no longer is a different construction that is consistent with the court's holding and available for adoption by the agency." *National Cable & Telecommunications Assn. v. Brand X Internet Services,* 545 U.S. 967, 1018, n. 12 (2005) (Scalia, J., dissenting). That view, of course, did not carry the day in *Brand X,* and the Government quite reasonably relies on the *Brand X* majority's innovative pronouncement that a "court's prior judicial construction of a statute trumps an agency construction otherwise entitled to *Chevron* deference only if the prior court decision holds that its construction follows from the unambiguous terms of the statute." *Id.,* at 982.

In cases decided pre-*Brand X,* the Court had no inkling that it *must* utter the magic words "ambiguous" or "unambiguous" in order to (poof!) expand or abridge executive power, and (poof!) enable or disable administrative contradiction of the Supreme Court. Indeed, the Court was unaware of even the utility (much less the necessity) of making the ambiguous/nonambiguous determination in cases decided pre-*Chevron,* before that opinion made the so-called "Step 1" determination of ambiguity *vel non* a customary (though hardly mandatory) part of judicial-review analysis. For many of those earlier cases, therefore, it will be incredibly difficult to determine whether the decision purported to be giving meaning to an ambiguous, or rather an unambiguous, statute.

Thus, one would have thought that the *Brand X* majority would breathe a sigh of relief in the present case, involving a pre-*Chevron* opinion that (*mirabile dictu*) makes it *inescapably clear* that the Court thought the statute ambiguous: "It *cannot* be said that the language is *unambiguous*." *Colony, supra,* at 33 (emphasis added). As today's plurality opinion explains, *Colony* "said that the taxpayer had the *better* side of the textual argument," (emphasis added)—not what *Brand X* requires to foreclose administrative revision of our decisions: "the *only permissible* reading of the statute." 545 U.S., at 984. Thus, having decided to stand by *Colony* and to stand by *Brand X* as well, the plurality should have found—in order to reach the decision it did—that the Treasury Department's current interpretation was unreasonable.

Instead of doing what *Brand X* would require, however, the plurality [revises] *yet again* the meaning of *Chevron*—and [revises] it *yet again* in a direction that will create confusion and uncertainty.... But in order to evade *Brand X* and yet reaffirm *Colony,* the plurality would add yet another lopsided story to the ugly and improbable structure that our law of administrative review has become: To trigger the *Brand X* power of an authorized "gap-filling" agency to give content to an ambiguous text, a pre-*Chevron* determination that language is ambiguous does not alone suffice; the pre-*Chevron* Court must in addition have found that Congress wanted *the particular ambiguity in question* to be resolved by the agency. And here, today's plurality opinion finds, "[t]here is no reason to believe that the linguistic ambiguity noted by *Colony* reflects a post-*Chevron* conclusion that Congress had delegated gap-filling power to the agency." The notion, seemingly, is that post-*Chevron* a finding of ambiguity is accompanied by a finding of agency authority to resolve the ambiguity, but pre-*Chevron* that was not so. The premise is false. Post-*Chevron* cases do not "conclude" that Congress wanted the particular ambiguity resolved by the agency; that is simply the *legal effect* of ambiguity—a legal effect that should obtain whenever the language is in fact (as *Colony* found) ambiguous.

Does the plurality feel that it ought not give effect to *Colony*'s determination of ambiguity because the Court did not know, in that era, the importance of that determination—that it would empower the agency to (in effect) revise the Court's determination of statutory meaning? But as I suggested earlier, that was an ignorance which all of our cases shared not just pre-*Chevron*, but pre-*Brand X*. Before then it did not really matter whether the Court was resolving an ambiguity or setting forth the statute's clear meaning. The opinion might (or might not) advert to that point in the course of its analysis, but either way the Court's interpretation of the statute would be the law. So it is no small number of still-authoritative cases that today's plurality opinion would exile to the Land of Uncertainty.

Perhaps sensing the fragility of its new approach, the plurality opinion then pivots (as the *à la mode* vernacular has it)—from focusing on whether *Colony* concluded that there was gap-filling authority to focusing on whether *Colony* concluded that there was any gap to be filled: "The question is whether the Court in *Colony* concluded that the statute left such a gap. And, in our view, the opinion ... makes clear that it did not." How does the plurality know this? Because Justice Harlan's opinion "said that the taxpayer had the better side of the textual argument"; because it found that legislative history indicated "that Congress intended overstatements of basis to fall outside the statute's scope"; because it concluded that the Commissioner's interpretation would "create a patent incongruity in the tax law"; and because it found its interpretation "in harmony with the [now] unambiguous language" of the 1954 Code. But these are the sorts of arguments that courts *always* use in *resolving* ambiguities. They do not prove that no ambiguity existed, unless one believes that an ambiguity resolved is an ambiguity that never existed in the first place. *Colony* said unambiguously that the text was ambiguous, and that should be an end of the matter—unless one wants simply to deny *stare decisis* effect to *Colony* as a pre-*Chevron* decision.

Rather than making our judicial-review jurisprudence curiouser and curiouser, the Court should abandon the opinion that produces these contortions, *Brand X*....

◆ JUSTICE KENNEDY, with whom JUSTICE GINSBURG, JUSTICE SOTOMAYOR, and JUSTICE KAGAN join, dissenting.

... In [*Brand X*], the Court held that a judicial construction of an ambiguous statute did not foreclose an agency's later, inconsistent interpretation of the same provision. This general rule recognizes that filling gaps left by ambiguities in a statute "involves difficult policy choices that agencies are better equipped to make than courts." There has been no opportunity to decide whether the analysis would be any different if an agency sought to interpret an ambiguous statute in a way that was inconsistent with this Court's own, earlier reading of the law.

These issues are not implicated here. In *Colony* the Court did interpret the same phrase that must be interpreted in this case. The language was in a predecessor statute, however, and Congress has added new language that, in my view, controls the analysis and should instruct the Court to reach a different outcome today. The Treasury Department's regulations were promulgated in light of these statutory revisions, which were not at issue in *Colony*. There is a serious difficulty to insisting, as the Court does today, that an ambiguous provision must continue to be read the same way even after it has been reenacted with additional language suggesting Congress would permit a different interpretation. Agencies with the responsibility and expertise necessary to administer ongoing regulatory schemes should have the latitude and discretion to implement their interpretation of provisions reenacted in a new statutory framework. And this is especially so when the new language enacted by Congress seems to favor the very interpretation at issue. The approach taken by the Court instead forecloses later interpretations of a law that has changed in relevant ways. The Court goes too far, in my respectful view, in constricting Congress's ability to leave agencies in charge of filling statutory gaps....

* * *

Points for Discussion

1. *Statutory Language*: What was the language at issue? What did each party want that language to mean? What meaning did the plurality and dissent adopt?

2. *Theories*: In this case, the plurality and dissent tried to determine whether the *Colony* Court had found the statute ambiguous. The plurality considered all of the sources considered by the *Colony* Court, including text, legislative history, absurdity, and subsequent acts. The dissent stopped when the *Colony* Court said the language was "not unambiguous."

3. *Brand X*: Let's make sure you understand how *Brand X* and *Home Concrete* interact. Why does *Brand X* apply to the issue in *Home Concrete*? And what analysis should you perform to determine whether the Treasury had the *power* to change the interpretation?

4. *Colony's Holding*: According to the Court in *Colony*, the text of the statute was "not unambiguous." So why was that not the end of the plurality's analysis under *Brand X*? Is step one of *Chevron* a search for textual clarity, as Justice Scalia argues, or is it a search for congressional intent using all the sources (or tools) of statutory interpretation, as Justice Stevens said in footnote 9 of *Chevron*? Assuming the latter, what other sources did the *Colony* court consider?

5. *Justice Scalia's Concurrence*: Justice Scalia lamented that the plurality used the wrong analysis to conclude that the *Colony* Court had determined that there was

no gap for the agency to fill. The plurality, he said, relied on the types of arguments that are typically used to resolve ambiguity. Instead, he argued, the plurality should have focused solely on the *Colony* Court's statement that the text was "not unambiguous." Is not Justice Scalia simply disagreeing, once again, about the nature of the inquiry at *Chevron* step one?

6. *Justice Kennedy's dissent*: Did the dissent disagree with the plurality's decision that *Brand X* applied or with the plurality's application of *Brand X*? How would the dissent have resolved the issue? The dissent concluded that *Brand X* was inapplicable because the statute was different from the statute the *Colony* Court had interpreted. The statute had been amended. The plurality's response to this "amendment" argument was omitted. Hence, the dissent simply applied *Chevron* to the agency's interpretation of this new statutory language and concluded that the new interpretation was reasonable.

   Alternatively, the dissent could have reached the same outcome by applying *Brand X*, concluding that the agency had the *power* to interpret the statute differently, and then applying *Chevron* to evaluate the new interpretation. The dissent would then have to conclude either (1) that Congress had now directly spoken to the precise issue before the Court given the new language (step one) and the agency's interpretation matched Congressional intent, or (2) that the agency's new interpretation was reasonable given the new language (step two). Do you understand how the dissent could have reached the same result using any of these three approaches?

7. *Legislative Correction*: On July 31, 2015, Congress enacted H.R. 3236, Surface Transportation and Veterans Health Care Choice Improvement Act of 2015. Section 2005 of the Act amended 26 U.S.C. § 6501(e)(1), which is the exception to the three-year statute of limitations at issue in *Colony* and *Home Concrete*. The amendment provides: "An understatement of gross income by reason of an overstatement of unrecovered cost or other basis is an omission from gross income." This amendment legislatively overruled both *Colony* and *Home Concrete & Supply*. Would the IRS be able to change its interpretation of this statute after the amendment?

* * *

Problem 19C

Assume that after *Chevron v. Natural Defense Resources*, the Environmental Protection Agency (EPA) promulgated a new regulation using notice and comment procedures interpreting the term "statutory source" to mean each individual, pollution emitting device, rather than the plant as a whole. In other words, the EPA changed its prior rule. When industry challenges the agency's interpretation of the statute in the new regulation, how should a court rule?

* * *

Chapter 20

Conclusion: The Linear Approach to Statutory Interpretation

A. Introduction to This Chapter

While there is more than one way to approach interpretation, the linear (or moderate textualist) approach appears to be gaining ground. For this reason, the outline below provides one possible step-by-step approach to convincing a court to interpret a statute in a way that would benefit your client. Because of the uncertainty in this area, however, it is not the only approach to try. Remain flexible and realize the depth of possible arguments that may be available to you.

The Linear Approach

- *Step 1*: Identify the language of the statute at issue
  - What do you want the language to mean?
  - What does your opponent want the language to mean?
- *Step 2*: Determine the ordinary or technical meaning of that language
  - Determine whether ordinary or technical meaning was intended
    - "words and phrases shall be construed according to the commonly approved usage of the language"
      - Ordinary meaning differs from definitional meaning
        - Ordinary meaning is narrower than dictionary meaning
        - Dictionary meaning is broader, including all ways words are used
        - Consider which dictionary to use
    - "technical words and phrases as have acquired a peculiar and appropriate meaning shall be construed accordingly"
      - Technical meaning was rarely intended
      - Exception: words with legal meaning
- *Step 3*: Determine whether the ordinary meaning is ambiguous
  - Ambiguity
    - Commonly defined: 2 or more reasonable people disagree
    - More accurately defined: 2 or more equally plausible meanings

- *Step 4*: Determine whether there is a reason to reject the ordinary meaning
  - Absurdity
    - Narrowly defined: would frustrate purpose/intent
    - Broadly defined: would shock the general moral/common sense
  - Scrivener's error, or
  - Constitutional avoidance doctrine
- *Step 5*: Determine whether other intrinsic sources are relevant to meaning
  - Grammar & Punctuation
    - Grammar and punctuation matter unless they contradict the ordinary meaning
    - Doctrine of last antecedent
  - Linguistic Canons
    - *In pari materia*
      - Whole act aspect
      - Related code aspect
    - The presumption of consistent usage and meaningful variation
    - The rule against surplusage, or redundancy
    - *Noscitur a sociis* (listed words)
    - *Ejusdem generis* (general words & catch-alls)
    - *Expressio unius est exclusio alterius*
  - Textual Components
    - Titles
    - Preambles, findings, purpose clauses
    - Provisos/exceptions
    - Non-severability/severability clauses
- *Step 6*: Determine whether extrinsic sources are relevant to meaning
  - Other Laws
    - Conflicts within a jurisdiction
      - Harmonize if possible, if not
        - Specific statutes trump general statutes
        - Later-enacted statutes trump earlier-enacted statutes
        - Repeal by implication is disfavored
    - Conflicts across jurisdictions
      - Preemption

- Borrowed Acts
- Model & Uniform Acts
- Timing
  - Pre-enactment context
    - Legislative history
      - The legislative process
        - Bicameral passage
        - Presentment
      - Legislative record
        - Bill drafts
        - Committee reports & hearings
        - Floor debates
        - Conference committee reports
        - Presidential signing statements & veto messages
    - Purpose, or spirit
  - Post-enactment context
    - Subsequent legislative acts (statutes)
    - "Subsequent" legislative history
    - Super-strong *stare decisis* & legislative acquiescence
    - Agency Interpretations: Standard of Review
      - Regulations
        - *Auer* = plainly wrong
      - Statutes
        - *Chevron* step zero
          - *Skidmore* = power-to-persuade test, or
            - No congressional intent to defer
          - *Chevron* = two step analysis
            - Congressional intent to defer
            - Has Congress spoken to the precise issue before the court?
            - If not, is the agency interpretation reasonable?
        - *Brand X*
          - Agency power to interpret after a court interprets a statute
- *Step 7*: Determine whether policy-based sources are relevant to meaning
  - Canons based on the constitution

- ▪ Penal Statutes
  - · The rule of lenity
  - · *Ex post facto* prohibition
- ▪ Clear Statement Rules
  - · Federalism
  - · American Indian lands
  - · Preemption
  - · Sovereign Immunity
- ▪ Canons based on prudential considerations
  - · Statutes in derogation of the common law are narrowly construed
  - · Remedial statutes are broadly construed
  - · Implied causes of action & remedies

B. The Linear Approach in Action

In the case below, see if you can identify the linear approach and each source the court examines. Are there any sources that you think should have been used but were not?

People v. Spriggs

Court of Appeal of the State of California
224 Cal. App. 4th 150 (2014)

◆ LEVY, ACTING P.J.

While stopped in heavy traffic, Steven Spriggs pulled out his wireless telephone to check a map application for a way around the congestion. A California Highway Patrol officer spotted him holding his telephone, pulled him over, and issued him a traffic citation for violating Vehicle Code section 23123, subdivision (a), which prohibits drivers from "using a wireless telephone unless that telephone is specifically designed and configured to allow hands-free listening and talking, and is used in that manner while driving." Spriggs contends he did not violate the statute because he was not talking on the telephone. We agree. Based on the statute's language, its legislative history, and subsequent legislative enactments, we conclude that the statute means what it says—it prohibits a driver only from holding a wireless telephone while conversing on it. Consequently, we reverse his conviction.

After Spriggs was cited for violating ... section 23123(a), he contested the citation.... The traffic court commissioner subsequently found Spriggs guilty of violating section 23123(a) and ordered him to pay a $165 fine....

On appeal, Spriggs asserts [that] he was not "using" the wireless telephone within the meaning of the statute because the statute applies only if a driver is listening and talking on a wireless telephone that is not being used in a hands-free mode. The People contend the statute is much broader and applies to all uses of a wireless telephone unless the telephone is used in a hands-free manner....

DISCUSSION

1. The applicable principles of statutory construction are well-settled.

... The principles of statutory construction are clearly established. "Our task is to discern the Legislature's intent. The statutory language itself is the most reliable indicator, so we start with the statute's words, assigning them their usual and ordinary meanings, and construing them in context. If the words themselves are not ambiguous, we presume the Legislature meant what it said, and the statute's plain meaning governs. On the other hand, if the language allows more than one reasonable construction, we may look to such aids as the legislative history of the measure and maxims of statutory construction. In cases of uncertain meaning, we may also consider the consequences of a particular interpretation, including its impact on public policy." Moreover, "[r]eviewing courts may turn to the legislative history behind even unambiguous statutes when it confirms or bolsters their interpretation."

To resolve [an] ambiguity, we rely upon well-settled rules. "The meaning of a statute may not be determined from a single word or sentence; the words must be construed in context, and provisions relating to the same subject matter must be harmonized to the extent possible. Literal construction should not prevail if it is contrary to the legislative intent apparent in the statute.... An interpretation that renders related provisions nugatory must be avoided; each sentence must be read not in isolation but in light of the statutory scheme; and if a statute is amenable to two alternative interpretations, the one that leads to the more reasonable result will be followed." We must interpret a statute in accord with its legislative intent and where the Legislature expressly declares its intent, we must accept that declaration. Absurd or unjust results will never be ascribed to the Legislature, and a literal construction of a statute will not be followed if it is opposed to its legislative intent.

2. Section 23123(a) is reasonably construed as only prohibiting a driver from holding a wireless telephone while conversing on it.

a. Statutory language

Section 23123(a) provides: "A person shall not drive a motor vehicle while using a wireless telephone unless that telephone is specifically designed and configured to allow hands-free listening and talking, and is used in that manner while driving." The statute does not define the word "using" or any other term contained therein.

Spriggs contends the statute is clear: "It applies if a person is listening or talking on a wireless telephone while driving and while the wireless telephone is not being used in hands-free mode." He asserts this interpretation is bolstered by the words "telephone" and "hands-free listening and talking[,]" which demonstrate the focus of the statute is on talking on the wireless telephone and not some other use of the telephone, such as looking at a map application.

The People, however, assert the statute clearly prohibits the act of "using a wireless telephone" while driving and, since the word "using" is not ambiguous, it encompasses all uses of the telephone. According to the People, the statute "allows 'using' a wireless 'telephone while driving if the telephone is specifically designed and configured to allow hands-free listening and talking, and is used in that manner while driving.' Otherwise, using a wireless telephone while driving is prohibited." The People reason that, because under section 23123(a) a "driver may not use *a cell phone unless it is used in a hands-free manner[,]" that section is violated when a driver holds a wireless telephone and looks at a map application while driving.*

While the statute may be interpreted, on its face, as the People assert, we agree with Spriggs that the statute is reasonably construed as only prohibiting engaging in a conversation on a wireless telephone while driving and holding the telephone in one's hand.... Had the Legislature intended to prohibit drivers from holding the telephone and using it for all purposes, it would not have limited the telephone's required design and configuration to "hands-free listening and talking," but would have used broader language, such as "hands-free operation" or "hands-free use." To interpret section 23123(a) as applying to any use of a wireless telephone renders the "listening and talking" element nonsensical, as not all uses of a wireless telephone involve listening and talking, including looking at a map application....

b. Legislative history

The legislative history of section 23123(a) supports our interpretation. Section 23123 was enacted ... as part of the California Wireless Telephone Automobile Safety Act of 2006 (the Act). A review of the legislative history ... reveals that, while the Legislature was concerned about hand-held use of wireless telephones, this concern was addressed by prohibiting drivers from engaging in conversations while holding the telephone in one's hand rather than prohibiting all hand-held uses of the telephone.

As explained in both the Senate and Assembly analyses of the bill, two distractions arise when one uses a cell phone while driving: (1) "the physical distraction a motorist encounters when picking up the phone, punching the number keypad, holding the phone up to his or her ear to converse, or pushing a button to end a call"; and (2) "the mental distraction which results from the ongoing conversation carried on between the motorist and the person on the other end of the line."

According to these analyses, the bill addresses the first distraction, i.e. the physical distraction of placing a telephone call and holding the phone to one's ear to converse. There is no mention in the legislative history of trying to prevent distractions that arise from other uses of a wireless telephone when driving, such as looking at a map application while holding the telephone....

c. Executive Branch actions

[S]tatements from the executive branch, while not controlling, further confirm the law was intended to only prohibit holding wireless telephones during conversations.... [I]n Governor Schwarzenegger's press release upon signing the bill, the Governor stated the "'simple fact is it's dangerous to talk on your cell phone while driving.'" The press release further commented: "Using a hands-free device while driving does not eliminate the distraction that comes with cell phones. Talking on the phone and dialing and hanging up the phone create a distraction. However, requiring drivers to use hands-free devices better ensures that drivers have two hands free to place on the wheel while driving."

4. The Legislature's subsequent enactments of sections 23124 and 23123.5 confirm it intended section 23123(a) to only prohibit a driver from holding a wireless telephone while conversing on it.

The Legislature's subsequent enactments pertaining to the use of wireless telephones and other electronic devices while driving confirm our conclusion. [The court explains that the legislature subsequently enacted two acts prohibiting drivers under age 18 and adult drivers from "from using a wireless telephone or other mobile service device even if used in a hands-free manner while operating a motor vehicle," including "talking, writing, sending, reading or using the internet, or any other function such a device may enable." Neither act would have been necessary if section 23123(a) were interpreted in the manner the state suggested.]

In sum, based on the legislative history of section 23123 and the statute's language, as well as the Legislature's subsequent enactments of sections 23123.5 and 23124, we conclude that section 23123(a) does not prohibit all hand-held uses of a wireless telephone. Instead, it prohibits "listening and talking" on the wireless telephone unless the telephone is used in a hands-free mode. Accordingly, Spriggs did not violate the statute when he held his cellular telephone in his hand and looked at a map application while driving and his conviction must be reversed.

* * *

Points for Discussion

1. *Statutory Language*: What was the language at issue? What did each party want that language to mean? What meaning did the court adopt?

2. *Theories*: Which theory did the court use? Did the court find ambiguity, absurdity, a constitutional question to avoid, or a scrivener's error?

3. *Linear Approach*: This opinion demonstrates the linear approach to interpretation that you have been learning. Notice how the court discusses the text first, then the legislative history, then subsequent executive and legislative acts to reach an interpretation. What sources are missing from this discussion that you believe are relevant?

4. *Smith v. United States*: Recall that in Chapter 5, you read *Smith v. United States*, 508 U.S. 223 (1993), in which the Supreme Court broadly interpreted the phrase "uses … a firearm" to include bartering a gun for drugs. In *Spriggs*, the California Court of Appeals narrowly interpreted the phrase "using a wireless telephone" to include only talking on the phone. Which court do you think more accurately discerned the ordinary meaning of the word use?

Problem 20

In 1951, after several well-publicized commercial airline crashes, the legislature of the State of Ames adopted the Aircraft Passenger Safety Law, which included the following provisions:[1]

Section 1. Findings and Purposes

(a) During the past year, four commercial airlines have crashed in Ames, injuring hundreds of persons, including passengers and persons on the ground in the crash sites.

(b) The airline crashes have caused millions of dollars of property damage in addition to personal injuries.

(c) Although the planes that have crashed were commercial airlines, smaller private aircraft can cause similar harm to individuals or property when such aircraft are not operated in a safe manner.

(d) Regulation of all aircraft under this law is necessary to protect the health, safety, and property of individuals in and around aircraft.

Section 2. Prohibited conduct

No person may operate a jet, biplane, turboprop, hot air balloon, blimp, helicopter, seaplane or any other aircraft in a reckless or careless manner so as to endanger the life or property of any person or the quiet enjoyment of any person's property.

Section 3. Licenses

(a) Except as provided in (b), no person may operate an aircraft unless that person obtains a license to operate an aircraft from the Ames Department of Aviation.

(b) This section does not require a license for the operation of a model airplane or other aircraft so long as it is operated solely by remote control.

Section 4. Penalties

Any person who violates any provision of this statute may be required to pay up to $10,000 for each violation and/or be imprisoned for up to six months. In addition, any person who violates any provision of this statute may be required to provide compensation to any person who is harmed by the violation of the statute for any personal injuries or property damage.

Section 5. Military Exception(added in 2005)

Nothing in this law applies to drones that are used for military purposes.

In January of this year, Jennifer McGill, a private attorney, was operating a drone (an unmanned flying device) to investigate the activities of the husband of a client she was helping with a divorce matter. McGill believed that the husband was involved

---

1. This problem was based on an exam question written by Professor Stephen M. Johnson. I am grateful to him for allowing me include a modified version in this text.

in an extra-marital affair, so she was using the drone to film evidence of the affair. Unfortunately, while McGill was operating the remote controls for the drone, an incoming call on her cell phone distracted her, and she crashed the drone into a grocery store window, injuring several shoppers and causing hundreds of dollars' worth of damage to the store. The Ames Attorney General, who enforces the Ames Aircraft Passenger Safety Act, filed a criminal complaint against McGill for violating Section 2 of the statute, seeking $10,000 in criminal penalties, in addition to compensation for the property damage the drone caused.

McGill would like to challenge the government's decision to prosecute. While unmanned aerial vehicles (often referred to as drones) were originally used in the United States by the military for surveillance and for combat purposes, civilians have used smaller versions of the devices for recreational purposes for many years, and businesses are beginning to use them for commercial purposes, including aerial photography, filming movies, inspecting wind farms, herding cattle, and tracking people, among other purposes. Indeed, Amazon and Google have begun to explore the use of drones to deliver packages to customers. Most of the non-military drones are operated at altitudes of 5 feet to 35 feet above the ground and most of the drones that are not used for commercial purposes weigh less than 55 pounds. While the drones are relatively quiet (sounding much like a buzzing wasp's nest), they can cause harm to persons or property (due to their speed and size) if they are operated in a careless or reckless manner. McGill has been using drones in furtherance of her business for several years and would like to continue to use them without being subjected to *criminal* prosecution for accidents that she might cause. She is perfectly willing to pay the costs of any injuries and damages she might cause.

McGill asked you for help. You do some research and discover the following information in the legislative history of the statute. When the bill was first introduced in the Ames Senate, Senator Hardy, the sponsor of the bill, introduced it as the *Aircraft Noise Reduction Act,* and indicated that the major purpose of the law was to reduce the noise caused by the proliferation of aircraft in residential neighborhoods. At that time, Section 2 prohibited only the operation of aircraft in a manner that interfered with the quiet enjoyment of property. Shortly after the bill was introduced, however, it was referred to the Senate Transportation Committee. At a hearing on the bill in committee, Senator Isakson suggested that it seemed nonsensical to work on legislation to address the noise caused by aircraft when aircraft passengers were being injured in crashes at an alarming rate in Ames. He argued that the legislature should focus on protecting the safety of airline passengers. The Transportation Committee changed the title of the bill to the *Aircraft Passenger Safety Act,* changed the language in Section 2 to prohibit the operation of aircraft in a manner that endangers the health or safety of any individual or interferes with the quiet enjoyment of property. With the changes approved, the committee reported the bill to the full Senate, which passed the Bill 50 to 6.

In the Ames's General Assembly, the Senate version of the bill was referred to the General Assembly's Aviation Committee. While the committee approved the bill, the committee report indicated that, despite the title of the bill, the purpose of the Act was to protect persons and property that might be harmed by aircraft, regardless of whether they were passengers on the aircraft. When the bill reached the General Assembly floor, Representative Walton raised concerns that the bill seemed broad enough to regulate model airplanes as aircraft, an outcome that he considered unwise, because the bill required licenses for operators of all aircraft. Representative Tattnall, whose district included the leading national producer of model airplanes, responded, in a statement on the floor, that a licensing requirement for model airplanes would be absurd. He stated that the term "aircraft" clearly did not include model airplanes, arguing that because a string of common law court decisions in Ames had protected persons who operated model airplanes and remote controlled aircraft from liability for nuisances or trespass, it would be inconsistent with these decisions for the bill to require licenses or impose other limitations on the operation of model airplanes or remote controlled aircraft in Ames. Nevertheless, to be safe, Tattnall proposed an amendment to Section 3 of the bill that exempted model airplanes and other remote controlled aircraft from the licensing requirements of the statute. After the amendment passed, the bill passed 256–9.

After these different versions of the bill passed both chambers, a conference committee reconciled the versions to produce the law above and issued a report. The conference committee report included the following statement: "In order to protect the health and safety of persons and property, broad regulation of aircraft used for commercial purposes is appropriate."

You also discovered that the bill that was modeled on a 1950 Mississippi statute and was identical to that statute. The Mississippi statute included an exemption in its Section 2 for the operation of model airplanes and remote controlled aircraft that was similar to the exemption the version from the general assembly had added to Section 3. The Mississippi statute, including the findings and purposes section, was identical to the statute Ames adopted.

Further, you discovered that in a 1973 case, *Ames v. Baldwin*, the Ames Supreme Court held that a model airplane that was being used for recreational purposes was not an aircraft for purposes of Section 2 of the Ames Passenger Safety Act. That decision has not been overruled, and the Ames legislature did not in response amend the law to expand the definition of aircraft in Section 2; however, the legislature did consider five different bills that would have amended the Ames Aircraft Passenger Safety Law to overrule *Baldwin*, but none of the bills passed both chambers.

In 2005, when the State of Ames began to produce drones for the military, the Ames legislature amended the Ames Aircraft Passenger Safety Law to include a new Section 5, which provides "Nothing in this law applies to drones that are used for military purposes." The amendment did not define "drones."

In 2010, the Mississippi Supreme Court concluded, in *Mississippi v. Wyatt*, that drones operated by civilians are exempt from the prohibitions in Section 2 of the Mississippi law, because they are remote controlled aircraft, regardless of whether they are operated for recreational or commercial purposes.

In 2011, the Ames legislature enacted the "Protect Our Parks" statute, which was designed to protect state parks from over-use by recreational outfitters. The legislature concluded that hang-gliding, helicopter tours, and various other activities were interfering with the aesthetics of the parks, increasing access to and traffic in areas of the parks that were formerly wilderness areas, and degrading the environment of the parks. Accordingly, the Act prohibited the operation of aircraft in state parks, except in accordance with regulations established by the State Parks Commissioner. The Protect Our Parks Act defines aircraft broadly to include "model aircraft, drones of all types, and many other remote controlled aircraft."

In addition to all of the research outlined above, you conclude that the term "aircraft" is defined currently, by Dictionary.com as "any machine capable of flying by means of buoyancy or aerodynamic forces, such as a powered glider, helicopter, or airplane." The New American Dictionary, which was published in 1951, defined aircraft as "a machine capable of transporting persons through the air." Finally, you learn that within the toy manufacturing industry, drones are included within that industry's definition of "aircraft."

If McGill concedes that her operation of the drone was reckless or careless, what arguments can you make on her behalf that Ames cannot impose criminal penalties?

Assume instead, that the Aircraft Passenger Safety Law is a federal law, rather than a state law, that all references in the preceding question to the Ames legislature refer to Congress, that all references in the preceding question to the Ames Supreme Court refer to the U.S. Supreme Court, and that the Federal Aviation Administration ("FAA") enforces the Act, instead of the state Attorney General. In addition, assume that the law includes the following provision, in addition to the provisions above:

Section 6. Federal Aviation Administration

The Federal Aviation Administration may issue such regulations as are necessary to interpret and implement this statute and conduct hearings on the record as necessary to enforce this act.

Assume the following additional facts:

In 2006, after the Aircraft Passenger Safety Act was amended to exempt military drones from regulation as "aircraft" under Section 5 of the law, the FAA posted a policy statement to its website. The policy statement provided, "Although the 2005 amendment only explicitly exempts military drones from regulation as 'aircraft' under the Aircraft Passenger Safety Act, civilian drones do not pose any threat to health, welfare, or the quiet enjoyment of property, so we do not intend to regulate them as 'aircraft' under the law, regardless of whether such civilian drones are used for recreational or commercial purposes."

By 2010, however, there was a significant increase in the use of drones for commercial purposes, and the FAA determined that they posed a significant risk of harm to persons and property if operated in a careless or reckless manner. Accordingly, in 2011, the FAA adopted rules, using notice and comment rulemaking procedures, that defined "aircraft," in the Aircraft Passenger Safety Act, to include drones operated by civilians. In the preamble to its final rule, the FAA explained, "Although many organizations commented that the FAA should exempt civilian drones from regulation and although Congress exempted military drones from the definition of 'aircraft' under the law, most of the operations of military drones take place outside of the United States or in areas that are not heavily populated. Drones operated by civilians, on the other hand, are routinely used in the United States and are frequently used in heavily populated areas. Thus, it is reasonable to regulate them as 'aircraft,' even though military drones are exempted from regulation as 'aircraft.'"

If Jennifer McGill is prosecuted for violating Section 2 of the statute for the conduct described earlier, how would your analysis of the statute differ, if at all, from the analysis you provided earlier?

Appendix A

Glossary

Absurdity doctrine — when interpreting a statute according to its ordinary meaning would lead to absurd results, courts can avoid the ordinary meaning

Act — a bill that Congress has passed and the president has signed; an enacted bill

Adjudication — agency action that is similar to civil litigation; can be very informal

Administrative Procedures Act — the statute that governs the procedural activities of federal agencies

Agency — "each authority of the Government of the United States ... not include[ing Congress, the courts, state governments, etc.]"

Ambiguity — when reasonable people understand words to have more than one meaning

Amendment by Implication — when the legislature does not indicate expressly that it is amending a statute, but the judiciary assumes that the legislature intended to amend the existing statute

Appropriations Bill — a bill that authorizes the government to spend money

Auer (Seminole Rock) **Deference** — judicial deference to agency interpretations of regulations; the standard is plainly wrong

Bargaining Theory — a legislative process theory that focuses on furthering the compromises that lead to a bill's passage

Bicameral Passage — the Constitutional requirement that both chambers of Congress pass a bill in identical form before it can become law; also required in almost all states

Bill — a law that Congress or the President has or is considering but is not yet an act

Borrowed Statutes — statutes that are taken, in whole or in part, from another jurisdiction

Cabinet — the collective heads of the Departments, who have served to guide the president in years past

Canons of Interpretation — rules of thumb, or guides, judges use when interpreting statutes

Chevron's **two step deference**—judicial deference to agency interpretations of a statute; requires that the court look first to see if Congress has spoken on the precise issue, and then if not, to defer to any reasonable agency interpretation

Clear Statement Rules—courts require the legislature to make a clear or plain statement when a statute will impact important rights such as federalism, because the court assumes that a legislature would not make such a major change without being absolutely clear

Cloture—the process in which sixty senators agree to defeat a filibuster

Codification—the process of consolidating statutes into subjects, forming a legal code

Committee of the Whole—the largest committee in the House, which is made up of all representatives and was formed to debate proposed bills

Conference Committee—an ad hoc committee of select senators and representatives who try to resolve differences in bills the House and Senate pass

Conflicting statutes—statutes that cannot exist harmoniously

Contextualism—the process of using the context to determine why the legislature acted or to determine what a statute means

Delegation Doctrine—the doctrine by which the Supreme Court determines whether intelligible principles sufficiently constrain the power delegated to agencies from Congress

Derogation of the Common Law—a statute that partially repeals or abolishes existing common law rights or otherwise limits the scope, utility, or force of that law

Dog-Does-Not-Bark Doctrine—the canon that directs that silence in the legislative history about a particular subject is generally not a good guide to meaning

Dynamic Interpretation—a theory of interpretation that encourage judges to be flexible and consider what the enacting legislature would have wanted given common day realities

Ejusdem Generis—the linguistic canon that general words should be limited to include only things similar in nature to the specific words near the general words

Enacting Clause—a section of a bill that is statutorily required. Components following enacting clauses are codified. Components preceding enacting clauses are not codified.

Engrossed Bill—a bill that one chamber of Congress has passed and forwarded to the other Chamber

Enrolled Bill—a bill that both chambers of Congress have passed in identical form and have forwarded to the president for signature

Enrolled Bill Rule—the rule that once a bill is filed, it is conclusively presumed to have been validly adopted

Executive Agency—an agency that is subject to presidential control for the head serves at the pleasure of the president

Executive Order—statements from a president or governor directing agencies and officials in the execution of legislatively granted authority

***Ex Post Facto* Law**—a law that redefines what is criminal conduct or increases the penalty for criminal conduct; the *Ex Post Facto* Clause of the U.S. Constitution prohibits such laws

Expressio Unius Est Exclusio Alterius —the linguistic canon of negative implication such that the inclusion of one thing means the exclusion of another

Extrinsic Sources of Meaning—materials outside of the official act, but within the legislative process that created the act

Filibuster—a delaying tactic used in the Senate to prevent a vote on a bill

Formalism—an approach the Supreme Court uses in separation of powers cases to maintain three distinct branches of government with constitutionally defined powers

Functionalism—an approach the Supreme Court uses in separation of powers cases to balance the inevitable overlap among the branches

Funnel of Abstraction—a v-shaped diagram Professors Eskridge and Frickey generated that depicts the sources of interpretation on one side of the v and the concreteness of that source on the other side of the v to explain pragmatic theory

General Assemblies—the name for state legislatures

Germaneness Rule—the rule in the house that permits amendments to bills only if the amendments are germane

Golden Rule Exception—the absurdity doctrine; the idea that if interpreting a statute according to its ordinary meaning would lead to absurd results, a court can avoid the ordinary meaning

Imaginative Reconstructionism—a theory of interpretation in which a judge would try to imagine what the enacting legislature would have intended had the precise factual problem before the court been raised during the enactment process

Implied Causes of Action and Remedies—causes of action and remedies that are not expressly provided for in the statute, but that the court implies based on the goals of the legislature

Independent Agency—a type of agency that is independent from the president because it is headed by a multi-member, bi-partisan board, serving terms.

Initiative Process—a form of direct democracy in which a certain minimum number of registered voters sign a petition to force a public vote on a proposed issue

In Pari Materia —a linguistic canon that identifies the statutory material that judges can legitimately look at to discern meaning, including the entire act and other statutes with similar purposes

Inseverability Provision—a provision in a bill or act that indicates a legislature's expectation that if any provision in the act is unconstitutional, the act as a whole must fail

Intentionalism—a theory of statutory interpretation that focuses on finding the specific intent of the enacting legislature

Intrinsic Sources of Meaning—sources of meaning from the official act being interpreted, also called textual sources

Journal Entry Rule—a rule in states that allows judges to determine whether constitutional enactment requirements were met by looking at the bill's journal entry

Last Antecedent, Doctrine of—a grammar canon that directs that a limiting or restrictive clause in a statute is generally construed to restrict the immediately preceding clause unless a comma separates the two

Last Enacted Rule—the doctrine that when two statutes conflict and cannot be harmonized, the last in time controls

Legislative Acquiescence—the reasoning that the legislature's failure to take action in response to a judicial interpretation of a statute means that the legislature agreed with, or acquiesced to, the judicial interpretation

Legislative History—the written record of deliberations surrounding and preceding a bill's enactment, including committee reports and hearing transcripts, floor debates, recorded votes, conference committee reports, presidential signing and veto messages, etc.

Legislative Inaction—when the legislature takes no action in response to a judicial interpretation of a statute

Legislative Intent, General—the purpose of the enacting legislature for enacting a bill

Legislative Intent, Specific—the intent of the enacting legislature on the specific issue before the court

Legislative Rules—rules an agency enacted via informal or formal rulemaking processes (legislative rulemaking is the process of enacting legislative rules)

Lenity, Rule of—a canon of interpretation based on due process concerns that judges should narrowly interpret penal statutes

Lobbyists—individuals who are generally paid to represent a particular point of view for a specific industry or organization

Mischief Rule—the idea that statutes should be interpreted to further their purpose or to limit the mischief the statute was designed to remedy

Model Acts—proposed acts that the National Conference of Commissioners on Uniform State Laws or the American Law Institute developed to address multijurisdictional issues; uniformity is not central

New Textualism—a form of textualism credited to former Justice Antonin Scalia

Non-legislative Rule—a rule an agency enacted without using informal or formal rulemaking procedures (non-legislative rulemaking is the process of issuing a non-legislative rule)

Noscitur a Sociis—the linguistic canon that when a word has more than one meaning, the appropriate meaning should be gleaned from the words surrounding the word being interpreted; generally used when the statute contains a list of words

Notice and Comment Rulemaking—another name for informal rulemaking required under the administrative procedures act; an agency publishes notice of a proposed rule, then seeks public comment on the rule

Ordinary Meaning—the commonly understood meaning of a word or phrase often arrived at by consulting a dictionary

Override—Congress's ability to overcome a president's veto of a bill, requires 2/3 positive vote from each chamber of Congress

Penal Statute—a statute that has a punitive effect

Plain Meaning Rule—a canon that allows judges to presume that words in a statute have their "plain," or "ordinary," meaning

Pluralist Theories—theories of legislative process that focus on the role special interest groups play in setting legislative policy, such as bargaining theory and public choice theory

Pocket Veto—if the president does not sign an enrolled bill for ten days during which Congress adjourns, the bill is vetoed

Policy-Based Sources of Meaning—sources of meaning that are extrinsic to both the statutory act and the legislative process; generally based on the Constitution or policy considerations

Preambles—a component in a bill that often precedes the enacting clause and explains the reason the statute is being enacted; a purpose clause

Preemption—the displacing effect that federal law has on conflicting or inconsistent state law

Presentment—the Constitutional requirement that a bill be presented to the president and be signed before it becomes law

President *Pro Tempore*—usually the most senior senator in the majority party

Proviso—a clause in a statute that creates an exception to or otherwise limits the effect of another provision; provisos often start with "provided that," "except for," and "provided however"

Public Choice Theory—a legislative process theory that statutes are the result of compromises among legislators and various competing private interest groups

Purpose—the reason the statute was enacted, the mischief that was designed to be remedied, also called the spirit of the law

Purposivism—a theory of statutory interpretation that focuses on the purpose of the statute and looks at all sources of meaning

Recodification—to codify again

Referendum — a popular form of democracy that allows voters to approve or reject legislation a legislature pass

Regulation — a rule an agency enacted via its rulemaking procedures

Remedial Statutes — statutes that are *in aid* of the common law or create new rights and remedies rather than being in derogation of the common law

Repeal by Implication — when the legislature does not indicate expressly that it is repealing a statute, but the judiciary assumes that the legislature intended to repeal the existing statute, in part or in full, because it cannot exist in harmony with a conflicting statute

Retroactive — statutes that govern both past and future conduct; generally statutes only govern future conduct

Rules Committee — the committee in the House or Senate that determines the rules governing debate on proposed bills

Scrivener's Error — a doctrine that permits judges to correct obvious clerical or typographical errors

Separation of Powers — the notion that the powers of government should be split among the various branches of government

Session Laws — legislative enactments for an annual period that have been bound chronologically; federal session laws can be found in the U.S. Statutes at Large

Severability Provision — a provision in a bill or act that indicates a legislature's expectation that if any one section of an act is unconstitutional, then it shall be severed so that the rest of the act may be saved

Signing Statements — statements a president or governor issues when a bill is passed, often to impact the law in some way

Single Subject Rule — the rule in most state constitutions that bills may only include one subject

***Skidmore* Deference** — judicial deference to agency interpretations that do not receive *Chevron* deference; agency interpretations receive deference to the extent that they have the power-to-persuade the court

Slip Laws — a legislative enactment that is published separately and promptly after passage, which can be used and cited in temporary form until it is published in a more permanent form by the Government Printing Office or state equivalent

Sovereign Immunity — a judge made doctrine that a government or sovereign may not be sued without its consent

Speaker of the House — the leader of the House of Representatives

Spirit of the Law — the purpose of the statute

Stare Decisis — the policy of the court to respect prior precedent

Statute — a written law enacted by a legislative body and the executive, a section or piece of an act

Statutes at Large (U.S.) — a chronological compilation of all enacted acts

Strict Construction — a theory of interpretation similar to textualism that strictly construes words in the statute

Super-Strong *Stare Decisis* — a heightened form of *stare decisis* the Supreme Court (and occasionally lower courts) uses for its statutory interpretation decisions

Technical Meaning Rule — a corollary to the plain meaning rule: the technical meaning rule is a canon that a word or phrase that has acquired a technical or particular meaning in a particular context has that meaning if it is used in that context

Textualism — a theory of statutory interpretation that focuses on the text and intrinsic sources of meaning

Unicameral — a legislature like Nebraska's that has only one chamber

Uniform Acts — proposed acts the National Conference of Commissioners on Uniform State Laws or the American Law Institute developed to address multijurisdictional issues; uniformity is central across jurisdictions

Uniform Statute & Rule Construction Act — a uniform act the National Conference of Commissioners on Uniform State Laws drafted to unify statutory interpretation

Veto — the president's rejection of a bill

Vetogate — a term Professors Eskridge and Frickey coined to describe the chokepoints in the legislative process that can prevent a bill from becoming law, such as committee votes

Whip — legislators who try to ensure that the party's members vote as the party leadership desires

Whole Act Rule — a component of the *in pari materia* canon that a court may look to the entire act when construing a statute

Whole Code Rule — a component of the *in pari materia* canon that a court may look to the entire code, so long as the statutes have similar purposes, when construing a statute

Appendix B

House Bill 916

110TH CONGRESS   H.R. 916 Union Calendar No. 88
1ST SESSION
[Report No. 110-148]

To provide for loan repayment for prosecutors and public defenders.

IN THE HOUSE OF REPRESENTATIVES
FEBRUARY 8, 2007

Mr. SCOTT of Georgia (for himself, Mr. GORDON of Tennessee, Mr. LEWIS of Georgia, Mr. PAYNE....) introduced the following bill; which was referred to the Committee on the Judiciary

MAY 14, 2007

Additional sponsors: Mr. LINCOLN DAVIS of Tennessee, Mr. COOPER, Mr. CHANDLER, Mr. UDALL of Colorado....

MAY 14, 2007

Reported with an amendment, committed to the Committee of the Whole House on the State of the Union, and ordered to be printed

---

A BILL

To provide for loan repayment for prosecutors and public defenders.

Be it enacted by the Senate and House of Representatives of the United States of America in Congress assembled,

SECTION 1. SHORT TITLE.

This Act may be cited as the "John R. Justice Prosecutors and Defenders Incentive Act of 2007".

SEC. 2. LOAN REPAYMENT FOR PROSECUTORS AND DEFENDERS.

Title I of the Omnibus Crime Control and Safe Streets Act of 1968 (42 U.S.C. 3711 et seq.) is amended by adding at the end the following:
"PART JJ—LOAN REPAYMENT FOR PROSECUTORS AND PUBLIC DEFENDERS

"SEC. 3111. GRANT AUTHORIZATION.

"(a) PURPOSE. — The purpose of this section is to encourage qualified individuals to enter and continue employment as prosecutors and public defenders.

"(b) DEFINITIONS. — In this section:

"(1) PROSECUTOR. — The term 'prosecutor' means a full-time employee of a State or local agency who —

"(A) is continually licensed to practice law; and

"(B) prosecutes criminal or juvenile delinquency cases (or both) at the State or local level, including an employee who supervises, educates, or trains other persons prosecuting such cases.

"(2) PUBLIC DEFENDER. — The term 'public defender' means an attorney who —

"(A) is continually licensed to practice law; and

"(B) is —

"(i) a full-time employee of a State or local agency who provides legal representation to indigent persons in criminal or juvenile delinquency cases (or both), including an attorney who supervises, educates, or trains other persons providing such representation;

"(ii) a full-time employee of a non-profit organization operating under a contract with a State or unit of local government, who devotes substantially all of such full-time employment to providing legal representation to indigent persons in criminal or juvenile delinquency cases (or both), including an attorney who supervises, educates, or trains other persons providing such representation; or

"(iii) employed as a full-time Federal defender attorney in a defender organization established pursuant to subsection (g) of section 3006A of title 18, United States Code, that provides legal representation to indigent persons in criminal or juvenile delinquency cases (or both).

"(3) STUDENT LOAN. — The term 'student loan' means —

"(A) a loan made, insured, or guaranteed under part B of title IV of the Higher Education Act of 1965 (20 U.S.C. 1071 et seq.);

"(B) a loan made under part D or E of 20 title IV of the Higher Education Act of 1965 (20 U.S.C. 1087a et seq. and 1087aa et seq.); and

"(C) a loan made under section 428C or 23 455(g) of the Higher Education Act of 1965 (20 U.S.C. 1078-3 and 1087e(g)) to the extent that such loan was used to repay a Federal Direct Stafford Loan, a Federal Direct Unsubsidized Stafford Loan, or a loan made under section 428 or 428H of such Act.

"(c) PROGRAM AUTHORIZED. — The Attorney General 5 shall, subject to the availability of appropriations, establish a program by which the Department of

Justice shall assume the obligation to repay a student loan, by direct payments on behalf of a borrower to the holder of such loan, in accordance with subsection (d), for any borrower who—

"(1) is employed as a prosecutor or public defender; and

"(2) is not in default on a loan for which the borrower seeks forgiveness.

"(d) TERMS OF LOAN REPAYMENT.—

"(1) BORROWER AGREEMENT.—To be eligible to receive repayment benefits under subsection (c), a borrower shall enter into a written agreement with the Attorney General that specifies that—

"(A) the borrower will remain employed as a prosecutor or public defender for a required period of service of not less than 3 years, unless in voluntarily separated from that employment;

"(B) if the borrower is involuntarily separated from employment on account of misconduct, or voluntarily separates from employment, before the end of the period specified in the agreement, the borrower will repay the Attorney General the amount of any benefits received by such employee under this section; and

"(C) if the borrower is required to repay an amount to the Attorney General under subparagraph (B) and fails to repay such amount, a sum equal to that amount shall be recoverable by the Federal Government from the employee (or such employee's estate, if applicable) by such methods as are provided by law for the recovery of amounts owed to the Federal Government.

"(2) REPAYMENT BY BORROWER.—

"(A) IN GENERAL.—Any amount repaid by, or recovered from, an individual or the estate of an individual under this subsection shall be credited to the appropriation account from which the amount involved was originally paid.

"(B) MERGER.—Any amount credited under subparagraph (A) shall be merged with other sums in such account and shall be available for the same purposes and period, and subject to the same limitations, if any, as the sums with which the amount was merged.

"(C) WAIVER.—The Attorney General may waive, in whole or in part, a right of recovery under this subsection if it is shown that recovery would be against equity and good conscience or against the public interest.

"(3) LIMITATIONS.—

"(A) STUDENT LOAN PAYMENT AMOUNT.—Student loan repayments made by the Attorney General under this section shall be made subject to the availability of appropriations, and subject to such terms, limitations, or conditions as may be mutually agreed upon by the borrower and the Attorney General in an agreement under paragraph (1), except that the amount paid by the Attorney General under this section shall not exceed—

"(i) $10,000 for any borrower in any calendar year; or

"(ii) an aggregate total of $60,000 in the case of any borrower.

"(B) BEGINNING OF PAYMENTS.—Nothing in this section shall authorize the Attorney General to pay any amount to reimburse a borrower for any re-payments made by such borrower prior to the date on which the Attorney General entered into an agreement with the borrower under this subsection.

"(e) ADDITIONAL AGREEMENTS.—

"(1) IN GENERAL.—On completion of the required period of service under an agreement under subsection (d), the borrower and the Attorney General 7 may, subject to paragraph (2), enter into an additional agreement in accordance with subsection (d).

"(2) TERM.—An agreement entered into under paragraph (1) may require the borrower to remain employed as a prosecutor or public defender for less than 3 years.

"(f) AWARD BASIS; PRIORITY.—

"(1) AWARD BASIS.—The Attorney General shall provide repayment benefits under this section—

"(A) subject to the availability of appropriations; and

"(B) in accordance with paragraph (2), except that the Attorney General shall determine a fair allocation of repayment benefits among prosecutors and de-fenders, and among employing entities nationwide.

"(2) PRIORITY.—In providing repayment benefits under this section in any fiscal year, the Attorney General shall give priority to borrowers—

"(A) who, when compared to other eligible borrowers, have the least ability to repay their student loans (considering whether the borrower is the beneficiary of any other student loan repayment program), as determined by the Attorney General; or

"(B) who—

"(i) received repayment benefits under this section during the preceding fiscal year; and

"(ii) have completed less than 3 years of the first required period of service spec-ified for the borrower in an agreement entered into under subsection (d).

"(g) REGULATIONS.—The Attorney General is authorized to issue such regula-tions as may be necessary to carry out the provisions of this section.

"(h) REPORT BY INSPECTOR GENERAL.—Not later than 3 years after the date of the enactment of this section, the Inspector General of the Department of Justice shall submit to Congress a report on—

"(1) the cost of the program authorized under this section; and

"(2) the impact of such program on the hiring and retention of prosecutors and public defenders.

"(i) GAO STUDY. — Not later than one year 1 after the date of the enactment of this section, the Comptroller General shall conduct a study of, and report to Congress on, the impact that law school accreditation requirements and other factors have on the costs of law school and student access to law school, including the impact of such requirements on racial and ethnic minorities.

"(j) AUTHORIZATION OF APPROPRIATIONS. — There is authorized to be appropriated to carry out this section $25,000,000 for each of the fiscal years 2008 through 2013."

Appendix C

Companion Senate Bill to H.R. 916

John R. Justice Prosecutors and Defenders Incentive Act of 2007 (Reported in Senate)

S 442 RS

Calendar No. 113

110th CONGRESS

1st Session

S. 442

[Report No. 110-51]

To provide for loan repayment for prosecutors and public defenders.

IN THE SENATE OF THE UNITED STATES

January 31, 2007

Mr. DURBIN (for himself, Mr. SPECTER, Mr. LEAHY, Mr. SMITH, Mr. KERRY, Ms. COLLINS, Ms. LANDRIEU, Ms. SNOWE, Mr. BIDEN, Mr. COCHRAN, Mr. KENNEDY, Mr. FEINGOLD, Mrs. FEINSTEIN, Mr. SCHUMER, Mr. WHITE-HOUSE, Mr. COLEMAN, Mr. KOHL, and Mr. HARKIN) introduced the following bill; which was read twice and referred to the Committee on the Judiciary

April 10, 2007

Reported by Mr. LEAHY, with amendments

[Omit the part struck through and insert the part printed in italic]

———

A BILL

To provide for loan repayment for prosecutors and public defenders.

Be it enacted by the Senate and House of Representatives of the United States of America in Congress assembled,

SECTION 1. SHORT TITLE.

This Act may be cited as the "John R. Justice Prosecutors and Defenders Incentive Act of 2007".

SEC. 2. LOAN REPAYMENT FOR PROSECUTORS AND DEFENDERS.

Title I of the Omnibus Crime Control and Safe Streets Act of 1968 (42 U.S.C. 3711 et seq.) is amended by adding at the end the following:

"PART JJ—LOAN REPAYMENT FOR PROSECUTORS AND PUBLIC DEFENDERS
"SEC. 3111. GRANT AUTHORIZATION.

"(a) Purpose—The purpose of this section is to encourage qualified individuals to enter and continue employment as prosecutors and public defenders.

"(b) Definitions—In this section:

"(1) PROSECUTOR—The term "prosecutor" means a full-time employee of a State or local agency who—

"(A) is continually licensed to practice law; and

"(B) prosecutes criminal *or juvenile delinquency* cases at the State or local level*(including supervision, education, or training of other persons prosecuting such cases).*

"(2) PUBLIC DEFENDER—The term "public defender" means an attorney who—

"(A) is continually licensed to practice law; and

"(B) is—

"~~(i) a full-time employee of a State or local agency or a nonprofit organization operating under a contract with a State or unit of local government, that provides legal representation to indigent persons in criminal cases; or~~

"*(i) a full-time employee of a State or local agency who provides legal representation to indigent persons in criminal or juvenile delinquency cases (including supervision, education, or training of other persons providing such representation);*

"*(ii) a full-time employee of a nonprofit organization operating under a contract with a State or unit of local government, who devotes substantially all of his or her full-time employment to providing legal representation to indigent persons in criminal or juvenile delinquency cases, (including supervision, education, or training of other persons providing such representation); or*

"(ii)*(iii)* employed as a full-time Federal defender attorney in a defender organization established pursuant to subsection (g) of section 3006A of title 18, United States Code, that provides legal representation to indigent persons in criminal *or juvenile delinquency* cases.

"(3) STUDENT LOAN—The term "student loan" means—

"(A) a loan made, insured, or guaranteed under part B of title IV of the Higher Education Act of 1965 (20 U.S.C. 1071 et seq.);

"(B) a loan made under part D or E of title IV of the Higher Education Act of 1965 (20 U.S.C. 1087a et seq. and 1087aa et seq.); and

"(C) a loan made under section 428C or 455(g) of the Higher Education Act of 1965 (20 U.S.C. 1078-3 and 1087e(g)) to the extent that such loan was used to repay a Federal Direct Stafford Loan, a Federal Direct Unsubsidized Stafford Loan, or a loan made under section 428 or 428H of such Act.

"(c) Program Authorized—The Attorney General shall establish a program by which the Department of Justice shall assume the obligation to repay a student loan, by direct payments on behalf of a borrower to the holder of such loan, in accordance with subsection (d), for any borrower who—

"(1) is employed as a prosecutor or public defender; and

"(2) is not in default on a loan for which the borrower seeks forgiveness.

"(d) Terms of Agreement—

"(1) IN GENERAL—To be eligible to receive repayment benefits under subsection (c), a borrower shall enter into a written agreement that specifies that—

"(A) the borrower will remain employed as a prosecutor or public defender for a required period of service of not less than 3 years, unless involuntarily separated from that employment;

"(B) if the borrower is involuntarily separated from employment on account of misconduct, or voluntarily separates from employment, before the end of the period specified in the agreement, the borrower will repay the Attorney General the amount of any benefits received by such employee under this section;

"(C) if the borrower is required to repay an amount to the Attorney General under subparagraph (B) and fails to repay such amount, a sum equal to that amount shall be recoverable by the Federal Government from the employee (or such employee's estate, if applicable) by such methods as are provided by law for the recovery of amounts owed to the Federal Government;

"(D) the Attorney General may waive, in whole or in part, a right of recovery under this subsection if it is shown that recovery would be against equity and good conscience or against the public interest; and

"(E) the Attorney General shall make student loan payments under this section for the period of the agreement, subject to the availability of appropriations.

"(2) REPAYMENTS—

"(A) IN GENERAL—Any amount repaid by, or recovered from, an individual or the estate of an individual under this subsection shall be credited to the appropriation account from which the amount involved was originally paid.

"(B) MERGER—Any amount credited under subparagraph (A) shall be merged with other sums in such account and shall be available for the same purposes and period, and subject to the same limitations, if any, as the sums with which the amount was merged.

"(3) LIMITATIONS—

"(A) STUDENT LOAN PAYMENT AMOUNT—Student loan repayments made by the Attorney General under this section shall be made subject to such terms, limitations, or conditions as may be mutually agreed upon by the borrower and the Attorney General in an agreement under paragraph

(1), except that the amount paid by the Attorney General under this section shall not exceed—

"(i) $10,000 for any borrower in any calendar year; or

"(ii) an aggregate total of $60,000 in the case of any borrower.

"(B) BEGINNING OF PAYMENTS—Nothing in this section shall authorize the Attorney General to pay any amount to reimburse a borrower for any repayments made by such borrower prior to the date on which the Attorney General entered into an agreement with the borrower under this subsection.

"(e) Additional Agreements—

"(1) IN GENERAL—On completion of the required period of service under an agreement under subsection (d), the borrower and the Attorney General may, subject to paragraph (2), enter into an additional agreement in accordance with subsection (d).

"(2) TERM—An agreement entered into under paragraph (1) may require the borrower to remain employed as a prosecutor or public defender for less than 3 years.

~~"(f) Award Basis; Priority—~~

~~"(1) AWARD BASIS—Subject to paragraph (2), the Attorney General shall provide repayment benefits under this section on a first-come, first-served basis, and subject to the availability of appropriations.~~

~~"(2) PRIORITY—The Attorney General shall give priority in providing repayment benefits under this section in any fiscal year to a borrower who~~

"(f) Award Basis; Priority—

"(1) AWARD BASIS—Subject to paragraph (2), the Attorney General shall provide repayment benefits under this section—

"(A) giving priority to borrowers who have the least ability to repay their loans, except that the Attorney General shall determine a fair allocation of repayment benefits among prosecutors and public defenders, and among employing entities nationwide; and

"(B) subject to the availability of appropriations.

"(2) PRIORITY—The Attorney General shall give priority in providing repayment benefits under this section in any fiscal year to a borrower who—

"(A) received repayment benefits under this section during the preceding fiscal year; and

"(B) has completed less than 3 years of the first required period of service specified for the borrower in an agreement entered into under subsection (d).

"(g) Regulations—The Attorney General is authorized to issue such regulations as may be necessary to carry out the provisions of this section.

"*(h) Study—Not later than 1 year after the date of enactment of this section, the Government Accountability Office shall study and report to Congress on the impact of law school accreditation requirements and other factors on law school costs and access, including the impact of such requirements on racial and ethnic minorities.*

"~~(h)~~*(i)* Authorization of appropriations—There are authorized to be appropriated to carry out this section $25,000,000 for fiscal year 2008 and such sums as may be necessary for each succeeding fiscal year."

Calendar No. 113

Appendix D

Senate Report 110-051

PROVIDING FOR LOAN REPAYMENT FOR PROSECUTORS AND PUBLIC DEFENDERS

VIII. ADDITIONAL VIEWS

ADDITIONAL VIEWS OF SENATORS KYL AND HATCH

While the bill reported by this Committee will help reduce the burden of the heavy law-school student loans borne by many young prosecutors and public defenders, this legislation treats only the symptoms, not the source, of this problem. The source of the problem—the cause of the excessive cost of becoming eligible to practice law in the United States today—was identified in testimony before this Committee by George B. Shepard, an associate professor of law at Emory University School of Law. In his testimony on February 27, Professor Shepard endorsed the John R. Justice Act, but went on to note that:

> we need to recognize that passage of the Act is necessary partly because of the [law-school] accreditation system; without the accreditation system, many more students would graduate from law school with no loans or much smaller ones, so that they would not need to use the benefits that the Act provides. With the accreditation system, the Act will, in effect, transfer much taxpayers' money from the federal government to overpriced law schools.

Professor Shepard went on to describe exactly how the American Bar Association's law-school accreditation rules substantially and unnecessarily increase the cost of becoming eligible to practice law:

> The ABA's accreditation requirements increase the cost of becoming a lawyer in two ways. First, they increase law school tuition. They do this by imposing many costs on law schools. For example, accreditation standards effectively raise faculty salaries; limit faculty teaching loads; require high numbers of full-time faculty rather than cheaper part-time adjuncts; and require expensive physical facilities and library collections. The requirements probably cause law schools' costs to more than double, increasing them by more than $12,000 per year, with many schools then passing the increased costs along to students by raising tuition. The total increase for the three years of law school is more than $36,000.

The impact of the increased costs from accreditation can be seen by comparing tuition rates at accredited schools and unaccredited schools. Accredited schools normally charge more than $25,000 per year. Unaccredited schools usually charge approximately half that amount. One example of the many expensive accreditation requirements is the ABA's requirement that an accredited school have a large library and extensive library collection. Insiders confirm that the ABA requires a minimum expenditure on library operations and acquisitions of approximately $1 million per year. This is more than $4,000 per student in an averaged-sized school.

The second way that the ABA requirements increase students' cost of entering the legal profession is as follows. The ABA requires students to attend at least six years of expensive higher education: three years of college and three years of law school. Before the Great Depression, a young person could enter the legal profession as an apprentice directly after high school, without college or law school. Now, a person can become a lawyer only if she can afford to take six years off from work after high school and pay six years of tuition.

The requirement of six years of education is expensive. The sum of the tuition payments and foregone income can easily exceed $300,000, or more. For example, a conservative estimate is that attending a private college and law school for six years would cost approximately $25,000 per year for a total of $150,000. In addition, let's assume conservatively that a student who could qualify for college and law school would have earned only $25,000 per year if the student had not attended college and law school. The amount of income that the student sacrifices for six years to become a lawyer is $150,000. The total is $300,000.

In addition to the John R. Justice Act, there are two other means by which the problem of the excessive cost of becoming eligible to practice law in this country could be addressed. First, the states themselves could liberalize their law-school accreditation requirements. This would directly reduce the cost of becoming a lawyer in all cases, not just for prosecutors and public defenders. In his February 27 testimony, Professor Shepard recommended that:

> the accreditation system's restrictions should be loosened. For example, law schools might be permitted to experiment with smaller libraries, cheaper practitioner faculty, and even shorter programs of two years rather than three, like business school. Or the requirements might be eliminated completely; students without a degree from an accredited law school would be able to practice law.

Removing the flawed, artificial accreditation bottleneck would not in fact be a drastic change, and it would create many benefits but few harms. The current system's high-end qualities would continue, while a freer market for variety would quickly open up. To Rolls-Royce legal educations would be added Buicks, Saturns, and Fords. The new system would develop a wider range of talent, including lawyers at $60, $40, and even $25 an hour, as well as those at $300 and up. This would fit the true diversity of legal needs, from simple to complex. With cheaper education available to more people, some lawyers for the first time would be willing and able to work for far less than at present.

The addition of many more lawyers would produce little additional legal malpractice or fraud, and the quality of legal services decline little, it at all. Private institutions would arise within the market for legal services to ensure that each legal matter was handled by lawyers with appropriate skills and sophistication. For example, large, expensive law firms would continue to handle complicated, high-stakes transactions and litigation. However, law companies that resembled H&R Block would open to offer less-expensive legal services for simple matters. Accounting and tax services are available not only for $300 per hour at the big accounting firms, but also for $25 per hour at H&R Block. The new law companies would monitor and guarantee the services of their lawyer-employees.

Elimination of the accreditation requirement is a modest, safe proposal. It merely reestablishes the system that exists in other equally-critical professions, a system that worked well in law for more than a century before the Great Depression. Business and accounting provide comforting examples of professions without mandatory accreditation or qualifying exams. In both professions, people may provide full-quality basic services without attending an accredited school or passing an exam. Instead, people can choose preparation that is appropriate for their jobs. A person who seeks to manage a local McDonald's franchise or to prepare tax returns need not attend business school or become a CPA first. Yet there is no indication that the level of malpractice or fraud is higher in these fields than in law. Likewise, there is no indication that malpractice and fraud were any more frequent during the century before accreditation and the bar exam, when lawyers like Abraham Lincoln practiced. Lincoln never went to law school.

Second, in response to those who have turned to Congress to address this problem, I would note that Congress already *has* acted. It acted in 1868, by enacting the Privileges and Immunities Clause of the Fourteenth Amendment. That Clause was understood at the time of the nation's founding 'to refer to those fundamental rights and liberties specifically enjoyed by English citizens and, more broadly, by all persons.' *Saenz* v. *Roe*, 526 U.S. 489, 524 (Thomas, J., dissenting)—a meaning that carried over to the Fourteenth Amendment as well, see *Id.* 526–27. Legal scholars and civil-rights organizations such as the Institute for Justice have in the past presented compelling arguments that the fundamental rights and liberties protected by the Privileges and Immunities Clause include a right to pursue a career or profession. And that right is in clear tension with the apparently protectionist nature of the current accreditation regime. As Professor Shepard noted in his testimony:

> Strict accreditation requirements are a relatively recent phenomenon, having begun in the Great Depression. What seems normal now after 70 years was in fact a radical change from a much more open system that had functioned well for more than a century before then. Until the Great Depression, no state required an applicant to the bar to have attended any law school at all, much

less an accredited one. Indeed, 41 states required no formal education whatsoever beyond high school; 32 states did not even require a high school
diploma. Similarly, bar exams were easy to pass; they had high pass rates.

* * *

During the Depression, state bar associations attempted to eliminate so-called
'overcrowding' in the legal profession; they felt that too many new lawyers were competing with the existing ones for the dwindling amount of legal business. They attempted to reduce the number of new lawyers in two ways. First, they decreased bar
pass rates. Second, they convinced courts and state legislatures to require that all
lawyers graduate from ABA-accredited law schools.

The protectionist nature of the current accreditation regime not only is at odds
with the Privileges and Immunities Clause; it also has a disproportionate impact on
the very minority groups that the Fourteenth Amendment was originally designed
to protect. Several of the witnesses who testified before the Committee emphasized
the negative effects that escalating tuition costs have on minority participation in the
legal profession and on access to legal services in minority communities. Jessica Berge-
man, an Assistant State's Attorney for Cook County, Illinois, stated:

> I truly believe that it is good for the communities of Chicago to see Assistant
> State's Attorneys of color. Unfortunately, it is often we who are most burdened
> with educational debt. People like me who are forced to leave the office be-
> cause they cannot afford to stay cannot be categorized as just a personal
> career set-back, but rather it has the potential to further the divisions between
> the prosecutors and so many of the people they prosecute.

Professor Shepard seconded this point in his testimony, noting that 'the system
has excluded many from the legal profession, particularly the poor and minorities.
It has raised the cost of legal services. And it has, in effect, denied legal services to
whole segments of our society.'

Simple legal planning plays an important role in individuals' efforts to provide for
their families, start businesses, and plan for their economic futures. Lower and mid-
dle-income citizens' lack of access to legal services makes it more difficult for them
to make the informed choices that will improve their lives. And existing law-school
accreditation requirements play a significant role in driving up the cost of legal services.
Recognizing the significance of these phenomena, the Committee adopted an amendment to this legislation that will require the Government Accountability Office to report to Congress on the impact that law-school accreditation requirements have on
law-school tuition, including the effect that the elevated cost of legal services has on
members of minority groups.

The bill reported by this Committee addresses a real problem. It is a problem,
however, that should also be addressed by other, more direct means.

JON KYL.
ORRIN G. HATCH.

Index